The American Presidents

Revised Edition

The American Presidents

Revised Edition

Editor, First Edition
Frank N. Magill

Associate Editor, First Edition
John L. Loos
Louisiana State University

Editor, Revised Edition
Tracy Irons-Georges

SALEM PRESS, INC.
Pasadena, California   Hackensack, New Jersey

Editor in Chief: Dawn P. Dawson
Project Editor: Tracy Irons-Georges
Research Supervisor: Jeffry Jensen
Photograph Editor: Karrie Hyatt
Production Editor: Cynthia Beres
Layout: William Zimmerman

∞ The paper used in these volumes conforms to the American National Standard for Permanence of Paper for Printed Library Materials, Z39.48-1992 (R1997).

Library of Congress Cataloging-in-Publication Data
The American presidents / editor, first edition, Frank N. Magill ; associate editor, first edition, John L. Loos ; editor, revised edition, Tracy Irons-Georges. — Rev. ed.
   p.   cm.
  Includes bibliographical references and index.
  ISBN 0-89356-224-6 (alk. paper)
  1. Presidents—United States—History.   2. Presidents—United States Biography.
  3. United States—Politics and government.
  I. Magill, Frank Northen, 1907-1997. II. Loos, John L. III. Irons-Georges, Tracy.
E176.1.A6563   2000
973'.09'9—dc21   99-38924
                                           CIP

Second Printing

PRINTED IN THE UNITED STATES OF AMERICA

Contents

Publisher's Note vii
Preface to the First Edition ix
Introduction to the First Edition xv
List of Contributors xxiii

The American Presidency: An Overview 1
George Washington 18
John Adams 47
Thomas Jefferson 62
James Madison 85
James Monroe 105
John Quincy Adams 121
Andrew Jackson 135
Martin Van Buren 162
William Henry Harrison 177
John Tyler 182
James K. Polk 188
Zachary Taylor 210
Millard Fillmore 216
Franklin Pierce 222
James Buchanan 230
Abraham Lincoln 241
Andrew Johnson 277
Ulysses S. Grant 292
Rutherford B. Hayes 313
James A. Garfield 328
Chester A. Arthur 332
Grover Cleveland 338
Benjamin Harrison 351
William McKinley 358
Theodore Roosevelt 372
William Howard Taft 395
Woodrow Wilson 408
Warren G. Harding 433
Calvin Coolidge 440
Herbert Hoover 451
Franklin D. Roosevelt 467

Harry S Truman 504
Dwight D. Eisenhower 530
John F. Kennedy 553
Lyndon B. Johnson 571
Richard M. Nixon 600
Gerald R. Ford 629
Jimmy Carter 642
Ronald Reagan 658
George Bush 677
Bill Clinton 694

U.S. Constitution 711
Law of Presidential Succession 725
Time Line 726
Presidential Election Returns, 1789-1996 757
Vice Presidents 762
Cabinet Members by Administration 764
First Ladies 779
Presidential Libraries 781
Glossary 785
Bibliography 795

Index III

Publisher's Note

The late 1990's shone a bright and sometimes harsh light on the U.S. presidency. President Bill Clinton's impeachment led many people to question the nature of the office and the officeholder. Is the president a role model or simply a political leader? What is the true meaning of the presidential oath? How did the Framers of the Constitution envision the proper relationship between the executive and legislative branches? Despite such soul-searching and often-divisive debate, the survival of the presidency itself has never been in doubt. It has withstood controversy, scandal, resignation, civil war, and assassination. *The American Presidents, Revised Edition,* offers crucial context for such questions by examining the strengths and weaknesses, the successes and failures of each individual to assume the title of president.

The American Presidents, Revised Edition, updates and revises the previous 1989 edition of this work. It comprises biographical portraits of all forty-one U.S. presidents to date. New articles were commissioned for Presidents George Bush and Bill Clinton, and information has been updated in the essays on Richard Nixon, Gerald Ford, Jimmy Carter, and Ronald Reagan. Every bibliography was revised to include the most recent presidential scholarship. Many new photographs have been added, as have textual sidebars such as Jefferson's Declaration of Independence, the Monroe Doctrine, and Lincoln's Gettysburg Address. More than 225 illustrations appear in this edition.

In addition, all articles now begin with reference information regarding date and place of birth, date and place of death, political party, vice presidents, and cabinet members. The text that follows offers a comprehensive portrait of the life and times of the president, from birth through political rise, election, term of office, defeat or retirement, and death. The legacy of each administration is measured against the yardstick of U.S. history, and the evolution of the office and the country can be traced clearly. Every essay ends with Bibliographical References that provide important evaluative information about the sources listed. All articles are signed.

Numerous useful appendices have been added. The U.S. Constitution is reprinted to provide the full context of the duties and limitations of the office of president, as is the Law of Presidential Succession in the event of death or removal. A Time Line chronicles important events by administration. Presidential Election Returns from 1789 to 1996 are listed, including all major candidates with their political parties and tallies for both electoral and popular votes. Next come lists of Vice Presidents, Cabinet Members, and First Ladies for every administration from Washington to Clinton. Another appendix provides information about the location and holdings of Presidential Libraries. A Glossary of political terms, programs, and campaign slogans offers concise definitions. The general Bibliography lists books about the presidency, campaigns and elections, First Ladies and presidential families, presidential quotations, the White House, and each president to hold office. The comprehensive subject Index allows easy access to the wealth of historical information found in these essays.

The illuminating Preface by Dr. Frank N. Magill and Introduction by Dr. John L. Loos that follow the Publisher's Note were written for the original edition of this work in 1986. A list of all contributors and their affiliations follows. The essay on the American Presidency that begins the text provides a fascinating overview. We wish to thank Michael Witkoski, Kevin J. Bochynski, Daniel P. Murphy, and R. Baird Shuman for their efforts in expanding the scope of this edition and bringing it up to date.

Preface to the First Edition

"When in the Course of human events, it becomes necessary for one people to dissolve the political bands which have connected them with another . . . " are the twenty-four words that heralded the formal rupture of ties with the Mother Country, a condition which the American Colonists deemed necessary in order for the citizens of the Colonies to develop into a whole society based on elective principles that applied directly to those being governed.

The idea of a social body considering that ". . . all men are created equal . . . with certain unalienable Rights . . ." was another noble concept new to much of the world at the time (and indeed down through history), and it was not easy for England's power structure to take this pronouncement from the Colonies as a serious threat to the status quo.

Most of those who voluntarily left the security and relative comfort of Great Britain for the wilderness across the sea did so hoping to get a new start in a land not locked in a class structure where tradition and bloodline were all-important and unalterable. Thus, the arbitrary restrictions of Great Britain's "Colonial overseers" became more and more intolerable as new generations grew in the Colonies, and at last the breaking point was reached in 1773, when 342 chests of British tea were dumped into Boston Harbor from the decks of British merchant ships by some three score Bostonians garbed as "Mohawks," an action schoolchildren have since known as the Boston Tea Party. Not only were these hardy people who had braved the New World—and all that implies—ready to resist further encroachment on their freedom at the hands of autocratic oppressors, but also they were ready to take up arms in order to end such treatment. In little more than a year after the tea-dumping affair the Colonies and Great Britain were indeed locked in a shooting war. Destiny had waited long enough.

Warfare in the North American wilderness was not an activity to which the conventional British military forces were fully attuned. Furthermore, they were forced to transport much of what they required—men, guns, supplies—across three thousand miles of ocean; worst of all, the stubborn rebels never seemed to understand that they were poorly trained, badly equipped, undersupplied, and outgunned. All they had to offer was dedication to a cause and, eventually—for leadership—president-to-be George Washington.

The war surged back and forth inconclusively for several years. At last, with substantial and timely help from the French military establishment, as well as some inept strategy on the part of the British high command, Major General Lord Charles Cornwallis, the ranking British general within the Southern battle area, was trapped with his entire army in Yorktown, Virginia, in 1781, and forced to surrender in October of that year—to president-to-be George Washington.

This act of surrender signaled the end of George III's attempts to subdue the rebellious American Colonists by military force. Withdrawal of the English, however, left no political vacuum. Representatives of twelve of the thirteen colonies that had dared to challenge Great Britain had already met in 1774 and 1775 and codified their thinking, which eventually resulted in a Constitution through which, as amended, the emerging nation could be governed, uniformly and without favor to any special class. To administer the letter and spirit of this Constitution, an Office was carefully designed: It should be freely elective, subject to the will of the people; it should be temporary, subject to reiteration or change by the electorate every four years; it should be occupied by one who inspired the confidence of the electorate and commanded the respect of world leaders. The man the framers seemed to be describing was—George Washington.

Washington was duly elected as the first president of the United States and became known thenceforth to innumerable schoolchildren as The Father of Our Country. He promptly set the tone of the office, and the new nation could not have been more fortunate in the choice. His physical appearance and formal demeanor were ideal for the image required of the new leader, and the model has served well many future aspirants.

Washington did not disappoint his constituents. He already had some political experience, having served as a Virginia delegate to the first and second Continental Congresses in 1774 and 1775. His integrity and sense of honor were beyond reproach, and he had earlier demonstrated his lack of ambition to acquire power, through his widely praised act of resigning his commission as supreme commander after the war rather than hang on to it and form a military dictatorship. Indeed, Washington's reputation for favoring civilian power over the military helped the states decide to form a fairly strong federal government and surrender some of their powers to it because Washington was to head up that new power base. It was known that Washington believed that the threat of anarchy by the masses was a greater danger to democracy than a dictatorship would be; thus, the Federal government should have sufficient power and resources to protect itself from all threats.

The importance of George Washington's eight years as America's first president is of such significance that the reader is referred without further discussion here to Professor Charles Royster's article describing Washington's two terms in office.

John Adams, the second president, lacked the charisma of his predecessor, though his handling of the XYZ affair, and the peaceful accommodation with France that followed, prevented his term of office from being a complete failure.

The third president, Thomas Jefferson, was perhaps the brightest star of his time, and his two administrations served to upgrade the office of president to the level of esteem it had held under Washington. One of the major reasons for his popular success was the fact that, like Washington, Jefferson had become a national leader prior to achieving the presidency, through his brilliant writing, his ambassadorial service in France, and his vision for the development of the new nation, as exemplified in his contributions to the drafting of the Declaration of Independence. As president, his stature continued to grow through such accomplishments as the Louisiana Purchase, the expansion of public works, the founding of schools, and the signing of the act that closed the international slave trade (a premature hope). On balance, Jefferson must be rated high as a president, surely among our five or six greatest.

Thomas Jefferson's much admired friend, James Madison, followed him as the fourth president of the United States. Like Jefferson, Madison also was a brilliant man with much prior service to the new nation, including membership in the first four Congresses, where he was the author of the first ten amendments to the new Constitution—known as the Bill of Rights. Madison inherited a major problem which eventually resulted in the War of 1812 with Great Britain, primarily over the general issue of free trade on the open seas. England persisted in refusing to honor such a policy, seizing American ships and impressing American sailors at will. As a new member of the family of nations, the United States could not tolerate such abuse, and prepared for war. Although the British captured the city of Washington, burned the "White House," and almost captured the fleeing president, a dramatic victory by General Andrew Jackson over the British at New Orleans in January, 1815, assured that the Treaty of Ghent, signed two weeks earlier and ending the War of 1812, would be honored by Great Britain. Madison's long and fruitful career in government ended with James Monroe's election as president in 1817. Without question, President Madison had given his best to his country, and he lived with these memories for nineteen more years.

The last member of the Virginia Dynasty and the last of the generation of those revolutionary leaders who helped form the new nation, James Monroe became the fifth president on March 4, 1817. He was a true republican in thought and his belief in the ability of free men to govern themselves through voluntary mutual agreement was innate.

While still in his late teens, Monroe had fought with distinction in Washington's Continental army, being severely wounded in battle. He ended his military career as a major and with the expressed admiration of General Washington himself. Monroe's political career began at the age of twenty-four with his election to the Virginia House of Delegates. He was a delegate to the Continental Congress in 1783 and was elected to the United States Senate in 1790. Monroe's two terms as president were characterized by fiscal responsibility in government but deep economic problems for the people, marked by The Panic of 1819 which caused a depression in land prices and agricultural products, as well as severe unemployment. By 1821, however, the economy had recovered, some economics lessons had been learned, and the nation was headed for a decade

of prosperity. Meanwhile, territorial expansion had been going on. In The Territorial Treaty of 1819, Spain ceded Florida and the Oregon Country to the United States, adding greatly to the territorial extent and the unification process of the nation. Monroe had now concluded that the Western Hemisphere should be free from foreign intervention, especially by adventurous European rulers, and in 1823 he proclaimed what was to become known as the Monroe Doctrine. This edict stated that the American continents were "henceforth not to be considered as subjects for future colonization by any European powers," probably at the time the most grandiose uncalled political bluff in history—and a fitting climax to the genius of four Virginians and one New Englander who in less than fifty years had turned a disparate group of immigrant descendants into a cohesive, powerful nation that had earned the attention and respect of the world's powers.

The seventh president, Andrew Jackson, was first of all a superb military leader, without whom some of the political successes of his predecessors might have been more difficult. As a president, Jackson was lacking in some of the fine points of diplomacy and all that implies, but he was a fast learner and, in time, mastered the minimal intricacies of protocol required of him in his office. A born warrior, Jackson's national reputation was made in the Battle of New Orleans at the end of the War of 1812. His plan for the defense of the city was phenomenal, with casualties running 20 to 1 in his favor against seasoned British troops. Lacking an established political base, Jackson more or less stumbled into a vacuum and quickly caught on with noncommitted voters. As an outsider on the political scene even after his election, Jackson, always dedicated to democracy, was from the beginning on the side of the little man. Even such things as paper money seemed to him a ploy of bankers to cheat the average citizen. For such reasons, Jackson was the first president of the United

States with whom "the man in the street" (or the frontiersman) could relate. Thus President Jackson demonstrated to *all* Americans that even they could have a voice in their country's actions.

The six presidents mentioned above were acting often without precedents to guide them, and their administrations have been reviewed at some length here. The remaining thirty-four presidential figures included in this work are also important to the full researcher, and for specifics, the reader henceforth is referred directly to the individual scholarly article that covers the target president.

It is true that not all the presidents provoked the same degree of interest or exhibited the charisma that mesmerized audiences, but all of them projected something special or they would not have gained the high office. This work is meant to bring forward the distinctive qualities of each man in the office so that the user may find the level of interest that most appeals individually.

The presidential articles here presented are not offered as a type of "media overview" but as scholar-oriented historical essays written by professors with more or less a scholarly lifetime of interest in and study of the presidential figure about whom they have been asked to write. The objective has been to interpret the impact of the man on the office, to stress his contributions to the safety and welfare of the nation, and to show whether the tenor of the office was changed by his administration and if so, how it was changed.

While all the presidents of the United States have been important in one way or another, after Andrew Jackson the next most serious threat to the nation came in the administration of Abraham Lincoln, a crisis that had been long in the making and came to a head with the firing on Fort Sumter by Confederates on April 12, 1861. Professor Robert Johannsen's article delineates in masterly fashion the background and presidential career of Abraham Lincoln, who presided at the death and resurrection of the United States of America as he knew it, and whose deep travail over these events was ended only with his own assassination on April 14, 1865.

Others leaving indelible marks on the Office of the President include Woodrow Wilson, who, among other things, persuaded the American public in 1917 that it was our duty to help "make the world safe for democracy," rather than stand by and see our traditional allies enslaved by power-mad dictators. Without help from the United States, the Western European Allies would very likely have been defeated.

The only man to break George Washington's nonbinding precedent of only two four-year terms as president is Franklin D. Roosevelt. When he was voted into office in 1933, the country was deep in the grip of one of the nation's worst depressions. Through imagination, innovation, and dramatic "fireside chats" he began the slow process of getting the economy back to normal. His first term was full of economic trial and error, with some successes, some failures, but never a lack of effort. Such concern for the problems of the unfortunate earned for Roosevelt the deep gratitude of those he helped and the goodwill of most of the nation, impressed as it was by the fact that he was "doing something" for those needing relief. His popularity level with the electorate during his first term was extremely high and the margin of his victory for a second term was by far the greatest in American history. Professor Robert McElvaine's survey of Roosevelt's presidential years is highly recommended.

Upon Franklin D. Roosevelt's death on April 12, 1945, Vice President Harry S Truman became the thirty-third president of the United States. His date with destiny at Hiroshima shook the world to its core, and instantly changed forever the way military men even dare give passing thoughts to all-out war.

Following Truman, the nation underwent eight more or less tranquil years under Dwight D. Eisenhower; a sudden soul-searching shock in the brutal assassination of the thirty-fifth president, John F. Kennedy; several years of unprecedented civil upheaval under Lyndon B. Johnson—events which influenced his decision not to seek another term in office—and the brazen Watergate scandal that eventually caused Richard M. Nixon to resign from the presidential office to which he had been reelected in 1972.

The next president, Gerald R. Ford, attained the office without ever having been elected either to the vice presidency or the presidency, a unique circumstance that required not a single vote from any constituent anywhere. Ford's presidency was ended with the election of Jimmy Carter, of Georgia, as the nation's thirty-ninth president, a sincere, hardworking, inexperienced political figure who succumbed to the glitter of Ronald Reagan after one term.

George Washington's "tone of the office" has ebbed and flowed with the tide of passing events, but in the minds of the serious electorate the legacy of the first president's example remains a beacon on which Americans still focus as a reminder of who they are and from whence they have come.

The complete list of contributing professors, along with their academic affiliations, follows. I wish to thank each professor individually for their valued contribution to this work. I also wish to express my appreciation to the staff of researchers and proofreaders for their untiring efforts in the processing of the manuscripts.

We wish to thank the White House Historical Association for making available for reproduction the official presidential portraits. As a portrait of President Reagan has yet to be commissioned, his official presidential photograph has been reproduced at the beginning of the chapter on his presidency.

We also wish to thank Imagefinders, Inc., for locating and obtaining copies of the illustrations in this book. Below each illustration, we acknowledge the source from which it was obtained.

FRANK N. MAGILL
1986

Introduction to the First Edition

The president of the United States is the most powerful and influential popularly elected public official in the world. The only person who represents and speaks for all Americans, he serves as the nation's head of state, chief executive, principal administrator, and legislative leader, as well as commander in chief of its armed forces, director of its foreign affairs, and head of his political party. The Constitution of the United States entrusts some of these manifold duties and responsibilities to the president, but they have been expanded upon and others have been added through the efforts of the men who have held the office or because changes in the nature of the federal government or of America's role in the world necessitated them. Since World War II, the president has come to be not only the leader of the United States, but also of the Western alliance if not the entire non-Communist world.

Americans of the Colonial era would be surprised, and probably aghast, at such expansive presidential power. Their experience under British rule left them extremely suspicious of executive authority. The royal governors, as representatives of the British Crown, had been very unpopular with the colonists, who had looked to their elected assemblies to represent and protect their rights and interests. Thus, when during the Revolution the newly independent states established governments, they generally gave preeminent power to the legislature and strictly limited the role of the governor. They made his term of office very short—usually only one year—carefully restricted his eligibility for reelection, and in a few instances even gave the legislature the right

to elect him. In addition, the governor's few powers were essentially determined by the legislature, and, with one minor exception, he had no authority to veto its acts. The one noteworthy exception to this general condition of executive impotence was New York, where the governor was given "the supreme executive power and authority of the state." He was elected directly by the people, his term of office was three years, he was indefinitely eligible for reelection, he had broad veto and pardoning powers, and he was the commander in chief of the state militia.

In actual practice, the legislatively dominated state governments left much to be desired from the point of view of the conservative classes. They proved to be lacking in stability and energy and prone to adopting unwise and unfair laws designed to satisfy the demands of one faction or special interest group or another. They were considered by the propertied classes to be far too democratic.

The Articles of Confederation, the frame of national government under which the states operated after 1781, near the end of the Revolution, also reflected the Americans' suspicion of executive power. The Articles provided for only one governing body, a Congress in which each of the states was represented by between two and seven delegates but in which each had only one vote. Administrative and executive functions were performed by committees of Congress and a few administrative departments: foreign affairs, treasury, war, navy, and post office. Congress under the Articles could not govern the country effectively. Lacking the power to levy taxes (it had to rely for funds on requisitions on the states, which were largely ignored, and on borrowing, especially from abroad), it had difficulty paying the war debt and its operating expenses. Without the power to impose tariffs, it was unable to protect American merchants and manufacturers from ruthless foreign competition. Faced with the growing discontent and occasional uprisings of poor, debt-ridden farmers and workers, the Articles of Confederation could not maintain law and order and protect the interests of the conservative, propertied classes.

The perceived failings of both the legislatively dominated state governments and the Articles of Confederation led to a movement for a stronger, more effective central government which in 1787 culminated in the calling of the Constitutional Convention. Although summoned to correct the failings of the Articles of Confederation, soon after assembling the members of the convention decided instead of amending the Articles to draft an entirely new constitution which would embody the principle of separation of powers, with an independent executive, legislature, and judiciary. They were influenced in their decision and guided in their planning for such a government by the writings of great political philosophers, such as John Locke, William Blackstone, and Montesquieu, and by their knowledge of and experience with the colonial and recently established state governments as well as the Articles of Confederation.

Convinced of the need for a strong executive, in spite of the considerable opposition of those who represented the widespread fear of monarchy in the country, the Constitutional Convention voted to follow the example of New York and create a strong executive in the form of a single individual with enough power to instill the office with vigor that would reach throughout the land. To assure the executive's independence of the legislature, he was to be elected by special electors in each state who would be chosen as the state legislature should

direct. The framers rejected the idea of popular ejection of the executive because they considered the people to be too ignorant or too easily subject to being misled by designing persons to make a proper choice. The president so chosen was to serve for a fixed term of office—four years—and was to be eligible for reelection for an indefinite number of terms. (With the adoption of the Twenty-second Amendment in 1951, he could be reelected only once.) Neither the president nor any other member of the executive branch could be a member of Congress, thus preventing the possibility of the development of a cabinet system of government like that in England. The new Constitution gave the president certain stipulated powers as well as those he might be authorized by Congress to exercise.

Despite the constitutional framers' concern not to create an elective monarch, the powers conferred on the chief executive were great. They were in part influenced in bestowing such a generous grant of authority by the assumption that George Washington, the chairman of the convention, would be the first president. "When men spoke of the great national representative, of the guardian of the people, they were thinking in terms of the Father of His Country," declares the constitutional scholar Charles C. Thach, Jr. Article II of the Constitution, which deals with the executive, states broadly that "the executive Power shall be vested in a President of the United States." It specifically makes the president commander in chief of the armed forces and, with the consent of two-thirds of the senators, empowers that individual to make treaties and appoint the principal military, judicial, and administrative officers of the government. The president can also independently appoint other inferior officers of the government, grant pardons for offenses against the United States, call Congress into special session and recommend "measures" to it, and invoke a suspensive veto of all its enactments. The president is responsible for the execution of all the laws of the United States and can be removed only upon impeachment for and conviction by Congress of treason, bribery, or other high crimes and misdemeanors.

The executive provided for in the Constitution, declared James Wilson, the member of the convention who was the chief advocate of a strong executive, is "the man of the people"—representative of and responsible to them. Wilson also considered the American presidency to be "unique," a judgment in which Thach concurred nearly two centuries later when he concluded that it "has proved a governmental creation, differing from its predecessors and its derivatives in a most decisive fashion." For a brief review of the events leading to the presidential office, readers may wish to examine Professor Magill's preface.

As the framers of the Constitution assumed, Washington was unanimously elected the first president and was inaugurated on April 30, 1789. "The office," as the great authority on the presidency Edward S. Corwin has stated, "got off to a good start under a very great man." As president, Washington did not seek to be a popular leader; rather he was "an Olympian figure, above the fray—a symbol of American nationhood." He avoided personal involvement in political controversies and the deliberations of Congress, but his secretary of the treasury, Alexander Hamilton, did steer through that body a major economic program. Washington's administration also conducted important relations with the powers of Western Europe—Britain, France, and Spain—to settle problems growing out of the American and French revolutions. At home, the president acted decisively to assert the power of the federal government by suppressing the insurrectionary threat of frontier farmers who refused to pay the excise tax on the whiskey they sold. Through wise and judicious conduct, Washington by the end of his second term had established the presidency on very secure ground.

Washington's immediate successors, like him, came from the leaders of the Revolution and the struggle to create the new government. They were very able men, but in large part their historical reputations owe more to their accomplishments before they became president than to their performance as chief executives.

John Adams, the second president, although a great statesman and political philosopher, was an unsuccessful chief executive because, strong-minded and convinced of his moral superiority, he proved a poor political and popular leader. Relations with revolutionary France dominated his administration, and he considered the avoidance of all-out war with that country the principal achievement of his presidency.

When he took office in 1801, Thomas Jefferson brought to the presidency a new philosophy and style of government. Under him and his successors and friends from Virginia—the "Virginia Dynasty"—the president gave up most of his autonomy and, in deference to the republican principle of legislative supremacy, acquiesced in congressional domination of the national government. Jefferson was, however, an exceptionally shrewd and practical politician who, as the chief founder and leader of the first national political party, the Democratic Republicans, skillfully managed Congress by personal influence. Although having little success in protecting American rights on the high seas by economic means during the Napoleonic Wars, Jefferson was particularly proud of his purchase of Louisiana from France, which almost doubled the territory of the United States.

Lacking the political skill and will of his predecessor, James Madison, despite his well-established greatness as a political thinker and statesman, was a weak and ineffectual president. Unable, even unwilling, to lead Congress, he bungled into a war against England in 1812 for which the country was completely unprepared. Exercising the war power reluctantly and uncertainly, he proved to be a poor commander in chief. Nevertheless, the war, although not a military success, did inspire in the American people a feeling of nationalism such that it has been called the Second War for American Independence.

James Monroe, best known for his famous doctrine claiming American hegemony in the Western Hemisphere, was personally popular but, like his predecessor Madison, had no clearly articulated policy or program. A passive president, in most matters he deferred to Congress and took no legislative initiative.

Although a brilliant diplomat and the nation's greatest secretary of state, John Quincy Adams was an ineffective president. Self-righteous and opinionated, the second Adams to hold the office was, like his father, a poor popular, as well as legislative and political, leader. Despite his superb credentials, he even failed in his diplomatic endeavors. His power and authority were undermined by the supporters of Andrew Jackson, who, throughout Adams's term of office, waged a vindictive and relentless campaign to assure his defeat in 1828.

The new president, Jackson, was the nation's first truly popular leader. The "Jacksonian democracy" which he ushered in was marked by the extension of political power from the propertied aristocracy to virtually all citizens, which at that time meant only all adult, white males. Jackson spoke and acted as the representative of all the people and as the one person with the special duty of protecting their rights and liberties. He reasserted the independence of his office from Congress by reviving and expanding the removal and veto powers, and from the courts by claiming to have as much authority to interpret the Constitution as the judges. On at least one occasion he allegedly even refused to enforce a decision of the Supreme Court with which he disagreed. He threatened to use military force to compel

South Carolina to obey the federal tariff laws when her legislature presumed to nullify them. Neither at that time nor at any other, however, did Jackson challenge in any fundamental way the federal principle which recognized the broad rights and powers of the states.

Following Jackson, until Lincoln assumed the office in 1861, the nation had a succession of relatively weak and passive presidents—Martin Van Buren, William Henry Harrison, John Tyler, James K. Polk, Zachary Taylor, Millard Fillmore, Franklin Pierce, and James Buchanan—each of whom served for only one term or less. As the sectional crisis over slavery worsened, the people seemed to believe that a strong, assertive chief executive might threaten the delicate compromises and accommodations that were worked out in Congress in an effort to prevent a rupture of the Union. Moreover, they appeared to feel safer with leaders who had no pronounced views or strong national policies or programs. In some respects, the one exception among these eight undistinguished presidents was Polk, who led the country in a successful, though rather unpopular, war to obtain a large territory in the Southwest from Mexico and who was an effective administrator and commander in chief.

Abraham Lincoln, judged by many historians to be America's greatest president, raised the power and importance of the presidential office to heights far above those claimed for it by any of his predecessors and became in some respects a virtual dictator. With the secession of the Southern states and the threatened dissolution of the Union, Lincoln faced a situation which was not only unique in American history but the greatest crisis ever faced by the nation. To deal with it, he had, in his words, "to think anew and act anew," and he relied mainly upon the president's war power as commander in chief, an insurrection being deemed to be a war. At first he acted—calling out the militia, enlarging the regular army and navy beyond their legal limits, ordering a blockade of the southern coast, suspending the writ of habeas corpus—only until Congress could ratify and reinforce what he had done. Later, however, he acted without seeking congressional authorization and even in violation of the Constitution itself, as when he issued the Emancipation Proclamation or declared martial law in certain areas in the North. Lincoln justified all that he did on the ground that the people demanded it and the preservation of the Union required it. His actions, according to historian Clinton Rossiter, "raised the Presidency to a position of constitutional and moral ascendancy that left no doubt where the burden of crisis government in this country would thereafter rest."

During the tenure of the eight presidents who followed Lincoln in the last third of the nineteenth century—Andrew Johnson, Ulysses S. Grant, Rutherford B. Hayes, James A. Garfield, Chester A. Arthur, Grover Cleveland, Benjamin Harrison, and William McKinley—Congress again became the dominant branch of the national government. The strongest of these generally passive chief executives was Cleveland, the only president in the nation's history to serve two nonconsecutive terms of office. A "defensive" president, Cleveland, like the other presidents of his generation, believed in a laissez-faire role for the national government but tried, especially through the use of his veto power, to keep the government honest, fair, and impartial in its treatment of all elements of population.

In 1898, pressured by Congress and the public, Cleveland's successor, William McKinley, led the country into war with Spain. From this conflict the United States emerged as a world power with territorial possessions extending from the Caribbean to the western Pacific. This new status led to the substantial enhancement of the role of the president as the nation's acknowledged leader in the field of foreign affairs.

Theodore Roosevelt became the first of the "new" twentieth century presidents. A very popular chief executive, he brought color and excitement to the office. "He was," as Rossiter states, "a brilliant molder and interpreter of public opinion and an active leader of Congress." Roosevelt claimed to have the right and duty to do anything necessary for the public welfare unless such action was forbidden by the Constitution or laws. He conducted the nation's foreign affairs with vigor and took the lead in securing from Congress legislation to regulate big business. He was also the first president to act as a mediator in an industrial dispute, but he did not envision or advocate for the national government such a positive role in economic and social matters as that inaugurated by his distant cousin a generation later. Roosevelt's handpicked successor, William Howard Taft, had a much more modest view of the proper role of the president. He believed that the chief magistrate could do only those things which he was expressly empowered to do by the Constitution or the laws, and he was quite content to leave the legislative initiative to Congress.

The balance of power shifted again with the accession to the presidency of Woodrow Wilson, who was through most of his two terms a very strong chief executive. A popular leader, he was both a good administrator and an exceptionally shrewd head of his party. Wilson dealt most effectively with the legislative branch and achieved a high level of vigorous and responsible government. During World War I he obtained from Congress extensive emergency powers, especially over the economy. In the end, however, because of the excessively partisan spirit in which he conducted his office, serious health problems, and a stubborn and uncompromising stand on the Treaty of Versailles, he lost support with the people and Congress and failed as a leader in foreign relations.

Wilson, like other strong presidents in times of crisis, was followed by a succession of largely passive chief executives—Warren G. Harding, Calvin Coolidge, and Herbert Hoover—all of whom held a relatively modest view of the position and powers of the president and of the proper functions of the national government. Despite his belief in "rugged individualism," however, Hoover did propose to Congress some rather novel economic measures to deal with the economic crisis which began with the stock market crash in 1929.

The failure of Hoover's efforts to revive the economy helped ensure the victory in 1932 of Franklin D. Roosevelt, the only person to be elected to the presidency four times. During his long tenure of slightly more than twelve years, the nation experienced the greatest depression in its history and its greatest war. In dealing with these crises, Roosevelt significantly enlarged the powers of the president and of the national government. In attacking the Great Depression, Roosevelt claimed for the federal government a positive role of unprecedented proportions in the economic and social affairs of the nation, introducing the welfare, or social service, state, which rested upon the "idea that the government should be active and reformist rather than simply protective of the established order of things." In legislating this new order, Congress intruded as never before into areas that had been traditionally reserved to the states. At the same time, the president assumed a far larger role than ever before in the initiation and passage of legislation, and Congress endowed the president with extraordinary legislative powers. During World War II the president, as commander in chief, assumed still greater powers over the economy and the people, even to the extent of seriously violating, in the name of national security, the constitutional rights of the Japanese Americans who were living on the West Coast. The war and the accompanying emergence of the United States as the greatest power in the world also resulted in greatly increased presidential power in international affairs.

Inasmuch as the United States has remained the greatest economic and military power in the world since World War II, all the presidents since Roosevelt have had an unusually important role in conducting the nation's foreign affairs and in serving as spokesmen for the Western alliance and other non-Communist nations. Furthermore, since the dropping of two atomic bombs on Japan in 1945, the world has lived in a state of greater or less crisis which has served to magnify the role of the president as commander in chief as well as chief diplomat. Similarly, since the inception of the social service state under Roosevelt, the role of the national government and of the president in the social and economic life of the nation has remained large.

Harry S Truman, who succeeded Roosevelt near the end of the war, was a strong party leader and an active president. Foreign affairs dominated his administration and focused on three important decisions which he made: (1) to drop atom bombs on Hiroshima and Nagasaki (2) to pursue a "cold war" policy of containment toward the Soviet Union, and (3) to fight the North Koreans when they invaded South Korea. Although these decisions were generally popular, Truman's inability to bring the Korean War to a successful conclusion finally contributed decisively to the president's growing unpopularity and the defeat of his party in the 1952 presidential election.

Following Truman, Dwight D. Eisenhower, a wartime hero and great popular leader with a winning personality, was more than anything else a symbol of national unity. Not a party leader, Eisenhower sought in both legislative and foreign affairs essentially to maintain the status quo by drawing on the support of moderate and conservative elements in both major parties. In contrast to what some considered the staid style of Eisenhower, John F. Kennedy, a charismatic popular leader, projected an image of youth, vigor, and great confidence. Although he painted appealing visions of greatness for America, he was not an effective legislative leader, and his short administration was noteworthy more for its style than its substance. Even in the field of foreign affairs the record was mixed. The Soviets' construction of the Berlin Wall and the Bay of Pigs invasion fiasco diminished American prestige and influence, but the Cuban Missile Crisis was a defensive success.

Lyndon Johnson, Kennedy's successor, brought to the presidency great skill and experience as a legislative leader, and in the emotional aftermath of Kennedy's assassination he secured the passage of an impressive body of social and economic legislation which significantly enlarged the social welfare role of the national government with the avowed—though unrealized—goal of abolishing poverty in the United States. Although a great leader of Congress, Johnson failed in the all-important role of commander in chief. His inability to bring an end to the increasingly costly and discouraging war in Vietnam ultimately cost the president his popular support and forced his decision not to seek reelection.

As president, Richard M. Nixon was a vigorous aggrandizer of power. His presidency has been described as "imperial" in part, at least, because of his somewhat successful efforts to wrest power, especially in budgetary matters, from Congress and to concentrate the power of the executive branch more directly under his control. An active and shrewd diplomatic leader with a reputation as an ardent anti-Communist, he achieved a significant relaxation of tensions, or detente, between the United States and the Soviet Union, as well as initiating the establishment of diplomatic relations with the People's Republic of China. Reelected in a landslide, less than two years later he became the only president to resign his office. He did so under the threat of impeachment growing out of charges of criminal misconduct in connection with an attempted burglary of the Democratic National Committee headquarters in the Watergate apartment complex in Washington by persons associated with his reelection campaign.

With Nixon's resignation, Gerald Ford, who had been appointed vice president following Spiro Agnew's resignation from that office, became the nation's only president who had been elected to neither office. The presidency which Ford assumed, already weakened by the events of Nixon's second term that brought him to office, was further enfeebled by Ford's unpopular pardon of Nixon. Ford sought, for the most part, only to continue the Nixon policies and programs, but even though he had been a popular veteran congressman, he was not an effective legislative leader and played a largely negative role by vetoing many congressional measures which he deemed to be fiscally irresponsible.

Capitalizing on the Watergate scandal and a general public disaffection with the government in Washington, Jimmy Carter won election to the presidency as an outsider. Taking office with no clearly defined policies, having no strong power base in his party, and apparently unable to establish good relations with Congress, he proved an ineffective legislative leader. Even his limited successes in Middle Eastern diplomacy failed to produce a larger settlement of international problems in the region.

Under Ronald Reagan the presidency has recovered its strong leadership position. A remarkably talented and persuasive communicator, Reagan is the most popular president since Franklin D. Roosevelt. The first truly conservative president since Hoover, he has espoused a clearly articulated policy of reducing the role of the national government in the nation's social and economic affairs while strengthening its military posture. A pragmatist, he has succeeded in securing the enactment of substantial parts of his program by exhibiting a willingness to compromise in his dealings with Congress. Similarly, in relations with the Soviet Union, he began, in his second term, to move from a confrontational stance to one of negotiation with the goal of achieving lowered tensions and armaments reduction.

Today, nearly two hundred years after its creation, the office of president is perhaps stronger and more popular than it has ever been. Since the days of Washington, the presidential office has grown enormously in power and importance. This expansion has not been regular or steady, but has occurred primarily in times of crisis or emergency, such as depressions and wars. Regardless of the situation, the power and influence of the office has depended upon the personality of its occupant. Presidents who have enhanced the power of the office have been dynamic, popular leaders who have actively and energetically sought power with the purpose of making a lasting impact on the country, or even the world—of changing things in so fundamental a way that history would take note of them and what they had done. To accomplish their purposes they have actively courted and depended upon the support of the people. They have communicated their views and their goals to the citizenry, and they have claimed to act for them and their posterity. In the hands of lesser men with smaller ambitions and aims, the presidency has at times shrunk in importance and power, but in the long run the nation's thirty-nine presidents have succeeded in making this uniquely American political office the greatest instrument of democratic government in the world.

JOHN L. LOOS
Professor of History
Louisiana State University
1986

List of Contributors

Wayne R. Austerman
Staff Historian
USAF Space Command, Peterson
AFB

Robert A. Becker
Louisiana State University

Michael Les Benedict
Ohio State University

Kevin J. Bochynski
Independent Scholar

Mark T. Carleton
Louisiana State University

Daniel Feller
Assistant Editor, The Papers of
Andrew Jackson
University of Tennessee

James E. Fickle
Memphis State University

Gaines M. Foster
Louisiana State University

William E. Gienapp
University of Wyoming

Louis L. Gould
University of Texas at Austin

Hugh D. Graham
University of Maryland, Baltimore
County

Ellis W. Hawley
University of Iowa

Joan Hoff-Wilson
Indiana University

Robert W. Johannsen
University of Illinois

Burton I. Kaufman
Kansas State University

Joyce P. Kaufman
Whittier College

Ralph Ketcham
Syracuse University

Richard S. Kirkendall
Iowa State University

Richard N. Kottman
Iowa State University

Richard B. Latner
Newcomb College, Tulane
University

Anne C. Loveland
Louisiana State University

Richard Lowitt
Iowa State University

Robert M. McColley
University of Illinois

Donald R. McCoy
University of Kansas

Robert S. McElvaine
Millsaps College

Daniel P. Murphy
Hanover College

Burl Noggle
Louisiana State University

Allan Peskin
Cleveland State University

George C. Rable
Anderson College

Randy Roberts
Sam Houston State University

Charles W. Royster
Louisiana State University

Robert A. Rutland
Editor in Chief, Papers of James
Madison
University of Virginia

Terry L. Seip
University of Southern California

R. Baird Shuman
University of Illinois at
Urbana-Champaign

William C. Widenor
University of Illinois

Major L. Wilson
Memphis State University

Michael Witkoski
Independent Scholar

The American Presidency

An Overview

It was a formidable task to found the United States. Revolution and domestic turbulence gave way only slowly to an ordered and stable republic. From May 25 through September 17, 1787, fifty-five delegates met in Philadelphia to draft a constitution for a new nation. They had a number of difficult problems to resolve, most of them connected with the extent and distribution of powers in the federal government. A central concern was the office of chief executive: How much power was the president to have? What would be the relationship of the executive to the legislative and judicial branches? Perhaps most significant and far-reaching of all, how was the president to be chosen? The method on which the Founding Fathers finally agreed has served the nation for more than two hundred years, and the presidents elected by that method reflect the development of the United States.

The possibility of having the president elected by direct vote of the people was rejected. The delegates believed that popular elections would be an incentive to demagoguery on the part of potential candidates and factions among the electorate. In addition, the new nation was spread across the breadth of the continent, with travel slow and difficult; under such circumstances, it would be impossible to conduct a nationwide popular election that would not be subject to fraud or open to dispute.

A second possibility was to select the president by means of the various state legislatures, but again, practical difficulties were prohibitive. Would there be an electoral convention every four years? If the state legislatures convened in their separate capitals, how could they agree upon a candidate both known and accepted by a majority?

There was strong support for having the president elected by Congress, which was—at least in theory—the direct representative body of the people. This would give the general population the opportunity to participate in the election process yet would reduce the chance for emotionalism and mob rule. At the same time, this method would mean that the president was selected by the men with whom he would work most closely in governing the nation. Election by Congress, argued its supporters, would give the choice to the most qualified, most knowledgeable, and most concerned segment of the nation.

These very points were the ones raised by opponents to congressional elections. A president selected by the legislature would be dependent upon its members, seeking their favor before the decision and rewarding his supporters after it. As James Madison pointed out, there was agreement that the three branches of the national government would be independent and equal, their powers separate and distinct. If Congress elected the president, then inevitably the legislative and executive powers would be mingled.

The Electoral College
The convention turned to a compromise plan, one which allowed the people to retain a role in presidential elections but which built safe-

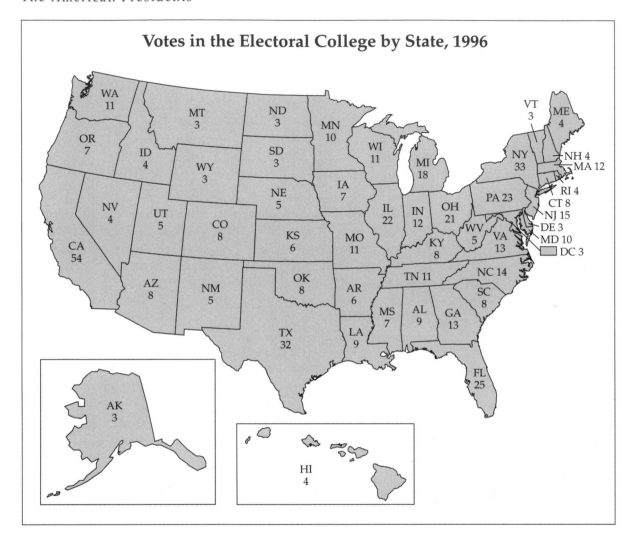

Votes in the Electoral College by State, 1996

guards around the choice. The method was to have a group of electors, chosen by each state, to cast the actual votes for president. These electors were to be chosen in a manner determined by the individual legislatures. Each state was entitled to a number of electors equal to its representation in Congress. Once the electors were chosen, they would vote for president, and the person with the majority of votes from this electoral college would be named to office. The person with the second highest total would be vice president. Should no candidate receive a majority for president, then the House of Representatives, voting by states, would make the decision. In this way, the con-

vention attempted to reconcile the varying interests of the small and large states.

This method was defended in *The Federalist* (number 68), probably by Alexander Hamilton, as having four points to recommend it. First, it did give the people a choice in selecting the president, even if this choice was indirect. Second, it reduced the possibility of corruption and bribery. Third, it removed the president from those persons who had put him into office, thus making favoritism and faction less likely. Finally, it ensured a capable, rather than merely popular, chief executive: "Talents for low intrigue, and the little arts of popularity, may alone suffice to elevate a man to the first honours of a single state; but it will require other talents, and a different kind of merit, to establish him in the esteem and confidence of the whole union."

Since the ratification of the Constitution, the electoral college has undergone several changes, some modifications the result of formal amendments, others from state legislative actions, and some from the evolutionary development of the American political system. In the election of 1796, for example, John Adams received the highest number of votes, and so was elected president; Thomas Jefferson, as the second-place candidate, assumed the office of vice president. Yet Adams and Jefferson were the leaders of rival parties; clearly such a situation was unacceptable. In succeeding elections party loyalty and discipline resolved this type of dilemma.

Party loyalty created its own difficulty in 1800, when all Republican (modern Democratic) electors cast their ballots for Jefferson and Aaron Burr. Their intention had been to elect Jefferson president and Burr vice president, but the ballots were not so marked, since the Constitution had no provision for the separate election of the vice president. The tie was decided by the House of Representatives after thirty-six ballots, and the troublesome issue was resolved by the Twelfth Amendment to the Constitution.

As the years passed, the states made changes in the manner in which electors were chosen. By 1836, all states but South Carolina had adopted some variety of the "general ticket" system, which gave the winner of a state's popular vote all of the state's electoral votes. This method continues to be used in modern elections.

There have been several criticisms of the electoral college: that it is outdated, that it is unnecessary, and that it can lead to the election of presidents who win enough large states to gain an electoral vote majority but who fall behind in the national popular vote. There have

been elections in which the candidate who took a majority in the electoral college did not also have a majority of the popular vote: James K. Polk, Abraham Lincoln, and Woodrow Wilson are three examples. Because this phenomenon occurs when third parties are involved (or, in the case of Lincoln, four contenders), it could be argued that the electoral vote system provides for a more objective measure of decisiveness than a simple count of the popular vote.

In any case, and with only relatively minor adjustments, the electoral college has remained intact for more than two centuries. Its presence has helped to shape the unique pattern and process of American presidential elections.

Washington and the Men of the Revolution

The first five presidents of the United States were of such distinction and accomplishment that they left a legacy of respect for the presidency which involves far more than its immense powers and responsibilities. From Washington through Monroe, these presidents set standards by which succeeding generations have measured chief executives. One of the aims of the Constitutional Convention had been to fashion a government that could remain beyond party politics and the dangers of faction; however, even the generation that had won the Revolution could not submerge the party instinct, which emerged during the first term of the first president.

Not that Washington approved of these forces; on the contrary, he consistently sought to forestall the dangers of faction. While he favored the views of Alexander Hamilton and the rapidly forming Federalist Party, Washington retained in his cabinet Thomas Jefferson and others of the emerging Democratic Republican (modern Democratic) Party. In politics as in war, Washington reached for coalition. His selection as president had been unanimous precisely because of that. Throughout the long and often difficult debate over the Constitution, all sides had tacitly agreed on one point: The first chief executive would be George Washington; there was simply no other figure so universally accepted, so completely trusted. Washington's shaping of the presidency began even before the position was created, and long before he assumed it; his impact was achieved not only through his own actions but through the collective belief and desires of his countrymen as well.

Although these beliefs and desires could find common ground in the person of Washington, their competing natures could not be reconciled within the office of the presidency. Party politics and personal rivalry were quickly and permanently established. Within a few years of the establishment of the new republic, Federalists and Republicans were fighting for local and national offices, drawing up competing agendas, and carrying their battles into the very councils of the president. Washington, fifty-seven and in poor health when he first assumed office in 1789, had originally intended to serve but one term; the increasingly bitter struggle between Hamilton and Jefferson forced him to change his plans, for he recognized his unique position in keeping the new government stable. Once Washington was gone, the rivalries could not be stilled. Washington was the only president elected by unanimous vote of the electoral college; in 1796, his successor, John Adams, only narrowly defeated Thomas Jefferson, 71 to 68. The brief national honeymoon was over.

Adams had an outstanding career in public service before becoming president; it did not save him from political attacks. In some ways, Adams drew these upon himself; he was a brilliant but prickly individual, strong in his belief in freedom but suspicious of too much liberty. Adams and the Federalist Party were mistaken in moving against the tide of Republican and Democratic sentiment: the Alien and Sedition Acts, for example, were a prime

political blunder. Jefferson and the Democratic Republicans instead built a broad-based party reaching from the local to the national level, a solid structure that has made the modern Democratic Party the oldest continuous political party in the world. Its power was felt as early as the election of 1800, when Jefferson exploited a split between Adams and Hamilton to take the White House. Jefferson's reelection four years later was a landslide and marked the beginning of the end for the Federalists.

It is with Jefferson that one can truly gauge the caliber of the nation's early leaders. Washington, even to his contemporaries, was almost more than human, the embodiment of the national ideal. Jefferson, on the other hand, was clearly a man, but a man of extraordinary talent and diversity: statesman, legislator, naturalist, educator, politician, artist, architect, philosopher. He excelled in all these roles, and in that he was unique; he was not unique, however, among his contemporaries, in assaying these various pursuits. A striking difference between the earliest presidents and those who followed is precisely this: From Washington to Monroe, the men were well rounded and experienced in many fields, and the presidency was but one form of their public service.

For Jefferson, Madison, or Monroe, the most pressing issue, that of slavery, was still held in abeyance. Madison's administration was deeply troubled by the unpopular and largely unsuccessful War of 1812, but the sectional dissension which led New England to talk of secession was seemingly forgotten with the election of James Monroe in 1816 and his reelection in 1820 with only one dissenting electoral college vote; the one vote against was cast so that no man might match Washington.

Yet, a look at Monroe's election reveals that the lingering days of revolutionary America were ending. The northern members of the Democratic Party were tired of domination by the Old Dominion. In the meetings of the party's congressional caucus, which then selected the nominee, there was a move to pick a candidate other than Monroe; it failed, but the caucus's lockhold on presidential nominations was seriously questioned. By the election of 1824, the power of the caucus to nominate would be severely weakened; by 1828, its choice would be ignored; and by 1832, the Democratic Party would hold its first national convention.

The Rise of Political Parties and the Coming of the Civil War

The selection of presidents from Monroe to Lincoln was determined by two factors: the rise of political parties and heightening tensions over slavery, which politicians sought to defuse by a series of increasingly desperate compromises. As political parties grew more dominant and professional and as conventions became the method of nominating candidates, there was a tendency to select the nominee most likely to win the election. The practical effect of this was that the least objectional man available was chosen, which frequently meant that the candidate not only had taken few controversial stands but also would be a weak president. Although the intent was to reduce tensions between North and South by avoiding the issue of slavery, the actual result was an escalation of the nation's drift toward conflict. In a sense—and with two notable exceptions—the elections from 1824 to 1860 represented the politics of presidential weakness.

The election of 1824 was a watershed in American political history. The Federalist Party had fallen apart, but the Democrats were in disarray: That year they could not agree on a candidate, and four men waged a vicious campaign for the presidency. John Quincy Adams, son of former president John Adams and himself a distinguished public servant, was perhaps the most experienced and accomplished. His opponents included Henry Clay and other notables, but the most famous was Andrew Jackson, hero of the Battle of New Orleans. Jackson was the first people's candidate, a man

who owed his support not to family or political connections but to his widespread popularity, especially in the South and the West.

This distinguished group promptly entered into a campaign in which personal attacks supplanted debate over public issues, and, when it was over, no one held a majority of electoral or popular votes, although Jackson had run ahead of the rest. The decision was left to the House of Representatives, which chose Adams; Henry Clay was named secretary of state. Jackson's supporters were quick to denounce this "corrupt bargain" and made it the main focus of the election of 1828. By then, Jacksonian forces had taken control of the Democratic Party and formed a majority in Congress. Having established firm discipline over the party organization, the Jackson Democrats conducted the first modern-style campaign, using popular election techniques such as songs, cartoons, symbols (hickory trees in honor of "Old Hickory," Jackson's nickname), mass meetings, and parades. The result was a 178-83 victory in the electoral college for Jackson; a trend had been set for American presidential campaigns.

Jackson was one of the two strong presidents between Monroe and Lincoln; he demonstrated this strength most notably in the stand he took with South Carolina in the nullification crisis of 1832. Had later presidents proved as firm, the drift to civil war might have been prevented, but few of the presidents who followed had Jackson's toughness. Martin Van Buren, his chosen successor, was a genius at party politics but hardly an inspiring national leader.

A new party, the Whigs, followed the lead of the Democrats by building their local base in preparation for an assault on the White House in 1840. They had a good issue—the economic crisis of 1837—and a popular candidate in William Henry Harrison, hero of the Indian wars, who stumped the country, making numerous appearances, and won the election.

Two traditional themes have determined

5

American presidential elections: economic conditions at home and dangers abroad. In 1840, the Whigs had economics on their side; in 1844, the Democrats returned to power over the issue of annexing Texas. The Democrats favored annexation; the Whigs were opposed. In its stand, each party followed the sentiment of the region where its strength lay: Democrats, the South, which wanted new land for slave states; Whigs, the North, which opposed spread of the system.

Two particular aspects of the 1844 election made it notable. The Democrats nominated James K. Polk, the first "dark horse" candidate. Polk had a distinguished career, including Speaker of the House of Representatives, but in 1844 he was only hoping for the vice presidential nod. When the Democrats could not choose one of their front runners, he was the convention's compromise choice. The second aspect was the impact of a third party. Harrison had died shortly after assuming office, but the Whigs had not nominated his successor, John Tyler, choosing Henry Clay instead. Tyler formed a new party to support his independent candidacy, and his efforts may have cost Clay enough votes to swing the electoral count in favor of Polk. Ever since, this spoiler effect has been the traditional role of third parties in American presidential politics.

Polk was the second strong president between Monroe and Lincoln, and he successfully conducted the Mexican War, adding enormous territory to the nation. Although the Whigs had been unenthusiastic about the war, they used it to win the White House in 1848, nominating General Zachary Taylor. It was neither the first nor the last time that success in combat would pave the way to the presidency. With a popular figure leading the ticket, the Whigs were able to dodge the increasingly divisive issue of slavery. The Democrats, on the other hand, were deeply split by the problem, and their division ensured the election of Taylor.

In the election of 1852, both Whigs and Democrats mirrored the nation, as they tried to find one more compromise to hold the sections together, while in each party increasingly strong factions pressed for an ultimate resolution. Seeking to restrain their firebrands, both parties nominated middle-of-the-road candidates. After fifty-three ballots, the Whigs selected Winfield Scott, another Mexican War general, while the Democrats went with Franklin Pierce of New Hampshire, chosen on the forty-ninth ballot. Pierce was a "doughface," a Northerner who sympathized with the South; he owed his victory to strong support in the South and residual Democratic strength in the North; it was the last election in which the fiction of compromise could be maintained.

The year 1856 was the first time an elected president was denied renomination by his party. Pierce had proven unable to reconcile the two sections of the Democratic Party, much less the nation, so the Democrats turned to James Buchanan, who had served in the House, the Senate, and as secretary of state. In spite of his impressive record, Buchanan was a weak and indecisive man. His opponent was no Whig, but the first nominee of the new Republican Party, John Charles Frémont.

For a new party, the Republicans made an outstanding effort; significantly, they presented a more coherent political philosophy than the Democrats, especially on the issue of slavery. While the Republicans were by no means total abolitionists, they were unified in their opposition to slavery, particularly its spread into new territories. By contrast, the Democratic Party was unable to confront, much less resolve, the issue. By 1860, the party had exhausted its moral and political reserve; like the nation, the Democrats had finally run out of compromises and evasions over slavery.

The Democrats met that year in Charleston, South Carolina. Their strongest candidate was Stephen A. Douglas, best known for his recent series of debates with Abraham Lincoln. Southern Democrats feared that he was not sufficiently committed to the protection and expansion of slavery; they deadlocked the convention. The Democrats left Charleston without a candidate and by the end of the summer had divided into three factions, each with its own nominee. This split virtually assured the election of the Republican candidate.

Before the Republican convention, it was generally thought that that nominee would be William H. Seward, the nationally known party leader. Seward, however, had liabilities: Some Republicans feared that he would be too soft on slavery, while others, recalling Seward's speech calling war between the sections an "irrepressible conflict," worried that his candidacy would wreck their chances in the vital border states. The Republicans who met in Chicago realized that they could nominate the next president, if they chose the right candidate. They chose Abraham Lincoln.

Abraham Lincoln

The election of 1860 was a four-man race that split along sectional as well as party lines. The Democrats divided into Northern and Southern branches, with Stephen Douglas heading the Northern faction and John C. Breckinridge as the nominee of the Southern Democrats. In addition, a hasty coalition named the Constitutional Union Party was formed, with John Bell as its candidate. Basically, these three candidates were competing for the same voters, with only Stephen Douglas having much opportunity to make inroads on Lincoln's potential strength.

The election revealed how deeply split the nation was. Bell carried the border states of Kentucky, Tennessee, and Virginia, while Breckinridge won the rest of the slave states. Douglas polled large amounts nationwide, but his totals were scattered so that he carried only Missouri. As for Lincoln, he won all of the Northern and Western free states, with the exception of New Jersey, and there he took four of the eleven electoral votes. This gave Lincoln 180 electoral votes, a majority, although his

popular vote total was less than 40 percent of all ballots cast. Lincoln had carried no Southern state and had hardly registered any votes in the region, since the Republicans were identified and feared as the vehicle of the abolitionists.

Although Lincoln made no attempt to hide his opposition to slavery and particularly its spread into new territories, he had certainly not campaigned on a platform of immediate abolition. The South, however, had virtually made the election a referendum on the continued existence of the Union, and the terms were quite simple: The election of Lincoln was unacceptable and would be regarded as cause for secession. In a sense, this was the final installment in a pattern of political blackmail in which the South had engaged for several generations. Feeling threatened and beleaguered, the South had convinced itself that any compromise on the slavery question would be fatal to its economic and social institutions. For years the rest of the country had acceded to this, preferring to retain the Union, imperfect as it was. The rise of the Republican Party had changed that, and Lincoln's election was a call for redefinition of the compact of the Union. Whether this could have been accomplished peacefully is a moot point, for the Southern states precipitated the war by secession.

As Lincoln's election in 1860 was a referendum on the Union, his reelection campaign in 1864 was a vote upon conduct of the war. After three years of struggle, the casualty lists were long, Union victories had not proved decisive, and there was a strong movement toward peace, through either compromise with the South or acceptance of an independent Confederacy. The Democrats had become known as the peace party, and it was widely believed that their nominee—General George B. McClellan, former commander in chief of the Union armies—would reach some accommodation with the South if elected. Lincoln's chances were linked with success on the battlefield and the will of the North to continue the struggle.

The fall of Atlanta in September was a signal of victory and reinforced Northern desire to see the conflict to a successful conclusion. Lincoln's resounding triumph, 212 electoral votes to 21, indicated that popular sentiment was in accord with the president's determination to preserve the Union, despite the costs and regardless of the burdens.

Lincoln, like Franklin D. Roosevelt, stands beyond the considerations of conventional politics. Both men took office at times when the nation seemed to have reached the end of its tether, and the American experiment was in danger of coming to an ignominious, perhaps violent, end. Yet both tapped resources that other, less visionary politicians had abandoned, and so preserved the nation.

The Aftermath of War
Following the Civil War, it might have seemed that the future of the Democratic Party was bleak; indeed, the Republicans won five of the next seven presidential elections. Yet only one was a decisive victory, and with the shifting of only a few thousand popular votes, the Democrats might have swept six out of the seven.

In 1868, the Republicans seemed to have the perfect candidate in Ulysses S. Grant. By contrast, the Democrats had no war hero, nor could they point to an unquestionable role in the conflict; they turned to party leader Horatio Seymour, hoping that he could assure the votes of his native New York, a rich electoral prize. In the campaign the Republicans first waved the "bloody shirt," recalling the suffering of the Civil War in order to associate the Democrats with the rebellion. Instead of the landslide that the Republicans had expected, however, the election was close, proving the surprising resilience of the Democratic Party.

By 1872, the corruption of the Grant administration was so excessive that an entire

wing of the party, the Liberal Republicans, bolted to join with the Democrats in nominating newspaper editor Horace Greeley. The regular Republicans renominated Grant; to repudiate a sitting president would mean admitting that the charges of their opponents were correct, the spoils of office had grown too tempting, and black votes from the Southern states under Reconstruction could be depended upon to provide the margin of victory.

By 1876, moderate Republicans welcomed the tradition against a third term as a method to force the choice of a candidate less tainted than Grant. Reformers and traditional party members deadlocked the convention, which turned to Rutherford B. Hayes, a third-term but otherwise obscure Ohio governor. During this period, such struggles for control of the Republican Party were frequent; they ended with a compromise candidate, reformers defused, and the money and big business powers securely in control of the party.

The Democrats chose Samuel J. Tilden, another New Yorker. Once again, the strength of the Democratic organization and the popular revulsion with the corruption of Grant's two terms were clear: The popular vote was solidly in Tilden's favor, and the outcome in the electoral college hinged on the contested votes from three Southern states, Louisiana, Florida, and South Carolina. If the Republicans lost any of these states, they lost the White House; only if they carried all three could Hayes win by a single electoral vote. The scene was set for a deal and a deal was made, revolving around the removal of federal troops from the South. A special election commission was formed to decide the disputed votes; it had eight Republicans and seven Democrats, and every vote was strictly along party lines. On March 2, 1877, only two days before inauguration, Hayes was finally declared president. It was during his term that the last federal troops were withdrawn from the South.

In 1880, control of the Republican Party was

again an issue, and when reformers and hard-liners had exhausted themselves after thirty-six ballots, Congressman James A. Garfield of Ohio was chosen. In many respects, Garfield was a typical Republican candidate of the period: A Civil War general with respectable service in state and congressional politics, he stressed that he had risen from a poor family, at one time working as a barge driver on Midwestern canals. This was the keynote in Garfield's campaign biography, *From Canal Boy to President*, written by that relentless chronicler of American opportunity, Horatio Alger. This election institutionalized the myth of humble beginnings for the presidential candidate. William Henry Harrison had made great play with his log cabin birthplace in 1840, and Lincoln's tenure as a rail-splitter had quickly entered election folklore; after Garfield, it became nearly essential that a candidate claim the supposedly ennobling experience of poverty in his youth as a prerequisite to the Oval Office. Such a view is in contrast to the backgrounds of earlier presidents, such as Washington, the Adamses, and the Virginians, who were established and well connected and who valued family traditions as much as individual initiative. American elections were moving toward a more populist and democratic system—at least on the surface, since the childhoods and characters of Garfield's backers and financial supporters went unrecounted in any campaign biography.

The Democrats selected Winfield Scott Hancock, whose war record more than matched his opponent's: Garfield had served honorably, but Hancock had played a decisive role at the Battle of Gettysburg. At the same time, the removal of federal troops had created the "Solid South," which would be a Democratic stronghold; the Republicans won not a single Southern state in 1880, nor would they until well into the twentieth century. The Democrats thus had an excellent opportunity, and out of some 9.2 million votes cast, Hancock came within 8,000 ballots of winning. His loss was largely attributable to a recurring situation in the American political system: a third party.

In American politics, third parties have tended to arise out of intense but short-lived dissatisfaction with a particular situation and the perceived failure of the two existing major parties to deal with it. Third parties are able to capitalize on voter frustration, but only for a relatively short period of time. They lack the organization and discipline needed for a sustained effort. In this sense, third parties are agents for political protest rather than political power, and in the national arena their effect has always been to deny the presidency to someone else rather than win it for their own candidates. Ironically, they frequently ensure the defeat of the candidate more attuned to their particular views. This was certainly the case in 1880, when the Greenback Party was active. Formed in opposition to the restrictive monetary policies of the Republicans, which had led to economic hardships for the middle and lower classes, the Greenbacks drew away voters who would otherwise have gone Democratic. Enough defected to make the difference in the electoral votes in key states to allow Garfield to win.

The campaign of 1884 was a study in contrasts. The Republicans chose James G. Blaine, the "Plumed Knight." Although a leader in the Senate and the party, Blaine was mistrusted by many, especially for his more questionable financial dealings. His opponent was Grover Cleveland, who had begun his political career as a sheriff in New York State and had gone on to become the honest, hardworking mayor of Buffalo and then governor of New York. Cleveland's honesty was almost painful and might have wrecked another man's political career; against Blaine, it was the Democrats' greatest asset.

The contest between the urbane, polished senator and the bluff, forthright governor was focused on two issues, economics and personal character. Economically, the two parties fol-

9

lowed their traditional platforms, with the Republicans favoring big business and special interests and the Democrats championing the small businessman, farmers, and the middle and lower classes. There was nothing new in this, and it has remained a constant party division even into contemporary elections. In 1884 the main issue was character. Blaine and his strategists sought to defuse mistrust over his character by attacks on Cleveland, making special use of the fact that the Democratic nominee, while a young man, might have fathered an illegitimate child. "Ma, Ma, where's my pa?" was the chant the Republicans used to keep the matter before the public. When Cleveland's managers asked what to say about the incident, Cleveland's reply was characteristic: "Whatever you do, tell the truth." Responding to such personal integrity, the voters gave Cleveland victory in November.

Four years out of power sharpened the appetites of the special interests that controlled the Republican Party. In 1888, their nominee was Benjamin Harrison, another Civil War general popular with veterans. Labor unrest offered the Republicans the opportunity to campaign against "anarchy." Seldom were the economic divisions between the two parties more clearly drawn, and in 1888 the configuration favored the Grand Old Party. Four years later, the same candidates and the same issues put Cleveland back in the White House. The difference was that the country had moved into a new era, leaving behind elections determined by memory of Civil War and entering a period of new economic and social forces.

The Modern Presidency Begins

With the presidency of William McKinley, American politics moved into the modern era. There had been professional politicians before McKinley—indeed, one of the strengths of the Democratic Party was its core of officeholders—and there had been organizations dedicated to the cause of a single candidate—again,

the Democrats had done it first, as far back as Andrew Jackson—but there had never been politicians and organizations such as those that placed McKinley in the White House in 1896. What made the difference was not McKinley's public service but his friendship with Marcus A. Hanna, an Ohio businessman. The two formed a potent combination: McKinley had popular charm and presence, and Hanna brought enormous financial resources and business connections. Together they fashioned strategies that made McKinley the inevitable nominee of the 1896 Republican convention.

By contrast, the Democrats selected their candidate because of circumstance, oratory, and the genius of the moment. The central issue of the campaign was economics, specifically hard currency, backed by gold, versus soft money, backed by silver. The Republicans followed the lead of big business and opted for gold: hard currency kept down inflation and raised profits. It also brought high unemployment and difficulties for small business, the farmers, and the working class—the natural constituency of the Democrats. The Democratic convention found its nominee when William Jennings Bryan delivered his famous "cross of gold" speech, and the resulting election pitted an impassioned but outmaneuvered Democratic crusade against a coolly organized and well-financed Republican onslaught.

The Democrats had ensured that they would continue to move in a more populist and progressive fashion. Although this led to defeat in 1896, it proved to be the course that would bring the Democrats to power during times when they would shape modern America. By contrast, the Republicans and big business further strengthened their ties, believing that only their union and hold on power brought national prosperity, but this philosophy was being undermined by growing popular resentment at the excesses of industry and capital. The strength of the progressive movement during the last decade of the century caused a shift in Republican strategy, as the link between the party and big business was masked, but not broken, especially during the presidency and election campaign of Theodore Roosevelt.

Roosevelt, who had come to the White House upon the assassination of McKinley, had a reputation as a progressive, a reformer who was prepared to support legislation that would put restraints upon the more high-handed actions of large corporations. This orientation was more image than substance, however, and during his election campaign of 1904, Roosevelt moved quickly to compromise his "progressive" views with Republican conservatives and their allies among the business community.

Roosevelt had ruled out another term in 1908, so his handpicked successor, William Howard Taft, was the Republican nominee. After Taft's election, it was not long before Roosevelt had broken with him and was busy seeking a third term. Publicly, the rift was caused by Taft's failure to follow in the progressive line; actually, the cause was Roosevelt's desire to return to power, and his recognition that 1912 was an excellent year for a progressive candidate.

Roosevelt was counting on the threat of a progressive split from the Republican Party if Taft were renominated, but Roosevelt had underestimated Taft's abilities, which proved quite formidable: Taft became the first sitting president to take part in the new primary process, and he did well enough to win renomination on the first ballot. Enraged, Roosevelt and his supporters bolted to form the Progressive Party, known to its friends as the Bull Moose Party and to more detached observers as the Moosevelt Party.

The split gave victory to the Democratic candidate, Thomas Woodrow Wilson, a scholar, author, and former president of Princeton University. He had come to politics relatively late, but once in office, as governor of New Jersey, Wilson became the nation's chief exponent of modern progressive thought; he was an intel-

lectual rather an emotional leader, but it was clear that the voters responded to his integrity and vision.

A Democratic majority in Congress allowed Wilson to put into place the key elements of his "New Freedom," a distillation of major populist and liberal ideals. The thrust of these reforms was blunted by the outbreak of World War I and the eventual involvement of the United States in the conflict. Having campaigned on a peace platform in 1916 ("He kept us out of war," was the Democratic slogan), Wilson considered the war a calamity, but he saw in the Allied victory an unparalleled opportunity to fashion a better world, guided by international cooperation secured through the League of Nations.

Fearful of further foreign entanglements, Republicans and conservative Democrats rejected the League, and controversy over it formed a large part of the 1920 campaign. The Republicans linked rejection with an even greater desire of the American people to return to "normalcy." The Republicans tapped this sentiment in their candidate, and after eight years of a high-minded and demanding professor, the American voter got Warren G. Harding.

Harding won by more than seven million votes, but his administration was the most corrupt since Grant's. The knowledge that cabinet officers had prostituted public trust for personal profit should have been an unbeatable issue for the Democrats in 1924, but the death of Harding removed much of the focus of the scandal, while the Republican nominee, Vice President Calvin Coolidge, was a walking, barely talking example of Yankee rectitude. Economic prosperity continued at an unprecedentedly high rate; little wonder that voters responded to the Republican slogan "Keep cool with Coolidge."

There is a tendency in the Democratic Party to move toward the populist, more liberal viewpoint and widen its base to include more of the electorate. This is especially true in defeat, and the party illustrated this tendency in 1928, when its members chose Al Smith of New York as the Democratic presidential nominee. Smith represented the urban voters, with their emigrant backgrounds, and his nomination was a signal that the Democrats sought to be an inclusive party. Smith represented change; Herbert Hoover, the Republican, was the embodiment of the status quo. Hoover's victory relied on the contrast between these two but was mainly based on good economic times—and those times were about to end, and end badly.

Franklin D. Roosevelt

Shortly after Franklin D. Roosevelt was elected president in 1932, a friend told him, "If you succeed, you will be the greatest president this country has ever had." Roosevelt replied, "And if I fail, I shall be its last."

When Roosevelt took office, the nation was in the midst of what has become known as the Great Depression: One quarter of the work force was unemployed; banks had failed throughout the country, wiping out the life savings of hundreds of thousands; breadlines and soup kitchens ministered to thousands of urban poor; and farm families were forced from their homes. In Washington, D.C., fifteen thousand work veterans camped on the banks of the Anacostia River, petitioning Congress for their bonus pay from World War I. President Hoover had the veterans dispersed and their camp destroyed by the Army. Across the nation there was real fear that the United States was sliding into revolution.

This was the situation when the Democrats convened in Chicago. The prime candidate was Roosevelt, then governor of New York. Roosevelt had already won recognition as the leader of the progressive wing of the party, and his efforts in New York to provide relief for victims of the Depression stood in stark contrast to the deadening inaction of the Hoover administration. Roosevelt was nomi-

nated on the fourth ballot. In a break with conventional protocol, he flew to Chicago to accept the nomination in person; it was the first indication of the dramatic, innovative nature of the coming presidency. Projecting energy and optimism, Roosevelt won handily, building an electoral college advantage over Hoover of 472 to 59.

Roosevelt's first term was a whirlwind of activity: Starting with the Hundred Days, FDR and the Democratic Congress pushed through a wide variety of measures, programs, and legislation called the New Deal. Some of these worked well; others were less effective; some, such as the National Recovery Act, were declared unconstitutional. While these activities did not end the Depression—it took the economic impetus of World War II to accomplish that—they did blunt its worst effects. Even more important, Roosevelt gave the country hope.

The country resoundingly approved FDR's efforts in 1936, when he was reelected in the largest landslide to that time: He carried every state except Maine and Vermont, and the Democrats increased their hold on Congress. One of the most enduring political legacies of Roosevelt's first term was the powerful coalition that he forged among old and new elements of the Democratic Party. The farmers in the West and South were won by federal programs supporting agriculture; blacks deserted the Republicans to join with the party that offered them equal economic opportunities in the new relief programs; ethnics, urban voters, and Catholics were also recipients of attention from the Roosevelt administration, after long years of neglect by the Republicans. Finally, organized labor, then just coming into its own, became a keystone in the Democratic edifice. This combination of forces not only allowed FDR to continue the programs of the New Deal but also established the American political landscape for a generation.

During Roosevelt's second term, focus

shifted from domestic issues to the growing threat of war. As Adolf Hitler moved to rearm Germany and expand in Europe, Roosevelt pressed for increased buildup of American might, and support for Great Britain. While these actions raised the ire of isolationists, they were applauded by a majority of Americans, including the 1940 Republican nominee, Wendell Willkie.

Willkie had taken the Republican nomination in an unexpected, grassroots campaign. A businessman, a liberal, and an internationalist, Willkie had few disagreements with Roosevelt or his efforts to aid Great Britain. The major issue in the campaign was the fact that Roosevelt was running for a third term; since Washington, there had been an unspoken prohibition against this, and the change troubled many, even some of FDR's strong supporters. Roosevelt's margin of victory shrank to five million votes, but he still carried the electoral college by a large majority, and the Democrats remained in control of the House and Senate.

War came to America in 1941, and Roosevelt turned from the New Deal to matters of strategy. During the conflict he was, in a literal as well as constitutional sense, the commander in chief of American forces, and the broad scope of American strategy, including the "Europe first" emphasis, was Roosevelt's. By 1944, the United States and its allies were on the verge of victory, and Roosevelt was nominated for a fourth term; he was reelected by his smallest margin, defeating Republican nominee Thomas Dewey by less than three million votes. Four months after his inauguration, Roosevelt was dead, a victim of a cerebral hemorrhage.

Roosevelt was a richly contradictory man: born to wealth, he became the champion of the poor and the needy; crippled by polio, he was tempered and deepened by his affliction; attacked by some as a dictator, he was among the most popular and democratic of presidents. His twelve years in office changed the presi-

dency and the nation more than any other presidency since Lincoln's.

The Contemporary Presidency

Post-World War II presidential elections have gone through two phases: a transition period under Harry S Truman and Dwight D. Eisenhower, and the subsequent rise of a new phenomenon in American politics, the permanent candidate. This second development was closely and perhaps inevitably linked with the spread of modern media, in particular television, which has transformed elections, the style in which they are conducted, and the candidates they favor.

Truman was vice president in 1944 largely through domestic political considerations. A product of the rough school of Missouri Democratic politics, Truman was generally regarded as honest and competent, but he was not believed to have any extraordinary qualities, especially when compared to Franklin D. Roosevelt. Hence, he surprised many by the statesmanlike manner in which he filled the office. The decision to use atomic weapons to end the war with Japan, his firm stance with the Soviets, and his sponsorship of the Marshall Plan to rebuild Europe were major accomplishments. Indispensable as these are to Truman's presidency, his place in American political history is assured by his dramatic reelection.

By 1948, Truman and the Democrats had fallen alarmingly low in the polls. Many Americans seemed ready for a change; the Democrats had been in office since 1932, and the country had weathered the most serious depression and greatest war in its history. Truman, by his connection with the Roosevelt presidency, suffered both by being linked to Roosevelt's failings and by comparison to FDR's successes. More than that, he seemed determined to continue the policies of change and innovation begun by the New Deal, leading in areas where even FDR had hardly entered, most notably civil rights.

13

In 1948, as in 1860, the Democratic Party split over the fundamental issue of blacks in American society. In 1860, the Southern Democrats had fought to preserve slavery; in 1948, they battled to continue segregation. The difference was that Truman and enough of the national Democrats refused to back away from their moral commitment, even when J. Strom Thurmond of South Carolina led disaffected Southerners into the short-lived Dixiecrat Party (officially known as the States' Rights Party). Standing firm on the civil rights plank was a courageous decision for Truman; he was facing a difficult election, and the votes of the traditionally Democratic South could easily be the deciding factor, especially since he had already alienated the more liberal wing of the party. Henry Wallace, whom Truman had replaced as vice president, had yoked various elements to form yet another progressive party, that perennial vehicle of American populist aspirations. Wallace would draw away many liberal voters; Thurmond would capture the Deep South; the national Democrats were in disarray, and Truman's own popularity was sinking—no wonder the Republicans sensed victory.

They renominated Thomas Dewey, who conducted a campaign that was basically a prelude to his inauguration. Truman took his cause directly to the American people. In a time before the electronic media brought the candidate into millions of living rooms, Truman literally crossed the country in person, conducting a whistle-stop campaign during which he lambasted the Republicans and richly earned his slogan, "Give 'em hell, Harry." His victory in November was a triumph of personal, traditional politics, with his popular vote total matching his rivals' combined strengths and his electoral vote count easily leading theirs.

The personal victory of Truman was repeated, but for different reasons, in the back-to-back triumphs of Dwight D. (Ike) Eisenhower. The popular hero of World War II, Eisenhower had been courted by both parties, but when it became apparent that his inclinations led him to the Republicans, there ensued yet another round in the struggle for control of the Grand Old Party. The true believers were lined behind Senator Robert A. Taft of Ohio, but the pragmatic professionals recognized that Taft would probably lose the election, whereas Eisenhower would almost certainly win. In the end, a potentially fatal convention battle was avoided and the Taft loyalists, while bitter, rallied behind Ike as the nominee.

Against a popular and victorious war hero, the Democrats probably had slight chance of retaining the White House; still, they nominated their best-qualified candidate: Adlai Stevenson, the governor of Illinois. Stevenson was brilliant, humorous, and eloquent, and has been described as "the best president the United States never had." He had no chance against Eisenhower, either in 1952 or when the two were rematched in 1956. The personal popularity of Eisenhower, the peace and prosperity which settled over the nation, and the simple desire to enjoy that peace were far more potent factors than any campaign issues devised by either party.

By 1960, the nation was on the threshold of a new style in presidential politics. There were several reasons for this shift: Eisenhower's personal popularity could not be transferred; even as president, he could not carry a majority in Congress, prompting one wit to remark, "There are no coattails on an Eisenhower jacket." There was also a consensus that it was time for American to get moving again; after all, it was the second half of the twentieth century. In addition, television had transformed the political process: It made elections faster, longer, and more calculated.

The candidate who exemplified this change was John F. Kennedy, and in a sense, he was the first of the permanent candidates, having decided in 1956 to run for the 1960 presidential nomination. There had been lengthy and well-devised campaigns before, but none conducted with the skill, tenacity, or flair of Kennedy's. Young, attractive, intelligent, and well financed, Kennedy edged out his party rivals who attacked him on traditional lines: that he was too young, that he lacked a record in the Senate, that he was a Catholic and could not carry the South or West. By accepting the challenge and making himself the focus of the campaign, Kennedy simply made most of these attacks irrelevant. In a similar fashion, the election itself, which pitted Kennedy against Vice President Richard Nixon, revolved around competing images.

Nixon was certainly no stranger to the politics of image; he had retained his spot on the 1952 Republican ticket with his famous Checkers speech, portraying himself as an honest man unfairly attacked. Nixon's problem, however, was that his talent for imagery was purely negative; he could not match Kennedy's optimistic visions and instead evoked the supposedly inevitable ruin that would follow a Democratic victory. It was a typical Nixon tactic and would work for him in 1968 and in 1972, when his opponents gave him enough substance to make his charges creditable. It failed in 1960, when the American voters narrowly preferred the politics of optimism and Kennedy's New Frontier.

The key point in Kennedy's victory was the style of his campaign. Although issues would change, the essential method was fixed: The successful candidate would establish an appealing image within a short period of time, mixing a shrewd combination of voters' perceptions and actual substance. The vehicle for the message was television, which presented short messages on the same theme, endlessly repeated. In a sense, the candidate became the image.

The first full-fledged example was in 1964. Lyndon Johnson had assumed the presidency after Kennedy's assassination and had replaced the New Frontier with the Great Society, an ambitious mélange of social, economic, and civil rights programs designed to rival the New Deal of Franklin D. Roosevelt. Johnson could rightly claim the image of a social progressive, a president of consensus. His rival, Barry Goldwater, was leader of the far-right wing of the Republican Party, which had taken control of the party after yet another internecine struggle. Aided by Goldwater's intemperate statements, Johnson and the Democrats had little difficulty in portraying the Republican as a dangerous, warlike individual who would reverse progress in civil rights and wreck Social Security. The result was a landslide for Johnson and what appeared to be a period of Democratic ascendancy. Yet, within four years, Johnson was practically driven from the White House and Richard Nixon had been elected president.

Once again, a campaign of images had been waged. The Democrats, badly split over the war in Vietnam, had seen their Chicago convention turn into a battle between delegates, demonstrators, and the police; worse, the entire country had seen it too, on their television sets. When Hubert Humphrey emerged as the nominee, his campaign was flawed by this burning image and the pain of an unsuccessful, apparently endless war in Southeast Asia. Nixon— the "new Nixon"—fashioned a persona that was presidential: He had a plan to end the war, he declared, but he could not reveal it. In a close decision, the American voters preferred vague Republican potential to the Democratic record.

Four years later, Nixon repeated the campaign of image, this time even more successfully, since it is fairly easy to appear presidential when one is actually the president. Unfortunately for Nixon and the Republicans, the image of a president ending wars and establishing peaceful relations with Communist China was replaced by that of a president engaging in third-rate burglaries and covering up crimes. So deep was the revulsion with Watergate across the country that the next successful candidate, Jimmy Carter, won in large part because he ran as an outsider, the candidate *not* from Washington, D.C.

Carter's theme and image were good ones, and he rode them to victory in 1976 against the hapless Gerald R. Ford, but in 1980 these very weapons were turned against Carter by a much more skillful player, Ronald Reagan. In a way, Reagan was the epitome of the post-FDR presidential candidate. He had enough background in government to demonstrate competence, but not so much as to be seen as merely another professional politician. He was skilled and at ease before the cameras, and appeared to believe, even if he did not fully understand, what he said. Finally, he was adept at discerning what image the American people seemed to desire and presenting it to them. This is a talent all successful politicians have possessed, but few have shown Reagan's mastery in demonstrating it so consistently and to such a vast audience. Not since Franklin D. Roosevelt has the country felt so close to one man.

Ronald Reagan and His Legacy

After surviving an assassination attempt early in his first term, Reagan first challenged organized labor by firing striking air traffic controllers who had followed their union off their jobs to protest working conditions. Despite the difficulties which followed, Reagan persisted and inflicted a severe blow on the American labor community. He then moved to dismantle much of the traditional machinery of government. His most ambitious, and far-reaching, goals were a series of drastic, across-the-board tax cuts and a rapid increase in military spending. The two combined to produce a spiraling federal deficit that, in a few years, moved the United States from the world's largest creditor nation to its greatest debtor. At the same time, however, the arms buildup forced the Soviet Union to increase its own military spending, eventually wrecking the Soviet economy.

The United States was spared a similar fate by its innate economic strength, but the growing deficit plagued Reagan's second term, causing turmoil on the stock market. Still, the president and his allies in Congress pledged to "stay the course" in their belief that the unfettered free market system would ultimately be vindicated. Even if minor problems were encountered, they argued, government properly had no major role to play in correcting them. Although Reagan often evoked the name of Franklin Delano Roosevelt, his two terms were largely dedicated to undoing much of the heritage of the New Deal. However, it was a legacy not to be undone, as Reagan gradually learned and which his vice president and successor discovered.

Elected in 1988 to continue the Reagan Revolution, George Herbert Walker Bush had boldly pledged, "Read my lips: No new taxes." However, after only one month in office he had to propose a plan to bail out the threatened savings and loan industry by raising taxes. Bush agreed to tax increases in 1990, which further incited the anger of Reagan loyalists. Bush also faced an increasingly stagnant economy, crippled by continued deficits. The bright spot for the Bush presidency was the brief Persian Gulf War, which united a coalition of European and Middle Eastern states against the aggression of Iraq under its leader, Saddam Hussein. However, even this victory paled as Americans realized that Hussein, although defeated, remained in power and a threat to U.S. interests in the area.

By 1992, the American electorate was restive, even rebellious. Bush found himself under scornful attack from the right wing of the Republican Party, challenged by wealthy independent candidate Ross Perot, and facing in Bill Clinton a Democratic candidate who had claimed the vital center ground of American politics. As Bush's reelection campaign foundered, he grew more shrill, trying to discredit Clinton's character and questioning his patriotism. Intensely partisan rhetoric had returned to the presidential election process; soon, it would spread to all aspects of national government.

After Clinton's election with a minority of the popular vote in 1992, Republicans set out to undo his victory. The proposed Clinton health care reforms drew the fire of the insurance and health care industries and eventually died. Meanwhile, congressional opponents demanded investigation of alleged Clinton offenses in what became known as "Whitewater," an old and tangled real estate development project in Arkansas. When Republicans gained control of the House and Senate in 1994 (the first time they had done so in forty years), their attacks on the president increased, finally resulting in the appointment of Independent Prosecutor Kenneth Starr, who used all means available to secure the president's impeachment. Despite, or perhaps because of, Clinton's easy reelection in 1996, the partisan attacks continued.

However, for many Americans clearly the partisanship had gone too far. In the 1998 congressional elections, the Republicans tried to make Clinton's impeachment the centerpiece of their campaigns. The result was a serious defeat that almost cost them their majority in the House and caused the resignation of their belligerent and abrasive Speaker, Newt Gingrich. Undeterred, Starr and House Republicans pushed on, finally bringing about President Clinton's impeachment on two counts, of perjury and obstruction of justice, on December 19, 1998. Ironically, the impeachment drama reached its end on February 12, 1999, just before President's Day weekend, when the Senate, sitting as a jury, found William Jefferson Clinton "not guilty" on both counts. Despite Republican control of the Senate, the House's impeachment articles could not even muster a simple majority. It seemed to many observers that the politics of partisanship had reached its inevitable conclusion. The country had simply had enough.

As the century neared its end and the United States prepared for the new millennium, the American presidency remained somehow the same, yet fundamentally changed. The office still retained immense power and prestige, despite the attacks its most recent occupants had endured. At the same time, the presidency increasingly had to share power with Congress, making its role something closer to that envisioned by the drafters of the Constitution. Perhaps most important, the presidency was increasingly seen as the only elective position for which all Americans can cast a vote, and therefore was regarded more than ever as uniquely "the people's office."

Michael Witkoski

George Washington

1st President, 1789-1797

Born: February 22, 1732
Bridges Creek, Westmoreland
County, Virginia
Died: December 14, 1799
Mount Vernon, Virginia

Political Party: Federalist
Vice President: John Adams

Cabinet Members

Secretary of State: Thomas Jefferson, Edmund Randolph, Timothy Pickering
Secretary of the Treasury: Alexander Hamilton, Oliver Wolcott, Jr.
Secretary of War: Henry Knox, Timothy Pickering, James McHenry
Attorney General: Edmund Randolph, William Bradford, Charles Lee

George Washington stands unique among presidents of the United States in the near unanimity with which politically influential Americans agreed that he should be elected. No other president has enjoyed a comparable degree of public confidence upon entering the office, and few if any other presidents have had equal scope for defining the chief executive's place in the federal government and the nation's life. The symbolic prestige attached to the presidency comes not only from its constitutionally defined powers but also from the implicit expectation that each new incumbent may achieve some of the unifying popular respect commanded by Washington.

The Character of a Leader: Ambition and Self-Control

Rather than deriving this respect from his position as president, Washington brought to the

Washington's official portrait. *(White House Historical Society)*

Washington and his family at home, by Currier & Ives. *(Library of Congress)*

office the esteem he had won personally by virtue of his character and career. Little in Washington's youth gave promise of the exceptional stature he later attained; yet, beginning in those early years, he developed the circumspection and reliability that became integral to his public career. Washington was born February 22, 1732 (New Style), in Westmoreland County on the northern neck of Virginia, near the Potomac River. His mother, Mary Ball Washington, was the second wife of Augustine Washington. Augustine's grandfather John had emigrated from England to Virginia in 1657-1658. George was eleven years old when his father died. Augustine's adult son by an earlier marriage, Lawrence Washington, filled some of the role of a father for George until Lawrence died in 1752. First by lease and then by ownership, Lawrence's estate, Mount Vernon, became

George's property and his preferred home for the rest of his life.

Washington grew to adulthood in an agricultural, slaveholding society that combined the stability of a self-perpetuating gentry leadership with the volatility of expanding settlement, immigration, and natural population increase. Through Lawrence's marriage to the daughter of Colonel William Fairfax, George came into contact with the comparatively cosmopolitan proprietary family, including Thomas Lord Fairfax, whose holdings included much of northernmost Virginia as far west as the Shenandoah Valley. The prospective value of this land lay in peopling it with tenants or buyers. Washington worked with a Fairfax surveying team in the Shenandoah Valley in 1748 and was appointed Culpeper County surveyor in 1749. Like other surveyors, the eighteen-year-old acquired land on his own account, in addition to inheriting Ferry Farm, which had belonged to his father. Washington was a home-taught and self-taught youth; he did not attend college. His reading tended toward history, biography, novels, and practical works on agriculture and the military. The ambition that Thomas Jefferson, James Madison, and John Adams manifested through intellectual self-development George Washington sought to realize in the world of plantation and military affairs.

In 1753 and 1754, as a major and then a lieutenant colonel in the Virginia militia, Washington became conspicuous in his activities as Governor Robert Dinwiddie's emissary to the chiefs of the Six Nations and to the French who were constructing a chain of forts from Lake Erie to the Ohio River. Washington's first skirmish with the French late in May, 1754, is often described as the beginning of the Seven Years' War. His military career during the war, although it attracted attention and won respect, was linked to several reverses: In July, 1754, he surrendered his command to a much larger French force from Fort Duquesne; in the summer of 1755 he served as an aide-de-camp with General Edward Braddock's expedition against Fort Duquesne, which ended in ambush and rout; as colonel and commander in chief of Virginia militia, he spent two frustrating years trying to protect the Shenandoah Valley and western Virginia with about three hundred men and inadequate supplies. Moreover, in 1755 and 1757 Washington stood for election to the Virginia House of Burgesses and was twice defeated. At the same time, he unsuccessfully sought a regular commission in the Royal Army.

After cooperating with the last expedition against Fort Duquesne in 1758, which ended in French withdrawal and the establishment of Fort Pitt at the forks of the Ohio, Washington returned to civil life. He won election to the House of Burgesses in 1758. In January, 1759, he married Martha Dandridge Custis, a wealthy widow, and settled with her and her children at Mount Vernon. For fifteen years he enjoyed the life of a family man, planter, colonial legislator, and justice of the peace; and yet, to decorate his home, Washington ordered portrait busts of Alexander the Great, Julius Caesar, Charles XII of Sweden, Frederick II of Prussia, Prince Eugene, and the Duke of Marlborough— all famous commanders. When his London agent could not get them, Washington declined to accept busts of poets and philosophers as substitutes. His own appearance was imposing: he was 6 feet, 3 inches tall and weighed 209 pounds. His shoulders were narrow, but his arms, hands, legs, and feet were large. He had great strength yet was graceful in posture and movement. He was an excellent dancer and an expert horseman. His large head had a prominent nose and a firm mouth. His eyes were gray-blue, and in his forties he began to use spectacles to read.

By the time that Washington attained national stature as commander in chief of the Continental Army in 1775, the character that buttressed his popular standing was well formed. As a young man, he was emotional, effusive, audacious, and ambitious. These traits remained with him throughout his life, but he schooled himself to keep these manifestations of his passionate nature under rigorous control. He had purposefully chosen a life of outward stability and inward disappointment. He gained the rewards of equanimity at the cost of curbing his strongest inclinations. The cost was high. Washington often said that he would not relive his life if given the chance.

As Revolutionary War commander and as president, George Washington won an unequaled public respect for integrity and reliability. He maintained this public, ideal character while remaining privately aware of the gap between his studied moderation of demeanor and his emotional preference for bold risks, high honors, impulsive attachments, and strong aversions. Without ever losing the enthusiastic temperament of his youth, he subjected it to the control of his will, so that his public expression of his deepest anxieties or strongest joys remained temperate. Only rarely—as in his occasional angry rages or in his effusive friendship with the marquis de Lafayette—did the young Washington and the inner Washington appear to others without being moderated by the mature, public Washington. After he became a general, he was asked whether he really had written the often-quoted lines from his report of his first skirmish with the French in 1754—"I heard the bullets whistle, and, believe me, there is something charming in the sound." Washington replied, "If I said so, it was when I was young."

Having worked so hard to build it, Washington set a very high value on his reputation. He distinguished his personal honor from the popular opinion of him: Praise did not make him overweening, nor did censure paralyze him, but he tended to believe that anyone who attacked his conduct or reputation thereby impugned his honor. Knowing that his public character was his own creation, maintained at the cost of great effort, he resented suggestions that it had flaws. At the same time, possessing a private distance from his public posture, he could see mistakes he had made and correct them, even when he did not want to admit them. Two of the most intimate views of Washington may provide the best brief summary of his character. Gilbert Stuart, who painted portraits of the public Washington, saw the private Washington clearly: "All his features were indicative of the most ungovernable passions, and had he been born in the forests . . . he would have been the fiercest man among the savage tribes." Lafayette, who knew the private Washington better than most, described the reliability of the public Washington: "Had he been a common soldier, he would have been the bravest in the ranks; had he been an obscure citizen, all his neighbors would have respected him."

The American Revolution: Commander in Chief

By the time that Americans' resistance to the British government's measures to levy colonial taxes and to tighten imperial administration had become armed conflict, George Washington was one of the most important Virginia politicians. On May 27, 1774, he joined the extralegal meeting of burgesses in the Raleigh Tavern in Williamsburg, after the royal governor had dissolved the House; and he was one of Virginia's delegates to the First and Second Continental Congresses in 1774 and 1775. He was not a theorist or propagandist of the political thought by which Americans explained their effort to win independence and to establish a republican form of government. Nevertheless, he understood the intellectual bases, as well as the moral vision, on which the American Revolution was undertaken. His wartime addresses to his soldiers went beyond the appeals to discipline and professional pride characteristic of the British commanders' orders to include brief summaries of the significance of civil liberties, self-government, and the prospect for America's greatness. He concluded in 1789 that the "sacred fire of liberty and the destiny of the republican model of government" depended "on the experiment intrusted to the hands of the American people." There were more learned, more philosophically profound, more articulate explicators of the American Revolution than Washington. His standing owed most to the personal reliability that had impressed Virginians before the war and that became integral to American victory.

The Continental Congress appointed Washington to command the American forces on June 15, 1775. The importance of unity among sections while most of the fighting was being done by New Englanders made a military veteran from the most populous colony especially appropriate. He remained commander in chief throughout the war, resigning his commission on December 23, 1783, in a ceremony before

Congress. His conduct during these eight years established his unique national fame, which led to his election as the first president of the United States. Three elements of Washington's wartime service underlay his success and the public esteem that he won: his unselfishness, his persevering constancy, and his restraint with power. The tableaux that Americans repeatedly celebrated were Washington's declining to accept a salary as commander in chief, Washington's holding the army together at Trenton or Valley Forge or other crucial times, and—above all—Washington's resigning his commission. These seemed to exemplify the civic-mindedness that should characterize the citizens of a republic, guaranteeing the new nation's survival.

As commander in chief, Washington aspired to be a victorious general who commanded a veteran regular army. He resorted to short-term soldiers, militia auxiliaries, and cautious Fabian strategy from necessity rather than preference.

Although he achieved some critical victories—especially the Battle of Trenton (December 26, 1776) and the capture of Lord Cornwallis's army at Yorktown (October 18, 1781)—his main accomplishment was the painstaking diligence with which he labored on what he called "minutious details" in the interest of supply, discipline, recruitment, and popular support of the war effort—all of which were in jeopardy during the war. The army's wartime difficulties, symbolized by the hardship of the winter at Valley Forge, Pennsylvania (1777-1778), but prevalent at many other times as well, Washington attributed to the deficiencies of the decentralized, state-oriented government under the Continental Congress and the Articles of Confederation ratified in 1781.

Although Washington grew convinced that the United States needed a stronger central government, he remained scrupulously deferential to civil authorities while he was a general. When a few officers, early in 1783, suggested

Washington Crossing the Delaware, an engraving by F. O. Freeman from the painting by E. Leutze. *(Library of Congress)*

that the army should defy Congress and refuse to disband until provision had been made for back pay and officers' pensions, Washington called a meeting of officers in camp at Newburgh, New York, to quell any attempt to use the army to influence Congress. Perhaps the most widely praised single act of Washington's life was his resignation. Most of the soldiers had already disbanded; Washington, far from contemplating a dictatorship, felt eager to return to private life. Nevertheless, his voluntary surrender of command—in contrast with generals since antiquity who had seized supreme power—stood for his contemporaries as proof that independence had been won without subversion of the political principles of the American Revolution. Here was confirmation that public-spirited citizens could wield power without being corrupted, that self-government could survive. The celebration of Washington's trustworthiness during and after the American Revolution did not glorify only one personality but also made a public character a basis for national unity.

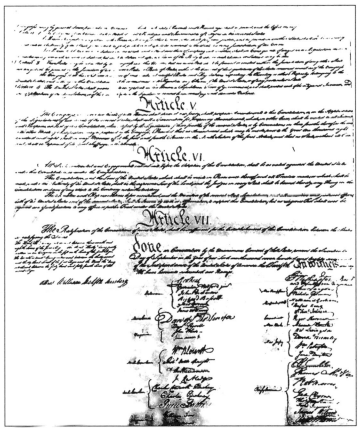

A page from the original copy of the U.S. Constitution. *(National Archives)*

The Drafting of the Constitution

The almost universal respect that Washington enjoyed after the war made him a pivotal figure in the establishment of the government created by the Constitution of 1787. Among Americans critical of the weakness of the Confederation government, the prospect of Washington as chief executive of a new government promised more effective central authority. Americans who were suspicious of the powers granted to the new federal government by the Constitution could not convincingly portray him as a potential dictator. The new institutions, like republicanism itself, were experimental, and Washington brought a proven record to a tentative undertaking.

Washington's reluctance was sincere as he wrote in April, 1789: "My movements to the chair of Government will be accompanied by feelings not unlike those of a culprit who is going to the place of his execution." He correctly anticipated that he stood a better chance of partly losing the "good name" he already possessed than of adding luster to it. He preferred private life to public power; yet he had taken an active part in the interstate political mobilization on behalf of a stronger federal government and had presided over the Philadelphia Convention of 1787 in which the Constitution was drafted. He supported ratification of the Constitution by the states and accepted the presidency because he believed that the weakness of the Confederation endangered American liberty and independence. The Continental Congress lacked the power to tax or to coerce. States' neglect denied Congress revenue. The opposition or absence of delegates from a few states could prevent major legislation, and the opposition of any one state could prevent Congress from expanding its powers. Hence, the central government could not pay its foreign or domestic debts; nor could it amass sufficient power to protect the expanding Western settlements from British forts or American Indian resistance. It lacked the power to retaliate against discriminatory foreign-trade regulations by European nations and to compel trade reciprocity. A state government confronted with unrest—such as Massachusetts when farmers in 1786 closed courts to protest heavy taxation—could not rely on a national government to maintain order. As Washington and other supporters of strong central government understood history, the prospect of anarchy was an even greater threat to republics than the danger of dictatorship. In fact, weak government would give way to mob rule, ending in tyranny. Washington entered the presidency keenly aware of the fragility of American unity and of the suspicion with which the conduct of the new government would be watched. Yet these centrifugal forces were the very influences that helped convince him to lend his influence to greater political centralization.

Establishing the Presidency

When Washington took the oath of office as president in New York City on April 30, 1789, two states—North Carolina and Rhode Island—had not yet ratified the Constitution. Furthermore, large numbers of Americans in such important states as Virginia, New York, and Pennsylvania had opposed adoption of the new form of government, thinking its powers too great. Political alignments within the states were highly complex and diverse. Some

states, such as New York, Rhode Island, and New Jersey, had two-party divisions of long standing. In Pennsylvania, the state constitution of 1776 divided political allegiances between its supporters and its critics. In most states, even those as different as Georgia and New Hampshire, political coalitions shifted according to personal, familial, and patronage loyalties. Small wonder that Washington, preparing to appoint federal officials, feared that a "single disgust excited in a particular State, on this account, might perhaps raise a flame of opposition that could not easily, if ever, be extinguished."

One of the first measures of the new government, designed to allay some of the concern provoked by its powers, was Congress's adoption, on September 25, 1789, of twelve amendments to the Constitution, of which ten were eventually ratified by three-fourths of the state legislatures. These amendments were an explicit recognition of rights reserved by the people, not to be violated by the United States government. They included prohibition of a national religious establishment and of federal abridgment of free speech, freedom of the press, peaceable petition and assembly, or the right to bear arms in the common defense. Other amendments prohibited arbitrary quartering of soldiers in private homes and regulated the procedures for the arrest and trial of persons accused of crime. The ninth amendment provided that other rights, not specified in this list, remained intact; and the tenth amendment read: "The powers not delegated to the United States by the Constitution, nor prohibited by it to the States, are reserved to the States respectively, or to the people." The ratification of these amendments—the Bill of Rights—was completed on December 15, 1791. Meanwhile, North Carolina had ratified the Constitution and joined the federal government on November 29, 1789. Rhode Island, under pressure from internal threats of secession, did so on May 29, 1790.

Despite the fact that Americans considered their country to be "the rational empire of human liberty and equality, founded upon the natural rights of mankind and sovereignty of the people," the first federal officeholders, including President Washington, devoted much attention to rituals of official behavior and to the mystique of precedent. The Federalists, as supporters of the Constitution called themselves, commanded a large majority in both houses of Congress. There were only three or four Antifederalist senators and no more than thirteen Antifederalist representatives. Some Federalists, especially in the Senate and above all Vice President John Adams, believed that the government needed not only the rational consent of its citizens but also the emotional attachment inspired by awe at its magnificence. Thus, senators proposed to exalt Washington with a quasi-monarchical title, such as "His Excellency"—the form of address often used while he was commander of the army—or "His Elective Highness." Washington himself addressed Congress in person and received congressional delegations with replies, as did the British monarch. He rode in state in a carriage with uniformed outriders; he did not accept invitations or return visits. All these proposals and practices excited comment, especially criticism from the more egalitarian-minded. The House of Representatives refused to adopt a special title for the president, and all holders of the office have since been addressed simply as "Mister President." The controversy was comparatively minor; yet, it first raised one of the fundamental issues of Washington's presidency and of early national period politics: a conflict between the attempt to establish a government that could command

The inauguration of Washington. *(Library of Congress)*

obedience and the fear that the American Revolution would be subverted by monarchical institutions.

George Washington probably overestimated the potential long-term significance of the precedents that he set, ceremonial or substantive. Thomas Jefferson, as president, abandoned Washington's social rules; Andrew Jackson abandoned Washington's practice of vetoing bills only when he deemed them unconstitutional. Washington's fundamental accomplishment was to inaugurate an executive office with strong—and potentially much stronger—authority among a people whose political life in part had long consisted of resistance to centralized executive power. Subject to the Senate's role in ratifying treaties and confirming nominees to office, the president conducted foreign relations, appointed diplomats, federal judges, and other federal officials, and commanded the nation's military forces, including state militias called into federal service. He held office for four years at a time when most state gubernatorial terms were one year or two, and there was no restriction on reelection of the president. He could prevent by veto the enactment of legislation that did not command a two-thirds majority in the House and the Senate.

Early in the first administration, Representative James Madison complained to Secretary of State Thomas Jefferson that Washington's followers "had wound up the ceremonials of the government to a pitch of stateliness which nothing but his personal character could have supported, and which no character after him could ever maintain." At the same time that Madison identified a drawback to Washington's distinctive position, he acknowledged its impact. The difficulties in fighting, recruiting, supplying, and financing the Revolutionary War effort had dramatized the deficiencies of state and continental governments with weak executives. No person embodied the impulse to constitutional change so emphatically as Washington. The "pitch of stateliness" supported by his "personal character" combined augmentation of power with the expectation that it would not be abused.

One of the clearest examples of Washington's personal importance as a nationalizing influence was his travel throughout the United States during his first years in office. In April, 1789, he traveled from Mount Vernon to New York to assume the presidency. In the autumn and winter of 1789-1790, he toured New England, crisscrossing Massachusetts and Connecticut and going as far north as Portsmouth, New Hampshire. In the spring of 1791, he completed an ambitious circuit of the Southern states that covered both the tidewater and the piedmont regions of Virginia, North Carolina, South Carolina, and Georgia. These progressions were an almost unending series of ceremonial addresses, parades, formal greetings,

fetes, and honors. Officials welcomed him; choirs serenaded him; girls strewed flowers in his path; tavern keepers played host to his entourage; volunteer companies of horsemen escorted him. After having passed through some of the areas where opposition to the Constitution had been strongest, Washington summarized the main lesson of his tour: "Tranquility reigns among the people, with that disposition towards the general government which is likely to preserve it. They begin to feel the good effects of equal laws and equal protection."

In establishing his administration, Washington neither foresaw nor desired the development of national political parties. Parties, or factions, because they were self-serving and self-perpetuating, were thought to be inimical to the public-spiritedness on which republican institutions were based. The balanced powers of the branches of government were designed to impede any attempt to unite control of the federal authority under one group. The electoral college, in theory, confided the selection of the president and vice president to a few of the best-informed and most judicious citizens. A nonparty ideal of government seemed to prevail at the opening of the Washington administration.

With James Madison, a central figure in the Constitutional Convention, as an especially prominent leader, the Congress in 1789 enacted legislation to establish the federal judiciary and the executive departments—not yet customarily called a "cabinet"—of State, Treasury, and War. The attorney general was legal counsel to the executive and not the administrator of a department. The Judiciary Act of 1789 established a Supreme Court, two circuit courts, and thirteen district courts, but left the state courts with original jurisdiction over most cases arising under the federal Constitution, laws, or treaties. The Supreme Court was given appellate jurisdiction over cases in which state courts decided against a claim of federal right.

This established the principle of federal judicial review of state legislation. Cases not falling under federal jurisdiction, however, could not be appealed beyond the state court systems. Washington appointed firm Federalists to the Supreme Court, with an eye to even geographical distribution and with John Jay of New York as chief justice. As secretary of state, Washington chose Thomas Jefferson, who had been minister to France since 1784. Edmund Randolph became attorney general. The secretary of war, Henry Knox, and the secretary of the treasury, Alexander Hamilton, were men whom Washington had measured during their service in the Continental Army.

Economic Policies: Hamilton's Guiding Vision

Secretary Hamilton took the initiative in defining a domestic legislative program for the administration. An intelligent, ambitious, hardworking man, Hamilton had a vision of governmental policy that encompassed a design for the future of the United States as a populous, industrially productive, powerful, centralized nation. In September, 1780, at a low point of the American effort in the War of Independence, Hamilton—then an aide-de-camp to Washington—had outlined the kinds of measures that he brought to fruition ten years later: executive authority in the hands of departmental administrators, more rigorous federal taxation, and a federally chartered bank that could loan money to the government and attract through the prospect of profits the support of rich men for the government. As secretary of the treasury, Hamilton submitted to Congress in 1790 three reports on provision for the support of the public credit. These contained his plan for funding the national debt, which consisted of approximately $11.7 million owed to Dutch bankers and to the governments of France and Spain, plus $40 million in securities held by foreign investors and by Americans. The Confederation government had been paying interest on the Dutch debt only by contracting additional loans and had allowed interest payments on the rest of the debt to fall into arrears, to a total of about $13 million. Hamilton proposed to convert the unpaid back interest to principal and to fund the total principal by an issue of interest-bearing securities, to the interest on which and to the redemption of which the government would permanently pledge part of its revenue.

The proposal not only was confined to the debt that had been contracted by the Continental Congress but also provided for the assumption by the federal government of the war debts owed by the states, which would add $25 million to the new national debt. In imitation of the British system by which Sir Robert Walpole had established his government's credit, the goal of the funding plan was not to retire the debt completely but to establish confidence that interest on government secu-

A portrait of Alexander Hamilton. *(Library of Congress)*

rities would be paid and that they could be sold or redeemed at or near their face value. When this situation prevailed, government securities could serve as collateral for private loans that expanded the credit available for business ventures.

Hamilton further proposed that Congress charter a Bank of the United States with a capital of $10 million, one-fifth of which would be subscribed by the government, the rest by private investors. One of the bank's functions would be to make short-term loans to the government. The income of the Treasury, primarily from import duties, fluctuated seasonally, whereas to maintain the value of its securities the Treasury needed a reliable, consistent source of cash. The bank's loans would serve this purpose. The government would deposit its money in the bank, which could also make its own private loans and issue bank notes that citizens could tender to the government at face value for the payment of taxes and other obligations. The notes of the Bank of the United States would be the principal currency in circulation.

Hamilton's conception of the government's responsibilities went beyond the management of its debts and finances. He sought, especially in his Report on Manufactures—submitted in December, 1791—to use federal power to shape the American economy. He wanted the United States to achieve the complex, internally balanced, self-sufficient economy toward which European nations were striving. Fearing that America's traditional trading partners would increasingly rely on their own and their colonies' resources and exclude American agricultural exports from their markets, Hamilton urged that the United States imitate this closed mercantilist system by developing the nation's industrial capacity to meet its domestic demand for manufactured goods, thereby diminishing dependence on Europe. His report proposed protective tariffs on some foreign manufactured goods, bounties for new Ameri-

can industries, and awards and premiums for improvements in productivity and quality. Such incentives would persuade capitalists that they could make greater profits from domestic manufacturing than from the traditional investments in shipping American agricultural products to Europe and selling European manufactures in America.

Not coincidentally, the features of Hamilton's proposals interlocked to foster one another. Holders of the public debt who stood to profit from the plan would lend their support to the federal government; the assumption of state debts would induce public creditors to look to the nation and not to the state for maintenance of the value of their holdings; relieved of their Revolutionary War debt, states would have less justification for levying taxes of their own, whereas the federal government would have more reason to assert its powers through taxation; such federal taxes could promote the growth of manufacturing by raising the cost of competing imports; an excise tax on liquor would not only raise revenue from large-scale distillers but would also establish the federal government's direct authority over backcountry independent distillers and backcountry opponents of federal power; a stable federal revenue would secure the confidence of investors in the public credit—they could then devote some of their profits and some of the credit newly available through the Bank of the United States to investment in manufacturing; the development of an integrated economy of agricultural suppliers, American manufacturers, and American consumers would promote the consolidation of the Union through ties of commerce; thus the United States could, by national policy, hasten the day of its becoming a great power.

Although Hamilton had an almost visionary enthusiasm for his conception of national greatness and did not seek to profit personally from the implementation of his program, the grand design, like the earlier system of Walpole, had as its motive power the pursuit of self-interest. If Hamilton were correct, the United States could enhance its international security, its domestic prosperity, its cultural unity, and its political stability by exploiting the selfishness of private advantage for the ends of national policy. In fact, Hamilton believed, the nation could achieve these goals in no other way.

President Washington took no hand in the drafting of Hamilton's program. Although Washington managed his own business affairs astutely and amassed a fortune through a lifetime of land transactions, he was not expert in the complexities of public finance. His support for Hamilton's policies, however, was crucial to their enactment by Congress. Hamilton said that Washington "consulted much, resolved slowly, resolved surely." In August, 1790, after prolonged debate and by a narrow margin, most of Hamilton's proposals were enacted, followed by the legislation for the Bank of the United States in February, 1791.

Opposition to Hamilton's Program:
Origins of the National Party System

Although almost everyone agreed that provision for the public debt was essential, Hamilton's plan excited strong, widespread opposition, which contributed to a lasting political division among the supporters of the Constitution. Some of the bases for opposition were highly specific. James Madison and his followers protested that most of the original holders of the public debt—people who had provided loans, goods, and services for the winning of independence, receiving the Continental government's paper money, loan office certificates, or promissory notes—had subsequently sold their claims to speculators for the fraction of the face value. Hamilton's plan would confer large profits on the monied men who now held the claims, while neglecting the patriots who had done most for the American Revolution. Madison proposed to divide the government's

repayment between the original and the ultimate creditors. Although congressmen joined Madison in commiserating with victimized widows, orphans, and veterans—denouncing greedy speculators—his alternative was too complex and entailed too much expense to attract much support in Congress.

The assumption of state debts aroused the opposition of congressmen from states that had contracted small debts or had paid off most of their debt since the war. Such states disliked the idea of now having to share in the cost of funding the debts of their less conscientious neighbors. To win support, the proponents of assumption had to add to the legislation federal grants to those states that would benefit least from assumption as well as special advantages for Virginia. Southerners, especially Virginians, were concerned by the fact that more than 80 percent of the holders of the national debt were Northerners and that most of the state debts were also in the North. Hamilton's system would increase the disparity of wealth and power in favor of the North. Hamilton obtained the additional votes needed to enact the funding and assumption plan by supporting the establishment of the national capital on the Potomac River in Maryland and Virginia, to take effect after a ten-year residence in Philadelphia.

Other bases of the resistance in Congress were broader concerns of principle, which became more urgent after Hamilton presented his plan for a national bank. To justify the demand for American independence, some proponents of the American Revolution had argued that British liberty was being undermined by the manufacturing economy and the politics based on self-seeking (or, as Americans said, corruption) that Hamilton now proposed to import to the United States. Urban concentrations of population, great disparities in wealth, the dependent status of wage workers, a powerful central bank whose resources lessened the reliance of the executive on the voters and their representatives, discriminatory taxes that used the government's power for the benefit of a few at the expense of the many—all these tendencies that made the British Empire seem a threat to liberty would systematically subvert a republican form of government in the United States. Far from sharing Hamilton's fear that a solely agricultural America would be at the mercy of Europe, his critics, especially Thomas Jefferson, contended that America's crops and raw materials were the foundation of the more industrialized nations' well-being. This fact made the United States more stable and secure than its trading partners. Moreover, Americans' buying the bulk of their manufactured goods from Europe left the evils of industrial society far away. Americans could aspire to perpetuate the independent-minded, public-spirited citizenry essential for the survival of self-government exactly because Americans remained self-sufficient farmers free from the economic and political engines admired by Hamilton.

Although Hamilton won enactment of his program, it became, with the divergent opinions on America's foreign relations, the source of a basic division leading to competing political mobilization in rival parties, called Federalist and Republican (or Democratic Republican). Political organizations, including long-standing two-party competition, were already well known in state politics, and many of these factions, or parties, were soon aligned in the new national party system. The Federalist and Republican parties, however, originated in Congress and among leading politicians. These men then encouraged a more general public alarm over governmental policy, which could best be influenced by systematic political cooperation. James Madison and Alexander Hamilton had collaborated in winning public ratification of the Constitution, and Hamilton had consulted Madison as he prepared his reports. Madison, however, became the parliamentary leader of opposition to Hamilton's system in the House of Representatives. Sec-

retary of State Thomas Jefferson, who did not take office until March, 1790, soon became the central figure in the nascent party, though not publicly its spokesperson. In the cabinet, Attorney General Edmund Randolph was an ally. In the Senate, the adept political organizer from New York, Aaron Burr, could be used, if not trusted. In the House of Representatives, the anti-Hamilton (or, by the time of Jefferson's resignation in December, 1793, the antiadministration) group was strongest, approaching a majority on some issues. Hamilton could count on a strong majority in the Senate, led by such able men as Oliver Ellsworth of Connecticut, Robert Morris of Pennsylvania, and Rufus King of New York. Representatives Fisher Ames and Theodore Sedgwick of Massachusetts and William Loughton Smith of South Carolina led pro-Hamilton members of the House, who controlled that body. Secretary of War Henry Knox allied with Hamilton in the cabinet.

For factions in the capital to become parties with national support, organized in even rudimentary networks, the concerns of the cabinet and Congress would have to become the concerns of influential men throughout the country and of voters who could change the composition of the House and, indirectly, the Senate, whose members were elected by state legislatures. One of the principal means of disseminating and intensifying these concerns was the partisan press, especially in Philadelphia after that city became the capital in 1790. The *Gazette of the United States*, edited by John Fenno, became the leading advocate of Hamilton's measures. Fenno dramatized and personalized his arguments by extravagant praise of Hamilton. To his critics, this was cause for alarm. George Washington was the most conspicuous example of the intimate connection between receiving fulsome adulation and possessing political power. Jefferson and Madison feared that the *Gazette of the United States* was exalting Hamilton similarly in order to make him the wielder of power that would overawe republican institutions. In 1791, to present the necessary warnings and to refute Fenno's support of the Hamiltonian program, Jefferson and Madison induced the poet and journalist Philip Freneau to undertake the editorship of a new paper, the *National Gazette*. In it, Freneau denounced Hamilton's conspiratorial designs and praised Jefferson for fidelity to the principles of the American Revolution. In practice, both editors were agents of the factions for which they spoke. They were responsible for organizing, clarifying, and exaggerating the opinions that would form one of the bases of party loyalty. Fenno's operations were supported partly by printing contracts from the Treasury Department and loans from Hamilton. Freneau received a clerkship in the State Department, which gave him an income with plenty of free time for his editorial labors. Hamilton wrote many of the attacks on Jefferson, published under pseudonyms, whereas Attorney General Randolph wrote defenses of Jefferson. As Hamilton's financial program and other issues attracted more widespread opposition and support, an avowedly partisan press developed in other cities, discussing not only local concerns but also the controversies originating in the capital.

George Washington felt strong concern about the increasingly bitter divisions within his administration. Both Jefferson and Hamilton offered to resign, but the president hoped for a nonparty government that would help attach the public to the Constitution. He wanted to keep Jefferson in office, but he refused to believe that Hamilton or any significant number of Americans were guilty of conspiring to introduce monarchy. Washington had accepted the presidency with sincere reluctance. Part of his reluctance came from the thought that, although his personal popularity might lend dignity to the government, political controversy might undermine the popular esteem for him. To his distress, he saw this happening, as criticism of Hamilton and of mon-

archists widened to touch the president himself. Washington set great store by the reputation of respect for republican institutions that he had established during the Revolutionary War. In 1789, he feared that accepting the presidency might look like ambition—reneging on the promise implied in his resignation of his commission—and he hoped to minimize any such suspicion by serving only one term. In 1792, at his request, Madison wrote a draft of a farewell address, with which Washington hoped to close his presidential term fittingly; but the growing political divisions, along with crises in the economy and in America's dealings with England and France, made Washington's continuance in office for a second term seem imperative to Hamilton, Jefferson, Madison, and many others. Even as Washington won reelection, however, the inchoate Republican Party gathered fifty electoral votes for Governor George Clinton of New York—as well as four for Jefferson and one for Burr—in an unsuccessful attempt to defeat the reelection of John Adams as vice president.

Having accepted a second term despite his own reluctance, Washington was keenly sensitive to accusations that he was arrogating power to himself and betraying his image as a civic-minded Cincinnatus who served only as long as the public needed him. When a newspaper called him a king and depicted him on a guillotine in 1793, Washington lost his temper in a cabinet meeting, which Jefferson recorded:

The President was much inflamed, got into one of those passions when he cannot command himself, ran on much on the personal abuse which had been bestowed on him, defied any man on earth to produce one single act of his since he had been in the government which was not done on the purest motives, that he had never repented but once the having slipped the moment of resigning his office, and that was every moment since, that *by god* he had rather be in his grave than in his present situation. That he had rather be on his farm than to be made *emperor of the world* and yet that they were charging him with wanting to be a king. That that *rascal Freneau* sent him three of his papers every day, as if he thought he would become the distributor of his papers, that he could see in this nothing but an impudent design to insult him. He ended in this high tone.

During his second term, Washington, though still deploring parties and aspiring to preserve his position as a figure of national unity, became increasingly a partisan, Federalist president.

The debate over Hamilton's program and the ensuing partisan rhetoric revealed that Americans had a source of political unity and authority at the national level other than respect for Washington: the Constitution. Despite the widespread opposition to its ratification, the document soon became an object of veneration and the appeal of last resort on controversial questions. Few men remained Antifederalists, and the developing parties of the 1790's had few significant continuities with the factions of the 1780's. The Constitution, almost everyone in political life agreed, defined the way to preserve an ever-vulnerable republican system of government. Contrary to the partisans' charges, Hamilton and the Federalists did not want to introduce monarchical tyranny; nor did Jefferson and the Republicans want to sabotage American unity and independence with anarchy or French revolutionary radicalism. In their deep disagreement, however, the two groups were appealing to a common source of authority for their claim to be patriots. They were constructing sharply divergent interpretations of the Constitution's ambiguous provisions.

For Hamilton, the main threat to American republicanism came not from the prospect of a tyrannical central government but from a weak federal government's inability to maintain its unity, solvency, and national independence. Thus, when Madison, Jefferson, and Randolph tried to persuade Washington to veto the bill establishing the Bank of the United States, on the grounds that the Constitution gave the federal government no such power, Hamilton disagreed. His defense of the constitutionality of the bank appealed to the last clause of Article I, Section 8 of the Constitution, which authorizes Congress to make laws that are "necessary and proper" for executing the powers vested in the government. In Hamilton's interpretation, which convinced Washington to sign the legislation, "necessary" meant not only essential for but also useful in or conducive to the execution of the government's duties. Since a bank would aid in collecting taxes, regulating trade, and providing defense—all of which the Constitution authorized—it was constitutional. This broad construction of the document's wording implied that the Constitution authorized an unlimited array of means whose use it did not specifically prohibit.

For Jefferson and the Republicans—at least until they took control of the federal government in 1801—the greatest threat to the republic was the use of what Jefferson called "props" for the government other than the freely given consent of the people. Such props would include officials' conspicuous military reputations, social and political rituals in imitation of European monarchies, concentrations of financial power aided by governmental policy, or displays of force through the taxing power, the judiciary, and other federal authorities. The Constitution, Republicans agreed, restricted the scope for abuses by confining the federal government to an essential minimum, keeping the remainder of governmental power at the state level, where it could be more closely supervised by the electorate.

The text of the Constitution could plausibly be construed along either of these lines. Its claim to delineate a dual sovereignty divided between federal and state governments and constituencies was theoretically ingenious and politically expedient but practically ambiguous. This ambiguity enabled the Constitution to function as a shared symbol of nationality and of successful self-government among people who deeply mistrusted one another's loyalty.

Despite their familiarity with state political factions, Americans were not accustomed to regarding as patriots those with whom they differed on fundamental questions of political principle, particularly when their opponents began to organize. Differences on immediate issues were quickly traced back to the basic issue of the American Revolution: the survival of liberty. Yet when differences were cast in these terms, it was difficult to credit opponents with patriotic intentions or republican sentiments. Instead, it seemed self-evident that a faction that was pursuing dangerous measures must be a conspiracy—at best, to serve the self-interest of its members; at worst, to subvert the American Revolution. The Federalists and the Republicans tended to see themselves, not as conscientious rivals over questions of official policy, but as combatants, each party claiming to be the rescuer of American independence from internal enemies of the republic. This antiparty outlook and this apocalyptic interpretation of partisans' motives remained influential in political discourse long after parties were no longer new in national politics.

Westward Expansion: Settlers and Speculators

Americans of the nineteenth and twentieth centuries have often portrayed the economy and society of late eighteenth century America as comparatively stable, traditional, almost decorous; yet, to people of the time, the country seemed volatile, potentially explosive. Even without massive immigration—though the importation of slaves continued legally until 1808—the population was almost doubling every twenty years. Both the growth of population and the economic ambitions of Americans focused attention on the lands west of the Appalachian mountain chain. Anticipating the rapid extension of settlement between the Appalachians and the Mississippi River, many American investors, including George Washington, speculated in Western lands. They acquired claims to vast holdings, which they hoped to sell at a profit to other investors, even before actual migration began on a large scale. Opponents of Hamilton's funding and assumption measures contended that the national debt could be retired without recourse to Hamilton's federal "engine" simply by selling parcels of the public domain to speculators and settlers—so sure were the migration and the resulting revenue. Under the influence of bribes given to state legislators, the state of Georgia sold sixteen million acres to three Yazoo land companies for $200,000—a vast tract of Georgia's Western lands in present-day Alabama and Mississippi. Robert Morris and his associates John Nicholson and James Greenleaf formed the North American Land Company, amassing claims to six million acres that they expected to resell at a large profit. Investors in the Potomac Company planned, with the help of a canal around the falls of the Potomac and a canal connecting the Ohio River network with the upper Potomac, to funnel much of the trade of the expanding West, from the Great Lakes to Tennessee, past the new national capital.

The vision and optimism of the speculators ran too far ahead of the actual settlements and purchases on which their hope for profits was ultimately based. Their market was soon impaired by the rising value of American government securities, which could be advantageously pledged in payment for land while they were depreciated but which became more expensive and less useful to speculators as the securities approached face value. Also, the outbreak of war in Europe in 1792 offered European capitalists more attractive returns on loans to belligerent powers than on purchases of American forests. Significantly, at the peak of speculative land values in the early 1790's, Washington, who had played this kind of game

General Wayne Obtains a Complete Victory over the Miami Indians, August 20th, 1794, by F. Kemmelmeyer. *(The Henry Francis du Pont Winterthur Museum)*

for thirty-five years and who needed money, was prudently selling some of his holdings while other men were still buying extensively. In 1795, the bottom began to drop out of the inflated market in Western lands. During the next fifteen years, a wide array of speculators found themselves insolvent. Several, including Robert Morris, went to prison at the suit of their creditors.

Indian Affairs: Benign Policies, Brutal Realities

Although the migration to Ohio, Kentucky, and Tennessee was well under way during Washington's administration, the intensive settlement that would eventually match the speculators' vision depended on more than population growth. The West already had a population—the diverse American Indian peoples, most of whom regarded the westward movement of

whites with alarm. Their leaders, especially Joseph Brant of the Mohawk and Alexander McGillivray of the Creek, hoped to confine white settlement within the narrowest possible limits, primarily near the major rivers. Great Britain and Spain, whose empires bordered the United States, also wanted to restrict American expansion. The British continued to occupy forts on territory ceded to the United States in 1783, acting as if Ohio were still British, and the Spanish in the Southwest encouraged American Indians to confederate and whites to separate politically from the United States.

Washington, like many of his successors, announced a policy of equitable dealings and peaceful relations with Native Americans. In 1791, he concluded a treaty confirming Indian title to most of the land granted by Georgia to the Yazoo land companies. He urged Congress to define legal ways for the transfer of land from Indians to whites, for the supervision of trade with Indians, and for the prevention of whites' attacks on Indians. Leaving out the question of the later governmental violations of treaties concluded during the Washington administration, this policy confronted immediate difficulties. First, the goal of most American Indians was not regional coexistence with whites under federal supervision but exclusion of whites from their ancestral lands. Second, the policy of coexistence was repeatedly violated by whites who settled on native lands. As one American officer reported, "The people of Kentucky will carry on private expeditions against the Indians and kill them whenever they meet them, and I do not believe that there is a jury in all Kentucky will punish a man for it." Third, the British and the Spanish encouraged American Indians to fight and provided them with arms and ammunition.

Early in 1790, attempting to exclude whites from the region north and west of the Ohio River, a group of Indians attacked, defeating Josiah Harmar's army at the Maumee River. In the autumn of 1791, General Arthur St. Clair, governor of the Northwest Territory, took the field with an ill-trained army. He fell into an ambush on November 4, 1791, with more than nine hundred of his men killed or wounded. White settlers in Ohio withdrew to Cincinnati and Marietta. President Washington privately received the news of St. Clair's defeat while guests were dining with him. His courteous, formal demeanor remained unchanged until the guests had left and Mrs. Washington had retired. Then, alone with his secretary, Tobias Lear, Washington's emotions mounted into a rage as he said, "It's all over—St. Clair's defeated—routed;—the officers nearly all killed, the men by wholesale; the rout complete—too shocking to think of—and a SURPRISE into the bargain!" Remembering his parting words to St. Clair in Philadelphia, Washington now spoke in a torrent, throwing his hands up several times, his body shaking:

Yes, HERE on this very spot, I took leave of him; I wished him success and honor; you have your instructions, I said, from the Secretary of War, I had a strict eye to them, and will add but one word—BEWARE OF A SURPRISE. I repeat it, BEWARE OF A SURPRISE—you know how the Indians fight us. He went off with that, as my last solemn warning thrown into his ears. And yet!! to suffer that army to be cut to pieces, hack'd, butchered, tomahawk'd, by a SURPRISE—the very thing I guarded him against!! O God, O God, he's worse than a murderer! how can he answer it to his country;—the blood of the slain is upon him—the curse of widows and orphans—the curse of Heaven!

St. Clair's defeat prompted the creation of the first congressional investigating committee, which reviewed the pertinent documents and blamed the outcome on army contractors who had failed to supply proper equipment. The government's Indian policy continued to entertain the prospect of a settlement by treaty until chiefs of the Six Nations, encouraged by the British, made clear in January, 1793, their insistence on an Ohio River boundary. Thereafter, despite some further negotiations, the administration concentrated on defeating resistance. Between 1790 and 1796, the Indian wars accounted for almost five-sixths of the federal government's operating expenses, eventually consuming a total of $5 million. To command in the West, Washington chose General Anthony Wayne, who reached Ohio in 1793. He carefully developed a trained, disciplined force, consisting of 2,000 U.S. Army soldiers and more than 1,500 Kentucky militiamen. In June, 1794, supported by British construction of Fort Miami on the Maumee River, 2,000 American Indians gathered there. Wayne began the march against them in August and met a force of 1,300 at Fallen Timbers, where he won a decisive victory on August 20, followed by the devastation of American Indian towns and crops. The British were discredited in Indians' eyes by their refusal to fight the Americans,

35

with whom they were officially at peace. Within a year, Wayne used his new power to dictate the Treaty of Greenville, removing all American Indians from the area that later became the state of Ohio, for which the United States paid $10,000.

Foreign Affairs: Internal Debate over Policies Toward France

The most difficult, divisive problem that confronted the Washington administration was the conduct of America's foreign relations. For its security, as well as its pride in being a republic, the new nation needed to demonstrate that it was not a temporary aberration. Markets abroad were essential to the prosperity of its maritime carrying trade, its commercial farmers, and its producers of raw materials. The nation owed money to European creditors; Britons who had made loans to Americans before the Revolutionary War still demanded payment. The eighteenth century had seen a series of European wars, which had extended to the overseas empires—wars that reached an unprecedented scale began during Washington's presidency. More so than many of its citizens desired, the United States was touched by events in other countries.

The greatest series of such events was the French Revolution. A sequence of bloody changes in the leadership of France, its transformation into a republic, and its war with other European powers forced the Washington administration to make choices, both internationally and among American politicians who differed in their reactions to these developments. Although the early phases of the French Revolution attracted extensive sympathy in the United States, by 1793 the rise of the Jacobins, the Reign of Terror, and the expanding war on behalf of atheistic republican revolution alarmed many Americans without destroying the pro-French sympathies of others. More than thirty local political groups, partly imitating the Jacobin clubs, formed into Democratic so-

cieties and Republican societies, which were among the first community political organizations in the United States emphasizing national and international concerns.

Washington and the members of his cabinet agreed that the United States should stay out of the war that France had declared against Britain, Holland, and Spain in January, 1793. Hamilton and Jefferson disagreed, however, on how this should be effected. Hamilton and many other Federalists were appalled at the revolutionary violence in France and at the Frenchmen's assertion that they were the vanguard of similar revolutions throughout the world. In a private letter in May, 1793, Washington, discreetly omitting the name of the country, wrote that France's affairs "seem to me to be in the highest paroxysm of disorder . . . because those in whose hands the G[overnmen]t is entrusted are ready to tear each other to pieces, and will, more than probably prove the worst foes the Country has." Hamilton argued early in April, 1793, that the Constitution authorized the president to proclaim neutrality and to enforce the policy against any Americans who might try to aid France. He wanted the United States to refrain from diplomatic relations with the revolutionary regime, giving France no grounds to invoke American aid under the terms of the 1778 treaty of mutual defense.

Jefferson did not want the United States to go to war, but he argued that since the Constitution gave to Congress the power to declare war, only Congress could declare neutrality. He wanted to delay a declaration of neutrality in the hope that the belligerent powers would grant more favorable terms of trade to Americans in order to keep the United States out of the war. Despite such calculations for American advantage, he believed that the survival of republicanism in France was essential for the security of republican government in the United States and for the future prospects of liberty elsewhere. In January, 1793, Jefferson expressed his regret that the executions in France had extended beyond "enemies" of the people to include friends of liberty, but he said of the French Revolution, "Rather than it should have failed, I would have seen half the earth desolated." On March 12, 1793, Jefferson instructed the American minister in Paris to recognize the National Assembly as the government of France.

Washington accepted Jefferson's recommendation that the United States recognize the new regime, but he accepted Hamilton's interpretation of the president's authority to proclaim neutrality. In his April 22, 1793, proclamation he omitted the word "neutrality" but declared a policy of "conduct friendly and impartial toward the belligerent powers." Republicans, including James Madison writing under a pseudonym, denounced the proclamation as an unconstitutional aggrandizement of the executive and a betrayal of Americans' moral obligations to their fellow republicans in France. Madison argued that "every nation has a right to abolish an old government and establish a new one. This principle . . . is the only lawful tenure by which the United States hold their existence as a nation."

The divisions among Americans over the French Revolution and the European war grew more intense as a result of the activities of Edmond Genet, the first minister to the United States from republican France. Genet, a Girondist, was politically out of favor at home by the time he reached America, as the Jacobins were replacing and liquidating the Girondists; but to many Americans, including Jefferson, he was an attractive representative of the fight for republicanism in France, with which they sympathized. On April 8, 1793, Genet landed at Charleston, South Carolina, where he received an enthusiastic welcome and began a month-long trip to Philadelphia. In Charleston and at stops along his route, Genet made arrangements with American supporters for raising armies to liberate Louisiana and Florida from Spain, as well as Canada from Britain. These grandiose plans came to nothing, but they showed Genet's intention to secure Americans' aid in France's wars, contrary to the policy of neutrality. The effusive public demonstrations of solidarity convinced Genet that his policy enjoyed more support than did Washington's. Jefferson, who asserted that 99 percent of Americans approved of the French Revolution, told Genet about the divisions within the cabinet and looked the other way when the French agent André Michaux sought to organize attacks on Louisiana and Canada.

Genet, in violation of Washington's proclamation, commissioned twelve privateering vessels to raid British shipping. Eighty British merchant ships were brought into American ports; they were condemned and sold—not by American admiralty courts, but by French consuls, for whom Genet claimed extraterritorial status. In July, 1793, Washington asked the Supreme Court to rule on the constitutionality of Genet's actions. The Court declined to do so. It asserted its equal status as a branch of government by refusing to act as counsel to the executive branch, confining itself to decisions in litigation. In 1794, in the case *Genet v. Sloop Betsy*, the Court ruled that Genet's consular courts were illegal and that any condemnation of prizes of war should take place in United States district courts, acting as admiralty courts. By August, 1793, Washington was ready to take action against Genet's operations. He prohibited the organizing of military units in America by belligerents. He forbade the privateers commissioned by Genet to enter American ports. The United States, however, had no navy and no army on its coast adequate to enforce these rules. Genet believed that he had sufficient popular support to defy Washington. He threatened to appeal "over Washington's head" to the pro-French sentiment of the American public. This threat was his undoing. Jefferson disassociated himself from Genet, and the government requested that France recall the minister. Since the Jacobins probably would have executed Genet, he was not forced to go home but was allowed to live in the United States as a private citizen.

Although Genet could not overthrow Washington, the controversy over his brief but excited tenure as minister clarified the deep division among Americans in their attitudes toward France. Washington could no longer aspire to preside over a people united in praise of him or over a nonparty government. In December, 1793, Jefferson resigned as secretary of state, to be succeeded by Edmund Randolph. Washington, during his second term, became decisively aligned with the developing Federalist Party, as his policies aroused more vigorous denunciation by Republicans.

Relations with Britain: Threats of War

The European wars did not give the United States the position of commercial advantage that Jefferson had imagined. On the contrary, the ports and the navies of the two main belligerents, France and England, both plundered the American merchant marine. Each stood to gain from trade with neutrals, but each also stood to gain from interrupting its enemy's neutral trade. France, beginning in 1793, confiscated cargoes in its ports. In June, Britain proclaimed a naval blockade of France, which became the basis for seizure of American cargoes headed there. In the autumn, when Britain undertook the conquest of the French West Indies, the government ordered the seizure of all ships trading with those islands—principally American—and kept its order secret until the concentration of ships for seizure was greatest.

Jefferson and the Republicans were troubled by the fact that 75 percent of American imports came from the British Empire and that most American exports went to Britain, even if the goods were subsequently reexported to the Continent. Such a pattern of trade might make the United States dependent on British policy and susceptible to the monarchical influence of Britain's reactionary policies, the Republicans feared. They hoped to establish a more extensive trade with France—indeed, to force American trade into French channels in order to destroy the influence over American politics arising from commercial ties with Great Britain.

Jefferson and the Republicans imagined that they could use the weapon of American trade against Britain and without fear of British military action against the United States. The Republicans opposed expenditures for an American military establishment on the scale that Federalists favored. In response to raids on American commerce by Algerian corsairs, Madison recommended that the United States hire the Portuguese navy to do the fighting. Washington, though he and the Federalists deprecated war with Britain, believed that the British might attack America as an ally of France. Moreover, the British seemed to be encouraging the activities of the Barbary pirates to drive American shipping out of the Mediterranean. In February, 1794, Congress authorized the construction of six frigates but also, during the same year, voted bribes to the dey of Algiers for the protection of American vessels.

Few people in government doubted, in the early months of 1794, that the United States and Britain would soon be at war. Hamilton and some Federalist senators believed, however, that the United States could persuade the British that America did not intend to wage covert war under the pretense of neutrality. To this end, these men urged Washington to send a special minister to Britain, charged with concluding a treaty that would avoid war and would settle such points of controversy as the continued presence of one thousand British troops on United States territory and the terms of American trade with Britain and the British West Indies. The Republicans, clinging to Jefferson's belief in commercial coercion of Britain, passed a bill in the House of Representatives prohibiting American trade with Britain. The bill lost in the Senate only by the casting vote of Vice President Adams. The ensuing compromise, an embargo keeping American ships in port, was lifted when it proved detrimental to the trade of the Southern states. Washington decided to send a minister plenipotentiary to Britain and chose Chief Justice John Jay. Hamilton, whose attachment to Britain matched that of Jefferson to France, drafted Jay's instructions. Jay was to secure British withdrawal from the American West, reparations for British seizures of American merchant vessels, compensation for the slaves that the British army had removed from the Southern states during the Revolutionary War, and a commercial treaty defining the Americans' trading rights with the British Empire.

Jay wanted a treaty and not war with Britain. He did not go to London to issue ultimatums. Even if he had wanted to hold out the threatening possibility that the United States might join with neutral European nations to enforce trading rights, he could not have done so because Hamilton, on his own initiative, had already assured the British minister in Philadelphia that the United States would not join the Armed Neutrality. Hamilton and Jay hoped to get the best results by a friendly approach. The British were primarily concerned with preventing any American friendship with France and keeping Anglo-American trade open to offset British merchant marine losses, crop failures, and falling government revenues. Nevertheless, they were disposed to make few concessions to the United States at the expense of British interests, as wartime mercantilist policy defined those interests.

Jay secured very little beyond maintaining peace with Britain. The British agreed to remove their troops from American territory by June, 1796, and allowed Americans to trade with India. American vessels of 70 tons or less could trade with the British West Indies but could not take molasses, sugar, coffee, cocoa, or cotton to ports other than American ones. Since a small, single-masted sloop might mea-

sure nearly 400 tons, this was a very limited concession. Other subjects of dispute—compensation for British spoliation of American commerce, British creditors' claims against American debtors, the location of the northwest international border—were referred to arbitration by joint commissions. Jay, who opposed slavery, did not even ask for compensation to slaveowners whose slaves had been freed by the British army. To secure these terms, Jay made a number of substantial concessions to Britain. He abandoned the American claim that neutrals had the right to trade freely with all belligerents, and he acquiesced in the British restrictions on neutral trade, including limitations on such commodities as naval stores and food. The treaty conceded Britain most-favored-nation status in American ports, thereby precluding American taxes and other legislation directed specifically against the British. The United States also conceded that it could not sequester money owed by Americans to Britons for private debts. Finally, the treaty guaranteed that American ports would not be open to the navies or the privateers of enemies of Britain; nor would prize vessels any longer be condemned in American ports.

The Federalists still had a commanding majority in the Senate; and, after removing from the treaty a prohibition on American export of cotton and the objectionable article on the West Indies trade, they were able to muster the two-thirds vote to ratify the treaty on June 24, 1795. Although the Senate undertook to deliberate in secret, Senator Stevens Thomson Mason of Virginia, an opponent of ratification, leaked a copy of the treaty, the terms of which were soon widely publicized. Jay's terms attracted bitter denunciation from Republicans: Mass meetings deplored the betrayal of American rights and national dignity; antitreaty petitions received many signatures. Workers in the port cities north of Baltimore were especially conspicuous in the protests organized by Republicans. The treaty was overwhelmingly unpopular among the political leaders of the Southern states.

Washington came near to leaving the treaty unsigned. He was especially provoked by learning, late in June, that the British had begun to seize American vessels carrying foodstuffs to France. In July, however, the British minister disclosed to the American government captured dispatches from the French minister in Philadelphia to his superiors. These convinced Washington that his secretary of state, Edmund Randolph, had sought bribes from the French. Washington decided to sign the treaty in order to assert that American policy was not subject to corrupt French influences. He feared that pro-French and anti-British sympathies among American politicians had already grown so great that only a treaty with Britain could forestall the degradation of the United States into a satellite of France. He required Randolph to execute the ratification before he revealed the captured documents to the secretary. When Randolph saw that his explanations did not convince Washington, he immediately resigned. Not until after the treaty went into effect did the British rescind the order for the seizure of American vessels.

Republicans decided to resist the implementation of the treaty in the House of Representatives by refusing to enact the legislation needed to carry its provisions into effect. They held the first congressional party caucus in order to mobilize their majority. Although this meeting did not produce consensus, it was an important innovation in disseminating a party policy and in seeking organized support. In March, 1796, the House called on the president to submit the documents pertaining to the negotiation of the treaty. This action implied that treaties need not be considered effective until the House approved them by its implementing legislation. Washington refused the request and asserted that the Jay Treaty was now the supreme law of the land. He cited as evidence of the House's error in its constitutional stance

the fact that the Constitutional Convention had voted down a proposal to give the House a role in treaty making. In rebuttal to Washington, Madison argued what became the prevailing view of constitutional interpretation: that the specific opinions of the framers of the Constitution were not binding on subsequent interpretations of it. The House endorsed Madison's argument by a majority that included some Federalists.

To counteract the Republicans' defiance and to solidify Federalists' loyalty to the administration, Hamilton—who had been succeeded as secretary of the treasury by Oliver Wolcott, Jr., on January 31, 1795, but who remained an influential party leader—set out to stimulate and dramatize protreaty public opinion. With the support of businessmen who wanted increased trade and closer ties with England, public meetings and petitions voiced support for Washington and the treaty. At the end of April, 1796, the supporters of the treaty narrowly won a vote in the House in favor of implementing it. The aftermath fulfilled the expectations of those interested in American commerce. Exports to the British Empire increased 300 percent within five years. In the same period, exports of American cotton rose from six million pounds to twenty million pounds. The rapid extension of this staple crop underlay the growth of a slave labor society in the Southern states. In 1796, British troops withdrew from the American Northwest, and the arbitration commissions in later years eventually settled the remaining issues.

The domestic agitation over the Jay Treaty promoted the coordination of party activities both in Congress and among the electorate, though the percentage of eligible citizens who voted remained small. Divisions over economic interests, the French Revolution, presidential power, sectional grievances, and competing visions of America's future came increasingly to be expressed through a partisan system. The Republicans enhanced the sophistication of their appeals to "the people"—that is, to many citizens whom the Federalists had not originally expected to have weight in matters of national policy. Newspapers, pamphlets, mass meetings, parades, local committees, and other techniques helped to expand the politically active population. The Federalists, though ultimately with less success, used similar methods on their own behalf.

Conspicuous in the denunciation of the Jay Treaty was bitter public abuse of President Washington. The Republican press charged him with affecting "the seclusion of a monk and the supercilious distance of a tyrant." He was called a "usurper" who was guilty of "political degeneracy" and who harbored "dark schemes of ambition." According to a writer in the *Philadelphia Aurora,* Washington had fought in the Revolutionary War only for power and personal glory. Another accused him of military incompetence. He was even charged—

correctly, as it turned out—with drawing his salary as president in advance. This meant, his critic said, that Washington intended to extract more than his allotted $25,000 per year from the Treasury—and he should therefore be impeached. Early in Washington's second term, Jefferson had noticed that the president was "extremely affected by the attacks made and kept up on him in the public papers. I think he feels those things more than any person I ever met with." Politically, Washington's reaction to the criticism was to ally himself more fully with the Federalists. After the resignation of Randolph, the cabinet had only Federalists in it: Wolcott as secretary of the treasury, Timothy Pickering as secretary of state, James McHenry as secretary of war, and Charles Lee as attorney general. All these men, as well as Washington, continued to be influenced by the advice of Hamilton, now an attorney in New York.

General George Washington Reviewing the Western army at Fort Cumberland the 18th of October 1794. (Library of Congress)

The Whiskey Rebellion and the Western Lands

The Washington administration confronted a domestic challenge to federal authority during the summer of 1794, while Hamilton was still in the cabinet. The secretary of the treasury took advantage of the occasion to dramatize his conception of the federal government's power. The challenge consisted of violent resistance in four western counties of Pennsylvania to the collection of the federal excise tax on whiskey. Private distilling of whiskey was common in the West, partly because it made corn crops a more readily exchangeable and transportable commodity. The federal tax struck many Westerners exactly as Hamilton intended it should—as a direct assertion of their subordination to the federal government. Many western Pennsylvanians decided to resist. They threatened excise officers, robbed the mails, stopped federal judicial proceedings, and seized United States soldiers who were guarding the home of an excise inspector. A general meeting threatened an attack on Pittsburgh.

Washington initially sent federal commissioners to the disturbed area; they were authorized to negotiate a peaceful settlement. Any federal use of force would have to rely on state militias called into federal service. Fearing more widespread defiance, the administration soon decided to use force. An army of thirteen thousand militiamen from Pennsylvania, New Jersey, Maryland, and Virginia was mobilized under the command of Governor Henry Lee of Virginia. Contrary to the Westerners' threats, the federal units met no resistance. Some leaders of the resistance fled, and the followers remained quiet when the army arrived. About twenty men were arrested, of whom two were later convicted and subsequently pardoned by Washington.

The president agreed with Governor Lee and other Federalists that the Pennsylvania unrest did not arise from reluctance to pay taxes.

It had been incited, Washington and his supporters charged, by the Democratic and Republican societies and by the inflammatory speeches of Republicans in Congress, who denounced the policies of the Washington administration. Madison, Jefferson, and their supporters protested that the administration was using its role as executor of the law to discredit conscientious critics by unjustly linking them with lawbreakers in western Pennsylvania. These Republican complaints had merit. Hamilton had acted provocatively in the spring of 1794 by proceeding with prosecutions of delinquent distillers in distant federal courts after the law had been revised to allow remote cases to be tried in the closest state courts. When Hamilton explained that he was accompanying the militia in Pennsylvania because Governor Lee "might miss the policy of the case," it is likely that he was referring to this opportunity to demonstrate federal power—an opportunity he had orchestrated. Ultimately, Hamilton's eagerness to use federal force and Washington's denunciation of Republican provocateurs backfired, as fellow Federalist Fisher Ames recognized. Ames said, "A regular government, by overcoming an unsuccessful insurrection, becomes stronger; but elective rulers can scarcely ever employ the force of a democracy without turning the moral force, or the power of public opinion, against the government." Washington's partisan interpretation of the Whiskey Rebellion helped establish him, in the eyes of the Republicans, as a thoroughgoing Federalist—a view that the Jay Treaty confirmed.

The volatility of western Pennsylvania exemplified a source of concern that had troubled American politicians since the Revolutionary War—the political cohesion of such a large, diverse country. The controversies over Hamilton's financial program and the Jay Treaty disclosed severe sectional divisions between Northern and Southern states. The expansion of trans-Appalachian settlement raised the threat of separatism and unrest among Western settlers. The Federalists preferred that the Western lands be settled gradually and comparatively stably. To this end, the Land Act of 1796 required that federal land be surveyed before purchase and settlement, that it not be sold for less than two dollars an acre, and that purchasers not receive extended credit. The effect of these provisions was to confine purchasing of federal land primarily to land corporations.

The Mississippi River was the obvious natural channel for the exports of the West, but its southernmost banks were under the control of Spain, the possessor of Louisiana. For Mississippi River trade to be feasible, Americans would have to be allowed to navigate the river through Spanish territory and to deposit their products temporarily near the mouth of the river while the goods awaited export. At the invitation of Manuel de Godoy of Spain, Washington sent Thomas Pinckney to Madrid in May, 1795, to negotiate a treaty on this matter as well as on the questions of the border between the United States and the Spanish colony of Florida and the role of the Spanish in stimulating Indian resistance in adjacent American territory.

French military successes against Spain meant that Spain would have to make territorial concessions to France from its empire. These would include returning Louisiana to France. In doing so, Spain could still undermine the security of France's imperial position by weakening the defensibility of Louisiana. Thus Pinckney found Godoy ready to offer the United States generous terms. In the Treaty of San Lorenzo, October 27, 1795, Spain granted the privilege of navigation of the Mississippi and the privilege of deposit, recognized America's claim to the thirty-first parallel as the border of Florida, and promised not to incite American Indians against the United States. Godoy evaded compliance with these terms until 1798 but left them as an encumbrance on French control of Louisiana thereafter.

Washington's Farewell Address: Three Lessons for the Young Nation

At the height of the scheming and political agitation in the presidential campaign of 1796—which turned on the choice of presidential electors and the attempts to influence the electoral college—Washington published his farewell address. In addition to declining to be considered for reelection, Washington sought to impress upon his fellow citizens three lessons that he considered crucial for the survival of the United States: The Union must be maintained by quelling sectional animosities; political parties threaten liberty by subordinating the people to factional leaders; and American interests are best served by avoiding intense attachments or intense aversions to other nations. Lacking the erudition and intellectual virtuosity of Hamilton or Jefferson, Washington also avoided the self-righteous dogmatism and immoderate enthusiasms to which the two younger men were susceptible. Washington asserted that the interests of the United States militated against exclusive attachment to one great power, even if that nation seemed to be the vanguard of liberty or the bulwark of civilization. Conversely, obsessive hostility toward any country clouded the pursuit of American interests by the preoccupation with the object of hatred.

Although most of the farewell address spoke in abstract terms—the president did boast of Pinckney's treaty and stressed the need to uphold the public credit—a reader could easily see that the address was in many respects a defense of Washington's policies as president as well as a condemnation of the behavior of his critics. Madison, who had helped with a draft in 1792, believed with other Republicans that the address was purely partisan and pro-British. Washington may have seen some vindication in the election of Vice President John Adams as his successor; but the circumstances were not very edifying, considered in the light of Washington's admonitions. Newspaper polemics reached new levels of personal abuse, whereas partisans, not content with denouncing their enemies, betrayed their allies, too. Jefferson's supporters mistrusted their own vice presidential candidate, Aaron Burr. Since electoral votes were cast for individuals, without specifying the office, Hamilton hoped to manipulate the Federalist electoral votes so that Thomas Pinckney rather than Adams would emerge as president. New England Federalists were as determined to check Pinckney as Virginia Republicans were to check Burr. In the outcome of the double crosses, Adams was narrowly elected president, and his Republican opponent, Jefferson, received the second largest vote and became vice president. Although the party organizations were obviously rudimentary, the election luridly demonstrated how little weight Washington's farewell advice carried in practice; nor did posterity heed his counsel on sectional antagonism or on foreign relations.

Washington did not expect his advice to prevail. He wrote that he hoped only that in the future the memory of his words might "recur to moderate the fury of party spirit, to warn against the mischiefs of foreign intrigue, to guard against the imposture of pretended patriotism." At the time of his retirement, there were many grounds for satisfaction. The governmental institutions had survived changes in officials; partisans had not destroyed the government; and states had not left the Union. Indeed, Vermont, Kentucky, and Tennessee had joined it as new states. Nevertheless, Washington's address had a note of detachment, even pessimism, in it. He was eager to retire to Mount Vernon, to take with him intact his personal honor and his public reputation—leaving his fellow citizens and their posterity to endure the consequences of the illusions he vainly warned them against. He said of his warnings, "I dare not hope they will make the strong and lasting impression I could wish—that they will control the usual current of the passions or prevent our nation from

running the course which has hitherto marked the destiny of nations." To Washington and his contemporaries, the course that nations had always run ended in the loss of their liberty and independence. The United States had a destiny no different from that of other countries; but he knew that, when it came, no one would be able to say that it was the fault of George Washington.

In 1799, resisting any hint that he should again be a presidential candidate, Washington wrote, "A mind that has been constantly on the stretch since the year 1753, with but short intervals and little relaxation, requires rest and composure." In retirement, he still had many visitors, took an active interest in the crises of the Adams administration, and accepted the nominal command of the special army established during the quasi-war with France. He censured the Virginia Resolutions against the Alien and Sedition Acts, urged Patrick Henry to come out of retirement as a Federalist candidate in Virginia, and rejoiced in the election of Federalist Virginians John Marshall and Henry Lee to the House of Representatives in 1798. Yet, despite the increasingly partisan role of Washington as an aegis for the Federalist Party—even including many eulogies of him in 1800—he remained an evocative symbol of American nationality. This stature grew even more conspicuous in the nineteenth century, after the alarms of the early national period had faded. The memory of Washington's unique strength of character and his providential achievements in the founding of the nation seemed to posterity to give promise that the United States enjoyed God's special favor. The historian George Bancroft wrote of him in 1858, "Combining the centripetal and the centrifugal forces in their utmost strength and in perfect relations, with creative grandeur of instinct he held ruin in check, and renewed and perfected the institutions of his country. Finding the colonies disconnected and dependent, he left them such a united and well ordered commonwealth as no visionary had believed to be possible."

Washington died as he had lived—practicing self-control, attending to details. In the early hours of December 14, 1799, he developed a severe inflammation of the throat, with labored breathing and much pain. During the day, he submitted quietly to a battery of medical treatments, including bleedings, blisters, and emetics; but he believed from the first attack that the disease was fatal. Finally, he said to his doctors, "I feel myself going. I thank you for your attention. You had better not take any more trouble with me; but let me go off quietly; I cannot last long." To his secretary, Tobias Lear, he said, "I am just going. Have me decently buried and do not let my body be put into the vault in less than two days after I am dead." When Lear did not reply, Washington asked, "Do you understand me?" Lear answered, "Yes, sir." Then Washington said, " 'Tis well." His last action, a few minutes later, was to take his own pulse as it fell.

Washington's Definitive Example: The Centrality of the Presidency

Like many subsequent presidents, Washington left office less popular and less influential than he entered it. Unlike other presidents, whom Americans have expected to be partisan, Washington lost some of his acclaim simply by developing a political affiliation. Compared, however, with the bitter experiences of his immediate successors—Adams, Jefferson, and Madison—Washington's presidency left him comparatively unscathed. The basic concern of the first president was to vindicate the proposition that republican institutions could function and survive. The specific tasks they faced seem much less complicated than those of many later presidents. The additional difficulty of the earliest chief executives was the uncertainty of maintaining the existence of the United States. In this undertaking no American could have inaugurated—or rather created—the office of president to such dramatic effect

as did George Washington. His use of his personal reputation to promote his policies of public credit, expanding commerce, international neutrality, and the extension of westward settlement largely succeeded. Later presidents, pursuing different policies or facing concerns unimagined by Washington, would continue to emulate his use of the presidency. Hardly anyone could imagine a republican America pursuing any course of policy without a president of the United States taking the initiative. In that presumption of the centrality of the office lies Washington's most lasting governmental legacy.

Charles Royster

Bibliographical References

The most thorough biography of Washington is Douglas S. Freeman, *George Washington*, completed by John A. Carroll and Mary W. Ashworth, 7 vols., 1948-1957. James T. Flexner, *George Washington*, 4 vols., 1965-1972, has been abridged in one volume under the title *Washington: The Indispensable Man*, 1979. Thomas A. Lewis, *For King and Country: The Maturing of George Washington, 1748-1760*, 1993, examines Washington's formative years. For an excellent one-volume study, see Marcus Cunliffe, *George Washington: Man and Monument*, rev. ed., 1982. Harrison Clark, *All Cloudless Glory*, 2 vols., 1998, is based solely on original sources from autobiographical materials that Washington left behind. Willard S. Randall, *George Washington: A Life*, 1997, a single-volume biography, focuses on Washington's triumphs over failure and adversity. Garry Wills, *Cincinnatus: George Washington and the Enlightenment*, 1984, perceptively explores Washington's use of power and his public image. Valuable analyses of Washington's administration appear in John C. Miller, *The Federalist Era, 1789-1801*, 1960, and in Forrest McDonald, *The Presidency of George Washington*, 1974. An important work on the policy debates among political leaders is Drew R. McCoy, *The Elusive Republic: Political Economy in Jeffersonian America*, 1980. Curtis P. Nettels, *The Emergence of a National Economy, 1775-1815*, 1962, analyzes many complex developments. Richard Brookhiser, *Founding Father: Rediscovering George Washington*, 1996, recounts Washington's heroic deeds in a quarter-century of public life and reflects upon his legacy. Fritz Hirschfeld, *George Washington and Slavery: A Documentary Portrayal*, 1997, chronicles the evolution of Washington's attitudes toward slavery as both statesman and slave owner. For an analysis of the politics and statecraft during the eight years of Washington's presidency, see Richard N. Smith, *Patriarch: George Washington and the New American Nation*, 1993.

John Adams

2d President, 1797-1801

Born: October 30, 1735
      Braintree, Massachusetts
Died: July 4, 1826
      Quincy, Massachusetts

Political Party: Federalist
Vice President: Thomas Jefferson

Cabinet Members

Secretary of State: Timothy Pickering, John Marshall
Secretary of the Treasury: Oliver Wolcott, Jr., Samuel Dexter
Secretary of War: James McHenry, Samuel Dexter
Secretary of the Navy: Benjamin Stoddert
Attorney General: Charles Lee

On September 19, 1796, President George Washington published his farewell address and revealed to the nation what he had decided privately months earlier, that he would retire from public life at the end of his second term. The news disappointed staunch Federalists, who hoped Washington would run again and thus avoid even the possibility that Thomas Jefferson might become president. It also delighted their opponents, who, not having to counter Washington's immense popularity, might be able to elect Jefferson president. Finally, it relieved Vice President John Adams, who wanted badly to be the Federalist candidate but who had, along with everyone else, to wait nervously until September to be certain Washington intended to retire after all.

Adams did not so much win the Federalist nomination in 1796 as inherit it. He had served

Adams's official portrait. *(White House Historical Society)*

Washington loyally as vice president for eight years, presiding quietly over the Senate, dutifully breaking tie votes in favor of Federalist economic and foreign policies when necessary (Adams broke twenty such ties, more than any other vice president in history). With the exception of Washington, no Federalist still active in national affairs rivaled his reputation with the public as an early and steady advocate of independence. No one still active, Federalist or otherwise, could bring with him to the presidency the long and successful experience in government and diplomacy and the reputation as a legislator, essayist, and speaker that Adams could. If he was not loved by the people at large as was Washington, he was at least genuinely and widely respected for his service to the American Revolution and the republic. In the minds of many Americans, and certainly in his own mind, Adams was Washington's heir apparent.

Lawyer, Revolutionary, Diplomat

Adams was born in 1735 to a middle-class farming family in Braintree (now Quincy), Massachusetts. His parents expected him to enter the ministry. He was graduated from Harvard in 1755 and taught school briefly in Worcester while he convinced himself that he would be far happier and much more successful disputing law before juries than dispensing piety from a pulpit. In 1758, he was admitted to the bar in Massachusetts and began practicing law in Braintree.

Public spirited and ambitious, Adams soon began writing essays for the Boston newspapers and was already established in a minor way as a public spokesperson when the Stamp Act crisis vaulted him into politics and prominence. Resolutions denouncing the stamp tax that he prepared for the Braintree town meeting were well received and circulated throughout the colony. Soon after, he joined James Otis in Boston to challenge the constitutionality of the Stamp Act in court, and he found himself being drawn into popular politics in the capital and into the nascent political party forming around Otis, Samuel Adams, John Hancock, and others. In 1768, Adams moved to Boston, and by the end of the decade his growing reputation as an opponent of British taxation and tyranny won for him election to the Massachusetts General Court.

Ill health forced his withdrawal from office for a while, but the Tea Act crisis brought him back into public view. In 1774, Massachusetts sent him to the First Continental Congress, where he urged a strong stand against English policy and opposed reconciliation on anything but colonial terms. Back in Massachusetts, he wrote a series of essays under the pseudonym of "Novanglus" refuting the Tory essays of Loyalist Daniel Leonard. The Novanglus essays circulated widely and began to build for Adams a national reputation in a nation not yet quite born. He returned to the congress after the war began, and in the spring of 1776 he was appointed to a committee to prepare a declaration of independence. Though Adams had little to do with drafting the declaration, he had much to do with wrestling Jefferson's text through an excited but nervous and often balky congress. In Jefferson's opinion, Adams was the declaration's "ablest advocate and defender" in the congress.

Adams began his diplomatic career in February, 1778, when the Continental Congress dispatched him to Paris to replace the discredited Silas Deane as a member of the American diplomatic team seeking French aid against England. For the next ten years, with only one brief hiatus during which he helped write Massachusetts's revolutionary constitution, Adams represented the republic abroad at Paris, Amsterdam, The Hague, and London on a variety of diplomatic missions: seeking recognition for the new nation, raising money, negotiating treaties of trade and alliance, and, most challenging of all, helping draft the Treaty of Paris, which finally brought the War of Independence, if not the American Revolution, to a formal close. In Paris, he acquired a healthy skepticism about French diplomats and a thorough dislike of Benjamin Franklin. Between 1785 and 1788, he served in London as the first United States minister to England. During his last two years abroad, he wrote *A Defense of the Constitutions of the United States of America*, which argued that bicameral (as opposed to unicameral) legislatures; the sharp separation of legislative, executive, and judicial functions in government; and a powerful executive with an absolute veto were all crucial elements of good constitutions. "The people's rights and liberties," he contended, could "never be preserved without a strong executive," for "if the executive power, or any considerable part of it, is left in the hands . . . of . . . a democratical assembly, it will corrupt the legislature as rust corrupts iron, or as arsenic poisons the human body." Such ideas would not be popular in America, he told Jefferson in 1787 (accurately, as it turned out), but he intended to publish his opinion anyway, "however unpopular it might be."

Adams returned home in 1788 and the following year won the vice presidency. It was not a particularly gratifying victory, since he received only 34 of the 69 electoral votes cast, and it placed him in a job he described halfway through his tenure as "the most insignificant office that ever the invention of man contrived or his imagination conceived." By 1796, then, Adams was determined either to move on to the presidency or, failing that, to retire to his law practice, his farm, and his family in Quincy.

The Campaign of 1796: No Electoral Mandate

The presidential campaign of 1796 was, by modern standards, a curious one. Both candidates thought it demeaning and unseemly to plead for votes, so neither campaigned. In Adams's opinion, and Jefferson's too, public

Abigail Adams *(Library of Congress)*

men should be called to office by an unsolicited electorate, very much as a minister was called to his pulpit by a congregation—a relaxed approach to presidential politics that would not survive Adams's presidency. Still, a campaign did take place in 1796, carried out mostly by newspaper essayists, editors, and political pamphleteers. Also, the election was expected to answer important questions. For example, what kind of government had the Philadelphia Convention of 1787 created? Or, put a little differently, where, precisely, was the limit of federal power with respect to the states? With England and France again at war, where did the best interests of the United States lie: as an ally of the revolutionary French Republic or as an ally in all but name of Great Britain? Did they lie somewhere in between?

Jefferson and his backers believed that Adams, Alexander Hamilton, and the Federalists had already perverted the Constitution and increased the powers of the central government at the expense of the states to a dangerous degree during Washington's two terms. Should Adams win, they warned, this assault on the Constitution and on the liberties of all Americans would doubtless continue. Adams, Republican essayists insisted, was a monarchist at heart who would reestablish in America the principles of monarchial government if he could. He was therefore unfit to govern a free people, and for proof they pointed to *A Defense of the Constitutions*.

From Adams's point of view, the creation of an effective national government with its powers properly distributed among its branches, and the imposition of order on licentious state governments prone to truckle to the whim of popular majorities, had been two important purposes of the Constitution. Two-thirds of the states, he thought, had constitutions so defective that they were, "as sure as there is a Heaven and an Earth," bound to produce "disorder and confusion." For Adams, Jefferson's election promised not liberty but licentiousness, not an ordered and orderly republic but the chaos and injustice inevitably born of weak government.

The two men differed as well over foreign affairs. Jefferson looked upon the War of Independence as the beginning of a revolution that would secure for Americans new liberties. He considered the American Revolution the first stage of an international movement that would topple monarchy throughout Europe as well as in America. Thus Jefferson and his Democratic Republicans welcomed the French Revolution and insisted that both America's revolutionary principles and its self-interest demanded close ties with France.

Adams and most Federalists, in contrast, looked on the War of Independence as the end of a revolution that had been fought, not so much to establish new liberties, as to preserve traditional ones. He thought of the Constitution as a means of securing these familiar liberties by returning order and authority to American

national government. Neither America's principles nor its self-interest, then, dictated an alliance with the architects of the Reign of Terror in France or their successors. If forced to choose between embracing the tricolor or the union jack (and unlike arch-Federalists such as Timothy Pickering and Alexander Hamilton, Adams did not believe that the nation *had* to choose one or the other), he would have preferred the British, whose balanced constitutional system (the recent perversions of George III and his henchmen aside) Adams rather admired. A Jefferson presidency, he feared, would draw the nation into a disastrous war with England and weaken the republic, perhaps fatally.

In the end, the clumsy maneuverings of Hamilton probably had as much to do with the outcome of the election as the often-hysterical debates conducted in the press. Even before Washington's farewell address, Hamilton hoped to find a way to prevent Adams's election without assuring Jefferson's. Adams was far too independent to work comfortably and closely with a man of Hamilton's arrogance and ambition. Hamilton eventually plotted to have Adams's vice presidential running mate, Thomas Pinckney of South Carolina, elected president, thus consigning Adams again to the limbo of the vice presidency. Since each elector cast two ballots, the scheme involved convincing a few Federalist electors to vote for Pinckney but not Adams. Presuming the Federalists won the election, Pinckney would have a few votes more than Adams and so would be president. He would, it was expected, accept with little protest Hamilton's advice on domestic and foreign affairs.

Inevitably, word of Hamilton's plot reached Adams. Angry about "treacherous friends" in his own party, he told his wife in December, 1796, that he was "not enough of an Englishman nor little enough of a Frenchman for some who would be very willing that Pinckney should come in chief." He predicted, however, that "they will be disappointed."

He was right. New England's eighteen Federalist electors, annoyed that Hamilton intended to steal the election from one of their own, voted solidly for Adams but gave no notes to Pinckney. South Carolina's eight electors voted for Pinckney but then cast all of their second-ballot votes for Jefferson. When the ballots were counted, Adams stood highest with 71 electoral votes, only two of which came from states south of the Potomac River. Jefferson stood second with 68 and so became vice president. Pinckney finished third with 59, and Jefferson's running mate, Aaron Burr of New York, polled only 30. Adams was president by three votes, a margin he found humiliating. Neither the Democratic Republicans nor his own pride would let him forget over the next four years just how narrow his victory had been. Unlike Washington, who had received every electoral vote in 1789, Adams was just barely president. He could hardly claim or even pretend, as Washington could, that he was president of all the people.

Adams as President: Under the Shadow of France

John Adams took the oath of office on Saturday, March 4, 1797. The new president was not a physically impressive man as he rose to deliver his inaugural address. Short and overweight, his hands occasionally trembling as the result of one of the vague illnesses that plagued him all of his life, he spoke with a lisp that made his words sometimes hard to follow. He praised Washington's policies and promised to continue them, and he tried to allay Republican-inspired fears that he might, by fiat presumably, alter the Constitution. He had, he insisted, no thought of making any changes in it "but such as the people themselves" might think necessary, and those only by amendment in the proper way. He hoped to "maintain peace . . . with all nations" and "neutrality . . . among the belligerent powers of Europe," and he professed (somewhat dishonestly) "esteem for the French nation" and (more truthfully) a determination to preserve Franco-American friendship by every reasonable means in his power, a pledge arch-Federalists thought uncomfortably Republican in tone. As the inauguration ended, a tired and relieved Washington told Adams, "Ay! I am fairly out, and you fairly in! See which of us will be happiest."

Adams began his term by trying to unite the nation and his own party behind his presidency. He offered a critical diplomatic mission to France to Thomas Jefferson, hoping to impress the French and to preempt Republican criticism of his foreign policy, but Jefferson refused the appointment. To foster unity in his own party, Adams kept Washington's cabinet officers: Timothy Pickering as secretary of state, James McHenry as secretary of war, Oliver Wolcott, Jr., as secretary of the treasury, and Charles Lee as attorney general. It was not, on the whole, a distinguished group. McHenry, for example, had been appointed only after a half dozen men declined to serve and Washington despaired of finding anyone more talented who would accept. Worse, most of the members owed their appointments and their influence in the party to Hamilton. McHenry and Pickering (and Wolcott more often than not) seemed determined to undermine the president's policies in order to implement Hamilton's in their place. McHenry went so far as to pass President Adams's queries to him on to Hamilton, who prepared replies that McHenry then passed back to the president as his own. At the head of a divided nation, a divided party, and a divided administration, Adams faced his first test as president.

Rarely in American history has a president been as completely preoccupied with a single issue throughout his term as Adams was with Franco-American relations. From his first day in office, the subject monopolized his time and destroyed his hopes for bipartisan support. It poisoned his already troubled relations with important leaders in his own party and crippled his attempts to earn the trust of his Republican opponents. Denounced throughout much of his term by the Jeffersonian left as a warmongering lackey of monarchist Federalists, and condemned by the Hamiltonian right as a cowardly panderer to American Jacobins, Adams followed his own independent policy, guided by his sense of integrity and his intuitive understanding of public opinion and the national interest. For four years no one, least of all Adams, knew whether his stubborn moderation in dealing with the French would succeed. In the end, when it did, Adams considered the results—enduring peace with France—the proudest achievement of his public life.

Even before Adams took office, it was clear that France and the United States were dangerously close to open war. Angered by President Washington's declaration of American neutrality (which helped England and hurt France), by the Jay Treaty (which did the same), and by Washington's recall of James Monroe as American envoy in Paris, the French reacted by ordering Monroe's replacement, Federalist Charles Cotesworth Pinckney, out of the country. Shocked again by Jefferson's defeat in 1797, the French began to treat the United States in many ways as an enemy state. French naval vessels and privateers began to capture American ships and confiscate cargoes bound to or from English ports, especially in the West Indies. Americans serving in the British navy—even those who had been forced to serve against their will—were declared pirates subject to execution on capture. As more and more American cargoes were seized, many on meager pretexts, the two nations began to drift into war.

Adams called Congress into special session in May, 1797, to deal with the crisis. His opening message warned France "and the world" that Americans were "not a degraded people, humiliated under a colonial spirit of fear and a sense of inferiority," fated to be "the miserable instruments of foreign influence." He recom-mended some limited military preparations in case war came and, equally important in Adams's view, to establish American credibility overseas. After all, on the day he took office, the regular army numbered less than three thousand men and it had its hands full on the frontier. The navy, politely so called, barely existed, boasting only a few light revenue cutters, though three substantial frigates were under construction. Congress agreed to build twelve new frigates, to put the militia on alert, to strengthen coastal fortifications, and to arm American merchants trading to the East Indies and the Mediterranean.

The XYZ Affair

Having begun to prepare for war, Adams also asked the Senate to sanction a special commission to France to preserve the peace if possible. He proposed sending John Marshall of Virginia and C. C. Pinckney of South Carolina, both moderate Federalists very much in Adams's mold, and (over the shrill protests of Timothy Pickering and the brooding suspicions of other high Federalists) anti-Federalist Elbridge Gerry of Massachusetts. The Senate somewhat reluctantly agreed. Congress adjourned in mid-July and the president and nation settled back to await the outcome. Everything depended on the commissioners' reception in France.

Early in March, 1798, Adams learned that not only had the ruling Directory of France refused to receive the commissioners officially but also that Talleyrand, the foreign minister, had demanded a bribe of 50,000 pounds sterling and a substantial loan for France as his price for merely beginning negotiations.

Talleyrand did not yet know (though he was about to learn) that whereas diplomacy in Europe might customarily be conducted by gentlemen in the privacy of their chambers, diplomacy in a popular republic could be conducted very differently. In the United States, the most sensitive diplomatic communications might even appear in the press and be hotly debated in the finest townhouses and the rawest frontier taverns if there were votes to be won as a result. Talleyrand also did not understand (though he was about to learn this, too) that new nations tend to be extraordinarily sensitive about their national honor and downright starchy about insults to the flag—and the United States in 1798 was still a very new nation.

After Secretary of State Pickering replaced the names of the French agents who carried Talleyrand's demands to the American commissioners with the letters X, Y, and Z, Adams sent the commission's dispatches to Congress. The Senate ordered them published in April, 1798, and the nation exploded with anger. Their publication, wrote Charles Francis Adams, "was like the falling of a spark into a powder magazine." Even some Republicans now denounced France and applauded C. C. Pinck-

ney's reply to the insulting demand for money: "No! No! Not a sixpence!" Adams, who normally walked the streets of Philadelphia without the public much noticing or caring, suddenly drew cheering crowds when he attended the theater or appeared in public. "Adams and Liberty" became a popular slogan, and overnight public opinion turned on France and rallied behind the president and the party that had long been suspicious of the French Revolution and that had warned that a French alliance was not in America's interest. The XYZ affair, as it came to be called, carried Adams and the Federalists to heights of popularity neither would ever know again. Almost as angry as the people he led, Adams promised Congress that he would "never send another minister to France without assurances that he will be received, respected and honored as the representative of a great, free, powerful and independent people."

A contemporary political cartoon of the XYZ affair, with Frenchmen trying to bribe "Madame Amerique." *(The Lilly Library, Indiana University, Bloomington)*

The Half-War with France

Protecting American commerce from French attack was the first priority. To that end, Adams asked Congress to create a department of the navy, to buy or build another twenty warships as soon as possible, to permit merchant ships to arm against French attack, and to abrogate all existing treaties with France. He also wanted the navy and American privateers authorized to prey on armed French ships (but not on unarmed vessels).

Many Federalists in Congress and out, such as Fisher Ames and Stephen Higginson, almost eager for a grand patriotic war, were pleasantly surprised by Adams's strong words. They assumed that he now saw the justice, the utility, and the inevitability of the war they were certain must come.

They could not have been more wrong. What Adams wanted was to force France to negotiate with the United States yet again, but this time on equal terms. The key to his plan was a fighting navy strong enough along the Atlantic coast and in the West Indies to neutralize French pressure on American commerce and to make the price of French belligerence at sea high enough that Talleyrand would seek a diplomatic end to the conflict. The Federalist majority in Congress, however, looked on the XYZ affair, the public rage it fostered, and the full war they expected to follow as a heaven-sent opportunity to destroy their Jeffersonian opponents by branding them traitors and as a chance to rid the country (as one of them put it) of "democrats, mobocrats and all other kinds of rats." Hamilton's allies in Congress and the cabinet pushed through a program of military preparation that went well beyond Adams's carefully measured response to French provocations. Congress approved raising an army of ten thousand men and enlisting another fifty thousand in a provisional army that could be quickly mustered into service following a declaration of war or a French invasion. Without consulting the president, the Federalist majority adopted a new series of taxes on houses, land, and slaves to pay for it all.

Adams had not asked for a large army to fight a declared war; he wanted a strong navy to prevent one. Yet he dared not veto the army bill. National unity, or at least the appearance of it, was crucial to Adams's plan. With the nation already engaged in an undeclared war with France at sea, he could not permit the angry brawl between the president and Congress that a veto would trigger.

Adams's lukewarm enthusiasm for the new army soon grew cooler. Many Federalists who were dissatisfied with Adams's leadership saw the army as a way to raise their preferred leader, Alexander Hamilton, to military glory and possibly to the presidency. Washington had converted success on the battlefield into a presidency. Perhaps Hamilton could too. Washington was the only possible man for commander in chief of the new army. Even Adams saw that, and he promptly offered him the post. The aging general, one of the few prominent Federalists who understood that Adams's goal was to establish peace rather than to promote a war and who thoroughly approved, accepted on two conditions. Happily retired at Mount Vernon, he did not want to take command in the field unless dire national emergency (presumably a French invasion of the South aimed at raising a slave rebellion) made his presence with the army absolutely essential. Also, he insisted he be allowed to name his own subordinate officers. "If I am looked at as the Commander in Chief, I must be allowed to chuse such as will be agreeable to me," he wrote to Secretary of War McHenry.

Washington, however, who had been privately lobbied by Hamilton and his supporters, including (unknown to Adams) Secretary McHenry, eventually insisted that Hamilton become his second in command and therefore, in effect, field commander of the army. He threatened to resign if he did not get his way.

By now, Adams despised Hamilton. He is, he wrote to Abigail Adams in January, 1797, "a proud Spirited, conceited, aspiring Mortal always pretending to Morality, with as debauched Morals as old Franklin." As President, however, Adams had little choice. Washington's resignation would divide the nation and turn a good part of the public against the administration. Angrily ("You crammed him down my throat," Adams complained later), he consented to Hamilton as the army's ranking major general.

The Alien and Sedition Acts

In the meantime, Congress laid plans to suppress enemy aliens and French sympathizers in America, to shield the government from divisive criticism during the war that was doubtless only months away, and to restrict the growth of the Republican Party. The Sedition Act of July, 1798, made libelous or false statements about public officials of the United States, or any statement fostering sedition or contempt for the government, federal crimes punishable by fine and imprisonment. Republicans denounced the law and warned that Federalists thought virtually all dissent seditious and all criticism treasonable. In the hands of partisan judges and prosecutors, they predicted, the law would be used to suppress the kind of public debate over men and measures that was essential in a free republic. Some of their fears were borne out as the editors of important Republican newspapers were prosecuted under the Sedition Act and several were jailed. Yet no Federalist editor went to prison for printing charges about Vice President Jefferson (presumably shielded from criticism by the law too) that were as false and malicious as any leveled at Adams.

The acts moved Jefferson and James Madison to introduce resolutions into the Virginia and Kentucky legislatures, arguing that the Constitution was, properly understood, a compact among sovereign states that were competent to judge for themselves whether federal laws were or were not constitutional. Jefferson went further, claiming that states could nullify federal laws they deemed unconstitutional.

The president had not asked for the Sedition Act, but he had no real objection to it either. For a public man, he was remarkably thin-skinned, and he would recall for years the pain and humiliation newspaper attacks on him produced. In his anger, he found it difficult to distinguish between partisan attacks on his integrity and seditious attacks on the presidency and the nation. "The profligate spirit of falsehood and malignity" in the press, he told the people of Boston at the time, threatened "the Union of the States, their Constitution of Government, and the moral character of the nation."

New alien laws, passed in the same session of Congress, gave Adams the power to expel enemy aliens during wartime and dangerous aliens in peacetime and increased the time an immigrant had to live in the United States before becoming a citizen from five years to fourteen. There is no need, said Harrison Gray Otis, summing up Federalist thought on the matter during an earlier debate over naturalization, "to invite hordes of wild Irishmen, nor the turbulent and disorderly of all parts of the world, to come here with a view to disturb our tranquility," especially, he might have added, when those Irishmen and their like voted Republican with alarming consistency once they became citizens.

The summer and fall following Congress's adjournment in 1798 was the worst time of Adams's presidency. His wife, Abigail, fell sick, and Adams, afraid she was dying, stayed with her in Quincy and conducted such affairs of state as he could by mail. In early October, he had to humble himself and agree to have Hamilton command the army under Washington. His plan to make the army acceptable to voters of all parties by appointing some prominent Republicans to high positions in it failed when

Washington and Congress combined to thwart him. Congressional Federalists argued that Jacobins and Republicans (synonymous terms in their opinion) could not be trusted to lead troops against their French friends—or against American rioters and rebels if it came to that. Of Washington's refusal to accept Republicans as staff officers, a still-bitter Adams wrote years later, "I was only Viceroy under Washington and he was only Viceroy under Hamilton." As the officer corps filled up with Federalists—and there were a lot of them, so many that eventually the new army had one commissioned officer for every seven men—the army began to resemble not so much a national force as a Federalist one.

Since Adams was in no particular hurry to enlist men for Hamilton to command, he delayed serious recruiting until 1799, well after the passions and inflamed patriotism of the XYZ affair had

An engraving of President Adams made by Amos Doolittle in 1799. Adams is surrounded by the coats of arms of the sixteen states in the Union at that time, and the eagle holds a banner with the motto Millions for Our Defence, Not a Cent for Tribute, a reference to the XYZ affair. *(Library of Congress)*

cooled. In 1798, the ostensible reason for creating the army (fear of a French invasion) had disappeared altogether when Lord Nelson's fleet defeated the French at the Battle of the Nile. Adams thought there was "no more prospect of seeing a French army here than there is in Heaven." As the possibility (it had never been a probability) of invasion receded month by month, more and more voters began to agree.

Hamilton, however, hoped to use the army for more than simply repelling invaders and

helping the British destroy the French Revolution, attractive though the idea was. He also dreamed of launching, in alliance with Britain, an invasion of Spanish America and of attaching Florida and Louisiana to the United States. When this scheme was presented to Adams (by third parties), he replied that the United States did not happen to be at war with Spain just then, so it was improper for the president even to receive such a proposal, much less act on it. Hamilton also thought it likely that the army would have to suppress insurrection in states such as Virginia, known to be teeming with unrepentant Jeffersonians who might take up arms to resist the Alien and Sedition Acts and the collection of federal taxes.

Adams thought Hamilton's immediate fears groundless, but he did not entirely dismiss the possibility of serious dissent. The large standing army, commanded exclusively by Federalists, and the resulting high taxes that Hamilton thought essential to preserve "domestic tranquility," Adams believed would be very likely to destroy it. If people are forced to pay for "a great army . . . without an enemy to fight," Adams told McHenry in October, 1798, there was no telling what might happen. The public, he warned Theodore Sedgwick early the next year, had so far "submitted with more patience than any people ever did to the burden of taxes, which has been liberally laid on, but their patience will not last always!" Americans had, after all, an uncomfortable amount of practical experience in subverting governments and overturning constitutions; they had done it twice in the last twenty-five years, once by convention and once by rebellion. When Jefferson and others argued in 1798 that laws clearly repugnant to the Constitution were not laws at all, and that they might be nullified by the states, they were speaking the language of revolution, the same language that had justified colonial resistance to the Stamp Act and the Intolerable Acts and had finally laid the groundwork for independence. Few who had lived throughout the American Revolution could have missed the resemblance.

By the end of 1798, protests over high federal taxes were increasing and petitions demanding relief were reaching Congress and the president. In Northampton County, Pennsylvania, three militant tax protesters were jailed for refusing to pay. A local auctioneer named John Fries then led a mob that captured a federal marshal and forced him to release the jailed men. Hamilton seemed almost happy at the news: Perhaps at long last his army would

have someone to fight and a rebellion to suppress. President Adams, calling on the rioters to disperse, sent the army in to restore order. The troops, however, found order already restored and no one to fight. Fries and two others were promptly arrested, tried, and convicted of treason. When they were sentenced to hang, they appealed to Adams for pardons, which he granted against the unanimous advice of his cabinet. Breaking three men out of jail, Adams reasoned, hardly amounted to treason. Also, hanging Americans for protesting taxes that Adams himself thought high and ill advised seemed neither just nor politic. Besides, when dealing with dissent, Adams preferred, if he could, to remove its causes rather than to treat its consequences. Events at home and abroad soon made it possible for him to do just that.

Peace Negotiations with France

By the summer of 1798 it was clear to Talleyrand that his attempt to obtain money from the American envoys and France's attempt to bludgeon the United States into a friendlier foreign policy had not only failed but also had driven the United States close to open alliance with England. The English were already accepting American vessels into their convoys and offering to lend the United States cannon to help fortify its coast. The last thing France needed in 1798 was another declared enemy. Talleyrand began to signal his desire to reopen negotiations. American ships being held in France were released. French privateers in the West Indies were reined in, and French courts there were ordered to stop condoning on the thinnest of grounds the seizure of American cargoes. Some of the most notorious judges involved were recalled to France.

In July, Talleyrand let Elbridge Gerry, the only American envoy still in France, know that any new negotiator Adams might wish to send to Paris would be respectfully received. He even claimed that the demand for a bribe had been instigated by underlings without his knowledge or approval—a lie John Adams found it as convenient to pretend to believe as Talleyrand found it prudent to tell.

In October, 1798, Gerry returned to America and reported to Adams Talleyrand's eagerness to negotiate. At the same time, letters from William Vans Murray, American minister to The Hague, came in reporting the same. Shortly thereafter, Adams told his cabinet that although he was still thinking about a declaration of war, he was also considering sending a new peace commissioner to France.

By February, 1799, the president had made up his mind to try negotiations again. Talleyrand's messages had much to do with his decision, but so did conditions at home. Anger over the Alien and Sedition Acts and the army taxes was on the rise and might get out of hand, and public opinion was beginning to turn against England. The English, too, were seizing American ships, and English admiralty court judges in the West Indies were condemning American cargoes just as enthusiastically as their French counterparts. Republican papers sarcastically recounted these "evidences of British amity." In February, 1799, the *Philadelphia Aurora* reported that in the last six months of the previous year, England had seized $280,000 worth of American goods, $20,000 *more* than France. Also, only the English stopped American ships routinely and hauled off able-bodied seamen to serve in the British navy, claiming that they were British nationals. Some doubtless were; others were not. Then, in November, 1798, HMS *Carnatic* stopped the American warship *Baltimore* en route to the West Indies and removed five crewmen as suspected British deserters. This act was a violation of American sovereignty (and honor, Republican papers happily pointed out) so raw that even Secretary of State Pickering, England's strongest advocate in Adams's cabinet, had to protest. By early 1799, then, to a growing number of Americans it was by no means as

clear as it had been that the English were friends and the French enemies.

On February 18, Adams regained control over foreign policy, which had been slipping by inches out of his hands and into the war Federalists' hands since the XYZ affair. At the same time, although he certainly did not intend to do so, he destroyed what remained of Federalist Party unity and probably his own chance for reelection. Without consulting his cabinet, he sent the Senate a brief message, which Vice President Jefferson, then presiding, read: "Always disposed and ready to embrace every plausible appearance of probability of preserving or restoring tranquility, I nominate William Vans Murray, our minister resident at The Hague, to be minister plenipotentiary of the United States to the French Republic."

The Senate was stunned. Astonished Republicans were puzzled, since they were still convinced that Adams lusted after a war. Federalist senators, expecting war and believing it necessary, were outraged. When the House of Representatives heard the news, wrote one eyewitness to the scene, "the majority acted as if struck by a thunderbolt."

High Federalists thought the proposal madness, but moderate Federalists rallied to Adams. John Marshall liked the idea, as did Benjamin Stoddert (secretary of the navy and the only cabinet member not left over from the Washington administration), Charles Lee, and Henry Knox. Most important of all, Washington, to whom Adams wrote explaining what he had done and why, approved—or at least he did not publicly disapprove. Nothing, however, could be done without Senate consent and militant Federalists there were determined to block new negotiations. Adams unbent far enough to add two more men acceptable to the Senate to the peace commission, but he hinted that if the Senate refused to consent to *any* commissioners, he might resign, leaving Thomas Jefferson as president. The Senate promptly approved a three-man peace commission.

Rumors that the peace might be saved turned into a growing hope that it would be and then into popular insistence that it must be. Adams, however, would not be rushed. Just as public bawling about avenging the nation's honor after the XYZ affair could not impel him to declare war, so now he would not be driven to conclude a peace "that will not be just or very honorable" by, as he put it, a "babyish and womanly blubbering for peace." "There is not much sincerity in this cant about peace," he told Washington. "Those who snivel for it now were hot for war against Britain a few months ago, and would be now if they saw a chance. In elective governments, peace or war are alike embraced by parties, when they think they can employ either for electioneering purposes." Presidents must lead, Adams believed, not follow either popular whim or party preference. Their function under the Constitution was to hold to the course they thought best to prevent the republic's changing direction with every shift in the public mood. The House of Representatives should reflect popular views, but all presidents should—and this president *would*—stand above all that.

Adams delayed sending the commission overseas for eight months, until he received "direct and unequivocal assurances" from the French government that it would be properly dealt with and, not incidentally, until several more American warships had been launched, increasing the nation's strength on the seas and its credibility at the bargaining table. At last, in November, 1799, the peace commission sailed for France. Months of intrigue by Hamilton, Pickering, and others to get Adams to change his mind, to stop the peace and save the war *somehow*, had failed. Adams held to his decision. They never forgave him for it.

The Campaign of 1800: Republican Slurs and Federalist Infighting

In May, 1800, a Federalist congressional caucus nominated Adams for reelection and C. C. Pinckney for vice president. A Republican caucus chose Jefferson and Aaron Burr. There followed eight months of brutal campaigning. Federalist writers and clerics denounced Jefferson as an atheist, a libertine, and a Jacobin whose election would trigger an epidemic of rape, riot, and infanticide across the land. Republicans countered that Adams was a monarchist, an aristocrat, and an enemy to the Constitution. It was rumored in Republican circles that he had intended to reestablish aristocracy in America by marrying one of his children to one of George III's, and that he had planned to become King John I of North America. Only Washington's threat to kill him if he tried it, the rumor went, had saved the republic. Other reports had Adams sending Pinckney to Europe to procure four mistresses, two for himself and two for the president. (If true, Adams quipped, "Pinckney has kept them all for himself and cheated me out of my two.")

Jefferson presented himself in the election as the defender of states' rights against overweening federal power, as the protector of civil liberties against the authors of the Alien and Sedition Acts, and as the advocate of fiscal responsibility against the profligate spending of tax-happy Federalists. Adams found these issues hard to handle. He knew by now that the Sedition Act had been a mistake, but his party had passed it, and had recently refused to repeal it, and he had signed it into law. He opposed a larger army and high taxes, but his party had championed both, and he had signed the resulting laws. He could not deny that federal spending during his term had nearly doubled or that taxes had soared, and he *did* think federal law and government were, and ought to be, superior to state law and government.

Adams, however, distanced himself from the more militant Federalists. It was obvious by election time that he wanted to avoid a declared war with France and to end the undeclared war at sea. Also, the Federalist majority in Congress, uneasily eyeing the coming election, had voted to begin reducing the army early in 1800. All that helped, but the nation did not learn that Adams's peace commission had reached an accommodation with France until the last days of the campaign, after nearly all the electors had already been chosen.

Finally, Adams had to fend off not only Jefferson but also a powerful segment of his own party. In May, he asked Secretaries McHenry and Pickering for their resignations on grounds of gross disloyalty to the president. When Pickering refused, Adams fired him. Hamilton and his allies understandably looked on another term for Adams as a disaster almost as great as a Jefferson presidency. They asked Washington to run again, and when he refused, they tried to arrange the election of Pinckney. Hamilton wrote a venomous pamphlet, intended only for influential Federalists and electors, denouncing Adams as unfit to govern. Republican editors got hold of a copy, printed it, and gleefully wondered aloud when Hamilton would be indicted under the Sedition Act.

Yet, with all his problems, Adams made a fight of the election and came close to winning. Much of the party's old leadership abandoned him, but the rank and file did not. The pivotal state was South Carolina, Pinckney's home state and the only Southern state with a vigorous Federalist tradition, but Republican campaign managers so skillfully distributed promises of federal patronage to the state legislature (which chose South Carolina's electors) that its eight votes went to Jefferson.

By December, Adams, who had just moved the government to the still-uncompleted Capitol at Washington, D.C., knew he had lost. When the electoral votes were tallied, Jefferson and Burr each had 73 (thus they tied for the presidency), whereas Adams had 65, Pinckney, 64, and John Jay, 1. Four years earlier, thirteen different men had received electoral votes. By 1800, the two national political parties so dominated presidential politics that no one but candidates they endorsed received any votes. (The

lone vote for Jay was deliberate, cast so that Adams and Pinckney would not tie for the presidency if the party won.)

Bitter and exhausted, like Washington before him, Adams longed to be free of the incessant, vicious, partisan wrangling that seemed to him now virtually part of the presidency. Yet he wanted badly to be reelected as a vindication of his first term and a public endorsement of his judgment, integrity, and character. He blamed Hamilton for his defeat and humiliation, and the end of Federalist rule.

As Congress wrestled over whom to declare president, Jefferson or Burr, and as it prepared for the inauguration to follow, Adams carried out his final duties as president—signing a new judiciary act and appointing John Marshall as chief justice of the United States were the two most important. Then, at four in the morning on inauguration day, he boarded a public stagecoach heading north. Somewhere near Baltimore, as Jefferson took his oath of office in the Capitol, John Adams's public career ended.

He retreated to Quincy, to farm and read (at last there was time enough), to write occasionally about history or law, and to correspond with friends. Not for thirteen years did his pain, humiliation, and anger fade enough to permit him to write again to his old enemy and older friend, Jefferson. As the years passed and the nation changed around him, he remained proud of his presidency and convinced that it had been a success. He would be happy, he said in later years, if his gravestone bore only this: "Here lies John Adams, who took upon himself the responsibility of the peace with France in the year 1800." He died on July 4, 1826.

Adams in Retrospect: "A Self-Made Aristocrat"

Throughout his public life, Adams displayed an almost cynical understanding of how and why men and governments do what they do.

"I have long been settled in my opinion," he told Jefferson in 1787, "that neither Philosophy, nor Religion, nor Morality, nor Wisdom, nor Interest, will ever govern nations or parties against their Vanity, their Pride, their Resentment or Revenge, or their Avarice or Ambition. Nothing but Force and Power and Strength can restrain them." As the foundation for the foreign policy of an infant republic in a world of monarchies, Adams's ideas had much to recommend them. As the foundation for policy and governance in a popular republic, they left much to be desired. His continued belief in them explains to some extent why as president he had more success in dealing with foreign adversaries than with his fellow countrymen.

He was, wrote historian Gilbert Chinard, "a self-made aristocrat." As such, he never completely understood the democratic strain in the American Revolution, and he never accepted fully its implications. As time and generations passed, the author of *A Defense of the Constitutions* seemed more and more alien to the increasingly democratic and populist mainstream of American thought, until in the minds of Americans Adams's memory was all but completely overshadowed by Washington and eclipsed by Jefferson.

Robert A. Becker

Bibliographical References

Good book-length accounts of John Adams's presidency are Stephen G. Kurtz, *The Presidency of John Adams: The Collapse of Federalism, 1795-1800*, 1949, and Ralph A. Brown, *The Presidency of John Adams*, 1975. For a brief but lively account, see John C. Miller, *The Federalist Era*, 1960, chapters 12-14. On Franco-American relations, see Alexander DeConde, *The Quasi-War: The Politics and Diplomacy of the Undeclared War with France, 1797-1801*, 1966. Manning J. Daur, *The Adams Federalists*, 1953, focuses on the party. Page Smith, *John Adams*, 2 vols., 1962, is a thorough biography. Peter Shaw, *The Character of John Adams*, 1976, is a controversial study. Joseph J. Ellis, *Passionate Sage: The Character and Legacy of John Adams*, 1993, is a perceptive study that focuses on Adams in retirement and examines his achievements and irascible personality. For an analysis of Adams's political and constitutional philosophy, see C. Bradley Thompson, *John Adams and the Spirit of Liberty*, 1998. For John Adams's writing, see Charles Francis Adams, ed., *The Works of John Adams*, 10 vols., 1856. The correspondence of Adams and Jefferson in Lester J. Cappon, ed., *The Adams-Jefferson Letters*, 2 vols., 1959, is fascinating. John Ferling, *John Adams: A Bibliography*, 1994, provides a comprehensive listing of primary and secondary sources on the life and presidency of John Adams.

Thomas Jefferson

3d President, 1801-1809

Born: April 13, 1743
      Shadwell, Goochland (now
      Albemarle) County, Virginia
Died: July 4, 1826
      Monticello, Albemarle County,
      Virginia

Political Party: Democratic Republican
Vice Presidents: Aaron Burr, George
    Clinton

Cabinet Members

Secretary of State: James Madison
Secretary of the Treasury: Samuel Dexter, Albert
    Gallatin
Secretary of War: Henry Dearborn

Secretary of the Navy: Benjamin Stoddert, Robert
    Smith
Attorney General: Levi Lincoln, John Breckin-
    ridge, Caesar Rodney

Jefferson's official portrait. *(White House Historical Society)*

The third president of the United States was the first to gain office by successfully challenging an incumbent. The orderly transfer of authority from John Adams to Thomas Jefferson was a novel success for the new American constitutional system. Jefferson was the only president to be followed by two trusted and loyal friends, James Madison and James Monroe. This "Virginia dynasty," lasting a full six presidential terms, remains unique in American history.

When Jefferson took office, the United States had more than five million inhabitants and extended from the Atlantic to the Mississippi and from the Great Lakes to the northern boundary of Florida. When Jefferson retired, the population had grown beyond eight million people, and American territory extended to the crest of the Rocky Mountains; indeed, the United States now pretended to have some claim to the Oregon Country on the Pacific Ocean. While

Monticello, Jefferson's home. *(Library of Congress)*

Jefferson was president, Robert Fulton, with the backing of Jefferson's political friend Robert Livingston of New York, succeeded in introducing steam navigation on the Hudson River. Eli Whitney, having failed to realize a fortune on his celebrated cotton gin, nevertheless prospered with a contract from Jefferson's War Department for manufacturing rifles with interchangeable parts in Springfield, Massachusetts. Native talent was continually being augmented by gifted immigrants, such as the radical English scientists Joseph Priestley and Thomas Cooper and the gifted architect Benjamin Latrobe, who helped design the public buildings of the new city of Washington, D.C.

A Child of the Enlightenment
With most developments in American society Jefferson was happily and deeply sympathetic. An optimistic child of the Enlightenment, he especially valued education, scientific inquiry, mechanical invention, and voluntary organizations for the improvement of humankind. He believed that government should not tax people to do these things for them but rather should create a climate in which such good things would be done at the people's initiative. Jefferson's maxim, "That government is best which governs least," was therefore not intended to encourage radical individualism but rather to encourage the widest and fullest possible participation in society.

Like many of the democratic heroes of the United States, Jefferson started life in the first rank of society. His father, Peter Jefferson, had worked hard and effectively to build an estate of nearly ten thousand acres around Albemarle County, which he had helped create. Peter was married to Jane Randolph, whose many-branched family was as wealthy and powerful as any in Virginia. He flourished as a tobacco planter, surveyor, militia officer, and justice of the peace. Thomas was born April 13, 1743, into a world, not of dignified leisure, but of bustling, wilderness-clearing, slavetrading, Indian-fighting activity. Among his father's associates were men who already yearned for the virgin lands of the Ohio Valley. Westward expansion, something closely associated with Jefferson until he retired from the presidency, was a family inheritance.

Educated in the local schools of two Anglican clergymen until he was seventeen, Jefferson rode down to the provincial capital of Williamsburg in 1760 to complete his liberal education and learn the law at the College of William and Mary. Such was his precocity that he soon found himself a regular guest at the table of the acting governor, Francis Fauquier. There, too, were Jefferson's favorite teachers, Dr. William Small from Edinburgh and the kindly and erudite lawyer George Wythe. Before he was twenty-one, Jefferson was accustomed to seeing the world through the eyes of learned, active, and powerful men.

Peter Jefferson had died in 1757, when Thomas was fourteen, and from then on Thomas took little interest in his family but much in his studies and in his friends. After six years of study in Williamsburg, he settled into the life of planter and lawyer and was reasonably successful at both occupations. In 1769, he won election to the House of Burgesses, where he quickly joined the majority there defending colonial rights against the supposed incursions of ministerial authority from England. In 1772, he married a wealthy widow, Martha Wayles Skelton, by most accounts an attractive and intelligent woman as well as a fine musician. She died only ten years later in 1782, leaving Jefferson with two daughters, Martha and Maria (Polly). Several other children had been stillborn or died in infancy.

A National Leader: From the House of Burgesses to the White House

Marriage added greatly to Jefferson's responsibilities, and so did the growing crisis between England and its colonies in America. The young burgess from Albemarle became familiar to radicals throughout the colonies through his fiery pamphlet of 1774, *A Summary View of the Rights of British America*. The next year, he attended the Continental Congress in Philadelphia, where his draft of "Causes for Taking Up Arms" was too strong for most of the other delegates but where his literary talents were fully recognized. This led to his appointment to the committee that drafted the Declaration of Independence. Though Congress made a few changes in it (which seemed much more significant to Jefferson than to most subsequent readers), the document remains an example of Jefferson's remarkable style, both for the force and felicity of its general philosophical statements and for the almost reckless élan with which the crimes of George III are cataloged.

Though established as a national leader, Jefferson left the Continental Congress in September, 1776, preferring to be closer to his wife and children. For three years, he worked tirelessly in the Virginia legislature, collecting all the laws of the colonial era and, with Wythe and Edmund Pendleton, forging a new legal code appropriate to a liberal planter's republic. He then served as governor for two terms, from 1779 to 1781, a period which unfortunately coincided with a sustained British invasion of the state. Jefferson was as helpless to prevent the marches and raids of Lord Cornwallis's army as other Southern governors had been. Still, some Virginia politicians tried for a time to blame Jefferson for the inability of the militia to turn the British away. Later, Generals George Washington and Comte de Rochambeau, not Jefferson, received the credit for finally defeating the British army in Virginia.

Retired from office with some feeling of relief, Jefferson wrote the only book he ever published in his lifetime, *Notes on the State of Virginia*, a work about the geography, products, and social and political life of eighteenth century Virginia.

The death of his wife left Jefferson temporarily despondent and aimless. Also, perhaps, it made him willing to serve away from home again. The year 1783 found him once again in the Continental Congress, where he was chiefly responsible for the new nation's system of weights and measures. As chair of a committee on Western lands, he also drafted an elaborate ordinance for the development of Western territories into eventual statehood. His draft included the provision that after a few years, no more slaves could be introduced into the West, a provision that failed to secure the needed support of nine states in the Congress. Before Congress finally acted to create the Northwest Territory, Jefferson had departed for Paris, initially to help John Adams and Benjamin Franklin with commercial negotiations and then, in 1785, to replace the aging and homesick Franklin as United States minister to France.

In Paris, Jefferson tried hard to strengthen commercial relations between France and the United States, but the feebleness of the Congress under the Articles of Confederation and the increasing ineffectiveness of the government of Louis XVI made such changes impossible. From a personal point of view, however, this was a very satisfying period. Jefferson's five years in Europe introduced him fully to the best minds, architecture, wines, and amenities of France. He was a close observer and, to a degree, even an unofficial adviser in the first stage of the French Revolution.

Back in the United States at the beginning of 1790, he accepted President Washington's invitation to become secretary of state. Within a year, however, he had begun to organize opposition to Alexander Hamilton, who as secretary of the treasury functioned as a sort of prime minister under Washington. Since Washington usually supported Hamilton, Jefferson eventually found his position untenable. At the end of 1793, he resigned after completing a report on American trade that indicted the British for unfair trading practices and urged closer ties with the chief ally of the United States, France. Jefferson then enjoyed three years of retirement in which he especially concentrated on building his mansion at Mon-

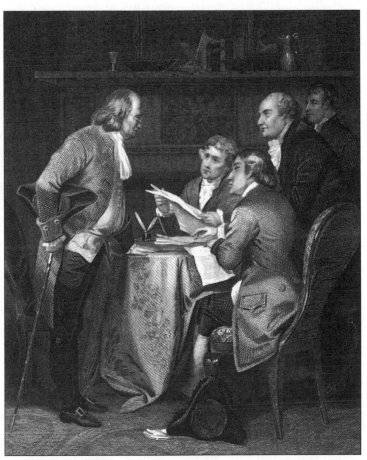

An 1866 engraving of the drafting of the Declaration of Independence, with (left to right) Benjamin Franklin, Jefferson, John Adams, Robert R. Livingston, and Roger Sherman. *(Library of Congress)*

The Declaration of Independence

In CONGRESS, July 4, 1776.

The unanimous Declaration of the thirteen united States of America,

When in the Course of human events, it becomes necessary for one people to dissolve the political bands which have connected them with another, and to assume among the powers of the earth, the separate and equal station to which the Laws of Nature and of Nature's God entitle them, a decent respect to the opinions of mankind requires that they should declare the causes which impel them to the separation.

We hold these truths to be self-evident, that all men are created equal, that they are endowed by their Creator with certain unalienable Rights, that among these are Life, Liberty, and the pursuit of Happiness—That to secure these rights, Governments are instituted among Men, deriving their just powers from the consent of the governed,—That whenever any Form of Government becomes destructive of these ends, it is the Right of the People to alter or to abolish it, and to institute new Government, laying its foundation on such principles and organizing its powers in such form, as to them shall seem most likely to effect their Safety and Happiness. Prudence, indeed, will dictate that Governments long established should not be changed for light and transient causes; and accordingly all Experience hath shewn, that mankind are more disposed to suffer, while evils are sufferable, than to right themselves by abolishing the forms to which they are accustomed. But when a long train of abuses and usurpations, pursuing invariably the same Object, evinces a design to reduce them under absolute Despotism, it is their right, it is their duty, to throw off such Government, and to provide new Guards for their future security.—Such has been the patient sufferance of these Colonies; and such is now the necessity which constrains them to alter their former Systems of Government. The history of the present King of Great Britain is a history of repeated injuries and usurpations, all having in direct object the establishment of an absolute Tyranny over these States. To prove this, let Facts be submitted to a candid world.

He has refused his Assent to Laws, the most wholesome and necessary for the public good.

He has forbidden his Governors to pass Laws of immediate and pressing Importance, unless suspended in their operation till his Assent should be obtained; and when so suspended, he has utterly neglected to attend to them.

He has refused to pass other Laws for the accommodation of large districts of people, unless those people would relinquish the right of Representation in the Legislature, a right inestimable to them, and formidable to tyrants only.

He has called together legislative bodies at places unusual, uncomfortable, and distant from the depository of their Public Records, for the sole purpose of fatiguing them into compliance with his measures.

He has dissolved Representative Houses repeatedly, for opposing with manly firmness his invasions on the rights of the people.

He has refused for a long time, after such dissolutions, to cause others to be elected; whereby the Legislative powers, incapable of Annihilation, have returned to the People at large for their exercise; the State remaining in the mean time exposed to all the dangers of invasion from without, and convulsions within.

He has endeavoured to prevent the population of these States; for that purpose obstructing the Laws for Naturalization of Foreigners; refusing to pass others to encourage their migrations hither, and raising the conditions of new Appropriations of Lands.

He has obstructed the Administration of Justice, by refusing his Assent to Laws for establishing Judiciary powers.

He has made Judges dependent on his Will alone, for the tenure of their offices, and the amount and payment of their salaries.

He has erected a multitude of New Offices, and sent hither swarms of Officers to harass our people, and eat out their substance.

He has kept among us, in times of peace, Standing Armies without the Consent of our legislatures.

He has affected to render the Military independent of and superior to the Civil power.

He has combined with others to subject us to a jurisdiction foreign to our constitution, and unacknowledged by our laws; giving his Assent to their Acts of pretended Legislation:—For quartering large bodies of armed troops among us:—For protecting them, by a mock Trial, from punishment for any Murders which they should commit on the Inhabitants of these States:—For cutting off our Trade with all parts of the world:—For imposing Taxes on us without our Consent:—For depriving us in many cases, of the benefits of Trial by Jury:—For transporting us beyond Seas to be tried for pretended offences:—For abolishing the free System of English Laws in a neighbouring Province, establishing therein an Arbitrary government, and enlarging its Boundaries so as to render it at once an example and fit instrument for introducing the same absolute rule into these Colonies:—For taking away our Charters, abolishing our most valuable Laws, and altering fundamentally the Forms of our Governments:—For suspending our own Legislatures, and declaring themselves invested with power to legislate for us in all cases whatsoever.

He has abdicated Government here, by declaring us out of his Protection and waging War against us.

He has plundered our seas, ravaged our Coasts, burnt our towns, and destroyed the lives of our people.

He is at this time transporting large Armies of foreign Mercenaries to compleat the works of death, desolation and tyranny, already begun with circumstances of Cruelty and perfidy scarcely paralleled in the most barbarous ages, and totally unworthy the Head of a civilized nation.

He has constrained our fellow Citizens taken Captive on the high Seas to bear Arms against their Country, to become the executioners of their friends and Brethren, or to fall themselves by their Hands.

He has excited domestic insurrections amongst us, and has endeavoured to bring on the inhabitants of our frontiers, the merciless Indian Savages, whose known rule of warfare, is an undistinguished destruction, of all ages, sexes and conditions.

In every stage of these Oppressions we have Petitioned for Redress in the most humble terms: Our repeated Petitions have been answered only by repeated injury. A Prince, whose character is thus marked by every act which may define a Tyrant, is unfit to be the ruler of a free people.

Nor have we been wanting in attentions to our British brethren. We have warned them from time to time of attempts by their legislature to extend an unwarrantable jurisdiction over us. We have reminded them of the circumstances of our emigration and settlement here. We have appealed to their native justice and magnanimity, and we have conjured them by the ties of our common kindred to disavow these usurpations, which, would inevitably interrupt our connections and correspondence. They too have been deaf to the voice of justice and of consanguinity. We must, therefore, acquiesce in the necessity, which denounces our Separation, and hold them, as we hold the rest of mankind, Enemies in War, in Peace Friends.

We, therefore, the Representatives of the United States of America, in General Congress, Assembled, appealing to the Supreme Judge of the world for the rectitude of our intentions, do, in the Name, and by Authority of the good People of these Colonies, solemnly publish and declare, That these United Colonies are, and of Right ought to be, Free and Independent States; that they are Absolved from all Allegiance to the British Crown, and that all political connection between them and the State of Great Britain, is and ought to be totally dissolved; and that as Free and Independent States, they have full Power to levy War, conclude Peace, contract Alliances, establish Commerce, and to do all other Acts and Things which Independent States may of right do.

And for the support of this Declaration, with a firm reliance on the protection of divine Providence, we mutually pledge to each other our Lives, our Fortunes, and our sacred Honor.

ticello. He still kept up a full political correspondence and became John Adams's chief rival for the presidency in the election of 1796. The Constitution as originally adopted did not anticipate the existence of political parties. Members of the electoral college voted for two candidates for president. The one receiving the greatest number of votes, if a majority, became president, and the one with the next highest number, vice president. Under this system in 1796 John Adams, a Federalist, was chosen president and Jefferson, a Democratic Republican, was elected vice president. While conscientiously presiding over the Senate during the next four years, Jefferson kept his political activities well concealed. They included writing Kentucky Resolutions of 1798, which asserted the right of the states to nullify acts of Congress—in this case, the Alien and Sedition Acts, which were intended to silence or remove from the country critics of the Federalist Party.

The election of 1800, in which Jefferson challenged the incumbent Adams, took place in a heated partisan atmosphere. Jefferson and the Republicans campaigned against Adams and the Federalists by portraying them as threats to the very notion of republican liberty. They had suppressed freedom, taxed heavily, and

created a dangerous military establishment, the Republicans charged. The people responded with wide support for Jefferson and his vice presidential candidate Aaron Burr, but again the voting in the electoral college produced an unintended result. The electors still did not distinguish between candidates for president and vice president and cast the same number of votes for Burr as they did for Jefferson. The Constitution dictated that the election was to be decided in the lame duck House of Representatives that had been elected in 1798. Many Federalist members in the House thought Burr the lesser evil and a man with whom they could work and cast their votes for him. After many ballots prolonged a stalemate well into February, 1801, a group of border state Federalists withdrew their support from Burr, and Jefferson was finally elected. Two years later, Congress, led by Republicans fearful of a repetition of the dangerous confusion of 1800, passed and the states quickly ratified the Twelfth Amendment to the Constitution, which provided for separate balloting for president and vice president.

The new president was close to his fifty-eighth birthday, but he still stood erect and lean, well over 6 feet tall, with red hair and a ruddy complexion. Always wise in his diet and drink and conscientious in taking exercise, Jefferson enjoyed exceptionally good health until his very last years. He had broken his right wrist in France and never quite recovered complete control of his right hand, but its effect on his violin playing was worse than on his writing. Otherwise, his only physical problem was an occasional severe migraine, which had a way of striking and prostrating him at times when he could scarcely afford to leave his work. Indeed, Jefferson was so industrious that the headaches may have been the way his system forced him to rest from time to time.

A Federalist Legacy of Peace and Prosperity

As John Adams's successor, Jefferson began his first term with several important assets. The United States was at peace with all the major powers, revenues exceeded expenditures, and trade was at an all-time high. So, too, were personal incomes. A good case can be made for saying that Jefferson inherited a strong and prosperous nation because the policies he had systematically opposed had nevertheless served the nation very well. In any case, Jefferson began his term in a conciliatory and generous mood. He came to his inauguration on March 4, 1801, dressed in homespun, as George Washington had done twelve years earlier. Although he owned a handsome carriage, he chose to ride to the Capitol on horseback, emphasizing the fact that he was an ordinary citi-

zen whom his fellow citizens had elected chief magistrate. "We are all Republicans, we are all Federalists," he asserted; the previous quarrels had represented mere differences of opinion and not fundamental differences of principle. Repeating ideas on foreign policy that had appeared in Washington's farewell address, he called for friendship with all foreign nations, "entangling alliances" with none. Disarming critics who charged that he would sell out to the French, Jefferson promised that he would not restore the Alliance of 1778. Furthermore, he was determined to continue the nation's profitable trade with England. He urged a harmony of interests in the Republic,

A copy of the original Declaration of Independence, as signed by John Hancock and the other delegates. (*National Archives*)

though he did assert the primacy of agriculture by describing commerce as "her handmaiden."

Jefferson enjoyed the advantage of having two devoted, loyal, and highly intelligent friends serve in his administration through its full eight years: James Madison as secretary of state and Albert Gallatin of Pennsylvania as secretary of the treasury. His other appointees were reasonably able and represented unavoidable political considerations. Thus his secretary of war, Henry Dearborn, came from the Maine district of Massachusetts and his attorney general, Levi Lincoln, came from Worcester, Massachusetts. Robert Smith, secretary of the navy, was from Maryland. Most of these men, and especially the trio of Jefferson, Gallatin, and Madison, were extremely attentive to the important details of administration.

Jefferson grasped instinctively that he was both chief administrator for the government and head of its majority party; he performed the latter role shrewdly and with masterful informality. Abandoning the formal levees held every week when Congress was in session by his predecessors—they were excessively monarchical for Jefferson's taste—the president entertained congressmen and members of the small diplomatic community in a series of dinner parties. Even there he abandoned protocol, letting each guest scramble for his seat at the table. Still, these were hardly potluck affairs; Jefferson had a fine French chef and a cellar of excellent wines. He had no taste for public oratory but a splendid gift for conversation. In the give-and-take around the president's dinner table, Jefferson quite pleasantly did most of the giving, and his ideas unfailingly filtered into the two chambers of Congress.

Reducing the Government's Reach: The Judiciary Act of 1802

With such promising men and methods at his disposal, Jefferson was, at the outset of his administration, still chiefly concerned with reducing, not expanding, the sphere of government. Economy and retrenchment were his paramount goals, and they required that something be done about the Judiciary Act of 1801. After losing the election of 1800, in an effort to retain control of the judicial branch, the Federalist lame ducks in Congress passed a bill greatly expanding the number of judgeships in the federal system. Besides its partisan purpose, the law wisely anticipated the future growth of the nation and the increasing need for federal courts. It also relieved the justices of the Supreme Court from riding circuit, and as these justices were likely to be men of advanced years, this change was both prudent and merciful. Just before leaving office, Adams appointed loyal Federalists to the new judgeships. The federal judiciary had thus become, as John Randolph of Virginia quipped, "a graveyard for decayed politicians."

With Jefferson's encouragement, the new Congress passed the Judiciary Act of 1802, which essentially repealed the act of 1801 and abolished all the new posts. Secretary of State James Madison further struck at the opposition by declining to deliver a number of certificates of appointment to office that Adams had made out the last night of his presidency and left for his successors to deliver. One of these made William Marbury a justice of the peace for the District of Columbia. Upon failing to obtain his commission, Marbury sued, asking the Supreme Court to issue a writ of mandamus ordering Madison to deliver it. In the celebrated case of *Marbury v. Madison*, the Court found that, although Marbury was entitled to have his commission, the Court could not force Madison to deliver it, for the section of the Judiciary Act of 1789 that empowered the Supreme Court to issue writs of mandamus under its original jurisdiction was unconstitutional. Although Jefferson and Madison were naturally pleased that Madison did not have to deliver to Marbury his commission, they found very unpalatable the Supreme Court's asserting the right of judicial review—that of nul-

Stephen Decatur fights the Barbary pirates of Tripoli. *(Library of Congress)*

lifying an act of Congress on the ground that it violated the Constitution.

Besides the Judiciary Act of 1802, the Seventh Congress, Jefferson's first, passed other measures that pleased a majority of Americans. With the end of Adams's Half-War with France in 1800, the Federalists had reduced the army and navy, but the Republicans cut them further. Also, with trade flourishing and customs receipts mounting, they declared that internal taxes were no longer needed and eliminated all of them, including a very controversial one on distilled liquor. The income from land sales alone permitted the government to meet all of its current expenses and to reduce the national debt significantly as well. It had as a further source of funds the income from the sale of its stock in the Bank of the United States. Even though Jefferson had argued against the constitutionality of the bank when it was char-

tered in 1791, the institution flourished and expanded during his presidency, and it saved the Treasury considerable sums by transferring funds from one part of the country to another at no charge.

War with the Barbary Pirates: To the Shores of Tripoli

There was one small exception to the general pattern of reduced federal activity under Jefferson's presidency. In 1801, the pasha of Tripoli declared war on the United States by the customary device of having his agents chop down the flagpole in front of the U.S. Legation. Such a declaration meant that warships of Tripoli would attack American merchant shipping in the Mediterranean, taking ships and cargoes as prizes and holding their crews for ransom. For several years, the Federalist administrations had paid subsidies and ransoms to three other North African potentates to protect American shipping and rescue its sailors. Now Tripoli was, in effect, demanding a generous payment. In the 1780's, Thomas Jefferson had advocated development of a powerful American navy, in no small part to relieve the United States of the necessity of paying blackmail to the piratical princes of the Barbary Coast. Without seeking authorization from Congress, President Jefferson dispatched a small fleet to the Mediterranean to protect American ships and, if necessary, attack the Tripolitans. Like his predecessors, Washington and Adams, Jefferson tended to disregard the clear prescription of the Constitution that the president make foreign policy with the advice and consent of the Senate. The war with Tripoli went badly until 1805 when, as a result of a combination of American naval pressure and diplomatic skill, the pasha was induced to sign a peace treaty, although the United States was required to pay $60,000 for the release of American prisoners.

Peaceful Expansion: The Louisiana Purchase

Jefferson presided over an era of peaceful growth in the Western territories of the United States. He eased out the old Federalist governor of the Ohio Territory, Arthur St. Clair, who had made many enemies by his indifferent administration and by his opposition to the admission of Ohio to statehood. Following his removal, Ohio became a state in 1803, adding strength to the Republican majorities in Congress. Meanwhile, Congress had authorized a government for the Indiana Territory, and Jefferson appointed William Henry Harrison, son of a former governor of Virginia, to be its governor.

About the same time, a series of events occurred that led to the greatest achievement of Jefferson's presidency and to the single largest addition to American territory, the Louisiana Purchase. In 1763, Bourbon France had reluc-

tantly transferred Louisiana to Spain as compensation for its loss of Florida. A succession of French ministries in the 1780's and 1790's pondered various schemes for reoccupying Louisiana but found none practical. By 1800, however, the king of Spain considered the area a burden rather than an asset. Its only purpose for him was to protect Mexico by offering a buffer against the notoriously expansionist English and Americans. By the secret Treaty of San Ildefonso (1800), Spain retroceded Louisiana to France, which promised in another document that the territory would not be alienated to a third power.

In 1802, news of the retrocession reached Jefferson, followed by the more alarming news that the Spanish governor had used the transfer as an excuse to close the Mississippi to American commerce. Worse still, Jefferson learned that Napoleon Bonaparte had sent a great fleet and army under General Charles Leclerc to reconquer the former French colony of Haiti, which had been the world's foremost producer of sugar before rebellious blacks succeeded in overturning their former masters. After he had reestablished French rule and slavery in Haiti, Leclerc was instructed to occupy Louisiana.

Jefferson responded by alerting his Western military commanders to the possibility of war with France in the Mississippi Valley. He also set in motion a plan he had first conceived as a member of the Articles of Confederation Congress in 1783: an expedition of expert observers and mapmakers to explore the uncharted trans-Mississippi West. This expedition, to be led by two veteran frontiersmen, Meriwether Lewis of Virginia, Jefferson's private secretary, and William Clark of Kentucky, when first projected by the president was intended as a reconnoitering of foreign and potentially enemy territory. At about the same time, Jefferson advised his representative in Paris, Robert Livingston, to inform Napoleon that the United States could not tolerate France's control of access to the Gulf of Mexico through the Mississippi River. The United States could accept moribund Spain's control of Louisiana and the mouth of the Mississippi, at least for a time, but with the French at New Orleans, the United States would be forced to seek a firm alliance with Great Britain and then attack Louisiana as soon as the next European war started. Livingston added, however, that the United States was prepared to buy New Orleans from France and thereby remove the major cause of future strife.

Livingston's threats would have been wasted on Napoleon had his campaign in Haiti succeeded, but it failed: The blacks, partly armed by British and American traders, fought ably, and Leclerc's men suffered dreadfully from tropical diseases. Though the French general succeeded by treachery in capturing the black leader, Toussaint-Louverture, other leaders arose and eventually drove out the French.

Having lost one army in Egypt and another in the West Indies, Napoleon decided to pursue his ambition closer to home. He determined to concentrate his efforts on the defeat of Great Britain, the perennial and formidable enemy of France. Without a single French soldier to defend it, Louisiana was no longer of any value to him, but he badly needed money. He therefore offered to sell the whole territory to the United States for $15 million, then a considerable sum of money. James Monroe, sent by Jefferson to help with negotiations, joined Livingston in accepting the emperor's offer. President Jefferson and Congress ratified their agreement and voted money for the purchase as quickly as possible. Recalling his belief in a strict construction of the Constitution and noticing that the document nowhere authorized the executive to purchase territory from foreign governments, Jefferson had at first suggested to his cabinet that it might be wise to propose an amendment specifically granting that power. Madison, however, pointed out that amendments, like laws, could not operate *ex*

A map of the United States in 1819 showing the Louisiana Purchase. *(Library of Congress)*

post facto. To propose an amendment would be virtually to admit that the purchase had been unconstitutional. Thus the Jeffersonians became self-conscious broad constructionists.

The Louisiana Purchase was enormously popular in the United States, but a remnant of Federalists, led by Timothy Pickering of Massachusetts, opposed the purchase bitterly, and with a degree of merit often overlooked. The territory, opponents pointed out, was not Napoleon's to sell. Why pay $15 million to an international swindler for stolen goods? If we had any right to Louisiana at all, it would have been better simply to occupy it and defy the French tyrant. Furthermore, the people who actually lived in Louisiana had not been consulted, and therefore the United States had no right to annex them unless they were willing to be annexed, according to the principle of the right of self-government so central in the Republican creed. In fact, Congress had, on Jefferson's advice, set up a special military government for Louisiana, which, though it treated the inhabitants fairly enough, allowed migrants from the older United States to move in and take control. Slavery was confirmed, which pleased the creole planters, but the African slave trade stopped, which angered some of them. Louisiana thus became another market for the surplus slaves of the upper South and especially valuable for Virginia, the largest and most populous of the slave-selling states.

Pickering now wrote a number of private letters proposing that the states without slavery explore the possibility of joining with Canada and the maritimes in a new and free confederation. None of his friends thought such a scheme feasible, including the strong-minded George Cabot of Massachusetts, the most influential member of the so-called Essex Junto. From that time to this, however, rumors have abounded of a New England secessionist conspiracy, waxing and waning from the time of Pickering's letters of 1804 down to the Hartford Convention of 1814.

Signs of Disunion: The Burr-Hamilton Duel and the Impeachment Trial of Samuel Chase

Many Federalists, though opposed to disunion, were again willing in 1804 to unite with Aaron Burr in the hope of regaining political power. Burr, when he realized that he would be replaced as Jefferson's candidate for vice president, sought that year to be elected governor of New York as a base from which to run for president. During his campaign, Alexander Hamilton, horrified at the proposed alliance between Federalists and Burrites, privately spread his opinion that Burr was a man of talent but no scruples. Burr subsequently lost the race for governor, although less because of Hamilton's comments than the strong tide in favor of Burr's former Republican allies that year. Nevertheless, Hamilton's remarks had found their way into print, which led Burr to challenge Hamilton to a duel in which he shot and mortally wounded Hamilton. Although his political career had come to an end, Burr completed his term as vice president.

With Burr no longer a viable candidate, the Federalists never found a serious challenger for the presidency in 1804. Some tried to gather votes for Charles Cotesworth Pinckney of South Carolina, but he had neither a program nor a network of supporters required for an effective campaign. Moreover, Jefferson had become extremely popular. Frugality in government, peace with foreign powers, general prosperity, and especially the Louisiana Purchase all served to heighten Jefferson's appeal. Even former president and Federalist John Adams allowed it to be known that he favored the Virginian's election. Only Connecticut, Delaware, and two electors from Maryland gave their votes to Pinckney; Jefferson carried the rest of New England and even his rival's home state of South Carolina.

During the period between the election and Jefferson's second inauguration, the Republicans proceeded with the impeachment trial of

The duel between Alexander Hamilton (left) and Aaron Burr. *(Library of Congress)*

Federalist Samuel Chase, an associate justice of the Supreme Court. It was, in fact, with this trial that Jefferson's fortunes as president began to change. Earlier the Federalists had been quite helpless to prevent the Senate's removal of John Pickering, a United States district court judge in New Hampshire, for that old Federalist was mentally incompetent and should have resigned. Since he was unwilling to do so, neither the Constitution nor the Judiciary Act prescribed a legal method of his removal.

Impeachment is limited to cases involving high crimes and misdemeanors, yet the House drew up a bill of impeachment for Pickering and the Senate mustered more than the needed two-thirds vote in 1804. Pickering was unable to appear in his own defense, nor did he send anyone to appear for him. Once again, the Jeffersonians were proving far less scrupulous

about the letter of the Constitution than they had been when out of power. The impeachment of Samuel Chase, however, was quite a different matter from that of Pickering. Although Chase had been an intensely partisan Federalist, accustomed to insulting Republicans from the bench, he had not lost his reason and was quite able to defend himself in a legal proceeding. A team of outstanding lawyers joined in his defense. With Burr presiding and John Randolph leading the prosecution for the House of Representatives, Chase received a fair and full trial before the United States Senate. Had he been found guilty and removed from office, the subsequent history of the United States might have been quite different, for after removing one partisan judge, Congress might more easily have removed others. The Senate, however, would not supply the needed two-thirds vote on a single one of the charges against

Chase. One reason was a continuing respect for the independence of the judiciary. Chase had clearly been guilty of bad manners, arbitrary conduct, poor taste, and partisan harangues in his courtroom. Yet none of these was in violation of federal statutes, and the Constitution makes no provision for removing unpleasant or even bungling judges. Chase had perhaps disgraced the bench, but he was no criminal.

Jefferson's Second Term: Optimistic Beginnings, Unforeseen Difficulties

If Jefferson felt any personal disappointment over Chase's acquittal, no trace of it appeared in his buoyant second inaugural address. He congratulated his countrymen on the success of pure Republicanism. "The suppression of unnecessary offices, of useless establishments and expenses, enabled us to discontinue our internal taxes," he declared. Then, warming to his theme of frugality, he continued, "It may be the pleasure and pride of an American to ask, what farmer, what mechanic, what laborer, ever sees a tax-gatherer of the United States?" Yet, thanks to good management, the day would soon dawn when all the debts of the federal government would be retired and the Treasury would enjoy a surplus. Would it not then be timely, "by a just repartition among the states, and a corresponding amendment of the constitution," to spend such surpluses on the improvement of "rivers, canals, roads, arts, manufactures, education, and other great objects within each state." Turning toward Native Americans, Jefferson declared that he had regarded them "with the commiseration their history inspires." He would continue his policy of introducing the domestic and agricultural arts of the United States among them and like his predecessors and successors would work to assimilate American Indians into the large and growing U.S. society. The address also contained a brief affirmation that the federal government should not meddle in religious institutions, and a rather surprising claim that, though a forebearance against libel and falsehood had been in itself a good thing, allowing truth to drive out error, nevertheless, "no inference is here intended, that the laws, provided by the State against false and defamatory publications, should not be enforced; he who has time, renders a service to public morals and public tranquility, in reforming these abuses by the salutary coercions of the law." The address ended with an appeal to the American people to sustain good government and with a dignified appeal to "that Being in whose hands we are, who led our forefathers, as Israel of old, from their native land, and planted them in a country flowing with the necessaries and comforts of life."

Jefferson's second term would end on a far more somber and uncertain note than his first term, but one can hardly blame him for his optimism on March 4, 1805. Indeed, the prosperity of the United States would continue until Jefferson himself curtailed it in 1808. A major source of American prosperity throughout the years from 1793 to 1812 was the neutral carrying trade during the French Revolution and Napoleonic Wars, which, for all its risks and inconveniences, expanded American opportunities for foreign enterprise—and attracted foreign capital to the United States—far more than was possible when all of Europe was at peace. A European peace did hold from 1801 until early 1803, and the trade of the United States declined somewhat as a result; but with the resumption of the European war, foreign trade again grew and in 1804 actually flourished under a most unusual condition: None of the belligerents placed any serious obstacles in the way of American involvement in the carrying trade. When the warring powers later undertook to prevent the United States from contributing significantly to their enemies' prosperity by trading with them, Jefferson and Madison tried to defend what had been the status quo of 1804, but this proved impossible.

Unaware of the difficulties into which European events must soon plunge him, Jefferson in 1805 pressed for further national triumphs. The Lewis and Clark expedition, launched in the spring of 1804, carried the American flag over the Rockies to the mouth of the Columbia River in 1805. Although failing to find the waterways that Jefferson hoped would link the upper Missouri to the Pacific, the expedition convinced Jefferson and his successors that the United States should span the continent. Before the return of Lewis and Clark, Zebulon M. Pike led an unsuccessful search for the source of the Mississippi River. In 1806-1807, he conducted a second expedition into the Spanish Southwest and brought back important information about that area. East of the Mississippi, Jefferson turned his attention to East and West Florida. They pointed, in George Dangerfield's useful simile, like a pistol aimed at New Orleans and the gateway to the heartland of North America. He urged his diplomats in Europe to persuade Spain that further retention of the Floridas was both costly and futile. They were of no use to Spain and belonged naturally to the territories already owned by the United States. Finally, Jefferson allowed the commercial terms of Jay's treaty with England to expire, trusting that the increased size and strength of the United States would enable him to secure a new treaty considerably more favorable to United States interests.

At first, negotiations over Florida went badly. Jefferson asked Congress for a secret appropriation of $2 million for the purchase of Florida. He then sent a public message to Congress taking a hard line against Spain, threatened Spain through diplomatic channels, and quietly suggested to Napoleon that if Spain could be influenced to sell Florida, the money could wind up in Paris. Napoleon and his agent Talleyrand took the position that they could not help the United States at this time because Spain was unwilling to sell, yet they left the impression that something might be done later. The following year, 1806, Jefferson sponsored

The Lewis and Clark expedition. *(Library of Congress)*

and Congress enacted a total embargo of American trade with the independent black nation of Haiti. This was partly to foster the goodwill of Napoleon, who still hoped to reconquer the former French colony, and partly in response to the racial attitudes of many congressmen. Even after currying favor with Napoleon, the Jefferson administration still did not acquire East or West Florida; the former was annexed only in 1810 and the latter in 1819.

Conflicts with Britain

The British, far from becoming more tractable during their new war with France, swiftly became more hostile to the United States than they had been at any time since 1783. The reason was the huge increase of American shipping after 1803. The British had encouraged American trade in the late 1790's because the United States was then engaged in an undeclared naval war with France and was in effect a British ally. In 1804, far from being at war with France, the United States was carrying a great deal of its shipping, as well as that of its reluctant ally, Spain. Bound by recent custom from attacking American merchant shipping, Britain saw more and more trade pass into American hands. Indeed, the demand for American shipping grew so rapidly that there were not enough ships and sailors to meet it. Foreign ships therefore transferred to American registry, and foreign sailors, including many Englishmen, took service on American ships.

By the summer of 1805, many Englishmen had come to resent the way the United States raked in profits while they bore the cost of protecting the Atlantic from the aggressive French emperor. Neutral rights were all very well; the American contribution to French prosperity was, however, profoundly unneutral.

Throughout the French Revolution and Napoleonic Wars, Britain had adhered to its unilaterally proclaimed Rule of 1756, which held that no trade normally prohibited in times of peace would be allowed—even in the hands of neutrals—in time of war. This rule was interpreted to mean that American vessels could not carry cargoes from the French West Indies to France since that trade had been proscribed before the war. Britain's Admiralty Court, however, modified this rule in 1800, when considering the case of an American merchant ship, *Polly*. If an American ship bought French colonial goods, carried them to the United States, and paid duties on them there, they might then reexport them to Europe, where the British would regard them as American goods and not subject to seizure under the Rule of 1756. This practice of the "broken voyage" was liable to fraud. American ships often sailed directly from the West Indies to Europe, pretending by means of forged papers to have completed a broken voyage via the United States.

In 1805, the British Admiralty Court in the case of the American merchant ship *Essex* rejected the broken voyage concept and reasserted the Rule of 1756 in its full vigor. British ships again claimed as prizes of war American vessels laden with French goods. Showing some discrimination, they seized only sixty American vessels, far fewer than they had in a similar crisis in 1793. Still, the use of British sea power to regulate American trade was galling, and no relief could be expected from Europe. In 1805, Horatio Nelson led his British fleet to a decisive victory over the combined fleets of France and Spain at the Battle of Trafalgar. Nelson died gloriously, and Napoleon remained from then until the end of his career a military threat only on land. Not since the days of Sir Francis Drake and Sir John Hawkins had Englishmen felt so superior, or acted so arrogantly, on the high seas. Now to prevent French goods sailing for Europe on American ships, they stationed their own warships just outside the major harbors of the United States, where they boldly stopped and searched American merchant vessels. Once at New York Harbor, an American ship refused to stop for a search by HMS *Leander*. *Leander* fired what was supposed to be a warning shot across the American ship's bow, but the shot struck and killed a sailor.

British commanders on the blockading ships looked for British sailors as well as French merchandise on American ships. Service in the British navy was hard, and the pay was poor. Many British tars had been drafted by a system little better than kidnaping. By the thousands they jumped ship and took berths on American merchant ships, where the service was easier and safer and the pay better. No matter how inhumanely they were recruited or treated, however, such men were deserters in time of war. England could not tolerate their loss, for if a few thousand desertions were winked at, the number would soon reach tens of thousands, and England's mighty fleet would stand unmanned.

To stop this drain on their manpower, ships of the Royal Navy stopped and searched American vessels, seized any deserters who were discovered, punished them, and returned them to service. Shorthanded British captains, however, often took not only deserters from the Royal Navy but also American citizens of English birth and Englishmen who had not served in the navy and had taken out papers applying for United States citizenship. Occasionally, they even seized native-born Americans. Americans differed over whether the United States should tolerate British searching of its ships for deserters. Those Federalists who were most sympathetic to Britain's struggle against Napoleonic France were inclined to allow the indignity. A large minority would tolerate the Rule of 1756 in its application against the French tyrant, but few could stomach British blockades of American harbors. The guns of *Leander* had given the United States grounds for war.

Jefferson wanted war even less than did his few remaining Federalist opponents. He was no pacifist, as he had most recently proved in fighting Tripoli. In the present crisis, however, Jefferson was above all an opportunist. Even with a galling semiblockade, American shipping enjoyed in 1806 its most profitable year ever. Warfare would increase the costs of government, reduce revenue, and yield no certain advantage in return. Convinced of the proposition that free ships make free goods (and free sailors), Jefferson and Madison decided to negotiate. They sent William Pinkney, a moderate Federalist lawyer from Baltimore, to assist the regular minister to England, James Monroe. Madison drew up instructions, which were expertly reasoned but hopelessly one-sided, demanding all possible advantages for American trade while offering the British nothing but goodwill in exchange. Departing from these instructions, Monroe and Pinkney negotiated a treaty in which England, although explicitly recognizing the right of American ships to carry cargoes from the West Indies to Europe if they had first stopped and paid a tariff in an American port, conceded nothing material on the matter of impressment. When the treaty reached the United States early in 1807, Jefferson refused even to submit it to the Senate for its ratification. Had the Senate learned the full contents of the agreement, along with the explanations of Monroe and Pinkney, it might have accepted the treaty.

Not long after, on June 22, 1807, the only new frigate commissioned under President Jefferson, the USS *Chesapeake*, under the command of Commodore James Barron, was sailing down Chesapeake Bay on its maiden voyage when the British frigate *Leopard* insisted on searching the ship for deserters from the Royal Navy. Barron quite properly refused, but his ship was in such poor order and his crew so little trained that he could offer no resistance when *Leopard* opened fire. After sustaining three dead and eighteen wounded and firing one shot for the sake of honor, Barron surrendered. The *Leopard*'s officers then removed four sailors from the *Chesapeake* and departed. At Halifax, the

British convicted and hanged one of these men. The other three, Americans who had volunteered to join the British navy, were also convicted but pardoned on the understanding that they would resume their service.

The British foreign secretary, George Canning, disavowed *Leopard*'s actions on the grounds that his government had never claimed the right to stop and search ships of the United States Navy. Canning also offered reparations for the dead and wounded. Even so, Jefferson might have had a declaration of war had he summoned Congress immediately and asked for one. The president, however, waited until October to summon Congress, while strengthening shore defenses, sending a number of stiff notes to the British government, and closing American ports to British warships. The latter move curtailed the warships' effectiveness markedly by forcing them to go either to Halifax or to Bermuda for supplies. Jefferson declined to accept the apologies and reparations offered by Canning unless Britain agreed to do much more. He wanted the government to punish Admiral Berkeley, who had ordered the affront and had since been transferred to another part of the world, and to promise to desist from all forms of impressment. Canning refused to negotiate further until the ban on British warships had been lifted. The question of reparations for the *Chesapeake* dragged on until 1811; by the time it was settled, other aggravations had made it seem a negligible matter.

Commercial Warfare: The Ill-Conceived Embargo

In the closing months of 1807, the United States found itself pressed by both Britain and France in a wholly new and uncomfortable way. After the defeat of Trafalgar, Napoleon had conceived the plan of ruining the British by cutting off all their trade with the continent of Europe. In his infamous Berlin Decree of November 21, 1806, Napoleon declared the British Isles

under a state of blockade, which he enforced by confiscating any ship found in European harbors carrying British goods. The British retaliated early in 1807 by extending their blockade to all European ports complying with the Berlin Decree. When Napoleon completed his "continental system" by bringing Russia into it, the British added Orders in Council, which declared that no nation might trade in Europe unless its ships first secured a license and paid duties in England. Napoleon's Milan Decree of December 17, 1808, then declared that any ships obeying the British orders would be confiscated.

Before the British and French had completed their measures for destroying each other's trade, Jefferson asked Congress to activate a limited Non-Importation Act first passed in 1806 but suspended during the Monroe-Pinkney negotiations. The act, aimed entirely at England, barred a number of importations that Americans could live without. Jefferson next persuaded Congress to adopt the Embargo Act, one of the most extraordinary acts in the history of American legislation. Not merely prohibiting trade with Britain and France, the Embargo Act required all American ships to stay at home and prevented the exportation of all American commodities. Although, in a way, a logical response to the de facto commercial warfare that the two greatest powers in the world had turned against the United States, unfortunately, it did more harm to America than it did to France and England. Hundreds of American ships sat idle and deteriorating in their harbors, the shipbuilding industry ceased, sailors were thrown out of work, New England fishermen lost their markets, and farmers lost outlets for their surplus grain, salt meat, and livestock. Tobacco and cotton planters, perennially short of cash, also suffered, but their commodities at least kept fairly well, and their chief capital—their slaves—continued to appreciate in value. Napoleon used the Embargo Act as an excuse to seize $10 million worth of American shipping.

As 1808 wore on, the act produced numerous complaints at home, but Congress supported the administration in a series of acts that served to make the ban more effective. It placed coastal shipping under strict controls and heavy bonds. It increased the size of the army and used small army detachments to patrol the long Canadian border where Americans were smuggling goods overland that they could not get out by sea. It also increased the "mosquito fleet" of gunboats, too small to challenge British warships but low in cost and useful for catching the small sailing craft that specialized in smuggling. After a trial of fourteen months, just before he retired from the presidency, Jefferson signed the act repealing the embargo. He also signed a new Non-Importation Act, which prohibited trade with France and Britain, but he promised to restore it with whichever power withdrew its decrees against neutral shipping. Since the new act permitted trade with all other nations and allowed American ships to return to the high seas, prosperity began to return.

Jefferson's handling of the nation's relations with France and England not only had been strongly criticized by the Federalists but also had alienated some of the members of his own party as well. One of the most important was John Randolph of Virginia. Randolph had been a loyal Republican throughout the president's first administration, chairing the powerful House Committee of Ways and Means in the interests of retrenchment and economy. In the 1790's, Randolph had been an ardent supporter of the French Revolution, believing, with many other educated Americans, that its cause was that of human freedom. By 1806, however, the self-proclaimed Napoleon Bonaparte ruled France by naked power and was launched on the conquest of Europe, whereas the British, however high-handed and selfish, were fighting for liberty. Randolph accordingly shifted his sympathies to Britain. He was highly displeased that Jefferson and Madison, although

they detested Napoleon, were quite willing to cooperate with him if they could gain advantages for the United States by doing so.

Randolph, supported by a small faction of the Democratic Republican Party called "Quids," turned even more strongly against Jefferson over the so-called Yazoo land claims. In 1795, the Georgia legislature had sold to the Yazoo land companies several million acres of its western lands in an area later ceded by Georgia to the United States. The next legislature rescinded the sale on the ground that it had been made fraudulently. Jefferson arranged a compromise settlement of the matter that would have satisfied Georgia and the Yazoo investors, many of whom were Northern Republicans whose support he sought. Randolph blocked the necessary legislation in Congress, charging that Jefferson had abandoned the states' rights principles of his party and become in essence a Federalist. The Yazoo claims were not settled until after Jefferson left office.

Internal Opposition: The Burr Conspiracy

In the meantime, Jefferson became involved in an imbroglio with his former vice president, Aaron Burr. Burr, thoroughly discredited because of his political machinations in New York and his killing of Alexander Hamilton in a duel, embarked on a scheme, the exact nature of which has never been clearly known. He visited the English minister to Washington, Anthony Merry, and proposed a plan for creating an independent Louisiana under British protection. Merry forwarded this proposal to his government with an enthusiastic endorsement; sager heads advised against plotting with Burr and soon recalled Merry to England. Meanwhile, Burr had been to see the Spanish minister with quite a different appeal. To forestall a planned invasion of Mexico, Burr proposed a *coup d'état* against Jefferson right in the District of Columbia. He would engage to organize

Aaron Burr *(Library of Congress)*

Jefferson himself had contemplated such a separation with equanimity in the 1780's, but his views were now quite different.

In August, 1806, Burr concentrated a force of sixty to eighty armed men and ten boats on an island in the upper Ohio River. As the expedition descended first the Ohio and then the Mississippi, Jefferson sent word to his Western commanders that Burr was leading an illegal expedition and should be arrested. Evidently, Jefferson had become convinced that such action was necessary on receiving an urgent warning from his military authority at New Orleans, General James Wilkinson, who later became the government's most important witness at Burr's trial. Burr and Wilkinson had plotted together in Philadelphia and later in New Orleans. Wilkinson, as it was later learned, had been a well-paid spy for Spain at various times. He collected more Spanish gold by pretending to save Mexico from Burr's military invasion. He then posed as protector of the United States, claiming that he was saving Louisiana from the menacing Burr. Whatever Burr may actually have had in mind, he knew that it would not work with Wilkinson now against him and a warrant out for his arrest. He tried to reach sanctuary in Florida by traveling overland but was recognized, arrested, and sent to Richmond to stand trial for treason.

A grand jury, with John Randolph as foreman, found ample grounds for indicting Burr, and he came to trial in August, 1807. Jefferson's attorneys gathered an enormous amount of evidence, but much of it was contradictory. To this day, no one really knows exactly what Burr had in mind or even if he knew himself. The trial did reveal that Jefferson was something less than an absolute civil libertarian, for he had published the government's case against Burr in advance of the trial and prejudged him guilty. Ironically, the Republican Judiciary Act of 1802 established procedures by which Jefferson's political enemy, John Marshall, sitting as a circuit court judge, presided at Burr's trea-

this with the help of money from Spain. No money was forthcoming, but Burr went on seeing people and making daring proposals. In Washington, Philadelphia, and especially in the new towns of the trans-Appalachian West, Burr built up a network of committed friends, most of whom believed that he was planning an expedition against Mexico.

By the early months of 1806, Jefferson had heard from many Western correspondents warning him of Burr's activities. These Westerners cared nothing for the rights of Spain in Mexico, but they did fear a secession plot, centered in New Orleans, where many citizens still grumbled at the American annexation. Such fears were plausible: From the earliest days of the United States, there had been Americans of independent minds and great ambitions who had believed that the Mississippi Valley, including its great tributaries, the Ohio and Missouri, must someday be the seat of an empire quite independent from the Eastern states.

son trial. In instructing the jury, Marshall narrowly defined treason as an overt act against the United States observed by at least two witnesses, and the jury found that Burr's guilt had not been proved. In the course of the trial, Jefferson invoked executive privilege by declining to answer Marshall's subpoena to appear as a witness. Jefferson, sorely disappointed at what he regarded as yet another instance of reckless Federalist obstruction to good government and believing Marshall's conduct on the bench to have been criminally wrong, sent the record of the trial to the House of Representatives, hinting that it might find grounds for the chief justice's impeachment. He also suggested amending the Constitution to make federal judges removable. Nothing came of these ideas.

Jefferson could at least take pleasure in the loyalty to the Union exhibited by almost all Westerners during Burr's scheming, arrest, and trial. Meanwhile, it was still possible to convict Burr for the lesser charge of violating the neutrality laws, which he had admitted doing while denying the charge of treason. Burr, however, jumped bail and fled to Europe, where he spent several years trying to sell chimerical schemes to the British and French governments. In 1813, he returned quietly to New York, where he prospered modestly as a lawyer until his death in 1836.

As the time for the election of 1808 approached, Jefferson decided that he would not run for a third term. Despite the failure of his foreign policy and the unpleasantness of the Burr conspiracy, no widespread political reaction occurred against the president and his party. Although the Republicans failed to duplicate their sweep of 1804, they still easily elected their candidate, Jefferson's friend James Madison, with 122 electoral votes compared to only 47 for the Federalist candidate, C. C. Pinckney. They also retained comfortable majorities in both houses of Congress. Only in New England did the Federalists reestablish

strong party organizations and win control of state governments.

Following the precedent of Washington and John Adams, Jefferson retired completely from public life at the end of his presidency. Returning to his beloved Monticello, he spent the last seventeen years of his life in "philosophical serenity," but in great financial difficulty. He always answered queries from Madison and Monroe fully and cordially, but he made no effort to influence them. The chief fruits of his long and active retirement were a philosophical correspondence with his ancient friend and sometimes foe, John Adams, and the founding of the University of Virginia. Jefferson and Adams both died on July 4, 1826, as citizens throughout the United States were celebrating the fiftieth anniversary of American independence. Jefferson had planned a small and elegant monument to himself at Monticello. Its inscription identified him as author of the Declaration of Independence and the Virginia statute for religious freedom and as founder of the university.

Jefferson's Record as President

Significantly, Jefferson did not list any of the public offices he had held. This was in part modesty, but it was also an expression of his lifelong fear of government's tendency to become too powerful and hence tyrannical. This fear, along with his urbane but retiring manner—he was never comfortable in public meetings—kept Jefferson from being one of the nation's most striking chief executives. The best and worst deeds of his administration—the Louisiana Purchase, the prosecution of Burr, and the enforcement of the Embargo Act—were all responses to major crises thrust on Jefferson and the nation. Otherwise, it was his wish that government should encourage constructive voluntary activity, and the years of his presidency were happily marked by the founding of new banks, the digging of canals, the laying of roads, the expansion of industries, the introduction of new inventions, the founding of schools, and the growth of population. Slavery, unfortunately, was spreading rather than declining, especially because of the acquisition of the sugar-growing province of Louisiana and the rapid spread of cotton as a major crop for export. Jefferson did sign, with satisfaction, an act that closed the international slave trade at the earliest moment the Constitution permitted, January 1, 1808.

Jefferson's style and methods were too subtle to be imitated, but he was a better president than the bare record suggests. Ideally, an American president must be the boss of a national political party, a ceremonial and ideological leader capable of reaffirming and adapting national values and ideals, and a tough-minded executive able to run the government and delegate authority to competent and honest subordinates. Very few presidents have done as well in each of these categories as Thomas Jefferson.

Robert McColley

Bibliographical References

The imposing *Papers of Thomas Jefferson*, edited by Julian P. Boyd, Charles T. Cullen, and John Cantanzariti, begun in 1950, reached to 1793 and 27 vols. by 1997. The presidency is represented in *The Writings of Thomas Jefferson*, 10 vols., edited by Paul L. Ford, 1892-1899, and *The Writings of Thomas Jefferson*, 20 vols., edited by A. A. Lipscomb and A. E. Bergh, 1903. Among biographies, Dumas Malone, *Jefferson and His Time*, 6 vols., 1948-1982, is outstanding; Merrill Peterson, *Thomas Jefferson and the New Nation*, 1970, is a competent single-volume biography. The astigmatic but penetrating views of the Adamses are in Henry Adams, *History of the U.S. During the Adminis-*

trations of Jefferson and Madison, 9 vols., 1891-1893. More straightforwardly critical is Leonard Levy, *Jefferson and Civil Liberties: The Darker Side*, 1964. Noble E. Cunningham, *The Process of Government Under Thomas Jefferson*, 1978, reveals how the administration functioned. Drew R. McCoy, *The Elusive Republic*, 1980, is an ideological study of Jefferson's foreign policy; more conventional studies include Bradford Perkins, *The First Rapprochement*, 1955, and *Prologue to War*, 1963; Burton Spivak, *Jefferson's English Crisis*, 1979; and Clifford L. Egan, *Neither Peace nor War*, 1983. David H. Fischer, *The Revolution of American Conservatism*, 1965, takes a fresh look at post-1800 Federalists, Thomas P. Abernethy explores *The Burr Conspiracy*, 1954, and Richard E. Ellis probes the problem of courts in a democracy in *The Jeffersonian Crisis*, 1971. Norman K. Risjord, *Thomas Jefferson*, 1997, is a brief biography which asserts that Jefferson's rhetoric was a matter of time and circumstance rather than absolute belief. Edwin S. Gaustad, *Sworn on the Altar of God: A Religious Biography of Thomas Jefferson*, 1996, examines Jefferson's dedication to the cause of religious liberty and the contradiction of his ownership of slaves. Annette Gordon-Reed, *Thomas Jefferson and Sally Hemings: An American Controversy*, 1997, is a thorough and even-handed examination of the evidence that Jefferson had a long-term affair and fathered children with one of his slaves. For a balanced reassessment of the life, career, and character of Jefferson, see Joseph J. Ellis, *American Sphinx: The Character of Thomas Jefferson*, 1997. Willard S. Randall, *Thomas Jefferson: A Life*, 1994, is a comprehensive single-volume portrayal of Jefferson's public and private life that explores the contradictions between his life and ideals.

James Madison

4th President, 1809-1817

Born: March 16, 1751
Port Conway, Virginia
Died: June 28, 1836
Montpelier, Virginia

Political Party: Democratic Republican
Vice Presidents: George Clinton,
Elbridge Gerry

Cabinet Members

Secretary of State: Robert Smith, James Monroe

Secretary of the Treasury: Albert Gallatin, George Campbell, Alexander J. Dallas, William H. Crawford

Secretary of War: William Eustis, John Armstrong, James Monroe, William H. Crawford

Secretary of the Navy: Paul Hamilton, William Jones, Benjamin Crowninshield

Attorney General: Caesar Rodney, William Pinckney, Richard Rush

No man ever came to the presidency with better credentials than James Madison. Most of his friends believed that Madison was among the most brilliant men in America. Indeed, Thomas Jefferson once spoke of him as "the greatest man in the world," by which he meant that his friend was second to none in his intellectual abilities. By the time he became president, his place as a great American statesman was already assured.

Madison was born on March 16, 1751, at Port Conway, Virginia, the home of his maternal grandparents, but he grew up at the Madison home in Orange County, Virginia. After preparatory training by tutors, he entered the College of New Jersey (Princeton) in 1769. He was graduated two years later and

remained for an additional year's study.

Madison first entered politics as a young delegate to the Virginia convention of 1776, which drafted the state constitution and declaration of rights. After serving as a member of the state assembly and governor's council, in 1780 he became a delegate to the Continental

Madison's official portrait. *(White House Historical Society)*

Congress. There he played a major role in creating the public domain out of the Western lands and worked to defeat Spain's efforts to close the Mississippi River to American commerce. Returning to Montpelier, his home in Virginia, at the end of the Revolutionary War, he was elected to the state house of delegates where he helped complete the disestablishment of the Anglican Church. During the turmoil that followed the American Revolution when the upper classes felt threatened by uprisings of the discontented poor farmers and workers, such as Shays's Rebellion in Massachusetts, it was Madison who sought, more actively than any other American, to replace the inadequate Articles of Confederation with a constitution providing for a stronger central government. The federal convention of 1787 was in a real sense Madison's handiwork, from its seedling moments in a commercial conference of delegates from Maryland and Virginia in 1785 to the actual gathering of the constitutional framers two years later. On the convention floor he was an able debater, and his Virginia Plan, introduced at the outset, gave the delegates a working draft of a plan of government that with many changes eventually became the Constitution. Madison's journal of the proceedings not only made him the ultimate authority on the Constitution but also preserved a record for history. He also played a major role in the struggle to secure state ratification of the new Constitution, producing along with John Jay and Alexander Hamilton a superb body of essays interpreting and explaining the Constitution, published as *The Federalist*.

The Jefferson-Madison Philosophy

Madison served in the first four Congresses under the new Constitution, where he proposed the first ten amendments to the Constitution—the Bill of Rights—in 1791. He was also instrumental in forming the political faction that grew into the Democratic Republican Party, which opposed Alexander Hamilton's Federalist policies. Working with Jefferson, Madison was, in fact, the most visible public opponent of Hamilton's program of funding the public debt, creating a national bank, and expanding American armaments. In 1797, Madison retired from Congress and returned to Montpelier. At home, he kept abreast of political developments and as coauthor with Jefferson of the Virginia and Kentucky Resolutions of 1798, which asserted the right of the states to nullify acts of Congress they considered to be unconstitutional, supplied a rallying point for the political opposition to Federalist programs.

When Jefferson became president in March, 1801, Madison, as expected, became secretary of state and served his chief for the next eight years as both a loyal party supporter and principal foreign policy adviser. The sorest trials faced by Jefferson and Madison grew out of the Anglo-French War that had begun in 1793. No problems were more vexing than those involving overseas trade. American maritime commerce had expanded rapidly, partly in response to the opening of lucrative wartime commodity markets. The British navy challenged this growth by impressing seamen from American ships on the ground that they were British citizens, and seizing ships bound for European ports under the control of France. Napoleon countered by seizing American vessels in the Caribbean or en route to British ports. The existence of hundreds of captured American vessels and thousands of impressed seamen testified to the weakness of the United States, if not its actual failure to have established itself as a true nation. No truly independent power could possibly accept such insults to its sovereignty.

Yet both Jefferson and his secretary of state acted with restraint when a declaration of war against either England or France would have been fully justified. On the one hand, as dedicated republicans, they believed war was the worst evil that could befall a nation. Wars meant

Montpelier, Madison's home. *(Library of Congress)*

large armies and navies, huge expenditures, and the loss of life. Peace, on the other hand, allowed government to maintain a low tax structure, even the retirement of the national debt and, for the most part, minimal interference in the life of the average citizen. In early agrarian times, American voters enthusiastically supported the Jefferson-Madison philosophy.

As Jefferson neared the end of his second term, he was urged by his supporters to stand for reelection but he declined, helping to set a two-term tradition that stood until Franklin D. Roosevelt successfully ran for a third term in 1940. Jefferson used his influence to secure the nomination by the Republican congressional caucus for his good friend and secretary of state, James Madison. The Federalist candidate in 1808 was Charles Cotesworth Pinckney of South Carolina. Madison defeated him easily, receiving 122 electoral votes to 47 for Pinckney. Six votes went to Vice President George Clinton, the candidate of a small number of disaffected eastern Republicans.

Madison as President: Inherited Conflicts

The new president was not physically impressive. Slender and only about 5 feet, 6 inches tall, he had a high forehead and a face so wrinkled by early middle age that he appeared to be much older. Madison, however, had considerable fame and he brought great political experience to the presidential office. Moreover, when he assumed office on March 4, 1809, he inherited a popular and generally unified political party from Jefferson.

The administration had reduced federal expenditures and lowered taxes, which contributed to Jefferson's and his party's wide acceptance. Yet, beneath the surface, factions had begun to form in the Democratic Republican Party. For the most part, in his last months in office Jefferson ignored the problem and tried to avoid any issue that would create discord. He had not been able to escape every confrontation, however, especially one with dissident senators from his own party. One of his last official acts was the nomination of his former secretary, William Short, as minister to Russia. The Senate's 31-0 vote against confirming Short's appointment was not only the most mortifying event of Jefferson's final days as president but also a warning to his successor not to risk similar humiliation; the senators would not accept a continuation of Jefferson's policy of rewarding enemies and neglecting friends.

In choosing the members of his cabinet, consequently, Madison was circumspect. Although wishing to make the able, Swiss-born Albert Gallatin his secretary of state, Madison was intimidated by the threat of Senate rejection into retaining him as secretary of the treasury, the post he had held under Jefferson. Similarly, bowing to pressure from Senate Republicans who professed to be his friends, he offered the State Department post to Jefferson's navy secretary, Robert Smith, brother of Senator Samuel Smith of Maryland. A worse choice could hardly be imagined. Congressman John Randolph gave the nomination backhanded approval by remarking that Smith knew "how to spell," but he neglected to add that Smith did not know how to write a dispatch or state paper. The president himself had to write most of his diplomatic correspondence. Finally tiring of Smith's incompetence, in 1811 Madison dismissed him and named his old friend and fellow Virginian James Monroe secretary of state. Madison replaced Smith in the Navy Department with Paul Hamilton of South Carolina. For secretary of war he chose Dr. William Eustis of Massachusetts, and he kept Caesar Rodney as attorney general.

Anglo-American Discord: False Hopes for Resolution

The chief problem facing the new president was the continuing dispute with Britain and France over American's right as a neutral on the high seas. Just before he took office, Congress repealed Jefferson's Embargo Act, which had banned carrying foreign goods in American ships, and replaced it with a law—the Nonintercourse Act of 1809—that forbade all trade with England and France but permitted a resumption of commerce with either power if and when it ceased to violate American maritime rights. This new piece of legislation pleased neither the War Hawks (the Western and Southern congressmen who favored war with England and the annexation of Canada and the seizure of Florida from Spain) nor the New England commercial classes, who wanted peace and unrestricted commerce with all nations. The situation seemed to change, however, when David Erskine, the British minister in Washington, hinted to Secretary of State Smith that he had the power to revoke the detested Orders in Council, under the authority of which the Royal Navy attempted to halt American trade with French-controlled Europe. Erskine, who had married an American, was perhaps overly zealous in his efforts to achieve an Anglo-American accord, whereas Madison was too eager to believe that Great Britain was suddenly ready to do what justice required. The president was undoubtedly influenced by the need to unclog American ports of their stockpiles of grain and cotton in order to bolster the prices of these commodities and end the agricultural depression. Furthermore, with foreign commerce at a standstill, income from import duties, the chief source of revenue for the federal government, had almost stopped. Consequently, Madison welcomed Erskine's overtures and accepted his assurances that the Orders in Council would be revoked. In return, under the provisions of the Nonintercourse Act, Madison issued a proclamation declaring that Americans could resume trading with England. Madison's achievement was acclaimed across the nation: Even the Federalist newspapers in Boston gave the president credit. Tough-talking congressmen from the Southwest grew silent, scores of ships loaded cargoes destined for British ports, and for a few weeks Madison basked in glory.

Madison's glory proved short-lived, however. When the British foreign secretary, George Canning, learned of Erskine's action, he repudiated it and ordered Erskine home. Erskine's instructions had stipulated that British concessions were dependent on American agreement to the right of the Royal Navy to intercept American ships bearing raw materials and goods for France. As historian Henry Adams has noted, Canning probably realized that such a brazen affront to American sovereignty would eliminate all chance for an accord.

The Madisons were enjoying a summer vacation at Montpelier when an express rider from Washington, D.C., arrived with word of Canning's action. Madison was forced to issue a humiliating counterproclamation repudiating his earlier one and acknowledging that nothing had changed. Not only did Canning recall Erskine but he also rubbed salt in the wound by appointing as the next minister to Washington, Francis James Jackson, the devious diplomat who earlier, as minister to Denmark, had spoken of peace to the Danes a few hours before the British bombarded their capital.

From the time Madison learned of Canning's rejection of the Erskine agreement, one could convincingly argue, the United States was set on a course for war with England. In a matter of weeks, the winds of diplomacy had forced American ships back into port and whipped up a storm of public outrage against Britain. "The late conduct of the British ministry has capped the climax of atrocity towards this country," observed the *National Intelligencer*, a Washington newspaper published by Madison's friends.

After learning from Secretary Gallatin that the new British minister appeared to have "nothing to say of importance or pleasant," the president decided to delay his return to Washington for a while. When he finally arrived there in late September, he had an interview with Jackson that was painfully short. In a subsequent conversation with the secretary

of state during which the nature of Jackson's instructions was discussed, a shouting match took place, ending with the exhaustion of American patience and Madison's refusal to have any further dealings with Jackson. His recall was sought early in January, 1810.

Testing the British and the French: Macon's Bill No. 2

War talk revived, although the military forces of the United States remained on a peacetime footing. Unwilling to accept the idea that a large military establishment gives strength to a nation's diplomacy, Madison adhered to the republican belief that in a time of crisis the militia could do America's fighting. Great Britain showed its contempt for American public opinion by leaving its ministry in Washington vacant after Jackson left. Meanwhile, Napoleon matched the British for arrogance by issuing the Rambouillet Decree in March, 1810, calling for the confiscation of all American ships in French-controlled ports that had violated the Nonintercourse Act. In doing so, the French emperor was ordering his navy to operate exactly as the British government had stipulated in its instructions to Erskine—but now France was going to seize the Yankee ships as prizes of war.

Madison, despite his generally antiwar disposition, was coming to believe that war was unavoidable. When, in 1810, the well-intentioned Pennsylvania Quaker George Logan prepared to undertake a private peace mission to England, Madison applauded Logan's motives but cautioned him, "Your anxiety that our Country may be kept out of the vortex of war, is honorable to your judgment as a Patriot, and to your feelings as a man. But the question may be decided for us, by actual hostilities agst. us or by proceedings leaving no choice but between absolute disgrace and resistance by force."

In the meantime, Gallatin worked with Nathaniel Macon, chair of the House Foreign

Affairs Committee, to draft legislation that would open the sea lanes to American ships but close all ports in the United States to belligerent vessels. Gallatin's object was to revive trade and increase lagging customs income so sorely needed by the federal Treasury. Although Macon's first bill failed in the Senate, Macon's Bill No. 2 passed and became law in 1810. Disarmingly simple, it repealed the Nonintercourse Act and removed all restrictions on American commerce, but, holding "up the honor and character of this nation to the highest bidder," the law stated that if England would repeal its Orders in Council, the United States would reimpose nonintercourse with France, and if France would withdraw its obnoxious decrees, the United States would reimpose nonintercourse with England.

Although Madison believed that the American people approved of Congress's action and of his relatively passive role in the management of the nation's foreign affairs, the Federalists, at least, were highly critical of the president's performance. Samuel Taggart, congressman from Massachusetts, observed, "Jefferson by a system of intrigue and low cunning managed the party. Madison is a mere puppet or a cypher managed by some chiefs of the faction who are behind the curtain." The radical Republicans, noted Taggart, overlooked French provocations while castigating England. "Because France burns our ships, confiscates our property, and imprisons our seamen they want to fight Great Britain."

Madison considered Macon's Bill No. 2 to be a poor successor to earlier legislative efforts to protect American rights on the high seas. "The inconveniences of the Embargo, and nonintercourse, have been exchanged for the greater sacrifices as well as disgrace, resulting from a submission to the predatory systems of force," he wrote William Pinkney, the American minister to London. Madison knew that the new law favored Britain, implicitly acknowledging its control of the seas. "She has now

a compleat interest in perpetuating the actual state of things, which gives her the full enjoyment of our trade and enables her to cut it off with every other part of the World," he told Pinkney. Napoleon, however, might "turn the tables on G. Britain" by announcing France's resumption of trade with the United States if the United States would renew nonintercourse with Great Britain, the president observed.

Madison proved to be a good prophet. On learning of the new American law, Napoleon instructed his foreign minister, the duke of Cadore, to write a letter to John Armstrong, the United States minister to France, stating that France was prepared to revoke its decrees effective November 1, 1810, and calling on the United States to issue a proclamation reopening trade with France alone unless the British revoked their Orders in Council. Madison was informed of the emperor's action while on a summer vacation in Virginia. A decent interval would be needed to discover whether Great Britain intended to follow suit, but meanwhile Madison felt relieved. Napoleon's action, he said, "promise us at least an extrication from the dilemma of a mortifying peace, or a war with both the great belligerents." Even so, Madison's position remained precarious. If Napoleon was insincere and had to be denounced as a liar, England would have no reason to change its policy. The result would be disastrous for American commerce and agriculture, for it would create a de facto monopoly for the British.

Assuming that the revocation of the French decrees was genuine, on the day following the date on which they were set to expire, Madison issued a proclamation reinstituting nonintercourse with Great Britain under the terms of Macon's Bill No. 2. Napoleon, however, then issued new decrees against American shipping in French ports, decrees equally as damaging as the earlier ones. In his annual message to Congress, Madison had to acknowledge that

France had acted in bad faith and, in effect, admitted that nobody in Washington knew the true situation in Europe.

Annexation of Florida

During this time, developments on the Southern frontier in that part of West Florida adjacent to the Mississippi River required a response from Madison. Following the purchase of Louisiana, Jefferson had quietly tried, without success, to purchase the region from Spain. In the fall of 1810, however, Americans in Baton Rouge revolted and asked to be annexed to the United States, and Madison quickly issued an executive order transferring all of West Florida to the Territory of Orleans, although the area east of the Pearl River was not effectively organized until 1812.

Federalists in Congress denounced the West Florida "invasion" as unconstitutional. Americans in the Southwest, on the other hand, were not satisfied because they wanted all of Florida. The territory still in Spanish hands was a refuge for runaway slaves and a base from which

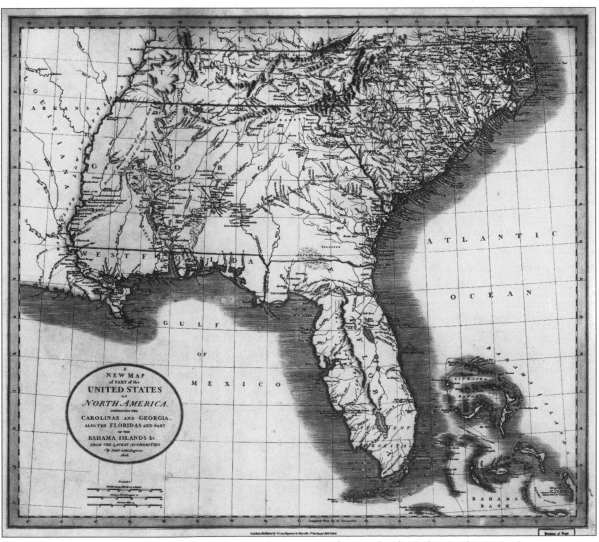

This 1806 map of the United States shows East and West Florida. *(Library of Congress)*

91

hostile American Indians mounted raids across the border. Besides, control of the rivers flowing through Florida into the Gulf of Mexico would give the farmers in the region easy access to outside markets for their products. Responding to their wishes, in January, 1811, Madison sent a secret message to Congress asking for authority to order a temporary occupation of East Florida if the Spanish would agree to it, or in the event of "an apprehended occupancy therefore by any other foreign power." After demurring for a while, Congress gave Madison such authority.

Although Madison was mainly concerned with foreign affairs, important domestic problems arose that also claimed his attention. In 1811, the charter of the Bank of the United States would expire. As a congressman, Madison had strongly opposed Congress's chartering of the bank in 1791, claiming that its action was unconstitutional. As president, though, he recognized the government's need of the bank to carry on its business efficiently. Despite Secretary Gallatin's pleading, however, so much Southern rhetoric had been spent excoriating the bank that Senate Republicans from Virginia and Maryland felt obliged to lead a drive to kill the institution. The recharter bill was defeated by the tie-breaking vote of Vice President George Clinton. Finding himself powerless in the situation, Madison was forced to watch the bank's dismantling.

Meanwhile, dispatch ships arriving from Europe during the spring and summer of 1811 brought no news of change in British or French policy. The president ordered the American minister to London, William Pinkney, home without naming anyone to take his place. Nevertheless, shortly after, Augustus J. Foster appeared in Washington, D.C., as Jackson's replacement as British minister. The only important news he brought was that the Orders in Council would remain in force until Napoleon withdrew his decrees in a verifiable manner.

Although having nothing to say about the French decrees, the new French minister in Washington did inform Madison that the emperor would not interfere if the Americans should seize the rest of Florida. Madison had already sent two American emissaries to East Florida with authority to take possession of the territory if conditions were favorable. By August, one of them, General George Mathews, a former governor of Georgia, reported that the area was ripe for plucking and that the price would be low—"two hundred stand of arms and fifty horsemen's swords," as he estimated. Still, Madison held back, apparently willing to recognize a *fait accompli* but not eager to order an invasion.

Acknowledging the urgency of the international situation, Madison moved the date for convening the forthcoming session of Congress forward thirty days. As the congressmen drifted into Washington, the British minister reported hearing talk of war, but he discounted it as more American hyperbole. Henry Clay, he noted, "talked to me of war as of a duel between two nations, which, when over, would probably leave them both better friends than they had ever been before." Another congressman, Robert R. Livingston, was far more blunt, warning Foster that he had only thirty days in which to pack and leave for home.

In his State of the Union message to the belligerent congressmen, Madison spoke with more confidence than he had in many months. Knowing that newspapers across the country would print his message in full, he wanted to make his case with the American people. The president reported that the British had been asked to match the French by withdrawing their hated Orders in Council but that the Royal Navy had replied by an even "more rigorous execution" of the obnoxious orders. British naval vessels hovered off the American coast in a provocative fashion, and an American frigate had fired on a vessel of the Royal Navy simply to maintain "the honor of the American flag."

The existing state of British-American relations, said Madison, had "the character, as well as the effect, of war on our lawful commerce."

Without saying so explicitly, Madison pointed out that Britain had pushed America as far as it could go. Yet the British minister so misperceived Madison's true feelings that he sent a message to London implying that the president was merely bluffing. Keep the Orders in Council, call the president's bluff, and the Republicans will lose the next election, counseled Foster.

Tippecanoe: Pretext for the War Hawks

Madison's message was being read at crossroads and in courtrooms across the land when a dramatic incident in the Indiana Territory helped build support for war. On November 7, 1811, General William Henry Harrison's troops beat back an American Indian attack near the confluence of the Wabash and Tippecanoe Rivers with heavy losses for the warriors led by The Prophet, brother of Chief Tecumseh. Frontier rumors connected the Shawnee leaders with British officials in Canada, leaving a conviction in the minds of most Americans that the attack had been inspired by redcoated Englishmen. While the young War Hawks in Congress rattled sabers for the folks back home, the secretary of state talked with the House Foreign Affairs Committee frankly about the prospects for peace. When he finished, one member concluded, "The present session will not be closed without *arrangement*, or an actual war with Great Britain." With only token opposition, the House approved bills increasing the army from six thousand men to an authorized thirty-five thousand regular troops supported by fifty thousand militiamen.

Before he would move to use these new troops, however, Madison waited for the return of the sailing vessel *Hornet*, which was bringing dispatches from the American chargé d'affaires in London. If they should reveal that the American government's recent actions had brought about no change in the British Orders in Council, Madison was ready to abandon all hope of peace. Still, in the spring of 1812, Republican antiwar views and Madison's indecisiveness combined to dampen the war fervor in Washington. Some angrily accused Madison of being more concerned about his reelection than about the issue of war or peace. As one Federalist congressman put it, "There is not a doubt entertained but the great pole star in the view of which he shapes all his measures, is his reelection to the presidency for the next four years."

Madison's attention was diverted from the imminent threat of war with England by disconcerting news of events in East Florida where in March, 1812, General Mathews reported that with a tiny American expedition he had seized Fernandina, at the mouth of St. Mary's River in the northeast corner of Florida, and had forced the Spanish commandant's surrender. Mathews requested instructions on what to do next. Instead of praising his action, however, the State Department rebuked the general, and Madison described his action, in a letter to Jefferson, as having been taken "in the face of common sense, as well as his instructions." Madison rightly thought that the Florida invasion placed his administration "in the most distressing dilemma." His actions repudiated by the American authorities, Mathews was forced to abandon his conquest while Madison turned his attention back to European affairs.

The government continued anxiously to await the return of the *Hornet* and news from England. Before its arrival, however, Madison learned that Spencer Perceval had the prince regent's support to become the new prime minister, which meant that no important change in British policy could be expected. "It appears that . . . they prefer war with us, to a repeal of their orders in Council," Madison wrote Jefferson. "We have nothing left therefore, but to make ready for it." When the *Hornet* finally arrived in late May, the dispatches it carried

The Battle of Tippecanoe. *(Library of Congress)*

revealed that indeed nothing had changed. The Orders in Council remained in effect. Only a cancellation of those orders would have prevented war. Even though Madison believed, "that war contains so much folly, as well as wickedness, that much is to be hoped from the progress of reason; and if any thing is to be hoped, everything ought to be tried," he now thought that all the peaceful options had been tried, leaving war as the only way to protect the nation's rights and honor.

Congress, acting as if it knew what Madison intended to do, voted to extend a sixty-day embargo, designed to keep American ships at home in case a war started, to ninety days so that merchant vessels on the high seas might have time to reach an American port in safety. Members of the Republican Party in Congress had already caucused and voted unanimously to support the president for reelection. He thus felt assured that they would vote for a declaration of war should he request it. Presciently, on May 25, Jefferson wrote Madison, "Your declaration of war is expected with perfect

calmness, and if those in the North [the antiwar New England Federalists] mean systematically to govern the majority it is as good a time for trying them as we can expect."

Madison, with the aid of Secretary of State Monroe, evidently worked on the president's war message to Congress for a week before he delivered it. The president wanted to present an unassailable argument, for he anticipated trouble from the New England Federalists and yearned for vindication in the forum of public opinion. His message was delivered to the clerk of the House of Representatives on June 1 and read at a secret session of Congress. Stripped of its rhetoric, the president's message declared that by virtue of Britain's actions in impressing American citizens into the Royal Navy, interfering with American trade, and inciting American Indians on the frontier, a state of war between the two countries already existed and Congress's duty was to recognize that fact officially. The House voted for the war resolution 79-49, but in the Senate the division appeared so close that votes had to be rounded up until the last minute. Although the antiwar Federalists stood firm, to the president's great relief the vote for war was 19-13. Madison signed one declaration of war on June 18. A few days later Augustus Foster, the British minister, called on Madison before departing for home. He subsequently recalled that in this last interview the president said he considered "that the war would be but nominal." Several months later, Washington learned that two days before the United States declared war Viscount Castlereagh had relented and told Parliament that the Orders in Council were being repealed. Reports of the British turnaround made some members of the administration hesitate to support the declaration until Madison let it be known that it was too late to undo Congress's action. Henceforth, hot lead and cold steel would decide the matter.

War with Great Britain

As the fighting began in the War of 1812, earlier predictions that Canada would quickly fall to the American invaders, and become a bargaining chip at the diplomatic tables proved to be exceedingly optimistic. General Henry Dearborn's army moved so slowly that his planned capture of Montreal turned into a fiasco. Even worse, General William Hull, after crossing the Detroit River into Upper Canada and advancing timidly toward Fort Malden, lost his nerve and withdrew to Detroit where he surrendered to the British without firing a single shot. Hull was later court-martialed and sentenced to be shot, but because of his fine Revolutionary War record, Madison pardoned him. American attacks on Canada at the western end of Lake Ontario also failed when militiamen refused to cross the Niagara River into Canada. At first the navy gave a good account of itself, winning a number of single-ship duels with British vessels, but the British preponderance of ships was so great that by the spring of 1813 the American navy was bottled up in port and the British had blockaded the American coast.

In the presidential election in the fall of 1812, following these military failures, Madison was challenged by DeWitt Clinton of New York, an antiwar Republican running with Federalist support. Even though the Republicans put Elbridge Gerry of Massachusetts on the ticket with Madison, the president carried only one New England state and garnered fewer than half the electoral college votes of the Middle Atlantic states, but he swept the South and West and received a total of 128 electoral votes to 89 for Clinton. New England's antiwar votes and its leading newspapers' harsh criticism of his administration bewildered Madison: He could not conceive of citizens placing pecuniary interest above patriotism.

Madison Begins a Second Term: A Beleaguered America

In his inaugural address following his reelection, Madison restated the nation's war aim as the restoration of American independence, but by the winter of 1812-1813 only an extreme patriot could have claimed progress in that effort. The Canadian invasion had failed on all fronts, the Royal Navy had clamped a tight blockade on American ports, and America's ally France was mired in an invasion of Russia and could do nothing to ease British pressure on the United States. Gallatin scrounged for funds to pay for weapons, blankets, uniforms, and food for the armies. In the face of so many problems and battlefield defeats, Secretary of War Eustis left the cabinet. His replacement, John Armstrong, former minister to France, started off badly by choosing the ill-starred James Wilkinson to command another Canadian invasion. After a short skirmish at Chrysler's Farm, on the north side of the St. Lawrence River, Wilkinson retreated. Commodore Oliver Hazard Perry's victory on Lake Erie and William Henry Harrison's triumph at the Battle of the Thames River in upper Canada in October, 1813, helped restore flagging American morale. When the Russian czar offered to act as a mediator in peace talks, Madison accepted and appointed three commissioners, led by Secretary of the Treasury Gallatin, to meet with the British at a neutral site.

The fighting continued, however, and developments in Europe left the Americans in an even more precarious position. After his great victory at Dresden in August, 1813, Napoleon began the long retreat that ended with his surrender to the British at Waterloo. The peace that followed in Europe released fourteen British regiments for service in the American theater. Britain continued to fight even though it had abandoned the practices of impressment and blockade that had originally led to war. Now with the best army in the world, the British decided on a series of attacks in North America that would end the war once and for all.

Totally inexperienced in military matters, and lacking an assertive character, Madison relied on his cabinet and a growing horde of generals to provide the leadership required to stop the British offensive. Unfortunately, problems plagued both the military effort and the cabinet itself. The American militia, despite all rhetoric, was no match for the well-trained British regulars. Furthermore, as England escalated its war effort, American commerce was swept from the seas and customs receipts, the main source of federal revenue, declined dramatically. With Gallatin's departure on the peace mission to Europe, William Jones, who had replaced the incompetent Paul Hamilton as secretary of the navy, assumed the extra burden of running the Treasury Department, and under his leadership financial crises were solved by expedients that offered only short-term relief. In the War Department, Secretary Armstrong, harboring presidential ambitions, made his decisions with an eye toward the 1816 election and consequently became an increasing liability to the administration.

When the American peace mission reached Europe, it soon discovered, as Gallatin reported from London, that British public opinion favored a continuation of the war. "They thirst for a great revenge," he observed, "and the nation will not be satisfied without it." With the American oceangoing navy shrunk to a single ship of the line, the venerable *Constitution*, the British were free to navigate at will along the Atlantic coast. Raids on American ports brought prize money that the Royal Navy crews shared, leading British sea captains to cast covetous eyes on Baltimore, New Orleans, and other depots of American commodities that would bring high prices in Europe. Thus in the British strategic planning for 1814, a major objective was the Chesapeake Bay region, where an attack on Washington in retaliation for the burning of York (Toronto) in 1813 was planned to accompany a raid for plunder on Baltimore.

The British plan for 1814 also included a pincers movement, with the northern prong striking at Lake Champlain and the southernmost one directed at New Orleans. A courageous American defense at Plattsburgh, New York, thwarted the British army coming down from Canada, however, and logistical delays hampered the New Orleans expedition. Meanwhile, a combined British army-navy task force moved up Chesapeake Bay toward the capital and Baltimore. The sudden appearance of the British fleet in rendezvous off Tangier Island near the mouth of the Potomac River forced the president to seek counsel in preparing a hurried defense of the capital. On July 2, he chose General William H. Winder to command a motley collection of regulars, marines, and gunboat crews totaling fewer than two thousand. On paper at least, some fifteen thousand militiamen were also armed and available for duty.

The British Take Washington: The Burning of the White House

The British commanders delayed their assault until August 18, but even with the extra time General Winder had still done little to thwart their plans. Confusion and incompetence were the order of the day: Monroe took the field with a small band of dragoons, Armstrong proved utterly incapable of issuing a sensible order, and Winder became *hors de combat* after falling off his horse. The British landing party continued toward the capital, panic broke out in Washington, D.C., and Madison took off on horseback with some of his staff and cabinet members. In the ensuing melee, Dolley Madison made her famous flight to the suburbs with most of the White House silver, some prized velvet curtains, a small clock, and a huge portrait of Washington loaded on a wagon driven by a faithful black servant.

Winder returned to action but the militia were overwhelmed at Bladensburg, Maryland, and the meager defense forces disappeared. Unmolested, the British troops walked into a nearly deserted Washington, D.C. on August 24. During the next twenty-four hours, they managed to burn the White House, Capitol, and several other public buildings, while the retreating Americans destroyed the navy yard. From different vantage points, the president and his wife viewed the glowing sky. Their intended rendezvous at a plantation house near McLean, Virginia, thwarted by delays in the president's party, they were finally reunited at Falls Church, Virginia, the next day.

That same day, August 25, a freak tornado struck Washington, D.C., adding to the devastation wrought by the British. Finding little of value to plunder, the British troops returned to their ships that night. Only two days after the enemy's initial attack, Madison returned to Washington, D.C., though not to the black-ened White House, which he never again occupied. The president instead took up quarters in a relative's house on F Street and looked for a place to hold a cabinet meeting. William Wirt, a fellow Virginian who saw the president at this time, found the sight distressing. "He looks miserably shattered and woe-begone," noted Wirt. "In short, he looked heart-broken."

With the British fleet and troops still somewhere below the city, Madison assembled his cabinet to decide on a course of action. When the president expressed to Secretary Armstrong his disappointment at the collapse of the capital's defenses, Armstrong took affront and soon resigned amid rumors from Baltimore that Senator Samuel Smith had taken charge of that city's defenses. Reports from Richmond, Philadelphia, and elsewhere that the people's reaction to the news of the British attack on the capital was one of defiance rather than depression helped to restore the administration's morale. Only in certain parts of New England, it seemed, did the leading citizens think that Madison got the drubbing he deserved. Early in 1814, resolutions were already circulating

The 1814 engraving by G. Thompson entitled *The Taking of the City of Washington in America. (Library of Congress)*

at a number of town meetings calling for an end "to this hopeless war" and abandonment of a wartime embargo on trade. Madison tried to mollify the dissidents by convincing Congress on April 14 to repeal the embargo. Only half satisfied by this concession and goaded by the high Federalists, the Massachusetts legislature sent out a call for a general convention, to meet at Hartford, Connecticut, in December for a discussion "by any or all of the other New England states upon our public grievances and concerns." To secede or not secede from the Union was, in the minds of some extreme Federalists, the main question.

The news was not all bad, however. Along with the information that Baltimore had repelled a British attack, Madison had learned of the beginning of negotiations between British and American diplomats in Ghent, Belgium. Castlereagh, who had turned down the czar's mediation offer, agreed to talk directly with the American envoys. On the other hand, the country's financial condition remained precarious. The Treasury held large quantities of private banknotes, mostly from Southern institutions, which Northern bankers would not accept, and Boston financiers refused to buy Treasury notes unless they were heavily discounted. To keep the army paid and fed, as well as to prevent the bankruptcy of the federal government, would be no mean feat. Madison had to find some way to keep an army in the field in order to keep England at the negotiating table.

In September, 1814, with the smell of burnt furniture still in the air, the Madisons moved to John Taylor's Octagon House on New York Avenue, not far from the ruins of the White House. While his wife worked at decorating the house and attempted to create a pleasant atmosphere there, the president sent Congress, reassembled in temporary quarters in the patents and post office building, a message full of foreboding. If "the negotiations on foot with Great Britain" should lead to something con-

crete, he stated, money would be needed to implement "a return of peace." In view of what had happened in the last month, however, intensive hostilities seemed more likely than peace. In either case, the nation's Treasury needed an immediate infusion of cash, for it held only $5 million at the start of the fiscal year in July. Failure to find "pecuniary supplies" and provide for an adequate military force, Madison warned, would threaten "our national existence." The full extent of the financial crisis was revealed later when Acting Treasury Secretary George W. Campbell explained that a shortfall of some $50 million could be expected during the coming year unless Congress found a way to raise the money. Congress decided that the Treasury Department needed a more resourceful head and suggested to the president Gallatin's friend Alexander J. Dallas for the post. Madison, accordingly, nominated Dallas on October 5, and the Senate confirmed the nomination the next day.

Despite the serious interference of the war with the nation's commerce, the government continued to derive a substantial part of its income from the tariff, especially after Congress raised the rates. Also, in spite of the aversion to such sources of taxation as "unrepublican," near the end of the war some revenue was raised through an excise tax and a stamp duty. Congress also tried, with indifferent success, to levy a direct tax on the states, which it had no power to enforce. Two-thirds of the cost of the war was met by loans. As a result, by the end of the conflict the national debt amounted to well over $100 million. Although the nation's financial situation was grim indeed, in his State of the Union message in December, 1814, Madison managed to note a ray of hope in the military situation to the south. General Andrew Jackson's Tennesseeans, he reported, had scored a victory over the Creek Indians at Horseshoe Bend, Alabama, which eliminated the possibility of a successful alliance between that tribe and the British. Almost as Madison's message was read, Jackson's forces repulsed a British attack on Mobile, which American forces had seized in 1813. In a matter of weeks, reports of a British expeditionary force in the West Indies, probably headed for New Orleans, brought Jackson to Madison's attention this time as the logical leader of the Southern port's defenses.

Meanwhile, the negotiations at Ghent, Madison learned early in October, were continuing, although the British were confident that they would prevail after Napoleon's downfall. They demanded the exclusion of American fishermen from British territorial waters, pressed for the cession of part of Maine to Canada, and urged the creation of an Indian barrier state in the West south of the Great Lakes. British negotiators also sought some agreement on naval vessels on the Great Lakes, fixing the northern boundary of the United States at the source of the Mississippi, and an acknowledgment of the British right to use that river. Although some of these demands had the stamp of British arrogance, Madison seemed to be encouraged by the progress of the talks. In any event, he decided to make the British peace terms public. A storm of opposition arose from Republican newspaper editors, who screamed that the propositions called for abject surrender, while the party's patron saint at Monticello ticked off the demands one by one and concluded: "In other words . . . she reduces us to unconditional submission."

New England Separatists: The Hartford Convention

In New England, the November, 1814, elections seemed to indicate that a majority of voters there still favored a policy of appeasement toward England and whatever additional action the Hartford Convention, which was soon to convene, might endorse to restore the region's prosperity. Madison looked back at the actions of the New Englanders and saw a pattern of behavior very close to treason itself—smug-

gling to avoid the embargo, a refusal to send the state militia forces to fight when Canada was invaded, insults to recruiting officers, and niggardly support for the anemic federal Treasury. He hoped that these actions represented the views of only a minority of the people of the region.

Besides the official delegations from Massachusetts, Connecticut, and Rhode Island who gathered at Hartford in December were three informal representatives from New Hampshire and Vermont. The delegates decided to hold their sessions behind locked doors. As Henry Adams has noted, this "excess of caution helped to give the convention an air of conspiracy." Although Madison decided against trying to interfere with the convention's deliberations, as a precaution he sent a loyal recruiting officer to Connecticut to observe the situation and instructed him to ask for aid from neighboring states if overt acts of treason should occur. Some of the extremists among the delegates, such as Timothy Pickering of Massachusetts, talked of preparing the way for "the separation of the northern section of the states" from the rest of the Union. More moderate Federalists, such as Harrison Gray Otis, whom Madison had known from their days together in Congress, played a moderating role and prevented any radical action. The convention proposed seven amendments to the Constitution intended to limit Republican influence and protect the interests of their section. After three weeks, the delegates adjourned but voted to meet again if the Congress did nothing to satisfy their grievances, in which event they would presumably recommend a more extreme course of action.

With the approach of Christmas, 1814, Madison appeared to have little to celebrate. Ghent and Hartford were ominously silent, while in Washington the president's party chieftains bickered over ways of carrying on the war in 1815. Not the least of Madison's worries came from rumors out of the South.

The Hartford Convention or *LEAP NO LEAP.*

A political cartoon of the Hartford Convention showing Massachusetts, Connecticut, and Rhode Island contemplating a leap into the arms of King George III. *(Library of Congress)*

Some of the duke of Wellington's Waterloo veterans, it was reported, were on board British vessels waiting for the winds to carry them to New Orleans. There the townspeople were at odds with General Andrew Jackson over his preparations for the city's defense. So dark were the American prospects that Timothy Pickering gloated, "From the moment the British possess New Orleans, the Union is severed."

Dramatic Reversals: Victory at New Orleans, a Peace Treaty at Ghent

The new year soon brought a dramatic change in Madison's and the nation's fortunes. First came the breathtaking reports brought by an express from the South. New Orleans was saved. Jackson's men had swept the British invaders from the field, inflicting twenty-six

hundred casualties to a mere handful for the defenders. The manner in which the British retreated meant they would not try another attack. Church bells tolled their joyous refrain as well-wishers called at the president's house to offer congratulations. At the same time, a stagecoach from Hartford unloaded three delegates from the secret convention ready to hand the president their demands, but the delirium created by Jackson's victory left them no stomach for the business. In an ill humor, they trudged off to await a better opportunity.

Their opportunity never came, for ten days after the news of Jackson's victory at New Orleans a messenger arrived in Washington with the preliminary peace treaty from Ghent. The war was over, if the Senate ratified the treaty, and the nation had lost not an inch of territory or conceded a major right to the enemy. Unsolved matters of fishing rights off the coast of Canada and boundaries were left to the future arbitration of special commissions. Since the nadir of the American cause had been reached a few months earlier, this unexpected news appeared to be something of a miracle. Torchlight parades and banners extolling the president testified to his sudden popularity in every section of the country save one. Madison saw two of the Hartford delegates at a social gathering shortly after and was mildly amused by their obvious embarrassment. Suddenly, what New England thought or did was of little or no concern to the president.

The scenario for Madison's final years as president seemed to have come from the pen of a guardian angel. On February 18, 1815, he sent Congress a special message with his version of the war's origin and end. "The late war, although reluctantly declared by Congress, had become a necessary resort to assert the rights and independence of the nation," he declared. Ignoring the militia failures, the inept military leadership, and the constant search for dollars as he exulted in the outcome, Madison observed, "The Government has demonstrated the efficiency of its powers of defense, and . . . the nation can review its conduct without regret and without reproach."

In his eagerness for national unity, Madison even glossed over the wartime dissent of New England. No sign of vindictiveness was evident in his retrospective view of "Mr. Madison's War," as the high Federalists on Beacon Hill chose to call it. Madison must have read the public letter sent from a Boston meeting of Republicans with particular pleasure. It thanked him for "maintaining the honor of the American Flag against those who had arrogantly assumed the Sovereignty of the Ocean." Of all the accolades Madison received, however, none could have been more welcome than Jefferson's. "I sincerely congratulate you on the peace; and more especially on the éclat

with which the war closed," Jefferson wrote. With peace restored, Jefferson hoped his old friend would push hard for a return to Republican principles, particularly in the field of foreign affairs, where Americans had so much to learn. "We cannot too distinctly detach ourselves from the European system, which is essentially belligerent," Jefferson advised, "nor too sedulously cultivate an American system, essentially pacific."

Never had the blessings of peace been so apparent to Madison as in the days that followed. The nation's mood was euphoric, and more than one observer realized that something fundamental had happened in America as a result of the war. With the peace and with the licking administered the British at the Battle of New Orleans, the young republic had proved something to itself. A sense of nationhood, which even Washington's administration had failed to nourish, began to flower. Returning to his adopted land after the diplomatic mission, Gallatin perceived the change. The people, he observed, "are more American; they feel and act more like a nation."

One of the first manifestations of the surge in national pride was the Mediterranean expedition dispatched to attack the Barbary pirates of North Africa. The American warships devastated the pirate vessels. So thoroughly did they accomplish their task that the dey of Algiers sued for peace and promised to promptly free the American prisoners he was holding for ransom. Further action at Tunis and Tripoli brought a similar response, ending in a complete American triumph. Henceforth, the American flag was respected by the Barbary pirates, who had for decades contemptuously extracted an annual tribute from the United States Treasury.

The new nationalism that followed the war also found expression in domestic policy. Madison, in a sharp reversal of his earlier advocacy of states' rights and a federal government of strictly limited power, called for a strong military establishment, a uniform national currency, a tariff that would protect new American industries, a federally subsidized system of roads and canals, and a national university. The experiences of the war amply justified Madison's request for a stronger military establishment, and Congress responded by authorizing an army of ten thousand men and appropriating $8 million for the construction for fifteen new naval units. While emphasizing the basic financial soundness of the nation, the president conceded that some alternative to the inadequate state banks was needed to provide for a stable public credit and a uniform national currency and expressed a willingness to support a bill chartering a Second Bank of the United States.

When a bill creating such an institution with a twenty-year charter passed Congress, Madison promptly signed it into law. How much the political parties had reversed themselves was evident as Republicans pushed the bank bill forward while Federalists, who had pleaded for the First Bank of the United States in 1791, made an earnest but feeble effort to defeat it. When Congress passed another measure appropriating $1.5 million to pay for the bank's charter, and all future dividends on government-owned stock in the bank to create a permanent fund to support the construction of roads and canals, Madison vetoed it, but only on constitutional grounds. He believed that a constitutional amendment was required to enable Congress to exercise such power.

To protect new industries established just before and during the war from the competition of cheap foreign, and especially British goods, being dumped on the American market, Congress passed and Madison signed a protective tariff bill that maintained or increased the wartime duties.

Madison's proposal for a national university, which was to be repeated by John Quincy Adams when he became president, was in both instances ignored by Congress.

Madison enjoyed his final year in office as Congress, under the leadership of Henry Clay and John C. Calhoun, worked through his legislative program. He spent a leisurely summer and fall at Montpelier, looking forward to the election of his successor. The Republican congressional caucus had selected his choice, Secretary of State James Monroe, as the party's candidate. The Federalist candidate was Rufus King of New York. His party badly weakened by its near-treasonous opposition to the war, King carried only three New England states with a total of 34 electoral votes to 183 for Monroe. The succession of presidents from Virginia—the "Virginia dynasty"—would continue.

Madison's last months in Washington, D.C., were marked by a civility and popularity he had rarely known during forty years of public service. A veritable procession of well-wishers called at the temporary presidential residence on Pennsylvania Avenue. In his valedictory State of the Union message in early December, 1816, Madison described the chief achievement of his eight years in office in a single sentence: "I have the satisfaction to state, generally, that we remain in amity with foreign powers." All the travail of two wars with England, the quasi-war with France during the Adams administration, the battles with the Barbary pirates, and the long squabble with Spain over the Mississippi River and Florida was subsumed in Madison's terse announcement. America was at peace with the world. Taking the Constitution as the palladium of American liberty, Madison predicted the continuation of "a Government pursuing the public good as its sole object" and one "whose conduct within and without may bespeak the most noble of all ambitions—that of promoting peace on earth and good will to man."

John Adams was one of the two Americans who best understood Madison's feelings as he left the presidency. "Notwithstanding a thousand Faults and blunders," Adams wrote Jefferson, Madison's "administration has acquired more glory, and established more union, than all his three predecessors . . . put together." The former president's gracious remarks undoubtedly reached Montpelier, and for the next decade when Madison visited with Jefferson (who kept up a lively correspondence with Adams) there was a mingling of thoughts of self-congratulation among the three founding fathers. Only they understood all the difficulties a president faced, and only they knew how much America had needed the sense of nationhood it finally achieved in 1815.

Madison in Retirement

Madison's achievements of eight years in the presidency can be succinctly summarized as having given the nation a stronger loyalty to the idea of republican government and a full awareness of American nationhood. As the Madisons traveled homeward in 1817 only one problem remained as a stain on American independence: slavery. Up to 1817 Madison's energies had been devoted to preserving independence and the civil liberties it guaranteed to the American people. As a Virginian, a slaveholder, and a planter, it was beyond Madison's capability to shape a solution for the slavery issue that was beginning to crystallize. In his retirement, which lasted for another nineteen years, Madison worried more about political threats to the Union—nullification and later secession—than about the corrosive effects of slavery on the national character. Until his dying day, Madison never claimed that slavery was right—only that its abolition was beyond his power.

During the remainder of his life, Madison experienced his share of trials and triumphs. The dissolute conduct of his stepson, John Payne Todd, was a constant problem as Madison tried to shield the young man's shady character from public view. Madison once estimated that he had spent more than $20,000 trying to keep Todd out of jail or other scrapes. Family

matters aside, Madison's health remained as fragile in retirement as during his active days. His medicine chest must have taken up a large part of his living quarters at Montpelier, where he alternately tended to his aged mother, watched as Dolley lost her good looks and comely figure, and wrote checks to cover Payne Todd's indiscretions.

Despite a reduction in his standard of living (his salary of $25,000 annually while president had no equivalent in farming income later), in retirement Madison and his wife were still noted for their hospitality. Famous visitors and ordinary citizens who called at Montpelier always found a dining table loaded with a variety of meats, vegetables, sweetcakes, breads, cider, and wine. During his last years, the expenses outran income and Madison was forced to sell some slaves—an experience common to many planters after the 1819 panic—which he excused by saying that the blacks were simply going from his plantation to that of a relative.

At Jefferson's urging, Madison became involved in the founding of the University of Virginia and served briefly as its rector. His remarkable friendship with Jefferson ended when black crepe shrouded Monticello in 1826. Madison spent his last decade arranging personal papers, with an eye toward creating a legacy for the nation and for Dolley Madison, for he realized that the cash value of his notes of the federal convention alone would provide a financial cushion for his widow.

When Madison became ill in June, 1836, well-meaning friends and relatives suggested that drugs might prolong his life until the Fourth of July, so that he might expire on Independence Day as had Adams, Jefferson, and Monroe. Madison dismissed the suggestion outright. He looked on July 4, 1776, as the beginning of a new era and saw no value in an artificial reminder of one of humankind's most glorious moments. He died on June 28, 1836.

Robert A. Rutland

Bibliographical References

Despite many shortcomings, Irving Brant's *James Madison*, 6 vols., 1941-1961, is valuable for its originality and sympathetic treatment. For an excellent short biography, see Harold S. Schultz, *James Madison*, 1970, which is factually sound and full of important insights. Standing somewhere in between these works are Ralph Ketcham's readable *James Madison: A Biography*, 1971, and Robert A. Rutland, *James Madison and the Search for Nationhood*, 1981. A meritorious work is Merrill Peterson, *James Madison: A Biography in His Own Words*, 1974.

Although the tendency in Henry Adams's classic *History of the United States: During the Administrations of Jefferson and Madison*, 9 vols, 1889-1891, is to regard Madison as a failure as an administrator, there is much merit and sound information in this interpretive work. Madison's political thought is central to the theme of Drew R. McCoy, *The Elusive Republic: Political Economy in Jeffersonian America*, 1980. Also by Drew R. McCoy, *The Last of the Fathers: James Madison and the Republican Legacy*, 1991, explores the human side of critical political and cultural issues during tests to the survival of the republic. Madison's role in the formation of one of the great political parties is recounted in Noble E. Cunningham, Jr., *The Jeffersonian Republicans: The Formation of Party Organization,*

1789-1801, 1957. Virginia Moore's *The Madisons*, is rather uncritical but contains valuable information on Dolley Madison and the complex genealogy of the Payne and Madison families. Two works by Adrienne Koch deserve a place in any library. Her *Jefferson and Madison: The Great Collaboration*, 1950, and *Madison's "Advice to My Country,"* 1966, are books written with profound scholarship and affection.

For the specialists, J. A. C. Stagg, *Mr. Madison's War: Politics, Diplomacy, and Warfare in the Early American Republic, 1783-1830*, 1983, offers monumental research and a forthright view of Madison as a wartime president. Conover Hunt-Jones, *Dolley and the "Great Little Madison,"* 1977, emphasizes Madison's interests in architecture and decoration, with additional essays on his intellectual pursuits. Richard K. Matthews, *If Men Were Angels: James Madison and the Heartless Empire of Reason*, 1994, examines Madison's worldview, humanity, and vision of the future. William L. Miller, *The Business of May Next: James Madison and the Founding*, 1994, puts Madison in context of the moral and intellectual foundations of the American nation. Robert A. Goldwin, *From Parchment to Power: How James Madison Used the Bill of Rights to Save the Constitution*, 1998, details Madison's transformation from skeptic to advocate of a bill of rights.

James Monroe

5th President, 1817-1825

Born: April 28, 1758
    Westmoreland County,
      Virginia
Died: July 4, 1831
    New York, New York

Political Party: Democratic Republican
Vice President: Daniel D. Tompkins

Cabinet Members

Secretary of State: John Quincy Adams
Secretary of the Treasury: William H. Crawford
Secretary of War: George Graham, John C. Calhoun
Secretary of the Navy: Benjamin Crowninshield, Smith Thompson, Samuel Southard
Attorney General: William Wirt

The day began auspiciously for a new administration and a new era. March 4, 1817, inauguration day for President James Monroe, dawned mild and radiant. Some five to eight thousand citizens witnessed the simple yet impressive ceremony. It was held outdoors, on the steps of the so-called Brick Capitol, a temporary structure for Congress located on the present site of the Supreme Court. Everywhere there were signs of the steady progress that had been made since British troops left the nation's capital in fiery ruins. The newly renovated President's House, soon to be called the White House, would be ready for occupancy in six months, and the Capitol would be usable in December, 1819.

The Virginia Dynasty

The vision of the American republic rising from the ashes of war formed an appropriate backdrop to Monroe's inauguration. The new presi-

Monroe's official portrait. *(White House Historical Society)*

105

dent was the last of the generation of revolutionary heroes to head the nation, a member of what John Quincy Adams called a special "race of men." He was also the last of the three great members of the Virginia Republican dynasty to lead his country in the early years of the nineteenth century.

Born of Scottish and Welsh ancestry in Westmoreland County, Virginia, on April 28, 1758, Monroe came from a family of modest estate. With the support of his mother's brother, however, an influential member of the Virginia ruling aristocracy, Monroe entered the College of William and Mary in 1774. In Williamsburg, he was swept up in revolutionary activity, joined the Third Virginia Infantry, and in the fall of 1776 was fighting with Washington's army in New York. His military record was distinguished, and at the Battle of Trenton, he was severely wounded in a daring charge that succeeded in capturing the enemy's cannons.

Monroe emerged from the fighting with the rank of major, the esteem of General George Washington, and the fixed ideal of serving the worldwide cause of liberty. He thoroughly identified the principles of the American Revolution with "free republican government," and he considered the success of America's republican experiment essential to the spread of liberty everywhere. He therefore turned to the study of law as preparatory to a career in politics. Significantly, his teacher and mentor was the wartime governor of Virginia, Thomas Jefferson, and thus began a lifelong association that brought social and intellectual, as well as political, rewards. It was also Jefferson who introduced Monroe to James Madison. Monroe's friendship with these men was occasionally strained, but it endured and, as president, he continued to solicit their advice.

Beginning in 1782 with his election to the Virginia House of Delegates, Monroe began a political career in which success and accomplishment were punctuated by periods of disappointment. He served as a delegate to the Continental Congress in 1783, where he sought to strengthen the Confederation government and to uphold the rights of the West to navigate the Mississippi River. Nationalism and expansionism would continue to be keynotes of his political thinking. He also attended the Virginia ratifying convention (he was a moderate opponent of the Constitution) and then, in 1790, was elected to the United States Senate.

A Precocious Diplomat

In 1794, Monroe, who was now identified with the Democratic Republican Party, was appointed by Washington as minister to France, but he was soon recalled by the president for being overly pro-French. The political tide was flowing in a Republican direction, however, and Monroe soon reentered public life, first as governor of Virginia in 1799 and, in 1803, as President Jefferson's special envoy to France to conclude the Louisiana Purchase agreement.

Monroe's triumph in France was not followed by further success as minister to England and envoy to Spain. When a treaty with England was not even submitted to the Senate for ratification, Monroe returned to the United States in late 1807, his political fortunes temporarily impaired. Yet the growing crisis with England again brought a need for his services, and after a short period as a state legislator and governor, he returned to national office as Madison's secretary of state. Monroe's experience and skill proved so valuable that during the War of 1812, he also took over the War Department when its previous occupant proved woefully incompetent.

By the time Madison's presidency drew to a close, Monroe's record of public service made him the Republicans' heir apparent. It came as little surprise that in March, 1816, the Republican congressional caucus nominated him. With the Federalist Party moribund, Monroe won an overwhelming presidential victory with 183 electoral votes against only 34 for his opponent, Rufus King.

The Virtues of Nonpartisanship

The president-elect was an impressive figure, both in height (he was about 6 feet tall) and bearing. His clothing resembled Revolutionary-period fashion, often a dark coat, knee-length pantaloons, and white-topped boots. His hair was cut short in front, powdered, and gathered in a queue behind. It was, however, his plain, honest, and virtuous character that most struck contemporaries. As Adams noted, Monroe did not possess brilliance, but rather "natural prudence and good sense, a tact, and a knowledge of men, which eminently fitted him for a successful politician." Somewhat slow and cautious in forming judgments, he was firm and energetic in upholding them. Others reached a conclusion more rapidly, another cabinet member observed, "but few with a certainty so unerring."

Monroe had his imperfections. Overly sensitive to criticism and given to brooding over alleged slights, he never won the kind of passionate devotion that some presidents have. Yet his modesty and warmth were major assets and account for his continued popularity in the midst of heated controversy.

The country that Monroe now headed was, under the beneficent sway of peace, undergoing a period of rapid change that would, in a few short years, make the world of his birth appear as quaint as Rip Van Winkle's phlegmatic Dutch community. Settlers poured into the West, advancing the frontier and adding six new states to the Union between 1812 and 1821. Planters and farmers in the South rushed into more fertile lands, spreading slavery in their wake. In the North, particularly in New England, the pace of industrialization quickened as capital flowed into manufacturing. Meanwhile, a revolution in transportation was under way, primarily involving the construction of canals but also embracing steam navigation and river and road improvements. Jeffersonian agrarian ideals inevitably faded, but the national pride and prosperity that immediately followed the War of 1812 helped ease the strains of adjustment to these new conditions.

Monroe's political philosophy admirably suited this period of transition. He was not a Jeffersonian ideologue, but rather a pragmatic and moderate nationalist ready to adjust Republican limited government principles to the demands of commerce, communications, and manufacturing. A more doctrinaire president would likely have added to, rather than muted, the difficulties of post-1815 America.

Monroe's inaugural address established the "liberal and mild tone" of his administration. Following Republican tradition, he celebrated the intelligence and virtue of the people, pledged "economy and fidelity" in government, and promised to discharge the national debt. Monroe also added new emphases to Republican doctrine. He endorsed the "systematic and fostering care" of manufacturing and spoke of the "high importance" of internal improvements, the construction of roads and canals, which he wanted to "bind the Union more closely together." Finally, he underlined the need for a large-scale program of fortifications and the improvement of the militia and navy.

Monroe's thinking about political parties and the presidential office constitutes one of the most fascinating aspects of his administration. More than any president except Washington, Monroe scorned political parties and acclaimed the virtues of nonpartisanship. He believed that political parties were neither necessary nor desirable in a free society. Indeed, he considered them a "curse" and thought government should be based instead on the people's "virtue."

Monroe recognized that the elimination of parties would have to take place gradually. In the meantime, he had no intention of reviving Federalism by appointing Federalists to office. For the present, the country needed to depend on its friends, Republicans, whose loyalty would be jeopardized if former enemies received political favor, but Monroe hoped that the effects of peace, the spirit of "moderation," and the absence of great political excitement would eventually bring an end to parties.

Monroe sought to place his administration on "national grounds," and his search for unity and harmony was most conspicuously demonstrated in his famous tour of the East and Northwest in the spring of 1817, and, two years later, of the South. Everywhere—from Baltimore to Portland, from Detroit to Pittsburgh—Americans hailed the new president with a burst of "national feeling" and demonstrations of respect for the Union and its "republican institutions." It was during his visit to Boston that the phrase "Era of Good Feelings" originated to become a label for the two terms of Monroe's presidency. The expression captured the patriotic hopes of its president that Americans would "all unite" to secure the success of self-government.

Monroe has generally been considered a weak president, content to drift with outside events and to follow the lead of Congress. Only in the realm of foreign policy has his more active contribution been acknowledged. This picture has some validity. He was, by temperament and circumstance, a less activist president than Jefferson or Andrew Jackson.

Yet Monroe was a surprisingly effective and able executive. His model was Washington, the disinterested, moral, and patriotic leader who was above class, party, or section. He was, therefore, not a passive president. Within the executive branch, he controlled the cabinet and the power of appointing officials. His frequent cabinet meetings—about 180 sessions in eight years—provided him with information and ideas and also enabled him to develop a consensus on policy. Monroe realized that in the absence of party loyalty, the agreement of powerful cabinet members more readily assured support for measures in Congress and the countryside. He also used his annual presidential message to help set the nation's political

agenda, and he often exerted a strong behind-the-scenes influence on Congress when controversial matters were before it. Considering the political obstacles confronting him, Monroe was quite successful in shaping the course of events.

The cabinet Monroe selected was, according to a leading authority, "one of the strongest that any President had assembled." He appointed Massachusetts's brilliant and dour John Quincy Adams as secretary of state. After failing to find a prominent Westerner to accept the War Department, he eventually settled on the young and talented South Carolinian John C. Calhoun. For Treasury secretary, Monroe maintained continuity with the past by reappointing William H. Crawford of Georgia, a "giant of a man," popular and exceedingly ambitious. Rounding out the cabinet were Benjamin Crowninshield of Massachusetts as secretary of the navy, a holdover from the Madison administration, and William Wirt of Maryland, an accomplished lawyer and man of letters, as attorney general. The cabinet was unusually stable, the most notable turnover occurring in 1818, when Crowninshield resigned and was replaced by the New Yorker Smith Thompson.

Monroe paid a heavy price, however, for the excellence of his selections. Without the constraint of party discipline, its leading members ambitiously jockeyed for position in the hope of succeeding Monroe. Monroe remained in charge of his administration, but the harmony of the first years gradually evaporated and with it a portion of his effectiveness in dealing with Congress.

Domestic Initiatives
With his cabinet in place, the new president grappled with the substantive issues of politics. Buoyed by the country's prosperity, Monroe recommended in 1817 the repeal of internal taxes, and Congress enthusiastically responded. Prosperity also enabled Monroe to reduce the public debt. Despite problems

caused by a drop in revenue during his first term, the debt was progressively lowered and Monroe could happily report by the end of his first term that nearly $67 million had been paid. By his last year in office, further reductions permitted Monroe to entertain a "well-founded hope" that the entire debt would be discharged within a decade. His wish was realized during Jackson's presidency.

Reducing government burdens was not undertaken at the expense of national needs. In keeping with his long-standing concern for national defense, Monroe forwarded with "zeal and activity" the system of coastal fortifications begun in Madison's administration. Congress appropriated substantial sums throughout his first term, and in December, 1819, Monroe announced the virtual completion of a survey of coastal defense as well as "considerable progress" in the construction of fortifications. By 1820, some $650,000 had been spent on various projects.

The panic of 1819 and consequent political maneuvering temporarily reduced expenditures, but once the economy rebounded, Monroe successfully urged larger annual appropriations. He could be satisfied when he left office that the nation's defense was considerably stronger than in the period before the War of 1812.

Much more problematic was the establishment of an acceptable policy toward internal improvements. This issue aroused competing sectional and constitutional claims. For Monroe himself, the desirability of such projects clashed with traditional Jeffersonian scruples about excessive federal power and violations of states's rights. In his first annual message, Monroe seemed to rule out active federal participation by asserting that members of Congress "do not possess the right" to establish a system of internal improvements without a constitutional amendment. His sentiments provoked a House debate that provided much heat but little light on the subject. A combination of declining revenue, congressional opposition, and presidential caution effectively handcuffed internal improvements legislation during Monroe's first term.

During his second term, the issue again came to the fore in a way that gave Monroe an opportunity to present his full views on the subject. In April, 1822, Congress passed a bill authorizing the construction of tollgates and the collection of tolls to keep the Cumberland, or National, Road in repair. This impressive project had received the support of previous Republican presidents, and Monroe had approved bills for its extension westward toward the Mississippi River. He vetoed this bill on May 4, 1822, however, asserting that it unduly infringed on states' rights. Again denying Congress the power "to adopt and execute a system" of improvements, he now proclaimed that Congress had unlimited power to raise money and could "appropriate" it for "purposes of common defense and of general, not local, national, not State, benefit."

Monroe's compromise, which left the door open to federal assistance for national projects, satisfied neither extreme opponents nor proponents of internal improvements, but it managed to balance demands for better transportation with fears of excessive federal power and the dangers of opening the Treasury to competing sectional and local interests. In 1824, he signed both a bill subscribing to stock in the Chesapeake and Delaware Canal Company and a general survey bill authorizing a comprehensive survey of routes for roads and canals of national importance. The lasting impression made by Monroe's formula became evident in 1830, when President Jackson referred to it as a precedent for his famous Maysville Road veto.

The Panic of 1819 and the Missouri Crisis

The favorable circumstances attending the start of Monroe's presidency were shattered by two

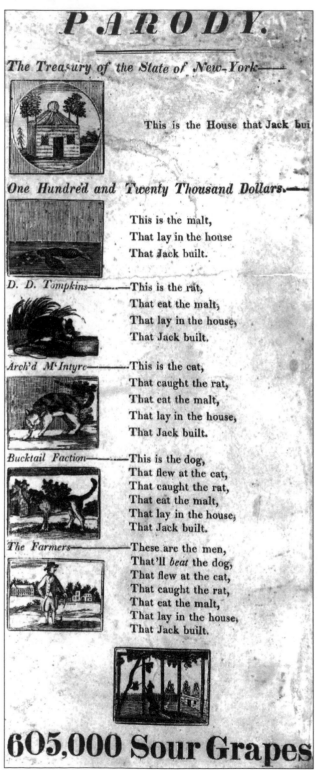

"The House That Jack Built" as a parody of the Panic of 1819. (*Library of Congress*)

major upheavals during his first term, the panic of 1819 and the Missouri crisis. The economic and sectional unrest unleashed by these events acted like a corrosive to national harmony and the one-party political system. The issues raised at this time would help shape the course of national politics for a generation, but their full impact would become evident only after Monroe left office.

The postwar economic boom proved short-lived, and by early 1819, the country was immersed in a full-scale depression. The price of land and agricultural commodities plunged; laborers were discharged; factories, businesses, and banks failed; and farms came under the sheriff's gavel. The South and West were especially hard hit. By 1821, the economy was recovering, and a period of economic expansion that would last into the 1830's marked the remainder of Monroe's presidency.

Monroe was concerned about the nation's "pecuniary embarrassments," but he tended to discount the panic's severity and to adopt a traditional moral posture that such setbacks served as "mild and instructive admonitions" for Americans to return to their republican habits of "simplicity and purity." The solution for economic ills lay with the people and Providence, not government.

In fact, however, the government did undertake various measures to improve conditions. The Second Bank of the United States, which had irresponsibly aggravated the boom-bust cycle from 1815 to 1819 by its restrictive financial policies and had mismanaged its affairs, was being called the "Monster" by angry citizens. Monroe, who considered a national bank essential for the country's stability and growth, helped the bank weather the storm. He forced the resignation of the bank's incompetent president, William Jones, and approved the appointment of Jones's successors, first Langdon Cheves and then, in 1823, Nicholas Biddle. Under their management, the bank was placed on a sound footing and became an increasingly useful instrument in the government's monetary and fiscal transactions.

The panic also made imperative an adjustment of the nation's land policy. Fueled in part by liberal credit terms, a tremendous speculative boom had preceded the depression. When land prices tumbled, land purchasers owed the federal government $22 million and faced the prospect of losing their lands. Congress first responded in 1820 by abolishing credit purchases and selling land for cash only. This reform reduced speculation, but made land purchases more difficult. Monroe came under considerable Western attack for signing this Land Act of 1820.

The president consequently recouped some favor from critics by recommending "a reasonable indulgence" to relieve land debtors. Congress soon approved a relief bill that allowed buyers to apply their previous payments to portions of their claims, relinquishing those portions for which they could not pay. The Relief Act of 1821 slashed the land debt in half and eliminated this issue as a national concern. Westerners, however, continued to agitate for cheaper land for the next decade.

Hard times also set off a wave of sentiment in favor of reducing expenditures. This movement gained momentum in 1821, then peaked and evaporated the following year. It was particularly unwelcome to Monroe because it severely undercut his efforts to strengthen the nation's defense. Congress reduced the army from ten thousand to fewer than six thousand men, cut naval appropriations, and slowed the fortifications program. Efforts to reduce civil salaries, however, ground to a halt when cuts were proposed in the salaries of members of Congress.

The economy drive had political overtones as the supporters of Henry Clay, Crawford, and Calhoun sought to turn the movement against their rivals, sometimes embarrassing Monroe as well. More than politics, however, was involved. Many people, especially in the South, encouraged retrenchment as part of a larger campaign to reassert limited government principles. These "Old Republicans" warned that Monroe's moderate nationalism dangerously swelled federal powers and jeopardized liberty and states' rights.

The panic of 1819 stimulated sectional and political disaffection with the course of national affairs. So, too, did the famous Missouri crisis that erupted suddenly in February, 1819, when representative James Tallmadge, Jr., of New York, introduced an amendment to a bill permitting Missouri to form a state government that would have gradually abolished slavery in the future state of Missouri.

Once raised, the slavery question flared into heated controversy that brought the possibility of violence and civil war. The House, where the North predominated, passed the restriction amendment in a sectional vote, but the Senate, where slave and free states were balanced, rejected it. Congress adjourned in March, 1819, without resolving Missouri's fate.

When the Sixteenth Congress convened the following December, Maine was applying for statehood and opponents of slavery restriction promptly announced that they would block Maine's admission until antislavery forces agreed to Missouri's admission with slavery. After considerable debate, a sufficient number of Northern representatives (called doughfaces) retreated and a compromise was adopted that, in effect, admitted Maine and Missouri, without restriction, to the Union. In addition, slavery was prohibited in all the Louisiana Purchase territory north of 36 degrees 30 minutes, the Southern boundary of Missouri. By early March, 1820, the Missouri crisis was over.

Blinded to the genuine antislavery convictions involved in the restriction movement, Monroe believed that its leaders merely sought increased political power by rallying the non-slaveholding states against the South. Like many Jeffersonians, Monroe disliked slavery, but he was determined not to sign any bill that incorporated the principle that Congress could impose slavery restriction on a state, as distinct from a territory. He therefore drafted a veto message in case the restriction measure passed both houses of Congress.

Since Monroe "never doubted" Congress's power to regulate the territories, he supported the compromise. When the House approved the bill, he called his cabinet together to develop a consensus in support. The entire cabinet agreed that Congress could prohibit slavery in the territories, but there was considerable wrangling about whether that prohibition extended into statehood. Adams, who had strong antislavery convictions, ardently maintained against the rest of the cabinet that the restriction applied to future states. The impasse was finally resolved when the cabinet agreed to a vague and modest statement that the compromise was not unconstitutional. Monroe "readily assented" to this formulation, and on March 6, 1820, he signed the Missouri enabling bill.

Monroe was heartened by the "auspicious" resolution of the sectional contest, and he applauded the "patriotic devotion" of those who had put the nation's welfare above local interests. He considered the slavery issue as "laid asleep" but the Missouri crisis, in reality, boded ill for the future. Many Northerners were disappointed at the setback to the cause of freedom, whereas the Old Republicans in the South condemned the acknowledgment of Congress's power over slavery in the territories and grew more vocal in their complaints against federal aggrandizement. In Monroe's own state of Virginia, there was powerful opposition to his renomination because he signed the compromise, a telling sign of the resurgence of sectionalism and the erosion of Republican Party unity in the wake of the Missouri dispute.

Foreign Affairs: Relations with Spain

Although domestic issues had dramatic consequences for the nation, Monroe's most striking achievements as president were in foreign affairs. His objectives were to preserve amicable relations with other nations, to protect and encourage American commercial operations, and to expand American boundaries. Perhaps most conspicuously, he wanted to make the United States a respected and recognized power in world affairs. "National honor is national property of the highest value," he lectured his countrymen.

Ironically, Anglo-American relations proved to be considerably smoother than before the War of 1812. Great Britain was now eager to cultivate American goodwill and the American marketplace. Monroe and Adams were therefore able to resolve some thorny issues.

In July, 1818, negotiations began to resolve fishing and boundary differences, which resulted in the Convention of 1818, Monroe's first treaty. The agreement compromised the complex fisheries issue by restoring American fishing liberties "for ever" to limited areas of British North America. The treaty extended the boundary line of 49 degrees between Canada and the United States westward from the Lake of the Woods to the Rocky Mountains, securing to the United States an area of the Midwest rich in farmland and natural resources. The Oregon Country was left open to both sides for ten years, neither side renouncing its claim. Finally, it left to arbitration the issue of compensation for slaves taken by British troops during the War of 1812, and renewed the commercial convention of 1815 for trade between the two countries. The Convention of 1818, Monroe declared, gave "great satisfaction" and firmed the rapprochement between Britain and the United States.

Relations with Spain were probably the most engrossing problem of Monroe's presidency. The disintegration of Spain's empire not only posed problems for the United States in

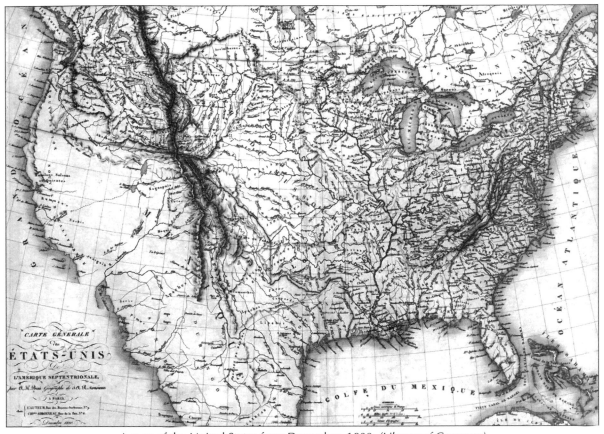

A map of the United States from December, 1820. *(Library of Congress)*

dealing with the struggling Latin American independence movement but also gave opportunities for expanding American boundaries at Spain's expense. Astutely combining patience and boldness, Monroe capitalized on this situation to gain Florida, further establish American claims as a continental nation, and announce a special American role in the Western Hemisphere.

Americans were naturally sympathetic to the cause of Latin American independence, and this sentiment was seized on by Henry Clay, who eloquently demanded American recognition of the newly independent states. Monroe's position was delicate. He, too, favored the revolutionaries, but he warned that premature recognition might provoke the European powers to intervene against them. Instead, he adopted a policy of neutrality, but a neutrality that gave

the rebels belligerent status. To Monroe, this gave them "all the advantages of a recognition, without any of its evils."

Withholding recognition also gave Monroe a lever to loosen Spain's hold on East Florida, an area he had long coveted, and to define the western boundary between Spain and the United States. Spain contended that the dividing line was the Mississippi River and that the Louisiana Purchase was invalid. Negotiations between the Spanish minister, Don Luis de Onís, and Adams initially proceeded slowly, but in December, 1817, they were given a new impetus when Monroe ordered General Andrew Jackson to put down Seminole border disturbances and authorized him to pursue the Indians into Florida if necessary.

Jackson responded with his customary energy, and by June, 1818, he had routed the

Seminoles, overwhelmed the Spanish posts of St. Marks and Pensacola, executed two British subjects for allegedly aiding American Indians, and engaged in a dispute with the governor of Georgia over the killing of some of his Indian allies. He was also ready, he informed the president, to take Cuba, if that were desired.

Whether Jackson had Monroe's permission to seize Florida is still in dispute. Jackson contended that Monroe had signaled his approval; Monroe categorically denied it. Although Monroe was probably right, it is also evident that the administration took no action to caution or restrain a general whose expansionary appetite was well-known.

When word reached Washington, D.C., of Jackson's exploits, the whole cabinet, with the exception of Adams, favored disavowing him. Adams thought the general entirely justified and even argued at first against restoring the posts to Spain. Monroe, employing "candor and good humor" in these exciting deliberations, skillfully built a consensus around his own views. Out of respect for Congress's war power and to deny Spain an excuse for war, he would return Spanish posts and acknowledge that Jackson had exceeded his instructions. Yet in justice to Jackson and to turn the incident "to the best account of our country," he refused to repudiate or censure Jackson. Instead, he alleged that the misconduct of Spanish officials justified Jackson's actions.

Monroe's refusal to repudiate Jackson supplied the "pressure" for Spain to conclude a treaty. The Transcontinental Treaty of 1819 ceded Florida to the United States and defined the western and northern boundary between the countries by drawing a line to the Pacific at 42 degrees north latitude from the source of the Arkansas River, thereby granting to the United States Spain's claim to the Oregon Country. The United States agreed to assume up to $5 million of American claims against Spain and to yield its pretensions to Texas. Although ratification was delayed until Feb-ruary, 1821, the treaty was a major triumph for the administration. It not only acquired Florida, Monroe's primary objective, but also gained international recognition of the United States as a continental nation.

Final approval of the treaty, coupled with significant military victories by the revolutionary armies in Latin America in 1821, tipped Monroe toward the side of recognition. In March, 1822, he informed Congress that La Plata (Argentina), Colombia, Chile, Peru, and Mexico ought to be recognized as independent. Congress agreed, and the United States became the first nation outside Latin America to recognize the new Latin American states.

A Second Term: The Monroe Doctrine

In March, 1821, Monroe was inaugurated for a second term. He humbly accepted his overwhelming reelection—only one electoral vote was cast against him—as a sign of national unity, not as a personal victory. He hoped that similar accord could be reached on all national questions. Like other presidents, however, he would find that his second term would present less cause for satisfaction than his first.

The course of affairs in Europe seemed to pose an increasingly serious threat of foreign intervention to restore Spain's former colonies. The autocratic rulers of Europe, organized as the Holy Alliance, helped oversee Europe's post-Napoleonic arrangements. Increasingly, they interpreted their charge as the suppression of revolutionary challenges to established regimes. In late 1822, after a revolution broke out in Spain, France was authorized by the Holy Alliance to restore the deposed Spanish monarch to the thorne, and in April, 1823, French troops marched into Spain. That the Holy Allies, using the French navy, would next intervene in Latin America seemed a distinct possibility to Americans in the summer of 1823.

In reality, the chance of military intervention was remote, largely because Britain, with George Canning as foreign secretary, utterly

The Monroe Doctrine

This doctrine was announced during President James Monroe's message to Congress on December 2, 1823:

"In the discussions to which this interest has given rise, and in the arrangements by which they may terminate, the occasion has been deemed proper for asserting as a principle in which rights and interests of the United States are involved, that the American continents, by the free and independent condition which they have assumed and maintain, are henceforth not to be considered as subjects for future colonization by any European power. . . . We owe it, therefore, to candor and to the amicable relations existing between the United States and those powers to declare that we should consider any attempt on their part to extend their system to any portion of this hemisphere as dangerous to our peace and safety. With the existing colonies or dependencies of any European power we have not interfered and shall not interfere. But with the governments who have declared their independence and maintain it, and whose independence we have, on great consideration and on just principles, acknowledged, we could not view any interposition for the purpose of oppressing them or controlling in any other manner their destiny by any European power in any other light than as the manifestation of an unfriendly disposition toward the United States."

opposed the use of force in Latin America. In August, 1823, Canning sought to bolster his anti-intervention stance by proposing to America's minister, Richard Rush, that the United States "go hand in hand with England" and issue a joint declaration on Latin American policy. This overture was forwarded to Washington, D.C., in early October.

Although initially inclined to meet the British proposal, Monroe favored rejecting Canning's offer by the time he convened his cabinet in early November, 1823, to deal with the European crisis. Adams vigorously supported this course. It was better for the United States to avow its principles independently, he argued, rather than "come in as a cock-boat in the wake of the British man-of-war." Adams recommended a systematic formulation of policy that would apply not only to the Holy Alliance but also to British pretensions in the Northwest and possibly Cuba, as well as to Russian claims on the Pacific Coast.

Adams advised the use of private diplomatic letters to Britain and Russia as the ap-

propriate medium to convey American views. Monroe, however, desired to broadcast American ideals and principles to the world. Thus while the cabinet deliberated on the wording of the diplomatic correspondence, it also considered Monroe's draft on foreign policy for his annual message.

The Monroe Doctrine—the term itself was first applied in the 1850's—was announced in Monroe's message of December 2, 1823. Its crystallization of basic foreign policy tenets owed much to Adams, but its rhetoric and inspiration were indeed Monroe's. The document asserted the principle of noncolonization (the concept was Adams's) that the American continents "are henceforth not to be considered as subjects for future colonization by any European powers." It also affirmed the principle of nonintervention, whereby the United States disclaimed any intent to interfere in the internal concerns of Europe and declared that any attempt by the European powers to extend their systems to this hemisphere was "dangerous to our peace and safety."

Although somewhat toned down from Monroe's original draft, which had seemed to Adams like a summons to arms against the Holy Alliance, the message was a high-minded expression of American nationalism. Issued before word reached Washington, D.C., that an agreement between Britain and France had entirely removed any threat of European intervention in Latin America, it courageously and independently avowed American aspirations in both North and South America.

An attempt at a display of America's diplomatic muscle on the long-standing West Indies trade issue, however, backfired. During Monroe's first term, Congress had passed retaliatory legislation against British restrictions on American trade in the West Indies. These Navigation Acts of 1818 and 1820 had indeed struck hard at West Indies prosperity, and Parliament, in 1822, yielded significant concessions by opening certain West Indies ports to American ships. Preference was still given, however, to British colonial trade. Monroe and Adams insisted that Britain do away with its system of imperial advantage and abandon intercolonial preferences. In March, 1823, Congress passed legislation granting the president authority to levy new discriminatory tariffs until Britain eliminated imperial preferences. Monroe quickly imposed the duties, the British retaliated, and by the close of his presidency, the West Indies trade remained restricted, a token of the administration's overzealous assertion of the principle of equal commercial opportunity.

Failure to Abolish the Slave Trade: The End of Republican Unity

Equally unsuccessful, though for different reasons, were efforts to reach an agreement to

In this painting by Clyde Deland, Monroe (standing) discusses the policy known as the Monroe Doctrine with his cabinet, (left to right) John Quincy Adams, William H. Crawford, William Wirt, John C. Calhoun, Samuel Southard, and John McLean. *(Library of Congress)*

An engraving depicting the horrors of the slave trade. Monroe supported strong legislation to punish those who participated in this practice. *(Library of Congress)*

abolish the odious international slave trade. Great Britain, the foremost agent in the campaign against the trade, urged adoption of a proposal that would have granted a reciprocal right to search vessels and established tribunals to judge cases. Monroe and Adams both wanted to end the trade, Monroe calling it "an abominable practice," but they vividly recollected previous British violations of American shipping. They therefore rejected the proposal as "repugnant to the feelings of the nation and of dangerous tendency."

Instead, the United States acted unilaterally. In 1819, Congress provided for the use of armed vessels to patrol the African coast, sometimes in cooperation with British patrols, and the following year legislation declared the participation of American citizens in the trade piracy was punishable by death.

These measures proved ineffective, and continued British pressure and growing public outrage at the trade brought stronger demands for international cooperation. The administra-

tion therefore modified its previous stand. The United States would in effect permit the right of search by declaring the slave trade piracy—pirates were not protected by a flag—without conceding the general principle of freedom of the seas.

In March, 1824, a slave trade convention was concluded with Britain, which declared the African slave trade piracy, and authorized the search, seizure, and punishment of offenders. In the Senate, however, Crawford supporters and Southerners anxious about cooperating with British antislavery forces rallied in opposition. An "astonished" Monroe urged ratification, but its foes were sufficiently strong to add crippling amendments that led Britain to reject the convention. Not until 1862, after the South seceded, did the United States sign a treaty suppressing the slave trade.

The trouble over the slave trade treaty was indicative of the problems posed during Monroe's second term by the political scuffling associated with the breakup of the Democratic

Republican Party into personal factions. Three of the five major presidential contenders were in Monroe's cabinet—Adams, Crawford, and Calhoun. The other two leading candidates were Clay and Jackson. Personal relations among cabinet members cooled, and an "embittered violent spirit" was often evident among their congressional followers. Monroe expressed "embarrassment and mortification" at the maneuvering of the candidates. He adopted a strict neutrality among them, but this only allowed the flames of factionalism to spread unchecked.

The end of Republican unity brought the demise of the congressional caucus. It met for the last time in February, 1824, when a small group of congressmen nominated Crawford. The other candidates disregarded the decision and condemned the caucus as undemocratic. The ensuing contest among Jackson, Adams, Crawford, and Clay—Calhoun dropped out to seek the vice presidency—ended without a majority selection. The decision went to the House of Representatives in February, 1825, where John Quincy Adams received the votes of a majority of states. When he chose Clay as his secretary of state and likely successor, the Jackson men cried "corrupt bargain" and organized an opposition that would, four years later, bring Old Hickory to the White House. The one-party system was dead, and the second American party system was emerging.

In the midst of this feverish presidential activity, Monroe gained a modest triumph when, in May, 1824, he signed a tariff bill providing for increased protection for manufactures. He had continually recommended that Congress encourage manufacturing, which he considered essential to national security, unity, and prosperity. Congress at first agreed, and in 1818 raised duties on iron and textiles, but the panic of 1819 and the Missouri controversy sparked hostility to protection, particularly in the South. In the spring of 1820, a new bill failed in the Senate by one vote, as the South and Southwest showed stiff opposition.

Despite this setback Monroe persisted. In early 1824, with the ardent protectionist Clay once again in the speaker's chair, Congress passed legislation providing additional support for iron, wool, hemp, cotton bagging, and textiles. Although the new rates were moderate, they were distinctly protective, and a howl of protests arose from the South. Southern spokespeople denounced the tariff as unjust and, even more ominously, as unconstitutional. The vote on passage resembled the sectional alignment over Missouri, an omen of the bitter tariff battles that lay ahead.

Expansion and Other Euphemisms: Indian Removal

Monroe's second term also marked an important turning point in Indian relations. Previous policy included a number of different and sometimes conflicting programs: Efforts to encourage American Indians to adopt white ways, inducements to remove tribes to Western lands, and efforts to cede only portions of the Indian domain to land-hungry white frontiersmen. Under Monroe, the confusion of multiple programs continued, but his administration brought a new vigor in all areas, particularly to Indian removal.

Monroe's interest in expansion and concern for national security led to the conclusion of a number of cession treaties, sometimes moving all or a portion of tribes westward. Treaties virtually cleared the old Northwest of American Indians and opened millions of acres of fertile land in the South. At the same time, Monroe urged a continuation of efforts to extend the "advantages of civilization" by encouraging education, religious training, and the individual ownership of land. Beginning in 1819, Congress appropriated $10,000 annually to this program, and by December, 1824, Monroe claimed that American Indians were making "steady" progress.

Despite Monroe's humanitarian intentions, it was increasingly evident that American Indian relations were reaching a crucial juncture. The problem was brought to a head by the state of Georgia, which stridently complained that the federal government had failed to live up to an 1802 agreement to extinguish the Indian title in the state. Both the Creek and Cherokee tribes stood fast against ceding any more land or moving westward, and when Monroe informed Georgia officials of this situation, the state's congressional delegation delivered a protest in March, 1824, demanding the eviction of American Indians and reproaching the government for encouraging them to stay. Monroe considered the protest an "insult," defended his efforts to gain cession treaties, but refused to consider the forcible removal of tribes as "unjust" and "revolting."

Nevertheless, the controversy with Georgia resulted in a new emphasis on removal as a means of saving the tribes and furthering their acculturation to white ways. In the last year of his presidency, Monroe called for the adoption of some "well-digested plan" of removal whereby civilization efforts could proceed "by degrees." He again rejected force, relying instead on such inducements as secure land and financial compensation to secure American Indian approval. Congress, however, failed to implement Monroe's recommendation before his term expired. Monroe's struggle with the Indian problem ended on a sour note when, on the day before he left office, he submitted a treaty with the Georgia Creeks so fraudulently negotiated that President John Quincy Adams was compelled to withdraw it and negotiate another.

Despite the discord evident at the close of Monroe's administration, he, as well as the nation, regained a sense of the nationalistic euphoria that marked its beginning when the marquis de Lafayette returned to the United States in August, 1824, and undertook a nationwide tour that extended through and beyond the remainder of his term. The outpouring of affection for the "Guest of the Nation" recalled the great revolutionary cause of liberty and the "blessings" derived from it. With Monroe's active promotion, Congress granted Lafayette $200,000 and a township of land to alleviate his financial embarrassments.

Monroe's Presidency: Steadiness in a Period of Change

Monroe left office on March 4, 1825, in a period of rapid social change and of political and sectional conflict. Yet throughout his presidency, his personal character and presidential style conveyed a sense of dignity, unity, and national purpose that eased the country's transition into the more dynamic and complex world of the nineteenth century. As Adams later wrote in a fitting tribute, "By his mild and conciliatory policy . . . a large and valuable acquisition of territory was made; the foundations for national prosperity and greatness were laid; and . . . the American Union was advancing, with the vigor and stride of a giant, on its path to true glory and fame."

Monroe retired to his Oak Hill plantation, where he busied himself largely with farming and personal matters. He avoided partisan activity but did not entirely neglect politics. During the late 1820's, he condemned disunionist proceedings in the South and reiterated his support of internal improvements and protective tariffs. He also defended his record from misrepresentation, particularly on the issue of his ordering Jackson's invasion of Florida. Retirement did not erase a lifetime habit of public service, either. He was an active member of the Board of Visitors of the University of Virginia, and until ill health forced him to resign, he served as president of the Virginia constitutional convention of 1829-1830, characteristically working to effect a compromise between conservative planters and Western demands for a greater voice in government.

Monroe left the White House in serious financial distress, having accumulated over his public career a debt of about $75,000. Selling his Albemarle estate provided some relief, but he concentrated his efforts on gaining congressional reimbursement for his past public expenses. A portion of this bill was paid to him in 1826, but not until five years later did Congress, in response to public sympathy, appropriate another substantial sum, enabling Monroe to pay off most of his debt.

In the fall of 1830, after his wife's death, a distressed and enfeebled Monroe moved from Virginia to New York to live with his younger daughter and family. There, on July 4, 1831, he died. Throughout the country, Americans commemorated the passing of a leading figure of their revolutionary past.

Richard B. Latner

Bibliographical References

Those wanting to find out more about the life of James Monroe should consult the authoritative biography by Harry Ammon, *James Monroe: The Quest for National Identity*, 1971. Monroe's style of presidential leadership is explained deftly by Ralph Ketcham, *Presidents Above Party: The First American Presidency, 1789-1829*, 1984; see also James Sterling Young, *The Washington Community: 1800-1828*, 1966. For Monroe's administrative contribution, see Leonard D. White, *The Jeffersonians: A Study in Administrative History, 1801-1829*, 1951. A provocative view of Republican Party doctrine is given in Drew R. McCoy, *The Elusive Republic*, 1980. The period of Monroe's presidency is wonderfully captured in two books by George Dangerfield, *The Era of Good Feelings*, 1952, and *The Awakening of American Nationalism: 1815-1828*, 1965; see also Frederick Jackson Turner, *Rise of the New West*, 1906, 1962. The sectional battle over Missouri is chronicled in Glover Moore, *The Missouri Controversy: 1819-1821*, 1953, whereas the revival of states' rights sentiment in the South is discussed by Norman K. Risjord, *The Old Republicans: Southern Conservatism in the Age of Jefferson*, 1965. Ernest R. May provides the domestic and diplomatic context for the Monroe Doctrine in *The Making of the Monroe Doctrine*, 1975, and Dexter Perkins, *A History of the Monroe Doctrine*, rev. ed., 1963, traces its origins and history. A fascinating account of diplomacy during Monroe's presidency is found in Samuel F. Bemis, *John Quincy Adams and the Foundations of American Foreign Policy*, 1949. Biographies of leading figures are an excellent means of understanding the era. Among the best are Robert V. Remini, *Andrew Jackson and the Course of American Empire: 1767-1821*, 1977, and *Andrew Jackson and the Course of American Freedom: 1822-1832*, 1981, and Charles M. Wiltse, *John C. Calhoun: Nationalist, 1782-1828*, 1944. Two first-rate studies of Indian policy are Francis Paul Prucha, *American Indian Policy in the Formative Years: The Indian Trade and Intercourse Acts, 1790-1834*, 1962, and Bernard W. Sheehan, *Seeds of Extinction: Jeffersonian Philanthropy and the American Indian*, 1973. Finally, one can become immersed in the day-to-day richness of politics and personalities in the appropriate volumes of the readily available *Memoirs of John Quincy Adams, Comprising Portions of His Diary from 1795 to 1848*, 1874-1877, edited by Charles Francis Adams. For a thorough examination of Monroe's presidency, see Noble E. Cunningham, *The Presidency of James Monroe*, 1996, a single-volume study in the University Press of Kansas series on American presidents. Harry Ammon, *James Monroe: A Bibliography*, 1991, provides a detailed listing of primary and secondary resources.

John Quincy Adams

6th President, 1825-1829

Born: July 11, 1767
Braintree, Massachusetts
Died: February 23, 1848
Washington, D.C.

Political Party: National Republican
Vice President: John C. Calhoun

Cabinet Members
Secretary of State: Henry Clay
Secretary of the Treasury: Richard Rush
Secretary of War: James Barbour, Peter B. Porter
Secretary of the Navy: Samuel Southard
Attorney General: William Wirt

No American, it can safely be said, ever entered the presidency better prepared to fill that office than John Quincy Adams. Born in 1767 in Braintree, Massachusetts, he was the son of two fervent revolutionary patriots, John and Abigail Smith Adams, whose ancestors had lived in New England for five generations or more. When John Quincy was seven years old, his father wrote Abigail of their duty to "Mould the Minds and Manners of our children. Let us teach them not only to do virtuously but to excel. To excel they must be taught to be steady, active, and industrious." Already drilled in these traits, John Quincy wrote at this time, in his earliest surviving letter, that he was working hard on his studies (emphasizing ancient history) and that he hoped to "grow a better boy." A year later, in an event he often recalled, he

held his mother's hand as they stood on a hill near their farm and saw the fires of Charleston and heard the cannon of the Battle of Bunker Hill. Experiencing the battles of the Revolutionary War around Boston in 1775-1776, and reading his father's letters from Philadelphia

Adams's official portrait. *(White House Historical Society)*

121

about the tense struggle to declare independence, John Quincy Adams was literally a child of the American Revolution. He absorbed in his earliest memories the sense of destiny his parents shared about the new nation born when he was a precocious nine-year-old.

At age ten, he entered public service, in a way, by accompanying his father on a dangerous winter voyage to France. On the crossing, the ship was struck by lightning (killing four of the crew), survived a hurricane, and fought off British vessels. Returning a few months later, John Quincy perfected his own French by teaching English to the new French minister to the United States and to his aide, François de Barbé-Marbois, who, twenty-five years later as Napoleon's foreign minister, would negotiate the sale of Louisiana to the United States. When his father was appointed a commissioner to negotiate peace with Great Britain, he again took John Quincy to Europe, this time as his private secretary. When their ship sprang a serious leak, John Quincy, with the other passengers, manned the pumps as the unseaworthy vessel barely reached the Spanish coast. A fascinating but grueling journey of two months across Spain and France finally returned them to Paris in February, 1780. After a year at school in Holland, at age fourteen he was appointed secretary to Francis Dana, American commissioner to the Russian court. John Quincy thus took two more long, eye-opening, and hazardous journeys across Europe, in between which he wrote and translated for Dana and pursued his own studies of history, science, and the ancient languages. He spent three more years in Paris and London as his father helped negotiate the peace treaty of 1783 with Great Britain and then served as first American minister to the former mother country.

When, in 1785, at age eighteen, he returned to America to enter Harvard College, John Quincy Adams had already been five years in public employment, knew four or five modern languages, as well as Greek and Latin, and

had shared in the most important diplomacy of the American Revolution. A bright, handsome, and serious youth, he never failed to impress the renowned American, French, Dutch, Russian, and British statesmen whom he met during his seven years abroad. His proud father declared him "a Son who is the greatest Traveller of his age, and without partiality, I think, as promising and manly a youth as in the whole world." Though the office was not yet created, he had also served an ideal apprenticeship for being president of the United States.

After graduation from Harvard and a few years as law student and young barrister, Adams resumed his preoccupation with public affairs by engaging with his father in strenuous newspaper polemics over the French Revolution. President Washington returned him to the public service in 1794 by appointing him minister to Holland. His skill in negotiations there and in London and his brilliant reports to the American government on the wars and revolutions convulsing Europe earned for him Washington's praise as "the most valuable public character we have abroad." Before he returned to the United States in 1801, he served four years as American minister to Prussia, translated a long German poem into English, wrote letters warning of the ambitions of Napoleon Bonaparte (Adams called him "the Corsican ruffian"), and married Louisa Catherine Johnson, the daughter of a Maryland merchant then acting as American consul in London.

In eight years at home, John Quincy served briefly in the Massachusetts Senate and then for five years in the United States Senate, where he was an increasingly unorthodox Federalist. He approved of the Louisiana Purchase (1803), refused to take a pro-British stance as the Napoleonic Wars reached their climax, and increasingly aligned himself with the policies and views of Secretary of State James Madison. Adams's adherence to his own principles in supporting the Embargo Act (1807) at once earned for him the gratitude of the Jeffersonian Republican administration, the bitter hostility of the Federalists (who forced his resignation from the Senate), and—150 years later—a place in John F. Kennedy's *Profiles in Courage*. In 1806, he was made professor of rhetoric and oratory at Harvard (his lectures were soon published in two volumes), and three years later he argued the landmark *Fletcher v. Peck* case before the Supreme Court. These distinctions were enough to earn for him in 1810 an appointment from President Madison to the Supreme Court, which the pressure of other tasks forced him to decline.

The proffered appointment reached him in St. Petersburg, where he was American minister to Russia in the final years of the Napoleonic era. He represented critical American interests there for four years as he and his young family endured the rigors of Russian winter and marveled, half in horror, at the dazzling court of the czar. From 1813 to 1815, he traveled about Northern Europe seeking a negotiated end of the War of 1812, an effort capped by Adams and other American commissioners when they signed the Treaty of Ghent, ending the war respectably if not triumphantly, on Christmas Eve, 1814. Adams concluded his long and brilliant career as a diplomat in Europe (he had lived there for more than twenty years between 1778 and 1817) by serving for two years as American minister to Great Britain, a post his father had held at the end of an earlier war with Britain and in which both Adamses stood staunchly for a dignified equality between mother country and former colony that would assure lasting peace between them.

John Quincy Adams was President James Monroe's widely approved choice to be secretary of state in the new administration. His service there, from 1817 to 1825, has rightfully earned for him standing as the premier secretary of state in American history. He guided negotiations with Great Britain that resolved the remaining disputes between the two coun-

tries and began an era of friendly relations between the two nations. Included in the settlement was a prohibition on armaments along the border with Canada that made it the longest (and longest-lasting) unfortified national boundary in the world. He also arranged for the purchase of Florida from Spain and negotiated a transcontinental treaty with that nation which established the boundary between Spanish and American possessions from the Gulf of Mexico to the Pacific Ocean. He adopted a posture of benevolent neutrality toward the independence movements in Spain's New World possessions and guided the joint British-American resistance to European efforts to thwart independence that resulted in the Monroe Doctrine in 1823. Adams was proud of these signal accomplishments in the State Department, regarding them as fulfilling the goals of the new nation he had seen form in the battles around Boston a half century earlier: equal standing in the family of nations, security within transcontinental boundaries, and sympathy for the national independence and republican aspirations of all the countries of the New World.

The Election of 1824: The Era of Sectionalism

Though Adams devoted his energies mainly to the large tasks of the State Department, he also was heavily engaged in the politics of the misnamed "Era of Good Feelings." The Federalist Party had disappeared and Monroe's elections as president were virtually unanimous, but factions seethed within his National Republican Party (a faction of the Democratic Republican Party). The able members of his cabinet jockeyed for position to succeed Monroe. Secretaries William H. Crawford and John C. Calhoun had respectable aspirations for the presidency, as did House Speaker Henry Clay and the hero of New Orleans, General Andrew Jackson. Adams nevertheless regarded himself as the legitimate heir apparent: The patriotic

The engraving *Lockport, Erie Canal* by W. Tombleson after the painting by W. H. Bartlett. Adams was a champion of federal funding for internal improvements such as canals. *(Library of Congress)*

history of his family, his own long, brilliant public service, and his success in the usual stepping-stone position as secretary of state made him the obvious choice—or at least so he thought. During Monroe's second term, the politics of his succession increasingly dominated conversation and alignments in Washington, D.C. Adams still accepted the ideal of the antiparty presidency held by Monroe and his predecessors, yet he was intensely ambitious and did all he could "backstage" to further his interests. His detailed diary, kept faithfully during these years, is by far the fullest account available of the intense, increasingly bitter politicking.

The jockeying among potential candidates mirrored in many ways the changes and traumas of the years following the War of 1812. Though a burst of national pride and enthu-

siasm followed immediately on the conclusion of the war, during the Monroe administrations rancorous disputes accumulated. New manufacturing interests grew in New England and the mid-Atlantic states. Settlement of the West accelerated. Canals, turnpikes, and, soon, railroads increasingly connected the country and provided myriad sources of conflict. The Missouri Compromise controversy polarized slave and nonslave states. The power of the reenfranchised Second Bank of the United States heightened animosities in the nation's financial system. Perhaps most aggravating of all, a severe depression afflicted the nation as it sought to adjust to the post-Napoleonic era. Farm prices fell sharply as war-fueled demand for grains in Europe subsided; the price of flour, which was $15 per barrel in Baltimore in 1817, had fallen to less than $4 by 1821. Low-priced manufactured goods from Great Britain threatened to overwhelm fledgling American producers. As hardship spread, competition intensified, and bankruptcies threatened, the rancor within the political system grew apace.

As these animosities burgeoned, the old political parties, which might have contained and modulated them, largely ceased to function as effective national organizations. The Federalist Party had disappeared by 1824, and the Republican Party was so incoherent that only 68 of its 261 members in Congress participated in its presidential nominating caucus in February of 1824. The effect was to give free rein to the always-potent sectional divisions within the country, divisions reflected in the regional strengths of the leading presidential aspirants. Jackson and Clay had strength mainly in the West, Crawford and Calhoun principally in the South, and Adams's support was confined largely to New England and some of the mid-Atlantic states. This properly named "Era of Sectionalism" was especially unwelcome to Adams because his own earlier career and strong sense of national purpose led him to denigrate regional biases—although his opponents, and, indeed, much of the country, saw him as very much the Northeastern sectional candidate.

After this failure of the National Republican caucus to nominate a majority candidate, the aspirants set out to gain as much support in the states as possible. Calhoun soon dropped out to assure his election as vice president. It appeared, too, that Clay and Crawford would lag well behind Jackson and Adams in both popular and electoral votes. When the returns were in, Adams was clearly behind Jackson in both tallies: He had 84 electoral votes to Jackson's 99 and only 114,000 popular votes to Jackson's 153,000 (in states where the electors were chosen by popular election). Nevertheless, the 41 electoral votes for Crawford and 37 for Clay threw the decision into the House of Representatives, where each state would

have one vote for any of the three leading candidates. The final contest was between Jackson and Adams, and both maneuvered for support from Clayites and Crawfordites. The Jackson forces, with their clear pluralities in the popular and electoral votes, thought the contest was rightfully theirs. Adams's solid base of six New England states plus enough support elsewhere (much boosted by Clay's efforts to throw his strength to Adams), though, gave him the victory on the first ballot in the House of Representatives, thirteen states to seven for Jackson and four for Crawford.

Thus, despite his splendid preparation for the office and earnestly nationalistic outlook, John Quincy Adams entered the presidency on March 4, 1825, with distinctly minority backing, which was decidedly sectional as well. Furthermore, even before his inauguration, Jackson's backers charged that Adams and Clay had entered a "corrupt bargain" in which Clay supported Adams's election in the House of Representatives in exchange for a promise that he become secretary of state in the new administration. There probably was an agreement of sorts between the two men, but not one that either regarded as corrupt. They were generally aligned in their more nationalistic views, as opposed to the more states' rights stand of the other candidates, and each regarded the other as an able and distinguished public servant. Clay thought Adams infinitely more qualified to be president than Jackson, and Adams believed Clay would be an excellent secretary of state. Nevertheless, the charges of corrupt bargain persisted, and Jackson's supporters began immediately to oppose and thwart Adams in every way they could, looking ahead to the 1828 election. Adams entered the White House, then, with severe and debilitating political liabilities.

A National President, Above Party

Adams announced his energetic, nationalist, nonpartisan outlook and program in his inaugural address and in a remarkable first annual message to Congress. As he assumed office, Adams acknowledged to the American people that he was "less possessed of your confidence in advance than any of my predecessors," but he promised to make up for this with "intentions upright and pure, a heart devoted to the welfare of our country, and the unceasing application of all faculties allotted to me to her service." Then, on a note of self-delusion or wishful thinking, he assured his audience that ten years of good feelings had "assuaged the animosities of political contention and blended into harmony the discordant elements of public opinion." He condemned party rancor and regional biases in appealing to all Americans to unite behind a common program for the public good. He hinted at his approach to promoting it by endorsing federal support for internal improvements and other energetic uses of national power. The address approached pure fantasy as the president doggedly asserted his active, above-party idea of leadership and public purpose in a political landscape where sectional disputes, contentions over states' rights, and party factionalism blossomed on all sides.

Adams returned, in detail and lofty rhetoric, to his theme of broad national purposes in his first annual message in December, 1825. "Were we to slumber in indolence or fold up our arms and proclaim to the world that we are palsied by the will of our constituents," the earnest and Puritan-descended president intoned, "would it not be to cast away the bounties of Providence and doom ourselves to perpetual inferiority? . . . The great object of the institution of civil government," Adams asserted, echoing a theme he had found in Aristotle, Cicero, and other advocates of good government through the ages, "is the improvement of the condition of those who are parties to the social contract. . . . No government . . . can accomplish [its] lawful ends . . . but in proportion as it improves the condition of those

over whom it is established." Within this conception Adams had little use for strict constructionist, states' rights, special interest dicta that denied deliberate, effective pursuit of the common national good.

In particular, the president recommended establishment of a national university and national naval academy to help train the wise and patriotic leadership he thought the country needed. He also advocated an extensive system of internal improvements (mostly canals and turnpikes, but railroads were also clearly in the offing) to be paid for out of increasing revenues from Western land sales and a continuing tariff on imports. He called, too, for the establishment of a uniform system of weights and measures and the improvement of the patent system, both to promote science and to encourage a spirit of enterprise and invention in the land. In a further effort to support science and spread its benefits to the nation and to the world, Adams advocated not only an extensive survey of the nation's own coasts, land, and resources but also American participation in worldwide efforts for "the common improvement of the species." "[Are] we not bound," the president asked, "to contribute our portion of energy and exertion to the common stock?" He urged American initiatives to explore the South Seas (partisan bickering largely thwarted attempts to launch an American expedition) and erection of an astronomical observatory, "light-houses of the skies," so the United States could make at least one such contribution to the advancement of knowledge to supplement the 130 observatories that had already been erected in Europe.

In general, Adams proved himself completely out of step with Congress, and perhaps the nation as well. His proposals were greeted with scorn and derision, regarded as so many efforts to enlarge the national power under his control and to create a national elite that would neglect the common people and destroy the vitality of state and local governments.

Senator Martin Van Buren complained of the "most ultra-latitudinarian doctrines" in Adams's message, and former President Thomas Jefferson condemned some of the proposals as unconstitutional (echoing disputes he had had with John Adams a quarter century or more earlier). With Congress dominated by an unruly collection of his political enemies and the mood of the country preoccupied with the release of its diverse sectional and individual energies, Adams had virtually no legislative success with his programs and found himself increasingly isolated, apparently living in a bygone age.

Adams sought to further his nationalistic, nonpartisan outlook through the design of his cabinet and in other appointments to office. He intended to retain as much as possible Monroe's cabinet, he said, to sustain a sense of continuity and national unity and to avoid implications that he would fill offices with his own friends and supporters. Samuel Southard agreed to remain as secretary of the navy, John McLean as postmaster general (not yet a full cabinet office), and William Wirt as attorney general. When the ailing William H. Crawford declined to stay as secretary of the treasury, Adams appointed an able and politically sympathetic Pennsylvanian, Richard Rush, to the office. This opened up the post of minister to Great Britain for a New Yorker, first offered to DeWitt Clinton, who declined, and then accepted by the aged Federalist Rufus King. Adams intended the War Department, vacated by Calhoun's election as vice president, for Andrew Jackson, but the general's contempt for the Adams administration precluded a formal nomination. Adams then gave the office to James Barbour, a Virginian and supporter of Crawford. The appointment of Clay to the State Department completed an able cabinet with a reasonable balance of men from the various sections of the country, which was, however, with the exception of Rush, filled with people friendly to other presidential aspirants.

Nevertheless, owing to Adams's obvious intention to act in the national interest and his effectiveness as an administrator, and also to Clay's great personal affability, the cabinet functioned with harmony and good humor for most of its four-year existence.

Adams professed indifference to this political disarray because he was determined to exclude partisanship from the presidency. He was well aware, though, as his diary attests, that he was to face debilitating political quarrels in the years to come. In other appointments he renominated, as his predecessors had, "all against whom there was no complaint." He refused, he said, to make "government a perpetual and intermitting scramble for office." Throughout his term of office, he removed only twelve incumbents from federal jobs, and those for gross incompetence. While his enemies intrigued around him and used appointments for blatantly political purposes, Adams adhered strictly to his above-party ideology. He presented a paradoxical picture of a president intent on ignoring, even to the point of apparent naïveté, party politics, while surrounded by some of the most avid, factious political warfare in American history. Thus unenviably positioned, he turned his attention to the day-to-day problems of his presidency. Bald, of average height, erect in bearing, somewhat stern visaged, with a rather long, sharp nose and tending toward the stoutness that characterized his family, Adams gave the impression of a man determined to do his duty as he saw it.

Foreign Affairs: Trade Agreements and the Collapse of Spain's New World Empire

Adams sought in his conduct of foreign relations (which he expected to be the dominant concern of his administration) to further the Jeffersonian goals of competitive world trade and access to foreign markets under terms favorable to American trading interests. This meant reciprocal trade agreements, giving the

United States most-favored-nation status in peacetime and protection of neutral's rights on the high seas in time of war, all objectives of critical concern to the nation since its founding and which had been the substance of Adams's long diplomatic career. With Secretary of State Clay, he negotiated general commercial treaties that improved American relations with Britain, France, the Netherlands, Sweden, Austria, Portugal, Turkey, and Mexico. Though Adams and Clay accepted less-than-ideal terms in some of these treaties, in each case American interests were furthered and a precedent set for amicable trade relations likely in the future to be beneficial to each nation. Meanwhile, trade with the growing number of newly independent nations of Latin America, released at last from the constrictions of Spanish regulation, remained unsettled and often chaotic.

More troublesome were the administration's efforts to remove the longstanding burdens imposed on American trade with European colonies in the Western Hemisphere, especially with British possessions in the West Indies. Continued efforts by Britain to monopolize trade with its North American possessions and, it seemed as well, to sustain a century-long preference for its West Indian merchants and planters at the expense of mainland producers of food and lumber resulted in irritating and sometimes insulting strictures on United States trade. Patient efforts by Adams and Clay to protect American interests and at the same time open up profitable trade, however, became entangled in domestic politics. Pro-Jacksonians, based in the South and West, alleged that the rigidity of the New England-biased administration in defending American merchants led to neglect of the needs of staple exporters. Britain sought to take advantage of the dissension by framing its regulations to favor first one side and then the other, and then ridiculing American negotiators caught in the political cross fire. As a result, there was no satisfactory

The signing of the Independence of Venezuela, one of several colonies to gain freedom from Spain during the Adams administration. *(Library of Congress)*

agreement, and the Adams administration was blamed for inaction. The problem found its long-range solution in the diminishing importance of United States trade with the British West Indies.

Looming beyond the diplomacy of commerce were the ideological and geopolitical implications of the near demise of Spain's New World empire. Using rhetoric echoing Thomas Paine and Jefferson, John Quincy Adams welcomed the end of Spanish tyranny in Latin America and hoped the newly independent nations would become both kindred republics and partners in the economic growth of the New World. "The natural rights of mankind, and the sovereignty of the people were . . . fundamental maxims which we from our cradle first proclaimed," Adams averred, should become the foundation of all the nations of the Americas, as "the will of kings" was expelled from the hemisphere. He shared as well, though, his father's reservations about whether the former Spanish colonies, untutored in any of the habits of self-government, would be able to establish stable republican institutions. Disputes among factions in the former colonies, incessant efforts by European powers to interfere for their advantage, and the difficulty of exercising any United States influence without also seeming to interfere or dominate complicated the fluid and volatile situation. The prospect that Spain might retain control of Cuba and Puerto Rico, the possessions of most strategic interest to the United States, added further complications. American efforts to encourage republican independence in Mexico, Central America, Colombia, and La Plata (Argentina) were inconclusive and left the Adams administration with more problems than resolutions. Yet, circumstances seemed to call for United States leadership.

The issue came to a head when, shortly after Adams became president, the United States received an invitation from Colombia and Mexico to attend an "assembly of Pleni-potentiaries" of the newly independent Latin American states to be held in Panama. Britain and the Netherlands, who along with the United States had opposed the reactionary designs of the Holy Alliance to reestablish Spanish power in its former colonies, were also invited. Adams, with Clay's enthusiastic support, favored American attendance, though both were aware of many difficulties. Would the United States be drawn into the wars still going on between Spain and its former colonies or drawn into wars with European powers? Would American commercial interests be better protected by bilateral negotiations with the new nations than by an international congress with an unpredictable agenda? Most complicated of all, what about Cuba and Puerto Rico? The United States preferred continued (weak) Spanish control to British or French domination of the islands, to conquest of them by Colombia or Mexico, and most of all to a slave revolt that would plunge Cuba and Puerto Rico into the Haitian nightmare of bloodshed and black domination. Yet, strong sentiment existed in the United States for both independence (under white settler control) and annexation of the strategic islands.

All these possibilities were aired in Congress and the press when Adams appointed American commissioners to the Panama congress and requested funds for their mission. Political opponents denied the president's authority to respond to the invitation without consulting Congress, pictured the whole enterprise as another federal-presidential power grab, and insisted that it betrayed the already hallowed injunctions of Washington and Jefferson against "entangling alliances." Southerners feared the Panama congress would act against slavery and encourage black revolt and tumult in the Caribbean. As a result the approval of the American commissioners was so delayed that they missed the congress (one of them died en route of tropical fever), and all the world could see that political discord within the United States would prevent the country from taking any leadership role. The congress, in any case, failed to reconvene for its second session, so the whole idea of a Pan-American union died. Adams had a certain sympathy for the idea and wanted the United States to encourage republican self-government in Latin America, but his political weakness and the continuing volatility there prevented significant results. Altogether, Adams and Clay were unable to respond constructively to the opportunity opened by the demise of Spanish power in Latin America.

Domestic Policies: The "American System" and the "Tariff of Abominations"

Even more than in foreign affairs, political liabilities and ineptitude vitiated the domestic policies of the Adams administration. Both the president and his secretary of state sought to translate their belief in active guidance of national development by the federal government into what Clay called the "American System." Essentially, it entailed protective tariffs to encourage American industry, land and Indian policies designed to hasten settlement of the West and provide revenue for internal improvements, the enlargement of markets for Western grains and Southern cotton, federal support of internal improvements to bind the nation together for the benefit of all, and the strengthening of the national bank as a device for guiding the economy of the country. Adams liked especially the grand design of the American System: its encouragement of growth in all sections of the country, its planned use of the resources of the nation, and the important role it gave to the federal government in organizing and fostering the common welfare. To him, such a design fulfilled, in a deliberate and coherent way, the purposes of the American Revolution and what he often saw as "the hand of Providence" in American history and his own ideas of the active,

above-party role of the nation's leader.

During Adams's administration, he, Clay, and Secretary of the Treasury Richard Rush spoke eloquently about the American System and managed to push many measures for federal subsidy of canals, harbors, and roads through Congress. Support for them, though, arose more from local enthusiasm for particular projects than from any sense of national purpose. The administration also broadened the effectiveness of the National Bank, but again criticism of administration policies by various sectional interests foreshadowed crippling controversies to come. Adams continued policies of removal of Eastern Indians to new reservations in the West (more humanely than would be characteristic of later Jacksonian administrations) and of a carefully controlled, revenue-producing sale of frontier lands. In both areas, however, Southerners and Westerners saw prejudice against their interests in favor of those of the Northeast and the middle states extending westward from Pennsylvania to Ohio and Kentucky.

Most troublesome of all was the question of protective tariffs. Adams repudiated the argument "that the Congress of the Union are impotent to restore the balance in favor of native industry destroyed by the statutes of another realm" and saw the advantages of fostering domestic manufactures, but he misjudged the degree of Western and Southern hostility. Jacksonians in Congress, moreover, saw an opportunity to manipulate the tariff issue in a way most damaging to the administration. In 1828, they maneuvered through Congress a tariff bill that gathered together various objectionable and contradictory features advocated by special interests—and then blamed the legislation on the administration, which had backed a revision of the tariff. The "Tariff of Abominations," as the act was called, became a rallying point of opposition to the administration and played a significant part in the campaign of 1828.

The Growing Strength of the Party System

The Adams presidency in its last years became increasingly engulfed in administrative tangles, quarrels within and between the armed forces, and, worst of all, the swirling political forces gathering around the popular but combative figure of Andrew Jackson that were determined to push Adams and all he stood for out of office. As the tariff legislation illustrated, proposals and alliances in Congress were calculated according to their likely effect on the next presidential election. Appointments to office were blocked or shifted in Congress according to their political colorations. Everywhere the burgeoning energies of the nation created new and often centrifugal forces and political alignments that thwarted or bypassed Adams's earnest, systematic efforts at orderly national development.

Adams was caught, as he perceived but could do nothing about, in one of the key transformations in American political history. He still sought, as the first five American presidents had done, to be a leader in the style of "civic republicanism" that harked back to the standards of good government, nonpartisan citizenship, and active pursuit of the public welfare he had learned from his study of Aristotle, Cicero, Plutarch, and other classical writers. Thus he regarded political parties as inherently corrupt because they were parts, or factions, of the whole. A president who celebrated, led, or even condoned parties was, *ipso facto*, not what a good national leader should be. Adams sought to sustain the apparent demise of the rival parties during Monroe's presidency and instead to include all political energy within a national republicanism that sought an inclusive public good.

Sectional and economic interests became more diverse, vociferous, and effective as access to politics broadened under the democratizing reforms (particularly within the states) of the 1820's, transforming the public life of the country into the vigorous, bewildering arena of "factions" that Madison had predicted, in *Federalist No. 10*, would be the fruit of freedom. Adams understood and accepted this in a way and did not oppose the enlargement of political participation, but he was deeply disturbed by the decline of active pursuit of the common good.

Jacksonian partisans, particularly Martin Van Buren, articulated and brought into existence a new, positive idea of political party. They saw political parties as manifestations of the needs and interests of the people of a free society. The job of the party and its leaders was to accept, enlarge, and fulfill the aspirations of the multitude of factions in the country and mold them into a political instrument (that is, party) that could gain national power. Instead of this goal being corrupt or partisan as Adams and his predecessors thought, to Van Buren it represented the triumph of democracy. The party would stand for certain principles and coordinate diverse interests, defining the public good in the only way suited to a free and pluralistic nation. The continuing competition between the parties would be "the life blood of democracy," providing policy alternatives to the citizens and a ceaseless criticism and honing of public needs.

Within this framework the president had the responsibility of leading and sustaining his political party as a necessary part of the machinery of a democratic society. It would be proper for a president to welcome the support of various interest groups, to campaign for office, to build party organization, to encourage party discipline in Congress, and even to use appointments to office to strengthen the party, all on the grounds that strong political parties were good for democracies. Van Buren declared that party disputes would "rouse the sluggish to exertion, give increased energy to the most active intellect, excite a salutary vigilance over public functionaries, and prevent that apathy which has proved the ruin of Republics."

131

Englishman Robert Cruikshank shows his disapproval of American democracy in his depiction of a House of Representatives debate over the "gag rule" against discussing slavery. Adams fought the gag rule during his presidency and afterward, as a member of the House. *(Library of Congress)*

The Election of 1828: Triumph of the Jacksonians

Under this new ideology of party, Van Buren and others organized the Jacksonian party, beginning before Adams's inauguration in 1825. Resting on solid Western and Southern opposition to Adams's alleged Northeastern bias, responsive to a wide diversity of interests, and gathering the forces of Calhoun, Crawford, Van Buren, and all the other anti-Adams politicians, the Democratic Party came into being around the objective of electing Andrew Jackson president in 1828. At the same time, it rejected not only John Quincy Adams but also all the older conceptions of good government and national purpose for which he stood. Calhoun and other pro-Jacksonians held "opposition" meetings even before Adams entered the White House.

The Tennessee legislature nominated Jackson for the presidency in October, 1825, and Van Buren traveled about the country putting the party machinery together. Proadministration forces were active as well, especially Clay and his supporters, in seeking local support and fostering newspaper advocacy of Adams's programs. The president himself, however, held stiffly aloof from what he regarded as "politicking," which was beneath the dignity of his office, though he earnestly wanted to be reelected and did what he thought permissible behind the scenes to further his cause.

By mid-1828, the campaign became increasingly rancorous, and it was clear that the tide was running strongly for the Jacksonians. The pro-Adams press—operating without Adams's support, encouragement, or often even his approval—played up scandalous charges about Jackson's marriage, whereas the pro-Jackson press dredged up stories about Adams's alleged aristocratic airs and misuse of public funds on his missions abroad. One newspaper even charged that Adams had acted as "a pimp" in arranging for one of his servants, while he was in Russia, to be the czar's mistress. New England and some of the mid-Atlantic states remained faithful to Adams, but the Jacksonians successfully enlisted the burgeoning sectional and democratic energies of the country and benefited from the skillful party-building efforts of Van Buren and others. When the returns were in, Jackson had gained a 178 to 83 victory in the electoral college and had a 647,276 to 508,064 margin in the popular vote. The heroic general swept every state in the South and West (both he and his running mate, John C. Calhoun, were slave-owning planters) and even managed to win Pennsylvania and more than half the electoral votes of New York. The gloom and illness in the Adams administration as it prepared to leave office during the winter of 1828-1829 and the joyous, tumultuous celebrations of the Jacksonians as they inaugurated their leader in the White House on March 4, 1829, measured the decisive change that had taken place in the nation's political life.

Adams and the Presidency: An Uncompromising Vision of Good Government

To Adams his defeat marked nothing less than the end of the noble aspirations of his first annual message that an active, above-party president and government might lead the nation in deliberate, coordinated pursuit of the public good. Five days after Jackson's inauguration, Adams wrote bitterly that the new administration would "be the day of small things. There will be neither lofty meditations, nor comprehensive foresight, nor magnanimous purpose." Henceforth, Adams complained a few years later, national development would depend on "the limping gait of State legislatures and private adventure, and the American Union is to live from hand to mouth, and to cast away, instead of using for the improvement of its own condition, the bounties of Providence." Grand purposes and rational ideals, such as the planned development of national resources or the gradual abolition of slavery (a cause Adams fostered courageously during a unique and remarkable eighteen-year, post-presidential career in the House of Representatives), were to give way to what he regarded as the often shortsighted, selfish interests and designs of the increasingly diverse peoples and sections of the nation.

The John Quincy Adams presidency, then, somewhat like that of his father, ended in frustration and a sense of having lost a vital battle to new and, to the Adamses, unwelcome political forces. Though sometimes regarded as antidemocratic (so the Jeffersonians in 1800 and the Jacksonians in 1828 charged), the Adamses are more properly seen as upholding a different model, or style, of republican leadership. John Quincy Adams accepted earnestly the idea of government by consent. He hoped as well that inspired national leadership in the public interest, eschewing the divisive forces of faction and party, might enlist support among the people. This would sustain what Adams regarded as the vital principle of good (wise, virtuous) government even in a democratic era. He despised his Jacksonian opponents, not because they were democrats, but because they assumed that partisanship and the clash of sectional and economic interests would by themselves result in the common good. Yet, this new ideology of liberal, private enterprise, suited to the energies that would develop the frontier and absorb millions of immigrants, seemed the wave of the future, and it did in fact characterize American growth and public life in the century to come. In the years before his fatal stroke on the floor of the House of Representatives on February 23, 1848, Adams refused to approve the "new politics" of the nation. He continued to believe that his own presidency had been a worthy, though perhaps futile, effort in sustaining a more purposeful and virtuous public life in the nation he had seen born in the revolutionary battles and diplomacy of his youth.

Ralph Ketcham

Bibliographical References

The basic source for the life and presidency of John Quincy Adams is the *Memoirs of John Quincy Adams . . . 1795 to 1848*, edited by C. F. Adams, 12 vols., 1874-1877. New editions of *The Papers of Henry Clay*, 8 vols. 1959, and *The Papers of John C. Calhoun*, 15 vols., 1959, also furnish abundant source material. Three biographies are essential. Samuel F. Bemis, *John Quincy Adams and the Foundations of American Foreign Policy*, 1949, and *John Quincy Adams and the Union*, 1956, are excellent on Adams's pre- and postpresidential careers. For a biography that draws on Adams's extensive diaries and explores his complex nature, see Paul C. Nagel, *John Quincy Adams: A Public Life, a Private Life*, 1997. Lynn H. Parsons, *John Quincy Adams*, 1998, is a concise biography that chronicles Adams's life from boyhood in 1778, when he accompanied his father to France on a diplomatic mission, to his last years. Marie B. Hecht, *John Quincy Adams: A Personal History of an Independent Man*, 1972, gives a full account of his family life and is also very good on his career in the House of Representatives, from 1831 to 1848. Leonard L. Richards, *The Life and Times of Congressman John Quincy Adams*, 1986, also details his career as a representative. Mary Hargreaves, *The Presidency of John Quincy Adams*, 1985, is a detailed, scholarly account of his presidency, especially thorough in its recording of the economic and political context of Adams's presidency. Ralph Ketcham, *Presidents Above Party: The First American Presidency, 1789-1829*, 1984, explains the place of Adams's administration in the history of the American presidency, and Daniel W. Howe, *The Political Culture of the American Whigs*, 1979, surveys the ideas and practices of the party closest to Adams. Lynn H. Parsons, *John Quincy Adams: A Bibliography*, 1993, is a comprehensive listing of resources by and about Adams and his personal and public life.

Andrew Jackson

7th President, 1829-1837

Born: March 15, 1767
   Waxhaw area, South Carolina
Died: June 8, 1845
   the Hermitage, near Nashville,
   Tennessee

Political Party: Democratic
Vice Presidents: John C. Calhoun, Martin
  Van Buren

Cabinet Members

Secretary of State: Martin Van Buren, Edward Livingston, Louis McLane, John Forsyth

Secretary of the Treasury: Samuel Ingham, Louis McLane, William John Duane, Roger B. Taney, Levi Woodbury

Secretary of War: John Henry Eaton, Lewis Cass, Benjamin Butler

Secretary of the Navy: John Branch, Levi Woodbury, Mahlon Dickerson

Attorney General: John M. Berrien, Roger Taney, Benjamin Butler

Postmaster General: William Barry, Amos Kendall

Andrew Jackson is one of the great mythic characters of American history. Acclaimed a hero for his military prowess, he became the dominant political figure of the half century between Thomas Jefferson and Abraham Lincoln. He was the first president elected from west of the Appalachians and the first to rise from humble origins to the White House. He became a symbol of the new opportunities open to the common people in nineteenth century society and of the triumph of the democratic principle in American politics. While serving as president, he fashioned his personal following into the Democratic Party, the longest sur-

viving of all American political organizations. Jackson lent his name first to a movement, then to a party, and finally to an era in American history.

Jackson's official portrait. *(White House Historical Society)*

Jackson—"The Brave Boy of the Waxhaws," by Currier & Ives. *(Library of Congress)*

A Leader Formed on the Frontier

Jackson was born on March 15, 1767, in the Waxhaw settlement, a community of Scotch-Irish immigrants located along the North Carolina-South Carolina border. His father died just before Andrew's birth, and his mother and her three small boys moved in with her nearby relatives, the Crawfords. Growing up in the Crawford household, Andrew received a satisfactory elementary education and perhaps a smattering of higher learning. According to later remembrances, he was a tall, lanky, and high-spirited youth.

The Revolutionary War shattered Jackson's placid childhood and wiped out his remaining family. Fighting in the Carolina backcountry was particularly savage, a nightmare conflict of ambushes, massacres, and sudden skirmishes. The Jacksons devoted themselves wholeheartedly to the American Revolution.

Andrew's oldest brother, Hugh, enlisted in a patriot regiment and died, apparently of heatstroke, on the battlefield. Too young for formal soldiering, Andrew and his brother Robert fought with American irregulars. In 1781, they were captured and contracted smallpox, of which Robert died soon after their release. Shortly afterward, Jackson's mother also succumbed to disease contracted while trying to retrieve two nephews from a British prison ship.

Alone in the world at the war's end, a combat veteran at the age of fifteen, Jackson drifted for a time, taught school, then read law in North Carolina. Completing his studies in 1787, he soon accepted a friend's offer to serve as public prosecutor in the newly organized Mero District west of the mountains. The seat of the district was Nashville on the Cumberland River. Founded in 1780, it had a population of only five hundred but excellent prospects for growth, and it offered fine opportunities for an aspiring young lawyer of small education but already much experience of the world. In Nashville, Jackson rose rapidly. He was ambitious, energetic, shrewd, and an agreeable companion. He did not know much law, but neither did anybody else, and a frontier town that was awash in bad debts and disputed land titles provided plenty of business. Jackson built a large private practice to supplement his public duties, entered into trading ventures, and began to acquire slaves. He also ingratiated himself with the leaders of Nashville society and with Tennessee's leading politician, William Blount, who became governor when the district was set off as a federal territory in 1790.

Jackson solidified his rising status in Nashville by marrying Rachel Donelson Robards, daughter of the late John Donelson, one of the city's founders. The circumstances of the marriage caused much controversy during Jackson's presidential campaign many years later, for at the time of their union, Rachel's estranged first husband, Lewis Robards, had initiated but not yet completed his divorce proceedings against her. Frontier Nashville, however, saw nothing wrong in the marriage. To ensure its legality, Andrew and Rachel performed the ceremony again after Robards finalized his divorce.

Despite its haste, Andrew's marriage to Rachel was perhaps the happiest event of his life, for the union proved an enduring success. It brought Jackson into an extensive and influential Tennessee clan and provided countless in-laws to replace his own lost family. The couple's youthful ardor matured into a devotion that deepened as they grew older. Lengthy periods of separation, the loss of Rachel's girlish beauty, and her increasingly religious, sometimes hysterical temperament could not shake Jackson's affection for her. Not surprisingly, in view of his violently attenuated childhood,

Jackson was a man of fierce and, at times, uncontrollable emotions. He carried a reputation as a hellion from some youthful escapades, and explosive quarrels surrounded him well into middle age, but his passions and inexhaustible energies never swayed him from his attachment to Rachel. Their mutual affection and utterly conventional domestic life furnished a needed emotional anchor throughout his turbulent military and political career.

Only one misfortune marred their marriage. Though Jackson loved children and desperately desired some of his own, the couple remained childless. Rachel's brothers and sisters obligingly provided a corps of nieces and nephews for the Jacksons to stand godparent to, and one, Andrew Jackson, Jr., son of Rachel's brother Severn, for them to adopt.

Jackson's adherence to Governor William Blount brought him rapid political preferment in the 1790's. Chosen a delegate in 1795 to Tennessee's state constitutional convention, he was then elected the state's first congressman and shortly promoted to senator. After a year, he resigned to take a job closer to home, as judge of Tennessee's superior court. Meanwhile, he was undertaking large-scale land speculations in partnership with John Overton. Still a very young man, Jackson seemed destined for greatness, but the next few years brought a series of setbacks that halted his meteoric rise and threatened to close out his political career.

The Blount faction fell from power at the turn of the century, and Jackson fell with it. Over his head in land speculations, Blount entered into a conspiracy to seize Spanish Florida and Louisiana for the British. The conspiracy came to light; Blount was expelled from the United States Senate in 1797 and died in 1800. Governor John Sevier, commanding a rival faction, replaced him as Tennessee's most powerful politician. Jackson and Sevier quarreled first in 1797, when Jackson was in Congress. The dispute was patched over, but it reopened in 1802, when Jackson challenged Sevier for election as major general in command of the Tennessee militia. Jackson won the post, but the aftermath brought the two men to a showdown in the streets of Knoxville, followed by preparations for a formal duel. No one was hurt, but his estrangement from the now-dominant Sevier faction shut Jackson off from further political advance in Tennessee. His subsequent angling for a federal appointment in Louisiana also came to nothing.

The Sevier feud inaugurated a series of quarrels, over matters both vital and trivial, between Jackson and a variety of Tennessee foes. The most notorious of these, in 1806, began with a minor misunderstanding over a horse race and ended with a duel in which Jackson shot young Charles Dickinson dead after taking Dickinson's own bullet in his chest. A coterie of close friends—most notably John Coffee, John Overton, and the Donelson clan—stood by Jackson (and sometimes fought in his behalf) through these troublous affairs, but they made

for him many other enemies and earned for him a reputation as a bellicose and perhaps unstable man.

Financial reverses accompanied the collapse of Jackson's political prospects. In the course of his freewheeling speculations, Jackson had carelessly endorsed the notes of one David Allison of Philadelphia. The notes came due, Allison defaulted, and Jackson found himself hard pressed by creditors. He met his obligations, but only by unloading some of his holdings and exchanging his Hunter's Hill plantation for a less-developed property named the Hermitage. In subsequent years, Jackson recouped his losses by raising cotton at the Hermitage and breeding and racing horses. He also continued his ventures in trading and storekeeping, though without much success. The Allison episode, however, taught him prudence. Henceforth, he trusted no one in money matters and avoided debt at all hazards—lessons that he later labored in vain to impart to his spendthrift adopted son, Andrew, Jr.

The Hermitage, Jackson's home. *(Library of Congress)*

In 1804, Jackson relinquished his judgeship, and for the rest of the decade he focused his ambition on military rather than political objects. Still holding his militia command, he yearned for the war that would bring honor, glory, and a vent for his relentless energy. He also had old scores to settle—with the British who had destroyed his family, with American Indians who had once terrorized Tennessee and still hovered over its Western and Southern borders, and with their aiders and abettors, the Spanish in Florida and Mexico. Jackson's thirst for action led him to befriend Aaron Burr when the latter came through Nashville in 1805, seeking recruits for his shadowy schemes of Southwestern conquest. Jackson cut loose from Burr in time to avoid implication in his alleged treason, but he was still eager for war against the Spanish. In the following years, Jackson busied himself with militia reorganization plans, and he volunteered himself and his troops for service at every hint of Indian trouble. He also watched with mounting indignation the government's inept efforts to win redress from Great Britain for violations of American neutral shipping privileges.

The War of 1812: The Making of a National Hero

In June of 1812, the United States at last declared war on Great Britain. Jackson immediately tendered his services, but the government had no use for him. In November, however, orders arrived for a Tennessee force to proceed to New Orleans, and Governor Willie Blount (William's half brother) designated Jackson to command. Jackson gathered two thousand volunteers and led them as far as Natchez, where he received a curt War Department order dismissing him and his troops. Fuming and raging at the government's imbecility, Jackson marched his command back to Nashville, where it dispersed. Throughout the summer of 1813, he awaited orders. In the interlude, he fell into another quarrel about nothing, this time with the Ben-ton brothers, Jesse and Thomas Hart, the latter of whom had recently completed services as a colonel under Jackson's command. The affair terminated in a street brawl; Jackson took a bullet that nearly cost him his left arm.

In September, 1813, American Indian hostilities finally brought an end to Jackson's inactivity. Summoned to punish the Creeks for frontier massacres, he regathered his volunteer force and invaded the Creek homeland in northern Alabama. In a series of engagements culminating at Horseshoe Bend in March, 1814, Jackson annihilated the main hostile Creek force. In subsequent treaty negotiations, he exacted a huge cession of land—more than twenty million acres—from the vanquished tribe. The Creeks would never again be a formidable power.

Jackson's success in the Creek War made him a minor national hero; his defense of New Orleans was to make him an icon. In May, 1814, he was commissioned United States major general and given command of the Southern frontier. The British were planning an attack on New Orleans, strategic gateway to the American interior. Jackson beat off a preliminary assault at Mobile Bay, then raided eastward to destroy the British base at Pensacola before returning to New Orleans. In December, a British seaborne invasion force made landfall and reached the Mississippi ten miles below the city. Jackson blocked their advance upriver. For two weeks, the British probed his position astride the Mississippi. Failing to find an exploitable weakness, on January 8, 1815, British general Sir Edward Pakenham ordered a direct frontal assault on Jackson's lines. The attack was a complete failure. Pakenham's men advanced over exposed and difficult terrain toward Jackson's fortified position and were mowed down by American artillery and rifle fire. The British suffered more than two thousand casualties, including Pakenham, dead on the field; Jackson's losses were thirteen killed, fifty-eight wounded and missing.

The Battle of New Orleans *(Library of Congress)*

Almost simultaneously with the word of Jackson's incredible victory came news that British and American commissioners in Europe had signed a peace treaty two weeks earlier. Though unconnected, the two events fused in the public mind to make Jackson appear as the agent of deliverance from a mismanaged and nearly disastrous war. After a series of defeats and disappointments that sorely tried their patriotism and their patience with the government, Americans hailed Jackson and his frontier soldiers with unrestrained adoration. For a generation of patriots, Jackson became the symbol not only of American military prowess but also of the superior republican virtue that produced it.

Jackson had begun the War of 1812 as major general of Tennessee militia, amateur commander of an amateur force. He ended it as a regular major general, second highest rank-

ing officer in the United States Army. After failures at trading, storekeeping, and land speculation, and a promising but stunted political career, he had at last found an occupation that matched his talents. Though no master strategist, Jackson for that time and place was a very good general. He lacked formal military training, but he knew the prerequisites for successful frontier warfare. His judgments were always decisive and his movements energetic. Most important, he understood the role of supply in waging wilderness campaigns and the necessity for discipline in leading half-trained, often-insubordinate soldiers. He commanded the full confidence of his troops and the absolute loyalty of his subordinate officers.

Jackson stayed in the army when the war ended. Its main peacetime job was to protect the frontier against American Indians, a task that suited his tastes exactly. He had long believed that white settlers and "savage" Indian nations could not coexist in peace; and as the former represented a higher civilization, American Indians must abandon their nomadic habits and settle down as individuals in white society or remove westward beyond the advancing frontier. Jackson's dual position as army commander and treaty commissioner gave ample opportunity to implement those views, and in the years after the war, he extracted major cessions of land from the Chickasaw, Choctaw, and Cherokee.

In December, 1817, Jackson received orders to subdue the Seminoles, who were raiding across the border from Spanish Florida. Liberally interpreting his vague instructions, Jackson effected a lightning conquest of Florida itself, in the process capturing, trying, and summarily executing two British nationals whom he accused of encouraging the Seminoles. Jackson's invasion brought foreign protests and domestic calls for his court-martial or congressional censure, but he successfully rode out the storm. Spain soon ceded Florida to the United States, thereby accomplishing his ulterior object. Jackson defended himself by claiming that he had merely carried out the real but unstated desires of President James Monroe and Secretary of War John C. Calhoun. This was a defense of much merit but in later years, as the controversy continued to smolder, Jackson weakened it by fashioning (with the help of compliant friends) a chain of evidence to show that Monroe had expressly authorized the campaign. Monroe denied it on his deathbed; whether Jackson believed his own concoction is difficult to say.

On the conclusion of the Florida cession treaty in 1821, Monroe offered the governorship of the new territory to Jackson. He accepted, but after presiding in stormy and controversial fashion over the installation of American authority there, he resigned and came home to Tennessee. There, his friends

were beginning to promote him as a candidate for the presidency in 1824.

Presidential Aspirations

James Monroe, heir to Thomas Jefferson and James Madison in the Virginia presidential dynasty, was now in his second term, and he had no obvious successor. Three seasoned statesmen vied for the post: Secretary of State John Quincy Adams of Massachusetts, Treasury Secretary William Harris Crawford of Georgia, and Henry Clay of Kentucky, speaker of the House of Representatives. Jackson's own candidacy was first floated to serve the local purposes of his friends in Tennessee, but it quickly caught on elsewhere. In the absence of party opposition from the moribund Federalists, the machinery for fixing on a single Republican candidate had broken down, leaving a vacuum to be filled at the polls by personal popularity. The returns made it plain that Jackson's military heroics had a far greater hold on the public imagination than the civil attainments of Adams, Crawford, or Clay. Jackson was the only candidate whose strength transcended a regional base. He gathered a plurality of popular votes, carrying eleven states out of twenty-four, including Pennsylvania, New Jersey, and the Carolinas, along with the entire Southwest. No one received a majority of electoral votes, however, so the contest among Jackson, Adams, and Crawford was thrown into the House of Representatives. There, speaker Clay announced his support for Adams, and his influence, together with a general suspicion of Jackson's unfitness for the presidency by both temperament and training, enabled Adams to win the requisite majority of states on the first ballot. He promptly appointed Clay secretary of state. Jackson cried that a "corrupt bargain" had swindled him out of the presidency and began planning for a rematch in 1828.

The four years of John Quincy Adams's presidency really constituted one long, increasingly acrimonious, and, in the end, one-sided presidential campaign. To Jackson's own tremendous popularity was added widespread outrage against the method of Adams's ascension to power. While Adams floundered in Washington, D.C., alienating key constituencies with indiscreet policy statements, Jackson drew around him a deft group of organizers and publicists to manage his campaign. They avoided discussion of issues and credentials and focused their propaganda on Jackson's mystique: his rise from humble origins, his heroism in war, his indomitable patriotism. As Jackson's candidacy gathered strength, powerful regional leaders swung to his side: Vice President John C. Calhoun of South Carolina, deserting the administration to accept the same post on Jackson's ticket; Martin Van Buren of New York, marshal of the former Crawford men; and Thomas Hart Benton, Jackson's former antagonist, now a senator from Missouri. In the end, the combination of a superior candidate and superior management produced a rout. In the 1828 election, Jackson carried the entire West and South, plus New York and Pennsylvania.

Hard on the news of this victory came personal sorrow. In its latter stages, the presidential campaign had turned ugly, as editors and pamphleteers mercilessly exposed the private lives of the candidates. Adams's publicists scrutinized the peculiar circumstances of Jackson's marriage, labeling him a wife stealer and Rachel a bigamist. As if in response to this torrent of abuse, Rachel withered and sickened. On December 22, she died at the Hermitage. For days, Jackson was inconsolable.

An Outsider in the White House

Jackson's victory in 1828 represented a radical break from tradition in the young republic. He was a genuine outsider in Washington, D.C., the first such to be elected president, and this fact was to color his perceptions and actions throughout his presidency. His election in-

spired trepidation among veteran politicians and bureaucrats, for he was, as Henry Clay warned, a "military chieftain" rather than an accomplished statesman. Jackson's predecessors in office had undergone extensive apprenticeships in national politics and diplomacy. Jackson had less formal education than any of them; he had acquired a little experience in Congress and almost none in public administration. Further, he had on occasion in his military career displayed an apparent contempt for civil authority. Though prominent men had attached themselves to his candidacy, his real political strength came from the mass of voters, who seemed not to care about his lack of traditional qualifications. Some established politicians admired Jackson; many feared him; few knew him well. They could only guess at what he might do in office.

Many doubted whether he could even survive his term. He was sixty-two, the oldest president to take office up to that time. Despite age and infirmity, Jackson's appearance was still striking: He carried his lean body erect, and his firm countenance and direct gaze won immediate respect, while his frank but dignified manners inspired admiration. He had, however, recently sustained a devastating blow in the death of his wife of thirty-seven years. He still carried bullets from Charles Dickinson and Jesse Benton in his chest and arm, and he suffered from persistent cough, wracking headaches, and debilitating digestive troubles.

His first task was to choose a cabinet. The chief place, the State Department, went to Martin Van Buren of New York, who had contributed vitally to Jackson's election and commanded the reigning political machine in the nation's largest state. The rest of Jackson's choices were weak and, to many of his supporters, alarming. Treasury Secretary Samuel Ingham of Pennsylvania, Navy Secretary John Branch of North Carolina, and Attorney General John M. Berrien of Georgia were politicians of modest reputation who brought no great strength to the administration. As all these men were practically strangers to Jackson, he saved the last post, the War Department, for a trusted confidential friend. The nod went to John Henry Eaton, a senator from Tennessee and Jackson's campaign biographer. Ironically, it was the appointment of Eaton—the safest one, in Jackson's mind—that eventually brought the whole cabinet down.

Reforming the Federal Bureaucracy: Jackson and the Spoils System

Having selected his cabinet, Jackson began a housecleaning at the second level of federal officeholders—the Washington bureau chiefs, land and customs officers, and federal marshals and attorneys. During the campaign, he had cried loudly for "reform," charging the Adams bureaucracy with fraud and with working to thwart his election. Now as president, Jackson implemented a policy of removals designed to eliminate the corruption, laxity, and arrogance that he associated with long individual tenure in office. Haste and naïveté in naming replacements did much to confuse Jackson's purpose. Under the guise of reform, many offices were doled out as reward for political services. Newspaper editors who had championed Jackson's cause came in for special favor. Jackson denied that he was injecting political criteria into the appointment process; yet he accepted an officeholder's support for Adams as evidence of unfitness, and in choosing replacements he relied exclusively on recommendations from his own partisans, few of whom shared his own concern for honest and efficient administration.

Some of Jackson's early appointments were truly appalling. He made John Randolph of Virginia, the most undiplomatic man in the United States, minister to Russia, and he placed an alcoholic editor at the head of the General Land Office. He raised the postmaster generalship to cabinet rank and filled it with William Taylor Barry of Kentucky, a genial bungler who reduced the postal system to chaos. Several of Jackson's land office appointees defaulted for large sums. Most damaging to his administration's reputation—he ignored warnings from Van Buren and Ingham—was the appointment of an old comrade, Samuel Swartwout, as collector of the New York Customhouse, through which passed nearly half of the federal government's revenue. Swartwout absconded with more than $1 million in 1838.

Jackson is usually charged with bringing the "spoils system" into American politics. That was the result, though not his intent. He always claimed, and evidently believed, that he had introduced greater efficiency and economy into government. He had, indeed, broken the hold of a bureaucratic clique on federal offices and thrown them open to all comers. The result was a democratization of public service at a temporary sacrifice in efficiency and honesty, though Jackson later found capable subordinates who instituted important administrative reforms. Jackson claimed the credit for returning the opportunity for office to the people at large, but he also deserved the responsibility for opening the way to manipulation of the federal bureaucracy for purely partisan purposes.

Indian Affairs: An Aggressive Policy

With his purge of the officeholders under way, Jackson bent his energies toward removing American Indians, particularly the powerful Southern tribes, beyond the frontier of white settlement. In its Indian relations, the federal government had hitherto continued the early practice of treating with the tribes as though they were foreign nations, while reserving to itself the abstract right of ultimate sovereignty. As a frontier negotiator, Jackson had protested this anomaly, claiming that the treaty form clothed the tribes with the trappings of an independent sovereignty that they did not really possess. Nevertheless, the practice continued. Jurisdictional conflict between the tribes and the government was avoided simply by inducing them to remove whenever white advances created a demand for their land and threatened their tribal integrity. Just as Jackson took office, the underlying issue was finally joined. The Cherokees, having acquired many of the attainments of white civilization, asserted sovereignty over their territory in Georgia and adjacent states and called on the federal government to defend them under treaty obligations. Georgia countered by formally extending its laws over all the state's Cherokee domain. Alabama and Mississippi followed by extending state jurisdiction over their Choctaw, Chickasaw, and Creek lands.

Faced with a direct contradiction between federal treaty stipulations and state sovereignty, Jackson came down unhesitatingly on the side of the latter. The government had no right to intercede on the Cherokees' behalf against Georgia, he announced; if the Indians wished to retain their tribal government and landownership, they must remove outside the state. To facilitate the removal, Jackson induced Congress in May, 1830, to pass a bill empowering him to lay off new American Indian homelands west of the Mississippi, exchange them for current tribal holdings, purchase the Indians' capital improvements, and pay the costs of their westward transportation. With this authority, Jackson departed for Tennessee in June to conduct the initial negotiations in person.

To American Indians, Jackson presented a simple alternative: Submit to state authority or remove beyond the Mississippi. The Chickasaws met Jackson near Nashville and agreed to emigrate. The Choctaws followed in September, treating with Jackson's intimates John Henry Eaton and John Coffee. The Creeks and Cherokees refused to come in, preferring to seek judicial support for their treaty rights, but after holding out two more years, the Creeks capitulated in March, 1832.

Only the Cherokees resisted to the bitter end. In *Cherokee Nation v. Georgia* (1831) and *Worcester v. Georgia* (1832), the Supreme Court upheld the Cherokees' independence from state authority, but the decisions pointed out no practical course of resistance to Georgia's encroachments. Tacitly encouraged by Jackson,

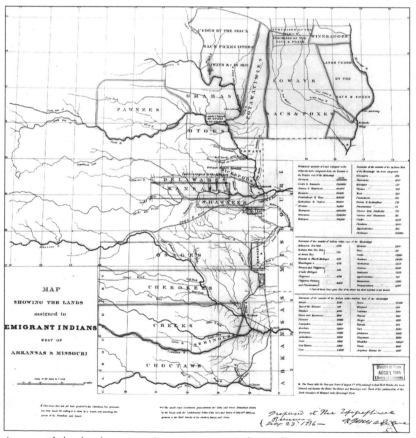

A map of the lands assigned to American Indian tribes in 1836. *(Library of Congress)*

Georgia ignored the rulings. Still, the Cherokees, led by Chief John Ross, refused to remove. Jackson cultivated a minority faction within the tribe, and with this rump he negotiated a removal treaty in 1835. Under its authority, the resisting Cherokees were rounded up and removed by force after Jackson left office in the infamous Trail of Tears.

Meanwhile, dozens of similar treaties closed out the remaining pockets of American Indian settlement in other states and territories east of the Mississippi. A short military campaign on the upper Mississippi quelled resistance by Black Hawk's band of Sacs and Foxes in 1832, and in 1835, a long and bloody war to subdue the Seminoles in Florida began. Most of the tribes went without resistance.

Granted the coercion and sometimes trickery that produced them, most of the removal treaties were fair, even generous. Their execution was miserable. The treaties included elaborate provisions to ensure fair payment for American Indian lands and goods, safe transportation to the West and sustenance on arrival, and protection for the property of those individuals who chose to remain behind under state jurisdiction. These safeguards collapsed under pressure from corrupt contractors, unscrupulous traders, and white trespassers backed by state authorities. Federal officials' efforts to protect the tribes were further hamstrung by the Jackson administration's drive for economy and its desire to avoid confrontation with state governments. For this abysmal record, Jackson bore ultimate responsibility. Even under the best of circumstances, the logistics of the gigantic removal operation would have taxed the federal government's limited resources. Jackson did not countenance its inadequacies, but he did little to prevent or correct them. Though usually a stickler for the precise performance of formal obligations, he allowed his administration to enter into engagements with American Indians that it was manifestly unprepared to fulfill.

The precepts of Jackson's Indian policy differed little from those of his predecessors. Like previous presidents, he regarded American Indians as children and believed that only through an extended tutelage in quarantine from white society could they absorb civilization and thus escape ultimate extinction. Yet while his predecessors undertook to uproot the tribes only in response to pressing white demand for their land, Jackson anticipated that demand, and by his posture he did much to encourage it. He made removal of American Indians, a peripheral concern in previous administrations, a central priority of his own. Inevitably, his impatience to remove the tribes encouraged other men who desired the same end and were not scrupulous as to means.

Petticoat Politics and the Nullification Controversy

Meanwhile, Jackson's cabinet was embroiling him in difficulties. Shortly before the inauguration, John Henry Eaton, his secretary of war, had married Peggy O'Neale, the daughter of a Washington boardinghouse keeper. Peggy's previous husband, a naval purser, had committed suicide under suspicious circumstances only shortly before her marriage to Eaton. Scandalous rumors circulated about Peggy's sexual promiscuity, and Washington's formal society refused to accept her. Among those who collaborated in snubbing her were the wives of cabinet secretaries Ingham, Branch, and Berrien.

Jackson came charging to Peggy's defense. Believing her innocent, he divined a deeper plot to drive Eaton from his cabinet, isolate himself among strangers, and control his administration. At first, he blamed Henry Clay's partisans, but his suspicions soon fixed on his vice president, John C. Calhoun, whose wife, Floride, was among Peggy's persecutors. To cement Jackson's convictions, the old controversy over his Seminole campaign of 1818 suddenly flared up again. In the spring of 1830,

Jackson learned that Calhoun, as secretary of war under Monroe, had privately advocated disciplining Jackson for exceeding his orders while publicly posturing as his defender. Jackson now accused Calhoun of treachery, initiating an angry correspondence that ended in the severance of social relations between the two chief officers of the government.

Secretary of State Van Buren, who had no wife to contend with, also sided with Peggy Eaton's defenders, and the controversy over her morals became the vehicle for a struggle for supremacy in the administration between him and Calhoun. Both men were aspirants to the presidential succession; further, they represented competing, though loosely defined, branches of the Jackson electoral coalition. Both opposed the nationalizing "American System" policy of a protective tariff and federal subsidies for road and canal construction (known as internal improvements) espoused by Henry Clay and embraced by the previous Adams administration, but their opposition rested on very different grounds.

Calhoun represented a group of politicians, in his home state of South Carolina and throughout the plantation South, whose opposition to the American System rested on essentially sectional motives. The central burden of their complaint was the protective tariff. They saw it as the culprit for all the South's economic ills, especially the stagnation in cotton prices, and as a humiliating reminder of their inferior and threatened position in the Union. An unheeding Congress had raised the tariff in 1824 and again in 1828 despite their anguished protests. As they saw it, the affront was not only to their pride and pocketbooks but also to their very way of life, for the emergence of a small but vocal Northern antislavery movement had raised the specter of a strong central government controlled by a sectional antislavery majority. Though the Calhounites sought refuge in states' rights, they were not doctrinaire strict constructionists. They op-

posed internal improvement expenditures mainly because these created a demand for tariff revenues, and some of them defended the constitutionality of the federally chartered Bank of the United States.

Against the tariff menace, Calhoun had conceived of a procedural remedy. He and his radical cohorts considered the current tariff unconstitutional; although federal taxation of imports was clearly authorized by the Constitution, the underlying purpose—to foster American manufactures—in their opinion was not. Building on the Jeffersonian notion of a state's right to protect its own citizens from federal tyranny, Calhoun elucidated a process by which a state could formally nullify an unconstitutional federal law and prevent its enforcement. Though he had not yet publicly avowed his nullification doctrine, Calhoun was known as its author by 1830.

Van Buren's opposition to the American System came from a different quarter. He was not against a protective tariff; indeed, he had helped engineer the tariff of 1828 that so outraged the plantation South. Van Buren's political musings lay in the direction of resurrecting the old transsectional Jeffersonian Republican Party. To do so would require conciliation on the tariff, but the key in Van Buren's mind would be to return to Jeffersonian strict constructionism—in particular, to the party's traditional antagonism to federal internal improvements and a national bank.

Where Jackson stood on these questions no one yet knew. His electoral coalition had embraced not only all the American System's opponents but also many of its staunch advocates in Pennsylvania and the Northwest. Jackson himself had ducked the tariff and internal improvement issues in the 1828 campaign, and his previous record was hard to read. He claimed allegiance to the old Republican Party and its strict constructionist doctrines. As a Westerner, a strident nationalist, and a military man, however, he had also in the past supported a protective tariff to make the United States industrially self-sufficient in wartime, along with internal improvements to strengthen the frontier and facilitate military movements.

Actually, Jackson's private views were quite close to Van Buren's. Like Van Buren, he accepted the constitutionality and, within limits, the wisdom of protective tariffs. He also nursed a deep animus against the Bank of the United States. Though in other areas he had once inclined toward constitutional latitudinarianism, the transgressions of the Monroe and Adams administrations convinced him of the urgent need to return the government to its original simplicity and purity. That meant clamping the lid on mushrooming internal improvement expenditures and returning to strict economy in government. Jackson craved the honor of presiding over the extinction of the national debt, already much reduced by previous administrations from its high following the War of 1812.

Hence, as petticoat politics threw Jackson and Van Buren together, they found grounds of agreement that extended far beyond their common faith in Peggy Eaton's moral character. Though a cotton planter and slaveholder himself, Jackson decried Calhoun's brand of narrow sectionalist politics. Nullification he regarded as incipient treason, a prelude to disunion and civil war. At a political dinner in April, 1830, he pronounced his ban on it by staring at Calhoun and toasting, "Our federal Union: *It must be preserved.*"

Jackson's first move to clarify his policy came in May, 1830. When Congress convened the previous December, he had urged moderation on both the tariff and internal improvements, and on sectional conciliation in general. Ignoring his plea for restraint, the majority in Congress pushed through several major internal improvement subsidies, including three in the form of purchases in the stock of private road and canal companies. Jackson vetoed all three, singling out for an explanatory message

the most politically vulnerable, a bill to subscribe $50,000 for construction of the Maysville Road in Henry Clay's home state of Kentucky. Van Buren helped write the veto message, which questioned the constitutionality of internal improvement subsidies and complained that they would exacerbate sectional tensions and postpone payment of the national debt. Southern antitariffites greeted the veto with apprehensive applause. They approved its tendency but suspected quite correctly that Jackson was not entirely in their camp. Indeed, his compromise proposal to distribute some federal funds directly to the states for their own use struck Calhoun and many Southerners as even more objectionable than direct federal internal improvement spending.

Calhoun's estrangement from Jackson deepened with the establishment of the *Washington Globe* in December, 1830, as the administration's newspaper office. A different paper, the *United States Telegraph*, had done excellent service as Jackson's campaign organ and had

John C. Calhoun *(Library of Congress)*

hitherto served as his official mouthpiece, but the *United States Telegraph*'s editor, Duff Green, was wholly devoted to Calhoun, and Jackson thought that his columns displayed too much sympathy with nullification and the Bank of the United States. To supplant him, Jackson brought in Francis Preston Blair of Kentucky. Closely associated with Blair in founding the *Washington Globe* was another Kentuckian, treasury auditor Amos Kendall. Blair and Kendall were not Van Buren's men, but like Van Buren, and unlike Green or Calhoun, they gave Jackson their complete loyalty and won his confidence in return. Together with a few other intimates—most notably Jackson's nephew and private secretary, Andrew Jackson Donelson, and his political manager, William B. Lewis— they formed a ring of confidential advisers who gave Jackson invaluable assistance in formulating his policies and presenting them to the public. Jackson's foes derisively dubbed them the Kitchen Cabinet.

A New Cabinet and a New Conception of the Cabinet's Role

While Jackson drew closer to Van Buren, the Eaton controversy smoldered on. Jackson's own household split over Peggy's acceptability, and his niece, White House hostess Emily Donelson, was banished to Tennessee for refusing to call on her. Her husband, private secretary Donelson, was at one point reduced to communicating by letter with Jackson even while living with him at the White House. Finally, to avoid utter paralysis of the administration, Van Buren and Eaton offered to resign in the spring of 1831. Jackson seized the occasion to demand the resignations of the opposing secretaries, Ingham, Branch, and Berrien. In their place, he appointed an entirely new cabinet.

The consequences of this move were momentous. Van Buren remained in Jackson's confidence as chief counselor and expected running mate in 1832. Calhoun and his faction were formally cast out. After two years of distraction and division, the administration was now prepared to steer a direct and unimpeded course. No less important, Jackson had liberated himself from the cabinet intrigues that had ensnared his own and previous administrations. Henceforth, his official advisers would be men he chose to implement his own ideas, not factional emissaries planted there to influence him. The most successful of Jackson's later cabinet secretaries—Roger Taney, Lewis Cass, Levi Woodbury, and Amos Kendall—were workhorses who administered their departments efficiently, offered advice when asked, accepted direction when given, and stood clear of political intrigue. Those who could not harmonize with administration policy were expected to keep quiet, invited to resign, or, if necessary, simply dismissed. For the remainder of his tenure, Jackson dominated his administration as no president had before, and he pioneered for future generations the conception of the cabinet as a subordinate agent of the presidential will.

Jackson vs. The Bank of the United States

The cabinet reconstruction of 1831 cleared the way for Jackson's next major policy move—his assault on the Bank of the United States. The bank had received a twenty-year charter from Congress in 1816. It was a private corporation, created for public purposes. The government held one-fifth of its stock and one-fifth of the seats on its board of directors. The bank's notes were legal tender for debts due the United States, and its branches served as exclusive federal depositories in their respective cities. The charter obliged the bank to perform various services, including transferring and disbursing federal funds without charge; in return, the charter guaranteed that Congress would create no competing institution.

Since its creation, the bank had provided a national currency through its notes, and in other ways had made itself useful to the Treasury. Jackson, however, was one of many who had never become reconciled either to the bank's constitutionality or to its financial power. Over his cabinet's objections, Jackson announced his opposition to a recharter of the bank in his very first message to Congress, and he had since recommended replacing the existing bank with a wholly governmental agency.

The bank's charter was due to expire in 1836. In January, 1832, its president, Nicholas Biddle, determined to apply for a recharter under the urging of Senators Daniel Webster of Massachusetts and Henry Clay of Kentucky, who were looking for an issue against Jackson in the pending presidential race. The recharter bill duly passed Congress, and on July 10, Jackson vetoed it.

The veto message, one of the most significant state papers in American history, was less an argument directed at Congress than a political manifesto to the American people. Jackson recited his constitutional objections to the bank and introduced some peculiar economic arguments against it, chiefly criticizing foreign ownership of some of its stock. (On any rational grounds, foreign investment in the underdeveloped American economy was to be welcomed, not scorned.) The crux of the message, however, was its attack on the special privileges that accrued to the bank's stockholders from their official connection to the government. Jackson did not attack wealth as such—he issued no call for class warfare or redistribution of private assets—but he condemned the addition of public privilege to private advantages. He also set forth an alternative vision of the government as a neutral arbiter in the economy, neither assisting nor obstructing the accumulation of private fortune, intervening only where necessary to protect basic rights. Jackson's earlier congressional messages and the Maysville Road veto had intimated this fundamental theme; the bank veto stated it powerfully and definitively.

Historians have debated whether Jackson attuned his blast against the bank to the ears of Western farmers, Northeastern mechanics and laborers, or rising entrepreneurs. In fact, it was aimed at no particular class or section. Rather, it was an appeal to all of society's outsiders—to anyone who had to make his way without benefit of inherited fortune; to those who worked with their hands, owned no stock in corporations, and to whom no congressman hearkened; to those outside the commercial community that connected every city and town and that in Jackson's mind had controlled the country before his election. It was a convincing appeal because it was heartfelt. Though Jackson's own success qualified him for admission to the existing centers of political and economic power, he had never felt at home there. He had run for president in 1824 against the regular political establishment, and even in 1828, his candidacy had secured only the grudging approval of some of its members. Not a member of the bankers' circle himself, he felt the outsider's resentment against its manipulation of public power for private purposes. Hence it was with no sense of incongruity that Jackson, a well-to-do planter and slaveholder, cast himself as the tribune of the people against the aristocracy of wealth and power.

Jackson and his opponents alike seized on the bank veto as the central issue of the 1832 presidential campaign. The American System supporters, under the name of National Republicans, nominated Henry Clay and savaged the veto for its display of economic ignorance, its demagogic appeal to the masses, and its obstruction of the people's will as expressed through their elected representatives in Congress. The campaign was complicated by the participation of two splinter groups: the anti-Masons in the Northeast, whom the National Republicans vainly tried to absorb, and the Southern antitariffites. After failing to substitute Philip Barbour of Virginia for Van Buren as vice presidential candidate, most of the latter supported the Jackson ticket, but South Carolina ominously refused its vote to any of the national candidates.

The election returns spelled a virtual repeat of 1828. Jackson again carried New York, Pennsylvania, and all the West and South, except South Carolina and Clay's home state of Kentucky. Whether the bank veto—or any other specific issue—cost or gained Jackson votes is uncertain. His foes traced their defeat solely to his untouchable personal popularity; Jackson himself read it as a popular ratification of his policies.

A Challenge from South Carolina: Resolving the Nullification Crisis

Jackson planned a further attack on the Bank of the United States, but before he could pursue it he faced a crisis in South Carolina. There, within days after the election, a state constitutional convention formally declared the tariff laws null and void and initiated steps to prevent the collection of customs duties within the state.

Nullification was a desperate move. A series of congressional ploys against the tariff in Jackson's first term had all failed, and South Carolinians no longer saw hope for relief from Washington, D.C. Congress had indeed reduced some duties earlier in the year, and with the national debt approaching extinction, Jackson now called for still further reduction. Even as it lowered some rates, however, the tariff of 1832 enshrined the protective principle, and a majority in Congress apparently regarded the issue as settled. South Carolinians felt themselves thrown back on their own resources.

To Jackson and to most Americans, including a majority of antitariffites outside South Carolina, nullification was an inadmissible recourse. Inclined by nature to personalize every dispute, Jackson traced South Carolina's action to Calhoun's corrupt ambition to rule at home if he could not rule in Washington, D.C. Still, Jackson also saw clearly the fundamental principle at stake. Calhoun claimed that nullification would actually save the Union, by providing a method short of state secession for resisting the federal government's unconstitutional excesses. To Jackson, this was nonsense. He was a strict constructionist, an advocate of limited government, and, to that extent, a states' rights advocate. The reserved rights of the states, however, did not in his opinion extend to defying legitimate federal authority. The tariff was an act of Congress duly and lawfully passed, and its constitutionality, though denied by South Carolina, had never been doubted by Congresses, presidents, or the Supreme Court. If a state could unilaterally repudiate federal laws and ban the collection of federal taxes, then the Union was no Union at all. To Jackson, nullification was tantamount to secession, and secession was treason.

Jackson was prepared to uphold federal authority in South Carolina at the point of a gun, but he preferred peaceful remedies or, if there were to be violence, that the state should strike the first blow. He quietly prepared for military action yet also pointed the way to accommodation. He again urged Congress to reduce the tariff, then followed with a proclamation warning South Carolinians to abjure their folly. In ringing phrases, the proclamation enunciated Jackson's conception of the United States as an indissoluble nation, not a mere league of sovereign states. Jackson followed up the proclamation by asking Congress for legislation to enforce the collection of customs duties over South Carolina's legal obstructions.

With Jackson applying pressure from all sides, the issue was successfully compromised. Congress passed a "force bill," giving Jackson the coercive powers he requested, but it simultaneously adopted a new tariff, which reduced duties to a uniform low rate over the next nine years. South Carolina accepted the new tariff and rescinded its ordinance of nullification. The adroit solution allowed all sides to claim victory, while Jackson basked in public acclaim throughout the North for his firmness in preserving the Union. What popularity he gained in the North, however, he lost in the South. The proclamation and the force bill angered Southern states' rights advocates. They gave credit for resolving the crisis, not to Jackson, but to Clay, who had introduced the compromise tariff bill, and to Calhoun, who had supported it.

Jackson's Second Term: The Bank War

The resolution of the nullification crisis in March, 1833, brought Jackson's first term to an end. His record thus far was one of signal success. He had survived the incapacitating Eaton affair and established control over his administration, set the removal of American Indians in train, won a resounding reelection over the opposition's best candidate, and maneuvered his man Van Buren into position to succeed him. More important, by circumscribing internal improvements and orchestrating the tariff settlement, he had finally got clear of the sectional wrangling that had paralyzed the Adams administration and threatened to rip apart the Union. He had presided over the extinction of the national debt and revitalized the old Jeffersonian doctrine of strict construction and limited government.

Yet, in Jackson's mind, his tack was only half finished. His victories thus far were merely personal and incomplete. He had yet to convert his own electoral mandate into an effective instrument of policy. Congress was uncooperative. Politicians of varying creeds were all too willing to attach themselves to his name, and Jackson had repeatedly endured the frustration of seeing men elected under his banner defy his most cherished recommendations. The Senate had rejected a string of important appointments, including even Van Buren himself for minister to Great Britain after the cabinet breakup of 1831. Congress's eagerness to spend and susceptibility to lobbying pressure had

forced Jackson to employ vetoes as his chief instruments of policy.

Jackson never doubted that the American people were on his side. He expected popular vindication for everything that he did, and thus far his confidence had been justified. In the face of his own resounding public support, Congress's ungovernability demanded explanation. By early 1833, Jackson had identified the culprit and had begun to see all of his myriad political antagonists as instruments of one central foe. The reconciliation of Clay and Calhoun, which he had anticipated long before, confirmed his suspicions; though directly opposed to each other on the sectional issues of Jackson's first term (with Jackson himself in the middle), they were both in his mind instruments of the concentrated economic and political power directed by that "hydra of corruption," the Bank of the United States.

News of the bank's activities since his veto of its recharter in 1832 outraged Jackson. The bank had been created and endowed with monopolistic privileges to serve the government's own needs, not those of its stockholders or directorate. As a creature of the government, the bank, therefore, in Jackson's eyes, had no right to an independent political character, no right to attempt to influence public policy even in defense of its own existence. Yet the bank had lavishly pamphleteered in its own defense (and implicitly against Jackson's reelection) in the 1832 campaign and had lent freely to congressmen and newspaper editors. Despite the election verdict of 1832, informants warned Jackson that bank president Nicholas Biddle still aimed to procure a recharter.

Jackson determined to draw the bank's fangs. The bank's enormous economic and political leverage stemmed largely from its role as the depository of federal funds. The government deposits augmented the bank's own capital and enabled it to restrain the lending of state banks by gathering and presenting their notes for redemption in specie. Jackson there-

The Bank War—"Downfall of the Mother Bank." *(Library of Congress)*

fore fixed on withdrawing the deposits as the surest way to disarm the bank for the three years remaining under its original charter.

Removing the deposits was a maneuver that required some delicacy. Legal authority to do it lay with the treasury secretary, not the president, and the House of Representatives had only recently voted by 109 to 46 that the deposits were safe where they were. In the spring of 1833, Jackson carefully canvassed his cabinet and confidential advisers on removal; most of them opposed it, but he got the support and arguments that he needed from Attorney General Roger Taney. Jackson next dispatched Amos Kendall on a mission to recruit state banks to accept the federal deposits. On Kendall's return, Jackson announced to the cabinet his decision to begin depositing federal revenues with selected state banks, simultaneously drawing down the government's balances in the Bank of the United States.

Here, a sticking point appeared. Treasury Secretary William John Duane, who alone possessed legal authority to order the change, refused to do it. He also refused to resign, so Jackson dismissed him and put Taney in his place. Taney duly issued the necessary order, and the drawdown, or removal, commenced on October 1. It was largely complete by the time Congress convened in early December.

The obstreperousness that Jackson had met from previous Congresses was nothing to the fury that he encountered in this one. A majority in Congress had supported the bank's recharter, but even many of its enemies there could not countenance Jackson's method of proceeding against it. Under the law, the secretary of the treasury, though an appointee of the president and member of his cabinet, was a distinct agent who, unlike other department heads, reported directly to Congress. Jackson's dismissal of Duane therefore looked like a bold stroke to draw all power over the federal purse into his own hands, and his hasty removal of the deposits seemed calculated to preempt action by Congress on a matter rightfully under its own authority. Moreover, Jackson appeared to be recklessly tampering with the nation's finances, removing control over the money supply from the responsible and lawfully sanctioned hands of the Bank of the United States to an untried, unregulated, and perhaps thoroughly irresponsible collection of state bankers. Jackson himself spoke of the arrangement with the state banks as an "experiment." Naturally, the removal forced the bank to curtail its widespread loans, and whereas Jackson and his allies accused it of exaggerating the contraction for political effect, the commercial community blamed the resulting distress on the president himself.

In the 1833-1834 congressional session, known as the "panic session," the deposit issue finally prompted Jackson's enemies to coalesce into a coherent political grouping. They called themselves Whigs, the name of British opponents of royal prerogative, to denote their opposition to Jackson's executive sway. Although political expediency obviously influenced the cooperation of men so different in principle as Clay and Calhoun, a genuine unity of outlook underlay the anti-Jackson coalition. The Whigs saw in Jackson the same danger that he saw in the bank—the threat of an unbridled centralized power, wielding sufficient money and influence to overawe or corrupt the opposition and ultimately to destroy the substance, if not the form, of republican government. It was true that Jackson claimed both popular mandate and constitutional sanction for his actions—but tyrants have ever spoken in the name of the people. Also, Jackson's assertions of presidential authority, though made familiar to the modern ear by later experience, sounded positively dangerous to men accustomed to legislative supremacy in government.

Fortunately for Jackson, his adversaries overplayed their hand. While denunciations raged in Congress, Biddle carried the bank's financial contraction beyond what was necessary, in an undisguised effort to force a recharter on Congress and the president. The maneuver served only to confirm Jackson's strictures against the bank's unwarranted power over the national economy. The House of Representatives refused to support either recharter or the restoration of the deposits, forcing the Whig majority in the Senate to wage battle on peripheral ground. The Senate rejected Jackson's nominations for the government seats on the bank's board of directors, rejected Taney as secretary of the treasury, and on March 28, 1834, adopted Clay's resolution that "the President, in the late Executive proceedings in relation to the public revenue, has assumed upon himself authority and power not conferred by the Constitution and laws, but in derogation of both."

To this unprecedented censure, Jackson returned a formal protest, complaining that the Senate had neither specified the grounds of his offense nor followed the constitutional process of impeachment. The Senate rejected the protest as an abridgment of its own freedom of expression. The Whigs, however, could do no more. The panic eased as the congressional session closed, and the bank, defeated, began preparations to wind up its affairs.

The Bank War aroused violent political passions on both sides. The future not only of the bank but also of the American system of government seemed to ride on the outcome. For Jackson, his struggle took on even religious significance; he saw himself serving "the Lord" against "the worshippers of the golden Calf." Partisans on both sides attributed the vilest motives to their adversaries. Biddle privately referred to the president and his advisers as "these miserable people," whereas Jackson raged against "reckless and corrupt" United States senators.

The right and wrong of the Bank War are difficult to sort out even today. The verdict depends more on one's point of view than on any dispute over facts. The bank's defenders, then and later, argued that its management had been prudent and responsible. The bank had regulated credit and the currency precisely as Congress had chartered it to do, and did it far more efficiently than any substitute Jackson was prepared to offer. To the Whigs, the president's wanton destruction of the one great stabilizing influence in the economy was thus unpardonably ignorant at best, criminally vicious at worst.

To Jackson, such arguments were essentially irrelevant. Useful or not, the bank was illegitimate: a private institution, unsanctioned by the Constitution, employing public funds and public power to serve the ends not of the government or the people but of its own wealthy, privileged stockholders. Jackson believed that the country could do without the bank, but his fundamental grievance against it was political, not economic.

Between these opposing views no real accommodation was possible. The bank's dual public and private functions provided endless ground for misunderstanding. If it expanded its loans, Jackson accused it of political bribery; if it contracted, of blackmail. The bank's dealings with congressmen and editors, damning evidence of corruption in Jackson's eyes, were from a less malign viewpoint simple and sound business transactions. Jackson demanded reports of the bank's transactions from the government directors, in fulfillment of their public office; to the rest of the directorate, the reports were violations of bankers' confidence that justified excluding the government directors from participation in the bank's deliberations and access to its books. In these circumstances, a true noninvolvement in politics, to which Biddle had originally adhered, proved impossible to maintain, and if the bank were not the partisan agency that Jackson claimed it to be at the beginning of the Bank War, it had certainly become so by its end.

Solidifying the Democratic Party

The Bank War furnished the opportunity Jackson and his advisers had long been seeking to shape his adherents into a unitary political organization. Opposition to the Bank of the United States became the first test for membership in the new Democratic Party, and as Jackson's own thinking on monetary policy progressed, that test was expanded to include opposition to any central bank, then to banking in general. Jackson himself by mid-1834 had come to advocate stripping banks of their monetary function entirely, and replacing their notes of small denomination with gold and silver coin as the medium of everyday exchange. Banks, said Jackson, were essentially swindling machines, whose obscure transactions and erratic currency fluctuations bilked the common man of the rightful fruit of his labor.

On the banking issue thus broadly defined, the Democrats went to the people. Theirs was, again, an appeal to the outsiders in society, to the simple producers—farmers, laborers, mechanics—who did not comprehend the mysteries of banking and finance and resented the commercial community's use of them to control the economy. It was a powerful appeal, for improvements in transportation were transforming the American economy, making it more stratified and specialized, more dependent on regional and national markets. Some Americans heralded the new complexity and the opportunities it created, but to others, it foretold the loss of control over their lives, the end of their economic independence and political freedom. To these men, Andrew Jackson stood forth as the champion of their liberties and of the old, simple, republican virtues. As Democrats carried his message to the state and local level, they broadened it to appeal to other outsiders as well, especially to ethnic and religious groups (most notably Irish Catholics) outside the native Protestant mainstream.

Simultaneously, Jackson's men conducted a purge of the party apparatus in the states. The chief instrument of the purge was a campaign to compel the Senate to expunge the censure of Jackson from its journal of proceedings. Thomas Hart Benton of Missouri made an expunging motion in the Senate, and resolutions supporting it were promptly introduced in state legislatures. Legislators and senators who opposed expunging were thrust out of the party. With this weapon, Jackson's lieutenants forced several senators from their seats and finally brought the rebellious Senate to heel. On January 16, 1837, Benton's motion passed the Senate, and the censure was formally expunged.

Foreign Policy

While the expunging campaign progressed, the administration suddenly found its attention diverted to foreign affairs. In dealing with overseas nations, Jackson had contented himself with negotiating trade openings and settling commercial damage claims, mostly left over from the Napoleonic Wars. In these routine endeavors, he had succeeded well. His agents had secured recognition of American claims against Denmark, Spain, France, and Naples, and they had concluded commercial treaties with Turkey, Austria, Russia, Siam (Thailand), Muscat (Oman), Venezuela, and Chile. Jackson's repudiation of the Adams administration's negotiating position in order to win an agreement with Great Britain on the West Indian colonial trade in 1830 provoked partisan attack, but otherwise his overseas diplomacy was not controversial.

His attempt to collect American claims against France, however, brought the country to the brink of war. In an 1831 treaty, France had agreed to pay 25 million francs for Napoleonic depredations on American shipping. The first installment was due in February, 1833,

but the French Chamber of Deputies refused to appropriate the funds. When another year went by without payment, Jackson lost patience and asked Congress to authorize reprisals should France stall any further. The insulted French then demanded explanation of this threat as a condition of payment. Jackson responded in effect that what he said to Congress was none of a foreign power's business. The impasse deepened throughout 1835; ministers were recalled and military preparations begun. Finally, under British urgings, the French decided to construe a conciliatory passage in a later message to Congress as sufficient explanation. France paid the debt, and the crisis, once resolved, left no repercussions.

The same could not be said of Jackson's dealings with Mexico. Jackson had craved Texas for the United States ever since his days as a Tennessee militia general, and he made its purchase from Mexico the first priority of his presidential diplomacy. Given the instability of Mexico's government and its suspicion of American designs, a Texas negotiation required extreme patience and discretion to have any hope of success. The agent Jackson chose, Anthony Butler of Kentucky, possessed neither of those qualities, and Jackson's own careless instructions encouraged Butler's clumsy dabbling in the diplomatic underworld of bribery and personal influence. Butler's machinations, combined with the flow of American settlers into Texas, served only to arouse Mexican apprehensions that the United States was bent on fomenting a revolution there. In 1835, American emigrants in Texas did revolt successfully against Mexican authority. Jackson prudently declined to back the annexation of the new Texas republic to the United States, or even to recognize its independence from Mexico without prior congressional approval, but his earlier inept efforts to purchase the province had helped to sow the seeds of mutual distrust that erupted into war between the two countries a decade later.

The Rise of the Whigs

Jackson's primary concern as his administration drew toward its close was to ensure that his policies, and particularly his hard-money and antibanking campaign, would continue beyond his own retirement to the Hermitage. He had long before settled on Martin Van Buren as the man best qualified to carry on his work, and he now bent every effort to secure Van Buren's nomination and election to the presidency. It was a difficult battle, for Van Buren was as roundly distrusted as Jackson was loved and revered. Rivals resented Van Buren's closeness to the president, and Democrats and Whigs alike considered him an artful schemer and flatterer. Further, Jackson's own forthright stance on every prominent issue of his long administration, and his vigorous and unprecedented conduct of the executive office itself, had aroused opposition at one time or another in many quarters. Men who could not bear—or did not dare—to disagree directly with Jackson himself were quick to assign responsibility for their grievances to Van Buren. He had become, unwittingly, the universal scapegoat of the Jackson administration.

Given his initial unpopularity and the weight of accumulated complaints against him, Van Buren needed the full weight of Jackson's influence behind his candidacy. Jackson wrote letters, attended political functions (which he had shunned during his own campaign), threatened reprisals on dissenters, and oversaw the Democratic convention that nominated Van Buren in May, 1835. The Whigs, who lacked a central directing head and hence lagged behind the Democrats in party organization, capitalized on the diversity of disgruntlement with Van Buren by encouraging the candidacies of regional favorites. William Henry Harrison of Ohio emerged as their main candidate, but Daniel Webster of Massachusetts and Hugh Lawson White of Tennessee also received Whig backing. Tennessee deserted the Democrats for White, a former Jackson intimate who had gradually fallen out of his confidence. The defection mortified Jackson, and he poured out his bitterest denunciations against White and the Democratic apostates who backed his candidacy.

Van Buren won the election. Even without a national candidate against him, however, he garnered a bare majority of the popular vote, and the real message of the campaign was the rise of the Whigs and Jackson's failure to pass on his own personal popularity to his Democratic successors. The party Van Buren inherited was better disciplined and more clearly focused than the diffuse coalition that had swept Jackson into office eight years before, but it was also smaller. Henceforth, Whigs and Democrats would do battle on nearly equal terms.

A Debased Currency

While working to ensure the succession, Jackson also refined and extended his campaign for hard money. His destruction of the Bank of the United States had inadvertently encouraged the spread of bank currency, as state governments proceeded to fill the void by chartering new banks that issued notes without any central restraint. There was an eager demand for this capital, for a decade of general growth and prosperity had begun to culminate in a speculative land boom. Federal revenue from Western land sales, which had previously hung at $2 to $3 million annually, leaped to $11 million in 1835 and to $24 million in 1836. Unwanted banknotes of dubious convertibility poured in, producing an embarrassing treasury surplus.

Jackson was appalled at this debasement of the currency, so contrary to his own intentions. He viewed the problem as essentially moral, tracing the profusion of banknotes not to impersonal economic forces but to the unrestrained spirit of speculation and avarice. He called again for the stricter regulation of banking and for the elimination of notes of small denomination, and in July, 1836, he directed the issuance of a specie circular, which required payment in coin for federal lands. In June, Congress did provide statutory regulation of the federal deposit banks and limited their issuance of notes, but, by the same act, disbursed the deposits among a much larger number of banks, then unloaded the treasury surplus by returning it to the state governments as a "deposit"—in form, a loan; in effect, a gift. These measures merely forced a shifting of balances among the banks. Even had they understood it to be necessary, neither Jackson nor Congress possessed the tools for the delicate and perhaps impossible task of easing down an overheated economy. As Jackson prepared to leave office, the nation's financial structure teetered on the edge of a deflationary collapse.

The Impact of Jackson's Presidency

Jackson's quiet departure from the White House in March, 1837, stood in sharp contrast to his tumultuous entrance eight years earlier. The administration's final weeks were calm, almost spiritless. Age and an accumulation of bodily ailments had finally caught up with Jackson; during his last congressional session, he was practically an invalid. Before retiring, however, he roused his strength for one more veto—of a bill overriding the specie circular—and for a farewell address, issued on the day of Martin Van Buren's inauguration as president.

The very act of delivering such an address bespoke Jackson's understanding of the extraordinary importance of his presidency. No chief executive since George Washington had departed office with a formal valedictory. Jackson began humbly, thanking the people for their confidence. In fatherly phrases, he admonished them to cherish the Union, avoid sectional divisions, and preserve the Constitution in its original purity.

Jackson's mood shifted sharply as he went on to discuss banking and currency. He condemned paper money as an engine of oppression in the hands of the bankers. In dark tones, he warned of a conspiracy of "the money power" to control the state and federal governments and subvert the liberties of the people.

In eight years, Jackson had fundamentally reordered the American political landscape. He entered the presidency at the end of a decade when the stresses and hardships of economic development had given rise to sectional conflict over the issues of the tariff and internal improvements. More than any politician of his day, Jackson stood above sectional feelings. Seeing that sectional antagonisms jeopardized the permanence of the Union, he sought with remarkable success to quiet the issues that prompted them. Though the ultimate sectional issue—slavery—began to intrude into politics during his term, the economic questions of the previous decade lost most of their divisive force under his conciliatory influence.

Jackson, however, substituted a new set of demons for the old. In the place of sectional opponents, he identified a new threat to the republic in the commercial oligarchy of bankers, speculators, and chartered corporations. Like many Americans, he was alarmed by the growing complexity and interdependency of the national economy. Interpreting it as a corrupt conspiracy rather than an economic process, he appealed in vivid language for the American people to redeem their traditional liberties and virtues from this alien power.

Jackson's attack on the money power set the tone for a generation of Democratic politicians. At the same time, his conduct of the presidency reshaped the structure of American politics. Elected president on a wave of popular enthusiasm, he had interposed his will against Congress, vetoing more bills than all of his predecessors put together. For justification, he appealed over the head of Congress directly to the mass of people, in the unshakable conviction that they would support him. Reversing a tradition in American politics, he claimed that he as president represented the people directly, whereas Congress represented only special interests. To make this claim effective, to transform his personal popularity into a workable instrument of policy, he and his advisers labored to shape his following into a political party. In thus forging a link between the highest and lowest levels of government, between the people and the president, Jackson elevated the importance of the presidential office and reduced the importance of Congress—especially the Senate—by bringing its members within reach of the party apparatus. At the same time, Jackson's bold measures and political innovations prompted his foes to coalesce into an opposing partisan organization. The Democratic Party was Jackson's child; the antebellum two-party system was his legacy.

Yet with all of his importance to the development of the American political system, Jackson's dominance of an era rested as much on his forceful personality as on his particular achievements. His character, which combined tremendous strengths with appalling weaknesses, inspired devotion from his friends, loathing from his enemies. Contemporaries disagreed violently in their assessment of Jackson, and historians have followed in their paths.

Concluding Perspectives: Jackson the Man

Jackson cut such a titanic figure that both admirers and detractors reckoned him an elemental force rather than a human being. Henry Clay likened him to a tropical tornado. Jackson's determination and willpower impressed friends and enemies alike. Intimates marveled at his fortitude. He suffered constant pain, and he often appeared so feeble that friends feared for his life; yet he met the demands of a brutal work and social schedule. He seemed to keep himself alive by sheer determination, an awesome domination of the will over the flesh.

His moods, like the weather, were unpredictable. His violent rages were legendary, yet he could be perfectly cool when the occasion required. White House visitors who were expecting to see a growling monster were charmed by his courtly demeanor and pleasant conversation.

Jackson radiated a magnificent self-assurance. Both as a general and as a president, he never admitted the possibility of defeat and never suffered it. His faith in his own ability to master the task at hand, no matter how formidable, mesmerized his associates. He seemed to be without weakness and without fear. Jackson's confidence in himself was an important political asset. It enabled him to overawe his enemies, for few men could face him without blinking; and it drew to his side weaker men, less sure of themselves, who found their strength in him.

Yet Jackson upheld this tremendous strength of character only at great cost in flexibility. He was indeed indomitable, but not infallible; yet, like many of his admirers, he tended to confuse the two. Though he condemned flattery, he was an easy mark for it. He could not take criticism, and he was extraordinarily sensitive to imagined personal slights. He viewed himself entirely too seriously to enjoy or even permit a joke at his own expense; indeed, he seemed to find little humor in anything. Though he made many errors in his long career, he could not acknowledge them, even to himself. He never apologized and rarely explained. His self-righteousness, combined with a wholly unwarranted confidence in the accuracy of his own memory, trapped him in one pointless personal controversy after another, and when he was in the wrong he sometimes stooped to substitute bluster for truth.

Throughout his life, Jackson wore a pair of moral blinders. He saw his own path of duty marked clearly ahead and followed it rigorously, but no alternative perspectives or courses of action ever entered his field of vision.

He simply believed that whatever he did was right. Hence, he never learned to accept political disagreement with the equanimity of a Henry Clay or Martin Van Buren. He took all opposition as a personal affront. Trusting as much in the people's virtue as in his own, he ascribed every victory of an opposition candidate to fraud or deception. Jackson was neither gracious in adversity nor magnanimous in triumph. He railed bitterly after his own defeat in 1824 and Van Buren's in 1840, and he exulted at Whig president William Henry Harrison's sudden death after only one month in office.

Trapped inside his own clear but narrow view of the world, Jackson failed to see the contradictions in his own career, which critics wrongly attributed to conscious hypocrisy. He thought himself modest and humble, though he was neither. He repeated so often the myth that he had never sought public office that he apparently came to believe it, even though his whole career bespoke otherwise. Although outraged at violations of his own confidence, he willingly read others' private mail when it was shown to him. He excoriated the Adams administration for corruption and partisan manipulation of the patronage, failings that were much more evident in his own. Opposed to a strong central government, he greatly strengthened the presidency, its most concentrated locus of power.

The depth of Jackson's emotional engagement in his political career, his unremitting search for personal vindication and for victory over his foes, suggest a character controlled by some deeply seated animus. His enemies—and some later historians—appraised him as a driven, vengeful, self-obsessed man. Yet the traits they condemned were fused with others that inspired reverence and devotion from those who knew him well.

Jackson was a faithful husband and a loving and indulgent father. He lavished affection on the wife and children of his adopted son, Andrew, Jr., and he exhibited endless patience with Andrew's own serious failings. Curiously, Jackson found it much easier to forgive personal shortcomings than political transgressions, and from those who gave him their loyalty he could tolerate almost any fault. He had many wards—relatives and children of deceased comrades—and he gave freely of money for their education and advice to guide their careers. Examples of his private generosity and kindness are legion. Widows and orphans found him an easy touch. He demanded good treatment for his slaves and dismissed overseers who handled them too roughly.

Though he did not join the Presbyterian church until very late in life, Jackson was a religious man. He cared little for doctrine, but he enjoyed hearing sermons and found consolation in the Bible and devotional literature. He coupled an unquestioning faith in his own destiny with a humble, almost fatalistic submission to the workings of Providence. A simple Christian charity was the centerpiece of his religious practice.

Jackson's mind was quick and forceful, but not subtle. His associates marveled at his ability to cut through to the heart of a difficult subject—which indeed he could do if the argument were reducible to a simple principle of direct action. More complex and sophisticated expositions eluded his comprehension; he dismissed them as trickery. Firm in his political convictions, he saw no need to explore them through systematic thought. With the great moral and intellectual dilemma of his era—the problem of slavery—he never concerned himself; he simply accepted the institution. Characteristically, he interpreted the rising abolitionist agitation as a political ploy to disrupt the Union and the Democratic Party, and on that ground he condemned it.

Jackson had few intellectual or cultural pursuits, though he liked to attend the theater, and few diversions other than horse racing, to which he was passionately devoted. He read mainly newspapers. He had acquired the gentleman planter's expensive tastes in food and wine, along with a sufficient veneer of higher learning to scatter classical allusions (sometimes misplaced) throughout his letters. Contemporaries attested his extraordinary abilities as a conversationalist, but they left little hint of what he talked about besides politics.

Jackson's writing lacked polish, but he had a gift for vigorous expression. He was best with maxims: "Our federal Union: it must be preserved" and "Ask nothing that is not right; submit to nothing that is wrong" were classics, and he repeated them often. With the help of Andrew Jackson Donelson, Jackson kept up a voluminous private correspondence. For aid in formal composition, he relied on Donelson, Van Buren, Kendall, and Blair, plus other advisers of the moment. The nullification proclamation was largely Edward Livingston's work; the farewell address, Roger Taney's. Most of Jackson's major presidential papers were group productions. They were always intended for the public eye, even when addressed to Congress. Measured against the florid standards of that era, Jackson's state papers were masterpieces of clarity and lucidity.

Throughout Jackson's presidency, he yearned for a quiet retirement at the Hermitage, but when the time for it came, he found that he could not let go of politics. Indeed, he was as unprepared as ever to lead the withdrawn life of a country gentleman. He yearned to see his policies carried through and what he called "my fame" upheld. In the financial panic that broke as Jackson left office, President Van Buren required guidance and fortitude. Jackson willingly supplied both. He demanded a complete divorce of the government from the banks and badgered Van Buren and Francis Preston Blair with advice, exhortations, and warnings. He summoned all of his failing energies in behalf of Van Buren's independent treasury plan and his reelection bid in 1840.

William Henry Harrison's defeat of Van Bu-ren staggered Jackson, but he soon found cause for rejoicing in Harrison's death and his successor John Tyler's reversion to Democratic principles on banking and the tariff. To his great satisfaction, Jackson's influence was again required from Washington, D.C., this time in behalf of the annexation of Texas. Ever eager for Texas, Jackson enlisted avidly in the annexation cause and when Van Buren declared against it, he helped set in train the movement to jettison Van Buren in favor of Tennessean James K. Polk for the 1844 Democratic nomination. Before Jackson died, he reaped the final vindication of seeing his loyal disciple Polk installed in the presidency to carry on his work.

Honors and tributes enriched Jackson's retirement. He was the living apostle of democracy, and an endless parade of well-wishers journeyed to the Hermitage to do him homage. Jackson welcomed them all. Though he accepted public tributes with an air of diffident humility, he never tired of them, and in 1840, he dragged himself to New Orleans for an exhausting celebration of the twenty-fifth anniversary of his great military triumph. Conscious of his historical importance and jealous of his reputation, Jackson occupied much of his spare time in arranging his papers and overseeing preparations for Amos Kendall's projected biography.

Financial worries darkened Jackson's final years. The luckless Andrew, Jr., conjured up debts without end and meeting them gradually drained away Jackson's assets. In the end, despite his horror of indebtedness, the old chief was driven to borrowing large sums from the faithful Francis Preston Blair. Jackson died in comfort but with his once ample estate heavily encumbered by debt.

Gradually, the weight of age, illness, and worry bore down on Jackson. For years, his health had been precarious, yet he had recovered from the brink so many times that friends half seriously questioned his mortality. Jackson knew better. He had long anticipated death, and he faced it without fear. In the spring of 1845, his condition worsened, and on June 8 he died, surrounded by family and friends. He was buried at the Hermitage, next to Rachel.

Daniel Feller

Bibliographical References

Andrew Jackson has had several biographers. Robert V. Remini's three-volume *Andrew Jackson*, 1977-1984, is an adoring portrait that has been condensed into a single volume edition as *The Life of Andrew Jackson*, 1988. Marquis James, *Andrew Jackson*, 1933-1937, makes lively reading, as does Remini's one-volume *Andrew Jackson*, 1966. Arthur Schlesinger, Jr., *The Age of Jackson*, 1945, presents the most provocative and influential view of Jackson's historical significance. For critical psychological assessments, see Michael P. Rogin, *Fathers and Children*, 1975, and James C. Curtis, *Andrew Jackson and the Search for Vindication*, 1976. The earliest and biggest scholarly biography, by James Parton, *Life of Andrew Jackson*, 1860, is still in many ways the best. There is extensive recent literature on some of the chief topics of Jackson's administration—Indian removal, nullification, and the Bank War. John F. Marszalek, *The Petticoat Affair: Manners, Mutiny, and Sex in Andrew Jackson's White House*, 1997, examines Jackson's defense of Peggy Eaton and the results of the controversy on the Jackson administration. For a thorough examination of Jackson's presidency, see Donald B. Cole, *The Presidency of Andrew Jackson*, 1993, a single-volume study in the University Press of Kansas series on American presidents.

The Papers of Andrew Jackson, edited by Sam B. Smith, Harriet C. Owsley, and Harold D. Moser, began publication in 1980. With five volumes to date, they have reached to 1824 and are part of a projected edition of fifteen volumes. John S. Bassett's *Correspondence of Andrew Jackson*, 1926-1935, though less thorough, presents an excellent selection. No one interested in Jackson's presidency should fail to consult his state papers, collected in James D. Richardson, *Messages and Papers of the Presidents*, 1896-1899. Remini's *Andrew Jackson: A Bibliography*, 1991, provides a comprehensive listing of primary and secondary sources on the life and presidency of Jackson.

Martin Van Buren

8th President, 1837-1841

Born: December 5, 1782
Kinderhook, New York
Died: July 24, 1862
Kinderhook, New York

Political Party: Democratic
Vice President: Richard M. Johnson

Cabinet Members

Secretary of State: John Forsyth
Secretary of the Treasury: Levi Woodbury
Secretary of War: Joel R. Poinsett
Secretary of the Navy: Mahlon Dickerson, James K. Paulding

Attorney General: Benjamin Butler, Felix Grundy, Henry D. Gilpin
Postmaster General: Amos Kendall, John M. Niles

Van Buren's official portrait. *(White House Historical Society)*

On March 4, 1837, Martin Van Buren became the eighth president of the United States. It was a beautiful early spring day, and great numbers turned out for the occasion. Some lined the route from the White House to the Capitol to see Van Buren and the outgoing president ride by in an open carriage; many others gathered at the East Portico to witness the inaugural ceremonies. Yet a dramatic happening at the end of the ceremonies showed that the crowds belonged to the old president and not the new one: As the inaugural party returned to the carriage, Andrew Jackson was greeted with thunderous cheering and applause. "For once," Thomas Hart Benton later recalled, "the rising was eclipsed by the setting sun." Three days later, President Van Buren escorted Jackson to the rail station, where the old hero began the first leg of his journey back to the Hermitage. Only then, many felt, did the new presidency begin.

Or was it the "third term" of Jackson? Most observers supposed that Van Buren had become president through Jackson's influence and had bound himself to defend the heritage. His preelection pledge "to tread generally in the footsteps of President Jackson" was thus welcomed by Democrats and understood by Whigs in the same light, even though they would at times indulge the temptation to taunt Van Buren for a "footsteps administration." The central domestic measure of his presidency, the independent Treasury, followed logically from the policy of his predecessor: Jackson's Bank War had separated the Treasury from the national bank; in response to the panic of 1837, Van Buren divorced Treasury operations from the state banks as well. To him also fell much of the burden for carrying out Jackson's policy of Indian removal. In other ways, however, Van Buren pursued a distinctly different course. More cautious than Jackson, he kept the peace at a time when problems with Mexico and Great Britain might have drawn a bolder spirit into war. With a keen awareness of the sectional tensions generated by abolitionism, he worked, in like manner, for sectional peace. After the stormy events of Jackson's administration, moreover, the new president sought to give the nation a period of repose. A review of Van Buren's earlier career shows that he had helped to shape the heritage he vowed as president to defend.

The Fox of Kinderhook

The long road Van Buren followed from Kinderhook, New York, to the White House also dramatized the remarkable achievements of a self-made man. He was born on December 5, 1782, into the household of Abraham and Hannah Van Buren, both of respectable if undistinguished Dutch stock. From his father, a somewhat improvident farmer and tavern keeper, the son received an amiable temper, robust health, and Republican politics, but not the means for a good education. Ending his formal schooling at fourteen, the young Van Buren read law for the next seven years and

then began his own practice in Kinderhook. Once established in the law, he married a childhood playmate, Hannah Hoes, and began a family amounting to four sons before her untimely death in 1819. (Though there were later flirtations and the rumor of a union with Thomas Jefferson's granddaughter, he never remarried.) Meanwhile, a move to Hudson and then to Albany marked growing success in his profession, earning for him a comfortable estate, the respect of his fellow lawyers, and consideration in the 1820's for appointment to the Supreme Court. In default of higher education, the law provided the basic discipline for his mind and served to deepen a conservative instinct to accept the existing arrangements of society. As a public official he was ever disposed, as in his law practice, to react to specific events rather than to shape them.

Politics, along with the law, engaged Van Buren from an early day and opened the pathway to power. Political talk in his father's tavern, revolving around the dramatic struggles in the 1790's between Federalists and Republicans, fired a lifelong passion. During the next two decades, he exhibited a sure instinct for the winning side among the warring factions in New York and reaped, as a reward, appointment as a county judge, election to the state senate, and the commission of attorney general. Attributing his success to the shady arts of management and intrigue, foes condemned him as a "politician by trade," a low-class upstart presuming to enter the political sphere once reserved for gentlemen. Close associates of Van Buren, by contrast, pointed to a keen knowledge of human nature which enabled him to penetrate the motives and foil the designs of his enemies. He possessed as well a remarkable capacity for self-control, a suavity of manners, and a smoothness of style that helped him conciliate friends and relate with good sportsmanship to opponents.

Personal appearance added to the force of his style and lent some measure of support to the image foes cast of him as a "red fox" or "little magician." Fashionably dressed, meticulously groomed, and endowed with grace of movement, he struck most observers as shorter than 5 foot, 6 inches, and this impression remained as obesity overtook him later on. Even more striking was his large round head, bald by the middle years and framed by thick sideburns of sandy red and gray hair. Giving further feature to his countenance were big blue penetrating eyes and the ever-present trace of a smile, suggesting benign contentment to some and calculating guile to others. It was the face of a man who might be expected, as one contemporary observed, "to row to his object with muffled oars." Others found in it an explanation for his "noncommittalism," that is, his knack of drawing out the views of others without revealing his own. Van Buren often chuckled at this charge and included one outrageous example of it in his autobiography. When asked if he thought the sun rose in the east, he replied, "I presumed the fact was according to the common impression, but, as I invariably slept until after sun-rise, I could not speak from my own knowledge."

Political success for Van Buren ultimately depended on the power of party. By the first quarter of the nineteenth century, two developments—the triumph of egalitarian ideals and the extension of suffrage to all adult white males—rendered increasingly obsolete older patterns of deference and rule by patrician elites. Permanent party organization and techniques of mass appeal were a response to the new democratic realities, providing a means for mobilizing voters, defining issues, and choosing officials. Politics became a profession and "new men" of politics embraced the opportunity to participate in the governing process. As one of the new men, Van Buren played a central role in party organization. During the decade after the War of 1812, he and close associates forged a disciplined party based on spoils, the secret caucus, and an ethos of absolute loyalty to majority rule. With this organization, soon to be known as the Albany Regency, they were able to challenge their patrician adversary, DeWitt Clinton, and lay a solid base for controlling the state. Claiming lineal descent from Jefferson, they also embraced the old republican ideology.

Elected to the United States Senate in 1821, Van Buren went to Washington, D.C., with the aim of reviving party competition at the national level. The demise of the Federalist Party after the War of 1812 ushered in the so-called Era of Good Feelings, hailed by many as a return to the normal state of affairs. Van Buren, however, saw it as an era of bad feelings: The breakdown of party competition across state and sectional lines fragmented political conflict, led to the Missouri controversy, and assured the election of neo-Federalist, John Quincy Adams, in the disputed presidential contest of 1824. He thus sought to resuscitate the old party alliance of Southern planters and the plain republicans of the North on which Jefferson had built the old Republican Party. As a spokesperson for states' rights and strict construction, Van Buren warned of the consolidationist tendencies in the policies Adams proposed. Meanwhile, he took a leading role in the coalition behind Andrew Jackson to foil the bid of Adams for reelection. He was especially anxious to harness Jackson's enormous popularity for party purposes and to make the election of 1828 a rerun of earlier contests between Federalists and Republicans. Van Buren also ran for governor of New York in 1828 to help the national ticket, and the favorable returns confirmed the wisdom of this move.

After a tenure of three months as governor, Van Buren resigned the post in Albany and returned to Washington, D.C., in early 1829 to join the Jackson administration. There he served in turn as secretary of state, minister to England, and vice president in the second term. As a diplomat he succeeded in opening trade with the British West Indies and in in-

An 1837 cartoon lampoons Van Buren's indecisiveness about his Treasury policy and the influence of former president Andrew Jackson. *(Library of Congress)*

itiating the negotiations that led to French payment of past claims. In domestic affairs, Van Buren exerted little influence over specific policies other than Jackson's opposition to internal improvements. His greatest influence came in the role as confidant to the president, as political interpreter of events, and, most of all, through his efforts to shape Jackson's perception of the presidency in party terms. All earlier presidents, however political and partisan, had clung to the old ideal of the president above party, but starting with Jackson the president began to see himself as the leader of a party as well as the leader of the nation. In the midst of the tumultuous Bank War, out of which the Whig opposition finally formed, Van Buren summarized for Jackson the statesmanship of a politics of conflict. "Their hatred is the best evidence of your orthodoxy," he assured the

president, "and the highest compliment that can be paid to your patriotism." Van Buren saw that party competition was both the inescapable product of a free society and the best means to keep it free.

The great influence Van Buren enjoyed in Jackson's administration predictably inspired opponents to charge that the little magician was at it again. How else, they asked, could a suave New York "politician" gain favor with the "border captain" except by management and intrigue? It was true that Van Buren was not unversed in the arts of flattery; solicitude for Jackson in their private correspondence was matched in public statements with praise for the old hero's virtues. Yet there was something in the relationship that did credit to both men. For all his prudence and caution, Van Buren at times expressed genuine admiration for Jackson's boldness and unflinching courage, his intuitive sense of public opinion, and his ability to command the trust of the people. Jackson also derived great benefit from the relationship. With sensitivity and good taste, Van Buren served as friend and comforter to an often ill and lonely old man. Jackson also depended on his counsel in assessing political situations. While Van Buren was in England, Jackson complained that one adviser could never say no and another "knows nothing of mankind." Most of all, Van Buren was loyal, supporting Jackson's decisions once made with "immovable constancy." Though he initially opposed the Bank War, he assured Jackson in the midst of the battle that "I go with you agt. the world." If this sounded like shameless sycophancy, it expressed even more clearly a political ethic of subordinating private judgment to the will of the party. Even before the political fireworks in Washington, D.C., brought about the fall of John C. Calhoun, whom many took to be the heir apparent, Jackson had privately confided to a friend that Van Buren was worthy of the succession.

The Jackson Succession

With Jackson's support Van Buren was chosen by the Democratic Party convention in 1832 to be the vice presidential running mate, and four years later he was nominated to succeed Jackson as president. While thus treading in Jackson's steps, he was also following some of his own, for he had done much to shape the party that chose him. A number of political circumstances in 1836 also indicated that he would need to take other steps on his own. Many elements contributed to a pervasive sense of restlessness in the nation. The arising incidence of mob action was directly linked by the Whigs to the Caesarian personality of Jackson and his stormy policies. At the same time a new and strident voice of abolitionism arose in the North. Among other things its petitions to Congress and the distribution of

"inflammatory" propaganda through the mails brought tensions in the South to a new level. One response was the storming of the Charleston post office by a mob; another and more fateful one was the emergence of the argument for slavery as a positive good.

The movement of economic forces enhanced the sense of restlessness and lent new urgency to political debate. A cycle of economic expansion after 1830 mounted to a speculative boom by 1835 and then by the middle of the following year, began to give way to the opposing forces of contraction. Whigs pointed a finger at Jackson's war on the national bank which, in their view, had exerted a stabilizing influence over the state banks and the currency. More serious for Van Buren was a division within his own party over banking and currency. Senator Thomas Hart Benton spoke for the "hard-money" Democrats who blamed the economic fluctuations on the state banks, a number of which were being used by the Treasury as depositories. He believed that a greatly enlarged circulation of specie would serve to keep bank paper in check and stabilize the economy. Other Democrats, soon to be called Conservatives, defended the state banks, believing that if properly managed by the Treasury they could at once stabilize the currency and sustain a desirable level of economic growth. Personal ambition gave an added dimension to these intraparty differences. Senator William C. Rives of Virginia, one of the leading Conservatives, felt bitter because he had been passed over for the vice presidential nomination, which went instead to a Western hero of sorts, Colonel Richard M. Johnson of Kentucky, the reputed slayer of the American Indian chief Tecumseh.

Whig strategy in 1836 exploited Van Buren's problems. Instead of uniting behind one candidate, Whigs supported three in the hope that the sectional appeal of each—Senator Hugh Lawson White of Tennessee, General William Henry Harrison of Ohio, and Senator Daniel

Webster of Massachusetts—might keep Van Buren from winning an electoral majority and thereby throw the choice of president into the House of Representatives. Making a virtue of their diversity, moreover, Whigs invoked old antiparty ideals for the purpose of condemning Van Buren as a spoilsman politician and the handpicked puppet of Caesar. Finally, they spoke a various language in different parts of the country. In the South, they pictured Van Buren as a covert abolitionist; in the West, as a foppish sycophant in contrast to Harrison, who had defeated the Indians at Tippecanoe; and in the Northeast, as a proslavery champion and a "Loco Foco," that is, a hard-money man scheming to wreck banking and commerce. Happily for Van Buren, his 170 electoral votes, compared with 124 votes for all of his foes, foiled the Whig strategy.

Van Buren as President: A Call for National Repose

Van Buren entered the White House in 1837 determined to give the nation a breathing spell or, as one adviser put it, to "let the troubled waters subside." To the surprise of many, who considered him the prince of spoilsmen, he made no outright removals from office. If sensitive to the spoilsman charge, he also feared that the competition for jobs might deepen intraparty divisions. He likewise decided to retain Jackson's cabinet which, in any case, he had played a large role in selecting. For the one vacancy, secretary of the War Department, he turned first to Senator Rives, hoping by the appointment to reassure the South and mollify the senator's disappointment. When Rives refused the appointment, Van Buren gave it to Joel R. Poinsett, a Unionist leader in South Carolina during the nullification crisis.

Van Buren's inaugural address can also be read as a call for national repose. Fifty years after the Constitution was written, he observed, the "great experiment" had proved a success. Most of the dangers that the Founding Fathers feared might wreck the Union had been overcome; now it remained only for the sons to "perpetuate a condition of things so singularly happy." The heroic Fathers had won freedom on the battlefield, ordered it by "inestimable institutions," and left to later generations the task of preservation. To dramatize the unheroic role of preservation remaining to the sons, Van Buren pictured himself as a lesser figure of a later age and invited others to share his reverence for the illustrious predecessors "whose superiors it is our happiness to believe are not found on the executive calendar of any country." If seen as a bow to the conventional pieties of the day, his self-deprecating position must also be taken as a statesmanlike effort to assess the point at which the nation had arrived.

In this light, he saw only one great danger that remained, namely, the disorganizing effect of abolitionist agitation. Addressing the danger, he reaffirmed a campaign pledge to veto any measure of Congress touching slavery in the District of Columbia. John Quincy Adams, back in the House after his term as president, called Van Buren a "northern man with southern feelings." Van Buren, however, saw himself as a Northern man with national feelings, driven by the conviction that the federative Union fashioned in a spirit of concession and that compromise was the highest good.

Maintaining sectional harmony was one of the important achievements of Van Buren's presidency. As the leader of a party, he worked for an accommodation between its Northern and Southern members, and the course he charted while vice president continued after he entered the White House. On the one side, he enlisted the support of Northern Democrats against abolitionism. In concert with leaders in New York, he orchestrated protest meetings condemning the new wave of antislavery agitation. While presiding over the Senate, he cast the deciding vote for Calhoun's bill giving postmasters discretionary power in handling "inflammatory" materials. Behind the scenes in the Capitol, he also supported the so-called gag rule, a procedural rule in the House by which abolitionist petitions would be admitted into the chamber but then tabled.

On the other side, Van Buren persuaded party spokespeople from the South to yield for the time their desire for the annexation of slaveholding Texas. Poinsett, a former minister to Mexico, and Secretary of State John Forsyth of Georgia were among those strongly in favor of Texas, but as good party men they recognized the volatility of the issue in the North and the need to harmonize party councils. When the Texas minister formally requested annexation in August of 1837, Secretary Forsyth served as Van Buren's polite but firm voice against it.

Foreign Affairs
Van Buren's efforts for sectional harmony were matched by his efforts for peace with foreign countries. The bad state of relations with Mexico at the end of Jackson's term required immediate attention. Bent on the annexation of Texas, Jackson had mounted pressures on Mexico to pay old claims, threatening reprisals and delivering a final ultimatum from a naval vessel. Van Buren reversed these priorities, dropped the idea of annexation, and sought peace with Mexico. The response of Mexico to his first effort at negotiation in 1837 was not acceptable, but he quickly agreed to a counterproposal made in April, 1838, for submitting the claims issue to an arbitration commission. The president went an extra mile with Mexico, moreover, patiently indulging delays that held up the formation of a commission until August, 1840. The final award of $2 million to the United States came after he left the White House, but peace was for him of greater value.

Two crises with Britain posed a greater threat to peace. One rose out of the rebellion in Canada, which began in the lower provinces and spread by the end of 1837 to the upper part. Sympathy for the rebels among Americans along the border led many to send aid

and others to enlist for action. In this context the *Caroline* affair in late December seemed to make war imminent. The *Caroline*, a small craft supplying rebels out of Buffalo, was seized by British forces on the American side of the Niagara River and sunk with the loss of one life. Yet the drums of war in western New York sounded much fainter in Washington, D.C., where two quick decisions by President Van Buren signaled a peaceful intent. He filed a formal demand for explanations from the British minister, Henry Fox, but indicated a willingness to wait for the response from the home government. He then issued a proclamation, warning Americans that any violations of neutrality would forfeit their right to protection by the government.

A second flare-up came in October, 1838, when Americans joined the rebel invasion of Canada in the Detroit area and at Prescott on Lake Ontario. Strong British forces easily repelled the attacks, in the process of which more than two score of Americans were killed and a larger number captured. News of the defeat cooled enthusiasm for the rebels, as did a second and more strongly worded proclamation from the president in November. By the following year, the promise to Canada of more self-government contained in Lord Durham's report substantially ended the rebellion. Van Buren never received an apology for the *Caroline* incident from the British, but the blessings of peace disposed him, as one close acquaintance observed, to "let sleeping dogs lie."

A second and more serious crisis arose in early 1839 over the disputed Maine-New Brunswick boundary. Possessing little geographical knowledge of the area, the treaty makers at Paris in 1783 probably expected the boundary to be fixed by later negotiation. From the 1790's through the Jackson administration, however, a number of efforts brought agreement on only one thing—that the lower part of the St. John, a river that flowed in a southeast direction from the St. Lawrence highlands to the Bay of Fundy, belonged to New Brunswick. With regard to the upper St. John, profound differences emerged. Americans claimed it all—the main Aroostook tributary on the south side closest to the Maine settlements and the Madawaska tributary farther up the St. John on the north side. For diplomatic reasons Britain also claimed it all, but Britain's primary concern was the Madawaska, the control of which was vital for an overland military road from the Bay of Fundy to Quebec during the winter when the St. Lawrence was frozen. Complicating the prospects of compromise was the political situation in Maine, where each party sought to outmatch the other in opposition to any concessions to the British. By the time Van Buren became president, incidents on both sides had raised tensions to a new level. The presence of Maine census takers in the Madawaska alarmed New Brunswick, and timber poachers from New Brunswick in the Aroostook area threatened one of Maine's vital interests.

The crisis came to a head in February, 1839. Without prior consultation with the president, Governor John Fairfield ordered the Maine militia northward to the Aroostook; in response, British forces at the Madawaska went on the alert. Van Buren moved quickly and evenhandedly to regain control of the nation's relations with Britain. While calling on Congress for added means to defend the nation, he sternly warned Maine that the central government would assume no responsibility for the aggressive actions of the state militia. He then worked out the essentials of a truce with the British minister in Washington to keep the peace until the home governments reached a final settlement of the boundary. By its terms, the Madawaska would be considered in the New Brunswick "sphere of influence," while Maine retained control over the Aroostook. To secure the truce Van Buren then sent General Winfield Scott to the troubled area and by the end of March, Scott was able to announce that the

governors of Maine and New Brunswick had agreed to the truce. Van Buren thus achieved his goal of "peace with honor." He also paved the way for a final settlement three years later: The terms of his truce defined the basic boundary provisions of the Webster-Ashburton Treaty.

The Indian Question

The question of peace or war was also involved in another matter of concern—the removal of the Southern Indian tribes to Oklahoma. In 1830, Jackson had pushed enabling legislation through Congress for that purpose, and by the end of his term all the tribes had moved or were in motion, except the Cherokees and the Seminoles. The Cherokees were the larger tribe, numbering from fifteen to twenty thousand and scattered over the states of North Carolina, Georgia, Alabama, and Tennessee. Under the Treaty of New Echota, made in December, 1835, they were to move the following year, but the repudiation of the treaty by many of the chiefs was among the reasons for delay. With a new deadline fixed for May, 1838, Van Buren called on General Scott to supervise the removal. Using some regular army units and a larger number of state militia, he began the process of rounding up the Cherokees from their scattered villages and directing them to three staging areas on the upper Tennessee River. Low water caused by a summer dry spell held up the process until fall, at which time the Cherokees began the long and painful journey over the "Trail of Tears." Van Buren had more personal doubts about removal than Jackson, yet he accepted it as a commitment that had to be honored. Given the anguish and suffering involved, the removal was a relatively peaceful and orderly process for which Scott won Van Buren's praise.

The Seminoles of Florida posed a far different problem. Along with other reasons for resisting removal was the presence of hundreds of blacks, many of them runaways from Georgia and Alabama plantations. Their language skills and knowledge of farming gave them added influence with their hosts, and they used this influence in opposing the government's policy, fearing that the removal of the Seminoles would leave them behind for reenslavement. Tensions, mounting as the December, 1835, deadline neared, finally erupted in violence with the ambush of more than one hundred United States troops in the Tampa area. With an occasional truce the war dragged on for seven years. Difficult terrain, a wretched climate, and the scattering of the Seminoles made it a "dirty war," marked by search-and-destroy missions, treachery, and truce violations on both sides. One of the most publicized instances was the capture of Chief Osceola under a flag of truce. George Catlin's sympathetic portrait of him languishing in prison surely expressed the ambivalent feelings of many at the time.

The back of the war was broken under General Philip Jesup during the first two years of Van Buren's term. His strategy was to detach the blacks and to stage the Seminoles at Tampa Bay for removal by way of New Orleans. An undetermined number of blacks did fall into the hands of slaveholders, but as many as four hundred accompanied the Seminoles to Oklahoma. Key statistics summarize what Van Buren's last annual message regarded as a sad and distressing affair: In removing 3,500 to 4,000 Indians, the United States suffered 1,500 casualties and expended upward of $30 million in treasure.

The Panic of 1837

Meanwhile, the livelihood of all Americans was being affected by two basic economic events in the Van Buren presidency—the panic of 1837 and, after a brief recovery, the severer downturn two years later. Several forces contributed to a cycle of expansion after 1830 and then a countermovement of contraction. One was the rapid growth of banks—from 330 to 788—and the loose practices many of them followed. In

earlier days, banks had extended credit mainly in the form of discounts on short-term commercial paper, and this fairly liquid asset, along with adequate specie held in their vaults, had secured the notes they put in circulation. The spirit of enterprise, however, and a growing hunger for capital began to pressure even sounder banks to make long-term loans and keep less specie in their vaults. A second force at work after 1830 was an inflow of English credit, much of it used for bank capital in the Southwest and elsewhere for state projects of internal improvement. Although supporting new economic growth, this credit also exerted a specifically inflationary effect on the currency. By paying for the excess of imports over exports, it kept specie from flowing abroad and thus removed a powerful check on the banks. Another inflationary force was a surplus in the Treasury, which began to mount rapidly with the retirement of the national debt. Placed on deposit in selected state banks after Jackson cut the Treasury's ties with the national bank, these funds provided the basis for further loans. In a circular fashion, finally, a mania of speculation greatly increased government land sales and added to the surplus.

The power of English credit to stimulate economic expansion was also the power to take away. In the third quarter of 1836, the Bank of England raised the interest rate to strengthen its own specie reserves. The resulting curtailment of credit to Americans ended the pattern of the preceding years and caused specie to start flowing out of the country. Eastern banks were affected first, and two actions by the government increased the pressures on them. One was the specie circular, an order from the Treasury requiring that after December, 1836, only specie would be received in payment for government lands. It had the effect of keeping specie in the West against the otherwise natural tendency of specie to flow eastward into the channels of trade. At the same time, an act of Congress ordered the Treasury to distribute its mounting surplus among the state governments. This meant that considerable sums would have to be withdrawn from the big Eastern deposit banks, particularly those in the New York area, where about two-thirds of the nation's import duties were collected. Under this pressure, the Eastern banks greatly curtailed their loans and thereby created severe money pressures in the mercantile community.

Political foes placed all the blame on the specie circular and called on the new president to rescind Jackson's order. Politically, however, Van Buren did not feel free to undo the pet measure of his predecessor. He believed, moreover, that specie in the West helped to shore up the deposit banks there. It was probably too late, in any case, to check the forces of contraction that led New York banks on May 10, 1837, to suspend, that is, to cease paying specie on demand to their depositors and the holders of their notes. Within a week, almost all other banks across the country followed the New York example.

Suspension put the federal government in a difficult position. By law, the Treasury could pay and receive only in specie or the notes of specie-paying banks, and it could deposit its funds only in such banks. Except for a small amount of specie at the Mint, however, the only funds available to the Treasury were the notes of the suspended deposit banks. Nor was much specie likely to flow into the Treasury very soon, for many import merchants were already behind in paying their duty bonds. Faced with these problems, President Van Buren called for the new Twenty-fifth Congress to meet in special session on September 4, 1837. When it assembled, Congress quickly passed a number of relief measures proposed by the president. The banks and import merchants were given additional time to make good on their obligations; the further distribution of the surplus revenue was postponed; and an issue of $10 million in Treasury notes was authorized. Used to pay creditors of the government and made receivable at par for import

"Bank-oh's! Ghost": The panic of 1837 recast by a political cartoonist as a new *Macbeth*. *(Library of Congress)*

duties, these notes entered quickly into circulation.

Beyond the measures for immediate relief, Van Buren set before the special session, as his basic response to suspension, the proposal to divorce the Treasury from the state banks. He therefore asked Congress to provide permanent facilities for the Treasury to keep and disburse its own funds, and to make the divorce a total one, he further proposed that the Treasury receive and pay only in specie and not in bank notes. The idea of divorce was considered at the time Jackson withdrew government funds from the national bank, but it was rejected as too radical a departure from previous practice. The panic of 1837 created a new political situation, however, and made divorce the next logical step for Van Buren and his party to take. Only by divorce, Democrats now argued, could the funds of the government be made safe and secure. Whigs answered this part of the new debate with their old cry of Caesarism, warning that an independent Treasury would in fact become a giant government bank which, by uniting purse and sword, would give tyrannical power to the executive.

Of far greater importance in the debate over the divorce proposal, however, was the impact it was expected to have on the currency. All agreed that divorce would be deflationary, but differences arose over the extent and desirability of this effect. Clearly, the funds held by the Treasury would not be available to banks for new loans and discounts. The steady demand for specie to pay government dues would be another constraint. The added specie put in circulation by Treasury disbursements also meant less specie in bank vaults to serve, by some multiple, as the basis for further note issues. In a less tangible way as well, the refusal of the Treasury to receive bank notes took away the credit the government could bestow on them. In sanguine moments, radical hard-money Democrats professed to believe that the withdrawal of government credit from the credit system of banking would wreck it and create at last an exclusively metallic currency. Moderates such as Van Buren hoped that a larger amount of specie in circulation could stabilize the currency.

Opponents of the divorce proposal in the special session invoked the spirit of enterprise and put themselves forward as the champions of the credit system. Exaggerating the deflationary effect of divorce, they damned the president for making war on the banks and leading the nation backward, as one put it, to a primitive economy of "Dorian purity, iron money, and black broth." Unique circumstances and not any basic flaw, according to Senator Rives, had temporarily thrown the state banks "out of gear." Although most Whigs privately favored a national bank, they publicly lent support to Rives and other Conservative Democrats on behalf of renewing the connection of the Treasury with the state banks. In mock fashion, Daniel Webster exclaimed that Van Buren's proposal made him feel as if he were on another planet. For him, the power and the interests of the government should be mingled in a benign and nurturing way with the interests of its citizens, particularly on behalf of a well-regulated paper currency. In like fashion, Henry Clay saw Americans as a "paper money people" and a mildly inflationary currency under government patronage as the basic need for economic recovery and growth.

Politically, the divorce issue served to give greater coherence to party lines and to mature what has come to be called the "second party system." During the Bank War in 1834, Jackson's assorted foes—including John C. Calhoun's Nullifiers and Clay's Nationals—came together under the new Whig banner on a platform condemning Jackson as a Caesar. Three years later, an important realignment took place as Calhoun left his Whig allies to support the divorce proposal and many Conservatives, led by Rives and Senator Nathaniel P. Tallmadge of New York, broke with Van Buren and moved toward the Whigs. The combined vote of Conservatives and Whigs defeated the divorce proposal at the special session and held firm against his renewed efforts in the two regular sessions of the Twenty-fifth Congress.

Van Buren nevertheless persisted in his course. The trait of "Dutch stubbornness" some saw in him was rather, a close associate felt, his "firmness of principle." It reflected, in any case, his concept of the presidency as based on party. He took the divorce proposal to be an irreversible commitment of his party, one that was consistent with its past experience and contributed to its evolving creed. If a politician by trade, he was also an ideologue of party, keenly aware that adherence to basic principles gave direction and corporate identity to his party which, he profoundly believed, spoke the voice of the nation. Having helped to place Jackson's presidency on a party basis, he was resolved to govern the same way. Private convictions about banking and currency also reinforced this sense of party need. Actions taken during his earlier career had consistently come down on the side of restraint: As a state senator for eight years, he voted for only one new bank charter; as governor, he signed into law a measure setting up a safety fund for New York banks and creating a state regulatory commission. The resumption of the state banks by summer, 1838, also strengthened Van Buren's will to persevere. Encouragement from Washington, D.C., and pledges of financial backing in New York contributed to resumption, but the basic cause was recovery in England and a new flow of credit to the United States.

The Independent Treasury: A Second Declaration of Independence

Paradoxically, however, a new round of bank suspensions by the last quarter of 1839 paved the way for passage of Van Buren's central domestic measure, the independent Treasury. With a second and far more austere policy of retrenchment in England, the flow of credit to the United States virtually ceased. On October 9, the old national bank, under a Pennsylvania charter since 1836, suspended specie payment, and before long almost all other banks to the west and south of Philadelphia took the same action. The new suspension, unlike that in 1837, was followed not by a quick recovery but by a profound economic downturn that lasted for four years.

In his message to the new Twenty-sixth Congress in December, 1839, the president renewed his proposal for divorce and skillfully linked it to recent events. The second suspension clearly strengthened his claim that the funds of the government could only be safe if held as specie in the Treasury's own vaults. On the currency side of divorce, he argued that the inherent fluctuations of bank note issues were greatly aggravated by the ebb and flow of English credit. Indeed, the "chain of dependence" forged by that credit ultimately tended to place the freedom and fortunes of the nation in the power of its ancient enemy. With "Spartan firmness," as one admirer noted, Van Buren advised the nation to pay off its old debts and incur no new ones. Freed from the artificial way in which English credit maintained an imbalance of imports over exports, the nation would be compelled to buy no more than it sold and to make up any yearly imbalance by the export or import of specie. As a complement to the policy of divorce, foreign trade in real goods for real money would exert a salutary and steady check on banks in the United States. These views clearly embodied Van Buren's more general belief that a laissez-faire posture for the government would allow the natural forces of economic equilibrium to work for enterprise at a sound and sober pace. Beyond present distress he looked to a future relatively free of violent fluctuations.

Democrats in Congress applauded Van Buren's message and supplemented its force with debate over two related matters. The first was

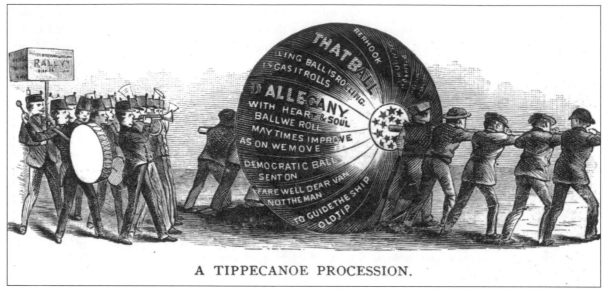

A TIPPECANOE PROCESSION.

The 1840 election featured the first campaigning for the presidency by a candidate, William Henry Harrison ("Old Tippecanoe"). *(Library of Congress)*

a proposal for a federal bankruptcy act that would set up machinery for closing any state bank that suspended specie payments. Strong opposition never allowed the measure to come to a vote, but it did reveal the desire to secure a sound bank currency. Democrats succeeded in a second matter, that of defeating the call of the Whigs for the federal government to assume the debts that the states owed to England. Communications from London bankers suggested that a pledge of the federal revenues to pay old debts might soon induce the flow of new English credits to the United States. This, however, was precisely what Democrats did not want, namely, to be linked in the chain of dependence once more. Although Whigs were reconciled to the passage of the independent Treasury bill, their delay tactics in the House held up the final vote until the end of June, 1840. Because of the timing, President Van Buren waited until July 4 to sign the bill, and the party paper in Washington hailed it as the "Second Declaration of Independence."

Unhappily for Van Buren, the second declaration of independence did not assure him a second term in the White House. Deepening

depression by summer, 1840, made even more appealing Whig praises for the credit system and the Whigs' promise of increasing the currency. Support in Congress for an insolvency law, in place of the Democrats' bankruptcy bill, also identified Whigs with the spirit of enterprise. By this means a debtor would be able to initiate action with his creditor and gain freedom to start over again. Clearly, the Whig view of government as a benign means for bringing recovery and economic growth contrasted with what they called the Spartan counsels of Van Buren. With cries of "Van, Van, a used up man" and "Martin Van Ruin," they pointed to a central issue in the presidential campaign of 1840.

The Campaign of 1840: "Tippecanoe and Tyler Too"

Enhancing the force of Whig economic views were a new sense of party unity, a popular candidate, and effective appeals to the voters by a "log cabin" campaign. Whig antiparty ideals and three separate candidates in 1836 gave way to a united convention that passed over Clay and Webster in favor of General William Henry Harrison, the hero of Tippecanoe, and John Tyler of Virginia. Although Tyler was not chosen as running mate for euphonious reasons, his name did lend itself nicely to the slogan "Tippecanoe and Tyler Too." Taking shameless liberties with the truth, Whig campaigners pictured Harrison, scion of an old Virginia family, as a simple farmer at North Bend living in a log cabin with the latchstring always out. Van Buren, by contrast, was presented as a foppish dandy luxuriating in the aristocratic trappings of the White House, sipping French wine, eating from golden spoons, and preening like a peacock before mirrors larger than barn doors. Van Buren became so enraged by the exposure of his lifestyle, one editor mischievously observed, that he "actually burst his corset!"

Harrison struck another democratic note by becoming the first candidate ever to campaign openly for the presidency. His presence often sparked a final element of frenzy generated at mass rallies by torchlight parades, the raising of a log cabin, and group singing in the mode of Methodist revivals. Democrats unctuously deplored the humbuggery of it all, forgetting the hickory poles and other devices used earlier on Jackson's behalf. The second party system had clearly come of age. In a moment of exasperated candor, one Democratic editor exclaimed, "We have taught them how to conquer us!"

Conforming to the practice of past presidents, Van Buren took no active role in the campaign. Occasional letters in response to inquiries indicated his willingness to stand on his record and party principles, but by September, he later wrote, he had resigned himself to defeat when he realized that the Whigs would leave no expedient untried in their determination to win. On the face of the returns, he suffered an overwhelming defeat: He won 60 electoral votes from seven states, while Harrison received 234 electoral votes from the remaining nineteen states. Some consolation doubtless

came with the knowledge that he received 400,000 more popular votes than in 1836 and that a shift of about 8,000 votes in four large states would have brought him a majority in the electoral college. At last, however, he suffered the fate of most incumbents in time of economic downturn, and the pattern of the vote points to the crucial issue of currency in the campaign. The seven states that supported Van Buren—Missouri, Illinois, New Hampshire, Virginia, South Carolina, Alabama, and Arkansas—were less integrated into the market economy, and they were less imbued with the spirit of enterprise than the other states.

Van Buren accepted defeat in a spirit of good sportsmanship that had always characterized his political career. Visitors at the White House found nothing in his cheerful demeanor to suggest that he was about to relinquish the highest office in the land. When Harrison came to Washington, D.C., in early 1841, Van Buren paid a social call at his hotel, invited him to the White House as guest of honor, and even offered to vacate the executive mansion so Harrison could move in early. Had he been invited, he would also have attended Harrison's inaugural ceremonies; only later did it become the custom for the outgoing president of a different party to attend the inauguration of his successor. In any event, Van Buren did not see defeat as fatal either to himself or to his party. Profoundly convinced that there could be only one genuinely popular party, he expected the "sober second thought" of the people to see through the delusions of the log cabin campaign and restore Democrats to their rightful place.

The Achievements of Van Buren's Presidency

Informed with this belief, Van Buren's last message to Congress proudly summarized the achievements of his presidency and reaffirmed its principles. The nation remained at peace and enjoyed relatively secure frontiers. Here, it might be added, Van Buren had resisted the Machiavellian advice of some who would have him divert attention from ills at home by precipitating war abroad. The past obligations of the government had also been met, including the difficult and costly task of Indian removal. In spite of a "formidable" political opposition and "pecuniary embarrassments," moreover, he had met these obligations without incurring a new debt or raising taxes. Silence on slavery, the only specific issue raised in his inaugural, likewise spoke of success in maintaining sectional harmony. Although recognizing that individuals had experienced derangement in their economic pursuits, he believed that the independent Treasury would contribute to a sound recovery and to stable enterprise. In larger perspective his policy of divorce completed the work of Jackson's presidency in bringing government back to its simple republican tack. As if looking to future elections, finally, he warned that vigilance would be required to preserve these principles: "The choice is an important one, and I sincerely hope that it will be made wisely."

The sequel of events provides a final perspective for assessing Van Buren's presidency. Opposition to the annexation of Texas in 1844 denied Van Buren a third nomination for president by his party. It went instead to James K. Polk on a platform of territorial expansion to the Pacific. War with Mexico in the wake of Texas annexation realized this "manifest destiny," but it also opened in fateful form the sectional controversy over slavery expansion. By the mid-1850's the deepening debate sundered the second party system Van Buren had helped to shape and had used so well to contain sectional tensions, and by the time of his death on July 24, 1862, the sectional conflict had become a civil war that was to transform the federative Union he wanted to save into a consolidated nation. His independent Treasury lasted longer, remaining in operation until the Federal Reserve System was established. Recurring booms and panics in the last half of the nineteenth century belied his hopes that it would bring stability to enterprise. There is no reason to believe, however, that a national bank would have served much better at taming the spirit of enterprise in a rapidly expanding economy. Van Buren began his presidency with the hope of bringing repose to the nation; relative success in achieving this goal constituted a modest but real act of statesmanship.

Major L. Wilson

Bibliographical References

Three older biographies are still useful for examining Van Buren's earlier career: Edward M. Shepard, *Martin Van Buren*, 1889; Denis T. Lynch, *An Epoch and a Man: Martin Van Buren and His Times*, 1929; Holmes Alexander, *The American Talleyrand*, 1935. Two later biographies—John Niven, *Martin Van Buren: The Romantic Age of American Politics*, 1983, and Donald B. Coles, *Martin Van Buren and the American Political System*, 1984—are more complete and evenhanded. For an examination of the importance of Van Buren's law career to his later political success, see Jerome Mushkat and Joseph G. Rayback, *Martin Van Buren: Law, Politics, and the Shaping of Republican Ideology*, 1997. Further perspective on his great contribution to party development can be found in Robert V. Remini, *Martin Van Buren and the Making of the Democratic Party*, 1951, and Richard Hofstadter, *The Idea of a Party System*, 1969. Two volumes devoted primarily to the presidential years are James C. Curtis, *The Fox at Bay: Martin Van Buren and the Presidency, 1837-1841*, 1973, and Major L. Wilson, *The Presidency of Martin Van Buren*, 1984. All direct quotations in this entry are drawn from the latter work. The interested reader will also want to consult Martin Van Buren, *Inquiry into the Origin and Course of Political Parties in the United States*, 1867, and *The Autobiography of Martin Van Buren*, 1920.

William Henry Harrison

9th President, 1841

Born: February 9, 1773
near Charles City, Virginia
Died: April 4, 1841
Washington, D.C.

Political Party: Whig
Vice President: John Tyler

Cabinet Members

Secretary of State: Daniel Webster
Secretary of the Treasury: Thomas Ewing
Secretary of War: John Bell
Secretary of the Navy: George E. Badger
Attorney General: John J. Crittenden
Postmaster General: Francis Granger

Indian Fighter, Legislator, Diplomat

In 1791, Harrison entered the army serving in the campaigns against American Indians in the

William Henry Harrison was the oldest man to serve in the presidency until the inauguration of Ronald Reagan in 1981. Sixty-eight years old at the time of his inauguration, in 1841, Harrison served only one month before he died from pneumonia. His early death made Harrison's presidency the shortest in the history of the United States and provided the final irony in a life full of color and controversy.

The son of a signer of the Declaration of Independence, Harrison was born in 1773 at his family's famous Berkeley Plantation in Virginia. He attended Hampden-Sydney College, and briefly undertook the study of medicine under the noted physician Benjamin Rush.

Harrison's official portrait. *(White House Historical Society)*

TECUMSEH

(Library of Congress)

of Indian lands, however, and in 1809, he negotiated a treaty with Indian leaders that transferred some 2.9 million acres in the vicinity of the White and Wabash rivers to the United States. This cession exacerbated the tensions between Indians and white men in the Northwest and triggered the activities on which Harrison's fame and later career were founded.

Given the uneasy relationship between the United States and Great Britain, many Americans assumed that the "Indian troubles" of the interior were encouraged and fomented by the British. In reality, the growing hostility of the Western tribes was largely an indigenous reaction to the constant encroachments on their lands by white settlers. The Indians' frustrations were finally focused through the leadership of two Shawnee half brothers, the chief Tecumseh and a one-eyed medicine man called The Prophet. Tecumseh developed the concept of a great Indian confederation, arguing that American Indian lands were held in common by all the tribes and could not be bargained away without their unanimous consent. The Prophet promoted a puritanical religious philosophy, and as his following grew, religion and politics gradually merged.

Harrison developed a healthy respect for the brothers' abilities, and he hoped at first that they could be placated. Finally, however, in what must be considered an aggressive move, Harrison marched a force of about one thousand men north from his capital at Vincennes toward Indian lands in northwestern Indiana. On November 7, 1811, Harrison's encampment near an Indian settlement called Prophetstown, near the confluence of the Tippecanoe and Wabash rivers, suffered an early morning surprise attack. Tecumseh was in the South organizing the tribes of that area, so the Indians who attacked Harrison were led, or at least inspired, by The Prophet. Harrison's forces beat back the attackers and later burned the Indian settlement.

Northwest Territory and eventually becoming a lieutenant and aide-de-camp to the commander, General Anthony Wayne. With the conclusion of peace, he remained on garrison duty in the vicinity of Cincinnati. Harrison resigned from the army in 1798 and accepted an appointment as secretary of the Northwest Territory, from which he was elected first delegate to Congress in 1799. With the division of the Northwest Territory into the territories of Ohio and Indiana, Harrison was appointed governor of the Indiana Territory.

Harrison was given a nearly impossible mission: to win the friendship and trust of American Indians and to protect them from the rapaciousness of white settlers, yet to acquire for the government as much land as he could secure from the Western tribes. Apparently, Harrison had a genuine concern for the plight of American Indians, ordering a campaign of inoculation to protect them from the scourge of smallpox and banning the sale of liquor to them. He actively pursued the acquisition

Almost immediately, controversy arose concerning the particulars of the Battle of Tippecanoe and Harrison's performance. Were his troops prepared for the Indian attack? Why had they camped in a vulnerable position? Had Harrison or his companion officers actually commanded the defenses? Were Harrison's men outnumbered? What, in fact, was the size of the attacking Indian force? In the face of such critical questions, Harrison, who was not a paragon of modesty, and his supporters immediately began to construct the legend of a "Washington of the West" who represented the bravery and ambitions of Western Americans.

During the War of 1812 with Great Britain, Harrison served in several military positions and eventually became supreme commander of the Army of the Northwest. He broke the power of the British and the Indians in the Northwest and in southern Canada, with the culminating victory in early October, 1813, at the Battle of the Thames. Again controversy followed Harrison's military performance, although his reputation among the general public was apparently enhanced. In May, 1814, he resigned from the army and took up residence on a farm at North Bend, Ohio, on the bank of the Ohio River near Cincinnati.

At North Bend, Harrison engaged in farming and several unsuccessful commercial ventures, and the foundation for another aspect of his public image was established. Harrison's home at North Bend was a commodious dwelling of sixteen rooms, but it was built around the nucleus of a log cabin and became one of the misrepresented symbols of "Old Tip's" 1840 presidential campaign. In 1816, Harrison was elected to the United States House of Representatives, serving until 1819 with no real distinction. In 1825, he was elected to the United States Senate by the Ohio legislature. He became chair of the Military Affairs Committee but resigned in 1828 to accept an appointment as United States minister to Colombia. His career as a diplomat was not particularly suc-cessful, but when he was recalled after about a year by President Andrew Jackson it was largely for political reasons.

Following his return from Colombia, Harrison experienced a continuing series of financial and family misfortunes and supplemented his resources by serving as clerk of the Cincinnati Court of Common Pleas. He was observed at this time by a French traveler who described him as "a man of about medium height, stout and muscular, and of about the age of sixty years yet with the active step and lively air of youth." A visitor to the "log cabin," on the other hand, considered Harrison "a small and rather sallow-looking man, who does not exactly meet the associations that connect themselves with the name of general."

The Election of 1840: "Tippecanoe and Tyler Too"

During the height of Jacksonian democracy, many displayed a growing concern about the alleged pretensions of "King Andrew" Jackson, which contributed to the emergence of the Whig Party. Old National Republicans, former Anti-Masons, and various others who reacted strongly against the president or his policies began to work together, and in 1836 the Whigs made their first run for the presidency against Jackson's chosen successor, Martin Van Buren. William Henry Harrison ran as the candidate of Western Whigs, showed promise as a vote getter, and thus became a leading contender for the nomination in 1840.

By now widely known as "Old Tippecanoe," Harrison the military hero presented an obvious opportunity for the Whigs to borrow the tactics of the Democrats who had exploited "Old Hickory," Andrew Jackson, to great success. Harrison's position on key issues of the day—banking policy, internal improvements, the tariff, abolition—was almost irrelevant, for the old general was to be nominated as a symbol of military glory and the development of the West. The Whigs wanted a candidate who

A souvenir from the first modern presidential campaign. *(Smithsonian Institution)*

would appeal to a broad range of voters and who was not too closely identified with the issues of the Jacksonian era. They did not offer a real platform, only a pledge to "correct the abuses" of the current administration. If the campaign were successful, the real decisions in a Harrison administration would be made by Whig leaders in Congress.

Harrison's age and health became immediate issues in the campaign, and he traveled from Ohio to Virginia so that he could be seen and "counteract the opinion, which has been industriously circulated, that *I was an old broken-down feeble man*." One observer who met the candidate described him as "about 5 feet 9 inches in hight [*sic*], very slender and thin in flesh, with a noble and benignant expression—a penetrating eye, expansive forehead and Roman nose. He is not bald but gray, and walks about very quick, and seems to be as active as a man of 45." During a later trip that Harrison made through New Jersey, a news-

paper reported that "his appearance is that of a hale, hearty Ohio Farmer, of about fifty years of age."

The tone and lasting fame of the campaign were established during the battle for the nomination when a partisan of one of his Whig rivals suggested that Harrison should be allowed to enjoy his log cabin and hard cider in peace. An opposition party paper then picked up the idea and said, "Give him a barrel of hard cider and a pension of two thousand a year . . . he will sit the remainder of his days in a log cabin . . . and study moral philosophy." Whig strategists knew a good thing when they read it, and they created a winning campaign around the portrayal of Harrison as a man of the people, a wise yet simple hero whose log cabin and hard cider were highly preferable to the haughty attitude and trickery of "Old Kinderhook" Martin Van Buren. In the process, the Whigs waged the first modern presidential campaign as they sold souvenirs, published and widely distributed campaign materials, flooded the country with speakers, and employed songs, slogans, and verses, the most famous being their cry of "Tippecanoe and Tyler Too."

A One-Month Presidency and Its Lasting Consequences

Harrison's presidency was anticlimactic. He traveled to Washington, D.C., before his inauguration and was well received both by his former opponent, President Van Buren, and by members of Congress. His inaugural address was widely praised, even though it lasted more than two hours, but it had unexpected results. The day was cold and rainy, and the new president caught a cold, which continued to nag him. Harrison was besieged by people who wanted favors and offices, and he attempted to escape from this pressure by immersing himself in minor details. He visited various government offices to see if they were operating efficiently, and he even concerned himself with the routine matters of running and purchasing supplies for the White House. The development of a legislative program was left to Whig leaders in Congress, and settlement of the *Caroline* affair with Great Britain, growing out of American involvement in an abortive Canadian rebellion in 1837, the only major problem of his brief tenure, was entrusted to the hands of Secretary of State Daniel Webster.

On a cold March morning, the president ventured out to purchase vegetables for the White House. He suffered a chill, which aggravated the cold he had contracted on inauguration day. The cold developed into pneumonia, and on April 4, 1841, Harrison died in the White House. His body was returned to North Bend for burial. Old Tippecanoe had virtually no direct impact on the office of the presidency itself, yet the method of his election and the circumstances of his death were of lasting importance. The 1840 campaign had established a new style of presidential campaigning, and Harrison's death forced the nation for the first time to experience the elevation of a vice president to the Oval Office, an event that established a landmark constitutional precedent.

James E. Fickle

Bibliographical References

The major biographies of William Henry Harrison are Freeman Cleaves, *Old Tippecanoe: William Henry Harrison and His Times*, 1939, and Dorothy B. Goebel, *William Henry Harrison: A Political Biography*, 1926. Robert G. Gunderson, *The Log-Cabin Campaign*, 1957, is the major work describing the election of 1840. James A. Green, *William Henry Harrison, His Life and Times*, 1941, is a laudatory popular account. For a thorough examination of Harrison's presidency, see Norma L. Peterson, *The Presidencies of William Henry Harrison and John Tyler*, 1989, a single-volume study in the University Press of Kansas series on American presidents. Kenneth R. Stevens, *William Henry Harrison: A Bibliography*, 1998, provides a comprehensive listing of primary and secondary sources on the life and presidency of Harrison.

John Tyler

10th President, 1841-1845

Born: March 29, 1790
    Greenway, Charles City
    County, Virginia
Died: January 18, 1862
    Richmond, Virginia

Political Party: Whig
Vice President: none

Cabinet Members

Secretary of State: Daniel Webster, Hugh S. Legaré, Abel P. Upshur, John C. Calhoun

Secretary of the Treasury: Thomas Ewing, Walter Forward, John C. Spencer, George M. Bibb

Secretary of War: John Bell, John C. Spencer, James M. Porter, William Wilkins

Secretary of the Navy: George E. Badger, Abel P. Upshur, David Henshaw, Thomas Gilmer, John Y. Mason

Attorney General: John J. Crittenden, Hugh S. Legaré, John Nelson

Postmaster General: Francis Granger, Charles A. Wickliffe

John Tyler is one of the least-known yet most controversial presidents in American history. The first vice president to succeed to the presidency upon the death of a chief executive, Tyler established the precedent that in such circumstances the new president holds the office both in fact and in name. Public and political opinion about Tyler was badly divided in his own time, and later historians have continued to debate his motives, ability, and performance. President Theodore Roosevelt said, "Tyler has been called a mediocre man, but this is unwarranted flattery. He was a politician of monumental lit-

tleness." He is often portrayed as a stubborn, vain, and inconsistent leader who was one of the worst presidents. Other writers portray him as a president with strong principles and great integrity who remained true to his beliefs despite tremendous political pressure. They say that even though Tyler was the first president threatened with impeachment and the only one to be formally expelled from his own political party, he deserves recognition as a competent and courageous chief executive.

A Singular Political Course

Tyler was born March 29, 1790, in tidewater Virginia near Richmond, the son of a distinguished Virginian who served as governor, as speaker of the Virginia House of Delegates, and as a judge. His father was a strict constructionist Jeffersonian Republican. John absorbed and remained deeply imbued with this philosophy throughout his life. He was reared in an atmosphere of aristocratic privilege and refinement, becoming something of a stereotypical representative of the tidewater aristocracy in his beliefs and values.

Upon his graduation from the College of William and Mary, where he had been an excellent student with a growing interest in political theory and practice, Tyler at the age of seventeen began to read law under his father. He was admitted to the Virginia bar in 1809. At the age of twenty-one he was elected to the Virginia House of Delegates. After brief military service in the War of 1812, he returned to politics and was elected to the United States House of Representatives in 1816. As a congressman, Tyler stood for strict interpretation of the Constitution and limitation of the powers of the federal government. He resisted national internal improvements because they might extend the power of the federal government, and he opposed the first Bank of the United States for the same reason, as well as on constitutional and other grounds. He did not favor the slave trade, but he voted against the Missouri Compromise, believing that time and the social climate would eventually doom the "peculiar institution." Defeated in an election for the United States Senate at the age of thirty-one, Tyler served briefly as chancellor of William and Mary, and then as governor of Virginia. He was finally elected to the Senate in 1827 and began to achieve a degree of national prominence.

Remaining true to his constitutional principles, Tyler found himself in an ambiguous political situation. As a Republican, he supported William H. Crawford for the presidency in 1824 and was elected to the Senate as an anti-Jacksonian. He was repelled both by Old Hickory's authoritarianism and by the rising influence of Jacksonian democracy. Tyler was very cordial and effective when dealing with members of his own class, but common folk and their heroes made him un-

comfortable. "The barking of newspapers and the brawling of demagogues can never drive me from my course," said Tyler. "If I am to go into retirement, I will at least take care to do so with a pure and unsullied conscience." Nevertheless, in 1828 Tyler supported Jackson and agreed with his opposition to the rechartering of the Bank of the United States. Tyler's principles, however, led him to split with Jackson and the Democratic Party.

Although Tyler favored the positions the president took on certain key issues, he considered Jackson's methods unacceptable, particularly in the nullification crisis and in dealing with the bank. Nullification became an issue during Jackson's presidency because of the linkage of two developments affecting the South. First was the tariff. In 1828, Congress

Tyler's official portrait. *(White House Historical Society)*

passed a high protective tariff, which Southern planters, dependent on an export economy, strongly opposed. They called it the "Tariff of Abominations," and Tyler was among the senators who spoke and voted against it. Second was the fact that with the increasing political integration of the Northwest and Northeast, Southerners were coming to constitute only a minority in national politics. Some Southerners were beginning to talk about separation from the Union in order to escape from the tyranny of the majority. Vice President John C. Calhoun of South Carolina understood Southern frustration, yet he wanted to preserve the Union, and therefore developed the theory of nullification as a permanent protection for minority sections within the Union.

Nullification and the tariff were linked when South Carolina threatened to declare the Tariff of Abominations null and void within its borders if it were not repealed by Congress. Despite passage of a new compromise tariff, South Carolina began the nullification process. President Jackson issued an extremely strong proclamation rejecting South Carolina's position, and Congress passed the Force Act, authorizing the president to use force to make sure that federal laws were obeyed. Even though South Carolina eventually backed down and the crisis passed, Tyler found himself in a troubling situation. He shared the general Southern opposition to high tariffs, but he did not agree with the theory of nullification. Still, he believed that Jackson's nullification proclamation was a violation of the Constitution, and he was the only senator to vote against the Force Act. Further, he was repelled by the vehemence of Jackson's reaction to South Carolina's challenge.

The bank question raised similar contradictions for Tyler. Like Jackson, he opposed the attempt to recharter the Bank of the United States, on constitutional as well as on other grounds. Yet, when Jackson attempted to destroy the bank before its charter expired by removing the federal government's deposits from its vaults, Tyler supported resolutions in the Senate condemning the president's action. When the Virginia legislature ordered him to vote for a motion to expunge the resolutions, Tyler resigned from the Senate and left the Democratic Party.

Tyler was now in strange political territory. He had left Andrew Jackson's party and had begun drifting along with other Southern expatriates into the ranks of the emerging Whig Party, which was coalescing in opposition to the executive tyranny of "King Andrew." Yet Tyler had not departed from his constitutional or political principles, and these were not consistent with those of many Whig leaders. The Whig Party was a loose coalition of diverse groups, however, and seemed at first to accommodate considerable philosophical latitude. Defeated in a Senate election in 1839, Tyler was nominated for the vice presidency on the ticket with William Henry Harrison, "Old Tippecanoe," the following year, in an obvious effort by the Whigs to attract Southern states' rights advocates.

Succession to the Presidency: A Historic Precedent

The Virginia politician whose name became part of the most famous campaign slogan in American political history—Tippecanoe and Tyler Too—had matured into a dignified and appealing figure. Although remaining distant from the masses, Tyler was a polished and effective orator. He was patient, considerate, good-humored, and friendly. Even his political enemies found it difficult to dislike him. Tyler was scrupulously honest and had no major vices. He drank, but always in moderation, and he used profanity, but only of the mildest sort. Physically striking, he was 6 feet tall and slender. He was very fair, with a high forehead and aquiline nose, brilliant eyes, and a ready smile. Observers said he reminded them of a Roman statesman or of Cicero. Some said he

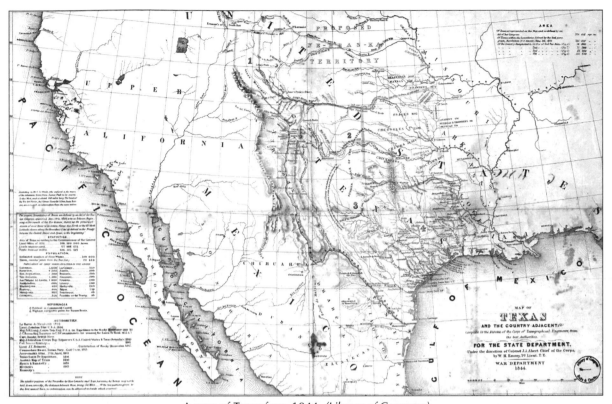

A map of Texas from 1844. *(Library of Congress)*

was vain, but he did have some justification for vanity.

The Harrison and Tyler ticket won the election easily, but within a month of his inauguration "Old Tippecanoe" was dead. Supposedly, his dying words, intended for the vice president, were "Sir—I wish you to understand the true principles of Government. I wish them carried out. I ask nothing more."

Were William Henry Harrison's principles shared by Tyler? Despite the Virginian's long political career and philosophical and constitutional consistency, contemporary observers professed not to know. Tyler had scarcely known Harrison and had not particularly liked what he knew of him. Tyler was a close friend of Henry Clay, and many, probably including Clay, believed that he would support the programs, including plans for a new central bank, that the Kentuckian planned to introduce in Congress. Tyler's oratory in the campaign had

been sufficiently vague to offer some justification for such a belief. Yet within a short period of time Clay would be a political enemy, attacking Tyler as a traitor to the Whig Party.

The first question was fundamental. What was Tyler's status upon Harrison's death? The Constitution is vague, saying that "in case of the removal of the President from office, or of his death, resignation, or inability to discharge the powers and duties of the said office, the same shall devolve on the Vice President. . . . " Does this mean the office itself, or simply the duties of the office? No precedents existed, and in this important crisis Tyler, the strict constructionist, interpreted the Constitution very broadly and claimed all the rights and privileges of the presidency. Although there was some criticism of his interpretation, it has been accepted and followed since that time.

Tyler kept the Harrison cabinet members, reinforcing the Whig perception that little would change. Almost immediately, Clay submitted a legislative program calling for a new Bank of the United States and a higher tariff. Clay quickly discovered that he had badly misread the situation. When Congress enacted legislation creating the new bank and a higher tariff, the president vetoed both, in language reminiscent of Andrew Jackson. Some charged that this was treachery; others held that Tyler was jealous of Clay's assumption of leadership. In fact, Tyler was simply being consistent with the strict constructionist, Southern agrarian views that he had held all along. He stood firm despite recriminations from Clay, tremendous pressure from majoritarian Whigs, and outcries from the public, including a rock-throwing mob that attacked the White House.

Conflicts with Congress: A President Without a Party

Tyler argued that the proposed bank violated constitutional principles and also posed the threat of an economic monopoly. He suggested a modified "exchequer system" as a compromise, but the Whigs in Congress forged ahead with another attempt to create a bank, thinly disguised as a "fiscal corporation." Tyler vetoed that too, and the situation rapidly deteriorated into open warfare between the Whig president and his colleagues in Congress. After Tyler, using the veto as actively as Jackson, struck down Clay's distribution program and other legislation, the Kentuckian resigned from the Senate in frustration. There were public demonstrations against the president, he was burned in effigy, and the entire cabinet, with the exception of Secretary of State Daniel Webster, who was involved in sensitive negotiations with Great Britain, resigned. They were replaced by men like Tyler himself, former Democrats who shared his views. In January, 1843, the Whigs brought impeachment charges against the man they now called "His Accidency." They failed, but proceeded formally to expel Tyler from the Whig Party, which was in shambles.

The president, now a man without a party, continued to perform the duties of his office, loyal to his principles and in apparent good humor. He actually managed to achieve some successes and even considered an attempt to retain the presidency in the 1844 campaign as an independent candidate. In 1841, he approved the Preemption Act, which made land more accessible to settlers rather than to speculators and stimulated the development of the Northwestern states of Iowa, Illinois, Wisconsin, and Minnesota. He helped to end the Seminole War in 1842. The same year, the dispute with Great Britain over the boundary between the United States and Canada in the Northeast was resolved through the Webster-Ashburton Treaty, and in 1844 the United States signed a treaty with China opening that country to American commerce for the first time. Although Tyler did not occupy the limelight in these diplomatic matters, he wielded considerable influence behind the scenes.

The president built his hopes for election in 1844 on the Texas annexation question. Originally a province of Mexico largely populated by slaveholding American settlers, Texas successfully rebelled in 1836 and hoped for annexation to the United States. The issue was troublesome because of the growing sectional controversy over slavery, and so for several years Texas remained an independent republic. Tyler genuinely believed that the annexation of Texas would be good for the United States, and he was hopeful that advocacy of such an action would generate support for his candidacy in the Southern slave states. He correctly anticipated the developing expansionist impulse in the country, but his personal ambitions were ill founded. When significant support failed to materialize, Tyler withdrew and endorsed Democrat James K. Polk, who ran on an expansionist platform and won. Following the election, Congress passed and Tyler signed a joint resolution of annexation for Texas. Two days later, during his last full day in office, the Virginian signed a bill admitting Florida to the Union.

Tyler then retired to his plantation home on Virginia's James River. He was coolly received by his neighbors, many of whom were Whigs, but his graciousness, character, and obvious goodwill gradually won them over. The former president became an honored citizen, and as the passions of sectional turmoil built in the 1850's, he was an influential sectional leader. Loyal to the Union, he attempted to promote compromise but finally voted in favor of secession as a delegate to the Virginia secession convention. He served in the provisional Congress of the Confederacy and was elected to the Confederate House of Representatives, but he died on January 18, 1862, before taking his seat. He was buried in Richmond.

Tyler's Achievements: A Reassessment

The first vice president to inherit the presidency upon the death of a president, the first chief executive to face impeachment charges, and the only one to be officially expelled from his party, John Tyler has been remembered primarily as a historical footnote. He deserves better. Although one can disagree with his reasoning on the issues, it is difficult to conclude that he acted out of malice or political expediency. Tyler remained true to his constitutional and political principles, displaying a consistency and courage rare in political leaders. He achieved some positive accomplishments despite the turmoil of his presidency, and he significantly shaped the theory of vice presidential succession under the United States Constitution.

James E. Fickle

Bibliographical References

The standard biography of John Tyler is Oliver Perry Chitwood's dated *John Tyler, Champion of the Old South*, 1939. Robert Seager II, *And Tyler Too*, 1963, is a joint biography of Tyler and his second wife, Julia Gardiner Tyler. Similarly titled, Donald B. Chidsey, *And Tyler Too*, 1978, is a brief general biography. Tyler's presidency is the focus of Robert J. Morgan, *A Whig Embattled*, 1954, of Oscar D. Lambert, *Presidential Politics in the United States, 1841-1844*, 1936, and of Frederick Merk, *Fruits of Propaganda in the Tyler Administration*, 1971. Tyler's role in the 1840 presidential campaign is discussed in Robert G. Gunderson, *The Log-Cabin Campaign*, 1957. Daniel Walker Howe analyzes the anti-Jackson movement in *The Political Culture of the American Whigs*, 1979. For an analysis of Tyler's presidency, see Norma L. Peterson, *The Presidencies of William Henry Harrison and John Tyler*, 1989.

James K. Polk

11th President, 1845-1849

Born: November 2, 1795
       Mecklenburg County, North
        Carolina
Died: June 15, 1849
       Nashville, Tennessee

Political Party: Democratic
Vice President: George M. Dallas

Cabinet Members
Secretary of State: James Buchanan
Secretary of the Treasury: Robert J. Walker
Secretary of War: William L. Marcy

Secretary of the Navy: George Bancroft, John Y.
    Mason
Attorney General: John Y. Mason, Nathan Clif-
    ford, Isaac Toucey
Postmaster General: Cave Johnson

Polk's official portrait. *(White House Historical Society)*

James Knox Polk was elected in November, 1844, and held office for one term, from March 4, 1845, to March 3, 1849, at age forty-nine the youngest president until that time. He declined to be considered for reelection. Although he was not widely known at the time of his election, he had served fourteen years in the House of Representatives (four of them as speaker) and one term as governor of his home state of Tennessee. As a protégé of Andrew Jackson (he was often called Young Hickory), Polk had represented the interests of the Jackson administration in the lower house of Congress and was recognized as the floor leader in securing Jacksonian legislation. His presidency was the strongest and most vigorous of those between Jackson and Abraham Lincoln. Besides being a loyal Jacksonian Democrat in matters of domestic policy, Polk shared the expansionist fervor of his generation and as president presided over the nation's most dramatic period of territorial expansion. In the brief space of three years, Texas was annexed, the Oregon Country was acquired, and a half-million square miles of Mexican territory was ceded to the United States as a result of the Mexican War. As America's first wartime president since James Madison, Polk did much to define the role of the president as commander in chief. The Mexican War dominated his administration and has influenced his reputation ever since. In spite of the controversy that has often been aroused over Polk's involvement in the war, he has fared well in presidential evaluations, as historians consistently place him among the top ten or twelve presidents of the United States.

Early Life

James K. Polk was born on November 2, 1795, in Mecklenburg County, North Carolina. His family, of sturdy Scotch-Irish stock and staunchly Presbyterian, had been in America since the seventeenth century, settling first in Maryland, moving to Pennsylvania, and from there sweeping southwestward with the great migration of Scotch-Irish to up-country North Carolina. Fiercely independent, the Polks resented British rule and were among the earliest to support separation from the mother country. Many of them served in the Continental Army. By the late eighteenth century, the family was among the most prominent in the region.

James K. Polk was the eldest of the ten children of Samuel and Jane Knox Polk. His father was a well-to-do farmer and, like the rest of the family, strongly Jeffersonian in politics. His mother, said to be descended from the Scottish religious leader John Knox, was a tenacious Presbyterian whose life revolved around the Bible and the teachings of the church. Nurtured on tales of America's War of Independence, Polk derived from his parents a strong patriotism, a keen interest in politics, and deep religious convictions.

Like so many North Carolinians following the Revolutionary War, members of Polk's fam-

ily invested heavily in land in the state's western district, later the state of Tennessee. In 1806, when Polk was eleven years old, his parents moved to a farm in the Duck River Valley, near Columbia in Maury County, Tennessee. His father expanded his interests from farming to mercantile activity and continued to engage in land speculation during the economic boom that followed the War of 1812.

Because of his frail health, Polk began his formal education later than most youths of his generation. After preparation in Presbyterian academies in Tennessee, he entered the University of North Carolina in Chapel Hill in 1815 as a sophomore, where he studied the classics and mathematics, two subjects he believed would best discipline his mind. He was graduated first in his class in 1818. The following year, he took up the study of law in the office of Felix Grundy, a successful Nashville lawyer and former congressman, and in 1820 was admitted to the bar. Polk established his practice in his hometown of Columbia and prospered almost immediately, thanks to the business his family placed in his charge.

It was not the law, however, but politics that stirred Polk's interest. The times were filled with opportunity for an aspiring politician. The panic of 1819 awakened the American people, jolting them out of their indifference and ushering in a period of change and uncertainty that would lead to new political alignments. In Tennessee, as elsewhere, the economic distress aroused demands that the government be more responsive to the needs of the people. A "new politics" (however vaguely defined) was called for. Symbolizing the rising dissatisfaction with the existing system was Andrew Jackson, the hero of New Orleans.

In 1819, Polk assumed his first political post, that of clerk of the state senate, and four years later he was elected to the lower house of the Tennessee legislature. His academic background, readiness in debate, and persistent application quickly marked him as a promising young leader in Tennessee politics. He supported legislation that would relieve the banking crisis in the state and bring order to its tangled land problems, and in 1823 he voted for Jackson for United States senator. At the same time, he married Sarah Childress, daughter of a well-to-do farmer and Murfreesboro businessman, a well-educated, refined, and cultured woman who would be an important asset to his career. She would become one of the most respected First Ladies to occupy the White House.

Polk's success as a legislator led him to seek election to Congress. The presidential election of 1824 promised to be one of the most important in years. Jackson had been nominated by the Tennessee legislature two years before, and his election to the Senate further boosted his candidacy. Although his triumph seemed sure, the results of the contest indicated otherwise. Jackson received more electoral and popular votes than any other candidate, but none of the four contenders—Jackson, William H. Crawford, John Quincy Adams, and Henry Clay—received the required majority. The election was placed before the House of Representatives, where in February, 1825, Adams was elected. The cry of "bargain and corruption" was immediately raised by the outraged Jacksonians. Polk shared the belief not only that Jackson had lost because of a nefarious plot involving Adams and Clay but also that his defeat had robbed the people of their choice. The outcome of the election gave new meaning to Polk's campaign for Congress; in August, 1825, he was easily elected from his four-county district in south central Tennessee.

Jacksonian Congressman

Although Polk proved extraordinarily successful in his appeals for the votes of his constituents—he served in the House of Representatives for seven successive terms, fourteen years—he lacked the charismatic quality that brought so many Americans to the side of Jack-

son. Of somewhat less than middle height, unprepossessing in demeanor, he often gave the appearance of dullness. He had but few intimate friends. Formal and stiff in his bearing, he was always concerned to maintain his dignity. When he presided over the House of Representatives as speaker during the last four years of his service, it was said that he appeared "in the chair as if he were at a dinner party." Thoughtful and reserved, his speaking style reflected his personality. His political statements lacked the ornamental flourishes common to early nineteenth century political rhetoric; instead, they were plain, sincere, and convincing, demonstrating a command of facts and principles and exhibiting a practical common sense.

John Quincy Adams once characterized Polk's speaking ability as having "no wit, no literature, no point of argument, no gracefulness of delivery, no elegance of language, no philosophy, no pathos, no felicitous impromptus; nothing that can constitute an orator, but confidence, fluency, and labor." Adams spoke as an opponent; others were more charitable.

The charge that Polk had no philosophy was unfair. The aftermath of the panic and the outcome of the presidential election brought his views into sharper focus. The Jeffersonian convictions he had absorbed from his family and the intellectual discipline he had derived from the Presbyterian influence formed the basis on which he built his political outlook. His exposure to moral philosophy at Chapel Hill gave him a well-defined sense of republican virtue and of the obligations that rested on citizens of a republic. The troubled atmosphere of the 1820's, however, revealed the need for something more. Polk found the missing ingredient in the new democratic currents of his time.

Polk prized individual freedom, the rights of the states against the centralizing tendencies of the national government, and a strict interpretation of the Constitution. The sovereignty

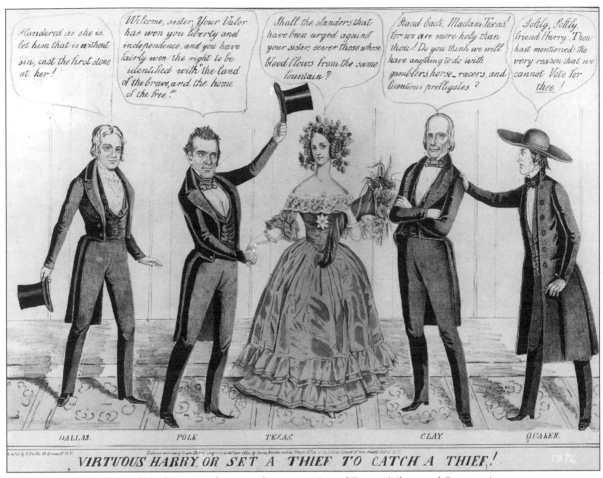

A political cartoon favoring the annexation of Texas. *(Library of Congress)*

of the people, he believed, was unquestioned and absolute. In one of his first pronouncements as a congressman, Polk declared his faith in the popular will. "That this is a Government based upon the will of the People," he stated, "that all power emanates from them; and that a majority should rule; are, as I conceive, vital principles in this Government, never to be sacrificed or abandoned, under any circumstances." He would return America's republican government to its beginnings: "I would bring the Government back to what it was intended to be—a plain economical Government."

Polk entered Congress in December, 1825, determined to vindicate Jackson from his defeat by the Adams-Clay combination. One of his first actions was to support the effort to amend the Constitution to prevent future presidential contests from being decided in the House of Representatives. He proposed that the selection of presidential electors be made uniform throughout the country and argued that election by districts was the fairest, most democratic mode. He agreed with some that the electoral college should be abandoned altogether in favor of a direct vote for president but realized the futility of proposing such a radical change.

Although the movement to amend the Constitution did not succeed, it enabled Polk to express his views on the nature of the presidential office. The president, he believed, was the chief executive of all the people, the only federal officer to be elected by all the people, and the only elected official whose constituency was the entire nation. More than any other officer, the president best reflected the popular will; therefore, he was responsible only to the people.

Polk's course in the House of Representatives established him as a loyal, orthodox Jacksonian. When Jackson defeated Adams in 1828, Polk felt that the people had been vindicated. The election was fought, he wrote, "between the virtue and rights of the people on the one hand and the power and patronage of their rules on the other."

Before long, Polk was recognized as the voice of the Jackson administration in the House of Representatives. He remained in close correspondence with the president, and Jackson frequently sent him directives and thinly veiled suggestions as to the course the House should pursue. Polk proved a trustworthy lieutenant. He waged continual war on Henry Clay's American System ("falsely called," said Polk) and warned against the "splendid Government, differing . . . only in name from a consolidated empire" that Clay's program would create. He fought efforts to fund internal improvement projects with federal money, and when the celebrated bill providing for a road from Maysville to Lexington, Kentucky, came before the House, he was assigned the task of leading the administration forces against it. The bill passed but was struck down in the first of Jackson's important vetoes. On the question of the protective tariff, Polk supported the reduction of duties without ever totally rejecting the principle of protection. When the nullification crisis pitted South Carolina against Jackson and the federal government, Polk was quick to side with the president. He assisted in drafting a compromise tariff that he hoped would placate South Carolina, but when his effort was superseded by Clay's compromise bill, he gave the Kentuckian his full support.

Polk was consistent in his stand on behalf of the Union, even though some have found in his support of Jackson's position a contradiction of his Old Republican views.

Polk's appointment to the House Ways and Means Committee and his subsequent designation as its chair placed him in an advantageous position to defend Jackson's assault against the Second Bank of the United States. In early 1833, Polk took exception to the committee's report declaring the bank's soundness and prepared a minority report in which he detailed the weakness and irresponsibility of the institution. A year later, as chair of the committee, he issued a report sanctioning Jackson's removal of deposits from the bank; its adoption by the House of Representatives was a death-blow to the probank forces. In one of his most powerful speeches as a congressman, Polk inveighed against the "despotism of money" and warned that, if not checked, the power of money would soon "control your election of President, of your Senators, and of your Representatives." To Polk, the forces of money and privilege constituted the gravest threat to America's republican system of government.

Polk's election as speaker of the House of Representatives during his last two terms in Congress, from 1835 to 1839, was a tribute to his leadership, his party loyalty, and his administrative ability. As speaker, Polk demonstrated the same relentless devotion to the responsibilities of the post that he exhibited in other offices he had held. During Martin Van Buren's troubled administration, he tried desperately (and not always with success) to hold the Jacksonian coalition together. He wielded a tight and virtually absolute control over the deliberations of the House, for which he was frequently criticized by his opponents. When he left the speakership, he boasted, without exaggeration, that he had decided more difficult and complex questions of parliamentary law and order than had been decided by all of his predecessors.

Polk preferred to remain in the House of Representatives and could easily have been reelected in 1839. Instead, he was persuaded to run for governor of Tennessee, a move his associates believed would redeem the state from Whig control, weaken the opposition, and influence the 1840 presidential election. Polk was elected, but his term of office (two years) was anticlimactic and uneventful. It was not a good time for Democrats, as much of the public's attention was focused on the effects of the panic of 1837. The party's position in the state was not strengthened. Polk was defeated for reelection in 1841, and two years later he was defeated again. The magic of the Jacksonian appeal was gone, the voters had turned away from the party of their hero, and Polk suddenly seemed an anachronism. At the age of forty-eight, after almost twenty years of public activity and service to his state and nation, his political career appeared to be over.

"Who Is James K. Polk?"

Nine months after his second defeat for the governorship of Tennessee, in an incredible turnaround of his political fortunes, Polk was nominated for president of the United States by the Democratic Party. "Who is James K. Polk?" asked startled Whigs. Historians, taking this cue, have explained the unexpectedness of Polk's nomination by insisting that he was the nation's first "dark horse" candidate. In fact, Polk was not unknown (the Whigs knew very well who he was), nor was he so dark a horse.

A political cartoon from 1846 examines the Oregon boundary dispute with Great Britain. Polk and the hawkish "General Bunkum" (on the right) negotiate with Queen Victoria, Prince Albert, and the duke of Wellington (on the left), while Irish leader Daniel O'Connell, Russian czar Nicholas I, and French king Louis Philippe look on. *(Library of Congress)*

When the delegates gathered at the Democratic National Convention in Baltimore in May, 1844, the name of James K. Polk was hardly mentioned. To be sure, Polk's ambitions for a place in the nation's executive branch had been aroused, but it was for the vice presidency, not the presidency. Four years before, as the parties maneuvered for the 1840 election, his name was paired with that of Van Buren. The Tennessee legislature nominated a Van Buren-Polk ticket, friends worked for his nomination among party leaders in Washington, D.C., and Andrew Jackson gave it his endorsement. Polk's place on the ticket, it was thought, would offset Van Buren's lack of popularity among Southerners. Polk, however, was not nominated, giving way to Kentucky's Richard M. Johnson, and Van Buren lost the election. Both men set their sights on 1844.

Van Buren was the leading contender for the nomination in 1844, long before the convention met. His nomination seemed a foregone conclusion. His delegate strength mounted as state conventions pledged their support (although often without enthusiasm). The presidential race, as everyone seemed to expect, would be run between Van Buren and Clay. Whigs were confident that they would be able to repeat their triumph of four years before.

As Van Buren's candidacy became more and more certain, Polk revived his quest for the vice presidential nomination. Someone acceptable to both the West and the South, he thought, would be sought, and who better to fill the need than himself? Once again, the aid of his friends, including the aged and ailing Andrew Jackson, was enlisted. Polk's record in the House of Representatives as a steadfast and "unterrified" defender of Jacksonian democracy was publicized. His supporters doubled their efforts to advance Van Buren's candidacy for the presidential nomination under the assumption that Polk would get the second position. By the spring of 1844, it appeared that the efforts on Polk's behalf would fall short, as they had four years before, and that Richard M. Johnson would likely be the candidate a second time.

Then on April 27, a bombshell was tossed into the campaign. On that day, Washington newspapers carried letters from both Clay and Van Buren announcing their opposition to the immediate annexation of Texas to the United States, on the ground that such a move would constitute aggression against Mexico. Van Buren's statement threw his party into confusion, desertions from his ranks began, and his opponents were handed an issue with which to defeat his nomination. The hopes of Van Buren's rivals were raised, and some sent out feelers to Polk seeking the latter's endorsement in return for the vice presidency. To Polk and his supporters, however, Van Buren's downfall suggested a different strategy.

From one of his closest friends, Polk received the suggestion that "if Van Buren is to be thrown over . . . we must have an entirely new man." There was no doubt who that new man should be. Jackson, both disappointed and angered at Van Buren's statement, insisted that the presidential candidate "should be an annexation man and reside in the Southwest" and suggested that Polk would be the "most available." Of one thing Polk was sure: If Van Buren's name were withdrawn, the balance of power in the convention would be held by his supporters; they would be able to control the nominations. "I have never aspired so high," Polk assured his friends, but while he reiterated his ambition for "the 2nd office," he made it clear that they could use his name in any way they thought fit.

Polk's credentials as a Jacksonian were impeccable, as his record in the House of Representatives attested. That he also shared Jackson's strong desire to see Texas annexed to the United States was without question. Ever since Texas's break with Mexico during the last year of his presidency, Jackson had favored annexation, although he declined to make any move in that direction because of the dangers it might create for the Union. By the early 1840's, however, the question could no longer be repressed. "It is the greatest question of the *Age*," declared one political leader, as Americans in the West and South gathered in rallies and demonstrations to demand government action. With an eye on the 1844 election, President John Tyler promoted annexation, and Democratic leaders carried the demand into Congress. Even before Van Buren's fateful statement, Texas annexationists in the West had been looking for another candidate.

Jackson joined the cry with a letter to one of Polk's close friends in which he urged immediate annexation. Although the letter was not made public until a year later, his position was well-known to Polk. A few days before Van Buren's letter was published, Polk made his views known in response to an inquiry from a committee of Ohio Democrats. Like Jackson, he strongly favored the immediate annexation of Texas, arguing that Texas had been a part of the United States before John Quincy Adams had given it up to Spain in the Adams-Onís Treaty of 1819. He feared, as did many Western Democrats, the rise of British influence in Texas and placed his argument in the broader context of hemispheric security. Unlike Jackson, Polk linked his demand for Texas with the demand that the authority and laws of the United States be also extended to the Oregon Country.

Democratic delegates gathered in Baltimore amid fears that the party would be seriously divided over the Texas issue and Van Buren's candidacy. Although commanding the support of a majority of the delegates, Van Buren faced a growing opposition from the West and South, and when his opponents succeeded in reaffirming the rule requiring a two-thirds majority for the nomination, his chances diminished rapidly. After several inconclusive ballots, on the convention's third day Polk's name was formally presented to the body as a candidate

for the presidential nomination, and before the day ended, he had received the necessary two-thirds vote.

Polk's nomination was a compromise between the opposing camps. It was acceptable to the Van Buren forces (one of Van Buren's most trusted lieutenants declared Polk to be his second choice), in part because his nomination denied the prize as well to Van Buren's rivals. The steadfastness with which Polk himself stuck to his support of Van Buren (hoping to get the vice presidential nomination) was impressive. It was New England, notably Massachusetts delegate George Bancroft, which first put his name before the convention. Polk's nomination, however, upset many rank-and-file Van Buren supporters; because it was unexpected, stories of intrigue and chicanery were circulated. Charges that his nomination had been hatched in the Hermitage were made, and the Whigs were quick to exploit them. With Polk's nomination, however, the Democratic Party acquired a candidate whose orthodoxy was above reproach—"a pure, whole-hogged democrat," as one delegate put it. Polk was also an unequivocal proponent of Texas annexation, and in 1844, that is what counted most.

The remainder of the convention was anticlimactic. For vice president, the delegates' first choice was New York's Silas Wright, but Wright refused the nomination. The weary delegates then turned to George M. Dallas of Pennsylvania. With the nominations completed, the platform was adopted almost as an afterthought. To a traditional statement of Jacksonian principles—strict construction, states' rights, opposition to a national bank, a high tariff, and federally funded internal improvements—the convention added one new plank. The title of the United States to "the whole of the Territory of Oregon" was "clear and unquestionable"; "the reoccupation of Oregon and the reannexation of Texas, at the earliest practicable period, are great American measures, which this convention recommends to the cordial support of the democracy of the Union."

The Whigs, who had already nominated Henry Clay, were startled at the turn taken by the Democrats, unbelieving and joyous that their opponents had made such a "ridiculous" nomination. Clay, in a fit of arrogant self-confidence, regretted that a person "more worthy of a contest" had not been chosen.

Clay need not have worried, for the campaign of 1844 was a hard-fought and bitter contest. The parties were evenly matched, a sign that the party system had reached a stage of maturity. Clay was moved to acts of desperation, which in the end cost him dearly. At the last minute, he experienced a sudden change of heart on the Texas question and joined the annexationists, and his efforts to dissociate himself from Northern abolitionists drove their support away, especially in New York. There, the Liberty Party candidate, James G. Birney, took enough voters away from the Whig column to give the state to Polk; it was Polk's victory in New York, in turn, that gave the Democrats their electoral majority.

Polk won the presidency with 170 electoral votes to Clay's 105. His popular vote exceeded that of Clay by only 38,000 out of a total of almost 2,700,000 votes cast. Polk's nomination and election, following so quickly after his failures to win the governorship of Tennessee, has been judged well-nigh miraculous. Although many unique circumstances involving issues, partisanship, and power contributed to his success, Charles Sellers, Polk's biographer, gives the larger share of credit to "the behavior of a remarkably audacious, self-controlled, and prescient politician" who shaped his course "with impressive skill and coolness."

A Continental Vision

Polk's inaugural address was in sharp contrast to the gloomy, rainy weather in Washington on March 4, 1845. It was a message of hope and confidence for a youthful nation from a president who was younger than any of his predecessors. A paean to America's republican system, it exhibited the ardor that many people felt toward the nation's future. The United States, "this Heaven-favored land," he declared, enjoyed the "most admirable and wisest system of well-regulated self-government among men ever devised by human minds." It was the "noblest structure of human wisdom," wherein burned the fire of liberty, warming and animating "the hearts of happy millions" and inviting "all the nations of the earth to imitate our example." Under the benign influence of their government, the American people were "free to improve their condition by the legitimate exercise of all their mental and physical powers."

The sheet anchor of American republicanism was the Union; to protect and preserve the Union was the sacred duty of every American. Warning against the forces of sectionalism that would disturb and destroy the Union, Polk struck out at those "misguided persons" whose object was the "destruction of domestic institutions existing in other sections," a reference to the abolitionists. The consequences of their agitation could only be the dissolution of the Union and the "destruction of our happy form of government." Preserved and protected, the Union was the guarantee that the "blessings of civil and religious liberty" would be transmitted to "distant generations." "Who shall assign limits to the achievements of free minds and free hands under the protection of this glorious Union?" he asked.

In a confession of his Jacksonian faith, Polk called for a strict adherence to the Constitution and a scrupulous respect for the rights of the states, each sovereign "within the sphere of its reserved powers." The government must be returned to the "plain and frugal" system intended by its founders. There was no need for national banks "or other extraneous institutions"; in levying tariff duties, revenue must be the object and protection only incidental.

More than a third of his address was devoted to the new spirit of continental expansion. He rejected the pessimistic view of some Americans that the nation's system of government could not be successfully applied to a large extent of territory. On the contrary, Polk insisted, the "federative system" was well adapted to territorial expansion, and as the nation's boundaries were enlarged, it acquired "additional strength and security." The annexation of Texas, "once a part of our country" that was "unwisely ceded away," was of first importance, and Polk lauded Congress for taking the initial steps to effect the reunion of Texas with the United States. To the settlement of the Oregon question, he stated, he was no less dedicated. America's title to the region was "clear and unquestionable." Thousands of Americans, moreover, were establishing their homes in this far-flung corner, and the extension of the jurisdiction and benefits of the country's republican institutions to the area was an inescapable duty.

Whereas the inaugural address provided the general direction of the course that President Polk had charted for himself, a statement made to the historian George Bancroft supplied the specifics. He intended, he told Bancroft at the time of his inauguration, to accomplish four great measures during his administration. Two of them related to his vision of continental expansion: the settlement of the Oregon boundary question with Great Britain and the acquisition of California. (It is interesting to note that aside from a general concern over the fate of California and the impulsive capture and brief occupation of Monterey by American naval forces in 1842, California had not been seriously mentioned as a target for American expansion.) The third was the reduction of the tariff to a revenue level, and the last was the establishment of the independent Treasury system, the Democrats' alternative to a third national bank. The independent Treasury had

been created by Congress in the waning days of the Van Buren administration, only to be repealed by the Whigs in 1841.

It was a large order for the new president, the more so since he had pledged to serve only a single term. Following his nomination, Polk made the promise in order to secure the support of Van Buren's leading rivals, men such as Lewis Cass, James Buchanan, and John C. Calhoun, whose hopes would be dashed if they had to wait eight more years to pursue their presidential ambitions. Concerned lest he appear to be favoring one or another for the succession, Polk refused to select any presidential aspirant for his cabinet. His appointees were to be men devoted to him and not to their own, or someone else's, advancement. He later regretted that he had taken at face value the disclaimer of Buchanan, whom he appointed secretary of state. Polk would thread his way carefully through the cliques and factions of the party, determined to maintain his independence. "I intend to be myself President of the U.S.," he wrote a friend.

Missing from Polk's list of intended achievements was the annexation of Texas, for by the time he was inaugurated, the annexation had already been set in motion. As president-elect, Polk played an important part in the movement. His election in November, 1844, was viewed as a mandate for annexation, and steps were immediately taken in the short session of Congress that followed. Polk himself favored a settlement of the issue before he should be inaugurated. The only question to be resolved was which plan to effect annexation would be adopted—a House resolution to annex simply by a joint resolution of Congress or a Senate bill that called for the appointment of commissioners to negotiate an agreement with Texas. Although he favored the former, Polk sought to avoid an impasse by proposing a compromise, whereby the two modes would be combined as alternatives, with the president empowered to choose between them. The assumption was that the decision would be made by the new president, Polk, rather than by John Tyler, the outgoing president. The measure passed Congress in the last days of the session and was signed by Tyler on March 1. To Congress's surprise, however, it was Tyler who acted quickly to exercise the option; he dispatched a messenger to Texas with the offer of annexation.

It remained only for Polk to complete the process following his inauguration. He could have reversed Tyler's decision (and some senators expected him to do so), but Polk let it stand. In the face of mounting public excitement for annexation in both the United States and Texas, the Texas government assented, but only after the American emissaries (and Polk) agreed to recognize Texas's claim to the Rio Grande boundary and to provide military protection to Texas as soon as annexation had been accepted. On July 4, a Texas convention voted to accept annexation and proceeded to draw up a state constitution; later in December, Congress admitted Texas to the Union as a state. Polk's role in the annexation of Texas has been closely scrutinized by historians, and some have argued that his insistence on the Rio Grande boundary and his dispatch of troops into Texas were part of a deliberate scheme to provoke Mexico to war and thus open the way for the acquisition of California. Certainly, relations between the United States and Mexico, which had been deteriorating for years, worsened, as the Mexican government charged the United States with an act of aggression against Mexico and recalled its minister from Washington.

With the Texas issue moving toward a resolution, Polk turned his attention to the Oregon boundary question. Although the Democratic platform and Polk's inaugural statements brought the question to a head, the dispute with Great Britain had been of long duration. Unable to settle their conflicting claims to the region, the two countries had negotiated a joint occupation agreement in 1818, at the time the boundary between the United States and British North America east of the Rocky Mountains was drawn along the forty-ninth parallel. The agreement, originally to run for ten years, was renewed for an indefinite period in 1827, with the proviso that either country might terminate the agreement by giving the other country one year's notice. Repeated efforts were made to resolve the dispute, the United States offering to extend the forty-ninth parallel to the Pacific and the British insisting on the Columbia River as the boundary. Neither side was willing to give in to the other.

British fur-trading interests were active in the Oregon Country during the early years of the century, but no attempts to settle it permanently were undertaken. Little was done by the United States to challenge the British presence, even though sentiment favored the ultimate extension of American sovereignty to the region. The situation changed in the 1830's when American missionaries arrived in Oregon; their reports were widely publicized and did much to arouse public feeling in support of an American occupation of the far Northwest. Indeed, the missionary efforts were responsible for the first movement of permanent settlers to Oregon's western valleys. The distress experienced by Western farmers in the aftermath of the panic of 1837 turned further attention to Oregon's rich soil and salubrious climate. Before long, an "Oregon Fever" raged, especially in the Mississippi Valley; people gathered in meetings and demonstrations to sing the praises of the new land and to voice their demands that the United States act quickly to extend its laws and institutions to Oregon's growing population.

Each year, large numbers of families gathered in their wagons in Independence, Missouri (the jumping-off point), and prepared to make the long trek over the Oregon Trail to the Pacific Northwest. As the population of Oregon grew, the settlers became increasingly impatient with

Immigrants walk the Oregon Trail. *(Library of Congress)*

the apparent reluctance of the United States government to recognize their needs. Beginning in 1841, they took steps to establish a provisional government of their own that would at least provide a semblance of law and order, but their uppermost desire was to be reunited with their country. The expansionist fervor of Western Democrats, fueled by the movement of Americans to Oregon, found expression in the repudiation of Martin Van Buren's candidacy and in the election of Polk to the presidency.

Following the 1844 election, the Oregon question became a heated national issue, as its supporters moved to the more radical demand that all of Oregon be acquired, meaning all that territory from the forty-second parallel north to 54 degrees 40 minutes. "Fifty-four Forty or Fight" became a new rallying cry. Polk seemed to endorse this new extreme in his inaugural address, although privately he still believed that the extension of the forty-ninth parallel, America's traditional position, was the

most feasible solution. The British government became alarmed at the bellicose tone of the American demands and feared that war might break out between the two countries.

Polk had no more intention than the British of fighting a war over the Oregon Country, but he was not above using the more radical demands to strengthen his efforts to settle the boundary dispute. As in the case of the Texas issue, the Tyler administration had taken steps to settle the question, and Polk's first actions were based on those of his predecessor. In July, he offered once again to draw the line along the forty-ninth parallel, without at the same time surrendering the American claim to the whole of Oregon. The offer was categorically rejected by the British minister in Washington without transmitting it to his government in London. Polk was both shocked and furious. He had made the offer, he said, out of deference to his predecessors; the offer was withdrawn, and the claim to all of Oregon was reasserted. The ball was now in the British court.

Polk was playing a dangerous game. Amid fears that his unyielding attitude would involve the United States in a war with Great Britain, Polk refused to back down. "The only way to treat John Bull," he confided to his diary, "was to look him straight in the eye." At the same time, the issue assumed an added urgency. Relations with Mexico were approaching a crisis, and Polk's attention was divided between the two situations. As with his Texas policy, there were hints that California was in his mind. The settlement of the Oregon question might deter Great Britain from acquiring California (perceived as a real threat in 1845), leaving the way open for an American acquisition through negotiations with Mexico.

Polk's course was bold and daring; at the same time, he was convinced that it was a peaceful one. In his first message to Congress, in December, 1845, he asked Congress to provide the one year's notice that the United States was terminating the joint occupation agreement with Great Britain. Furthermore, he asked that jurisdiction be extended over the Americans living in Oregon and that steps be taken to provide military protection to emigrants along the route to Oregon. Finally, he restated the Monroe Doctrine against any further colonization of North America by a European power, a reference to the British designs on California. Congress responded but not until the spring of 1846, when the one year's notice resolution was finally approved.

As Polk had expected, the passage of the resolution spurred the British government to make a new offer to the United States. It was tantamount to a surrender to the traditional American position. An extension of the boundary along the forty-ninth parallel was proposed, with the provision that British settlers south of that line could retain title to their lands and that the great fur-trading organization, the Hudson's Bay Company, would be allowed the free navigation of the Columbia River. The latter stipulation was not crucial,

for by 1846 the company had moved its operations to Vancouver Island in anticipation of the boundary settlement. Polk stood firm but offered to seek the advice of the Senate. When the Senate advised the president by an overwhelming vote to accept the terms, Polk relented, and on June 15, 1846, a treaty was signed by the two powers that brought an end to the boundary dispute.

The settlement of the Oregon boundary has often been seen as a compromise between the United States and Great Britain. Insofar as the United States receded from its extreme demand for all of Oregon, it perhaps was. In the perspective of the long history of negotiations, however, the treaty was clearly a diplomatic victory for the United States—and that is how Polk viewed it. He had secured all that he initially sought; his firm stance had paid off. Western expansionist Democrats saw the result as neither a victory nor a compromise; to them, it was an abject surrender of an unquestioned American claim. Some of them never forgave Polk.

Within fifteen months of his inauguration, Polk had presided over the addition of two immense regions to the United States, Texas and Oregon, not only fulfilling the pledge in the Democratic platform on which he was elected but also bringing his dream of continental expansion closer to reality. There still remained the acquisition of California. That too had been set in motion; one month before the Oregon treaty was signed, Polk announced to Congress that war between the United States and Mexico had begun.

Relations with Mexico

In both Texas and Oregon, Polk carried to fruition problems that he had inherited from a previous administration to the ultimate advantage of the United States. The same was true with the deteriorated state of American-Mexican relations. Ever since Mexico had won its independence from Spain in the early 1820's, relations between the two countries had been on a downward slide. The initial enthusiasm expressed by Americans over the organization of a sister republic waned as Mexico became a country wracked by revolution and plagued by instability. The perception of Mexican irresponsibility (an attitude fomented among Europeans perhaps to a greater extent than among Americans) and of Mexico's inability to provide a sound and efficient republican system grew, and it was easy for critics to explain the situation in racial terms.

Two issues brought relations between the two countries to a crisis in the Polk administration: the claims issue and the issue of Texas annexation. With independence from Spain, Mexico freed itself from the restrictive policies of Spanish mercantilism and opened its borders to foreign commercial activity. The frequency of revolution, exacerbated by an inability by foreigners to appreciate cultural differences, often resulted in the loss of property (and sometimes lives) by foreign nationals. Claims for compensation were lodged against the Mexican government; when it became obvious that Mexico was unable to pay, the claimants appealed to their governments—principally Great Britain, France, and the United States— for support. That the claims were often exaggerated did not lessen the determination of the governments to intervene on behalf of their aggrieved citizens.

The British and French solution was to exact payment by force. The French landed soldiers at Vera Cruz and fought a brief engagement (known as the Pastry War) with Mexican troops; Great Britain followed with a blockade of the Mexican coastline. Both Great Britain and France, with Spanish support, concluded that only the establishment of a monarchy in Mexico, headed by a European prince, could stabilize Mexico. The prospect horrified Americans.

Although Jackson had once threatened war against Mexico over the claims issue, the course of the United States had been a peaceful one. The issue was submitted to arbitration, the size of the claim was scaled down by two-thirds, and Mexico agreed to make payments to the United States. After only a few installments, Mexico defaulted. The claims issue continued to fester. By 1845, when Polk was inaugurated, it had become a major source of contention between the two countries. Fears, fed by rumors, that California would be either ceded to or seized by the British in payment for the Mexican debt became magnified. To many Americans, California seemed suitable payment for Mexico's unpaid debt to the United States, especially since large numbers of emigrants were now crossing the plains and mountains to settle in California's interior valleys.

It was the annexation of Texas, however, that had a more immediate impact on American relations with Mexico. Ever since Texas had won its independence in 1836, Mexico had nurtured plans for regaining the region. When Texas gave up its independence to accept integration into the American Union, such plans suffered a major setback. The issue became involved in Mexico's domestic politics, and no Mexican leader could ignore the rising anti-American sentiment in the country. Although the hard-line government of Antonio López de Santa Anna had been ousted by a coup in 1844 and replaced with the more liberal administration of José Joaquín Herrera, Mexico could ill afford to recognize the loss of Texas. On the contrary, the passage of the annexation resolution early in March, 1845, was viewed as equivalent to "a declaration of war against the Mexican Republic" and "sufficient for the immediate proclamation of war" on Mexico's part. The Mexican minister to Washington was recalled, and diplomatic relations between the two nations were broken off.

The volatility of the claims and Texas issues had never been so great as when Polk assumed office. His initial actions regarding Texas, the recognition of the Rio Grande boundary and the promise of military protection to the Texans, only aggravated the situation. United States Army troops, commanded by Zachary Taylor, entered Texas and took up positions at Corpus Christi, on the south bank of the Nueces River. Mexico responded by ordering an increase in the size of the Mexican army and threatened war against the United States as soon as the annexation process should be completed.

In the face of the heightened tension, Polk sent a personal representative, William S. Parrott (probably a poor choice inasmuch as Parrott was one of the largest claimants against the Mexican government), to probe the possibility of reopening diplomatic relations. When Parrott reported that the Herrera government would receive a qualified commissioner to negotiate the differences between the two countries, Polk moved to the next step. He chose John Slidell, congressman from Louisiana, to go to Mexico with instructions to secure Mexican recognition of the Rio Grande boundary in exchange for the cancellation of the claims and to offer to purchase California and New Mexico for an undetermined sum of money. The threat of British seizure of California seemed real: Parrott had emphasized it in his report from Mexico City, and Polk was determined to frustrate it.

Slidell went to Mexico, however, not only as a commissioner to negotiate a settlement of the disputes but also as a fully accredited minister, an effort on Polk's part to reopen diplomatic relations but one that would place Herrera in jeopardy if accepted. Slidell's arrival in Mexico was greeted by an outburst of anti-American activity as reports spread that Slidell intended to secure for the United States not only Texas but also the northern Mexican borderlands. Under the circumstances, the Herrera government could not receive Slidell; the rebuff, however, did not save it. A revolution forced Herrera out of office, and his place was taken by General Mariano Paredes, a monarchist who almost immediately contacted European powers with the intention of establishing a monarchy in Mexico as the only way the country could be saved from the United States.

Texas was admitted to the Union as a state in December, 1845, and shortly afterward, Taylor's army was ordered to new positions along the Rio Grande; by the end of March, 1846, he had arrived opposite the Mexican town of Matamoros. In the meantime, Slidell applied for recognition to Paredes, but with no different result. If Slidell should be rejected a second time, Secretary of State Buchanan had written, "the cup of forbearance will then have been exhausted." Nothing remained, he stated, "but to take the redress of the injuries to our citizens and the insults to our Government into our hands."

In rejecting Slidell, the Paredes government reiterated the position that the annexation of Texas was a cause for war between the two countries. Paredes followed with an order to mobilize Mexico's armed forces and to reinforce Mexican troops on the south bank of the Rio Grande. Taylor had been told to regard any Mexican attempt to cross the Rio Grande as an act of war, whereas the Mexican commander viewed Taylor's refusal to pull back as an act of war. Paredes further emphasized the Mexican position by declaring a "defensive war" against the United States in April. There matters between the two countries stood in the spring of 1846. Sentiment for war was on the increase in both countries. With European encouragement, Mexico was led to believe that a conflict with the United States would result in easy victory, and Americans, gripped by an expansionist fervor, resentful of supposed insults to their sovereignty and threats against their republican system, were equally persuaded that a war against Mexico would be quick and smooth.

With the arrival of news in Washington, D.C., that Slidell's mission had failed, Polk was prepared to adopt "strong measures towards Mexico" but delayed until the Oregon question, then reaching its climax, should be settled. When Slidell returned to the capital and reported to the president, Polk agreed that action against Mexico must be taken. After securing cabinet approval, he decided to recommend a declaration of war to Congress. That night, he received a dispatch from General Taylor. Mexican forces had crossed the Rio Grande and had engaged American troops, resulting in some loss of life. To Polk, there no longer was any question as to what policy should be followed.

On May 11, 1846, Polk sent his war message to Congress. "The grievous wrongs perpetrated by Mexico upon our citizens," he declared, "remain unredressed, and solemn treaties pledging [Mexico's] public faith for this redress have been disregarded." The United States, he continued, in what some regarded as an exaggeration, had "tried every effort at reconciliation" but to no avail.

The cup of forbearance had been exhausted even before the recent information from the frontier of the Del Norte [Rio Grande]. But now, after reiterated menaces, Mexico has passed the boundary of the United States, has invaded our territory and shed American blood upon the American soil. . . . As war exists, and, notwithstanding all our efforts to avoid it, exists by the act of Mexico herself, we are called upon by every consideration of duty and patriotism to vindicate with decision the honor, the rights, and the interests of our country.

Two days later, Congress, by a decisive vote, recognized a state of war between the United States and Mexico, empowered the president to use the army and navy against Mexico, appropriated $10 million for military purposes, and authorized the enlistment of fifty thousand volunteer troops. A short time later, Polk told his cabinet that "in making peace with our adversary, we shall acquire California, New Mexico, and other further territory, as an indemnity for this war, if we can."

The War with Mexico

The war with Mexico was a short war, as wars go, yet it was an extremely important conflict for the United States. Stung by the taunts of European powers that republics were ill equipped to fight wars and, because they eschewed professional standing armies, helpless to defend themselves, Americans saw in the war an opportunity to strengthen republicanism, both at home and abroad. Those who were uncomfortable with a conflict between two republics were also aware that Mexico's republican institutions had never been allowed to work, that repeated revolution and turmoil had destroyed their effectiveness, and that, in fact, the nation, through much of its life, had been ruled as a military dictatorship. Thus the war for many assumed an idealistic character.

At the same time, it was clear that the United States would benefit greatly by a victory over Mexico. Polk's continental vision would become a reality and his dream of adding California to the nation would be fulfilled. The war was a natural outgrowth of the expansionist feeling of the 1840's, a feeling that Polk shared. Although he denied that it was being fought for conquest, the circumstances of its origin suggested otherwise. As a result, Polk's role has been a controversial one in American historiography, as some historians have insisted that he deliberately provoked an unjust war in order to satisfy his lust for more territory.

Following the call for volunteers, a wave of war excitement passed over the country. Men flocked to the colors, many more than could be handled, and the quotas assigned some of the states were oversubscribed. The war, fought in a distant exotic land, held a romantic appeal for those who volunteered, an appeal that soon faded as the fighting began. The response to the volunteer calls, however, confirmed the belief that the republic could rely on its citizen-soldiers during times of crisis.

The problems faced by the Polk administration in fighting the war were enormous; that they were met and for the most part solved was a tribute to the president's administrative ability. For the first time, the country was compelled to raise large numbers of troops in a short time, to train, equip, and move them quickly to distant points. Knowledge of Mexico was sketchy and the means for gathering intelligence either nonexistent or crude. War material had to be produced on an unprecedented scale, and quartermaster stores (everything necessary to support an army in the field) had to be provided without delay. Ships were built, purchased, or chartered to carry the men to the battle areas. The need to coordinate naval and land operations and to direct the movement of troops in enemy territory placed a premium on military skill and ingenuity.

Military operations were mounted in three areas. General Zachary Taylor crossed the Rio Grande and moved into northern Mexico, fighting a desperate and costly battle for Monterrey in September, 1846, and achieving one of the greatest victories of the war at the Battle of Buena Vista in February, 1847. A second army, commanded by General Stephen Watts Kearny, moved west from Missouri over the Santa Fe Trail, occupying New Mexico and, in conjunction with naval forces, taking possession of California. A third front was opened in the spring of 1847 when General Winfield Scott, in the greatest amphibious operation to that time, landed twelve thousand soldiers at Vera Cruz. Marching inland along the route of Hernán Cortés's sixteenth century invasion, Scott's army fought several sharp engagements, including a series of battles in the vicinity of Mexico City, before occupying the Mexican capital in September, 1847. With the occupation of Mexico City, the fighting came to an end, except for sporadic guerrilla activity along the lines of supply.

In his administration of the war, Polk con-

The landing of U.S. troops at Vera Cruz during the Mexican War. *(Library of Congress)*

tributed significantly to a definition of the president's role as commander in chief, and his exercise of military power became a model for future presidents. He assumed full responsibility for the conduct of the war, taking the initiative in securing war legislation and finance, deciding on military strategy, appointing generals and drafting their instructions, directing the supply efforts, and coordinating the work of the various bureaus and cabinet departments. He insisted on being informed of every decision that was made by his cabinet officers. Polk was, as one author has written, "the center on which all else depended."

There were problems, however, on which Polk faltered. He was bothered by the fact that the two senior officers in the army, Winfield Scott and Zachary Taylor, were both Whigs. He had no choice but to rely on them, in spite of the uncomfortable prospect that their exploits would advance their prestige and lead to presidential ambitions. To allay his doubts, he made a clumsy effort to persuade Congress to revive the rank of lieutenant general so that he might appoint a Democrat to this high-ranking post. Congress refused. His dislike for Scott was deep seated, culminating in Polk's unfair treatment of the general at the end of the war when Scott was relieved of his command and recalled to face a military inquiry. At the same time, Polk made some disastrous appointments of civilians to military commands, the most notorious being that of his former law partner, Gideon Pillow. On balance, however, Polk's conduct of the war was good. There were limits to even his endurance, and the long hours he devoted to his task and his intense application of energy eventually undermined his health.

When Polk delivered his war message to Congress, he anticipated a short conflict. Indeed, he expected Mexico to sue for peace in the very first weeks and months of the war, but the Mexican government, in spite of an unbroken series of military defeats, refused to give up. Almost as soon as the war began, Polk was seeking ways to end it. He made overtures to the Paredes government in the summer of 1846, but without success. At the same time, he entered into discussions with Santa Anna, exiled in Havana, offering to help restore the former Mexican leader to power in return for a peaceful settlement of the conflict. Santa Anna gave his assurances, and Polk foolishly believed him. Following his return to Mexico, Santa Anna assumed personal command of the army, increased its size, and took the field against the Americans.

With the failure of his peace efforts, Polk decided to open an offensive against Mexico City from Vera Cruz and reluctantly placed Scott in charge. Confident that this operation would bring the war to an end, he appointed Nicholas Trist, chief clerk of the State Department, to accompany Scott and granted him authority to suspend hostilities and enter into peace negotiations whenever Mexico might appear receptive. His instructions called for the cession of Upper and Lower California and New Mexico, the cancellation of the claims, and the payment of $15 million to Mexico.

Trist's task was not an easy one. He became involved in bitter personal quarrels with Scott, who resented the encroachment on his own authority, although relations between the two men later improved. Mexico was still unwilling to end the war, and Trist's efforts to lure Mexican representatives to the peace table, including an abortive plan to bribe Santa Anna, proved futile. It was not until the end of the summer, with Scott's army in the environs of Mexico City, that Santa Anna finally appointed commissioners to deal with Trist. Still, there was no meeting of the minds. Polk's impatience mounted. Extreme expansionists in the United States were demanding all of Mexico, and Polk himself apparently concluded that more territory should be taken from Mexico. Finally, in October, 1847, frustrated and at the end of his patience, Polk recalled Trist.

Trist, however, was determined to conclude a peace treaty with Mexico. He disregarded Polk's order and remained in touch with his Mexican counterparts, confident that no one else Polk might send could do better than he. The discussions continued, Polk became exasperated at Trist's arrogance, and Scott began making preparations to resume military operations. British diplomats urged the Mexican government to make peace; the country was rapidly falling into disarray. Santa Anna finally relented at the end of January, 1848.

The Treaty of Guadalupe Hidalgo, named after the town in which the document was signed, followed Trist's original instructions (except for the cession of Lower California). Mexico agreed to recognize the Rio Grande as the boundary of Texas and to cede New Mexico and Upper California to the United States; the United States assumed all the claims against Mexico and agreed to pay Mexico $15 million. Although Trist negotiated and signed the settlement without diplomatic authority, Polk accepted it and in late February transmitted the treaty to the Senate for ratification. By the end of May, the treaty was ratified by Mexico. Dispatched by special messenger to Washington, D.C., the document was delivered to Polk on July 4, when he proclaimed an end to the war amid the festivities celebrating America's independence.

When Polk submitted his fourth and last annual message to Congress in December, 1848, he pointed proudly to the fulfillment of America's expansionist destiny. The acquisition of California and New Mexico, the settlement of the Oregon boundary, and the annexation of Texas, he declared, "are the results which . . . will add more to the strength and wealth of the nation than any which have preceded them since the adoption of the Constitution." Within less than four years, almost 1,200,000 square miles of territory had been added to the United States, an area half as large as the nation before the acquisition. The geographic configuration of the country had undergone a profound change, for "the Mississippi, so lately the frontier of our country, is now only its center."

The war with Mexico, he continued, belied the assertions of Europeans that the United States was a weak and ineffective power. The United States had demonstrated "the capacity of republican governments to prosecute successfully a just and necessary foreign war with all the vigor usually attributed to more arbitrary forms of government." There could no longer be any doubt that a "popular representative government" was equal to any emergency likely to arise. The war had increased American prestige abroad, and even at that moment, Polk declared, European countries were struggling to erect republican governments on the American model.

"Peace, plenty, and contentment reign throughout our borders, and our beloved country presents a sublime moral spectacle to the world. . . . We are the most favored people on the face of the earth."

Slavery

With the advantage of hindsight, one can now wonder at Polk's optimistic faith in the future of his country, for although the Mexican War resulted in the addition of vast new regions to the republic, it also raised an issue that would rock the nation to its foundations.

It was inevitable that the question of territorial expansion would become involved with that of slavery. The first warning had in fact been sounded in 1819 when Missouri applied for admission to the Union as a slave state. The Missouri Compromise of 1820 resolved the issue, but few Americans believed it to be finally settled. The emergence of a militant abolition movement in sections of the North was a clear indication that the problem would only become more acute. Northern antislavery and abolitionist elements, a small but growing minority, strenuously opposed the annexation of Texas on the ground that it would strengthen the institution of slavery. Later, they took a strong stand against the Mexican War, in the mistaken belief that the war was a grand plot of the slave power to extend the institution to new areas, and they vented their spleen against Polk as one of the leading conspirators. Although their cries were drowned out in the enthusiasm that followed the opening of the war, they constituted a formidable political force.

It was not an abolitionist, however, but a disgruntled Pennsylvania Democratic congressman who first interjected the slavery issue into the deliberations on the war. David Wilmot, who believed that the Western territories should be reserved for free white settlers but who also had clashed with President Polk over the latter's tariff and internal improvements policies, introduced a resolution in August, 1846, that would bar slavery forever from all territory taken from Mexico. The so-called Wilmot Proviso, attached to an appropriation bill, became a rallying point for antislavery people and a focus for opposition to the war itself.

Although Polk was a slaveholder with plantations in Tennessee and Mississippi, he had never actively defended the institution. As a member of Congress, he had deplored the persistent agitation of the issue and believed that it only hampered the deliberation of more important questions. He had supported the gag rule, by which antislavery petitions were automatically tabled without being read, and as speaker of the House of Representatives he had enforced it. At the same time, he viewed slavery as an evil that affected not only the South but the entire nation as well, insisting that slaves were a species of property with a difference, inasmuch as they were also rational human beings. Although abolitionists believed otherwise, Polk had never linked his continental vision with a desire to extend slavery throughout the West.

Polk was shocked and dismayed by Wilmot's move, calling the resolution a "mischie-

vous & foolish amendment." He feared that it would only entangle and frustrate his efforts to make peace with Mexico. "What connection slavery has with making peace with Mexico," he confided, "it is difficult to conceive." Still, the issue would not go away. Although it was never adopted by both houses of Congress, the Wilmot Proviso was raised in the following years, gathering momentum and strengthening the antislavery forces that were opposed to the war. Discussions in Congress became more heated, and Polk worried lest they sidetrack needed war legislation and jeopardize the acquisition of California and New Mexico. The question, he argued, was an abstract one, for not only had Mexico abolished slavery in the territory in question, but also slavery could never exist there. He blamed the "ultra" Northerners and the "ultra" Southerners for placing the Union in danger by their demands. "There is no patriotism on either side," he wrote, "it is a most wicked agitation that can end in no good and must produce infinite mischief."

With the end of the war and the ratification of the Treaty of Guadalupe Hidalgo, the discussion shifted to the question of providing territorial governments for the new lands. In August, 1848, Congress, after much debate, finally agreed on a bill organizing a territorial government for Oregon, with slavery prohibited in keeping with the wishes of the population, and Polk signed it into law, pointing out that the territory lay wholly north of the Missouri Compromise line.

Governments for California and New Mexico were not so easily established. Polk would have been happy to see the Missouri Compromise line extended to the Pacific, but Northern antislavery elements had already defeated that proposal. He was strongly opposed to the Wilmot Proviso's prohibition of slavery in the area because he believed that it would divide the nation, not because he was anxious to see slavery spread. At the same time, he tried to point out that the slavery question involved much more than a matter of property rights to the people in the South. The question "ascends far higher, and involves the domestic peace and security of every family." By the time Congress was able to agree on the organization of governments for California and New Mexico, Polk had not only left office but had also died.

Young Hickory

Although Polk's administration was dominated by territorial expansion and the war with Mexico, other matters on his agenda also demanded his attention. As a lifelong disciple of Andrew Jackson, he was determined to reinstate the Jacksonian program that had suffered erosion under the Whigs following the election of 1840. The modification of the tariff and the establishment of the independent treasury system, both mentioned to Bancroft, formed the core of his domestic program. Equally important was his determination to enforce Jacksonian scruples against the passage of internal improvements legislation by Congress. His program constituted a full-scale attack on Henry Clay's American System.

He succeeded in all three areas. Following the guidelines Polk set forth in his first message to Congress in December, 1845, new tariff legislation was introduced that would reduce the rates established by the Whigs in 1842 and place them on an ad valorem basis. In keeping with Jacksonian orthodoxy, the tariff was designed for revenue only, with protection merely incidental. Polk kept a close eye on the bill's progress, exerted pressure on wavering congressmen, and held numerous conferences with Democratic leaders. In August, 1846, the bill passed and was signed. Almost simultaneously, legislation restoring the independent Treasury system, or constitutional Treasury, as Polk called it, became law. The system, Polk hoped, would end all connection between the government and banks, whether state or national. Henceforth, the government would be the custodian of its own funds, depositing revenues in treasury vaults and disbursing them as the government's business might require. Polk placed great emphasis on these achievements, commenting that "the public good, as well as my own power and the glory of my administration" depended upon their success.

The question of internal improvements had long been a source of contention between the parties. For the Whigs, it served as an important element in their platform, alongside the protective tariff and the Bank of the United States. Although Andrew Jackson had not always been consistent in the matter, he made opposition to internal improvements projects that were essentially local in nature a primary characteristic of Democratic Party ideology. Polk shared Jackson's conviction that internal improvements bills were violations of constitutional authority.

In 1846, the same year in which the tariff and independent Treasury bills passed Congress, a comprehensive river and harbors bill, to which scores of internal improvement projects had been added, was enacted. Polk promptly vetoed it in one of the most important actions of his administration. The legislation, he insisted, was not authorized by the Constitution. "The whole frame of the Federal Constitution," he wrote, "proves that the Government which it creates was intended to be one of limited and specified powers." An interpretation of the Constitution as broad as that argued by the bill's supporters, he warned, would head "imperceptibly to a consolidation of power in a Government intended by the framers to be thus limited in its authority."

Polk's veto aroused a fierce opposition among many Democrats, especially in the Western sections of the country where internal improvements were deemed essential to economic development, but Polk was unmoved by their protests. The principle behind the question of internal improvements struck at his concept of limited national government and strong states' rights. "I am thoroughly convinced," he wrote, "that I am right on this subject."

Polk stood by his pledge to serve only one term as president and, in spite of the appeals of many of his friends, refused to allow his name to be presented to the Democratic convention in 1848. He also declined to express a preference for his party's nominee. The conflict over the extension of slavery to the Mexican cession continued to worry him, and as it became clear that the party was seriously divided on the question, concern gave way to depression. All that he had worked to achieve seemed threatened by an issue that he had not foreseen. The pressures of the presidential office began to take their toll on his health. When Zachary Taylor won election as president, Polk confided his deep regret to his diary. Taylor, he feared, had no opinions of his own; he would be wholly controlled by the leaders of the Whig Party. "The country," he was sure, "will be the loser by his election." On March 5, 1849, Taylor assumed the reins of government (March 4 had fallen on a Sunday), and that evening Polk and his wife began their journey home.

Polk returned to Tennessee physically exhausted and in ill health. On June 15, 1849, barely three months after he left office, he died unexpectedly. He was fifty-four years old.

Although lacking in charisma and judged by many of his contemporaries to be dull and colorless, Polk brought to the presidency a dynamic quality that few occupants of the office have had. He devoted his full energy to his duties, working tirelessly to achieve his goals. He put in long hours; twelve-hour days were not uncommon. "I am the hardest working man in this country," he once remarked. Polk seldom left the national capital and during his four years as president took only one brief vacation. "No President," he insisted, "who performs his duty faithfully and conscientiously can have any leisure." He maintained a constant surveillance over the departments of the government and kept in constant touch with the leadership in Congress. Polk was his own man, made his own decisions, and seldom allowed them to be changed. Even Jackson found that he could not influence Polk.

Polk left behind a monument to his energy and his dogged determination. Seldom has a president carried out such an ambitious and far-reaching program as did Polk in the brief space of four years. To George Bancroft, one of Polk's devoted supporters and friends, he was "one of the very foremost of our public men and one of the very best and most honest and most successful Presidents the country ever had." To another, a political leader who had tangled with Polk on more than one occasion, he was "the partisan of a principle—of a system of measures and policy which he believed to be essential to the purity and perpetuity of our republican institutions . . . [who] consecrated his life to the cause, and staked his fortunes on the result."

Robert W. Johannsen

Bibliographical References

Indispensable to a study of Polk's presidency is the diary he maintained during his administration, *The Diary of James K. Polk During His Presidency, 1845 to 1849*, 4 vols., 1910. Charles G. Sellers, Jr., has written two volumes of a definitive biography, *James K. Polk: Jacksonian, 1795-1843*, 1957, and *James K. Polk: Continentalist, 1843-1846*, 1966. An early biography is by Eugene I. McCormac, *James K. Polk: A Political Biography*, 1922. A study of Polk's conduct of the presidency is Charles A. McCoy, *Polk and the Presidency*, 1960. Sam W. Haynes and Oscar Handlin, *James K. Polk and the Expansionist Impulse*, 1997, deals with Polk's views on territorial expansion. For a documentary examination of Polk's life and presidency, see *Correspondence of James K. Polk*, 9 vols., edited by Herbert Weaver and others, 1969-1996, which reach to 1845. For a thorough examination of Polk's presidency, see Paul H. Bergeron, *The Presidency of James K. Polk*, 1987.

Zachary Taylor

12th President, 1849-1850

Born: November 24, 1784
Orange County, Virginia
Died: July 9, 1850
Washington, D.C.

Political Party: Whig
Vice President: Millard Fillmore

Cabinet Members

Secretary of State: John M. Clayton
Secretary of the Treasury: William M. Meredith
Secretary of War: George W. Crawford

Secretary of the Navy: William B. Preston
Attorney General: Reverdy Johnson
Postmaster General: Jacob Collamer
Secretary of the Interior: Thomas Ewing

Zachary Taylor entered the White House as a former professional soldier who had never voted in an election or run for public office before the presidential election of 1848. Although he died before completing even half of his term, he exhibited strong leadership during a dangerous period of domestic crisis.

Taylor's official portrait. *(White House Historical Society)*

A Military Heritage

Born at Montebello, Orange County, Virginia, on November 24, 1784, Taylor could claim descent from distinguished forebears. One ancestor arrived in North America on the *Mayflower*, and James Madison was the Taylors' second cousin. The family also counted Robert E. Lee as a distant relative. One of seven children born to Revolutionary War veteran Lieutenant Colonel Richard Taylor and his wife, Sarah Dabney Strother Taylor, young Zachary was still an infant when the family moved to Jefferson County, Kentucky. He grew up on a farm near Louisville with the benefit of little formal schooling.

In 1808, Taylor was commissioned a lieutenant of infantry and won promotion to captain two years later in the minuscule regular army of the United States. During the War of 1812, he repeatedly distinguished himself in action. In September, 1812, his determined defense of Fort Harrison in the Indiana Territory won for him a brevet promotion to major. In 1814, he led troops against a superior force of British soldiers and American Indians at Credit Island on the Mississippi, attacking aggressively before being forced to withdraw in the face of overwhelming enemy strength. It was the first and last time that Taylor retreated during his military career.

In 1832, Colonel Taylor again served in combat during the brief and tragic Black Hawk's War, which he regarded as a needless waste of lives and resources in a dubious cause. The conquered Chief Black Hawk later recalled Taylor's kind treatment of his people with great gratitude. From 1837 through 1840, he battled the Seminoles in Florida Territory. An ill-managed conflict fought under appalling conditions, the war brought Taylor brevet promotion to brigadier general as the result of his victory over the Seminoles at Lake Okeechobee in 1837. He finished his tour of duty in Florida as commander of all the troops in the territory, having won a reputation for resourcefulness and dogged determination.

In 1810, Taylor married Margaret Mackall Smith, the daughter of a prominent Maryland family. She gave birth to five daughters and one son between 1811 and 1826 before becoming an invalid. In 1835, one of their daughters, Sara Knox Taylor, married Mississippian Jefferson Davis against her father's wishes. Three months later, she died of malaria and Taylor remained embittered against Davis for more than a decade. Taylor's son, Richard, grew up to become one of the most prominent generals in the Confederate army. A second daughter, Mary Elizabeth, served as official hostess of the White House during Taylor's presidency.

Despite his frequent absences on campaign or frontier service, Taylor remained a devoted husband to his ailing wife and an affectionate father to his children.

The Mexican War
In 1845, the sixty-year-old Taylor was well known in the army but still little known in the nation as a whole despite his victories in two wars. He was placed in command of the American troops stationed at Corpus Christi, Texas, that year and instructed to guard against Mexican incursions into the newly annexed state. Early in 1846, his "Army of Observation" marched south to the disputed territory between the Rio Grande and the Nueces River and encamped on the eastern bank of the Rio Grande across from Matamoras, Mexico. Fighting erupted in April, 1846, when Mexican troops ambushed an American patrol on the north bank of the Rio Grande. On May 8 and 9, Taylor met and defeated a Mexican army in pitched battles at Palo Alto and Resaca de la Palma. The enemy fled across the Rio Grande, leaving Taylor a new national hero in the United States while giving open justification to President James K. Polk's call for a declaration of war against Mexico.

An aggressive commander, Taylor chose to maintain the momentum of his success by pursuing the beaten Mexicans across the Rio Grande and driving south against the city of Monterrey, a key city in the northern portion of the country. It fell to his troops after fierce fighting raged through the suburbs and streets from September 21 to 23. The defeated defenders were allowed to withdraw their forces under a truce granted by Taylor. This act of chivalry angered President Polk, who desired the swiftest possible conclusion to the war while fearing Taylor's potential rise as a political rival to candidates of his own Democratic Party.

Polk's concerns led him to choose General Winfield Scott rather than Taylor to lead the main American offensive aimed at the conquest

Taylor leads U.S. troops to victory in the Battle of Buena Vista. *(Library of Congress)*

of Mexico City. A large portion of Taylor's command was taken from him and assigned to reinforce Scott's expeditionary force as it prepared to drive inland to the west after making an amphibious landing at Vera Cruz on the Gulf coast. Taylor was left to secure control of northern Mexico with a badly depleted army.

From February 21 to 23, 1847, General Antonio López de Santa Anna learned of the enemy forces' division and decided to strike north to destroy Taylor before turning to face Scott's thrust from the coast. Santa Anna attacked Taylor at Buena Vista, a stretch of rugged, hilly terrain south of Saltillo. Although some of the American volunteers panicked under fire, Taylor masterfully held his line together and bloodily repulsed the enemy assaults with musketry and skillfully handled artillery. The five thousand Americans inflicted heavy casualties on the twenty thousand Mexicans and forced Santa Anna to withdraw in frustration.

Buena Vista was the most spectacular victory of Taylor's military career, and it had more to do with his subsequent election to the presidency than any single factor.

Scott successfully captured Mexico City at the climax of his offensive, and a peace treaty was signed at Guadalupe Hidalgo early in 1848. The United States had won vast new southwestern territories extending from the Rio Grande to the Pacific, and Taylor returned home a hero despite Polk's attempts to belittle his fame.

Taylor as President: Free States and Threats of Secession

The Whig Party had last won the White House in 1840 with William Henry Harrison, a part-time soldier with enduring political aspirations. In June, 1848, the Whigs eagerly nominated Zachary Taylor, an even more glamorous military figure, as their presidential candidate.

"Old Rough and Ready," as his soldiers called him, was the perfect candidate for the times. His earthy, unassuming personality and reputation for courage and decisiveness were complemented by an obscure record on the prevailing political issues. His ancestry and ownership of slaves and a cotton plantation made him attractive to Southern voters, while his lack of prior political involvement meant that he had said or done nothing to offend groups in other parts of the country.

The Democrats countered with Lewis Cass of Michigan, a colorless party figure. Cass joined Taylor in conducting a campaign that was purposely vague on the pressing issues of the day: slavery and the future of the new Western territories. Even before the war had ended, debate had raged in Congress over whether slavery should be permitted in the new territories won from Mexico. Many Northern abolitionists demanded a permanent prohibition against slavery in the new lands, whereas moderates favored the concept of popular or "squatter" sovereignty, which would allow the residents of those territories to make independent decisions on the issue. Neither Taylor nor Cass openly committed himself to either side of the debate, a prudent attempt to win votes by not antagonizing any group in the electorate.

The campaign was complicated by the appearance of the Free-Soil Party. Its candidate, Martin Van Buren, continually agitated against the expansion of slavery westward and attempted to goad his opponents into confronting the issue in a decisive manner. Taylor won a narrow victory, with 1,360,967 popular votes to 1,222,342 for Cass and only 291,253 for Van Buren. In the electoral college, Taylor received 163 votes to 127 for Cass and none for Van Buren. It is probable, however, that Van Buren deflected enough Democratic votes from Cass in New York to throw the contest to Taylor.

Taylor was the first man to enter the White House with no previous political experience or training. He was also the first professional soldier to hold the office. Although a Southerner and a slaveholder on his Louisiana plantation, he had acquired a national outlook from his military service and was no friend to sectional extremists of any stripe.

Congress had failed to provide any form of civil government for the new territories before Taylor's election, and he disliked the prospect of administration by military governors. The new president wanted both California and New Mexico brought promptly into the Union. Once they had achieved statehood they could dispose of the slavery issue as their citizens desired.

California, where the Gold Rush had resulted in a rapid rise in population and demands for statehood, quickly adopted a constitution that prohibited slavery. When Congress convened in December, 1849, Taylor urged California's admission while calling for popular sovereignty in New Mexico—that is, allowing the people, acting through their legislature, to decide whether the territory should permit slavery. His recommendations were ignored by the bitterly divided Congress. Southern legislators feared that the admission of California would weaken their position in the Senate, and numerous other sectional issues began to be joined with that of what to do about slavery in California and New Mexico.

Determined abolitionists wanted slavery barred from the District of Columbia. Southerners countered that only the state of Maryland could authorize such a measure, for it had donated the land from which the district was organized. Even if Maryland consented to the prohibition, the South could not countenance an act that would place a national stigma on its "peculiar institution."

Southerners were also nettled by Northern sympathy and aid extended to runaway bondsmen. Northern state laws—personal liberty laws—that barred courts and law enforcement agencies from assisting Southerners in finding and returning runaways led them to agitate for a strictly enforced national law which would require Northern assistance in such efforts. This proposal, seen as an attempt to force complicity in slavery, deeply angered abolitionists.

Another sensitive issue arose over Texas's claim to the eastern part of New Mexico Territory. Texans fought what they considered an attempt to annex a portion of their domain to another state and asked the national government to assume their share of the debt which they had incurred in fighting the Mexican War. Antislavery Northerners opposed their claims in an effort to reduce the size of at least one slave state.

The South as a whole was angered and alarmed by the possibility of a new bloc of free states entering the Union. In 1849, the number of free and slave states was equally balanced at fifteen. Only in the Senate did the South retain numerical equality in representation. Moreover, Southerners resented the affront to their honor implied by the enactment of any national law prohibiting slavery in the territories. Many talked of secession, and members of Congress appeared armed in its chambers and corridors. President Taylor faced a major crisis of the Union as 1850 began.

Taylor chose nation over section in his response to the crisis. Supported by most of his fellow Whigs on the issues, he took a firm stand in dealing with the volatile mixture of Democrats and Free-Soilers in Congress. Speaking for the South, John C. Calhoun demanded full rights for the slaveholders in the West and protection for their property in the East. Abolitionists, such as William H. Seward and Salmon P. Chase, decried any compromise with slavery, talked of a higher law than the Constitution—the law of God, which slavery contravened—and demanded that slavery be prohibited in all the territories. Henry Clay, meanwhile, joined by Daniel Webster and Stephen A. Douglas, led moderate Northerners in seeking a compromise.

Clay's compromise proposals met with continued Southern opposition, but President Taylor persisted in his insistence that California be admitted to the Union before other issues were considered. He made it clear that Southern recourse to secession would be met with force, and that he was willing personally to lead troops against his native section if it should become necessary to preserve the Union. The stalemate in Congress persisted, but Taylor's blunt response had effectively called the South's bluff on the threat to secede.

As Congress remained deadlocked, Taylor was suddenly stricken with a violent stomach disorder following an attack of heat prostration. He died on July 9, 1850, and was succeeded by Vice President Millard Fillmore. Taylor's death may have sobered the sectional and antislavery zealots in the government, for an amended version of Clay's original "omnibus bill" was eventually agreed upon by Congress and enacted by mid-September. Passed as five separate measures, the Compromise of 1850 provided for: the admission of California as a free state; the creation of New Mexico Territory without reference to slavery and the payment of $10 million to Texas for relinquishing to New Mexico its claim to the disputed area east of the Rio Grande; the formation of the Territory of Utah without reference to slavery; a strong fugitive slave act; and the abolition of the slave trade in the District of Columbia. With the achievement of this compromise the survival of the Union was assured for another troubled decade.

In contrast to strife and turmoil on the domestic scene, foreign affairs during Taylor's brief administration were calm and uneventful. The only happening of significance was the signing of the Clayton-Bulwer Treaty with Great Britain. By its terms the two nations agreed to join in promoting a canal across Central America which neither nation should ever fortify or put under its exclusive control. Furthermore, neither party was ever to occupy or claim sovereignty over any part of Central America.

Taylor's Legacy

Zachary Taylor was an able and dedicated soldier. His intelligence, ingenuity, and aggressiveness served the United States well from the War of 1812 through the Mexican conflict. Although he cannot be rated as one of the truly great captains cast in the mold of Robert E. Lee, Ulysses Grant, or Dwight D. Eisenhower, his skillful handling of a greatly outnumbered American force at Buena Vista averted what could have been a costly defeat and a serious setback to the achievement of national aims in the Mexican War. At a time when many Americans suspected the officer corps of harboring aristocratic pretensions, Taylor's simple dignity and lack of pomp won the popular confidence in both his person and his profession.

As president, Taylor left no great body of legislation behind him. He coined no ringing slogans and led the nation on no great crusades. His major contribution as president was his firm and resolute adherence to the old Union. A slaveholder himself, he had no desire to interfere with the practice where it already existed, but he was determined that it be permitted neither to expand nor to imperil the Union. A Southerner, but also a son of the Western frontier and a staunch nationalist, he displayed great moral courage in defending the Constitution against domestic as well as foreign enemies.

Wayne R. Austerman

Bibliographical References

A useful biography of Taylor is Brainerd Dyer, *Zachary Taylor*, 1946. Also of value is Holman Hamilton's study, *Zachary Taylor*, 1941. The military phase of Taylor's life is ably dealt with in such works as K. Jack Bauer, *The Mexican War, 1846-1848*; K. Jack Bauer, *Zachary Taylor: Soldier, Planter, Statesman of the Old Southwest*, 1985; Robert S. Henry, *The Story of the Mexican War*, 1950; and Otis A. Singletary, *The Mexican War*, 1960. Taylor's own correspondence during the period from 1846 to 1848 is preserved in *Letters of Zachary Taylor, from the Battlefields of the Mexican War*, 1908. The Taylor presidency and related matters have inspired an extensive literature. Milo M. Quaife edited *The Diary of James K. Polk During His Presidency*, 1910. This four-volume work contains useful insights on Taylor's Mexican War role and his subsequent rise to political prominence. Hamilton's valuable *Prologue to Conflict*, 1964, deals with the events surrounding the Compromise of 1850 and Taylor's impact on the sectional crisis. Elbert B. Smith, *The Presidencies of Zachary Taylor and Millard Fillmore*, 1988, is an analysis of the presidency of Taylor and his successor.

Millard Fillmore

13th President, 1850-1853

Born: January 7, 1800
　　　Summerhill, New York
Died: March 8, 1874
　　　Buffalo, New York

Political Party: Whig
Vice President: none

Cabinet Members

Secretary of State: Daniel Webster, Edward Everett

Secretary of the Treasury: Thomas Corwin
Secretary of War: Charles M. Conrad
Secretary of the Navy: William A. Graham, John P. Kennedy
Attorney General: John J. Crittenden
Postmaster General: Nathan K. Hall, Sam D. Hubbard
Secretary of the Interior: Thomas McKennan, A. H. H. Stuart

Fillmore's official portrait. *(White House Historical Society)*

Millard Fillmore has been characterized as a "handsome, dignified man of no great abilities." Although perhaps harsh, this comment underscores the truth that Fillmore was a man of unrealized expectations. He became president by a tragic fluke of fate, and although possessing some genuine administrative ability, he never displayed the leadership qualities of his predecessor, Zachary Taylor.

An Education in Practical Politics

Fillmore was one of the few prominent nineteenth century American politicians who could truthfully boast of having been born in a log cabin. The second of six children born to a poverty-stricken family in Cayuga County, New York, Fillmore entered the world on the bitter winter day of January 7, 1800. His father apprenticed him in boyhood to a cloth-dressing and carding business in the hope that he would learn a useful trade.

Young Fillmore felt the stirrings of higher ambition and purchased a release from his apprenticeship to pursue an education. While still working at the textile mill, he had already enrolled as a part-time student at an academy in Mount Hope, New York. In 1819, his father obtained for him a clerkship in the office of Judge Walter Wood in Montville, New York. Fillmore clerked for Wood's firm and for another firm in Buffalo, New York, for several years. He also supplemented his meager income by teaching school. In 1823, he was admitted to the state bar and began his own practice in East Aurora, New York. As his business prospered, he hired a student clerk, Nathan K. Hall, who would subsequently become his law partner, political associate, and presidential cabinet member. In 1826, Fillmore married Abigail Powers, the daughter of a Moravia, New York, clergyman and the sister of a local judge. They had a daughter in 1828 and another in 1832. The marriage endured until her death in 1853. Fillmore remained a widower until 1858, when he married a wealthy widow from Albany, Caroline Carmichael McIntosh. Her income allowed the Fillmores to live fashionably in a handsome mansion on Niagara Square in Buffalo.

In 1826, Fillmore joined the Anti-Masonic Party. This, the first organized third party in American history, originated in the 1820's in western New York in opposition to the Society of Freemasons and other secret, exclusive, and presumably undemocratic organizations. Fillmore soon became closely linked to the movement's leaders, William H. Seward, Thurlow Weed, and Francis Granger. Marked as a rising figure in local politics, Fillmore rode the Anti-Masonic fervor to win three terms in the state assembly. An amiable legislator, he gained some distinction by sponsoring a bill to abolish imprisonment for debt.

In 1830, Fillmore moved to Buffalo and became a prominent member of the Unitarian Church while continuing to enjoy a thriving legal partnership with Hall. A popular figure in Erie County, he won a seat in Congress in 1832, still upholding the Anti-Masonic banner. By 1834, he was following Weed's leadership as a newly converted Whig but declined the party's congressional nomination for fear of alienating his Anti-Masonic supporters at home. He astutely strengthened his political base by securing the editorship of the *Buffalo Commercial Advertiser* for a close associate.

Reelected to Congress in 1836 as a Whig, he enjoyed three consecutive terms before declining to run again in 1842. Fillmore was a convinced protectionist and used his position as chair of the Ways and Means Committee to secure passage of the 1842 tariff bill through the House of Representatives.

Spurred by his increasing ambition, Fillmore began to chafe at Weed's continued dominance of the New York Whigs. He supported Granger, Weed's rival, for the state governorship in 1838, only to see him lose the nomination to Seward, a Weed ally. Fillmore subsequently declined Seward's offer of a post with the state but secured for Granger the office of postmaster general in the Harrison administration.

Although Fillmore was a liberal Whig and leader of the party's antislavery faction, he opposed interference with the institution where it already existed, even as he staunchly opposed its expansion elsewhere. Like many New Yorkers, Fillmore was preoccupied by the perceived threat of massive foreign immigration, and he led the nativist opposition against fellow Whigs such as Seward and Weed, who saw the influx of foreigners as a way to forge new alliances and win added support for the party.

The Taylor-Fillmore Ticket

Accepting the gubernatorial nomination in 1844, Fillmore lost to his Democratic opponent. He blamed his defeat on "abolitionists and foreign Catholics" and accused Seward and Weed of having placed him in a doomed contest. Serving as state comptroller in 1847, Fillmore sponsored internal reforms in the office and designed a currency system that later served as a model for the National Banking Act of 1863. The following year he returned to the national stage as Zachary Taylor's vice presidential running mate. It was a purely pragmatic move by the Whigs, for Taylor's nomination had antagonized Henry Clay's supporters and antislavery partisans. Fillmore was viewed as a healing agent and assured winner for the ticket in New York State.

The 1848 election gave the Whigs a slim victory in a climate of rising sectional tension as debate flared over the westward expansion of slavery. Fillmore mistakenly believed that the Whigs' victory had ended "all ideas of disunion." The Taylor-Fillmore administration was instead witness to the greatest domestic political crisis the nation had faced since that over the admission of Missouri to the Union as a slave state in 1820. In addition, Fillmore's experience with the traditional frustrations associated with the vice presidency was made even more bitter by internal bickering within the Whig Party. A patronage struggle between Fillmore and Seward ended with Taylor supporting Seward's rival and awarding him control of all patronage appointments in the state of New York. It was typical of Fillmore that he should be personally involved in such minor matters as the nation began to divide ever more deeply along sectional lines.

The long-simmering dispute over slavery threatened to boil over in the wake of the Mexican War. The Wilmot Proviso of 1846 had never become law, but its proposed ban on the importation of slaves into the territories won from Mexico was still a popular rallying point for antislavery Northerners in Congress. Southern demands for a stringent fugitive slave law, Northern attacks on the existence of slavery in the District of Columbia, and a Texas claim on portions of New Mexico created a sharply divided body when Congress convened in December, 1849.

The House of Representatives numbered 112 Democrats, 105 Whigs, 12 Free-Soilers, and 1 Native American. Sectional rivalry prevented any party from forming a stable majority, and a deadlock resulted whenever an attempt was made to determine the status of the new territories or their eventual acceptance into the Union as slave or free states. Frustrated Southerners spoke openly of convening a secession convention the following June.

The nation's political leadership offered a variety of proposals to defuse the crisis. President Taylor pressed for the immediate admission of California as a free state, while warning that any attempt at secession would be suppressed with the full force of the government. John C. Calhoun led the South in demanding equal rights for slaveholders in the West and blanket protection for the institution where it already existed. Henry Clay of Kentucky joined Daniel Webster of Massachusetts and Stephen A. Douglas of Illinois in sponsoring a compromise settlement. Fillmore joined Taylor in opposing any extension of slavery and hoped to avoid an open breach in the Union. He was disturbed by Seward's adamant refusal to support any compromise with slaveholders.

In May, 1850, Clay's "omnibus bill" presented the compromise package to a restive Congress. Clay proposed that California be admitted as a free state, that in the rest of the Mexican cession territorial governments be formed without restrictions on slavery, that Texas yield its land claims in New Mexico in exchange for compensation, that the slave trade, but not slavery itself, be abolished in the District of Columbia, and that a strict fugitive slave law be passed.

Earlier versions of this compromise had sparked violent debates in Congress, and sectional suspicions still made agreement over Clay's simplified version difficult.

A parade in San Francisco celebrates California's admission as the thirty-first state in 1850. *(Library of Congress)*

Inheriting the Presidency: The Compromise of 1850

President Taylor's death in July, 1850, thrust the burden of leadership upon Fillmore, and although he lacked the blunt forcefulness of his predecessor, the unqualified support he and his cabinet gave to Clay's efforts proved decisive. Fillmore's choice of John J. Crittenden as attorney general and Webster as secretary of state, both moderates, was open indication of his desire for a compromise. His August message to Congress called for indemnification of Texas in exchange for that state surrendering its claim to New Mexico Territory. Understanding the importance of give and take, however, Fillmore also sought to placate the South by including an affirmation of states' rights in his first annual message. Such gestures helped to win passage and acceptance for the Compromise of 1850 while soothing the inflamed feelings of the South.

The Compromise of 1850 can rightfully be called the apogee of Fillmore's presidency and public career. In other matters, his administration emphasized national economic development by fostering internal improvements and the growth of overseas trade. Commodore Matthew C. Perry used diplomacy and the implicit threat of his warships to secure open commerce with Japan, which enhanced American interest in Asia and the Pacific. The patronage issue remained a domestic irritant, causing further conflict with Seward and his allies in the party as Postmaster General Hall used his influence to weaken their hold on the system in New York State so that more conservative Whigs could gain posts.

A Career in Decline

In 1852, Fillmore enjoyed strong support from Southern and Northern conservative Whigs for the presidential nomination, but Webster's bid also gained conservative and moderate strength, dividing the party. General Winfield Scott claimed the nomination as the antislavery faction's candidate. Denied renomination by his own party, a disappointed Fillmore went home to Buffalo in 1853 after the inauguration of his successor, Franklin Pierce, and became the chief spokesperson for the rapidly growing nativist Know-Nothing Party. The rise of the avowedly sectionalist Republican Party concerned him, but his 1856 candidacy for the Know-Nothings saw him finish far behind James Buchanan of the Democrats, the victor, and John C. Frémont of the Republicans.

Realizing that his national political career was over, Fillmore watched the nation drift toward disunion with mounting alarm. He deplored Abraham Lincoln's election in 1860 and saw little hope of averting a violent Southern response. Although Fillmore remained loyal to the national government during the Civil War, he blamed the Republicans for what he considered a needless tragedy. In 1864, he supported Democrat George B. McClellan against Lincoln. After the war, when the Radical Republicans attacked Andrew Johnson, he sympathized with the embattled president.

Domestic and local affairs also occupied much of Fillmore's attention after leaving the White House. He was the first chancellor of the University of Buffalo, serving from 1846 until his death. He also helped to establish Buffalo General Hospital and was a patron and first president of the Buffalo Historical Society. His wife became a chronic invalid during the 1860's, which made further demands on Fillmore's time, but their marriage remained stable and happy. Fillmore remained the well-spoken and kindly retired politico until he suffered a paralytic stroke in February, 1874. A second stroke followed, and Fillmore died on March 8, 1874.

Millard Fillmore was a skilled and insightful practical politician. He understood the psychology of his own New York electorate and grasped how issues and personalities could be molded to reach effective compromises in the flow of politics. Well-read and surprisingly devoid of the overweening egotism that afflicted many of his fellow politicians, Fillmore was essentially a good man of limited perceptions and talents. He was generous and public spirited among his native New Yorkers, but he feared the influx of foreigners and joined in the persecution of the Masons. Animated by both moral and pragmatic sentiments in his opposition to slavery, he sought accommodation and not confrontation in dealing with Southern threats of secession over the issue. Sadly shortsighted on the major issues of his day, Fillmore was at least skilled and fortunate enough to delay the Union's dissolution by a decade while avoiding a genuine confrontation with the ills that beset it. Unlike Zachary Taylor, he habitually chose the path of least resistance.

Wayne R. Austerman

Bibliographical References

Fillmore's papers reside in the Buffalo Historical Society. They have also been edited for publication by Frank H. Severance in the *Buffalo Historical Society Publications*, vols. 10 and 11, 1907. Among the notable biographies are William E. Griffis, *Millard Fillmore*, 1915, and Robert J. Rayback, *Millard Fillmore, Biography of a President*, 1959. Dorothea L. Dix, *The Lady and the President: The Letters of Dorothea Dix and Millard Fillmore*, 1975, edited by Charles M. Snyder, is a collection of correspondence between the president and an advocate of reform. Edward Everett Hale, *William H. Seward*, 1910, is a useful study of Fillmore's chief rival. Ulrich B. Phillips's study *The Southern Whigs, 1834-1854*, 1910, provides insights on the rise and fall of Fillmore's party. Ray A. Billington, *The Protestant Crusade, 1800-1860*, 1938, treats Fillmore's involvement with the Know-Nothings in an evenhanded manner. Holman Hamilton, *Prologue to Conflict*, 1964, is an invaluable aid to understanding the skein of issues, people, and events surrounding the Compromise of 1850. Useful general studies of the period can be found in Avery O. Craven, *The Growth of Southern Nationalism, 1848-1861*, 1953, and Allan Nevins, *Ordeal of the Union: Fruits of Manifest Destiny*, vol. 1, 1947. Benson L. Grayson, *The Unknown President: The Administration of Millard Fillmore*, 1981, and Elbert B. Smith, *The Presidency of Zachary Taylor and Millard Fillmore*, 1988, are detailed accounts of the Fillmore presidency.

Franklin Pierce

14th President, 1853-1857

Born: November 23, 1804
Hillsborough, New Hampshire
Died: October 8, 1869
Concord, New Hampshire

Political Party: Democratic
Vice President: William R. D. King

Cabinet Members
Secretary of State: William L. Marcy
Secretary of the Treasury: James Guthrie
Secretary of War: Jefferson Davis

Secretary of the Navy: James C. Dobbin
Attorney General: Caleb Cushing
Postmaster General: James Campbell
Secretary of the Interior: Robert McClelland

Pierce's official portrait. *(White House Historical Society)*

Franklin Pierce was probably the most obscure man ever elected president. Although he had served in both the House and the Senate, he had been out of national politics for a decade when he was nominated in 1852 and was barely known outside his native state of New Hampshire. Indicative of his lack of national stature, the president-elect stopped in New York City on his way to Washington, D.C., for the inauguration and strolled down a crowded Broadway without once being recognized.

Pierce's unexpected nomination grew out of the deep divisions within the Democratic Party. Factionalism, personal rivalries, and divisions over a number of issues including the expansion of slavery and the Compromise of 1850 increasingly plagued the party. As a result the 1852 Democratic convention deadlocked, with none of the leading contenders able to secure the necessary two-thirds vote for nomination. In this situation a number of dark horse possibilities were brought forward, and on the forty-ninth ballot the delegates in a stampede named the little-known Concord lawyer. Lacking any knowledge of Pierce or his principles, most delegates blindly accepted assurances that he was sound on the Compromise of 1850 and would be evenhanded in distributing patronage.

Born in 1804, the Democratic nominee was the son of General Benjamin Pierce, a prominent New Hampshire politician. In 1824 he was graduated from Bowdoin College, where he formed a lifelong friendship with Nathaniel Hawthorne. Five years later, aided by his name (which the family pronounced "purse"), Pierce entered the state legislature. He subsequently served three terms in the House of Representatives, where he was a strong supporter of Andrew Jackson, and was elected senator in 1836. The youngest member of the Senate, he was a dogged party man, hardworking but unimaginative. Pierce resigned in 1842 before the end of his term. His decision to leave national politics stemmed in part from his wife's dislike of political life and his inability to resist the temptations of Washington society. Genial and well-liked, Pierce was fond of liquor, for which he had a low tolerance and which earned for him a certain notoriety. He became a temperance advocate in the 1840's and struggled the rest of his life with varying success to forgo stimulants. Indeed, his wife, remembering his earlier behavior, collapsed when news arrived of his nomination for president.

Following his retirement from the Senate, Pierce resumed his career as a lawyer, but he reentered public life during the Mexican War as a brigadier general in the army. His military career was also undistinguished, its most notable aspect being his fainting after his horse fell during the Battle of Contreras. On his return home, he resumed his place as a leader of the state Democratic Party but did

A flyer in 1855 announces a meeting for antislavery "Free-Soilers" in Kansas. *(Library of Congress)*

not hold public office again until his election as president.

An Ill-Starred Administration

Pierce scored a clear victory in the 1852 election. Carrying every state but four, he won a majority of the popular votes, which was increasingly an unusual feat. Pierce's triumph was soon scarred by tragedy, however, as his only surviving child, Benjamin, was gruesomely killed in January, 1853, in a train wreck before his horrified parents' eyes. Plagued for years by religious self-doubt, Pierce was haunted by guilt over his son's death, which he feared was punishment for his own religious shortcomings. A pall of tragedy hung over the entire gloomy Pierce presidency, with the First Lady in mourning and social life held to a cheerless minimum. The accident undermined Pierce's none-too-large self-confidence at the crucial beginning of his ill-starred term in the White House.

When he assumed office, Pierce was forty-eight, the youngest chief executive the country had ever elected. His program to reunite the Democratic Party was twofold. First, he planned to use the federal patronage to heal the rifts in the party. He announced that the past would be forgotten and all factions recognized in appointments. In particular, the president intended to welcome back into the party's good graces the Van Burenite barnburners, who had bolted in 1848 and helped defeat Lewis Cass, the party's presidential candidate, and the radical states' rights men in the South, who had advocated secession following passage of the Compromise of 1850.

His second policy was territorial expansion, which he believed was generally popular and would especially appeal to Democrats. Ignoring the deep divisions that the territorial question had recently produced, Pierce confidently announced in his inaugural address, "My administration will not be controlled by any timid forebodings of evil from expansion." His major goal was to acquire Cuba, long an object of desire for American expansionists and proslavery men. He also hoped to gain more territory southward, especially from Mexico. That slavery would be suitable in most if not all of this territory seemed to Pierce, who had long denounced abolitionists and believed the slavery issue had no place in national politics, an unimportant consideration.

Physically unimposing, Pierce was only 5 feet, 9 inches tall and of wiry build, but he was a genuinely handsome man, with pale coloring, thin features, and a full head of hair.

Graceful and well-mannered, he exuded a boyish charm mingled with a good dose of vanity. For all of his personal attractiveness, however, his flawed character was inadequate to meet the challenge before him. Known as Frank to his intimates, he was a weak and indecisive person, without intellectual depth and excessively optimistic, who when challenged took refuge in stubborn inflexibility. The new president knew few Democratic power brokers when he took office, and the party's real leaders, especially in the Senate, were unwilling to defer to one they considered a nonentity. Social and affable, Pierce desperately wanted to be liked, and rather than confront those he disagreed with, he preferred to seem to endorse whatever policy was recommended to him regardless of whether he agreed with it. Men who left believing that Pierce concurred with them only to see him ultimately adopt a different course naturally accused him of disingenuousness and came to distrust him thoroughly.

Pierce's inexperience and ineptitude came to the fore immediately. He wanted an old friend, John A. Dix of New York, a barnburner who had reluctantly bolted the Democratic Party in 1848, to head his cabinet as secretary of state, and he offered Dix the post. When Southerners and anti-Van Burenites objected, rather than insisting on his right to name his cabinet and on the necessity for all party members to accept his policy of reconciliation, Pierce backed down and withdrew the tendered appointment. Keen-sighted politicians saw that Pierce lacked the inner strength to command acceptance of his policies and could be intimidated.

As finally constituted, Pierce's cabinet was not without talent. Its leading members were Secretary of State William L. Marcy; Secretary of the Treasury James Guthrie, a leading advocate of accepting the barnburners back into the regular party organization; Secretary of War Jefferson Davis, who represented the anti-Compromise Southern wing of the party; and

Attorney General Caleb Cushing, a man of distinguished intellectual ability but without any firm political principles. Pierce intended that Marcy, the most politically experienced and capable of the group, be the premier, but the New Yorker was quickly shunted aside in the administration's councils by Davis and Cushing. This development was one pregnant with potential disaster, especially under a weak and vacillating leader such as Pierce. Davis and Cushing were efficient subordinates, but they were too extreme to be given any important say in policy. More and more, they directed the administration along a pro-Southern, proslavery course that badly weakened the party in the North. Pierce's diplomatic appointments were equally unfortunate; they included a gang of romantic adventurers, bumptious representatives of the proexpansion Young America movement, whose antics brought ridicule on the administration, involved the country in a series of unnecessary imbroglios, and helped undermine the president's foreign policy. Compounding Pierce's problems was his failure to put the administration organ, the *Washington Union*, in loyal hands. Of its two editors, A. O. P. Nicholson, a Cass man, feuded with several members of the cabinet, whereas the talented John W. Forney was personally loyal to James Buchanan and deserted Pierce in 1856.

Repeal of the Missouri Compromise: The Kansas Crisis

Problems were not long in developing. The administration's patronage policies satisfied no one. Not enough jobs existed to buy off every faction, and in any event men resented recognition of their rivals. Such problems plagued the party in virtually every state, although the situation in New York was the most intractable and ominous for the party's future. There dissident Democrats refused to accede to the administration's appointment of former Free-Soilers and ran a separate state ticket in 1853,

thereby handing control of the nation's leading state back to the Whigs.

Such was the condition of the Democratic Party, with its ranks in complete disarray and the party seemingly rudderless, when Congress assembled in December, 1853. Some men, such as Stephen A. Douglas of Illinois, believed that without vigorous new leadership the party would soon fall apart, whereas a number of powerful Southern senators saw in the existing political chaos a chance to impose new policies and erect a new test of party orthodoxy for Pierce's despised Free-Soil nominees, who had to be confirmed in the upcoming session. The Missouri Compromise of 1820 had forever prohibited slavery in the remaining portion of the Louisiana Purchase, but Southerners now demanded that the principle of popular sovereignty—that the residents of the territory (at some unspecified time) decide whether they wanted slavery—be applied to this region. To be confirmed, Pierce's barnburner nominees would be required to endorse this policy, a bitter pill since they had earlier favored the Wilmot Proviso, which sought to bar slavery from all the territory acquired from Mexico.

Under pressure, Douglas, who was preparing a bill to organize the Kansas and Nebraska territories, agreed to repeal the time-honored Missouri Compromise, but the Illinois senator wanted the administration's endorsement before proceeding with such a controversial move. In a rare Sunday interview at the White House on January 22, 1854, Douglas and a group of Southern leaders induced Pierce to accept the proposed repeal of the 1820 compromise as the unspoken price to get his appointments through the Senate. Knowing the president's unreliability, Douglas insisted that Pierce put his support in writing. In taking this step, Pierce ignored Marcy's advice and was influenced instead by Davis and Cushing, the latter of whom convinced him that the Missouri Compromise was unconstitutional anyway; he was also eager to repel the damaging accusation that his administration was Free-Soil in its sympathies. Pierce's acceptance of the repeal of the Missouri Compromise was the most fateful day of his presidency. It not only made a mockery of the 1852 platform's pledge not to reopen the sectional controversy but also precipitated a series of problems that ultimately drove Pierce from office.

Once committed, Pierce threw the power of the administration behind the Kansas-Nebraska bill. No record remains of the specific means used to secure support for the bill, but aided by these efforts the bill finally passed the House in early May by a vote of 113-100, with Northern Democrats evenly divided. Hailing it as the first great measure of his administration, Pierce signed the bill on May 30. Compounding this error, the *Washington Union* officially announced in another serious blunder that support of the law was a test of party regularity. A number of Northern Democrats refused to support the law and bolted in the fall elections; before long, many of these dissidents would join the new Republican Party, which the Kansas-Nebraska Act spawned. The Nebraska issue contributed to the Democratic Party's crushing defeat in the 1854 elections; the party lost sixty-six Northern seats and control of the House of Representatives, dooming Pierce's legislative program.

Trouble soon erupted in the Territory of Kansas. Southerners believed that an unspoken agreement existed that Kansas would be a slave state and Nebraska free, and Pierce certainly acted as if this were the case. Northerners opposed to the repeal of the Missouri Compromise, however, had no intention of conceding Kansas to slavery. Almost immediately a race developed between pro- and antislavery elements to settle the region, and elections in the territory were marred by massive illegal voting by Missourians. When Pierce upheld the fraudulently elected proslavery territorial legislature, which expelled the legally elected free state members, enacted a thoroughly unfair

election law, and passed a harsh legal code to protect slavery and silence critics, free state men organized their own "state" government, defied the territorial authorities, and petitioned Congress for admission as a free state. With two governments in existence, fighting soon erupted and flared off and on for the next two years.

What would have been a disorganized situation anyway was made worse by Pierce's unfortunate territorial appointments, headed by the volatile Samuel Lecompte, an aggressively proslavery Southerner, as chief justice, and Andrew Reeder, a local Democratic politician from Pennsylvania of no significance and without administrative experience, as governor. Tactless and erratic, Reeder was soon at odds with the legislature, and in response to heavy Southern pressure Pierce finally replaced him with former Governor Wilson Shannon of Ohio, an even worse choice. Shannon was incompetent and a tool of the proslavery interests in the territory. In 1856, with the territory ablaze, he resigned and fled in panic. That more capable governors could have completely forestalled the violence in the territory is perhaps doubtful, but poor leadership unquestionably made the situation worse.

Pierce's one-sided response to the Kansas crisis greatly contributed to the welling anger in the North as well. In his discussions of territorial affairs, Pierce took the Southern side and blamed all the troubles on Northern efforts to colonize the territory and on the illegal free state movement. These criticisms were not completely misdirected, but to overlook or excuse the illegal voting by Missourians, the unconstitutional laws passed by the territorial legislature, and the acts of violence by Southerners destroyed whatever influence Pierce might have exercised. Events reached a climax in May, 1856, with the caning of Senator Charles Sumner by the fiery-tempered Preston Brooks, a member of Congress from South Carolina, for a speech Sumner delivered on

Senator Charles Sumner, who was assaulted by Congressman Preston Brooks for delivering an antislavery speech on Kansas in 1856. *(Library of Congress)*

affairs in Kansas and the raid on Lawrence, Kansas, headquarters of the free state movement, by a proslavery band. These two events dealt the final blow to Pierce's fading chances for renomination.

Democratic leaders recognized that Kansas could not continue to bleed until the 1856 presidential election. They exerted pressure to force the administration to retreat from its plan to try free state leaders for treason. More important, Pierce finally selected in John W. Geary a man capable of handling the duties of territorial governor. Energetically governing in an evenhanded manner, Geary brought some semblance of law and order to the territory for the first time. By then, however, Pierce's political career had been irreparably destroyed. More than anything else, bleeding Kansas sank

Pierce and almost sent the Democratic Party with him.

In domestic matters, Pierce adhered to the limited government philosophy of the Democratic Party. He vetoed several internal improvement bills, as well as a proposal to dedicate part of the proceeds from public land sales to care for the insane. Pierce's unwillingness to use government power to encourage economic development alienated many business interests, especially in the North. The president and his advisers displayed a positive genius for needlessly making enemies and letting chances to gain friends slip through their fingers.

The Decline of Manifest Destiny

Pierce's foreign policy was equally controversial. Cuba remained the main object of desire. Initially, the administration quietly encouraged the schemes of the proslavery filibusterer John Quitman of Mississippi, who endlessly planned to invade the island, but suddenly in 1854 Pierce shifted to a policy of acquiring Cuba through diplomacy. His program ran athwart his foreign appointments. Prodded by Pierce, three American ministers, led by the theatrical Pierre Soulé, in 1854 drafted the Ostend Manifesto, which urged that the United States offer up to $120 million for Cuba and if Spain refused to sell, seize the island by force. The memo was intended to be secret, but its contents soon became public, and in the ensuing outcry the administration felt compelled to repudiate it. A public relations disaster, the manifesto discredited the doctrine of manifest destiny in the eyes of many Americans by linking it to naked aggression, and it exposed the administration as a group of bumbling incompetents. At the same time, it reinforced the idea of an aggressive slave power bent on using any means to strengthen slavery and expand the institution's domain. The renewal of sectional agitation rendered any effort to obtain Cuba futile for the remainder of the decade.

More successful were his efforts to secure additional territory from Mexico. Pierce's negotiator, James A. Gadsden, a South Carolina railroad promoter, was unable to gain Lower California or a port on the Gulf of California as Pierce desired, but he did obtain territory south of the Gila River, which afforded the best route for a Pacific railroad from New Orleans. Critics charged that the administration bought the land to facilitate selection of a southern rather than a central or northern route, but as with other programs the growing sectional conflict blocked all efforts to construct a transcontinental railroad. The Senate ratified the Gadsden Treaty only after reducing the amount of territory annexed.

It is clear in retrospect that these efforts marked the decline of manifest destiny until after the Civil War. A growing number of Northerners opposed expansion, since it would inevitably be to the south and thus would strengthen slavery. Although the seeming endorsement of the use of force alienated a minority of antebellum Americans, it was the fear of slavery expansion rekindled by the Kansas-Nebraska Act that doomed the administration's program of territorial acquisition. Pierce's failure to recognize this consequence when confronted with the demand for the repeal of the Missouri Compromise is testimony to his lack of political acumen.

The High Cost of Pierce's Presidency

Pierce actively sought renomination in 1856, but party leaders realized that a new choice was necessary for the party to beat back the

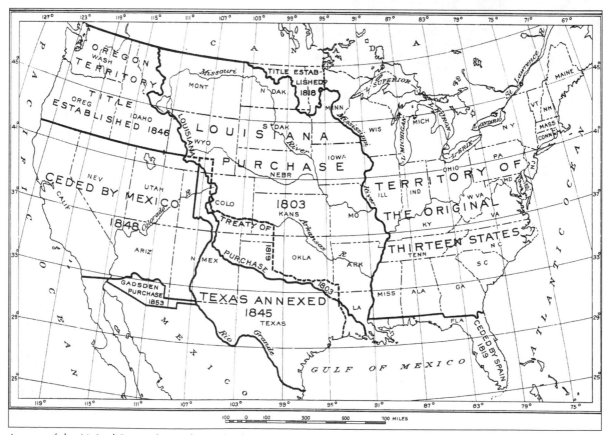

A map of the United States shows the nation's expansion across the continent through territorial acquisitions from 1803 to 1853. (*Library of Congress*)

challenge of the suddenly powerful Republican Party. At the Cincinnati convention, Pierce had some support among Southern delegations, but his strength soon melted away, and in the end the party nominated James Buchanan. So unpopular had Pierce become in the North that had he been renominated, he almost certainly would have been defeated. Few presidents have squandered so much goodwill at the beginning of their term in such a short time. Pierce became the first elected president not to be renominated by his party.

Pierce did not play an active role in politics after he left the White House. When war broke out in 1861, he tepidly backed the Union cause, but he became a strident critic of the Emancipation Proclamation and the Lincoln administration's regulation of civil liberties. He died in 1869, largely a forgotten man without influence.

Although Pierce's impact on the office of president was negligible, his role in American history was crucial. Taking office at a time when the slavery issue was declining in force, he recklessly reopened the sectional conflict, and his ill-advised policies made the crisis steadily worse. By such actions, he significantly contributed to the events that led to civil war. Pierce should be ranked a failure as president.

William E. Gienapp

Bibliographical References

Pierce apparently destroyed most of his personal papers relating to his presidency, and hence its history must be written from widely scattered sources. In general, historians have been too charitable in evaluating his performance. Roy F. Nichols, *Franklin Pierce: Young Hick-*

ory of the Granite Hills, 2d rev. ed., 1969, is a full-length biography based on a wide knowledge of the sources. Nichols displays a sure grasp of the intricacies of Democratic politics, but he is overly generous in his judgments and does not create a vivid portrait of Pierce's character and personality. The most important reminiscence is by Pierce's private secretary, Sidney Webster, *Franklin Pierce and His Administration*, 1892. Three members of the Pierce cabinet have modern biographies: Claude Feuss, *The Life of Caleb Cushing*, 2 vols., 1923; Ivor D. Spencer, *The Victor and the Spoils: A Life of William L. Marcy*, 1959, a good study; and Clement Eaton, *Jefferson Davis*, 1977. A thorough discussion of the origins of the repeal of the Missouri Compromise is Roy F. Nichols, "The Kansas-Nebraska Act: A Century of Historiography," *Mississippi Valley Historical Review* 53 (September, 1956): 187-212. Histories of the coming of the Civil War perforce devote considerable attention to Pierce's term in office. Of particular importance are Allan Nevins, *Ordeal of the Union*, 2 vols., 1947, the second volume of which covers Pierce's administration, and David M. Potter, *The Impending Crisis, 1848-1861*, completed and edited by Don E. Fehrenbacher, 1976. These works will guide the interested reader to many specialized studies of American history during this period. Larry Gara, *The Presidency of Franklin Pierce*, 1991, explores Pierce's rise from obscurity and evaluates the Pierce presidency. Wilfred J. Bisson and Gerry Hayden, *Franklin Pierce: A Bibliography*, 1993, is an annotated list of manuscripts, archival resources, articles, biographies, Pierce's published writings, and commentary on his life and times.

James Buchanan

15th President, 1857-1861

Born: April 23, 1791
      Mercerburg, Pennsylvania
Died: June 1, 1868
      Lancaster, Pennsylvania

Political Party: Democratic
Vice President: John C. Breckinridge

Cabinet Members
Secretary of State: Lewis Cass, Jeremiah S. Black
Secretary of the Treasury: Howell Cobb, Philip F. Thomas, John A. Dix
Secretary of War: John Floyd, Joseph Holt

Secretary of the Navy: Isaac Toucey
Attorney General: Jeremiah S. Black, Edwin M. Stanton
Postmaster General: Aaron V. Brown, Joseph Holt, Horatio King
Secretary of the Interior: Jacob Thompson

Buchanan's official portrait. *(White House Historical Society)*

Few men have entered the presidency with as much political experience as James Buchanan. A veteran of more than forty years of public service, the Pennsylvania leader had served in the state legislature, in both houses of Congress, as secretary of state in the Polk administration, and most recently as minister to Great Britain under Franklin Pierce. With legislative, administrative, and diplomatic experience, Buchanan seemed eminently qualified to be president.

He had been born in 1791 of Scotch-Irish ancestry, the son of a Pennsylvania farmer and merchant. Hardworking and ambitious, he compiled an excellent record at Dickinson College and then trained for a career in the law. He was a successful lawyer, and through diligence, thrift, and shrewd investments amassed a fortune of some $300,000 during his lifetime. In 1819, his life was forever altered, however, when his fiancée, who had broken off their

Buchanan and his cabinet. *(Library of Congress)*

engagement after a quarrel, suddenly died. In reaction, Buchanan vowed that he would never marry; he became the first bachelor president in American history.

Buchanan commenced his political career as a Federalist, but he eventually became a loyal follower of Andrew Jackson and steadily rose in the ranks of the Democratic Party. A loyal party man, he shrank from controversy and built up a large personal following through a voluminous correspondence. After several unsuccessful attempts to gain the party's presidential nomination, he finally secured the prize in 1856, in large measure because he had the good fortune to be out of the country in 1854 and 1855 and was not identified with either the repeal of the Missouri Compromise or the troubles in Kansas. Party managers turned to Buchanan, who seemed a safe, experienced, conservative choice.

Buchanan and the Forces of Sectionalism: A Failure of Understanding

To Buchanan, the main issue of the 1856 contest was the Union. The Democratic standard bearer viewed the Republican Party as a fanatical organization and predicted that if the party carried the election, disunion "will be immediate and inevitable." Aided by the division of the opposition, Buchanan was elected despite winning only a plurality (45 percent) of the popular vote, but the Union had had a narrow escape. In its first national campaign, the sectional Republican Party had come very close to electing a president, and in the aftermath of his victory Buchanan indicated that his major goal as president would be to defuse the territorial crisis and "destroy" the Republican Party, which was the main threat to the Union.

Tall and heavyset, with a large head, snow

231

white hair, and a ruddy complexion, the fifteenth president was a gentleman of the old school. He dressed impeccably but in an old-fashioned style, cultivated courtly manners, and had a well-developed taste for fine liquor and cigars. Because of a vision defect, he tilted his head forward and sideways in conversation, which reinforced the impression of great courteousness. He was rather fussy and vain—those in Washington, D.C., dubbed him "Miss Nancy"—and was extremely sensitive to criticism or personal slights. Lonely and never completely adjusted emotionally, he was stiff and formal and allowed little familiarity; he had few close friends and rarely revealed his feelings on controversial matters to anyone. He had a peculiar relationship with Senator William R. King of Alabama, with whom he lived

for many years when in Washington, that led one Tennessee congressman to refer to them as "Buchanan and *his wife*." Ill at ease with confrontation, he was timid and indecisive and often relied on stronger men, yet in spite of his conciliatory nature he could be petty and vindictive when attacked. Like many insecure men, Buchanan was unable to admit that he had been wrong, and once he made up his mind he tenaciously held to his position.

Buchanan's greatest handicap was not his irresolute character but his lack of understanding of the conflict between the North and the South. Although he termed slavery a wrong in his memoirs, he felt no great moral indignation over the institution, harbored a deep hatred of abolitionists, and had long contended that Northern agitation of the slavery question

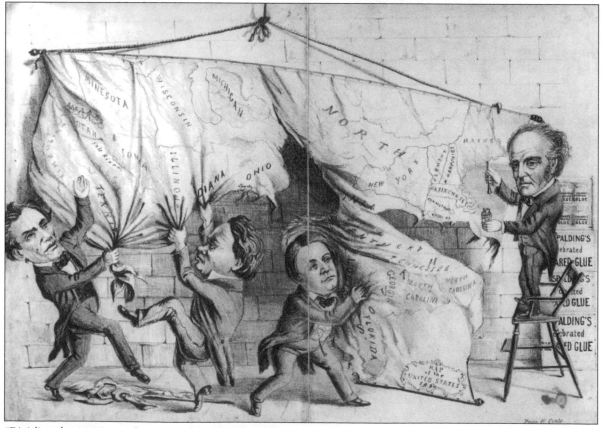

"Dividing the Map"—as they enter the campaign of 1860, Lincoln and Douglas struggle for the West, Breckinridge captures the South, and Bell tries to repair the damage. *(The Lilly Library, Indiana University, Bloomington)*

was solely responsible for the sectional crisis. Few Northern politicians were so pro-Southern in their policies and feelings, and for many years his closest friends had been Southerners. Willing to see slavery expand, he had wanted to annex more territory from Mexico in 1848 while secretary of state, and he had signed the infamous Ostend Manifesto in 1854, which advocated that the United States acquire Cuba by force if necessary. He had not witnessed at firsthand the Northern protest over the Kansas-Nebraska Act and had no appreciation of how much Northern public opinion had changed in a few years. Devoid of any real comprehension of the Republican Party or the reasons for its success, he was intellectually and emotionally unsuited to deal with the forces of sectionalism in American politics.

Less than two months shy of his sixty-sixth birthday when he took the presidential oath, Buchanan, who was uncomfortable around men of intellectual distinction, surrounded himself with an undistinguished cabinet. The only member of national stature was Secretary of State Lewis Cass, who was indolent and no longer mentally alert; Buchanan intended to direct foreign policy himself. A few of the other members had some experience in national politics, but they were all men of limited vision and talent. The strongest personalities in the cabinet were Secretary of the Treasury Howell Cobb of Georgia, Secretary of the Interior Jacob Thompson of Mississippi, and Jeremiah S. Black, an old political associate from Pennsylvania who was attorney general. Cobb and Thompson were strongly proslavery, and Black, although no advocate of the institution, usually sided with them on narrowly legalistic grounds. Together they dominated the cabinet and with it the president, who normally followed the collective will of his advisers, although the idea that they constituted a "directory" and ran the government virtually without consulting him is exaggerated. The president's closest adviser outside the cabinet was Senator John Slidell

of Louisiana, who despite his New York origins was an ardent Southerner, ready with Cobb and Thompson to push extreme measures to protect the South. None was a very astute judge of Northern public opinion or of the political consequences of their policies, and unfortunately Buchanan lacked the ability to compensate for their shortcomings.

The Dred Scott Decision

Most presidents have had a period of time to get their administration organized before dealing with major problems. Buchanan enjoyed no such luxury. His term began in controversy. Two days after his inauguration, the Supreme Court handed down its decision in the famous Dred Scott case. The Court majority (five Southerners joined by one Northerner) ruled that blacks could not be citizens of the United States, that Congress had no power to prohibit slavery from the territories, and that the Missouri Compromise of 1820, which had banned slavery from most of the Louisiana Purchase territory and which had been repealed by the Kansas-Nebraska Act, was unconstitutional. Republicans were incensed, for not only did the Court ignore countless past precedents in propounding this ruling but the opinion also negated the party's platform.

Buchanan, in fact, had played an important and highly improper role in the decision. Secretly informed of the Court's deliberations, he urged a Northern justice who was undecided to support the majority point of view. Then, knowing that the decision would be favorable to slavery, he announced in his inaugural address with seeming innocence that the Court was about to rule on the question of slavery in the territories and lectured that all good Americans would cheerfully acquiesce in the decision "whatever it may be." In the ensuing outcry, Republicans bitterly denounced the Court and its decision, and, although not informed of his intervention in its deliberations, accused Buchanan of conspiring to extend slav-

Dred Scott. *(Library of Congress)*

ery. Contrary to Buchanan's naïve expectations, the decision did nothing to quiet agitation over slavery or heal sectional animosities. That he thought the decision would have such an effect revealed how little he understood the nature and causes of the sectional conflict.

A second event in 1857 that weakened the administration was the onset in August of a depression. The economic downturn severely reduced government revenues and produced a growing clamor in the North to raise the tariff duties, both as a means to stimulate American manufacturing and to increase government revenues to meet expenditures. Pennsylvania, long a center of protariff sentiment because of its coal and iron industry, was especially prominent in demanding greater protection. Democratic leaders recognized that loss of the state, which Buchanan had carried in 1856, would be a devastating blow. In a rare display of political acumen, Buchanan favored revising tariff duties upward to what they had been under the 1846 Walker tariff, both to increase government revenue and to cool dis-

content in his home state. His Southern advisers, however, headed by Cobb in the Treasury, were inflexibly opposed to any increase. In their messages to Congress in December, 1857, Buchanan and his secretary assumed opposite positions on the question, prompting Cobb's famous remark, often cited as evidence of Buchanan's weakness, that "Old Buck is opposing the Administration." Unwilling to impose his views on his subordinates, the president failed to muster the resources of his administration behind revision of the tariff, and all efforts at tariff reform failed during his term. Failure to increase the tariff alienated certain groups, especially in the business community, that up to this time had largely opposed the Republican Party.

The Kansas Controversy: A Disastrous Decision

The greatest problem that bedeviled Buchanan in his first year in office, however, was the continuing turmoil in Kansas. Buchanan was determined to bring Kansas into the Union and end the bitter controversy over the status of slavery in that territory. To accomplish this task he selected Robert J. Walker, his colleague in the Polk cabinet and one of the most talented politicians of his generation, to be territorial governor. Knowing Buchanan's tendency to waffle on disputed questions, Walker got the president to pledge in advance support for the policy of submitting the state constitution, which a convention was about to draft, to a fair vote of the territory's residents.

Once he took up his new post, the diminutive governor soon found himself enmeshed in a host of difficulties. Meeting in Lecompton, the constitutional convention, which had a proslavery majority because the free state men refused to vote despite Walker's pleas, drafted a constitution that protected slavery. Then, contrary to Walker's announced policy, the delegates submitted only the slavery clause rather than the entire constitution for popular ratification. Residents could vote for the constitution with more slavery or for the constitution with only the slaves already in the territory, but they could not vote against the entire constitution nor could they vote to abolish slavery. Denouncing the convention's action, Walker hurried to Washington and warned Buchanan that the Lecompton constitution was a fraud and represented the wishes of only a small minority of the residents of Kansas.

Buchanan was now caught in a dilemma. Reaffirming his earlier pledge to Walker, he had written the governor in July that he was willing to stand or fall "on the question of submitting the constitution to the bona fide residents of Kansas." Now he confronted a growing demand from the South and from his Southern advisers that Walker be removed. Their anger increased when the governor threw out obviously fraudulent returns in the legislative election, thereby handing control of the legislature to free state men for the first time in the territory's existence. Through a series of procedures that were outwardly legal, Southern Democrats had the opportunity to make Kansas a slave state, and they desperately grabbed at this chance. Walker, however, gained a powerful ally in Senator Stephen A. Douglas, who insisted that the Lecompton constitution made a mockery of popular sovereignty and demanded a full and fair vote on the constitution. In a stormy interview, Douglas warned Buchanan that endorsement of the Lecompton constitution would destroy the Democratic party in the North. Nursing a cordial hatred for the aggressive Illinois senator and badly overestimating his power to enforce party discipline, Buchanan affirmed his support for the constitution and warned Douglas, who considered the president a political pygmy, that he would be crushed if he opposed it.

Buchanan, the Democratic Party, and the nation now stood at the crossroads on the road to civil war. The president was about to make the most disastrous decision of his presidency.

Warned by his governor that a large majority of the residents of the territory opposed the Lecompton constitution and wanted Kansas to be a free state and warned by the most popular Northern Democratic leader that the party could not carry the burden of the fraudulent Lecompton constitution in the free states, Buchanan nevertheless plunged ahead, swayed by his Southern sympathies and his obtuse advisers. Abandoned by the president, a disgusted Walker soon resigned. The referendum called by the constitutional convention produced a large majority in favor of the Lecompton constitution and slavery, but a separate vote a few weeks later scheduled by the antislavery legislature demonstrated quite clearly that a majority of the people of Kansas opposed the constitution. Nevertheless, in a special message in February, Buchanan urged Congress to admit Kansas under the Lecompton constitution.

The stage was now set for a titanic struggle in Congress in which Douglas openly opposed the administration. In this fight, Buchanan showed none of his customary indecisiveness. He bent every power to force the Lecompton constitution "naked through the House," as he phrased it, discharging opponents of Lecompton from federal offices, extending patronage to wavering congressmen, and even offering outright cash to secure the necessary votes. Northern representatives were more sensitive to public opinion, and in the end enough Northern Democrats defected to defeat Lecompton in the House by a tally of 120-112. At this point, the administration agreed to a face-saving compromise, which provided for the residents of the territory to vote on whether they would accept admission under the Lecompton constitution with a reduced land grant. On August 2, 1858, with the free state men participating, the voters of Kansas rejected the land grant and with it the Lecompton constitution by a vote of 11,812 to 1,926. The struggle over Kansas was at an end. Slavery was doomed there, and it was only a matter of time until the territory would have sufficient population to enter the Union as a free state (as it did in January, 1861).

Buchanan insisted that the immediate admission of Kansas under the Lecompton constitution would end the territorial controversy and destroy the appeal of the Republican Party. In reality, Buchanan's ill-advised policy had precisely the opposite effect. It strengthened the Northern belief in the slave power and linked the president directly to an alleged conspiracy to force slavery on the unwilling people of Kansas. It broadened the Republicans' appeal by allowing them to pose as the defenders of cherished democratic principles and procedures. Finally, it badly divided the Democratic Party, with Douglas the symbol of this division. The Democratic Party paid this heavy price needlessly, for even Buchanan realized that the South would not have seceded over this question.

The fall elections were a debacle for the administration and the Democratic Party. Republicans scored gains in a number of key Northern states, and Northern congressmen who had supported the Lecompton constitution went down to defeat in droves, while those who had stood with Douglas generally won reelection. The new House had an anti-Democratic majority. More ominous was the loss of Pennsylvania, which foreshadowed an impending Republican victory in 1860 unless there was a radical change in policy. To all of this Buchanan remained oblivious. His advisers dismissed the losses as the result of temporary causes rather than the administration's pro-Southern policies, and the president, unwilling to confront the harsh political truth, eagerly embraced this explanation.

Desperately needing to shore up the Democratic Party's support in the North, Buchanan instead alienated additional Northern groups by adhering to his outmoded Jacksonian economic principles. As he grew older, Buchanan became increasingly inflexible on economic matters, and during his presidency he consistently opposed using the federal government to promote economic growth. Southerners blocked all attempts to revise the tariff, and Buchanan vetoed several internal improvement bills that got through Congress, which angered popular opinion, especially in the Northwest. He also vetoed a homestead bill designed to appease Western sentiment. Another bill, which donated public land to states to found agricultural colleges, met a similar fate. These vetoes enabled Republicans to picture him as a tool of Southern interests, who used their stranglehold over the federal government to block Northern progress and development, and his actions further damaged the Democratic cause in the free states.

More successful was his handling of the growing difficulties with the Mormons in the Utah Territory. When not entirely accurate reports reached Washington that the Mormons under the leadership of Brigham Young were defying federal authority, Buchanan moved with uncharacteristic firmness. He dispatched twenty-five hundred troops to subdue the rebellious saints, but before they arrived in Utah his emissary negotiated a peaceful settlement under which the Mormons would not be interfered with in their religion but in temporal matters the federal government would be supreme. The so-called Mormon War thus came to an end without bloodshed and with federal authority intact.

In foreign affairs, Buchanan's primary goals were to expand the national domain and check foreign influence in the New World. He did get the British to abandon some of their territorial aspirations in Central America, and he managed to secure commercial treaties with both China and Japan. His efforts to acquire additional territory, however, were doomed to failure. He was rebuffed by Congress when he requested the power to establish protectorates over the northern provinces of Mexico and when he sought authority to invade Mexico to gain redress for wrongs committed against American citizens. In addition, in 1860 the Senate rejected a treaty the administration negotiated with Mexico that would have given the United States the right of unilateral military intervention. Republican senators believed that the treaty's real purpose was to seize additional territory from Mexico and expand slavery. Buchanan also continued to push for the acquisition of Cuba, and in 1859 he backed a bill to appropriate $30 million for negotiations with Spain. Although it could have passed the Senate if brought to a vote, the bill stood no chance in the House, and its introduction was simply a futile gesture. Thus Buchanan's diplomatic record, while not a total failure, fell far short of the goals he had set when entering office.

Administrative Corruption: Damaging Revelations

More damaging to Buchanan's reputation were the revelations of a House committee chaired by John Covode of Pennsylvania, which was appointed to investigate charges of administrative corruption. Covode and his colleagues ferreted out massive amounts of evidence of wrongdoing. Indeed, when the investigation was completed, it was clear the Buchanan had presided over the most corrupt administration in American history up to that point. Testimony revealed that patronage and even money had been offered to editors and congressmen for their support, that campaign contributors had been rewarded with lucrative federal contracts, and that the huge profits from the public printing had been partially diverted to Democratic candidates. Evidence also came to light that completely discredited Secretary of War John Floyd, who had used his office to reward his friends and was criminally lax in his management of accounts. This was not all. It would later be discovered that Floyd had endorsed bills for army supplies before Congress appropriated the money and that he had continued this illegal practice even after Buchanan ordered him to stop. Moreover, some of these notes had been exchanged for $870,000 worth of bonds stolen from the Interior Department by one of the secretary's kinsmen. Although Floyd's malfeasance brought him into complete disgrace, he defiantly refused to resign when Buchanan through an intermediary asked him to do so, and the president meekly backed down. Buchanan had not profited personally from these activities, but the evidence fully documented his weakness of character and lack of judgment.

Buchanan's performance put the Democratic Party badly on the defensive in 1860, and party unity was essential if the Republican challenge were to be turned back. Motivated by narrow personal considerations, Buchanan refused to make any effort to heal the breach with Douglas. The senator's supporters were proscribed or removed from federal office and some of his most bitter enemies appointed in their stead. Buchanan also threw the power of the administration against Douglas's bid to win the 1860 Democratic presidential nomination. Pressure was applied to federal officeholders to get anti-Douglas men elected to the national convention, and some of the president's closest associates went to Charleston for the sole purpose of defeating the Illinois senator. In the end the Democratic Party split, with the Northern wing nominating Douglas and the Southern wing Buchanan's vice president, John C. Breckinridge of Kentucky. Buchanan, who had not sought renomination, endorsed Breckinridge and the Southern platform, which demanded a federal slave code for the territories. With the Democratic Party hopelessly divided, Abraham Lincoln was easily elected the nation's first Republican president in November.

The Secession Crisis

With four months remaining until the end of his term, Buchanan now confronted the most serious crisis of his life. Following Lincoln's election, as the states of the Deep South began making preparations to leave the Union, Buchanan's cabinet, which had been noted for its harmony, became a deeply divided and quarrelsome body. Its Northern members, led by Black, heatedly denounced secession, whereas Southern members defended it and denied that the federal government could coerce a state to remain in the Union. Some members, most notably Cobb and Thompson, were merely waiting for their states to act before leaving the administration. Still attached to these men by feelings of affection, Buchanan could not

bring himself to dismiss them and reorganize his administration on a pro-Union basis. Instead, he presented to the world the folly of maintaining in office men who now openly advocated disunion. Buchanan rationalized that their dismissal would strengthen secession sentiment in the South, but more revealing was his refusal to break with his personal organ, the *Constitution*, edited by William E. Browne, who was an outspoken secessionist. Not until January, 1861, did Buchanan cut off the paper's official patronage. He even gave his blessing for Thompson, who was still in the cabinet, to go to North Carolina as the representative of the seceded state of Mississippi. Never was his weakness more forcefully demonstrated.

This division in his official family badly paralyzed Buchanan, under whom decisions had usually been a joint effort. Never the most decisive of men, he was now a lame duck, and the recent election had deprived him of most of his political influence. The president immediately grasped the seriousness of the situation. He recognized that the South's fundamental grievance was the continuing agitation over slavery, and the main problem was its accompanying threat of insurrection. He had, however, no constructive ideas on how to deal with this crisis. He considered issuing a proclamation announcing his intention to enforce the laws in the South, but backed off from this idea because of the split in his cabinet. In his annual message of December 3, 1860, he again entirely blamed the North for the crisis and recommended that Congress call a constitutional convention to deal with Southern complaints. Embracing the most extreme Southern demands, he urged passage of amendments to secure the return of fugitive slaves and to protect slavery in the states and territories. The recent election had thoroughly repudiated this last idea,

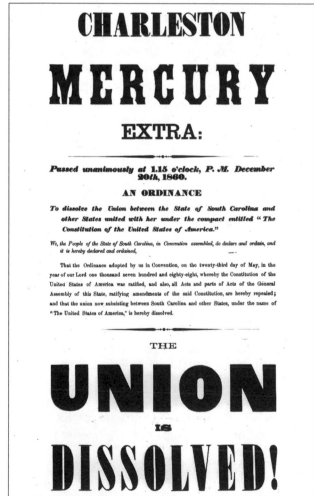

A notice announcing South Carolina's secession from the Union on December 20, 1860. *(Library of Congress)*

and Congress ignored his suggestions.

On the constitutional question of secession, the president's message was hopelessly inadequate. Devoted to Andrew Jackson's concept of a perpetual Union, Buchanan argued that secession was unconstitutional, but he went on to declare that he had no power to prevent it. The federal government, he asserted, could not coerce a state, but he mitigated the force of this statement by reaffirming his sworn duty to enforce the laws. Buchanan's message produced a chorus of indignation in the North. His constitutional argument was specious, since the federal government did not have to coerce states at all but could direct its authority against individuals. Although Buchanan vainly hoped that Congress would devise some sectional settlement, the day of compromise had passed. Neither secessionists nor Republicans were interested in compromise, and although Buchanan might have been more vigorous in promoting a solution, in the end his efforts would not have made any difference. Buchanan's policy was simply to hang on until his term was over without legally recognizing secession or starting a civil war.

Of fundamental importance in Buchanan's eventual response to the secession crisis was the reorganization of his cabinet. In little more than one month, beginning in early December, the secessionists in the cabinet resigned and were replaced by staunch Union men. Black, who took over the State Department, now emerged as the guiding force of the administration; he gained powerful allies in Edwin M. Stanton, who assumed Black's old post as attorney general, and Postmaster General (and subsequently Secretary of War) Joseph Holt. Together these men stiffened Buchanan's resolve not to surrender federal property or to forswear the use of force.

The major point of conflict ultimately was Fort Sumter in the middle of Charleston Harbor with its small federal garrison under the command of Major Robert Anderson. Influenced by Black, Stanton, and Holt, Buchanan resisted intense Southern pressure to abandon the fort, and on December 31 he authorized sending a relief expedition. The relief ship was driven off by batteries on the South Carolina shore, but the president was now fully committed to the doctrine, which he outlined in his special message to Congress on January 8, that he had the right to use military force defensively to protect federal property and enforce the laws. South Carolina officials now undertook to starve out the garrison, and Buchanan decided not to send any further supplies or reinforcements until Anderson requested aid. The stalemate that had developed in Charleston continued for the remainder of Buchanan's term. Up until Buchanan's last day in office, Anderson reported that he did not need any supplies or reinforcements.

On March 4, a relieved Buchanan turned the reins of government over to Lincoln. He had managed to leave office without compromising his successor by legally recognizing disunion or precipitating a war. "If you are as happy in entering the White House as I shall feel on returning [home]," he confessed to Lincoln, "you are a happy man indeed."

The Judgment of History

Buchanan retired to his estate, Wheatland. He came under heavy attack by partisan journalists during the war, but he publicly supported the war effort and opposed the peace plank in the 1864 Democratic platform. He was largely out of the public limelight, however, and he spent his retirement writing his memoirs. Published in 1866, they presented a full-scale defense of his actions as president. Finally, on June 1, 1868, death came to the former president at the age of seventy-seven. The day before he died, he told a friend, "I have always felt and still feel that I discharged every public duty imposed on me conscientiously. I have no regret for any public act of my life, and history will vindicate my memory."

Historians have not been as charitable as Buchanan prophesied. Few administrations present such an unbroken record of misjudgments, shortsightedness, sordid corruption, and blundering. Ill-equipped to handle the sectional conflict and blind to the realities of Northern public opinion, Buchanan pursued a course that drove the sections further apart, ruptured his own party, and made a Republican victory all but inevitable in 1860. His incredible belief that the Supreme Court's Dred Scott decision would solve the crisis, his endorsement of the fraudulent Lecompton constitution, his destructive vendetta against Douglas, his zeal to add slave territory to the United States, and his obstruction of much desired economic legislation all aided the Republican Party to varying degrees. Desirous of healing the sectional breach, Buchanan instead promoted policies that escalated the crisis to the point where no compromise was possible. His failure as president had unprecedented tragic consequences for the nation.

William E. Gienapp

Bibliographical References

The best biography of Buchanan is Philip S. Klein, *President James Buchanan*, 1962. Although cognizant of his subject's shortcomings, Klein presents the most convincing defense possible of Buchanan and his policies. George T. Curtis, *Life of James Buchanan*, 2 vols., 1883, prints some important documents and correspondence but is tedious. Sally S. Cahalan, *James Buchanan and His Family at Wheatland*, 1988, details Buchanan's family life in Pennsylvania. A brief, balanced treatment of Buchanan's presidential years is Elbert B. Smith, *The Presidency of James Buchanan*, 1975. John B. Moore, *The Works of James Buchanan*, 12 vols., 1908-1911, is a valuable selection of Buchanan's writings. Essential for understanding Buchanan's point of view and his limited insight into the crisis he confronted are his memoirs, *Mr. Buchanan's Administration on the Eve of the*

Rebellion, 1866. Buchanan's presidency understandably has attracted considerable attention from historians of the sectional conflict. Allan Nevins, *The Emergence of Lincoln*, 2 vols., 1950, contains a full treatment of these crucial four years. Nevins is hostile to Buchanan and views him as a prisoner of the cabinet Directory, which, he argues, set policy. More balanced is Roy F. Nichols's magisterial *The Disruption of American Democracy*, 1948, a thorough examination of the politics of the Buchanan administration. Nichols provides the best analysis of the impact of the Lecompton issue on the Democratic Party. The last half of David M. Potter, *The Impending Crisis, 1848-1861*, 1976, edited and completed by Don E. Fehrenbacher, is a superb analysis of the political developments of this period. Michael J. Birkner, ed., *James Buchanan and the Political Crisis of the 1850's*, 1996, is a compilation of essays which evaluate Buchanan's presidency and examine the political climate of the 1850's. David E. Meerse, "Presidential Leadership, Suffrage Qualifications, and Kansas: 1857," *Civil War History* 24 (December, 1978) 293-313, challenges the view that Buchanan changed his mind on submitting the Lecompton constitution to the voters of Kansas. The best study of the Dred Scott decision is Don E. Fehrenbacher, *The Dred Scott Case*, 1978, an exhaustive analysis that takes a broad view of its subject. For the Covode investigation and the scandals of Buchanan's administration, see David E. Meerse, "Buchanan, Corruption, and the Election of 1860," *Civil War History* 12 (June, 1966), 116-31. Kenneth M. Stampp, *And the War Came: The North and the Secession Crisis, 1860-61*, 1950, presents an acute analysis of Northern public opinion in the secession crisis. Indispensable on this crisis is Horatio King, *Turning on the Light*, 1895, the recollections of Buchanan's assistant postmaster general. Frederick M. Binder, *James Buchanan and the American Empire*, 1994, explores foreign relations during the Buchanan presidency.

Abraham Lincoln

16th President, 1861-1865

Born: February 12, 1809
near Hodgenville, Kentucky
Died: April 15, 1865
Washington, D.C.

Political Party: Republican
Vice Presidents: Hannibal Hamlin,
Andrew Johnson

Cabinet Members

Secretary of State: William H. Seward
Secretary of the Treasury: Salmon P. Chase, William P. Fessenden, Hugh McCulloch
Secretary of War: Simon Cameron, Edwin M. Stanton
Secretary of the Navy: Gideon Welles
Attorney General: Edward Bates, James Speed
Postmaster General: Horatio King, Montgomery Blair, William Dennison
Secretary of the Interior: Caleb Smith, John P. Usher

Popular consensus and polls taken of American historians have named Abraham Lincoln as the country's greatest president. Yet at the time of his election, he was not well known to the American people. Only after 1858 was his name recognized beyond the borders of his state, and even then he was known primarily as the challenger of one of the nation's leading political figures. A politician of some local reputation, he had held national office

Lincoln's official portrait. *(White House Historical Society)*

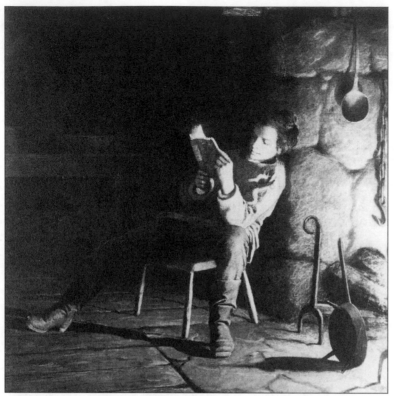

The Boy Lincoln, by Eastman Johnson. *(Library of Congress)*

a line from Thomas Gray's popular "Elegy Written in a Country Churchyard": "The short and simple annals of the poor."

At the age of two, Lincoln was taken to a hardscrabble farm on nearby Knob Creek, which his father later purchased. The circumstances of Lincoln's early years were not as poor as he had people believe. His father owned three farms, totaling in excess of six hundred acres, and augmented his farm income with work as a skilled carpenter. Although he never learned to read and could barely sign his name, Thomas Lincoln instilled in his son an appreciation for the value of education. He was a responsible citizen, serving on juries and on the county slave patrol, supervising road construction, and guarding prisoners, and he provided for his family in a manner that placed them among the better-off members of the community. Lincoln's relationship with his father has long puzzled historians. In later years he preferred not to speak of him and rarely mentioned him in anything he wrote; although the distance was not great, Lincoln never visited him, even when his father lay dying.

In 1816, the Lincolns left Kentucky and moved across the Ohio River to southern Indiana. Although Lincoln later recalled that the move was made in part because of Thomas's dislike of slavery, a series of damaging lawsuits over defects in his land titles was probably more important. It was in Indiana, on a farm that had to be hacked out of the woods on Little Pigeon Creek near Gentryville, that Lincoln spent his adolescent years. It was there also that his mother, Nancy Hanks, died two

only once, a single term in the House of Representatives, and had never occupied an administrative office (unless one counts his brief stint as postmaster of New Salem, Illinois). Compared with his predecessors in the presidency, Lincoln may well have been the least prepared president in the history of the republic.

Early Life

Lincoln was a product of the frontier, born near Hodgenville, Kentucky, on February 12, 1809. Grandson of a settler who was murdered by American Indians as he worked in his fields, son of an uneducated laborer and farmer, he epitomized the struggle between civilization and wilderness that has so often been eulogized by American romantics. Lincoln himself found little romance in his early life and was always reluctant to speak of it. To one of his early biographers, he summed up his childhood with

years after the family moved. Although books seem to have been available to the young Lincoln, the opportunities for a more formal education were meager. There was nothing in that frontier environment, he later wrote, "to excite ambition for education." His attendance in school was sporadic, probably amounting to no more than a year in the aggregate. What learning he acquired, he secured through his own exertions. "The little advance I now have upon this store of education," he recalled proudly, "I have picked up from time to time under the pressure of necessity."

After living fourteen years in Indiana, during which time Thomas remarried, the Lincolns were on the move again, lured to Illinois by glowing reports of the state's fertility. Stopping first on the Sangamon River a few miles west of Decatur, the family moved in 1831 to a farm in Coles County, near Charleston, this time without Abraham. Twenty-two years old, ambitious, and anxious to leave the hard frontier life behind him, Lincoln struck out on his own.

In 1828, Lincoln made a trip to New Orleans, traveling down the Ohio and Mississippi Rivers on a flatboat loaded with farm produce, and three years later, in the spring of 1831, he made a second trip to New Orleans for an Illinois merchant who offered him employment in his store in the village of New Salem. In each instance, Lincoln returned in style by steamboat. The trips opened his eyes; for the first time he was brought into contact with a life and culture he had hardly imagined back home on the farm.

Lincoln's decision to settle in New Salem, located on the Sangamon River not far from Springfield, marked his transition from rural to urban America and opened a new and significant period in his life. The town was growing and, with the anticipation of a river trade, seemed to have a bright future. Its people were congenial because, like Lincoln, most of them had migrated from the border South. His thoughts and plans now found new directions,

as he distanced himself from his background and placed his feet on the pathway upward to social and economic success.

Whig Politician

Lincoln was drawn almost immediately to the pursuit of politics, which to him was the means not only for bringing civilization to the frontier but also for achieving the prestige he so anxiously sought. Seven months after his arrival in the village, he announced his candidacy for the Illinois state legislature. From this moment on, with only rare exceptions, his life was dominated by a quest for office. His decision to follow a political career not surprisingly carried with it a determination to study and practice law. The role of the lawyer was an important one in developing societies, and Lincoln was quick to sense its advantage to an aspiring politician. Lawyers traveled, sometimes extensively, and were able to establish contacts beyond the limits of their own communities. Clients, moreover, and members of juries all voted; if they could be won over by legal arguments, political support would not be far behind. Receiving encouragement from other lawyer-politicians, Lincoln borrowed law books, and he applied himself diligently to their study. In 1836, he was licensed to practice without having passed an examination, an unusual circumstance even in the informal atmosphere of the time, and in the following year he entered his first partnership. Although he knew very little law, was not inclined to read further once he had received his license, and later conceded that he was "not an accomplished lawyer," Lincoln developed a highly successful and lucrative practice by the 1850's.

Lincoln's first political platform was derived from his own experience. Partisan alignments had not yet hardened in Illinois, but it was clear that the popular figure of Andrew Jackson (then seeking reelection to the presidency) had little appeal for Lincoln. Rather, his Kentucky beginnings drew him to the side of Henry Clay, his "beau ideal of a statesman," and when Clay formed the Whig Party, Lincoln joined the ranks. To Lincoln, the political issues of the 1830's were essentially economic issues. He found in Clay's American System—internal improvements, a protective tariff, and a sound financial structure—the route to national strength and to the material progress that was essential to the development of his region. Whigs believed that the national government was the proper instrument for the promotion of the national welfare and that all interests would be harmonized by a vigorous use of national power to advance the material well-being of the country. Especially appealing to Lincoln was the Whig insistence that progress could be realized only through an orderly and rational development. In one of his later platform statements, he affirmed the "stake in society" principle, insisting that only those who shared the burdens of government, that is, those who owned property and paid taxes, should share in its governance. He rejected the romantic democracy of Andrew Jackson, embraced by most of his fellow Illinoisans, and like many Whigs accepted the principle of universal suffrage only reluctantly.

Lincoln's first bid for the state legislature ended in defeat, but he ran again in 1834 and was elected. From that time on, he never lost a legislative race, serving four terms altogether. In the legislature, he supported internal improvement bills, defended the state's banking system, and voiced his fears for the security of persons and property against the "mobocratic spirit" he associated with Jacksonian democracy. One of his most important early political statements and his clearest exposition of conservative Whig philosophy was his address before the Springfield Lyceum, "The Perpetuation of Our Political Institutions," in January, 1838. In a vigorous call for law and order, Lincoln warned that the gravest threat to the Republic lay in the "wild and furious passions" of the mob that tore at the

foundations of government and made it easy for a man "of the loftiest genius" to subvert republican government (he had Andrew Jackson in mind). It was the government's responsibility, Lincoln urged, to protect its "good men" (those who loved tranquillity and obeyed the law) by securing the ordered, regulated society that was essential to economic and social progress. The Republic would be saved, he declared, only by a reverence for the Constitution and the laws and the subordination of passion to "cold, calculating, unimpassioned reason." Let this become, he concluded, the "*political religion* of the nation."

Illinois was a heavily Democratic state, which limited the opportunities for Whigs such as Lincoln. Within the state's Whig organization, however, Lincoln achieved a position of leadership; by the 1840's, he was recognized as a member of the "Springfield Junto," the small group in the state capital that pulled the party strings. In 1846, by prearrangement with other leading Whigs, Lincoln was nominated and elected to Congress from the Springfield district, the only sure Whig congressional district in the state, and seventeen months later, in December, 1847, he took his seat in the Thirtieth Congress.

Lincoln's single term in the House of Representatives is remembered mostly for his stand against the Mexican War, an opposition he hoped would bring him distinction within the party. Lincoln's response to the war, however, suffered from the same ambiguity that plagued Whigs generally. When the war was declared in 1846, he voiced no opposition to it; on the contrary, he urged prompt and united action against Mexico. He had been indifferent to the annexation of Texas, yet later argued that the United States must, under "a sort of necessity," take territory from Mexico. As a congressman, he voted supplies to the army and expressed his pride in the victories that the volunteers had won in Mexico. It was not until he took his seat in the House of Representatives, when the war was won and only awaited the signing of the treaty, that Lincoln expressed his opposition to it, insisting that it had been unconstitutionally begun by President James K. Polk and that Polk had deceived the American people in his war message two years before. Lincoln's speech merely echoed arguments Whigs had been making since the war had begun and did not bring him the prominence he had hoped to achieve.

It was as an Illinois Whig that Lincoln first formed his views on the nature of the presidency and of presidential power. Molded in the turbulent politics of the Jacksonian era, his position was antithetical to Jackson's belief that the president, as the only direct representative of all the people, must be a strong and powerful figure. Lincoln's warning against the rise of a "lofty genius" who would use his popular support to undermine the institutions of republican government was echoed in later statements. He once likened the Jacksonian presidency to a "great volcano . . . belching forth the lava of political corruption." Whigs—and Lincoln—argued instead for a weak executive and a strong legislative branch. The "legitimately expressed will of the people," he believed, must be filtered through their congressional representatives, who, mindful of the need for order and stability, would temper their wishes according to the best interests of the nation.

The presidential veto power, so dramatically employed by Jackson, threatened the separation of powers and, as Lincoln believed, clothed the chief executive with a legislative function that properly belonged to Congress. Lincoln contended that the nation's legislation should rest exclusively with Congress, "uninfluenced by the executive in its origin or progress, and undisturbed by the veto unless in very special and clear cases." That Lincoln believed such cases would be rare was obvious. The notion that the president can "know the wants of the people, as well as three hundred other men, coming from all the various localities of

the nation" was "a pernicious abstraction."

As a member of the Whig Party's central committee in Illinois, Lincoln took an active part in the presidential campaigns, organizing the party, planning the strategy, and issuing platform statements. Although Whigs had staunchly opposed the organization of political parties as obstructions to good government, they came to realize by 1840 that only by adopting the party structure of the Jacksonians could they hope to achieve success. Lincoln was no exception, although he came later than most to an acceptance of the party system. He developed an organizational framework for the party in Illinois that extended to the precinct level and campaigned vigorously that year for William Henry Harrison, the very model of the Whig weak executive. Later he urged the adoption of the convention system, first initiated by the Democrats, while still expressing doubts about its validity. In an 1843 address to the party, he suggested that "while our opponents use it, it is madness in us not to defend ourselves with it."

In 1844, Lincoln had the opportunity to support his idol, Henry Clay, for election to the presidency. Once again, as a leading Whig in Illinois, he urged that limitations be placed on the power of the presidential office. The veto power, he declared, should be restricted "so that it may not be wielded to the centralization of all power in the hands of a corrupt and despotic Executive." Furthermore, he proposed that presidents be limited to a single term, that all executive officers refrain from interfering in local and state elections, and that the president's power of appointment be significantly reduced.

Clay was not elected in 1844. The victor, James K. Polk, a Democrat and protégé of Jackson, became a target for Lincoln's attack on unchecked presidential power. He denounced Polk's "high-handed and despotic" exercise of the veto power as reflecting an "utter disregard of the will of the people." Polk's refusal to approve measures passed by Congress "for the good and prosperity of the country," principally Congress's bills for extensive river and harbor improvements, constituted in Lincoln's view an abuse of presidential authority.

As a Whig member of Congress, Lincoln was most disturbed by Polk's role in the coming of the Mexican War. In his maiden speech in January, 1848, he placed full blame for the war squarely at Polk's feet, charging the president with deception and falsehood in his effort to justify the conflict. In an emotional outburst that revealed the depth of Lincoln's feeling, he likened Polk's arguments to the "half insane mumbling of a fever dream" and charged that the blood of the war would cry out to heaven against him. More important, Lincoln was convinced that Polk had exceeded his constitutional authority in forcing the war upon the country. He lashed out at the view, held by many of the war's supporters, that the president may "without violation of the Constitution, . . . *invade* the territory of another country" if he thought it necessary to the national defense. To allow the president that power, he warned, was to "allow him to make war at pleasure." The Constitution clearly gave the war-making power to Congress, not the president. Polk's actions, Lincoln stated, were contrary to the principles of republican government, for they placed "our President where kings have always stood."

Lincoln's stand against the extension of presidential prerogative was carried into the 1848 campaign, when the Whigs sensed an opportunity to oust the Democrats from the executive branch. He abandoned Henry Clay in favor of Zachary Taylor, the hero of the Mexican War, apparently for no other reason than that Taylor had the better chance of winning. It was an ironic twist, for it may have cost Lincoln an appointment to a federal office following Taylor's election. Lincoln campaigned strenuously for Taylor, both within and outside the state of Illinois, urging a return to a Whig presi-

dency, a reassertion of congressional supremacy, and the enactment of the party's economic program. Following the election, he fully expected to be rewarded with a federal appointment but was disappointed when Taylor, anxious to mend relations with Clay, gave the office Lincoln sought to an Illinoisan who had remained faithful to the Kentuckian.

Lincoln's adherence to Whig Party doctrine is extremely important to an understanding of his later political positions, for his outlook continued to be flavored by his Whig approach to the nation's problems. Yet Lincoln was no doctrinaire. His thinking always contained a strong streak of pragmatism and expediency, reflected in an ability to shift and modify his stands according to changing circumstances. In this sense, he was a typical Western politician of the early nineteenth century. It was this flexibility and the balance between pragmatism and principle on which it rested that provided strength to his efforts to meet the great crisis of civil war in later years. Lincoln revealed, in these early years, many of those traits that would enable him to carry the nation through its most troubled time—an understanding of human behavior and an ability to use that understanding to achieve his ends, a shrewdness of judgment that made him a master at manipulation and maneuver. An opportunist in the best sense of the word, he was able to seize the moment and bend it to his own purposes. In 1849, however, the full demonstration of these traits lay yet in the future.

The Politics of Slavery

Following his term in Congress, Lincoln returned to Illinois. Rebuffed by the Taylor administration, unable to seek reelection, he saw his political prospects dim. For the next five years, he devoted himself to his law practice while continuing to keep his hand in Whig Party affairs.

The passage by Congress of Stephen A. Douglas's Kansas-Nebraska Act in 1854 abruptly ended Lincoln's "retirement." The organization of two new territories in the nation's heartland on the basis of popular sovereignty (allowing the local population to decide for or against slavery), thereby repealing the Missouri Compromise, so aroused and angered Lincoln that it altered the direction of his life. Douglas's act provoked a storm of protest from antislavery and abolitionist elements and provided the opportunity for Lincoln's return to the political arena.

Lincoln was not a new convert to an antislavery position. He had always opposed slavery on principle but admitted that until 1854 it had been only a "minor question" for him. Confident that the institution had been contained by the Missouri Compromise, he apparently felt little need to argue against it. Furthermore, he had always opposed militant abolitionism as a threat to law and order. The Kansas-Nebraska Act shattered this confidence when it opened a vast new territory to the expansion of slavery. No longer on the defensive, as Lincoln had assumed, slavery had moved to the offense. From 1854 on, his thinking and the direction of his career were dominated by the slavery issue.

Lincoln's opposition to slavery, as it evolved in the 1850's, rested on a foundation of moral principle. If slavery was not wrong, he once said, then nothing was wrong. In his public statements following the passage of Douglas's act, he defined his opposition. He hated the institution because of its injustice and because it negated the promise of the Declaration of Independence, violated the free-labor underpinnings of his political thought, and rendered America's republican example a mockery. To allow the expansion of slavery would be to derail America's mission, to convert progress into "degeneracy," and to make hypocrites of all Americans who proclaimed themselves the "friends of Human Freedom." He called upon his countrymen to put the nation back on track by returning it to the ideals that had given it

birth. "Our republican robe is soiled, and trailed in the dust," he declared. "Let us repurify it . . . in the spirit, if not the blood of the Revolution. . . . If we do this, we shall not only have saved the Union; but we shall have so saved it, as to make, and to keep it, forever worthy of the saving."

Lincoln's declarations, however, were balanced by a keen sense of pragmatism. He recognized the complexity of the slavery problem and did not fault Southerners for failing to do what he himself would not know how to do. He was aware of the legal protections that slavery enjoyed and of the practical difficulties involved in any effort to deal with it. What could be done? Like Clay, he leaned toward colonization as the ideal solution but conceded that this was impractical. Free the slaves and treat them as "underlings"? That, he believed, would not improve their condition. Free them and treat them as political and social equals? This too he rejected, for "my own feelings will not admit of this; and if mine would, we well know that those of the great mass of white people will not." Lincoln's solution—the only practical course—was to prevent slavery from expanding. By restricting slavery to the states where it already existed, he believed the institution would be placed in a condition of "ultimate extinction." Rejecting the immediacy of abolition, he favored a vague and indeterminate gradualism. Even so, he knew that the question was so fraught with danger to the Union that he was uncertain which was the greater evil— disunion or slavery, "Much as I hate slavery," he conceded, "I would consent to the extension of it rather than see the Union dissolved, just as I would consent to any GREAT evil, to avoid a GREATER one."

In the years following 1854, Lincoln's voice mingled with the protests of others. Their impact on the party system proved fatal. Whigs became split beyond recovery, Democrats tried vainly to maintain national unity, and a new sectional party with an unabashed anti-Southern and antislavery platform emerged. Lincoln, hoping at first that the Whig Party could be refashioned into an antislavery force, gradually identified himself with the new party and its slavery-restriction demands; by 1856, he was calling himself a Republican. The thrust of the slavery question in politics gave new incentive to his political ambitions. He was elected to the Illinois legislature in 1854 but resigned soon afterward to run for a seat in the United States Senate, only to be defeated by an anti-Nebraska Democrat. Although deeply disappointed, he lost no time in building his candidacy for the Senate in 1858, when Douglas himself would seek reelection.

Lincoln's arguments against slavery became less equivocal and ambiguous as he became more active politically. His views were not only refined but also considerably sharpened in his vigorous campaign against Douglas in 1858. Meeting Douglas in seven joint debates, he sought to discredit the Illinois senator in the eyes of Southern Democrats while at the same time emphasizing his own credentials as a spokesman for the Northern antislavery position. His language assumed a stronger moral tone as he portrayed Douglas as a man without moral scruples. "The real issue in this controversy," Lincoln concluded in the final debate, "is the sentiment on the part of one class that looks upon the institution of slavery *as a wrong*, and of another class that *does not* look upon it as a wrong."

Douglas won the election, but in losing Lincoln finally gained what had eluded him before—national prominence and visibility. Republicans in other states sought his assistance in their local campaigns, whereas his frequent mention as a candidate for the presidency in 1860 kindled his ambition for the nation's highest office. By the time the election year began, Lincoln's prospects for the Republican nomination were amazingly good for someone whose name was barely known outside his own state only two years before.

If Lincoln's prospects were good, those for the Union were not. The sectional conflict over slavery had reached formidable proportions. Several Southern states had made thinly veiled secession threats, John Brown's trial and execution were fresh in the South's memory, a long and frustrating speakership contest in the House of Representatives threatened a breakdown in Congress, and Jefferson Davis's demand for federal protection of slavery in the territories was matched by new extremes of invective from the abolitionists.

Lincoln himself contributed to the tension of the election year when he delivered his address at Cooper Institute in New York City, warning Republicans against seeking a middle ground between right and wrong and urging them to stand fast in their moral opposition to slavery.

The Presidency, Secession, and War

When the Republicans gathered in their nominating convention in Chicago in May, 1860, Lincoln was ready to do battle against his rivals. New York's distinguished Senator William H. Seward had the greatest support among the delegates, and he might have won the nomination had it not seemed likely that Douglas would receive the Democratic nomination. Seward's position on slavery smacked too much of radicalism. Republican strategy dictated the selection of someone whose views were perceived as moderate, someone who could woo Northern voters away from Douglas and at the same time appeal to the old Whig element in the party. Lincoln was the logical choice. He won the nomination after only three ballots. To satisfy those Republicans with Democratic antecedents and to balance the ticket geographically, the convention nominated Hannibal Hamlin of Maine for vice president.

The presidential election of 1860 was the most critical in the history of the United States. It marked the final breakdown of the existing party system, as the Democratic Party (the only remaining national party) split and presented two candidates: Stephen A. Douglas and John C. Breckinridge. A fourth candidate, John Bell, was presented by the Constitutional Union Party, a collection of old Whigs and former Know-Nothings. The campaign belied the election's importance in its relative calm. By September it was clear that Lincoln would win. The Republicans had carefully calculated their chances and knew they could elect their candidate without carrying a single Southern vote. Lincoln won in November by a decisive majority in the electoral college, but he carried only 39 percent of the popular vote.

With Lincoln's election, only the executive branch of the government was won by the Republicans. The Democrats would have majorities in Congress (although the party was badly split), and the Supreme Court was firmly controlled by a Democratic proslave majority. All arguments, however, that the South would have nothing to fear from Lincoln were to no avail. On the contrary, Southerners had reason to fear the worst from Lincoln's election; nothing could stay their course toward secession.

Republicans, Lincoln included, did not fully appreciate the depth of Southern feeling. They saw no need to meet or even to understand Southern grievances. Lincoln steadfastly refused to believe that secession was popular, and he blamed disunion on a slave-power conspiracy. He refused to sanction compromise as a means for saving the Union and urged all Republicans in Congress to reject any proposals that would inhibit the party's platform. "The tug has to come," he wrote, "and better now than later." It is obvious that he had no idea that such a stand might result in a war between the sections.

Lincoln assumed the responsibilities of the presidency under the most inauspicious circumstances. Between December 20 and February 1, seven states of the Union seceded, the entire Deep South from South Carolina to Texas. On February 4, their delegates met at

Montgomery, Alabama, to organize a new nation—the Confederate States of America. Hopeful that Lincoln's silence meant that they would be allowed to remain at peace, they were anxious to have the new government organized and functioning by the time Lincoln was inaugurated.

On inauguration day, March 4, Washington, D.C., had the appearance of an armed camp. Rumors that Lincoln would be assassinated, that the South would never allow the president to be sworn in, and that a Southern-led coup would overturn the government had been circulating for days. The air was thick with tension. Soldiers were everywhere in evidence, in the streets, along the route of the inaugural procession, on the Capitol grounds, and in the windows of the Capitol overlooking the gathering crowd. A battery of artillery was drawn up on the grass. The military character of the scene on the day Lincoln began his term of office forecast the character of his administration. It would be dominated, from the first day to the last, by war, with all its horror and bloodshed. Lincoln would never know what it was like to preside over a country at peace.

To say that Lincoln was unprepared to cope with the crisis would be an understatement, although he sensed the magnitude of the difficulties that lay in his path. "No one, not in my situation," Lincoln told Springfield's citizens when he bade them goodbye on February 11, "can appreciate my feelings of sadness at this parting." With an almost eerie prescience, he continued, "I now leave, not knowing when, or whether ever, I may return, with a task before me greater than that which rested upon Washington." Following his election there had been little time to contemplate the crisis, let alone develop a response to it. Republican office seekers, rejoicing in their first presidential victory, descended on Lincoln, eager to share the rewards of his success.

Lincoln's first concern was to shape a cabinet that would reflect the diversity of the Republican Party while satisfying the party's leaders. It was a task that demanded a tactful and careful balancing act. To William H. Seward of New York, his principal rival for the party's nomination, Lincoln assigned the State Department. Another presidential aspirant, Salmon P. Chase of Ohio, representing the radical antislavery element in the party, was appointed to the patronage-rich Treasury Department. For attorney general, Lincoln chose Edward Bates, an old Whig from the border slave state of Missouri, and for postmaster general he selected Montgomery Blair of Maryland, a member of the influential Jacksonian family of Francis Preston Blair. Gideon Welles of Connecticut represented both New England and the Democratic element in the party as secretary of the navy. Two cabinet members—Simon Cameron of Pennsylvania and Indiana's Caleb Smith—were appointed (secretaries of war and the interior, respectively) to honor deals Lincoln's managers had made at the Chicago convention.

Lincoln continued to grapple with patronage problems during the early stages of his presidency, a distraction from the pressing questions of disunion and war that should have held his full attention. "There is a throng here of countless spoilsmen who desire place," complained one member of Congress. Thousands of office seekers were "fiddling around the Administration for loaves and fishes, while the Government is being destroyed."

As the crisis deepened during the winter of 1860-1861, Lincoln's Whig belief in a weak president began to wane. Although he confessed that his "political education" strongly inclined him against the "free use" of presidential power, he had in fact begun to move toward the Jacksonian conviction of strong presidential leadership. The seeds for Lincoln's shift were sown as early as 1849, when he had proposed that Zachary Taylor avoid the appearance of a "mere man of straw" and adopt some of Jackson's characteristics. "We dare not

disregard the lessons of experience," Lincoln warned.

As the slavery issue grew more explosive during the 1850's, Lincoln saw Jackson in a new light, praising his "decision of character" in dealing with South Carolina's defiance of federal authority in 1832. With slavery threatening the nation's moral fiber as well as the Union, Lincoln's early suggestion that the people, through Congress, should "do as they please" now seemed dangerously out of place. It was precisely the weakness of the presidents—Franklin Pierce and James Buchanan—and the near breakdown of order in a Congress dominated by the South that encouraged the aggressions of the slave power.

Following the presidential election, Americans were assured that Lincoln, of whom so many people knew so little, was endowed with the same "sagacity, honesty, and firmness" that characterized Andrew Jackson; printmakers even made Lincoln look like Jackson. Jacksonian phrases crept into Lincoln's rhetoric, and many supporters urged Lincoln to follow Jackson's example in dealing with the South. Lincoln was sustained during the dark days of the "secession winter" at least in part by the spirit of Old Hickory.

Lincoln's inaugural address on March 4, 1861, was eagerly awaited by Americans in both the North and the South, for it would be the new president's first public response to the secession of the seven lower South states and the creation of the Confederate States. No one knew for sure what he would say. Southern leaders had already made it clear that nothing Lincoln could say would induce their states to return to the Union; many Northerners, however, were hopeful that he would propose some policy that would mend the rift in the Union peaceably.

Although he held out assurances to the Southerners that they need have no fears for their peace, property, and personal security under his administration, Lincoln was firm in his rejection of secession. He offered little hope for a peaceful solution to the crisis and indeed recognized a war between the sections as a possibility. "The Union of these states is perpetual," he declared. No state on its own motion can lawfully withdraw from the Union; therefore the "Union is unbroken." Echoing Jackson's statements (and those of Buchanan just two months before), he asserted his strong resolve to see the laws of the nation enforced in all the states, including those that had seceded, and he warned the South that he would use his power to "hold, occupy, and possess" the property of the United States within those states. Once again, he placed the differences between North and South on a moral foundation; the only point of dispute, he said, was the question of slavery's rightness or wrongness. He believed that the people in their intelligence, patriotism, and devotion to God would surely find a way out of the "present difficulty," but he gave no hints on how this

might be accomplished. Lincoln ended with both a challenge to the South and an expression of hope that all might yet be put right. "In *your* hands, my dissatisfied fellow-countrymen, and not in *mine*, is the momentous issue of civil war. . . . You can have no conflict, without being yourselves the aggressors." Reasserting his faith that reason must ultimately prevail over passion, he hoped that the "mystic chords of memory" that united all Americans would "yet swell the chorus of the Union, when again touched, as surely they will be, by the better angels of our nature."

Some elements of conciliation could be found in Lincoln's statement, but they did nothing to allay the crisis. He recognized that many "worthy, and patriotic citizens" sought to save the Union by amending the Constitution, and he favored giving the people an opportunity to act on their proposals, without committing himself to any one of them. Men such as

The bombardment of Fort Sumter, 1861. *(Library of Congress)*

Douglas, who still thought compromise possible, took heart, but neither Lincoln nor his party followed up the suggestion. Southerners reacted to the address with predictable outrage, viewing it as tantamount to a declaration of war against the South.

Of the fifteen slave states in the Union, seven withdrew from the Union in response to Lincoln's election. To the people in the remaining eight, the election of a Republican to the presidency by itself was not sufficient cause for disunion. In turning down secession, however, some of the states issued clear warnings that future action would depend on Lincoln's policy toward the seven. If, as some expected, Lincoln attempted to coerce those states back into the Union against their will, others would have no alternative but to leave the Union as well. Their decision was not long in coming.

Immediately following his inaugural, Lincoln confronted the problem of retaining two small pieces of land in the South that still remained in federal hands: Fort Pickens, near Pensacola, Florida, and Fort Sumter, in the harbor of Charleston, South Carolina. Of the two, Fort Sumter was the more sensitive, largely because of its location. To South Carolinians, the continued federal occupation of Fort Sumter was more than merely insulting to their new nation; it was regarded as a continuing act of hostility against the South. To people in the North, the fort became a symbol of United States authority in the seceded states; evacuation would be a humiliating retreat. Informed only hours after his inauguration that provisions were running low at Fort Sumter and that the garrison could not hold out longer than a few more weeks, Lincoln was forced to make one of the most important decisions of his administration. Consistent with the policy suggested in his inaugural address, he decided to send provisions to the beleaguered fort, but only after some vacillation and confusion resulting from contradictory advice and mixed-up orders. Unwilling to allow this sym-bol of United States authority to continue to be maintained, Confederate leaders ordered the batteries in Charleston harbor to open fire on the fort early on April 12. Thirty-three hours later the federal garrison capitulated. The Civil War had begun.

The bombardment and surrender of Fort Sumter produced an intense war excitement in both North and South. The tensions and uncertainties of the preceding months were swept away. The air was cleared and there no longer seemed any doubt as to the course every American should take. In the North, an impressive show of unity gave Lincoln the strength to mobilize the nation against the rebellion. On April 15, the day after the surrender, he issued his first wartime executive proclamation. Seventy-five thousand militia troops, to serve ninety days, were summoned to suppress the resistance to federal authority. At the same time, Lincoln called Congress into special session to meet on July 4 "to consider and determine, such measures, as, in their wisdom, the public safety, and interest may seem to demand." It was Lincoln's hope (shared by many in the North) that the emergency would be short-lived and that Southern resistance would be successfully quelled by the time Congress should meet.

Lincoln's call for troops was the signal for which the other slave states had been waiting. In response to what they maintained was a deliberate policy of coercion against the seceded states, four more states—Virginia, Tennessee, Arkansas, and North Carolina—withdrew from the Union, swelling the size, population, and resources of the Confederate States. The Southern nation now comprised eleven of the fifteen slave states, one-third of the total number of states in the Union. The loyalty of the four border slave states—Delaware, Maryland, Kentucky, and Missouri—was of continuing concern to Lincoln, and his determination to retain their loyalty strongly influenced the direction of his wartime policies.

Attack on Fredericksburg, December, 1862, by Alonzo Chappel. *(Library of Congress)*

War and the Power of the Presidency

The months following the surrender of Fort Sumter revealed the firmness with which Lincoln would meet the crisis of civil war, as he embarked on policies that contrasted sharply with his earlier Whig views on the nature of presidential power. The period has been labeled the "Presidential War" and Lincoln's role that of a "constitutional dictator" as he single-handedly placed the nation on a wartime footing, acting wholly without congressional sanction. The situation was desperate. Washington, D.C., during those first weeks was virtually isolated from the rest of the country. Telegraph lines were cut, railroad bridges destroyed, and a section of the rail line to the West had fallen into rebel hands. Some of the first troops to arrive in the capital had been attacked as they marched through Baltimore. Desperate measures were called for to meet the crisis; by postponing the meeting of Congress for three months, Lincoln indicated that he did not want

his action to be inhibited by an endless debate over "constitutional niceties."

In defining the nature of the conflict, Lincoln adopted a deliberate ambiguity, giving flexibility to his policy making. Regarded as an insurrection for some purposes, the conflict became a war between belligerent powers for others. Two proclamations were quickly issued establishing a naval blockade of the Southern coastline, an action that normally followed a congressional declaration of war in a conflict between the powers of equal status. The legality of these actions was later upheld by the Supreme Court by the narrowest of margins. Four justices, including the chief justice, argued that Lincoln had exceeded his constitutional authority, that the president's power to deal with insurrection was not equivalent to a war power, and that only Congress was authorized to declare or recognize a state of war. Perhaps to meet such constitutional objections, Congress in mid-July did recognize a state of war between the United States and the Confederate States but by doing so contradicted Lincoln's assertion that the conflict was a domestic insurrection.

Early in May, 1861, Lincoln issued a call for forty-two thousand volunteer troops (the first of a number of such calls) and at the same time ordered an increase in the strength of the regular army and navy, actions that were regarded as congressional rather than executive powers (although Congress later sanctioned Lincoln's moves as if they had been done under congressional authority). He authorized the requisition and arming of ships "for purposes of public defence" and made arrangements for the transportation of men and supplies, in each instance working through private individuals rather than the appropriate government agencies. To meet the military expenses, Lincoln ordered the payment of funds out of the national treasury, even though the Constitution forbade the disbursement of money without a congressional appropriation.

Finally, in one of his most drastic steps, Lincoln authorized the suspension of the privilege of the writ of habeas corpus in all instances in which resistance to federal authority was suspected, an action that left a wide area of interpretation to military officers. Initially limited to specific locations, the suspension was expanded in September, 1862, to encompass all persons who discouraged enlistments, resisted the draft, or were guilty of disloyal practice, wherever found. The chief justice of the United States ruled in May, 1861, that Lincoln had overstepped the constitutional bounds of his office in suspending the writ, but Lincoln brushed his objections aside. In the spring of 1863, Congress ended all constitutional doubts by sanctioning Lincoln's practice.

The constitutional limits of presidential power were a source of constant concern, both to Lincoln and to his critics. He was sensitive to the objections raised against his actions and uneasy in his own mind about the constitu-

tional question. He was aware that some of his actions were of doubtful legality, but he always believed that the seriousness of the crisis justified them. The Constitution, Lincoln argued, authorized the president to determine the existence of an insurrection and to take steps to suppress it, no matter how extreme. "It became necessary for me," he explained, "to choose whether, using only the existing means, agencies, and processes which Congress has provided, I should let the government fall at once into ruin, or whether, availing myself of the broader powers conferred by the Constitution in cases of insurrection, I would make an effort to save it with all its blessings for the present age and for posterity." If his actions sometimes exceeded even those "broader powers," he pointed out, they were taken because the preservation of the government demanded them.

Lincoln's task was made easier by his knowledge that the people supported him. What he did, he did "under what appeared to be a popular demand, and a public necessity." Like Jackson, he justified his actions by linking them to the popular will. The constitutional power of the president, he believed, was variable, dependent on circumstances. Certain actions, he wrote, "are constitutional when, in cases of rebellion or Invasion, the public Safety requires them, which would not be constitutional when, in the absence of rebellion or invasion, the public Safety does not require them."

Lincoln insisted, as Jackson did before him, that his oath of office allowed him to exercise power that under ordinary circumstances would not be legitimate. In his inaugural address, he reminded the South that he had taken a "most solemn" oath to preserve, protect, and defend the Constitution. This oath, "registered in Heaven," became a source of power in itself, independent of the Constitution. Must the government be allowed to fall, he asked, lest he be charged with violating its laws? Would not his oath be broken "if the government should be overthrown, when it was believed that disregarding the single law, would tend to preserve it?" Lincoln clarified his position in 1864: "My oath to preserve the Constitution imposed on me the duty of preserving by every indispensable means that government, that nation, of which the Constitution was the organic law. Was it possible to lose the nation and yet preserve the Constitution? . . . I felt that measures, otherwise constitutional, might become lawful by becoming indispensable to the preservation of the Constitution through the preservation of the nation." The Constitution must, under some circumstances, be violated in order to preserve it.

Furthermore, Lincoln maintained that he could exercise power that constitutionally belonged only to Congress on the grounds that Congress could always ratify his action after the fact. "It is believed," he stated in reference to his decrees in the spring of 1861, "that nothing has been done beyond the constitutional competency of Congress." Thus, in the crisis, with Congress out of session, the president held legislative as well as executive power. As the war continued, Lincoln moved even beyond this position when he declared that his function as commander in chief enabled him to do things that were constitutionally denied to both Congress and the president. His power, he came to feel, was virtually unlimited, as long as it was wielded in defense of the Constitution and the Union. "As Commander-in-Chief," he stated, "I suppose I have a right to take any measure which may best subdue the enemy." He held the authority to "do things on military ground" that could not be done constitutionally any other way, and indeed this was precisely the justification he offered for his Emancipation Proclamation.

No president brought the executive's war power to so careful and reasoned a definition. That he should grasp the nature of presidential power in a time of crisis so quickly and so astutely was nothing short of remarkable, considering his lack of experience in office. Critics during the war exaggerated his use of power when they denounced him as a dictator and a despot. He exercised the authority of his office with considerable restraint, cautiously weighing the alternatives and consequences, and never losing sight of his larger values. Although he carried presidential power to unprecedented heights, he did so only after he was persuaded that his ends could be accomplished in no other way. Lincoln himself suggested that whereas he may have used extraordinary and unconstitutional means, he had never misused the assumed power. The power, he stressed, was coterminous with the war and would expire with the conflict.

Lincoln's relations with Congress were surprisingly tranquil throughout the war, and on only a few occasions did they reach open disagreement and confrontation (and then, ironically, Lincoln faced the hostility of members of his own party). He made almost no use of the veto power, although he was not hesitant to threaten its use when it suited his purposes. Ever since the tumultuous sessions of the late 1850's, Congress's reputation for calm and efficient deliberation had suffered, and Lincoln shared the distrust that many Americans felt toward the legislative branch. During his administration, Congress served as an arena in which his critics did not hesitate to work their mischief. A standing investigation of the administration and of Lincoln's prosecution of the war by the Joint Committee on the Conduct of the War bordered at times on downright harassment, while a well-orchestrated effort by Senate Republicans to seize power from the president in late 1862 failed only because of Lincoln's skill at maneuver and manipulation. When Lincoln confronted Congress in 1864 on the question of Reconstruction, he had to endure some of the most vicious attacks ever hurled at a chief executive by members of his own party. It is not surprising that Lincoln

The Emancipation Proclamation

By the President of the United States of America:
A Proclamation.

Whereas on the 22d day of September, a.d. 1862, a proclamation was issued by the President of the United States, containing, among other things, the following, to wit:

"That on the 1st day of January, a.d. 1863, all persons held as slaves within any State or designated part of a State the people whereof shall then be in rebellion against the United States shall be then, thenceforward, and forever free; and the executive government of the United States, including the military and naval authority thereof, will recognize and maintain the freedom of such persons and will do not act or acts to repress such persons, or any of them, in any efforts they may make for their actual freedom.

"That the executive will on the 1st day of January aforesaid, by proclamation, designate the States and parts of States, if any, in which the people thereof, respectively, shall then be in rebellion against the United States; and the fact that any State or the people thereof shall on that day be in good faith represented in the Congress of the United States by members chosen thereto at elections wherein a majority of the qualified voters of such States shall have participated shall, in the absence of strong countervailing testimony, be deemed conclusive evidence that such State and the people thereof are not then in rebellion against the United States."

Now, therefore, I, Abraham Lincoln, President of the United States, by virtue of the power in me vested as Commander-in-Chief of the Army and Navy of the United States in time of actual armed rebellion against the authority and government of the United States, and as a fit and necessary war measure for suppressing said rebellion, do, on this 1st day of January, a.d. 1863, and in accordance with my purpose so to do, publicly proclaimed for the full period of one hundred days from the first day above mentioned, order and designate as the States and parts of States wherein the people thereof, respectively, are this day in rebellion against the United States the following, to wit:

Arkansas, Texas, Louisiana (except the parishes of St. Bernard, Plaquemines, Jefferson, St. John, St. Charles, St. James, Ascension, Assumption, Terrebonne, Lafourche, St. Mary, St. Martin, and Orleans, including the city of New Orleans), Mississippi, Alabama, Florida, Georgia, South Carolina, North Carolina, and Virginia (except the forty-eight counties designated as West Virginia, and also the counties of Berkeley, Accomac, Northhampton, Elizabeth City, York, Princess Anne, and Norfolk, including the cities of Norfolk and Portsmouth), and which excepted parts are for the present left precisely as if this proclamation were not issued.

And by virtue of the power and for the purpose aforesaid, I do order and declare that all persons held as slaves within said designated States and parts of States are, and henceforward shall be, free; and that the Executive Government of the United States, including the military and naval authorities thereof, will recognize and maintain the freedom of said persons.

And I hereby enjoin upon the people so declared to be free to abstain from all violence, unless in necessary self-defense; and I recommend to them that, in all cases when allowed, they labor faithfully for reasonable wages.

And I further declare and make known that such persons of suitable condition will be received into the armed service of the United States to garrison forts, positions, stations, and other places, and to man vessels of all sorts in said service.

> And upon this act, sincerely believed to be an act of justice, warranted by the Constitution upon military necessity, I invoke the considerate judgment of mankind and the gracious favor of Almighty God.

was happiest when Congress was in recess. When Congress was in session, he followed an independent course without much heed to congressional reaction. No president, historian James G. Randall has concluded, carried the "power of presidential edict and executive order," independently of Congress, as far as Lincoln did.

War Aims: Union and Emancipation

For Lincoln the Civil War held a significance that extended beyond the preservation of the nation. His scrupulous use of his war power was always conditioned by that broader significance; he was determined that nothing he might do should compromise the meaning that America had for the rest of the world. On the contrary, he felt a deep responsibility to preserve America's mission and to find in the war the means for advancing it.

The romantic attachment that early nineteenth century Americans felt toward their revolutionary beginnings touched Lincoln as well. The meaning of the American Revolution first emerged for Lincoln from the pages of Parson Weem's popular biography of George Washington, which he read as a youth. It took shape in his 1838 Lyceum address, but it was not until he joined the antislavery crusade that Lincoln brought to full flower his dedication to the principles of the Revolution. From then on, the American Revolution and the Declaration of Independence it inspired formed the bedrock of his ideas. The Revolution, he believed, provided the "germ" from which the "universal liberty of mankind" would find nurture. The United States alone of all the nations represented the "advancement, prosperity and glory, of human liberty, human right and human nature." He spoke movingly of the spirit of America that was embedded in the country's charter of freedom. The Declaration of Independence was that "electric cord . . . that links the hearts of patriotic and liberty-loving men together, that will link those patriotic hearts as long as the love of freedom exists in the minds of men throughout the world."

Lincoln's faith in America was reflected in his inaugural address, but it was not until later that he fully articulated the relationship between the war and the American mission. The issue, he told Congress in his message on July 4, 1861, "embraces more than the fate of these United States." The war was a test, before "the whole family of man," whether a constitutional republic, or democracy, "a government of the people, by the same people," could maintain itself "against its own domestic foes." The fate of democratic government everywhere depended on the outcome of the conflict. "Is there," he asked, "in all republics, this inherent, and fatal weakness? Must a government, of necessity, be too *strong* for the liberties of its own people, or too *weak* to maintain its own existence?" Popular government, he stated, was yet an experiment. Americans had successfully demonstrated that they could establish and administer it; now they were being asked to show the world that they could also maintain it "against a formidable attempt to overthrow it."

The war, Lincoln declared, was a "People's contest." Its goal was to maintain in the world "that form, and substance of government, whose leading object is, to elevate the condition of men—to lift artificial weights from all shoulders—to clear the paths of laudable pursuit for all—to afford all, an unfettered start, and a fair chance, in the race of life." The ideas were not new to the mid-nineteenth century, but few Americans expressed them so well.

To Lincoln, then, the war was being fought to preserve the Union and, by extension, the Union's world mission. In his inaugural address, he disclaimed any intention of interfering with the institution of slavery in the states where it existed, and in his first wartime message he assured the South that his mind had not changed. Looking ahead to the course the government would follow after the rebellion was suppressed, he promised that he would be guided simply by the Constitution and the laws. His understanding of the relations between the states and the nation, he added, would not differ from the sentiments expressed in his inaugural.

Little more than two weeks later, on July 21, Union and Confederate armies fought their first major engagement at Bull Run, about twenty-five miles from Washington, D.C. The result was a defeat and disorderly retreat for the Union army, a shock to Northerners who had expected a quick and easy triumph. On the following day, Congress, sobered by the defeat, authorized the enlistment of five hundred thousand volunteers for a period of three years. At the same time, it issued the first formal declaration of war aims, the Crittenden Resolution, echoing Lincoln's earlier assurances to the South. The war, according to the statement, was not being waged for conquest or subjugation or to overthrow or interfere with the established institutions of the state; rather, it was being fought simply "to defend and maintain the *supremacy* of the Constitution, and to preserve the Union with all the . . . rights of the several States unimpaired." Congress thus joined the president in disavowing any intention to interfere with slavery in the states where it existed.

Yet the slavery question could not be put aside. Many antislavery Americans believed that the war was the long-awaited opportunity

to rid the nation of the hated institution and that with his war power Lincoln had the authority to emancipate the slaves. Convinced (as was Lincoln himself) that the slavery issue had precipitated the crisis, they believed it the height of folly to fight for the preservation of the Union with slavery left intact.

Lincoln found it increasingly difficult to counter these arguments, but counter them he felt he must. Although he was willing to bend the Constitution and expand his war power in other areas, he was insistent that all the constitutional and legal guarantees be observed when it came to slavery. Four slave states remained in the Union, and he was determined to retain their loyalty, almost at any cost. Any action taken against slavery, he was persuaded, would drive some or all of them into the waiting arms of the Confederate States, rendering a Union victory more difficult if not impossible. Furthermore, he believed that action against

Confederate president Jefferson Davis. *(Library of Congress)*

slavery would alienate a large segment of Northern opinion, represented in the Democratic Party and among the more conservative members of the Republican Party. His purpose was to draw these elements to his side in support of the war, not to drive them into an opposition to the war. Finally, Lincoln realized what many antislavery people apparently did not, that nothing could ever be done to emancipate the slaves unless the Union were preserved first. The war must be won before slavery could be dealt with; to win the war required the support of all political constituencies. Lincoln's hatred of slavery was well known, his desire to see the institution eliminated deeply felt. Pragmatic considerations, however, outweighed his convictions.

Despite his well-founded intentions, the question of slavery demanded his attention from the moment the war began. Not only was Lincoln's position challenged by a growing number of Americans, but events also revealed the ambiguity of his stand. The Fugitive Slave Act was still in force (it would not be repealed until 1864), necessary legislation to the loyal slave states but ridiculous when applied to the seceded states. The result was that Union field commanders were frequently forced to deal with the practical problems of slavery in the absence of direction from the president. Lincoln's dilemma only worsened.

The issue was confronted early in the war when General Benjamin F. Butler, commander at Fort Monroe in Virginia, refused to return slaves who came into the Union lines to their owners. Instead, he declared them "contraband of war," in effect treating them as captured enemy property. Other field officers, such as Ulysses S. Grant in the West, gathered escaped slaves in camps where they could be cared for and in some instances organized for paramilitary labor. Their status was uncertain, for they were no longer slaves yet neither were they free. The situation was only partially clarified in August, 1861, when Congress enacted

its first (or "halfway") confiscation act, providing for the seizure of enemy property, including slaves, that was used for hostile purposes. It was not until the spring of 1862 that military personnel were prohibited from returning escaped slaves to their owners.

Lincoln's policy met its first test in August, 1861, when General John C. Frémont declared martial law in Missouri, ordered the confiscation of the property of persons who supported resistance to the government, and freed their slaves. Frémont's action, aimed at slaveholders in a loyal state, raised an immediate storm of protest in the North. Lincoln, fearing the defection of neighboring Kentucky, was appalled. "I think to lose Kentucky is nearly the same as to lose the whole game," he confided to a friend. Lincoln directed Frémont to change his order to bring it into conformity with the terms of the confiscation act, thus revoking the general's attempt to emancipate the slaves, and later removed him from his command. Where would constitutional government be, he asked, if a "General, or a President" should be allowed to "make permanent rules of property by proclamation"? Abolitionists who rejoiced at Frémont's edict turned their anger on Lincoln.

Lincoln was compelled to act a second time in May, 1862, when General David Hunter, commanding Union-occupied bits of Georgia, Florida, and South Carolina coastline, declared all the slaves in his department to be free. Lincoln intervened once again, countermanding the order lest it damage support for the war. This time he made it clear that military emancipation could not justifiably be left to the decision of field commanders; rather, it was a responsibility he reserved to himself. Lincoln had already begun to move, if ever so slightly, toward the exercise of presidential authority over slavery.

Republicans in Congress, however, were not willing to wait. They began chipping away at slavery, believing not only that the institution must be a casualty of the war but also

This photograph by Mathew Brady was made in October, 1862, as Lincoln visited General George B. McClellan at his headquarters in Antietam, Maryland. *(Library of Congress)*

that action taken against it would weaken the South and hasten Union victory. In April, 1862, slavery was abolished in the District of Columbia with compensation to the slaveholders, and in June it was abolished in the nation's territories without compensation (and in defiance of the Supreme Court's decision in the Dred Scott case). The following month, Congress took the next logical step when it passed the second confiscation act, one of the most important and far-reaching legislative enactments of the war. All property held by persons who supported the rebellion (by definition encompassing all the people in the eleven seceded states) was declared forfeit and subject to confiscation. To make the intent of the act clear, Congress explicitly declared that "all slaves of persons who shall hereafter be engaged in rebellion against the Government of the United States, or who shall in any way give aid thereto . . . shall be forever free." One year after the passage of the Crittenden Resolution, Congress had reversed itself; slavery was no

longer to remain untouched by Union victory.

Lincoln could not ignore the growing sentiment in favor of emancipation. Pressure to take presidential action increased following the failure of General George B. McClellan's spring campaign against Richmond. More drastic measures against the South were demanded. The foreign situation, moreover, was deteriorating. England and France were providing aid to the Confederacy and seemed to be moving closer to a recognition of Confederate independence. Only an unequivocal emancipation policy, it was thought, could halt this trend. More and more people in the North came to believe that Lincoln's hesitancy stemmed from a lack of understanding of the crisis, and they began to question his competence as president. Lincoln, anguished by military defeat and the growing strength of the Confederacy abroad, searched for a course of action that would meet the objections of his critics and at the same time hold the support of all Northern elements. It was not an easy task.

Still clinging to his constitutional scruples, Lincoln recognized only two means for ridding the nation of slavery: by individual state action or by a constitutional amendment. With one-third of the states out of the Union, the latter was a remote possibility. In a special message to Congress in March, 1862, he revealed his solution to the slavery issue. Abolition, he suggested, must be by state action, it should be gradual rather than sudden (which he believed "is better for all"), and it should be accompanied by compensation "for the inconveniences public and private, produced by such a change of system." The cost to the federal government, he pointed out, would be less than the cost of continuing the war. He hoped to persuade the loyal border states to abolish slavery under his plan, and he even drafted sample legislation that would achieve that goal. The end of the war, he was convinced, would follow soon thereafter.

Lincoln met with border-state representatives and later called them to a conference in the White House in the hope that he might interest them in his proposal. He pleaded with them to carry it to their respective states and to work for its adoption. Lincoln's desperation was apparent. "The pressure," he told them, "is still upon me, and is increasing." He appealed to their patriotism and statesmanship to help save the government "to the world" and vindicate its "beloved history." To make their decision easier, he argued strongly for the colonization of the freed slaves outside the United States, and he later tried to sell the idea to a delegation of blacks. Lincoln's pleas, however, were unavailing. His proposal was rejected by the border states.

The demands of the abolitionists became more intense, and it was obvious that Lincoln would not be able to resist them much longer. To a group of visiting churchmen he expressed doubts that a presidential proclamation emancipating the slaves could be effective. The world would recognize it as "inoperative," in a class

with the "Pope's bull against the comet." He urged once again that the preservation of the Union must be the first priority. When Horace Greeley, the outspoken antislavery editor of the *New York Tribune*, denounced Lincoln's recalcitrance and pointed out the inconsistency of putting down the rebellion while upholding its cause, Lincoln replied publicly in one of his best efforts to link the slavery question with the cause of the Union

> My paramount object in this struggle *is* to save the Union, and is *not* either to save or destroy slavery. If I could save the Union without freeing *any* slave I would do it, and if I could save it by freeing *all* the slaves I would do it; and if I could save it by freeing some and leaving others alone I would also do that. What I do about slavery and the colored race, I do because I believe it helps to save the Union; and what I forbear, I forbear because I do *not* believe it would help save the Union.

The statement was of great import, for it was the first time that Lincoln conceded publicly that he might free either all or some of the slaves. Any emancipation policy he might adopt, he was saying, would rest on expediency and would be tied to the greater good of the Union.

Without the knowledge of Greeley and the visiting churchmen, Lincoln had already decided on just such an expedient policy, a decision known only to members of his cabinet. On July 22, five days after Congress's passage of the second confiscation act, Lincoln placed before his cabinet a document he had prepared that would emancipate all the slaves in the rebellious states. The border states had rejected his pleas for state emancipation; whatever damage might be done to their loyalty by a presidential proclamation had already been done by Congress's action. The proclamation was the last option open to him. On Seward's advice, however, he set the document aside. To issue it on the heels of military defeat, Seward argued, would be to deprive the policy of its sincerity in the eyes of the world. He proposed that Lincoln hold it until the military situation should improve.

Following McClellan's failure to take Richmond in the spring of 1862, Confederate forces commanded by Robert E. Lee advanced northward toward the Potomac. To stop them Lincoln turned to John Pope, who had enjoyed some small successes in the Western campaigns. It was an unfortunate choice. The two armies clashed on the last days of August in the Second Battle of Bull Run, another defeat and disorderly retreat for the Union army. Emboldened by his success, Lee decided to carry the war into the Union, hoping that an invasion would liberate Maryland, capitalize on Northern war weariness, and influence the coming congressional elections, thus forcing the Lincoln administration to negotiate an end to the war. On September 5, Lee's forces crossed the Potomac and moved into central Maryland. In desperation, Lincoln restored McClellan to his command and charged him with stopping Lee's advance. The result was the Battle of Antietam on September 17, the bloodiest single day of fighting in the entire war. Lee's invasion was halted and his forces withdrew into Virginia, but McClellan failed to follow up his advantage. It was, however, the best that Lincoln could hope for. Five days later, he issued his preliminary Emancipation Proclamation.

Lincoln's move was a masterstroke, perhaps the most important turning point in the war. He preserved his priorities and left his constitutional scruples undamaged, quieted the opposition from his own party, and at the same time fulfilled a long-held desire. He reiterated his conviction that the purpose of the war was the restoration of the Union and repeated his proposal for financial aid to any slave state that might adopt a plan for gradual abolition. Lincoln, however, now believed that military emancipation was necessary for the preservation of the Union. All slaves living in areas

that would still be in rebellion on January 1, 1863, he declared, were "then, thenceforward, and forever free." On that day he issued the final Emancipation Proclamation, listing those areas still in rebellion in which the slaves were freed.

Lincoln rested his action on his power as commander in chief. It was, he said, "a fit and necessary war measure" for suppressing the rebellion, an act of justice "warranted by the Constitution, upon military necessity." The proclamation could have no force beyond the termination of the war. Limited in duration, it was also limited in scope. Slaves living in the four loyal slave states and in those areas occupied by Union forces were excluded; the United States was not at war with those areas and therefore Lincoln's war power could not apply. Indeed, it has been suggested that Lincoln's Emancipation Proclamation fell short of Congress's emancipation in the second confiscation act and that Lincoln acted as if in ignorance of all the actions that Congress had taken earlier. At the same time, the congressional legislation was ineffective without the cooperation of the president. Thus it was Lincoln's proclamation that altered the nation's war aims and changed the course of the war; it was Lincoln's action that committed the American people to the abolition of slavery. With the proclamation, in the words of Allan Nevins, the war became a revolution.

The significance of the Emancipation Proclamation can hardly be exaggerated. Much of Lincoln's historical reputation and the perception of Lincoln as a folk hero rests on his role as the "Great Emancipator." Was he, however, a reluctant liberator, as some have maintained? When viewed from the perspective of his convictions and of his responsibilities as a war leader, it is clear that he was not. The proclamation did not weaken the will of the Southerners to continue their fight for independence, and the war would drag on for another two and a half years. From the point of view of one Confederate general, however, it was not only a great political triumph for Lincoln but also the greatest victory yet for the North.

That Lincoln did not regard his proclamation as the final solution to the vexing question of slavery became evident even before it went into effect. A president had no more power than a general, he had written, to make permanent rules of property by proclamation. In his message to Congress on December 1, 1862, a month before the final Emancipation Proclamation, he returned to the plan he had urged many times before. He proposed that Congress consider a constitutional amendment that would provide federal aid to those states that would adopt a gradual abolition of slavery. Gradual (until 1900, he suggested), compensated emancipation by state action still remained his favored course of action.

As the war continued, however, Lincoln came to recognize the necessity of a constitutional amendment that would simply abolish slavery wherever it existed in the United States.

The patchwork manner in which the question was treated—by congressional acts, including the important second confiscation act, and by presidential proclamation—and the limited and confusing policies that declared some slaves free but not others were unsatisfactory. Doubts concerning the effectiveness, as well as the legality, of the Emancipation Proclamation (shared by Lincoln himself) demanded more uniform and unambiguous action. After one unsuccessful attempt to pass a constitutional amendment abolishing slavery (without gradualism and compensation), Congress finally approved the Thirteenth Amendment to the Constitution in January, 1865. Although it was not the amendment he had preferred, Lincoln pushed strongly for its passage, especially after his reelection to the presidency in November, 1864, arguing again that the abolition of slavery was "among the means" to secure the "maintenance of the Union." The amendment was not finally ratified until after Lincoln's death.

Company E of the Fourth U.S. Colored Troops, 1865. *(Library of Congress)*

The Emancipation Proclamation added a new dimension to the meaning that the Civil War held for Lincoln. He appealed to Americans to overcome their qualms and to accept the commitment to freedom for the slaves. "The dogmas of the quiet past," he urged, "are inadequate to the stormy present." The times called for new thoughts and actions. "We must disenthrall ourselves, and then we shall save our country." In granting freedom to the slave, he declared, "we *assure* freedom to the *free*," thus saving "the last best, hope of earth." Lincoln returned to this theme a year later, in November, 1863, when he dedicated the military cemetery on the field of the great Battle of Gettysburg. The war, he said on that occasion, was a test of whether a nation "conceived in liberty, and dedicated to the proposition that all men are created equal" could "long endure." He urged all Americans to join in resolving "that this nation, under God, shall have a new birth of freedom—and that government of the people, by the people, for the people, shall not perish from the earth." Few Americans ever defined the nation's mission so effectively.

Political Opposition
Lincoln's Emancipation Proclamation eased the pressure from members of his own party, but it did not subdue Republican opposition to his prosecution of the war. Since the opening days of the conflict, when Lincoln deliberately postponed calling Congress into special session, members of that body had been attacking his policies. His proclamation removed one of the areas of contention for a time but left untouched the growing feeling among many in his party that he was incompetent to deal with the immense task that lay before him. Indeed, one of the darkest moments in the war for Lincoln came in December, 1862, between his preliminary and his final Emancipation Proclamation, when Republican opposition was exacerbated by another serious defeat for the Union army.

Lincoln had no military experience when he assumed the presidency (one can hardly count his brief experience in Black Hawk's War), nor had he ever shown any interest in military history. The Mexican War had been of little concern to him, except as a vehicle for registering his opposition to Polk's use of presidential power. Yet his administration was dominated from the day he took office until its end by a bloody war, and he was required, to an unusual degree, to make military decisions that would have taxed even the most experienced of leaders. In the absence of trustworthy commanders, he had to develop military strategy and plan military movements on a large scale with little information and skill. Furthermore, Lincoln's policy of recognizing Democrats as well as Republicans in his military appointments angered members of his own party and made him the object of continuing attack.

The initial defeat of the Army of the Potomac, commanded by General Irvin McDowell, at the First Battle of Bull Run in July, 1861, forecast a long and costly war. In the first of a series of command changes over the next three years, Lincoln replaced McDowell with George B. McClellan, an officer of Democratic antecedents who would cause Lincoln more moments of anxiety than any other general. In November, Lincoln further advanced McClellan to the office of general in chief, in place of the aged and infirm Winfield Scott. Hopes that McClellan would make a successful advance against the enemy, however, faded as it became apparent that the general lacked confidence, was overly cautious, and seemed reluctant to commit his men to battle. To make matters worse, McClellan did not hide his scorn for Lincoln or his impatience at being subject to a commander in chief whom he hardly trusted. He made a habit, moreover, of advising Lincoln on matters of policy, including the question of slavery.

As the nation chafed at McClellan's delay

and the pressure on Lincoln to mount an offensive against the enemy increased, Union troops suffered another costly setback at the Battle of Ball's Bluff in October, only a few miles up the Potomac River from Washington. The defeat, in which a prominent Republican senator and close friend of Lincoln was killed, spurred Congress to action. A congressional committee, including members of both houses, was formed "to inquire into the conduct of the present war." Dominated by radical anti-slavery Republicans, the Joint Committee on the Conduct of the War maintained a continuing surveillance of Lincoln's administration, often interfering in his military appointments and engaging in investigative practices that bordered on harassment of both the president and the military.

McClellan quickly became a principal point of opposition between Lincoln and congressional Republicans. Responding to their pressure, Lincoln ordered McClellan to open his long-awaited offensive in late February, 1862, but it was not until the following month that McClellan's army began to move. At the same time, Lincoln replaced McClellan as general in chief with Henry Wager Halleck, a former West Point professor whom Lincoln once characterized as a "first-class clerk." After an excruciatingly slow advance up the peninsula between the York and James Rivers, McClellan's army was turned back in a series of bloody encounters known as the Seven Days' Battles. Following McClellan's failure to take Richmond, relations between the two men deteriorated as attacks against both mounted in intensity. Lincoln had no choice but to reduce McClellan's authority and to bring in another general, in this case the arrogant and inept John Pope, whose appointment had been urged by the joint committee.

Following Pope's defeat at the Second Battle of Bull Run and Lee's invasion of Maryland, Lincoln turned in desperation to McClellan once again. Republicans were furious. Combined with their increasing indignation over Lincoln's apparent reluctance to take action against slavery and the frustration of military defeat, the restoration of the Democrat McClellan seemed the last straw. The governors of Massachusetts and Pennsylvania called a conference of Northern loyal governors to discuss Lincoln's prosecution of the war, fearful that the country would soon come to ruin if something were not done. The Battle of Antietam and Lincoln's subsequent Emancipation Proclamation, followed by his final dismissal of McClellan early in November, temporarily eased the situation, and the conference ended on a positive note.

Lincoln's reprieve did not last long. His choice to succeed McClellan, General Ambrose E. Burnside (whose lack of self-confidence was widely known), proved no more able to defeat Lee than had his predecessors. His ill-advised attack on Lee's army at Fredericksburg in December resulted in needless casualties, created open dissension among the officers in the army, and plunged Northern morale to new depths of despair. "We are going to destruction as fast as imbecility, corruption, and the wheels of time, can carry us," moaned one Republican senator. Lincoln was attacked more bitterly than before, as his critics blamed the military disasters on his "utter incompetence." Impressive Democratic victories at the polls in the congressional and state elections the month before underscored the need for drastic changes in Lincoln's administration. *The New York Times* blamed the crisis on Lincoln's inefficiency and concluded that the president was temperamentally unfit to deal with the "stern requirements of deadly war." The influential *Chicago Tribune* wondered if the rebels could ever be beaten with Lincoln at the helm.

Three days after the Battle of Fredericksburg, Senate Republicans met in caucus and voted to force Lincoln to reorganize his cabinet, presumably a first step toward asserting congressional control over the executive branch.

Their target was Secretary of State Seward, whom they believed to be the "evil genius" behind Lincoln's decisions, and in seeking his removal they had the support of Lincoln's Treasury secretary, Salmon P. Chase. Rumors swept the capital that the entire cabinet would resign, and some thought that Lincoln himself would give up his office. For Lincoln it was a crisis of the first magnitude. If the Republican senators should succeed, he would lose control of his administration. "What do these men want?" he asked a friend. "They wish to get rid of me, and I am sometimes half disposed to gratify them. . . . We are now on the brink of destruction. It appears to me the Almighty is against us, and I can hardly see a ray of hope."

There was hope, however, and it lay in Lincoln's political acumen and his masterful ability to manipulate his adversaries. Through a series of deft maneuvers, he was able to thwart the senators' attack, and by assuming the initiative he forced them to back off. Having received Seward's resignation, Lincoln so embarrassed Chase that he too offered his resignation. Lincoln emerged the winner when the senators, chagrined and frustrated, decided that Chase's loss from the cabinet was too great a price for Seward's removal. The crisis ended and the integrity of the executive branch was preserved. The Republican leadership in Congress, however, was not mollified and continued to harbor feelings of rancor and bitterness toward Lincoln.

Lincoln's troubles were far from over. While he was warding off the opposition from his own party, he faced an increasing opposition from the Democratic Party. Only a month after his encounter with the Senate Republicans, he told a visitor to the White House that he feared "the fire in the rear," meaning the Democratic opposition, more than he did the Union army's chances.

The coming of the war had had a disastrous impact on the Democratic Party. With the se-cession of eleven Southern states, Democratic strength in Congress was reduced, leaving the Republican Party with comfortable majorities in both chambers. The death of Stephen A. Douglas in June, 1861, left the party leaderless, creating a vacuum at the top that was never filled. Lacking effective leadership, the party never became a responsible opposition party to the Lincoln administration. The stresses of secession and war also left its ranks divided. Some Democrats moved into the Republican Party; others supported Lincoln's prosecution of the war while trying to maintain an oppo-sition to the administration on the traditional party issues. These were the War Democrats, and it was from their ranks that Lincoln made many of his appointments. Still others—the Peace Democrats, or more derisively, the cop-perheads—not only opposed Lincoln's han-dling of the war but also opposed the war itself. By early 1863, their opposition had de-veloped into a full-fledged peace movement.

Democratic opposition rested initially on traditional conservative grounds: a defense of states' rights against the consolidation of power on the national level implied in the Whig-Re-publican position, and of laissez-faire econom-ics against those elements of the old Whig plat-form that seemed to favor business and industrial interests over those of the rest of the population. Of more importance, however, were Lincoln's moves to extend presidential prerogative into those gray areas where con-stitutionality was in doubt.

Lincoln's proclamation of martial law and his suspension of the writ of habeas corpus following the fall of Fort Sumter, although lim-ited in scope and obviously supported by most Americans, were challenged by those who be-lieved only Congress had that power. The belief was confirmed by Chief Justice Roger B. Taney's ruling that Lincoln had violated the Constitution. That Lincoln was undeterred by the decision became evident when he expanded the suspension in September, 1862, a week after the Battle of Antietam, to cover the entire United States. To a growing number of Democrats, Lincoln appeared to be launching a full-scale attack on constitutional civil liberty, using the exigencies of the war as an excuse. When Congress sought to remove all constitutional doubts by ratifying Lincoln's moves in the Habeas Corpus Act of March, 1863, Democratic fears were hardly allayed. Thousands of individuals (the number is uncertain) suffered arbitrary arrest, and some Democratic newspapers were suspended.

The Emancipation Proclamation, issued only a few days before Lincoln's extension of the suspension of the writ of habeas corpus, brought Democratic opposition to a peak. The proclamation, it was charged, was further evidence of Lincoln's disregard of the Constitution. Furthermore, it violated the Republican Party's 1860 platform and Lincoln's often-repeated pledges never to interfere with slavery in the states where it existed. By enlarging the war aims, Lincoln, critics maintained, had altered the nature of the war. The charges became entangled with deep-seated antiblack prejudices in many parts of the North as Lincoln's opponents pointed out that while he was impairing the civil rights of whites, he was enhancing the rights of blacks.

Lincoln succeeded in doing with the Emancipation Proclamation what Robert E. Lee had failed to do with his invasion of Maryland, that is, to arouse a political opposition to the Republican administration of the war. The seriousness of the opposition was revealed in the results of the November elections. Although the Republicans retained their control in the House of Representatives, Democratic strength almost doubled. In addition, Democrats made substantial gains in states that the Republicans had carried just two years before, including Lincoln's own state of Illinois. To one leading Republican paper, the election results constituted a vote of no confidence in Lincoln's leadership.

The Battle of Fredericksburg, which had stimulated Republican opposition to Lincoln, also pushed Democrats to a more extreme stand. A congressman from Ohio, Clement L. Vallandigham, emerged as the leader of a peace movement that demanded an end to the useless slaughter of young men. From his seat in the House of Representatives, he denounced the war as cruel and wicked and charged Lincoln with attempting to erect a Republican despotism on the ruins of slavery. He attacked the Emancipation Proclamation as illegal, unconstitutional, and even immoral and urged resistance to Lincoln's broadening of the war aims. Vallandigham's condemnation of Lincoln's actions invited the action of the military. In May, 1863, he was arrested, tried by a military commission, and sentenced to imprisonment for the duration of the war. Lincoln was appalled at the arrest, for it gave Vallandigham the martyrdom he sought; in June, Lincoln commuted Vallandigham's sentence to removal beyond the Union lines.

Vallandigham's protests encouraged others to speak out against the war. The passage of the Habeas Corpus Act and of the nation's first Conscription Act in the spring of 1863, along with another Union army defeat at the Battle of Chancellorsville, gave force to the Democratic charges. In the Midwest (including Illinois), legislators called for the cessation of hostilities, the withdrawal of the Emancipation Proclamation, and a negotiated peace with the Confederacy. New York's Governor Horatio Seymour attacked the Conscription Act as a violation of civil liberty in a speech that contributed to the celebrated draft riots in New York City in early July.

Lincoln's distress at the opposition from both Republicans and Democrats was suddenly relieved in midsummer. Military events came to his rescue when two simultaneous and decisive Union victories were won at Gettysburg and Vicksburg. A turning point in the war had been reached. Military success, together with an economic recovery that soon became an unprecedented boom, gave Lincoln the strength to press the war to ultimate victory. With a Union victory at the Battle of Chattanooga in November, the Union's soldiers stood poised on the threshold of the Confederacy's heartland. A new general emerged who demonstrated an ability to win. When Ulysses S. Grant was brought to the East and placed in command of all the military forces of the United States, it seemed only a matter of time before the war would end.

The Election of 1864: The Issue of Reconstruction

With the Union army victories in 1863 marking a turn in the military fortunes of the North, the attacks on Lincoln from both Republicans and Democrats subsided. Lincoln's Gettysburg Address in November revealed a new confidence in the eventual triumph of the Union cause. In March, 1864, Ulysses S. Grant was promoted to the rank of lieutenant general (held by only two officers before him, George Washington and Winfield Scott) and was appointed general in chief of all Union armies, an office that Lincoln himself had filled in practice ever since the Battle of Antietam. As Grant began laying plans for a spring campaign against Lee's army, Lincoln believed that he had at last found his general. All the signs pointed to a quick end to the war.

At the same time, the nation gained the economic strength necessary to push the war to victory. The economic dislocation of the first two years of the conflict, brought on by the disruption of secession and war, had been overcome. With Lincoln's support, the government became an active partner in promoting an economic growth and development that by 1863 seemed unprecedented in its dimensions. Congress passed a series of tariff bills, raising protective duties higher and higher in response to the needs and demands of an expanding industrial establishment. A new national bank-

ing system to stabilize and strengthen the country's financial order was created by Congress, a move that, with the issuance of more than $400 million worth of unbacked paper money, made it possible to finance the war. A railroad was begun that would link the Pacific coast with the rest of the nation, the construction to be aided by large-scale government largesse, and a second transcontinental railroad was planned in 1864. Agricultural expansion was boosted with the passage in 1862 of the Homestead Act and of the Morrill Land Grant Act, providing free land to America's farmers and enabling the states to promote agricultural education and research. Never before had the United States government played so active a role in the nation's economic affairs.

The new prosperity and the turn in military fortunes strengthened Lincoln's hand and gave him the power and prestige he needed to save the Union. Toward the end of 1863, the poet Walt Whitman spoke for many Americans when he confessed that "I have finally got for good, I think, into the feeling that our triumph is assured" and that the president "has done as good as a human man could do." Lincoln began the critical presidential election year of 1864 with optimism and hope; his reelection hardly seemed in doubt.

Lincoln's opponents, however, were simply biding their time. Some Republicans still questioned Lincoln's competence to see the struggle through to its conclusion: The Democrats, disturbed by the infringement on civil liberty and shocked by the horrendous loss of life that accompanied Grant's Virginia offensive, still believed that the bloodshed could be halted and the Union preserved by peaceful negotiation. Both sides looked to the presidential election as the opportunity to achieve their ends legally and constitutionally.

As early as the fall of 1863, a number of Radical Republicans, convinced that Lincoln's administration was a failure, promoted the candidacy of Treasury Secretary Salmon P. Chase.

The Gettysburg Address

Fourscore and seven years ago our fathers brought forth on this continent a new nation, conceived in liberty and dedicated to the proposition that all men are created equal.

Now we are engaged in a great civil war, testing whether that nation or any nation so conceived and so dedicated can long endure. We are met on a great battlefield of that war. We have come to dedicate a portion of that field, as a final resting-place for those who here gave their lives that that nation might live. It is altogether fitting and proper that we should do this.

But, in a larger sense, we cannot dedicate, we cannot consecrate, we cannot hallow this ground. The brave men, living and dead, who struggled here have consecrated it far above our poor power to add or detract. The world will little note nor long remember what we say here, but it can never forget what they did here. It is for us the living rather to be dedicated here to the unfinished work which they who fought here have thus far so nobly advanced. It is rather for us to be here dedicated to the great task remaining before us—that from these honored dead we take increased devotion to that cause for which they gave the last full measure of devotion—that we here highly resolve that these dead shall not have died in vain, that this nation under God shall have a new birth of freedom, and that government of the people, by the people, for the people shall not perish from the earth.

Support for Chase, never strong, collapsed in the following spring, when the secretary himself tried to assure Lincoln that he was not involved in the movement. Later, an effort was made to advance the candidacy of John C. Frémont, but it proved to be a small affair (although Frémont took it seriously).

Lincoln had little reason for concern. The Republican convention, in an effort to expand its appeal to the War Democrats by calling itself the Union Party, easily nominated Lincoln for reelection to the presidency and selected the Tennessee Democrat Andrew Johnson as his running mate. The platform endorsed Lincoln's wartime policies, urged that the war be pressed to its ultimate military conclusion, and called for the passage of a constitutional amendment that would abolish slavery.

Events that followed in the summer of 1864, however, gave encouragement to Lincoln's critics and raised the hope that even yet he might be removed from the presidency. In the first place, the military situation took a turn for the worse. After pushing southward in Vir-

ginia, maintaining a relentless pressure on the depleted manpower resources of the Confederacy, Grant was stopped by Lee's army at Petersburg, a few miles south of Richmond. By mid-June he had settled down to a long and frustrating siege that would extend into the early months of 1865. In the meantime, Confederate General Jubal Early swept out of the Shenandoah Valley and reached the outskirts of Washington, D.C., threatening the capital and apparently demonstrating the weakness of the Union command. In the West, General William Tecumseh Sherman's advance into Georgia was stopped by Confederate forces at Atlanta. The promise of victory, so evident at the beginning of the year, had given way to stalemate, and by the late summer the North was plunged into another abyss of defeatism and despair.

More critical to Lincoln's relationship with his party was the discord that burst into the open over Reconstruction policy. Lincoln began thinking early in the war about the terms that would govern the return of the seceded states to the Union, and as the Union army occupied larger portions of the Confederacy the need for a policy became more urgent. Before December, 1863, Lincoln groped for a workable plan that could be applied to the occupied areas. In approaches to both Tennessee and Louisiana, he proposed certain vague steps toward the organization of new governments but seemed uncertain about how to reconcile the Emancipation Proclamation with a desire "to have peace again upon the old terms under the Constitution." When Congress met in December, 1863, with Union victory on the horizon, Lincoln issued his program for the restoration of the states to the Union in a Proclamation of Amnesty and Reconstruction.

Lincoln based his plan on two assumptions: first, that since secession was not recognized either in law or in the Constitution, the states had not left the Union; and second, that it was the responsibility of the president and not of Congress to devise and oversee the steps by which the states would resume their former places in the Union. The seceded states, he believed, were simply out of their practical relation with the other states. His plan looked to a speedy, easy resumption of that practical relation. Concerned primarily with the status of the states in the Union, Lincoln was more anxious for their restoration than he was for their reconstruction. Any internal changes would follow once the states had been restored to their former positions; furthermore, Lincoln appeared ready to allow Southerners a role in the formulation of these changes.

Lincoln was insistent that the authority to restore the states to the Union was his by virtue of his war power as commander in chief and of his constitutional authority to grant pardons. In his exercise of this authority, he argued for flexibility, expediency, and a forward-looking practicality. He had little patience for delay.

In his proclamation, Lincoln promised pardon to all in the seceded states who would take an oath to support, protect, and defend the Constitution and Union and to support all the actions of Congress and the president relating to slavery. Barred from the oath-taking were several categories of high-ranking Confederate civil and military officials. When 10 percent of the eligible voters in any state should have taken the oath and received the pardon, they could establish a new state government. Lincoln urged but did not require the new states to declare permanent the freedom of those who had been slaves. Once the states had fulfilled his conditions, they would presumably be restored to their former relations with the other states, although Lincoln conceded that Congress would have the final determination whether their representatives should be seated in the legislative body.

Lincoln's 10-percent plan was implemented in Arkansas and Louisiana in the spring of 1864 and in Tennessee later in the year, but not without confusion and uncertainty. Republicans in Congress, especially the radicals, responded bitterly to Lincoln's initiative. Not only did they believe that the terms of his plan were far too liberal, but also they resented Lincoln's contention that Reconstruction was the president's responsibility. After months of debate, they passed the Wade-Davis bill, in which their own Reconstruction program was outlined. Congressional intentions became clearer when the elected representatives from Louisiana and Arkansas were denied seats, in effect destroying Lincoln's plan.

The Wade-Davis bill replaced Lincoln's terms with harsher and more stringent provisions. An alternative oath was prescribed that gave assurance of the oath taker's past loyalty, and the 10 percent figure was raised to 50 percent. The new states were required to abolish slavery and to repudiate their Confederate debt. The bill, designed to postpone Reconstruction until after the war by making it virtually impossible for the Southern states to comply with its terms, revealed the gulf that existed between the president and Congress.

The confrontation widened when Lincoln expressed his opposition to the bill by exercising the seldom-used pocket veto. In a curious move, however, he issued a proclamation detailing his objections (no message is required for a pocket veto) that only incensed Congress the more. He was, he wrote, unwilling to be "inflexibly committed to any single plan of restoration," suggesting that he was not fully committed to his own plan. Furthermore, he was unwilling both to set aside the governments that had already been established in Louisiana and Arkansas and to concede to Congress the power to abolish slavery in the states. Having registered his objections, Lincoln then declared that he was "fully satisfied" with the bill as representing "one very proper plan." Finally, he offered the seceded states a choice between his plan and that of Congress, a meaningless gesture inasmuch as the latter had been pocket vetoed.

If Lincoln's proclamation was an effort to unify support for his reelection, it fell wide of the mark. Instead, it solidified Republican dissatisfaction with his leadership. Outraged and puzzled by his statements, the authors of the bill issued a fierce diatribe against his action—the Wade-Davis Manifesto. Arguably no president has had to endure such vilification from his own party. Lincoln's action was denounced as a political attack on the friends of the government, a "grave Executive usurpation," and a "studied outrage on the legislative authority of the people." He was charged with subverting the Constitution in the interest of his personal ambition. The manifesto concluded with a thinly veiled warning against Lincoln's use of presidential power. "The authority of Congress," Lincoln was reminded, "is paramount"; the president must "confine himself to his executive duties—to obey and execute, not make the laws."

The confrontation between Lincoln and the Republicans in Congress, with the defeatism that swept the North following the military stalemate, revived demands among some leading Republican spokespeople that Lincoln be replaced. Lincoln, declared one prominent editor, could no longer be reelected. Only another ticket (Grant or Sherman was suggested) could save the country "from utter overthrow." Plans were made for another Republican convention to find a new candidate "who commands the confidence of the country."

The furor had a dispiriting effect on Lincoln, and he began to doubt his own chances for reelection. The military impasse on top of the army's heavy losses encouraged the Peace Democrats, and once again demands were made for an end to the war through peace negotiations with the South. Lincoln's call for an additional five hundred thousand volunteers intensified the protests against the further needless sacrifice of lives. Even some Republicans, such as Horace Greeley, urged the president to explore every possible avenue toward a peaceful end to the conflict. Lincoln, by late August convinced that he would be beaten, exacted a pledge from his cabinet that they would cooperate with the president-elect to save the Union between the election and the inauguration, for it could not possibly be saved afterward. A week later, the Democratic convention nominated George B. McClellan for the presidency and placed him on a platform that demanded that hostilities cease immediately and that peace be restored "on the basis of the Federal Union."

Within days, however, the entire picture suddenly changed. Admiral David Glasgow Farragut forced his way into Mobile Bay and sealed off one of the last Southern ports open to the outside world. On September 2, General Sherman's army marched into Atlanta on the heels of the retreating Confederate force, and later General Philip Sheridan ended Confederate resistance in the Shenandoah Valley, freeing the national capital of any further threat from the enemy. Northerners, with victory once more in sight, rallied to the side of Abraham

Lincoln. A nervous John C. Frémont withdrew his candidacy, and the plans for a Republican convention were abandoned. McClellan strongly endorsed the prosecution of the war to ultimate Union victory. Lincoln was rescued by military events, and on election day in November he coasted to an easy victory in both the popular vote and the electoral college.

The End of the War and Assassination
Lincoln's reelection ended all doubts that the war would continue until the nation's goals were achieved. The Republicans not only won the presidency but also swept the congressional elections, increasing their majority in the lower house of Congress and maintaining their strong lead in the Senate. With their triumph as a mandate, they succeeded in passing the Thirteenth Amendment to the Constitution, abolishing slavery throughout the United States. General Sherman's army moved out of Atlanta and began its march across Georgia; by Christmas it had reached the sea at Savannah and, turning northward, began its movement into the Carolinas.

In the Confederacy, the desire for peace reached a peak. Jefferson Davis, partly to mollify his critics, agreed to meet with Northern representatives to negotiate a peaceful end to the bloodshed. Lincoln also agreed to take part, although, like Davis, he had no faith that such an endeavor could succeed. The conference was doomed before it started; Davis wrote of a meeting "to secure peace to the two countries," whereas Lincoln indicated a readiness to bring "peace to the people of our one common country." A Southern delegation headed by Vice President Alexander H. Stephens met with Lincoln and Seward aboard a Union transport vessel in Hampton Roads, off Norfolk, Virginia, on February 3, 1865. Lincoln presented his terms for an end to the war: the restoration

The surrender of Robert E. Lee and his army at Appomattox Court House to General Ulysses S. Grant on April 9, 1865. (*Library of Congress*)

of the Union, the abolition of slavery, and the disbanding of all military forces hostile to the United States. It took only four hours for the Southerners to realize that they were not going to dissuade Lincoln from his position.

One month later, Lincoln delivered his second inaugural address. In a brief, sensitive statement, he reiterated his belief in the sanctity of the Union and the necessity for its preservation and attributed to God's will the end of slavery through "this mighty scourge of war." He ended on a note of forgiveness and goodwill, as he looked ahead to the war's conclusion:

> With malice toward none; with charity for all; with firmness in the right, as God gives us to see the right, let us strive on to finish the work we are in; to bind up the nation's wounds; to care for him who shall have borne the battle, and for his widow, and his orphan—to do all which may achieve and cherish a just, and a lasting peace, among ourselves, and with all nations.

The end now came swiftly. In the latter part of March, Lincoln met with Generals Grant and Sherman to plan the final campaign. He expressed his desire for a quick end to the bloodshed and urged each general to offer generous terms of surrender to the Southern troops. As Sherman's force advanced through the Carolinas, Grant broke the siege of Petersburg with a swift flanking movement. Petersburg fell, and on April 3 Grant's army entered Richmond. The Confederate government was in flight. Within a few days Lee asked Grant for his surrender terms, and on Sunday, April 9 at the Appomattox Court House, the conditions were agreed on by the two commanders. With Lee's surrender, the Civil War, for all practical purposes, was at an end.

While the nation rejoiced, Lincoln's attention was focused on the question of Reconstruction as he sought some way out of the tangle into which his plans had fallen. Earlier, in February, he had revealed that he still preferred a form of compensated emancipation, even in the face of the Thirteenth Amendment, when he proposed to his cabinet that the government pay $400 million to the Southern states in proportion to their slave populations, a kind of recompense for the loss of slavery but also a form of federal aid to their economic reconstruction. The cabinet was not enthusiastic and the matter was dropped. Governments established under Lincoln's 10-percent plan were functioning in three of the states, but they were feeble and shaky, owing their existence to Union occupation troops. Lincoln had hoped that some limited form of black suffrage might be adopted and urged the states to provide for the education of the freedmen.

Two days after Lee's surrender, on April 11, Lincoln was serenaded at the White House by a crowd of jubilant citizens. He defended his Reconstruction policy and alluded in some detail to its operation in Louisiana, which he regarded as the showcase of his program. He emphasized that the "sole object" of the government should be the restoration of the states to their "proper practical relation" with the Union. The question whether the states were in the Union or out of it he believed to be nothing more than a "pernicious abstraction." "Finding themselves safely at home," he declared, "it would be utterly immaterial whether they had ever been abroad." Lincoln urged again that flexibility be maintained. This situation was "so new and unprecedented" that "no exclusive, and inflexible plan can safely be prescribed." That his own views were still evolving became apparent. "It may be my duty," he told his audience, "to make some new announcement to the people of the South. I am considering, and shall not fail to act, when satisfied that action will be proper."

What that "new announcement" was to be, whether he intended to ease the confrontation with Congress or exacerbate it, will never be known. Three days after his address, feeling relaxed for the first time in years, Lincoln de-

The assassination of Lincoln. (Library of Congress)

cided to spend an evening at the theater with his wife.

Abraham Lincoln's assassination at the hand of John Wilkes Booth as he sat in the presidential box at Ford's Theater on the night of April 14, 1865, struck the North like a thunderbolt. All the rumors of impending attacks on the president that had swept through Washington, D.C., from the day of his first inauguration had hardly prepared the public mind for the actual deed. The murder of the president seemed inconceivable, and Americans had difficulty comprehending the horror of the act. Reports circulated wildly that the assassination had been planned in Richmond and that Jefferson Davis himself had been involved in its execution.

Booth and the cluster of characters he had gathered about him acted out of an obsessive and irrational hostility toward Lincoln's war-

time politics. A strong and devoted supporter of Southern independence and slavery, Booth had denounced Lincoln as an oppressor and a tyrant, charging the president with subverting liberty and justice and trying to uplift blacks at the expense of whites. The plot evolved from a bizarre scheme to kidnap Lincoln and hold him hostage, but the war's end dashed Booth's hope that the plan could help the Confederacy win its independence. The decision to murder Lincoln rather than kidnap him was apparently made on the spur of the moment; some of Booth's conspirators demurred, whereas others took part in only a halfhearted manner.

The significance of the assassination to the course of Reconstruction cannot be minimized. Coming only five days after Lee's surrender at Appomattox, Lincoln's murder had a profound effect on the Northern psyche. The great wave of rejoicing and jubilation that had followed the news of the surrender was turned abruptly into deep sorrow and grief. The assassination was widely viewed as the last, crowning act of treachery by the South against the Union. It called out for vengeance. There was no more conclusive proof, declared one Northern intellectual, that the Union's cause had been the cause of humanity against barbarism. Any story of Southern wickedness now became believable.

To many Americans, the assassination was a sign of God's intervention, but why, they asked, had God intervened? Ministers sought to explain God's action from their pulpits for weeks and months following the deed. Lincoln, it was said, had failed to appreciate the real evil of the South and of slavery; he had spoken of leniency and charity when sterner, harsher measures were necessary. Lincoln had served as God's instrument for the preservation of the Union; that task was accomplished. God removed Lincoln so that abler, firmer hands could take over the task of Reconstruction. The tragedy was God's way of arousing the North from its complacency, of reminding the people that the struggle against the South was not over yet. God had snatched up Lincoln in the moment of his glory and had made him a martyr, a "citizen of the ages." The apotheosis had begun.

When George Bancroft, America's first great historian, delivered his memorial address on Abraham Lincoln less than a year after the assassination, the dimensions of the demigod and folk hero were already taking shape. Lincoln, he pointed out, had been God's agent in carrying out His will that the United States should live. Guided by God's light and obeying the eternal truths of liberty, he had brought the nation through its peril to safety. Through his faith in the perpetuity of the Union and the righteousness of its mission, he had renovated the nation's moral purpose and unity.

Lincoln was called to this task, Bancroft continued, because he was the very embodiment of America. His humble origins, his identification with the frontier, and his self-education and intuitive wisdom were "altogether American." Lincoln "lived the life of the American people, walked in its light, reasoned with its reason, thought with its power of thought, felt the beatings of its mighty heart, and so was in every way a child of nature, a child of the West, a child of America."

One need not indulge in the rhetoric of mid-nineteenth century America to concede Lincoln's greatness. Few today challenge the judgment of the nation's scholars that Lincoln was America's greatest president. That he was able to surmount the obstacles placed in his path and to carry to triumphant conclusion the goals he had set for himself and for his country must certainly point to qualities of greatness, although he was also at times the beneficiary of fortuitous military and economic events. Lincoln's faith in himself, in human beings generally, and in his country ran deep; it never wavered, even during the darkest days of the war. His grasp of America's meaning to the world, of its moral destiny, and of the quality of its mission was firm and unequivocal.

Robert W. Johannsen

Bibliographical References

An indispensable guide to all aspects of Lincoln's life is Mark E. Neely, Jr., *The Abraham Lincoln Encyclopedia*, 1982. Two other useful works by Neely are *The Last Best Hope for Earth: Abraham Lincoln and the Promise of America*, 1993, and *The Lincoln Family Album*, 1990. For a pictorial biography, see Philip B. Kunhardt, Jr., Philip B. Kunhardt III, and Peter W. Kunhardt, *Lincoln: An Illustrated Biography*, 1992. Lincoln has been the subject of countless biographies; among the best are Benjamin P. Thomas, *Abraham Lincoln*, 1952, and Stephen B. Oates, *With Malice Toward None: The Life of Abraham Lincoln*, 1977. For analysis of Lincoln's Illinois years, see Paul Simon, *Lincoln's Preparation for Greatness: The Illinois Legislative Years*, 1989; Elizabeth

W. Matthews, *Lincoln as a Lawyer: An Annotated Bibliography*, 1991; and Douglas L. Wilson, *Lincoln Before Washington*, 1997. David H. Donald, *Lincoln*, 1995, is an illuminating biography that draws extensively on resources not previously available, including Lincoln's personal papers. Lincoln's presidency is treated in depth by James G. Randall, *Lincoln the President*, 4 vols., 1945-1955, with vol. 4 completed by Richard N. Current. Current has skillfully summarized those aspects of Lincoln's life that remain in shadow in *The Lincoln Nobody Knows*, 1958. For Lincoln's own words, see Roy P. Basler et al., eds., *The Collected Works of Abraham Lincoln*, 9 vols., 1953, supplement, 1974. See Gary Wills, *Lincoln at Gettysburg: The Words That Remade America*, 1992, for an extensive analysis of the circumstances and impact of Lincoln's historic speech. Lois J. Einhorn, *Abraham Lincoln, the Orator: Penetrating the Lincoln Legend*, 1992, is a rhetorical analysis of Lincoln's speaking skills and includes a collection of his major speeches and an extensive primary and secondary bibliography. William C. Harris, *With Charity for All: Lincoln and the Restoration of the Union*, 1997, maintains that Lincoln's efforts to restore the Southern states to the Union began long before the end of the war and Reconstruction.

Andrew Johnson

17th President, 1865-1869

Born: December 29, 1808
　　　Raleigh, North Carolina
Died: July 31, 1875
　　　near Carter Station, Tennessee

Political Party: Republican
Vice President: none

Cabinet Members

Secretary of State: William H. Seward
Secretary of the Treasury: Hugh McCulloch
Secretary of War: Edwin M. Stanton, Ulysses S. Grant, John M. Schofield
Secretary of the Navy: Gideon Welles
Attorney General: James Speed, Henry Stanbery, William M. Evarts
Postmaster General: William Dennison, Alexander Randall
Secretary of the Interior: John P. Usher, James Harlan, O. H. Browning

Born on December 29, 1808, in Raleigh, North Carolina, Andrew Johnson was the third child of Jacob and Mary Johnson, illiterate tavern servants. Jacob Johnson died when Andrew was three, leaving his wife to eke out a living by sewing and taking in laundry. This hardscrabble existence and an unwise second marriage forced Mary Johnson to apprentice Andrew and his older brother William to a Raleigh tailor. Johnson was an able and diligent worker but also headstrong and possessed with a burning passion for education and self-improvement. By listening to the reading of famous American speeches in the tailor shop, Johnson was encouraged to learn to read. For reasons now obscure, in 1825 Andrew and William ran away from their apprenticeship. They drifted into

South Carolina, failed in business, grew homesick, and returned to Raleigh but could not pacify their irate employer.

At the age of seventeen, Johnson fled from his background of poverty and from the aristocratic pretensions of Raleigh society to begin

Johnson's official portrait. *(White House Historical Society)*

a new life on the Tennessee frontier. He settled in the small town of Greeneville and there became a successful tailor. After his marriage to Eliza McCardle in 1827, both Johnson's personal and business life prospered. The Johnsons had five children, three sons and two daughters. Johnson read avidly, learned to write with his wife's help, and was a stalwart participant in a local debating society.

From Tailor's Shop to Congressional Chambers

Andrew Johnson used his connections made in the tailor shop and his natural speaking ability to enter politics. Elected alderman in 1829 and mayor of Greeneville in 1831, by 1835 he had moved on to the state legislature. At 5 foot, 10 inches and 175 pounds, the dark-haired, dark-eyed Johnson was already an impressive stump orator. An admirer of Andrew Jackson, Johnson early displayed a dogged commitment to strict constitutional construction regardless of political consequences. Although his own East Tennessee constitutents were clamoring for improved transportation, the new legislator opposed state aid to railroads, thereby paving the way for his own defeat at the next election. After that, Johnson returned to Nashville in 1839, having modified his opposition to state-supported internal improvements. By this time, he had become an avid advocate of hard money and a stridently partisan Democrat, ready on all occasions to lash out at Whig policies and candidates.

Elected to Congress in 1842, Johnson served five consecutive terms in the House of Representatives. Reflecting his impoverished background, he quickly elevated public parsimony into the highest of virtues. The Smithsonian Institution and both military service academies became for him symbols of government extravagance and aristocratic privilege. Johnson loyally supported the expansionist and war policies of Democratic president James K. Polk, but he never got along well with the presidents during his congressional service because of dissatisfaction with their patronage policies. Johnson saw himself as a special defender of the common people's interest and long pushed for the abolition of the electoral college in favor of direct popular election of the president. Most politicians, in his view, were selfish timeservers, and he made few friends of any kind in Washington, D.C. He especially resented the arrogance of certain Southern politicians such as Mississippian Jefferson Davis, who in Johnson's mind represented "an illegitimate, swaggering, bastard, scrub aristocracy." Despite this largely negative philosophy, Johnson was a strong supporter of one forward-looking measure—a homestead bill. He saw this as a way to serve the real people—the small farmers—and to prevent the growth of concentrated economic power based on the ownership of land and slaves. Johnson's unsuccessful fight for 160-acre homesteads during the early 1850's gave him his first taste of national prominence.

As a Southerner in the midst of growing sectional conflict, Johnson occupied an anomalous position. Although an orthodox defender of slavery and himself a small slaveholder, the Tennessee congressman was no fire-eater. Like his hero Andrew Jackson, Johnson was a staunch Union man and saw sectional agitation as both dangerous and unnecessary. He voted for all the provisions of the Compromise of 1850, except for the bill that abolished the slave trade in the District of Columbia.

Successful as a spokesperson for small farmers and sectional peace, Johnson suddenly encountered the realities of politics in a state that neither party effectively controlled. In 1852, the Whig-dominated legislature gerrymandered him out of his congressional seat. This proved to be a temporary and perhaps fortunate setback because Johnson won election as governor of Tennessee in 1853. In that office, he successfully pushed for a tax to support education, but for the most part he quarreled with a legislature that contained enough Whigs to stymie any gubernatorial initiatives. Frustrated by the time spent on administrative detail, he nevertheless successfully ran for reelection in 1855, braving the Know-Nothing tide then sweeping across the nation.

Johnson in the Senate: The Secession Crisis

By 1857, Democrats had regained control of the legislature and awarded Johnson the prize he coveted most, a seat in the United States Senate. Johnson the senator was little different in outlook or approach from Johnson the young member of the House. He seemed less willing to compromise on sectional questions than he had been in 1850, but he was hardly a Southern radical. He bitterly accused Northern Republicans of incendiary agitation during the debates over John Brown's raid at Harper's Ferry, but in 1860, Johnson still saw himself as a possible compromise presidential candidate for a badly divided Democratic Party. Yet he was curiously passive, and although the Tennessee delegation supported his candidacy for thirty-six ballots at the tumultuous Charleston convention, Johnson refused to instruct them on a possible political truce with Northern Democratic leader Stephen A. Douglas. The disruption of the Democratic Party, opposition from Southern Democrats to his beloved homestead bill, and the more and more strident sectional rhetoric of politicians such as Jefferson Davis made Johnson increasingly uncomfortable. He belatedly agreed to stump for John C. Breckinridge, the presidential candidate of the Southern Democrats, but considered preserving the Union more important than winning an election.

The secession crisis marked the final break between Johnson and the Southern Democratic leadership. In blistering rhetoric on the Senate floor, he condemned disunionists as traitors, accused them of wishing to destroy not only the Union but also political democracy, and even called for their swift and condign punishment. For his efforts, Johnson received warm denunciations from many Tennessee Democrats but equally fervent applause from the state's Whigs and from Northern Republicans. Despite threats against his life, in April, 1861, Johnson returned to Greeneville to take part in a last desperate round of speechmaking in an effort to hold Tennessee in the Union.

When his state seceded in June, however, Johnson returned to Washington, D.C., and defended the policies of the new Republican president, Abraham Lincoln. Johnson had always been a committed Unionist; still, when Lincoln put Johnson in charge of distributing patronage for the administration in East Tennessee, he could weld political principle to long-standing personal ambition. When the Confederate defense of Tennessee collapsed in 1862, Lincoln appointed Johnson military governor of the state. In this post, Johnson found it difficult to remain patient with plodding Union generals in Tennessee and was continually frustrated by the lingering spirit of disunion there. Johnson treated the Confederates in his jurisdiction harshly and put great store in administering loyalty oaths to would-be penitents.

Considering Johnson's strongly Unionist record and the Republican desire to build bipartisan support for Lincoln's war policies, party leaders asked Johnson, a lifelong Democrat and former slaveholder, to become the vice presidential nominee in 1864 on the "Union" ticket. By the end of this grueling campaign, Johnson was exhausted and ill. On Inauguration Day, he drank some whiskey to fortify himself for the occasion and as a consequence delivered a rambling and incoherent address filled with boastful references to his "plebeian" origins. Although Lincoln stood by him, many Republicans began to doubt Johnson's fitness for high office. Also, Johnson never seemed to realize that he owed his position not only to his own courage in standing up to the secessionists but also to the Republican Party. When Lincoln was assassinated on April 14,

279

1865, this great symbol of Southern Unionism who breathed fire against Confederates and who would now be the nation's chief executive was unknown to many Americans and an enigma to politicians, North and South.

Johnson as President: An Enigma in the White House

Johnson's long experience in the rough-and-tumble of Tennessee politics had ill prepared him to be president during a period of revolutionary upheaval. Johnson shared Lincoln's belief in the primary responsibility of the president for reconstructing the Union. Indeed, he pledged to carry out the martyred president's policies, but these were hardly clear at the time, and historians are still debating what Lincoln would have done after the war. Some Radical Republicans believed that Johnson's harsh wartime statements about punishing traitors meant that he would support their plans for a thoroughgoing reconstruction of the South. Yet Republicans of all stripes and Democrats as well courted the new president and sought to shape the course of his administration.

Initially, Johnson was greatly influenced by Secretary of War Edwin Stanton, especially in dealing with Lincoln's murderers. Both men believed that leading Confederates, including Jefferson Davis, were behind the actions of John Wilkes Booth and the other conspirators. The assassination undoubtedly presented Johnson with an opportunity to punish traitors as he had often promised to do, and he issued a proclamation offering a reward for the capture of Davis and other supposed rebel conspirators. Johnson signed the execution orders for those convicted by the military commission established to try the case, but, apparently, he did not see the recommendation of mercy for Mary Surratt, mother of conspirator John Surratt. Johnson was probably following the advice of Stanton and Judge Advocate General Joseph Holt when he approved her execution, but historians remain divided over whether Stanton

and Holt intentionally kept him from seeing documents that might have saved Mrs. Surratt's life.

The influence of Stanton, who favored black suffrage, was less evident when Johnson began to outline his plans for reconstructing the South than for punishing the alleged assassins of Lincoln. In a series of proclamations in the spring of 1865, Johnson demanded neither black suffrage nor any other dramatic change in the Southern political order. The president announced that he would appoint provisional governors for each of the Southern states, who in turn would call for constitutional conventions to set up new state governments. Johnson promised amnesty and therefore the right to vote in these proceedings to Southerners who would take a prescribed oath. He did exclude from this general amnesty high civil and military officials of the Confederacy and—reflecting his continued hostility toward Southern aristocrats—rebels who held more than $20,000 in property. Even these men, though, could take an oath, petition for special pardon, and, if it were granted, regain the franchise. Johnson's approach thereby put more emphasis on loyalty oaths, as if the very act of swearing allegiance could blot out past sins, than on efforts to remold Southern institutions.

Johnson was apparently pleased at having old political enemies assume the attitude of supplicants, and he spent an inordinate amount of time—sometimes almost all of his working day—poring over pardon applications. The pardon policy also affected the government's attitude toward the recently freed slaves, because a presidential pardon meant the restoration of confiscated property to former Confederates. This brought an end to the wartime experiment of dividing up confiscated plantations among the freedmen. Although all of this seemed to indicate a conservative policy, the several proclamations that the president issued were general enough to gain support from various factions, and their meaning would clearly depend on how they were administered and interpreted. Radicals such as Congressman Thaddeus Stevens and Senator Charles Sumner were worried about the direction of Johnson's policies, but most Republicans in the summer of 1865 were prepared to be very patient with the new president.

In dealing with the provisional governors he had appointed to carry out his policies in the "states lately in rebellion," the president made it clear that the constitutional conventions meeting in them would have to ratify the Thirteenth Amendment to the United States Constitution, declare their ordinances of secession null and void, and repudiate the Confederate debt. Johnson suggested that the states might enact a qualified form of black suffrage but did not insist on it. Indeed, his failure to press the new state governments in the South to protect the civil rights of the recently freed slaves proved to be a fatal weakness in this conciliatory approach to the problems of Reconstruction. Southern politicians took advantage of Johnson's liberality and made as few concessions as possible to Northern opinion.

Johnson highly valued constitutional consistency, and his policy reflected an unbending belief that secession had never taken place. In his view, individuals, but not states, could commit treason. The president alone could deal with these individuals; Johnson saw only a secondary role for Congress in restoring the Southern states to their full constitutional relations. Thus, he could be stern with individuals while being very lenient with states—not recognizing that the restoration of loyalty was an institutional as well as an individual problem. Ironically, Johnson maintained the fiction of state sovereignty while at the same time attempting to reshape the state governments in the South.

In his first annual message to Congress in December, 1865, the president claimed that his policy was working well and that full restoration of the South to the Union was nearly complete. He based these assertions on fragmentary evidence gathered by several Northern emissaries, including General Ulysses S. Grant, who had recently visited the Southern states, but he ignored reports of other travelers who had found many signs of continuing rebellion in the South. Congressional Republicans remained skeptical, particularly after elections in several Southern states revealed a clear voter preference for selecting former Confederates to important offices, and refused to seat representatives and senators from the South.

Reconstruction

Republican leaders, unhappy with Johnson's efforts, decided to try their own hand at Reconstruction and formed the Joint Committee on Reconstruction to investigate conditions in the former Confederate states. Johnson believed that the critics of his policy constituted a radical minority who could be isolated if met with executive firmness. Yet in vetoing a bill extending and expanding the Freedmen's Bureau, he outraged moderate Republicans and actually strengthened rather than isolated the radicals. The president claimed preeminent authority over Reconstruction policy and objected to the bureau as unconstitutional and discriminatory to whites. He mistakenly believed that the Joint Committee on Reconstruction constituted a radical "cabal" bent on undermining administration policy. Johnson and his critics began to show signs of paranoia—both sides seeing in the actions of their opponents vile conspiracies against freedom and the public good. Addressing a crowd of Washington serenaders on February 22, 1866, Johnson claimed the radicals were as much a threat to the Union as the secessionists and denounced Charles Sumner, Thaddeus Stevens, and Wendell Phillips by name. In a speech filled with personal references and pathetic appeals for public sympathy, Johnson portrayed himself as the popular defender of constitutional principles against unscrupulous conspirators.

Johnson quickly followed this remarkable performance with a veto of a civil rights bill that would have extended citizenship and legal protection to the freed slaves. This veto all but made inevitable a final break between Johnson and the Republican majority in Congress. Moderate Republicans could not accept Johnson's states' rights version of the Constitution and increasingly considered him a major, if not dangerous, obstacle to restoring loyalty in the Southern states. For Johnson, Congress (he drew no distinction between moderate and Radical Republicans) was the enemy. He ignored the advice of some cabinet members and other supporters to be more accommodating to Congress and instead established a totally inflexible position based on what he thought to be sacred constitutional principles and the popular will.

It came as no surprise, therefore, when Johnson publicly denounced the proposed Fourteenth Amendment, which would have made blacks citizens, forbade the states from denying to any citizen "due process" or "equal protection" of the laws, reduced representation for states not adopting universal manhood suffrage, and barred leading former Confederates from holding public office. For the president, this marked the culmination of a scheme by congressional Republicans to control the government by destroying the sovereignty of the states. Any amendment at this time was inappropriate, Johnson claimed, because the Southern states remained without representation. If this all sounded like the rhetoric of a Northern Democrat, there was little doubt that Johnson was steadily moving back toward his old party allegiance. He could never admit it, but his course had thrown the moderate and Radical Republicans together; by the summer of 1866, only the most conservative members of the party stood with the president.

The more Southerners and copperheads found to praise in Johnson's policies, the more unpopular the administration became in the North. When a bloody race riot broke out in New Orleans in July, 1866, Republicans blamed the president for not using military force to protect the lives of Southern Union men and blacks and thought the violence the logical result of the president's stubborn and mistaken course.

Johnson sought to rally his supporters behind a National Union Party, which would serve as a campaign vehicle against congressional Republicans in the fall election campaign. From the first, this jerry-built coalition of Southerners, conservative Republicans, and Northern Democrats showed both weakness and division. Republicans denounced the meeting of these desparate elements in Philadelphia as a conclave of copperheads and rebels, and several cabinet members were decidedly unenthusiastic about the National Union movement. Johnson, on the other hand, hyperbolically described the National Union meeting as the most important convention in the United States since 1787 and remained oblivious to his increasingly precarious political position.

Democrats supported Johnson to promote their own party interests but would do little more; moderate Republicans resented the seeming Democratic control of the National Union movement and were even more embittered when the president began wholesale removals of Republican officials—offices then handed over to ungrateful Democrats. Although some historians have suggested that Johnson would have been better advised to divide his opposition by broadening his campaign to include the currency and tariff questions, there is little evidence to suggest that including these complex and badly understood issues could have salvaged the situation.

With his political coalition about to collapse, Johnson turned to what had always worked for him before—the stump speech. He took his case to the people on a "swing around the circle" from New York to Missouri. In Cleveland, Ohio, he delivered a series of ill-considered impromptu remarks to a rowdy crowd. Johnson accused Congress of plotting to break up the government and, losing all sense of presidential dignity, exchanged crude remarks with hecklers. In several speeches, he bragged of his plebeian origins, compared his pardon policy with the forgiveness of Jesus Christ, and portrayed himself as a martyr to constitutional principles. Johnson appeared foolish (several Republican newspapers charged that he was drunk during the trip) and probably lost more support for his policy than he won.

As Northern voters prepared to cast their ballots, Johnson sought to move against Stanton, the cabinet member who appeared to be most sympathetic to his political enemies. In a complex maneuver, the president sought to send General of the Army Grant on a diplomatic mission to Mexico and bring General William Tecumseh Sherman to Washington, D.C., to become the new secretary of war. Grant, however, refused to go, and Sherman was averse to becoming mixed up in Washington politics.

The fall elections spelled disaster for the administration. The Northern voters undoubtedly shared Johnson's desire for a speedy restoration of the Union but also sought to keep the former rebels from resuming political power while providing minimal rights for the freedmen. The Republicans gained two-thirds majorities in both houses—what amounted to a vetoproof Congress—and could thank the political blunders of Andrew Johnson for their success. Yet the president ignored his advisers' suggestions for a conciliatory approach to Congress and still expected Northern opinion to turn against the radicals. In his annual message to Congress in December, 1866, Johnson called for the readmission of the Southern states to representation and made no concessions to his opponents. He did not even mention the proposed Fourteenth Amendment.

There was some talk of a possible compromise between Congress and the president based on Southern ratification of a modified version of the Fourteenth Amendment, but Johnson ended it when he encouraged the Southern states to reject the amendment. His intervention both demonstrated his longtime commitment to states' rights and testified to his firm belief in white supremacy and belligerent opposition to black suffrage. Johnson, the enemy of the large slaveholders, had never been the friend of the slave. In a passionate wartime speech, he had promised Tennessee blacks to be their Moses, but this signified little beyond a general commitment to Lincoln's emancipation policy. He considered moderate black leader Frederick Douglass to be a dangerous incendiary. Johnson never overcame the prejudices of his background and class and failed to recognize the revolutionary changes in race relations wrought by the Civil War.

Congress Rebels: The Tenure in Office Act

When the lame duck session of the Thirty-ninth Congress assembled in December, 1866, most Republicans were at last ready to build a more thoroughgoing Reconstruction policy based on abolishing the Southern state governments and establishing black suffrage. Outraged by the president's intransigence, Southern foot dragging, and growing violence against blacks and Union men in the South, on March 2, 1867, Congress passed the first Reconstruction Act, which placed the South under military rule until "loyal" state governments could be established. As expected, Johnson vetoed the bill, warning of its dangerous and revolutionary character. He also appealed to racial fears by unfavorably contrasting the bill's enfranchisement of blacks to its disfranchisement of whites.

While putting forward a new Reconstruction plan, the Republicans in Congress also sought to limit the president's ability to subvert their policy. Still stinging from Johnson's use of patronage against loyal Republicans, the congressional majority pushed through the

Tenure of Office Act. This measure prohibited the president from removing officials whose appointment had been confirmed by the Senate unless that body approved the removal. Unable to agree on whether the act should cover cabinet members, the Republicans included an ambiguous clause, which stated that cabinet officers "shall hold their offices . . . during the term of the President by whom they may have been appointed, and for one month thereafter, subject to removal by and with the advice and consent of the Senate." Some observers thought this provision was meant to protect Stanton, and during a cabinet discussion, Johnson cleverly induced his secretary of war to denounce the bill as unconstitutional. Congress also attached a rider to the Army Appropriations Act, forcing the president to issue military orders through the general of the army, Grant, and forbidding him to remove the general's headquarters from Washington, D.C.

These laws demonstrated the ironic fact that the success of congressional Reconstruction depended on executive cooperation. Johnson allowed Grant to select the commanders of the military districts established by the Reconstruction Act and seemed unwilling to risk a confrontation with Congress by failing to enforce the law. Although politically weakened, Johnson still possessed the power of his office. Indeed, the Republicans had given the president an opportunity to influence Reconstruction by their slipshod and hasty drafting of the Reconstruction Act (defects only partly remedied by a second Reconstruction Act, which was passed by the new Fortieth Congress on March 23, 1867).

Johnson might have recouped some of his lost power and prestige by turning the nation's attention to matters other than the condition of the South. Despite his own firm belief in paying off the national debt quickly and reducing government expenditures, however, his administration failed to devise a financial policy that could please both Western interests, who demanded currency inflation, and Easterners, who favored protective tariffs and hard money. Traditionally, presidents have recouped political prestige by diplomatic triumphs, and Secretary of State William H. Seward was as skillful and loyal in serving Johnson as he had been in serving Lincoln. When Seward managed to purchase Alaska from Russia at a bargain price, even rabid enemies of Johnson, such as Charles Sumner and Thaddeus Stevens, approved. Johnson failed to make the most of these accomplishments.

The Southern question would simply not go away. The Reconstruction Acts had only vaguely defined the qualifications for voting, and the powers of district commanders in the South were also poorly delineated. Attorney General Henry Stanbery issued opinions in May denying the power of the district commanders in the Southern states to remove civil officials and also limiting their power to disfranchise voters. Although Grant instructed the district commanders that the attorney general's opinion was not an official order and Johnson refused to press the matter further, Congress drafted a bill for yet a third Reconstruction Act in July, 1867, which closed up the loopholes Stanbery had found in the first two acts. Both Grant and Stanton worked with the more radical district commanders, particularly General Philip Sheridan, to administer the Reconstruction Acts in the South with a broad and liberal view of congressional intent.

The Stanton Affair

Johnson was furious at Sheridan, military governor of Louisiana, for his many attempts to remove Democratic civil officials in Louisiana and his apparent willingness to defy presidential orders. The president also received new reports supporting a long-held suspicion that Stanton was in frequent consultation with congressional radicals. Johnson therefore decided to remove Sheridan, suspend Stanton, and make Grant secretary of war ad interim. The cabinet had been cool to the idea of removing Sheridan, and so Johnson decided not to consult it on the Stanton matter. Stanton had earlier refused a direct presidential request to resign and now only yielded to what he pointedly described as "superior force." Stanton undoubtedly believed that he had remained in office to protect the interests of the army and the loyal citizens of the United States. Yet he had often acted disingenuously, if not deceptively, toward Johnson, especially in cabinet meetings. Andrew Johnson, however, for all his tenacity on fine points of constitutional law, could be very indecisive. Evidence of Stanton's "disloyalty" to the administration had been accumulating for more than a year, but the president had failed to replace Stanton earlier when he could have removed him without a serious confrontation with Congress.

Grant at first protested Sheridan's removal but finally acquiesced. Johnson also moved swiftly to remove radical General Daniel Sickles from command in the Carolinas. Increasingly, Grant saw Johnson as an obstruction, not only to Reconstruction in the South but also to his own political future; the general feared that Johnson would continue to interfere in the operations of the army or might attempt to use him in a battle with Congress. Newspaper speculation arose during the fall about additional cabinet changes, including the replacement of Seward and Secretary of the Treasury Hugh McCulloch, but Johnson refused to dismiss these faithful cabinet officers.

Indeed, the president's prospects brightened considerably when the Democrats did well throughout the North in the 1867 state elections. Johnson interpreted that success as vindication and perhaps envisioned the Democrats making him their nominee in 1868. Still, he feared the radicals might grow desperate as their political prospects dimmed and might attempt to impeach him.

The prospects of impeachment, however, had faded, at least for the moment. As early as December, 1866, radical congressman James Ashley of Ohio had introduced an impeachment resolution, accusing the president of abusing his patronage powers and delivering the country back into the hands of the rebels. Ashley and Benjamin F. Butler of Massachusetts even believed that Johnson had been involved in the conspiracy to assassinate Abraham Lincoln and apparently attempted to suborn perjury to prove this wild charge. During the spring and summer of 1867, the House Judiciary Committee called several witnesses, collected Johnson's public speeches, and even examined the president's bank accounts, but the committee could not discover any "high crimes or misdemeanors." All of this simply roused Johnson's seldom dormant persecution complex, and he continued to press Grant over whether the general would cooperate with Congress in placing him under arrest during an impeachment trial.

When the Judiciary Committee in December, 1867, suddenly voted articles of impeachment, the cabinet advised Johnson to resist any attempt to place him under arrest during a Senate trial. In his annual message to Congress, Johnson issued another blast against the "unconstitutional" Reconstruction Acts and ominously warned that a situation might occur in which the president would have to stand firm against any congressional attempts to encroach on the constitutional prerogatives of his office. Despite the president's inflammatory document, Republican moderates helped handily defeat an impeachment resolution in the House.

Although the performance of Sheridan's successor in Louisiana, the conservative general Winfield Scott Hancock, and the removal of General John Pope from command in Georgia, Alabama, and Florida caused some irritation in Congress, the attempt to remove Stanton remained the outstanding source of conflict between the executive and legislative branches. In a carefully prepared message in December,

FAC-SIMILE OF TICKET OF ADMISSION TO THE IMPEACHMENT TRIAL.

A ticket to Johnson's impeachment trial in the Senate. *(Library of Congress)*

1867, Johnson outlined in detail Stanton's duplicitous behavior. He asserted his authority as president to remove a cabinet official but studiously ignored the Tenure of Office Act, despite the fact that he had, to that point, followed its provisions in the Stanton case. On January 13, 1868, the Senate voted overwhelmingly not to concur in Johnson's suspension of Stanton.

This decision left Grant in a most uncomfortable position. Johnson expected Grant to hold onto his office in defiance of Congress or at least turn the office back to the president in time to prevent Stanton from resuming his position. He believed that Grant shared his understanding, but there had apparently been no firm agreement. As it happened, Grant handed the key to the office back to the acting adjutant general, who in turn gave it to Stanton. A series of meetings and, finally, a lengthy and public exchange of letters followed, in which

Grant and Johnson in essence called each other liars. To some extent, Grant had deceived Johnson, and certainly the president had shown a lack of firmness and direction throughout his troubles with Stanton. Grant succeeded brilliantly in protecting himself from being caught between the president and Stanton while at the same time promoting his own political interests. The radicals now applauded Grant, and Johnson once again emerged as a bumbling and hesitant leader.

Impeachment

With Stanton back in the cabinet, Johnson searched desperately for someone else to replace his wily secretary of war. Sherman was clearly his first choice, but Sherman hated Washington, D.C., despised politics, and adroitly avoided being trapped in the War Department morass. Johnson at last settled on the garrulous, occasionally besotted, and increasingly senile adjutant general, Lorenzo Thomas. On February 21, the president sent a message to the Senate, which announced the removal of Stanton and the appointment of Thomas as secretary of war ad interim. Thomas tried to assume the post, but Stanton refused to yield it. To moderate Republicans, the entire Reconstruction program seemed to be in danger; the House hastily and overwhelming voted to impeach the president.

Both sides feared a possible civil war. Stanton stayed in the War Department and posted armed men in the basement. Johnson believed that Congress might attempt to place him under arrest during the trial in the Senate. Radicals heard rumors that Johnson had ordered the blowup of the Capitol with nitroglycerin and that the old rebel cavalry chieftain John Mosby was about to descend on Washington, D.C. Stanton arranged to have Thomas arrested for violating the Tenure of Office Act but quickly had the charges dropped, perhaps fearing that he had inadvertently provided the judicial test of the law's constitutionality that Johnson apparently wanted.

On February 24, the day the House voted on his impeachment, Johnson sent a message to the Senate nominating Hugh Ewing, Sr., to be secretary of war. Thomas continued in his bumbling way to try to take the war office from Stanton, but even the president paid little attention to him. Johnson had blundered through the Stanton affair, first acting too slowly, then indecisively, and in the end too hastily and without consulting his cabinet. Whether he had been guilty of "high crimes and misdemeanors" remained for the Senate to decide, but he had clearly shown political ineptitude on a colossal scale.

The House appointed Thaddeus Stevens, Benjamin F. Butler, and five other Republicans to present the case for Johnson's removal to the Senate. The first eight articles of impeachment set forth detailed charges against the president for violating the Tenure of Office Act in attempting to remove Stanton and appoint Thomas in his place. A ninth article charged that Johnson had attempted to induce General William H. Emory to carry out orders that had not been properly sent through Grant. Butler added an article about Johnson's various speeches questioning the authority of Congress, and Stevens drafted a general article summing up the other ones and, for good measure, accusing the president of failing to execute faithfully the Reconstruction Acts. Ironically, it is this clause, added almost as an afterthought, which some historians have argued was the strongest and most serious charge against the president.

With Chief Justice Salmon P. Chase presiding, the Senate eventually allowed Johnson sixteen days to prepare his case. After weighing the possibility, Johnson fortunately decided not to appear before the Senate in person to defend himself. He hired five attorneys, including Henry Stanbery and prominent Republican William M. Evarts of New York. They had a difficult client—one inclined to speak too freely with reporters and to question the advice of his own lawyers. Stanbery and Evarts skillfully prevented the president from destroying their carefully planned defense strategy with some final public blunder.

Johnson fully believed that he would be vindicated and even expected the Supreme Court to declare the Reconstruction Acts unconstitutional; indeed, he saw impeachment as the final effort by his enemies in Congress to destroy the Constitution. Johnson's attorneys, however, concentrated on getting their client acquitted rather than proving the wisdom of his Reconstruction policies. By focusing on relatively narrow legal questions, they tried to defuse, at least partially, the political dynamite inherent in the trial.

Stanbery and Evarts carefully dissected the issues surrounding the attempted removal of Stanton and the appointment of Thomas. They argued that the Tenure of Office Act was unconstitutional and surpassed the House managers in piling up legal precedents to buttress their point. More important, however, they showed that regardless of whether the tenure law was constitutional, it did not protect Stanton. The cabinet proviso of the act specified that cabinet members should hold offices during the term of the president who had appointed them. Since Stanton had been appointed by Lincoln, he could be removed by Johnson. Although the managers quibbled about the meaning of the word "term" in the law, Johnson's attorneys had discovered and vigorously exploited the weakest point in the prosecution's case.

The other defense arguments were not as strong. The contention that Johnson had not violated the law because Stanton remained in office could not stand close scrutiny. The assertion that Johnson had only removed Stanton so that the constitutionality of the tenure law could be tested in the courts could hardly excuse the chief executive from faithfully executing the law. In describing impeachment as a judicial rather than a political process, the president's attorneys entered a constitutional thicket. In the opinion of some scholars, the Constitution's "high crimes and misdemeanors" are not confined to indictable criminal offenses. By its very nature, impeachment is a political process conducted by politicians. Chief Justice Chase's attempts to run the impeachment trial as a judicial proceeding angered many Republicans, who believed that he biased the process in Johnson's favor.

Both sides turned the contest into an oratorical marathon. The president's lawyers called witnesses to prove that Stanton himself had declared the tenure law unconstitutional and that Johnson simply intended to bring the matter to a judicial test. Moreover, they cited statements from Republican senators made in February and March, 1867, which declared that the tenure law did not protect Stanton. The House managers and a majority of Republican senators decided to exclude some of this defense evidence, especially testimony from General Sherman and Secretary of the Navy Gideon Welles. To some moderates, this seemed patently unfair, as did Butler's badgering of old General Thomas on the witness stand.

Acquittal

During the trial, the president uncharacteristically acted with discretion, allowing his attorneys to carry the rhetorical burden of proof. Their appeal was clearly to the Republican Party center. If they could convince seven Republican senators of Johnson's innocence, the president would escape removal from office. If Johnson were removed, the president pro tempore of the Senate, Benjamin F. Wade of Ohio, would become president. Moderate senators, such as William Pitt Fessenden of Maine and Lyman Trumbull of Illinois, detested Wade and had been skeptical about impeachment from the beginning. The president sought to assuage Republican fears by promising to nominate moderate general John M. Schofield to be the new secretary of war. He also dropped some careful hints that he would do nothing to undermine the course of Reconstruction if he were acquitted. Johnson grew more confident of acquittal, especially as news of dissension among the Republicans spread through the capital. In the end, only two impeachment articles came to a vote, and Johnson escaped conviction by one vote on each of the articles. For once, Johnson's mercurial temper was not in evidence, and he received the news with equanimity but undoubted relief.

Most historians have argued that Johnson's acquittal was justified because the president, whatever his political ineptitude, had committed no impeachable offenses. Although some scholars have argued that Johnson's removal would have set a dangerous precedent, the circumstances of Reconstruction were extraordinary and the weight of such a precedent doubtful. The impeachment illustrated the deadly serious nature of the debate over Reconstruction policy, the revolutionary nature of the era, and the tendency of both the president and the Radical Republicans to color opponents in the darkest possible hues.

The Radicals lashed out at the seven "recusant" Republicans who had voted "not guilty," and Butler made wild charges of bribery against them, but most Republicans simply wanted to forget impeachment as quickly as possible. The nomination of Grant as the party's presidential candidate, coupled with the president's fulfillment of his promise not to use the army to interfere with the Reconstruction process, pacified the country. Yet Johnson had abandoned his opposition to congressional Reconstruction; he vetoed bills readmitting seven Southern states under the terms provided by the Reconstruction Acts.

The president's hope for popular vindication lay in capturing the Democratic presidential nomination. Although he claimed not to be "ambitious of further service," he hoped for a popular groundswell in his favor and believed that he could defeat Grant in November. He timed a general amnesty proclamation to coincide with the opening of the Democratic National Convention in July, 1868. Johnson's friends opened negotiations with New York Democrats whose prime interest was in federal patronage. The president considered currying Democratic favor by removing McCullough, but the secretary's hard money policies were popular with many conservative Democrats. Johnson likewise refused to get rid of Seward. He could never understand why the Democrats would not readily hand him the nomination if they approved of his presidency as much

ELEVATION—At the White House.　　　DEPRESSION—At the Tribune Office.

EFFECT OF THE VOTE ON THE ELEVENTH ARTICLE OF IMPEACHMENT.

One cartoonist's depiction of the reaction to Johnson's acquittal. *(Library of Congress)*

as they claimed that they did. The continuing attacks of the Radical Republicans should, in Johnson's view, have made him even more deserving of the prize. Despite some Southern support on the early ballots, the Democrats did not think Johnson was either astute or trustworthy enough to run under their banner. Instead, they nominated former governor Horatio Seymour of New York.

The remainder of the Johnson presidency was surprisingly busy. Seward worked on completing arrangements for the purchase of Alaska, and the president personally received a delegation from China at the White House. Congressional hostility to Johnson had occasionally spilled over into the conduct of foreign policy, and key Republican leaders blocked Seward's plans for additional territorial acquisitions in the Caribbean.

Johnson paid only passing attention to these diplomatic developments; he was much more interested in the election campaign and what he hoped would be Grant's defeat. He begrudgingly recognized the ratification of the Fourteenth Amendment and appointed conservative generals to command the troops in the recently readmitted Southern states. As the early state elections pointed to a Republican victory, the president grew discouraged, his only comfort being a steady faith in the eventual triumph of his political principles.

In his last annual message to Congress, Andrew Johnson condemned the Reconstruction Acts yet again. He also criticized selfish bondholders and proposed scaling down the interest on the national debt. Ever the democrat, he called for the direct popular election of the president, vice president, and United States senators. The president and Congress continued to squabble over minor matters for the rest of his term. Johnson moved his family out of the White House before Grant's inauguration, stayed at the capital signing bills on Inauguration Day, and rode off in a carriage without even speaking to the new president.

When Johnson left Washington, D.C., for East Tennessee, he did not abandon politics; he still yearned for vindication and refused to fade away into retirement. He campaigned for conservative candidates in the summer of 1869 and was nearly elected to the United States Senate by the legislature. Although Johnson remained popular in Tennessee, many former Confederates as well as Republicans could not forgive his past. In 1872, he entered an at-large congressional contest by running as an independent but finished third behind a former Confederate general and the victorious Republican candidate. His political career seemed over. Friends reported that Johnson drank heavily, and he was stricken by cholera in 1873. He recovered, however, in both body and spirit by working hard to get back his old Senate seat. In 1875, he won a close fight in the legislature and prepared to return to Washington. Attending a special session of the Senate in March, he was at last able to get a measure of revenge against Grant. In his last public speech, Johnson denounced the president for using troops to support the carpetbag government of Louisiana, emphasizing his favorite themes of "military despotism" and constitutional government. He returned to Tennessee apparently with political plans laid, but at his daughter's farm, he collapsed with a paralytic stroke and died two days later, on July 31, 1875.

Johnson's Presidency in Perspective

Johnson's historical reputation has fluctuated dramatically ever since. It remained low until a flood of works after World War I elevated him to the status of a courageous patriot who fought against the Radical Republicans to preserve sacred constitutional principles. In the 1950's, Reconstruction scholars began to reexamine critically Johnson's presidency. These historians pointed to the obvious defects in Johnson's character: his stubbornness, indecisiveness, and lack of good judgment. Other historians portrayed Johnson as a racist who attempted to subvert needed constitutional reforms and to return the Southern states to conservative control.

Johnson's honesty and reverence for the Constitution (at least as he defined it) are unquestioned. Certainly, he worked as hard as any president since Polk. Johnson, however, could never transcend his background in the frontier politics of Tennessee. Unlike Abraham Lincoln, who showed enormous capacity for growth during his presidency, Johnson attempted to apply the same crude style of stump-speaking politics to Washington, D.C., that he had used so often back home. More important, he failed to see that the problems of Reconstruction demanded flexibility of both means and ends. Like many of his opponents, he was far too quick to equate opposition with evil intent and therefore wasted several opportunities to work with moderate Republicans to build a national consensus on Reconstruction. Even his friends conceded that Johnson's political judgments were often defective, and he failed to see that the war had wrought enormous changes in race relations and in the power of the national government. In the end, Johnson largely failed. His presidency was characterized by lost opportunities but also by perpetual conflict with Congress and, eventually, constitutional crisis. When Johnson returned to Tennessee in 1869, he left behind a presidency much weaker than the office he had inherited from Abraham Lincoln.

George C. Rable

Bibliographical References

The best introduction to Johnson's life and career is in Leroy P. Graf and Ralph W. Haskins, eds., *The Papers of Andrew Johnson*, 14 vols. to date, 1967-1997. A brief but sound modern biography is James E. Sefton, *Andrew Johnson and the Uses of Constitutional Power*, 1980. For a full-length treatment, though now badly outdated, see Robert W. Winston, *Andrew Johnson: Plebeian and Patriot*, 1928. Another older work still valuable for its enormous quantity of information is George F. Milton, *The Age of Hate: Andrew Johnson and the Radicals*, 1930. More recent biographies are Fay W. Brabson, *Andrew Johnson: A Life in Pursuit of the Right Course, 1801-1875*, 1972, and Hans L. Trefousse, *Andrew Johnson: A Biography*, 1989. A solid synthesis of modern scholarship on Johnson's presidency is Albert Castel, *The Presidency of Andrew Johnson*, 1979. For a perceptive interpretive account of the Johnson presidency, see Eric L. McKitrick, *Andrew Johnson and Reconstruction*, 1960. Also useful are Martin E. Mantell, *Johnson, Grant, and the Politics of Reconstruction*, 1973; Howard P. Nash, *Andrew Johnson: Congress and Reconstruction*, 1972; and James E. Sefton, *Andrew Johnson and the Uses of Constitutional Power*, 1980. For the impeachment, see Michael L. Benedict, *The Impeachment and Trial of Andrew Johnson*, 1973; Hans L. Trefousse, *Impeachment of a President: Andrew Johnson, the Blacks, and Reconstruction*, 1975; Gene Smith, *High Crimes and Misdemeanors: The Impeachment and Trial of Andrew Johnson*, 1977; and William H. Rehnquist, *Grand Inquests: The Historic Impeachments of Justice Samuel Chase and President Andrew Johnson*, 1992. Richard B. McCaslin, *Andrew Johnson: A Bibliography*, 1992, lists more than two thousand primary and secondary sources and includes an extensive chronology of Johnson's life.

Ulysses S. Grant

18th President, 1869-1877

Born: April 27, 1822
Point Pleasant, Ohio
Died: July 23, 1885
Mount McGregor, New York

Political Party: Republican
Vice Presidents: Schuyler Colfax, Henry
Wilson

Cabinet Members

Secretary of State: Elihu B. Washburne, Hamilton Fish

Secretary of the Treasury: George S. Boutwell, William A. Richardson, Benjamin H. Bristow, Lot M. Morrill

Secretary of War: John A. Rawlins, William Tecumseh Sherman, W. W. Belknap, Alphonso Taft, James D. Cameron

Secretary of the Navy: Adolph E. Borie, George M. Robeson

Attorney General: Ebenezer R. Hoar, Amos T. Akerman, G. H. Williams, Edwards Pierrepont, Alphonso Taft

Postmaster General: John A. J. Creswell, James W. Marshall, Marshall Jewell, James N. Tyner

Secretary of the Interior: Jacob D. Cox, Columbus Delano, Zachariah Chandler

Grant's official portrait. *(White House Historical Society)*

Cold fog enveloped the city in the gray morning. Shivering in the damp were army units: Marchers from Irish, German, and other clubs, the firemen, veterans' groups, the Boys in Blue, Lincoln Zouaves, and other Republican clubs tried to organize their formations along Pennsylvania Avenue, beyond the White House toward Georgetown. Carriages carrying the justices of the Supreme Court, the judges of the court of claims, foreign ambassadors, presidential electors, and other dignitaries searched for their places, found them, and milled about, their drivers huddled miserably against the chill rain. Tens of thousands of visitors slogged through the mist, lining the route General Ulysses S. Grant and the rest of the procession would take down Pennsylvania Avenue to the Capitol, where he would be inaugurated the eighteenth president of the United States.

At 10:45 a.m., Grant emerged from his headquarters and the parade lurched toward its destination. At the Capitol, Grant and Vice President-elect Schuyler Colfax went to the Senate chamber, where Colfax was sworn in and delivered his short inaugural speech. Then Grant, Colfax, the senators, the members of the House of Representatives, and other dignitaries marched to the special platform erected on the east front of the Capitol. Chief Justice Salmon P. Chase stepped forward, turned to Grant, and administered the oath of office. The artillery boomed and bells began to ring all over Washington, D.C. An immense cheer went up from the crowd, and the sun broke through the clouds.

Ulysses S. Grant entered the White House on March 4, 1868, at the age of forty-six the youngest man elected to the presidency to that time. A veteran of the Mexican War and, more recently, the Civil War, Grant was known as the hero of the Union: It was to Grant that the Confederate general Robert E. Lee had surrendered at Appomattox Court House on April 9, 1865. Grant subsequently was appointed to the new post of general of the armies of the United States. Admired by a nation just beginning to recover from the ravages of war, Grant inspired the confidence of the nation.

This Silent Man

Ulysses Grant has been an enigma to biographers. An apparent failure before the Civil War, in that great struggle he demonstrated a command of tactics and strategy, a talent for organization, and an ability to inspire confidence that enabled him to succeed where all others had failed. He rode an avalanche of popularity and respect into the presidency, but most historians have considered his administration a disaster. A later Pulitzer Prize-winning biog-

rapher decided that the secret to Grant was that there was no secret—he was a completely ordinary man thrown by accident into a situation where his few real talents and some of his characteristics proved of crucial value.

Such a judgment surely would have surprised most of Grant's contemporaries. It parallels that of the small group of reformers who blasted away at Grant for most of his presidential career and afterward. From the time he became commander of the Union armies, however, most Americans perceived greatness in him. Many came to detest him; many more continued to idolize him; none questioned his stature.

By the nature of things, the journalists, litterateurs, and scholars who have written about Grant have been part of an intellectual community that has shared a set of expectations about how men of conscious intellect behave. When a man makes a great public reputation, one expects him to demonstrate an interest in public events, to leave a record of his views and explanations of his actions.

Grant disappoints such expectations. His leading characteristic was his taciturnity. Future president James A. Garfield, college professor-soldier-politician, who delivered speeches all over the United States and who left books and diaries and a huge correspondence filled with his views, marveled that "no man . . . carried greater fame out of the White House than this silent man." That silence could be disconcerting. "He has a wonderful capacity of letting you talk, without moving a muscle and then saying nothing himself," a young lion of Boston's intellectual society recorded in his journal after meeting him.

Others, in contrast, found him genial. Another future president, Rutherford B. Hayes, noted that "after he warms up he is . . . cheerful, chatty, and good natured. . . . I feel just as much at ease with him as I do with intimate friends." The great black leader Frederick Douglass likewise remembered, "Many who approached him told me he was a silent man. To me, he was one of the best conversationalists I have ever met."

The simple fact was that Grant felt no compulsion to talk. He did not break into conversations, and if a visitor out of nervousness or egotism felt obliged to carry the conversation, Grant would let him, silently listening until the speaker felt positively foolish.

This pattern carried over into the way Grant made decisions. He encouraged his subordinates to discuss matters before him, or to present him with clear statements of the case and proposed courses of action. "[T]he suggestions of others were presented simply, and either accepted or rejected as his judgment dictated," one of his aides remembered. He barely explained his reasons, and woe to the man who argued. "He was never persuaded."

That stolidity frustrated those whose suggestions he rejected. Among that number was the most reform-minded member of Grant's early cabinet, Jacob D. Cox, who watched his influence being undermined by men of far lesser intellect. "A certain class of public men adopted the practice of getting an audience and making speeches before him, urging their plans . . .," he recalled. "They would then leave him without asking for any reply, and trust to the effect they had produced." Cox wanted to know Grant's objections to his proposals; he wanted to explain why those objections were mistaken. He wanted to persuade. He never had a chance.

Grant was no more forthcoming in public. His public speeches would not fill a pamphlet. His messages to Congress were brief requests to consider a course of action, with almost no effort to persuade. His call for legislation to suppress violence in the South in 1871, a major reversal of policy raising difficult constitutional issues, consisted of four short paragraphs, taking up about one-third of a page in James D. Richardson's *Messages and Papers of the Presidents* (1896-1899). His veto of the inflationary Currency Act of 1874, the most controversial of his presidency, on an issue of utmost importance to the public, ran about two and a half pages.

No volume of public speeches and addresses of President Grant exists. The collections of correspondence between him and his family and friends attend hardly at all to public matters. When Grant did write *Personal Memoirs of U. S. Grant* (1885-1886), the book consisted almost entirely of his descriptions of tactics and battles. It is a classic of the genre, but it contains almost nothing about his political career or the reasons that motivated his actions; nor is his private correspondence more enlightening.

From West Point to Appomattox

Grant simply did not care much about abstractions. He retained facts easily. Naturally, he grew bored with the mere recitation that made up most teaching in the early nineteenth century, but he disliked debate and argument, in which young scholars honed their critical abilities. Romantic novels and travel fired his enthusiasm. He was born Hiram Ulysses Grant in Ohio on April 27, 1822. He devoured books and was surely the best-traveled boy in his small Ohio town, taking every excuse to replace his father on business trips, despite his inexperience. Still, even he was fooled by his disinterest in formal schoolwork into thinking that he was stupid. His father perceived Grant's potential better than young Ulysses himself. He finagled an appointment to West Point for his son, who was convinced that he would embarrass himself and his family by failing the entrance examinations. Instead, he passed without trouble; in fact, he found academics at West Point easy, never reviewing his texts once he had read them, and he finished in the upper quarter of his class. His ambition was to teach mathematics for a while at West Point and then spend the rest of his life as a college professor.

These plans did not materialize. After Grant served a short tour of duty near St. Louis, where he became engaged to (and later married) Julia Dent, the sister of a West Point classmate, the United States precipitated war with Mexico. To his surprise, Grant found that he enjoyed war and that he had a talent both for command and organization. At the same time, the war gave him another opportunity to travel. Mexico was the most exotic place he had ever visited, and he etched his experiences with photographic precision in his memory.

Unlike the majority of West Point graduates, Grant delayed leaving the army at war's end. He was plainly unwilling to turn to his own or his wife's family for support, although both were in comfortable, if not plush, circumstances. Assigned to remote frontier outposts in the Northeast and in California, he looked for business opportunities that would permit him to support his wife on the level to which she was accustomed. He rose to captain, a high rank in the peacetime army of the 1850's, but finally resigned in 1853 without achieving his goal. Forced to turn to his family after all, Grant tried farming his father-in-law's land in Missouri, went into business as a debt collector in St. Louis, and finally moved up the Mississippi River to Galena, Illinois, to join two brothers in a leather and harness business set up by his enterprising father.

Living throughout the trying years from 1853 to 1861 in better circumstances than most Americans, Grant and his wife still surely were dismayed at their reverses. Writing Julia just as he left the army, he described "the *downs* of all I have done. (Before this I had never met with a down.)" In Galena, he slowly established himself as a respected member of the community, living in a brick house (a mark of gentility) near other rising men. When Southerners fired on Fort Sumter, beginning the Civil War, the townspeople called on him, as a nonpartisan newcomer, to preside at a mass meeting to reaffirm their loyalty to the Union.

The last photograph of General Grant taken in the field by Mathew Brady, August, 1864. *(Library of Congress)*

The war made it possible for Grant to return to the field in which he felt most confident and in which it slowly became clear that he excelled. In battle, Grant eschewed the theories that dominated strategic and tactical thinking at the time. Clockwork field maneuver and polished dress and drill meant little to him. Battles were won by securing the best ground, bringing to bear a stronger force than that of the enemy, and then using it to kill until the opposing army broke. Such an approach took a fearful toll of both enemy and friendly forces; it required superior organization so that one could move immense numbers of men and amounts of material quickly. Most of all, such generalship required an iron serenity, an ability to ignore the frightful possibility that one's opponent had acquired a stronger force or had put into effect some brilliant plan of attack. General after general on the Union side failed this test, paralyzed into inaction at crucial moments, until President Abraham Lincoln found Grant.

As one of his aides described it, after Grant made a decision, he "settle[d] in." "He had done what he could, and he gave himself no anxiety about the judgment or the decision." Grant himself told an interviewer, "I never get excited, and I have made it a rule through life never to borrow trouble or anticipate it. I wait until it reaches me." The aide explained, "This confidence engendered composure. . . . This was the secret of his courage and of the steadiness which held him to his purpose." Others thought that Grant's incredible stolidity suggested lack of imagination. Meeting him at a particularly trying time during his presidential administration, Garfield noted in his diary, "His imperturbability is amazing. I am in doubt whether to call it greatness or stupidity." It was Grant's peculiar greatness. His calm in crisis inspired all around him, especially during the Civil War, when the nation's existence lay in the balance. He was a rock in a sea of uncertainty, and that was the source of the hold he had on those who served with him.

The Election of 1868

At the war's end, Grant was commanding general of all the Union armies, at the pinnacle of his military career. After Abraham Lincoln, he was the most popular man in the victorious North. As customary in nineteenth century America, Grant eschewed political ambition. Offices were supposed to seek the man, not the man the office; even the most blatantly ambitious politicians honored this ritual. During the Reconstruction crisis, both the Democrats and the Republicans wooed him, and Grant carefully kept his options open and his opinions to himself—an easy accomplishment for a man who disliked argument.

In the Reconstruction controversy, he found himself in closest sympathy with the moderate Republican leaders in Congress. Intensely practical, he was not moved by the devotion of President Andrew Johnson and his Democratic supporters to the principle of states' rights—certainly not when the practical consequence was to revive the power of the old leaders of the Confederacy. Furthermore, he was no more receptive to Radical Republican commitment to the abstract principle of racial justice. Such enthusiasm led men into impracticalities and interfered with the business of administering a government (or an army). Like other conservative Republicans, he finally endorsed equal suffrage as the best way out of the Reconstruction muddle. He came to see it as a practical solution to the problem of how to guarantee civil rights to the freedmen: Let them protect their own rights through their influence as voters.

By 1868, Grant had broken with Johnson and was the favorite of the Republican conservatives for their party's presidential nomination. Moreover, he had the support of leading intellectuals, who insisted that the war had settled the slavery issue. What the country now needed was stable, expert leadership to reform the financial and civil service systems, precisely the sort of leadership one could expect from this most practical and stable man. Radical Republicans, however, were suspicious of him.

As the popularity of the Republican Party waned in 1867-1868, Radical Republican hostility to Grant's nomination collapsed. Without Grant as its candidate, the Republican Party would risk defeat. "Let us have peace," he wrote in his terse letter of acceptance. After twenty years of conflict over slavery, it was what most Americans wanted to hear. To the audience at his inauguration, the transition from Johnson's administration to Grant's was as cheering as the burst of sunlight that accompanied it.

As Grant entered the White House, Americans faced public problems in a variety of areas. First was what most Americans expected to be the winding up of Reconstruction. Virginia, Texas, and Mississippi had not yet complied with the conditions that Congress had set for restoration to the Union—ratification of the Fourteenth Amendment and new state constitutions guaranteeing civil and political equality between the races. In each state, radicals had tried to impose further conditions that more conservative Republicans and Conservatives (former Democrats and Whigs who opposed the Republicans) resisted. Moreover, the Georgia state legislature had expelled its black members, disrupting Reconstruction there. Finally, in several of the restored states, so much antiblack and anti-Republican violence remained that the more radical Republicans were demanding some national action to stop it.

In the area of foreign affairs, the most important task was to settle the bitter dispute between Great Britain and the United States over tacit British support of the Confederacy. Americans were demanding reparations for destruction of American shipping wreaked by Confederate ships built in Great Britain and permitted to use British ports during the war. The Johnson administration had negotiated a settlement of these so-called *Alabama* claims

(named after a Confederate cruiser built by a British shipyard), but in the first months of his administration, Grant and Congress rejected it as too conciliatory. Bellicose Republicans, such as Nathaniel Banks and Benjamin F. Butler, spoke of war, and even more moderate Republicans hankered after Canada as a suitable compensation.

Beyond that, many Americans were demanding that Spain give up control of Cuba, where it maintained a slaveholding regime against perennial Cuban insurrection. In general, many Americans continued to believe that it was the nation's "manifest destiny" to become the dominant power in the Caribbean basin.

The Currency Crisis

Most Northerners probably thought that the linked questions of funding the national debt, controlling the amount of currency in circulation, taxation, and banking were the most im-

Grant and his cabinet, 1869. *(Library of Congress)*

portant matters facing the country. They directly affected the economic vitality of the nation. To finance the war, Republicans had dramatically increased both internal taxes and tariffs on imports. They had issued paper money, or "greenbacks," which they made legal tender for the payment of all debts, even though they were not redeemable in gold or silver. Congress had borrowed an immense amount of money by selling bonds bearing high rates of interest and, to help their sale, had exempted them from state or national taxation. It also created a national banking system, forcing new and preexisting banks to secure national banking charters and making such charters conditional on banks buying government bonds. National banks were authorized to issue banknotes, which would be legal tender, in proportion to their holdings of government bonds. Soon all the bonds earmarked for banks were sold. Naturally, people hoarded gold (not much silver was available), and the value of both greenbacks and banknotes fell below that of specie. As a consequence, the Civil War was a time of inflation in prices and, to a lesser degree, wages.

With the end of the war, powerful interests demanded a return to the "specie standard"—that is, a system where all paper money could be converted into gold or silver. Backed by most theoretical economists, they insisted that only specie had real value and that it was impossible to plan business properly if the value of currency were unstable. Most Republicans agreed, and in 1866 they authorized the secretary of the treasury to withdraw greenbacks from circulation at his discretion by exchanging them for government bonds. The practical effects of this, however, aroused strong opposition. By contracting the amount of currency in circulation, the government raised the value of that remaining, forcing prices down and interest rates up. Republicans were forced to repeal the contraction program.

By the time Grant became president, Ameri-

cans were completely divided on the currency, tax, and banking questions. Most of the national banks were in the Northeast, thus most of the banknotes were issued there. With plentiful money, Northeasterners did not feel the effects of contraction so severely. Other regions, particularly the West (Indiana to California) and the South, had few banks and therefore fewer banknotes in circulation. Moreover, banks themselves in these areas had to borrow money in the Northeast to secure money to lend, raising interest rates far above those in the more favored region. Also, as contraction caused prices to fall, it became harder to make enough money to pay one's debts.

Worse, from the standpoint of Westerners and Southerners, they bore an unfair burden in paying for the system. Since Northeasterners were richer than other Americans, they had bought more bonds, which were exempt from taxation. Moreover, tariffs enabled American manufacturers, mostly based in the Northeast, to raise prices without fear of foreign competition.

To remedy the inequity and promote economic growth, most Westerners and Southerners called for increasing the number of greenbacks in circulation. They demanded the elimination of the national banking system, or the establishment of "free banking," whereby the Treasury Department would be obligated to sell bonds to any newly organized bank. Many Westerners demanded that the interest and principal on government bonds be repaid in greenbacks rather than gold, reducing the taxes it would take to pay them off and increasing the amount of currency in circulation. They called for reduction of tariffs. Finally, many Westerners insisted that the "bloated bondholders" pay taxes on their bonds. Northeasterners generally opposed all these proposals and demanded contraction of the currency and a return to specie payments. Although the dominant division was sectional, Western and Southern Republicans tended to be more moderate in their demands for contraction, and some even favored taxation of government bonds.

The reform-oriented intellectuals in the Republican Party took extreme positions on these issues, based on what they thought were fundamental principles. They demanded the quickest possible return to "hard money"—that is, gold. A paper money system permitted the government to manipulate the money supply and therefore enabled political majorities to affect the value of the dollar. The complaints of Westerners and Southerners, these intellectuals contended, were simply those of people who did not want to pay their debts at full value. Refusal to redeem government bonds in gold or silver would be dishonest and immoral. They agreed, however, with Westerners and Southerners on the tariff. Tariffs artificially redistributed wealth by forcing consumers to pay more for goods so that owners and workers in a protected industry could make more money. Seeing the issues as ones of principle, they viewed compromise on them as immoral.

These reformers were the supporters of civil service reform. They worried that an active government—one that promoted economic development through manipulation of the currency, protective tariffs, subsidies for transportation, and similar legislation—invited corruption. Those seeking such help inevitably would try to secure it through their influence with the government, not by mere persuasion. Already Washington, D.C., and the state capitals were full of "logrolling lobbyists," exercising improper influence and even bribing government officials. Politicians tolerated this because all they were interested in was gaining office. Political parties were more and more turning into "machines," which secured votes, not on issues, but through strong organizations cemented by "patronage"—that is, government offices given in exchange for service to the party rather than on the bsis of merit. A reform of the civil service, making appointment to office

dependent on ability rather than politics, would end corruption and also remove the main pillar sustaining machine politicians. This would enable the reformer intellectuals—the "best men"—to wield more influence in politics.

Finally, the reformers wanted a quick end to Reconstruction. Eliminate the radical proposals in Virginia, Texas, and Mississippi that were delaying these states' readmission to the Union, force Georgians to readmit black state legislators, and then turn to other matters, they insisted. Black Southerners, protected by their right to vote, would have to work out their own relationship with their former masters. This would enable the government to turn to the more important matters of finances, tariff reduction, and civil service reform. Moreover, it would weaken the hold of Republican machine politicians, who kept the support of Republican voters by stressing the dead Reconstruction issue.

Grant's Conception of the Presidency

Although Grant had been so reticent, or perhaps because he had been so reticent, many thought that they knew where he stood on some of the issues. On Reconstruction, they presumed that he shared the views of his strongest supporters, the moderate and conservative Republicans. Reformers happily took his slogan "Let us have peace" to mean that he, too, regarded Reconstruction as settled. In foreign affairs, they expected a hard line on the *Alabama* question from the former chief of the Union forces, and his rejection of the proposed settlement seemed to confirm their expectations. Grant's financial views were less certain, but most of his conservative and reform Republican allies were committed to following his lead.

Finally, reformers expected Grant to take the lead in breaking the power of Republican politicos. One of his greatest strengths as military leader was his ability to identify capable commanders, such as William Tecumseh Sherman and Philip Sheridan, and his willingness to remove incompetent ones, even if politically powerful, such as Benjamin F. Butler. Organization and administration were his strong points. Surely he would demand skilled government officers, selected on merit.

These expectations assumed an active president, committed to establishing policies that he favored, but in fact, as he entered the presidency, Grant did not see his role that way. Grant was succeeding three presidents—James Buchanan, Lincoln, and Johnson—who not only had sought to push their programs through Congress but also had used all the powers of the presidency to overcome opposition. By 1869, all Northerners perceived Lincoln's greatness, but he had exercised his leadership in a time of crisis, when constitutional niceties and traditional divisions of power were at discount. Buchanan's and Johnson's peacetime efforts had proved disastrous. Buchanan's attempt to impose a Southern solution on the question of slavery in the territories had disrupted his party and precipitated the Civil War. Johnson had paralyzed the government, been impeached, and escaped removal by one vote. In his inaugural address, Grant assured his audience that "on all leading questions agitating the public mind I will always express my views to Congress and urge them according to my judgment." Final decisions would rest with Congress. "I shall on all subjects have a policy to recommend, but none to enforce against the will of the people." As to appointments, reformers were cheered. "The office has come to me unsought," he reminded the crowd. "I commence its duties untrammeled." He owed nothing to the party on whose ticket he had been elected; he had no debts to pay with offices.

In fact, Grant did seem to perceive himself as a man above parties. He chose his cabinet from among the least partisan and most conservative of Republicans, so much so that Re-

publicans in Congress rebelled. He made the mistake of nominating for secretary of the treasury Alexander T. Stewart, a leading importer and former ally, asking Congress to repeal a law prohibiting appointment of anyone doing business subject to departmental oversight. Republicans refused, at the same time making plain their unhappiness with Grant's cabinet choices. He smoothed things over by appointing the influential Massachusetts Republican politico George S. Boutwell to the Treasury position. At the same time, senate Republicans blocked repeal of the Tenure of Office Act, passed to limit Andrew Johnson's control over government appointments. This meant that Grant would not be able to remove government officers permanently unless the Senate confirmed their successors. Refusals to confirm would restore the old officers, giving senators a crucial vote in the distribution of patronage.

As a consequence of the brief, sharp struggle, Grant essentially withdrew from patronage matters. He insisted that a few government positions go to personal friends and relations. (His father was appointed postmaster in Covington, Kentucky, for example.) For the rest, he delegated the job of selection of government officers to his cabinet. Some, like Boutwell and Postmaster John A. J. Creswell, another traditional politician, followed customary practices in distributing offices. They consulted the Republican congressional delegations about appointments in their states and generally accepted their recommendations. Others, like Cox, repudiated the traditional pattern and sought to establish one based on merit rather than partisanship.

In like manner, despite the promise of his inaugural address, Grant did little in the way of devising and pressing policies on Congress. The division in the cabinet over the criteria for appointments was one example. Reformers expected Grant to require all cabinet members to reform the process, to introduce merit as the main criterion. They were dismayed when he failed to force Boutwell and Creswell into line.

Reconstruction provided another example. In April, 1869, after Congress deadlocked on the question, Grant acted on Reconstruction. Over the objections of radicals and Conservatives, he issued a proclamation, which permitted the people of Virginia, Mississippi, and Texas to vote separately on the provisions of their proposed state constitutions. With the administration evidently taking a conciliatory approach to former Confederates, Republicans in those states and in Tennessee divided, some joining Conservatives to support conservative Republicans against regular Republican nominees for state offices.

Grant refused to take a position. He permitted some cabinet members to sustain the regular Republican nominees and others to remain neutral. Without guidance from the administration, Republican newspapers and officeholders in the affected states felt free to bolt the Republican ticket, while Northern Republican newspapers were divided in their sympathies. As as consequence, the bolters and Conservatives won control of the governments in Virginia and Tennessee, and dissident Republicans in other Southern and border states, especially Georgia, Missouri, and West Virginia, were encouraged to fashion similar alliances with Conservatives.

In Georgia, too, the administration failed to take a clear stand, as a few influential Republicans joined Conservatives to oppose the Republican governor, claiming that they better reflected the administration's conciliatory position than the party regulars did. The result was a bitter struggle both in Georgia and in Congress over how to deal with the expulsion of the black legislators, as a consequence of which the divided Republicans lost control of the state.

Rather than promoting programs, Grant concentrated on administration, something at which everyone thought he excelled. As he had in the army, he proceeded by finding capable subordinates and then advising without instructing them. In fact, with the exception of the soon-replaced secretary of the navy, all the cabinet members whom he appointed in the first month of his presidency were excellent administrators. All observers recognized the improvement.

The Taint of Corruption: Currency Reform and Black Friday

The Treasury Department earned the highest praise. As high tariffs brought in more gold than the government needed to pay its expenses (in fact, most government spending was in greenbacks), Boutwell creatively interpreted existing laws to permit him to sell gold for greenbacks. He then used the greenbacks to buy outstanding government bonds, reducing the national debt. In the first four months of the new administration, Boutwell proudly reported, the debt had been reduced by $50 million.

At the same time, by withdrawing some of the greenbacks from circulation and replacing them with gold, Boutwell brought the value of the two currencies closer together, an essential step in restoring specie payments without totally disrupting the economy. It had the effect of lowering prices somewhat within the country and raising the cost of American exports. This slowed the economy, especially in the South and West, whose farmers depended on exporting their crops and where money was in shorter supply.

In the spring of 1869, two aggressive, young speculators, Jay Gould and Jim Fisk, joined with Grant's brother-in-law and the assistant treasurer in New York, in charge of selling gold for greenbacks, to try to take advantage of the system. Through the brother-in-law, Gould lobbied to convince Grant that the value of greenbacks and banknotes should be lowered to enable the farmers to get better prices for their crops and at the same time make them cheaper on the international market. To accomplish this, all that was necessary was for the government temporarily to stop withdrawing greenbacks from circulation through its gold sales. Thinking they had convinced Grant, Gould and Fisk then bought up gold futures, driving the price of gold ever higher and "cornering" the outstanding gold. People who had agreed to sell them gold at low prices would have to pay them high prices to get it, or default on their contracts. As the price of gold soared on "Black Friday," September 24, 1869, hundreds of brokers and financial institutions faced bankruptcy and begged Grant and Boutwell to have the government sell gold to lower its price. Finally, Grant and Boutwell did so, breaking the conspiracy as the price of gold plummeted.

Although Grant plainly had no part in the conspiracy, his brother-in-law and a key government appointee were proved corrupt, and even Julia came under suspicion. Boutwell's continued reduction of the national debt, through purchases of outstanding bonds and exchange of old, high-interest bonds for new, lower-interest ones, continued to earn praise, but Black Friday was the first of many instances where Grant's administration would be tarnished by corruption near the top.

While Boutwell worked assiduously to reduce the national debt, the administration took no position on the tariff issue and played no active role in the fight over free banking, expansion or contraction of the currency, or efforts to redistribute currency to the South and West. This inaction dismayed reformers and regular Republicans alike.

Foreign Affairs: The Santo Domingo Initiative

Under the Constitution, the president has primary responsibility for foreign affairs, so it is natural that the Grant administration most actively promoted particular policies in that area. The Cuban issue caused the most trouble, because Grant's advisers were divided. His close friend John A. Rawlins, secretary of war, endorsed the groundswell of public support for tough action against Spain. His respected secretary of state, Hamilton Fish, backed by Charles Sumner, the chair of the influential Senate Foreign Relations Committee, urged moderation. They succeeded in preventing hasty action, and after Rawlins died in September, 1869, Fish was able to turn Grant into a bulwark against reckless attacks on the Spanish holdings in the Caribbean.

Allies on the Cuban question, Sumner and Fish differed widely on relations with Great Britain, and Grant backed Fish. Sumner tried to persuade the administration to claim such large damages from Great Britain for its conduct during the war that cession of Canada would be an appropriate setoff. That policy risked war, and many Americans would have welcomed it, despite the damage the British were likely to inflict on foreign trade. When Fish and Grant rejected such a risky course, Sumner tried to impose his own foreign policy through his authority in the Senate, which would have to ratify any settlement, and his influence with the American ambassador to Great Britain John Lothrop Motley, who owed Sumner his appointment. Motley violated the instructions that he received from Fish, who was forced to try to take away from him the primary responsibility for dealing with the British on the issue.

At the same time, Grant enthusiastically endorsed efforts by his close friend and private secretary, Colonel Orville E. Babcock, and several American and Dominican speculators to annex the Dominican Republic, which the Americans called Santo Domingo, as a new state in the Union. Without much enthusiasm Fish cooperated. Sumner promised Grant personally to give the matter his deepest consideration, affirming that he was "an administration man" and sympathetic to its desires. When the annexation treaty came before the Senate early in 1870, however, Sumner attacked it bitterly, violating what Grant had interpreted as a promise of support. Opinion became divided all over the country, and the treaty stalled.

By 1870, it was clear that neither the Grant administration nor the Republican Congress had any firm policies to offer the people. While Grant's Santo Domingo initiative sputtered, Republicans divided over the currency question, tariff reform, and civil service reform. Southern Republicans reported that organized bands, generally known as the Ku Klux Klan, were waging campaigns of increasing violence against them, but the administration and Republican leaders in Congress, afraid to reopen an issue that was "settled," rejected all proposals to intervene. Republicans seemed adrift, and the reformers openly urged voters to defeat Republicans who stood in the way of tariff reduction, contraction of the currency, and civil service reform. Their sympathizers in the cabinet, especially Cox, urged Grant to unify his administration on the reform side.

Matters came to a crisis in the summer of 1870. In Missouri and West Virginia, dissident Republicans bolted the party nominations and joined Conservatives to put forward Liberal Republican tickets for state offices. They called for the reenfranchisement of former rebels to settle finally the Civil War issues. Seeking the support of reform elements in the Republican Party, they also called for tariff and civil service reform. Reformers declared the Missouri election a test of strength for control of the Republican Party and demanded that Grant's administration stay neutral, as it had in similar conflicts of 1869.

Grant's inability to secure Republican support for his Santo Domingo treaty finally convinced him that something had to be done to unify party ranks. Regular Republicans, cleverly supporting the Santo Domingo annexation, warned him that the party faced disaster in 1872 if it did not rally around some popular issue and discipline bolters. To begin to unify the cabinet, he nominated Attorney General

Ebenezer R. Hoar to the Supreme Court. When senators rejected the nomination to punish Hoar for his refusal to agree to follow their patronage recommendations, Grant accepted his resignation from the cabinet. When Cox tried to force Grant's hand by refusing to honor the custom of assessing campaign contributions from employees in the Interior Department and refusing to give them leave to return to vote, Grant forced him out. In state after state, the administration began to remove federal government employees accused of being lax or inept partisans. None of this could save Missouri or West Virginia, which elected the Liberal Republican tickets, but it committed Grant to fulfilling his responsibility as party leader. In response, most Republican leaders, who had been critical of him, now came to support his renomination in 1872. To allay suspicions that he had completely abandoned civil service reform, Grant named a civil service commission, led by a respected reformer, to suggest changes in the system.

Grant hoped to rally Republicans around his proposal to annex Santo Domingo. To show that he meant business, he replaced Sumner's friend Motley as minister to Great Britain. Then, when Sumner bitterly attacked Grant in the Senate and refused to associate with Secretary of State Fish, Senate Republican leaders stripped Sumner of his chairmanship of the Foreign Relations Committee.

All of this alienated the reformers, and Sumner's removal so shocked Republican voters that it became impossible to pass the Santo Domingo treaty. His and Motley's removals, however, did facilitate settlement of the *Alabama* claims dispute with Great Britain. In May, 1871, the British and Americans agreed to establish a tribunal to arbitrate all claims.

This did not, however, revive Republican fortunes. Still unable to unite on the tariff and currency questions, afraid that civil service reform would destroy the party machinery, the divided Republicans seemed to be careening toward disaster despite Grant's efforts to unify the party. They were saved by the issue that had created their party—the issue of North versus South.

The Ku Klux Klan Act

Committed to revitalizing their party, Republican leaders could no longer ignore the efforts of such organizations as the Ku Klux Klan to terrorize it out of existence in the South. Prepared to let the reformers leave the party rather than continue to disrupt it, the leadership no longer feared to alienate them by reopening Civil War issues. In the spring and summer of 1871, urged on by a brief message from Grant, Republicans passed an act to enforce the Fourteenth and Fifteenth Amendments, popularly dubbed the Ku Klux Klan Act, which authorized Grant to impose martial law in Southern counties where violence had overawed state authorities.

As Republicans documented the atrocities the Klan had committed in the South, the effect was electric. Reformers lamented the sacrifice of "real" issues, such as tariff and civil service reform, to the "dead" one symbolized by the "bloody shirt" that outraged Congressman Benjamin F. Butler brought to the floor of the House to illustrate Klan cruelty. Throughout the North, however, Republicans rallied to protect the fruits of Northern victory in the Civil War. Democrats denounced the imposition of martial law in scattered counties of South Carolina and the use of federal troops elsewhere as gross violations of civil liberty, but they were also forced at last to give up their open hostility to equal rights and black suffrage. Announcing a "new departure," they promised to accept the finality of the Thirteenth, Fourteenth, and Fifteenth amendments.

The new departure enabled Democrats, reform Republicans, and some Republican poli-

An ambush by the Ku Klux Klan, c. 1869. *(Smithsonian Institute)*

ticians who had lost power in their party to unite against Grant's reelection. Calling themselves Liberal Republicans, the dissident Republicans met in Cincinnati in June, 1872, to frame a platform and name a candidate whom the Democrats would endorse. The nominee, newspaper editor Horace Greeley, was, however, more the candidate of dissatisfied politicians than of the reformers. Incredibly, he was an advocate of high tariffs and only shakily committed to civil service reform. Worse, he was an outspoken advocate of temperance legislation. That made him anathema to German Americans, whom Liberals had counted on for political support. All of his life, Greeley had been a trenchant critic of the Democratic Party; it would be hard to persuade rank-and-file Democrats to vote for him.

Greeley agreed with the reformers and Democrats primarily on the need to lay the Civil War issues to rest. Ironically, this difference between Republicans and Liberals on war issues became the main focus of the campaign. The war issues united the Republicans, whereas Greeley's position on the tariff and temperance divided the Liberals and Democrats. Grant swept to reelection in an immense victory.

Grant's Second Term: A False Spring

At the inauguration of his second term in 1873, Grant was at the high point of his career. The savior of his country in war, he was hailed for his accomplishments in peace. He had settled its dangerous dispute with Great Britain. He had been forceful in suppressing violence in the South, yet all knew that he bore no malice toward the brave people whom he defeated in the field.

Grant seemed equally successful in his economic policies. The Treasury Department's steady hand had made a significant dent in the national debt and fostered economic recovery from the depression of 1867 to 1869. Grant instituted a few measures of civil service

reform, appointing a commission to make recommendations, and the civil service seemed more efficient than it had been under Johnson and prewar Democrats. Nevertheless, such disasters lay ahead that most historians still count Grant among America's least successful presidents.

The Panic of 1873

Six months into Grant's second term, panic struck the stock market. Prices, especially of railroad stocks, collapsed. Leading financial institutions that had invested in them were forced to close. Although the Treasury Department immediately began to add small amounts of currency to the circulation by buying bonds, it was not enough to reverse the economic slide. Desperately, businessmen pressed Grant to stimulate the economy by increasing the amount of money in circulation. Others, especially the doctrinaire reformers and academic economists, insisted that the economic depression was the natural consequence of the artificial prosperity induced by the already inflated currency. The only way to secure stable prosperity, they insisted, was to return to the gold standard as quickly as possible. Unable to decided between the two extremes, Grant seemed paralyzed.

Without administration leadership, Congress was left to try to deal with the depression itself. Both parties were divided on the issue, with Easterners still tending to favor contracting the currency and Southerners and Westerners calling for inflation and free banking. Farmer and labor organizations demanded that government take responsibility for restoring prosperity and joined the call for inflation. After their initial panic, most businessmen turned against the movement, fearing the growing militancy of farmers and workers. Reformers and businessmen joined in great rallies protesting inflation proposals, but in April, 1874, Congress nevertheless passed legislation adding $64 million to the circulation.

Reformers and businessmen lobbied Grant to veto the bill. Hit from all sides, Grant continued to vacillate; finally, he came down on the side of the contractionists, vetoing the bill. Now he at last articulated a firm policy. He urged the repeal of the Legal Tender Act, which had created the greenbacks; he wanted a law requiring that all contracts made in the future be payable in coin; he wanted all greenbacks of under ten dollars withdrawn from circulation; and he wanted Congress to authorize the Treasury to exchange government bonds for all the greenbacks still in circulation. Western and Southern Republicans were stunned by Grant's course. As Democrats in those regions swung firmly behind inflation, Republicans faced political disaster.

Fraud and Corruption

At the same time, Republicans were plagued by renewed charges of corruption. The most important scandal was the exposure of the Crédit Mobilier fraud. Investigation showed that during the 1860's the men whom Congress had authorized to build the Western Union Railroad had subcontracted the work at inflated prices to a company they themselves had organized, the Crédit Mobilier. To prevent any embarrassing questions, their representative, Congressman Oakes Ames, had spread stock in the company among important members of the House of Representatives. As the shock spread, congressmen voted themselves a retroactive $7,500 raise in salary.

None of this directly involved the administration, but there was a Republican majority in the offending Congress, the "salary grab" was managed in the house by Grant's ally, Massachusetts's congressman Benjamin F. Butler, and the episodes reminded the people of Black Friday and allegations of corruption in the civil service. The perception was strengthened when Grant nominated Alexander H. Shepherd to be governor of the territorial government that administered Washington, D.C. As building

commissioner, Shepherd had undertaken a massive building campaign in the city, beginning its transformation from a sleepy Southern town to a monumental capital. He had financed the change by borrowing, issuing bonds authorized in referenda in which poor black citizens far outvoted wealthier, taxpaying whites. In the opinion of many Americans, this paralleled the activities of New York's corrupt Tammany Hall, and Shepherd's promotion raised a tremendous outcry.

Reformers seized on the concern to renew their challenge to the machine politicians, calling again for civil service reform and insisting that corruption was the natural consequence of the present patronage system. Grant, however, was now firmly allied with the regular politicians in his own party. They depended on their patronage-disciplined organizations, and he depended on them. Grant ignored the recommendations presented by his civil service commission, and when key members resigned in the spring of 1873, advocates of change attacked him as the main obstacle to reform. In early 1874, yet another scandal broke, this time centering on F. B. Sanborn, an ally of Butler, the reformers' favorite target.

Despite mounting criticism, Grant began to think about an unprecedented third presidential term. He had given up his military commission; he had never been successful in private business; he must have wondered how he would support his family if he left the White House. At the same time, the regular Republican politicians faced a serious challenge from the reform elements of the party. With Grant as president, they could maintain their patronage-based organizations. Besides, who knew who might succeed him? If a new president allied with the reformers, cutting off the regulars' patronage, they would be in serious trouble.

Grant's veto of the inflation bill may have been aimed at securing support of the business community for a third term and reducing reformer hostility. He also tried to restore the good feeling that had existed between him and former Confederates when he had first entered the White House. He had the Justice Department drop prosecution of arrested Klan members. He refused to intervene on behalf of Texas and Arkansas Republicans, who claimed that they had been defeated only by fraud and violence in the 1872 elections. The Justice Department worked out a compromise between rival Democratic and Republican claims for control of the Alabama state legislature. He openly dickered with Virginia and South Carolina Conservatives. As violence flared anew in Alabama and Mississippi, he ignored the calls of their Republican governors for United States troops. Only in Louisiana, where his brother-in-law was a leading Republican, did Grant seem to side actively with Republicans in a dispute over who had won the 1872 state elections. Even there he urged Congress to relieve him of the responsibility by passing legislation to deal with the matter.

One political cartoonist's view of the corruption in the Grant administration: Hawaiian king Kalakaua tattoos a list of scandals on Grant. *(Library of Congress)*

In the summer of 1874, however, Conservative Southerners forced Grant's hand. Emboldened by his inaction, they formed "White Leagues" in Alabama, Louisiana, and Mississippi. In each of the states, they terrorized their Republican opponents. In rural Louisiana and Mississippi, they violently overthrew Republican city and county governments. In the course of the confrontations, numerous black and some white Republicans were murdered. Still, Grant resisted calls for troops until after violence had broken out. Finally, in September, 1874, the Conservatives of New Orleans rose against the Republican state government, defeated the state police in a pitched battle, and replaced Republican state officials with Conservatives. A coup d'état of this magnitude was too much even for the most sympathetic of reformers, and Grant intervened forcefully to restore the Louisiana Republicans to power. Southern Conservatives attacked him violently for doing so, and in the countryside, Conservatives continued to wrest power from Republicans by force.

By the summer and fall of 1874, as most states held congressional and local elections, the Grant administration and the Republican Party were completely on the defensive. In the North, Democrats blamed them for the depression and stressed corruption and the salary grab. In the South, Conservatives blasted Grant's support for local Republicans and his intervention in local affairs. They warned that Republicans in Congress were preparing a new civil rights bill, which would guarantee blacks equal access to schools, churches, hotels, streetcars, and other public facilities. Reformers determined to prove their power by urging their supporters to back Democratic candidates or to refrain from voting at all. In many states, Democrats and reformers made the question of a third term for Grant a key issue of the campaign. Elect Republicans, they warned, and it would be taken as a sign of Grant's popularity and make his renomination certain.

The results were disastrous for the Republicans. They were routed nearly everywhere. The Republicans lost ninety seats in the House of Representatives; the Democrats gained eighty, with the rest going to fourteen independent inflationists. In New York, where the Democrats ran almost entirely on the issue of a third term for Grant, Samuel J. Tilden defeated the popular Republican incumbent by thirty thousand votes, a shift of eighty thousand since 1872.

The Democratic landslide of 1874 not only demolished Grant's hopes for renomination, but it also discredited him with much of the party. Republican vice president Henry Wilson lamented, "Grant is now more unpopular than Andrew Johnson in his darkest days." He was a "millstone around the neck of our party that would sink it out of sight."

Charges of corruption dogged Grant throughout the rest of his second term of office. To restore confidence in the administration's financial policy and to add a Southerner to his cabinet, Grant named Benjamin H. Bristow secretary of the treasury, with a mandate to clean house. Immediately, Bristow and his subordinates began to investigate the "Whiskey Ring," which involved Treasury employees who had taken bribes to permit whiskey to go untaxed. When the trail led to personal friends whom he had appointed to government positions in St. Louis, Grant backed away from his commitment to reform. When Bristow and his investigators told him that his close friend

and personal secretary, Babcock, was involved in the ring, Grant could not believe it. As reformers began to boom Bristow for the 1876 Republican presidential nomination, Grant decided that the investigations were designed merely to discredit his administration, and he began to undermine Bristow's efforts. By careful maneuvering and dogged resistance, Grant managed to prevent Babcock's conviction on fraud charges and then forced Bristow's resignation. His reputation for rectitude was now in shambles. When investigators learned that Secretary of War W. W. Belknap had accepted kickbacks from contractors, his impeachment in 1876 merely confirmed the popular perception of a generally crooked administration.

Grant was not much more fortunate in his economic policies. For a brief moment, he considered pressing for a program of government works to ease unemployment, but that notion was far too radical for his advisers and the dominant molders of public opinion. Instead, Grant adhered to the idea that restoration of the gold standard would somehow revive business confidence. He took no strong role in the bitter fight over financial policy that wracked Congress in the 1874-1875 winter session. To restore party unity on the divisive issue, congressional Republicans finally compromised on a resolution calling for the resumption of specie payments by 1879, but it was to be done not by contracting the amount of money in circulation but by building up the government's reserve of gold. As a result of the compromise, the Republicans clearly became the party of hard money; the Democrats remained badly divided. The benefits became clear in the fall of 1875 when Republicans used the money issue to defeat squabbling Democrats in key Northern state elections. Grant, however, could claim little credit for the accomplishment.

Reconstruction: A Continuing Struggle

The most intractable problem that Grant faced remained Reconstruction. By 1875, Northern sympathy for Southern Republicans had largely dissipated. Southern Republicans had undertaken expensive projects designed to improve public facilities and promote economic growth. Moreover, they had responded to their mostly black constituency by opening schools and other state institutions to them. Like Shepherd in Washington, D.C., they had paid for the programs by issuing bonds, greatly increasing their state debt and tax rates. Southern Conservatives complained that propertyless blacks sustained these policies over the objections of white taxpayers. They charged that Republicans stole much of the money or spent it on expensive "jobs" put up by corrupt political supporters. Many Northern Republicans came to believe that their Southern allies were no better than Tammany Hall. Grant himself had little use for them and had tried to distance his administration from them in 1873-1874.

As president, however, Grant could not permit their overthrow by violence. Having prevented one such coup d'état in Louisiana in September, 1874, he faced another a few months later. Both Republicans and Conservatives in Louisiana claimed to have elected a majority of the state legislature in 1874. When the legislature met in January, 1875, the Conservatives took control by force, seating conservative claimants from disputed districts and ousting Republicans. Acting on their own initiative but under Grant's general orders, United States troops entered the legislature and purged the offending Conservatives, restoring the preexisting balance of parties.

Throughout the North, Democrats and reform Republicans organized meetings to protest the purge. It had been undertaken without any judicial authorization, by presidential fiat, they complained. It suggested military despotism; it destroyed states' rights. Republicans were stunned at the depth of the feeling. When the military authorities in Louisiana formally reported the circumstances, however, a favorable reaction set in among Republicans. Grant

urged Congress to pass legislation authorizing him to protect voters in the South from violence and to reverse Conservative victories in Arkansas and Louisiana based on intimidation, but such bold steps were too risky for the Republicans in the wake of the shattering defeat of 1874. Lame duck Republicans in Congress passed a new civil rights bill, but they allowed a new Force Act to die.

Such caution encouraged Southern Conservatives to continue their campaign of violence. In 1875, Mississippi Conservatives incorporated violence as an integral part of their election strategy. Grant vacillated as the Republican governor pleaded for troops to protect Republican voters. Northern Republicans lobbied Grant to reject the request, fearing to raise the military interference issue during the election season in the North. Grant agreed and told his attorney general to reject the request for protection. Exaggerating Grant's sentiments in order to win reform support in the North, the attorney general wrote cruelly, "The whole public are tired out with these annual autumnal outbreaks in the South, and the great majority are now ready to condemn any interference on the part of the government," as if the fault lay with the victims rather than the perpetrators of the violence.

The Election of 1876

By 1876, Grant's administration had been generally discredited. The only chance most Republicans believed they had to win the presidential election of 1876 was to nominate a candidate not identified with Grant and to hope that Northerners remained unwilling to trust pro-Southern Democrats. Reformers took advantage of Republican doubts to push Bristow as the Republican most identified with reform. Former House speaker James G. Blaine cleverly distanced himself from Grant and sought the nomination as a hard-money reformer. Other candidates closer to the administration found little support outside their states and a few pockets of the South. Finally, the Republicans turned to Rutherford B. Hayes, who had won the gubernatorial election of 1875 in Ohio by stressing the hard-money issue and who had diligently cultivated good relations with leading Republican reformers.

The nomination was a repudiation of Grant, although Hayes wisely remained silent on exactly how far he would go in changing administration policy. Hayes's victory would do little more to vindicate Grant's administration than his defeat. Grant did little to help Hayes, perhaps because Republicans thought his vocal support would do more harm than good.

Yet Grant did not work to subvert Hayes's campaign, as some Republican reformers feared that he would. In fact, regular Republicans went all out to secure victory. Grant permitted the campaign managers a strong say in matters of patronage and did his best to harmonize feuding party factions. During the campaign, Republicans began cautiously to point to the accomplishments of his administration. Stressing Democratic untrustworthiness and instability, they contrasted these qualities to Grant's steadiness. By the end of the canvass, many Republican critics were once more speaking of Grant almost with affection. "Unpopular as the later years of his administration have been," wrote one of the bitterest, "he will go out of office amid general good will."

Grant played a critical role during the crisis that followed the election. Neither Hayes nor the Democratic candidate, Samuel J. Tilden, had a clear majority of the electoral votes, with those of three Southern states claimed by both. As each side warned of the danger of violence, Grant calmly maintained order in the capital and in the disputed Southern states. Grant's firmness played an important role in convincing Democrats that they could not simply have the House of Representatives name Tilden president, as they insisted it had the right to do. At the same time, Grant pressured Hayes's supporters to compromise with Democrats, hinting that he would not sustain their claim with military force if it came to that. By the time the electoral commission created by the compromise ruled in favor of Hayes, all had come once more to appreciate Grant's steadiness in times of crisis.

Grant in Retirement

On leaving the presidency, Grant decided to satisfy his lifelong love of travel. Two months after stepping down, he and Julia launched themselves on a world tour. Everywhere he went—from Great Britain to the Continent to the Orient—he was feted as the representative type of the self-made American man. As correspondents reported triumph after triumph, Grant's popularity in the United States climbed to the same level that he had enjoyed after Appomattox. By 1879, his allies in the Republican Party determined to make him president for a third term and thus to recover their own positions of party leadership. Reform Republicans bitterly resisted, aided by Hayes's allies in the party. At the 1880 Republican National Convention, slightly more than three hundred delegates—some seventy short of the required majority—stood by Grant through thirty-five ballots, until his enemies combined to defeat him.

His political career at an end, Grant cast about for an occupation. Always a plunger in business, seeking quick riches, Grant put all of his money into a banking and financial partnership with his son and his son's friend, Ferdinand Ward. Ward, however, was a charlatan, inflating his business with borrowed money, and when the pyramid collapsed, Grant lost everything he had. Refusing to accept gifts, Grant scrimped along on small loans from personal friends.

To recoup his fortune, Grant accepted a long-standing invitation to write his memoirs. Harnessing his remarkable memory, he recalled his days as a young lieutenant in the war with

Mexico. In straightforward style, he limned his Civil War battles, modestly disavowing his talent as a tactician or strategist and demonstrating surprising deftness in characterizing friends and foes. As he wrote, he began to suffer from terrible pain in his jaw. Doctors diagnosed cancer, and with grim determination Grant labored to provide for his destitute family by finishing his work before he died. His biographers have described the agonizing effort as the greatest personal accomplishment of his life—equal in its way to his great wartime triumphs. He completed *Personal Memoirs* on May 23, 1885; he died on July 21, once again a great American hero, beloved of the nation.

Assessing Grant's Presidency: The Need for Balance

Historians and political scientists have generally considered Grant's administration of the presidency to be a failure. He has consistently been ranked among the country's worst presidents. Scholars have felt revulsion for the corruption that surrounded Grant as president; they have perceived his economic policies to be unfairly favorable to big business; and until recently, they have considered him unwise in trying to protect black rights in the South.

This assessment, however, is probably too extreme. A considerable amount of corruption actually occurred in Grant's administration, and Grant did not take a strong interest in rooting it out, but much of what scholars have called corruption was merely the dominant mode of choosing government officials through the patronage system. Scholars have tended to accept the judgment of the anti-Grant reformers that this system was inherently corrupt, but that is a very questionable conclusion,

and reformers had ulterior, political motives for making the charge.

Once one gets beyond the corruption issue, Grant's administration emerges in a better light. With the exception of the controversial Santo Domingo treaty, his foreign policy was one of recognized achievement. His economic policies certainly did not challenge the dominant economic wisdom of his time, but he can hardly be blamed for that; in fact, he carried them out so efficiently that by the end of his term it was possible to set a definite date for the return to a specie-based currency, a significant achievement in the opinion of most contemporaries.

Grant's effort to protect the rights of black and white Republicans in the South did fail, not because it was misguided, but because of the recalcitrance of Southern whites and waning support in the North. Most analysts now consider Grant correct in making the attempt and wonder whether he manifested enough commitment to it. There can be no doubt that Grant wavered in the face of mounting political opposition to intervention in the South. Nevertheless, Grant remained committed to pro-

Grant's tomb. *(Library of Congress)*

311

tecting civil and political rights in the South after most Republican leaders had given up. Given the capacities of the national government at that time and considering the degree of suppression of normal civil and political liberties that a firmer policy would have required, it is doubtful that any president could have succeeded where Grant failed.

Overall, Grant's administration was neither an abject failure nor a great success. A great general, he made an adequate president. Intending to play only a modest role in the making of policy, he seems a pale figure compared with such giants as Andrew Jackson, Lincoln, or the Roosevelts. Still, he dominated his era, a stronger president than most have recognized.

Michael Les Benedict

Bibliographical References

The best general biography of Grant is William S. McFeely, *Grant: A Biography*, 1981. It has much new information and is very well written. The reader, however, should be cautious in accepting McFeely's intuitive judgments about Grant's personal motivations and psychological makeup. Readers should compare McFeely's assessments with those of John A. Carpenter, *Ulysses S. Grant: His Life and Character*, 1898. William B. Hesseltine, *Ulysses S. Grant, Politician*, 1935, concentrates on Grant's

post-Civil War career. It provides a fuller description of specific events than McFeely's work. Frank J. Scaturro, *President Grant Reconsidered*, 1998, argues for a positive reassessment of Grant's presidency as one of strength, achievement, and principle. Also useful is William Gillette, *Retreat from Reconstruction, 1869-1879*, 1979, and Brooks D. Simpson, *Let Us Have Peace: Ulysses S. Grant and the Politics of War and Reconstruction*, 1991, both of which concentrate on the Grant administration's Reconstruction policy. Allan Nevins, *Hamilton Fish: The Inner History of the Grant Administration*, rev. ed. 1957, is based largely on the diaries of Grant's conservative secretary of state.

Many of Grant's associates wrote biographies of him or described their association with him. Of these, Adam Badeau, *Grant in Peace: From Appomattox to Mount McGregor, A Personal Memoir*, 1887, is the most informative, furnishing insight into Grant's character as seen by an associate and friend. James R. Arnold, *Grant Wins the War: Decision at Vicksburg*, 1997, focuses on Grant's strategy in that decisive siege. Grant's own *Personal Memoirs of U. S. Grant*, 1885-1886, offers an insight into his character but attends only slightly to his presidential years. Geoffrey Perret, *Ulysses S. Grant: Soldier and President*, 1997, details both Grant's military and his political careers.

Rutherford B. Hayes

19th President, 1877-1881

Born: October 4, 1822
       Delaware, Ohio
Died: January 17, 1893
       Fremont, Ohio

Political Party: Republican
Vice President: William A. Wheeler

Cabinet Members

Secretary of State: William M. Evarts
Secretary of the Treasury: John Sherman
Secretary of War: George M. McCrary, Alexander Ramsey
Secretary of the Navy: Richard W. Thompson, Nathan Goff, Jr.
Attorney General: Charles A. Devens
Postmaster General: David M. Key, Horace Maynard
Secretary of the Interior: Carl Schurz

Rutherford Birchard Hayes was born five years after his parents, Rutherford and Sophie Birchard Hayes, moved from Vermont to the central Ohio community of Delaware and less than three months after the death of his father. He was left in the care of his mother, a strong-willed and protective woman, and her bachelor brother, Sardis Birchard, who became the dominant male influence in his life. A bright but frail child, "Ruddy" grew up in a sheltered world, his early years marked by a close attachment to his sister Fanny, the only other sibling to survive childhood.

With financial help from Birchard, an established businessman in Lower Sandusky (later Fremont), Rutherford attended private grammar schools and a college preparatory school in Connecticut before enrolling at Ken-

yon College in Gambier, Ohio. Studious and intense, he gained a reputation as a mediator of campus disputes, began to dabble in Whig politics, and was graduated first in the class

Hayes's official portrait. *(White House Historical Society)*

313

of 1842. A bachelor of law degree from Harvard in January, 1845, capped a good formal education for the young Hayes.

After a less than satisfying law practice of four years in Lower Sandusky, late in 1849 Hayes moved south to the bustling river city of Cincinnati. As he quickly rose to become one of the city's leading barristers, he courted Lucy Ware Webb, and they were married late in 1852. From their union would come eight children—of whom four boys and one girl would survive childhood. Bright, well-educated, gregarious, and an excellent hostess, Lucy became her husband's faithful confidante and companion in the political trials and triumphs that lay ahead.

As the sectional crisis broke up the Whig Party during the mid-1850's, Hayes moved into the new Republican coalition. Never radically antislavery, he worked quietly in the party as his interest in local politics grew. In 1858, the city council appointed him city solicitor—a post to which he was elected the following year. He worked at the local level for the election of Abraham Lincoln in 1860 but admitted that he could not "get up much interest in the contest." His seeming indifference to the ensuing secession crisis disappeared with the firing on Fort Sumter in April, 1861, and early in June he readily accepted a commission as major in the Twenty-third Ohio Volunteer Infantry.

The Twenty-third spent most of the next four years in West Virginia, one of the more rugged minor theaters of the Civil War. Holding the area, as historian T. Harry Williams put it, involved "small and nasty work—fighting in pygmy battles, chasing guerrillas, patrolling lonely mountain roads, repressing civilian sympathizers of the South." On only two occasions did the Twenty-third take part in the major battles of the East—at Antietam in 1862 and with General Philip Sheridan in his Shenandoah Valley campaign of 1864. A regimental and brigade commander, Hayes compiled a good record and steadily advanced in rank to brigadier general of volunteers by 1864. He adapted easily to army life; combat brought out his leadership qualities, and the experience made him more assured and ambitious.

Hayes's war record helped launch his postwar political career. Through the influence of a prominent Cincinnati editor, Hayes was nominated for Congress in 1864. Rather than take a furlough to campaign, he remained at the front and in October easily overwhelmed his Democratic opponent. Seated in December, 1865, and reelected the following year, Hayes served during the critical period when Congress rejected President Andrew Johnson's conservative Reconstruction policy and formulated its own.

Although some historians classify Hayes as a moderate "Centrist" in the Republican-dominated House, his voting record on most Reconstruction issues was similar to that of Radical leaders. He privately expressed reservations about harsh treatment for the former Confederate states, but he quietly supported congressional efforts to wrestle control over Reconstruction from Johnson. He voted for the Fourteenth Amendment, the final congressional plan of Reconstruction, and toward the end, he sided with those calling for Johnson's impeachment.

By the time Johnson was brought to trial, Hayes was serving the first of three terms as governor of Ohio. Nominated for the position in June, 1867, he resigned from the House the following month and won a narrow victory over Allen G. Thurman, Ohio's popular chief justice. He enhanced his reputation as a vote getter two years later when he took the "sound" money ground and won reelection over George H. Pendleton, a prominent proponent of the "Ohio Idea" to pay off the Union war debt in depreciated greenbacks.

Hayes's first two gubernatorial administrations (1868-1872) were clean and untroubled, and demonstrated his commitment to reform.

He helped secure Ohio's ratification of the Fifteenth Amendment, called for a state civil service system and state regulation of railroads, and won the enactment of a coal-mining safety code. He also recommended upgrading the state's prisons and mental hospitals, and he convinced the legislature to establish a new agricultural college, which became Ohio State University in 1878.

Hayes declined to run for a third term and refused entreaties to become a candidate for fellow Republican John Sherman's seat in the U.S. Senate. Also, when several close political friends joined the Liberal Republican revolt against President Ulysses S. Grant in 1872, Hayes stayed with the regular Republican organization even though he was troubled by the Grant administration's record. In that year, Hayes reluctantly but dutifully accepted an unwanted nomination for Congress, only to suffer defeat by a narrow margin.

Out of public life for the first time since 1858, Hayes moved his family to Fremont in 1873, and early in the following year Sardis Birchard died, leaving the bulk of his estate including his fine home, Spiegel Grove, to Hayes. At fifty-two years of age in 1874, Hayes looked the part of a settled, successful man. Of medium height, with his 180 pounds distributed over a stocky frame, Hayes had dark blue eyes, a ruddy complexion, and a once reddish full beard, which was now touched with gray. Of moderate tastes and conciliatory by nature, Hayes had a dignified yet open and friendly manner. Always close to his family, he enjoyed traveling, reading history, and tracing his genealogy. Hayes had done well with his own investments and, with the property inherited from Birchard, he would leave an estate of nearly a million dollars at his death.

On his return to Fremont, Hayes avowed that his public career was over. It proved to be an opportune time to be retired from Republican politics. Much troubled by corruption, a failing policy of Reconstruction, and economic depression following the panic of 1873, the Republican Party lost heavily in the elections of 1874. Still, when Republican leaders asked him to enter the gubernatorial race against incumbent Democrat William Allen in 1875, Hayes assented and conducted a vigorous campaign on the issues of sound money and free schools.

The Election of 1876: Disputed Returns

Hayes's close victory over Allen in October, 1875, and his attractive record as a moderate reformer catapulted him into the national spotlight as a possible presidential contender in 1876. As his friends began to organize in his behalf, Hayes shrewdly maintained a pose of public silence and detachment, while privately he conceded his availability and carefully avoided alliances with any of the more prominent candidates for the nomination.

The leading contender, James G. Blaine of Maine, was the three-time speaker of the House of Representatives and leader of the so-called Half-Breed faction, which at least gave lip service to reform. Grant supposedly favored New York Senator Roscoe Conkling, an avowed enemy of Blaine and the recognized leader of the Stalwart faction of machine politicians and spoilsmen. Another, somewhat milder Stalwart aspirant, Senator Oliver P. Morton of Indiana, was a favorite of Southern Republicans because of his continuing advocacy of Reconstruction. A third faction in the party, the Liberal Republican element which had bolted the party in 1872, favored reformer Benjamin H. Bristow of Kentucky.

At the national convention in June, Hayes's supporters worked quietly and effectively to make him the second choice of delegates favoring other candidates. As the front runner, Blaine became the target for all other contenders and failed to receive a first-ballot nomination. On that ballot Hayes ran a weak fifth but he moved up steadily. When Morton, Bristow, and Conkling were withdrawn on the seventh ballot, Hayes was the primary beneficiary and won the needed majority to defeat Blaine. To balance the ticket, the convention turned to New York Representative William A. Wheeler.

Two weeks later, the Democrats chose reform governor Samuel J. Tilden of New York as their standard bearer with Thomas A. Hendricks of Indiana as his running mate, and what would turn out to be a long and bitter struggle for the presidency began. As was traditional, neither Tilden nor Hayes made public speeches in the canvass, although Hayes did help bring Liberal Republicans fully back into the party with a call for civil service reform in his letter accepting the nomination. Despite the clean images and reform postures of both Hayes and Tilden, however, the campaign was intensely partisan, and as the returns came in on the evening of November 7, Hayes's chances looked dim. Tilden had won the popular vote by about 250,000, and he had 184 electoral votes—just one shy of the 185 needed for victory. In addition, Democrats felt assured of victory in South Carolina, Florida, and Louisiana—the last three Southern states with Republican regimes at the time of the election. With a certain claim to only 166 electoral votes, Hayes returned late in the evening believing that he had lost the election.

In reality, however, the contest had just entered a new phase—thanks to a sudden aggressiveness at Republican campaign headquarters in New York. Party leaders, seeing the critical importance to Hayes of the three Southern states with their 19 electoral votes, asked prominent Republicans in each state if they could hold their states in the Republican column. When the positive replies came in, party chair Zach Chandler released his famous statement, "Hayes has 185 electoral votes and is elected."

Representatives of both national parties hastened South to secure the disputed states in their interest. Republicans, certainly the more active, collected affidavits charging Democrats with intimidation, and the Republican-controlled state returning boards threw out returns from counties or parishes where it was apparent that Democrats had "bulldozed" Republican voters. By early December, the returning boards ruled that Hayes had carried the disputed states. The Democrats immediately charged the returning boards with partisanship and fraud and submitted a second set of returns signed by the minority (Democratic) members of the boards proclaiming victory for Tilden. In addition, the Democrats challenged one of Oregon's three Republican electors on the grounds that he had been a federal employee at the time of the election.

The Republican Senate and Democratic House quickly deadlocked on procedure for determining which set of returns should be accepted, and the impasse was not broken until January 29, 1877, when Congress, much to the displeasure of Hayes, agreed to form an electoral commission as a mechanism for resolving the dispute. To be composed of five members from each house of Congress and five from the Supreme Court, the commission was to hear arguments and decide which sets of returns were valid. As anticipated, the House chose three Democrats and two Republicans to sit on the commission; the Senate, three Republicans and two Democrats; and the supposedly nonpartisan Court, two known Democrats and two known Republicans. The final Court seat on the commission was to go to David Davis of Illinois, thought to be an independent, but Davis was disqualified when the Illinois legislature selected him for the Senate. With Davis eliminated, the justices chose Joseph P. Bradley, a Republican appointee, as their fifth member, and although all fifteen members were to act impartially, Hayes's chances suddenly improved.

In the interim there were some Democratic threats of insurrection if Tilden were not chosen, almost constant behind-the-scenes dealing among party partisans, and rampant speculation and rumors. For his part Hayes avoided any public statements but kept in close communication with Republicans in Washington, D.C., especially Ohioans Stanley Matthews, James A. Garfield, and John Sherman. In comparison with the Republicans, Tilden and his managers appeared ill organized and inactive—much to the distress of Southern Democrats, who feared that Southern Republican regimes might be reinforced if Tilden lost. With that eventuality in mind, some Southern Democrats conducted a useful flirtation with a handful of Northern Republicans throughout the crisis. A few Southerners, amply assisted by lobbyists for Thomas A. Scott's Texas and Pacific Railroad, wanted pledges that Hayes, if elected, would favor further subsidies for the completion of Scott's Southern transcontinental railroad. Still others wanted Southern representation in the Hayes cabinet, and there was some loose talk of Southern Democrats allowing Republicans to organize the next House with Garfield as speaker. The parties to these talks were few, however, and overall these side issues were of little consequence in helping to resolve the dispute. Of paramount importance to the South were Republican guarantees to withdraw federal support from Republican regimes in South Carolina and Louisiana—the last two Southern states in which Republicans were still contending for control, Florida having peacefully inaugurated a Democratic administration in January.

Against this backdrop the electoral commission began work on the first of February with hearings and deliberations on Florida. Within a week, the commission decided by a partisan 8-7 vote to accept the returning board's decision to award the state to Hayes. The 8-7 margin soon became familiar, with the commission awarding Louisiana, the disputed Oregon vote, and finally, on February 28, South Carolina to Hayes.

Although only one house of Congress had to accept the commission's decisions for them to take effect, the Democratic majority in the House frequently held up the count throughout February with dilatory motions and filibustering. Yet Southern Democrats could not maintain the delaying tactics alone, and the Northeastern Democratic leadership, under pressure from settlement-minded businessmen, haunted by their overwhelming endorsement of the electoral commission idea, and sensing the futility and danger of resisting its decisions, were noticeably reluctant to promote a filibuster. It was in this atmosphere that Southern Democrats sought final assurances from Northern Republicans that Hayes, once inaugurated, would agree to "home rule" for South Carolina and Louisiana.

Those assurances came in meetings between a handful of Southern Democrats and several of Hayes's close friends, and with the acquiescence of Northern Democrats, the filibustering efforts ended on March 1. The count proceeded; at 4:10 a.m. the next day, Congress declared Hayes elected with 185 electoral votes to 184 for Tilden. Hayes learned of the decision on his way to Washington, D.C., and on the evening of March 3, he privately took the oath of office in the presence of the chief justice and Grant.

Hayes in Office: Efforts Toward Reconciliation

On a cool and overcast March 5, Hayes became the nineteenth president of the United States, amid some concern for his safety. He calmly delivered a short inaugural address that stressed the "supreme importance" of settling the Southern question, repeated his call for "thorough, radical, and complete" civil service reform, and promised to work for specie resumption—making all currency redeemable in gold or silver—to hasten the return of prosperous times. Overall, the address was a quiet, nationalistic appeal to lay aside partisan differences and unite once again for the common

The arrival of freedmen and their families in Baltimore. *(Library of Congress)*

good. The president, he said, should "be always mindful of the fact that he serves his party best who serves the country best."

As he noted in his diary during the electoral crisis, Hayes wanted a cabinet with no holdovers from the Grant administration, no "presidential candidates," and no appointments to "take care" of anybody. Although he did not live up to these criteria fully, the nominations he sent to the Senate reflected his interest in reform and his independence from the Stalwart faction of the party. The three key nominees were William M. Evarts of New York, a distinguished lawyer and a longtime opponent of Conkling, as secretary of state, Senate Finance Committee Chairman and close friend John Sherman as secretary of the treasury, and reformer Carl Schurz of Missouri, who had led the Liberal Republican revolt against Grant in 1872, as secretary of the interior. Of less import were Charles A. Devens, a Massachu-

setts Supreme Court judge, as attorney general, Congressman George M. McCrary of Iowa as secretary of war, and Richard W. Thompson of Indiana, a protégé of Senator Oliver P. Morton, as secretary of the navy. Finally, as a concession to the South, Hayes chose Senator David M. Key of Tennessee, a Democrat and former Confederate, as postmaster general.

The nominees, particularly Schurz, Evarts, and Key, quickly aroused the ire of leading Senate Stalwarts, who had been denied any voice in the selection process. There was talk of blocking approval of the whole cabinet, with Zach Chandler raging that Hayes had "passed the Republican party to its worst enemies," but reform-minded Republicans and independents supported the nominees and Hayes won the first of many clashes with congressional Stalwarts.

The most immediate problem facing the new administration was what to do about rival claimants for power in Louisiana and South Carolina. In Louisiana both Republican Stephen B. Packard and Democrat Frances T. Nicholls claimed to be duly elected, and a similar standoff existed in South Carolina between Republican Daniel Chamberlain and Democrat Wade Hampton. De facto authority, however, lay with the Democrats—the Republicans controlled little beyond their respective state houses, which were protected by small contingents of federal troops under orders to maintain the status quo.

Like most Northerners, Hayes had become increasingly disillusioned with the use of military force to prop up Southern Republican regimes. "There is to be an end to all that," he had written Carl Schurz in February; still, he had to move slowly. Southern Republicans beseeched him not to abandon them, congressional Stalwarts, already irked because of his cabinet appointments, urged him to support Packard and Chamberlain, and old Northern Radicals and abolitionists readily joined the chorus. After several weeks of delay, Hayes extracted pledges from Hampton to safeguard the rights of all South Carolina citizens, and when he removed the soldiers from the state house on April 10, Chamberlain reluctantly relinquished the governor's office to Hampton. Ten days later, after securing promises from Nicholls in Louisiana that blacks and other Republicans would be protected in their rights and not prosecuted "for past political conduct," Hayes withdrew the troops from the Packard-held state house, and Reconstruction was over—much to the relief of Southern conservatives and most Northerners.

Removal of the troops was only the first part of Hayes's broader Southern strategy to attract former Whigs and "respectable" Democrats to the Republican standard through a conciliatory posture and a nonpartisan patronage policy. Working with Key and other advisers, Hayes went out of his way to appoint Democrats to federal positions in the South—one-

third of his Southern appointments during the first five months went to conservatives. To demonstrate further his good will, in September, 1877, Hayes and a large party toured several Southern states—accompanied most of the way by Governor Hampton of South Carolina. The entourage received enthusiastic receptions and Hayes returned much encouraged.

Other signs, however, were not as positive. Democrats who had accepted patronage positions remained Democrats and sometimes turned even more vehemently on Republicans in their areas. When the new Forty-fifth Congress met in October, 1877, no Southern Democrats voted to help Republicans organize the House—allegedly violating a promise given during the electoral crisis. (Shortly after this, Hayes came out directly against further federal subsidies for the Texas and Pacific Railroad, and another frail compromise agreement fell by the wayside.) Moreover, in local elections in November, the South went heavily Democratic.

Criticism of Hayes's policy from within the party steadily increased as prominent leaders charged him with destroying what remained of the Southern Republican Party and abandoning the freedmen to the care of brutal Redeemers. By early 1878, party support for his Southern policy had evaporated, and in the November elections fraud, violence, and widespread intimidation of black voters created as solidly a Democratic South as the nation had yet seen. Only four Republicans remained in the sixty-three-man Southern delegation to the House, and Democrats won control of the Senate for the first time since before the war.

In an interview after the election, Hayes lamented the Southerners' failure to live up to their promises to protect black voters and reluctantly admitted "that the experiment was a failure." In fact, his Southern strategy was a pipe dream that showed no understanding of the depth of racial prejudice and the degree to which party loyalty had become an article of faith among white Southerners. True to his Whiggish background and lifelong desire for harmony, Hayes had tried conciliation to ease out of Reconstruction, but his naïve and misplaced faith in Southern conservatives led to failure. In his defense, his alternatives were perhaps nonexistent—given the failure of coercion, the pervasiveness of Southern racism, and the absence of continued Northern commitment to safeguarding the rights of Southern blacks.

Forced after the elections of 1878 to take a harder line against the South, Hayes called for larger appropriations to enforce the election laws, but the lame duck Congress failed to take action. When the new Congress met in 1879, the Democrats, now in control of both Houses, attached riders repealing federal election laws to appropriation bills, but they were stopped by five separate Hayes vetoes—much to the pleasure of congressional Republicans

and the party press. As a result, Southern repression of the freedmen, made all the more evident by the plight of black "Exodusters" leaving the South, served to reunite the various Northern Republican factions in the campaign of 1880 against a solidly Democratic South—the reverse of what Hayes had initially intended.

An Unfortunate Precedent: Federal Troops and the Railroad Strike of 1877

Whereas Hayes declined to use federal force in the South, he believed that he had to use it in the railroad strike of 1877. Railroad labor had, with good cause, been restive for some time. The ongoing depression had trimmed railroad revenues, less available work meant increased idle time with no pay for many employees, and several lines had cut the wages of their already hard-pressed labor force.

The crisis began on July 16, when a 10-percent wage cut was to go into effect on the

The Sixth Maryland militia opens fire on railroad strikers on July 20, 1877, killing twelve. *(Library of Congress)*

Baltimore and Ohio Railroad. Workers walked off their jobs and began stopping trains in Maryland and West Virginia. Strikes against other lines, marked by a considerable amount of looting, violence, and loss of life, soon followed. Some fourteen Midwestern and Northeastern states were affected, and at one point strikes closed all five major trunk lines from the East to the Midwest. Local police forces and state militia often proved incapable of controlling the situation; in a period of eight days the administration received requests for aid from nine governors. After cabinet debate, Hayes issued warnings against further disorder, sending federal troops to four states. The soldiers restored order without further bloodshed, and the crisis was over in a few weeks.

Although Hayes had avoided declaring martial law and sent troops only when the governors had convinced him that the situation was beyond their control, his actions set an unfortunate precedent for the use of the federal military to break strikes. As he confided to his diary, he knew that the workers' grievances deserved attention, but he made no recommendations for new work laws, and Congress showed little interest in legislation to ease the workers' plight.

The Currency Question

In part, the railroad strikes resulted from a troubled economy and a set of monetary problems that had plagued the government since the end of the Civil War. Forced off the gold standard in late 1861, the Union had resorted to nonspecie-backed currency (the "greenbacks"), which had quickly depreciated. Fiscal conservatives such as Hayes believed a gradual contraction of the currency necessary to return it to par with gold, but a banking panic in September, 1873, thrust the nation into an economic depression which spawned inflationist sentiment in both parties. In an effort to restore Republican Party unity on the money question, John Sherman and other hard-money advo-

cates pushed through the Resumption Act in early 1875. The act provided for gradual contraction of the greenbacks and directed the secretary of the treasury to build a gold reserve in preparation for the resumption of specie payments on January 1, 1879.

Hayes had advocated hard money and specie resumption in his gubernatorial campaigns, and his choice of Sherman to head the Treasury Department was a signal to businessmen and creditors that his administration would work to achieve resumption. Quite clearly, the contraction of the greenback circulation in preparation for resumption hurt the debt-ridden farmers in the South and West, and there were sound arguments that the nation needed a greater volume of currency. Hayes, however, believed that the nation's paper currency must be redeemable in gold: He considered resumption critical to restoring confidence in the economy and ending the depression. Through Sherman's diligent stockpiling of gold and shrewd management of bond issues, greenbacks reached par with gold late in 1878, and on January 2, 1879, greenbacks were favored over gold in New York markets. Most of the plaudits by financial and commercial interests went to Sherman, but his success was at least partially the result of Hayes's backing and persistence.

Meanwhile, many of those demanding an expansion of the monetary circulation had turned to silver as a new panacea for the nation's economic problems. Silver had originally circulated with gold (in a set 16-1 ratio in value) as legal tender, but owing to its increasing scarcity before the war, silver began commanding a premium in gold and generally disappeared from circulation. In 1873, Congress had quietly discontinued coinage of the silver dollar and restricted the legal tender power of silver to amounts not exceeding five dollars. This action, which later gained notoriety as the "Crime of '73," effectively demonetized silver. In late 1876, after considerable agitation by inflationists and silver-mining interests, the House passed Democrat Richard P. Bland's bill to renew coinage of the silver dollar and restore its legal tender status, but the Senate, in the midst of the electoral crisis, failed to take action.

When the new Congress convened in late 1877, the House repassed the Bland bill and sent it to the Senate, where Finance Committee Chair William Boyd Allison reported it with an amendment limiting government purchases of silver for coinage to between $2 million and $4 million a month. In the meantime, both houses had passed a concurrent resolution declaring that the principal and interest on the public debt might be paid in silver dollars. The chambers agreed to the Bland bill as modified by Allison's amendment and sent it to Hayes for his signature.

In the firm belief that gold should be the sole standard of value, Hayes vetoed the Bland-Allison bill, declaring that it would be "justly regarded as a grave breach of the public faith" to pay the public debt in silver coin. Both chambers quickly overrode the veto (the only successful override among Hayes's thirteen vetoes), and to the president's disappointment the nation went back to a limited extent on the bimetallic standard.

Fraud and Favoritism: Charges and Countercharges

As Hayes confided to his diary after Congress overrode his veto of the silver bill, "I am not much liked as a president by the politicians in office, in the press or in Congress." In addition to encountering opposition to his monetary and Southern policies, Hayes had just lost a round in his efforts to reform the New York Customhouse. To add to his troubles, later that spring House Democrats began to investigate new allegations that in 1876 Republicans had used fraud to secure a Hayes victory in Florida and Louisiana. Although Hayes was not directly implicated, the reputation of the men who served as his managers during the elec-

toral dispute were damaged by the revelations of the investigating committee headed by Clarkson N. Potter. Sherman suffered the most. Although he denied ever promising to "take care" of members of the Louisiana returning board as alleged, an inordinate number of tainted Louisiana Republicans later secured jobs in the Hayes administration—particularly in Sherman's Treasury Department.

It was an ordeal for Hayes, but his fortunes improved in October when the Republican *New York Tribune* decoded and published a series of secret telegrams sent by Democrats during the electoral crisis which implicated Democrats, including some close to Tilden, in corrupt dealings with the Florida and South Carolina returning boards. Much to the embarrassment of Democrats, House Republicans forced the Potter Committee to look into the "cipher dispatches." In the end, the involvement of Democrats in wrongdoing took much of the pressure off the Republicans, and Hayes himself later counted the Potter investigation as one of the "most fortunate" episodes in his administration. Still, the ongoing dispute over his title to the office haunted his presidency. The stinging epithets of "Rutherfraud" and "His Fraudulency" were favorites of a particularly abusive Democratic press, and many Republican editors, piqued over his appointments, Southern policy, antisilver stance, prohibition policy at White House functions, and the like, were often less than cordial until late in his term. Hayes endured the abuse and deprecation silently, rarely responding in public and taking solace in gatherings of family and friends and a wide range of White House activities and visitors.

Civil Service Reform: A Mixed Record

In his inaugural address, Hayes had stressed the pressing need for civil service reform—a plea repeated in his annual messages to Congress. Although Congress remained singularly unresponsive, Hayes took some significant steps on his own to start cleaning up the spoils system. His first executive order instructed officers in all departments of the government not "to take part in the management of political organizations, caucuses, conventions, or election campaigns" and prohibited the common practice of assessing officers and subordinates for political contributions. Enforcement of the order varied from department to department, and later "voluntary" contributions were permitted, but it was an important step toward reform. Believing that satisfactory officeholders should have security, Hayes removed fewer government employees than had most previous presidents. He also encouraged the use of competitive merit examinations for subordinate jobs, made extensive nonpartisan appointments, and resolutely avoided nepotism.

His own high-level appointments tended to be solid, able, and occasionally outstanding men—his placing of John Marshall Harlan of Kentucky on the Supreme Court is a prime example. He also won the applause of civil service reformers for appointing Schurz to the cabinet and allowing him an influential voice. Schurz effectively applied civil service standards in a four-year effort to clean up the Department of the Interior and was especially active in reforming the Indian Bureau, both in personnel and with new sets of regulations. Although American Indians suffered their last major defeats at the hands of the military during the Hayes years, Schurz's reforms lessened the bitterness and helped launch a new era in American Indian relations.

Still, Hayes's appointment record was a mix of reform impulses and partisan and personal considerations that often frustrated civil service reformers outside the administration. His appointment of Southern Democrats to federal offices was done in a spirit of reconciliation and nonpartisanship, but it also represented an effort to build the Republican Party in the South. Similarly, his choice of black leader Frederick Douglass as marshal for the District of Columbia was at least partially intended to disarm critics who claimed that he was abandoning the freedmen. He rewarded key people who had worked for his nomination and election and served his interests during the electoral crisis, and he received a substantial amount of criticism late in his term for nominating Stanley Matthews to the Supreme Court. The press saw the nomination, admittedly personal, as a reward for Matthews's work during the electoral crisis, and the Senate rejected the nomination. Finally, despite hints of wrongdoing, neither Hayes, Key, nor Horace Maynard, who became postmaster general late in the administration, probed deeply enough to uncover the ongoing corruption in the postal service inherited from the Grant administration. The problem, which erupted as the notorious Star Route frauds after Hayes had left office, became the only major blot on his administrative record.

Hayes's mixed motives, his caution as a reformer, and his battle to win back some control over federal appointments from entrenched Stalwart senators were evident in his celebrated effort to reform the New York Customhouse. Most of the more than one thousand customhouse employees owed their positions to the patronage of Senator Roscoe Conkling's Stalwart faction of the New York Republican Party, and there was ample evidence of favoritism to New York merchants, bribery, fraud, and inefficiency.

Hayes decided early to make the customhouse a showcase for civil service reform, but it also presented an opportunity to strike at Conkling's machine while perhaps elevating the opposing faction to which Secretary of State Evarts belonged. After an investigation detailed customhouse "irregularities" in late May, 1877, Hayes asked for the resignation of Collector Chester A. Arthur and Naval Officer Alonzo B. Cornell. Both refused and Cornell openly defied Hayes's executive order forbidding political activity. Rather than removing them forthwith as reformers wished, Hayes waited until Congress returned in October to recommend anti-Conkling replacements. Conkling quickly lined up Senate opposition on the grounds that Hayes was trampling over the "right" of senators to control patronage, and all but six Republicans voted with the majority to reject the nominees.

After Congress adjourned for the summer of 1878, Hayes struck back and replaced Arthur with Surveyor Edwin A. Merritt and Cornell with Deputy Naval Officer Silas W. Burt, long a favorite of reformers. Although the new appointments were less obnoxious to the Stalwart faction, Conkling renewed the fight when Congress reconvened in December. A majority of Republican senators still voted against the appointments, but Hayes finally won approval for them in February, 1879, after a two-year struggle—thanks to Democratic support, the switch of a few more Republican votes, and some astute lobbying by Sherman. Most important, Merritt and especially Burt took seriously Hayes's instructions to organize the customhouse in a more efficient and business-like manner. Although problems remained with political activity, the operation of the customhouse under Merritt and Burt pleased reformers and showed that civil service reform would work.

Foreign Relations

In contrast to the troubles at home, foreign relations were relatively peaceful during the Hayes years. The major ongoing problem involved Mexico, where Porfirio Díaz had overthrown the established government in 1876. Because counterrevolutionary activity kept Díaz from preventing Mexican and Indian raids on United States soil, Hayes withheld diplomatic recognition and, in June, 1877, authorized army commanders in Texas to pursue the raiders back across the border. Although Hayes finally extended diplomatic recognition in April, 1878, the "hot pursuit" policy remained

in effect until Díaz was able to suppress the raids to Secretary of State Evarts's satisfaction early in 1880.

In another area, violent anti-Chinese demonstrations in San Francisco during the summer of 1877 prompted Congress to pass a bill restricting Chinese immigration in early 1879. Hayes personally favored restriction, but he feared that the congressional bill, which revoked part of the Burlington Treaty with China, might lead the Chinese to abrogate the entire treaty. Rather than risking the loss of the commercially favorable treaty and possibly creating a situation endangering Americans in China, Hayes vetoed the bill and quickly sent a commission to China to negotiate a new treaty. The Chinese agreed to a new commercial agreement and another treaty, approved in early 1881, to regulate immigration as the United States desired.

A final diplomatic problem emerged in 1879 when Ferdinand de Lesseps, the French engineer who had built the Suez Canal, unveiled a plan to construct a canal across the Panama isthmus. While trying to secure French support, de Lesseps also offered construction company stock to Americans. In a strong message to the Senate, Hayes declared that the United States would not surrender control of the canal project to foreign powers, nor would it support a private building company backed largely by foreign capital. With neither French nor American backing, de Lesseps began the project in the early 1880's, but his company collapsed later in the decade. In the meantime, Hayes had helped shape American policy for eventual control of the isthmian canal.

When he accepted the Republican nomination in 1876, Hayes had expressed his "inflexible purpose" to retire after only one term. As the election year of 1880 approached, he was tired of the office—yet perhaps disappointed that no party leader encouraged a draft movement that he could then decline. He took no part in the process of selecting a Republican

Hayes welcomes Chun Lan Pin, the first Chinese minister to the United States, in 1878. *(Library of Congress)*

candidate and made no endorsements. Garfield's nomination pleased him, but instead of campaigning he left the White House in late August for an extensive tour of the Far West and did not return until the day before the election. Garfield's victory and the return of both houses of Congress to Republican control, which Hayes viewed as a vindication of his policies, brightened his last months in office. He relished the final White House functions and the tributes paid his administration by friends and former opponents, but as he noted in his diary, he looked forward to "retiring from this conspicuous scene to the freedom, independence and safety of our obscure and happy home in the pleasant grove at Fremont."

After Garfield's inauguration the Hayes family returned to Fremont where Hayes immersed himself in community organizations, worked to improve his Spiegel Grove estate, and traveled extensively with Lucy and his family. He seldom missed the annual reunions of Civil War veterans. In the belief that education offered the best hope for resolving the South's racial problem, he served as a trustee of the Peabody Educational Fund for the South and as president of the Slater Fund for black education.

Although he maintained a private interest in politics, he removed himself completely from the public political scene and had little association with those still active in the party. With the exception of appearing at funerals for Garfield, Grant, Arthur, and others, he disappeared, largely forgotten, from the public eye. What is most interesting, his political philosophy changed in his later years. Strongly influenced by the social criticism of Henry George, Mark Twain, and William Dean Howells, he worried about the emergence of monopolies, the decline of fair competition, the deteriorating condition of labor, and the general corrupting influence that "vast accumulations of wealth" had on society.

As he lamented the course the country was taking, Lucy suffered a stroke in June, 1889, and died a few days later. Although the shock of her passing affected him deeply, he busied himself with a heavy regime of travel and work. While in Cleveland on business in January, 1893, he suffered a sharp chest pain and his son hurried him back to Fremont. Bedridden, he talked of plans to travel, yet knew that he was "going where Lucy is." He died late in the evening of January 17.

Hayes's Presidency in Retrospect

Despite the political turbulence that marked his years in office, historians have tended to view the Hayes administration as something of a calming, transitional regime during which the nation withdrew from the turmoil of Reconstruction and settled down after the Grant years. Reconstruction was ended—with bitterness and acrimony in some quarters, with relief in others. After five years of depression the economy revived and stabilized, perhaps aided, as Hayes believed, by specie resumption. The nation continued its emergence as an industrial power, with all the attendant problems of business concentration, labor unrest, and market expansion.

In their periodic evaluations of presidential performance, historians and other commentators have consistently ranked that of Hayes toward the top and more recently in the middle of the "average" category. Hayes might well have been satisfied with this ranking given the difficulties he faced. Handicapped from the beginning by his disputed title, Hayes entered the office of the presidency in the midst of economic depression and would have to preside over the bitter end of Reconstruction. With the exception of a Republican Senate during the first two years of his administration, he had to work with a hostile Democratic Congress, and he often faced considerable congressional opposition from within his own party. Some of his problems, however, were of his own making. Hayes proved far more adept at seeking the office than in occupying it effectively. Once in the presidency, he was often too independent and high-minded for his own good, too much the nonpartisan nationalist and too little the pragmatic party politician. At times he appeared to lack the drive and a good sense of the best means of achieving his often laudatory goals. In the case of civil service reform, he seemed content to do what he could on his own and to make general recommendations to Congress, but he never pushed vigorously, working and lobbying with Congress, for specific reform legislation. At other times, as in the case of his Southern policy, he was too abrupt in choosing his course and then too resolute in adhering to it. Often he would have been better served if he had listened to others than his cabinet advisers and worked with party leaders to make adjustments in his programs and policies. In an age of close party divisions in Congress, he also needed to establish a working relationship with powerful factions in the party, but on the whole he failed to do so.

These factors and others clearly limited his performance. His two primary goals when he entered the office—to promote sectional reconciliation and civil service reform—were achieved only to a limited extent. Some recent historians have been particularly harsh in evaluating his Southern policy—especially his misplaced trust in southern conservatives to treat African Americans fairly. Yet even in retrospect viable alternatives are not apparent given the overriding racial problems. Although Congress ignored his pleas for civil service reform and he often failed to live up to his own standards in appointments, he did lay some important groundwork for later reform efforts. With his attempts to win greater control over appointments from Congress and his vetoes of the Democratic riders, he also restored some of the independence and power to the executive branch that had been lost beginning with the presidency of Andrew Johnson. Finally, Hayes worked diligently to restore respectability and a measure of dignity to the office. This was perhaps his chief legacy when he left the presidency in 1881.

Terry L. Seip

Bibliographical References

The standard biography is Harry Barnard, *Rutherford B. Hayes and His America*, 1954, but the White House years are covered more thoroughly in Kenneth E. Davison, *The Presidency of Rutherford B. Hayes*, 1972. Hayes's wartime experiences are perceptively treated in T. Harry Williams, *Hayes of the Twenty-Third: The Civil War Volunteer Officer*, 1965. Hayes's wife is the subject of Emily A. Geer's detailed *First Lady: The Life of Lucy Webb Hayes*, 1984. For an overview of the Hayes presidency, see Ari A. Hoogenboom, *The Presidency of Rutherford B. Hayes*, 1988, and also by Hoogenboom, the biography *Rutherford B. Hayes: Warrior and President*, 1995. The complex, behind-the-scenes negotiations during the electoral dispute are detailed in C. Vann Woodward, *Reunion and Reaction: The Compromise of 1877 and the End of Reconstruction*, 1951, but Woodward's emphasis on economic dealings is questioned in Keith I. Polakoff, *The Politics of Inertia: The Election of 1876 and the End of Reconstruction*, 1973, and sharply disputed in Michael L. Benedict, "Southern Democrats in the Crisis of 1876-1877: A Reconsideration of Reunion and Reaction," in *Journal of Southern History* 46 (November, 1980), 489-524. A consistent diary keeper, Hayes left a valuable record of his administration, which Williams edited as *Hayes: The Diary of a President, 1875-1881*, 1964. Vincent P. De Santis, *Republicans Face the Southern Question: The New Departure Years, 1877-1897*, 1959, and Stanley P. Hirshson, *Farewell to the Bloody Shirt: Northern Republicans and the Southern Negro, 1877-1893*, 1962, cover Hayes's Southern policy. A more recent critical view of the Hayes presidency and his policy toward the South is William Gillette, *Retreat from Reconstruction, 1869-1879*, 1979. Since 1976, the *Hayes Historical Journal: A Journal of the Gilded Age*, published semiannually by the Hayes Presidential Center, has featured scholarly articles on Hayes and his times.

James A. Garfield

20th President, 1881

Born: November 19, 1831
Orange Township, Ohio
Died: September 19, 1881
Elberon, New Jersey

Political Party: Republican
Vice President: Chester A. Arthur

Cabinet Members
Secretary of State: James G. Blaine
Secretary of the Treasury: William Windom
Secretary of War: Robert Todd Lincoln
Secretary of the Navy: William Hunt
Attorney General: Wayne MacVeagh

Postmaster General: Thomas James
Secretary of the Interior: S. J. Kirkwood

Garfield's official portrait. *(White House Historical Society)*

It was hardly a coincidence that one of James Abram Garfield's campaign biographies was written by Horatio Alger. The last president to have been born in a log cabin, Garfield seemed to have stepped out of the pages of one of Alger's novels. Born in Orange Township near Cleveland, Ohio, on November 19, 1831, left fatherless as an infant, reared in rural poverty by his plucky mother, canal boy, carpenter, student (at what would later be Hiram College and then at Williams College in Massachusetts), preacher in the Disciples of Christ denomination, professor of ancient languages, Civil War hero, and eight-term congressman, he combined in one career the politically potent themes of home, mother, school, church, and country. Above all, he seemed to embody the American dream of upward mobility. As Rutherford B. Hayes put it, "The boy on the tow path has become in truth the scholar and the gentleman by his own unaided work. He is the ideal candidate because he is the ideal self-made man."

The real James A. Garfield was more complex than this caricature. A scholarly, introspective man, lacking in self-confidence, he projected an aura of amiability that misled some into dismissing him as a shallow backslapper. Actually, he was a misplaced intellectual cast into the world of action. Gifted with a prodigious memory and a fanatic capacity for sustained intellectual effort, he seemed more at home in the classroom or library than in the rough-and-tumble of the political arena. Yet he never lost an election in his life, and in a political environment characterized by blood feuds and bitter personal vendettas, he stood out as a man virtually without enemies.

It was this quality of accommodation as much as anything else that led to his surprise nomination for president in 1880. Garfield had come to the Republican National Convention in Chicago as the floor manager for Ohio's John Sherman. The leading candidate was Ulysses S. Grant, whose third-term bid was led by New York's haughty and imperious boss, Roscoe Conkling. A great hater, Conkling was not even on speaking terms with James G. Blaine, Grant's leading competitor for the nomination, nor had he ever forgiven Sherman for his role in firing Conkling's protégé, Chester A. Arthur, from his post as collector of the port of New York. Riven by such deep personal and factional fissures, the convention deadlocked, with neither the friends of Grant (the so-called Stalwarts) nor his opponents willing to yield to the other. On the thirty-sixth ballot, the convention spontaneously and dramatically turned to Garfield, who was not an avowed candidate but who was the one man acceptable to all elements of the party. Arthur was chosen as his running mate as a sop to the Stalwarts.

The Republican presidential nominee had all the makings of an attractive candidate: muscular, 6 feet tall, with a full beard (though balding) and a golden voice. He would have been an eloquent, persuasive campaigner had not nineteenth century convention dictated that presidential candidates should pretend not to

electioneer on their own behalf as did candidates for lesser office. Garfield ingeniously evaded this restriction by inventing what would later be called the front porch campaign: staying at home in Mentor and greeting visiting delegations with noncampaigning campaign speeches.

His victory in November was the closest on record: only a 7,368 vote plurality over the Democratic candidate, Winfield Scott Hancock, less than one-tenth of 1 percent of the total vote cast. This narrow margin dramatized the necessity for party unity. Had any Republican other than Garfield been nominated, he very likely would have lost the votes of some members of the rival faction and thereby lost the election. The cultivation of Republican unity, therefore, became Garfield's first order of business as president.

An Aborted Presidency

The new president tried his best, but the gap between Republican factions was too wide to be bridged by good intentions. The first signs of trouble appeared even before the inauguration with the construction of the cabinet. When the choice post of secretary of state was offered to Blaine, Conkling demanded the right to choose the equally prestigious secretary of the treasury. His choice was unacceptable to Garfield. Rather than compromise, Conkling attempted to force his followers to boycott the ungrateful administration. With remarkable patience, the president persisted in his attempts to placate Conkling and his friends by offering them other offices.

Now it was Blaine's turn to be alarmed. He induced Garfield to appoint William H. Robertson as collector of the port of New York. Since Robertson was a Conkling foe, it was hardly surprising that the New York senator strongly opposed the appointment. Realizing that he was being whipsawed between the rival factions of his party, Garfield attempted to reach an understanding with Conkling, but the

The assassination of Garfield. *(Library of Congress)*

been in decline. The impeachment trial of Andrew Johnson represented the low point of that decline. The passive presidential style of Grant and the clouded title of Hayes had not appreciably strengthened the office. Now, by accepting the challenge of a powerful senator, Garfield was making a dramatic test of the potential power residing in the White House.

His victory was complete. Not only was the Robertson appointment confirmed, but also Conkling and his fellow New York senator, Thomas Platt, resigned their seats in protest. By destroying Conkling, Garfield had dramatically enhanced the power of his office and set the presidency on the road to the twentieth century.

Although the struggle against senatorial courtesy overshadowed all else, there were other significant activities in the early days of the Garfield administration. Since the House of Representatives was not in session, no legislation could be introduced, but the executive departments were off to a strong start. Postmaster General Thomas James was considering a plan to reform the patronage abuses of the postal system. Discovery of an earlier abuse of the so-called Star Route postal service spurred Attorney General Wayne MacVeagh to launch an investigation, even though the suspects were highly placed Republicans. Secretary of Treasury William Windom triumphantly refunded the national debt, and Secretary of the Navy William Hunt took the first significant steps since the Civil War to rebuild the decaying United States Navy. The most vigorous activity came from the State Department, where Blaine was attempting to reorient American foreign policy rom its traditional emphasis on Europe

arrogant senator rejected any compromise and declared war on his own party's leader. This drove Garfield firmly back into Blaine's camp, where his inclinations probably would have led him in any event.

What had begun as a petty patronage squabble now escalated into a struggle for the soul of the Republican Party. Conkling represented machine politics in its most narrow and retrogressive form; Blaine and Garfield were groping for a more modern national organization capable of promoting industrial growth and an aggressive foreign policy.

When Conkling undertook to block Robertson's appointment by invoking the hallowed principle of "senatorial courtesy," the struggle took on the aspect of a constitutional crisis. Garfield's stand could now be portrayed as a struggle for presidential independence from congressional dictation. Ever since the Civil War, the power of the presidential office had

to a greater concern with what today would be called the Third World, especially Latin America.

The president's energies were largely consumed by patronage matters. With more than a hundred thousand government offices needing to be filled, with office seekers hovering around him as eager as "vultures for a wounded bison," he had time for little else. "My services ought to be worth more to the government than to be thus spent," he wearily concluded, and he began to consider schemes for general civil service reform. He was also considering a fresh approach to the perennial Southern problem, which would feature federal aid to education as the solution for black economic and political handicaps.

Nothing came of any of these initiatives. On July 2, 1881, after only 120 days in office, Garfield was cut down by a crazed religious fanatic, Charles Julius Guiteau. The president lingered for another eighty days amid the glare of morbid public curiosity and died on September 19.

What sort of president Garfield might have become had he been spared can never be determined with certainty. John Hay, Abraham Lincoln's private secretary, thought that Garfield had entered office with better training and greater intellectual endowments than any president for more than half a century. After a shaky beginning, his administration was beginning to live up to that glowing assessment, until Guiteau's bullets brought it to an abrupt end, leaving it to enter history only as a question mark.

Allan Peskin

Bibliographical References

After a spate of campaign and memorial biographies in 1880 and 1881, Garfield was neglected until the 1925 publication of Theodore C. Smith's monumental but careless *The Life and Letters of James Abram Garfield*. It was finally superseded by the simultaneous appearance in 1978 of Margaret P. Leech and Harry James Brown, *The Garfield Orbit*, and Allan Peskin, *Garfield*. Garfield's inner life is presented with remarkable candor in Brown and Frederick D. Williams, eds., *The Diary of James A. Garfield*, 1967-1981. The fourth (and final) volume deals with the presidency. Also on the presidency is Justus D. Doenecke, *The Presidencies of James A. Garfield and Chester A. Arthur*, 1981. For an insight into Garfield's courtship and marriage and details of his daily life between 1853 and 1881, see John Shaw, ed., *Crete and James: Personal Letters of Lucretia and James Garfield*, 1994. Other biographical treatments are Richard O. Bates, *The Gentleman from Ohio: An Introduction to Garfield*, 1973, and Hendrik Booraem, *The Road to Respectability: James A. Garfield and His World, 1844-1852*, 1988. For a highly readable survey of the politics of the Gilded Age, see H. Wayne Morgan, *From Hayes to McKinley*, 1969. Robert D. Marcus, *Grand Old Party*, 1971, traces the growth of party organization during those years, and Ari Hoogenboom, *Outlawing the Spoils*, 1961, clarifies Garfield's split with Conkling. James C. Clark, *The Murder of James A. Garfield: The President's Last Days and the Trial of His Assassin*, 1993, recounts Garfield's death. For a detailed annotated list of primary and secondary resources, see Robert O. Rupp, *James A. Garfield: A Bibliography*, 1997.

Chester A. Arthur

21st President, 1881-1885

Born: October 5, 1829
      Fairfield, Vermont
Died: November 18, 1886
      New York, New York

Political Party: Republican
Vice President: none

Cabinet Members

Secretary of State: Frederick T. Frelinghuysen
Secretary of the Treasury: Charles J. Folger, Walter
    Q. Gresham, Hugh McCulloch

Secretary of War: Robert Todd Lincoln
Secretary of the Navy: William E. Chandler
Attorney General: Benjamin J. Brewster
Postmaster General: Thomas James, Timothy O.
    Howe, Walter Q. Gresham, Frank Hatton
Secretary of the Interior: Henry M. Teller

Arthur's official portrait. *(White House Historical Society)*

In American political folklore, the career of Chester Alan Arthur reads something like Hans Christian Andersen's tale of the Ugly Duckling. In this fable, Chet Arthur, a faintly corrupt, highly partisan politician, is magically transformed into a competent, dignified, mildly reformist president, much to everyone's delight and astonishment. As a contemporary put it, "No man ever entered the Presidency so profoundly and widely distrusted as Chester Alan Arthur, and no one ever retired from the highest civil trust of the world more generally respected, alike by political friend and foe."

A Victorian Gentleman

In truth, however, this alleged transformation was not as startling as it has been portrayed. The prepresidential Chet Arthur was not the ugly spoilsman that many believed him to be, nor was President Arthur quite as successful as some have painted him. Instead of the two

Arthurs of folklore, there was only one: an exceedingly competent, intellectually limited Victorian gentleman, ponderous and self-centered but loyal to the code of whatever station he found himself called upon to occupy.

Chester Alan (rhymes with salon) Arthur was born on October 5, 1829, in a remote corner of Vermont, close enough to the Canadian border to give rise to later charges that he was actually born on the wrong side. He was the fifth child and the first son of William Arthur, a college-educated Baptist minister with abolitionist leanings who had emigrated from Ulster almost a decade earlier.

Young Chester dutifully pursued a traditional course of study at Schenectady's Union College, taught school briefly, and then studied law. A mildly successful attorney who occasionally defended runaway slaves, he naturally gravitated to the infant Republican Party. Latching onto the coattails of New York's governor, Edwin D. Morgan, Arthur joined his staff and on the outbreak of the Civil War was appointed quartermaster general of the state, a position that enabled him to use the politically potent title of General in later years.

Energetic and efficient, Arthur made himself useful to the state and to his party, fitting himself so smoothly into the New York Republican machinery that when the imperious Roscoe Conkling assumed its control after the war, he inherited Arthur along with the party organization. By this time, Arthur had become a family man, with two children from his marriage to Ellen Herndon, the musically gifted daughter of a naval captain who had heroically gone down with his ship.

Family and private life, however, took a back seat to politics. Arthur was the perfect organization man, loyally working his way up to the powerful and lucrative position of collector of the port of New York. Arthur himself was impeccably honest. "If I had misappropriated five cents," he once said, "and on walking down-town saw two men talking on the street together, I would imagine they were talking of my dishonesty, and the very thought would drive me mad." The post over which he presided, however, was such a foul nest of corruption and blatant partisanship that when Arthur was fired by President Rutherford B. Hayes, it could be portrayed as a blow for honest government. Conkling and his friends did not see it that way, and Arthur's dismissal only widened the breach between these so-called Stalwarts and the rest of the Republican Party.

Garfield's Assassination

Arthur's surprise nomination as vice president in 1880 did not heal that breach. Conkling soon turned his wrath upon the new president, James A. Garfield. Arthur loyally stood by his old friend as they tried to bring down the administration of which Arthur was vice president. Conkling and Arthur roomed together and plotted together and were associated in the public mind. When Garfield was shot, in July of 1881, that association almost destroyed Arthur's reputation. It did not help matters that the crazed assassin, Charles J. Guiteau, exulted, "I am a Stalwart! Arthur is now president!"

Had Garfield died instantly, it is unlikely that the public would have accepted Arthur, but during the eighty days in which the wounded president clung to life, Arthur displayed such tact and dignity that his star began to rise. In fact, the low esteem in which Arthur had been held may actually have worked in his favor. After such initial low expectations, any sign of competence on his part would be greeted with pleased surprise.

The new president was far from incompetent, and he well realized the delicacy of his situation. Like William Shakespeare's Prince Hal, once he assumed power, he abandoned the disreputable companions of his youth. When Conkling pressed him to continue the feud with Garfield's followers, Arthur repudiated his former benefactor, which earned for him a place on Conkling's lengthy list of enemies. To balance the score, Arthur also removed from the cabinet Conkling's prime enemy, Secretary of State James G. Blaine, along with all the other holdovers from Garfield's cabinet, except for Secretary of War Robert Todd Lincoln. This posture may have been intended to demonstrate manly independence, but its practical result was to alienate Arthur from all the factions that constituted the Republican Party. Arthur had assumed not only the presidency but also the leadership of a bitterly divided party. Rather than healing those divisions, his policies only excerbated them.

Such a course might seem strange in a man whose whole life had been devoted to politics, but, as historian H. Wayne Morgan perceptively notes, "Arthur was less a politician than an organizer and administrator." Essentially a technician, he was incapable of building a personal following or generating grass-roots appeal. A languid, urbane, intensely private man, Arthur lacked the common touch.

Under his supervision, the White House attained an elegance that it had not known for generations. The mansion itself was refurbished in high Victorian style under the direction of Louis Tiffany. The president, a portly 6-footer with well-combed sideburns, made a striking host. Because of the death of his wife early in 1880, the president's sister, Mrs. John McElroy, served as official hostess, planning the twelve-course meals that her gourmet brother enjoyed. For the first time since the Grant administration, wine flowed freely at the White House. When a temperance spokeswoman urged him to continue the abstinence policy of "Lemonade Lucy" Hayes, Arthur frostily replied, "Madame, I may be President of the United States but my private life is nobody's damned business"—a remark that fairly summed up his attitude toward the office he held.

A Passive Conception of the Presidency

Presidents in the nineteenth century were not supposed to be bold or innovative statesmen. Except during wartime, they were expected merely to staff and administer the executive departments, enforce the laws, and generally follow the lead of Congress. This passive conception of the presidency was congenial to Arthur's temperament as well as to his political philosophy. Consequently, it is hardly surprising that his list of domestic accomplishments (including his chief pride—lowering the cost of first-class postage from three to two cents) seems meager by present-day standards.

Arthur was not devoid of ideas, but he seldom pursued them vigorously. He advocated government control of the railroads, but he was content to make the suggestion and then let the matter drop. He flirted with tariff reform and even appointed a commission to study the matter. It recommended a general reduction of duties, but Congress was otherwise inclined. It passed the Mongrel Tariff of 1883, which increased the duty level for most goods. The president passively signed the bill into law. On two occasions, Arthur did bestir himself to veto significant bills but then failed to follow through. When Congress passed a Chinese exclusion act, contradictory to the spirit of existing treaties, Arthur interposed his veto. The revised legislation made only minor changes, but the president professed himself to be satisfied and allowed the bill to become law. A pork-barrel rivers and harbors appropriation bill also proved unpalatable to the president. This time, Congress contemptuously overrode his veto. Content with having made a gesture, Arthur pulled no strings to ensure that his veto would be sustained.

Constitutionally, presidents have more leeway in foreign affairs than in domestic matters, so it is hardly surprising that more activity was displayed by the State Department than by many other branches of the executive arm. Yet, even here, the activity was essentially negative—to undo the innovations inaugurated by Blaine.

Protected by its oceans, preoccupied with its internal development, the United States had stood aloof from the rest of the world ever since the end of the War of 1812. The State Department made do with only a few dozen permanent employees, and the secretaryship was often a refuge for influential, gentlemanly politicians. According to Hayes's secretary of state, William M. Evarts, "There are just two rules at the State Department: one, that no business is ever done out of business hours; and the other is, that no business is ever done *in* business hours."

Garfield's secretary of state, the dynamic, ambitious James G. Blaine, could hardly be expected to conform to this leisurely pace. He busied himself especially with Latin America, injecting American influence into the many and various quarrels that were then upsetting the continent's peace. Dissatisfied with these piecemeal adjustments—"patching up a peace treaty between two countries today, securing a truce between two others tomorrow"—he determined to institute a more comprehensive continental policy to be inaugurated at a grand pan-American conference. Plans for the conference were under way when Garfield was shot. Blaine attempted to secure Arthur's approval for the project, but when no satisfactory answer was forthcoming, he resigned from the cabinet. He was succeeded by Frederick T. Frelinghuysen, a cautious New Jersey aristocrat who promptly repudiated all of Blaine's flamboyant initiatives and set American foreign policy back on its traditional unenterprising course.

The activities of most of the other executive departments were equally lackluster. At the Justice Department, Attorney General Ben-

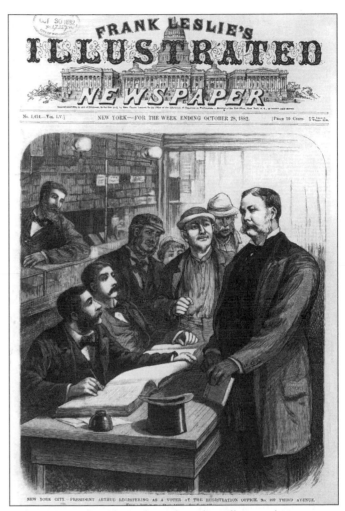

A drawing on the cover of *Frank Leslie's Illustrated Newspaper* shows Arthur registering to vote in New York City in October, 1882. *(Library of Congress)*

jamin J. Brewster botched the prosecution of the Star Route case, a scandalous post office fraud dating from the Hayes administration that involved some of Arthur's former cronies. The other cabinet posts were managed with routine competence, with the most notable flashes of energy coming from the Navy Department where New Hampshire's William E. Chandler vigorously laid the foundation for the new navy. It was badly needed. In the early 1880's, the American war fleet was so weak, obsolete, and impotent that some officials feared even a fourth-rate power such as Chile

A political cartoon shows a crowd of corrupt politicians protesting Arthur's attempts at civil service reform. *(Library of Congress)*

readjusters, greenbackers, maverick Democrats, and independents. He came tantalizingly close to success in some states, but nowhere was he able to break the grip of the white Democrats. The Solid South remained solid.

Political problems dogged the Arthur administration in the North and the West as well as in the South. The midterm elections of 1882 produced some of the worst Republican setbacks of the decade. Aided by a faltering economy and a rudderless opposition, the Democrats not only recaptured the House of Representatives but also enjoyed a comfortable margin of more than eighty seats. The New York canvass was an especially bitter defeat for the president. He had personally intervened in the gubernatorial contest, pulling all the administration's strings to secure the nomination of his crony Charles J. Folger and so alienated his party in the process that Folger was inundated by a margin of more than two hundred thousand votes. This result was not only a personal repudiation of Arthur's leadership, but it also gave a boost to the meteoric rise of the victorious Democratic governor, Grover Cleveland.

could sweep it from the seas. By the 1890's, the seeds Chandler had planted would blossom into the fleet that would win for the United States an empire from Spain.

Chandler was equally active in politics, having been given the task of rebuilding the shattered Republican organizations in the Southern states. In this assignment, success eluded him, but not for want of trying. With the abandonment of Reconstruction in the mid-1870's, the Bourbon Democrats were everywhere resurgent, creating the "Solid South." Southern blacks, the backbone of the Republican Party in the region, were intimidated, demoralized, and disfranchised. Seeing no hope for success from that quarter, Chandler bypassed the largely black, regular Republican Southern organizations and relied instead on alliances with dissident Southern whites. There was no consistency in his program other than "Anything to beat the Bourbons!" He tried alliances with

The Pendleton Act: The Death of the Spoils System

After these reversals, the lame duck Republican Congress was receptive to new issues that might win back its disaffected electorate. Reform of the civil service held attractive political potential. The cause had steadily been gaining popular support ever since the Grant administration, and after the assassination of Garfield by a crazed job seeker, it even had a sanctified martyr. If the Republicans could get credit for enacting the reform, independent voters might turn to the party out of gratitude; if, despite all, the Democrats should win the 1884 election, then civil service reform would lock thousands of Republican officeholders into their jobs, safe from Democratic dismissal. Democrats, not surprisingly, sniffed at civil service reform as poisoned bait, even though one of their own, Ohio's Democratic senator George Pendleton, had given his name to the measure. Enough of them voted for it, however, to enable it to pass Congress and be sent to the president for his signature.

Signing the Pendleton Act is generally regarded as the greatest accomplishment of the Arthur presidency, and some have found a delicious irony in the fact that a once-notorious spoilsman presided over the death of the spoils system. Actually, the bill was not the sort of civil service reform that Arthur had in mind when he had earlier recommended "discreet reform." Like all presidents, Arthur was anxious to support any measure that would relieve him of the frightful pressure exerted by hopeful office seekers, but, like all politicians, he was distrustful of competitive examinations and lifetime tenure. He supported the Pendleton Act with misgivings; a man with his past to live down could hardly afford to oppose it.

Personal ambition played no part in Arthur's action. In 1882, he learned that he was suffering from Bright's disease and had at best only a few years to live. He kept his fatal condition secret from the world and even went through the motions of seeking renomination. Even had he been in perfect health, it is unlikely that he would have been nominated by the Republican Party, all of whose factions he had managed to alienate. Instead, the party turned to his chief rival and longtime foe, James G. Blaine. Arthur became only the third incumbent president, after Millard Fillmore and Franklin Pierce, to be so humiliated by his own party. He sat out the rest of the election on the sidelines, taking grim satisfaction in Blaine's narrow defeat.

Arthur's last official act as president was signing the bill that restored pension rights to his dying predecessor, Ulysses S. Grant. Arthur soon followed Grant to the grave, dying on November 18, 1886, only twenty months after the conclusion of his own competent but undistinguished presidency.

Allan Peskin

Bibliographical References

Thomas C. Reeves, *Gentleman Boss: The Life of Chester Alan Arthur*, 1975, is perhaps the last word on Arthur's life. It thoroughly supersedes the former standard biography by George F. Howe, *Chester A. Arthur*, 1934. Arthur's administration is detailed in Justus D. Doenecke, *The Presidencies of James A. Garfield and Chester A. Arthur*, 1981. The most important event of Arthur's presidency is thoroughly examined by Ari Hoogenboom, *Outlawing the Spoils*, 1961. For foreign policy, see David M. Pletcher, *The Awkward Years: American Foreign Relations Under Garfield and Arthur*, 1961. For Southern affairs, see Vincent P. De Santis, *Republicans Face the Southern Question*, 1959. The best and most readable survey of Gilded Age politics can be found in H. Wayne Morgan, *From Hayes to McKinley*, 1969.

Grover Cleveland

22d President, 1885-1889

24th President, 1893-1897

Born: March 18, 1837
    Caldwell, New Jersey
Died: June 24, 1908
    Princeton, New Jersey

Political Party: Democratic
Vice Presidents: Thomas A. Hendricks,
    Adlai E. Stevenson

Cabinet Members (1st Administration)
Secretary of State: Thomas F. Bayard
Secretary of the Treasury: Daniel Manning,
    Charles S. Fairchild
Secretary of War: William C. Endicott

Cleveland's official portrait. *(White House Historical Society)*

Secretary of the Navy: William C. Whitney
Attorney General: A. H. Garland
Postmaster General: William F. Vilas, Don M.
    Dickinson
Secretary of the Interior: L. Q. R. Lamar, William
    F. Vilas
Secretary of Agriculture: Norman J. Colman

Cabinet Members (2d Administration)
Secretary of State: Walter Q. Gresham, Richard
    Olney
Secretary of the Treasury: John G. Carlisle
Secretary of War: Daniel S. Lamont
Secretary of the Navy: Hilary A. Herbert
Attorney General: Richard Olney, Judson Harmon
Postmaster General: Wilson S. Bissel, William L.
    Wilson
Secretary of the Interior: Hoke Smith, David R.
    Francis
Secretary of Agriculture: J. Sterling Morton

Stephen Grover Cleveland was a notably confident man during an age when confidence came naturally to prosperous men. An observer could read Cleveland's personal and political

338

philosophy in his body and face. He was a big man and grossly overweight. He moved slowly, cautiously, and often with great effort. Sitting behind a desk, however, he was tireless, capable of working continuously for twenty-four hours or more at exacting mental labor. His face was stoic and phlegmatic. A walrus mustache and several chins hid his lower face from the world. Only his eyes, surprisingly innocent and kind, gave a hint at the man inside. In public he seldom spoke, but when he did it was with confidence and conviction. He had faith in his beliefs, and he never doubted—indeed, he may never have questioned—that he was right.

"The Mugwump Party" and Cleveland, by G. Y. Coffin, 1884. *(Library of Congress)*

A Man of Definite Convictions

Faith and confidence were his at birth. Richard Cleveland, his father, was a Yale-educated preacher. Born in Caldwell, New Jersey, on March 18, 1837, Grover, the fifth of nine children, inherited his father's strong and unquestioning Presbyterian faith. Richard Cleveland was a kind, gentle man, but not a prosperous one. He died when Grover was sixteen, and he left his son little more than the fruits of conscientious rearing.

Financial pressures forced Grover Cleveland to find a job. For a year he lived in New York City and taught at the New York Institute of the Blind, a task he found as unrewarding mentally as financially. Like many men of his generation, he then decided that his fortune and future waited in the West. His western trek ended abruptly, however, in Buffalo, New York, where his wealthy uncle, Lewis P. Allen, who exerted considerable influence in the Buffalo area, soon found Cleveland a job as a clerk in a solid and respectable local law firm. After four years of study, Cleveland, in 1859, was admitted to the bar. For the next twenty-three years, he practiced law in virtual public anonymity. Never a showman, he disliked appearing in the courtroom and instead tried whenever possible to settle a case before it went to court. Hardworking, fair, and possessing absolute integrity, Cleveland aptly and conscientiously mastered the details of each case and plodded his way toward a just settlement.

Life in Buffalo suited him. He had his work and his friends, and he seldom expressed much interest in the world around him. Even the Civil War failed to excite him greatly. He was unsympathetic with the crusade against slavery, although he believed the Union should be preserved. He did not, however, feel impelled to take up arms to save the Union. He had a mother and several sisters to support; these were concrete duties in his mind. Thus while two of his brothers enlisted, Grover hired a substitute for $150.

Cleveland never expressed regret over his decision not to enlist. Nor did he ever lament his relatively uneventful years in Buffalo. He enjoyed an unimaginative social and intellectual life. Work and duty compelled him to study law; simple curiosity never pushed him much further. Outside of the poetry of Alfred, Lord Tennyson, he had no love for literature and was strikingly uneducated in the classics. He was similarly uninterested in attending church or working his way into Buffalo's genteel society.

A bachelor until late in life, Cleveland enjoyed the company of other men. Although not a heavy drinker, he was drawn to the nightlife offered at cozy street-corner saloons. A plate of pickled herring, Swiss cheese, and chops suited his appetite. A quart of beer quenched his thirst. A day of hunting or night of card playing satisfied his entertainment needs. There were women in his life, but they were not the kind he thought of marrying. With one,

a widow named Maria Halpin, Cleveland may have fathered a son. Although Cleveland doubted that he was the father, he did accept financial responsibility for the child.

The Veto Mayor

However unimaginative and dull Cleveland seemed, something nevertheless burned inside him. Perhaps it was personal ambition, perhaps it was a desire to make Buffalo a better place. Probably it was a combination of the two. Whatever it was, it pushed him into politics. In 1863 he was elected a ward supervisor and then assistant district attorney of Erie County. Seven years later, at the age of thirty-two, he was elected sheriff of Buffalo County. The job paid well, and Cleveland performed well. As sheriff he showed the strengths on which he would later base his political career. He worked hard and he strove to make his post a model of honesty and efficiency. Nor did he balk at difficult tasks. When he had to press the lever to hang two convicts, he did so. In 1873, when his three-year term as sheriff ended, he went back to his law office.

He returned to politics in a much larger role in 1881. In that year the Democratic Party nominated him to run for mayor of Buffalo. Wealthy, influential Democrats turned to Cleveland because they wanted to rid their city of inefficiency and corruption. Cleveland, who had an unassailable reputation for honesty and hard work, certainly spoke their language. "We believe," he said, "in the principle of economy of the people's money, and that when a man in office lays out a dollar in extravagance, he acts immorally by the people." With the Tweed Ring still a haunting memory, Cleveland's words also struck a soothing chord with the voters, and he was elected mayor. As always, Cleveland proved to be a man of his

"Another Voice for Cleveland"—a reference to his alleged illegitimate child. *(Library of Congress)*

word. He was quick to veto all inappropriate or corrupt appropriations. Overly legalistic, he never exceeded delegated authority, but he did provide Buffalo with efficient and honest leadership. He even made small gains in the area of public health by expanding Buffalo's inadequate sewer system.

Cleveland's political ambitions and fortunes rose fast. Less than one-half year after becoming mayor of Buffalo, he was seeking support for a bid at the governorship of New York. Again backed by the wealthy Democratic business community and favored by incredible luck, Cleveland moved forward. When the Republicans nominated machine-controlled Charles J. Folger for governor, the Democrats saw their chance. Popular sentiment was against urban machines, the corruption and inefficiency of which were well publicized. Clearly, Cleveland was free of machine ties and as honest as Boss Tweed was corrupt. He was the right man at the right time in the right place. The powerful and wealthy New York Democratic organizer William C. Whitney realized this. As he told Democratic state chairman Daniel Manning, "The man who can defeat the Republicans worst is that buxom Buffalonian, Grover Cleveland. You up-State Democrats want to unite with the New York Democracy on Cleveland, and we'll not only elect him Governor this fall but President a little later."

The two Democratic groups united, and in the fall Cleveland was swept into office in a landslide. Both Democrats and reform-minded Republicans voted for the largely unknown candidate. They wanted honest government, efficient government. This—and little more—Cleveland was prepared to give them.

Cleveland took office on January 3, 1883. Before his inauguration he penned a telling and worried letter to his brother, the Reverend William N. Cleveland. He wrote that he wanted "to do some good to the people of the state. I know there is room for it, and I know that

I am honest and sincere in that desire to do well, but the question is whether I know enough to accomplish what I desire." His concern was well founded. As governor his honesty and ignorance led him to political triumphs and social failures.

In the governor's office, as he had in the mayor's office, Cleveland used his veto power freely. Poorly drafted bills and bills of questionable constitutionality Cleveland quickly sent back to the legislature. His faith was in the letter of the law, not the spirit, and he used this strict interpretation of the Constitution to veto a wide range of socially progressive bills. He vetoed the popular five-cent fare bill, a measure aimed at reducing the cost of riding on the New York City elevated railroad, and he vetoed another bill that attempted to establish maximum hours for the conductors and drivers of horse-drawn streetcars. As a lawyer for corporations, he believed in an individual's freedom of contract. As governor he continued to act on those beliefs to block any regulation of working hours or wages.

The poor and the manual laborers were little served by Cleveland. Business leaders, however, found much to applaud. Cleveland did bring order, economy, and efficiency—"good government"—to the state. His appointments were made to improve government, not to satisfy the desires of political machines. This position brought Cleveland into conflict with Tammany Hall, New York's most powerful machine. It also split the Democratic Party in New York. The short-term results of Cleveland's actions, however, pleased wealthy reformers. They had found their champion in the honest and conservative politician from Buffalo.

The Campaign of 1884: Bourbon Democrats and Mugwumps

By late 1883 Cleveland certainly had his eyes on the White House. His future in New York State politics was problematic at best. By alienating Tammany Hall, he had badly hurt the state Democracy, and it is doubtful if he could have restored it to health. It was better and easier for Cleveland to move up the political ladder. Again fortune was on his side, for national Democratic leaders were looking for a candidate of Cleveland's beliefs and abilities. For most of the last third of the nineteenth century, Bourbon Democrats controlled the party. They spoke for the businessmen and railroad men, extolling the virtues of free enterprise and laissez-faire economics and fighting the demands of urban wage earners and farmers. They believed that government should be efficient and honest, but most of all they thought it should be inexpensive. This entailed restricting such government giveaways as the Civil War pensions and reducing such special favors as the high protective tariff. For the Bourbons, Cleveland's record as governor, and his conservative nature, were irresistible.

Cleveland's stock rose further after the Republicans chose James G. Blaine to carry their banner in 1884. In most ways an admirable and effective politician, Blaine's reputation still suffered from railroad scandals in which he had been involved during the 1870's. His nomination split the Republican Party. A group of "good government" reformers known as mugwumps vowed to vote for an honest Democrat rather than Blaine. Sensing their opportunity, Bourbon Democrats pushed through the nomination of Cleveland.

The 1884 campaign was notable for its circuslike atmosphere and mudslinging. Democrats and mugwumps reminded the voters of Blaine's dishonest past, harping on his unethical dealings with the Little Rock and Fort Smith Railroad and his duplicitous attempt to escape condemnation. In turn, Republicans unearthed Cleveland's indiscretions before he became mayor of Buffalo. Although no political or financial scandals clouded Cleveland's past, there was his illicit affair with Maria Halpin. "Ma, Ma, Where's My Pa?" became the Republican chant.

In truth, the campaign focused on personalities largely because of the parties' unwillingness to take stands on the major issues of the day. Neither Democratic nor Republican Party leaders wanted to alienate voters by talking too much about tariffs, monopolies, or the money question. In an age when presidential elections were always very close, a strong stand on a major issue could lead to defeat at the polls. It was easier instead to focus on Blaine's financial dealings and Cleveland's sexual life. As far as the Democrats were concerned, a mugwump summarized the campaign and the issues most clearly:

> We are told that Mr. Blaine has been delinquent in office but blameless in public life, while Mr. Cleveland has been a model of official integrity but culpable in his personal relations. We should therefore elect Mr. Cleveland to the public office which he is so well qualified to fill, and remand Mr. Blaine to the private station which he is admirably fitted to adorn.

In the end, the election may have been decided by several unwise political decisions Blaine made during the closing days of the campaign. On the morning of October 29, 1884, an exhausted Blaine met with a group of clergymen, whose spokesman told the Republican candidate that the Democratic Party was one of "Rum, Romanism, and Rebellion." Democrats seized on this remark, which Blaine did not challenge, to drive a wedge between Blaine and his Irish supporters. That night Blaine committed another mistake. He attended a fundraising dinner at Delmonico's that was attended by two hundred of the wealthiest men in America. Dubbing it the "prosperity dinner," newspaper editorialists and cartoonists used it to emphasize Blaine's support for the monied interests in America. A *New York World* cartoon showed "Belshazzar Blaine" eating terrapin and canvasback duck and sipping champagne while a starving family begged for crumbs.

Less than a week later, Cleveland won a

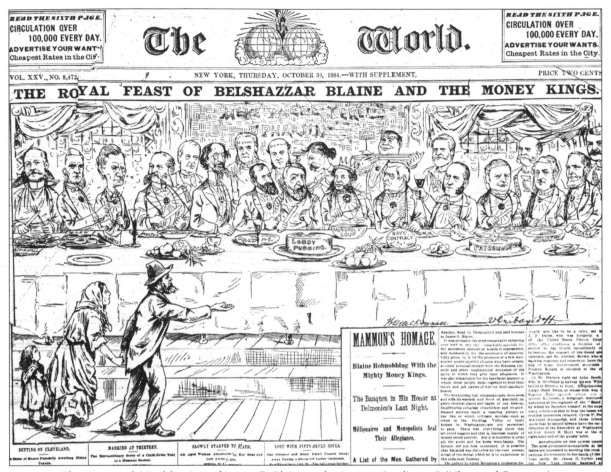

The *New York World*'s view of James G. Blaine at the "prosperity dinner." *(Library of Congress)*

narrow victory. The election was particularly close in New York, which Cleveland carried by a plurality of only 1,149 votes. Mugwump support, Bourbon politics, and Blaine's own mistakes had carried a Democrat into the White House, the first to make his home there in twenty-four years.

First Administration: Pensions, Tariffs, and the Nation's Currency

Cleveland was forty-eight when he took office. Short but weighing more than 250 pounds, he was clean-shaven, except for a mustache, during an age when most politicians wore beards. Close friends found him a boon companion on hunting and fishing trips, but in public he was cold and distant. Intellectually, he was much the same man that the citizens of Buffalo had elected mayor in 1881. His goals still included governmental efficiency and economy, and he was more than ever the friend of business. His cabinet reflected his leanings. Although it contained Bourbon Democrats from every section of the country, it contained no voice for farmers, wage earners, or blacks. For Cleveland and his cabinet, there would be no conflicts between "good government" and good business.

Cleveland never forgot his promise. He strived mightily to bring order, efficiency, and economy to every office under his control. Although he used his patronage power to reward Democrats, he appointed only well-qualified persons, and his cabinet members achieved commendable successes. Friend, adviser, and supporter William C. Whitney, who became Cleveland's secretary of the navy, proved particularly able. He worked closely with Cleveland and the leaders of American steel companies to construct a modern steel navy.

Nor were his business ties severed. He did not use his office to enrich his business friends, but his approach to most problems implicitly demonstrated a probusiness mentality. The Dawes Act of 1887, which Cleveland supported, aptly illustrates this. In a sincere attempt to integrate American Indians into American life, the act encouraged them to own land as individuals rather than as tribes. Of course, as free agents in a free country, they were then free to lease their land to loggers and real estate agents. Cleveland was not unethical or Machiavellian, but his policy soon proved disastrous for the tribal system.

Even Cleveland's approach to reform was influenced by his probusiness mentality. In his inaugural address, he had promised "reform in the administration of government, and the application of business principles to public affairs." This was not idle rhetoric. Cleveland saw no reason why government should not be run like a profitable business. Trim the fat and streamline the process—if it worked for the giant meatpackers in Chicago, Cleveland reasoned, it should work for the government in Washington, D.C.

Given the Republican tradition of high protective tariffs, liberal land grants and subsidy payments to railroads, and generous pension plans for veterans, Cleveland discovered plenty of fat to trim. He moved first against pension waste. Since the end of the Civil War, Grand Army of the Republic supporters in Congress had pushed through more than half a million pension bills, many involving cases of questionable merit. Cleveland was determined to stop this raid on the public treasury. Unlike presidents Grant and Hayes, he read carefully all the private pension bills that Congress

passed and sent on for his signature. What he read sickened him. About a fourth of the bills were based on fraudulent claims. Some of the more flagrant examples were cited by Allan Nevins:

> One claimant explained that he had been registered "at home" and had set out on horseback *intending* to complete his enlistment, that on the way his horse had fallen on his left ankle, and that he was thus entitled to a cripple's pension. A widow whose husband had been killed by a fall from a ladder in 1881 traced this to a slight flesh-wound in the calf of 1865! . . . One gallant private claimed that a disease of the eyes had resulted from army diarrhea.

These and more than two hundred like claims Cleveland unhesitatingly rejected, although he also signed nearly fifteen hundred private pension bills.

Cleveland moved beyond private pension bills in early 1887. In January of that year Congress passed a piece of legislation dubbed the "pauper's bill." It "offered pensions to all disabled veterans who had served honorably for at least ninety days and were dependent upon their own efforts for support." A veteran's disability did not have to be the result of his wartime activities; old age disabilities and nonmilitary injuries also qualified a veteran for a pension. Cleveland predictably vetoed the bill. Government, he implied, was not in the charity business.

Pension corruption was not the only pressing financial problem that Cleveland confronted. Currency and tariff issues proved to be more vexing and complex—and more important problems. Although in early 1885 some politicians feared that the Treasury's gold reserve was falling too low, by 1886 it had a surplus. Indeed, by 1888 the surplus amounted to $255 million, or $125 million in excess of what was needed to support the currency in circulation. The effect of this surplus was to depress the economy, and unless the government did something to reduce it, financial experts predicted there would be a depression.

Opportunities for disposing of the surplus abounded. Veterans and their supporters certainly wanted more and higher pensions. Other special interest groups also were anxious to get on the government's payroll. Some politicians wanted the government to purchase the telegraph business. Others sought to spend more money on harbors, internal improvements, and education. Still others wanted to reduce the excise taxes on whiskey and tobacco.

Cleveland rejected all these proposals. He and his advisers decided that the best way to reduce the surplus was to lower the tariff, thereby reducing the government's income. High protective tariffs, he maintained, taxed consumers for the benefit of protected industrialists and other producers. Lower tariffs would help rid America of specially privileged groups and enhance economic egalitarianism; it would force American producers to act in an economically efficient manner and reduce the cost of goods to consumers.

In 1887, Cleveland devoted his annual message to Congress exclusively to the need for tariff reform. This was the first time in history that a president's annual message concerned only one issue. He called for reductions on major consumer items and on the raw materials used to produce those items. In a moderate tone, he explained that laborers would benefit from his proposed reforms and that manufacturers would not be hurt.

Most people applauded Cleveland's speech, but such demonstrations of support did not move Congress. With an election less than a year away, most politicians did not want to run the risk of alienating any of their supporters. Never a strong leader and unpopular with most Democrats in Congress, Cleveland was unable to push through legislation to reform the tariff.

At the end of his first term in office, Cleveland's record was mixed. In an age marked by political manipulation and graft, he had returned a certain dignity to the office of the presidency. Honest and hardworking, he had tried with some success to impose those quali-

A crowd in Buffalo, New York, celebrates Cleveland's nomination for president. *(Library of Congress)*

ties on his administration. As a politician, however, he often had been tactless and closed-minded. He had lectured Congress rather than led it, and he had paid little attention to the urgent cries of hard-pressed farmers and laborers. Too often he had seen only Bourbon solutions to problems and had been impatient with even honest opposition.

The greatest event in Cleveland's personal life during his first term was his marriage. On June 2, 1886, the forty-nine-year-old president wed Frances Folsom, an attractive and well-educated woman twenty-six years his junior. Frances was the daughter of Oscar Folsom, Cleveland's friend and law partner, who died in 1875. The marriage was destined to be a happy one and one that helped to enhance Cleveland's social graces. Unfortunately, it did not seem to improve his skill as a politician.

The Campaign of 1888: Defeat Despite Victory in the Popular Vote

The Democratic Party renominated Cleveland at its 1888 convention. It could hardly do less. But while doing so, the party and its nominee did attempt to soften the president's earlier antiprotectionist position on the tariff. The Republicans, however, nominated as their candidate an ultraprotectionist, Benjamin Harrison of Indiana, and forced the tariff issue into the forefront of the campaign. Republican propagandists portrayed Cleveland's tariff stand as one that was overly friendly to free-trade-loving England and dangerous to American businessmen, industrialists, farmers, and laborers. They equated high tariffs with high wages and low tariffs with economic disaster. Forced on the defensive, Cleveland's political ineptitude became all the more apparent.

Although the tariff was the major issue, other factors also figured in the campaign. For many Americans, prohibition or Civil War pensions as well as regional, ethnic, or religious prejudices outweighed purely economic concerns. Cleveland's attempt to return captured

Confederate flags to the South enraged many Northerners. Of even greater importance, however, was the Murchison letter affair. This letter, released to the press in Los Angeles a few weeks before the election, was a Republican trap. It baited Sir Lionel Sackville-West, the British minister in Washington, D.C., into writing that in effect a vote for Cleveland was a vote for England. Given the anti-English sentiment in America, especially among Irish Americans, the letter's impact was obvious. Cleveland failed to carry New York, and although he won a plurality of the popular vote, he lost the election.

Cleveland did not leave office with a whimper. In his last State of the Union address in December, 1888, he issued some stern warnings to Americans. In many ways it was the most important address Cleveland ever gave. He spoke openly about the growing gulf between rich and poor in America, and he lashed out against the powerful trusts, combinations, and monopolies. With a voice seldom heard before, he sympathized with the plight of farmers and urban laborers. In the end, he condemned all special privileges—especially the tariff. Unfortunately, Cleveland saw the problems in a much clearer focus than the solutions.

The Harrison Administration: Free-Spending Republicans

The period between 1889 and 1892 took more the form of a hibernation for Cleveland than a retirement. Cleveland returned to New York and resumed the practice of law, although he handled few cases. He maintained his ties with politicians through letters rather than personal meetings. He enjoyed summers in his cottage at Buzzards Bay and winters in New York City. He fished and hunted and attended Broadway plays and exclusive parties. All in all, he followed a pleasant routine. Later, he said that these years were the happiest of his life.

Perhaps with some satisfaction he watched the new administration wrestle with some economic problems that his had faced. The Republicans' answer to the Treasury surplus was to spend it. A substantial portion went to the veterans. The Dependents' Pension Act more than doubled the number of pensioners. Congress also spent money on upgrading coastal defenses, building schools, and improving rivers and harbors. In 1890 the reserve was $190 million; by 1893 it had dropped to $108 million. In addition, Congress passed the McKinley tariff, which raised rates on both farm and industrial products to the highest levels ever. Finally, Congress pushed through the Sherman Silver Purchase Act, which required the Treasury to purchase 4,500,000 ounces of silver each month and angered sound money supporters such as Cleveland.

Unfortunately for the Republicans, their spending and support of various special interests came at a time when the economy began to turn downward. Predictably, they paid the price. Democrats and agrarian independents made remarkable gains in the 1890 elections. More important for Cleveland, the prospects looked bright for a Democratic presidential victory in 1892. Next to the extravagant Republicans, the tightfisted Cleveland took on a certain luster of sagacity. "Good government," tariff reform, and the gold standard were seen by many Americans as the proper cure for the nation's ills.

Cleveland's Second Administration: A Shift in Public Sentiment

Between the 1890 elections and the 1892 Democratic convention, Cleveland regained leadership of the Democratic Party. Although publicly he said he would not campaign actively for the presidency, he worked industriously for it behind the scenes. At the Chicago convention, Cleveland was nominated on the first ballot,

TO AMEND BUT NOT DESTROY.
UNCLE SAM. "How much o' that dew ye calkelate ter take off?"
G. C. "The rough edges, merely."

Cleveland's 1887 message to Congress on tariff reform won applause but not votes. *(Library of Congress)*

and Adlai Stevenson of Illinois was chosen as his running mate. The platform committed the party to tariff and currency reform. After four years of Republican spending, the country was once again ready for Cleveland's frugal policies. In November, Cleveland defeated Harrison by a margin of 132 electoral votes, and the Democrats regained control of both houses of Congress.

The victory celebration ended quickly. No sooner had Cleveland taken office than the financial panic of 1893 began. Depression racked the country. Thousands of businesses failed, and hundreds of banks suspended operations. In the cities, unemployment rose and charities were unable to ease the suffering of millions of homeless and hungry Americans. State and federal officials ignored the anguished pleas of the urban and rural poor. The governor of New York spoke for many in government: "In America, the people support the government; it is not the province of the government to support the people."

Cleveland blamed the depression on the Sherman Silver Purchase Act and the McKinley tariff. To deal with it, he concentrated his efforts on repealing the Republican legislation. First he went after the Sherman Silver Purchase Act, which he believed was rapidly draining the Treasury's gold reserves. Essentially, the depression had driven politicians into one of two financial camps. Cleveland, Bourbons, and conservative Republicans called for a return to the gold standard, while Agrarian Democrats and Republicans and Populists demanded the free coinage of silver in order to inflate the currency and raise prices.

It was a time of high drama. On June 30, 1893, Cleveland summoned a special session of Congress to convene on August 7, to repeal the Sherman Silver Purchase Act. About the same time, he noticed a rough spot on the roof of his mouth, which medical experts soon diagnosed as cancer. The very day he called for the special session of Congress, Cleveland boarded a private yacht to undergo surgery. The operation was a success, as was a later one to provide him with an artificial jaw of vulcanized rubber. As biographer Horace Samuel Merrill noted, "Neither his facial appearance nor the quality of his voice was thereby altered. But he seemed less rugged and more irritable, and he weighed less."

The operation was performed under a cloak of secrecy. The public did not learn of the event until twenty-five years later. The battle over the Sherman Silver Purchase Act, however, was waged in the open. Cleveland refused to compromise. Finally, in late October, 1893, he prevailed, and the act was repealed. The gold standard was saved, but Cleveland and the

Bourbon Democrats paid dearly for their victory. The issue split the Democratic Party, a division that eventually led to the defeat of the Bourbon element within the party. In addition, the repeal neither ended the financial crisis nor restored public confidence.

The Treasury reserve continued to decline. After other efforts to maintain the reserve by selling bonds for gold failed, finally in 1895 the president asked the major New York bankers for help. A banking syndicate headed by J. P. Morgan agreed to buy $65 million in bonds at a special discount and to use its influence to keep the gold from being withdrawn from the Treasury. Although this move helped the situation, it was roundly condemned by the agrarian population of the South and West especially as a crooked deal with Wall Street.

Politically weakened by the fight over the money question, Cleveland found the struggle for tariff reform all the more difficult. The Wilson bill that emerged from the House provided significant reductions, but it was badly mauled in the Senate. The resulting Wilson-Gorman bill was only slightly less protectionist than the McKinley tariff. Cleveland was bitterly disappointed and accused Congress of "party perfidy and party dishonor." The bill became law without his signature.

Unpopular with professional politicians, Cleveland, by 1894, was equally unpopular with the American people. The depression exposed the heartlessness of his economic beliefs. "While the people should patriotically and cheerfully support their Government," he wrote, "its functions do not include the support of the people." He did not believe the government should be in the relief business. It violated every principle he held. It was uneconomical, favored a special interest, and went beyond the scope of the Constitution. Thus when Jacob S. Coxey led his ragtag army on a march toward Washington. D.C., in an effort to encourage government public works relief legislation, Cleveland showed no sympathy.

When the "petitioneers in boots" arrived at the Capitol in 1894, they were rudely dispersed.

Strikers received similar treatment from Cleveland. In the spring of 1894, four thousand workers in the Pullman Company of Chicago went on strike. The American Railway Union, headed by the able Eugene V. Debs, soon supported the strikers and boycotted Pullman cars. Cleveland and his attorney general, Richard Olney, a former railroad lawyer, acted quickly. They used the excuse of protecting the mails to come to the aid of the railroad managers. Over the protest of the governor of Illinois, the government sent two thousand troops to the Chicago area, and a federal court issued a blanket injunction which virtually ordered the union leaders to do nothing to continue the strike. Debs and his associates were convicted of defying the injunction and were im-

prisoned, and the strike ended. Some industrialists and businessmen cheered Cleveland's and Olney's high-handed methods, but labor was bitter.

While wrestling with intractable economic problems, Cleveland also had to deal with foreign policy matters. A staunch anti-imperialist, he blocked the annexation of Hawaii because he believed American sugar interests on the island had been involved illegally in the request. He also refused to involve America in Cuba's war for independence from Spain. Yet, as his first administration's efforts to build a modern steel navy attested, Cleveland still supported an active role for the United States in certain situations. In 1895, he intervened in a long-standing dispute between England and Venezuela over the boundary between British Guiana and Venezuela. When gold was dis-

The first shipment of meat leaves the Chicago stockyards under escort by the U.S. cavalry during the Pullman Strike of 1894. *(Library of Congress)*

covered in the disputed territory, Britain pressed its case. Cleveland took the position with the British foreign office that its claim violated the Monroe Doctrine. When Cleveland's offer to arbitrate the dispute was rudely refused by Britain, the president secured authority from Congress to locate the boundary and force the British to recognize it. For a few tense months, war seemed a possibility. Then Britain yielded. The matter was settled by arbitration largely in Britain's favor. Certainly, Cleveland's actions enhanced the Monroe Doctrine and bolstered America's international prestige, but the dispute hardly warranted Cleveland's bellicose actions.

By 1896, Cleveland was a defeated man. Most Americans disagreed with his handling of the depression and even the majority of his own party now rejected his conservative fiscal policies. Silver Democrats, who favored the free and unlimited coinage of silver, wrested control of the party from the Bourbons. Speaking for the new power in the Democratic Party, William Jennings Bryan intoned, "We have petitioned, and our petitions have been scorned; we have entreated, and our entreaties have been disregarded; we have begged, and they have mocked when our calamity came. We beg no longer; we entreat no more; we petition no more. We defy them." At the national convention that summer, Democrats nominated Bryan to carry their banner.

Tired, bitter, and defeated, Cleveland retired from active politics. He bought a modest house in Princeton, New Jersey. He wrote and delivered a few speeches, and he fished and hunted. Even in retirement he lived a full and active life. In time the bitterness of the mid-1890's died, and the nation's attitude toward him softened. Then on June 24, 1908, in the middle of the convention season, Cleveland died.

Cleveland's Record: Honesty and Inflexibility

As for his performance as the nation's chief executive, Cleveland was honest and courageous, and he gave the American people an honest, efficient, and courageous administration. During an age of shabby political dealings, Cleveland helped to restore prestige to the office of the presidency. He was, however, narrow and inflexible. He could never identify with the suffering farmers in the South and West or the struggling laborers in the growing cities. When the economic situation demanded flexibility and empathy, Cleveland was found wanting. His failure contributed to the people's sufferings in the mid-1890's and led to the permanent decline of the Bourbons in the Democratic Party.

Randy Roberts

Bibliographical References

The fullest biography of Cleveland is Allan Nevins, *Grover Cleveland: A Study in Courage*, 1932. More recent and more critical is Horace S. Merrill, *Bourbon Leader: Grover Cleveland and the Democratic Party*, 1957, and Rexford G. Tugwell, *Grover Cleveland*, 1968. Together the books provide a full picture of Cleveland and his times. Robert McElroy, *Grover Cleveland: The Man and the Statesman*, 1923, remains of interest for the scholar.

Cleveland's most important writings are collected in Nevins, *Letters of Grover Cleveland, 1850-1908*, 1933. Richard E. Welch, *The Presidencies of Grover Cleveland*, 1988, provides an in-depth analysis of Cleveland's terms as president. For bibliographies on Cleveland's life and presidency, see Robert I. Vexler, *Grover Cleveland, 1837-1908: Chronology, Documents, Bibliographical Aids*, 1968, and John F. Marszalek, *Grover Cleveland: A Bibliography*, 1988.

Benjamin Harrison

23d President, 1889-1893

Born: August 20, 1833
North Bend, Ohio
Died: March 13, 1901
Indianapolis, Indiana

Political Party: Republican
Vice President: Levi P. Morton

Cabinet Members

Secretary of State: James G. Blaine, John W. Foster
Secretary of the Treasury: William Windom, Charles Foster
Secretary of War: Redfield Procter, Stephen B. Elkins
Secretary of the Navy: Benjamin F. Tracy
Attorney General: W. H. H. Miller
Postmaster General: John Wanamaker
Secretary of the Interior: John W. Noble
Secretary of Agriculture: Jeremiah M. Rusk

Benjamin Harrison, the twenty-third president of the United States, became the first grandson of a former president to hold the office. His grandfather, William Henry Harrison, died only one month after his inauguration, and whereas "Little Ben" served a full term, cynics sneered that he had no more impact on the office than "Old Tippecanoe." If this were true, it was not because Harrison lacked motivation or intelligence.

Born August 20, 1833, on his grandfather's famous farm at North Bend on the Ohio River near Cincinnati, Benjamin Harrison was the son of a farmer and two-term congressman who was skeptical about the motivation of the typical political officeholder. Benjamin, a short, stocky boy, was reared in bucolic surroundings.

He attended private schools and was graduated from Miami University in Oxford, Ohio. After reading law in a Cincinnati firm, young Harrison was admitted to the bar in 1854 and soon moved to Indianapolis to practice.

Harrison's official portrait. *(White House Historical Society)*

"Little Ben": Idealism and Intolerance

Harrison's family lineage was Whig, and its long identification with the political life of the old Northwest gave Benjamin an immediate advantage when he entered local politics in Indianapolis. From the beginning, he exhibited a strong streak of idealism, demonstrating a genuine concern for the plight of slaves and identifying with the new Republican Party as it rose during the 1850's. Deeply religious, Harrison became an elder in the Presbyterian Church and a strong supporter of local philanthropies.

After holding local and state office as a Republican, Harrison fought in the Civil War as commander of an Indiana brigade, rising to the rank of brigadier general on merit. His supporters referred to him as General Harrison throughout the remainder of his public life. After the war, he returned to an increasingly lucrative law practice in Indianapolis, substantial activity in philanthropic causes, and a steady rise up the Republican political ladder. An ardent supporter of Radical Republicanism during Reconstruction, he later became known as a member of the party's progressive wing, supporting civil service reform, labor legislation, railroad regulation, the protective tariff, and liberal veterans' pensions. In 1876, Harrison ran unsuccessfully for governor, but four years later he became influential in the national party as chair of the Indiana delegation to the Republican convention. Elected to the United States Senate, he served from 1881 to 1887 and chaired the committee on territories, demonstrating a strong interest in the admission of the Western territories to statehood.

By 1887 Harrison was being pushed for the Republican presidential nomination to run against the incumbent, Grover Cleveland. Although one of his major assets was his name, there was more to Benjamin Harrison than that. He had developed a well-deserved reputation for ability and integrity, and both in his political career and as a Civil War commander he had demonstrated courage, compassion, and solid judgment. Yet although he had earned respect, he was never the recipient of great affection, even from his political allies and supporters. His nickname, Little Ben, referred to his small stature—he was only about 5 feet, 6 inches tall—but it certainly was not an affectionate sobriquet. Although Republican campaigners sang that "Grandfather's Hat Fits Ben," they were unable to dispel the cold aura the candidate generated.

Despite this image, Benjamin Harrison was a very convincing speaker when addressing large crowds. He spoke in a forceful manner and exuded dignity, presence, and ability. His speeches were characterized by clarity, common sense, and excellent organization. Eschewing rhetorical bombast, Harrison illustrated his addresses with appropriate similes and never talked down to his audiences. Even political skeptics were impressed by the effectiveness of Harrison's public style.

It is ironic that, although a forceful and effective public speaker, Harrison was miserably unsuccessful in dealing with individuals. Both critics and friendly observers agreed that "he could charm a crowd of twenty thousand . . . but he could make them all enemies with a personal handshake." He was called "Mr. Harrison, the man who never laughs." Uncomfortable in social situations, he hated small talk and insincerity and was something of a loner. He was a well-known figure in Indianapolis social and legal circles but was not at all outgoing, speaking only when spoken to and certainly not courting familiarity. In part, this attitude was a result of his idealism. He had high standards and expectations and was intolerant of those who failed to measure up. His reputation as a cold individual may have been somewhat unfair. Harrison was comfortable with children and could apparently unwind when away from the pressures of office and public life. A friend once noted, "When he's on a fishing trip, Ben takes his drink of

PRESIDENT BEN? HARRISON.

HON. W.H.H. MILLER,
Attorney General.

HON. JAMES G. BLAINE,
Sec'y of State.

HON. JOHN WANAMAKER,
Postmaster General.

HON. W?? WINDOM
Sec'y of the Treasury

HON. JNO. W. NOBLE
Sec'y of the Interior.

HON. BEN? F. TRACEY,
Sec'y of the Navy

HON. REDFIELD PROCTOR,
Sec'y of War.

HON. J. M. RUSK,
Sec'y of Agriculture.

PRESIDENT HARRISON AND HIS CABINET.

COPYRIGHT 1889, BY CURRIER & IVES, N.Y.

Harrison and his cabinet, 1889. *(Library of Congress)*

whiskey in the morning, just like anyone else. He chews tobacco from a plug he carries in his hip pocket, spits on his worm for luck, and cusses when the fish gets away." This description would have amazed colleagues and subordinates, who were continually taken aback by Harrison's brusqueness, impatience, and icy manner.

In the 1888 campaign, President Cleveland remained aloof from the fray, believing campaigning to be beneath the dignity of his office. Harrison conducted a "front porch" campaign from his solid and comfortable home on North Delaware Street in Indianapolis. He spoke reasonably and clearly, and although he did not always tell his audiences exactly what they wanted to hear, they respected him. The professional politicians were surprised by the ef-

fectiveness of his speeches as he defeated Cleveland in the electoral college, even though he trailed Cleveland by 90,000 in the tally of the popular vote.

The Businessman's Cabinet

In his inaugural address, Harrison promised civil service reform, pensions for veterans, the free ballot for blacks, and continuation of the protective tariff. He immediately got off on the wrong foot with many of the party professionals. Matthew Quay, the Republican boss of Pennsylvania, reportedly reacted to Harrison's remark that he owed his victory to Providence with the comment that "Providence hadn't a damned thing to do with it." He supposedly said that "Harrison would never learn how close a number of men were compelled to approach the gates of the penitentiary to make him president where he could return thanks to the Almighty for his promotion." In any case, no evidence exists that Harrison was personally involved in the corrupt machinations of what was an extremely dirty campaign.

Harrison later recalled, "When I came into power, I found that the party managers had taken it all to themselves. I could not name my own Cabinet. They had sold out every place to pay the election expenses." Torn between the promises of his campaign and his personal integrity on the one hand and the pressures of party politics on the other, Harrison pleased no one. He extended the number of jobs under civil service and appointed the formidable Theodore Roosevelt as a civil service commissioner, dismaying the party bosses. He also, however, appointed Philadelphia merchant John Wanamaker as postmaster general in return for Wanamaker's heavy financial contributions to the presidential campaign. Wanamaker used this traditional position for patronage dispensation to carry out one of the largest and most blatant campaigns of spoils-oriented appointments in the nation's history. The members of Harrison's cabinet were generally noted for their status as geographical party bosses rather than for their integrity or suitability for office, and they collectively became known as the Businessman's Cabinet. Even Harrison's extension of the civil service system had a partisan aspect—now newly appointed Republican officeholders would be protected when the Democrats came back into power.

A Presidency of Restricted Scope

Like other presidents of the period, Harrison had a rather limited view of the parameters of his office. He believed that policy initiatives should come primarily from Congress, with the president responsible for their promulgation and general administration. During the first half of his term, the Republicans controlled Congress, and thus it would seem that Harrison

should have had a relatively positive experience. From the beginning, however, he was uncomfortable with the job and with the demands that it placed on his principles and his family.

He cherished privacy and had an essentially adversarial relationship with members of the press; neither did he like the policemen and other officials who were supposed to shield him from the public. The president rose early and often walked in the White House garden, in Lafayette Park, or, if not many people were about, along Pennsylvania Avenue. As in Indianapolis, he was a familiar figure with his Prince Albert coat and umbrella. One historian who has described the period notes that "in a close-fitting Prince Albert, with an erect stance and dead-level look, Harrison resembled a pouter-pigeon on parade in LaFayette Square or Dupont Circle. Returning to the White House, he would nod curtly at the historic columns: 'There is my jail.'" After praying and breakfasting with his family, he undertook what was usually a long day's work.

Harrison immersed himself thoroughly in the most minute administrative details of the government. The White House became a model of bureaucratic efficiency, of which the president was inordinately proud. He based decisions on thorough, factual information, never shirked or avoided the hard questions, and resented those who wasted his time or failed to measure up to his standards of competence. Visitors were seldom invited to take a chair, lest they stay too long, and stories of his brusqueness became legend. Harrison never complained about the burdens of office, taking it for granted that people would understand, and he had little toleration for those who complained. Clearly, his forte was administration, which he greatly preferred to the role of political leader. Just as clearly, Harrison's obsession with minor administrative detail, his inability or unwillingness to delegate authority, and a tendency toward overwork, which compounded his personal intolerance and curtness, combined to undermine the effectiveness of his leadership.

Perhaps in the political climate of the time no president could have completely risen above or taken command of the system, but Harrison failed to make a significant effort. Although later students of his presidency have given him credit for being his own man and trying to influence policy, the fact remains that the accomplishments of the time, even those that the president supported, owed their genesis and achievement to other leaders and forces. Other political figures were on the scene who were far more effective at using the system than was Little Ben. These expert politicians included William McKinley, the congressman from Ohio, later something of a disappointment in the presidency but an effective and powerful force in the Congress; Tom Platt and Matthew Quay, the political bosses from New York and Pennsylvania; and above all, Thomas B. Reed of Maine, the speaker of the House of Representatives. Reed, a large and caustic man, presided over the House with an iron hand and became famous as "Czar Reed" became of his arbitrary ruling that members of Congress would be counted in determining a quorum even if they were present but not voting on a particular issue. This ruling limited the ability of the Democratic opposition to stymie the operations of the House, and it increased the power of the Republican majority. These men, and others like them, would have a greater effect in determining national policy than the dour Hoosier in the White House.

Significant Legislation: The Sherman Antitrust Act

Under such leadership, major legislation poured out of the Congress, much of it enacted in 1890. Among the more significant was the Sherman Antitrust Act, sponsored by Senator John Sherman of Ohio. By this time, public pressure was growing for governmental action to curb the power of the trusts, and several states had already attempted to deal with the problem at that level. The act (which outlawed every "contract, combination . . . or conspiracy in restraint of trade or commerce among the several states or with foreign nations") was passed with the support of both parties and the administration. It was the first national effort to deal with the problem of conspiracies in restraint of trade, and both its nature and its effectiveness have been disputed. Some have argued that the law was deliberately written to be vague and unenforceable; others hold that the failure of the law to have any major effect before 1901 was primarily a result of unfavorable interpretations by the Supreme Court. In any case, Harrison signed the bill into law, although it should be noted that, like other conservative chief executives of the period, he made little effort to enforce it.

Congress also moved to deal with the money question by passing the Sherman Silver Purchase Act, which required the Treasury to buy a stipulated amount of silver and pay for it in Treasury notes redeemable "in gold or silver coin." A compromise between those who wanted to increase the monetary supply by the coinage of silver and the hard money faction, which wanted a restricted monetary system and a return to the gold standard, the law had no significant effect and satisfied no one. It was based on a plan promoted by Secretary of the Treasury William Windom and supported only halfheartedly by the president, and it was designed at least in part to win the support of Western congressmen from silver-mining states for the high tariff duties that were so dear to Republican hearts.

The third legislative accomplishment of 1890 was passage of the McKinley tariff, the highest protective tariff in American history. It was designed primarily to protect United States industry, but to placate farmers, increased duties were also established for agricultural products. Consistent with Harrison's principles, the measure included a reciprocity provision, which he had promoted, that allowed the president to lower duties if other countries did the same. Harrison and Secretary of State James G. Blaine, anxious to increase trade with Latin America, used this provision to begin negotiating reciprocal trade agreements.

In cartoonist Joseph Keppler's 1890 parody of Edgar Allan Poe's *The Raven*, Grandpa's hat overwhelms Little Ben. *(Library of Congress)*

In his first message to Congress, Harrison recommended federal protection for black voters, improved conditions for railroad workers, and generous pensions for veterans. The first two recommendations came to naught, but in 1890 Congress passed a liberal Dependents' Pension Act, which broadened coverage to make eligible for pensions all disabled veterans, regardless of whether their disabilities were service-connected, and their dependents, and thereby opened the door to drastically increased governmental pension expenditures. These were accompanied by other government outlays for internal improvements, subsidies to steamship lines, and enlargement of the navy. The last two areas were pet projects of President Harrison, who wanted to build a two-ocean navy and promote the American merchant marine. The cost was enormous. The fifty-first Congress was the first to spend $1 billion in peacetime, but when the critics howled and the Democrats termed it the "Billion Dollar Congress," Speaker Reed simply responded that the United States was a billion-dollar country.

Foreign policy was dominated by Secretary of State Blaine. Long a power, presidential aspirant, and kingmaker in the Republican Party, Blaine was a man of ability who had helped to decide on Harrison's nomination. His stature was such, however, that he would dominate an administration. Harrison knew this and delayed for some time before offering the state portfolio to the "Plumed Knight." Nevertheless, in the final analysis Harrison had no other choice than to bring "the man from Maine" into the cabinet. Blaine would prove a productive secretary of state, although some disagreement exists about whether Blaine, Harrison, or both should receive the credit for his accomplishments.

In 1889, the first Pan-American Congress met in Washington, D.C., and promoted cooperation among hemispheric nations by, among other things, creating the Pan-American Union. Other diplomatic activities included an abortive attempt at the end of the term to annex Hawaii, an agreement to arbitrate the Bering Sea controversy with Great Britain over fur seals in that area, and the establishment of a joint protectorate over the Samoan Islands.

By the middle of Harrison's term, the rising tide of political protest was becoming stronger, and in the 1890 midterm elections the Republicans lost control of Congress. Strong popular reaction against the new McKinley tariff was partially responsible, but it was also true that the administration and Congress seemed to be out of harmony with the popular mood, and Harrison had not demonstrated an ability to lead the public or the legislature toward support of his policies. The emergence of the Populist Party, intervention by the federal government in the bloody strike at the Homestead works of the Carnegie Steel Company, and public concern about the dissipation of a sizable federal Treasury surplus through prodigal expenditures combined to seal Harrison's fate. The election year 1892 saw a replay of the 1888 presidential election, but the results were reversed. Benjamin Harrison was defeated by Grover Cleveland by more than 63,000 popular votes and 132 electoral votes, and he returned to Indianapolis and the practice of law. His last major public endeavor was to represent Venezuela in the arbitration of its boundary dispute with Great Britain in 1897. Little Ben died at his home on March 13, 1901, and was buried in Indianapolis.

An Instinctive Failure
Benjamin Harrison was a prime example of the fact that high marks for integrity, courage, and intellect do not necessarily make a good president. Harrison's inability or unwillingness to function within the glad-handing, give-and-take world of practical politics made it virtually impossible for him to influence legislators or other political constituents and power brokers, and achieve his goals; neither was he able to build a coterie of close personal associates or friends to help him through the political battles. Although recent historians have tended to give him more credit than did their predecessors, Harrison's was essentially a failed presidency. A recent biographer treats him very generously, yet concludes that he "seems to emerge greater as a man than as a president."

James E. Fickle

Bibliographical References
Harry J. Sievers, *Benjamin Harrison*, 3 vols., 1952-1968, is an extremely favorable biography. Matthew Josephson, *The Politicos*, 1938, is quite critical, as is Harold U. Faulkner, *Politics, Reform, and Expansion*, 1959. The best surveys of the period are H. Wayne Morgan, *From Hayes to McKinley, 1877-1896*, 1969; Morton Keller, *Affairs of State: Public Life in Late Nineteenth Century America*, 1977; and John A. Garraty, *The New Commonwealth, 1877-1890*, 1969. Homer E. Socolofsky and Allan B. Spetter, *The Presidency of Benjamin Harrison*, 1988, an analysis of the Harrison administration, is part of the University Press of Kansas series on the American presidency.

William McKinley

25th President, 1897-1901

Born: January 29, 1843
      Niles, Ohio
Died: September 14, 1901
      Buffalo, New York

Political Party: Republican
Vice Presidents: Garret A. Hobart,
      Theodore Roosevelt

Cabinet Members

Secretary of State: John Sherman, William R.
    Day, John Hay
Secretary of the Treasury: Lyman J. Gage

Secretary of War: Russell A. Alger, Elihu Root
Secretary of the Navy: John D. Long
Attorney General: Joseph McKenna, John W.
    Griggs, Philander C. Knox
Postmaster General: Joseph Gary, Charles E.
    Smith
Secretary of the Interior: Cornelius N. Bliss, E. A.
    Hitchcock
Secretary of Agriculture: James Wilson

McKinley's official portrait. *(White House Historical Society)*

William McKinley was born in Niles, Ohio, on January 29, 1843, and attended Allegheny College before enlisting in the Union army in 1861. He attained the rank of major and was known by that title during his political life. His combat record in the Civil War added to his public appeal in late nineteenth century America. After the war he became a lawyer and served as prosecuting attorney for Stark County, Ohio, from 1869 to 1871. He married Ida Saxton in 1871. Their two children died early in life, and Mrs. McKinley became a perpetual invalid on whom her husband lavished care and affection.

In 1876, McKinley, then a prosperous attorney in Canton, Ohio, was elected to Congress. He served there until 1891. He became identified with the protective tariff as an expression of the nationalism of the Republican Party, and he helped frame the McKinley tariff of 1890. Defeated for reelection in 1890 in a Democratic year, he ran successfully for governor of Ohio in 1891 and was reelected in 1893. His ability to carry this key Midwestern state and his broad national popularity made him the front-runner for the Republican presidential nomination in 1896. The friendship and support of the Ohio industrialist Marcus A. Hanna helped him secure the nomination, but it was McKinley's appeal to the broad mass of the GOP that made him the party's standard-bearer.

William Jennings Bryan won the Democratic nomination as the champion of inflationary solutions to the depression of the 1890's. His advocacy of "free silver" at a ratio of sixteen to one with gold and his youthful energy made him a formidable adversary as he stumped the country for the Democrats and the farmer-based People's Party. McKinley campaigned from his front porch in Canton. More than three-quarters of a million people heard his deft speeches that attacked inflation and praised the protective tariff as the Republican cure for hard times. While the candidate reached the electorate in controlled circumstances that conveyed an image of dignity and calm, the Republicans, with Hanna as campaign chairman, sent out 250,000,000 pamphlets and documents that echoed McKinley's themes. The Republicans did not buy the election of 1896 with their ample campaign treasury. They used the money that Hanna raised from wealthy contributors to conduct a "campaign of education." In the end, the voters went decisively for McKinley's pluralist, inclusive doctrine. He received 271 electoral votes to Bryan's 176 and the largest plurality in the popular vote since Ulysses S. Grant in 1872.

McKinley was fifty-four when he came to the presidency. A British journalist who observed him in 1896 noted that he had a "strong cleanshaven face" with "clear eyes, wide nose, full lips—all his features suggest dominant will and energy rather than subtlety of mind or emotion." He was 5 feet, 6 inches and sought in dress and posture to appear taller than he really was. Because McKinley wrote few personal letters and rarely shared intimate thoughts with friends, he was not an easy man to know. Enemies called him irresolute and cautious. Those who worked with him knew better. "He was a man of great power," said Elihu Root, "because he was absolutely indifferent to credit. His great desire was 'to get it done.' He cared nothing about the credit, but McKinley *always had his way.*"

McKinley's First Term: The Power of the Presidency Revitalized

When McKinley took the oath of office on March 4, 1897, the presidency was still weak relative to Congress, and the institution lacked the modern mechanisms that enable a chief executive to govern. Grover Cleveland had asserted presidential prerogatives to deal with the economic crisis of the decade, but his inept handling of Congress, his party, and public opinion had pushed the presidency lower in popular esteem. The nation's first citizen seemed aloof and remote from the average American. During his four and a half years in office, McKinley laid the basis for the modern presidency and revitalized the institution's power. The Spanish-American War accelerated this process, but even before that conflict the new president showed his intention to reassert his authority.

The cabinet that he assembled was a conventional official family. It reflected the geographical balances within the Republican Party in its selection of John D. Long of Massachusetts as secretary of the navy, Joseph McKenna of California as attorney general, and Joseph Gary of Maryland as postmaster general. Lyman J. Gage, an Illinois banker, went to the Treasury Department, and Cornelius N. Bliss of New York served in the Interior Department. Two weak choices flawed the cabinet. Russell A. Alger of Michigan became secretary of war because of his service to the party and popularity with fellow Civil War veterans. McKinley failed to ask how he might perform in the event of war.

The choice of secretary of state became entangled with the problem of a reward for Mark Hanna. After Hanna declined to be postmaster general, the possibility arose that Senator John Sherman of Ohio might be persuaded to take the State Department and thus make a vacancy to which Hanna could be appointed by the governor of Ohio. Later talk of a deal overlooked that McKinley approached another senator first about the State Department and that Sherman himself wanted the appointment. The problem was that Sherman's mind was failing and he was not up to his new duties. That a friend of the president, William R. Day, would be Sherman's assistant and keep an eye on him did not overcome the basic error of naming Sherman. When Hanna was appointed to the Senate, the whole topic gained unfortunate public attention. Sherman was a poor choice who had to be ignored while in office and eased out once the war with Spain began.

The new administration pursued varied political and diplomatic initiatives in its first year. McKinley called Congress into special session on March 15, 1897, to revise the tariff, and the protectionist Dingley tariff became law on July 24. Although the Dingley law raised customs duties, it also contained language that authorized the president to seek tariff reciprocity treaties with trading partners. McKinley used these provisions to seek a lowering of trade barriers from 1897 onward.

Negotiations with France and Great Britain for an international agreement to promote a wider use of silver in world commerce began with promise but collapsed in October, 1897, over British opposition to any breach in the gold standard. Following that result, McKinley moved toward an endorsement of gold that led eventually to the passage of the Gold Standard Act of 1900.

In foreign affairs, the administration addressed the long-standing disputes with Great Britain and Canada over fur seals, Newfoundland fisheries, and the Alaskan boundary question with Canada. A joint high commission began considering these interrelated questions in 1898; these talks were also part of a general improvement in Anglo-American relations that marked the McKinley years.

More difficult was the perennial problem of Hawaiian annexation. Republicans had long favored acquiring the islands, and tension with Japan over Japanese immigration and that nation's ambitions in the Pacific led to the writing of a treaty of annexation. The Senate received the pact at the end of the special session in June, 1897, but a vote could not come until Congress reconvened in December. McKinley exercised presidential persuasion on behalf of the treaty in early 1898, but opposition from Southern Democrats, whose states competed with Hawaiian sugar, stalled the administration short of the two-thirds majority needed. It was decided to pursue the approach of a joint resolution of annexation once the foreign policy crisis with Spain was concluded.

The president also sought to revitalize his office in 1897. The White House, surrounded by sentries and detectives in Cleveland's final years, became easier to visit. McKinley also traveled extensively in a manner that publicized the openness of his administration and gave him a means to influence public opinion. He devoted equal attention to relations with the press. Newsmen were given a table on the second floor where those assigned to the White House had seats. McKinley allowed no formal interviews, and direct quotation of the president was also forbidden. The chief executive was, however, an adept leaker, and he served as a much better news source for the administration than students of his presidency have realized.

McKinley used his staff and cabinet in ways that anticipated modern practices. The president's secretary, John Addison Porter, and his assistant, George B. Cortelyou, worked out a system to manage the release of official speeches and statements that made the White House a more important center for news. As the efficient Cortelyou supplanted Porter and became more influential, his role in arranging McKinley's tours and supervising the flow of business made him a forerunner of the twentieth century White House staff. McKinley employed his cabinet as a sounding board for policy but left no doubt as to who was in charge. John Sherman said that the meetings were "not a free exchange of opinions but rather the mandates of a paramount ruler." The quality of the cabinet improved when John Hay joined it as secretary of state in 1898 and Elihu Root became secretary of war in 1899.

At the end of his first year in office, McKinley had made important progress toward a revitalized presidency. He had established good relations with the press, publicized his office through travel, and expanded his influence with Congress. In the government he had tested his associates and reasserted formal procedures for decision making that brought power back to the presidency. All these accomplishments would be needed as McKinley confronted the foreign policy crisis that would determine the nature of his remaining years in the White House and the way history has depicted him.

The front page of the New York *World* for February 17, 1898, depicts the explosion of the *Maine* in Havana. *(Library of Congress)*

The Spanish-American War

The Spanish-American War, which began in April, 1898, is most often characterized as an unnecessary conflict that McKinley did not want but lacked the courage to prevent. It is rarely recognized that real issues separated the United States and Spain in these years. In 1895, a rebellion against Spanish rule broke out in Cuba. The Cuban rebels sought independence from Madrid and refused to contemplate a negotiated settlement of the war. Spain regarded Cuba as part of the Spanish nation, and committed several hundred thousand men to subdue the uprising. The Spanish people would never have tolerated a resolution of the fighting that took the "Ever Faithful Isle" away from Spain without a war. No basis for a compromise existed between these two adversaries.

Grover Cleveland followed a course that allowed Spain the chance to put down the rebellion and preserve its sovereignty over Cuba. The administration hoped that Spain would improve conditions on the island, prevent European intervention, and maintain its hegemony. Cleveland's policies persuaded Madrid that the United States would not impose a deadline and that procrastination on American demands might eventually produce success in Cuba. Because of the unpopularity of Cleveland's approach in Congress and the country at large, the United States had no viable policy toward Cuba when McKinley took office.

The new president decided that Spain must have a chance to end the rebellion, but that military action could not continue indefinitely without result. Moreover, Spain must conduct the war within humane limits and not use "fire and famine to accomplish by uncertain indirection what the military arm seems powerless to directly accomplish." Finally, any settlement must be acceptable to the Cuban rebels. McKinley wanted to convince Spain, by a process of gradual diplomatic pressure, to relinquish Cuba peacefully. Such a decision would, he believed, serve Spain's own interests. The Americans hoped that Spain would yield Cuba; the Spanish vowed never to do so. If both sides stood firm, in the end war was inescapable.

Through the second half of 1897, the McKinley administration believed that its policy of intensifying diplomatic pressure was altering Spanish behavior. In November, the Madrid government ended the practice of moving Cubans into "reconcentration" camps and announced an autonomy plan for the island. The Cubans obtained more home rule, but Spanish sovereignty remained in place. Nevertheless, the direction of Spanish action seemed positive as the year ended. In his annual message to

Congress in early December, McKinley called it "a course from which recession with honor is impossible."

Events deteriorated in January, 1898. On January 12, riots against the new autonomy program occurred in Cuba that persuaded McKinley that Spain could not live up to its promises. As the situation worsened, the administration decided to send a warship to Havana harbor, and the battleship *Maine* arrived on January 25. On February 1, the Spanish reiterated their view that their sovereignty over Cuba must be preserved and any foreign intervention resisted. President McKinley received this information on February 9.

That same day American newspapers proclaimed that the Spanish minister to the United States, Enrique Dupuy de Lome, had written a private letter, intercepted and published by the Cubans, that called the president "weak and a bidder for the admiration of the crowd." Such insulting language led to Dupuy le Lome's recall. More significant were his words which indicated that Spain was stalling for time in its negotiations with Washington and not acting in good faith.

Six days later, on February 15, the *Maine* blew up in Havana harbor, killing more than 260 officers and men. Modern research has shown that the explosion had an internal cause, probably spontaneous combustion in a coal bunker. Public opinion at the time believed that the cause was external and that Spain was either responsible or negligent in allowing the explosion to occur. For McKinley the problem was to retain control of the situation in the face of public excitement and to determine the cause of the tragedy. A naval court of inquiry was set up, and the president knew that when it reported, he would face a deadline for action. While the country awaited the court's verdict in mid-March, 1898, the administration sought to bolster national defense and explored, without success, the idea of buying Cuba from Spain.

Time ran out for McKinley's policy as the month concluded. Senator Redfield Proctor of Vermont told the Senate on March 17 of conditions in Cuba in a speech that moved public attitudes closer to intervention. Two days later, the president learned that the naval board had concluded, based on the physical evidence and scientific knowledge then available, that an external explosion had destroyed the *Maine*. When he submitted the report to Congress four or five days later, pressure for war would mount.

Over the next several weeks, McKinley pressed Spain to grant an armistice or to accept American mediation leading to Cuban independence. In response to the first initiative of the United States, extended in late March, Spain refused to contemplate independence for the island, either at once or through negotiations. Under intense pressure from Congress for war, McKinley tried to buy time to allow Spain to see the wisdom of relinquishing Cuba peacefully. Spain's negative answer to the American proposals, which reached the White House on March 31, 1898, meant that the president had to lay the matter before Congress. He prepared to send a message to the lawmakers during the first week of April.

McKinley's message went to Capitol Hill on April 11. Many historians believe that Spain had in fact capitulated to American demands by the time the president acted, making war unnecessary. This judgment is incorrect. What Spain did on April 9 was agree, under the prodding of its European allies, to ask for a suspension of hostilities in Cuba. Unlike an armistice, this break in the fighting did not involve a political recognition of the rebels. It would gain time for Spain to defend Cuba against the United States, especially since the length of the pause would be determined by the Spanish military commander in the field. Spain still balked at Cuban independence, and on the key American conditions had not capitulated at all.

The argument that McKinley's "weakness" prevented a peaceful settlement rests on a false premise. Spain had not yielded, and the president had not missed a chance for a negotiated peace. His message to Congress, read by a clerk, asked for presidential authority to end the hostilities in Cuba through the use of armed force. "The war in Cuba must stop," he concluded. He mentioned Spain's proposed suspension of hostilities at the end but gave it little weight.

A cartoon from June, 1898, questions the fate of the Philippines after the Spanish-American War. *(Library of Congress)*

Congress spent the next week debating its response. It adopted the Teller Amendment, which disclaimed any goal to control Cuba, but voted down efforts to accord political recognition to the rebels. On April 19, Congress passed a resolution that McKinley could accept, giving him the authority to intervene militarily. The president signed it on April 20. Spain broke diplomatic relations on the same day and declared war on April 24. Congress said on April 25 that a state of war between the two nations had existed since April 21. In the end, the Spanish-American War took place because both countries believed that their cause was just. McKinley had sought a diplomatic solution until that option was clearly impossible, and he conducted the negotiations with Spain with more tenacity and courage than his critics have been willing to recognize.

The Spanish-American War lasted a little more than three months, and it was a decisive military triumph for the United States. For the president, it became a test of his leadership ability as he played a crucial part in directing military operations and shaping diplomatic policy to end the fighting. The most important event in the war's initial stage was the overwhelming victory that Commodore George Dewey and his naval squadron won at Manila Bay in the Philippines on May 1, 1898. The American navy was in the Asian archipelago to further war plans that had been developed since 1895. The celebrated telegram that Assistant Secretary of the Navy Theodore Roosevelt sent Dewey on February 25, 1898, was an element in this large process, not a decisive departure from it.

Acquisition of the Philippines

After Dewey's success, the McKinley administration sent American troops to the Philippines in May, 1898. This military commitment reflected the president's intention to keep a United States option to acquire the islands as a result of the war. In the opening weeks of the conflict, McKinley thought that a port in the islands might be all that the country would need, but he intended to preserve flexibility. "While we are conducting war and until its conclusion we must keep all we get," he wrote privately. "When the war is over we must keep what we want."

The emerging United States policy in the summer of 1898 brought tensions with Filipinos, led by Emilio Aguinaldo, who were in revolt against Spain in pursuit of national independence. McKinley instructed Dewey and the army officers in the islands not to have any formal dealings with the Filipino forces. At the same time, he pushed anew for the annexation of Hawaii and employed presidential influence and lobbying to get an annexation resolution through the House in June and the Senate in July. The Hawaiian Islands would be an important supply link for a military campaign in the Philippines.

The primary focus of the fighting against Spain was Cuba. Proponents of war had argued that taking the island would be easy. In fact, however, raising an army, moving it to Cuba, and winning the battles proved to be a task that required McKinley to exercise close presidential supervision and leadership of the war effort. There was no shortage of volunteers to fight in this most popular conflict, and the army, along with Secretary of War Alger, was ill-prepared to cope with the sudden flood of eager recruits. Nearly 280,000 men saw active duty in the war. Many of them complained about shortages of supplies, ammunition, and the quality of the food in their rations. An experiment with canned roast beef produced an inedible meal and a major postwar controversy. By the time the fighting had ended, the War Department and the secretary had resolved most of the logistic problems that marked the early weeks of the fighting. Nevertheless, the impression of confusion and ineptitude lingered in the public mind and made Alger the subject of scathing press criticism.

Initially, the administration expected to fight a naval battle for Cuba. It became clear, however, that troops on the ground would be required to ensure political control of Cuba's fate and forestall any prospect of European intervention. An invasion of Cuba was planned for May. Then the focus of the assault became the harbor and city of Santiago de Cuba, where the Spanish fleet, under Admiral Pascual de Cervera, had been bottled up by June 1. American troops, commanded by General William R. Shafter, got ashore in late June, after a series of delays.

From the War Room in the White House, McKinley followed closely the combat that ensued. A switchboard with twenty telegraph lines, maps, and a staff of clerks gave the president the capacity to communicate with Shafter within twenty minutes, projecting a presidential presence directly to the battlefield. On July 1, American ground forces defeated the Spanish defenders at San Juan Hill; on July 3, the navy destroyed the Spanish fleet outside Santiago harbor. With these victories the focus shifted to securing the surrender of the Spaniards in Cuba and bringing the war to an end. Over the next two weeks, the president kept the pressure on his commanders to achieve Spanish capitulation, which came on July 17. At the same time, American forces under General Nelson A. Miles captured Puerto Rico. The most significant danger to the United States military in the Caribbean was the prospect of tropical disease, especially malaria and yellow fever.

As Spain's military position collapsed in mid-July, 1898, the Spanish government asked France to approach Washington about peace negotiations. In discussions that began on July 26, McKinley insisted that Spain give up Cuba and Puerto Rico and that the Philippines be the subject for the peace conference that would follow the end of the fighting. The president stood firm even though he knew that the physical condition of his army in Cuba was deteriorating. Word leaked out to the press about sickness in the army in early August, but the news did not have an adverse effect on the American negotiating position. Reluctantly accepting the terms of the United States, Spain agreed to an armistice on August 12, 1898.

In the immediate aftermath of the armistice, the administration arranged for soldiers from the Cuban expedition to come home at once. Sickness in Cuba and the United States killed more than 2,500 soldiers; battle deaths in the war reached a total of 281 officers and men. To meet the public outcry over the condition of the army, McKinley created a commission under Grenville M. Dodge, a Union army veteran and railroad owner, to investigate the War Department and its leadership. This body enabled the president to avoid a congressional investigation and to diffuse the political impact, during an election year, of problems in the conduct of the war. The Dodge Commission also promoted reform in the army through the recommendations for change it made in its report.

Although governing Cuba remained a large task after the fighting ended, the fate of the Philippines was a central concern for McKinley in the autumn of 1898. The president had replaced John Sherman as secretary of state with William R. Day when the war began. Now Day was replaced by John Hay, who was to lead the American delegation to the peace talks with Spain in Paris. To that body, McKinley added three senators who would vote on any treaty they negotiated. The president knew that the issue of the Philippines was exacerbated by increasing tension between American troops and the Filipinos. He was also aware of German and Japanese interest in the islands should the United States depart. McKinley had already decided against an independent Philippines under an American protectorate, but the administration did not yet go beyond retaining one island, Luzon, in the archipelago. The prospect that the United States might take all the Philippines and acquire an overseas empire

The Rough Riders on San Juan Hill, Cuba. *(Library of Congress)*

had aroused opposition from those who styled themselves anti-imperialists, and an important political battle was imminent as the peace negotiations went forward.

To rally support for his foreign policy, President McKinley made a speaking tour of the Midwest in October. Ostensibly nonpolitical, the junket helped Republican candidates in the congressional elections and allowed McKinley to sound themes that prepared the nation for the acquisition of all the Philippines. In Iowa, he said that "we do not want to shirk a single responsibility that has been put upon us by the results of the war." The president used the publicity weapons of his office to set the terms of the debate and to move opinion in the direction he desired.

Later in the month the question of the Philippines became crucial at the Paris talks. The American delegates asked on October 25 for precise instructions, and McKinley responded three days later. He could see "but one plain

path of duty—the acceptance of the archipelago." The celebrated anecdote that has McKinley seeking guidance from God through prayer at this pivotal juncture is implausible and represents one of those cases of embroidered reminiscence that attach themselves to presidents who have died in office. The decision to take all the Philippines was a logical outgrowth of the policy McKinley had followed since Dewey's victory in May.

Spain and the United States signed a peace treaty on December 10, 1898, by which the victor gained the Philippines, Puerto Rico, and Guam. Spain relinquished Cuba and received a $20 million payment. McKinley's political task was to secure Senate ratification of the treaty. Over the next two months, he used the extensive array of methods open to a strong president. In the South, where Democratic senators represented a key bloc of votes, McKinley made public appeals in December. The administration wooed other lawmakers with promises of patronage and exerted pressure on the state legislatures, which in those days elected senators. Support for approval of the pact from William Jennings Bryan and divisions among its opponents also helped McKinley. All these elements helped bring ratification of the Treaty of Paris on February 6, 1899, by a vote of 57 to 27, one more vote than necessary.

On the day of the vote, Americans knew that fighting had begun in the Philippines between United States soliders and Filipino troops under Aguinaldo's command. Relations had been increasingly tense in December and January, as it became evident that the United States intended to exercise political control over the islands and to assert its sovereignty. McKinley sent a commission to the islands in late January, 1899, to establish a civil government. Before that body arrived, the fighting had begun. McKinley asserted that the United States had "no imperial designs" on the Philippines, but intended to carry out the obligations assumed under the peace treaty. Anti-imperialists and Filipinos saw the question differently, and the president faced domestic opposition to the fighting even in its earliest stages.

In the wake of the Spanish-American War, McKinley had an array of foreign policy issues to confront during 1899 and 1900. The struggle in the Philippines was the most urgent. Militarily, the Americans gained an ascendancy over the Filipinos in the spring of 1899 in a series of conventional battles. During the rainy season from May to October, the Philippines Commission tried to establish a civil government within the president's framework that put American sovereignty at the center of any political arrangements. The Filipinos refused to accede to American plans. In the meantime, the anti-imperialists at home criticized the army's policy of censoring news from the islands as well as the way the war was being waged. By the end of the year, the army had defeated the Filipino forces in regular warfare.

Aguinaldo now decided to shift to guerrilla tactics. With the combat situation improving, McKinley sent a second Philippines Commission in early 1900 under William Howard Taft, to pursue the goal of civil government.

Critics of McKinley at the time and since have alleged that American soldiers pursued a genocidal policy toward the Philippine natives and were also guilty of war crimes and atrocities in combat. The first charge is not true. The second has a basis in fact. Though official policy neither condoned nor approved the mistreatment or killing of prisoners, American troops did violate the rules of war and army regulations in the Philippine fighting. The nation that had condemned the harsh tactics of Spain in Cuba now found itself using the same techniques in its own colonial war.

American Interests in Central America

The fate of Cuba was of almost equal importance to the McKinley administration in 1899-1900. The president believed that the Teller Amendment had to be respected, but he also wanted to ensure that Cuba remained free from interference by nations—such as Germany—with ambitions in the Caribbean. During 1899, a military government ran the islands. The soldiers improved the economic situation of the war-ravaged country and oversaw the disbanding of the rebel army. Once McKinley selected Elihu Root to be secretary of war in July, 1899, the task of establishing a civil government got under way and went forward throughout 1900. At all times, however, the president made clear that Cuba would have political and military links to the United States.

The outcome of this process was the Platt Amendment of 1901. Attached to an army appropriation bill, the amendment prohibited Cuba, once it became independent, from allying itself with a foreign power. It also gave the United States the right to intervene to preserve a stable government in the island and granted American rights to have naval bases on Cuban soil. The amendment, which McKinley shaped, reflected apprehensions about Germany's intentions in the region at the turn of the century and was designed to prevent a recurrence of the events of 1898. Instead, it became a permanent source of Cuban-American friction until it was abrogated in the 1930's.

President McKinley addressed other issues arising out of the war in these months. To achieve a route for a canal across Central America required an agreement with Great Britain to revise the Clayton-Bulwer Treaty of 1850, which barred both countries from having exclusive control of a canal. That goal in turn required a resolution of the controversy over the boundary between Alaska and Canada. The McKinley administration could not settle the boundary issue, which was left to Theodore Roosevelt to end in 1903. The president and John Hay did negotiate a treaty with Great Britain that allowed the United States to build an unfortified canal that all nations could use even in time of war. Because of these provisions, the first Hay-Pauncefote Treaty encountered strong opposition in the Senate and had to be renegotiated in 1901 before it achieved approval after McKinley's death.

American Interests in China: The Open Door Notes

In Asia, the president was aware of European efforts to dominate China through economic and political spheres of influence. Anxious about American trade with China and concerned to preserve that nation's territorial integrity, the administration, through Secretary Hay, issued what were called the Open Door notes in September, 1899. These messages asked the European countries active in China to safeguard trading privileges, local tariffs, and other economic rights that gave the United States a chance to compete for markets. As diplomatic statements, the Open Door notes had less significance at the time they were sent than they later had as an assertion of American

interests in China that rationalized involvement in Asia in the twentieth century.

Domestic issues produced less presidential activism than foreign policy had done during McKinley's first term. On the subject of race relations, the president emphasized sectional reconciliation between North and South ahead of the preservation of black rights. Little was done to offset the impact of segregation and violence on African Americans in those years. The problem of trusts and industrial mergers gained increasing public attention after 1897, but the administration responded slowly to pleas for a greater federal regulatory role. By 1899, McKinley grew more aware of the problem, and he asked Congress for additional action on trusts in his annual message. His record on trusts was cautious in his first term; he expected to do more in his second.

In the area of civil service, McKinley drew back from the reformist position of Cleveland in his second term and expanded, in an order of May 28, 1899, the list of positions to which competitive examinations did not apply. On the whole, however, the administration's record on honesty and efficiency in the federal service was creditable. Criticism in the first half of 1899 also focused on the War Department and the record of Secretary Alger. The hearings of the Dodge Commission produced some public outcries over allegations of "embalmed beef" in the soldiers' rations. The handling of the canned beef that the troops received had been inept, but no corruption or conspiracy was involved. The most constructive result of the hearings was recommendations for changes in the structure of the army and pressure on McKinley to replace Alger. He finally did so in the summer of 1899 when the secretary endorsed a political opponent of the president in McKinley's home state. Alger's replacement, Elihu Root of New York, was an excellent choice.

In the autumn of 1899, President McKinley made another tour of the Midwest, continuing the public advocacy of his positions that characterized his first term. Republican successes in the off-year elections seemed to forecast a victory for the GOP when McKinley ran again in 1900. Only the death of his vice president, Garret A. Hobart, in November, 1899, complicated the president's political future, and talk quickly arose that Theodore Roosevelt should be his next running mate.

The session of Congress that convened in late 1899 proved more troublesome than McKinley had anticipated. In his annual message, he said it was the nation's "plain duty" to extend free trade to Puerto Rico. This proposal struck at the Republican policy of tariff protection, and opposition arose within the president's party. McKinley shifted his ground, accepted a modest tariff on Puerto Rican goods, and used his influence to push the compromise measure through Congress. He also withstood Senate opposition to the Hay-Pauncefote Treaty and attacks on tariff reciprocity treaties the administration had negotiated with the nation's trading partners. It was a difficult session, but McKinley emerged with his prestige intact.

The Campaign of 1900: McKinley's Mandate Confirmed

As the Republican national convention neared, the most important political decision for McKinley was the choice of a running mate. The governor of New York, Theodore Roosevelt, was popular with the Republican rank and file. An easterner who was strong in the West, he represented a good balance for the president. The White House would probably have preferred someone less volatile and more conventional than Roosevelt, but no good alternative emerged. When it became clear that the Republican convention was likely to nominate Roosevelt anyway, McKinley stopped efforts of others to thwart the New Yorker's election. As a result, the GOP put forward its strongest possible ticket against William Jennings Bryan, who made his second race for the Democrats.

When McKinley accepted the party's nomination in mid-July, the nation was looking with concern at the fate of Westerners trapped in China by the Boxer Rebellion. Though the United States was not at war with China and Congress was not in session, the president sent several thousand American soldiers with the China Relief Expedition to Peking. It was another example of McKinley's innovative use of the war power to support the foreign policy of his presidency. He was equally surefooted in seeing that the soldiers left China as soon as possible after the safety of the Westerners was guaranteed.

In 1900, McKinley observed the tradition that prevented incumbent presidents from campaigning for reelection, and he let Roosevelt do most of the actual speaking. The president's speech of acceptance and his letter of acceptance set the tone for the Republicans. With the tide of economic prosperity running their way and the foreign policy successes of the administration, the Republicans easily defeated their opponents. McKinley increased his popular vote margin over 1896, and he won by a margin of 292 to 115 in the electoral college. "I am now the President of the whole people," McKinley said after his victory.

In the congressional session of 1900-1901, the president secured approval from the lawmakers, through the Spooner Amendment, of his authority to govern the Philippines once the insurrection had been quelled. This achievement was additional proof of McKinley's dominance of Capitol Hill. The capture of Emilio Aguinaldo in March, 1901, was another positive sign for the American side, though all resistance did not end for several years after the president's death. During this session, Congress also worked out the Platt Amendment for Cuba. One newspaper said that "no executive in the history of the country" had exercised greater influence on Congress than had McKinley.

The assassination of McKinley. *(Library of Congress)*

McKinley's Assassination: An Anarchist's Bullet

As the second term began on March 4, 1901, William McKinley was very much the strong president. "You are going to see an Emperor in a dress suit," a French visitor was told before he went to the White House. Under Cortelyou's adroit direction, the size of the presidential staff had expanded and the business of the executive office had become more standardized. Relations with the press reflected Cortelyou's desire for order and system in the treatment of newsmen. For McKinley himself, a routine of hard work and diligent attention to policy characterized his approach to the presidency after a full term in office. As one journalist put it, "The power originally vested in the executive alone has increased to an extent of which the framers of the Constitution had no prophetic vision."

In his second term, McKinley intended to travel more widely and even had plans to break precedent by leaving the continental boundaries for a trip to Cuba or Puerto Rico. First he wanted to pursue the program of tariff reciprocity that he had been quietly preparing for several years. His aim was to achieve gradual, controlled reductions in the protective system

that would help the United States secure foreign markets. To that end, the administration had pushed for Senate ratification of reciprocity treaties in 1900. With a mandate from the electorate, McKinley now prepared to argue for reciprocity again and challenge the protectionists in his own party in Congress. During the spring of 1901, he prepared to make speeches for the treaties on a western tour, but an illness of Mrs. McKinley cut the trip short. The president decided to resume his campaign when he traveled in September to Buffalo, New York, to see the Pan-American Exposition.

On September 5, 1901, he told his audience that "the period of exclusiveness is past," and contended that "the expansion of our trade and commerce is the pressing problem." The speech signaled the president's intentions for his second term, including a desire to lead his party in a new and more constructive direction. A day later, on September 6, while standing in a receiving line in the Temple of Music, McKinley was shot by Leon Czolgosz, an anarchist. Eight days later, on the morning of September 14, 1901, William McKinley died. Eulogizing him in 1902, John Hay said that the president "showed in his life how a citizen should live, and in his last hour taught us how a gentleman could die."

McKinley and the Modern Presidency: An Important Historical Role

McKinley's historical reputation declined in the 1920's as disillusion over the war with Spain led to charges that he lacked the courage to preserve peace. Perceived as a conservative Republican in the era of the New Deal, he became a byword for reaction and weakness in the presidency. Since the 1960's, however, newer appraisals have given him due credit for his strength and purpose as a foreign policy leader. He was the first modern president, and he laid the foundation on which Theodore Roosevelt and Woodrow Wilson expanded. In his use of the war power, fruitful relations with Congress, deft management of the press, and shrewd handling of public opinion, he acted as would imperial chief executives in the century that followed. William McKinley was an important figure in the history of the presidency, and his historical significance is likely to increase.

Lewis L. Gould

Bibliographical References

Because he wrote few letters and left only traces of his thinking on key issues, McKinley presents problems for biographers. Charles S. Olcott, *Life of William McKinley*, 2 vols., 1916, was the official life, based on materials that George B. Cortelyou had collected. Margaret Leech, *In the Days of McKinley*, 1959, is thorough and interesting on both the president and his wife. H. Wayne Morgan, *William McKinley and His America*, 1963, is the best full biography. For an illustrated biography, see Richard L. McElroy, *William McKinley and Our America: A Pictorial History*, 1996. For an examination of McKinley's attitudes on territorial expansion, foreign relations, and the Spanish-American War, see Lewis L. Gould, *The Spanish-American War and President McKinley*, 1982, and Brian P. Damiani, *Advocates of Empire: William McKinley, the Senate, and American Expansion, 1898-1899*, 1987. Gould and Craig H. Roell, *William McKinley: A Bibliography*, 1988, lists primary and secondary sources for further study of McKinley. Gould, *The Presidency of William McKinley*, 1980, develops in more detail the argument of this essay.

Theodore Roosevelt

26th President, 1901-1909

Born: October 27, 1858
New York, New York
Died: January 6, 1919
Oyster Bay, New York

Political Party: Republican
Vice President: Charles W. Fairbanks

Cabinet Members

Secretary of State: John Hay, Elihu Root, Robert Bacon
Secretary of the Treasury: Lyman J. Gage, Leslie M. Shaw, George B. Cortelyou

Secretary of War: Elihu Root, William Howard Taft, Luke E. Wright
Secretary of the Navy: John D. Long, William H. Moody, Paul Morton, Charles J. Bonaparte, Victor H. Metcalf, T. H. Newberry
Attorney General: Philander C. Knox, William H. Moody, Charles J. Bonaparte
Postmaster General: Charles E. Smith, Henry C. Payne, Robert J. Wynne, George B. Cortelyou, George von L. Meyer
Secretary of the Interior: E. A. Hitchcock, James R. Garfield
Secretary of Agriculture: James Wilson
Secretary of Commerce and Labor: George B. Cortelyou, Victor H. Metcalf, Oscar S. Straus

Roosevelt's official portrait. *(White House Historical Society)*

There was something about Theodore Roosevelt that endeared him to his contemporaries and gave him while still living a cult following new in the annals of American political history. He won the presidential election of 1904 by a plurality wider than anyone before had ever achieved, and the succeeding generation of Americans saw fit to enshrine his memory in the granite of Mount Rushmore in the rather exclusive company of George Washington, Thomas Jefferson, and Abraham Lincoln. The reputation of "America's President" is, however, somewhat in eclipse, among both historians and the general public. That can be attributed in part to the fact, so neatly encapsulated by John Morton Blum's decision to entitle his 1954 study *The Republican Roosevelt*, that the name Roosevelt is now more likely to evoke images and memories of Franklin Delano than of Theodore. There are also other reasons, both more important and more revealing.

As exemplified in Richard Hofstadter's critical essay "The Conservative as Progressive," historians have had difficulty finding an appropriate political classification for Theodore Roosevelt. He once playfully described himself as a conservative radical, but such a category has little resonance in either American political or intellectual tradition. Although practically all historians recognize that he was a major figure in the evolution of the presidential office and in the structure of the national government and find some of his achievements noteworthy and admirable, few have been inclined to endorse him wholeheartedly. Historians with a conservative political orientation usually praise his foreign policy but are less attracted to his efforts at domestic reform. Their accounts tend to emphasize his personal ambition, his demagoguery, and his attempt to usurp congressional, judicial, and state powers and concentrate all the reins of government in his own hands. Historians with a leftist political orientation usually praise his domestic policies (though most believe that he could have done more, that his progressivism was too limited) but are likely to execrate his foreign policy for its imperialistic and nationalistic overtones and to feel, as Stuart Sherman once put it, that "he can never again greatly inspire the popular liberal movement in America." The point is that Roosevelt does not fit conventional political categories, and hence modern critics are not as comfortable with him as were his contemporaries.

If Roosevelt were to have an opportunity to answer his critics, he would undoubtedly

The young Roosevelt as frontiersman. *(Library of Congress)*

try to explain that his domestic and foreign policies were complementary and that in both realms he operated on the basis of a well-defined philosophy of history and politics. Privately, Roosevelt might even have been willing to acknowledge the basic truth of H. L. Mencken's observation that he believed more in government than he did in democracy. Though not quite *sui generis* in the American political system (he was, after all, the product of a regional class and culture with Federalist antecedents and sympathies), Roosevelt's views are probably more understandable when placed in a European context. His intellectual affinity with members of the British upper classes attracted to social imperialism and with Otto von Bismarck, who looked favorably on reforms that might strengthen the German national state, is marked. Roosevelt not only adhered to and preached an aristocratic value system but also tended toward the European aristocratic view that both capital and labor were to be made subservient to the state.

Distressed by the deepening divisions between capital and labor that threatened the country internally, and attuned to the equally fundamental struggle for world power and position, Roosevelt envisioned a new kind of federal executive power to control the complex processes of the modern American industrialized state and at the same time advance the interests of that state in the international arena. Seeing more strength and promise for the American future than danger in the new industrialism, Roosevelt was not wont to advocate reform for the mere sake of reform. His first interest was in increasing the strength and cohesion of the American national state, and reform was often a means to that end, but he never had any intention of destroying or even seriously impairing the kind of corporate system that had brought the United States to the threshold of world power. The interests of the state were paramount, and both capital and labor had to be made to understand that. In a country where both the Left and Right have been historically suspicious of many aspects of governmental power and in a country that, as Georg Wilhelm Friedrich Hegel once observed, had no tradition of the state and was not yet a "real state," such views were what set Theodore Roosevelt apart from traditional American politics.

A Patrician in Politics

In the absence of a hereditary aristocracy, some historians have made the mistake of describing Theodore Roosevelt's family as upper middle class. Patrician is probably a much more meaningful class description. Only in comparison with the fortunes of the magnates of the new late nineteenth century industrialism could his family have been considered other than a very wealthy one. Roosevelt, the second of four children and the first son, was born on October 27, 1858, in Manhattan (one of the few American presidents to have been born in a large city). He was the product on his father's side of an old, longtime affluent Knickerbocker family and was descended from families all of whom had been established in America by 1764 and most in the seventeenth century. Though his lineage on his father's side went directly back to Klaes Martenszen Van Rosenvelt, who arrived at New Amsterdam in 1649, it is important to note that Theodore Roosevelt was actually only one-fourth Dutch and that the family had forsaken their traditional Dutch Reformed Church for a more fashionable Presbyterian Church.

His father, Theodore Roosevelt, Sr., was not only a merchant and banker in the family tradition but also a socially prominent philanthropist and reformer. His mother was Martha Bulloch, the daughter of a well-to-do and socially distinguished Georgia planter, a woman who was beautiful and socially adept, who was steeped in the manners and mores of the Old South, but otherwise rather ineffectual. Young Theodore was reared in a family that was self-consciously aristocratic, devoted to values that transcended those of mere money making, but a family nevertheless accustomed to power and influence. Such families, with their traditions of public service and noblesse oblige, had only scorn for upstart industrialists but had begun to discover that power in the United States was gravitating toward those with the great new fortunes, however rude their antecedents. Much of what Theodore Roosevelt did in later life can be seen as an effort to preserve a place in American public life for the patrician virtues with which he was imbued as a child and to neutralize the power of those who did not respect those virtues. It was precisely the peculiar social and political conditions attendant on nineteenth century American industrialization that could turn a conservative into a reformer.

The stories are legion about how young

Theodore, a frail, nearsighted, severely asthmatic child, acting on the urging of the father whom he idolized, built up his body to the point where he could endure incredible physical hardship. His has become a staple American success story, as much part of American folklore as Lincoln's rail splitting. It is very tempting, and many observers have succumbed to the temptation, to explain not only Roosevelt's devotion to the philosophy of the strenuous life but also the sum total of his political thinking and his conduct of the presidency in terms of his childhood personality development. Though useful, such an approach is not sufficient. It does help to explain certain facets of his personality—his courage, his confidence, his determination, and certainly his hyperactivity, but it is not nearly so compelling when it is used to explain the ends toward which his activity was directed. For that purpose, one must plumb his intellectual development and place him in his social context.

Roosevelt was educated primarily at home by private tutors. Two year-long trips to Europe and the Near East significantly broadened his horizons. He attended Harvard College, where he distinguished himself in natural history, a subject that in the age of Charles Darwin was pregnant with political implications, and his overall record was good enough to merit election to Phi Beta Kappa. When, in later years, he tended to denigrate his undergraduate educational experience, it was probably because little at Harvard caused him to question the viewpoint of the class from which he came. He tended to judge his fellow students by whether they were gentlemen, and his own antecedents made easy for him the ascent of Harvard's social terraces—the Dicky, the Hasty Pudding Club, and the Porcellian, the last probably America's most exclusive undergraduate social club.

Although it is tempting to think of Roosevelt as unique in personality and viewpoint, his early views were common among his class.

Neither the doctrine of the strenuous life nor that of the wisdom of cultivating military virtues was personal to Roosevelt or even of his own devising, but was rather the generational response of a group of patrician intellectuals profoundly influenced by the psychic legacy of the Civil War and at odds with the value system of business America. These men tried to counter the current business ethic with a social ethic of public service and a noncommercial lifestyle. Related to this was an attempt to reinvigorate the Federalist tradition in American history and to knock the Jeffersonian tradition from the pedestal it had so long occupied. Roosevelt's very first book, *The Naval War of 1812*, begun while he was an undergraduate and published when he was only twenty-four, strongly reflects this point of view. Though extremely technical in its discussion of naval maneuvers, it is also strongly anti-Jeffersonian and reflective of a lifelong commitment to preparedness and the necessity for leadership and the cultivation of the military virtues. As Richard Hofstadter put it, Roosevelt began his career as a member of an "American underground of frustrated aristocrats" who constantly complained of the alienation of education, intellect, and family reputation from significant political and economic power.

Though Roosevelt flirted with the idea of becoming a naturalist, as a result of interests he developed as a young child and cultivated all of his life, one suspects that he ultimately decided that such a life was too contemplative and too removed from what his generation regarded as the battle for America's soul. He chose to attend law school (which he never completed) and to pursue what he probably hoped would be a lifetime of public service. What he never contemplated was a career in business. A triggering event may very well have been the Senate's refusal to ratify President Rutherford B. Hayes's appointment of his father as collector of the port of New York. Roosevelt was extremely close to his father, had long since taken him as a model for his own conduct, and was desperately shaken by his father's death while he was still an undergraduate. Equally important may be the fact that on his father's death he inherited about $200,000, certainly sufficient in those days to allow him to do whatever he wanted with his life.

Despite the counsel of his social set, who tended to assume a condescending aloofness toward ordinary politics, Roosevelt quickly joined the local regular Republican organization in New York City and before long was a successful candidate for the state assembly. Here personal traits of determination, ambition, and an aggressive hyperactivity may well have been decisive; Roosevelt was constitutionally incapable of sitting on the sidelines. "I intended," he said, "to become one of the governing class"; and if he could not hold his own with the rough and vulgar men who then dominated that class, "I supposed I would have to quit, but I certainly would not quit until I had made the effort and found out whether I was too weak to hold my own in the rough and tumble." Though sometimes dismissed for his dandyism, Roosevelt really had little trouble holding his own, and in the process he did much to recapture political power for the cultivated and to make politics once more an attractive career for well-educated, talented men and women who thought of public service in terms other than personal aggrandizement. He virtually rehabilitated the idea of the patrician in politics; the result was not accidental but consciously intended. As Hofstadter has written, he was "the first reformer to understand how much the stigma of effeminacy and ineffectuality had become a handicap to reformers" and also the first to show others how that stigma might be overcome, to blaze a path by demonstrating and dramatizing the compatibility of education, social status, and reform with energy, vitality, and Americanism.

The energy he poured into sport, scholarship, politics, and even actual physical combat in the next two decades made him something of a national legend long before he became president and early gave him an unusual ability, as his friend Henry Cabot Lodge expressed it, to command the popular imagination. Even if there was no calculation in his early decision to try ranching in the then untamed Dakota territory (and he was not the only aristocrat attracted by adventure in the West), his identification with the West and with the outdoor life in general soon became a part of his political style, a means of identifying himself with an energetic, manly, and uncorrupted way of life, with the straightforward politics Americans idolize and yet never seem to achieve. Stories about his feats in the West eventually became a part, not only of his own personal political capital, but also of the American political legend. Roosevelt hunted grizzlies and cougars in the Rockies, matched shooting skills with American Indians, captured armed thieves, and knocked out a tough in a brief barroom brawl. In real life he seemed to demonstrate precisely the frontier virtues he tended to idolize in his historical writing.

Roosevelt's energy was always prodigious. For example, in the twenty years between his graduation from Harvard and his accession to the presidency, he wrote nine books, including two serviceable biographies, *Thomas Hart Benton* (1887) and *Gouverneur Morris* (1888), and, while governor of New York, an extremely self-revelatory study, *Oliver Cromwell* (1900). He also published a major four-volume history of the early trans-Appalachian West, *The Winning of the West* (1889-1896), which was well received by professional historians and, though far from pro-Indian in point of view, demonstrated a considerable interest in and understanding of American Indian culture.

None of this caused him to neglect politics and government service. He served three terms in the New York State legislature, where he developed a reputation as an exposer of corruption and a battler for the public interest. Though conventionally conservative in most respects, he did advocate state regulation of business in a few limited areas, and he early developed an aversion for both the judiciary's narrow devotion to laissez-faire economics and its seeming inability to understand the necessity of according priority to the public interest.

In 1886, he ran unsuccessfully for mayor of New York City in a famous three-cornered race with Abram Hewitt and Henry George, and he was appointed to the United States Civil Service Commission by President Benjamin Harrison in 1889. He was reappointed by Grover Cleveland, a Democrat, four years later and continued to serve in that capacity until appointed head of the New York City Board of Police Commissioners in 1894. On both commissions, he managed to attract national attention and add to his reputation as an active and effective reformer. He proved to be a singularly adept administrator, combining a mastery of detail and careful planning with bold vision. Above all, he was a master at dramatizing the need for reform and using the press skillfully to that end. At the same time, he dramatized himself, and as early as 1895 some of his friends were predicting that he would eventually come to high national office, perhaps even the presidency itself. His political skills were especially apparent in his ability to establish a reputation for principled, nonpartisan administration of the law while keeping his fences within his own party carefully mended.

TR and the Rough Riders: The Spanish-American War

Through the advocacy and mediation of high-placed political friends, Henry Cabot Lodge foremost among them, Roosevelt was next appointed assistant secretary of the navy in 1897 by President William McKinley, for whom he had conducted an extensive speech-making tour of the Northeast and the West. Long an advocate of naval expansion and preparedness, Roosevelt regarded this as a position of considerable substance and challenge. Handicapped by a public opinion and an administration that did not share his priorities, he nevertheless did much to prepare the navy for the struggle with Spain, which he not only foresaw but for which he fervently wished. Owing to Secretary John Davis Long's having taken the day off, Roosevelt found himself in actual control of the United States Navy on February 25, 1898, ten days after the destruction of the battleship *Maine* in Havana Harbor. Acting on his own and with great dispatch, he ordered the Pacific fleet, commanded by Commodore George Dewey, whose appointment Roosevelt had been instrumental in securing, to stand by at Hong Kong prepared for combat with the Spanish fleet in the Philippines to prevent its movement across the Pacific toward the American mainland. He thereby set the stage for the Battle of Manila Bay and eventual American annexation of that large Asian archipelago.

Once the war that Roosevelt so long and vehemently advocated was declared, he, acting against the advice of friends and family, resigned his office and helped to organize a voluntary cavalry unit (under the command of Leonard Wood with Roosevelt as his second) composed of a few hundred cowboys, a good number of Ivy League football players, a few New York City policemen, fifteen American Indians, and assorted other adventurer types. Roosevelt strongly believed in leadership by example (a style not frequently cultivated in the United States): If one advocated a course of national conduct that entailed sacrifices, then one should be foremost in one's willingness to incur those sacrifices. The First Cavalry Regiment, quickly dubbed "The Rough Riders" by the press, with Lieutenant Colonel Theodore Roosevelt as battle commander, saw brutal action in the hills overlooking Santiago, Cuba, and suffered extraordinary casualties.

TR with members of the Rough Riders, 1898. *(Library of Congress)*

Though undoubtedly brash on the field of battle, Roosevelt proved an excellent leader; he was not only a good motivator but also extremely solicitous of his men's welfare when it came to provisions. He himself was in the forefront of the unit's military engagements, and perhaps the wonder is that he managed to survive. In the parlance of the day, the war was a "splendid little one," and Roosevelt and his Rough Riders were soon returned to Montauk Point on Long Island. While still waiting to be mustered out in August of 1898, Roosevelt began to receive political visitors within a few hours of disembarkation. The year 1898 was thought to be a Democratic one in New York because of the charges of corruption that were rocking the current Republican regime. Roosevelt, owing to his wartime fame, was deemed to be the only Republican with even a chance of success. As a result, the bosses came to Roosevelt, an event unlikely under other circumstances, and Roosevelt became the GOP gubernatorial standard-bearer. He conducted an extremely vigorous canvass, seldom

appearing without a vanguard of Rough Riders and never reluctant to talk about his recent military exploits. The result was a narrow victory and a two-year stint for Roosevelt as governor of the nation's most populous state.

Nothing short of the White House could have been a better testing ground for his ideas and abilities than was the governorship of a state such as New York, certainly urban and industrial but otherwise almost as diverse as the nation. Roosevelt's methods were by now familiar: He walked a fine line between consultation with the Republican bosses and the maintenance of his integrity and independence; he held almost daily news conferences and used the press as a means of getting advance reaction to proposals and of putting his own ideas constantly before the people; and he regularly sought the advice of experts in all areas of projected legislation. He popularized the idea of the neutral state—neutral, that is, between capital and labor but positive in promoting the general welfare. In but two short years, he had boasted a considerable achievement, generally improving the quality of state administration by a series of excellent appointments and getting through a boss-ridden legislature bills extending the civil service system, treating franchises as real estate for tax purposes, increasing the power of factory inspectors, licensing sweatshops more rigorously, and regulating the hours of drug clerks and of employees on state work. Though by no means successful in all of his reform efforts, it is the opinion of the closest student of his governorship that he developed an excellent grasp of the mechanics of political power and had as governor already "worked out a philosophy and a program by which his party could attack the great domestic problems of the day."

Roosevelt certainly wanted at least a second term as governor, but that was not to be. By a congruence of circumstances as unusual as those that made him governor, he was chosen to run with McKinley as the vice presidential nominee in 1900. Thomas C. Platt, boss of New York Republicanism, clearly wanted him out of the state; a reformer so adept at politics was a definite menace to his power. Equally important, Roosevelt already had a strong national following and was particularly popular in the West where William Jennings Bryan, the likely Democratic nominee, had his greatest strength. The powers in the Republican Party regarded Roosevelt, not with affection, but as a considerable asset to the national ticket and so he proved, conducting a campaign exceeded in vigor—miles logged and speeches made— perhaps only by the exertions of Bryan himself. McKinley was reelected by a comfortable margin, and Roosevelt began to settle into a job, the vice presidency, so lacking in power and work to do that he expected to be bored and even contemplated a renewal of his legal studies.

President by an Act of Fate: Restoring the Stature of the Office

Then, less than a year later, in September, 1901, at the Pan-American Exposition in Buffalo, yet another assassin changed the course of American political history by killing President McKinley and putting Theodore Roosevelt, that "damn cowboy" as Mark Hanna called him, in the White House. Roosevelt, not yet quite forty-three, was the youngest man ever to hold the office, and the powers that ruled the Republican Party had certainly never intended him to do so. Yet, he was almost supremely qualified; he had extensive administrative experience and was extremely well read and well traveled. Moreover, he was a serious thinker about major contemporary issues, both domestic and foreign, and he had both the makings of a program and the confidence that he knew what the country needed.

TR refused to shoot a cub during a bear hunt in 1902. Cartoonist Clifford Berryman used this incident to invent the "teddy bear." *(Library of Congress)*

At home and abroad, his task was a formidable one. In domestic affairs, the Republican Party had long since abandoned its Federalist and Whig antecedents and now stood for weak government, especially in the economic arena. The judiciary dominated American policy making on economic matters, and the judiciary in this period was disposed to interpret the Constitution narrowly and reserve for the states all powers not expressly granted to the federal government. The problem was that the states were incapable of regulating the new giant economic concerns that spanned the nation. The revolution in business organization, production, and marketing that had so drastically changed the face of the nation in the last several decades had rendered archaic a constitutional and legal system that still assumed that the trusts were exercising private power in the same manner as had the small entrepreneurs who serviced local communities in earlier eras. Competition was no longer free; a few very large interstate corporations were too powerful to permit that, but they had a vested interest in pretending that conditions were still the same. The matter was complicated by the fact that Americans had no tradition of the state (even the Constitution was antistatist and restrictive of government power in philosophy) and had historically been susceptible to much antigovernment demagoguery. In addition to these factors, Roosevelt faced a congressional coalition of conservative Republicans. As representatives of the interests of the new mammoth corporations, these conservatives opposed a derogation of power from the judiciary and the states and Southern Democrats, who feared any enlargement of federal power for their own regional and racial reasons. As Roosevelt saw it, his primary task was to reestablish the legitimacy of federal power, even of federal executive power, for neither the courts nor the legislative branch of the federal government was doing the job of protecting the American people from ravages of unrestrained corporate power. If he could not gain widespread popular support for federal restraint of this new great private power, the alternative appeared to be some form of socialism and that, he believed, was likely to inhibit the growth of American economic power and hence interfere with the growing international power of the American nation.

It has become fashionable to denigrate Roosevelt's achievements, especially in legislation, by means of invidious comparison with those of such successors as Woodrow Wilson and Roosevelt's cousin Franklin D. Roosevelt. The opposition to Theodore Roosevelt's plans, however, were formidable and so deeply entrenched that one should probably be more impressed by his actual achievements than by what historians writing in retrospect see as having been left undone. Certainly, he made the presidency once again, for the first time since Abraham Lincoln, a meaningful institution for most Americans, and certainly he not only greatly increased the scope of federal power but also did much to shape the nature of the modern American presidency. Wilson, who as a political scientist had once detailed the workings of what he called congressional government, drastically revised and upgraded his estimate of the power inherent in the presidency as a direct result of witnessing Roosevelt's conduct of the office.

In his efforts to gain popular support for a larger federal role in the economy, Roosevelt was his own best asset; his enormous talent for publicity served him especially well. His was one of the great commanding personalities of American political history. Even his enemies were usually charmed. Moreover, as recent studies have shown, he was assiduous in his cultivation of the press and an absolute master at managing the news and securing headlines when it so served his purposes. As important as his management abilities was the fact that he literally reveled in the presidency. He enjoyed being president, he said; "I like the work and I like to have my hand on the lever." He also considered the White House (he changed the name from the more formal Executive Mansion) a bully pulpit, and he preached from that pulpit with great frequency and with considerable effect. He was one of the great exhorters of American history and was able to rivet the country's attention on Washington, D.C., and, not incidentally, on himself. As George Will has written, "Because politics is 95% talk, and the Presidency is 98% talk, there's nothing the President can do on his own except move the country, and by moving the country with his rhetoric move Congress, and once Congress is moved, then, but only then, can he govern." No one understood that better than Theodore Roosevelt.

As Roosevelt himself later wrote, apart from his belief in the need for more and better government, he did not enter the presidency with any deliberate planned and far-reaching scheme of social betterment. He offered no panacea or all-encompassing idea; indeed, he had an abiding distrust of those who did. He simply persuaded the voters that he had a conscience, that he would be fair, and that he knew how to lead. In domestic politics as in international politics, there were no final solutions; politics was only a means of reconciling conflicting interests. He was forever engaged in a delicate balancing act, gathering support by excluding from the national consensus only those at the extreme ends of the American political spectrum. As Richard Hofstadter commented, "The straddle was built, like functional furniture, into his thinking." He despised the idle rich, but he also feared the mob. The abuses of big business aroused his ire, but that did not mean that he was in favor of indiscriminate trust-busting. He favored reform, but that impulse was mitigated by the fact that he disliked the personality and methods of the militant reformers. Roosevelt coined the name "muck-raker" and it was not meant to be complimen-

tary, yet there was some truth to House Speaker Joseph G. Cannon's charge that TR himself was the chief muckraker, a master at arousing the indignation of progressives against the practices they considered antisocial. He never attacked the violent Left on one side but what he also execrated the plutocracy, the "male-factors of great wealth," on the other side. He often deliberately and publicly offended the big businessmen who contributed to his campaign, but at the same time he distanced himself from what he called "the La Follette type of fool radicalism on the left." This made for excellent political strategy under American political conditions, for he was telling the vast American middle class precisely what it wanted to hear. In performing this balancing act Roosevelt was doing two things, suggesting that somewhere was a golden mean and also that he was the one person best equipped to discover it. He had long since convinced himself that only someone of his class and background could stand above the fray, serving as a kind of impartial arbiter devoted to the national good and ensuring that right and justice would always prevail. One can applaud the effort without believing that he or anyone else is that capable of transcending his or her own interests.

Moral Government: High Ideals and Political Realities

For Roosevelt's generation, the key to national consensus was moral government. The moral element always dominated his political rhetoric; he fancied his role as being that of "national moralist," and he once defined progressivism as "the fundamental fight for morality." He often claimed that "we are neither for the rich man, nor the poor man as such, but for the upright man rich or poor." He pushed this insistence on morality so far sometimes that one of his advisers was once tempted to quip, "What I really admire about you, Theodore, is your discovery of the Ten Commandments."

Roosevelt was a champion of conservation. Here he stands with naturalist John Muir at Glacier Point, above California's Yosemite Valley. *(Library of Congress)*

surprising that both Roosevelt's major political programs, the initial Square Deal and the later New Nationalism, had a certain ambiguity about them.

His attacks on the corporate plutocracy were both vigorous and moderate. In his first annual message to Congress he declared, "There is a widespread conviction in the minds of the American people that trusts are in certain of their features and tendencies hurtful to the general welfare. This is based upon the sincere conviction that combination and concentration should be, not prohibited, but supervised and within reasonable limits controlled; and in my judgment this conviction is right." The following year he informed Congress, "Our aim is not to do away with corporations; on the contrary, these big aggregations are an inevitable development of modern industrialism, and the effort to destroy them would be futile unless accomplished in ways that would work the utmost mischief to the entire body politic. . . . We draw the line against misconduct, not against wealth." He thereby practically invited Finley Peter Dunne's famous burlesque of his remarks, "The trusts says he are heejous monsthers built up be the enlightened interprise iv th' men that have done so much to advance progress in our beloved country, he says. On won hand I wud stamp thim undher fut; on the other hand not so fast." Though gaining a reputation as a trustbuster, Roosevelt, when confronted by the complexities of antitrust, often shifted from one foot to the other, moving to break up an unpopular holding company in the Northern Securities case and permitting United States Steel to take

In all of this, the similarity with Woodrow Wilson is readily apparent, but an important distinction needs to be made. Whereas Wilson thought that morality was God-given and that he was chosen to interpret it to the American people, Roosevelt, less the believer though nevertheless religious, usually thought of morality in terms of a cultural consensus—in other words, in political terms. Progressivism for Roosevelt was always little more than a search for standards of justice that all Americans could accept.

What worked well in generality was not necessarily that helpful when it came to concrete legislation. As a result it should not be

over a competitor in the Tennessee Coal and Iron case.

His attitude toward the labor movement was also rather ambiguous. The federal government had previously intervened in labor disputes, but heretofore as a strikebreaker for the employers. Roosevelt moved to make the government an impartial arbiter instead. His interest was not so much in strengthening the unions per se (though he thought strong unions a necessary countervailing power) as in strengthening the government. As in his dealings with the corporate plutocracy, he wished government to be paramount over the conflicting economic forces and neutral between their struggles. To his way of thinking, strengthening the state was the only way of achieving social responsibility in an increasingly impersonal society. The large corporations had already corrupted (and the unions were on their way to doing the same thing) the old Jeffersonian individualistic ideal, and the result was not only an undemocratic society but also a chaotic and conflict-ridden one. Jeffersonian weak government was no longer sufficient. Democratic ends and national cohesion could now only be accomplished by Hamiltonian means, by more and stronger government.

Roosevelt was always cautious in confronting private power. He did not aim at breaking the trusts but at satisfying public concern about corporate power and hence heading off socialism. His solution from the start was regulation rather than dissolution. As TR explained in his *Autobiography*, it was the only workable solution:

> One of the main troubles was the fact that the men who saw the evils and who tried to remedy them attempted to work in two wholly different ways, and the great majority of them in a way that offered little promise of real betterment. They tried (by the Sherman-law method) to bolster up an individualism already proved to both futile and mischievous; to remedy by more individualism the concentration that was the inevitable result of the already existing individualism. They saw the evil done by the big combinations, and sought to remedy it by destroying them and restoring the country to the economic conditions of the middle of the nineteenth century. This was a hopeless effort, and those who went into it, although they regarded themselves as radical progressives, really represented a form of sincere rural toryism. . . . On the other hand, a few men recognized that corporations and combinations had become indispensable in the business world, that it was folly to try to prohibit them, but that it was also folly to leave them without thoroughgoing control.

Roosevelt wanted to work out methods of controlling the big corporations without paralyzing the energies of the business community. He feared the politics of big business, not its size. If government could get the upper hand, all would be well. He envisioned a new kind of federal executive power to control the complex processes of an industrialized state. In this, demonstrating considerable vision, he anticipated the methods of the future, the methods for the positive government of an industrialized society that began to emerge in the 1930's under his kinsman Franklin. Roosevelt always saw more strength than danger in the new industrialism and never preached reform for reform's sake alone. His first interest was in increasing the strength and cohesion of the American national state, and reform was a means to that end. He never had any intention of destroying the kind of corporate system that had given the United States the economic leadership of the industrialized world.

Roosevelt was a consummate political tactician. A master of the symbolic act, he chose both his issues and his enemies very carefully and always with an eye toward what actions were likely to advance his cause and which were likely to prove detrimental. He began his presidency very cautiously, assuring a worried business community that he not only would retain McKinley's cabinet but also would continue his policies for the peace and prosperity of the country. Before long, however, he had a well-nigh perfect issue on which to distinguish his administration from his predecessor's.

In 1902, J. P. Morgan contrived a massive merger of E. H. Harriman's Union Pacific with James J. Hill's northern railroads in an effort to control rail transport in a vast section of the Middle and Far West. Morgan offered Roosevelt a perfect target, the public having been sensitized to the trust issue by his recent spectacular consolidation of the steel industry. Roosevelt had his attorney general file suit against the Northern Securities Company, the holding company Morgan established to accomplish his ends, for violation of the Sherman Antitrust Act. The suit was successful and was even upheld in a 5-4 decision by the Supreme Court, which had to admit, however reluctantly, that the railroad industry was engaged in interstate commerce and hence subject to federal power. Roosevelt himself viewed this successful Northern Securities prosecution as the most important achievement of his first administration, not because one further consolidation had to be prevented, but because the president had been able to thwart several of the country's leading business tycoons. In putting Morgan in his place, Roosevelt did what no recent president had been able to accomplish, and also gave considerable impetus to his plans for making business subordinate to government. When he went after other trusts, such as Standard Oil and the tobacco and meat trusts, he chose his targets well (all were already unpopular) and to the same end.

He had another opportunity to discipline monopolistic business in the summer and fall of 1902 as a result of the intransigence of the country's coal mine operators and their determination to crush the United Mine Workers. This was more than a fight between miners and a few coal operators. Seventy percent of the anthracite mines in the country were owned by six railroad companies, which were themselves controlled by the country's largest financial houses. Public sympathy was generally with the miners, not only because so many homes were heated by coal but also because George Baer, president of the Reading Railroad and spokesperson for the mine owners, had the audacity to declare that "the rights and interests of the laboring man will be cared for, not by the labor union agitators, but by the Christian men to whom God, in his infinite wisdom, had given control of the property interests of the country." Roosevelt had his foil, and he yearned for some means of taking control of the industry in the public interest, the more so as a prolonged strike would likely damage Republican prospects in the November elections. He even seriously contemplated using federal troops to operate the mines; he realized he had no constitutional authority to do so, but he let it be known that he was prepared to invoke the higher imperatives of government. He may have been bluffing, but J. P. Morgan got the message and twisted the appropriate arms. The result was an agreement on a presidentially appointed commission to arbitrate a settlement, but without any recognition of the mine workers union. The step was a small one; still, never before had there been a similar kind of federal government intervention in industrial life.

By 1903, public unhappiness with the nation's corporate hierarchy had become so great that Roosevelt was able to challenge another right that American business once considered sacred. Against the bitterest conservative opposition, he secured the passage of legislation that established a Department of Commerce and Labor and, within it, a Bureau of Corporations authorized to investigate and publicize suspect corporate dealings. Though the legislation had no real teeth and rested on the idea of inhibition under the threat of adverse publicity, it served to establish a public and governmental right to know as a means of holding private economic power accountable.

The Election of 1904: A Roosevelt Landslide

Roosevelt had to spend a good portion of his first term endeavoring to sidetrack a possible conservative challenge to his renomination. Mark Hanna was the most likely alternative, but the threat evaporated with Hanna's untimely death. Then in the fall of 1904, Roosevelt beat the Democratic nominee Alton Parker by a huge margin of 2.5 million votes, up to that time the largest plurality ever recorded, and he truly became president in his own right. Just when his power appeared to be at its height, he undercut it by announcing that he would under no circumstances be a candidate for reelection to a third term in 1908. Most of his advisers regarded that announcement as his greatest political blunder, and most historians agree. It may, however, have served his purposes rather well. Like strong presidents before him (Andrew Jackson, for example), he was probably more politically vulnerable to the charge of usurpation of power than to any other. In fact, Roosevelt had lived through an era of American history in which images of governmental usurpation had been regularly presented to the public by special interests trying to preserve their immunity from any form of public control. Moreover, as Richard Abrams has suggested, Roosevelt's action may not only have served to blunt such criticism but may also in his own mind have freed him morally to stretch the Constitution whenever his own view of the national interest seemed to require it.

By the end of his second term, the conservatives in Congress had fought Roosevelt to a standoff, and he was forced to choose his issues carefully, eschewing tariff reform, for example, as not only divisive for his party but likely to detract from his own priorities as well. Nevertheless, his legislative achievements in

the first years of his second term were considerable, even remarkable given the political complexion of the Congress.

Domestic Achievements: Conservation and Other Topics of Progressive Legislation

The year of 1906 was the high-water mark for Roosevelt's brand of progressive legislation. The passage of the Meat Inspection, Pure Food and Drug, and Hepburn Railroad acts demonstrated the president's political adroitness in the management of Congress and considerably advanced his larger purposes. These acts established the federal government as a major power in the direction of the nation's economic life, and taken together they might well be considered as marking the birth of the modern regulatory state. Each served to bring order to the economy by increasing the power of independent regulatory commissions, which alone, in Roosevelt's view, could provide the requisite "continuous disinterested administration." Each established a federal agency with not only investigatory powers but also the authority to fix at least some of the conditions under which goods could be transported and sold across state lines. The federal government's constitutional power to regulate interstate commerce was now stretched to include the supervision of the production of certain merchandise that entered that commerce. In the case of the Hepburn Railroad Act, the passage of which taxed all of Roosevelt's tactical and promotional talents, the Interstate Commerce Commission was even given limited rate-making powers, which meant in reality a form of price control unprecedented for the federal government. In retrospect, it is easy to minimize Roosevelt's achievements, both because only limited segments of the economy were made subject to governmental supervision and because in all three cases he had substantial support from business groups that had been placed at a disadvantage by the chaotic conditions and unfair competition that had previously prevailed, but all three acts established significant precedents and were an integral part of his long-range plans for shifting the nexus of power in American society.

Perhaps Roosevelt's greatest triumphs and most significant achievements lay in the area of the conservation and regulation of the nation's natural resources. Though Presidents Cleveland and McKinley had made some effort to stem the tide, for years private interests, assuming it was their right, had been laying waste the timber, mineral, soil, and water resources of the West, just as they had once done in the older settled regions of the continent. Vast stretches of public land had been allowed to slip into the control of private interests under conditions of considerable corruption and without thought of preventing destructive use, requiring replenishment of renewable resources, or preserving portions for public recreational use. In this, as in so many other areas, Roosevelt sought expert advice. He was strongly influenced by an educated elite of new, self-conscious professionals (engineers, scientists, and public servants), spearheaded by Gifford Pinchot and Frederick Newell, men with the vision to see that the long-term national interest required that the depletion of the nation's natural resources be stopped. The ideas (multiple-purpose irrigation projects for the development of water and land resources, forest replenishment, parks for recreation and the preservation of wildlife) certainly did not originate with Theodore Roosevelt, but without his ability to publicize them and invest them with the kind of moral imperative that captured the popular imagination, the results would probably have been rather meager. No doubt Roosevelt was sometimes demagogic in appealing to the public's antimonopoly sentiments and often simplistic in characterizing the conservation cause as a clear-cut struggle between special interests and the people, but here, too, Roosevelt's purposes were larger

than assumed. Conservation was important per se, but the cause took on added significance because it was an area in which the business ethic and the social ethic were so clearly in conflict. Thus, Roosevelt was provided with a convenient vehicle for convincing the country of the desirability of increased federal power in the name of a higher public ethic.

Much was accomplished by way of legislation. The Newlands Reclamation Act of 1902, which earmarked revenues from the sale of public lands for the construction of irrigation projects, was an important beginning. During Roosevelt's tenure in office, more than thirty such projects, including Roosevelt Dam in Arizona, were launched. Congress also agreed in 1905 to establish the Forest Service with broad powers to manage the country's forest reserves. Roosevelt named Pinchot chief forester and, acting in tandem, they withdrew countless areas of public land from the clutches of private exploiters. In fact, the whole conservation movement depended to a large extent on the president's use of executive orders and other administrative prerogatives. Especially toward the end, Roosevelt was forced to achieve his purposes by some quick-footed maneuvering before Congress's efforts to restrict such orders could take legal effect.

Whereas some historians, their views colored by the legislative achievements of Wilson and Franklin D. Roosevelt, fault TR for not having accomplished more as president, others see in his actions the seeds of the abuses of presidential power that came to mark what has been dubbed the imperial presidency. The charges are somewhat contradictory. Roosevelt could be arrogant and arbitrary in his use of power (as in his peremptory discharge of a company of African American soldiers accused of a raid on the "good, white citizens" of Brownsville, Texas), and he certainly took both the Republican Party and a conservative Congress further in a progressive direction than they ever wanted to go. It is very unlikely that under prevailing political circumstances anyone could have done more (as subsequent events confirmed, the conservatives were very deeply entrenched in their control of the Republican Party), and despite all of Roosevelt's efforts and achievements, the power that resided in the presidency when he left office was still remarkably small.

Foreign Policy: Imperialism and Noblesse Oblige

Like all presidents, Roosevelt had more latitude when it came to the conduct of foreign policy, and that aspect of his presidency has been more severely criticized than any other. Not atypical is the comment of John Morton Blum that Roosevelt's

> belief in power and his corollary impatience with any higher law presumed that governors . . . possessed astonishing wisdom, virtue, and self control. As much as anything he did, his direction of foreign policy made that presumption dubious.

Critics, dominating historical discourse, have regularly derided his imperialism and his bellicosity, described by the appellation "Big Stick Diplomacy," and with almost equal vigor have denounced his supposed racist assumptions and the secret understandings he contracted with other powers. Even his manifest accomplishments have been minimized by reducing his own role in them. Such criticism has two wellsprings: Americans have never been able to agree about the basis on which the United States should conduct its foreign policy, and Roosevelt had some clear-cut ideas about how American foreign policy ought to be conducted and, moreover, tried to put them into practice. He probably deserves much better marks in this area than he has received.

By the time the mantle of the presidency descended on Roosevelt's shoulders, the United States, by reason of its great economic resources alone, was already a world power. By no stretch of the imagination, however, could it have been deemed a responsible world power. Severely hampered by an incompetent foreign service, impeded by a Congress lulled by America's safe position in the world into regarding foreign policy issues as little more than the sources of possible domestic advantage, and faced by a people who clung tenaciously to the isolationist shibboleths of the past rather than face the realities of a complex, interdependent, modern world, Roosevelt was nevertheless determined to make the United States a responsible force in international affairs.

Roosevelt presents historians with special problems; because he is considered a modern president, one tends to expect him to share modern values. He was, however, the product of an age whose values differed markedly. He was, for example, an imperialist, even a rather belligerent one, and no doubt he was also a militarist, in some senses of the word. He found it easy to divide the world into "civilized" and "barbarian" countries, and strongly believed that peace would never prevail "until the civilized nations have expanded in some shape over the barbarous nations." Like Walter Lippmann, he thought in terms of parceling out among the civilized nations stewardships over those who had not yet reached that stage, and he had no qualms about the use of military force to accomplish such ends. The American Civil War had demonstrated for his generation the necessity of sometimes using military force to accomplish moral ends; only northern military superiority had saved the Union and abolished slavery. Moreover, many commentators of his generation and the coming of World War I have emphasized its widespread willingness to risk or accept war as a reasonable solution to a whole range of problems, political, social, and international.

Roosevelt's imperialism was also of a special variety; it was almost naïvely idealistic and was dominated by a strong sense of noblesse oblige. He sincerely believed that the United

States should endeavor to take civilization to the rest of the world, much as his father had organized Bible classes in the slums of New York City. The United States, as a specially advanced and privileged nation, had a moral obligation to play a major role in modernizing the backward peoples of the world. He strongly and publicly eschewed the imperialism of economic exploitation and was determined to make American administration of the Philippines a model, a means of showing the more exploitation-minded Europeans how it really ought to be done.

Though his successes were limited by a Congress intent on protecting local and regional agricultural interests, he expended considerable effort in trying to push through tariff arrangements that would give the Filipinos and the Cubans advantages in the American market likely to encourage their own rapid economic development. Moreover, he regarded imperialism as bound to be beneficial for Americans, not economically but morally. It would divert Americans from their preoccupation with material gain and set up a standard of conduct for a generation of idealistic young Americans who would administer dependent areas in such a selfless way as to remove even the possibility of the charge of American economic exploitation.

It has been fashionable to label Theodore Roosevelt a racist, but modern usage does not do justice to the complexity of Roosevelt's thinking. He was a historian, well attuned to the fact that the world's great civilizations had all eventually succumbed, whether to the vagaries of human nature or to superior military force. Though he proclaimed the superiority of Anglo-Saxon civilization in his world and celebrated its spread across the Earth's surface, he had a strong sense of the fact that such developments were not fixed for all time. His estimate of nations and peoples was always strongly conditioned by considerations of power. Although his attitude toward the Chi-

nese, for example, was always one of condescension bordering on scorn, he was reacting much more to Chinese weakness than to Chinese racial characteristics, though it must be admitted that he sometimes had difficulty maintaining a rigid distinction between the two. Moreover, he never begrudged respect for individuals, regardless of race or ethnic origin, when he thought it warranted by achievement or character. The friendships he cultivated with foreigners and his appointments of African Americans and other minority group members to federal office all attest that fact.

Particularly revealing in this regard was his attitude toward the Japanese. For them he had only great respect, a respect based almost entirely on their rapid economic development and especially on their demonstrated military prowess. In fact, Roosevelt, contrary to the views of most Americans, was quite willing to assign to the Japanese responsibility for civilizing and policing major portions of East Asia, likening Japan's paramount interest in the area surrounding the Yellow Sea to that of the United States in the area of the Caribbean. Not only did he believe that Japan deserved to control Korea but he also thought that it had a world historical role to play in bringing China "forward along the road which Japan trod" toward membership in the exclusive club of great civilized powers.

Much criticism has been directed against Roosevelt's actions in Central America and the Caribbean. Some of the criticism is justified, especially that concerning means (called by some, "Big Stick Diplomacy"), but here as elsewhere it is important to understand that his object was not simply to advance the interests of the United States but to stabilize the region in the interest of peace and world order as well.

The Panama Canal

Roosevelt considered the building of the Panama Canal to be his greatest achievement in office and in later years was once so bold as to claim that he "took" Panama. His actions came under considerable criticism at the time; the Democratic Party took up Roosevelt's treatment of Colombia as a political issue, and the United States Congress later acknowledged its guilt by paying Colombia additional monies, if only after Roosevelt's death and in an effort to pave the way for American oil leases. The whole affair had its immediate cause in the publicity surrounding the ocean-to-ocean dash of the USS *Oregon* around Cape Horn in 1898 in a futile effort to bolster the American fleet before the Spanish-American War ended. The epic underscored the necessity for a canal across the Central American isthmus for security reasons. The idea had gained currency about the middle of the nineteenth century for economic reasons, and its attractiveness had grown as Californians and Westerners chafed under the transportation charges exacted by the great transcontinental railroad companies.

After the eruption of a volcano in Nicaragua lessened the attractiveness of that route, the Isthmus of Panama became the logical choice. A French company had once made an effort in that area and still held a valid charter. Panama had always been an unruly province of Colombia. During the course of the nineteenth century, Colombia had to cope with more than fifty insurgencies there aimed at secession, and at least four times Colombia had called on the United States, under an 1846 treaty in which the United States pledged to help assure safe transit across the isthmus, to assist in repressing Panamanian rebellions.

Colombia was never averse to the construction of a canal across the isthmus (in fact, it initiated negotiations in 1900), but as American interest peaked it was prepared to exact a price. In January, 1903, Roosevelt offered Colombia $10 million plus a quarter of a million a year for a ninety-nine-year lease of a 6-mile-wide canal zone. Congress also authorized a $40 million payment to the French Panama Canal Company to assume the company's rights to the route. The Hay-Herran Treaty embodying these terms was quickly negotiated and as quickly ratified by the U.S. Senate. It was, however, turned down by the Colombian Senate, acting under instructions from the Colombian dictator, who normally dispensed with his legislature entirely but had summoned it to con-

Roosevelt visits the construction site for the Panama Canal in 1906. *(Library of Congress)*

389

sider the treaty while permitting it to pursue no other business. Basically, the Colombian dictator wanted to exact more money, which raised Roosevelt's dander and resulted in a flow of expletives directed at the Colombians, "homicidal corruptionists" being among the milder of them. To Roosevelt's way of thinking, such behavior lessened the regard he needed to pay to Colombia's sovereign prerogatives; moreover, he determined not to let legal technicalities stand in the way of the more fundamental moral imperatives wrapped up in the march of civilization.

Although it is true that Roosevelt contemplated a direct seizure of the isthmus, that action proved unnecessary. The Panamanians, with their own interest in the construction of a canal, soon rebelled against Colombian authority. The United States did not make the Panamanian Revolution, nor did it create the conditions that engendered the rebellion against Colombia's authority. The Panamanians, however, had good reason to believe that the United States would smile on their efforts. Roosevelt's instructions to the acting secretary of the navy were "to prevent the landing of any armed force, either Government or insurgent," and although this was technically in accord with the American obligation (under the 1846 treaty) to preserve transit across the isthmus, its effect was to block Colombian military efforts to suppress the new insurgency instead of aiding those efforts as had sometimes happened in the past. Roosevelt hastily recognized the Republic of Panama and quickly negotiated a canal treaty with that new country, the terms of which were even more favorable to the United States than those previously negotiated with Colombia. Years later, in his autobiography, Roosevelt boasted, "I took the Isthmus, started the canal and then left Congress not to debate the canal, but to debate me." Certainly, his methods were somewhat high-handed, but the construction of the canal was a great achievement, and without

Roosevelt's actions it might have been long delayed.

The canal (though not completed during TR's presidency) solved the country's major strategic problem by permitting the quick passage of the American navy from one major ocean to the other. It also occasioned new concerns. The European powers had just completed their division of Africa and were casting longing eyes at Latin America; blocking their encroachment into the Caribbean (into the area that controlled the approaches to the projected vital canal) became a matter of high national priority. The most likely threat was posed by European powers moving into the area in an effort to collect debts owed to European creditors by impecunious countries or their dictators.

The problem was that the United States was having difficulty invoking the Monroe Doctrine against European intervention in the absence of any willingness to assume responsibility itself. The idea that power and responsibility went hand in hand was in fact the principal rationale for the Roosevelt Corollary to the Monroe Doctrine; as Roosevelt told his friend George Otto Trevelyan, "We cannot perpetually assert the Monroe Doctrine on behalf of all American republics, bad or good, without ourselves accepting some responsibility in connection therewith." In taking such an approach (now criticized as paternalistic), Roosevelt was doing little more than meeting the demands of the Europeans, perhaps best expressed in Lord Salisbury's reply to President Cleveland's rather peremptory note during the Venezuelan crisis of 1895. Salisbury's point was that "the Government of the United States is not entitled to affirm as a universal proposition, with reference to a number of independent states for whose conduct it assumes no responsibility, that its interests are necessarily concerned in whatever may befall those states simply because they are situated in the Western Hemisphere."

Chastened by German bombardment of the Venezuelan coast in 1902 (an incident that was contained by the dispatch of an American squadron under Admiral Dewey and a private warning to the kaiser), Roosevelt decided that the only way to prevent such dangerous incidents in the future was for the United States to step in first, so that there would be no pretext for European intervention. In the interest of national security and peace in the region, he told Congress that the United States had to see to it that order prevailed and that just obligations were met. When internal disorders threatened payments on the Dominican Republic's foreign debt, Roosevelt, acting on his authority as commander in chief, took over the Santo Domingo customhouse and soon established that country on a sound financial footing.

Historians have usually assumed that Roosevelt coveted additional territory in Latin America and was widely resented there for assuming the role of hemispheric policeman. In fact, he did not desire the annexation of either Cuba or Santo Domingo (in his ever-colorful language this was expressed as having "about the same desire to annex" another island "as a gorged boa constrictor might have to swallow a porcupine wrong-end-to"). Moreover, American prestige was exceptionally high under Theodore Roosevelt. He was held in great esteem for his role in the war for the liberation of Cuba and even more highly regarded for his honoring of the American pledge to withdraw from Cuba in 1903 and for the limitations that he imposed on subsequent interventions. Roosevelt usually resisted the temptation to preach to Latin Americans, and in turn many of them saw him, not as a Yankee imperialist, but as their protector against European ambitions.

Roosevelt's Diplomacy in Retrospect

Roosevelt was actually one of the United States's premier diplomat presidents, often serving as his own secretary of state while nevertheless making distinguished appointments (John Hay and Elihu Root) to that office. He was the first president in a long time who could be called a cosmopolitan man: He had traveled extensively in Europe as a child and had a wide circle of European friends and correspondents, and a few non-European ones as well. Despite his reputation for brashness and vigorous speech, he was extremely sensitive to the feelings of other countries and to those of their diplomats, several of whom (for example, Jules Jusserand of France, Speck von Sternberg of Germany, and Cecil Spring Rice of Britain) were among his innermost circle of friends. Historians, in their emphasis on the "big stick" aspect of Rooseveltian diplomacy (and in their reference to Roosevelt's thinking that demonstrations of military force and diplomacy went hand in glove), have frequently neglected the other aspect of Roosevelt's aphorism: He always talked of speaking softly, while carrying a big stick, and his most insistent complaint about his fellow countrymen was that they tended to want to "combine the unready hand with the unbridled tongue." Although pursuing a substantial naval building program, he was invariably punctilious in his treatment of the Japanese. Many of his countrymen (including too many of their representatives in Congress), in contrast, sought every occasion to insult the Japanese yet were nevertheless eager to cut naval appropriations.

Not since the early years of the Republic had an American president held such a firm grasp on the geopolitical realities of world politics. Unlike most Americans, TR recognized the oneness of the early twentieth century world. He once told the U.S. Congress that "the increasing interdependence and complexity of international political and economic relations render it incumbent on all civilized and orderly powers to insist on the proper policing of the world." The United States could no longer shut itself off from the rest of the world.

"The Busy Showman"—TR making peace in Morocco. *(Library of Congress)*

sphere, but in all major diplomatic decisions." Even those who like to speak of Roosevelt's "imperial internationalism" have had to admit that his role in world politics was eminently constructive. He took risks and often incurred domestic political disadvantage, but his achievement becomes clear when set against his successors' inactivity during the second Moroccan crisis in 1911 and during the fateful summer of 1914.

Howard Beale contends that Roosevelt had a particularly noteworthy concern with power relationships: "He was intrigued with power, with problems of power, and with rivalries for power." Indeed, Roosevelt himself once confessed that he believed in power, though it is important to note that the full quotation states, "I believe in power, but I believe that responsibility should go with power." Often in American history such thoughts have been sufficient to condemn someone, and just as often they have been used to obscure the truth. Roosevelt understood that idealism was not a self-fulfilling proposition and that what he had done could have been accomplished only from a position of strength. In fact, he was extremely proud of the things he had done to make the United States into a major military power, and he was inclined to put his doubling of the size of the U.S. Navy at the very top of his list of accomplishments. He wanted to increase the power of the United States in the international arena for many of the same reasons that he sought to increase the power of the federal government and of the presidency in the domestic arena. Only such power, he

Its security depended on maintaining the balance of power both in Europe and Asia (and Roosevelt was acutely aware of how closely interrelated the two were). Moreover, Roosevelt believed that as a great power the United States had commensurate international responsibilities and obligations; it was in the interest of the United States to work actively for world peace. This he did most effectively; his work at the Portsmouth Conference, mediating between Russia and Japan to end their recent war, earned for him the Nobel Peace Prize, and he also played a major role behind the scenes in the Algeciras Conference, which smoothed over a potentially volatile Franco-German conflict over Morocco. As Frederick Marks had written, "For the first time, America was taken into account by world leaders, not only in questions affecting the Western Hemi-

thought, could establish order both at home and abroad. It was important that this great new power be accumulated in the right hands, but whether in his hands or in those of the United States, Roosevelt did not doubt that either he or the United States was playing a progressive and righteous role.

Thanks to the innovative work, bridging psychology and history, of Kathleen Dalton, who studied the countless letters that Roosevelt received from the proverbial man and woman in the street, historians are coming to understand precisely what it was about Theodore Roosevelt that endeared him to so many Americans and gave him while still living a cult following new in the annals of American history. Dalton argues that Roosevelt understood that the symbolism of harmonious social unity and equality drew the public to him and that he consciously intended to portray himself in his 1899 book *The Rough Riders* "as a leader who could unite an odd assortment of American types—cowboys, polo-players, derelicts, football stars, Indians, and Wall Street lawyers." The question remains whether TR used his talents simply to secure power for himself or in an effort to reunite a very fragmented society and imbue it with a new sense of purpose. One suspects that in his own mind at least the distinctions between the two were blurred, but it also cannot be denied that by the time he stepped down in 1909, he had established the basic conditions under which the American state would eventually assume its modern responsibilities.

At fifty, he was still a young man when he retired from the presidency. His initial intentions were the best; he went off on a long African safari in order to permit his successor, William Howard Taft, to put his own stamp on the presidency. He found it very difficult, however, to stay out of the political limelight. Upset by some of Taft's policies, particularly in foreign affairs, antitrust enforcement, and conservation, Roosevelt, in 1912, challenged his renomination. When Taft defeated TR at the Republican convention, Roosevelt bolted the party and sought to rally his followers in a third-party bid for the presidency. In a race against Taft, the Democrat Woodrow Wilson, and Socialist Eugene V. Debs, Roosevelt campaigned on a platform that accepted the existence of big business but called for federal regulation to prevent abuse of its power and that endorsed federal social welfare legislation such as workers' compensation and child labor laws. Roosevelt finished a strong second to Wilson, who won partly because of the split within Republican ranks. World War I broke out in Europe two years after the election, and Roosevelt became an ardent supporter of preparedness and a vocal critic of Wilson's policy of neutrality. When Wilson finally took the nation into war in 1917, Roosevelt sought but failed to receive Wilson's approval to raise a division and lead it into combat. Roosevelt remained critical of the Wilson administration but nevertheless became a vitriolic supporter of the war effort. By 1918, he had begun to lay plans for another try at the Republican nomination for president, but he died on January 6, 1919. In his treatment of Taft and harsh attitudes toward those who were not as enthusiastic as he was about aligning the United States with Great Britain during World War I, Roosevelt had often succumbed to his less generous impulses. Nevertheless, it is likely that had he lived, he could not have been denied the Republican presidential nomination in 1920. Had that happened, Republicanism in the 1920's would have had an entirely different tenor, and American history probably would have taken a markedly different course.

William C. Widenor

Bibliographical References

Roosevelt needs to be read to be understood. Indispensable are his own *Autobiography*, 1913, and Elting E. Morison, John Morton Blum, and Alfred D. Chandler, Jr., eds., *The Letters of Theo-

dore Roosevelt, 8 vols., 1951-1954. His fascinating childhood has received an enormous amount of attention, both from historians and professional writers. Practically definitive in this area is Carleton Putnam, *Theodore Roosevelt: The Formative Years, 1858-1886*, 1958. Very readable are Edmund Morris, *The Rise of Theodore Roosevelt*, 1979, and David McCullough, *Mornings on Horseback*, 1981; the latter contains some intriguing speculation about the effect of TR's asthma on his personality development.

The best single biography is still that of William H. Harbaugh, *The Life and Times of Theodore Roosevelt*, Rev. ed. 1975, but Harbaugh should be supplemented by the insightful interpretations of Blum, *The Republican Roosevelt*, 1954, H. W. Brands, *T.R.: The Last Romantic*, 1997, and Nathan Miller, *Theodore Roosevelt*, 1992. More specialized studies are David Burton, *Theodore Roosevelt: Confident Imperialist*, 1968; Howard Hurwitz, *Theodore Roosevelt and Labor in New York State, 1880-1900*, 1943; G. Wallace Chessman, *Governor Theodore Roosevelt*, 1965; George W. Mowry, *The Era of Theodore Roosevelt*, 1962; and *Theodore Roosevelt and the Progressive Movement*, 1946. For detailed accounts of Roosevelt's military career, see H. Paul Jeffers, *Colonel Roosevelt: Theodore Roosevelt Goes to War, 1897-1898*, 1996, and Peggy Sa-

muels, *Teddy Roosevelt at San Juan: The Making of a President*, 1997. An excellent effort in comparative biography is John Milton Cooper, Jr., *The Warrior and the Priest: Woodrow Wilson and Theodore Roosevelt*, 1983, which uncovers some striking similarities between Wilson and Roosevelt. Edward J. Renehan, Jr., *The Lion's Pride: Theodore Roosevelt and His Family in Peace and War*, 1998, explores the bond between Roosevelt and his children and contrasts his heroic war exploits with the tragic experiences of his four sons in World War I.

Howard K. Beale, *Theodore Roosevelt and the Rise of America to World Power*, 1956, is a comprehensive study of Roosevelt's foreign policy. More sympathetic to Roosevelt's conception of the world and to his manner of conducting the nation's foreign policy are Frederick W. Marks III, *Velvet on Iron: The Diplomacy of Theodore Roosevelt*, 1979, and William C. Widenor, *Henry Cabot Lodge and the Search for an American Foreign Policy*, 1980. Albert B. Hart, Herbert R. Ferleger, and John A. Gable, eds., *Theodore Roosevelt Encyclopedia*, rev. 2d ed., 1989, is a comprehensive reference. For an extensive analysis of Roosevelt's presidency, see Lewis L. Gould, *The Presidency of Theodore Roosevelt*, 1991.

William Howard Taft

27th President, 1909-1913

Born: September 15, 1857
      Cincinnati, Ohio
Died: March 8, 1930
      Washington, D.C.

Political Party: Republican
Vice President: James S. Sherman

Cabinet Members

Secretary of State: Philander C. Knox
Secretary of the Treasury: Franklin MacVeagh
Secretary of War: Jacob M. Dickinson, Henry L. Stimson
Secretary of the Navy: George von L. Meyer
Attorney General: George W. Wickersham
Postmaster General: Frank H. Hitchcock
Secretary of the Interior: Richard A. Ballinger, Walter L. Fisher
Secretary of Agriculture: James Wilson
Secretary of Commerce and Labor: Charles Nagel

William Howard Taft, by background, training, and experience, was ideally suited to serve as the twenty-seventh president of the United States. His father, a distinguished lawyer and judge in Cincinnati, served in Ulysses S. Grant's cabinet briefly as secretary of war and as attorney general. Several years later, President Chester A. Arthur appointed him minister to Austria-Hungary and then transferred him to the Russian capital of St. Petersburg. Taft, one of five children, was born September 15, 1857, and was reared in a privileged, urbane, and Republican family. His entering public life, while not inevitable, was certainly assured after he was admitted to the bar in 1880. After attending public schools in Cincinnati, Taft en-

tered Yale in 1874 and then the Cincinnati Law School. He was an excellent student, first in his class in grade school, salutatorian in his high school class, and second in his class at Yale, where he delivered the class oration. While attending law school he was a part-time court reporter for the *Cincinnati Commercial*.

Taft's official portrait. *(White House Historical Society)*

Taft Before the Presidency

His political rise, if not as meteoric as Theodore Roosevelt's, his predecessor and mentor, was nevertheless remarkable and distinguished. He achieved the presidency without previously being elected to any legislative or executive office. Conservative by background, by training at Yale where he was greatly impressed by the laissez-faire views of William Graham Sumner, and by preference, Taft was president as the progressive reform impulse crested throughout the United States. He much preferred and was more at home in sedate judicial chambers among legal brethren discussing and resolving crucial questions predicated on the logic of the law, uninfluenced by clamorous and noisome public pressures. The fact that when he entered the presidency at the age of fifty-two he was more than 6 feet tall and weighed 332 pounds might also help explain his preference for an ordered, traditional, and precedent-bound approach to both his public and private life. So too might a weakness for procrastination help explain Taft's preference for the law, which was a rather casual mistress for some practitioners. Yet his entire career, aside from his brief stint as a journalist and five years as a practicing lawyer, was devoted to public service, a not unexpected endeavor given his abilities and his father's prominence in the Republican Party.

Shortly after receiving his LL.B degree in 1880 from the Cincinnati Law School, Taft was appointed assistant prosecuting attorney of Hamilton County, Ohio. Then in rapid succession, except for a short stint in the 1880's when he practiced law, Taft was appointed collector of internal revenue in Cincinnati (1882-1883), assistant county solicitor (1885-1887), and superior court judge in Cincinnati (1887-1890). He was appointed to the court by Governor Joseph Foraker to fill an unexpired term. He successfully ran for election to the office but was invited to serve as United States solicitor general by President Benjamin Harrison in 1890 before the conclusion of his judicial term.

In Washington, D.C., Taft first met Theodore Roosevelt, then a young, ambitious civil service commissioner. After two years, Taft returned to Cincinnati as a United States circuit court judge, a post he held until 1900, when President William McKinley recruited him to bring civil order to the newly acquired Philippine Islands. As a federal judge, Taft exhibited surprising sympathy for the concerns of working people, recognizing, for example, their right to organize and to strike and ruling that employers could not plead contributory negligence by workers when statutory safety provisions had been violated. In an important case involving the Sherman Antitrust Act, Taft decided that a combination of cast-iron pipe manufacturers was restraining trade and issued an injunction to curb the practice.

When he accepted the presidency of the Philippines Commission, Taft for the first time became an executive and administrator. His performance did much to enhance his reputation. As president of the Philippines Commission (1900-1901) and as governor general (1901-1904), Taft supervised the establishment of civil government ending military rule on the islands. Encouraging education, pacifying still-rebellious natives, and resolving the troublesome issue of the friars' lands were among the important goals he achieved. In the last instance, Taft in 1902 conferred with Pope Leo XIII in Rome and concluded an agreement in which the United States paid $7.2 million for the friars' lands, which then became available for sale to residents at fair prices. Before his return to the United States in 1904, Taft devoted his energies to improving the economic status of the Philippines and also toward establishing limited self-government.

While in the Philippines, engrossed in his challenging job, Taft twice declined appointment to the Supreme Court. In 1904, satisfied that his work on the islands could be relinquished to another, Taft joined the Roosevelt administration as secretary of war. He quickly became a close adviser, friend, and troubleshooter for the president, Taft's genial conservatism balancing the more impulsive Roosevelt. In 1904, he went to the Canal Zone to launch the actual construction of the Panama Canal. Two years later Roosevelt hurriedly sent Taft aboard a cruiser to Cuba to forestall a threatened revolution. In the end, Taft helped impose a provisional American government under the terms of the Platt Amendment to the Cuban constitution, which permitted the United States to intervene.

Roosevelt's declaration after his decisive victory in 1904 that he would not run again, plus Taft's increasingly prominent role in government and his growing friendship with the president, brought Taft's name to the fore as a successor to his chief. Few, if any, seemed better qualified than he to follow Theodore Roosevelt as president of the United States. Late in 1907, Roosevelt publicly let it be known that Taft was the person he wished to succeed him. Vigorously campaigning as Roosevelt's man, he was easily victorious in 1908, defeating William Jennings Bryan, who was seeking the presidency for the third time, by more than a million votes (Taft, 7,637,636; Bryan, 6,393,182) and with 321 electoral votes to his opponent's 162. Bryan carried no Northern state and only three (Nebraska, Colorado, and Nevada) in the West. His other votes came from the "Solid South."

Taft in Office: Frustrated Hopes

Much was expected of Taft as president; he would continue the Roosevelt policies and thereby enhance, in the words of the Republican platform, "justice, equality, and fair dealing" among the American people and further the nation's standing as a world power seeking stability and peace in a world where the balance of power was most tenuous. Unfortunately for

Theodore Roosevelt and his successor, Taft. *(Library of Congress)*

Taft and his party, however, which had dominated the national government since the defeat of Bryan in 1896, his administration turned out to be an abject failure, paving the way for the election of Woodrow Wilson in 1912. Taft failed because, despite a genial personality and a keen sense of humor, he was unable to project, as his predecessor could, the image of the presidency as an institution that could further the goals and aspirations of the American people. He could not articulate with memorable words or phrases either the goals of his administration or what the people were striving to achieve. Few could identify with him, and very quickly it became evident that he was unable to lead and guide his own party and mobilize public opinion behind his legislative program. As the head of his party, as the chief spokesperson of the American people, and as the chief legislator who outlined a program he wished the Congress to translate into law, Taft's presidency was a failure, notwithstanding the fact that more significant legislation was enacted during his term of office than during any presidency since Abraham Lincoln occupied the White House. At the end of Taft's tenure, he and Roosevelt were hurling barbed epithets at each other. Theirs was a friendship that split the Republican Party.

At the outset, however, few if any observers could foresee these developments. Roosevelt literally had groomed Taft as his successor. He was nominated on the first ballot with almost no opposition. Also, he inherited a most prosperous nation. His party's platform proudly proclaimed, "The United States now owns one-fourth of the world's wealth and makes one-third of all modern manufactured products. In the greatness of civilization, such as coal, the motive power of all activity; iron, the chief basis of all industry; cotton, the staple foundation of all fabrics; wheat, corn, and all agricultural products that feed mankind, America's supremacy is undisputed." So confident was his party in providing "equal opportunities for all" that its platform declared unequivocally for tariff revision by a special session of Congress immediately following the inauguration. Here was a time bomb, one that Roosevelt had avoided, which marked the start of Taft's difficulties. When Taft and Roosevelt rode up Pennsylvania Avenue on March 4, 1909, however, it was the first time since Andrew Jackson and Martin Van Buren had passed that way, more than seventy years before, that a retiring president would not have preferred another seatmate than the one the fortunes of politics had thrust upon him. Owing to a violent snowstorm and wind, the two men rode in a closed carriage, and the ceremony was held in the Senate chamber instead of its customary place on a platform in front of the Capitol. The inaugural parade and other festivities were greatly curtailed. Numerous celebrants were unable to reach Washington, D.C., which was almost cut off from the outside world by the downing of telegraph wires.

Roosevelt soon departed for Africa to hunt game, and Taft assumed the reins of office by summoning a special session of Congress to convene on March 15 to consider tariff revision, a matter he considered of the most pressing importance. Taft said in his inaugural address that the revised tariff should secure an adequate revenue and at the same time adjust duties in such a manner as to afford labor and industry, whether of the farm, factory, or mine, protection equal to the difference between the cost of production abroad and at home. Taft envisioned that such a tariff would "permit the reduction of rates in certain schedules and will require the advancement of few, if any." What he got was almost a six-month debate. The bill was not passed until August 5. It was strenuously opposed, especially in the Senate, by Republicans who asserted that the platform pledge called for greater reduced rates than Taft's bill proposed. These Republicans and their constituents, primarily in the Midwest and the West, saw the tariff as a means of providing a more equitable distribution of wealth by curbing the special privileges protection afforded large corporate interests, popularly called trusts.

Largely overlooked in the debate and the furor that accompanied it was a section in the tariff act that imposed a 1-percent tax on all joint-stock companies enjoying net earnings or profits in excess of five thousand dollars a year. By imposing this tax, Congress assumed the right to ascertain the earnings of corporations and to prescribe the forms of return, a long step toward federal control and supervision of large corporations whose business encompassed more than one state. The rates, however, were higher than Taft had initially envisioned, owing to the efforts in the Senate of Nelson W. Aldrich, an extreme high-tariff advocate. Though at one time during the long-drawn-out debate Taft had considered vetoing the measure, instead he made himself its defender, signed the bill, and in September began a speaking tour lasting two months and covering every state in the Union. He defended and even extolled the Payne-Aldrich Tariff Act while taking on a broad range of issues. On October 15, he defied tradition and crossed the Rio Grande, formally calling on the president of Mexico on Mexican soil. When he returned to Washington, D.C., the contours of his presidency were evident. There was a deep and growing fissure within his own party, and Taft, unlike his predecessor, was aligning himself with the old-guard, stand-pat wing of the Republican Party, a situation that ran counter to public opinion in many parts of the nation and from which the Democrats, who had not controlled a branch of Congress since 1894, stood to benefit greatly.

By itself, since it came early in Taft's tenure, the political damage done through his handling of the tariff issue might have been repaired. Yet more was to come, and in the course of his managing a conservation issue Taft alienated his mentor, Theodore Roosevelt. On January 7, 1910, the president dismissed Gifford Pinchot, chief forester of the United States, after Senator Jonathan P. Dolliver read a letter from Pinchot on the Senate floor endorsing charges leveled by subordinates against the secretary of the interior, Richard H. Ballinger, of opening for private sale a tract of valuable coal land in Alaska, acreage that Roosevelt previously had withdrawn from the market. Before his appointment to the cabinet, Ballinger had been the attorney for the syndicate seeking the Alaska coal lands. Taft, when the subject was brought to his attention, made public a letter in September, 1909, exonerating Secretary Ballinger and dismissing from office the chief field inspector of the Interior Department for filing misleading information against his superior officer. Thus when Pinchot's letter was made public, the controversy attracted widespread attention and further convinced Congress that an investigation of the charges was necessary. Since Pinchot was a friend of Roosevelt, the controversy opened a breach between the former president and his successor and widened the fissure in the Republican Party, despite the fact that the congressional joint committee later in the year on a closely divided vote exonerated Secretary Ballinger.

Taft was now seen as an enemy of conservation, and public criticism within a year led to Ballinger's resignation and the cancellation of the Alaska coal land claims. Yet Taft's record in withdrawing from public sale water power sites and mineral and forest lands was every bit as impressive as Theodore Roosevelt's. He also endorsed the expenditure of public monies to further reclamation projects in the arid regions. Since he had exacerbated tensions over policy, however, controversies and feuding within various agencies in the Departments of the Interior and Agriculture continued unabated, and their ramifications boded ill for both Taft and his party. Still, an even greater crisis was in the offing.

Rebellion in the Party

On March 17, 1910, a relatively obscure Nebraska congressman, George W. Norris, precipitated a parliamentary revolution by introducing a resolution that successfully challenged the power of the speaker to appoint committee members by removing him from membership on the Rules Committee, which performed this assignment and which the speaker chaired. Since the Rules Committee also determined the order of business in the House of Representatives, depriving the speaker of membership seriously weakened his power. Although Taft was not directly involved in these events, Joseph G. Cannon, the speaker, championed the president's programs, as did the old-guard, stand-pat members of Congress. Norris and the insurgent members had opposed the Payne-Aldrich Tariff and had endorsed Pinchot in the conservation fight. For their refusal to go along, Taft had withdrawn their patronage. In opposing what they considered Speaker Cannon's autocratic use of power in the president's interest, the insurgents further aggravated divisions within the Republican Party and gave the Democrats, who supported the resolution to curb the power of the speaker, a chance to capitalize on Republican dissension and gain control of the House of Representatives in the November elections.

Popular discontent with the Republican leaders was quickly evident in a Massachusetts by-election where a Democrat was elected by a majority of nearly six thousand votes from a district that had been invariably Republican and where the late member in 1908 had beaten his Democratic opponent by fourteen thousand votes. Shortly after, in a by-election at Rochester, New York, a Republican stronghold, the Democratic candidate won an almost equally striking victory. Equally foreboding to Republican ascendancy was the impending retirement at the close of the existing (Sixty-first) Congress of Senators Nelson Aldrich of Rhode Island and Eugene Hale of Maine, who for many years had controlled the Senate in the interest of Republicanism and extreme protectionism.

Yet despite these developments, so ominous for the prestige of both the president and his beleaguered party, the results of the session seemingly helped restore the Republicans' credit with the American people. More constructive legislation was enacted than at any time since the Civil War. The Interstate Commerce Commission was granted further authority over railroad rates, and telephone as well as telegraph lines were brought within its jurisdiction. A court of commerce was created to allow carriers and shippers seeking judicial review of rates an opportunity for prompt consideration. New Mexico and Arizona were admitted as states of the Union. A system of postal savings banks was established, and the following Congress approved a parcel post system. A bureau of mines was created, and, in an important step toward the conservation of natural resources, the president was granted authority to withdraw public lands from sale, pending a decision by Congress on their use. A commission was established to inquire into the corporate practice of issuing stock in excess of assets, and another investigated the cost of production in the United States compared with that of foreign countries, with a view to readjusting tariff schedules. Also, candidates for Congress were henceforth to be required to publish particulars of their campaign costs. These accomplishments were largely the result of the president's influence—and the result of compromises that did little to resolve the divisions within the Republican Party.

These divisions became evident as campaigning got under way for the fall elections. Theodore Roosevelt, fresh from a triumphal tour of Europe following his successful venture in African big-game hunting, reentered politics. In various speeches he estranged Republican "machine" politicians by commenting, among other things, on industrial and social conditions in the anthracite coal region, advocating the conservation of natural resources, suggesting that social evils might be the result of a wrong system, indirectly attacking the Supreme Court, and formulating his "New Nationalism," which widened the breach with conservative elements in both parties and led many to believe that he was ready to lead the insurgents, now increasingly called Progressives, in an effort to head again the Republican Party. In almost all of his speeches, Roosevelt advocated increased federal control—over corporations, natural resources, wages and hours, and the conditions of rural life. Though he was careful not to criticize the president, and at times he praised Taft and some of his policies, Roosevelt's speeches were generally regarded as widening the breach in the Republican ranks. In three weeks Roosevelt traveled fifty-six hundred miles through fourteen states and had spoken in some twenty cities, besides addressing hordes of people from his railroad car.

Roosevelt's tour was only one indication of the troubles affecting the Republican Party in that election year. Insurgent candidates were successful in party primaries in several states, chiefly in the Midwest. The Vermont elections on September 6 showed a greatly reduced Republican majority; those in Maine, six days later, witnessed the election of a Democratic governor and two congressmen in that traditionally Republican state. Elsewhere tensions within the Republican Party also came to the fore as delegates selected candidates for the November elections.

The result was a great Democratic victory. For the first time since 1894 the Democrats would control the House of Representatives. Key states—New York, Ohio, New Jersey, Massachusetts, and Connecticut—elected Democratic governors, and insurgent or Progressive Republican senators increased their numbers as did the Democrats, drastically reducing the Republican working majority in the Senate. Throughout the country the president and his party suffered severe reverses. Theodore Roosevelt, writing in the *Outlook*, said the fight for progressive popular government had merely begun. It would continue despite roadblocks and the fact that the last two years of Taft's tenure would be marred by intense partisanship, ripping the Republican Party asunder and bringing a Democrat to the White House in 1912. Taft, never a president to exercise strong leadership, was rendered almost impotent during his remaining years in the White House. He was caught up in forces that he no longer could effectively control, but to his credit, he tried. Unfortunately, some of his efforts further contributed to the deteriorating political situation.

Taft's aspirations for an Anglo-American arbitration treaty, expressed at the meeting in Washington, D.C., of the Society for the Judicial Settlement of International Disputes on December 19, 1910, was soon crowned with a measure of success when in June of the following year a joint agreement among Great Britian, Russia, Japan, and the United States was announced that curbed the wanton destruction of the seal rookeries in the Bering Sea. Also, in August, 1911, the president was truly pleased when treaties of arbitration with Great Britain and France were placed before him for his signature. Unfortunately, the Senate refused to ratify them, and Taft again found himself at odds with his party. Earlier, on January 26, Taft had sent a special message to the Senate, making a powerful appeal for Canadian reciprocity. He insisted that the time was ripe "to facilitate commerce between the two countries and thus greatly to increase the natural

"Taking No Sides" in the rift between "regular" and "insurgent" members of the Republican Party—Taft at his desk with a Rooseveltian "teddy bear." *(Library of Congress)*

resources available to our people" and to "further promote good feeling between kindred peoples." In numerous speeches the president warmly supported the project. Yet it seemed likely that the Senate, despite its Republican majority, would not go along because those members from agricultural states, such as Iowa, Minnesota, the Dakotas, and Wisconsin, feared that their staple products might be adversely affected by the proposed free list or by reduced rates on competing Canadian agricultural products.

Rather than trying to achieve Canadian reciprocity through a treaty, which would require a two-thirds vote in the Senate, Taft sought an agreement necessitating majority approval in both chambers of the Congress. In this endeavor he was ultimately successful. During the debate in the House of Representatives, however, the speaker-designate of the next (Sixty-second) Congress, Champ Clark of Missouri, created a sensation when he expressed support for reciprocity because he hoped that Canada would become part of the United States. A Republican member from New York, William S. Bennet, followed by introducing resolutions favoring annexation. Taft was unable to secure congressional support at this time, but he called the new Congress into special session early in April. The Democrats, now controlling the House of Representatives, approved the measure before the month was out, and the Senate, several months later, followed suit. Taft, who had labored long and hard for the agreement, signed it on July 26, 1911. All his efforts came to naught, however, when, in September, the Canadian government of Sir Wilfrid Laurier, the Liberal Party premier, went down to defeat. Laurier had made the consummation of reciprocity the prime issue in his campaign for reelection. The new premier, Robert L. Borden, had depicted Taft as a duplicitous leader seeking Canadian annexation.

To embarrass the president further and to define an issue for the next presidential campaign, the Democrats in the House of Representatives introduced several low-tariff measures: a woolen bill, a cotton bill, and a farmers' freelist bill, which the Progressive Republicans in the Senate also endorsed, allowing these "pop" tariff bills to receive congressional approval. Taft vetoed them as haphazard measures of tariff reduction.

Trust-Busting and Dollar Diplomacy

In his broad view of the trust problem and in a wide-ranging application of the Sherman Antitrust Act, Taft used an approach that truly entitled him, rather than his predecessor, to the title of trust buster. Whereas Theodore Roosevelt invoked the Sherman Act to further his political and national goals in a sparse number of instances, Taft seemed to interpret the law literally, and his attorney general, George W. Wickersham, launched a vigorous attack. The wire trust was compelled to dissolve; the electric trust dissolved itself after an adverse legal decision. Proceedings were also initiated against the lumber trust, the ice trust, the magazine trust, and others for unlawful combination and conspiracy in restraint of trade. The steel trust in October, 1911, announced its intention to cancel its lease of Minnesota iron range ore lands and to reduce the ore rates on its railroads. Nevertheless, the government instituted proceedings against it for violating the Sherman Act by monopolist practices. Earlier in the year the Supreme Court in suits against the Standard Oil and tobacco trusts ordered their dissolution but at the same time reassured business interests that "reasonable" restraint of trade was not illegal.

The suit against the steel trust seemingly violated an agreement Roosevelt had formulated during the panic of 1907 sanctioning the purchase of a controlling interest in the Tennessee Coal and Iron Company by the United States Steel Corporation to prevent the failure of the smaller firm, the largest iron and steel producer in the South, and to help curb the financial panic. Taft's action in this instance further widened the breach with his predecessor. Roosevelt, in opposing Taft's trust policy of initiating court action as a means of securing reasonable and legal competition, advocated legislation for supervision and control of the companies.

In a significant way Taft's major thrust in foreign policy also differed significantly from that of Roosevelt. Although accepting the nation's commitment as a world power, Taft pursued this approach largely through a policy of Dollar Diplomacy, encouraging economic interests in pursuing national interests. He described it as a policy of "substituting dollars for bullets" and sought to persuade American bankers to enter international consortiums to refinance Nicaragua's foreign debt and to support railroad building in China. Taft said that his approach was "frankly directed to the increase of American trade upon the axiomatic principle that the Government of the United States shall extend all proper support to every legitimate and beneficial American enterprise abroad." Although there was nothing new or original about Taft's approach, in the heated political climate of the latter part of his administration it aroused intense debate and controversy involving anti-imperialists, progressives and others critical of the role of large banking firms, and followers of Theodore Roosevelt who viewed national interests in much broader terms. Moreover, before Taft's presidency there had been little American investment in China.

Dollar Diplomacy, in the case of the Caribbean and Central America, would provide the means for helping those countries achieve stability by rehabilitating their finances, establishing sound monetary systems, securing efficient administration of customhouses, and establishing reliable banks. Such policies, Taft envisioned, would curb revolutions, further secure the Panama Canal, and avoid the danger of international complications brought about by foreign creditors. In addition, in 1912 the Senate approved a resolution that in effect extended the Monroe Doctrine to include an Asiatic power and foreign corporations that sought control over potential military or naval sites.

Roosevelt's Challenge: The Race in 1912

The year 1912 marked the disintegration of Taft's presidency, exhibited the acceptance of the reform spirit in both major parties, and split the Republican Party asunder in the fifty-eighth year of its existence. By the end of 1911 Senator Robert M. La Follette, creating the Progressive Republican League, announced his intention of seeking his party's presidential nomination. Also, early in the new year a movement in favor of Theodore Roosevelt's nomination was clearly evident, despite his disclaimer in 1904 of ever again seeking the presidency. By the end of February, Roosevelt openly acknowledged that he would challenge Taft for the nomination. The widening breach between these two former friends helped complete the rending of their party. Roosevelt declared Taft's support of the arbitration treaties "an unworthy and, however unconsciously, a hypocritical move against the interests of peace and the honor and interests of the United States and civilization." Taft, for his part, in a speech on Lincoln's birthday described the insurgents and Progressives as "political neurotics" whose proposals threatened to reduce the country to conditions paralleled only in the history of South America or in the French Revolution. Later their barbs became more direct and personal.

In seeking the nomination, Roosevelt endorsed a program of reform that included the recall by popular vote of judicial decisions, the initiative and referendum, presidential primaries, and an amendment calling for the direct election of United States senators. He later included woman suffrage. Taft had reservations about the entire reform program, but, along with most conservatives, he was particularly adamant about Roosevelt's endorsement of the recall of judicial decisions. Roosevelt's managers, however, appealed to the public by denouncing the Taft administration as lacking in leadership, destroying the Republican Party, disheartening the country, and bewildering business. Roosevelt himself charged Taft with being an oligarch, the friend of reaction and privileged minorities.

In the few states, fifteen out of forty-eight, with presidential primaries, most of the delegates endorsed Roosevelt. With the Republican convention scheduled to meet in Chicago on June 18, the leading candidates engaged in much reciprocal vituperation, with Taft accusing Roosevelt of deliberately misrepresenting his speeches and actions, of knowingly making false statements about him, of distorting his views, and more. He supported some of his charges by reading from his private correspondence with "My dear Theodore." Roosevelt responded in kind, describing Taft as "biting the hand that fed him" and yielding through feebleness to the "bosses" and the "interests" and attacking him for presenting confidential correspondence without permission.

As the primary results became known, it was evident that Roosevelt had real popular support, although New York decisively and Massachusetts rather uncertainly declared for Taft. Ohio, the president's home state, selected an overwhelming majority of Roosevelt delegates. When Republican delegates headed for Chicago in June, it was estimated that Taft and Roosevelt had secured anywhere from 400 to 450 delegates apiece. The outcome was centered on the contesting delegations, chiefly from the Southern states, consisting mainly of officeholders and African Americans, individuals holding patronage appointments in areas where Republican strength was small or virtually nonexistent. The task of deciding these contests fell to the Republican National Committee, which met in Chicago on June 6. On June 16, the result of its deliberations was an-

nounced. Taft was awarded 235 seats; 20 went to Roosevelt delegates. Taft's renomination was now assured. Roosevelt, charging that the president was a receiver of stolen goods, no better than a thief, called on his followers to bolt the convention and to form a new party dedicated to progressive reform principles and proposals. On August 6, the Progressive Party meeting in Chicago nominated Theodore Roosevelt by acclamation.

Roosevelt's candidacy and that of Woodrow Wilson, selected by the Democrats at their convention in Baltimore, prompted the widely held view that Taft had little chance of reelection. Roosevelt and Wilson both championed the cause of reform. Nevertheless, the platform of the Republican Party contained numerous progressive planks, including regulating by law the working conditions of women and children, workmen's compensation, simplifying judicial procedures, further conservation measures, and a federal trade commission to curb monopoly practices. It was so progressive that several prominent Republicans favorable to reform refused to support Roosevelt and remained loyal to their party.

During the campaign, Taft talked about the integrity of the Constitution and maintaining prosperity through a moderate and scientific tariff. Roosevelt, he intimated, was seeking to aggravate and exploit unrest in his own interest, whereas Wilson was a dangerous idealist who would break up the Constitution. Progressives and Democrats, he charged, were increasing popular dissatisfaction with talk of evils they had trouble defining and appeared incompetent to cure.

When Congress recessed at the end of August, Taft vetoed several tariff and appropriation bills, one of which indirectly abolished the Interstate Court of Commerce. He approved several reform measures, however, adding to the body of significant legislation enacted during his administration. One called for an eight-hour day for all government work-

Taft (center) on the Supreme Court, 1921. *(Library of Congress)*

ers and for employees on the Panama Canal after completion was approved; another prohibited the manufacture of white phosphorous matches. The third session of the Sixty-second Congress, the last of the Taft administration, would convene in December after the results of the vehement and hardfought presidential campaign were known.

An indication of what was to come was evident after the Vermont election on September 2, usually regarded as a political barometer. The Republicans lost heavily to the Progressives, while the Democrats gained in this traditional Republican state which, nevertheless, was carried by Taft. A week later, Maine, also a traditional Republican state, went for Wilson. In all, Taft carried one additional state, Utah, in the November elections for a total of 8 electoral votes to 88 for Roosevelt and 435 for Wilson. Taft also trailed Wilson and Roosevelt in the popular vote. In addition, the Republicans lost control of the Senate and failed to regain

control of enough states, so that the Democratic Party prevailed in a majority of state houses as well. Taft and his party were discredited and repudiated in the election of 1912, a complete reversal of the situation in 1908, when Taft was overwhelmingly approved by the voters as Theodore Roosevelt's successor.

Taft's Achievements

The election results meant that Congress in the last months of Taft's presidency would accomplish little in the way of significant legislation. Both were "lame ducks" waiting for their terms to end. Yet policies launched by the Taft administration continued to be implemented in the early months of 1913, before the inauguration of Woodrow Wilson. The campaign against trusts continued in the courts. Officials of the National Cash Register Company, for example, were fined and some were jailed after being convicted of violations of the Sherman Antitrust Act. In the House of Representatives, a subcommittee reported evidence of the existence of a "money trust," a few great banking firms controlling through interlocking directorships vast enterprises capable of depriving rival or competing concerns of their ability to secure adequate access to capital.

Among the pieces of legislation approved by Congress were several that added to the body of progressive measures during Taft's administration. Included were laws calling for the "physical valuation" of railroads so that rates would reflect the actual properties and not the paper (security) value of the enterprises and for the creation of a department of labor. Before Taft left office, the Sixteenth Amendment to the Constitution, calling for a federal income tax, secured the necessary support of three-fourths of the state legislatures. Soon after, the Seventeenth Amendment, providing for the direct election of United States senators, was ratified. Both were approved by Congress during Taft's presidency.

The Taft administration had been unfortunate in many ways. It had failed to achieve tariff reform; it had been weakened by a dispute over conservation policy and by the traditional association of the Republican Party with big business and organized capital. Countries in Latin America had been alarmed by Dollar Diplomacy, and the consortium designed to take the Manchurian railways out of politics had been ill received. It had also blundered in its reciprocity campaign. Still, Taft had done his best to provide international arbitration, and he had signed into law much useful legislation. The executive branch, moreover, had combated trusts with energy and success. Yet when he left office, his party was in shambles and he had suffered a humiliating defeat, which he accepted with dignity. Though well liked as an individual, his deficiencies as a politician and a leader made his four years in the White House a trial and an ordeal. More than any previous president, he escaped from Washing-

ton whenever he possibly could. In four years he traveled a total of 150,000 miles, a record for a president, crisscrossing the country, appealing in effect for a reversal of the popular verdict against his administration. He retired with dignity to a professorship at Yale Law School.

His later career was more suited to his talents and provided infinitely more satisfaction than his presidency. During World War I, he returned to Washington to serve as joint chairman of the National War Labor Board. Then on June 30, 1921, President Warren G. Harding rewarded Taft and gratified his heart's desire by selecting him for the highest official honor ever to be given to a former president, an office that he coveted far more than the presidency itself—the chief justiceship of the United States. Here Taft's abilities as a coordinator and conciliator could function in a more meaningful and harmonious atmosphere. Taft died on March 8, 1930.

Richard Lowitt

Bibliographical References

An older although in many ways the best biography is by Henry F. Pringle, a two-volume study, *The Life and Times of William Howard Taft*, 1939. Paolo E. Coletta, *The Presidency of William Howard Taft*, 1973, is a thorough and sound study. Dollar Diplomacy and international affairs are carefully examined by Walter Scholes and Marie V. Scholes in *The Foreign Policies of the Taft Administration*, 1970. Ralph E. Minger, *William Howard Taft and United States Foreign Policy: The Apprenticeship Years, 1900-1908*, 1975, explores Taft's political career prior to the presidency.

The relationship between Taft and his predecessor in the White House is reviewed by William Manners in *TR and Will: A Friendship That Split the Republican Party*, 1969. Equally valuable in understanding Taft is Archibald W. Butt, *Taft and Roosevelt: The Intimate Letters of Archie Butt, Military Aide*, 2 vols., 1930. For an insight into the insurgency movement that plagued Taft's presidency, see Richard Lowitt, *George W. Norris: The Making of a Progressive, 1861-1912*, 1963, and Kenneth S. Hechler, *Insurgency: Personalities and Politics of the Taft Era*, 1940. Two studies examine Taft from widely different perspectives: Donald F. Anderson, *William Howard Taft: A Conservative's Conception of the Presidency*, 1973, and Judith I. Anderson, *William Howard Taft: An Intimate History*, 1981, an attempt at psychobiography. Coletta, *William Howard Taft: A Bibliography*, 1989, provides a comprehensive listing of primary and secondary sources on Taft's life and presidency.

Woodrow Wilson

28th President, 1913-1921

Born: December 28, 1856
    Staunton, Virginia
Died: February 3, 1924
    Washington, D.C.

Political Party: Democratic
Vice President: Thomas S. Marshall

Cabinet Members

Secretary of State: William Jennings Bryan, Robert Lansing, Bainbridge Colby
Secretary of the Treasury: William Gibbs McAdoo, Carter Glass, David F. Houston
Secretary of War: Lindley M. Garrison, Newton D. Baker

Secretary of the Navy: Josephus Daniels
Attorney General: James C. McReynolds, Thomas W. Gregory, A. Mitchell Palmer
Postmaster General: Albert Burleson
Secretary of the Interior: Franklin K. Lane, John P. Payne
Secretary of Agriculture: David F. Houston, E. T. Meredith
Secretary of Commerce: William C. Redfield, J. W. Alexander
Secretary of Labor: William B. Wilson

Wilson's official portrait. *(White House Historical Society)*

Thomas Woodrow Wilson was born on December 28, 1856, in Staunton, Virginia. His father, Joseph Ruggles Wilson, a Presbyterian minister, was a powerful influence on his son "Tommy," as Woodrow Wilson's parents called him until he declared one day in his twenty-second year that he wished to be known as T. Woodrow Wilson (the initial quickly disappeared). He, along with his older sisters Annie and Marion and his younger brother Joseph, Jr., was brought up by a mother and father who nurtured him and shaped his personality and temperament in profoundly significant ways. From his father, Wilson gained a heady sense of confidence and of duty to fulfill his destiny as one of God's elect. He also developed an abiding moral intransigence, a stubborn self-righteousness that dogged him throughout his career.

Intensely ambitious for her son and completely uncritical of his faults, his mother made him feel intellectually and morally superior to his classmates and colleagues. Often ill herself, she helped develop in Wilson a preoccupation with his health. During his life he had a number of serious ailments; from the age of thirty-nine until his death in 1924, he suffered from cerebral vascular disease. In 1896 a stroke left him with a marked weakness in his right hand. Another stroke in 1906 weakened his right arm and left him almost blind in his left eye. In addition to periodic stress and related bouts of debilitating headaches and stomach problems, he continued to suffer from carotid artery disease, which caused a massive stroke in October, 1919, completely paralyzing the left side of his body and affecting his mental attitude and personality.

Wilson was also a dyslexic. He was nine before he knew his letters and eleven or so before he could read. Nevertheless, he was a good if not brilliant student. In 1873 he enrolled as a freshman at Davidson College, a tiny Presbyterian school near Charlotte, North Carolina. He stayed for two semesters at Davidson, where he played second base on the freshman baseball team and was active on the campus debating team. After spending the next year with his parents in Wilmington, North Carolina, Wilson entered Princeton in 1875. He had given up any plans he may once have had to enter the ministry and looked ahead to a political or literary career.

Following his graduation from Princeton, Wilson enrolled as a law student at the University of Virginia in the autumn of 1879, but he quickly developed a distate for legal studies and grew depressed about his career. Wilson left the university after a year, reentered in the autumn of 1880, but then, in December, withdrew again and went home to Wilmington.

He remained at home for some eighteen months. In the fall of 1882, he passed the Georgia state bar examination and set up practice in Atlanta. Yet his heart was not in his work, and he grew increasingly restless. He wanted to become "a master of philosophical discourse, to become capable and apt in instructing as great a number of persons as possible, . . . a speaker and writer of the highest authority on political subjects. This I *may* become in a chair of political science." In 1883, therefore, Wilson gave up his law practice and gained admission to The Johns Hopkins University in Baltimore, where the "seminary" of Herbert Baxter Adams was the very citadel of political scholarship in the United States. Soon after his arrival at Johns Hopkins, Wilson began writing his first book, *Congressional Government*. Drawing on earlier essays he had written and borrowing much from the British essayist Walter Bagehot, he finished the work in October, 1884. In it, Wilson described how laws were made, how Congress operated, and how the legislative branch dominated the government. Based on little original research, the book was full of glib generalizations and stylistic infelicities and sorely remiss in its depiction of economic realities in Gilded Age America. Yet in the book Wilson expressed some of the basic principles of political action that he would himself put into practice as president of the United States, and this alone makes *Congressional Government* Wilson's most noteworthy book. His *Constitutional Government in the United States* (1908) is a gloss on the earlier book. *The State* (1889) is a mediocre textbook. *Division and Reunion* (1893) is a short and derivative history of the country from 1829 to 1889. *George Washington* (1896) is a potboiler that Wilson, in haste and carelessness, wrote to pay for a new home. *A History of the American People* (1902), in five volumes and profusely illustrated, he also did in a hurry and for money.

By the spring of 1884, nearing the end of his first year at Johns Hopkins, Wilson wanted to leave. He wanted to marry Ellen Axson, the daughter of a minister in Rome, Georgia, whom he had met the year before, but to do so he had to have a job. In January, 1885, he found one: teaching at Bryn Mawr, a new Quaker college in Pennsylvania for women. On June 24, 1885, he and Ellen were married.

During the next twenty-nine years, besides giving birth to three daughters—Eleanor Randolph, Jessie Woodrow, and Margaret Woodrow—Ellen Axson gave Wilson unflagging devotion and constant affection, even tolerating a brief romance that Wilson suddenly developed in 1907-1908 with Mary Allen Hulbert Peck, a vivacious and talented, if vain and frivolous, woman whom he met while he was on vacation (without Ellen) in Bermuda. In 1914 Ellen Axson died. A few months later, at the age of fifty-eight, Wilson fell passionately, boyishly in love with Edith Galt, a forty-two-year-old widow of statuesque beauty and sexual magnetism, and in December, 1915, he married her.

Woodrow Wilson may never have reached the White House or any height of professional achievement without the women in his life to sustain him. He may also never have reached the presidency without the particular ascent he followed from college teaching to the presidency of Princeton University to the governorship of New Jersey. From 1885 to 1888, Wilson taught at Bryn Mawr College, then at Wesleyan University for two years, and from 1890 to 1902 he was professor of jurisprudence and political economy at Princeton. In 1902 he became president of Princeton and at once inaugurated some bold changes at the university. He revised the curriculum, established a preceptorial system of guided study, and brought in a number of promising young teachers and scholars. In 1906-1907 he tried—and failed—to abolish undergraduate eating and social clubs. In 1909-1910 he lost a bruising fight over the establishment and control of a graduate college. Wilson's successes at Prince-

ton brought him to the attention of New Jersey politicians, who asked him to seek the Democratic nomination for governor in 1910. His failures at Princeton, along with his old aspirations for high political office, prompted him to seize the opportunity to move from the halls of ivy to the corridors of political power.

New Jersey in 1910 was controlled by a corrupt alliance of political bosses and railroad and public utilities magnates. Republicans had held the governorship since 1896. Democratic bosses hoped to regain the office by putting forth as gubernatorial candidate a prominent citizen they could control, who would run on a liberal platform they could disregard. Wilson, at the time of his nomination, was a political conservative with little awareness of the great Progressive reform movement sweeping through American (and New Jersey) politics since the turn of the century. Quick to grasp the chance for nomination, Wilson was equally quick to adopt some of this reform program as his own. Repudiating the machine that nominated him, he swept into the governorship by a fifty-thousand-vote majority. He then openly broke with the state bosses, established his own firm control over the Democratic Party in the state, and pushed through a reform program—a direct primary system, corrupt practices legislation, workers' compensation, strict state control of railroads and public utilities—that soon provoked an intensive campaign by Democratic progressives to make him the party's presidential nominee in 1912.

The 1912 Campaign

Wilson himself thirsted for that nomination, and early in 1911 he began his campaign to gain it. Up and down the country he went, seeking delegates, speaking incessantly. His chief rival for the nomination was James B. ("Champ") Clark of Missouri, elected to Congress in 1892 and elected speaker of the House in 1911. When all the 1,088 delegates to the Baltimore convention had been chosen, 436 had

A Wilson campaign van. *(Library of Congress)*

pledged to Clark and 248 had pledged to Wilson, with the remaining 400 or so unpledged or pledged to Oscar Underwood of Alabama and other minor candidates. Clark, on the early balloting, held a substantial lead. On the fourteenth ballot, the veteran presidential candidate and powerful voice in the party, William Jennings Bryan, a delegate from Nebraska, spoke out against Clark and voted for Wilson, but his move caused little change in the balloting. After a riotous and bitter fight, the convention finally chose Wilson on the forty-sixth ballot. The progressive wing of the Democratic Party, as demonstrated by Wilson's recently developed progressivism and the support for him by old agrarian reformers such as Bryan, now controlled the party. It remained for Wilson to win the election, a challenging task.

Except for Grover Cleveland's two terms, from 1885 to 1889 and from 1893 to 1897, Re-

publicans had controlled the presidency since Lincoln's election in 1860. In 1912 the Republicans renominated William Howard Taft, who had already served one term. A progressive faction of the Republican Party, rebelling against the Taft nomination, chose Theodore Roosevelt as candidate on the Progressive, or "Bull Moose," ticket. Roosevelt was formidable opposition. During his tenure in the White House, from 1901 to 1909, he had dramatically transformed the office and powers of the presidency, altered the course of American politics, and shaped the Republican Party into an instrument of progressive reform. In 1912, Roosevelt, not the Republican Taft (and not Eugene V. Debs, nominated on the Socialist Party ticket), was Wilson's chief opponent.

Roosevelt's program in 1912 bore the label the New Nationalism. Wilson countered with the New Freedom. The veteran journalist William Allen White once described the difference between the two as that between Tweedledum and Tweedledee. If by this reference to *Alice's Adventures in Wonderland* White meant that there was no difference at all, he was nearly but not quite right. On some issues the two candidates took remarkably similar stands, but they also displayed significant, if subtle, differences. Both men minimized two important issues of 1912—woman suffrage and racial discrimination—since neither man cared about them. Both were white racists, the New Yorker Roosevelt more so than the Southern-born Wilson. Wilson neither supported nor opposed woman suffrage; Roosevelt endorsed nationwide suffrage but only to gain support from reformers such as Jane Addams. Differences between the candidates showed up most clearly in the matter they discussed most: the role of the federal government (and the president) in exercising controls over the economy. Each man advocated federal controls under a strong chief executive. Roosevelt thought concentration of wealth and economic power in commerce and industry inevitable and even desirable, and he would use federal regulation and direction to help rationalize economic growth while seeking social justice for the powerless masses victimized by the system. Wilson talked of using federal power to break up certain economic conglomerates, to restore competition, and to provide the small entrepreneur with a better chance to compete against the existing economic giants. Also, Wilson opposed any kind of special interest legislation.

As he campaigned, Wilson's speeches glowed with phrases about social righteousness and economic justice. Roosevelt, although he ran a strong race, failed to draw progressive Democrats from Wilson and failed to draw Old Guard Republicans from Taft. Wilson polled 6,293,019 popular votes; Roosevelt, 4,119,507. Taft received 3,484,956 votes; Debs, 901,873. Wilson received less than half the popular vote, but in the electoral college he won by a land-

slide—435 votes to 88 for Roosevelt and 8 for Taft. The Democrats also won control of both the House and the Senate.

The Administration

Few if any political figures in American history have made, so late in life, such a meteoric ascent from comparative obscurity to the pinnacle of power that Wilson reached with his inauguration as twenty-eighth president on March 4, 1913. Yet he felt no heady sense of triumph on the occasion. In his inaugural address he declared, "This is not a day of triumph; it is a day of dedication." Two weeks later, he wrote in a private communication,

> I am administering a great office, no doubt the greatest in the world, but . . . it is not me, and I am not it. I am only a commissioner, in charge of its apparatus, living in its offices and taking upon myself its functions."

Such "impersonality," he said, perhaps robbed the office of intensity, of pride, and even of enjoyment, but it "at least prevents me from becoming a fool, and thinking myself IT.

If Wilson in March, 1913, felt neither pride in having gained the office he occupied nor enjoyment from it, he found abundant joy in the Wilson family that now lived in the White House. Besides his wife and three daughters, who made up his immediate family, there were other women around the house. Wilson's widowed sister, along with several female cousins and honorary cousins, visited often. Wilson once joked that he was "submerged in petticoats." In the intimacy of his family, this trim and slender man, with refined face and aggressive jaw, with penetrating blue-gray eyes that narrowed behind his pince-nez when he talked, this austere public figure with the wintry smile could play the fool, wag his ears, do droll and skillful mimicries, joke and tease, and, on medical advice, sip an occasional Scotch. Except for golf, which he played often ("ten or eleven holes . . . almost every day" was his estimate in August, 1913), Wilson cared little for entertainment and social ceremonies outside his beloved family circle. He dispensed with the traditional inaugural ball. He refused to join the Chevy Chase Country Club, to which presidents before him had belonged as a matter of course. He had no interest in meeting smart or rich or distinguished people. Even for advice and information on affairs of state, he scarcely reached out beyond his own private world. In fact, he cared not for information or advice but for comfort and reassurance, and this he derived largely from the women in his family, but even they played no important part in the political decisions he made.

Wilson's White House entourage consisted of his secretary, Joseph Tumulty, his personal doctor, Admiral Cary T. Grayson, and Colonel Edward M. House, a wealthy Texan with a consuming interest in politics who functioned as a manipulator and emissary behind the scene rather than as a conspicuous occupant of elective office. House became Wilson's intimate friend and one of the most important figures in Wilson's administration. House was one of the few men—perhaps the only man—to whom Wilson ever turned for advice, although it was loyalty and spiritual support more than advice that Wilson wanted from House. Because he understood Wilson and handled him shrewdly, House enjoyed Wilson's confidence and affection from 1912 until 1919, when amid the terrible tensions and perplexities of the postwar peace conference, Wilson abruptly ended their friendship.

As Wilson began to plan the legislative program he would ask Congress to implement, he commissioned House to find candidates for the cabinet. Wilson named William Jennings Bryan secretary of state, a surprising choice in view of Bryan's insularity and inexperience in foreign affairs. Wilson did not remotely anticipate the enormous foreign problems he would face. He remarked just before his inauguration, "It would be the irony of fate if my administration had to deal chiefly with foreign affairs." In 1915, after Wilson had begun to deal much if not chiefly with foreign affairs (although that stage would soon begin), Bryan resigned in protest over Wilson's policies toward Germany. Wilson replaced him with Robert Lansing, who shaped American foreign policy even less than Bryan. That policy, from 1913 to 1921, remained largely in the hands of Woodrow Wilson, who was in essence his own secretary of state.

William Gibbs McAdoo became Wilson's secretary of the treasury in 1913. He also became Wilson's son-in-law in May, 1914, upon marriage to Wilson's daughter Eleanor—a marriage that, to some observers, made McAdoo "Crown Prince." McAdoo was a forceful, loyal, and successful member of the cabinet as well as the director-general of railroads during World War I. In 1920 his relationship to Wilson would hinder rather than help him in his bid for presidential nomination.

For attorney general, Wilson first considered Louis D. Brandeis, a renowned and controversial lawyer from Kentucky by way of Boston, who had been the major source of ideas for Wilson's New Freedom campaign in 1912. Instead, Wilson listened to Colonel House and gave the job to James C. McReynolds, a native Kentuckian practicing law in New York. In 1914, Wilson named the irascible and unlikable McReynolds to the Supreme Court, where in time he became one of the "Fearsome Foursome" who in the 1930's ruled, automatically and absolutely, against the New Deal in cases brought before the Court. Wilson replaced McReynolds in the cabinet with Thomas W. Gregory, a Texan, under whose direction the Justice Department during World War I would do whatever seemed necessary to keep opponents of "Mr. Wilson's War" in line. In 1916, in a courageous move that provoked a grueling fight over confirmation, Wilson named Brandeis to the Supreme Court, the first Jewish appointment ever made to that bench.

For secretary of war, Wilson chose Lindley M. Garrison, a New Jersey chancery court judge. An able and forthright man and a superb administrator, he chose to resign rather than compromise during a battle over preparedness in 1916. Wilson replaced him with Newton D. Baker, who had gained a certain fame as progressive mayor of Cleveland, Ohio. Josephus Daniels, editor of the *Raleigh* (North Carolina) *News and Observer* and Wilson's chief supporter in the state, became secretary of the navy. Daniels would suffer ridicule for his alleged ignorance of naval affairs and for his attempts, in the name of reform and his version of Methodist morality, to close down red-light districts near naval stations and to eliminate the navy's traditional grog ration. Nevertheless, Daniels and Baker, who also felt the sting of critics for his supposed incompetence, were to be instrumental in the creation of the U.S. Army and Navy that fought in the war that Wilson led the nation into in 1917.

Albert Burleson of Texas, who became postmaster general, used the patronage system to strengthen the Democratic Party in the states. During the war, he banned antiwar literature from the mail and exercised other powers of repression and censorship that were extralegal and arbitrary and that showed no consideration for traditional freedom of speech and press.

The remaining four secretaries left no major mark on Wilson's administration. Franklin K. Lane, a Californian whom Wilson named secretary of the interior, was the chief gossip of the cabinet. David F. Houston, a native North Carolinian who was president of Washington University in St. Louis in 1913, became secretary of agriculture. William B. Wilson, Democratic congressman from Pennsylvania mining country and a veteran union organizer, was an apt choice to head the recently established Labor Department. William C. Redfield became secretary of commerce. A congressman from Brooklyn, Redfield used his office to serve and protect business.

Domestic Program: Enacting the New Freedom—and More

As president, Wilson was in command of the executive branch. He was leader of his party in the Congress and the nation and had in mind a program that he wanted to see enacted and implemented. To do so, however, he had to unite his rather badly divided party behind him. The party was made up of a "Solid South" of conservative white agrarians, strong ethnic coalitions of reformers in the industrialized, urbanized North, and urban and rural Western progressives, all of them hungry for power to achieve reforms, to further their special interests, or to cash in on patronage after years in the political wilderness. Each of these factions and large interest groups had a spokesperson or two in the cabinet, and each had representation in the Congress. It was up to Wilson to work with and unite the discrete Democratic representatives in the Congress, himself initiating and guiding through to passage a legislative program that would gain enactment of his New Freedom program and turn the Democrats into the nation's majority—and progressive—party.

Immediately after his inauguration, Wilson called Congress into special session and on April 8 appeared in person to deliver a message—the first president since John Adams to make such an appearance. The next day, April 9, he went to the Capitol and held the first of many conferences with Democratic leaders. He asked Congress for tariff revision and got it, after heavy lobbying by private interests and a strong and dramatic attack on them by Wilson. The Underwood-Simmons Tariff Act lowered rates to levels not seen since before the Civil War. To make up for the loss of tariff revenue, Congress added to the tariff bill a provision for a graduated income tax, the first such tax under the Sixteenth Amendment, which was ratified on February 25, 1913.

Next, Wilson and Congress took up the major objective of the New Freedom: banking and currency reform. Everyone informed on the subject—bankers, businessmen, economists, leaders of both political parties—agreed that the existing banking system, one first established during the Civil War, needed drastic overhauling. It lacked any effective central control. Banking reserves were inadequate and the money supply too inelastic to allow the system to cope with periodic crises. No public agency had any voice in determining such critical matters as the money supply, the location of banking facilities, and the links that banks had with business corporations. Southern and Western farmers complained that all of the money was locked up in Eastern banks, which charged farmers exorbitant interest rates on loans. Reformers wanted federal control over the money supply. Bankers themselves wanted to increase the money supply and wanted a more centralized (yet private) system, one that could pool reserves and shift them about to meet unusual demand. One Democratic faction, with William Jennings Bryan as spokesperson, wanted to create a centralized, government-owned bank. Another faction, with Congressman Carter Glass of Virginia as spokesperson, wanted a loose association of private banks.

Wilson knew practically nothing about the details of the matter. His primary goal was some form of public supervision over a private banking system. In June, 1913, Wilson went before Congress and called for creation of a presidentially appointed Federal Reserve Board to supervise a private banking system. The nation would be divided into twelve Federal Reserve regions, with a Federal Reserve bank—a "bankers' bank," it came to be called—in each region. The Federal Reserve System would issue paper currency, in the form of Federal Reserve notes. Besides shifting currency reserves about the country to meet demands, the board could exercise other controls over the flow and supply of money, primarily by raising or lowering the "rediscount rate" it charged to private member banks when the

Reserve banks issued Federal Reserve notes (currency) to these banks in exchange for the commercial and agricultural paper the banks had taken in as security from borrowers.

Late in December, 1913, after six months of debate, Congress passed the Federal Reserve Act, called by one Wilsonian authority the "greatest single piece of constructive legislation of the Wilson era." Constructive it was, radical it was not. Interlocking directorates still existed. Private bankers still largely controlled the supply and availability of money. The Federal Reserve Bank of New York dominated the system. The Federal Reserve Board did not control the nation's bankers, and the board used its influence over discount rates sparingly until after the crash of 1929. A new and flexible currency had been created, and the private banking system had been retained—but under a degree of federal regulation, with potential for more in crises to come.

Late in 1913, as the Federal Reserve bill neared passage, Wilson began to consider one or two antitrust measures he might support. Most Democratic Party leaders wanted simply to amend the Sherman Antitrust Act of 1890 and enumerate and outlaw specific unfair trade practices. A minority of Democrats, however, agreed with Theodore Roosevelt that it would be impossible to draw up such a list. Louis Brandeis and other progressive Democrats wanted to see Wilson establish a powerful, independent trade commission, one with broad powers to investigate business activities and issue "cease and desist" orders suppressing unfair competition whenever and however it arose. Wilson had to choose between his own proposal of 1912 and that of Theodore Roosevelt. He also had to consider the outcry from Samuel Gompers and his American Federation of Labor, which had supported Wilson in 1912, that the Clayton antitrust bill then before Congress did nothing to exempt labor unions from antitrust prosecution. Wilson agreed to see added to the Clayton bill a few mild—and essentially useless—provisions to protect labor. Congress passed the Clayton bill in June, 1914, and labor unions proclaimed it their "Magna Charta," which, however, it was not.

Wilson, meantime, all but ignored the Clayton Act, even before its passage, and threw his support behind a Federal Trade Commission bill, one drafted partly by Louis Brandeis that came closer to Roosevelt's New Nationalism than to Wilson's New Freedom. The bill that became law on September 10 established the Federal Trade Commission, composed of five members appointed by the president and charged with preventing the growth of new monopolies by seeing to it that businesses competed fairly and openly—although the law did not specify in detail what this meant. Implementation of the commission's powers would depend on the inclinations of the members named to the commission, most of whom in the years to come showed little disposition really to go after business monopolies.

After passage of the Federal Trade Commission bill and the Clayton antitrust bill, Wilson announced that his New Freedom program was completed. He had thus far opposed any special interest legislation—for manufacturers, bankers, laborers, farmers, or children. As much as possible, government should, in the tradition of Democratic Party liberalism, keep hands off, giving favors to no one. Wilson opposed establishment of rural banks that would provide long-term loans at low interest rates to needy farmers. He opposed a bill to abolish child labor, saying that "domestic arrangements" were for states, not Washington, D.C., to supervise. Yet within the Democratic Party, as well as among Roosevelt Republicans of 1912, a great many reformers were demanding even more changes than Wilson's New Freedom legislation had wrought in the system by 1915. Since the turn of the century, when reformers had first begun to give voice to the proposals, slogans, programs, and aspirations that would collectively be labeled "progres-

sivism" by historians, diverse groups of reformers had called for various reforms: stringent regulation of industry, woman suffrage, child labor legislation, government aid to labor, farmers, and the unemployed, public health programs, prohibition, even laws against profanity. In his first two years in office, Wilson had satisfied some, but by no means all, of these reformers. In the state and congressional elections of 1914, the Democrats lost control of several key states they had carried in 1912 and saw their House majority reduced from seventy-three to twenty-five. Fearful that he and his party would lose control in 1916, Wilson set out to bring all progressives, all reform elements, Democrat or Republican, into the party.

When the new Congress convened in December, 1915, Wilson took command again, and under his leadership Congress enacted a sweeping and progressive program, one that could more easily bear the label New Nationalism than New Freedom. Between December, 1915, and September, 1916, Congress created a tariff commission, established a shipping board to regulate and aid merchant seamen, established the Federal Farm Loan Board, which extended long-term loans to farmers, prohibited child labor in interstate commerce (through the Keating-Owen Act that the Supreme Court would nullify in 1918), provided an eight-hour day for railroad workers (the Adamson Act), sharply increased income and inheritance taxes on the rich, and even passed a bill providing federal aid for highway construction. One Wilson scholar called 1916 "the year of the new progressive dispensation." Another declared that Wilson took over Roosevelt's New Nationalism "lock, stock, and barrel." Practically every important proposal that Roosevelt or his supporters made in 1912 had now become law—with Wilson's blessings. Although the 1916 measures included no laws comparable in importance to the Federal Reserve Act, and although he had exercised less planning, perseverance, and mediation in 1916 than he had displayed in 1913-1914, Wilson went to the country in 1916 claiming that the Democratic Party was also the progressive party, the party of social justice for all.

The 1916 Campaign

By campaign time, 1916, the war in Europe, which had begun in August, 1914, threatened increasingly to provoke American entry. Since Wilson had struggled for two years to keep America out of the war, he could campaign in 1916 as a progressive Democrat and also with a slogan (one he did not coin and did not like, because of the false hopes it seemed to raise): "He kept us out of war." Roosevelt, who had moved back to Republican orthodoxy since his defeat in 1912, was now supporting the regular Republican candidate and attacking Wilson for not having at once gone to war on the British side against "the beastly Hun." Roosevelt's tactic simply increased Wilson's support. Wilson's Republican opponent, the estimable Charles Evans Hughes, entered the campaign enjoying the respect and admiration of many Democratic journals, but his petty criticism and his failure to offer constructive alternatives to Wilson's policies earned for him the nickname Charles "Evasive" Hughes. As Wilson campaigned around the country, he did not mention that he had opposed a national woman suffrage amendment and had done little to abolish or even to restrict Jim Crow practices in his administration, but he did speak of what he had done for labor, farmers, and children. Prominent Progressives who had supported Roosevelt in 1912 came out for Wilson. Thousands of urban, ethnic voters who had preferred Eugene Debs in 1912 also swung to Wilson. The 1916 presidential contest revealed an almost perfect alignment of Democratic progressives versus Republican conservatives. The election was a cliff-hanger. Wilson received only 23 more electoral votes than Hughes (277 to 254). The popular vote was 9,129,606 for Wilson and 8,538,221 for Hughes. Even so, Wilson received nearly three million more votes in 1916 than he did in 1912 and by winning in 1916 became the first Democrat since Andrew Jackson to win reelection for a second consecutive term. If Wilson's first term had been a spectacular success, however, his second term would prove to be a tragedy.

The nemesis of Wilson's second term was revolution and war. Policies he had formulated in confronting these great cataclysmic forces in his first term led him inexorably toward entrance into World War I in April, 1917, toward intervention in the Russian Revolution in the summer of 1918, and toward a tragic denouement of World War I, the Versailles peace settlement of 1919.

Relations with Mexico

Three years before Wilson took office in March, 1913, revolution erupted in Mexico. Wilson was ignorant of, even indifferent to, the Mexican Revolution and to foreign affairs generally when he became president. Nevertheless, in 1913 and thereafter he held fast to certain provincial and arrogant notions about the world beyond America. He assumed the superiority of Anglo-Saxon people and their political and religious institutions. He formulated foreign policies, not in light of the exigent and the expedient, but in light of what were, to him, eternal verities. He could not conceive of a people who did not share his moral principles, who did not want for themselves the kind of government that the United States enjoyed. Again and again, in matters of diplomacy and war, Wilson played missionary, trying to do to and for other people what he thought was right and good and moral—by his definition. Whatever else may have been involved in Wilson's foreign policy—naïveté, protection of American economic interests, imperialistic ambition, military security—Wilson was driven by two principal motives: to advance the cause of international peace, even if, as in 1917, it meant going to war in Europe to end war and achieve peace, and to give other people the blessings of American-style democracy and Protestant Christianity, even if they did not want them. A case in point in Wilson's first term is his policy toward the revolution in Mexico.

The Mexican Revolution of 1910 was like a volcanic explosion that released decades of pent-up feelings. By 1910, when he abdicated power in Mexico and fled into exile in Paris, Don Porfirio Díaz had ruled the country for thirty-six years. Díaz had imposed law and order for the benefit of the propertied, both Mexican and foreign, making Mexico the best-policed country in the world. Through bribery and force Díaz controlled the state. By paying his officers well and by drafting young malcontents into the enlisted ranks, he controlled and used the army. He made Mexico a virtual colony of foreign capital ("Díaz held Mexico while foreigners raped her"). American, and to only a somewhat lesser degree British, capital developed railroads, sugar and rice and coffee plantations, oil wells, and gold and silver mines. Americans owned millions of acres of good land, and among Mexicans themselves less than three thousand families owned nearly 50 percent of the nation's land. By contrast, in some Mexican states between 95 and 99 percent of the Mexican people owned no land at all. The presidential election of 1910 brought to a head a quarter century of discontent by landless, exploited, oppressed Mexicans.

Francisco Madero, a liberal landowner from the state of Coahuila, ran for the presidency against Díaz in what the latter regarded as a farcical election. Predictably, Díaz won, but then Madero issued a *pronunciamiento*, a manifesto that demanded free and orderly elections. Madero proclaimed himself provisional president and designated November 20, 1910, as the day on which Mexicans should rise up in revolution against the oppressive Díaz regime. When several local leaders in Mexico—among them Francisco ("Pancho") Villa, Emiliano Za-

pata, and Venustiano Carranza—rallied to Madero, Díaz fled into exile, saying, "Madero has unleashed a tiger; let us see if he can control him."

Madero did not, could not, control the tiger of revolution. President William Howard Taft extended Madero diplomatic recognition, but the American ambassador to Mexico, Henry Lane Wilson, entered into a plot with several European ambassadors to oust Madero and replace him with General Victoriano Huerta, a man cut closer to the Díaz model of authoritarian caudillo and one partial to foreigners and their Mexican investments. In February, 1913, Madero was assassinated and Huerta became provisional president. Taft refused to recognize Huerta, but his refusal did not reflect a judgment on Madero's murder. Rather, on the advice of his State Department, Taft planned to use, or anticipated Wilson's using, recognition as a bargaining weapon for settling certain disputes over the rights and property of Americans in Mexico.

As soon as Wilson took office, he came under heavy pressure to recognize Huerta—from Ambassador Henry Lane Wilson in Mexico, from foreign service officials in the State Department, from the American colony in Mexico City, and from powerful financial interests in the United States. Wilson refused. Recognition of Huerta would sanction government by assassination. "I will not recognize a government of butchers," said Wilson. If not Huerta, then, whom should Wilson recognize? Wilson began sending personal agents into Mexico to contact Villa, Carranza, Zapata, and other revolutionaries who had supported Madero and were now opposing Huerta. He hoped to determine which, if any, one of these might be worthy of obtaining American support to oust Huerta and form a "legitimate," a "constitutional," Mexican government.

Wilson's agents gave him conflicting advice, some wanting him to support Carranza, some recommending Villa. All of them denounced

Huerta, but not all of them recommended actual military intervention of U.S. troops against him—although it finally came to that. From the State Department itself Counselor John Bassett Moore advised Wilson that European nations, which had promptly recognized Huerta, were correct in recognizing de facto regimes such as his and that such recognition was traditional American policy. Wilson, however, believed that to recognize a government's existence was to approve it as moral.

Wilson was in a quandary. He refused to approve of Huerta, but he was unable to come to terms with any other Mexican leader. He made an incredible proposal to Carranza and his so-called Constitutionalist Army that the United States join Carranza in a war on Huerta if Carranza would confine the revolution to orderly and constructive channels. Wilson felt responsible for the lives and property of American citizens in Mexico caught up in the Revolution, which by 1914 had become civil war between Huerta and several other forces, some of them fighting Huerta and some of them fighting one another as well. Wilson even felt pressure from Britain to recognize either Huerta or a successor who would protect Britain's considerable investment in Mexican petroleum, an investment of critical importance to Britain on the eve of war in Europe. One scholar has judged Wilson to have been in a state of "righteous paralysis," drifting and uttering platitudes.

In April, at Tampico, a chain of events began that led to overt American intervention in the Mexican Revolution, to Huerta's downfall, to Carranza's rise to power—and to still another American armed intervention that ended just short of an American-Mexican war. U.S. Navy ships were stationed in force in Tampico Bay to protect American property in the city and along the coast. On April 10, a colonel in Huerta's army unit holding Tampico arrested the paymaster and several crew members of the USS *Dolphin* when they came ashore to pick up the mail and inadvertently ventured beyond prescribed limits. The Americans were promptly released, and the Huertistas in Tampico at once apologized to Admiral Henry T. Mayo, ranking American officer in the area. Mayo, dissatisfied, demanded a twenty-one-gun salute and court-martial of the colonel who had arrested the Americans. Huerta, when notified of the incident, refused to accede to Mayo's demand. Wilson, when notified, chose to support Mayo. Declaring America's "honor" at stake, Wilson accused Huerta of deliberately insulting the United States and asked Congress for authority to use military force to obtain redress. Armed conflict broke out the next day, but at Vera Cruz, not at Tampico.

Wilson learned that a German steamer loaded with arms consigned to Huerta was about to land at Vera Cruz. Without waiting for congressional response to his earlier request, Wilson ordered the U.S. Navy to occupy Vera Cruz and prevent the German vessel from docking. Nineteen invading Americans and three hundred Mexicans who resisted the invasion died in the landing. The German ship simply docked and unloaded at a port farther down the coast. Appalled at the deaths, Wilson accepted an offer from Argentina, Brazil, and Chile to mediate, although he insisted that he would accept only a settlement that removed Huerta from power. Huerta condemned the American invasion, as did Carranza, who by now was pressing his Constitutionalist Army closer and closer to Mexico City. His funds exhausted and under pressure from the oncoming Constitutionalists, Huerta abdicated in July, 1914. In August Carranza marched into Mexico City, but the Mexican Revolution—and Wilsonian interference—abated not at all.

Since Carranza spurned his offers of support, Wilson now turned to Pancho Villa, when the great primitive guerrilla bandit revolted against Carranza and sought control over the revolution for himself. For a year or more, Carranza and his gifted military leader Álvaro

Pancho Villa. *(Library of Congress)*

Obregón fought Villa and Zapata for control of the revolution. Finally, Carranza won. Villa retreated north to his stronghold in Chihuahua. Finally aware that Carranza could be deposed neither by support for his rivals nor by Wilsonian rhetoric, and ever more concerned with the European war, Wilson in October, 1915, extended de facto recognition to Carranza.

Then Villa reentered the picture. Deflated and resentful, he tried to provoke an American intervention that would allow him to pose as hero against the Yankee invaders. In January, 1916, his forces killed sixteen American engineers taken from a train in Sonora. In March, 1916, Villa raided the small border town of Columbus, New Mexico, killed nineteen Americans, and vanished into the Mexican desert. Wilson ordered General John J. Pershing at Fort Bliss in El Paso, Texas, to lead a punitive

expedition into Mexico in pursuit of Villa. Carranza agreed to the proposal that a small detachment of Americans cross the border for this purpose, but when Villa, eluding Pershing, raided Glen Springs, Texas, Wilson mobilized the National Guard along the border and the U.S. Army prepared for a full-scale invasion of Mexico. When Pershing's troops moved more than three hundred miles into Mexico, Carranza ordered his generals to resist any further southward movement by the Americans. Neither Carranza nor Wilson wanted war. Carranza was preoccupied with the revolution in Mexico and Wilson with the war in Europe. Also, Wilson had evidence that Germany was trying to stir up trouble between the United States and Mexico along the border and preoccupy Wilson there to discourage him from intervening in the European war against Germany. In January, 1917, Wilson ordered the Pershing expedition to withdraw from Mexico. In March Wilson extended Carranza de jure recognition.

Wilson in 1913 had set out to rid Mexico of Huerta and teach the Mexicans "to elect good men." The Vera Cruz occupation played a part in Huerta's downfall, but the U.S. Navy's intervention and the U.S. Army's thrust into northern Mexico in 1916 poisoned U.S.-Mexican relations for years to come. Wilson wanted an American-style democracy for Mexico, but Carranza, who finally after years of bloody civil war emerged as victor and obtained Wilson's recognition, was more dictator than democrat, although he and his Constitutionalists were also more bourgeois than revolutionary. They welcomed American trade and investments and, despite the rhetoric of the Mexican constitution they drew up in 1917, they had no intention of ousting American oil companies from Mexico. Some of those oil interests, along with Catholics and professional patriots, had pressured Wilson to intervene far more than he did. Wilson refused to make open war on Mexico, although in the spring of 1916 he came perilously close to doing so. American outrage over Villa's border raids and over combat deep in northern Mexico that saw Americans captured by Mexicans led Wilson on June 27 to begin preparing a war message to Congress. The next day the prisoners were released, and telegrams, ten to one against any form of war, poured into the White House. Wilson had come close to a war he did not want out of a mistaken belief that national sentiment as well as national policy demanded it. Colonel House told Wilson, "The people do not want war with Mexico. They do not want war with anybody." Neither did Wilson. In 1916 he avoided war in Mexico. In 1917 he entered war in Europe.

World War I

When the Central Powers (Germany and its allies) went to war against the Allied Powers (Britain, France, and their allies) in August, 1914, Wilson issued a routine proclamation of neutrality and a few days later made an appeal to Americans not to take sides, to be "neutral in fact as well as in name, impartial in thought as well as in action." To Wilson the outbreak of war in Europe was simply another manifestation of the immorality and power politics of the Old World, to which America stood in shining contrast. He knew little and cared less about the origins or the causes of the war. The conflict, he said, was "like a drunken brawl in a public house," disgusting, although as between the antagonists his sympathies in 1914 lay more with Britain and France than with Germany.

Although calling for neutrality in thought and deed in 1914, Wilson soon began to change his mind. By early 1915, he had begun to plead for "the rights of a neutral," for the "rights" of Americans to continue to trade with and travel to Europe. When that trade and travel (and the British blockade) provoked German submarine attacks on Allied shipping and Americans drowned, Wilson declared America

"too proud to fight." In April, 1917, in his war message to Congress, he declared, "Right is more precious than peace." He had decided that America's "moral purposes" should be fulfilled, not by remaining aloof but by going to war. He would go to war not to win it but to end it, and, with the moral leverage he gained thereby, write a treaty that would end war forever. A "just and lasting peace," a Wilsonian peace, would follow a war fought to end all wars.

Parallel to this lofty Wilsonian rationale and vision, and working reciprocally with it, ran more mundane day-to-day exigencies: British propaganda that fell on the receptive ears of Anglophile Americans in the Wilson administration, British naval blockades and search-and-seizure episodes, German submarine attacks, American loans to Britain and France made to help the Allies pay for the American trade and commerce that increased from $800 million in 1914 to $3 billion in 1917 (whereas it dropped from $170 million to $1 million with the Central Powers in the same period).

Practical, nagging questions about Wilson's neutrality policy arose at the very beginning of the war: Was true American neutrality possible? Did neutrality mean continued trade with both sides? Britain, however, could not allow American trade with Germany, and to ask the British to stop using their surface blockade of Germany would be like asking Germany to stop using its army. Did neutrality mean prohibiting trade with both sides? Such prohibition would not have maintained true neutrality, since Britain was far more dependent than was Germany on international exchange. A Wilsonian embargo in 1914 on all foreign trade would have harmed Britain and helped Germany. On August 6, 1914, Secretary of State Bryan informed the Allies and the Central Powers that American neutrality did not mean it was unlawful to export goods in the ordinary course of commerce. Neither the British nor the Germans, however, agreed with this policy.

The British used their navy to stop shipment of goods to Germany, and the Germans used their submarines to stop shipments to Britain. Wilson, despite some controversies, came to accept the British blockade as legitimate, but German submarines were another matter, since they did not and could not follow the established rules of search and seizure that Britain followed. The Germans torpedoed vessels and drowned passengers; the British ordered vessels into port, searched them, seized contraband, and sometimes but not always even paid compensation for what they seized ("the British were thieves, but the Germans were murderers," was one bitter contemporary distinction).

In May, 1915, off the Irish coast a German submarine fired a single torpedo and sank the *Lusitania*, a British liner carrying 1,257 passengers, 128 of them Americans. In a series of notes Wilson warned the Germans that he would hold them to "strict accountability" for any more such incidents. Germany eased off submarine warfare, but then on August 19, a submarine, without warning, sank the *Arabic*, a large British liner, with two Americans listed among the forty-two casualties. Wilson let it be known that if Germany did not give satisfactory response to the incident he would contemplate a break in diplomatic relations. Germany pledged that "liners will not be sunk by our submarines without warning." On March 24, 1916, a submarine, without warning, torpedoed the British liner *Sussex* and eighty men drowned, among them four Americans. Wilson issued Germany an ultimatum: Unless the German government abandoned "its present practices of submarine warfare," America would sever diplomatic relations altogether. Germany agreed to suspend unrestricted submarine warfare, conditional on American efforts to compel the British to abandon their

The front page of *The New York Times* for May 8, 1915, reports the sinking of the British liner *Lusitania* by a German submarine. *(The New York Times)*

blockade of Germany. If the British blockade continued, so might the German submarine campaign. Late in January, 1917, Germany announced that after February 1, German submarines would sink without warning all ships, belligerent and neutral, found in a zone around Britain, France, and the eastern Mediterranean. The Germans knew they were risking war with the United States, but they believed that through loans and trade America was already an ally of Britain and France and an opponent of Germany. Perhaps an intensive all-out submarine campaign could cut off supplies coming to Britain and France and drive them to surrender before the United States declared war—or at least before America, even if it did declare war, could effectively mobilize and train an American army and bring it to the Western Front.

When the Germans announced resumption of submarine warfare, Wilson promptly broke diplomatic relations with them, yet held on to hopes of mediating and bringing the war to an end short of an American entry. He announced to Congress that he wished no conflict with Germany. Then on February 25, he learned that German foreign minister Alfred Zimmerman had instructed the German minister in Mexico City to propose a German-Mexican alliance against the United States if Germany and America went to war. To one New York newspaper, the Zimmerman note was "final proof that the German government has gone stark mad." Wilson, however, still committed to his peculiar interpretation of neutral rights, ordered guns and naval crews placed on board American merchant ships; he also ordered that the crews shoot on sight any submarine observed. On March 18, German submarines sank without warning and with heavy loss of life three American merchant vessels. At mass meetings throughout the country Americans demonstrated and called for war on Germany, although advocates of peace also held mass rallies and demanded that Americans stay out of the war zone and called for a general strike if war were declared.

As war tensions mounted in the United States, revolution erupted in Russia in February and March, the first of two great Russian revolutions in 1917, this one overthrowing the czarist regime, which, in alliance with Britain and France, had gone to war against Germany in 1914. With the czar replaced now by a constitutional monarchy—and one that pledged to carry on the war against Germany—Americans found it easier than before to believe that the war in Europe was a war between good and evil, between freedom and despotism.

Wilson still agonized over what to do. He learned that the Allies were in desperate straits and that only American intervention could save them. On March 21, he called Congress into special session for April 2, "to receive a communication concerning grave matters of national policy." On March 24, he ordered Secretary of the Navy Josephus Daniels to begin coordination of American naval operations with those of Britain. On March 25 and 26, he called National Guard units into federal reserve. Wilson, seeing no alternative, was clearly moving toward war. He was trapped by his own pronouncements. In 1916 he had said, "I shall do everything in my power to keep the United States out of war. . . . But if the clear rights of American citizens should ever unhappily be abridged or denied [by a warring power], we . . . have in honor no choice as to what our course should be." Wilson could not consent "to any abridgement of the rights of American citizens in any respect. The honor and self-respect of the nation is involved. We covet peace, and shall preserve it at any cost but the loss of honor."

On February 2, 1917, Wilson had told his cabinet that he did not care which side won the war, that both sides were wicked. Only weeks later, driven to find moral justification for what he was about to do, he decided that Germany was not merely wicked but had chal-

Wilson announces the United States' official break with Germany before Congress in February, 1917. *(National Archives)*

lenged America's honor as well. He still distrusted the Allies and did not believe they genuinely cared about democracy and self-government as much as he did, but by joining with them in war on Germany, he would save them all. He would save the world. He would enter the war and make it "a war to end all wars," a war that would end in "a just and lasting peace," a war that would "make the world safe for democracy."

On April 2, 1917, Wilson went before a joint session of Congress and asked for a resolution of war. On April 4, the Senate adopted the resolution, 82 to 6. On April 6, the House concurred, 373 to 50, and on April 7, Wilson signed the resolution. A headline in *The New York Times* read, "America in Armageddon."

Wilson had led the country into war, but the country was not yet ready for war. Neither Wilson nor his administrators nor the Congress in April, 1917, was prepared for the great economic mobilization they would finally achieve. Congress, however, quickly gave virtual dic-

tatorial power over the economy to Wilson, who promptly delegated it to administrators he named as directors of new administrative boards he created, such as the War Industries Board, the War Labor Board, the U.S. Food Administration, and the Emergency Fleet Corporation. Wilson launched his crusade for democracy abroad with a push toward autocracy at home. Rationalizing the economy, standardizing parts and production, even in a few cases nationalizing elements of the economy for the duration became Wilsonian tactics and strategy. A network of agencies throughout the country—state and local but mostly federal—produced the greatest concentration of public bureaucratic power Americans had ever experienced, a bureaucracy that oversaw the production of massive supplies of ships, arms, goods, and food for America and America's allies.

When Wilson asked for war and Congress declared it, neither he nor they envisioned mobilizing a great American army to send to

Europe to fight, but after six weeks of impassioned debate over how to raise an army, Congress, on May 18, passed the Conscription Act of 1917. Through that act's selective service system and through other more voluntary means, some four million Americans entered the American armed forces. Some entered with reluctance. Since the Conscription Act offered them little leeway, twenty thousand conscientious objectors underwent actual induction. About sixteen thousand of them changed their minds, or were persuaded to do so, after reaching camp. Four thousand absolutists refused to change their views. Some thirteen hundred of these finally went into noncombat units, about twelve hundred more gained furloughs to do farm work, and some five hundred suffered courts-martial and imprisonment. Conscientious objectors were a tiny minority when compared with some seventeen thousand draft evaders—"slackers" they were called in 1917—and compared with the millions inducted into the armed forces. With varying degrees of enthusiasm, chauvinism, and romanticism, two million Americans went off to France to fight in the Great War, some imbued with Wilson's own sense of mission, some regarding it all as a "great adventure," and some bewildered and painfully ignorant about the war and what it meant to them and to America. More than fifty thousand Americans died on the battlefield in France from wounds received there; fifty-six thousand more died from disease. Thousands of those who returned home vowed never to wear a uniform again, and when Wilson lost the peace he sought to achieve after the war, they began to doubt the justification Wilson had made for the war they had fought.

If American military mobilization reflected a spectrum of doughboy experience and outlook ranging from unqualified enthusiasm for "service" (a term stressed by Wilson) to absolute and principled refusal to serve, American civilians at home reflected a comparable range of attitude and behavior. As war began, Wilson said, "It is not an army that we must train for war, but a nation." To carry out that task, to mobilize minds as well as men and matériel, the Wilson administration, assisted by the Congress and by private citizens, turned the nation into a virtual surveillance state. The Committee on Public Information, chaired by Wilson's appointee George Creel, set 150,000 workers to the task of publicizing and propagandizing the virtues of America and its allies and the heinous crimes and cruelties of Germany. Wilson's postmaster general, with the president's approval, banned antiwar literature from the mail. Wilson's attorney general, with the president's approval, prosecuted cases arising under the Espionage Act of 1917 and the Sedition Act of 1918, acts designed to silence, and if necessary to imprison, critics of the war. Eugene V. Debs wound up in Atlanta federal penitentiary, following his arrest and conviction for speaking out in opposition to the war.

When the United States entered the war, Wilson told a friend that war "required illiberalism at home to reinforce the man at the front" and that a "spirit of ruthless brutality" would enter American life. Required or not, illiberalism and brutality came, and the Wilson administration did little to hinder their coming. Alongside the Wilsonians, carrying on their censorship and repression, ran private vigilante groups—the Boy Spies of America, the Sedition Slammers, the Terrible Threateners, the Knights of America—who tarred and feathered and otherwise harassed and sometimes even murdered Americans who seemed pro-German, or who were merely critics of the war, or who refused to buy war bonds, or who refused to stand up when the national anthem was played. While some Americans were ostensibly fighting for democracy abroad, others were undermining it at home. The wartime hysteria over things German turned into hysteria over things Russian in 1919-1920, and Wilson paid no more attention to violations of civil liberties in the Red Scare after the war than he paid to violations during the war. During Wilson's second term in the White House, progressivism was perverted into suppression. Abroad, however, America's contribution of men and matériel to the Allies on the Western Front was crucial in the last months of the war, and when the war ended on November 11, 1918, Wilson announced from the White House, "Everything for which America fought has been accomplished. It will now be our fortunate duty to assist by example, by sober, friendly counsel and by material aid in the establishment of just democracy throughout the world."

The Peace Settlement

For many weeks Wilson had worked for the armistice now reached. Early in October, the German government had asked Wilson "to take steps necessary for the restoration of peace." Through October and into November, Wilson had maneuvered his fellow Allies and the defeated Germans into accepting an armistice on Wilsonian terms. Both the Allies and the Germans entered the armistice understanding that Wilson's Fourteen Points of January, 1918, along, with his subsequent statements of principles, would provide the basis for peace negotiations soon to begin in Paris.

Months before the war ended, Wilson began to concentrate on formulating the postwar peace settlement. After November, 1918, the task came more and more to possess him until, finally, he all but abdicated leadership at home in desperate pursuit of his diplomatic goals abroad. Between December, 1918, and July, 1919, Wilson spent only ten days in the United States, so preoccupied was he with the peace conference in Paris. He came home for good in July, but in September he suffered a stroke that left him partly paralyzed, and for the next seven months he was bedridden and out of touch with the nation as it stumbled through 1919-1920 toward the "normalcy" of Warren

G. Harding. In December, 1919, a veteran newspaperman wrote that in Washington there was "no government, no policies. . . . The Congress is chaotic. There is no leadership worthy of the name." It is far from certain that a more healthy and active Wilson could have prevented the national spiral downward from armistice exhilaration and hopes for postwar reconstruction reforms to the brutal suppressions of the Red Scare of 1919-1920, but clearly Wilson did nothing to halt the country's drift rightward. Yet if Wilson defaulted on leadership at home after the war, he became in international politics a figure of renown.

On November 18, 1918, when Wilson announced that he was going to Paris, debate broke out at once over his decision. Criticism ranged from trivial to telling: His trip was unconstitutional, unprecedented, unseemly; Wilson would be a poor negotiator in Paris, where he would become enmeshed in personal quarrels, but an able one in Washington, where he could remain aloof and yet influential. Many Republicans resented Wilson's presumption that in Paris he would speak for all of America. Wilson had campaigned for a Democratic majority in the recent congressional election and had made the forthcoming peace conference a party issue, only to see his party lose heavily to the Republicans. Out of partisanship if not from conviction, Republicans now declared Wilson repudiated, and they objected to his presence in Paris. Wilson intensified this Republican partisanship—and made all but inevitable the Republican opposition to the treaty that he brought home in July, 1919—when he failed to take Republican advisers with him to Paris, although even had he done so he would have given them scant heed, just as he mostly ignored the Democrats who did accompany him. This was to be, essentially, Woodrow Wilson's great and solitary mission.

On December 4, 1918, Wilson embarked for Europe aboard the *George Washington*. In London and in Paris he received frenzied and spontaneous acclaim from huge, delirious crowds that pressed about his carriage. Wilson, as John Maynard Keynes expressed it in a famous essay, was "the man of destiny, who, coming from the West, was to bring healing to the wounds of the ancient parent of his civilization and lay for us the foundations of the future." If Wilson had a messiah complex when he arrived in Europe, his reception heightened it. The masses in England and France who adored Wilson, however, also hated the Germans and were set on revenge and recompense, and British prime minister David Lloyd George and French premier Georges Clemenceau, the two men who with Wilson thrashed out the Paris peace treaty, were far more responsible to their own people than to Woodrow Wilson.

Both Clemenceau and Lloyd George found Wilson boring and exasperating, with his prim, missionary manner, his thoughts for the day typed out on his own typewriter and delivered as from a pulpit—his "sermonettes," Clemenceau called them—and above all his points and principles that he brought to every meeting of the peace conference. Clemenceau grumbled that dealing with Wilson was like dealing with Jesus Christ. A more caustic observer saw Wilson, in his dealings with Lloyd George and Clemenceau, behaving like "a long-faced virgin trapped in a bawdy house and calling in violent tones for a glass of lemonade." As one historian has said, more prosaically and accurately, the moment Wilson set foot in the same room with Clemenceau and Lloyd George he was doomed, "overborne by their infinitely nimbler wits, their irresistibly stronger wills, . . . two of the most determined and resourceful politicians in history."

Between January and June, 1919, in the Paris suburb of Versailles, Wilson and the Allied representatives—except for Russians—hammered out the Treaty of Versailles. Russia sent no representative spokesperson to Paris, but Bolshevik Russia hovered like a specter over the Paris proceedings. By January, 1919, when the peace

conference opened, Wilson had spent more than a year groping for a policy toward Russia. When the February, 1917, revolution overthrew the czarist government, Wilson promptly recognized the new provisional regime and even dispatched a goodwill mission to Russia in the spring of 1917. When the Bolsheviks—V. I. Lenin, Leon Trotsky, and company—seized control of Russia in October, 1917, Wilson chose not to extend diplomatic recognition. United States-Russian relations began immediately to deteriorate, so much so that some analysts have located the beginnings of the Cold War of mid-century in this period following the Bolshevik Revolution of 1917. In the summer of 1918, Wilson ordered American forces into Russia. Some five thousand U.S. troops landed at Archangel on the Baltic, alongside twenty-four hundred British and nine hundred French troops. Nine thousand more Americans moved into Vladivostok on the Pacific coast of Russia, as did seventy-two thousand Japanese troops. Speculation over these landings has been abundant ever since they occurred, with five or six basic interpretations put forward: Wilson intervened to help the anti-Bolshevik forces in Russia regain power and crush the Bolshevik Revolution; he intervened to resume the eastern front war against Germany, since the Brest-Litovsk Treaty of March, 1918, between the Germans and the Bolsheviks had ended war in the east; he intervened in the name of self-determination of peoples, hoping that the American troops in Vladivostok, for example, would help rescue several thousand Czech prisoners of war who had escaped and were trying to get back home and fight the Germans; he intervened in Siberia to keep an eye on the Japanese and to guarantee a continued Open Door policy in Asia at the end of the war; he intervened in Archangel because the British and the French—openly and sharply anti-Bolshevik—wanted him to, and he was anxious to maintain good relations with these Allies as peace talks drew near; he intervened to strike at the Bolsheviks because he believed they were actually German agents.

Wilson and his advisers may never have developed a "policy" toward the Russian Revolution. They may have been confused and uncertain of just what they were doing, as well as why they were doing it. Rather than a deliberate and reasoned scheme, Wilson's Russian diplomacy may have been a day-to-day matter, turning on the contingent and the unforeseen, although perhaps in retrospect moving in one direction more than in another. Whatever the motive or design that had driven Wilson to order troops to Russia, his attitude toward the Bolsheviks was inseparable from his goals and strategies at the peace conference. Wilson's aims and methods at Paris ran head on into conflict with those of Lenin, who, although not invited to Paris and scornful of its deliberations, was as vital a figure in those deliberations as any one at the conference. Wilson proposed to change Europe, if not the entire world, into an American image (or at least Wilson's image of America), to the advantage of

liberal capitalism everywhere. Lenin was trying, by revolutionary violence, to bring about a new social and economic order that in theory held no place for capitalism, liberal democracy, or nation-states—the very things Wilson came to Paris to sustain and to spread.

Wilson in Paris confronted Lenin in absentia. He confronted Lloyd George and Clemenceau face to face. Although they, too, were perhaps haunted by the specter of bolshevism, they were patently scornful of Wilson's sermonettes and the kind of peace settlement he wanted to make with Germany. Again and again, from January when the conference opened to June when it ended, Wilson found himself forced to compromise one after another of his Fourteen Points. His slogan about the self-determination of peoples, his plea to exact no punitive indemnities from the Germans, his call for "open covenants of peace openly arrived at," his cry for a peace between equals ran up against the hard realities of European history, as read and lived and remembered by Clemenceau and Lloyd George. Wilson also

At the peace conference in Versailles (left to right): British prime minister David Lloyd George, Italian prime minister Vittorio Emanuele Orlando, French premier Georges Clemenceau, and Wilson. *(Library of Congress)*

from time to time in his negotiations stumbled into compromise unwittingly, owing to his own ignorance. When he promised Italy the South Tyrol, he did not know its population was Austrian. When he approved the boundaries of the newly created Czechoslovakia, he did not know that two million Germans lived within those boundaries. Other compromises he knew he was making. Each time he compromised, each time he accepted French occupation of German territory, British and French mandates over former German and Turkish territory, British and French demands for heavy reparations from Germany, or creation of national boundaries in Eastern Europe that did violence to his principle of national self-determination, he fell back in desperate hope on his fourteenth point, a League of Nations. He had envisioned drawing up at Paris a "peace without victory," a term that prompted one pundit to remark that there were three sides at Paris: the winners, the losers, and Wilson. Each compromise he made rendered the peace settlement less just and hence more certain to fail, to lead to war, not peace. A League of Nations, with the United States as an essential member, became an obsession with him. Owing to the treaty's imperfections, Wilson needed the League of Nations to forestall the wars that the treaty's terms might engender, and without a lasting peace he had no justification for having led his country into war.

Wilson agreed that Britain and France could, by treaty, demand massive reparations from Germany and in the infamous Article 231, the "war guilt" clause of the treaty, assign Germany full responsibility for starting the war. In return for these blatant compromises with his Fourteen Points, Wilson received support for his proposed league. His obsession about the league may have developed not only because of the compromises he had struck with his principles but also because of his sickness of body and mind. On April 3, he suffered an attack of coughing, vomiting, and high fever that may have been caused by a cerebral vascular occlusion, complicated by a viral inflammation of the brain. Whatever his illness, he became a changed man after the attack: He was forgetful. He stumbled. He was paranoid about his French servants. He groped for ideas, worried needlessly about trivial matters, was irascible. He held some of his ideas ever more rigidly, especially about the league. He had compromised enough. On the league he would not budge. The league would be his and the world's salvation.

On June 28, 1919, a German delegation, after waiting for days in a Paris hotel, signed the Treaty of Versailles. Wilson returned to the United States and on July 10, 1919, presented the treaty to the Senate for its consideration. If the Senate ratified it by the necessary two-thirds vote, America's war with Germany would officially end and, more significantly, the United States would become a member of the League of Nations. Wilson, by way of a league constitution or "covenant" written into the treaty, had managed to make ratification of the treaty inseparable from American membership in the league. It was this inseparability of treaty and league that led to Wilson's undoing.

While Wilson and the Europeans had entered into their parlays, running from January to June, Americans demobilized, readjusted from war to peace, moved toward the Red Scare, and from time to time talked about the peace conference. Even before the peace conference opened, the league became an acrimonious issue. Republican Senator William E. Borah of Idaho voiced his objections as early as December, 1918. Borah did not propose to surrender to a league "the power to say when war shall be waged," the power to "conscript American boys and take them to Europe to settle differences." Borah was close to the archetypal isolationist. Republican Henry Cabot Lodge of Massachusetts, chair of the Senate Foreign Relations Committee and arch enemy of Woodrow Wilson, was a fervent expansionist, who objected to the league not because it would involve the United States in world affairs but because it would, in his view, restrain American freedom of action in the world.

Neither Lodge nor Borah spoke for the majority of the Senate. When Wilson presented the treaty to that body for consideration, forty-three Democrats and one Republican proposed ratification, without qualification. Fifteen Republicans supported the treaty except for a few "mild reservations." Twenty Republicans expressed "strong reservations" with regard to the treaty's terms, mostly about the league.

Twelve Republicans and three Democrats were "irreconcilably" opposed to the treaty in any form, and Borah vowed war to the death on "the unholy thing with the holy name." On September 10, 1919, the Senate voted on the treaty with numerous amendments and reservations attached. Wilsonian Democrats defeated them all. Again in November the Senate voted, again with various reservations attached (Lodge puckishly offered fourteen of them), and again the treaty failed to pass.

Wilson had opposed every reservation raised. He was convinced of his own rectitude and convinced that the treaty was the best one he could have negotiated in the circumstances. Above all, he regarded ratification and American entry into the league as a matter of his and America's moral salvation. Having failed to gain approval from the Senate, Wilson went to the people. While on a westward tour in the fall of 1919 trying to arouse support for the treaty, he collapsed in Pueblo, Colorado, and was brought home to the White House where he remained, sick and all but shut off, for seven months, from the nation and from the Senate deliberations over the treaty. Suffering from an occlusion of the right middle cerebral artery, he was completely paralyzed on his left side and had lost vision in the left half fields of both eyes. His voice became weak and his speech lost its resonance and fluency. As a result of the stroke, Wilson developed what neurosurgeon Edwin Weinstein, in a recent medical biography, analyzes as anosognosia—literally, "lack of knowledge of disease." Wilson did not deny that he was physically ill, but he did deny that he was unable to continue carrying on his duties.

In November, 1919, the Senate cast its second vote on the treaty, as amended by numerous reservations including the fourteen from Lodge, and following Wilson's directive the Senate Democrats joined with Republican irreconcilables and rejected it. In March, 1920, for a third time the Senate voted on the treaty with reservations attached; Wilson again ordered his loyal followers to reject and once more the treaty failed to pass. On May 15, 1920, by joint resolution, Congress repealed its war resolution of April, 1917, against the Central Powers and reserved to the United States all rights expressed in the Treaty of Versailles. Wilson vetoed the resolution. The United States did not ratify the Treaty of Versailles and did not enter the League of Nations.

Wilson clung to his belief that the United States should and would enter the league. During the 1920 presidential campaign, he expressed the hope that the election would be a "solemn referendum" on the league, a vote for Democrat James M. Cox registering a vote for the league and a vote for Republican Warren G. Harding a vote against it. Harding drubbed Cox in the election, but it would be a distortion to say that his lopsided victory reflected American opposition to the league. Neither candidate had taken a distinctive position on the league, and a number of prominent Republicans, such as William Howard Taft, were outspoken in support of it. Yet if the election was not the solemn referendum on the league that he had hoped for, it was a cruel referendum on Woodrow Wilson. Some five weeks before Harding's election, Herbert Hoover wrote to a friend, "Since the Armistice, the present administration has made a failure by all the tests that we can apply. . . . The responsibilities of government should now, therefore, be transferred." "The people," wrote one historian, "were tired of star-reaching idealism, bothersome do-goodism, and moral overstrain. . . . Eager to lapse back into 'normalcy,' they were willing to accept a second-rate President—and they got a third-rate one." On March 4, 1921, Wilson and Harding rode down Pennsylvania Avenue to the inauguration of normalcy, the careworn face and wracked condition of the great retiring president in stark contrast to that of his handsome, bumbling, smiling, inept successor.

The Last Years

For four years after his retirement Wilson lived in a house on S Street in Washington, D.C. Although he regained his sense of humor and his interest in language, he turned down offers to write articles and refused all offers to speak. In 1923 his health worsened and he became almost blind. He grew extremely depressed, became upset at any mention of death, and was obsessed with fears of abandonment. Late in January, 1924, he weakened badly. His personal physician, Dr. Cary Grayson, found him in extremis and called in two medical colleagues. As they were about to enter his room, Wilson whispered, "Be careful. Too many cooks spoil the broth." It was his last jest. He died on the morning of February 3, 1924.

The distinguished Wilson scholar Arthur S. Link once wrote, "There is no more tragic and searing story in history and mythology than the ordeal of Woodrow Wilson." Perhaps so. Yet to be placed by historians in the company of Washington, Lincoln, and Roosevelt as one of America's great presidents is success and not failure, victory and not defeat, triumph and not tragedy.

Burl Noggle

Bibliographical References

The Wilson authority for this and any other generation of scholars is Arthur S. Link. He is editor in chief of *The Papers of Woodrow Wilson*, 1966-1993, published by Princeton University Press in some sixty-nine volumes, covering Wilson's life from 1856 to 1924. Supplementary volumes to the Wilson papers are a personal memoir by his brother-in-law and close friend, Stockton Axson, *"Brother Woodrow: A Memoir of Woodrow Wilson,"* 1993, and Arthur S. Link and John E. Little, eds., and Niels Thorsen, *The Political Thought of Woodrow Wilson, 1857-1910*, 1988. Link, *Woodrow Wilson and the Progressive Era, 1910-1917*, 1954, a volume in the New American Nation Series, is indispensable.

John Morton Blum, *Woodrow Wilson and the Politics of Morality*, 1962, is a succinct biographical essay. John Mulder, *Woodrow Wilson: The Years of Preparation*, 1978, focuses with sympathy and insight on Wilson's religious and intellectual development to about 1910. John M. Cooper, *The Warrior and the Priest: Woodrow Wilson and Theodore Roosevelt*, 1983, is an engrossing analysis of the contrasts and comparisons in two parallel careers. Patrick Devlin, *Too Proud to Fight: Woodrow Wilson's Neutrality*, 1974, is a definitive and exhaustive study of Wilsonian diplomacy from August, 1914, to April, 1917. Other works dealing with Wilson's foreign policies are David M. Esposito, *The Legacy of Woodrow Wilson: American War Aims in World War I*, 1996; Derek B. Heater, *National Self-determination: Woodrow Wilson and His Legacy*, 1994; and Thomas J. Knock, *To End All Wars: Woodrow Wilson and the Quest for a New World Order*, 1992. Edwin A. Weinstein's *Woodrow Wilson: A Medical and Psychological Study*, 1981, is a fascinating study by a neurosurgeon who has worked closely with Link in bringing the discipline of history and the findings of medical science and psychiatry to bear on the life of Wilson. Robert Ferrell, *Woodrow Wilson and World War I, 1917-1921*, 1985, a volume in the New American Nation Series, is a sequel to Link's volume in that series. A. Lentin, *Lloyd George, Woodrow Wilson, and the Guilt of Germany: An Essay in the Pre-history of Appeasement*, 1984, is a brilliantly written essay on an old and troublesome issue. The early chapters of George F. Kennan's *Russia and the West Under Lenin and Stalin*, 1961, are a distillation of his magisterial two-volume work on United States-Russian relations, 1917, 1921, *Russia Leaves the War*, 1956, and *The Decision to Intervene*, 1958. For an overview of the Wilson administration, see Kendrick A. Clements, *The Presidency of Woodrow Wilson*, 1992. Robert M. Saunders, *In Search of Woodrow Wilson: Beliefs and Behavior*, 1998, examines the effectiveness of Wilson's leadership. For an analysis of the evolution of

Wilson's views on the constitutional separation of powers, see Daniel D. Stid, *The President as Statesman: Woodrow Wilson and the Constitution*, 1998.

Link and William M. Leary, Jr., *The Progressive Era and the Great War, 1896-1920*, 1978, lists hundreds of books and articles on Wilson and his era. Also useful is Peter H. Buckingham, *Woodrow Wilson: A Bibliography of His Times and Presidency*, 1990. Mulder, Ernest M. White, and Ethel S. White, *Woodrow Wilson: A Bibliography*, 1997, is a comprehensive guide to the secondary literature on Wilson.

Warren G. Harding

29th President, 1921-1923

Born: November 2, 1865
    Caledonia, Ohio
Died: August 2, 1923
    San Francisco, California

Political Party: Republican
Vice President: Calvin Coolidge

Cabinet Members

Secretary of State: Charles Evans Hughes
Secretary of the Treasury: Andrew W. Mellon
Secretary of War: John W. Weeks
Secretary of the Navy: Edwin Denby
Attorney General: Harry M. Daugherty
Postmaster General: Will H. Hays, Hubert Work,
    Harry S. New
Secretary of the Interior: Albert B. Fall, Hubert
    Work
Secretary of Agriculture: Henry C. Wallace
Secretary of Commerce: Herbert Hoover
Secretary of Labor: James J. Davis

Warren Gamaliel Harding was the twenty-ninth president of the United States. Born November 2, 1865, in Blooming Grove, Ohio, he grew up around Caledonia, Ohio. Harding was graduated in 1882 from a two-year college, Ohio Central, where he edited the school newspaper. After teaching school for a term, he settled in Marion, Ohio, selling insurance. In 1884, he and two partners bought the ailing *Marion Daily Star*. Harding soon gained full control of the newspaper, which he eventually made into a paying enterprise. His editorial policy was to boom Marion, the United States, and business development. In 1891, he married Florence Kling De Wolfe, an outspoken and formidable woman commonly referred to by

her husband and friends as the "Duchess." Her determination and ambition reinforced his drive for success.

Harding's official portrait. *(White House Historical Society)*

Harding became active in politics in the 1890's out of a growing conviction that Ohio Republicanism needed a younger generation of leadership. His admiration of wealth and power eventually led him to reach accommodation with his party's aging bosses, and his budding ability as an orator gained for him recognition among Republicans. In 1899, Harding was elected to the state senate; reelected in 1901, he became the senate Republican floor leader. Eager to become governor, he found that his ambition exceeded his influence. In 1903, therefore, he had to settle for the lieutenant governorship, in which he served only one term. Not until 1910 did he receive the Republican gubernatorial nomination. Running as the candidate of a badly divided party, Harding failed to win election. He remained in demand after his defeat, however, because of his oratorical talent, although that talent ran largely to uttering hollow if resounding platitudes. At the 1912 Republican National Convention, he was chosen to nominate President William Howard Taft, his fellow Ohioan, for reelection.

Despite Taft's overwhelming defeat in 1912, things went Harding's way. In 1914, he was elected United States senator. As a senator, Harding sponsored little legislation and had a poor attendance record. He did grow in status among Republicans, however, because of the roles he assumed as an able spokesperson for his party and an apostle of Republican harmony. This attitude led to Harding's selection as the keynote speaker and permanent chair of the 1916 Republican National Convention. Later, as he became a popular critic of the Wilson administration, he was mentioned as a possible contender for the 1920 Republican presidential nomination.

Harding's attractiveness to Republicans also lay in his stands on issues. Under the credo of "Prosper America First," he called for merchant marine subsidies, protective tariffs, immigration restriction, and territorial expansion.

He was generally probusiness and antiunion, although he endorsed an eight-hour day for workers. He accepted woman suffrage and Prohibition, and he warned against bolshevism and "creeping socialism." He favored ratification of the Treaty of Versailles but with reservations designed to protect American sovereignty.

A Perfect Nominee: The Election of 1920

By 1920, Harding had become Ohio's favorite son for the Republican presidential nomination. His ability to balance issues and to ingratiate himself with a variety of Republicans made it easy for his aides to secure many second-choice commitments from among delegates to the 1920 national convention. Harding did not rank among the front-runners for the nomination, comprising General Leonard Wood, Illinois governor Frank O. Lowden, and California senator Hiram Johnson. None of them, however, had enough votes to gain nomination. Consequently, when the convention delegates tired of the deadlock among the three leading candidates, Harding was able to attract enough votes to win nomination.

Harding turned out to be an almost perfect presidential nominee. His campaign was well pitched to appeal to those Republicans, independents, and even Democrats who were vexed by rising prices, labor problems, fears of depression, and the divisive issue of the League of Nations. He also shifted to championing positive action to cope with the nation's problems instead of indulging in carping criticism of the Wilson administration and Ohio governor James M. Cox, the Democratic presidential nominee. Harding's promise to return America to "normalcy" projected an image of an agreeable, conciliatory leader who was concerned with doing the right thing as a majority of voters saw it. As a result, he was elected on his fifty-fifth birthday in November, 1920, by the largest percentage of votes ever cast for a Republican presidential nominee.

The new president looked right for his job. Over 6 feet tall, Harding weighed 210 pounds, had gray eyes, a prominent forehead, silver hair, and a strong jaw. He was always well dressed. Moreover, in public he projected affability, moderation, or seriousness, but never meanness or pettiness. He was by nature easygoing. Nominally a Baptist, he was less devoted to religion than to playing poker or golf. He used tobacco and drank, though not to excess. Also, he had had affairs with women, ascribable to Florence Harding's frostiness on sexual matters, although the presidential couple otherwise got along well. Harding was not a disciplined thinker, tending to develop his opinions intuitively along lines suggested by copybook maxims. Intensely loyal to his friends, he was not often discreet enough in choosing or using them. The president worked hard in considering and acting on official business, although he often seemed frustrated by differences of opinion among his advisers.

Harding's cabinet was generally conservative, though well balanced in the personal and geographical background of the appointees. Several members of the cabinet, especially Secretary of State Charles Evans Hughes and Secretary of Commerce Herbert Hoover, were eminent and able men. Others, such as Attorney General Harry M. Daugherty and Secretary of the Interior Albert B. Fall, were men of dubious merit. Nevertheless, Senator Fall's appointment was so popular on Capitol Hill that the Senate confirmed him without going through the usual committee hearing.

Legislative Action: Domestic Policy

The president approached Congress soon after his inauguration in March, 1921. Calling a special session for April, he presented a long legislative agendum. He asked for higher tariffs, lower taxes, a national budget system, and action to ease the economic plight of farmers. Harding also called for strengthening the merchant marine, a national highway system, en-couragement of civil and military aviation, regulation of radio, establishment of a veterans bureau and a department of public welfare, government reorganization, expansion of hospital facilities, and maternity and antilynching legislation. On foreign affairs, the president requested formal action to end World War I, promotion of international cooperation outside the League of Nations to prevent war in the future, and aid for European economic recovery.

Harding enjoyed considerable legislative success in 1921 and 1922. The new high-tariff and low-tax legislation helped to combat America's postwar recession and to pave the way for later prosperity. The Budget and Accounting Act established the Bureau of the Budget and the General Accounting Office to make for better control and accountability in the appropriation and expenditure of federal funds. Moreover, these tools were crucial to the administration's outstanding success in fostering economy in government. The president scored well on foreign policy legislation and on measures to develop highways, hospital facilities, and aviation, and Congress substantially reduced immigration quotas, which he had long favored. Congress also enacted significant legislation to regulate agricultural markets, stimulate the growth of farm organizations, and reduce railway freight rates. These measures did not solve the nation's agricultural problems, but as a consequence of the legislation farmers' incomes lagged behind that of others in the economy less than it would have without such legislation.

There were also defeats. Harding lost on merchant marine subsidies, and the Senate killed his antilynching proposal. Although the president failed to secure authorization for a department of public welfare, Congress passed the Sheppard-Towner Act in 1922 to promote the health of mothers and children. The credit that he received for the establishment of the Veterans Bureau was offset by the development of scandal in that agency.

Harding issued a controversial pardon to Socialist Party leader Eugene V. Debs, who was jailed as a political prisoner during World War I. *(Library of Congress)*

The administration displayed more than legislative concerns. Harding showed his mettle in pardoning Eugene V. Debs, the socialist leader, and most other wartime political prisoners. The president also worked, especially with Commerce Secretary Herbert Hoover, to institute an eight-hour workday in the steel industry, encourage self-regulation of radio stations, and use federal action to counter the effects of the 1921-1922 recession. Harding was business-oriented, yet he promoted more enlightened operation of business to benefit the whole nation and sponsored some programs of interest to farmers and welfare advocates. He was less the instrument of business (or of the Senate) than it had been predicted that he would be.

If Harding was captive to anything, in fact, it was to his high-level appointees, although their advice so often was conflicting that he was not always their creature. He needed their help, though, in taking action. Sometimes he chose wrongly, as when he supported Attorney

General Daugherty's punitive injunction to end the railway shopmen's strike in 1922. This action earned for the president the enmity of many labor unions.

Foreign Policy: Soothing Troubled Relations

In foreign policy Harding generally followed the advice of Secretary of State Hughes. In 1921, his administration convinced Congress to terminate formally World War I hostilities and to ratify peace treaties with America's former enemies. Harding's and Hughes's boldest success was the Washington Conference of 1921-1922. This meeting of representatives of nine nations with interests in the Far East produced agreement on and ratification of treaties that substantially limited naval armaments and reduced tensions in the Pacific and the Far East. The Harding administration also enjoyed success in soothing the troubles it had inherited in Latin America. Negotiations were initiated to restore diplomatic relations with Mexico;

American intervention in Central America and the Caribbean was reduced; and Colombia's grievances against the United States stemming from the Panamanian Revolution of 1903 were settled. What Harding and Hughes set in motion with Latin America would be continued by Presidents Calvin Coolidge and Herbert Hoover and lead to the Good Neighbor era of Franklin D. Roosevelt. In dealing with European concerns Harding felt less confident, saying, "I don't know anything about this European stuff." Nevertheless, his administration edged its way into some cooperation with the League of Nations, set easier terms for European nations to pay their war debts to America, and negotiated some favorable commercial agreements. Harding also, contrary to Hughes's advice, sought to explore with the Soviet Union the restoration of diplomatic relations.

Harding's program was not among the most weighty offered by an American president. His legislative efforts, however, were respectable. Many of his administration's operations ranked well in efficiency, effectiveness, and es-

pecially economy. Yet Harding was beset by problems. There were the usual problems of patronage and congressional relations. In addition, agriculture was not satisfied with the administration's efforts on its behalf, organized labor was angered by Harding's favoritism toward business, and business wanted additional favors. The recession of 1921-1922 aggravated the situation. The administration's enforcement of Prohibition vexed wets, yet it was not active enough to satisfy many drys. Moreover, Harding's veto of a veterans bonus sorely irritated many World War I soldiers and sailors. The 1922 elections reflected the resulting reactions of all these groups and interests when Republicans retained only a bare majority in the two houses of Congress. Consequently, Harding would have far less legislative success during the rest of his presidency.

Failing Reputation, Failing Health

Harding liked the office of president, but he found that he had to work extremely hard. "I never find myself with all my work completed," he commented. He also worried about

Harding's secretary of state, Charles Evans Hughes (third from right), attends the Washington Conference on disarmament. *(Library of Congress)*

EXTRA! The Evening Star. EXTRA!

WASHINGTON, D. C., FRIDAY, AUGUST 3, 1923.   TWO CENTS

Apoplexy Kills President

PRESIDENT'S RECORD ONE OF TRIUMPHS IN MANY GREAT ISSUES

Arms Parley and Success of Budget System Outstanding Features of Career.

WARREN G. HARDING.

CAME TO PRESIDENCY SPLENDIDLY EQUIPPED

By Temperament and Training Mr. Harding Was Well Fitted for Highest Office.

BAY STATE LEADS IN RULE OF NATION

AN UNFORSEEN 'ATTACK BRINGS END SUDDENLY, WITHOUT WARNING

Mrs. Harding at His Bedside Reading Aloud When Fatal Attack Comes.

The front page of *The Evening Star* for August 3, 1923, announces the death of Harding. *(D.C. Public Library)*

the decisions facing him and the criticisms directed at his administration. Harding had no illusions about his presidential performance. "I cannot hope to be one of the great presidents," he said, "but perhaps I may be remembered as one of the best loved." He did not achieve this wish. Instead, he would go down as one of America's worst presidents.

After the disappointing 1922 election, Harding called a special session of Congress to pursue the remainder of his legislative program. Unfortunately, he chose to begin with the wrong legislation, a bill creating federal ship subsidies to make America self-sufficient on the high seas. Congress did not agree on the

need for such a measure, and as a result, much time and goodwill were lost before the Senate finally killed the bill in February, 1923. The administration's only noteworthy successes in 1923 would be the Agricultural Credits Act to make more farm loans available and the Government Reclassification Act to improve the civil service.

By 1923, Harding was being overwhelmed by his job. Illness and worry increasingly plagued him, but the scandals associated with his administration were probably what broke him. Almost from the beginning of his administration, rumors of malfeasance had circulated. Nothing of significance occurred until fall, 1922, when there was an unsuccessful attempt by the House of Representatives to impeach Attorney General Daugherty, specifying some fourteen improper and illegal actions. This was, however, only a straw in the wind.

Scandal soon became a serious concern to Harding. After corruption was uncovered at the highest levels in the Veterans Bureau, the president required the resignation of its director, Charles Forbes, in February, 1923. The next month, the bureau's general counsel, Charles F. Cramer, committed suicide because of his involvement in the wrongdoing. In May, a close and shady associate of Daugherty, Jesse M. Smith, also committed suicide. All of this contributed to Harding's unease. As he said, it was his friends, not his enemies, who "keep me walking the floor nights."

On June 20, Harding left Washington on a cross-country tour intended to solicit public support and to improve his own morale. He encountered favorable reactions, but the strain of the long tour cost him his life. He died in

San Francisco on August 2, 1923, probably of problems associated with high blood pressure. Harding may have died a well-loved president, but in 1924 additional evidence of corruption within his administration surfaced. Some of it related to Attorney General Daugherty, whom President Coolidge forced to resign. There was also evidence that led to Charles Forbes's conviction; proof of corruption by Alien Property Custodian Thomas Miller, who was imprisoned; and especially scandals over private oil leases at the government's Teapot Dome and Elk Hill reserves, which led to the conviction of former Secretary of the Interior Albert Fall, who had profited personally from the arrangement. The new scandals further besmirched Harding's reputation. Soon forgotten were his accomplishments.

Warren Harding was not an outstanding president. The Washington Conference and the budgetary actions were noteworthy but hardly earthshaking events in American history. Nor was he innovative; including the vice president in cabinet meetings cannot be deemed significant. The Harding administration did run very economically, and in 1921 and 1922 it enjoyed a considerable measure of legislative success. All of this is a record of some accomplishment but not of greatness. It appears substantially less when set against the disastrous scandals connected with Harding's presidency.

Donald R. McCoy

Bibliographical References

The most scholarly volumes on Harding's life are Randolph C. Downes, *The Rise of Warren Gamaliel Harding, 1865-1920*, 1970, and Robert K. Murray, *Harding Era: Warren G. Harding and His Administration*, 1969. Together they constitute a comprehensive biography of the man. Other valuable biographies of Harding are Andrew Sinclair, *The Available Man: The Life Behind the Masks of Warren Gamaliel Harding*, 1965, and Francis Russell, *The Shadow of Blooming Grove: Warren G. Harding in His Times*, 1968. Carl S. Anthony, *Florence Harding: The First Lady, the Jazz Age, and the Death of America's Most Scandalous President*, 1998, details the life and the important role of Mrs. Harding in the president's career. Robert H. Ferrell, *The Strange Deaths of President Harding*, 1996, is a detailed examination of Harding's sudden death in 1923.

Eugene P. Trani and David L. Wilson, *The Presidency of Warren G. Harding*, 1977, gives a good overview of the Harding administration, and James M. Giglio, *H. M. Daugherty and the Politics of Expediency*, 1978, ably deals with a key figure in Harding's political career. Harding's papers are located at the Ohio Historical Society in Columbus. Richard G. Frederick, *Warren G. Harding: A Bibliography*, 1992, is a comprehensive listing of resources on Harding's personal life and public career.

Calvin Coolidge

30th President, 1923-1929

Born: July 4, 1872
Plymouth, Vermont
Died: January 5, 1933
Northampton, Massachusetts

Political Party: Republican
Vice President: Charles G. Dawes

Cabinet Members

Secretary of State: Charles Evans Hughes, Frank B. Kellogg
Secretary of the Treasury: Andrew Mellon
Secretary of War: John W. Weeks, Dwight F. Davis

Secretary of the Navy: Edwin Denby, Curtis D. Wilbur
Attorney General: Harry Daugherty, Harlan F. Stone, John G. Sargent
Postmaster General: Harry S. New
Secretary of the Interior: Hubert Work, Roy O. West
Secretary of Agriculture: Henry C. Wallace, Howard M. Gore, William Jardine
Secretary of Commerce: Herbert Hoover, William F. Whiting
Secretary of Labor: James J. Davis

Coolidge's official portrait. *(White House Historical Society)*

Calvin Coolidge was an extraordinarily popular president. His popularity hardly waned whatever problems beset the nation, whatever the administration's ineptitude, whatever the impact of presidential actions or inaction.

Coolidge's popularity is hard to explain. A slightly built man, 5 feet, 9 inches tall, weighing only 150 pounds, with delicate features, he was neither physically imposing nor handsome. Alice Roosevelt Longworth quipped that he had the facial expression of one who had been weaned on a pickle. He never dominated a gathering with his mere presence. He lacked charisma. He had cultivated no particular interests. He did not enjoy spectator sports. He unenthusiastically attended the theater and concerts. Until late in his presidency, when he took up fishing, his only regular recreation was riding a mechanical horse that he kept in the White House. Much like his father, he was not a stimulating conversationalist. Although he could become garrulous, especially when discussing politics, he said little to visitors unless he knew them well. Coolidge, then, was not the typical outgoing, facile politician. His only traditional asset was his wife. Grace Coolidge exuded those qualities so lacking in her husband—charm, gregariousness, enthusiasm, and warmth.

Nor did Coolidge bring to the White House a renowned reputation, unless it was one for winning political office. Born on July 4, 1872, Coolidge grew up in the bleak and parochial rural world of Plymouth Notch, Vermont. (Named John Calvin for his father, he dropped the John when he became a young man.) Leaving Vermont in 1891, he attended Amherst College, where he was graduated in 1895. After college, he studied law in the office of a firm in Northampton, Massachusetts. In 1898, he opened his own law practice there, which he maintained for twenty-one years. Beginning with membership on the Northampton City Council in 1898, Coolidge rose rapidly in politics, becoming a member of the state legislature in 1906, lieutenant governor in 1915, governor in 1918, and Warren G. Harding's vice president in 1921. As a state legislator and governor, Coolidge was industrious, competent, and loyal to the Republican Party. He won national attention during the Boston police strike of 1919, when, to restore order in the city, he called out the National Guard and backed the police commissioner in his decision not to rehire any of the strikers, declaring, "There is no right to strike against the public safety, by anybody, anywhere, anytime." As vice president, Coolidge had virtually nothing to do. He presided over the Senate, read a good deal, took

his regular afternoon naps, and saved his money. Lonely, without power after years of exercising it in Massachusetts, he found the vice presidency a mockery. Rather than commanding respect pointing to a bright political future, in 1923 the idiosyncratic Coolidge had become in the eyes of many a capital "character" or "joke." Informed political observers even expected him to be dropped as Harding's running mate in 1924.

The tragic death of Harding was just the latest of many lucky breaks that accompanied Coolidge's political rise. Harding's death occurred when Coolidge was visiting his father in Vermont. There on August 2, 1923, his father awakened him with the news that he was president and, as a notary public in Plymouth Notch, Vermont, administered the oath of office to his son by candlelight in the house in which the new president had been born.

Extraordinary luck accounts in part for Coolidge's meteoric political rise, but it does not explain his continuing popularity. In the 1920's, Americans responded to a man who guilelessly argued that the national government should be as passive as possible, leaving people to pursue their economic interests largely free of government interference. The chief business of the American people, he declared in 1925, was business,

buying, selling, investing, and prospering in the world. I am strongly of the opinion that the majority of people will always find these are the moving impulses of our life. . . . In all experience, the accumulation of wealth means the multiplication of schools, the encouragement of science, the increase of knowledge, the dissemination of intelligence, the broadening of outlook, the expansion of liberties, the widening of culture.

For the individual and society to thrive, Coolidge believed, the federal government ought to be reduced in size and function, administered with greater economy, and kept ever alert to raids on the Treasury by groups whose proposals, if enacted, would restrict individual initiative. Government should be in no hurry to legislate.

The 1920's were generally prosperous, and in Calvin Coolidge the people had a president who articulated and symbolized traditional values, economic and moral. He came from a family of moderate means, from a poor state where work, thrift, and frugality were extolled and the hardship of privation endured. Certainly, his personality and lifestyle contrasted favorably with the profligate types in the Harding administration, and Americans apparently welcomed the safe, secure, and predictable following the twin traumas of war and corruption.

Coolidge and His Image: The First Master of the Media

The Coolidge image, however, was shaped largely by a very skillful manipulation of the public relations media, one orchestrated by the president himself. Discerning the crucial role of public opinion in a democratic government, Coolidge used the mass media to sell himself and the Republican program to the people and in the process developed techniques that his successors emulated or refined.

In doing so, Coolidge shrewdly exploited four available media—the press, radio, movie newsreels, and official government releases. Coolidge enjoyed a favorable press throughout his presidency, at a time when a president's primary link to the people was the newspaper. He consciously promoted amicable relations with the publishers of metropolitan dailies. Although the press conference was inaugurated by William Howard Taft, Coolidge was responsible for institutionalizing it. He held press conferences twice a week, using a format that allowed the president to control news dissemination. Questions were submitted in writing before the conference, only minimal dialogue between reporters and the president was allowed, and the president could not be quoted or identified as having been the source of the information.

In addition to the press, Coolidge used radio, then in its infancy, to communicate with the people. His initial State of the Union message, read in person to Congress in December, 1923, was the first such address to be broadcast to a near national audience. Other selected and campaign speeches were sent simultaneously over the airwaves, and on occasion Coolidge spoke from the White House only to a radio audience, an innovation that Franklin D. Roosevelt refined into his fireside chats. The newsreel also brought the president regularly before Americans, who had become avid moviegoers in the 1920's. Coolidge was keenly aware of the medium's public relations potential and used it with skill. Finally, the White House issued a large number of official releases. Coolidge sent birthday greetings and letters to prominent Americans, addressed messages to organizations holding conventions or celebrating anniversaries, and delivered patriotic statements on special days. There was, thus, no official "Silent Cal." However taciturn he may have been in private, the public Coolidge was loquacious, much in the news, the very symbol of a national leader.

Coolidge's Program: Domestic Policies and Legislative Achievements

Upon taking office, Coolidge kept the same cabinet that had served Harding, but he forced Attorney General Harry Daugherty to resign when it became clear that he had been involved in the scandals of the Harding administration. Although the cabinet met with him as a group twice weekly, Coolidge expected each secretary to administer his own department and make decisions. The dominant figure in the cabinet, and for that matter in Washington, D.C., during the decade, was Herbert Hoover, secretary of commerce. This ambitious subordinate not only expanded the budget, personnel, and functions of his own department but also had an influential voice in the formulation of many administration policies. James J. Davis, secretary of labor, Hubert Work, secretary of the interior, and William Jardine, after 1925 secretary of agriculture, deferred to his ambition. Coolidge relied much on Hoover's judgment, but their personalities, their work habits, and even their philosophies of government differed too greatly for the two ever to be close. Coolidge was not intimate with anyone, least of all a "shaker and mover" such as Hoover. Secretary of the Treasury Andrew Mellon, the other major figure in the cabinet, commanded Coolidge's utmost respect, if not awe. The president warmly embraced the Mellon tax program, the secretary's prescription for an expanding and increasingly prosperous economy. He saw a correlation between govern-

Crowded housing in a company-owned coal town. *(Library of Congress)*

ment fiscal policy and the nation's economic health. Eventually, Congress enacted most of the Mellon Plan, and the public, encouraged by Coolidge and other Republican politicians, came to believe that the secretary was orchestrating the decade's prosperity.

Coolidge deferred in foreign affairs to his secretaries of state, Charles Evans Hughes and Frank B. Kellogg, and to special emissaries Dwight Morrow (Mexico) and Henry L. Stimson (Nicaragua). He probably reposed greater confidence in Hughes, but he also approved most of Kellogg's recommendations.

Soon after taking office, Coolidge began to prepare for the 1924 election. Having control of the party machinery, he won nomination easily and chose as his running mate Charles G. Dawes, former director of the budget and author of the Dawes Plan for the settlement

of the German World War I reparations problem. The badly divided Democrats finally nominated John W. Davis, a conservative Wall Street lawyer from West Virginia, on the 103d ballot. The Progressive Party nominated Robert M. La Follette for president. Coolidge won a decisive victory, receiving 382 electoral votes compared with 136 for Davis and 13 for La Follette.

The program that Coolidge presented to Congress was minimal, essentially that inherited from Harding, and his success in guiding it through Congress was mixed. Revenue laws providing for reduction in the surtax on individual incomes constitute Coolidge's most popular legacy. Secretary Mellon proposed these reductions to spur high-risk investment by wealthy investors who otherwise would find tax-free securities the most attractive outlet for their capital. If they did concentrate their buying on government securities, economic growth necessary for the creation of jobs would be stunted, and the national Treasury would be denied the revenue that lower taxes would bring to it. Congress passed the key tax measure in 1926 when it lowered the maximum surtax (on incomes above $100,000) and the estate tax to 20 percent and abolished the gift tax entirely. Since the exemption for married taxpayers was $3,500, however, most Americans paid no federal income tax at all.

Other noteworthy laws were passed during the Coolidge presidency, laws that had Coolidge's approval if not the enthusiastic support accorded the administration's fiscal legislation. The Air Commerce Act of 1926 brought federal regulation to a chaotic industry that required order for development. Largely the idea of Hoover, the measure furnished aid to private enterprise through regulation of aircraft and pilots and the provision of weather information, auxiliary airfields, and subsidies for mail delivery; but it still envisaged that the investment should be private, not public as in Europe. Even the post office subsidies for air mail were only temporary. Once private airlines could carry the mail, in compliance with the Kelly Act of 1925 the government retreated from the scene. The Radio Act of 1927, also advocated by Hoover, created a radio commission to regulate that industry. The Railway Labor Act, an impressive achievement of the Coolidge administration, replaced the justly maligned Railroad Labor Board with a Board of Mediation for the resolution of disputes and guaranteed to railway workers the right of collective bargaining. The Boulder Canyon Project Act authorized the construction of a huge dam on the Colorado River between Arizona and Nevada. Since the development included production of vast amounts of electrical energy, which could be sold by the government to pay for flood control, irrigation, and water storage projects, Coolidge signed the measure without en-

thusiasm, his thinking paralleling that of private power companies, which opposed the project. Although accepting the Boulder Canyon bill, Coolidge pocket vetoed the Muscle Shoals bill, which provided for a similar public power development on the Tennessee River in Muscle Shoals, Alabama. Under Franklin D. Roosevelt, this project was carried out by the Tennessee Valley Authority.

Legislation passed in 1926 expanded American military aviation, both army and navy, although not enough to satisfy Colonel William Mitchell, outspoken advocate of military air power. Coolidge was no more disposed to spend government funds unnecessarily on the military than on any domestic scheme. For most of his presidency, he publicly discounted the pleas of both branches of the service that they were underfunded and that the country's security was being placed in jeopardy. The president's Aircraft Board, established by Coolidge in September, 1925, and chaired by Dwight Morrow, vindicated his judgment that the nation was not in immediate danger from an attack by air and, taking issue with Mitchell and his congressional supporters, opposed the creation of both a separate air force and a unified department of defense. The Morrow board did recommend action which when authorized by Congress in 1926 created new assistant secretaries for air in the War, Navy, and Commerce departments. Only after the abortive Geneva Disarmament Conference in 1927 did the president seek large sums from Congress for the construction of fifteen new heavy cruisers and one additional aircraft carrier. Previously, he had opposed the appropriations necessary to build the three cruisers authorized by Congress in 1924. Even then, Congress in 1929 brushed aside presidential wishes when it stipulated a time limit in building those sixteen new vessels.

Farm relief legislation precipitated the most intense struggle between Congress and the executive branch of the period. The decade of the 1920's brought depression to American agriculture, as farm prices in the aggregate fell while costs stabilized or increased. Farmers wanted the government to assure them of parity—the same prices for their commodities relative to their costs as they had enjoyed before the war. In response to this demand, Congress twice passed McNary-Haugen bills, which would have authorized the government, in an effort to support domestic prices, to buy the surplus of certain staple commodities, dispose of them at a loss on the world market, and make good the loss and administrative costs through an equalization fee to be paid by the farmers. Coolidge vetoed the legislation, the second time using uncharacteristically passionate and vitriolic language. A McNary-Haugen Act would have meant unprecedented peacetime intervention in the farm economy by government, necessitated an initial federal subsidy to carry the export program until the equalization fee made it self-sustaining, and included a price-fixing feature. Coolidge objected to the bill on philosophical and practical grounds. Such government involvement with agriculture, he held, "was dangerously socialistic in character" and contravened the American tradition of laissez-faire. Besides, the plan would not work, since it had no provision for production control. In fact, it would encourage greater production, more dumping of farm produce abroad, and foreign retaliation. Since Congress could not override the vetoes, stalemate ensued. Cooperative marketing, the administration's long-term answer to the problem, failed to satisfy farmers, their organizations' leaders, and their farm spokespeople in Congress.

Congress regularly failed to act on some of Coolidge's recommendations, as with his railroad consolidation legislation; it modified some of his proposals, as when it made the appropriation in the Flood Control Act of 1928 much greater than the president thought necessary; and it overrode some of his vetoes, of which there were fifty.

Coolidge's difficulties with Congress included not only legislation but also Senate confirmation of his appointments. The Senate refused to confirm as circuit court judge Wallace McCammant, the man who in 1920 had nominated him for the vice presidency. It also turned down two Interstate Commerce Commission nominees. The ultimate embarrassment, however, was its rejection in 1925 of Charles B. Warren as attorney general. Not since the presidency of Andrew Johnson had the Senate rejected a president's choice for a cabinet position. The administration argument that the president had the right to choose his subordinates conflicted with the belief of some senators that their advice and consent were legitimate constitutional prerogatives. The major concern of Senate progressives, both Democratic and Republican, was Warren's former ties to the sugar trust; they worried that his department might have to prosecute the corporation he at one time headed, which was under indictment. Such a conflict of interest never bothered the president, but it did certain progressive Republicans, who were smarting as well from the recent treatment accorded four of their progressive colleagues by the party regulars. Those senators had been stripped of their committee chairmanships and seniority because they had supported the third-party effort of Robert La Follette in 1924.

In fairness to Coolidge, it should not be inferred that had he been more forceful, Congress would have done his bidding on the Warren appointment or his legislative agenda. The most activist president would have had trouble with the politically independent Congresses of the 1920's. Party affiliation meant little, and both Republicans and Democrats were divided among themselves. After 1925 the division on key issues often was a fluid coalition of progressives and moderates against conservatives. A greater effort by Coolidge would likely not have produced much success. Nevertheless, he did try to influence the legislation. He met regularly with Republican leaders in Congress, kept abreast of issues and canvasses, and pressed congressmen to support the administration.

Coolidge had his greatest influence on the federal government by altering the ideological complexion of the courts and government agencies to conform to his economic philosophy. His only Supreme Court appointment, Harlan F. Stone, was superlative. He was less circumspect in his nominations to lower federal courts. Ignoring the views of Chief Justice William Howard Taft, even though he was a strong Coolidge supporter, the president nominated only persons of strong conservative leanings.

Coolidge effectively politicized the regulatory commissions and the tariff commission. He killed any chance that the tariff commission might help set rates to reflect the difference in the cost of producing an item in the United States and abroad. He simply replaced the moderates on the tariff commission with high protectionists regardless of party and exercised his power almost exclusively to raise, not lower, rates. He reduced duties on only five items recommended by the commission while raising those on thirty-eight. Twice he rejected its advice to lower schedules on sugar and linseed oil. Moreover, Coolidge never accepted the commission's quasi-judicial pretensions. To him it was only a fact-finding agency whose recommendations he was free to accept or reject as he pleased. In 1926, at the instigation of George W. Norris, the Senate investigated Coolidge's emasculation of the tariff commission, but nothing came of it. The commission remained a bastion of protectionism.

As for the regulatory commissions, Coolidge appointed railroad people to the Interstate Commerce Commission and enemies of business regulation to the Federal Trade Commission. In 1925 he named to the latter William E. Humphrey, a former Washington congressman who had for years vehemently attacked the FTC. Under his leadership the commission was transformed into a friendly adviser to business. The frustrated Norris saw no reason for the continued existence of the FTC since it had become an agent of those interests supposedly being regulated. Overall, then, the Coolidge administration preferred not to harass business enterprise, not to interfere with trade associations, and not to initiate antitrust suits unless there were compelling reasons to do so, but rather to use government mechanisms to promote, to refine, and to humanize business.

Support in 1925 for rent controls in the District of Columbia excepted, indications of a Coolidge sensitivity to society's less fortunate citizens are hard to find. Although in 1924 Hoover brought together United Mine Workers and management representatives who negotiated the Jacksonville agreement, which was designed to bring peace and improved living conditions to the coal-mining area of the central United States, the administration turned away from the industry when that agreement broke down in 1927 and workers went out on what proved to be a disastrous strike. A Senate investigation revealed shocking conditions in the company towns in Pennsylvania, West Virginia, and Ohio, where inhabitants were denied essential civil liberties and a feeling of hopelessness characterized those seemingly forgotten people. Washington had no more power to act here, Coolidge believed, than it did to regulate the stock exchange. The problem was for local and state authorities to correct. Similarly, he refused to address or to acknowledge signals of mounting industrial unemployment in American cities. The administration discounted the severity of the problem and denounced as partisan election rantings the efforts of Democratic Senator Robert Wagner of New York to have the government at least gather statistics to ascertain its magnitude.

Coolidge's greatest insensitivity was reserved for African Americans. He was not unusual in failing to see any moral or political urgency in the improvement of race relations. In 1924, James Weldon Johnson, the leading official in the National Association for the Advancement of Colored People (NAACP), paid a visit to Coolidge, after which he reported that the president seemed ill at ease and had little to say, not even raising issues of concern to African Americans. Coolidge's response to grievances that they most wanted redressed, segregation in federal employment and lynching, left African Americans frustrated. The NAACP informed Coolidge in detail of every lynching of an African American during the period and urged him to make an antilynching bill a legislative priority. The president was content simply to reprove the crime in his annual messages. He condemned the Ku Klux Klan in October, 1925, when its power had already begun to wane.

Foreign Policy: Involvement Without Commitment

Coolidge came to the White House with experience in local and state government, but he was quite ignorant of international politics. From the first, he deferred to professional policymakers in this area. In December, 1923, Coolidge expressed thoughts that excited the possibility of Washington's diplomatic recognition of the Soviet Union. Secretary of State Hughes quickly dashed the hopes of those Americans who favored that course, and Coolidge acquiesced. He, moreover, allowed the State Department to exploit the communist issue in its Central American endeavors. Robert Olds, undersecretary in 1926, and Kellogg tried to link Mexico and Nicaragua to a Kremlin threat to the Panama Canal, but Americans, however hateful they were of the Soviet experiment, failed to respond. Rather they welcomed the peaceful settlement of the dispute with Mexico over property rights of foreigners, particularly those of American petroleum companies, and an election in Nicaragua under the supervision of American military personnel

after the conclusion of that country's civil war. Unfortunately, American marines, whom Coolidge had returned to Nicaragua in 1926 after a brief withdrawal, soon found themselves warring against the forces of Augusto Sandino, a revolutionary committed to the complete withdrawal of American military forces from his country. The continued skirmishes precipitated a lively debate that saw George Norris in 1928 sponsor amendments to a naval appropriations bill that called for the partial or complete withdrawal of the marines and an accounting to the Senate if the president kept them in Nicaragua past the designated date. These antecedents of the War Powers Act, however, were voted down. Yet, under Coolidge, the United States retreated from its imperialistic past, anticipating the "Good Neighbor" orientation of Herbert Hoover and Franklin D. Roosevelt. Hughes's impromptu defense of intervention at the Sixth Inter-American Conference at Havana in 1928 constitutes the final assertion of that dubious American right.

The foreign policies associated with the Coolidge administration, then, were reasonably enlightened, if not always successful. Domestic imperatives limited the foreign policy initiatives the administration contemplated. For example, however wise World War I Allied debt cancellation or drastic reduction of intergovernmental obligations might have been, such action was in direct conflict with the fiscal commitment of the president. Even so, the United States pursued a lenient war debt policy, basing the agreement negotiated during the Coolidge presidency on the capacity-to-pay principle, in effect reducing the total debt through sharp curtailment of interest. The State Department did, however, threaten to disapprove private loans to citizens, corporations, or local governments of those nations that refused to negotiate debt-funding agreements.

The formulators of the Coolidge administration foreign policy discerned the importance

Coolidge signs the Kellogg-Briand Pact. *(Library of Congress)*

to American interests of European political and economic stability and the contributions the United States, through business and banking experts, should make to that stability. The Dawes Plan, involving loans by American banks to Germany to make possible reparations payments by that nation, expansion of American commercial markets abroad, and encouragement of private investments in Europe (although the State Department denied loans for certain purposes and to selected countries) were initiatives that carried with them no political commitments or obligations. The United States abstained from membership in the League of Nations and even refused to affiliate with the World Court. When the signatories raised questions about a reservation the Senate attached to American adherence to the court protocol, Coolidge adopted a take it or leave it attitude. Republican foreign policy managers developed a course best described as involvement without commitment. Within the confines of domestic restraints and the desire to maintain future freedom of action, the Coolidge years witnessed an American effort to stabilize Europe. A prosperous Europe would be a peaceful Europe. A prosperous and peaceful

Europe would be a lucrative market for exports of American goods and capital.

The Kellogg-Briand Pact, or the Peace of Paris, was the most memorable foreign policy legacy of the Coolidge presidency. Not wanting to become part of a French security system that might involve the United States in a future European conflict, Kellogg rejected the overture of Aristide Briand, the French foreign minister, for a Franco-American pact renouncing war as an instrument of national policy. Because peace groups embraced the idea, the secretary of state countered by proposing a multilateral treaty. All signatories (ultimately sixty-two), not only France and the United States, would renounce war. The treaty, however, provided for no enforcement machinery, no commitment of a signatory to any concrete action in the future. Washington concurrently ratified this pact and launched its naval arms program.

The most praiseworthy American initiatives during the Coolidge years were in East Asia. China was the scene of continual civil turmoil as various northern warlords vied for control of the central government in Peking, while rolling northward from Canton in the south was a coalition composed of Chinese Communists and a reorganized Kuomintang under Chiang Kai-shek. Victorious in 1927, with the northern armies in retreat, and with China nearly unified, the coalition collapsed when the Kuomintang turned on the Communists, launching another civil war that finally led in 1949 to the ouster of the Kuomintang from the mainland. Against this backdrop of conflict, facing the forces of revolution and nationalism, the Coolidge administration established ties with the new China, agreeing to discuss tariff autonomy, negotiating such an arrangement—thus recognizing the new regime in Nanking—and refusing to employ force to suppress emerging Chinese nationalism.

As Coolidge left office, the prized goal he failed to attain was a naval arms pact with Great Britain extending the Washington tonnage reduction formula to auxiliary ships. In early 1929, Anglo-American relations reached their lowest point in many years, with the United States embarked on an extensive naval construction program and many Britishers in agreement with Winston Churchill, who argued against renewed Anglo-American negotiations with a president who recently had expressed "the view-point of a New England backwoodsman."

An Unwarranted Complacence

Historians still debate the meaning of Coolidge's cryptic press conference release in 1927 that he chose not to run for president in 1928. Would he neither seek nor accept the nomination of his party, or was he angling for a draft? The more cogent judgment is that he intended to retire from the presidency and expressed that intention in the idiom of New England. According to Hoover, Coolidge worked for his nomination and he, Hoover, never questioned the statement's meaning. Several factors weighed heavily in Coolidge's decision. The death of Calvin, Jr., in 1924 at age sixteen—from blood poisoning contracted while playing tennis—was a blow from which neither he nor his wife ever completely recovered. Coolidge was also concerned about his health. In 1926, he may have suffered a heart attack. Grace Coolidge also suffered physically in Washington, D.C. Renomination and then reelection would have required a greater effort than the

president wanted to expend. He did not step down because he sensed impending economic disaster. He had, in his opinion, served his country well and it was time for a new administration. Coolidge bequeathed prosperity, peace, and public tranquility to his successor, who was committed to continuing the policies believed responsible for that state of the nation.

Richard N. Kottman

Bibliographical References

The starting point for any study of Coolidge is the three principal biographies. Claude M. Fuess, *Calvin Coolidge: The Man from Vermont*, 1940, is strong on his early life and career but treats the presidential years too favorably. William A. White, *A Puritan in Babylon: The Story of Calvin Coolidge*, 1938, although emphasizing the positive aspects of the Coolidge presidency, presents a sound analysis. Unfortunately, the book is flawed with numerous factual errors. Donald R. McCoy, *Calvin Coolidge: The Quiet President*, 1967, is the most balanced of the three

Coolidge declined to run for reelection in 1928. *(Library of Congress)*

biographies, reflecting research in numerous manuscript collections. For an examination of Coolidge's formative years, see Hendrik Booraem, *The Provincial: Calvin Coolidge and His World, 1885-1895*, 1994. J. R. Greene, *Calvin Coolidge's Plymouth, Vermont*, 1997, is a pictorial profile of Coolidge's birthplace. Robert Ferrell and Howard Quint have edited selections from Coolidge's press conferences entitled *The Talkative President: The Off-the-Record Press Conferences of Calvin Coolidge*, 1964. In his *Presidential Leadership of Public Opinion*, 1965, Elmer E. Cornwell, Jr., has an outstanding chapter on Coolidge and public relations. An overview of the period, but one with a thesis that throws significant light on Hoover and associational-ism, is Ellis W. Hawley, *The Great War and the Search for a Modern Order: A History of the American People and Their Institutions*, 1979. As for Republican foreign policy, L. Ethan Ellis, *Republican Foreign Policy, 1921-1933*, 1968, is traditional and factual, but Melvyn P. Leffler, *The Elusive Quest: America's Pursuit of European Stability and French Security, 1919-1933*, 1979, is more provocative and contains a more cogent and accurate analysis of Republican diplomatic efforts. Robert Sobel, *Coolidge: An American Enigma*, 1998, is a balanced biography that contradicts the popular image of Coolidge as an ineffectual leader. For an extensive analysis of the Coolidge presidency, see Robert H. Ferrell, *The Presidency of Calvin Coolidge*, 1998.

Herbert Hoover

31st President, 1929-1933

Born: August 10, 1874
West Branch, Iowa
Died: October 20, 1964
New York, New York

Political Party: Republican
Vice President: Charles Curtis

Cabinet Members

Secretary of State: Henry L. Stimson
Secretary of the Treasury: Andrew Mellon, Ogden L. Mills
Secretary of War: James W. Good, Patrick J. Hurley
Secretary of the Navy: Charles Francis Adams
Attorney General: William D. Mitchell
Postmaster General: Walter Brown
Secretary of the Interior: Ray Lyman Wilbur
Secretary of Agriculture: Arthur M. Hyde
Secretary of Commerce: Robert Lamont, Roy D. Chapin
Secretary of Labor: James J. Davis, William N. Doak

Herbert Clark Hoover, thirty-first president of the United States, assumed office on March 4, 1929, and relinquished it four years later after being defeated in the election of 1932. His name was long associated with the suffering and misery of the Great Depression, and in popular mythology and political rhetoric it still conjures up visions of a hard-hearted, stiff-collared reactionary mouthing individualist dogma to justify stingy relief expenditures and showing solicitude for the greedy rather than the needy. Recent scholarship on his presidency, however, has tended to portray him in a more positive light. It has moved toward vindicating those who have argued that he was both "the last of the old presidents and the first of the new." Increasingly, it has associated him with a variant form of political progressivism seeking to develop new managerial

Hoover's official portrait. *(White House Historical Society)*

capacities and social safety nets but insisting that this had to be done through government-encouraged private mechanisms and public-private partnerships rather than through expansion of the public sector.

Indeed, the experience of Hoover's presidency can be read as testimony both to the strength of this strain of progressivism in American political culture and to its inadequacy when subjected to severe tests. This progressivism underlay his designs for recovery, relief, and reform as well as his resistance to competing designs; and although it contributed to the failures that made him a one-term president, it also helped to put him in the office. Its appeal made his earlier career seem ideal preparation for serving national needs.

Prepresidential Career

Hoover was born on August 10, 1874, in the Quaker village of West Branch, Iowa, the son of blacksmith and farm implement dealer Jesse Hoover and his wife, Hulda. Reared as a Quaker, he would retain much of the austere demeanor and duty-bound industriousness associated with that faith. Even more important in shaping his personality, however, were the deaths of his father in 1880 and mother in 1884, his move to Oregon to live with relatives, and the insecurities, defensiveness, and determination to succeed thus instilled. By the time he entered Stanford University's "pioneer" class in 1891, he had become what one historian has called an "aggressive introvert," seeking ways to exert influence while staying in the background. While working toward a degree in geology, he became noted among close associates for his entrepreneurial, organizational, and manipulative talents.

Following graduation from Stanford in 1895, Hoover initially had difficulty in finding suitable employment, but in 1896 he entered the employ of San Francisco mining engineer Louis Janin, and this proved to be the starting point in a meteoric rise to fame and fortune.

In 1897 he was hired by the British company of Bewick, Moreing serving first as an evaluator and manager of mining properties in Western Australia and then, from 1899 to 1901, as the Bewick, Moreing man in the Chinese Engineering and Mining Company. On his way to China, he married Lou Henry, also a Stanford graduate, and in Tientsin, at the outbreak of the Boxer Rebellion, he directed construction of barricades to protect the foreign colony. In 1901 he became a partner in Bewick, Moreing, and subsequently played a key role in modernizing the company and establishing its reputation for financial probity and business progressiveness. In 1908 he left to pursue business interests of his own, particularly in Burmese tin and international oil exploration. Although calling himself a "mining engineer," he earned large fees and profits as a specialist in mining finance and the reorganization of failing enterprises. By 1914, he was both wealthy and internationally recognized.

In this rise to international prominence, one can also note three other behavioral patterns significant for Hoover's later career. One was an early and persistent interest in institutional reform and social betterment, manifested particularly in his managerial innovations, professional writings, and philanthropic projects, and leading him toward visions of a new capitalism ordered and kept productive and progressive through professionalized organizations accountable to informed public opinion. A second was his continued penchant for indirection and behind-the-scenes wire-pulling, evident not only in business dealings and "hidden-hand" philanthropies but also in public relations promotions such as that undertaken for the Panama-Pacific Exposition in 1913. A third was his considerable capacity for self-delusion when ventures and projects with which he was associated turned out badly. In such cases he tended to minimize his own role, find others to blame, and credit himself with a foresight and detachment not borne out by the record.

With the outbreak of World War I in 1914, Hoover quickly became involved in relief work, initially to rescue stranded Americans in Europe and then as organizer and director of the Commission for Relief in Belgium. In the public mind he became the "great humanitarian" as well as the "great engineer." When the United States entered the war in 1917, he became wartime food administrator, and he proceeded to develop a complex of public-private partnerships, community units, and governmental purchasing and publicity agencies through which production stimulants and distributive controls were administered. Some of the resulting arrangements would become models for the kind of societal and governmental machinery that he would advocate in the postwar period, and in operation they made him the best known and most widely acclaimed of Woodrow Wilson's war managers. To "Hooverize," meaning to economize for noble purposes, became a new addition to the American vocabulary.

Following the armistice in 1918, Hoover became director of American relief efforts in Europe, not only helping to feed millions and reconstruct wartorn economies but also engaging in heated controversies over policy toward Germany, Allied economic controls, and the use of food for political purposes. In September, 1919, he returned to the United States and in the months that followed became involved in a number of domestic developments and issues. He helped to organize the Federated American Engineering Societies, became its first president, and led it to take on projects for reducing waste and reforming managerial practice. He was vice chair of President Wilson's Second Industrial Conference, which offered schemes for solving the labor problem. He supported American membership in the League of Nations. Then, in 1920, he was an unsuccessful contender for the Republican presidential nomination. At that time he seemed to many liberals the best hope for revitalizing and advancing progressive causes.

During this same period, particularly in his engineering and political addresses and testimony at congressional hearings, Hoover was also working his way toward the variant of progressivism with which his future political career would become so firmly associated. It was a progressivism that accepted much of the era's managerial thinking. It saw, in other words, an emerging organizational society threatened by market and community failures and in need of new managerial capacities and ordering mechanisms if it were to remain progressive. Yet, at the same time, it rejected prescriptions that would meet these needs through a new managerial state or through schemes to suppress self-interestedness, accepting much of the era's antistatist and anticollectivist thought. The answer, this kind of progressivism claimed, lay in building the needed mechanisms into the social order itself, thus equipping organized social groups for responsible self-government, responsible use of their new social power, and responsible participation in the management of national progress. In this building process, envisioned as both corporate and professional, there was room for governmental work of a progressive sort.

In 1921, Hoover entered Warren G. Harding's cabinet as secretary of commerce, and over the next seven years under both Harding and Calvin Coolidge he transformed that department into a beehive of the kind of activity he had defined as progressive. It became the center of an ongoing whirl of conferences, campaigns, and committee meetings, from which emerged new structures and networks that spanned the public and private sectors and purported to give the nation new managerial capacities. The department devised new machinery for employment and business cycle stabilization, for improving the performance of problem industries, for promoting trade, efficiency, conservation, and ethical business behavior, for reducing industrial conflict and providing relief during natural disasters, and for implementing a variety of other social betterment projects. Never before, noted one commentator, had any cabinet officer engaged in "such wide diversity of activities or covered quite so much ground." Given the economic boom that developed after 1922, Hoover could claim that such activity was helping to solve long-standing national problems and speed national progress. Those who saw it as a cover for business domination, social injustice, or growing economic unsoundness were by 1928 very much in the minority.

Indeed, once Coolidge had decided against seeking reelection, there were many who wanted to make Hoover president. Both he and his progressivism were highly attractive in the context of 1928, particularly as presented by the public relations network now at his command. Once set in motion, the Hoover campaign machinery proved strikingly successful. Easily nominated at the Republican convention, Hoover crushed Democratic opponent Alfred E. Smith by carrying forty states and polling 58 percent of the popular vote.

Before the Crash

In the early months of his administration, Hoover continued to have a strongly favorable image. He was, many believed, precisely the kind of president that the nation needed, an expert, an engineer, a businessman, a "nonpolitician," a humanitarian, and a self-made success all rolled into one. He was also physically impressive, somewhat forbidding but large and athletically built, with an "outdoors" complexion, a square chin and firm facial features, and a general aura of efficiency, mastery, energy, and seriousness. His family life, as evidenced by an enduring marriage, a talented wife, and two promising sons, seemed exemplary. So did his capacity for administration, especially his proven knacks for choosing able and dedicated lieutenants and turning lethargic or failing organizations into thriving and dynamic ones. If his protective reserve, strong sense of privacy, and lack of skill in the oratorical and political arts made the political side of his job more difficult, many in 1929 still regarded these as virtues rather than defects.

In staffing the new administration, Hoover weighed and acted on two major kinds of considerations. First, there were political powers to be recognized and political debts to be paid, which meant that Andrew Mellon remained at the Treasury and that the War, Agriculture, and Post Office departments went, respectively, to James W. Good, Arthur M. Hyde, and Walter Brown, all of whom had played important roles during the campaign. Second, there was the need for men who shared Hoover's vision of the future and could help in building the kind of organizations through which it was to be realized. Two cabinet appointments of this sort were Ray Lyman Wilbur as secretary of the interior and Robert Lamont as secretary of commerce; and below the cabinet level were numerous other "Hoover men" anxious to participate in new "Hooverization" projects. In completing his cabinet, Hoover also chose Henry L. Stimson as secretary of state, William D. Mitchell as attorney general, James J. Davis as secretary of labor, and Charles Francis Adams as secretary of the navy.

During the campaign in 1928, Hoover had talked of a "new day," to be ushered in by the kind of organizational and fact-finding endeavors with which his name had become associated; and in the early days of the administration he initiated a variety of such projects. In existence within a few months were such agencies as the President's Research Committee on Social Trends, the Commission on the Conservation and Administration of the Public Domain, and the National Commission on Law Observance and Enforcement. Also under way were efforts to improve the performance of problem agencies, particularly the Indian, Veterans, Prisons, and Prohibition bureaus. In the planning stages were projects that envisioned

Black Tuesday, 1929, at the New York Stock Exchange. *(Library of Congress)*

a public-private economic council, a new series of economic studies and conferences, and a Hoover-type organizational complex engaged in rationalizing and coordinating the nation's welfare and social service activities.

An auspicious beginning was also made in efforts to develop better organization for an agricultural sector that had been depressed throughout the 1920's. The answer here, Hoover had long argued, was a properly developed set of marketing cooperatives that would make agriculture more businesslike while preserving the virtues inherent in rural individualism. In a special session of Congress convened in April, 1929, he was able to fend off other farm relief schemes and secure passage of an Agricultural Marketing Act based on his prescriptions. Under it a new Federal Farm Board, organized to represent the various interests in agriculture, was to become the

agency for building and financing a new set of marketing associations. It could provide technical and promotional assistance, make loans to facilitate orderly marketing, and form emergency stabilization corporations to deal with demoralized markets; and in operation it was soon busily engaged in such organization building.

Even as such projects got under way, however, involvement in other issues provided a foretaste of future political difficulties. Tariff revision, originally intended to facilitate agricultural adjustment, bogged down in the special session and had to be postponed. A national oil conference, intended to produce cooperative machinery for rationalizing oil production, produced little but criticism. Efforts to strengthen Prohibition enforcement, as demanded by dry supporters, brought worrisome clashes with urban politicians and civil libertarians. A

"Southern policy," seeking to consolidate Republican gains in the South, was successful only in alienating Northern groups. In these political arenas, where problem solving called for political artistry more than organization building, the administration was already gaining a reputation for ineptitude.

Battling the Depression

The Great Depression, which would become the central preoccupation of the Hoover administration, is generally regarded as having its roots in the economic imbalances, excessive speculation, and shaky financial structures of the 1920's. The event, however, that separated the prosperous 1920's from the Depression decade was the stock market crash of late 1929. In trouble from September on, the great bull market finally collapsed in an orgy of panic selling on October 29, a date that would be remembered as Black Tuesday. Although business and political leaders kept saying that the underlying economy was still fundamentally sound, the crash not only unmasked much unsoundness but also created an atmosphere of gloom that dampened both investment and consumer spending. There would be brief upturns, but the general drift of economic indicators during Hoover's remaining forty months was radically downward. From 1929 to 1933, the gross national product fell by 29 percent, while unemployment rose from 3 to 25 percent.

Through behind-the-scenes actions, Hoover had tried to generate warnings and secure more responsible business behavior. These efforts, however, had failed to have much effect. Following the crash, he joined those who viewed the underlying economy as fundamentally sound and moved to establish countercyclical organizations believed capable of curbing deflationary forces and getting expansion started again. By early 1930, three of these were in operation. A National Business Survey Conference, created as an adjunct of the Chamber of Commerce and making use of the administrative machinery of some 170 trade associa-

A breadline in New York City during the Great Depression. *(Library of Congress)*

tions, was seeking to dispel gloom and obtain compliance with pledges of wage maintenance and new investment. A National Building Survey Conference, similarly organized, was attempting to implement pledges of new or expanded construction. A Division of Public Construction was working to speed up federal building projects and obtain compliance with state and municipal pledges to increase public works expenditures.

In addition, Hoover was able to secure a temporary tax cut, a $400 million increase in federal public works appropriations, a "labor peace" pledge from union leaders, monetary expansion measures from the Federal Reserve Board, and special antideflation lending by the Federal Farm Board. Such measures were supposed to facilitate the work of the recovery organizations, and initially much optimism was expressed about their effectiveness. A "great economic experiment," Hoover declared in May, 1930, had "succeeded to a remarkable degree." As of June, however, it was becoming clear that many economic decision makers did not share this official optimism, and as summer gave way to fall, the economy reeled under the impact of new layoffs, shrinking investment outlays, worsening farm distress, mounting bank failures, and an intensifying international trade war aggravated by passage of the protectionist Smoot-Hawley Tariff. Recovery, it seemed, could not be organized in the way attempted. Refusing to concede this, Hoover tended to blame the deteriorating situation on foreign dumping, congressional politics, and irresponsible criticism.

Consequently, the administration's response to the developments of late 1930 was the creation of new Hoover-type organizations while resisting calls for governmental controls, federal relief, and legalized cartel agreements. In August, the administration formed the National Drought Committee to mobilize community relief machinery in distressed farm areas hit by the twin blows of depression and drought. From midsummer on, it mounted organized campaigns to reduce the acreage being planted to wheat. In October came the President's Emergency Committee for Employment (PECE), which was to serve as mobilizer, coordinator, and informational exchange for community-centered programs of relief and job creation. Modeled on the temporary relief organization that Hoover had helped to create in 1921, it was supposed to relieve suffering while preserving local and individual responsibility and saving the unemployed from the character-destroying effects of a dole.

In early 1931, as economic indicators turned slightly upward, Hoover again declared that "mobilized voluntary action" had "proved its strength." Again he spoke too soon. In May and June came the financial crash in Europe, making the Depression worldwide and having strongly adverse repercussions in the United States. Although Hoover took the lead in securing a one-year suspension of international debt payments, an arrangement known as the Hoover Moratorium, this failed to check a contraction that further discredited his policies, forced abandonment of further efforts to maintain wage rates and farm prices, and led him to replace PECE with a more business-oriented President's Organization on Unemployment Relief. Again, the contraction brought the monetary and banking system into jeopardy, leading Hoover to organize the National Credit Association through which stronger banks were supposed to aid the weaker ones. The relief thus provided proved minimal and short-lived.

Still, Hoover resisted the calls for government planning, welfare statism, and legalized creation of cartels, offering instead a program that would couple more emergency organization with supportive governmental credits and deficit-reducing fiscal action. This was the program presented to Congress and the public in late 1931, and by the summer of 1932 most of it had been implemented. A Reconstruction Finance Corporation, modeled on the War Finance Corporation of 1918, was established and authorized to make loans to needy banks and railroads and subsequently, under congressional pressure, to local relief and public works agencies. New economy and tax measures were passed. Lesser laws and actions expanded the lending powers of the Farm Loan and Federal Reserve systems, added a new system of home loan banks, tried to mobilize social pressures against hoarding, and created another network of banking and industrial committees to promote credit expansion and new investment outlays. Recovery, Hoover now held, awaited only the revival of credit and confidence.

Again, too, Hoover took the brief upturn in August and September of 1932 as evidence that his program was working. The worsening crisis of his last six months, he would argue then and later, was the result of business fears created by election uncertainties and Democratic flirtations with unsound monetary and fiscal proposals. In the eyes of most Americans, however, his recovery prescriptions and programs had now become thoroughly discredited. They were, it was being argued, based on highly fallacious assumptions about what could be done through associational action and public-private cooperation, and in operation they had only delayed recovery and prolonged suffering by blocking more effective forms of recovery action. Recovery had remained elusive despite Hoover's energetic search for it. The resulting experience had left him crippled politically and unable to prevent the forms of governmental intervention that he still held to be incompatible with a progressive national future.

A Frustrated Reformism

Meanwhile, the deepening of the Depression had also become a major factor in making Hoover's reformist and educational efforts a story of increasing frustration, lowered goals, and growing criticism. In the "new day" visions

of 1928 and 1929, the presidency was to become an instrument working to fill the informational and organizational gaps threatening further progress. As noted previously, the period before the crash had witnessed the launching of several such projects. After the crash, however, these projects were forced by recovery considerations to take a backseat; and although they were never totally abandoned, they accomplished relatively little and became, in the eyes of many, prime examples of gross inadequacy, unrealistic reasoning, and political ineptitude.

In the area of economic reform, for example, the early designs for filling organizational gaps were soon subordinated to the search for emergency recovery and relief mechanisms. In agriculture, the Federal Farm Board became involved in futile efforts to stabilize farm prices, lost the support of both farm and business groups, and left relatively little imprint on agricultural organization. In business, the administration's prescriptions for problem industries came under attack from antitrusters on one side and business protectionists on the other. They produced new kinds of associational machinery for the oil, lumber, coal, railroad, aviation, and cotton textile industries, but the machinery would prove fragile and little of it survived. In labor, the major reform, the 1932 Norris-LaGuardia Act outlawing "yellow dog contracts" and other antiunion weapons, emerged from Congress rather than from the administration. Hoover signed it somewhat reluctantly. In the shaping of overarching institutions, the administration's designs for a national economic council, continuing economic surveys, and new balancing mechanisms were never realized. The only agency that seemed a step toward their realization was a Federal Employment Stabilization Board established in 1931, and contemporaries saw this as part of Senator Robert Wagner's program rather than the administration's.

The outcome of conservation reform, an-

Hoover Dam. *(National Archives)*

other area in which Hoover had long been interested, was also frustrating. Here the administration was able to get the Hoover Dam project under way, expand the national park system, and conduct some valuable experiments in improved forestry and oil reserve management, but its hopes for a national waterway plan, improved developmental practices in the natural resource industries, and new partnership arrangements in administering the public lands were never fulfilled. It was also unsuccessful in bringing the kind of development it envisioned to the St. Lawrence and Tennessee River Valleys. Its treaty with Canada for St. Lawrence development was never ratified, and the stalemate it had inherited on Tennessee River development persisted. Hoover vetoed the Norris bill for development by a federal corporation, and its proponents blocked serious consideration of his scheme for a developmental agency composed of private sector and local government representatives.

Frustrating, too, were the efforts to fill organizational and informational gaps in the na-

tion's social service system. Here the Research Committee on Social Trends became an industrious amasser of social data, but its apolitical standing was in constant jeopardy, and the accompanying scheme for creating national coordinating and promotional agencies in the fields of housing, child welfare, recreation, education, and public health was in large measure abandoned. Only two of the projected national conferences, those on child welfare and housing, were ever held, and neither the follow-up machinery produced by these nor the promotional machinery of study groups examining the educational and medical systems ever accomplished what was originally intended. By 1932, moreover, a social service community once strongly supportive of Hoover had become highly critical. In its eyes the great problem had become one of shrinking funds, not inadequate information or organization. Increasingly, its solutions called for expanding the public sector in ways that Hoover still strongly opposed.

A similar pattern was also apparent in efforts aimed at improving the lot of racial minorities. A new leadership for the Bureau of Indian Affairs made a start toward modernizing its administrative structure and improving its services. Some concern also was shown for the need to improve black education, housing, and business opportunities and to develop a better basis for racial progress in the South. The Depression, however, kept programs that cost money to a minimum, and the administration's distaste for such militant groups as the Indian Defense Association and the National Association for the Advancement of Colored People (NAACP) heightened these groups' disenchantment with the administration's policies. They criticized it not only for niggardliness but also for having assimilationist attitudes toward American Indian cultures, discriminating against African American soldiers and Gold Star mothers, embracing "lily-whiteism" in its Southern policy, and doing essentially nothing about lynching atrocities in the South. Unknown at the time was Hoover's consideration of a plan for making federal troops available to assist local authorities, a plan finally shelved after administration lawyers questioned its constitutionality.

Two other reform projects were also disappointing in the results achieved. One was the effort to reorganize the executive branch in the interests of greater efficiency and rationality. This finally culminated in a series of reorganization plans proposed under a 1932 economy bill, all of which were rejected by Congress. The other sought to reduce lawlessness and improve the nation's law enforcement and judicial system. It led to altered appointment procedures and bureau reorganizations, limited reform of the prison system, new exercises in federal-local cooperation, and much fact-gathering by a National Commission on Law Observance and Enforcement. Political resistance blocked much that was attempted, however, and the tendency of the lawlessness issue to become intertwined with the Prohibition debate exacerbated the political difficulties and made for an increasingly negative press.

In all the areas noted, Hoover's can be regarded as a reform presidency, unsatisfied with things as they were, but the elitist, quasi-privatist, antistatist style of reform that he had identified as "truly progressive" was not well suited to the changing economic and political context of the early 1930's. The result was a frustrated reformism having unintended consequences, one achieving few of its objectives but having some significance as a conduit for

reform-minded professionals on their way to the New Deal and as a negative experience strongly indicating that effective reform would have to be sought along other paths.

Foreign Policies

The story of the Hoover administration's foreign policies is also largely one of frustrated hopes. It began with visions of completing the "American system" of the 1920's, a system that would use new fact-gathering, business, and legal mechanisms to achieve the ordered world prosperity that had not and could not be achieved through international politics, military interventions, or utopian peace movements. In particular, Hoover hoped to build on earlier progress toward curbing irrational arms races, developing international adjudication agencies, and bringing American-style business organization to the international economy. The Depression and the impact that it had on politics at home and abroad, however, would create a context increasingly hostile to such initiatives and turn most of them into exercises in futility and frustration.

One area in which Hoover hoped to build on the achievements of the 1920's was that of naval limitations. Here he did have some initial success. He offered a new "yardstick principle," which would "measure" navies by taking into account their ages, armaments, and other fighting capacities as well as their tonnage. This allowed the British to accept parity with the United States without giving up the larger cruiser tonnage on which they had long been insisting. The eventual result was the London Naval Treaty of 1930, extending the limitations agreed to at Washington in 1921 and adding a new set of limitations in the previously unrestricted categories of cruisers, destroyers, and submarines. The latter, however, was accepted only by Britain, the United States, and Japan. Efforts to bring France and Italy into the system were unsuccessful. In operation, the structure not only would prove shortlived but also would later be seen as a shortsighted legitimation of Japanese dominance in the western Pacific.

A second area to which Hoover devoted considerable energy was relations with the countries of Latin America. Before his inaugural he made a goodwill tour of the region, and early in his administration came actions upgrading the diplomatic service there, encouraging more inter-American economic cooperation and cultural exchange, and creating a special commission to arrange military withdrawal from Haiti. The Monroe Doctrine, moreover, was no longer to serve as justification for police actions in the area, and despite pressure from American investors Hoover rejected collection of debts by force and allowed the wave of debt repudiations and political disturbances accompanying economic contraction to run its course without American intervention. Some have interpreted his policies as an important shift from Gunboat Diplomacy to Good Neighborism. Others have noted a harder side, particularly his unsympathetic attitude toward debt relief and economic assistance proposals. By 1931, conditions in Latin America were making a mockery of the visions of growth and stability set forth earlier.

In Europe, too, initial appearances of diplomatic success soon gave way to conditions markedly at variance with what the Hoover administration had hoped to achieve. An international business committee headed by American industrialist Owen D. Young devised a new reparations settlement, and through the work of Elihu Root a formula emerged for American membership in the World Court. The resulting court treaty, however, was not ratified, and the Young settlement had no chance of survival after the Depression became worldwide. The need, so various analysts argued in 1931 and 1932, was for debt cancellation, emergency credits, tariff revision, and joint monetary actions, but the Hoover administration rejected such proposals and rebuffed Allied efforts to tie reparations reductions to reduc-

tions in the war debts owed the United States. Its willingness to provide relief was limited to the Hoover Moratorium of 1931 and a supplementary "standstill agreement" on repayment of private loans to Germany. These measures did not, as was hoped, allow the European nations to get their finances in order and their people and resources back to work.

In 1932, the Hoover administration urged arms reductions as a means of providing financial relief. Under the Hoover Plan, as proposed to the Geneva Disarmament Conference, all military forces would be reduced by one-third. This came to nothing—a victim, Hoover thought, of French attitudes and intransigence. Similarly unfruitful were the slowly developing plans for a world economic conference and Hoover's calls in late 1932 for a new debt commission to reconsider capacities to pay. All the debtor nations except Finland would repudiate their war debts, and the economic crisis would bring to power a German regime bent on scrapping the Versailles Treaty and the system it had established.

Even as the Versailles system crumbled in Europe, moreover, developments in the Far East shattered hopes that the Washington treaty system of 1921-1922 could provide a framework for stability and peaceful development there. In Japan the economic crisis and growing resistance to Japanese economic designs in China undermined the prestige of Western-oriented liberals. In September, 1931, the Japanese began a conquest of Chinese Manchuria followed by open defiance of Western efforts to invoke moral sanctions under the League of Nations, the Washington treaties, and the 1928 Paris Peace Pact outlawing aggressive war. The major American response was a doctrine of "nonrecognition" of "immoral" and "illegal" Japanese conquests, enunciated in early 1932 and generally known as the Stimson Doctrine. Stimson himself wanted to threaten economic sanctions, but Hoover feared that such a move would only strengthen the Japanese militarists, and he decided instead to offer assurances that no such sanctions would be used.

Viewed in terms of the goals set forth in 1929, Hoover's foreign policies must be regarded as failures. The visions associated with the American system were not realized, and nothing effective was done to curb or control the economic and political forces eventually responsible for another world war. Study of the period's diplomacy, however, has shown it to be less isolationist and more sophisticated than once thought; some historians have argued that in its perceptions of the limits of American power and its skepticism about political entanglements and military solutions, it showed more wisdom than the diplomacy that followed.

Changing Political Configurations

Meanwhile, the years of persisting depression, a frustrated reformism, and shattered diplomatic hopes had also become years of mounting political discontent, heated political controversy, and changing political allegiances and alignments. Ironically, a president who prided himself on being a nonpolitician, who tended to equate good government with decisions made outside or above politics, and whose projects for improving national life would in general diminish the roles played by professional politicians now found himself in an increasingly politicized environment. In this environment he did not fare well. His once-favorable image became increasingly negative, particularly among the newly politicized; his hopes for using his reputation to build an administration bloc in Congress were soon shattered; and his association with the Republican Party became a political liability for the party, helping to convert it from majority to minority status.

One aspect of the changing political situation was a growing reservoir of anti-Hooverism from which political opponents could draw. In part this reflected the need for a Depression scapegoat. In part it was systematically sown and nurtured by the Democratic Party's publicity apparatus. Also involved were the overselling done earlier, a breakdown of relations with the press, a growing gap between Hooverian values and those of a populace battered by Depression forces, a negative fallout from Hoover's deficiencies as a political leader, and a personality and temperament ill suited to coping with such adversities. By 1932, the president's image had become almost the reverse of that in 1929. He was perceived now as stony-hearted, incompetent, irritable, dogmatic, out of touch, and insensitive to human needs, a man concerned only with the "big fellows" and more with saving mules and cattle than with saving human beings.

Association with the president was clearly not an asset in the midterm elections of 1930 and the special elections of 1931. Identifiable Hoover men did badly, and the Republican Party lost control of the House of Representatives and became dependent on party irregulars for control of the Senate. The results reflected the strong tendency of newly politicized ethnic and labor groups to vote Democratic, the collapse of efforts to make Republicanism respectable in the South, and the growth of protest politics in the rural Midwest, all developments helping to transform the party system under which Hoover was elected and to usher in an era of Democratic Party dominance.

The rise of antiadministration forces in the electorate was also accompanied by a parallel development in Congress. Initially, an administration bloc had formed there, led by Hoover men such as Senators Henry J. Allen and Arthur Vandenberg and occupying a middle position between the Republican Old Guard and Western Republican insurgents, neither of whom had been happy about Hoover's rise to the presidency. Hopes of expanding the bloc's influence were soon shattered, however; and in the 1930 battle over Hoover's nomination of Judge John J. Parker to fill a vacancy on the Supreme Court, an antiadministration coalition formed and dealt administration forces a major defeat. Although an able jurist, Parker proved vulnerable to charges of racial and antilabor bias and could not be confirmed. His critics succeeded in putting together a winning senatorial alliance of Democrats and liberal Republicans.

In the lame duck session that followed the elections of 1930, this antiadministration coalition reappeared, particularly in the heated battles over drought relief and employment service legislation and in overriding the president's veto of a bonus bill authorizing federal loans to holders of World War bonus insurance certificates. After the Seventy-first Congress gave way to the Seventy-second, congressional rebellions became a regular feature of the political landscape. On most of its recovery program in 1932, the administration was able to secure the cooperation of the Democratic congressional leadership, but antiadministration rebellions forced significant modifications in the farm and relief programs, gave the administration much difficulty on the bonus issue, and turned back efforts to raise new revenue through a federal sales tax. The sales tax rebellion has been viewed as particularly significant, since it foreshadowed congressonal alignments that would be characteristic of much of the subsequent New Deal period.

Most of these legislative battles contributed to further growth of Hoover's negative image. Following congressional adjournment in 1932, a "bonus riot" incident did more damage. Involved here were the remnants of the "bonus army" of World War I veterans who had gathered in Washington, D.C., to lobby for immediate maturity-value redemption of their bonus insurance certificates. Although the lobbying failed, some had stayed on; and when efforts were made to remove a group of them from federal properties along Pennsylvania Avenue, the result was violence in which two veterans were killed. Hoover then decided to use federal troops, and on July 28 a special riot force under

General Douglas MacArthur proceeded to clear the riot area. Violating Hoover's orders, MacArthur also cleared and destroyed the veterans' camp at Anacostia Flats, an action that Hoover subsequently defended as necessary to deal with a dangerous group increasingly controlled by communists and criminals. The defense, however, was not persuasive, and the outcome tended to strengthen perceptions of Hoover as insensitive and paranoiac. Added to the image of hard-heartedness and dogmatism was that of a man who had turned the nation's arms against the very people who had saved the nation in 1918.

Defeat, Interregnum, and Postpresidency

At the Republican convention in 1932, Hoover encountered much pessimism but no serious challenges from other contenders. He and Vice President Charles Curtis were easily renominated. In the campaign that followed, he occasionally seemed convinced that economic upturns, concessions to the antiprohibitionists, proper education about his administration's achievements, and better appreciation of how he had saved the country from "chaos and degeneration" would somehow turn his political fortunes around. He also believed that in nominating Franklin Delano Roosevelt, the Democrats had provided him with the weakest of several possible opponents; and he tended to discount much of the Democrats' criticism as irresponsible political propaganda that would be ineffective with sensible portions of the citizenry.

Hoover's hopes for reelection, however, rested mostly on misperceptions. Roosevelt proved to be a confident and effective campaigner, able to unite his party, take advantage of the anti-Hooverism pervading the political scene, and associate himself with the Depression-bred values of compassion and economic morality. Hoover remained on the defensive, punctuating his speeches with warnings that a Democratic victory would delay sound recovery and imperil future progress, and employing an increasingly conservative rhetoric to mobilize groups fearful of where current political and social agitation could lead. Rhetorically at least, he was moving to the right, whereas much of the United States was moving in the opposite direction. The result was to diminish even further his political appeal. On election day he carried only six states for an electoral count of 59 to Roosevelt's 472; in the popular column he lost by a count of 27,821,857 to 15,761,841.

Hoover's last four months in office, a period generally known as the interregnum, saw the Depression reach its lowest point. Unemployment climbed to 25 percent, and a new banking crisis produced near paralysis of the nation's financial machinery. Many states were forced to declare bank holidays, closing the banks or severely restricting their functions. Since the lame duck president and the president-elect could not agree on the causes of or cures for the situation, no remedial program was forthcoming. For Hoover, confidence remained the key. In a series of exchanges with Roosevelt, he tried to commit the incoming administration to the program he believed necessary to restore confidence in the system and its future, a program consisting essentially of budget balancing, gold standard maintenance, war debt renegotiation, and banking law revision. These exchanges, however, came to nothing. As Roosevelt saw it, Hoover was not only out to trick him and tie his hands in making needed reforms but was also trying to shift the blame for the crisis to those who had defeated him at the polls.

Accordingly, the change of administrations on March 4, 1933, came at one of the nation's darkest economic hours; and partly because of the burst of activity and change of mood that followed, the Hoover administration entered public memory as a time of do-nothingness, despair, and defeatism. Largely forgotten were the activism and hopes with which it began, the optimistic innovativeness

with which it attempted to short-circuit the business cycle, and the numerous reform projects that remained a part of its agenda. Also badly distorted because these things were forgotten was the political philosophy that shaped its attitudes concerning proper and improper forms of governmental intervention and led to policies that in the eyes of some meant unnecessary misery and suffering.

After leaving the presidency, Hoover continued to play active roles in Republican Party politics and public policy debate and from 1933 through 1938 became an outspoken critic of the New Deal, especially in *The Challenge to Liberty* (1934) and in a series of "addresses upon the American road." He also gave much attention to Stanford University, particularly to its Hoover Institution, and as World War II approached, he worked to keep the United States at peace and tried unsuccessfully to establish a food relief program for populations in German-occupied countries. After the war, as both he and attitudes toward him mellowed, he assumed the role of elder statesman, was asked to head several special agencies, and served successively as coordinator of the European Food Program in 1947, chairman of the Commission for Reorganization of the Executive Branch from 1947 to 1949, and chairman of a second Commission on Reorganization from 1953 to 1955. In addition, he published his memoirs, wrote and published histories of Woodrow Wilson's "ordeal" and America's post-World War I relief operations in Europe, and worked on but failed to publish a history of communist influences on the West. He died on October 20, 1964, and is buried on a hillside in West Branch near his birthplace and the presidential library that houses his papers. Ninety years old at the time of his death, he lived longer than any president since John Adams.

General Assessment

Among historians of the Hoover administration, its nature and place in American history have been subjects of continuing controversy. Initially, the controversy was between those who contrasted it negatively with Roosevelt's New Deal and those who contrasted it positively, both seeing Hoover as an anti-Rooseveltian but the former deploring Hoover's stance against needed forms of government intervention and the latter deploring the nation's movement away from his wisdom. Yet from the beginning a few questioned the terms in which this debate was framed. The similarities and linkages between the Hoover and Roosevelt administrations, they argued, were as great as or greater than the differences and disjunctures. Both had been reformist-oriented, and both had rejected classical economic formulas for dealing with business crises and had attempted to develop new political and social machinery for that purpose. In this larger sense they had formed a continuum, with the dividing line between the old and the new coming in 1929 rather than in 1933.

Hoover visits children in Poland in 1946 as part of his humanitarian efforts following World War II. *(Library of Congress)*

As serious research on the period got under way, moreover, particularly in the 1960's, it tended to provide more support for those questioning the framework of the initial debate than for those engaged in it. Much of the research amounted to the rediscovery and documentation of the reformist, activist, interventionist side of the Hoover administration, the thinking that underlay this, and the heritages that it had bequeathed across the rhetorical divide of 1933. It found in the records a story at odds with the images of rugged individualism decried by pro-New Deal interpreters and idealized by their conservative rivals. As research and rethinking proceeded, the new scholarship began to alter the whole framework of the interpretive debate, undercutting the premises of established positions and bringing new questions to the fore.

Increasingly, although somewhat grudgingly, participants in the older debate have had to concede that Hoover's was a reform presidency, that it had attributes foreshadowing a new managerial role for the American presidency, and that its policies seem best explained by the Hooverian variant of progressivism that guided their formulation. Most interpreters, however, would still make fairly sharp distinctions between the Hooverian and New Deal orientations, both in the role of the state and the degrees of responsiveness to insurgent political groups and antiestablishment critics. Also continuing to generate debate were the suggestions of some reinterpreters that Hoover's progressivism had been wiser and potentially more capable of realizing liberal ideals than had the New Deal variety. This view had its supporters, particularly among certain critics of the New Deal state and its failures. Most studies of Hoover's system in action, however, have concluded that the mechanisms envisioned or created were inadequate to deal with the problems they were seeking to solve and that in some cases these mechanisms tended to evolve quickly toward the use of illiberal and undemocratic methods. Scholarship would seem to support the view that although the Hoover presidency was reformist, activist, principled, and intellectually sophisticated, it was also a failed presidency, economically, politically, and in its prescriptions for social distress.

Ellis W. Hawley

Bibliographical References

The best biographical works on Hoover are Joan Hoff-Wilson, *Herbert Hoover: Forgotten Progressive*, 1975; David Burner, *Herbert Hoover: A Public Life*, 1979; and George Nash, *The Life of Herbert Hoover: The Engineer*, 1983. Also valuable if used with caution are Hoover's *Memoirs*, 3 vols., 1951. His other major writings include *Principles of Mining*, 1909; *American Individualism*, 1922; *The Challenge to Liberty*, 1934; *The Ordeal of Woodrow Wilson*, 1958; and *An American Epic*, 4 vols., 1959-1964.

Book-length accounts of the Hoover administration include William Myers and Walter Newton, *The Hoover Administration*, 1936; Ray L. Wilbur and Arthur Hyde, *The Hoover Policies*, 1937; Harris Warren, *Herbert Hoover and the Great Depression*, 1959; Albert Romasco, *The Poverty of Abundance*, 1965; Gene Smith, *The Shattered Dream*, 1970; Edgar E. Robinson and Vaughn Bornet, *Herbert Hoover: President of the United States*, 1975; and Martin Fausold, *The Presidency of Herbert C. Hoover*, 1985. The best

balanced of these are the ones by Warren, Romasco, and Fausold. Other works that have engaged in the interpretive debates about the administration are Arthur M. Schlesinger, Jr., *The Crisis of the Old Order*, 1957; William A. Williams, *The Contours of American History*, 1961; Murray Rothbard, *America's Great Depression*, 1963; Ellis Hawley, "Herbert Hoover, the Commerce Secretariat, and the Vision of an Associative State," *Journal of American History*, June, 1974; J. J. Huthmacher and Warren Sussman, eds.; *Herbert Hoover and the Crisis of American Capitalism*, 1973; Martin Fausold and George Mazuzan, eds., *The Hoover Presidency*, 1974; Elliot Rosen, *Hoover, Roosevelt, and the Brain Trust*, 1977; and Mark Hatfield, comp., *Herbert Hoover Reassessed*, 1981. For an examination of Hoover's relationship with Franklin D. Roosevelt, both before and after Hoover's presidency, see Timothy Walch and Dwight M. Miller, eds., *Herbert Hoover and Franklin D. Roosevelt*, 1998.

Significant monographs illuminating various aspects of the administration include Alexander DeConde, *Herbert Hoover's Latin American Policy*, 1951; Robert Ferrell, *American Diplomacy in the Great Depression*, 1957; Jordan Schwarz, *The Interregnum of Despair*, 1970; Roger Daniels, *The Bonus March*, 1971; Craig Lloyd, *Aggressive Introvert: Herbert Hoover and Public Relations Management*, 1972; Robert F. Himmelberg, *The Origins of the National Recovery Administration*, 1976; James Olson, *Herbert Hoover and the Reconstruction Finance Corporation*, 1977; and Donald J. Lisio, *The President and Protest*, 1974, and *Hoover, Blacks, and Lily-Whites*, 1985. For an analysis of the treatment of Hoover by the press during the Depression, see Louis Liebovich, *Bylines in Despair: Herbert Hoover, the Great Depression, and the U.S. News Media*, 1994. Richard D. Burns, *Herbert Hoover: A Bibliography of His Times and Presidency*, 1991, is a comprehensive listing of resources on Hoover's personal life and public career.

Franklin D. Roosevelt

32d President, 1933-1945

Born: January 30, 1882
    Hyde Park, New York
Died: April 12, 1945
    Warm Springs, Georgia

Political Party: Democratic
Vice Presidents: John Nance Garner,
    Henry A. Wallace, Harry S Truman

Cabinet Members

Secretary of State: Cordell Hull, E. R. Stettinius, Jr.

Secretary of the Treasury: William H. Woodin, Henry Morgenthau

Secretary of War: George H. Dern, Harry H. Woodring, Henry L. Stimson

Secretary of the Navy: Claude A. Swanson, Charles Edison, Frank Knox, James V. Forrestal

Attorney General: H. S. Cummings, Frank Murphy, Robert Jackson, Francis Biddle

Postmaster General: James A. Farley, Frank C. Walker

Secretary of the Interior: Harold Ickes

Secretary of Agriculture: Henry A. Wallace, Claude R. Wickard

Secretary of Commerce: Daniel C. Roper, Harry L. Hopkins, Jesse Jones, Henry A. Wallace

Secretary of Labor: Frances Perkins

Franklin Delano Roosevelt was not born in a log cabin, and unlike many nineteenth century aspirants to the presidency, he never pretended that he had been. His birth took place instead in a modest mansion commanding a magnificent view of the Hudson River as it flows below Hyde Park, New York. The ten-pound baby to whom Sara Delano Roosevelt gave birth on January 30, 1882, entered a family of considerable means. Born in an era noted for its self-made men, Franklin Roosevelt never had an opportunity to "make" himself, at least not

Roosevelt's official portrait. *(White House Historical Society)*

in an economic sense. He was financially secure from birth. His childhood was anything but disadvantaged, and for one who chose to enter American politics, just such a privileged upbringing was potentially a distinct disadvantage.

In fact, however, Franklin Roosevelt's nurturance in an affluent society was one of the most important contributors to the character he would display as one of America's most important presidents. His father, James Roosevelt, was a man of impeccable lineage and substantial property. His income from coal and transportation holdings provided solid financial security for his family, but James Roosevelt never achieved acceptance into the select millionaires. He left an estate of $300,000, in itself enough to make his family secure, but his marriage to Sara Delano improved the family's financial position substantially. Her father, Warren Delano, had made a fortune in the China trade and established himself on the other side of the Hudson from Hyde Park. The Delanos were also across the political river from the Democrat Roosevelts. "I will not say that all Democrats are horse thieves," Franklin's maternal grandfather often proclaimed, "but it would seem that all horse thieves are Democrats." The $1 million he left his daughter helped to prepare a nonthieving Democrat— his grandson—for the nation's highest office.

The security that social station and wealth gave to the Roosevelts was a central fact in young Franklin's upbringing. His mother was twenty-six years younger than his father, who was fifty-four when Franklin was born. The child immediately became the center of attention in the family. He remained Sara's only child, and so never had his serenity upset by the intrusion of a new rival for the affection of his parents. A full platoon of servants supplemented the parents' attention. It would be difficult to disagree with his mother's assessment that Franklin "had many advantages that other boys did not have."

From the Hudson to Harvard
The "River families" of the Hudson were the closest parallel in post-Civil War America to the English or European country gentry. They taught their children not only the benefits to be enjoyed by their wealth and position but also the responsibilities that their position entailed. Franklin was reared, as his mother put it, to "grow up to be like his father, straight and honorable, just and kind, an upstanding American." If this was a rather vague aspiration, the future president showed in his undergraduate thesis, written in 1901, what he understood his heritage to mean. He ascribed the "virility" of the Roosevelts to their "democratic spirit": "They have never felt that because they were born in a good position they could put their hands in their pockets and succeed," he wrote. "They have felt, rather, that being born in a good position, there was no excuse for them if they did not do their duty by the community, and it is because this idea was instilled into them from their birth that they have in nearly every case proved good citizens."

Franklin Roosevelt's aristocratic upbringing and status as an only child gave him an extraordinary degree of self-confidence, optimism, and sense of noblesse oblige. The last quality was reinforced by at least one of the private tutors who guided his early education. It was further developed under the tutelage of Rector Endicott Peabody at Groton School, where Roosevelt enrolled at the age of fourteen. Peabody had founded the school a little more than a decade before as an American version of an exclusive English public school, one that would educate the children of the elite, giving them moral and physical training as well as any academic instruction for which they could find time. Roosevelt acquitted himself well enough in this new environment, but at no point in his schooling did he ever distinguish himself intellectually or show any particular interest in scholarship. The Groton experience with the rector's stern moralism and his father's annual holiday season readings of Charles Dickens's *A Christmas Carol* added to the sense of stewardship and social responsibility that Roosevelt had acquired on the banks of the Hudson.

In 1900, young Roosevelt moved on from Groton to Harvard and quickly settled into the Boston social scene. He clearly wanted to excel at something, but it was still not education that held his interest. He did his best at sports but was too slight to succeed at varsity athletics. Harvard society was ranked by the social clubs that students were invited to join. Despite his lineage and habit of quite literally sticking his nose in the air (by throwing his head back), Roosevelt was not asked to join Porcellian, the most prestigious of the clubs. This rejection was a bitter experience for a young man accustomed to having his way at all times. Some biographers see the episode as significant in adding to the future president's sympathy for less fortunate people, but this is probably placing too much importance on it.

Roosevelt found his opportunity for success on the college newspaper, winning the editorship at the end of his third year in Cambridge. Although still a casual student, Roosevelt could have graduated in three years but chose to stay a fourth in order to edit the *Crimson*. His concerns were nothing out of the ordinary for a college editor: school spirit, a winning football team, and more fire extinguishers in student residences. In his classwork, Roosevelt took several courses in history but absorbed little of the subject's import and managed to escape the burden of economic theories that would lose their credibility after 1929. All in all, though, his Hudson gentry heritage had a far greater impact on the future president than did his formal education.

Politics and Paralysis

By the time he left Harvard, Franklin Roosevelt had chosen both a career and a bride. For both

Eleanor Roosevelt in 1898. *(FDR Library)*

he looked no farther than his own family. He entered Columbia Law School, but not out of any desire to make a career in the law or to do as his mother wished and follow the path of his father, who had died while Franklin was a freshman at Harvard. Rather, young Roosevelt had decided to emulate his fifth cousin, Theodore Roosevelt, who was then president of the United States. The ambition was a lofty one, but Roosevelt was lacking in neither ambition nor self-confidence, and in his still boyish fantasizing he developed a career plan that had already been tested: Harvard, Columbia Law School, the New York state legislature, assistant secretary of the navy, governor of New York, and president of the United States. If a Republican Roosevelt could do it, why not a Democratic one? Roosevelt outlined these ambitions to friends at least as early as 1907. What was remarkable, however, was not that he should have such dreams but that, with only a few changes along the way, he was to follow the script all the way to its climax in the White House.

Franklin Roosevelt's admiration for members of the Oyster Bay branch of his family soon encompassed Theodore Roosevelt's niece as well as the president himself. Anna Eleanor Roosevelt, the daughter of Theodore Roosevelt's younger brother Elliott, suffered from a childhood as unhappy and insecure as Franklin's was happy and secure. Her mother, Anna Hall Roosevelt, made little attempt to hide her distaste for a daughter who had not inherited her beauty. Eleanor worshiped her father, but he slipped into alcoholism and followed his wife into an early grave, leaving Eleanor an orphan at the age of ten. Although parentless children of the Roosevelts' social position were spared the rigors of life in an orphanage, Eleanor Roosevelt did not fare well. The grandmother who took charge of her had no more liking for the girl than had her mother. The childhood rejections suffered by Eleanor Roosevelt helped awaken in her a lifelong feeling of compassion for those facing hardship.

As fifth cousins once removed, Franklin and Eleanor Roosevelt had played together at a few family gatherings in their early years. It was not until the latter part of his college career, however, that Franklin became reacquainted with the suddenly grown-up distant relative and quickly fell in love with her and determined to marry her. The cousins were married at an early 1905 ceremony in which the president stood in for his deceased brother and gave away the bride.

"Well, Franklin," Cousin Ted said to the groom after the ceremony, "there's nothing like keeping the name in the family"—nor, from Franklin's perspective, was there anything like joining more closely the family of his idol. As it turned out, though, Eleanor Roosevelt was to be a far greater asset in her own right than as a link to the presidential family. Her compassion and sense of social justice helped give

direction to her husband's political ambitions and amorphous sense of stewardship. The first decade of marriage, however, found Eleanor Roosevelt assisting her mate in the more traditional manner. Without inordinate complaint she bore six children and endured the domineering practices of her mother-in-law.

Franklin Roosevelt spent these years going through the early phases of the political career he had planned for himself. After being admitted to the New York bar, he left Columbia without completing his law degree. He took a position in a Wall Street law firm and could easily have slipped into a comfortable, conservative, respectable, but largely meaningless, upper-class life—but such was never his intention. He was awaiting his chance to get into politics. It came in 1910, when New York Democrats asked him to run for the Dutchess County seat in the state assembly. Roosevelt was enthusiastic but soon disappointed when the Democratic incumbent changed his mind and decided to seek reelection. Now if Roosevelt wanted to run, it would have to be for the state senate, in a larger, more Republican district. His supreme confidence leading him on, Roosevelt agreed to the greater challenge. Benefiting from a national split in the Republican ranks and his own flair for innovate campaigning—especially getting around to voters in a red Maxwell touring car—Roosevelt became only the second Democrat since before the Civil War to win in this senate district. His campaign was of the traditional upper-class sort: frequent calls for "clean government" but little in the way of the genuine social progressivism then sweeping the country.

In Albany, the twenty-eight-year-old freshman legislator rapidly made a name for himself by assuming leadership of a group of insurgent Democrats who opposed Boss Charles F. Murphy of Tammany Hall when he sought to name "Blue-eyed Billy" Sheehan as the new United States senator from New York (the state was one of those in which the legislature still picked the senators). Although eventually obliged to accept another Murphy-backed candidate, Roosevelt received nationwide publicity in the struggle against Tammany. Only later did he come to understand that the machine was not entirely evil and that some degree of accommodation was essential to successful political practice.

In 1912, Roosevelt backed the successful presidential candidacy of Woodrow Wilson. His reward was the post he most coveted at this point in his career: assistant secretary of the navy. Roosevelt loved ships almost as much as he loved following the trail of Cousin Ted. He proved to be a capable administrator and an advocate of a bold foreign policy and a big navy. His service in the Navy Department ran four times longer than had TR's, although this was not for the lack of trying to move on at the same pace as had his famous kinsman. Franklin made a disastrous attempt to win his party's U.S. Senate nomination in 1914. His heavy loss convinced him that he must learn to work with the better elements in the Tammany machine.

Ever since the days of Andrew Jackson—or, for that matter, George Washington—fighting in a war and gaining a reputation as a hero has been a most helpful step toward the presidency. When the United States entered World War I in 1917, Franklin Roosevelt tried once more to do as TR had done, this time by leaving Washington, D.C., in search of battle. President Wilson, however, insisted that Roosevelt was needed more in the Navy Department. Finally, toward the end of the war, Roosevelt persuaded his superiors to send him on an inspection tour to Europe, and he briefly came under fire before contracting double pneumonia during the terrible influenza epidemic of 1918.

When Roosevelt returned home in a weakened condition, his wife unpacked his luggage and discovered in it a group of love letters he had received from Eleanor's social secretary, Lucy Mercer. In fact, Roosevelt and Mercer had

been carrying on an affair for more than a year. Eleanor suggested divorce, and Franklin might have accepted had it not been for the realization that such a step would end his political career. Instead, Franklin and Eleanor agreed that she would remain his wife in public, but not in private, and that he would not see Lucy again. This contract was kept by only one partner. Franklin met Lucy Mercer Rutherfurd secretly from time to time throughout the remainder of his life.

Roosevelt's next political opportunity came in 1920, when he was the surprising choice of Democratic presidential candidate James M. Cox to be his running mate. It turned out, however, that Americans were tired of liberalism and Wilsonian internationalism, and they voted overwhelmingly for Warren G. Harding's promise of a return to "normalcy." Roosevelt chalked up the defeat to experience and settled down to wait for the political pendulum to swing back from conservatism.

While he waited, Roosevelt suffered a setback much worse than he had received at the polls. In the summer of 1921, while vacationing at the family's retreat at Campobello, Roosevelt was stricken with polio—then commonly called infantile paralysis. He was in excruciating pain for several weeks, and after the crisis his legs remained paralyzed. Had he been the "mama's boy" that many claimed he was, Roosevelt would at this point have retired quietly to the life of a wealthy invalid. Instead, his lifelong experience of having his own way gave him the optimism to struggle on. With the help of his wife, and political adviser Louis Howe, he worked through the 1920's to preserve his political career as he worked simultaneously to strengthen his legs.

Roosevelt's bout with polio ranks behind only his aristocratic upbringing, the influence of his wife, and the impact of the Great Depression in shaping his character as president. He was thirty-nine years old when he contracted polio; his basic character had long since been formed, but his previously vague sense of noblesse oblige now blossomed into a genuine understanding of suffering. Without his disability, a man with Roosevelt's background might never have had a true feeling for the hardships his countrymen underwent during the Depression, nor would Depression victims have been likely to have responded as warmly to Roosevelt's optimism had he not faced and overcome a terrible burden of his own.

From Albany to Washington

During the remainder of the 1920's, Roosevelt became a bit more liberal, in defiance of the popular movement toward conservatism, and waited for circumstances to push opinion in his direction. It is most ironic, though, that for all his planning Roosevelt took his decisive final step toward the White House with great reluctance. When New York governor Alfred E. Smith won the Democratic presidential nomination in 1928, he and state party leaders insisted that Roosevelt run for governor to help the ticket in upstate New York. Knowing that "Republican prosperity" was at high tide, Roosevelt feared that he would lose and that, should he win, he would be propelled toward the 1932 presidential nomination. Calculating that the conservative trend would not yet have waned by that time, Roosevelt thought it better to aim for 1936, but he could not risk the appearance of unwillingness to help the party, and he did not say that he would refuse to run if drafted. When he learned of his nomination, Roosevelt said, "Well, if I've got to run for governor, there's no use in all of us getting sick about it!" In November, 1928, Roosevelt won the governorship by a very narrow margin while Al Smith was losing his home state along with the nation as a whole.

As governor when the Depression hit in 1929, Roosevelt established a solid record as one of the leading liberals in America. His conservation programs carried forward the family tradition begun by TR, and his establishment

of a state relief program, wholly inadequate though it was in the face of the immense needs created by the Depression, served as a model for other states and for federal relief efforts after Roosevelt reached the White House. Yet one fact was brought home repeatedly as Governor Roosevelt sought to counter the effects of the Depression in New York: The economic disaster was a national problem, and no individual state could do much to solve it. Even so, the progressive measures supported by Roosevelt led him to a decisive reelection victory in 1930. His winning margin of 725,000 votes was more than twenty-eight times larger than his margin two years before, and Roosevelt showed great strength in the rural upstate counties where Democrats usually did poorly. He automatically became the favorite for his party's 1932 presidential nomination.

Although Roosevelt's perceptions of the early Depression were not unlike those of the Republican president, Herbert Hoover, the New York governor differed with the man in the White House in a fundamental way. Hoover was an idealist, but Roosevelt was by this time decidedly pragmatic in his approach to social problems. Although Hoover did not steadfastly reject government intervention in all areas, he was a firm believer in voluntarism. Roosevelt quickly came to see government as a necessary tool in dealing with the economic crisis. As governor, he demonstrated one more critical difference from Hoover: Roosevelt was able to put forth the image of a dynamic, caring leader who knew what needed to be done, or at least was willing to experiment. Hoover, in contrast, appeared to the public to be incapable and uncaring.

Before he could get into the ring with the opponent in the White House in the 1932 election campaign, Roosevelt would have to knock out his Democratic rivals. The problem here was that the party still required a nominee to win the backing of two-thirds of the delegates in the nominating convention. Roosevelt had no trouble getting a simple majority, but several other candidates held key delegations that kept Roosevelt short of two-thirds. One of those other candidates was Al Smith, who turned against Roosevelt as the latter began to overshadow him.

To win the nomination, Roosevelt became more daring in his rhetoric. Realizing that the American people had grown tired of the ineffective economic practices of the past and increasingly bitter toward big businessmen, bankers, and the rich in general, Roosevelt emphasized the traditional Democratic alternative to the Republican "trickle-down" approach to prosperity for all. In an April, 1932, radio address, the candidate called for plans "that build from the bottom up and not from the top down, that put their faith once more in the forgotten man at the bottom of the economic pyramid." Such rhetoric enraged Smith, but it seems to have pleased a large portion of the electorate.

The opposition to Roosevelt held firm on the first two ballots at the 1932 Democratic convention and came very close to turning the tide against him on the third, before the Roosevelt forces reached agreements with House Speaker John Nance Garner and influential publisher William Randolph Hearst and won the nomination for Roosevelt on the fourth ballot.

Roosevelt's flair for the dramatic was promptly displayed when he violated the tradition of waiting for weeks to be notified officially of his selection as his party's nominee and instead flew from Albany to Chicago to deliver an acceptance speech directly to the convention. He told the delegates that he intended his action to be symbolic of his willingness to break with "foolish traditions." The nominee denounced the "Tory" idea of helping the rich in hopes that "some of their prosperity will leak through, sift through, to labor, to the farmer, to the small businessman." Roosevelt pledged himself "to a new deal for the American people."

Certainly, that is what most Americans desperately wanted in 1932. The only thing they wanted more than a "new deal" was to put Herbert Hoover out of office. Franklin Roosevelt was the means to achieve both of these objectives, and he needed to do almost nothing in order to be elected over Hoover. Still, Roosevelt chose to undertake a strenuous campaign, demonstrating to the voters that he was physically capable of handling the duties of the presidency.

In his campaign speeches, Roosevelt hedged on most controversial questions. He shocked adviser Raymond Moley by looking at two drafts of a tariff speech, one favoring free trade and the other strong protectionism, and telling Moley to "weave the two together." Only in an address at San Francisco's Commonwealth Club did Roosevelt give a clear indication of the direction he would take as president. In other speeches the Democrat lashed at Hoover as a spendthrift and one who wanted "to center control of everything in Washington as rapidly as possible." Mostly, Roosevelt declined to take any forthright stand during the general election campaign. In one speech he refused to be specific about how he would eliminate the causes of poverty, saying that it was not proper to talk politics on Sunday. "You cannot quarrel with a single one of his generalities . . . ," reporter Elmer Davis wrote, "But what they mean (if anything) is known only to Franklin D. Roosevelt and his God."

None of this mattered. Hoover complained with some justification that his opponent was "a chameleon on plaid," but the American people wanted a change, and in a two-party system Roosevelt was their only other real choice. His overwhelming victory, with nearly 23 million votes to fewer than 16 million for Hoover and the electoral votes of forty-two states to the Republican's six, was more a repudiation of the incumbent than an endorsement of the vague "new deal" promised by the challenger.

FDR delivering the second fireside chat of 1934. *(FDR Library)*

Bold, Persistent Experimentation

Not since Abraham Lincoln had an American president taken office in the midst of a great national crisis such as that which prevailed when Franklin D. Roosevelt—or FDR, as he came to be known—repeated the oath on March 4, 1933. The Depression had grown steadily worse in the months since the election. One-fourth of the nation's workforce was unemployed; private charity and state and local relief funds were woefully inadequate; hunger was widespread; and the nation's banking system was in nearly complete collapse.

Although such conditions were horrible, Roosevelt could not have asked for a better scene at which to make his entrance. He immediately found himself in a position to accomplish more than any other peacetime president. His inaugural address began the process of restoring confidence to the shattered national psyche. This is just what Hoover had been saying was needed for three years, but he had been singularly unable to induce confidence in the people. Yet when Roosevelt intoned the words, "So, first of all, let me assert my firm belief that the only thing we have to fear, is fear itself—nameless, unreasoning, unjustified terror which paralyzes needed efforts to convert retreat into advance," the spirits of a downcast nation began to revive. Sensing the popular mood, Roosevelt took a few verbal swipes at the "money changers" and said, "This Nation asks for action, and action now."

He gave it action by calling the Congress into special session and closing all the nation's banks. Roosevelt could have obtained almost any banking legislation he wanted when the new, heavily Democratic Congress convened five days after his inauguration. It is therefore a measure of FDR's moderate approach that he endorsed an emergency banking bill that had been drawn up by Hoover appointees and bankers. The new president signed the measure into law eight hours after its introduction into Congress. Then Roosevelt demonstrated his abilities as the first media president by giving a "fireside chat" over radio to explain the banking crisis. He spoke in fatherly, soothing terms that his listeners—and, Will Rogers said, even bankers—could understand. As a result of FDR's assurances that those banks that were allowed to reopen were safe, people stopped their withdrawals and began again to make deposits. Raymond Moley exaggerated only slightly when he said, "Capitalism was saved in eight days." Part of Roosevelt's motive in remaining conservative on banking was his penchant for catching opponents off guard. By pushing the conservative banking measure and an even more conservative economy bill that would cut federal spending, Roosevelt pleased businessmen and paved the way for the most intense period of reform in American history.

The quick actions of Roosevelt's first week in office lacked substance, but they excited the public. The new president realized, though, that people would soon look for results. He was in the fortunate position of having goals that largely coincided with the public desires of the Depression years. Both the American people and Franklin D. Roosevelt had a vague desire for an economy based more on fairness, justice, and humanitarianism than had been the case in the past. This coincidence of goals was one of the reasons that Roosevelt was able to become such a successful leader. It is always easier to lead people in the direction they are already headed. FDR usually did this, although he sometimes had to move rapidly to catch up to his followers.

Roosevelt decided to continue the special session of Congress he had called to deal with the banking crisis, so that he could accomplish as much as possible while his own popularity was at its highest. Next to the banking question, the farm problem was most pressing. American agriculture had been in depression while much of the rest of the country was prospering in the 1920's. Roosevelt had argued during his campaign that the fundamental imbalance in the economy was attributable to the failure of farm income to rise sufficiently to enable farmers to buy the products of industry. Whatever the merits of this view as an explanation of the Depression, Roosevelt was determined to take steps to raise farm prices.

There was no lack of proposals for solving the agricultural problem. Roosevelt's goals were to satisfy as many different farm groups as possible and at the same time to produce a law that would give him maximum freedom to try different policies as he saw fit. Accordingly, he insisted that the leaders of the various farm groups agree among themselves to a bill

before he would endorse it. The result was the omnibus Agricultural Adjustment Act (AAA), an amalgam of contradictory farm panaceas. Like many of Roosevelt's measures, it was politically sound—but economically somewhat incoherent. The basic goal was to raise prices through induced scarcity. The president and the leaders of the newly created Agricultural Adjustment Administration could choose among a variety of means to achieve this end, but mainly they used government payments, financed by a tax on food processing, to farmers who reduced their acreage under cultivation.

Just what planned scarcity meant was soon apparent. Since controversies over portions of the agriculture bill kept it from becoming law until mid-May, the growing season was well under way and crops already planted had to be plowed under. Many people could not see the point of destroying food while millions were hungry. The economic system had failed to bring the food to those who needed it but could not pay for it. Roosevelt's hope was to stimulate recovery by putting more money in the pockets of farmers.

The plan did not work as hoped. Many farmers took their worst land out of production and worked their best acres more intensively. In many cases the end result was greater production than before the AAA went into effect. Thanks more to the massive drought that made a dust bowl of the Great Plains than to the AAA, farm prices rose by 50 percent during FDR's first term. This proved too little to have much of an effect on reviving the economy, and the farm problem continued to plague the administration into Roosevelt's second term.

While Congress considered the farm bill, the president continued to send other proposals to Capitol Hill. Among his firmest beliefs were the need for conservation and the desirability of giving urban youths the advantages of the rugged life of the outdoors. In both respects, he was a worthy successor to Cousin Ted. Here, too, was an appropriate concern for one brought up in the tradition of the country gentleman. The lord of the manor had a responsibility to care for the land as well as the people. FDR embodied these objectives in a bill he sent to Congress in the second week of the special session. Ten days later, Congress, on a voice vote, created the Civilian Conservation Corps (CCC). The agency took unemployed young men and put them to work at reforestation and other conservation tasks, sending most of their meager paychecks home to help their families. The CCC was one of the New Deal's most popular and successful programs, and Roosevelt's personal role in its founding was a source of great pride to him.

Roosevelt's personal popularity was enormous during the first Hundred Days of the New Deal. He took advantage of this circumstance to push through some of his favorite ideas. Along with conservation, FDR was committed to planned use of the land and to public electric power projects. He combined all three when he asked Congress in April, 1933, to create the Tennessee Valley Authority (TVA). The TVA was in part a proposed solution to the battle that had raged for more than a decade between progressives and conservatives in Congress over the disposition of the Wilson Dam on the Tennessee River in northern Alabama. Conservatives wanted the government-built facility at Muscle Shoals to be sold to private power interests, whereas progressives led by Senator George Norris of Nebraska insisted that it be operated by the government. Roosevelt had long been aligned with the public power advocates, but he now went far beyond the Wilson Dam controversy and called for a development program for "national planning for a complete river workshed."

The Tennessee Valley was one of the most depressed and underdeveloped areas in the United States. The TVA, which was created by large congressional majorities within five weeks of Roosevelt's proposal, was designed to invigorate the local economy by providing cheap hydroelectric power, to stop soil erosion and provide flood control, to uplift the people through education and recreation programs, and to provide a yardstick by which to measure the fairness of electricity rates charged by private companies. In almost all respects, the TVA was a great success—so much so that frightened private power interests loudly denounced it as a form of socialism in order to block Roosevelt's intention to create several similar regional development programs. Success, not failure, prevented the duplication of the TVA elsewhere.

Although Roosevelt was sincere in his desire for government economy and a balanced budget—he even called for slashing the monthly payments to war veterans totally disabled in civilian life from $40 to $20—he did not suffer from Hoover's single-mindedness. Roosevelt explained the contradiction of pressing for vast relief and recovery expenditures while calling for government economy by saying, "You cannot let people starve." This simple humanitarian pragmatism gave FDR the support of millions of people who had rejected Hoover's more consistent but less practical approach.

Like Hoover, Roosevelt always feared that a federal dole might destroy the self-reliance of recipients and make them dependent. Still, he also recognized that people had to be provided the basic necessities of life. On the same day that he sent the CCC bill to Congress, therefore, he asked for authorization to name a federal relief administrator and to provide federal grants to the states for direct relief payments to the jobless. Both houses responded quickly with heavy majorities in favor of this step into federal relief.

Roosevelt appointed Harry Hopkins, who had headed his relief program in New York, to oversee the Federal Emergency Relief Administration (FERA). Hopkins thought much as Roosevelt did—that direct relief was not desirable but was necessary. Hopkins said that a dole took from people "their sense of independence and their sense of individual dignity"—yet no short-term alternative existed. The relief administrator responded to the argument that one proposal would "work out in the long run" by noting that "people don't eat in the long run—they eat every day." Setting up a desk in a hallway, Hopkins spent $5 million in his first two hours on the job. Both Roosevelt and Hopkins saw the FERA as what its name implied—an emergency agency, not a long-term solution to poverty. Accordingly, Hopkins concentrated on distributing as much money to as many needy people as quickly as he possibly could. Some critics complained that such an approach wasted public funds, but there was surprisingly little waste or corruption in the FERA programs.

Another massive problem area emerging from the Depression led to an innovative pro-

posal from the Roosevelt administration during the Hundred Days when the president asked in April for legislation to assist home owners threatened with foreclosure. Foreclosures had reached the frightening rate of a thousand per day. The most basic part of the American Dream—home ownership—was being undermined. The Home Owner's Loan Corporation (HOLC) refinanced mortgages at lower interest rates and saved many home owners from foreclosure. Its greatest beneficiaries, though, were the bankers and other lenders, repayment of whose loans was now guaranteed by the federal government. Eventually, 20 percent of American homes came under the protection of the HOLC.

The special session of Congress was nearing its end, and Roosevelt had proposed no legislation to deal with what most people saw as the nation's most basic need: industrial recovery. The new president had sincerely be-

FDR visits the Norris Dam construction site in 1934 with Eleanor Roosevelt and TVA director A. E. Morgan. *(TVA)*

lieved that recovery in agriculture, combined with increased relief spending, would stimulate the economy sufficiently to reinvigorate industry. Many in Congress and the general public were less sanguine. Senator Hugo L. Black of Alabama introduced a bill, supported by the American Federation of Labor, that would limit the hours of all workers connected with interstate commerce to thirty per week. The Senate passed this work-spreading bill, and the House appeared likely to go along. Roosevelt was unhappy with Black's proposal, since it would not give the president the flexibility that other early New Deal measures provided.

It was the need to sidetrack the Black bill that led FDR to propose his own recovery legislation. The result was the National Industrial Recovery Act (NIRA), requested by Roosevelt on May 17 and enacted a month later. The goal, the president said in his message asking for passage of the bill, was "a great cooperative movement throughout all industry in order to obtain wide reemployment, to shorten the working week, to pay a decent wage for the shorter week and to prevent unfair competition and disastrous overproduction." This was a tall order, even for a New Deal law. The basic means by which the NIRA sought to achieve its multiple objectives were the establishment of codes that would establish minimum wages, maximum hours, and standards of working conditions in each industry. The underlying idea, though, was *self*-regulation, that is, action by the businesses themselves. The largest companies in each field dominated the creation of the codes for these industries.

Title II of the NIRA created a huge program of public construction projects, the Public Works Administration (PWA). To head the program, Roosevelt named his interior secretary, Harold Ickes. Ickes was nominally a Republican and fervently a progressive. He was absolutely committed to the efficient use of the public funds. As a result, the PWA had a remarkable

record of useful construction without any significant corruption. In contrast to Harry Hopkins, Ickes believed in going slowly and carefully when the public purse strings were opened. Consequently, the PWA never provided the rapid stimulus for economic recovery that Roosevelt had intended when it was paired with the National Recovery Administration (NRA).

The NRA was supposed to introduce a modicum of rationality and planning into the American free market economy. This was in no sense an antibusiness move. On the contrary, the law that Roosevelt called "the most important and far-reaching legislation ever enacted by the American Congress" created "a partnership in planning" between business and government. The NRA codes, in effect, put the federal government behind cooperative arrangements among separate businesses in each industry. This flouting of the antitrust laws was excused with the argument that such planning was necessary to bring about recovery and that concessions were also being given to labor. The latter were contained in Section 7(a) of the NIRA, which provided for collective bargaining, but this section was soon watered down by decisions of the National Labor Relations Board.

In fact, the NRA under the leadership of General Hugh Johnson became little more than an effort at cheerleading. The old Hoover idea of restoring confidence was pushed by parades, songs, advertisements, and the omnipresent NRA symbol, the Blue Eagle. It was all quite exhilarating, but it produced little in the way of lasting recovery.

A Liberal Conservative

The first hundred days of Roosevelt's presidency were marked by the "bold, persistent experimentation" that he had said the American people demanded. The actions were dramatic but lacking in consistency. Franklin D. Roosevelt was a politician, not an economist or a philosopher. As a political practitioner, he sought to please as many voters as possible. He was uninterested in general concepts; he preferred concrete problems and direct attempts to deal with them. He chose advisers and associates on the basis of personality and character, not ideology. The consequence was a wide variety of voices reaching the presidential ear in the first years of FDR's administration.

Yet presidents sometimes inspire more than they intend. Much as John F. Kennedy did three decades later, FDR launched a more liberal movement than he would initially have endorsed. The excitement engendered by the newly active government and the charismatic leader brought thousands of idealistic young men and women to Washington, D.C., to join the multiplying "alphabet agencies" of the New Deal. These tireless young New Dealers came firmly to believe in active government as a tool of the community's will. They gave the Roosevelt administration an increasingly liberal aura, even before the president himself made a decisive move to the left in 1935. They were so committed to active government that most of them would not tolerate a hint of corruption, and there was very little of it in the early years throughout the wide array of government agencies.

If the New Dealers were decidedly liberal, the same cannot so easily be said of the man whose shuffling of the cards inspired them—at least not during his first two years in the White House. In many respects, FDR's policies during the early New Deal resembled the classic conservatism of the eighteenth century British political philosopher Edmund Burke. This conservatism, to be sure, was a far cry from the ideas of those who had misappropriated the conservative label by the 1920's and 1930's. These people, principally wealthy businessmen, became the most bitter opponents of the New Deal. To them, conservatism meant a philosophy of egoism, the suppression of change,

and concern only for immediate self-interest, with little thought of interests of others in the present or of future generations.

If this is what one understands as conservatism—and it is what the word came to mean in the minds of most twentieth century Americans—plainly Franklin D. Roosevelt was no conservative; but if one looks to the classic conception of conservatism, the early New Deal nearly fits. In the first two years of his presidency, FDR sought—through such programs as the NRA—to achieve a consensus above the clamoring of interest groups. He attempted to promote cooperation among government, business, labor, farmers, and other groups. He did identify himself with those at the bottom of the economic pyramid, but not yet by opposing those at the top. President Roosevelt tried valiantly in these years to convince businessmen that change was necessary if the system from which they had so much benefited were to be saved. "Reform if you would preserve," he told them in the words of classic conservatism.

Despite the harsh rhetoric of his right-wing critics, Roosevelt was not moving in those early years in anything approaching a socialistic direction. With the sole exception of the TVA, Roosevelt resisted all suggestions of government ownership, remaining a firm believer in an economic system based on private ownership. What he sought was a wider distribution of property, not its elimination. Moreover, like classic conservatives, Roosevelt believed that each generation is entrusted with the society built by the past and is obligated to preserve and improve that society for those who will inherit it in the future.

Although Roosevelt possessed many of the characteristics and beliefs of the classic Burkean conservative, views that saved the capitalistic system and helped produce conditions that enabled business profits to rise rapidly, the right wing organized into a bitter, unflinching opposition to the president and his programs.

In a 1934 cartoon, FDR tries several "New Deal remedies" to treat an ailing Uncle Sam. *(Library of Congress)*

This opposition centered in the Liberty League, an organization launched in mid-1934 by some of the leading corporate executives in the nation joining forces with Al Smith and other anti-New Deal Democrats. Roosevelt could not understand the bitterness of these people. He summed up the situation with a parable: "In the summer of 1933, a nice old gentleman wearing a silk hat fell off the end of a pier. He was unable to swim. A friend ran down the pier, dived overboard and pulled him out; but the silk hat had floated off with the tide. After the old gentleman had been revived, he was effusive with thanks. He praised his friend for saving his life. Today, three years later, the old gentleman is berating his friend because the silk hat was lost." Roosevelt approvingly quoted a friend as saying that organizers of the Liberty League believed in two things: "Love God and then forget your neighbor."

This statement of what he opposed demonstrated the heart of Roosevelt's beliefs. Never a systematic thinker, he cannot accurately be placed in any philosophical category but perhaps can be best described as a pragmatic humanitarian. He placed the need for concern about the fate of one's neighbors above any philosophical consistency. He would try many different—apparently contradictory—approaches to improve the general well-being of the community. Both the classic conservatism of 1933-1934 and the modern liberalism of 1935 and later years were grounded in FDR's upbringing as a responsible country gentleman. His sense of stewardship was close to the essence of classic conservatism and became the main feature of the twentieth century liberalism that had started with Theodore Roosevelt and Woodrow Wilson and was crystallizing in the New Deal. The new liberalism that issued from Franklin D. Roosevelt's presidency combined the best elements of Burkean conservatism—elements that had been abandoned by most of those who took up the conservative banner in the twentieth century—and Jeffersonian liberalism. Following the path of Cousin Ted, Franklin D. Roosevelt came to see government in a democracy as a tool of the people, not as their enemy. He therefore was able to employ Hamiltonian means of big government to try to achieve Jeffersonian ends of the common good and wider distribution of private property.

Which Side Are You On?

Most presidents enjoy a "honeymoon" with the American people and the Congress in their early months in the White House, but never was a honeymoon more romantic and exciting—or as long-lasting—as that of Franklin D. Roosevelt. His brimming confidence, particularly in contrast to Hoover's sourness, combined with the terrible crisis to make Roosevelt a leader most people were prepared to follow almost without question. One congressman called FDR a Moses leading the nation out of the wilderness. Many, perhaps most, Americans had much the same impression. When he spoke, a Kansas man wrote of the president, "it seems as though some Moses had come to alleviate . . . our sufferings." A letter written in March, 1933, by several Brooklyn residents to Senator Robert F. Wagner summarized Roosevelt's effect on a dispirited citizenry: "It makes one raise the head and square the shoulders, feeling that now indeed we can place confidence in those chosen to lead the destiny of our Country. We now feel that in truth Washington is the throbbing heart of U.S.A. Fear has gone."

Roosevelt's popularity in 1933-1934 was in all likelihood among the greatest ever enjoyed by an American president. FERA investigator Martha Gellhorn filed a report from the Carolinas in 1934 reflecting the common view of FDR:

> Every house I visited—mill worker or unemployed—had a picture of the President. These ranged from newspaper clippings (in destitute homes) to large coloured prints, framed in gilt cardboard. The portrait holds a place of honor over the mantle; I can only compare this to the Italian peasant's Madonna. And the feeling of these people for the President is one of the most remarkable emotional phenomena I have ever met. He is at once God and their intimate friend; he knows them all by name, knows their little town and mill, their little lives and problems. And, though everything fails, he is there, and will not let them down.

Letters from ordinary Americans poured into the Roosevelt White House at a rate four times greater than they had during any other presidency. The great majority of these communications from the public were laudatory. Many put their perception of the Roosevelts' benevolence into concrete terms. "I do think you and the President is the Mother and Father of this Great USA," a Toledo resident wrote in a typical 1936 letter to Eleanor Roosevelt.

Franklin D. Roosevelt occupied a position that is the dream of every politician. A majority of the voters praised him for everything they liked in the New Deal and blamed others for what they disliked. Those writing to the Roosevelts often complained about economic conditions, relief policies, or other problems, but they usually went on to absolve the president, like the Californian who wrote, "You are wonderful. But surely this treatment is unknown to you." Roosevelt was such a masterful politician that many people who had a strong distaste for politicians excused his calling. "Your husband is *great*. He seems lovable even tho' he's a 'politician,'" a Denver woman wrote to Eleanor Roosevelt. "I wish him all the success in the world." Any endeavor is lifted to the level of an art when it can be made to seem effortless and natural. In these qualities, Roosevelt was the American politician who most deserves to be called an artist.

FDR's political artistry notwithstanding, his hopes to please everyone and achieve consensus government could not be realized for any lasting period. Terrible crisis may lead various groups and individuals to give up their separate interests for the duration of their extreme apprehension, but as soon as the crisis gives any sign of easing, the resuscitated businessman will begin to look for his silk hat, and his counterparts in other constituent groups will begin again to seek their own interests. Roosevelt's very success in lifting the hopes—and, to a lesser extent, the economy—of the United States meant that his consensus would be short-lived. Eventually, he would be obliged to heed the words of the union song that came out of the bitter labor conflict of Harlan County, Kentucky, in the early 1930's: "Which side are you on?"

That choice became imperative as Roosevelt's great popularity began to decline in late 1934 and early 1935. It was not that very many Americans outside the Liberty League were recoiling from the New Deal. The Democrats won an unprecedented victory in the congressional elections of 1934, reducing Republican representation to 25 in the Senate and 103 in the House—the first instance in modern American history in which the president's party gained congressional seats in a nonpresidential election year. Surely, these results were heartening to FDR, but there were also portents of trouble for him in the politics of 1934. When the choice before voters was a New Deal Democrat versus an Old Guard Republican, the Democrat almost invariably won. Signs appeared in 1934, however, indicating that the people were moving farther to the left than their president. A minimum of thirty-five candidates who preached the need to go beyond the New Deal were elected to Congress that November.

In Minnesota, the Farmer-Labor Party, led by Governor Floyd Olson, swept the state. Olson had declared that he was not a liberal but a radical, and implied that many businessmen were "burglars and thieves and pirates." In neighboring Wisconsin, the sons of Progressive hero Robert M. La Follette also took the third-party route to a point somewhat to the left of the New Deal and won. In California, veteran socialist novelist Upton Sinclair infiltrated the Democratic Party, proposed a radical program to "end poverty in California" by setting up a production-for-use economic system, and won the Democratic nomination for governor with a record number of votes. Although Sinclair finally lost in an extremely dirty campaign, the popularity of his essentially socialist proposals provided another indication of the leftward drift of American public opinion.

Numerous other signs of the same phenomenon surfaced. The year 1934 saw one of the largest waves of strikes in American history—eighteen hundred strikes involving almost one and a half million people were called in that turbulent year. In Toledo, Minneapolis, and San Francisco, huge strikes precipitated violent clashes that bordered on class warfare.

Wealthy residents of both Minneapolis and San Francisco, seeing strikers taking over their cities, fled out of fear that the revolution had finally come. There was little danger that it would go that far, but Roosevelt's bold economic actions seemed to have touched off a new spirit among American workers, a spirit that went beyond anything the president had intended. Workers, like voters in many parts of the nation, were restless in 1934 and demanding a more rapid move toward economic justice.

The same demand was picked up in one way or another by three nationwide movements led by charismatic figures. In the late 1920's, Father Charles Coughlin of Royal Oak, Michigan, had begun giving sermons over the radio to counteract the anti-Catholic activities of the Ku Klux Klan. By 1930, he had broadened his subject matter to include economic questions and had secured a network radio contract. Initially, Coughlin fixed his oratorical wrath on such immobile targets as communists, bankers, and Herbert Hoover. As the Radio Priest demanded "social justice," his audience grew rapidly until he had an estimated thirty million listeners in 1934 and 1935. For a time Coughlin wavered in his treatment of Roosevelt, but then more and more often he attacked the president. Although Coughlin later made his anti-Semitism and pro-Hitler views plain, at the peak of his popularity in the mid-1930's he seemed to be challenging the New Deal from the Left, not the Right.

In the fall of 1933, Francis Townsend, a retired physician living in California, launched a plan to end the Depression by paying $200 a month to every American above the age of sixty. Support for the Townsend Plan spread like wildfire, particularly among those older citizens who would be its greatest beneficiaries. Townsend proposed to finance his plan through what would have amounted to a massive sales tax. Although Townsend's lavish scheme was wholly unworkable, this fact deterred the movement not at all, and between 1934 and 1936 more than twenty million people signed petitions calling for the Townsend Plan. Pressure was mounting on politicians to endorse the plan or face the wrath of a very large group of voters.

As threatening as the Coughlin and Townsend movements were, the loudest claps of the mid-1930's thunder on the Left emanated from the hills and bayous of Louisiana. By preaching redistribution of wealth and attacking the Standard Oil Company, "Kingfish" Huey P. Long had become governor of the state in 1928. After securing virtual dictatorial powers there, Long moved on to the United States Senate in 1932. That year he helped Roosevelt win the Democratic presidential nomination, but Long's ambitions were too great for him to remain in the shadow of another politician. Early in 1934 he created the Share Our Wealth Society and demanded that the fortunes of the rich (whom he described as "pigs swilling in the trough of luxury") be divided among all Americans. This was an idea with great appeal in the Depression years, and tens of thousands of enthusiastic letters came into Long's Senate office each week.

Whatever the ultimate aspirations of such figures as Olson, Sinclair, Coughlin, and Townsend, no doubt whatsoever existed about where the Louisiana Kingfish had set his sights. The pond Huey Long sought to dominate was already occupied by Franklin D. Roosevelt, but by 1935 the Southern demagogue was picking up enough support around the country to make his goal seem realizable. There was no chance that Long could take the 1936 Democratic nomination from FDR or that he could win the presidency that year at the head of a third-party ticket. What worried Roosevelt and his aides was that Long might siphon off enough votes from the president's left flank to give a Republican victory in 1936. A secret poll commissioned by the Democratic National Committee in 1935 indicated that a Long candidacy

might win between three and four million votes. Roosevelt was not anxious to find out whether he would have that many to spare.

The president would have to choose sides if he wanted to avert a possible large defection of voters anxious for more rapid change toward egalitarianism than the New Deal had so far produced.

Tacking to the Port

Several forces combined to push Franklin D. Roosevelt to the left in 1935. One was the now-bitter attacks on him by businessmen who charged that he was a "traitor to his class." The president deeply resented these fusillades, and he wondered why such wealthy individuals could not understand that he was saving their necks—or at the very least the bulk of their stock portfolios. "One of my principal tasks," he said in 1934, "is to prevent bankers and businessmen from committing suicide." As the vicious and frequently personal abuse continued from the right, however, Roosevelt's patience wore thin.

Huey P. Long. *(Library of Congress)*

The Supreme Court gave FDR another shove toward the left when it invalidated several of the early New Deal programs. In the most noted of these decisions, the Supreme Court declared the NRA unconstitutional. Roosevelt protested loudly, charging that the Court had returned the Constitution to the "horse and buggy days," but the "nine old men" may have done him a favor by executing the terminally ill Blue Eagle.

In any case, the original New Deal concept of cooperation among government, business, and labor seemed no longer viable: Many businessmen would not cooperate, labor was restive, the NRA had not brought about sufficient recovery, and now the Supreme Court said the NRA violated the Constitution. Yet, by the time the Court issued its rebuke to the NRA, Roosevelt had already begun his decisive move to the left. His principal motive was to solidify his support among lower- and middle-class voters who wanted more change. In the spring of 1935, the president told adviser Raymond Moley that something must be done "to steal Long's thunder." That something clearly had to involve a turn to the left.

Such a shift materialized in the "second New Deal" of 1935. In the late spring and early summer of that year, FDR called for, and the heavily Democratic Congress enacted, a series of laws that rank the period with the Hundred Days of 1933 and Lyndon Johnson's Great Society programs of 1964-1965 as the three most significant spurts of reform legislation in twentieth century American history.

In April, Congress agreed to Roosevelt's request for an unprecedentedly large appropriation for relief. The Emergency Relief Appropriation Act of 1935 provided $4.88 billion, a figure representing 10 percent of the national income for the previous year. After Congress appropriated the funds, Roosevelt used a large portion of the money to launch a new work relief program, the Works Progress Administration (WPA), which he placed under the di-

rection of Harry Hopkins. Both Roosevelt and Hopkins had long been unhappy with direct relief payments to the jobless, a feeling they shared with most of the public and with most relief recipients. Everyone realized that working for relief payments helped to maintain a person's self-respect. The only drawback was the cost of work relief, but now that a new stimulus to the economy seemed advisable before the 1936 election year, the president agreed to try work relief.

Although the WPA was the target of much conservative criticism, it was a remarkably successful program. Under it, thousands of schools, hospitals, playgrounds, and other public facilities were constructed, and at the same time work, a degree of self-respect, and a subsistence wage were given to millions of Americans. Among the most daring of Hopkins's experiments was the use of a small part of the WPA funds to create programs that for the first time made the American government a patron of the arts. WPA projects for theater, art, music, and writing brought plays and live music performances to areas of the country that rarely saw them; put visual artworks in public buildings across the nation; preserved life-history narratives of workers, farmers, and former slaves; and wrote guidebooks to the states. The federal arts projects also fostered the careers of dozens of the most important figures in twentieth century American arts and letters.

Part of Roosevelt's shift to the left in 1935 meant stiffening his stand against the greedy. He was careful to point out that he was not condemning businessmen in general but only that minority who misused their positions for completely selfish ends. (Contrary to popular impression, many businessmen, especially in newer industries such as motion pictures and business machines, strongly supported Roosevelt.) Two of the developments of the second New Deal helped to draw the line Roosevelt sought to place between himself and such wealthy magnates. One was the Wheeler-Rayburn Act, which outlawed some public utility holding companies, although its final version failed to abolish them entirely. The other was a tax message that FDR sent to Congress in June. In it the president went a great distance toward stealing Huey Long's "soak the rich" thunder. Denouncing the "unjust concentration of wealth and economic power" in the United States, Roosevelt called on Congress to enact a series of new taxes aimed at the wealthy. The legislation that resulted was of little consequence, but Roosevelt had dramatically placed himself in opposition to the very wealthy.

The other two major laws of the second New Deal reemphasized FDR's stand as champion of the needy. The Wagner (National Labor Relations) Act and the Social Security Act were probably the two most important domestic accomplishments of FDR's presidency.

Roosevelt had never before been especially identified with the cause of organized labor. He had, nevertheless, been partly responsible for inspiring the hopes among workers that produced the upheaval from below in the mid-1930's. Others were more attuned to the sounds of this new force, and Roosevelt endorsed New York Senator Robert F. Wagner's bill to protect the rights of workers to form and join unions of their own choosing when it became clear that Congress would pass the legislation anyway. By making it possible for the new Congress of Industrial Organizations (CIO) to unionize most mass production workers, the Wagner Act helped to lift a large segment of American laborers into the middle class.

Of no less lasting importance was the creation of the Social Security system. Spurred by the Townsend movement, Roosevelt recommended an old-age pension plan in January, 1935. His August, 1935, signing of the Social Security Act, which made the United States the last major industrial nation in the world to establish a social insurance program giving protection against poverty among the aged and against unemployment among all ages, was the capstone of the second New Deal.

In mending his fences on the left, Roosevelt had prepared the way for his 1936 campaign for reelection. The basis of that campaign was to recognize the sharp class division that the Depression had created and to identify the president with the lower and middle classes. Early in the election year, Roosevelt linked himself with the image of Andrew Jackson and lashed rhetorically at "the forces of privilege and greed." The rest of the Roosevelt strategy for 1936 was simply to emphasize the president and the difference between the dark days of 1932 and the hopeful and relatively better days of 1936. On both counts, Roosevelt stood to fare extremely well. His opponent, Governor Alfred M. Landon of Kansas, was a moderate Republican who vacillated between endorsing parts of the New Deal and heeding the demands of Hoover and the Old Guard Republicans to attack the Roosevelt program savagely. The danger to the president from the left had subsided with Huey Long's assassination in September, 1935. Although the remnants of the Long, Coughlin, and Townsend movements joined to form the Union Party, they were unable to mount an effective campaign for their candidate, Representative William Lemke of North Dakota.

By the end of the campaign Roosevelt had turned his class rhetoric up to full blast. "Never before in all our history," he told a New York audience, "have these forces [of organized money] been so united against one candidate as they stand today. They are unanimous in their hate for me and I welcome their hatred."

The side with which Roosevelt had cast his lot—the victims of the Depression and those who believed in active government to improve social conditions—turned out massively on Election Day, giving him an electoral vote victory of 523 to 8, the largest in a contested election in American history.

A Second-Rate Second Term

With an immense mandate from the people and huge Democratic majorities in both houses of Congress, Franklin D. Roosevelt seemed to be in a perfect position to move on to new triumphs that would assist the "one-third of a nation" that, as he pointed out in his second inaugural address, remained "ill-housed, ill-clad, ill-nourished." As it happened, though, Roosevelt's second term proved to be far less significant than either his first or third term.

Huge election victories have often led presidents into mistakes based at least in part on the notion that the voters will support anything they propose. The 1936 victory seemed an expression by a large majority of Americans of personal faith in Roosevelt. It also represented a clear endorsement of the New Deal. One major obstacle, however, blocked the path of the president's reforms. The Supreme Court had invalidated a series of New Deal measures in 1935 and 1936, and with its personnel unchanged there seemed little reason to believe the Court would not continue to strike down social legislation. Roosevelt had served an entire term without the occurrence of a single vacancy on the high bench. He had for some time been considering taking some action to reform the Court. Now with his great mandate from the people, he decided the time for bold action had arrived.

In February, 1937, FDR startled both Congress and the public by presenting a proposal to permit the president to appoint a new justice for every member of the Court who failed to retire within six months of his seventieth birthday. Although no one doubted that his purpose was to create a court more favorable to the New Deal, Roosevelt did not admit this. Instead, he insisted that the reform was needed because the nine aging justices were overworked.

A storm of criticism broke almost immediately. Many people feared that the proposal would upset the balanced government created by the Constitution. Even those who had complete confidence in Roosevelt were concerned about what some future president might do with such power. In the age of Adolf Hitler, Benito Mussolini, and Joseph Stalin, Americans were particularly jealous of their democratic system and especially aroused at anything that hinted of dictatorship. Roosevelt's proposal was a long way from dictatorship, but a fear existed that it might be a step in that direction.

Roosevelt's frustration with the Court was understandable, but his poorly handled reform proposal proved to be one of his worst mistakes. It gave members of Congress who were anxious to show their independence but fearful

A political cartoon in the *San Francisco Chronicle* for March 24, 1937, criticizes FDR's Supreme Court proposal. *(FDR Library)*

of the president's popularity a legitimate issue on which to oppose him. The result was the reemergence of a conservative coalition of Republicans and Southern Democrats, a coalition that harassed New Dealers' attempts at further social reform during the remainder of FDR's presidency. What made the error of Court "packing" even more galling was that it was unnecessary. In the weeks following Roosevelt's proposal, the Court announced several decisions upholding New Deal legislation. Shortly after, one of the conservative judges retired, giving Roosevelt a chance to make a normal appointment. Still, the damage to Roosevelt's reputation was done, and he henceforth had to deal with a more recalcitrant Congress. Presidential hubris had done in lesser men than Franklin D. Roosevelt. The Supreme Court episode did not by any means finish him off, but it left him chastened.

Other problems followed in a year that had seemed to promise great success for Roosevelt. The president had never accepted the new economic doctrine propounded by John Maynard Keynes, calling for the purposeful creation of large budget deficits to stimulate a depressed economy. Roosevelt tolerated deficits as a necessary evil, the only way to avert mass deprivation, but his goal was to balance the budget as quickly as possible. With some improvement in the economy by 1937 (although unemployment still stood at 14 percent), FDR decided the time had come to cut back spending sharply. Drastic cutbacks were made in the WPA and PWA. In August, 1937, the economy took a new nosedive. For months this recession left Roosevelt bewildered. He began issuing statements on the fundamental strength of the economy. Such talk was distressingly reminiscent of the words of Herbert Hoover in the early 1930's.

The continuing decline left Roosevelt no choice. In the spring of 1938 he asked Congress for a massive new relief appropriation. This provided the stimulus that was needed to turn the economy around, but the improvements were still not sufficient to bring the nation out of the Depression. At no time before the military buildup for World War II was Roosevelt willing to prescribe a sufficiently large dose of deficit spending to cure the nation's economic illness. Instead, he kept injecting maintenance doses that kept the patient alive but allowed the sickness to continue.

Only one major reform of lasting impact was enacted in Roosevelt's second term. The president sought legislation that would define the minimum permissible wages and the maximum hours of labor per week. Opposition was intense, especially from Southern states with notoriously low wage rates. To get the bill passed, Roosevelt and its sponsors had to agree, as they had done in the case of Social Security three years before, to exclude from the bill farm and domestic labor, two major black occupations in the South. Thus made more palatable for some members of the Congress, the Fair Labor Standards Act of 1938 became law. In those occupations that fell under the law's coverage, wages of at least twenty-five cents per hour had to be paid, and workers' hours were limited to forty per week.

By this time, the majority coalition Roosevelt had constructed out of urban Democratic machines, the Solid South, farmers, African Americans, immigrants, organized labor, and intellectuals was showing cracks. The CIO unions had found a powerful weapon in the sit-down strike, in which workers occupied the factories rather than form picket lines outside. Although successful in bringing such corporate giants as General Motors to recognize the demands of their workers, the sit-down strike seemed to many Americans to be an assault on the rights of private property. Caught in a difficult position in such industrial disputes, Roosevelt tried to take a middle ground, and in the midst of a bitter steel strike in 1937 the president said of labor and management, "A plague on both your houses." This served only to add to the strength of his opponents on both sides.

The Court fight, the labor unrest, and the recession left Roosevelt in a mood to strike back at those who had opposed him. He was especially angry at big businessmen, with whom he believed the blame for the recession rested, and conservative Democrats who had deserted him on the Court issue and other important congressional votes. The president struck a blow at the first group in April, 1938, when he called on Congress to enact measures that would tighten laws against monopolies. Congress responded in typical fashion by appointing a committee to investigate concentration in the economy. Roosevelt's antimonopoly campaign soon fizzled out when heightened military production took precedence over concerns about business concentration.

When it came to punishing opponents within the party, Roosevelt made a much bolder move. During the first years of his presidency, FDR had tried to rule by consensus. In 1935 he had identified himself with the lower and middle classes and maintained that stance through his landslide reelection the following year. He had moved during the first term from bipartisanship to partisanship. In 1938 he tried to go beyond partisanship and realign the parties. There should be some meaning to party labels, he reasoned, and those Democrats who consistently opposed their president's programs had no place in the party. At the beginning of the summer, Roosevelt announced that he would support in primary elections the opponents of certain conservative Democrats.

Roosevelt's attempted purge (the word had especially sinister connotations at the time of Stalin's horrible purges in the Soviet Union) failed. The reasons were several: The president had started too late; his personal popularity was not easily transferable; and those he opposed made an issue of state pride in not allowing an "outsider" to "dictate" to them. The failed purge was followed by substantial Republican gains in the general election of 1938. The GOP, reduced after 1936 to a minuscule 88 seats in the House, rose to 170 seats and picked up 8 in the Senate. Although the Democrats still held large majorities in both houses, Roosevelt could hardly expect to achieve new social reforms from the incoming Congress when the previous, overwhelmingly Democratic one had not been cooperative. The innovative period of the New Deal was over.

The Depression was not. In 1939, unemployment still hovered around 17 percent. It is clear that the New Deal had not solved the nation's economic woes. Roosevelt's policies had, however, brought great relief to many of those suffering the ravages of the Depression, and they had produced substantial reforms that changed the United States in lasting ways. Where the New Deal had not succeeded was in the other R, recovery. This failure was, it can be argued, not one of policy so much as it was of courage. The sorts of programs Roosevelt pushed could have brought about recovery, but neither the president nor the Congress had the courage to push them far enough to end the Depression.

Roosevelt's constant fear of deficit spending was, according to this view, the greatest impediment to recovery. Had he—and Congress—been willing to spend on domestic social programs the way the government did for military purposes after the outbreak of World War II, it is very likely that recovery from the Depression would have been achieved at a much earlier date. As it was, World War II ended the Depression.

Toward War and Reelection
As the New Deal was sputtering to a standstill in Roosevelt's second term, the president was giving increasing attention to foreign affairs. The rise of Hitler to power a few weeks before FDR took office in 1933 was a cause for worry

from the outset of Roosevelt's presidency. In the early years of his administration, though, Roosevelt had to concentrate heavily on domestic economic matters. As Nazi Germany, Mussolini's Italy, and Japan started military adventures in the second half of the decade, Roosevelt became alarmed at the drift toward another world war. Not only were foreign problems becoming more pressing but also domestic ones had become so intractable that a turn to events abroad was a welcome change for the president.

Adolf Hitler addresses a crowd on April 14, 1938. *(Library of Congress)*

The barriers to serious diplomatic action were formidable. Isolationism, rooted both in American tradition and in the conviction that bankers and munitions manufacturers—"merchants of death"—had led the nation into World War I, was a powerful force in the nation at large and even more so in the Senate. In 1935, as Italy invaded Ethiopia, FDR agreed to a Neutrality Act that embargoed arms shipments to all belligerents. Early in 1936 Nazi troops moved into the Rhineland, violating the treaties of Versailles and Locarno. A few months later, Fascists under General Francisco Franco began a civil war to overthrow the Spanish republic. The American response was to extend the provisions of the Neutrality Act to cover civil wars, thus preventing aid to the beleaguered republic. In mid-1937, the Japanese began a full-scale war in China.

In October, 1937, Roosevelt decided to test American sentiment on aggression. In a speech in Chicago the president suggested that aggressor nations ought to be "quarantined" as were patients with contagious diseases. The quarantine speech amounted to running a bolder foreign policy up the flagpole to see how many would salute. Few did. "It's a terrible thing," FDR lamented, "to look over your shoulder when you are trying to lead—and to find no one there."

With the public adamant about not getting involved in overseas problems, Roosevelt could do little but watch as the dictators moved the world toward war. In March, 1938, Hitler seized Austria. Later in the year, he demanded that Czechoslovakia give him a large part of its territory. Hitler was of a mind to take the territory by force but was persuaded by Mussolini to invite the heads of the British and French governments to a conference at Munich, where the Western leaders would approve the German aggrandizement. Roosevelt's role in these maneuvers was minimal. When British prime minister Neville Chamberlain accepted Hitler's invitation to Munich, FDR wired, "Good man." The American president, however, had no illusions about Hitler. Seeing him for the madman that he was, Roosevelt was only waiting for American public opinion to catch up with him before taking a larger part in the world crisis.

Meanwhile, Hitler was tightening the noose around the Jewish people of Germany. Here was an area in which the American government could have taken humanitarian action of great consequence by allowing Jewish refugees to immigrate into the United States, but given the continued high unemployment rate, American public opinion ran strongly against easing the immigration quotas. When the Nazis went on a particularly terrible binge of destruction and assault against Jews in November of 1938, Roosevelt said, "I myself could scarcely believe that such things could occur in a twentieth-century civilization"—but 83 percent of the public opposed letting in more immigrants, and Roosevelt did not push to arouse the nation's conscience. It was not his finest hour.

In March of 1939, Hitler broke the pledge he had made at Munich five months earlier and seized the rest of Czechoslovakia. The next month Roosevelt sent cables to Hitler and Mussolini directly asking them whether they would promise not to attack thirty-one nations that the president listed. Hitler's response was delivered in a speech in which he sneeringly read the thirty-one names and indicated that the United States was a greater threat to peace than was Germany.

This occurred only four months before the Nazis signed a nonaggression pact with the Soviet Union, carving up Poland in the process and precipitating World War II. The sympathies of Roosevelt, like those of most Americans, were clearly on the side of the British and the French, but still the overwhelming majority of Americans wanted their country to stay out of the war.

As the European crisis deepened, an American election year approached. No president (except, under unusual circumstances, an earlier Roosevelt) had ever broken the precedent established by George Washington of not seeking a third term. FDR, however, had remained noncommittal about such a possibility. This was good politics, since it lessened the problems created by being a lame duck from which second-term presidents usually suffer. With the

war in Europe, the possibility grew that Roosevelt might run again.

If Roosevelt was to break the anti-third-term tradition, he would have to do so by answering the draft of his party and the people. In this way it could be said that he was not seeking a third term but was accepting a call to duty during a time of great crisis. Such a draft by the Democratic convention was inevitable with the president not having said he would refuse the nomination. God would provide a candidate, Roosevelt told his aides.

By the time Roosevelt was renominated in July, events in Europe had turned ominous. Hitler's Blitzkrieg had swept over Denmark, Norway, the Low Countries, and—shockingly—France. As the crisis worsened, Roosevelt took two defense-related steps that also were helpful to the cause of his reelection. In May he asked Congress for funds to build "at least 50,000 planes a year." This appropriation provided a sharp stimulus to the lagging economy and marked the beginning of the end of the Depression. By the first Tuesday after the first Monday in November, the economic improvement would be obvious. Late in June, just before the Republican Convention, Roosevelt appointed Henry L. Stimson, who had been Hoover's secretary of state, as secretary of war, and Frank Knox, the 1936 Republican vice presidential candidate, as secretary of the navy. The concept of bipartisan government in the face of international danger helped to blunt the third-term issue.

The Republicans nominated the previously little known Wendell L. Willkie, and for a time in the fall his chances of unseating Roosevelt looked promising. The British, with their backs to the wall, were pleading for American assistance. In September, Roosevelt announced an exchange of fifty overage American destroyers for long-term leases on bases in British possessions in the Western Hemisphere. It was a noble and courageous act on Roosevelt's part, for the political risks were great. Willkie approved of the idea, but he denounced Roosevelt for acting on his own, without congressional approval. The GOP nominee began charging that Roosevelt would lead America into the war. "If his promise to keep our boys out of foreign wars is no better than his promise to balance the budget," Willkie declared, "they're already almost on the transports."

Roosevelt waited until the last two weeks to campaign actively, but he did a masterful job. He contrasted Willkie's endorsement of some New Deal initiatives with the Republican policies of 1932, and he felt obliged to respond to Willkie's charges. "Your boys," the president flatly stated, "are not going to be sent into any foreign wars." With the solid backing of the lower classes, Roosevelt swept to easy victory, although Willkie was able to win eight states in addition to the two that Alfred Landon had carried four years earlier. The president was genuinely fearful of some of the right-wing elements behind Willkie. After the returns were in, FDR said to Joseph Lash, "We seem to have avoided a *Putsch*, Joe."

A Third Term and a Second World War
Even before his third term officially began, Franklin Roosevelt was faced with momentous decisions. The election results appeared to be an endorsement of his policy of providing material assistance to Great Britain but also an emphatic agreement with his promise to keep American boys out of foreign wars. On the other side of the world, tension was growing between the United States and Japan. Before the election, Roosevelt had decided to increase the pressure on the Japanese to stop their war against China. The president ordered an embargo on all shipments of scrap metal to the Far Eastern empire. American oil, which was absolutely vital to the Japanese, would still be made available to them.

The British need for war supplies was becoming desperate, but American neutrality legislation required that they pay for everything they received from the United States, and they were no longer able to do so. While cruising in the Caribbean in December, Roosevelt hit on an idea to break through this impasse. The result was the Lend-Lease program, by which the United States would make supplies available to the British as they needed them and would be repaid in kind when the war was over. In announcing the concept at a press conference, the president employed one of the simple illustrations for which he was famous:

Suppose my neighbor's home catches on fire, and I have a length of garden hose four or five hundred feet away. If he can take my garden hose and connect it up with his hydrant, I may help him put out his fire. Now what do I do? I don't say to him before that operation, "Neighbor, my garden hose cost me $15, you have to pay me $15 for it." What is the transaction that goes on? I don't want $15—I want my garden hose back after the fire is over.

Lend-Lease was a brilliant stroke for furnishing aid to Britain and, later, other nations fighting the Nazis. In 1941 the United States became, in Roosevelt's words in a fireside chat, "the great arsenal for democracy." This, he told the American people, was the best way to keep the nation out of the war. The Lend-Lease program still had to be accepted by isolationists in Congress, such as Burton K. Wheeler of Montana, who declared, "The lend-lease-give program is the New Deal's triple A foreign policy; it will plow under every fourth American boy." Overcoming such venomous attacks, Roosevelt obtained congressional approval of the Lend-Lease Act in March, 1941, and immediately asked for an unprecedented appropriation of $7 billion to fund the program.

Roosevelt had begun 1941 by presenting his vision of a just world. In the context of an economic bill of rights, the president said the world should be based upon Four Freedoms: freedom of speech, freedom of religion, freedom from want, and freedom from fear. Here, nearly a year before the United States entered World War II, FDR was presenting a shorthand formula for the ideals that the Allies should seek in the war. There was no longer much pretense of American neutrality. The United States had become an active nonbelligerent, clearly on the anti-Nazi side but not involved in the fighting. It was a strange situation. Roosevelt and other Americans were calling on other nations to give their all against the Nazi menace, which the Americans clearly perceived to be a threat to themselves as well as to others, while Americans remained at a safe distance three thousand miles from the fighting.

The Roosevelt and American position in the war became even more anomalous in the summer of 1941, when the president secretly went to Argentia Harbor, Newfoundland, for a conference with British prime minister Winston Churchill. The purpose of the meeting was to discuss war strategy—an odd undertaking for a country that was not supposed to be at war. As it happened, though, no important strategic decisions were reached at the Argentia Conference. Its impact came instead from a declaration of war aims, the Atlantic Charter, to which Roosevelt and Churchill agreed. The Atlantic Charter provided a general framework for the Allied vision of what the postwar world ought to be like. It was for Americans in World War II what Woodrow Wilson's Fourteen Points had been in World War I and in fact addressed some of the same ideals: equal access to world trade, freedom of the seas, "no territorial changes that do not accord with the freely expressed wishes of the peoples concerned," self-government for all nations under forms of their own choosing, a secure peace for all nations, and arms reductions. Partly reiterating Roosevelt's call for the Four Freedoms, the Atlantic Charter also looked forward to "the fullest collaboration between all Nations in the economic field with the object of securing, for all, improved labor standards, economic advancement, and social security."

Such an elaboration of war aims must surely be a prelude to American entry into the war. Not so, Roosevelt insisted. This insistence points up an important question about his leadership. As biographer James M. Burns has noted, "Roosevelt would lead—but not by more than a step. He seemed beguiled by public opinion, by its strange combinations of fickleness and rigidity, ignorance and comprehension, by rapidly shifting optimism and pessimism." Clare Booth Luce, Republican congresswoman from Connecticut and wife of *Time-Life-Fortune* publisher Henry Luce, said that the gesture that symbolized FDR was not Churchill's "V for victory" sign but a wet finger held in the air to judge the direction of the wind. Luce was no friend of Roosevelt, and her characterization may seem unduly harsh, but it was not very far from the mark. FDR's view of the role of leadership in a democracy was to stay close to public desires, to try to shape the attitudes of the people but never to alter them drastically. Far more than most people realized at the time, Roosevelt relied on scientific samplings of public opinion in reaching his decisions. Opinion analyst Hadley Cantril of Princeton University frequently provided the president with polling results. This is one of the many ways in which FDR set the tone for subsequent presidents, who have often been guided more by polls than by principles.

Roosevelt did have principles; he really believed in the Four Freedoms and the ideals stated in the Atlantic Charter. He also believed that the defeat of the Nazis was essential to the realization of those goals and that active American participation in the war would be necessary to achieve victory over the forces of evil unleashed by Hitler. In 1941, Roosevelt understood that the American people agreed with him on all of these points except the last. In the 1940 campaign, he had encouraged the belief that the United States could aid the Allies but stay out of the war. In 1941, he continued to go along with this popular impression. By the fall of that year, Roosevelt probably could have pushed a war declaration through Congress, but it would have left the country bitterly divided, and he had no desire to lead a disunited country into war. The president would wait for events that would solidify the public behind an all-out war effort.

Such events were not long in coming. Roosevelt had given his permission for American naval vessels in the Atlantic to transmit to their British counterparts the location of German submarines they encountered. Here was another distinctly unneutral act, but Hitler was anxious to postpone American entry into the war as long as possible, and he ordered his U-boat commanders to avoid hostile actions against American ships. In September, 1941, however, an American destroyer, the USS *Greer*, trailed a German U-boat for two hours, reporting its position to a British plane, which dropped depth charges at the submarine. Finally, the U-boat launched torpedoes at the *Greer*. They missed, but Roosevelt at last had an incident that gave him a pretext for widening American efforts against the Nazis. He declared that the United States Navy would guard the western half of the Atlantic and that if any German or Italian warships entered the region, American officers had orders to shoot on sight. This amounted to a declaration of naval war in a large part of the Atlantic and freed British ships to operate in the eastern half of the ocean. American ships would guard British ships to Iceland. Roosevelt called his new policy "active defense."

Still Hitler did not make a hostile move against the United States. He had already plunged himself into a two-front war in July when he broke his nonaggression pact with the Soviet Union and launched an invasion of that country. This new Nazi aggression had presented Roosevelt with an important choice. Should Lend-Lease assistance be made available to the Soviets, whose Communist government many Americans detested almost as much as they did Hitler's regime? Senator Harry S Truman of Missouri spoke for many when he said, "If we see that Germany is winning we ought to help Russia and if Russia is winning we ought to help Germany and in that way let them kill as many as possible."

Germany was winning, but Roosevelt had motives for extending aid to the Soviets other than that cited by Truman. Although the president had no liking for the communists, he realized that they did not at that time pose a serious threat to the United States. The Nazis did, and anyone who was fighting them deserved American assistance. Lend-Lease aid began to flow into the Soviet Union.

For all the concern over the Nazi horrors and the growing American participation in the Atlantic war, it was from the Pacific that the United States was to be drawn fully into the conflict. Roosevelt's short-term objective in the Pacific was to delay a showdown with Japan, but while Roosevelt sought to put off confrontation, time was running out for the Japanese. Militarists were insistent on bringing matters to a head. They were aware of the American military buildup, which would eventually tip the scales in favor of the United States. When Japan occupied the French colony of Indochina in July, President Roosevelt froze all Japanese credits in the United States, bringing trade between the two nations to a halt. Roosevelt also cut off shipments of high-octane gasoline to the Japanese. He was trying to blend conciliation and pressure into a policy that would bring concessions from Japan. It almost worked. Japanese prime minister Fumimaro Konoye sought a personal meeting with the president. Roosevelt would agree only if the Japanese would pledge in advance to withdraw from China. Although the civilian leaders of the island nation might have accepted this demand, they had to contend with the militarists. The latter convinced Emperor Hirohito to agree in the fall to a timetable that placed a strict limitation on diplomacy. If the diplomats had

The USS *West Virginia*, USS *Tennessee*, and USS *Arizona* on fire in Pearl Harbor on December 7, 1941. *(National Archives)*

not gained concessions from the Americans by the end of November, the military would take over and launch an attack.

Much of this was known to Roosevelt, because American cryptographers had broken the main Japanese diplomatic code. This fact has led some Roosevelt critics to charge that he knew in advance of the attack on Pearl Harbor and allowed it to occur in order to get the country into the war. This charge misses two important points. First, Roosevelt did want the United States to enter the war, but against Germany, not Japan. Second, Roosevelt knew only that the Japanese planned an attack in early December, not where that attack would take place. The assumption was that it would be against the Dutch West Indies, British Malaya, or the American Philippines. Few thought the Japanese would venture as far east as Hawaii.

The Japanese surprise attack on Pearl Harbor on December 7, 1941, produced a unified American nation. In mid-November, Congress had passed by very narrow margins a president-sponsored bill to arm American merchant ships. In the Senate, 37 voted nay; in the House, 194 members opposed the measure. Less than four weeks later, the Senate unanimously passed a declaration of war and only one member of the House voted against it.

Although this was the wrong war, Hitler solved that problem by abiding by his treaty with Japan and declaring war on the United States on December 11. Americans were united as they had never been before.

The Home Front

The war solved some domestic problems and exacerbated others. Most significantly, it ended the Depression. The effects of the economic collapse were still evident as Roosevelt's third term began. Of the first one million men drafted for military service in 1940 and 1941, 13 percent were rejected for reasons stemming from malnutrition. Unemployment still stood at eight million in 1940 despite the early military buildup. By 1944, it had fallen to 670,000, about 1 percent of a greatly enlarged workforce. Not only had almost all of those who had been unable to find work in the 1930's obtained jobs, but also millions of people, mostly women and minorities, had entered the labor market and found employment.

Production for military purposes soared to fantastic levels. Family incomes rose rapidly, and the share of the nation's income going to lower groups on the socioeconomic scale increased, as families that had previously had no employed wage earner sent two or more members into war plants.

All of this was mainly to the good, but problems also arose. The migration of people to the locations of defense plants disrupted communities and families and created critical housing shortages. The growth of consumer incomes at a time when consumer goods were in short supply threatened to produce runaway inflation. The unprecedented spending (the incomprehensible figure of some $100 billion in fiscal 1944) that cured the Depression would at the same time swell the national debt to record levels. The demand for labor made the task of union organizers easier, and membership jumped by six million during the war, reaching 25 percent of the labor force. Yet strikes could endanger the war effort. Also, the flow of rural Southern blacks into urban areas where jobs were available led both to a growing awareness of the disparity between the antiracist rhetoric of the war against Nazism and the reality of life for African Americans and to friction between black and white workers in war industries.

Roosevelt was forced to try to deal with these domestic problems at the same time that he was engaged in the largest war in human history. Before U.S. entry into the war, African Americans, angry at discrimination in defense industries and the armed forces, threatened a massive march on Washington, D.C., in the summer of 1941. Alarmed at what such a demonstration might do to America's image abroad, Roosevelt reluctantly agreed to issue Executive Order 8802, which called on defense employers and unions to treat everyone equally and created a Fair Employment Practices Commission (FEPC). The FEPC was a toothless organization, but its creation marked a turning point in the federal attitude toward racial discrimination, and Roosevelt deserves some credit for the step, even though he took it under duress.

The needs of the wartime economy led to a new proliferation of federal agencies and far more governmental regulation than had existed in the New Deal years. The activities of the Office of Production Management and the Office of War Mobilization organized the American economy with more efficiency than it had ever known before. The Office of Price Administration had to resort to rationing of scarce commodities, but it did a remarkable job of holding down the inflationary pressures inherent in a war economy. Roosevelt would have done more along these lines had Congress been willing to go along. The president was insistent that war profiteering be checked. His attempts to impose confiscatory taxes on the highest incomes—he said that during the war no one should be allowed to have an after-tax income in excess of $25,000—were rejected by Congress. Although taxes were raised substantially during the war, they did not come close to matching spending levels. That the resulting deficit produced full employment meant that an important legacy of the Roosevelt war years would be a much greater acceptance of Keynesian economics, although no evidence exists that FDR himself ever accepted the deficit doctrine.

On the whole, organized labor was cooperative during the war, but there were exceptions. Most notable was Roosevelt's longtime adversary, John L. Lewis. In 1943, the United Mine Workers' chief attempted to defy the president's wage and price stabilization program. Roosevelt responded by seizing the coal mines and threatening to draft striking miners.

One of the most important developments on the home front during World War II was the emergence of a permanent defense industry that would be needed to construct the sophisticated weapons of modern warfare. These complex weapons also required well-trained soldiers to operate them, which meant an ominous departure from the American democratic tradition against a large standing army in peacetime. It also marked the beginning of the military-industrial complex that Dwight D. Eisenhower would warn about nearly two decades later.

The dangers that a standing army and a military-industrial linkage posed to American democracy were real but not immediate. The worst blot on American democratic practice during World War II was the treatment of Japanese Americans. In the wake of the Pearl Harbor attack, anti-Japanese actions were to be expected, but few materialized at first (although someone did cut down several Japanese cherry trees around the Tidal Basin in Washington, D.C.). Soon, however, whites in California began to turn harshly against their neighbors of Japanese ancestry. Thirty-six incidents of "violent patriotism" against Japanese Americans had been reported by March, 1942. Some "patriots" chose odd ways in which to express their love of country. Along with seven murders and nineteen assaults were two rapes of Japanese American women. To protect these citizens against such attacks, but more to guard against the possibility of sabotage, President Roosevelt early in 1942 signed an order to evacuate all people of Japanese ancestry from the West Coast. Concern about sabotage was not based on any evidence. General John De Witt, who

oversaw the removal, admitted that no fifth column activities had occurred, but said, "The very fact that no sabotage has taken place is a disturbing and confirming indication that such action will be taken." The result of these essentially racial fears was that approximately 110,000 Japanese Americans, some 70,000 of whom were native-born United States citizens, were uprooted and placed in "relocation centers," which Roosevelt more forthrightly called concentration camps. Their only crime was their race.

No similar actions were taken against German or Italian Americans, although Roosevelt was worried about the former. "I don't care so much about the Italians," the president said privately. "They are a lot of opera singers, but the Germans are different, they may be dangerous." FDR was not enthusiastic about the internment of Japanese Americans, but he went along with one of the greatest assaults on the civil liberties of a group of American citizens in the history of the United States.

President Roosevelt's openness to new ideas led him into the greatest technological undertaking of the era. In 1939, a group of physicists who were alarmed at reports that scientists in Nazi Germany were making progress in the area of nuclear fission asked Albert Einstein to write to the president and explain to him the possibility of the construction of bombs with enormous explosive power. Einstein's letter was taken to Roosevelt by Alexander Sachs, a friend of the president, who persuaded him of the urgency of the matter and of the nearly incomprehensible danger should the Nazis succeed in developing atomic weapons before the democratic nations did. Roosevelt promptly started an exploratory program in nuclear fission. After American entry into the war, it expanded rapidly.

The Manhattan Project eventually employed 150,000 people at sites around the country. The secrecy of the undertaking required that Congress appropriate vast sums of money without knowing the nature of the project on which the funds were being spent. Great Britain and the United States cooperated in atomic research from the start, but Roosevelt was reluctant to inform the Soviets. By the time of the president's death in the spring of 1945, the Manhattan Project was nearing its awful climax, but no decision about using it for postwar cooperation had been made.

The Good War

The early months of American participation in World War II were not encouraging. Japanese forces swallowed up islands across the western Pacific. American troops in the Philippines fought valiantly, but they finally had to surrender. On the other side of the world, Hitler had been unable to knock the Soviet Union out of the war or to mount an invasion of England, but the Germans were still on the offensive and both of those feats still seemed possible.

Well before Pearl Harbor, President Roosevelt had settled on an "Atlantic first" strategy. He saw the Nazis as a more formidable threat than the Japanese. The latter would be held by delaying actions while American forces were built up to defeat Germany. Throughout the war, Roosevelt's primary goal was to win a decisive military victory in the shortest possible time, with the fewest possible American casualties. He was very much concerned with achieving his objectives for the postwar world, but he did not believe that he had a right to extend the war for these purposes.

This view was not shared by the leaders of the United States' chief allies. Both Churchill and Stalin always kept an eye on their postwar goals as they made wartime decisions. Stalin's desperate need in 1942 was the opening by the western Allies of a second front that would draw German troops away from the Soviet front. Churchill was in no hurry to do this favor for his communist ally, and it was not without reason that Stalin complained that the

British leader was willing to let the Soviets absorb the bulk of the Allied casualties. Roosevelt was more ready to provide relief for the hard-pressed Soviets and was also anxious to have American troops get into action against the Nazis. Churchill was adamant in insisting that the Allies did not yet have sufficient strength to risk an attack across the English Channel. The two leaders agreed on a fall, 1942, offensive in French North Africa. Operation Torch furnished little relief to the Soviets and was not of much strategic significance in winning the war, but it did give American forces a chance to engage the enemy.

As the North African campaign continued in late 1942, a more significant military development was occurring deep in the Soviet Union. The Red Army stopped the penetration of Hitler's troops at Stalingrad, held their ground in a horrible struggle, and finally began to push the Germans back. The Nazis were far from beaten, but they had ceased to advance.

In the late weeks of 1942, the tide also began to turn against the Japanese. American forces won a costly struggle with the Japanese on Guadalcanal, in the Solomon Islands. It was a long way to Tokyo, but like their Axis partners the Japanese were now on the defensive. There was cause for optimism when Roosevelt and Churchill met at Casablanca in January, 1943, to discuss strategy. In making the trip to Morocco, Roosevelt became the first American president to journey abroad during wartime and the first since Lincoln to enter a zone of war.

At Casablanca, Churchill gradually persuaded his American counterpart that a cross-channel invasion should be postponed in favor of an attack in the Mediterranean, into what the British leader termed the "soft underbelly" of the Axis. Although Roosevelt was always confident of his persuasive abilities in face-to-face meetings, it was Churchill who was usually successful in swinging the American president over to his way of thinking. Still, as the

Atlantic Charter had overshadowed strategic decisions at Argentia, it was a statement at the end of the Casablanca meeting that became its most significant product. At a press conference at the conclusion of the meetings, Roosevelt said, "The elimination of German, Japanese, and Italian war power means the unconditional surrender by Germany, Italy, or Japan." This policy had not been agreed on by the leaders at Casablanca, but Roosevelt's public statement made it Allied policy. Some have questioned its wisdom, suggesting that the demand for unconditional surrender stiffened enemy resistance and hindered efforts by German military leaders to overthrow Hitler. Roosevelt, however, well remembered how the armistice that ended World War I had given Hitler an opportunity to gain a following by falsely claiming that the German military had not really been defeated. When the courses of Germany and Japan after World War II are contrasted with that of Germany after the first war, Roosevelt's insistence on unconditional surrender appears to be vindicated.

Churchill continued to oppose a "premature" invasion of France and to argue instead for further adventures in the Mediterranean. The Anglo-Americans won a fairly quick victory in Sicily, and when they landed in Italy Mussolini was overthrown. Soon the Italian government surrendered, but German troops rapidly moved in and made the soft underbelly hard. The troops of the western Allies remained bogged down on the Italian peninsula through 1943 and into 1944. Meanwhile, the Red Army slowly advanced on the long Soviet front and Stalin's anger over the repeated postponements of the cross-channel invasion grew.

Tension between the Soviets and the West was high. The alliance was one of necessity, not choice. It was held together by the cement of a common enemy. Lesser, but still significant, differences existed between Roosevelt and Churchill. The British leader favored a division of much of the postwar world into spheres of influence dominated by the three major powers. Roosevelt, an old Wilsonian, preferred a greater reliance on an international peacekeeping organization. Roosevelt understood the forces of nationalism that were rising in Asia and believed that the principles of the Atlantic Charter should be applied to colonial possessions. He was particularly anxious to keep the French from returning to Indochina and to persuade the British to take steps toward Indian independence. Churchill made his opposing position clear: "I have not become the King's First Minister in order to preside over the liquidation of the British Empire." Roosevelt was on the correct side in opposing colonialism, but he was unwilling to increase the pressure on his friend and ally.

Stalin's reluctance to travel far from the fighting in his country and his anger at the failure of the allies to open a second front in France had led him to decline previous invitations to meet with Roosevelt. The first gathering of the Big Three took place in November, 1943, at Tehran. Roosevelt's confidence in his ability to deal with people in a face-to-face meeting was put to a great test. The president tried to win Stalin over by teasing Churchill. The Soviet dictator joined in the fun but was happy with Roosevelt only when the American agreed with him in opposing Churchill's desires for further peripheral actions in the Mediterranean. It was agreed at Tehran that the Anglo-American invasion of German-held France, named Operation Overlord, would begin in the spring of 1944. Roosevelt's emphasis on quick victory had finally prevailed over Churchill's strategic hopes for the postwar world.

Great differences among the Allies remained, and out of those differences the Cold War developed during the later stages of World War II. The greatest problem areas were the disposition of Eastern Europe (especially Poland), the scope and power of the international organization to be formed, and the treatment of the defeated Germans. All of these difficult issues were left unresolved at Tehran.

As the war continued, reports of Nazi atrocities mounted. In 1942 word reached the White House that Hitler had ordered the "final solution" of what he termed the "Jewish problem": the systematic slaughter of all Jewish people the Nazis could find. At the end of that year, Rabbi Stephen Wise gave FDR a paper outlining Hitler's "Blue Print for Extermination." In the summer of 1943 *The New York Times* published a story documenting the Nazis' systematic murder of at least 1.7 million people. Roosevelt could not plead ignorance of the Holocaust as an excuse for not taking more effective steps to counteract it.

Early in 1944, Treasury Secretary Henry Morgenthau asked his department's general counsel, Randolph Paul, to write a report on the situation. Paul's "Report to the Secretary on the Acquiescence of this Government in the Murder of Jews" pulled no punches. It charged that the United States State Department had failed to do what it could to rescue Jews and in fact had stood in the way of private efforts to do so. "One of the greatest crimes in history, the slaughter of the Jewish people in Europe, is continuing unabated," Paul correctly declared. Faced with this and other evidence, Roosevelt set up a War Refugee Board, but the president never took much effective action to halt the Holocaust. He steadfastly refused to seek changes in the immigration laws, worried about angering Muslims in the Middle East, and did not order the bombing of railroad tracks leading to the death camps. Roosevelt maintained that the rapid defeat of Hitler would be the most effective means of stopping the horror.

The decisive step toward ending the war came with the D day invasion on the beaches of Normandy in June of 1944. Once General Dwight D. Eisenhower's forces had established themselves on the Continent, it was only a matter of time until Hitler's armies were vanquished. With the exception of a startling Nazi counteroffensive in December, 1944 (the Battle of the Bulge), the Allied vise closed steadily on the Nazis from east and west.

During these final months of war in Europe, the American political calendar called for a presidential election. Roosevelt insisted that he wanted to retire, but he was determined to see the war through to a successful conclusion. There was no pretense of a draft in 1944; the president made it plain that he was available for a fourth term. His long tenure in the White House was no longer much of an issue. As a popular joke had it, "If he was good enough for my pappy, and good enough for my grandpappy, then he's good enough for me!"

The only serious questions concerned Roosevelt's health and his running mate. The sixty-two-year-old chief executive was noticeably older and less vigorous than he had been during his previous campaigns. He was suffering from an enlarged heart and high blood pressure. These particulars were unknown to the public, but his appearance was a cause for concern.

Vice President Henry Wallace was anathema to conservative Democrats, who considered him a leftist visionary. Roosevelt had forced Wallace on a reluctant party in 1940; he could do it again. As was his wont, FDR indicated to several prospective running mates that each had his backing. In the end the choice fell on Harry S Truman, a border state senator who had been faithful in support of the New Deal. As is the case with most decisions on vice presidential candidates, this one was made with political considerations in mind, not with a thought that the person chosen might soon become president.

The Republicans chose Thomas E. Dewey, the forty-two-year-old governor of New York, who was noted for his drive and lack of humor. Roosevelt's main tasks in the 1944 race were to demonstrate his health and to get people to go to the polls. The former was accomplished with a few good speeches and a lengthy open-air motorcade through a downpour in New York. This was surely of no benefit to the president's health, but it was a great help to the image of his health.

The job of getting people to turn out on Election Day was more difficult. The people most likely to vote for Roosevelt were often those least likely to vote, especially during the war, when so many were away from home in the armed services or had moved to different voting jurisdictions in search of defense industry employment. The consequence was a low turnout and the narrowest of Roosevelt's four national victories. The margin was comfortable, though: 3.6 million popular votes and 432 to 99 in the electoral college.

One result of FDR's reelection was that the American people seemed to have endorsed United States participation in a new world or-ganization. The structure of the United Nations was one of the major topics to be addressed when the Big Three convened at the Soviet Crimean resort of Yalta in February, 1945. The leaders did reach agreement on the United Nations. The major powers were to have vetoes over U.N. actions and resolutions, a point on which Stalin would not budge. The question of Poland was more perplexing. With a substantial number of Polish American constituents to consider, Roosevelt wanted a democratic government in Poland. Stalin, whose country had been invaded via Poland twice in less than thirty years, demanded a government in that country that would be friendly to the Soviet Union. Both positions were reasonable. Unfortunately, they were incompatible. The long history of Russian domination of Poland meant that any popularly elected

The D day invasion of Normandy as seen from a landing barge. *(National Archives)*

Polish government would be unfriendly toward Moscow. Since the Red Army was already in possession of most of Poland, there was little that Roosevelt and Churchill could do at Yalta but try to convince Stalin that he should broaden the communist-oriented government that he had already established in the country. This the Soviet leader finally agreed to do, but in terms so loose as to be nearly meaningless.

The leaders of the Big Three (left to right): Soviet premier Joseph Stalin, FDR, and British prime minister Winston Churchill. *(Library of Congress)*

Contrary to the later charges of his political opponents, Roosevelt did not "give Poland away" at Yalta, either intentionally or because of ill health. He never had Poland in the first place and had to accept the best deal he could get from Stalin. Moreover, Roosevelt did achieve one of his primary objectives at Yalta. Stalin agreed to declare war on Japan three months after the Germans surrendered. At the time of Yalta, American military analysts still expected the Japanese war to last a long time, and Soviet intervention was prized as a way to save tens of thousands, perhaps hundreds of thousands, of American lives.

Undoubtedly, Roosevelt was in poor health at the Crimean conference. This does not appear to have affected his judgment, but by the time he returned from the arduous journey he was very weak. After a halting report to Congress, delivered from a seated position, the president went to Warm Springs, Georgia, for a period of recuperation. While there on the afternoon of April 12, 1945, in the company of his former mistress, Lucy Mercer Rutherfurd, the president suffered a "terrific headache." Less than three hours later, the longest presidency in American history reached its end.

FDR and the American Presidency

The man Americans mourned in the spring of 1945, less than a month before the defeat of Germany and four months before the Japanese surrender, is generally acknowledged to rank with George Washington and Abraham Lincoln as one of the greatest presidents. Circumstances helped to provide opportunities for greatness for each of these leaders: precedent setting for Washington as the first president, preserving the Union during the Civil War for Lincoln, and meeting the two greatest crises of twentieth century America—the Great Depression and World War II—for Franklin D. Roosevelt.

"If during the lifetime of a generation no crisis occurs sufficient to call out in marked manner the energies of the strongest leader," Franklin Roosevelt's cousin Theodore once said, "then of course the world does not and cannot know of the existence of such a leader; and in consequence there are long periods in the history of every nation during which no man appears who leaves an indelible mark in history." That fate may, to a degree, have befallen Theodore Roosevelt, but Franklin Roosevelt did not lack challenges. "There is," he declared in his 1936 acceptance speech, "a mysterious cycle in human events. To some generations much is given. Of other generations much is expected. This generation of Americans has a rendezvous with destiny."

Crises may furnish an opportunity for greatness, but it is left up to the individual to deal with them in such a way that he or she will be judged a great leader. This FDR did. His confidence, humanitarianism, and dedication to democracy led the nation through hard times and war during an era in which democratic beliefs were besieged. Franklin D. Roosevelt is one of the few leaders of whom it can be said without hesitation that the world would have been a greatly different place had he not lived. Had a conservative been elected in 1932, conditions might have continued to deteriorate to the point of revolution; had a radical won, he might well have taken the nation toward socialism. American democracy is strong, but it needed a great champion in the 1930's and 1940's. Roosevelt filled that role admirably.

Certainly, FDR had many faults. Yet in the end what stands out about him is that he gave the United States the courage and outlook necessary for the country to survive its worst economic collapse and its largest international war and to emerge from both a stronger nation than it had been before those upheavals.

Roosevelt was not an intellectual. He always preferred to obtain information from people rather than books. He was a politician and a moralist, in the best sense of those words. His moralism grew out of his aristocratic heritage. He brought the sense of stewardship that was ingrained in people of his class to the national government. By thus blending morality with economics, responsibility with government, he met the desires of a people wracked by depression and in the process established a new role for the federal government. That role was not one of dominance but of caring.

Roosevelt's view of government was ex-

pansive. He believed that government in a democracy was an instrument of the people and should be used to meet their needs. He was certainly not a socialist, but he believed that making capitalism more humane through reform and government regulation was essential to saving the economic system.

Not only was Roosevelt not a socialist but also he was the antithesis of an ideologue. He loved to try to combine opposites, to experiment in an eclectic fashion to see what would work. He was guided by common sense rather than a coherent philosophy. Once he made a decision, he rarely looked back to second-guess it. His brand of leadership was to stay close to the wishes of the people. This can be criticized as government by opinion poll or weather vane, but it can also be praised as the essence of democratic government. Roosevelt was one of the best interpreters of public attitudes ever to sit in the White House. His personal popularity was extraordinary, even among people who were unsure of his policies. In 1938, at a time when Roosevelt's political rating had declined, polls indicated that 80 percent of all Americans liked him as a person and only 10 percent disliked him.

Roosevelt's style of administration was similar to his practice in other realms. He did not like to delegate too much authority to any one aide or administrator, preferred informal gatherings of advisers to formal use of the cabinet, and liked to draw advisers from differing perspectives and shift his favor from one to another. He also had the faults of his virtues. His practical, one-problem-at-a-time approach was helpful in resolving many issues, but it prevented long-range planning that might have been useful in dealing with both the economy and the war.

Roosevelt's failings, real though they were, pale when placed beside his accomplishments. Just before taking office, Roosevelt said that the presidency is preeminently a place of moral leadership. So it was during his long tenure in the White House. He made the office of president far more powerful and much more the center of national attention than it had ever been before. Lincoln may have decided the question of whether the term "United States" is singular or plural, but Franklin Roosevelt gave real meaning to the unity of the country. Most Americans after Roosevelt look to the federal government as a means of solving problems and look to the White House to offer possible solutions. Every president after Franklin D. Roosevelt lives, as historian William Leuchtenberg put it, "in the shadow of FDR."

Robert S. McElvaine

Bibliographical References

Comprehensive biographies of Franklin D. Roosevelt are James M. Burns's two-volume study, *Roosevelt: The Lion and the Fox*, 1956, and *Roosevelt: The Soldier of Freedom*, 1970. The most richly detailed studies of FDR and his times are Frank Freidel, *Franklin D. Roosevelt*, 5 vols. to date, 1952-1990, and Arthur M. Schlesinger, Jr., *The Age of Roosevelt*, 3 vols., 1957-1960. For a comprehensive fresh examination of Roosevelt's life, see Kenneth S. Davis, 4 volumes to date, *FDR: The Beckoning of Destiny, 1882-1928*, 1972; *FDR: The New York Years, 1928-1933*, 1985; *FDR: The New Deal Years, 1933-1937*, 1986; and *FDR: Into the Storm, 1937-1940*, 1993. Nathan Miller, *FDR: An Intimate History*, 1983, and Patrick J. Maney, *The Roosevelt Presence: A Biography of Franklin Delano Roosevelt*, 1998, are concise biographies. William E. Leuchtenberg, *Franklin D. Roosevelt and the New Deal*, 1964, and Robert S. McElvaine, *The Great Depression: America, 1929-1941*, 1984, provide interpretive surveys of FDR's first two terms. Robert S. Thompson, *A Time for War: Franklin Delano Roosevelt and the Path to Pearl Harbor*, 1991, argues that Roosevelt provoked war with Japan and Germany. Russell D. Buhite and David W. Levy, eds., *FDR's Fireside Chats*, 1992, gathers transcripts of thirty-one fireside chats delivered in the thirteen years of Roosevelt's presidency.

Three books that appraise Roosevelt's legacy are Philip Abbott, *The Exemplary Presidency: Franklin D. Roosevelt and the American Political Tradition*, 1990; Leuchtenberg, *The FDR Years: On Roosevelt and His Legacy*, 1995; and Mark J. Rozell and William D. Peterson, eds., *FDR and the Modern Presidency: Leadership and Legacy*, 1997. Joseph P. Lash, *Eleanor and Franklin*, 1971, is a biography of the nation's important First Lady, covering the years ending with her husband's death. Doris Kearns Goodwin, *No Ordinary Time: Franklin and Eleanor Roosevelt: The Home Front in World War II*, 1994, is a meticulously detailed biography of the Roosevelts from 1940 to 1949. Geoffrey C. Ward, *Before the Trumpet: Young Franklin Roosevelt, 1882-1905*, 1985, gives a detailed account of the future president's early years. On Roosevelt's foreign policy, see Robert Dallek, *Franklin Roosevelt and American Foreign Policy, 1932-1945*, 1979. Robert H. Ferrell, *The Dying President: Franklin D. Roosevelt*, 1998, chronicles Roosevelt's decline in health and speculates on the consequences of his incapacity during the final days of World War II. Robert Underhill, *FDR and Harry: Unparalleled Lives*, 1996, contrasts the dissimilar lives but similar destinies of Roosevelt and Truman.

Harry S Truman

33d President, 1945-1953

Born: May 8, 1884
Lamar, Missouri
Died: December 26, 1972
Kansas City, Missouri

Political Party: Democratic
Vice President: Alben W. Barkley

Cabinet Members

Secretary of State: James F. Byrnes, George C. Marshall, Dean Acheson

Secretary of the Treasury: Fred M. Vinson, John W. Snyder

Secretary of War: Robert P. Patterson, Kenneth C. Royall

Secretary of the Navy: James V. Forrestal

Secretary of Defense: James V. Forrestal, Louis Johnson, George C. Marshall, Robert A. Lovett

Attorney General: Tom C. Clark, J. Howard McGrath, James P. McGranery

Postmaster General: R. E. Hannegan, Jesse M. Donaldson

Secretary of the Interior: Harold Ickes, Julius A. Krug, Oscar L. Chapman

Secretary of Agriculture: C. P. Anderson, C. F. Brannan

Secretary of Commerce: W. A. Harriman, Charles Sawyer

Secretary of Labor: L. B. Schwellenbach, Maurice J. Tobin

Truman's official portrait. *(White House Historical Society)*

Often described as a man who was too small for the job, Harry S Truman believed that he was an unusually successful president. Proud of his knowledge of history, he maintained that he had learned the lessons of the past and avoided the mistakes that had been made in it. To him, the most relevant lessons were those taught by the history of the 1920's and 1930's. The mistakes of that past had resulted in the tragedy of the World War II. Faced with similar challenges, Truman had, in his own view, made the decisions required to avoid World War III.

The Path to Power

The apparent harmony between Truman's personality and the situation within the Democratic Party by 1944 had much to do with Truman's rise to the White House. Franklin D. Roosevelt had helped to make the party more complex and powerful by adding a New Deal wing to the party of the South and a few Northern urban machines, thereby converting the Democrats from the minority to the majority party. By 1944, the party was troubled by intense internal conflict over policy and control, with conservatives anxious to check the advance of the New Deal pitted against liberals eager to revive it as a force for reform. To many of the liberals, the vice president, Henry A. Wallace, seemed to be especially attractive, surely as a vice president and possibly as Roosevelt's successor. To Wallace's foes, James F. Byrnes of South Carolina seemed a better choice for the vice presidency, but although the party did discard the idealist who had been serving as vice president since 1941, it did not substitute the experienced Southern politician for him. Instead, the Democrats turned to a gregarious, pragmatic border-state senator whose personality seemed to fit the conditions inside the party.

Harry S Truman had not always been the gregarious person he was in 1944. Born in Lamar, Missouri, on May 8, 1884, the oldest of three children of John Anderson and Martha Ellen (Young) Truman, and reared in Grandview and Independence, he had been rather withdrawn as a boy. His poor vision and the thick glasses he wore had hampered his efforts to join the activities that other boys enjoyed. He had drawn close to his mother and had turned to books and the piano. Although not unhappy, his early years were far from satisfying. In spite of his great appetite for books, especially histories, he failed to graduate near the top of his high school class and did not go on to college. His poor eyesight frustrated his hope for an appointment to West Point and a career in the Army.

After high school, unsure of what he should do with his life, Truman moved to Kansas City, where he worked at several jobs. Then he returned to his grandfather's farm in Grandview, where his personality began to change. The large farm provided the young Truman a rich opportunity to prove himself, and he also became active in various organizations, such as the Masons and the National Guard. During World War I, he served as captain of an artillery battery and was very popular with his men. After the war, he owned and operated a men's store in downtown Kansas City. It became for him more than a place to make money, serving as a gathering spot for his friends and a base from which he moved about the city visiting other men and encouraging them to come to the store. Such activities culminated the slow transformation of the retiring boy into a very gregarious adult.

Truman's new personality provided a foundation for his political career. Politics now became attractive to him, for such a career offered great opportunities for association with people. He in turn became attractive to politicians as his popularity with voters became clear.

Truman had been born and reared a Southern Democrat. His ancestors had migrated to Missouri from Kentucky in the 1840's and had shown Confederate sympathies during the Civil War. Like his father, he had become active in Democratic politics in independent and rural Jackson County, an area with Southern ties and customs.

Truman, however, did not remain merely a Southern Democrat. He received much of his early political education as a member of an urban Democratic machine. While living on the farm, he joined Kansas City's Pendergast organization, which was trying to spread its influence into rural Jackson County. In 1922, recognizing that he was well liked outside the city, the machine threw its weight behind him in the race for eastern district judge of the county court (an administrative post). During the next twelve years as a county official, Truman did help the organization gain strength, accepting one of the basic rules of machine politics and appointing the machine's members to offices that he controlled. In 1934, Tom Pendergast, influenced again by confidence in Truman's popularity outside the city, asked him to run for the United States Senate and furnished essential support in his successful campaign.

Also in 1934, Truman added a new dimension to his point of view. He became a New Deal Democrat. Earlier, he had participated in efforts to use government for economic purposes (especially to build roads), had supervised welfare agencies, and had promoted regional planning, but he had been closer to "old deal" groups such as the Chamber of Commerce than New Deal ones such as labor unions. Now he campaigned for the Senate as a New Dealer, endorsing what had been done and promising to support further developments.

As a senator, Truman fulfilled his promises. He voted for major measures such as Social Security and the Wagner Labor Relations Act, backed the president in his unsuccessful attempt to increase the number of justices on the Supreme Court, investigated the malpractices of financial and industrial leaders, and championed federal regulation of transportation facilities. At the same time, Truman attempted to strengthen and protect the Pendergast machine. He obtained federal patronage for it and defended the organization against the rising tide of criticism that eventually overwhelmed it.

Truman also established close ties with leading Southern Democrats in Washington, D.C., including ones who were unhappy with Roosevelt and the New Deal. The Missouri senator seemed to place a higher value on developing and maintaining good relations with the various members of his party than on promoting the point of view of one of its factions.

To move higher in American politics, Truman needed to become a national figure, and he did so during World War II as head of a senatorial investigating committee soon known as the Truman Committee. The committee, which dealt with mismanagement and corruption in war production, helped to make him popular with a multitude of groups, especially the critics of big business and big government, as his investigations and reports frequently criticized the contributions of business and government to the war effort. At the same time, his concentration on the war programs enabled him to avoid identification with any one of the contending factions of the party. While he explored the construction of army camps, the procurement of airplanes, and the like, other figures who were rising toward the top of the party, such as Henry Wallace, were taking stands on the issues that divided the party and the nation. Everyone wanted to win the war, and Truman's work clearly contributed toward that goal. Not everyone wanted to revive the New Deal.

As a consequence of the ways in which he had functioned on the national stage, Truman was acceptable to all the major factions in the Democratic Party in 1944. The leading promoter of his nomination as vice president, Robert Hannegan, who had been a major figure in the Democratic organization in St. Louis and was now chairing the Democratic National Committee, represented the urban machine wing. He played an important part in convincing Roosevelt that the controversial Wallace would hurt the ticket, whereas Truman would not.

Although Truman's major support came from the party's urban machines, he would not have been nominated if he had not been acceptable to the other groups. The Southern faction accepted him, although its members preferred other candidates. These politicians consoled themselves with talk of Truman's Southern background and assurances that he was much more desirable than Wallace. New Dealers also accepted Truman, despite their preference for Wallace. They stressed Truman's senatorial voting record with its consistent support for the New Deal and his obvious—to them—superiority to Byrnes.

Thus Truman became president when Roosevelt died on April 12, 1945, because the Missourian had seemed to satisfy the needs of the party in 1944. As he had advanced in politics, he had not switched from being one type of Democrat to being another; rather, he had added one to another, layer by layer. By 1944, he contained within himself all three types, just as his party did, and thereby became an ideal choice to hold the parts together.

Although Truman's career so far had been dominated by domestic matters, his presidency would be controlled by foreign affairs, and he brought to his new responsibilities a distinct point of view on international matters that stressed political considerations, especially the distribution of power, the importance of the military factor, and the need to deal quickly and forcefully with aggressive nations. His own experiences as a soldier during World War I and as a reserve officer in the 1920's and 1930's, and the nation's experiences in world affairs since 1918, had shaped his fundamental ideas on American foreign policy. The nation's military weakness and its isolationism had, he was convinced, contributed significantly to the coming of World War II. Such mistakes of the past had to be avoided in the future. That was the clear lesson of history.

FDR's Successor

International affairs dominated Truman's first four months in office, a quite successful period for him. By April 12, the job of defeating Adolf Hitler's Germany was almost complete. The German armies had lost the war, but Hitler had not yet given up. On April 30, he committed suicide; on May 8, the new German government surrendered.

Determined to carry Roosevelt's projects to completion, Truman battled on behalf of a new international organization and American membership in it. On April 13, he promised that the San Francisco Conference to organize the United Nations would be held as scheduled. It was, and by June 26 it completed its work and Truman moved on to victory at home. On July 28, the Senate, by a vote of 89 to 2, ratified American participation in the new organization. Building on Roosevelt's preparations, Truman had avoided a repetition of Woodrow Wilson's failure in 1919-1920.

Truman next sought victory over Japan. American forces and their allies had gained control of nearly all of the Philippine Islands and had defeated the Japanese on Iwo Jima and Okinawa. Plans had been made, and approved by Truman, for an invasion of Japan, but recent victories purchased at heavy cost had strengthened convictions that the invasion would also be very costly for American forces.

The administration recognized that Japan had lost the war but also knew that the nation was not ready to surrender on American terms. Strategic bombing had severely damaged Japan's industry and inflicted heavy civilian losses, and American submarines had blockaded Japan so that the people could not get enough food. Its air and sea forces were nearly destroyed, and Japan had been cut off from the vital resources of Southeast Asia. A peace faction with substantial political strength sought a negotiated settlement, but Washington knew that it faced significant opposition, especially within the still strong army.

American leaders not only wanted Japan to surrender but also were determined to force great changes on Japan, including removal of the wartime leaders from power, demilitarization, democratization, and liberalization of the nation and destruction of its empire. Influenced by intense hostility toward a people who had attacked Pearl Harbor and believing such changes were needed to make the world

Truman with British prime minister Winston Churchill (left) and Soviet premier Joseph Stalin (right) at the 1945 Potsdam Conference at the end of World War II. *(National Archives)*

of the future a peaceful one, Washington was convinced that only massive military force could produce them.

By late July, however, an alternative to a large and costly invasion seemed to be available. The first test of an atomic device was made on July 16. The new weapon seemed capable of forcing Japan's unconditional surrender more quickly and at a much lower price than an invasion. Supplementary considerations also influenced the decision to use the new weapon; above all, there was hope that the bomb would limit Soviet expansion and alter the country's behavior, which, especially in Eastern Europe, had become alarming. The bomb, in sum—not American or Soviet ground forces—might bring about the unconditional surrender of the Japanese, do so more quickly than an invasion could, and do so without such heavy loss of life and without great gains to the Soviet Union in Asia.

Informed that two atomic bombs would soon be available, President Truman, on July 24,

ordered their use against Japan as soon after August 3 as weather permitted. The first bomb obliterated Hiroshima on August 6, the Soviet Union declared war on August 8 and quickly moved against the Japanese on the mainland, and the second bomb hit Nagasaki on August 9. Five days later, Japan accepted surrender terms that conformed to American specifications and opened the door to a revolution in Japan.

The Beginning of the Cold War

The victories from May to August ended World War II but did not prevent the emergence of a new and different type of international conflict, a cold war between the United States and the Soviet Union. The Cold War was nonviolent—a feature that distinguished it from what is customarily meant by war but which was no less intense, so intense as to be the dominant feature of the relationship between the two nations. The Cold War also affected virtually all other nations, imposing pressure on them to take sides.

Both ideological differences and economics contributed to the emergence of the Cold War but did not fully explain it. Of other factors, World War II was especially important. It had destroyed the power of the nations that had separated the Soviet Union and the United States, giving them new opportunities to clash with each other. It had increased the power of both. The United States, its economy stimulated by the war, had developed great military strength while suffering relatively light loss of lives and had obtained new influence in crucial places, especially Western Europe and Japan. The war had a more mixed impact on Soviet power. The war did inflict serious damage on the Soviet Union, taking many more lives than in any other country and wreaking heavy damage on the economy, but victory gave the Soviets new opportunities, especially in Eastern Europe and Germany, which they eagerly seized. The war also increased the self-confidence and sense of power of both countries, for they had triumphed over strong adversaries. Finally, the war reduced the influence of isolationism in both, convincing American leaders of its folly and persuading Soviet leaders that they must control Eastern Europe and Germany to be secure.

The Cold War emerged and escalated during late 1945 and through 1946 for several reasons. The ending of World War II reduced pressures on both nations to cooperate with each other. The atomic bomb increased the American leaders' sense of strength and alarmed the Soviets. Soviet behavior in Eastern Europe and Iran, where they maintained their military presence and sought to shape political developments, troubled Americans, as it contravened their ideas for the postwar world; seemed to violate agreements that Roosevelt, Winston Churchill, and Joseph Stalin had made at Yalta in February, 1945; and suggested that the Soviet Union might continue to expand as Germany and Japan had. Soviet pressure on Turkey in 1946 also contributed to the Cold War, and so

did rivalry over Germany. There, the two nations were locked into a system of joint control; they had promised reunification of Germany, but they now disagreed over the terms.

In this deteriorating international situation, Truman rejected Roosevelt's efforts to cultivate Soviet friendship and instead developed a "get tough" policy, insisting that he was "tired of babying the Soviets" and that they needed to be "faced with an iron fist and strong language," as the only language they understood was "how many divisions have you." The new policy sought to liberate Eastern Europe from Soviet control. It assumed that Roosevelt's objectives there had been correct but that his methods had been inadequate. The Yalta agreements had stated that free elections would be held, but the Soviet Union had refused to allow them. Therefore, Truman assumed, the United States now had to take a new approach to the Soviet Union in order to compel that nation to honor its agreements and bring political reality in Eastern Europe into harmony with American democratic ideals.

The United States did not use the military to force the desired changes. In fact, the nation reduced its military presence in Europe very rapidly after the end of World War II and carried out a large-scale program of demobilization, even though the president and most of his aides highly valued military power. Truman believed that the nation must have a powerful navy and air force and a strong army reserve "because only so long as we remain strong can we ensure peace in the world." The United States could not "on one day proclaim our intention to prevent unjust aggression and tyranny in the world, and on the next day call for immediate scrapping of our military might." In spite of Truman's belief that military weakness had been one of the great mistakes of the past that must not be repeated, the administration rapidly demobilized the armed forces, influenced by pressure to bring the boys home, a belief that the nation could rely on the United Nations for security, and concern, which Truman shared, about large-scale government spending. The United States retained and developed one powerful military resource, the atomic bomb, but did not threaten to use it and quickly learned that mere possession of it would not force the Soviet Union out of Eastern Europe.

The Cold War in its early stage was largely a war of words, each side employing verbal pressure against the other. They clashed over Eastern Europe, Italy, Germany, Iran, Turkey, and other places, one side seeking liberation and the other control of Eastern Europe, each side trying to prevent control of Germany by the other and pursuing other objectives. Washington hurled critical speeches and diplomatic protests at Moscow, charged that the Soviets were not behaving as they had promised at Yalta, and denied recognition to some of the new regimes the Soviet Union supported in Eastern Europe. "We shall refuse to recognize any government imposed on any nation by the force of any foreign power," Truman insisted. He and his lieutenants also tried to bargain with the Soviet Union and to convince the Soviets that the United States wanted governments that would be friendly to the Soviet Union as well as representative of all "democratic" elements. The Soviet Union, however, regarded American interest in Eastern Europe as a threat to its security and another attempt at encirlement by capitalist nations. Soviet leaders charged Washington with using threats and at the same time tried to persuade American officials to accept the new situation in Eastern Europe.

Although Truman achieved a few of his objectives in 1946, he failed in Eastern Europe. Concerned but not swayed by American power, the Soviets tightened their control. They tolerated noncommunist but friendly governments that were established in several countries, including Finland, Austria, and Hungary, and pulled their troops out of pluralistic Czechoslovakia. In other countries, such as East

An atomic bomb test in 1946. *(U.S. Navy)*

Germany, Poland, and Romania, however, the Soviets tightened their control, using police action to remove unfriendly politicians from office and to pave the way for large Communist Party victories at the polls.

As the Cold War escalated, Truman sought to unify his administration's position on foreign policy by removing dissenters. Henry Wallace, an advocate of toleration of Soviet behavior in Eastern Europe and renewed efforts at cooperation, had warned that American hostility toward the Soviet Union was leading to war. "The tougher we get, the tougher the Russians will get," he predicted. "Our interest in establishing democracy in Eastern Europe, where democracy by and large has never existed, seems to her," he advised, "an attempt to reestablish the encirclement of unfriendly neighbors which was created after the last war and which might serve as a springboard of still another effort to destroy her." After Wallace publicized these views in September, 1946, Truman fired him from his job as secretary of commerce.

The Emergence of Containment

In 1947, the Truman administration's strategy for waging the Cold War shifted from liberation to containment, and Washington began to draw more heavily on American economic power to accomplish its objectives. This shift was produced by the interaction of situations in Southern and Western Europe, including economic depression and communist pressure, and American perceptions. In spite of American aid, Europe had not recovered from the war, and the economic conditions encouraged communists to believe that they could enlarge their power and influence. In France and Italy, the large communist parties reversed their policy, established at the end of the war, of cooperation with bourgeois governments, and in Greece, Communist-led revolutionaries waged a guerrilla campaign against the government. Each side in the Greek civil war received military and economic help from outsiders, the revolutionaries from Yugoslavia, Bulgaria, and Albania and the government from Great Britain. The possibility of renewed Soviet pressure on Turkey also influenced development in the area, the Soviets having indicated in 1946 that they wanted air and naval bases in Turkey and a share in control of the Dardanelles. Finally, in February, 1947, the British, weakened by World War II, announced that they would be forced to withdraw their forces from Greece by the end of March and could no longer afford to provide financial assistance to Greece and Turkey.

By then, the Truman administration had a fixed perspective through which it viewed developments in Southern and Eastern Europe. It strongly emphasized the Soviet Union's role in the world's trouble spots. To Washington, the Soviet Union appeared to have unlimited ambitions and substantial power, and it seemed eager and able to draw Southern and Western Europe into its empire by prolonging and exploiting the economic crisis which had followed the war.

In addition, the administration regarded Europe as an area of major political and economic importance to the United States. The United States could not be secure if a hostile power dominated Europe and could not prosper if political or economic conditions in Europe prevented Americans from obtaining materials, investing capital, or selling products there and in areas linked with Europe.

American leaders also assumed that economic conditions exerted a powerful influence on politics: "The seeds of totalitarian regimes are nurtured in misery and want," Truman maintained. If Europe remained depressed, he believed, communism would triumph; if Europe became prosperous, communism would lose out.

Finally, administration leaders believed that the United States had the capacity and responsibility to tackle problems such as those in

The Berlin airlift. *(National Archives)*

Southern and Western Europe. Only the United States had the economic strength needed to help the nations there. Thus, the United States must act.

The old concept of the "American mission" reinforced Truman's perception of the lessons of history to produce this sense of responsibility. In explaining the administration's position, the president spoke in the language of that mission, interpreting world politics as a struggle between alternative ways of life:

> One way of life is based upon the will of the majority, and is distinguished by free institutions, representative government, free elections, guarantees of individual liberty, freedom of speech and religion, and freedom from political oppression. The second way of life is based upon the will of a minority forcibly imposed upon the majority. It relies upon terror and oppression, and controlled press and radio, fixed elections, and the suppression of personal freedoms.

The United States had a mission to guarantee that the first way of life survived and prospered.

It would best do so, the Truman administration decided, through the containment policy, with the Truman Doctrine and the Marshall Plan as its main features in 1947-1948. In March, 1947, Truman proposed that the United States should "support free peoples who are resisting attempted subjugation by armed minorities or outside pressure" and asked that $400 million be sent to Greece and Turkey. In June, Truman's secretary of state, General George C. Marshall, called on Europeans to get together and "draw up a program designed to place Europe on its feet economically" and suggested that the United States would supply "friendly aid in drafting a European program and later support of such a program so far as it may be practical for us to do so." The president and his top lieutenant on foreign affairs proposed that the United States play a role of crucial importance in world affairs: It should use its economic power to halt Communist expansion.

Although the administration's containment policy enjoyed wide popularity, even in the Republican-controlled Congress, it did encounter some opposition. Henry Wallace was especially critical of it. Wallace attacked "the Truman-led, Wall Street-dominated, military-backed group that is blackening the name of American democracy all over the world" by supporting "kings, fascists, and reactionaries." He charged that the Marshall Plan was "a plan to interfere in the social, economic, and political affairs of countries receiving aid" and that the administration was willing to help only those countries that would accept "our kind of government" and subordinate their economy to the American economy. Labeling it the Martial Plan, he warned that it would lead to war; he proposed that it be replaced with a program handled by the United Nations.

Senator Robert A. Taft of Ohio, the Republican leader in the Senate, was another significant critic. Reflecting his party's strong desire to reduce government spending, he argued that the administration's proposals were too costly and likely to wreck the American economy.

Several factors enabled the president to overcome the opposition of Wallace, Taft, and others and gain congressional approval of aid to Greece and Turkey in May, 1947, and of the plan for European recovery the following year. The administration employed dramatic rhetoric to argue persuasively about the dangers of the international situation and marshaled impressive evidence of the seriousness of Europe's plight, the ability of the United States to supply the required aid, and the economic and political benefits the nation would derive from it. The administration also carefully cultivated leaders in and out of Congress and gained the cooperation of some major figures, especially Senator Arthur H. Vandenberg of Michigan, chair of the Senate Foreign Relations Committee.

Although hardly intending to do so, the Soviets helped Truman win the adoption of his program. While most European nations joined together to plan a coordinated attack on their problems, the Soviet Union withdrew from these efforts and forced the Eastern Euro-

peans to follow suit, fearing that the Marshall Plan would enable the United States to interfere in the internal affairs of European countries, gain control of their economies, and restore Germany as a strong, dangerous power. Had the Soviet Union been included in the program, Truman would surely have encountered greater difficulties in persuading Congress to finance it. In addition, Communists, with assurances of support from the Soviet Union, seized complete control of Czechoslovakia in Feburary, 1948. This dramatic illustration of the Soviet Union's determination to tighten its control in Eastern Europe in 1947-1948 created especially great difficulties for Wallace, who claimed that liberals and Communists could work together. In Czechoslovakia, at least, they had not.

The consequences of Truman's policy of containment and economic aid were immediately apparent. The policy strengthened anti-Communist groups in Southern and Western Europe and aided progress toward the establishment of a West German republic. It also encouraged the Soviets to tighten further their control of Eastern Europe, a process that encouraged Yugoslavia to rebel and establish itself as an independent Communist country in 1948. Progress toward an independent West Germany persuaded the Soviets to impose a blockade on land and water traffic into Berlin, a city jointly controlled by the Soviet Union, the United States, Great Britain, and France but inside the Soviet zone of occupation, and the United States responded by airlifting supplies into the western sectors of the city, resuming the draft, enlarging the air force, and stationing two groups of long-range bombers in England and Germany.

The Cold War escalated rapidly in 1947-1948, and the United States, under Truman's leadership, took on a large role in Europe, relying heavily on economic power backed up by air power and the atomic bomb.

Avoiding Depression

Chiefly significant for his role in the history of American foreign policy, Truman did not accomplish nearly as much at home, yet he did enjoy some successes there. For one, he avoided a postwar depression, a possibility many people had anticipated and feared. Recognizing that the Great Depression was ended by the war, not by the New Deal or private enterprise, pessimists feared that by stopping massive government spending and reducing the size of foreign markets, peace would bring depressed conditions similar to those of the 1930's.

The federal government did cut spending sharply once the fighting stopped, and furthermore Truman had difficulty establishing a domestic economic program. Conflicts inside the administration hampered efforts to do so, as Truman, seeking broad support, staffed the administration with both liberals and conservatives. Clashes with Congress over economic policies were even more significant. Less than a month after the surrender of Japan, Truman delivered a major message on domestic policy that in effect called for a revival of the New Deal. In the next year, however, he failed to persuade Congress to accept his proposals for a fair employment practices committee, a housing program, and price controls. Congress did vote for the Employment Act of 1946, a response to the fear of depression. The act declared the government's responsibility for maintaining high employment and established the Council of Economic Advisors to assist the president in promoting that goal.

In November, 1946, the Republicans gained control of Congress for the first time since the early days of Herbert Hoover's presidency. The electorate's decision was influenced by the bitter struggles over prices and wages and by dissatisfaction with Truman. Dominated by Republicans determined to reduce the size and cost of the federal government as well as the power of organized labor, the Eightieth Congress clashed with the president in many economic areas, including welfare, price control, taxes, agriculture, reclamation, and labor.

In spite of the sharp cuts in spending and the difficulties in shaping economic policy, a postwar depression did not occur, and the president, as well as the federal government as a whole, deserves some credit for preventing one. Federal spending, however, remained well above prewar levels, and the government administered programs established during the Roosevelt years, especially Social Security and the G.I. Bill of Rights, that gave the unemployed money to spend and kept people out of the job market. Furthermore, the administration and the Congress agreed on a tax cut immediately after the war, and the government maintained foreign sales at a high level through overseas relief, loans, and aid, and it helped American firms gain access to raw materials abroad.

With the private sector contributing even more than government, the postwar years were quite prosperous. During the first year, the economy suffered from many strikes, shortages of consumer goods, an increase in unemployment, and inflation, but the nation avoided truly massive difficulties. After a brief transition period, the economy began to grow again and continued to do so until 1949.

An Unexpected Victory

In spite of the economic accomplishments of these years, Truman suffered many political troubles. He not only faced an apparently reviving Republican Party but also his own party seemed to be disintegrating. The Truman-Wallace clash over foreign policy resulted in the defection of a bloc of liberals into the Wallace camp. Late in 1947, the deposed cabinet officer announced that he would run for president in 1948 on a third-party ticket. Campaigning strenuously, Wallace emphasized several themes: Containment was a creature of Wall Street and the military, was imperialistic, and was leading to atomic war; reform at home depended on peace in the world; a return to reliance on Roosevelt's United Nations would permit a revival of his New Deal; the groups opposed to reform—big business and the big brass—also promoted international conflict, so their power had to be destroyed before policies could be changed.

While losing the support of Wallace and the Progressives, Truman also lost support in the South because of his efforts to improve race relations. He had entered the White House with an interest in this issue, as African Americans had been active participants in the politics of Kansas City and Missouri and had educated him on some of their problems, needs, and desires and made him somewhat receptive to their demands for change. An increase in Southern white violence against blacks also affected his thinking after he became president, as did his concern about the American image in the world.

Truman's interest in the African American vote also helped make him a more active advocate of change in race relations than any of his predecessors had been. The 1946 congressional elections suggested that Northern and Western blacks, a rapidly growing group as a consequence of black immigration from the South, were moving to the Republican Party, partly because of Truman's failure to persuade Congress to pass civil rights legislation. Following the 1946 elections Truman established a Committee on Civil Rights to investigate race relations and make recommendations for government action. As the 1948 election approached, his top political adviser, Clark Clifford, told him that he must act on civil rights. African American voters held the balance of power in several key states, and no policies "initiated by the Truman administration no matter how 'liberal' could so alienate

A triumphant Truman holds a copy of the early edition of the *Chicago Daily Tribune* for November 4, 1948. *(Library of Congress)*

the South in the next year that it would revolt."

In the Truman period the leading proponent of change in race relations was the National Association for the Advancement of Colored People (NAACP). The organization moved into the political arena on occasion to battle for laws against lynching; discrimination in employment, housing, and public accommodations; and the poll tax. More characteristic, however, were its struggles in the judicial arena aimed at persuading judges to enforce the Fourteenth and Fifteenth Amendments to the United States Constitution. By the Truman years, the organization had acquired a large amount of experience in the courts, had developed a high degree of skill, and had enjoyed some successes. It also had greater resources than ever before as a consequence of its growth during the war from 50,000 to 450,000 members. Furthermore, in the new climate in race relations it had more friends to call on for help, some of whom filed *amicus curiae*, "friend of the court," briefs in NAACP-sponsored cases.

Late in 1947, Truman's Justice Department became one of the NAACP's new friends when it filed an *amicus curiae* brief in a restrictive covenant case brought by the NAACP. A step that had been proposed by the Committee on Civil Rights, this marked the beginning of the department's participation in the Civil Rights movement. The Supreme Court, before which the NAACP argued this and other cases in the Truman years, was highly receptive to the group's arguments. It was composed of men who had been appointed by Roosevelt and Truman, who were highly critical of the tendency of the Court before 1937 to invalidate economic legislation, and who inclined toward a belief that the Court should be more concerned with noneconomic issues such as civil rights. Not dominated by precedent, they were often influenced by legal theories about the need for law to reflect social and economic realities. In the spring of 1948, this sympathetic Court announced two decisions on civil rights cases. One did not attack segregation per se, but ruled that a state must provide legal education for blacks "as soon as it does for any other group." The other, the case in which the Justice Department had entered a brief, ruled that judicial enforcement of real estate contracts designed to exclude, on the basis of race and other qualities, persons from living in residential areas—in other words, restrictive covenants—constituted state action and thus violated the equal protection clause of the Fourteenth Amendment.

By the time the Court spoke on restrictive covenants Truman had taken an even larger step. In line with Clifford's advice and with the bold report of the Committee on Civil Rights, he delivered a special message to Congress on civil rights in February. He called for national action, including legislation that would give federal protection against lynching, protect the right to vote, prohibit discrimination in interstate transportation, and establish a permanent fair employment practices commission.

Leaders in the South protested more vigorously than Clifford had anticipated. They charged that Truman's proposals "would destroy the last vestige of the rights of the sovereign states," and they began to organize in the hope of forcing party leaders to behave more conservatively. Feeling betrayed by Truman, they blamed his actions on a new interest in African American votes, and they threatened to deprive him of the white Southern votes he needed for reelection. Hostility toward the civil rights proposals and toward advocates of civil rights legislation was widespread in the South; Southerners seemed divided only on the question of the steps to be taken. Although some insisted that the South must continue to work within the Democratic Party, others proposed a bolt from it. The latter group hoped their threats would restrain the Democrats and encourage them to adopt a weak civil rights plank and nominate a foe of civil rights legislation.

The administration worked to limit the scope of the Southern revolt. Advisers most fearful of the loss of black votes and the Wallace threat urged new steps in civil rights, but Truman for the moment believed that loss of white Southern votes was the biggest problem and counseled caution. At the Democratic convention of 1948, a spokesperson for the White House proposed a civil rights plank for the party platform that ignored the specific proposals Truman had made in February. Anti-Wallace liberals, with Hubert H. Humphrey of Minnesota as one of the leaders, battled successfully for a stronger civil rights plank that made the president's stand in February the official position of the party, commended his "courageous stand on the issue of civil rights," and called on lawmakers "to support our President" in guaranteeing a set of clearly defined rights.

The civil rights plank produced the Southern bolt that the administration had feared. Following its acceptance, thirty-five delegates from Mississippi and Alabama withdrew from the convention, and shortly thereafter the bolters joined other Southerners in a conference in Birmingham that nominated Governor J. Strom Thurmond of South Carolina for the presidency and adopted a declaration of principles that expressed Southern resentments and fears. The leaders of this States' Rights Party expected to obtain the South's electoral votes, defeat Truman, restore Southern influence in the Democratic Party, and use that influence to maintain the "Southern way of life."

Truman now appeared certain to lose the election. Before the Democratic convention, he had seemed so unpopular that several groups of Democrats had tried to substitute Dwight D. Eisenhower as the party's candidate, and he had been saved largely by Eisenhower's refusal to run. By midsummer, the pollsters agreed that the Republican candidate, Governor Thomas E. Dewey of New York, would win.

Truman, however, avoided defeat, largely because of the Democrats' basic strength, developed under Roosevelt, and his long and strenuous campaign. In his campaign, Truman sought chiefly to persuade Democrats not to desert him. He attacked the "do-nothing" Eightieth Congress and linked his Republican opponent with his party's congressional leadership. The president portrayed himself as a crusader rallying the people to save the gains made under the New Deal and pictured the GOP as dominated by big business and a threat to New Deal programs. To combat Wallace, he argued that the administration's foreign policy promoted peace, charged that the Progressive Party was dominated by Communists, and advised liberals that they must unite to be effective. To contain defections to Thurmond, Truman reminded Southerners of their need for economic programs of the New Deal type and of the dangers of Republican rule. He seldom discussed civil rights.

Truman did discuss that subject in Harlem, however, and just before the campaign began

he issued two executive orders calling for changes in race relations in the armed forces and the federal government. The Committee on Civil Rights had recommended an end to Jim Crow in the military, and Truman in his civil rights message had promised to take such action. The Southern revolt and opposition from the army had encouraged delay, but African American leaders, above all A. Philip Randolph, head of the Brotherhood of Sleeping Car Porters, demanded action and issued their own threats. The Republican platform criticized racial segregation in the armed forces, and the Democratic civil rights plank added to the pressure. In this situation, several liberal leaders advised the president to do everything he could to carry out that plank, warning that otherwise he would lose the black vote. In response, Truman ordered equality of treatment and opportunity in the armed forces, and when confusion arose about the order's purpose, he stated that it was intended to end segregation.

Truman contributed to his own victory through other uses of presidential power. In May, he had recognized the new state of Israel; in July, he called Congress into special session to demonstrate that the Republicans would not enact legislation which their party platform endorsed. Throughout the campaign period he both clashed with the Soviets and pushed for negotiations with them over Berlin.

In spite of the divisions within his own party, Truman was reelected—but by a small margin. He held on to most but not all of the states where the Democrats were traditionally strong. He was somewhat weaker in the East and South than Roosevelt had been but slightly stronger in the Midwest and Far West than Roosevelt had been in 1940 and 1944.

Truman's victory maintained Democratic control of the White House but did not demonstrate great popular support for the president himself. He received less than 50 percent of the popular vote, won by the narrowest margin—4.5 percent—in any election since 1916, and drew a much smaller percentage of the voters to the polls than had voted in the presidential contests of the Roosevelt period. The Democrats recovered control of Congress. The result seemed to indicate voter approval of established programs but little demand for new ones, except among African Americans.

Although the campaign was waged chiefly on domestic issues, the outcome was especially significant for foreign policy. It gave added support to the administration's policy of containment. Three of the four presidential contenders—Dewey and Thurmond as well as Truman—endorsed that policy. The only one who challenged it—Wallace—was destroyed politically, receiving less than 3 percent of the popular vote.

Changes in Containment

In his second term, Truman militarized and expanded the containment policy. By 1949 the United States had substantial military power, much more of it than it had had before World War II, but it had reduced the size of the armed forces sharply since 1945—from twelve million to one and a half million persons. Truman's early defense policy relied heavily on atomic bombs and long-range bombers to deliver them—and strictly limited military spending. To increase the efficiency of the armed forces, Congress, pressed by Truman, passed the National Security Act of 1947, which partially unified the armed forces, but it turned down his proposal to build strength through a system of universal military training.

Budgetary considerations heavily influenced thinking on military policy among members of Congress as well as White House staff members and the president himself. After Louis Johnson replaced James Forrestal in the newly created position of secretary of defense in 1949, they came to dominate the Defense Department as well. The economizers assumed that the United States had a limited amount of money to devote to national purposes. They feared that if the government tried to spend too much it would hurt the American economy, and a strong economy was absolutely essential in the fight against communism. They also assumed that European economic recovery was more important than the development of a large army. Since European recovery cost several billion dollars each year, less than $15 billion appeared to be available for the development of American military power. Confidence in air power made lower defense expenditures seem acceptable. As the United States had a monopoly on atomic bombs and long-range bombers, it did not appear to need a large army. Equipped with the latest technology, the new air force could guarantee that Soviet armies would not move; Soviet leaders would not be foolish enough to provoke an American attack upon the Soviet Union.

The assumption about the limits on American economic resources also encouraged the administration to focus on Europe at the expense of Asia, even though the advance of the communists in the Chinese civil war threatened American hopes for the development of good United States-Chinese relations. Washington made several efforts to influence the Chinese revolution, including diplomacy designed to halt the civil war and establish a coalition government, but decided against massive economic aid.

Truman did not seriously consider large-scale military intervention in China either. Such intervention had no significant advocates in the United States and no significant popular support. Americans had traditionally opposed military engagements on the Asian mainland, and postwar military policy supplied an additional restraint. Furthermore, at the time the civil war reached a crisis stage, Truman simply did not have a large army to order into combat in China.

While the United States made a relatively small effort to exert its influence, the Chinese communists gained control of mainland China.

Their victory greatly affected international relations, leading to closer ties between the Soviet Union and China and greater conflict between the United States and China. The communists denounced the Americans harshly for their intervention, small though it was, and the United States refused to recognize the new regime or to permit it to become a member of the United Nations.

The United States did maintain a presence in Asia, which was especially important in Japan. There, the United States monopolized the occupation, refusing to allow any other nation to participate, and used its new power in the country to reshape its life and block communist efforts to give their own form to it. Although Japan had been the most powerful country in Asia, most Americans derived little comfort from their nation's accomplishments there, and developments in China engendered a sense of great frustration.

At the end of the 1940's and the beginning of the 1950's, these developments, continuing tension in Eastern Europe, and the Berlin blockade, along with the substitution of Dean Acheson for George Marshall as secretary of state, persuaded the administration to make changes in its policies. Acheson, especially, pressed for greater reliance on military power. The North Atlantic Treaty Organization (NATO), a Western defense alliance whose members promised to cooperate militarily if the Soviet Union moved against one of them, was the first result. NATO nations did not embark on a military buildup, but rather relied heavily on American atomic power to defend the West. Nuclear weapons had come to be central to the policy of containment.

The acceptance of the NATO treaty by a wide margin in the Senate in July, 1949, illustrated the significance of Truman's defeat of Wallace. Wallace opposed the treaty; so did Taft. The administration, however, helped once again by Senator Vandenberg, triumphed over the opposition even though the treaty marked a significant departure from the nation's traditional opposition to "entangling alliances" in peacetime. The treaty's champions insisted that NATO would convince the Soviets that military moves would be too risky and thereby serve to prevent war.

Further militarization of containment followed quickly after the establishment of NATO, chiefly because of the Soviet development of the atomic bomb, which was tested by the Soviets in August, 1949, and announced by Truman the following month. Soviet possession of the atomic bomb appeared to alter the military situation fundamentally, as it challenged the West's reliance on the American monopoly of atomic weapons. Congress responded by accepting an administration request for the establishment of a military assistance program that would use American economic power to promote the military development of the nation's allies. In further response to the Soviet atomic bomb, Truman decided early in 1950 to build an even more powerful weapon of mass destruction, a hydrogen bomb, which could also be delivered by the United States Air Force.

At the same time, the administration developed a plan for a huge buildup of American forces. National Security Council-68 (NSC-68)—the bureaucratic label for the plan—called for a great increase in the defense budget, including a substantial expansion of the army. Championed by Acheson and widely endorsed inside the administration by the late spring of 1950, the plan assumed that the Soviet Union's capacity to expand its sphere of influence had been increased significantly and would become even greater if the United States and its allies did not develop more military power. The plan also assumed that the United States could afford to spend much more money on its military forces. Administration economic views, as well as the conception of the importance of military power, had also changed, at least for the champions of NSC-68.

By June, 1950, however, Truman had not yet decided to press for a greatly increased program of military spending and the development of an expanded military establishment including a large army as well as a powerful air force. Restrained largely by political considerations, by his doubts that the people and the Congress were ready to endorse the spending envisioned in the plan, he did not make the decision to implement NSC-68.

The Korean War

In the last week of June, 1950, Truman clearly extended containment to the Asian mainland. He decided to intervene militarily after the forces of North Korea invaded South Korea. Truman's interpretation of history dictated his decision. Viewing North Korea as a puppet of the Soviets, he saw the invasion as a Soviet-backed move against the free world. The attack, he maintained, demonstrated that "communism had passed beyond the use of subversion to conquer independent nations and will now use armed invasion and war." This view encouraged him to see the Korean situation as similar to ones in the 1930's, such as the Japanese invasion of Manchuria, not as a civil war or as an attack by one small country on another. He was convinced that he must avoid the great American mistake of the 1930's: the refusal to get involved significantly at an early stage in the development of aggression. United States intervention would halt aggression, discourage Communist moves in other places, reassure America's allies about its reliability, and avoid a larger war. The fact that he had not avoided the mistake of military weakness did not inhibit him. The president believed that success in Korea would not require great effort. Thus, although the United States was not well prepared for the kind of ground war that was raging in Korea, Truman decided to intervene. He secured United Nations sponsorship for the police action in Korea and then intervened first with air and sea power and then with ground forces as the South Korean army fell back before the forces from the North.

Truman's doubts about the wisdom of a military buildup and popular and congressional opposition to it quickly disappeared. Although Washington limited the war to the Korean peninsula, the war became the largest military effort that United States had yet made in Asia. The war grew in a step-by-step fashion, but still involved heavy losses on both sides. Soon after the fighting began, the United States engaged in a military buildup along the lines that had been laid out in NSC-68. Annual expenditures on defense were pushed above $50 billion by 1952, and the armed forces grew to more than three million men. The army, which played the largest role in the war, experienced the most substantial growth. American military policy no longer emphasized budgetary restrictions or placed heavy reliance on the new weapons.

The Korean War led to an expansion of American involvement elsewhere in Asia, including American economic aid to the French to help them win their battle against revolution in Indochina. The administration, however, continued to regard Europe as more important than Asia to its containment policy. The decision to intervene in Korea had, in fact, been influenced by Truman's desire to demonstrate to his European allies that the United States could be relied on for Europe's defense and to convince the Soviets that they dare not move against any allies of the United States.

At the same time the Americans fought in Korea, the Truman administration stepped up its efforts to develop Europe's military strength, hoping thereby to restrain the Soviets. The United States pushed plans for a great expansion of NATO forces, enlarged the military assistance program, and sent additional American troops and an American commander, General Dwight D. Eisenhower, to Europe.

Truman's view that the Korean War was part of a larger picture, and far from the most important part, led him to reject a proposal for a much larger effort in the Korea-China theater, a rejection that contributed to a major civil-military clash.

American forces, led by General Douglas MacArthur, won a spectacular victory over North Korea in September, 1950. Rather than stop after enemy forces had been driven out of South Korea, Truman, eager to take advantage of an opportunity to destroy a communist regime and unite the peninsula under a non-communist government, sent his armies north to liberate the entire country from communism. MacArthur advised him that the Soviets and Chinese would not intervene, at least not effectively, but as American forces advanced toward the Chinese border, the Chinese, seeing the American advance as a threat to their security, attacked with a heavy concentration of troops and pushed the American and Korean troops away from China and out of North Korea before the end of the year.

MacArthur now proposed a much greater military effort. He urged the administration to throw more force against the Chinese in Korea and to carry the war into China itself, using American air and naval power and the troops of Chiang Kai-shek in Formosa. The United States should seek a decisive victory that would liberate North Korea, reunify the peninsula, cripple China, and prevent it from seizing other areas. He had confidence that the United States could succeed in these efforts and that it should and could defend every place in the world that was threatened by communism. To him, the administration placed too little value on Asia.

Truman rejected MacArthur's proposals, regarding them as costly, dangerous, and unnecessary. The potential dangers included all-out war with China and even the Soviet Union as well, should it conclude that it must come to the defense of China. "We are trying to prevent a world war—not to start one," Truman

U.S. troops in Korea, 1950. *(U.S. Marine Corps)*

explained. Furthermore, MacArthur's proposal could tie the United States down in an area of secondary importance and furnish the Soviets with new opportunities for expansion in Asia, which, the administration assumed, was the Soviet objective. MacArthur did not accept Truman's rejection of his proposal; rather, he appealed directly to the public and the Republicans in Congress for support. The president considered this action a threat to his authority as commander in chief as well as to his foreign policy and, in April, 1951, removed MacArthur from all of his commands. As Truman explained, he considered it "essential to relieve General MacArthur so that there would be no doubt or confusion as to the real purpose and aim of our policy."

The administration had returned to the original goal of the war, containment. Washington now sought a negotiated settlement, limited American military operations to Korea, and employed no more force than seemed necessary to gain terms it could accept. In spite of public discontent with the conduct of the war, which grew as the fighting became stalemated in 1951 and efforts at negotiation failed to produce a settlement, the administration persisted in pursuit of its goal, confident that the defense of South Korea had many desirable consequences. "The attack on Korea was part of a greater plan for conquering all of Asia," Truman insisted, but the enemy had "found out that aggression is not cheap or easy," and "men all over the world who want to remain free . . . know now that the champion of freedom can stand up and fight and that they will stand up and fight."

The Fair Deal

As the Truman administration changed American foreign and military policies from 1949 to 1953, Truman battled for a Fair Deal at home. Although based on the New Deal's assumption that the government should promote desirable social and economic change, the Fair Deal was more than a mere continuation of the New Deal. It sought to strengthen the labor movement; to expand benefits and coverage under Social Security; to raise the minimum wage; to increase public housing, slum clearance, public power, and reclamation; and to institute federal aid to education and national health insurance. Finally, the Fair Deal envisioned changes in the farm program that would serve the interests of consumers and provide the basis for a farmer-labor alliance, and it expressed more concern about civil rights than had the New Deal.

In his fight for the Fair Deal, Truman enjoyed victories but also suffered defeats. His major success was the Housing Act of 1949, which included a public housing provision and slum clearance. Congress also enacted legislation to expand public power, soil conservation, reclamation, and flood control; increased the number of people covered and the benefits paid by Social Security; and raised the minimum wage. Congress did not, however, enact the new farm program, federal aid to education, national health insurance, Truman's labor program, or the civil rights proposals.

The Truman administration did influence Supreme Court decisions in the area of civil rights. Continuing to cooperate with the NAACP, the Justice Department submitted "friend of the court" briefs that helped to persuade the Court to hand down decisions in 1950 attacking segregation in interstate commerce and higher education and coming close to ruling that separate educational facilities could never be equal. Two and a half years later, Truman's Justice Department, in one of its last acts, filed a brief that advised the Court to overrule the separate-but-equal doctrine as it applied to elementary and secondary schools.

As commander in chief, Truman had a much larger role in the desegregation of the armed forces than he did in the judicial attacks on discrimination and segregation. In 1949, however, he learned that a directive from the commander in chief was not enough. His earlier order had led the Navy and Air Force to adopt a policy of integration, but the Army offered strong resistance, arguing that it must conform to the customs of the larger society to be effective and that African Americans were not well suited for combat. This resistance forced the president to apply pressure on the Army to persuade it to adopt integration as a policy, but even that pressure did not end the practice of segregation. Rather, the high casualties of the Korean War, compelled the Army to send blacks into combat alongside whites to replace other whites who had been killed or wounded. Integration worked. Whites and blacks in combat units got along well together, and the blacks fought more effectively than they had in segregated units. The experience changed the minds of army officers and key Southern congressmen.

Several factors prevented Truman from enacting more of his Fair Deal legislation. He was not as interested in domestic matters as he was in foreign affairs, he was not as articulate and skillful in managing Congress as Roosevelt had been, and he relied quite heavily on conservative advisers and administrators who resisted his reform proposals.

Truman also worked in a situation that posed major difficulties for a reformer. Depression had generated support for innovation in Roosevelt's early years, whereas Truman functioned in a relatively prosperous period. He faced a powerful conservative coalition in Congress that had already demonstrated that it could frustrate a president, even one as skillful as Roosevelt. Furthermore, as an advocate of change in race relations, Truman had to contend with the filibuster. It was used by Southern senators who took advantage of the interest that Truman and other advocates of civil rights legislation had in other areas as well. Pro-civil rights senators could tolerate inaction by the Senate for only so long before they felt compelled to give up on their efforts on behalf of

civil rights in order to move forward in other areas. Powerful pressure groups, such as the American Farm Bureau Federation and the American Medical Association, only added to Truman's frustrations.

The Korean War proved an additional obstacle to reform efforts. It commanded the attention of the president and the Congress. They believed that no matter was more deserving of their time and energy. Also, it increased the importance of Southern Democrats, many of whom occupied major positions in the congressional committees concerned with military and foreign affairs. Furthermore, as a far-from-popular war, it helped the Republicans gain seats in the congressional elections of 1950.

The Red Scare

An escalating Red Scare, generated by a widely held belief that communists inside the United States constituted a serious threat to the nation, was another obstacle in the Fair Deal's path. The scare distracted attention from reform, put Truman on the defensive against charges that his administration had been seriously infected by the "Communist conspiracy" and was "soft on communism," completed the destruction of the radical Left, thereby depriving reformers of helpful support, and raised doubts about the loyalty of liberals. Anyone who suggested that American life needed to be changed in important ways seemed un-American to many people in the early 1950's.

Communist penetration of the federal government had been insignificant, but communism in American life nevertheless became a large issue. Some historians have blamed Truman and his aides for McCarthyism, the extreme version of the Red Scare. Truman did make contributions, but they were hardly the crucial factor in the rise of McCarthyism.

The Truman administration responded to an already developing phenomenon and contributed to its further growth. In 1947, the president established a loyalty-security program for the federal government, and the next year, the Justice Department moved against the leaders of the American Communist Party, obtaining their conviction for conspiring to overthrow the government by force and violence. Three years later, the United States Supreme Court upheld the convictions.

During the 1948 campaign, Truman sought to exploit the communist issue to his own advantage. He presented his party as the effective foe of communism and charged that the Republicans were "unwittingly the ally of the Communists in this country." In support of his claim about vigorous Democratic opposition to communism, he pointed to the "strong foreign policy" that he had developed and that checked the "Communist tide," the domestic programs of the Roosevelt-Truman administration that prevented the communists from making "any progress whatever in this country," and his loyalty program that made certain "that Communists and other disloyal persons are not employed by the Federal Government." On the other hand, he listed "considerable opposition" from Republicans in Congress to his foreign aid program and to his efforts "to strengthen democracy at home," and he charged that Republican investigations of communism lacked "the democratic safeguards of the loyalty program." He also contended that the Communists backed Wallace because they wanted a Republican victory. A Republican administration's "reactionary policies" would "lead to the confusion and strife on which communism thrives." Truman's rhetoric and actions distressed civil libertarians.

In the early 1950's, Truman became much more critical of those who fomented the Red Scare, believing that it had taken on dangerous proportions. The anticommunist crusade had in fact turned on him.

If Truman's earlier behavior contributed to the Red Scare, clearly other factors were more important to its growth. A series of frustrating developments after 1948, including the com-munist victory in China, the development of the Soviet atomic bomb, and the Korean War, stimulated its growth. It also was influenced by several spy cases, by the unhappiness of many conservatives, and by the needs of Republicans. Conservatives, especially conservative Republicans, were opposed to the domestic changes of the Roosevelt-Truman period and recent developments in foreign affairs. Feeling cheated of deserved victories in the last three presidential elections, they employed their substantial power in Congress against the executive branch.

By the early 1950's, Congress led the anticommunist crusade and had passed several pieces of anticommunist legislation. The lawmakers enacted the McCarran Internal Security Act of 1950, which supplied the government with a battery of weapons to use against communists and other radicals. In 1952, Congress passed the McCarran-Walter Immigration and Nationality Act, with provisions barring the immigration of "subversives" and permitting the attorney general to deport immigrants with communist affiliations even after they had become citizens.

Truman vetoed these bills, convinced that the anticommunist crusade had become a threat to American freedom. "Instead of striking blows at communism," the provisions of the McCarran bill would, he maintained, "strike blows at our own liberties and at our position in the forefront of those working for freedom in the world." He referred to the deportation provisions of the McCarran-Walter bill as "worse than the infamous Alien Act of 1798" and "inconsistent with our democratic ideals." Congress overrode the vetoes; its ability to do so testified to the great strength of the Red Scare.

Early in 1950, a Republican senator from Wisconsin, Joseph R. McCarthy, had emerged as the most promising figure in the crusade against domestic communists, and his needs and skills contributed to the rise of the movement that he came to personify. He supplied the American people with a conspiracy theory to explain recent history that pinned the blame for apparent communist successes on disloyal men in the Democratic administration, especially the State Department. Hurling such charges, he made himself into a major figure in American politics.

McCarthy successfully identified himself with frustrated conservatives. He expressed in his own way a view that had long had adherents in conservative circles and was now more widely endorsed as a consequence of the American struggle against the Soviet Union and China. It held that radicals constituted a serious threat to American institutions. He did not create this view, but he made it his own. Conservative Republicans rallied to his cause, supplying much of his active support.

McCarthy encountered opponents, including Truman, but they did not check his rise. McCarthy and others like him, according to the president, were "chipping away our basic freedoms just as insidiously and far more effectively than the Communists have ever been able to do," and they had "created such a wave of fear and uncertainty that their attacks upon our liberties go almost unchallenged." Such arguments failed to rally the public behind Truman, perhaps because he and his aides had so frequently preached the dangers of communists themselves. Still, given the forces working against him now, Truman might have been even less successful in rallying support if he had not had an anticommunist record to which he could point. He would surely have accomplished more if the Senate had supplied strong opposition to McCarthy. Only a minority of senators, however, opposed their Wisconsin colleague, many of the Democrats were quite

Senator Joseph McCarthy. *(Library of Congress)*

tolerant of him, and some senators feared him, as he participated strenuously in the congressional elections of 1950 and gained a reputation for great political effectiveness. Most of the active senatorial opposition came from a small band of liberals, most of whom were new to the Senate and incapable of leading it.

The Loss of Power

By 1952, another presidential election year, Truman had become an unusually unpopular president. Only 23 percent of the people, according to a public opinion poll in late 1951, approved of his performance. This was the lowest presidential rating in the history of scientific polling, then nearly two decades old, and would not be surpassed by any president, not even Richard Nixon in 1974, until Jimmy Carter in 1980. Along with his other problems, Truman faced mounting public criticism over the scandals in his administration. During his second term, officials in various federal agencies had been charged with corruption, and in April, 1952, Truman forced Attorney General J. Howard McGrath to resign because of lack of zeal in investigating these charges. That same month, Truman further undermined his popularity when he seized major American steel mills in order to prevent a strike. The president had become frustrated both with labor's demands for wage increases, which threatened his wartime efforts to curb inflation, and what he considered management's intransigence. Therefore, he placed the mills under federal control. When the Supreme Court ruled, in *Youngstown v. Sawyer*, that Truman's action exceeded presidential authority, he returned the mills to private control and acquiesced in an eventual rise in wages and steel prices that he thought inflationary.

In such a situation Truman felt compelled to withdraw as a candidate for reelection. He was not prevented by the Constitution from running again, but he concluded that he should take himself out of the race. Later, he would suggest that he would have won if he had run, just as he had in 1948. The situation, however, was much more difficult than in 1948, only in part because it now included a famous opponent with a very attractive personality, Dwight D. Eisenhower.

Truman's plight was illustrated by the difficulties he had in finding someone who would go before the country as his successor. Early in 1952, he turned to the governor of Illinois, Adlai Stevenson, but found him reluctant to make the race. Stevenson's reluctance was not a reflection of weaknesses in his personality but of political shrewdness. Stevenson did not want to be Truman's handpicked successor, and he tried as much as possible to avoid having that label pinned on him. This act testified dramatically to Truman's lack of success as a political leader. He had not demonstrated the skill in coalition politics that had been anticipated for him by his champions eight years before.

When Stevenson finally accepted the Democratic nomination, Truman worked hard for him even though he had grown unhappy with the Illinois Democrat. The president's vigorous efforts in the campaign duplicated what he had done in 1948, but this time they failed. Truman could not maintain Democratic control of the White House.

Eisenhower swept to victory by a wide margin in an election in which an unusually large percentage of the eligible voters went to the polls and in which many Democrats voted for him. Each of the major candidates attracted many more voters than had Truman four years earlier. Supported by all classes, Eisenhower made a breakthrough in the traditionally Democratic South, made significant gains in the large Northern cities where Democrats had dominated since 1928, swept the suburbs, and restored Republican domination of the towns and rural areas in the Middle and Far West. Unhappiness with the course of American foreign policy and the war, fears of communism, and concern about corruption and inflation influenced the outcome. A positive factor was the confidence in and affection for Eisenhower.

Discontent with Truman contributed to the outcome. Just before he left office to return to his home in Independence, Missouri, only 31 percent of the people approved of his performance in the White House. He, however, looked upon himself as having been an unusually successful president.

A Sense of Success

In his farewell address to the American people on January 15, 1953, Truman expressed a feeling of success, not failure as president. Describing the president's job as big and hard, he emphasized his role as decision maker. "The greatest part of the President's job is to make decisions. . . . The President . . . has to decide. He can't pass the buck to anybody. No one else can do the deciding for him. That's his job." To Truman, it seemed, he had played that demanding role well. "We feel we have done our best in the public service," he continued. "I hope and believe we have contributed to the welfare of this Nation and to the peace of the world."

Dealing only briefly with domestic accomplishments, he emphasized economic success, maintaining that "we in America have learned how to attain real prosperity for our people." He also pointed with pride to his civil rights record. "We have made great progress in spreading the blessings of American life to all of our people," he insisted. "There has been a tremendous awakening of the American conscience on the great issues of civil rights—equal economic opportunities, equal rights of citizenship, and equal educational opportunities for all our people, whatever their race or religion or status of birth."

The chief significance of his presidency, Truman asserted, lay in foreign affairs. "The menace of communism—and our fight against it" he called "the overriding issue of our time." Then he added, "I suppose history will remember my term in office as years when the 'cold war' began to overshadow our lives. I have had hardly a day in office that has not been dominated by this all-embracing struggle—this conflict between those who love freedom and those who would lead the world back into slavery and darkness."

Truman was proud of the manner in which he had dealt with the Soviet challenge, as he saw it, regarding his moves as "great and historic. . . ." He listed his accomplishments as the withdrawal of Soviet troops from Iran after the United States took a firm stand, the freedom and independence of Greece and Turkey as a result of American aid, "the Marshall Plan which saved Europe, the heroic Berlin airlift, . . . our military aid program," and the defense pacts in the North Atlantic region and elsewhere. "Most important of all," he insisted, "we acted in Korea." That decision was, he believed, "the most important in my time as president," and the right one. Referring to the invasion of South Korea as a "test," he argued, "We met it firmly. We met it successfully. The

aggression has been repelled. The Communists have seen their hopes of easy conquest go down the drain. The determination of a free people to defend themselves has been made clear to the Kremlin." Truman maintained that the policies which he had inaugurated had "set the course" that would "win" the Cold War and that the sign of victory would be the ultimate breakup of the Communist system. There was, he argued, a "fatal flaw" in the Communist world. "Theirs is a godless system, a system of slavery; there is no freedom in it, no consent. The Iron Curtain, the secret police, the constant purges, all of these are symptoms of a great basic weakness—the rulers' fear of their own people." This weakness guaranteed victory. "As the free world grows stronger, more united, more attractive to men on both sides of the Iron Curtain and as the Soviet hopes for easy expansion are blocked—then there will have to come a time of change in the Soviet world."

For his own time, however, Truman did not claim that "liberation" was at hand. Yet he did claim that his policies "averted World War III up to now, and we may already have succeeded in establishing conditions which can keep that war from happening as far ahead as man can see." He declared that the "whole purpose of what we are doing is to prevent World War III."

Truman believed that war had been a real possibility during his years as president and that he had successfully avoided it because he had learned the lessons of history and had not repeated the mistakes of the past. Those lessons and mistakes were found in the years between the two world wars.

Truman divided the interwar period into two eras, each with different lessons. The first period was the 1920's, which taught the need for cooperation and trade with other nations. The second period was the 1930's, which demonstrated the need to respond to aggressors. During the 1930's, Truman reminded his listeners, "the Japanese moved into Manchuria, and free men did not act. The Nazis marched into the Rhineland, into Austria, into Czechoslovakia, and free men were paralyzed for lack of strength and unity and will." These were "years of weakness and indecision," and World War II was the "evil result." Americans, he said, should compare the indecision and inaction of the 1930's with "the speed and courage and decisiveness with which we have moved against the Communist threat since World War II."

Truman pointed particularly to the situation in Korea. "Here was history repeating itself," he maintained, comparing the invasion of South Korea "to the 1930s—to Manchuria, to Ethiopia, the Rhineland, Austria, and finally to Munich." The invasion was "another probing action, another testing action." If he had behaved as leaders had in the 1930's and had "let the Republic of Korea go under, some other country would be next, and then another." The evil consequences would grow: "The courage and confidence of the free world would be ebbing away, just as it did in the 1930's. And the United Nations would go the way of the League of Nations." Finally, the United States would be forced to fight a large-scale war as it had from 1941 to 1945. The lessons, however, had been learned. "Where free men failed the test before, this time we met the test."

Truman had not behaved as had Hoover, Roosevelt, and other Western leaders. He, like them, had faced the threat of world war. Their actions had contributed to the coming of such a war, but his had avoided one. Because he had learned the lessons of history and avoided the mistakes of the past, he had been forced to fight only a limited war even though his situation had been as dangerous as theirs—even more dangerous, as he was the first president to serve in the atomic age and a third world war would be even more destructive than the first and second.

The significance of the Truman period and the Truman presidency was to be found, Tru-

man suggested, chiefly in its contrast with the years between the great wars. His incumbency as president would have been enormously important, he implied, even if nothing of importance had taken place at home. Failure and frustrations, it appears, could have been tolerated there, but not in international affairs. Mistakes there could have been fatal. International affairs were paramount in the Truman presidency, and they had been well conducted.

Richard S. Kirkendall

Bibliographical References

Truman told his own story in his *Memoirs*, published in 1955-1956, and his daughter, Margaret Truman, backed him up in a biography published in the year after his death, *Harry S Truman*, 1973. Bert Cochran, *Harry Truman and the Crisis Presidency*, 1973, sought to revise the official view, whereas Robert H. Ferrell, *Harry S Truman and the Modern American Presidency*, 1983, reflected the view of Truman as national hero which emerged in the 1970's. For a full-length biography by Ferrell, see *Harry S Truman: A Life*, 1994. Robert J. Donovan's two-volume *The Presidency of Harry S Truman*, 1977 and 1982, and Donald R. McCoy's book of the same title, 1984, offer balanced accounts. Harold F. Gosnell, *Truman's Crises*, 1980, is a substantial biography. For a balanced portrait of Truman's complex personality, see Alonzo L. Hamby, *Man of the People: The Life of Harry S Truman*, 1995. David G. McCullough, *Truman*, 1992, a substantial Pulitzer Prize-winning biography, explores Truman's rise from humble roots to the presidency, examines the key decisions of his administration, and emphasizes Truman's character and integrity.

For insights into Truman's decision to drop the atomic bomb on Japan, see Ferrell, ed., *Harry S Truman and the Bomb*, 1996; Dennis Wainstock, *The Decision to Drop the Atomic Bomb*, 1996; and Samuel J. Walker, *Prompt and Utter Destruction: Truman and the Use of Atomic Bombs Against Japan*, 1997.

For analysis of the presidential election of 1948, see Gary Donaldson, *Truman Defeats Dewey*, 1998, and Harold I. Gullan, *The Upset That Wasn't: Harry S Truman and the Crucial Election of 1948*, 1998. References on the Truman presidency include Richard D. Burns, *Harry S Truman: A Bibliography of His Times and Presi-* *dency*, 1984; Richard S. Kirkendall, ed., *The Harry S Truman Encyclopedia*, 1989; Donovan, *Conflict and Crisis: The Presidency of Harry S Truman*, 1996; and Dennis Merrill, ed., *Documentary History of the Truman Presidency*, 23 vols. to date, beginning in 1995.

Dwight D. Eisenhower

34th President, 1953-1961

Born: October 14, 1890
    Denison, Texas
Died: March 28, 1969
    Washington, D.C.

Political Party: Republican
Vice President: Richard M. Nixon

Cabinet Members

Secretary of State: John Foster Dulles, Christian A. Herter

Secretary of the Treasury: George Humphrey, Robert B. Anderson

Secretary of Defense: Charles E. Wilson, Neil H. McElroy, Thomas S. Gates

Attorney General: H. Brownell, Jr., William P. Rogers

Postmaster General: A. E. Summerfield

Secretary of the Interior: Douglas McKay, Fred Seaton

Secretary of Agriculture: Ezra T. Benton

Secretary of Commerce: Sinclair Weeks, Lewis L. Strauss

Secretary of Labor: Martin Durkin, James P. Mitchell

Secretary of Health, Education, and Welfare: Oveta Culp Hobby, Marion B. Folsom, Arthur S. Flemming

Eisenhower's official portrait. *(White House Historical Society)*

During his administration, Dwight David Eisenhower, the thirty-fourth president of the United States, was much criticized by news commentators, political pundits, and students of the presidency. Critics attacked him for his alleged blunders, blandness, and laziness in office. A common image of the president depicted him as a mumbling, bumbling, stumbling, fumbling leader who preferred a game of golf or a bridge foursome to the duties of his office. A series of stories and jokes, at Eisenhower's expense, circulated even while he was in office. One story claimed that if Eisenhower died, then Vice President Richard Nixon would become president, but if Sherman

Adams (Eisenhower's chief of staff, who supposedly ran the administration) died, then Eisenhower would become president. Another story described an Eisenhower doll as one that, when wound, did nothing for four years. One of Eisenhower's own speechwriters described the president as a "walking debate" and an "oaf."

Yet to the majority of Americans in the 1950's, Eisenhower was known simply as Ike, and, having elected him to office in 1952 by a comfortable margin, they reelected him in 1956 by an even greater margin and would probably have reelected him to a third term if the Constitution did not prohibit his running again. Politically, he was the most powerful president of the postwar era.

What accounted for Eisenhower's immense popularity in the 1950's, even as some critics, including the majority of professional historians, held him in such low esteem? Undoubtedly, one reason was that he was a national hero, a poor boy of humble origins from Abilene, Kansas, who had led the Allied armies to victory over Germany in World War II. Another reason was almost certainly Eisenhower's famous grin and winning personality, which often masked his short and fiery temper. The "I Like Ike" buttons of the 1952 and 1956 campaigns expressed the genuine sentiment of most Americans.

Equally important was the fact that his administration reflected many of the broad undercurrents and overarching themes of American life in the 1950's. It is too simplistic to dismiss the 1950's as a serene, rather passive, decade much akin to the 1920's in its political apathy, conformity, and materialism. Much more complex than that, the 1950's witnessed the escalation of the Civil Rights movement, the start of the space age, and the beginnings of America's involvement in Vietnam. The 1950's was also an anxious period when Americans, haunted by the fear of nuclear holocaust, seriously considered a proposal to build an air raid shelter for every family in the United States and when schoolchildren were instructed in the event of a nuclear attack to protect themselves by hiding their faces and assuming a fetal position under their desks.

Yet those who characterize the 1950's in terms of its crassness, mediocrity, and political conservatism would not be entirely wrong. The 1950's was above all a period of unprecedented prosperity, mass consumption, and planned obsolescence, when consumers, encouraged by mass advertising, chose from a seemingly endless variety of goods and gadgets, many of questionable durability. It was also a period of mass culture, when television invaded the homes of even America's poorest families (some still without indoor plumbing) and, along with radio and motion pictures, produced forms of entertainment characterized by their drabness and humdrum quality. Finally, the 1950's was a decade whose political leaders generally accepted the political goals, programs, and policies of the previous twenty years but who took few political initiatives or showed little imagination of their own.

The Eisenhower administration mirrored the climate of the times. As later historians have shown, President Eisenhower was not the indifferent, ineffectual leader that his contemporaries often accused him of being. He was an activist president and a shrewd organizer and coordinator of men and women. He had a keen and often penetrating intellect, and although he preferred to operate quietly behind the scenes, he was fully informed and completely in charge of his administration. The common image of Eisenhower, even when he was president, as an essentially inarticulate and incoherent leader who was controlled and manipulated by his cabinet is simply false.

Yet Eisenhower was not an original thinker or an intellect. "Eisenhower's mind is, like his personality, standard-American," one observer noted. "It is unschematic, distrustful of fine distinctions into the realm of matter and things, concerned with the effect of ideas rather than their validity." Also, Eisenhower was almost a father figure in the 1950's, a president who stood above the political fray and a leader whose purpose was to watch over and assure continuation of the status quo affluence. His was a middle-of-the-road presidency designed to assure the good life at a time when it seemed obtainable to the great majority of Americans. (African Americans, Latinos, other ethnic minorities, and the most destitute were largely ignored—African Americans until the end of the 1950's, and the others until the 1960's.) Advocating moderate policies and an economy of abundance, Eisenhower rejected both orthodox Republicanism and New Deal statism. Instead, he sought an authentic American center, which would assure freedom and security by accepting the basic economic and social tenets of the New Deal, even as he remained a fiscal conservative in most matters. At the same time, Eisenhower was a strident anticommunist who continued the nation's basic foreign policy of containment, with the added flourish of threatening massive retaliation in case of communist aggression, but who nevertheless followed policies in many ways more restrained than those of subsequent administrations. In short, Eisenhower reflected perfectly the temper of the times even as he led the country with good sense and much prudence.

A Midwestern Boyhood

The future president was born in Denison, Texas, on October 14, 1890, the third son of David and Ida Eisenhower. Both his parents were members of the River Brethren Protestant sect, descendants of German-born farmers who had first come to Pennsylvania in the eighteenth century and later migrated to the Middle West. They had met while students at Lane University, a small school in Lecompton, Kansas, operated by the River Brethren. They were married at the college chapel on September 23, 1885.

A family quickly followed. In 1886, Ida gave birth to the first of her six sons, Arthur. A second son, Edgar, was born in 1889, followed by David Dwight (Ida later reversed the names to avoid having two first-name Davids in the family), Roy in 1892, Paul (who died in infancy) in 1894, Earl in 1898, and Milton in 1899. Times were hard for the Eisenhowers. As a wedding gift, David's father, Jacob, a successful farmer from Abilene, Kansas, had given his son a 160-acre farm and two thousand dollars, but David lost everything in a business he had started after his partner absconded with all of his cash. Bankrupt after he had paid off his creditors, David found a ten-dollar-a-week job with the Cotton Belt Railroad in Denison, where Dwight was born. With three sons, little money, and few prospects, however, David was persuaded by his family in 1891 to return to Abilene, where he found work with a local creamery and later with a gas plant.

Making hardly more than he had in Texas, David Eisenhower's financial problems multiplied as his family grew, but the family managed. Although Dwight wore clothes handed down from his older brothers and sold vegetables to more prosperous families on the north side of town (his family lived in the poorer south side of Abilene) to make some pocket money, his younger years were generally typical of boys growing up in a small Midwestern town at the turn of the century. Dwight enjoyed listening to the old-timers tell about the days when Abilene, the northern terminus of the Chisholm Trail, had been a wild frontier town, which probably explains his later love for Western novels. He was also a natural athlete who loved sports, fishing, and hunting. At Abilene High School, he played football and baseball and was regarded as something of a football hero. It was in sports that he first displayed some of his later talent as a leader. He organized Saturday afternoon games of baseball or football and helped form the Abilene High School Athletic Association to purchase athletic equipment for the baseball and football teams. He also arranged camping and hunting trips with his friends, taking charge of their money and purchasing necessary food and supplies.

In school, Dwight was a good student, particularly in history. His class prophecy was that he would become a Yale University history professor, whereas his brother Edgar would become president of the United States. As a sophomore at Abilene High, Dwight first met Swede Hazlett, the son of a physician and pharmacist who lived in the more affluent north side of town. The two boys would later become lifelong friends. Even as president, Eisenhower would write Hazlett long, introspective letters in which he would lay out his most private thoughts on pressing issues before him.

At the time that Eisenhower was graduated from high school in 1909, he stood about 6 feet tall and weighed approximately 150 pounds, having blue eyes and light brown hair that had not yet begun to thin. He had the coordination and gait of an athlete. Sometimes shy with girls, he was, for the most part, popular, poised, and remarkably self-confident. From his father, a stern disciplinarian who sometimes displayed a fierce temper, he had acquired his own short temper, but his mother had passed on to her son her warm personality and ingratiating smile and, perhaps, Ike's later concern for organization. Ida was a born organizer, who had established a regular routine of chores for her sons that included cooking, cleaning, caring for the family chickens, and tending to the family garden.

From West Point to the White House
In 1911, Eisenhower entered the United States Military Academy at West Point after working for a year to help put his brother Edgar through his first year of college. He had been persuaded to apply to both West Point and the United States Naval Academy at Annapolis by Swede Hazlett, who himself had been appointed to the naval academy. Although the two young

men intended that Ike (Dwight's nickname since childhood) would join Hazlett at Annapolis, when Eisenhower was offered an appointment at West Point, he jumped at the opportunity. In June, he left Abilene to enter West Point as a member of the class of 1915, "the class on which the stars fell" (fifty-nine of the 164 graduates of the class of 1915 would rise to the rank of brigadier general or higher).

Eisenhower's career at the military academy was undistinguished. Although he did manage to graduate in the top third of his class in 1915, he was known more for his skill at coaching football than for anything else. He had planned to play football as a cadet, but he injured his knee in 1912 and had to leave the team. Instead, he became a cheerleader and a coach of the junior varsity team. Evaluations of his potential as an officer were mixed. One instructor recorded that Eisenhower would enjoy army life but not excel, whereas another wrote that he "was born to command." His career as a cadet, however, made a lasting impression on him. At West Point he had learned the importance of discipline and dedication, had been taught about the structure of command and the responsibilities of leadership, and had come to appreciate even more the value of teamwork, something he had already learned from playing and coaching football.

Commissioned a second lieutenant in the infantry, Eisenhower was assigned to Fort Sam Houston in San Antonio, Texas. There he met Mary Geneva Doud (nicknamed Mamie), the daughter of a well-to-do Denver couple, who was spending the fall and winter in Texas. Following a whirlwind courtship, Ike and Mamie were married in Denver on July 1, 1916. Fourteen months later, Mamie gave birth to a boy, Doud Dwight, whom she and Ike called Icky.

During the next few years, Eisenhower was assigned to various army posts in the United States. The new officer was greatly disappointed that he did not see service in Europe during World War I. Instead, he became an instructor in the use of a new weapon, the tank. In 1920, he and Mamie suffered a personal tragedy when Icky died following a bout of scarlet fever. Still grief stricken over the loss of his son, Eisenhower was assigned in 1922 to Camp Gaillard at the Panama Canal. Ike's two years at Camp Gaillard were important ones for him, primarily because he was greatly influenced by his superior, General Fox Conner, a man versed in military history and theory, who passed on to his young subordinate much of his own considerable knowledge about tactics, logistics, reconnaissance, and intelligence. Later, Eisenhower would refer to Conner as one who "held a place in [his] affections that no other, not a relative, could obtain."

In 1925, Eisenhower was selected to the Command and General Staff School (C&GS) at Fort Leavenworth, Kansas, generally considered an essential step for high command. Although he was graduated first in a class of 275 and was later appointed to the Army War College (another step toward higher command), his major posting during this period was as a member of the American Battle Monuments Commission from 1927 to 1929, hardly a choice assignment for an ambitious officer. Furthermore, having reached the age of forty in 1930, he still held only a major's rank.

In the war game exercises at C&GS and in his work for the Battle Monuments Commission, Ike displayed a mastery of detail, a capacity to work under pressure and as part of a team, and a talent for translating concepts and ideas into action. These abilities did not go unnoticed by his superiors or by such senior officers as General John Pershing, who headed the Battle Monuments Commission and who even asked Eisenhower to help him with his memoirs. This task brought him into contact for the first time with Colonel George C. Marshall, who as chair of the Joint Chiefs of Staff during World War II would help catapult him upward in his career.

In 1929, Eisenhower was assigned to the War Department in Washington, D.C., where he served under the army's chief of staff, General Douglas MacArthur. Ike's three years in the War Department afforded him excellent training in administration and personal diplomacy, which would be extremely important to him later. He worked closely with MacArthur, writing many of the general's speeches, reports, and press releases. He also lobbied Congress and helped prepare a national economic mobilization plan, during the course of which he visited industrial plants and met with business leaders throughout the country. He also had major responsibility for organizing the Industrial War College to train officers in supply, and he worked with a combined executive-congressional committee organized to determine "how to take the profits out of war."

Eisenhower impressed MacArthur enough that when he left for the Philippine Islands in 1935 he took Ike with him. Eisenhower's four years in the Philippines were generally not pleasant for him. Mamie and his son, John, who had been born in 1922, remained behind in Washington, D.C., for a year, and then when they joined him, Mamie frequently became ill. Moreover, Ike was anxious to serve with American troops, and his personal relationship with MacArthur, which had been close in Washington, became increasingly strained as he clashed more and more with the general over MacArthur's grandiose, but financially unrealistic, plans for building a Filipino army. By the time he returned home in 1939, each man was glad to be rid of the other.

While serving in the Philippines, Eisenhower was promoted to the rank of lieutenant colonel, but as he told his son after returning home, he did not expect to be made a full colonel until 1950, at which time he would be sixty years old and unlikely to make general. Yet within five years he would be a four-star general and an internationally known figure. What changed Eisenhower's destiny was World War II.

Eisenhower gives orders to his troops on D day, June 6, 1944. *(Library of Congress)*

Events moved rapidly for Eisenhower as the army expanded following the outbreak of war in Europe in 1939. In 1941, he was promoted to the rank of colonel. Three months later, he was made chief of staff of the Third Army, which soon thereafter participated in large-scale maneuvers in Louisiana. Ike's tactical skills in these maneuvers won for him a promotion to the rank of brigadier general and brought him to the attention of General Marshall, now the army chief of staff, who in March, 1942, passed over 350 senior officers to promote Ike to major general. Two months later, Marshall appointed him commander of the European theater of operations (ETO) and, shortly thereafter, put him in charge of the invasion of North Africa, America's first major combat mission in the war. Following victory in North Africa, Ike was put in command of the May, 1943, invasion of Sicily and then the invasion of Italy. Finally, in December, 1943, before the

Italian campaign had been concluded, he was named commander of Operation Overlord, the invasion of Europe across the English Channel. By this time, Eisenhower had already attained the rank of full general.

Several reasons accounted for Eisenhower's meteoric rise in less than four years from a relatively obscure brigadier general to commander of the largest military operation ever conceived. These were, for example, Ike's relatively young age, his unbounded energy, his poise under pressure, and his ability to take command of a situation and make hard decisions. When Marshall first recommended Eisenhower for promotion to major general in 1942, he was looking for relatively young and energetic commanders with considerable initiative. Ike seemed to display these qualities, as well as those of geniality and supreme self-confidence. Almost everyone whom Eisenhower met liked him and trusted him implicitly.

Even more important, Ike emphasized teamwork and was able to bring together and work successfully with military and political leaders from all the Allied nations. He was comfortable with world leaders, and he had shown in North Africa that he could run a combined British-American operation. President Franklin D. Roosevelt, who chose Eisenhower for Overlord, appreciated these qualities of leadership.

The successful invasion of Europe on June 6, 1944 (D day), and the victory over Germany less than a year later turned Eisenhower into a world celebrity. He enjoyed overwhelmingly favorable press coverage. More than any other person, except perhaps Prime Minister Winston Churchill of Great Britain, he was associated with victory in Europe. Returning to the United States from Europe in June, 1945, he made a round of triumphant appearances. Everywhere he received a hero's welcome, and the first talk began to be heard of Ike as future presidential candidate.

At that time, however, Eisenhower had no interest in politics. Indeed, he shared the military's general bias against politicians and claimed to be apolitical. "Your conclusions concerning my attitude toward politics are 100 percent correct," he wrote Swede Hazlett in March, 1946. "I cannot conceive of any set of circumstances that could ever drag out of me permission to consider me for any political post." Instead, he accepted an appointment by President Harry S Truman in November, 1945, as army chief of staff, a position he held until 1948 when he retired from the Army to become president of Columbia University. As chief of staff, he advocated a universal military training and unification of the armed forces. While at Columbia, he opposed loyalty oaths for faculty members, and he instituted several new programs, including an Institute of War and Peace Studies.

As Eisenhower confessed to Hazlett before accepting the position at Columbia, however, he knew "nothing about the workings of a great University," and after moving to Columbia, he found himself increasingly isolated from the faculty, many of whom had opposed his appointment because he had no advanced degree. At the same time, war had broken out in Korea in June of 1950, the world appeared in crisis, and Eisenhower felt secluded at Columbia. When President Truman asked him in the fall of 1950 to assume the command of the newly formed North Atlantic Treaty Organization (NATO), he readily accepted, taking an indefinite leave of absence from Columbia.

Eisenhower served as commander of NATO from 1951 to June, 1952, when he returned to the United States to run for president. As the military commander who had directed the liberation of Europe during World War II, he was a staunch proponent of a strong Atlantic alliance, and as head of NATO, he worked relentlessly in the cause of collective security. Indeed, had Senator Robert A. Taft of Ohio, the likely Republican nominee for president in 1952, supported NATO, he might not have opposed him for the presidency. In June, 1951, Eisenhower met with Taft to discuss the European alliance. Dismayed by the senator's talk of limiting the number of divisions in NATO and by what he sensed as growing isolationism in Congress, Eisenhower concluded that Taft's advocacy of such a "Fortress America" foreign policy indicated an ignorance of world affairs. He later claimed that, had Taft indicated any commitment to collective security, he, Eisenhower, would have withdrawn his own name as a candidate for the Republican nomination.

Eisenhower had been under growing pressure for several years to make a bid for president. Although he continued to deny any interest in the office, he left his options open, meeting politically influential people and making public appearances that only increased the demand that he run. He had never declared a political preference, but his own conservative views on most domestic issues inclined him toward the Republican Party. He was finally persuaded to seek the office in 1952 by a group of moderate Republicans, led by Senator Henry Cabot Lodge of Massachusetts, that was determined to prevent the right wing of the party from gaining the nomination for Taft and that saw in General Eisenhower an extremely popular alternative whose international orientation coincided with its own. Resigning from the army in June, Eisenhower returned home to campaign against the Ohio senator, and at the Republican National Convention in July, he was nominated on the first ballot. As his running mate, he selected Richard Nixon, a conservative senator from California favored by the Taft wing of the party. Focusing on the issues of Korea, communism, and corruption, and promising to go to Korea if elected, he easily defeated his Democratic opponent, Governor Adlai Stevenson of Illinois, in the November elections.

Cabinet and Staff: An Organizational Approach to the Presidency

Eisenhower took the oath of office on January 20, 1953. During his first administration, American society was, for the most part, affluent, complacent, and self-satisfied. The journalist Marquis Childs described what he perceived to be the national mood at mid-decade: "No American boy was being shot at anywhere, our taxes had been cut, and we were on our way to making eight million automobiles in a single year." Although undercurrents of change in both foreign and domestic policy were already present, the widespread mood in the nation was to leave matters pretty much as they had evolved since the New Deal of the 1930's. For domestic issues, this meant retaining the broad outlines of the social welfare state developed under Franklin D. Roosevelt and Harry S Truman but not going much beyond that. In foreign affairs, it meant continuing the essential policy of containing Soviet aggression developed after World War II, although the great majority of Americans were anxious to end the no-win war in Korea.

The new administration was committed to these basic principles, although President Eisenhower thought it essential that government spending be cut and a cheaper way be found to limit Soviet expansion than by relying on large military forces. Eisenhower was a fiscal conservative who had long believed in the need to limit government spending and authority. Even as a young military officer, he had expressed occasional disagreement with his younger brother Milton, then rising through the ranks of federal bureaucracy, who saw a much more positive role for government than he did. After Ike returned to the United States from Europe in 1945, he became good friends with many of the nation's richest and most powerful business leaders, whose staunch conservative views on fiscal and other issues he found congenial. Increasingly, he inveighed against statism and talked about the importance of following a middle course.

President Eisenhower characterized his domestic programs as dynamic conservatism, by which he meant that he would be "conservative when it comes to money and liberal when it comes to human beings." To help carry out his programs, the new president picked for his cabinet a group of successful businessmen. (One journalist quipped that Eisenhower's cabinet consisted of "eight millionaires and a plumber," the latter referring to Secretary of Labor Martin Durkin, former head of the Plumbers and Steamfitters Union.)

Unquestionably, the two most influential members of the cabinet were Secretary of State John Foster Dulles and Treasury Secretary George Humphrey. The former, a senior partner in the prestigious law firm of Sullivan and Cromwell, was a longtime spokesperson for the Republican Party on foreign policy. Articulate and strong-willed, Dulles rejected the Truman administration's strategy of containment in favor of a new and bolder stance in world affairs that included the "liberation" of "captive peoples" under communist control. Such a program would include the threat of nuclear retaliation against aggression at places of America's own choosing. Commonly referred to as massive retaliation, or brinkmanship (going to the brink of nuclear war), Dulles's program really represented a variant of containment, which was supposed to reduce defense costs by relying on American air power instead of costly conventional forces. In fact, the policy of massive retaliation was tempered by the unlikelihood of atomic warfare in situations of local conflict, whose relation to Soviet expansion was not always apparent. Eisenhower, however, shared Dulles's view of the Soviet threat to the West, and the two men developed a close working relationship.

Much the same was true with Treasury Secretary Humphrey. An Ohio industrialist who had supported Taft in 1952, Humphrey quickly

Eisenhower's secretary of state, John Foster Dulles. *(Library of Congress)*

became one of Eisenhower's closest and most trusted advisers. Friendly and gregarious like the president, he was extremely bright and conversant on most policy issues. On fiscal matters, he was even more conservative than Eisenhower. As Treasury secretary, he made the reduction of federal spending and the balancing of the budget his overriding concerns.

In addition to his cabinet, Eisenhower depended heavily on his White House advisers and developed an elaborate staff system and chain of command very much along the lines of a military command structure. To head his staff, he named Sherman Adams, a former governor of New Hampshire. A tireless administrator, Adams determined more or less who got to see the president and what was placed before him for his perusal. In 1958, Adams was forced to resign his position as a result of a scandal involving the peddling of influence on behalf of a Boston industrialist, Bernard Goldfine, in exchange for several gifts. Eisenhower would later refer to the Adams affair as the saddest event of his administration.

Eisenhower also looked to his brother Milton as an unofficial adviser. The intellectual of the family and president of The Johns Hopkins University, Milton normally spent three or four days a week at the White House. He was held in complete trust by his older brother, who regarded him as his possible successor. Generally more liberal than the president in economic and domestic affairs, Milton also played an important role in foreign affairs, especially in cultivating closer relations with Latin America.

Domestic Affairs: Limiting the Role of the Federal Government

The basic conservatism of the new administration became clear soon after Eisenhower took office. The president believed that federal involvement in developing electric power and natural resources amounted to "creeping socialism," which he was determined to end. One of his early acts as president, therefore, was to sign a Submerged Lands Act, pushed through by a coalition of Republicans and Southern Democrats, which turned over offshore oil rights to the seaboard states. Eisenhower also jettisoned a Republican proposal for the federal construction and operation of a huge hydroelectric complex in the Hell's Canyon area of the Snake River in favor of a project by the privately owned Idaho Power Company.

The most sensational episode in Eisenhower's attempts to limit the federal role in the development of electric power involved a proposal by Edgar Dixon and Eugene Yates to build a privately owned and operated generating plant to supply the power needs of the city of Memphis. This would allow the federally operated Tennessee Valley Authority (TVA), which provided power to Memphis, to divert electricity to a plant of the Atomic Energy Commission (AEC) in Paducah, Kentucky. Eisenhower preferred this option to the construction by the TVA of an additional facility to supply the AEC's needs. In 1954, Eisenhower instructed the AEC to negotiate a contract with Dixon and Yates. The opposition by public power adherents to the contract was immense, however, and became even more so when discrepancies in awarding the contract became public, including a conflict of interest and the failure to let out the contract for public bidding.

The Dixon-Yates issue played a role in the 1954 elections when the Democrats employed the slogan "Nixon, Dixon and Yates" to embarrass the administration. They might have embarrassed the White House even more had not Memphis announced that it would build its own power plant. Claiming that he favored this type of municipal initiative in the first place, the president ordered the AEC to cancel its contract with the Dixon-Yates combine. When Dixon-Yates sued to recoup its losses, the administration was placed in the uncomfortable position of having to state that the contract was invalid because of a possible conflict of interest in awarding it. Public power advocates could find satisfaction at the defeat of this alleged threat to the TVA.

Besides his opposition to federal public works projects, Eisenhower's basic conservatism was evident in other respects as well. He tried, for example, to overturn Democratic farm policy, based on price supports for certain agricultural commodities, through a flexible farm-price support program, but this proved a costly failure. In his first State of the Union message, he announced that he would soon end all controls on prices and wages and then proceeded to carry out that pledge. He also abolished the Reconstruction Finance Corporation, established during the Hoover administration to make loans to banks, railroads, and other businesses. He refused to sign a construction measure, believing that it interfered with local autonomy, and he opposed amendments to Social Security providing for medical insurance.

Yet Eisenhower thought of himself and his administration as belonging in the middle of the road, and he accepted the basic outline of the welfare state that had developed in the last twenty years. Thus he signed into law a measure providing for the biggest single expansion of the Social Security system in history, which brought the self-employed into the system. He also fought successfully for an increase in the minimum wage from seventy-five cents to one dollar an hour, and he favored limited expansion of federal activity in housing, medical care, and education. In 1955, he signed into law a measure providing for construction of forty-five thousand housing units over the following four years, and he pushed unsuccessfully for plans to subsidize private health insurance programs and to make federal grants to the states for school construction. In addition, his administration established the Department of Health, Education, and Welfare (HEW), and it obtained legislation providing for the construction with Canada of the St. Lawrence Seaway and for the building of a forty-two-thousand-mile interstate highway system, the largest program of its kind in the nation's history.

McCarthyism

One matter left over from the Truman administration, which caused Eisenhower considerable anguish during his first term, was the so-called Red Scare, or the national alarm over alleged communists in government, charges that were most closely associated with the name of Senator Joseph McCarthy of Wisconsin. On this issue, the president's record was less than admirable. Although Eisenhower detested McCarthy personally, he and other White House leaders shared the common belief that Soviet espionage in the United States had jeopardized national security. For this reason, the president allowed Julius and Ethel Rosenberg, convicted of giving atomic secrets to Soviet agents, to be executed as spies on June 13, 1953, despite worldwide pleas for clemency. He also issued an executive order permitting the firing of seven thousand federal employees as security risks, and he forced the Atomic Energy Commission to withdraw its security clearance from J. Robert Oppenheimer, often referred to as the father of the atomic bomb, even though no evidence existed to show that he was disloyal to the country.

By his own actions, therefore, Eisenhower seemed to give substance to Senator McCarthy's charges that the United States was faced with an internal communist conspiracy. As a result of the 1952 elections, which gave Republicans control of Congress, McCarthy was in a position to promote his accusations. Appointed chair of the Permanent Investigations Subcommittee on Government Operations, McCarthy intensified his hunt for alleged subversives in the executive branch. In doing so, he seemed to ignore the fact that a president and administration of his own party were in office.

McCarthy objected to the appointment of Charles Bohlen as ambassador to the Soviet Union because he had been Franklin D. Roosevelt's interpreter at the Yalta Conference of 1945 during which, the Wisconsin senator charged, the United States "handed over" Eastern Europe to the Soviets. He attacked the Voice of America because, he claimed, Communist Party sympathizers had schemed to locate two transmitters where their signals could easily be jammed by the Soviets. He sent two aides, Roy Cohn and G. David Schine, to Europe to locate and destroy "subversive" books (such as the works of Ralph Waldo Emerson and Henry David Thoreau) at the libraries of the United States Information Service. He accused the army of "being soft on Communism" by promoting to major and then giving an honorable discharge to a dentist, Irving Peress, who had once pleaded the Fifth Amendment when questioned about communist connections. Calling before his committee General Ralph Zweicker, Peress's commanding officer, McCarthy told the general that he was not fit to wear his uniform. He also summoned Army Secretary Ted Stevens to answer questions before his subcommittee.

Eisenhower was outraged by McCarthy's charges. At Dartmouth College in June, he spoke out against book burners. Also, when a McCarthy aide, J. B. Matthews, accused the Protestant clergy of communist leanings, Eisenhower released a telegram to the National Conference of Christians and Jews objecting to Matthews's article. For the most part, however, the president took the position that he would not denigrate his office by getting "into the gutter with that guy." He also did not want to cause a break with the Republican right wing.

In the end, Senator McCarthy brought about his own undoing. In response to McCarthy's accusations that the Army was coddling communists, the Army brought charges of its own against McCarthy, the most sensational of which was that McCarthy had tried to blackmail it into giving preferential treatment to McCarthy's aide, Schine, who had been recently inducted into the service. The subsequent Army-McCarthy hearings, which were televised nationally, showed McCarthy to be a bully and a bore who evaded issues and constantly pleaded points of order. Thereafter, the tide of opinion turned against McCarthy. On December 2, 1954, the Senate voted to condemn him for "conduct unbecoming a senator." Three years later, with little public support left, he died. As a result of his activities, a new word, "McCarthyism," was added to the English language to describe unsupported, demogogic accusations of disloyalty.

As for the Eisenhower administration, it felt vindicated in its policy of generally ignoring McCarthy until time and circumstances brought about his downfall. Still, like Truman before him, President Eisenhower by his own actions and timidity, bore some of the responsibility for the climate of fear that sustained McCarthy as long as it did.

Brown v. Topeka: Beginnings of the Civil Rights Movement

On the issue of civil rights, the White House's record was substantially better, but not all that it might have been. As a general proposition, Eisenhower believed that every American citizen was entitled to vote and to equal protection under the law. As a military commander in World War II, he had experimented with integrating several army units toward the end of the war, and one of his first acts as president was to order desegregation of facilities in federal offices and on military bases. At the same time, however, the president thought that responsibility for civil rights should be left to the individual states, and in his memoirs he later made clear that he had little regard for those who "believed that legislation could institute instant morality."

In 1954, the Supreme Court under Earl War-

Central High School in Little Rock, Arkansas, September, 1957. *(Library of Congress)*

ren, whom Eisenhower had appointed as chief justice eight months earlier, concluded unanimously in a landmark case, *Brown v. Board of Education of Topeka, Kansas*, that "in the field of public education the doctrine of 'seprate but equal' had no place. Separate educational facilities are inherently unequal." A year later, the Supreme Court ordered federal district courts to speed up the process of desegregation of public schools. By 1957, several Southern states and the District of Columbia had complied with the desegregation order, but many others, including Arkansas, had not. When several African American students tried to integrate Central High School in Little Rock in September, 1957, Governor Orville Faubus ordered the National Guard to block their entry. Faubus maintained that his order was necessary to prevent violence on the part of an unruly crowd of whites who had gathered in front of the school. When violence erupted after the National Guard had been removed in response to an order by a federal judge, Eisenhower, who was vacationing in Newport, Rhode Island, federalized the National Guard and sent in army troops to reopen the school, which had been closed. This was the first time since Reconstruction that the federal government had used military force to protect the rights of African Americans. Even so, two years would pass before Central High School was finally desegregated.

Throughout most of the crisis, Eisenhower had displayed a singular lack of leadership. Privately, he deplored the Supreme Court decision of 1954, and he later called his appointment of Earl Warren as chief justice "the biggest damn fool mistake I ever made." In the summer of 1954, he told a newsman that he could not "imagine any set of circumstances that would ever induce me to send federal troops . . . into any area to enforce the orders of a federal court," causing opponents of desegregation to believe that they could resist desegregation orders without fear of federal intervention. De-

spite the crisis (the most serious domestic matter of his administration), Eisenhower had continued to vacation in Newport instead of returning to Washington, D.C., to underscore the seriousness of this confrontation between federal and state authority. Even his decision to confer with Governor Faubus in Newport while the turmoil in Little Rock was building was probably unwise. The meeting settled nothing, for after Faubus returned to Little Rock from Newport, he made further efforts to delay school desegregation. Meanwhile, he and his cause received national attention, and Faubus became something of a hero among forces resisting desegregation.

Even before the events in Little Rock, the Civil Rights movement, encouraged by the *Brown* decision of 1954, had begun to gather momentum. In 1957, Congress approved, and the president signed, a civil rights bill establishing a Civil Rights Commission and a Civil Rights Division within the Justice Department and empowering the federal district courts to hear cases involving violations of a person's voting rights. Although a much-amended and weak measure, it was the first such civil rights legislation in eighty-two years. In 1960, Congress passed, and the president quickly signed, a second and stronger civil rights act authorizing the appointment of federal referees to investigate voting rights violations and providing for stiff fines and prison terms for those violating a person's voting rights or threatening to obstruct a court order.

Even more important than this legislation was the fact that African Americans themselves had begun to mobilize in nonviolent protests to gain their civil rights in the South. In 1955, in Montgomery, Alabama, a black woman, Rosa Parks, refused to give up her seat to a white man on a city bus as required by state law and local ordinances. After her arrest, African Americans in Montgomery, led by a twenty-five-year-old minister, Martin Luther King, Jr., began a successful boycott against the bus line, which cut patronage by a third and attracted nationwide attention. In 1956, the Supreme Court declared the Alabama laws unconstitutional.

The Montgomery boycott was only the first chapter in the direct protest movement. In 1960, a group of African American students from North Carolina Agricultural and Technical College staged a sit-in at a Woolworth store in Greensboro when they were refused service at the lunch counter. The technique caught on immediately, and within the next few months, similar demonstrations took place in cities throughout the South involving, by the end of the year, fifty thousand blacks and white supporters and leading to partial or total integration of public accommodations in 126 Southern cities. By this time, Martin Luther King, Jr., had emerged as the undisputed leader in the campaign of passive resistance.

The Civil Rights movement extended over the two terms of Eisenhower's administration. The civil rights measures of 1957 and 1960 were passed by a Democratic-controlled Congress and would not have become law had it not been for the efforts of Senate Majority Leader Lyndon B. Johnson, who, probably more than any other individual, was responsible for getting the two bills through the Senate despite strong opposition from Southern legislators.

The Democrats had captured both houses of Congress in the 1954 elections and increased their majority in the Senate and the House of Representatives in 1956 and again in 1958. Yet Eisenhower and his middle-of-the-road policies remained popular among the electorate. In 1956, he easily defeated Adlai Stevenson, who had been renominated by the Democrats, by an even greater margin than in 1952, despite the fact that Eisenhower had suffered a serious heart attack a year earlier. In the November elections, Eisenhower received more than 57 percent of the popular vote and 457 electoral votes to Stevenson's 73 electoral votes.

Foreign Policy

If Eisenhower accepted the basic tenets of the New Deal and Fair Deal in social welfare legislation during his two terms in office and practiced a policy of what he regarded as dynamic conservatism, so too did he follow an internationalist foreign policy much along the lines that had developed after World War II. The president, however, was a consummate Cold Warrior and a strident anti-Communist, an attitude he shared fully with Secretary of State Dulles. Together, these two men raised the pitch of the Cold War rhetoric and followed a policy of confrontation with the Soviet Union.

Eisenhower's most pressing problem after he took office in 1953 was to end the Korean War, which had been stalemated for almost two years. To break the deadlock in the armistice negotiations over the repatriation of prisoners of war (POWs), which alone prevented an end to the war, the president issued a threat to the Chinese Communists that the United States would not be held responsible for failing to withhold atomic weapons if a truce could not be arranged. Whether it was because they responded to this threat of nuclear war, the Communist negotiators in Panmunjom agreed to the United Nations position on POWs, which provided for the return of prisoners on a voluntary basis only. With this issue settled, an armistice was signed on July 27, 1953, establishing a demilitarized buffer zone between North and South Korea roughly along the thirty-eighth parallel.

As Secretary of State Dulles explained in a 1956 article in *Life* magazine, the threat of nuclear war was the type of brinkmanship that was sometimes necessary to prevent—or, in the case of Korea, to end—war. "You have to take some chances for peace, just as you must take chances in war," he stated.

Vietnam: The Background to American Intervention

In his *Life* article, Dulles cited two other instances besides Korea in which the Eisenhower administration had resorted to brinkmanship, both in Asia. The first of these came in Indochina (Vietnam), where the French had been waging war against communist guerrillas, known as the Vietminh and led by Ho Chi Minh, a Vietnamese communist and nationalist. At the end of 1952, the lame duck Truman administration had approved $60 million in support for the French effort. By 1954, the United States was paying almost four-fifths of the cost of the war. Still, Ho Chi Minh's forces had gained the upper hand and controlled more than half the country. In a last desperate effort to salvage victory, the French sent their best troops into an isolated garrison north of Hanoi called Dienbienphu and dared the Vietminh to come after them. The French were convinced that in a conventional battle they could defeat the guerrillas. The Vietminh, however, brought heavy artillery up the mountains that surrounded Dienbienphu and began to inflict heavy losses on the garrison. By this time, the French were tired of the war, and it was clear that the fall of Dienbienphu would mean the withdrawal of French troops from Vietnam.

President Eisenhower believed that the fall of Vietnam would mean a victory for communist aggression and the failure of containment. The president compared the fall of Vietnam to a row of dominoes. "You have a row of dominoes set up, and you knock over the first one, and what would happen to the last one was certainly that it would go over quickly. So you have a beginning of integration that would have the most profound influence." Eventually, Eisenhower implied, all of Southeast Asia might fall to the Communists if they were not stopped in Vietnam.

What to do? In the end, the administration did nothing, but not before giving serious consideration to American military intervention in the war. Several of Eisenhower's advisers, including Admiral Arthur Radford, chair of the Joint Chiefs of Staff, and Vice President Richard Nixon, recommended an air strike, including the use of atomic weapons, to relieve the garrison in Dienbienphu. Admiral Radford's plan, known as Operation Vulture, called for a strike employing tactical atomic bombs by sixty American B-298's stationed in the Philippines, supported by 150 American carrier-based fighters. The attack against the forces besieging Dienbienphu would devastate the enemy, Radford believed, and rescue the French from certain defeat.

Both Eisenhower and Secretary of State Dulles rejected the use of atomic weapons in Vietnam but considered a conventional air strike. Eisenhower, however, established certain preconditions without which he would not intervene. These included the support of Congress and the backing of America's allies in Europe. Congress itself would not approve American intervention, so soon after the end of the Korean War, without the firm support of the NATO allies, especially Great Britain. Eisenhower and Dulles also insisted that any American intervention in Vietnam be preconditioned on the French promise to give the states of Indochina their independence. None of these preconditions were met. Prime Minister Winston Churchill of Great Britain told Eisenhower that he was unable to obtain his cabinet's approval of military participation, and the French refused to state that independence would follow the success of its armed forces against the Communists. Without the support of America's allies, Congress also refused to give its approval to military intervention. As a result, Dienbienphu fell to the Communists on May 8, without American intervention.

Following the fall of Dienbienphu, a new government came into power in France led by Pierre Mendès-France, who was committed to ending the war in Indochina. At a conference in Geneva that had been meeting since February to discuss Far Eastern questions, the

French agreed to a truce and a temporary partition of Vietnam at the seventeenth parallel, with the French withdrawing south of that line. National elections were to be held within two years to elect a government for all of Vietnam. The French would administer the elections in the South, and the elections would be supervised by an international commission. Neither part of Vietnam was to join a military alliance or to allow foreign bases in its territory.

The United States regarded the Geneva accords, which it did not sign (although it did promise to support free elections for the unification of Vietnam), as a major setback for the West. Before Dienbienphu fell, the Eisenhower administration had gone to the brink of a war to save that outpost. Eisenhower had resisted unilateral involvement precisely because he was determined to avoid a second Korea, but he would have considered using nuclear weapons if the Chinese had intervened in the war and if Congress and America's European allies had consented. On May 26, the president approved recommendations by the Joint Chiefs of Staff that called for "employing atomic weapons, whenever advantageous . . . against those military targets in China, Hainan and other Communist-held offshore islands" in case of Chinese intervention in Indochina. The threat of atomic warfare if the Chinese should expand the conflict or attempt to spread their control throughout Southeast Asia was transmitted to the Chinese through John Foster Dulles.

To forestall the possibility of further communist expansion in Southeast Asia, Dulles helped organize the Southeast Asia Treaty Organization (SEATO), an Asiatic defense community that included Pakistan, Thailand, and the Philippines, as well as the United States, Great Britain, France, Australia, and New Zealand. Although the organization existed only on paper and its members had no obligations except to consult in the event of threatened subversion, the United States included Cambodia, Laos, and Vietnam under its umbrella

in violation of the Geneva accords. Also, the United States began dealing directly with South Vietnam instead of through the French and sent huge amounts of military and economic assistance to bolster the government of Ngo Dinh Diem, a member of the Catholic minority and a staunch anticommunist who had spent several years in exile in the United States.

In effect, the United States replaced France as the principal guardian of Southeast Asia against communist expansion. By the summer of 1955, the French had left Vietnam. Ngo Dinh Diem announced that elections would not be held in 1956, realizing that he would lose a fair election against Ho Chi Minh. The United States fully supported Ngo in this decision, for the fact was that, although Eisenhower had avoided American intervention in Vietnam, he had made a commitment to a separate South Vietnam and to the Ngo Dinh Diem government that would shackle subsequent administrations.

Cold War Crises: Quemoy, the Suez, and the Hungarian Uprising

No sooner had the armistice in Vietnam been arranged than the administration was faced with another crisis, this time involving a threat by the Chinese Communists to "liberate" the small offshore islands of Quemoy and Matsu, controlled by the Chinese Nationalists. The crisis began in September, 1954, when the Chinese Communists started to shell the island of Quemoy, killing two Americans and raising the threat of an invasion. The Communists also talked about an early liberation of Taiwan (Formosa). In January, 1955, the shelling of Quemoy (and the nearby island of Matsu) intensified. In response, Eisenhower asked for and received from Congress the Formosa Resolution, which was virtually a blank check authorizing Eisenhower to take whatever steps were necessary to protect Formosa and the Pescadore Islands against attack, including the protection "of closely related localities."

Intermittent bombardment of Quemoy continued, and a major war scare ensued. In March, Secretary Dulles informed Eisenhower that the situation in the Formosa Straight was "far more serious" than he had realized. The administration gave serious consideration to using nuclear weapons against mainland China and might have done so had the Chinese actually launched an invasion of the islands. On March 12, Dulles went public with his threat of atomic reprisal. In a statement, the secretary spoke of "new and powerful weapons of precision which can utterly destroy military targets without endangering unrelated civilian centers." At a press conference a few days later, President Eisenhower said much the same thing.

These warnings evidently had a sobering effect on the Chinese Communists, for on April 23, Foreign Minister Chou En-lai spoke of Chinese friendship with the Americans and suggested a conference to discuss Far Eastern matters, "especially the question of relaxing tensions in the Taiwan area." In August, negotiations got under way in Geneva between American and Chinese diplomats. Although the conference settled none of the outstanding differences between the two countries, Chinese pressure on Quemoy and Matsu lessened, and the crisis subsided.

A similar crisis developed in 1958, after Chiang Kai-shek, the Chinese Nationalist leader, reinforced Quemoy and Matsu with one hundred thousand men, and the Chinese Communists began shelling the islands once more. At first, Eisenhower pledged to defend the islands, but under heavy criticism at home and abroad from those who did not believe that the islands were worth the risk of war, the administration backed down and compelled Chiang to renounce publically the use of force to regain control of the mainland of China. In return, the Peking government agreed to a de facto cease-fire.

Despite the policy of brinkmanship that the administration had followed in the Korean War,

Vietnam, and the Quemoy and Matsu crisis, Eisenhower feared a nuclear war and sought to avoid conflict with the communist world. Also, the president was alarmed at the high cost of the Cold War. In a speech in 1953, he remarked, "Every gun that is made, every warship launched, every rocket signifies, in the final sense, a theft from those who hunger and are not fed. . . . The cost of one heavy bomber is this: a modern brick school in more than 30 cities."

Eisenhower sought therefore to reduce tensions with the Soviet Union, and for that purpose he agreed to meet with the Soviet leaders in Geneva in July, 1955. Winston Churchill had urged such a conference after the death of Joseph Stalin in 1953, and a series of conciliatory gestures by the Soviet Union, most notably an agreement to end its military occupation of Austria, convinced Eisenhower to go to Geneva. Meeting from July 18 to 23, delegations from the United States, Great Britain, France, and the Soviet Union discussed the issues of German reunification, European security, disarmament, and East-West trade. None of these issues was resolved, and the main accomplishment of the meeting was an agreement to have each country's foreign minister consider these same questions at a meeting in the fall. Reporters, however, talked of a "spirit of Geneva," and the meeting did seem to represent a thaw in the Cold War, at least until October, when the foreign ministers' meeting ended in deadlock.

Indeed, relations between Moscow and Washington reached another low point in the fall of 1956 as a result of a new crisis, this time in the Middle East, and a revolution against Soviet control in Hungary. The crisis in the Middle East developed in July, 1956, when Gamel Abdel Nasser of Egypt nationalized the Suez Canal following the cancellation of American, British, and French pledges of aid to Egypt for the construction of the huge Aswan Dam on the Nile River. Nasser seized the canal partly to pay for the dam. About the same time, Nasser, an Arab nationalist, made threatening gestures against Israel. Great Britain and France, both large stockholders in the canal company, plotted with Israel, which wanted to launch a preemptive attack against Egypt, to retake the canal. On October 29, Israel attacked across the Sinai Desert toward the Suez. As prearranged, Great Britain and France demanded that Egypt and Israel stop fighting and withdraw from the area of the canal. When Nasser refused, they destroyed what remained of the Egyptian air force and occupied the northern third of the waterway.

Furious that the allies had not consulted with him before launching their attack and anxious that it might cause the Arab states to move closer to the Soviet Union, Eisenhower went to the United Nations. Along with the Soviet Union, the United States introduced a resolution condemning the action of its own allies.

It also applied pressure against Great Britain and France to stop the fighting by cutting off badly needed oil supplies from Latin America. (Mideast oil could no longer reach Europe through the Suez Canal.) Humiliated and resentful toward the United States, Great Britain and France had little choice but to agree to withdraw their forces from Egypt. As a result, Egypt maintained control of the canal, for which it paid $81 million. Nasser became a hero throughout the Arab world, and the Soviets increased their influence in the Middle East, even agreeing to build the Aswan Dam.

One reason Eisenhower had been so upset by the developments in the Middle East was that they distracted world attention from Eastern Europe, where the Soviet Union was putting down a revolution by Hungarian students and workers against its control. At the Twentieth Party Congress in February, Nikita Khrushchev, the new leader of the Soviet Union,

Soviet tanks in the streets of Budapest, Hungary, in 1952. *(Library of Congress)*

had shocked the world by attacking Joseph Stalin for his crimes against the Soviet people and by indicating a liberalization of Stalinist restrictions. Several months later, riots broke out in Poland against the ruling Politburo, and leadership was transferred to Wladyslaw Gomulka, an independent Communist. News of Gomulka's success spread to Hungary, and the students and workers took to the streets, demanding that longtime Stalinist leader Erno Gero be replaced by Imre Nagy. The Soviets gave in to these demands, but when Nagy announced that Hungary was withdrawing from the Warsaw military pact, which bound it to the Soviet Union, this proved too much for Moscow. Khrushchev sent tanks into Budapest and brutally crushed the revolution.

President Eisenhower hailed the Hungarian uprising as "the dawning of a new day" in Eastern Europe, and frequent talk by Secretary Dulles and others about "liberating" the captive countries of Eastern Europe and "rolling back" communism had given some leaders of the revolution cause to believe that they could depend on the United States for military assistance. There was never a chance, however, that Eisenhower would risk World War III by giving military support to the Hungarians, even if the United States had been militarily able to do so, which it was not. Talk about liberation was nothing more than that—talk. Taken together, the disarray among the Western allies caused by the Suez crisis and the failure of the United States—indeed its military incapacity—to come to the aid of the Hungarians made the fall of 1956 one of the bleakest for the United States in the history of the Cold War.

The Suez crisis revealed also the potency of Third World nationalism and the danger of growing Soviet influence among Third World nations. For the remainder of his administration, therefore, Eisenhower made the containment of communist expansion in the Third World one of his highest priorities. This meant continuing attention to developments in the Middle East and new emphasis on relations with Latin America.

As a result of the Suez crisis and the Soviet Union's expanded influence in the Middle East, Dulles and Eisenhower managed to get through Congress, in 1957, legislation authorizing the president to use military forces if deemed necessary to defend Middle Eastern nations that requested such aid from overt Communist-inspired aggression. This became known as the Eisenhower Doctrine. Employing the doctrine, Eisenhower in April gave King Hussein of Jordan $10 million and shifted the Sixth Fleet to the eastern Mediterranean in order to prop up Hussein's government during a period of political and economic instability.

The next year, the president sent American troops into Lebanon under the provisions of the Eisenhower Doctrine to forestall a threatened communist coup similar to one in Iraq. Actually, the unrest in Lebanon was internal, but in a television address, Eisenhower suggested to the American people that Lebanon was about to become a victim of indirect communist aggression. Eventually, fourteen thousand troops were landed in Lebanon, but their activity was restricted to Beirut and the adjoining airport. When the coup failed to materialize, the administration was subjected to criticism at home and to further complications in the Middle East, largely as a result of the fact that the Eisenhower Doctrine took little account of Arab nationalism.

Revolution in Cuba

After 1958, President Eisenhower showed increased concern about developments in Latin America. Largely ignored by the United States during Eisenhower's first term in office, Latin America had been almost totally excluded from such programs as economic assistance under the United States' foreign aid program. A series of developments culminating with a riot during

Vice President Nixon's visit to Venezuela caused the administration to review its Latin American policy. In 1958, the White House came out in support of regional economic aid for Latin America, central to which was the establishment of an Inter-American Development Bank. The basis for the Alliance for Progress program of the Kennedy administration was traceable to the Eisenhower administration.

Yet the administration's new sense of urgency in Latin America came too late to prevent a revolution in Cuba, led by Fidel Castro, from turning bitterly anti-American. Cuba had long been a haven for American investment and a playground for American tourists, but the president of Cuba, Fulgencio Batista, was a cruel dictator, and in 1959, Castro overthrew the Batista regime. Washington extended prompt recognition to the new Cuban government and made several friendly gestures. Castro, however, would not forgive the United States for its support of Batista and other dictators in Latin America. Relations between Havana and Washington deteriorated after Castro began to confiscate land and other properties owned by American citizens, conducted kangaroo courts and mass executions of former Batista officials, and leaned closer and closer to views held by communist supporters. By 1960, Eisenhower determined that Castro was a communist (which he certainly was by this time if not earlier) and gave the Central Intelligence Agency permission to plan for an invasion of Cuba by a group of anti-Castro exiles with the purpose of overthrowing the Castro regime. Preparations for the invasion were still incomplete when Eisenhower left office in 1961,

but by this time Khrushchev could boast that the Monroe Doctrine had "died a natural death." As one of its final acts, the Eisenhower administration severed diplomatic relations with Cuba in 1961.

The U-2 Affair

Eisenhower's administration ended on a somber note in another way as well. In November, 1958, the Soviets precipitated a crisis over Berlin by stating that negotiations on European security, a nuclear-free Germany, and the end of four-power occupation of Berlin had to begin within the next six months or Moscow would conclude a separate peace treaty with East Germany, which would then control access routes into West Berlin. The status of that city had posed a dilemma for the Soviet Union for many years. An estimated three million East Germans had escaped into and through West Berlin since the end of World War II. The glowing prosperity and glittering life of West Berlin was in marked contrast to the depressed state of affairs in East Berlin. Also, West Berlin was a center of espionage activity directed against the Communist world. What made Khrushchev decide to move against West Berlin in late 1958, however,

Fidel Castro at the United Nations on September 22, 1960. *(United Nations)*

In 1958, Eisenhower watches as the six members of the President's Commission on Civil Rights are sworn in. *(Library of Congress)*

was the placement in West Germany of American bombers capable of carrying nuclear warheads and the knowledge that American forces in Germany were equipped with tactical nuclear weapons.

In the United States, some in the administration wanted to increase the armed services and prepare for war against the Soviet Union. Eisenhower rejected such advice but held firm against the Soviet ultimatum. Fearful of provoking a nuclear war, Khrushchev began to back down. He extended the deadline in stages until the end of 1961. He also visited the United States in September, 1959, and arranged with Eisenhower for a summit meeting in Paris, scheduled for May, 1960.

The summit meeting never took place. On the eve of the conference, an American U-2 spy plane was shot down over Soviet territory. At first, the United States denied that it was

a spy plane, but when the Soviet Union released details of the flight and displayed the pilot, who had been captured alive, the American government was caught in a lie. Although Khrushchev, who wanted the Paris summit to take place, gave Eisenhower every opportunity to dismiss the U-2 incident, Eisenhower made full disclosure of the spy flights and implied they would continue. Furious, Khrushchev canceled the meeting.

It is perhaps not surprising, therefore, that the Democratic candidate for president in 1960, John F. Kennedy, harped on the accusation that the United States had lost much of its prestige and influence under Eisenhower. The Democratic candidate also accused Eisenhower of letting the United States fall behind in the development of intercontinental ballistic missiles (ICBMs). As Kennedy would find out after he took office, a missile gap existed, but it involved the Soviets lagging far behind the Americans. To a large number of Americans, however, the time was right to put a younger man in office, one who promised to revitalize the United States and bring it back to its paramount position in the world.

Yet the Eisenhower administration was not the do-nothing, standpat administration that some had accused it of being, and the 1950's was not the dull, dreary, and uneventful decade that others charged. Each of these accusations contained an element of truth but not the whole truth. Eisenhower had accepted and, in some respects, extended, the basic tenets of the social welfare state that had been established since the 1930's, and although he did not go much beyond the Cold War clichés of the previous administration, he was guided by the policy of containment with its burden of international responsibilities. Also, if relations with the Soviet Union were not much better when Eisenhower left office than when he entered in 1953, neither were they worse. It is also to Eisenhower's credit that he ended one war (Korea) and prevented the United States from becoming militarily involved in another (Vietnam) when many of his advisers were urging such a course. The Eisenhower administration gave the United States seven and a half years of relative peace, more than his predecessor and successor.

The Last Years

In January, 1961, Eisenhower, the oldest president in the nation's history up to that time, was succeeded in office by John F. Kennedy, then the nation's youngest elected president, after Kennedy narrowly defeated Vice President Nixon. Retiring to his farm in Gettysburg, Pennsylvania, Eisenhower continued to be consulted on foreign policy questions by the new president and then by his successor, Lyndon Johnson. He

also lived to see his former vice president elected to the presidency in 1968. Eisenhower appears to have become somewhat politically more conservative during the last years of his life, and he continued to advocate a strong anticommunist foreign policy. At the 1964 Republican National Convention, which nominated the right-wing Barry Goldwater for president, Eisenhower joined the right-wing extremists in excoriating the media for allegedly biased political reporting. He also supported the expansion of America's involvement in Vietnam after 1965 as essential to prevent further communist aggression. At the same time, he preferred Governor William Scranton of Pennsylvania or some more moderate Republican to Goldwater in 1964, and he remained committed to a broad internationalist foreign policy, which included considerable sympathy for the political and economic aspirations of Third World nations and an ex-

Soviet premier Nikita Khrushchev examines the wreckage of the U-2 spy plane shot down over the Soviet Union in May, 1960. *(Library of Congress)*

panded program of American foreign aid for less developed countries.

In 1968, the former president's health deteriorated rapidly after he suffered two major heart attacks, the second on the day after he addressed the Republican National Convention in August from his suite at Walter Reed Hospital. Although Eisenhower managed to live another seven months, he died peacefully on March 28, 1969, after giving his final command: "I want to go; God take me."

Burton I. Kaufman

Bibliographical References

The definitive biography of Eisenhower is Stephen E. Ambrose, *Eisenhower: Soldier, General of the Army, President-Elect*, 1983, and *Eisenhower: The President*, 1984. Still very good, however, are Kenneth S. Davis, *Soldier of Democracy: A Biography of Dwight Eisenhower*, 1945, and Herbert S. Parmet, *Eisenhower and the American Crusades*, 1972. Two illustrated biographies are Michael R. Beschloss and Vincent Virga, *Eisenhower: A Centennial Life*, 1990, and Douglas Kinnard, *Ike, 1890-1990: A Pictorial History*, 1990. A fine study of the Eisenhower family is Steve Neal, *The Eisenhowers*, 1984. Daniel D. Hold and James W. Leyerzapf, eds., *Eisenhower: The Prewar Diaries and Selected Papers, 1905-1941*, 1998, gives insights into Eisenhower's development as a military and political leader. Also well worth reading is Eisenhower's cor-

respondence with Swede Hazlett, which has been conveniently edited and annotated by Robert W. Griffith in *Ike's Letters to a Friend, 1941-1958*, 1984. Two standard treatments of the Eisenhower presidency are Charles C. Alexander, *Holding the Line: The Eisenhower Era, 1952-1961*, 1975, and Elmo Richardson, *The Presidency of Dwight D. Eisenhower*, 1979. For a brief evaluation of Eisenhower's foreign policy, see Robert A. Divine, *Eisenhower and the Cold War*, 1981. For more detailed coverage, consult Peter Lyon, *Eisenhower: Portrait of the Hero*, 1974. More critical is Blanche Cook, *The Declassified Eisenhower*, 1981. Robert R. Bowie and Richard H. Immerman, *Waging Peace: How Eisenhower Shaped an Enduring Cold War Strategy*, 1998, evaluates the long-term effect that Eisenhower's New Look strategy has had on American foreign policy. A highly acclaimed evaluation of Eisenhower's leadership style is Fred I. Greenstein, *The Hidden-Hand Presidency: Eisenhower as Leader*, 1982. Other surveys of the Eisenhower presidency are Chester J. Pach and Elmo J. Richardson, *The Presidency of Dwight D. Eisenhower*, rev. ed., 1991; Shirley Anne Warshaw, ed., *Reexamining the Eisenhower Presidency*, 1993; and Michael S. Mayer, ed., *The Eisenhower Presidency and 1950's*, 1998. Alton R. Lee, *Dwight D. Eisenhower: A Bibliography of His Times and Presidency*, 1991, is a comprehensive list of primary and secondary sources for further study.

John F. Kennedy

35th President, 1961-1963

Born: May 29, 1917
Brookline, Massachusetts
Died: November 22, 1963
Dallas, Texas

Political Party: Democratic
Vice President: Lyndon B. Johnson

Cabinet Members
Secretary of State: Dean Rusk
Secretary of the Treasury: Douglas Dillon
Secretary of Defense: Robert McNamara
Attorney General: Robert F. Kennedy
Postmaster General: J. Edward Day, John A. Gronouski
Secretary of the Interior: Stewart L. Udall
Secretary of Agriculture: Orville Freeman
Secretary of Commerce: Luther Hodges
Secretary of Labor: Arthur Goldberg, W. Willard Wirtz
Secretary of Health, Education, and Welfare: Abraham Ribicoff, Anthony Celebrezze

John Fitzgerald Kennedy, the thirty-fifth president of the United States, was the first Roman Catholic to occupy the White House and the first president born in the twentieth century. With his victory in 1960 at the age of forty-three, he became the youngest American elected to the presidency. A native of Boston and a 1940 graduate of Harvard University, he saw combat as a naval officer in the South Pacific during World War II. Elected in 1946 to the U.S. House of Representatives from Boston's Eleventh Congressional District, he served three terms and was elected to the Senate in 1952, where he served until his presidential victory in 1960.

Kennedy's official portrait. *(White House Historical Society)*

The Kennedy administration was noted for its atmosphere of youthful vigor and intellectual sophistication, which inspired comparisons with the popular Arthurian myth of Camelot. Its foreign relations were early dominated by the disastrous Bay of Pigs invasion of Cuba in 1961 and then by the Cuban Missile Crisis of 1962, wherein Kennedy successfully confronted the Soviet threat of Caribbean-based nuclear rockets. Domestic issues were characterized by a summons to a New Frontier of change, symbolized by such dramatic initiatives as the Peace Corps, but characterized more by a series of reform proposals, most of which failed to pass the Congress—such as federal aid to education, Medicare, civil rights laws, and tax reduction. Kennedy's presidential victory over Republican Richard Nixon in 1960 had been so narrow that he lacked a working majority for his programs in Congress. His administration's hopes for a major reelection victory in 1964, with a strong congressional mandate, were shattered by his assassination in Dallas on November 22, 1963.

Childhood to Manhood

John Fitzgerald "Jack" Kennedy was born in Boston, Massachusetts, on May 29, 1917, the second of the nine children of Joseph P. and Rose Fitzgerald Kennedy. Grandson of a poor Irish immigrant, Joseph represented the emergence of the successful third generation, whose family fortunes had prospered through a shrewd and industrious combination of tavern keeping, banking, and Democratic machine politics. Joseph himself considerably multiplied the family wealth while acquiring a deserved reputation for shrewd intelligence, creative enterprise, and political savvy as well as for unprincipled self-aggrandizement and ruthless manipulation. In 1937, he became President Franklin D. Roosevelt's ambassador to the Court of St. James, but he had an even greater ambition: The office of the president for his firstborn, Joseph P. Kennedy, Jr.

When Joseph, Jr., died in combat during World War II, John Kennedy became heir apparent to the Kennedy clan's political ambition. Unlike his athletic, gregarious older brother, Jack was a sickly, quiet, and shy child. Struck by scarlet fever when he was three, Jack remained a frail boy whose athletic contribution to the robust Kennedy image took the less physical forms of sailing and swimming. The Kennedy boys attended mostly elite, Protestant-affiliated boarding schools, the better to equip them for the challenge of Harvard and the Yankee-dominated world beyond. Young Jack attended Dexter, Riverdale Country Day, Canterbury, and Choate, prestigious prep schools where he was frequently ill and a mediocre student at best. Yet if he was more of a loner, less pushy and calculating than the favored older brother with whom he was invariably compared, Jack's introspection took a more subtle, thoughtful form. His illnesses reinforced a bookish tendency, and his lack of brilliance disguised a persistent and wide-ranging intellectual curiosity.

At Harvard, after Joe was graduated, Jack emerged toward his own mature individualism, his career there culminating in a published honors thesis that illustrated many of the attributes of the mature man's character. Originally titled "Appeasement at Munich," his senior thesis was awarded magna cum laude and then was quickly published as a book that achieved considerable celebrity, selling eighty thousand copies under the Churchillian title *Why England Slept* (1940). Its analysis was grounded in the lessons of history and reflected a Whiggish cast of mind that lamented the slowness and uncertainty of democracies when threatened by authoritarian regimes.

Kennedy's assessment in *Why England Slept* of the danger of unpreparedness was widely praised as balanced and objective rather than argumentative and as clearly independent of his father's more rigid isolationism (and alleged anti-Semitic tendencies). The Harvard senior's

The Kennedy family: Caroline, JFK, John, Jr., and Jackie. (*JFK Library*)

thesis also reflected Kennedy's elite advantages, including professional stenographic dictation and typing and editorial assistance from such journalistic notables as Arthur Krock and Henry Luce. His father provided personal access to such leaders as Sir Winston Churchill, the duke and duchess of Kent, Cordell Hull, Harold Ickes, William Bullitt, Herbert Feis, and Charles ("Chip") Bohlen. His thesis research in Harvard's Widener Library was reinforced by well-connected travels through Europe, the Soviet Union, the Balkans, Turkey, and Palestine. Being the wealthy son of Ambassador Kennedy had pronounced advantages, and Jack was beginning to enjoy the limelight.

World War II

Graduated from Harvard in the spring of 1940 with his career goals uncertain, Kennedy considered Yale Law School, briefly attended the Stanford School of Business Administration,

and then took an aimless tour through Latin America. American entry into the war, however, brought an ensign's commission and, through Ambassador Kennedy's timely and typical intervention with Admiral James V. Forrestal and Massachusetts Senator David Walsh, a stint in naval intelligence in Washington followed by assignment to PT boat training and combat duty in the South Pacific. On the night of August 2, 1943, commanding officer Kennedy's *PT 109* was rammed at night and sunk by the Japanese destroyer *Amigari*. Throughout the ensuing week of shipwreck and suffering, during which two of his crew died, the young lieutenant showed an extraordinary combination of courage, determination, stamina, and cool leadership that merited the intense loyalty of his men and a mantle of wartime heroism that even his subsequent detractors could not tarnish. During this ordeal, he also caught malaria, and his terrible night of swimming, tow-ing wounded comrades with the towrope in his teeth, compounded both his chronic back problem and an old adrenal insufficiency that dangerously weakened his resistance to disease throughout his life.

Congressman Kennedy

Ambassador Kennedy once explained to his biographer with characteristic bluntness the necessary transfer of presidential ambitions from Joe to Jack: "I got Jack into politics, I was the one. I told him Joe was dead and that it was therefore his responsibility to run for Congress. He didn't want it. He felt he didn't have the ability and he still feels that way. But I told him he had to." As President Kennedy recalled to journalist Bob Considine, "I was drafted. My father wanted his eldest son in politics. 'Wanted' isn't the right word. He demanded it. You know my father." Both the ambassador's claim and his son's deference underestimated Jack's ambition, but the patriarch's drive was a major determinant of the extraordinary family's political fortunes.

Jack Kennedy's path to the White House was marked from the beginning by a unique combination of advantage, tragedy, and luck—the latter taking the form in 1946 of Congressman (and former Massachusetts Governor) James Michael Curley's decision to relinquish his safe Democratic seat in the blue-collar Eleventh Congressional District and run for mayor of Boston. The formidable Kennedy campaign discouraged all serious opposition, and freshman Representative Kennedy entered the Republican-controlled Eightieth Congress with no particular mandate on the issues and with little discernible program beyond a call for federal housing assistance for veterans.

Congressman Kennedy's three terms in the House were curiously aimless and lackluster for a dashing wartime hero with alleged presidential ambitions. On domestic issues his voting record reflected an unimaginative, bread-and-butter New Dealism that befitted his blue-collar constituency. This included support for such standard items of the liberal Democratic agenda as the closed shop, an increased minimum wage, continued price and rent controls, and public housing. His major committee appointment was to Education and Labor, where he cordially joined fellow freshman and war veteran Richard Nixon. Foreshadowing their presidential rivalry to come, and also Kennedy's dilemma as a Catholic president, Kennedy supported federal aid to education, but only if it included such auxiliary services for parochial schools as school transportation, lunch, textbooks, and health care.

Democrat Kennedy dutifully opposed the Republican Eightieth Congress's Taft-Hartley Act to counterattack the New Deal's empowerment of organized labor, including support for President Truman's unsuccessful veto. Kennedy, however, sympathized with much of the Republican stir over "industrial communism," which mainstream Democrats called Red-baiting the unions, and he shared with Nixon and Wisconsin's Joe McCarthy an anticommunist fervor that was muted in his rhetoric, unlike theirs, but that found resonance among his constituency of ethnic Catholics.

To liberal Democratic loyalists, Jack Kennedy was an intriguing disappointment. They were troubled by his obliviousness to the demagogic danger they saw in McCarthyism, and they were irritated by his cronyism with fellow Irish Catholic McCarthy and by his and his father's poorly concealed support in 1948 of Nixon's successful challenge to California's liberal senator, Helen Gahagan Douglas. Furthermore, Kennedy's abiding intellectual interests were in foreign affairs, where the House provided little outlet. He appeared to be a part-time congressman, compiling one of the poorest attendance records in the House.

Not content to work as part of his party's minority team in Congress, he seemed a self-centered loner, noted for escorting beautiful women to elite social affairs. He was also notable for his extremely gaunt, sallow appearance and the crutches he used to ease the constant pain of an unforgiving back. If he often appeared lethargic and bored, the public was unaware of the terrible diagnosis made in 1950 that he had Addison's disease, a debilitating adrenocortical insufficiency that required daily injections of the steroid deoxycorticosterone (DOCA) through pellet implantation in his thighs. Kennedy told Joseph Alsop that he expected to die in his forties.

Senator Kennedy

Political prudence had dictated in 1948 that freshman Congressman Kennedy not run against the formidable Senator Leverett Saltonstall when the Yankee Republican sought reelection from Massachusetts. Yet in 1952 Kennedy did challenge the reelection of the aristocratic Republican Henry Cabot Lodge, Jr. In spite of the massive Eisenhower tide that year, Kennedy still defeated Lodge in a race determined less by sharply contested political issues than by Kennedy's maturing appeal as a candidate and the superiority of the Kennedy political organization. This victory marked a transition in the Kennedy staff from Joseph Kennedy's political operatives to Jack's own younger loyalists. The new, able lieutenants, most of whom remained with Kennedy through the White House years and came to be known as the Irish Mafia, included younger brother Robert, Lawrence O'Brien, Kenneth O'Donnell, and, after his recruitment as the new senator's legislative assistant in Washington, Nebraskan Theodore Sorensen.

Kennedy's Senate career began auspiciously in 1953 with his marriage to the elegant Jacqueline Lee Bouvier. Physically, however, his back miseries dangerously incapacitated him, and politically his refusal to take a stand on the Senate censure of Joe McCarthy in 1954 alienated the dominant liberal wing of his party. In 1955 he published *Profiles in Courage*, a collection of essays that celebrated courageous

statesmen in American history and that captured for Kennedy the Pulitzer Prize in biography the following year. Although Kennedy clearly bore responsibility for the original concept and ultimate content of the book, *Profiles in Courage* was primarily researched and written by an eclectic group of aides and consultant academics, most significantly the gifted Sorensen. Moreover, the Pulitzer committee had overridden its jury for biography, which had not even ranked *Profiles in Courage*. Nevertheless, the book was widely read and praised, and Kennedy's reputation as an eloquent and visionary young statesman was greatly enhanced.

In 1956 the Democrats renominated Adlai Stevenson to challenge the popular Dwight Eisenhower, who had suffered a heart attack in 1955. In retrospect it was fortunate for Kennedy's ambitions that his hard run for the vice presidential nomination, which Stevenson had thrown open to his party, was blocked by Senator Estes Kefauver of Tennessee. With a recovered Eisenhower presiding over peace and prosperity in 1956, Kennedy tried to aid his party's doomed ticket by making a nationwide speech-making tour, effectively promoting his expertise in foreign affairs. In 1957, he won a coveted seat on the Senate Foreign Relations Committee, where he attracted international attention for his anticolonialism, including criticism of French policies in Algeria and Indochina, as well as for his traditional Cold War appeals for a stronger defense against Soviet imperialism.

The year 1957 was a watershed one for Jack Kennedy's presidential ambitions. With Eisenhower ineligible to run for a third term in 1960, the Republican administration was jarred by a sharp recession, by corruption scandals centering on senior presidential adviser Sherman Adams, and by the Soviet launch of *Sputnik*. In the 1958 congressional elections, Kennedy easily defeated a weak Republican candidate, and nationally the Democratic Party tightened its congressional control with a stunning gain of fifteen seats in the Senate and forty-eight in the House.

By 1959, Kennedy was strategically positioned for the presidential contest ahead. He possessed not only a beautiful wife and a growing family but also a compelling public style and a striking persona in the new age of television. Cortisone treatments had greatly improved his health and spirits, and a minor side effect of facial puffiness had also transformed the old gauntness into a handsome visage. His talented staff continued to produce a cascade of speeches and essays that were published under his signature.

Moreover, as a sure-handed and now-veteran politician, Kennedy had skillfully neutralized the more dangerous domestic issues. On civil rights, he supported Senate Majority Leader Lyndon Johnson's leadership toward a centrist compromise in the Civil Rights Act of 1957. He thereby earned surprising support among Southern Democrats, who preferred his moderation to the strident liberalism of his Senate colleague, Hubert Humphrey of Minnesota. On labor, although his brother Robert had aggressively led the Senate staff investigation of labor racketeering, Jack Kennedy demonstrated expert command of the issues on the Senate's labor subcommittee. He steered a safe path between attacks on labor bossism to protect union members and the Republican administration's antiunionism, as embodied in the Landrum-Griffin Act of 1959. To reassure liberal Democrats, Kennedy fought the loyalty oath provision of the National Defense and Education Act of 1958. To reassure Protestants, he opposed general aid to parochial schools as a violation of constitutional separation between church and state.

Early in 1959, Kennedy quietly authorized Sorensen to begin organizing an academic brain trust out of Cambridge, including Paul Samuelson, Arthur Schlesinger, John Kenneth Galbraith, Archibald Cox, Walt Rostow, and Jerome Wiesner. He also flatly rejected considering the vice presidency and opened his files to James M. Burns, the Pulitzer Prize-winning biographer of FDR, whose sympathetic campaign biography of Kennedy pointed toward the presidential contest of 1960.

The Presidential Campaign and Election of 1960

Because President Eisenhower was barred from a third term in 1960 by the Twenty-second Amendment, the Republican standard fell to Vice President Richard M. Nixon. The Democratic field, in contrast, was wide open, with Governor Stevenson, the party's titular leader, having been twice defeated. American voters had historically turned to their governors for presidential candidates, but by 1960 the growth of federal authority since the New Deal, and the postwar prominence of foreign affairs, had focused the nation's political attention increasingly on Washington and especially on the Senate, with its treaty authority and international jurisdiction. For the Republicans, both Nixon and his ultimate running mate, Henry Cabot Lodge, Jr., had been senators (Lodge, Kennedy's victim in 1952, had been appointed by Eisenhower as ambassador to the United Nations). Among the Democrats, four senators vied for their party's presidential nomination.

First to announce his candidacy was Hubert Humphrey, the liberal champion, who was promptly challenged by Kennedy in a string of state primaries during the spring of 1960. The other two, Stuart Symington of Missouri and Majority Leader Lyndon Johnson of Texas, avoided the primary battles, hoping to bargain in a deadlocked convention. The amply financed and well-organized Kennedy organization, however, crushed Humphrey in a series of primaries beginning with Wisconsin on April 5, where the Catholic-Protestant voter split was salient, and running through Illinois, Massachusetts, Pennsylvania, Indiana, and Nebraska. The primary battle culminated in heavily Protestant West Virginia, where Kennedy forcefully declared his political independence from religious obligations and drove Humphrey from the contest with an impressive majority of 60.8 percent of the primary vote. By July, when the Democratic nominating convention met in Los Angeles, Kennedy's momentum was unstoppable. He climaxed his first-ballot victory with a surprise announcement that Johnson would be his running mate. (It was a dual surprise, with political veterans expressing astonishment that Johnson would relinquish the powerful majority leadership for the vice presidency.) On July 15 Kennedy's acceptance speech proclaimed a New Frontier of challenge to "get America moving again."

In the ensuing campaign against the Nixon-Lodge ticket, Kennedy stressed economic stagnation at home and declining U.S. prestige abroad. He especially criticized the incumbent Republican administration for allowing a "missile gap" to develop between the Soviet and American arsenals (current intelligence reports supported the alleged gap, but subsequent evidence has disproved it), and he chided the administration for allowing the transformation of Cuba into a Soviet base. The fall campaign featured four televised debates between Nixon and Kennedy, in which Kennedy performed impressively, especially on the first debate on September 26, when Nixon appeared tentative and insecure.

Kennedy met the religious issue head-on, opposing "unconstitutional" federal aid to parochial schools and telling the Houston Ministerial Association on September 12 that "I believe in an America where the separation of church and state is absolute—where no Catholic prelate would tell the President (should he be a Catholic) how to act and no Protestant minister would tell his parishoners for whom to vote." He met the medical issue

JFK with his brother and attorney general, Robert F. Kennedy. *(JFK Library)*

head-on also, falsely denying that he had Addison's disease but legitimately displaying a healthy constitution that bore up well under the punishing campaign.

On Election Day a record 68,838,979 Americans cast presidential ballots, and Kennedy emerged with a tiny plurality of just over 110,000. Nixon had carried twenty-six states to Kennedy's twenty-three, but Kennedy still won in the electoral college with a substantial margin of 303 to 219. The Catholic issue that had doomed Democrat Al Smith in 1928 had cost Kennedy an estimated one and a half million votes, but his huge Catholic majorities in the urban-industrial states had given him narrow pluralities there and hence large electoral totals. Also, Lyndon Johnson's tireless railroad campaign across the South—the train was nicknamed the "Cornpone Special"—had helped hold losses from the more conservative and Protestant South to such border states as Tennessee, Kentucky, and Oklahoma. Although Kennedy's campaign had largely avoided the controversial issues of labor and civil rights reform, he had successfully courted the African American vote, telephoning Martin Luther King, Jr.'s wife to express his sympathy when King was jailed in Georgia in October.

The overall result of the campaign was a shrewdly orchestrated presidential victory that kept intact the Democrats' classic but volatile post-New Deal coalition of labor, liberals, Catholics, African Americans, and Southerners. Kennedy's victory did little to help other Democrats; the party lost two seats in the Senate and twenty in the House. In many cases, these losses resulted from a recapture of normally Republican seats lost in the Democratic tide of 1958, although the Democrats were still left with safe margins in both the House (263 to 174) and the Senate (64 to 36). Such partisan majorities, however, did not easily translate into legislative program majorities, especially when such controversial issues as desegregation and civil rights divided the old Roosevelt coalition down the middle.

Presidential Transition: The Kennedy Team, Style, and Agenda

Kennedy aide Adam Yarmolinsky referred to the president's new cabinet as consisting of "nine strangers and a brother." The brother was, of course, thirty-six-year-old Robert Kennedy, who had finished the University of Virginia Law School but had never practiced law. Bobby's appointment as attorney general embarrassed senior Democrats but satisfied the demands of Ambassador Kennedy, who also engineered in Massachusetts the appointment of a seat warmer to hold Jack's vacated Senate

seat for Edward "Teddy" Kennedy in 1964. The leading stranger was Dean Rusk, whose appointment as secretary of state surprised a nation that had for the most part never heard of him, and revealed many of the determining characteristics of the Kennedy style of leadership.

Popular speculation for secretary of state had centered on Adlai Stevenson, but Kennedy had little belief in Stevenson's political acumen and toughness, and he offered him instead what the disappointed Stevenson privately called the "errand boy" position of ambassador to the United Nations. Kennedy's early favorite for secretary of state was Senator J. William Fulbright of Arkansas, the intellectually formidable chair of the Senate Foreign Relations Committee. When Fulbright's appointment was blocked by opposition from a combination of labor and civil rights forces who objected to the Southerner's support for right-to-work laws and racial segregation, and by Jewish insistence on a more stalwart ally of Israel, Kennedy turned to the little-known Rusk of the Rockefeller Foundation, who was a competent and loyal professional. President Kennedy, in effect, had chosen to become his own secretary of state.

The other cabinet "strangers" served political and constituent needs in the modern fashion, in which presidents attempt to govern primarily through their expanded and loyalist White House staffs, and "cabinet government" becomes a myth served largely through rhetoric. Orville Freeman for Agriculture, Luther Hodges for Commerce, Arthur Goldberg for Labor, Abraham Ribicoff for Health, Education, and Welfare (HEW)—all were visible Democrats who were politically well matched to their constituencies. For Treasury, Kennedy picked an Eisenhower Republican, Douglas Dillon, to reassure the business community. Kennedy's major new find was Ford Motor Company president Robert McNamara, who promised to get a grip on defense, was a Republican, and was not a Catholic.

Kennedy's cabinet reflected the tenor of the new administration. The secretaries were not liberal ideologues but rather safe, competent, elite men of influence. Together with Kennedy's energetic young lieutenants on the informally structured White House staff—Sorensen, O'Donnell, O'Brien, and Myer Feldman—who radiated (and cherished) a self-conscious toughness to lend muscle and respect to the romantic myth of Camelot, they made a formidable team.

When President Kennedy took the oath of office on January 20, 1961, his moving inaugural address, which owed a heavy debt to the talented pen of Theodore Sorensen, intoned the new litanies:

> Let the word go forth from this time and place, to friend and foe alike, that the torch has been passed to a new generation of Americans—born in this century, tempered by war, disciplined by a hard and bitter peace, proud of our ancient heritage. . . . Let every nation know . . . that we shall pay any price, bear any burden, meet any hardship, support any friend, oppose any foe, to insure the survival and the success of liberty. . . . So let us begin anew—Let us never negotiate out of fear. But let us never fear to negotiate. . . . And so, my fellow Americans: ask not what your country can do for you—ask what you can do for your country.

The New Frontier and the Eighty-seventh Congress

The New Frontier that nominee Kennedy had proclaimed in Los Angeles and that President Kennedy enunciated in his inaugural address and state messages in early 1961 reflected far more a tone and spirit than a specific legislative program. Kennedy's first one hundred days were characterized by superbly performed press conferences, where the charismatic young president with the arresting Boston accent charmed millions of television viewers with his crisp sense of command and his witty spontaneity. Not legislative bills and congressional lobbying but executive orders set the tone: appoint more African Americans, launch the Peace Corps, negotiate on nuclear arms control. Jacqueline Kennedy redecorated the White House, and the Kennedys graced it with Nobel laureates and artists of world renown.

Given his executive style and weak political margin in the Eighty-seventh Congress, Kennedy was generally successful on Capitol Hill in exercising his presidential prerogatives in foreign affairs and unsuccessful in his domestic initiatives. His early victories included establishing the Peace Corps and the Alliance for Progress, creating the U.S. Arms Control and Disarmament Agency, achieving five-year loans for developing nations, gaining U.S. membership in the Organization for Economic Cooperation and Development. Kennedy also greatly increased the budget appropriations of the National Aeronautics and Space Administration (NASA) for the moon-shot race with the Soviets (from $915 million in fiscal 1961 to $3.7 billion in fiscal 1963) and especially for the Pentagon (topping $48 billion by fiscal 1963, an increase of $8 billion since fiscal 1961). An instinctive fiscal conservative, he nevertheless pursued expansionist fiscal and monetary policies, increasing federal expenditures from $81.5 billion in fiscal 1961 to $94.3 billion in fiscal 1963. In the second congressional session he added the major Trade Expansion Act of 1962 and a United Nations bond authorization.

In domestic policy, Kennedy's successes were largely confined to incremental increases in traditional New Deal programs that held special appeal to an overwhelmingly Democratic Congress, whose new public works projects and federal appointments would be controlled by a Democratic president and traditional patronage arrangements. These achievements included raising the minimum wage to $1.25 an hour, aiding depressed areas (as promised in the crucial West Virginia primary), increasing Social Security benefits, expanding the interstate highway and water antipollution programs, creating seventy-three new federal judgeships, and passing a $4.9 billion omnibus housing bill. Kennedy's congressional achievements also included the 1962 establishment of the Communications Satellite Corporation, the legislation for which was passed by invoking the first cloture on a Senate filibuster since 1927 (the administration ironically sought cloture against filibustering Senate liberals, who were objecting to a "giveaway" of the public's airwave rights).

Still, Kennedy failed to make a major breakthrough in domestic legislation, and by the end of the Eighty-seventh Congress routine defeats of his major program initiatives were becoming embarrassing. These included such key initiatives as federal aid to education, a Department of Urban Affairs (which promised to the cabinet the first African American, Housing and Home Finance Administrator Robert Weaver), Medicare, urban mass transit, youth unemployment programs, and a change in Senate Rule 22 to make filibusters easier to terminate. In 1961 and 1962 Kennedy submitted nine executive reorganization plans, and Congress rejected four of them. In the face of a burgeoning Civil Rights movement with increasingly explosive potential, Kennedy did not even offer the country a civil rights bill; he merely mildly endorsed efforts to ban the poll tax and reduce the disfranchising effects of literacy tests in federal elections.

The explanation for these failures lies in a combination of Kennedy's beliefs and style, congressional circumstances, and public opinion. Given the president's dominant interest in foreign affairs, his lack of interest in liberal domestic reform, and his tendency to offer and explain programs to Congress but not to lobby hard for them, the senior congressmen's powerful committees felt free to ignore his more controversial importunings. The White House legislative staff under Sorensen and O'Brien was superior, but Kennedy withheld from the

congressional fray both himself and his redoubtable vice president and former legislative wizard, Lyndon Johnson. Yet his selection of Johnson, so crucial to his narrow victory, had led to the appointment of the mild-mannered Mike Mansfield of Montana as Senate majority leader. In the more troublesome House, where the conservative coalition between Republicans and Southern Democrats was stronger, Kennedy persuaded the powerful speaker, "Mr. Sam" Rayburn of Texas, to pack the twelve-member House Rules Committee by adding two Democrats and one Republican, loosening the obstructionist grip of the gateway committee's conservative chair, Democrat Howard Smith of Virginia. Rayburn, however, died of cancer in November, 1961, and the new speaker was John W. McCormack of Massachusetts, whose coolness toward the Kennedys was stronger than his grip on the House.

The classic example of Kennedy's dilemma in domestic politics was his repeated and embarrassing failure to secure passage of his promised bill to aid education. Despite the pressures of *Sputnik* and the baby boom, the Kennedy administration was unable to overcome the whiplash of opposition generated by three interlocked issues: religion, school desegregation, and federal control. This translated politically into fear of taxpayer support of parochial (especially Catholic) schools, financial coercion in school desegregation, and control of local school curricula by federal bureaucrats. Such fears created an unlikely coalition of Roman Catholics, Southern Democrats, and conservative Republicans that blocked all efforts at federal school aid throughout the Kennedy administration and symbolized the administration's fecklessness in domestic affairs.

The Bay of Pigs, the Berlin Wall, and the Cuban Missile Crisis

Kennedy's early performance as an untested world leader was judged less by what he formally proposed to the American people and to Congress than by the consequences of his covert initiatives and the aggressive probings of the Soviet Union. The first international crisis broke early and disastrously when on April 17, 1961, a force of twelve hundred anti-Castro refugees trained by the Central Intelligence Agency (CIA) invaded Cuba at the Bay of Pigs. Despite Kennedy's insistence on a covert operation, American participation was widely known even before the invasion. Partly for that reason, Kennedy reduced the three air strikes planned for the operation to one (and cut the number of planes in it) and refused to approve additional air support once the invasion began. Fidel Castro's army and militia of two hundred thousand men easily crushed and captured the inept invaders and humiliated the new American president. Kennedy had inherited the project from Eisenhower and had yielded to the

assurances of CIA Director Allen Dulles that Castro could be overthrown as easily as the Arbenz Communists in Guatemala in 1954. Kennedy cut his losses by an early admission of defeat and responsibility, and paradoxically his popularity rating soared in the face of the Cuban debacle. He had, however, executed the implausible invasion plan, formally denied U.S. complicity, misled Ambassador Stevenson, and resisted not only the warnings of such liberal advisers as Stevenson, Chester Bowles, and Arthur Schlesinger but also the cautions of such old-school statesmen as Dean Acheson, Fulbright, and Rusk. Thus humiliated by the despised Castro, Kennedy replaced Dulles at the CIA with another Republican conservative, John A. McCone, and approved a clandestine anti-Castro operation code named Mongoose, which included bizarre attempts to assassinate

JFK examines the combat flag of the 2506th Cuban Landing Brigade from their mission during the Bay of Pigs invasion in April, 1961. *(National Archives)*

JFK at the Berlin Wall, June 6, 1963. *(JFK Library)*

Another Soviet probe involved the placement of Soviet missiles in Cuba. On October 22, 1962, Kennedy told the American people that offensive missile sites were being prepared in Cuba "to provide a nuclear strike capacity against the Western Hemisphere." He then boldly announced a naval blockade of offensive weapons into Cuba. Khrushchev broke the tension on October 27 by agreeing to remove the missiles under U.N. supervision (which the angry Castro blocked) in return for a U.S. pledge not to invade Cuba, which Kennedy agreed to but never formalized. Kennedy also terminated Operation Mongoose.

the Cuban leader using Mafia hit men and exploding cigars.

The Soviet probes began at a summit meeting between Kennedy and Communist Party Chairman Nikita Khrushchev at Vienna in early June, 1961, and then tested the unity and will of the North Atlantic Treaty Organization (NATO) at vulnerable Berlin. Kennedy responded with a firm statement of American resolve to defend West Berlin, a call for civil defense measures in the United States, and an increase in U.S. and NATO readiness. In early August Khrushchev boasted of a new 100-megaton nuclear warhead, and the Communists erected a barbed-wire fence, which was quickly replaced by a concrete wall, along the border between East and West Berlin, effectively stopping the flow of refugees out of the East. The president then sent fifteen hundred American troops along the autobahn from West Germany to West Berlin in order to demonstrate American commitment to the city. The Soviets did not challenge the convoy, and the crisis eased without any real resolution of the issues.

In facing the crisis and publicly facing down Khrushchev, Kennedy had resisted pressure from his military advisers to bomb the missile sites. His intelligence sources had convinced him that Khrushchev's main goal was to prevent an American invasion of Cuba, and that the Soviets had neither the intention nor the preparedness to risk nuclear war over such an issue.

Kennedy's prestige soared in the wake of his bold and successful maneuver, which removed much of the sting from the Bay of Pigs fiasco and the subsequent need to pay ransom for Castro's 1,113 prisoners. In the congressional elections of November, the Democrats evenly traded four lost seats in the House for four gains in the Senate and were quick to claim the lightest midterm losses since 1934. Republicans had counted heavily on the Cuban issue and complained bitterly that Kennedy's timing in announcing the missile site discovery was politically targeted toward the fall elections. As the Kennedy administration entered

1963 and the Eighty-eighth Congress, the Soviets had been faced down by a determined and sure-handed young president, the economy was quickening, and renewed Democratic majorities dominated the Congress.

Soviet Détente and the Indochinese Quagmire

In 1963 Kennedy was to reverse dramatically the deteriorating relations with the Soviet Union that had occasioned such dangerous confrontations over Berlin and Cuba. At the same time, however, U.S. efforts to prevent the communist takeover of Laos continued to falter. By the end of 1963, the American client regime in Vietnam was collapsing, despite the infusion of ten thousand American military personnel as "advisers."

Kennedy's inaugural address had been criticized as an eloquent but saber-rattling Cold War challenge and the combination in 1962 of Khrushchev's new 100-megaton warheads and Kennedy's missile blockade had alarmed Western leaders. In 1963, hardening relations with Peking inclined Moscow to a more conciliatory attitude toward Washington, which was then reciprocated. On June 10, President Kennedy expressed a new and less bellicose tone in a speech at American University: "Let us reexamine our attitude toward the Cold War," he said. "We must deal with the world as it is, and not as it might have been had the history of the last eighteen years been different. We must, therefore, persevere in the search for peace in the hope that constructive changes within the Communist bloc might bring within reach solutions which now seem beyond us."

In that speech he announced that the United States, the Soviet Union, and Great Britain would begin new talks on a nuclear test ban. On July 25, a limited agreement was initialed in Moscow, and the Senate ratified the Nuclear Test Ban Treaty on September 24. It pledged the signatory nations not to conduct tests of nuclear weapons underwater, in the atmos-

phere, or in outer space. That summer a hot line was installed linking the White House and the Kremlin. In addition, President Kennedy proposed a joint U.S.-Soviet manned flight to the moon and authorized negotiations for the private sale of $250 million in surplus wheat to the Soviet Union.

In Southeast Asia, however, conditions continued to deteriorate. Attention had concentrated primarily on Laos during 1961 and 1962. Kennedy chose not to take a military stand against communist insurgents there but instead agreed to negotiations that led to a neutral government. The agreement soon collapsed, however, as the Communist-backed Pathet Lao pummeled the neutralist forces of Premier Souvanna Phouma, and the United States and China exchanged heated charges. In neighboring South Vietnam, Kennedy rejected the idea of negotiations but also refused to commit American forces to a direct combat role. Instead he sought a "limited partnership" in the defense of that nation against Communist insurgency and invasion from North Vietnam. Nevertheless he continued and even escalated American involvement there. During his administration, the number of American military advisers in South Vietnam increased from about three thousand to more than sixteen thousand. In 1963, South Vietnam began to dominate the news, as the Catholic regime of Premier Ngo Dinh Diem cracked down hard on protesting Buddhists, and grisly scenes of self-immolating Buddhist priests appeared on American television. Protests broke out across the United States against the widely reported repression and corruption associated with Ngo, his brother and secret police chief, Ngo Dinh Nhu, and his wife, Madame Nhu—the infamous "Dragon Lady." This coincided with a marked cooling in U.S.-South Vietnam relations and led to a military coup on November 1, in which Diem and Nhu were killed. Frustrated by America's inability to move South Vietnam toward political and social reforms, the Kennedy administration actively abetted the plotters, then was unable to prevent the murder of the Ngo brothers. The military junta that replaced Ngo Dinh Diem was short-lived, and local Viet Cong successes continued in the countryside. This was the crumbling legacy that Lyndon Johnson was to inherit.

The Belated Commitment to Civil Rights Reform

When campaigning for president against Nixon in 1960, Kennedy was quick to accuse the Eisenhower administration of failing to bar racial discrimination in federally assisted housing "with the stroke of a pen." Once elected, however, Kennedy avoided the penstroke for almost two years, until safely after the elections of 1962. Like Franklin D. Roosevelt, he saw his high-priority legislation held potentially hostage by powerful Southern Democrats in Congress. Such key bills as the trade and tax

measures, federal aid to education, and Medicare were too important to risk with a civil rights fight that would invite the enmity of such powerful Southern legislators as James Eastland of Mississippi and Robert Kerr of Oklahoma in the Senate and Wilbur Mills of Arkansas and Howard Smith of Virginia in the House.

During the fall of 1962, the turmoil associated with the admission of a black law student, James Meredith, to the all-white University of Mississippi taught both Jack and Bobby Kennedy the necessity of dealing firmly with bitter-end resistance by such defiant Southern politicians as Governors Ross Barnett of Mississippi and George Wallace of Alabama. On February 28, 1963, Kennedy proposed his first civil rights bill, which concentrated on voting and excluded controversial provisions for equal employment machinery or open public accommodations. In early April, in Birming-

Civil rights leaders Fred L. Shuttlesworth, Dr. Martin Luther King, Jr., and Ralph D. Abernathy hold a press conference in Birmingham, Alabama, in May, 1963. *(Library of Congress)*

ham, peaceful demonstrators led by the Reverend Martin Luther King, Jr., were shown on television being attacked by police dogs and fire hoses under the aggressive direction of police chief Eugene ("Bull") Connor. The demonstrations spread to hundreds of towns and cities throughout the spring and summer of 1963, and on June 11, in a nationwide television address, President Kennedy said, "We are confronted primarily with a moral issue." He called for an omnibus civil rights bill, including a ban on segregated restaurants, hotels, and other public accommodations.

On August 28, more than two hundred thousand black and white Americans converged peacefully in the March on Washington for Jobs and Freedom. Kennedy had crossed the Rubicon on civil rights, as had a bipartisan coalition in the House, where the Judiciary Committee with strong administration support reported out a comprehensive civil rights bill in early November. The main test lay ahead in the Senate, where a conservative and Southern-led filibuster was certain—and had never failed in the past.

JFK signs a nuclear test ban treaty on October 7, 1963. *(National Archives)*

John F. Kennedy and the Eighty-eighth Congress

President Kennedy's decisive commitment to civil rights was paralleled by a major initiative for an economy-boosting tax cut. In January, 1963, he called for an "urgent" and politically unorthodox $10.3 billion cut in personal and corporate taxes, even though the administration budget projected a deficit of $8.3 billion for fiscal 1964. Kennedy's Keynesian tax cut bill, shorn of its earlier tax reform initiatives but increased to $11.1 billion, was reported out by the House Ways and Means Committee on September 13, and passed the House on September 25. Senate passage was hoped for early in 1964.

These major Kennedy initiatives, however, pointing as they did toward the harvest of the Kennedy legacy by President Lyndon Johnson in 1964, should not obscure a further deterioration in Kennedy's record with the Congress. Except for his initiatives in civil rights and the tax cut, Kennedy's accomplishments remained few and marginal. They included a new federal program supporting community treatment centers for the mentally ill, grants and loans for college and medical school construction, and modest expansion of air pollution and manpower retraining programs. Both the tempo and the output of Congress in response to administration proposals was further reduced in the Eighty-eighth Congress. Although the first session ran through December 30, 1963, for a near record 356 days, it completed only four of twelve annual appropriations bill (even though the fiscal year had ended the previous July). Its adoption of 44.3 percent of administration proposals in 1962 dropped sharply to 27.2 percent in 1963.

In foreign affairs, President Kennedy, by the fall of 1963, had achieved a measure of balanced firmness and détente with the Soviets that had earned for him high regard in American and indeed world opinion. His belated commitment to civil rights followed an apparently irresistible tide of domestic opinion, fueled by the televised brutality of Southern all-white police forces. Yet like all controversial measures, the civil rights bill had a polarizing effect that drove Kennedy's Gallup ratings downward markedly. He was already gearing up for the reelection campaign in 1964, hoping for the Republicans to nominate hard-line conservative Senator Barry Goldwater rather than a more centrist candidate such as Governor Nelson Rockefeller of New York or Governor George Romney of Michigan. A rightist Goldwater campaign would provide Kennedy with an opportunity to argue the issues sharply and enter the Eighty-ninth Congress with a clear mandate and strong program majority. To do this he needed first to patch and mend the tattered Democratic coalition, where his drives for education aid and civil rights reform had especially rent the political fabric.

It was such a mending trip that took him to Dallas, Texas, on November 22, 1963, where an assassin gunned him down. The assassination investigatory commission, headed by Chief Justice Earl Warren, concluded that President Kennedy had been murdered by Lee Harvey Oswald acting alone—a finding that has been much disputed by competing conspiracy theories but that stands as a formal and public judgment in the absence of conclusive evidence to the contrary.

Camelot and Martyrdom: The Kennedy Legacy

Martyrdom powerfully ennobled the memory of Abraham Lincoln, and its impact on the reputation of the captivating young Kennedy was equally stunning. The world naturally views his presidential legacy through the mythic prism of a Camelot whose hero had fallen—and in truth the martyred leader was uncommonly blessed with youth, grace, and charm, an ironic and spontaneous wit, and a probing political intelligence that was enriched by a superior education. The courage and character he had demonstrated in war bore the hallmark of genuine heroism. His ability to master the new political demands of the age of television was matched only by Franklin D. Roosevelt's command of radio, and it was unsurpassed in his own time. The profound loyalty, respect, and affection that he commanded from his able lieutenants signaled a rare devotion and was reflected in the worldwide grief that marked his untimely passing. That same grief was echoed thirty-six years later, in 1999, with the tragic crash of a small plane piloted by the charismatic John F. Kennedy, Jr., who many had hoped would continue his father's political legacy.

Romantic myths such as Camelot reinforce their darker underside by implicitly denying it. Critics charged that the nation's charmed intellectuals and captivated media practiced a double standard—they blinked at character flaws in John Kennedy that they would savage with relish in a Johnson or a Nixon. Kennedy's inherited wealth and his father's connections bought his career, they said, and ghosted and helped publish his books and essays. His sexual and marital indiscretions were reputedly sustained even through the White House years, with consorts ranging over a wide spectrum. Also, Kennedy had lied to the American people about his Addison's disease.

Beyond Camelot and the alleged contradictions of the personal character of its hero, what were the unique and lasting contributions of President Kennedy's thousand days in office? Clearly, high rank must be accorded to his effective destruction of the powerful myth that a Roman Catholic is unfit for the American presidency. His consistent opposition to direct federal aid to parochial schools helped to doom his education bill, but it confirmed the historic primacy of a secular presidency.

In Kennedy's preferred domain of foreign affairs, one may compare the adventuresome fiasco at the Bay of Pigs with the subsequent triumph over Khrushchev in the Cuban Missile Crisis, and also the hawkish ring of his inaugural address with his conciliatory American University speech, and conclude that his growth as president ultimately moved the republic away from the brink of nuclear war. His Arms Control and Disarmament Agency and Nuclear Test Ban Treaty nourished a successful legacy of détente, especially in Europe. Throughout his thousand days, the United States kept the peace, however uneasily.

In contrast, Kennedy's fascination with counterinsurgency, his early approval of the Cuban invasion and Operation Mongoose, and later his military escalation in Vietnam and his involvement in the toppling of Ngo Dinh Diem, all left a legacy that led toward the disastrous American war in Vietnam. The overthrow and murder of Ngo fundamentally changed America's Vietnam commitment. The president and his senior administrators were appalled by the assassinations, but their role in the coup assigned to them a heavy measure of responsibility for what followed. It seemed as if the military-dominated governments that ruled South Vietnam for the rest of the war were inherited by the United States—unruly American offspring to whose fate and ultimate defeat Kennedy's successors remained tightly and tragically bound.

In domestic policy Kennedy has generally been accorded high marks for promoting economic growth through the expansion of world trade and the pump-priming tax cut.

The latter achievement was signed by President Lyndon Johnson, and its economic impact was even greater than its proposers had hoped. It constituted the first of a triple harvest that Johnson freely acknowledged as fulfilling the Kennedy promise: the tax cut and the civil rights bill of 1964, and federal aid to education in 1965. Yet Johnson achieved the first two, in addition to launching his War on Poverty, with essentially the same Congress that had so consistently defeated most of Kennedy's legislative proposals throughout his administration.

It was Johnson, of course, who enjoyed the landslide over Goldwater and who translated those majorities into the extraordinary burst of new Great Society programs that so dwarfed Kennedy's legislative achievements for the New Frontier. To speculate how Kennedy might have fared with a Goldwater challenge and beyond is to engage in dreams of what might have been. Perhaps it is best that Kennedy is most singularly and warmly associated in the public memory with the concrete achievement of the Peace Corps—whose meaning, like that of its mentor, is derived less from its demonstrable impact than from an abiding spirit of youth and hope.

Hugh Davis Graham

Bibliographical References

The standard scholarly biography is the two-volume study by Herbert S. Parmet, *Jack: The Struggles of John F. Kennedy*, 1980, and *JFK: The Presidency of John F. Kennedy*, 1983. Kennedy's White House chief of staff, Theodore C. Sorensen, published the most comprehensive memoir in *Kennedy*, 1965, as well as an evaluation of Kennedy's impact in *The Kennedy Legacy*, 1993. Other profiles by presidential aides include Arthur M. Schlesinger, Jr., *A Thousand Days: John F. Kennedy in the White House*, 1965, and Pierre Salinger, *John F. Kennedy, Commander in Chief: A Profile in Leadership*, 1997. Garry Wills, *The Kennedy Imprisonment*,

1982, provides a wide-ranging, sometimes savage critique of the Kennedy legend. Kennedy's public and private life are examined with a focus on his youth and indiscretions in Nigel Hamilton, *JFK: Reckless Youth*, 1993, and Seymour M. Hersh, *The Dark Side of Camelot*, 1997.

For a case study of Kennedy and the civil rights crisis, see Carl M. Brauer, *John F. Kennedy and the Second Reconstruction*, 1977. Similar analyses in foreign affairs are William J. Rust, *Kennedy in Vietnam*, 1985; Noam Chomsky, *Rethinking Camelot: JFK, the Vietnam War, and U.S. Political Culture*, 1993; and Orrin Schwab, *Defending the Free World: John F. Kennedy, Lyndon Johnson, and the Vietnam War*, 1998. For a detailed examination of the Cuban Missile Crisis, see Robert S. Thompson, *The Missiles of October: The Declassified Story of John F. Kennedy and the*

Cuban Missile Crisis, 1992, and Ernest R. May and Philip Zelikow, eds., *The Kennedy Tapes: Inside the White House During the Cuban Missile Crisis*, 1997.

There are numerous books on the Kennedy assassination, but some of the more useful are James P. Duffy and Vincent L. Ricci, *The Assassination of John F. Kennedy: A Complete Book of Facts*, 1992; Gerald Posner, *Case Closed: Lee Harvey Oswald and the Assassination of JFK*, 1993; Michael Benson, *Who's Who in the JFK Assassination: An A to Z Encyclopedia*, 1993; and William E. Scott, *November 22, 1963: A Reference Guide to the JFK Assassination*, 1999.

For a balanced portrait of Kennedy's term, see James N. Giglio, *The Presidency of John F. Kennedy*, 1991. For a comprehensive bibliographic overview of the Kennedy years, see Giglio, *John F. Kennedy: A Bibliography*, 1995.

Lyndon B. Johnson

36th President, 1963-1969

Born: August 27, 1908
       Gillespie County, Texas
Died: January 22, 1973
       near Stonewall, en route to San
       Antonio, Texas

Political Party: Democratic
Vice President: Hubert H. Humphrey

Cabinet Members

Secretary of State: Dean Rusk
Secretary of the Treasury: Douglas Dillon, Henry H. Fowler, Joseph W. Barr
Secretary of Defense: Robert McNamara, Clark Clifford
Attorney General: Robert F. Kennedy, N. de B. Katzenbach, Ramsey Clark
Postmaster General: John A. Gronouski, Lawrence F. O'Brien, W. Marvin Watson
Secretary of the Interior: Stewart L. Udall
Secretary of Agriculture: Orville Freeman
Secretary of Commerce: Luther Hodges, John T. Connor, Alexander B. Trowbridge, C. R. Smith
Secretary of Labor: W. Willard Wirtz
Secretary of Health, Education, and Welfare: Anthony Celebrezze, John W. Gardner, Wilbur J. Cohen
Secretary of Housing and Urban Development: Robert C. Weaver, Robert C. Wood
Secretary of Transportation: Alan S. Boyd

At one o'clock on the afternoon of November 22, 1963, John F. Kennedy died from gunshot wounds received while riding in a motorcade through Dallas,

Texas. Lyndon Baines Johnson became the thirty-sixth president of the United States. A little more than two and a half hours later, aboard *Air Force One* on a runway at a Dallas

Johnson's official portrait. *(White House Historical Society)*

571

airport, Johnson took the oath of office. Immediately thereafter, the plane took off for the flight back to Washington, D.C., carrying the new president as well as the body of the slain one. During the next four days, amid the ceremonies marking Kennedy's burial, a Kennedy legend was born that, for some people, would cast a shadow over Lyndon Johnson's presidency. For them, Johnson remained always the usurper, the unsophisticated Texan who never matched the glamour and vigor and promise of Kennedy. The man who flew back to assume the power of the presidency, however, had first left Texas for Washington a long time before, and his experience in the capital had shaped his attitudes and goals.

Rise to Power

Lyndon Johnson's life began in Texas, southwest of Dallas in the hill country, a beautiful but deceptively rugged land. There he was born on August 27, 1908, to Rebekah Baines and Sam Ealy Johnson, Jr. Sam Johnson owned a fairly prosperous farm and served the people against the special interests in the Texas state legislature. Johnson served only a few terms in the legislature, however, and went broke at farming in the early 1920's. He then moved his family to nearby Johnson City, where Lyndon grew up. Except for displaying an intense interest in his father's political activities, Lyndon had a not-uncommon small-town Texas childhood. He did, however, develop a fierce determination to succeed and to escape the rigors of the hill country. The young Lyndon also acquired a deep sense of insecurity, perhaps because of his relations with his parents or the embarrassment of his father's financial difficulties.

After high school, Lyndon escaped to California, but a little more than a year later, he returned to Texas and took a job on a Johnson City road crew. Soon he enrolled at Southwest State Teachers College in nearby San Marcos, where he was graduated in 1930. Johnson had

to work his way through school and took a year off to teach in Cotulla, Texas, a small, poor, primarily Mexican American community south of San Antonio. He dedicated enormous energy to his job and exercised a demanding paternalism, but still became exceedingly popular with his students and the community. Years later, when he was president, Johnson cited his year among the poor of Cotulla as the origin of his commitment to oppose racism and eradicate poverty. After graduation, Johnson returned to teaching, this time in Houston, but soon quit to become assistant to the newly elected congressman from Texas's Fourteenth District, Richard M. Kleberg.

In December, 1931, at the age of only twenty-three, Lyndon Johnson arrived in Washington, D.C., for the first time. He never severed his ties to Texas nor lost his love for the hill country, but except for a two-year stint as director of a federal agency in Texas, neither did he live there again until he left the White House in 1969. He never ran for state office. The capital served as his escape from the hill country and became the stage upon which he played out his ambitions. His life as a Texan in Washington, a provincial in the capital, only exacerbated his insecurities. Johnson at once envied and felt patronized by the better-educated, more sophisticated residents of the capital, especially the intellectuals from the Northeast.

As a young congressional aide, Johnson worked incredibly hard and quickly mastered his job. He cajoled the conservative Kleberg into voting for much of the New Deal, excelled at constituent services, learned everything he could about how the government worked, and cultivated people in high and low places within it, especially a friend of his father, Congressman Sam T. Rayburn. While still working for Kleberg, in 1934 Johnson met Claudia Alta Taylor, a recent graduate of the University of Texas, daughter of a well-to-do merchant from Karnack, and descendant of Alabama gentility. The young aide courted Lady Bird, as she was already known, with the same intensity with which he had taught school or managed Kleberg's office. Within a few months, she agreed to marry him. A woman of great consideration for others and considerable business and political acumen, Lady Bird Johnson displayed unquestioning loyalty to and unending patience with her husband.

After a year of marriage, the young couple returned to Texas. Johnson had used his connections in Washington, D.C., to secure the post of Texas state director of the newly created National Youth Administration (NYA). He did an excellent job of administering this New Deal relief program, some said the best job of any state director. After only two years, Johnson resigned in order to run for the Tenth Congressional District seat when the incumbent died. He campaigned as a devoted disciple of Franklin D. Roosevelt and his New Deal, stressing that he would vote for the president's then-controversial plan to add members to the Supreme Court. In a ten-man race, Johnson won a plurality of the votes, all that was necessary in a special election. Shortly after Johnson's victory, Roosevelt visited Texas, and Johnson took the opportunity to ingratiate himself with the president. Roosevelt naturally welcomed such a loyal supporter, and he soon developed a real fondness for him.

In 1937, Lyndon Johnson returned to Washington as congressman from the Tenth District of Texas, which included the hill country and the capital of Austin. With his experience in Washington, the tutelage of influential House member Rayburn, and, most important, the favor of President Roosevelt and the assistance of his influential aides, the young Texan quickly became a very effective congressman. Most of the measures of the New Deal had already passed, though Johnson arrived in time to cast a vote for the first minimum wage law. Johnson's success, however, came not from his voting record or his role in floor debates—in fact, he rarely made speeches or introduced bills—

LBJ with Lady Bird Johnson, 1936. *(LBJ Library)*

but rather, from his skill at serving constituents and at securing federal benefits for his district: millions of dollars in Works Progress Administration and Public Works Administration construction, one of the first four federal housing projects, and, after Roosevelt's intervention, a Rural Electrification Administration loan that at least brought electricity to the Texas hill country. Johnson ran unopposed in the next two elections.

In 1941, Johnson lost a special election for a vacated Senate seat but remained in the House, where he became, under Roosevelt's influence, an avid supporter of military preparedness and of an activist foreign policy. Except for seven months in uniform, Johnson remained in Congress during World War II. After the war, he became a bit more conservative than he had been in the 1930's. Roosevelt, his liberal hero and patron, had died. The nation as a whole had become more conservative. Most important, Johnson had begun to position himself for a statewide race and realized that postwar Texas would accept less liberalism than had the Depression-struck Tenth District. Although he supported President Harry S Truman on most foreign policy matters, he sometimes voted against him on domestic issues, most prominently in voting for the Taft-Hartley Act designed to limit the influence of organized labor.

In 1948, Johnson ran again for the Senate. Campaigning by helicopter, he waged a determined race in the Democratic primary that stressed his anticommunist credentials and opposition to unions. He won a runoff by only 87 votes, and his opponent and others charged that voting irregularities in South Texas accounted for the margin. Indisputably, one voting box had been stuffed and its ballots burned before investigators could check them. Whether Johnson stole the election or whether it was stolen for him by others unconnected to him or even whether the stealing on his side only balanced theft by the other side remains unclear. In any case, a close vote in the state executive committee placed Johnson's name on the ballot as the Democratic nominee, and therefore at that time in Texas as the winner, and clever arguments by Johnson's lawyers in federal courts defeated his opponent's attempt to overthrow that decision.

Lyndon B. Johnson—teased as "Landslide Lyndon" because of the closeness of the vote and tainted by the accusations of fraud—joined the Senate in 1949. He very quickly became an influential member through the same means he had employed in the House: incredibly hard work, mastery of the system, and cultivation of an influential elder, in this case Senate leader Richard Russell of Georgia. Johnson kept the voters of Texas happy, again through dedicated constituent services but also by his opposition to civil rights and organized labor and by his unswerving support of oil and gas interests. While protecting his position in Texas, he moved rapidly into a leadership position within the Senate. In 1951 he became Democratic whip and in 1953, after the defeat of the incumbent, minority leader. In 1955, when the Democrats regained control of the Senate, Johnson became majority leader. By 1958, he had established himself as one of the ablest majority leaders in Senate history.

His success owed something to his use of money and influence. As early as 1940, Johnson served as a conduit of campaign contributions to national politicians from the oilmen and other wealthy individuals of Texas. As majority leader, he craftily built support through his control of committee assignments and office space. He also performed various personal favors and kindnesses. Ultimately, however, his power in the Senate rested on two things: his ability to convince individual senators to vote with him and his masterful use of legislative tactics.

Johnson rarely moved his colleagues through inspiring oratory. The majority leader never won an argument on the floor, one observer commented, and never lost one in the cloakroom. His method in the latter place came to be called the Johnson "Treatment," best described by newspapermen Rowland Evans and Robert Novak:

> Its tone could be supplication, accusation, cajolery, exuberance, scorn, tears, complaint, the hint of threat. It was all of these together. It ran the gamut of human emotions. Its velocity was breathtaking, and it was all in one direction. Interjections from the target were rare. Johnson anticipated them before they could be spoken. He moved in close, his face a scant millimeter from his target, his eyes widening and narrowing, his eyebrows rising and falling. From his pockets poured clippings, memos, statistics. Mimicry, hu-

mor, and the genius of analogy made The Treatment an almost hypnotic experience and rendered the target stunned and helpless.

Critics called such efforts "arm twisting"; Johnson rightly preferred the term "seduction." He rarely asked a senator to vote against his constituents on an issue important to them and always tailored his argument to the political or personal needs of the man or woman he confronted. Along with the amazing force of his presentation, therefore, his success owed much to his awesome ability to understand what the object of his seduction desired, needed, or responded to—an ability derived partly from instinct, partly from the hard work of intelligence gathering that produced an accurate profile of each of the senators.

That intelligence system also provided the majority leader remarkably accurate vote counts. The Senate rarely surprised him, and he had a sure sense of when and how to present a bill. Johnson himself kept his own counsel, rarely making speeches or even publicly explaining his position. In fact, he often emphasized a bill's conservative nature with Southerners and its progressive intent with liberals. Such an approach allowed him to build the diverse coalitions central to his success. It also helped that he worked with a phenomenally popular Republican president, Dwight D. Eisenhower. Johnson usually supported Eisenhower on foreign affairs and occasionally on domestic matters as well. He especially delighted in portraying himself and his party as allied with the president in a fight against the ultraconservatives of the president's own party.

Johnson, in short, excelled as a legislative tactician rather than as a strategist, as his aide George Reedy put it. The majority leader never tried to establish a Democratic agenda. Indeed, he scorned senators who sought to do so through impassioned public or Senate speeches—"show horses" he called them. He preferred "workhorses," senators of whatever ideological belief or party affiliation who worked quietly and steadily to pass legislation. He and his workhorses passed a number of measures, many of them surprisingly liberal for the conservative 1950's: an increase in housing subsidies for the poor, a moderate (more moderate than the liberals wanted) rise in the minimum wage, and an expansion of Social Security coverage, including the establishment of benefits for the disabled. Johnson was also instrumental in the start of the space program, and he played a major role in the censure of Senator Joseph McCarthy and the passage of the 1957 Civil Rights Act.

Beginning in 1950, but exploiting an already widespread and intense fear of internal communist subversion, McCarthy commanded national attention with reckless attacks on the loyalty and patriotism of many individuals within and outside government. Only in 1954 did the majority leader decide that the popular McCarthy had become vulnerable and then quietly mobilized the Senate establishment against him. The Senate soon voted to censure McCarthy, and under Johnson's leadership every Democrat voted in favor. McCarthy's influence and career quickly declined.

The majority leader's role in the passage of the Civil Rights Act of 1957 proved more public than his role in the fall of McCarthy. Until that time Johnson's record on racial issues had resembled that of many Southern moderates of the era. He only occasionally resorted to race-baiting and aided African Americans when he could do so without attracting public attention, but he never attacked segregation and consistently voted against federal intervention in Southern race relations. By 1957, though, Johnson figured the time had come for federal legislation. The Supreme Court decision against school segregation and the Montgomery bus boycott had created a climate for action. Many African Americans had voted Republican in 1956, and Johnson believed that the Democratic Party had to woo them back.

Moreover, he knew that he himself needed to escape his identification with Southern racial practices if he were to realize his growing ambition to be president.

In 1957, Johnson set out to pass a civil rights bill without provoking a Southern filibuster that had blocked earlier civil rights legislation and that he feared would divide his party. Working from a strong bill proposed by the Eisenhower administration, Johnson made significant concessions to the Southerners to convince them to allow a vote (though they still voted against the bill) and yet persuaded enough senators to agree to the compromise to pass the act in what some described as a "legislative miracle." Although weak and ineffective, the Civil Rights Act of 1957 was the first federal civil rights law since Reconstruction, it placed the federal government on record as supporting black voting rights, and it opened the way for the far more effective legislation enacted during Johnson's presidency. Finally, the bill passed without a seriously divisive confrontation over a filibuster and therefore with minimal damage to the Democratic Party and sectional relations.

Response to Johnson's role in both the McCarthy censure and the passage of the Civil Rights Act typified opinions held about the majority leader. Many observers considered both major successes and praised Johnson as a master tactician who secured legislation few could have passed. Others, particularly in the liberal wing of the Democratic Party, questioned why he had waited so long to attack McCarthy and condemned the Civil Rights Act as a sellout to Southern racists. They minimized Johnson's legislative accomplishments and believed that he refused to take a valiant liberal stand in the face of sure defeat because of his own conservatism. Their antipathy limited Johnson's chances of securing the Democratic nomination for president just as surely as his success as majority leader made him a likely candidate.

Exactly when Johnson decided that he wanted to be president remains unclear. Some seem to believe that he reached the decision in his mother's womb. Clearly, the thought had crossed his mind as early as 1940 and never entirely passed from it. He always minimized his chances, though, because he believed that no Southerner could be elected. Nevertheless, from 1955 on, he thought of it more and more, and in 1960 he made a halfhearted, poorly conceived attempt to secure the Democratic nomination. He failed; John F. Kennedy easily won nomination on the first ballot at the convention. The new nominee then offered Johnson the vice presidency.

Some maintained that Kennedy only offered the majority leader the second spot on the ticket because he expected him to say no. More likely, the tough-minded politician realized that Johnson could help him in the crucial state of Texas as well as in the rest of the South. In either case, when the liberals heard of Kennedy's offer, many balked at the idea of Johnson on the ticket, and Kennedy wavered in his decision. During that period, Robert Kennedy, the nominee's younger brother, went to Johnson and asked him to withdraw. Johnson then called John Kennedy, who told him that Bobby was out of touch and reassured him that he was the nominee. Out of the confusion and Bobby's visit, however, emerged animosity between Johnson and the younger Kennedy, which only grew with time.

If some observers could not believe that Kennedy had offered the job to Johnson, others were astonished that Johnson accepted it. The vice presidency offered no challenge and less real power than the post of majority leader. Johnson believed that he could help the ticket, and as a loyal Democrat may have felt a duty to do so. Johnson may also have seen the vice presidency as a means to free himself of his sometimes troublesome ties to conservative Texas and thereby enhance his chance for a later run for the presidency. Moreover, with his astute sense of political timing, Johnson may have realized that he would not retain the power that he had as majority leader if either Kennedy, an activist within his own party, or his opponent, Richard M. Nixon, a very different Republican from Eisenhower, became president. Perhaps, too, Johnson believed that he could invest the office with real power.

That fall Johnson campaigned very hard for the ticket and clearly helped Kennedy carry Texas and possibly other states as well. Once in office, Johnson did try to increase the power of the vice president, sending a memo to the White House outlining considerable authority for himself and seeking a role in the Senate Democratic caucus. Summarily rebuffed in both attempts, Johnson found himself becoming a typical vice president. Kennedy, who always treated him well, asked Johnson to chair the President's Committee on Equal Employment Opportunity and the National Aeronautics and Space Council. As head of the latter, Johnson urged Kennedy to undertake the program to land an American on the moon. Kennedy also sent Johnson on eleven trips abroad, during which he visited thirty-three countries. On a courageous trip to West Berlin during a Soviet-American crisis over access and on a fact-finding mission to South Vietnam, Johnson performed well and served a useful function. He turned many other trips into American-style campaign stops, sometimes winning friends for the United States but often generating unflattering press reports of his folksy ways and unreasonable demands on the diplomatic staff. Such stories only increased the derision of Johnson as "Uncle Cornpone" by many within the Kennedy camp. By 1963, rumors circulated, which Johnson apparently believed, that he would be dropped from the ticket in 1964. They were untrue, but the powerlessness and ignominy of the vice presidency took their toll. In what was for him an amazing act of self-restraint, Johnson never publicly aired his resentments or criticized Kennedy.

He remained a most loyal vice president but an increasingly miserable one.

Assuming Power

With the assassination, Johnson escaped his exile in the vice presidency and assumed the awesome burdens of the presidency at a most difficult time. As he flew back from Dallas, the new president realized that he had to reassure the nation and the world that the government would continue. He also knew that he had to convince both of the legitimacy of his power. His career thus far had left LBJ, as he was often called during his presidency, particularly suited to do so. He knew the ways of Washington, D.C., and the means of power as well as anyone. Using his experience, Johnson quickly established his control over the government and his intention of carrying out Kennedy's goals. Turning on The Treatment, he convinced the Kennedy cabinet and staff to remain with him, though he began bringing in his own advisers as well. Two days after Kennedy's burial, Johnson delivered a sentimental but hugely successful televised address to a joint session of Congress. He began by saying, "All I have I would have given gladly not to be standing here today" and closed by quoting from "America the Beautiful." In between, he promised to carry out Kennedy's plans for the nation and, echoing Kennedy's inaugural rhetoric of "let us begin," urged "let us continue."

To ease public concern over a possible plot against the government, Johnson appointed a panel of distinguished Americans, headed by Chief Justice Earl Warren, to investigate the Kennedy assassination. The Warren Commission, as it came to be called, in September, 1964, issued a reassuring report that Lee Harvey Oswald had acted alone in killing Kennedy. That conclusion has not been disproven, though critics have established the commission's lack of thoroughness and have raised serious questions about its findings.

Throughout the transition, Johnson performed masterfully. He calmed the nation's fears and reassured people of the continuity in government. LBJ also quickly moved to enact two measures that Kennedy had proposed but failed to convince Congress to pass, a tax cut and a civil rights bill. In doing so, Johnson sometimes invoked Kennedy's memory but always relied on the skills that he had developed in Congress. The old legislative wizard advised his aides on how to manipulate the Congress and used his telephone, a favorite instrument, to administer The Treatment to wavering congressmen. As he had in the Senate, he often compromised, but as president LBJ displayed a greater willingness—to use his analogy—to push in his whole stack. He soon won more than a few pots.

Kennedy's Keynesian advisers had recommended a tax cut, despite a budget deficit, in order to stimulate a stagnant economy. Johnson concluded that to pass the tax cut he would have to reduce the proposed budget, thus low-ering the potential deficit and making the cut easier for fiscal conservatives to accept. He ordered a rigorous review of the already planned budget and pared it significantly, primarily through cuts in defense spending. By the end of February, 1964, Congress had passed a substantial reduction in personal and business taxes, which, most economists contend, provided the desired stimulus to the economy.

Congress moved more slowly on the civil rights bill. From the first, Johnson made clear his determination not to compromise the strength of the bill. Unlike in 1957, he knew a filibuster could not be avoided and resolved to wait it out. Violent white Southern response to nonviolent black protest, particularly in demonstrations in Birmingham, Alabama, led by Martin Luther King, Jr., had helped create a national consensus that something had to be done. LBJ used that consensus, the Kennedy legacy, and whatever else he could think of to pass the bill. He worked especially hard to create a "hero's niche" for Senate Republican leader Everett Dirksen, whose support Johnson realized would be crucial in invoking cloture as well as in passing the bill. Dirksen admirably filled the niche, though only after securing certain compromises the Republicans wanted. With his and other Republican support, the Senate voted cloture and then passed the bill. On July 2, 1964, Johnson signed the Civil Rights Act of 1964 outlawing segregation in public accommodations and discrimination in employment as well as authorizing federal suits to ensure school desegregation. A strong measure,

Johnson is sworn in as president following the assassination of John F. Kennedy. (LBJ Library)

it served as the legal basis for the destruction of the rigid system of segregation that had ruled the South for seventy years or more.

In addition to the tax bill and Civil Rights Act, Johnson worked for passage of a comprehensive antipoverty bill. The idea for such legislation originated in the Kennedy White House, though Kennedy had not finally decided or publicly declared his intention to seek it. Shortly after Kennedy's assassination, his economic advisers approached Johnson with their ideas and received quick approval to proceed, no doubt partly because LBJ believed, given Kennedy's lack of public comment, that he could make the poverty program "his." In his State of the Union address that January, the president announced, with typical understatement, "This administration today, here and now, declares unconditional war on poverty in America." At first LBJ left planning to the White House economists but later created an independent agency, the Office of Economic Opportunity, to oversee the battle. The bill it presented to Congress had something for everyone: work study, financial aid for college students; the Job Corps, a training program for the unemployed; VISTA, an agency to sponsor volunteers to work in depressed areas; and loans for small businessmen and farmers. The measure also included the Community Action Program (CAP). Johnson later claimed that he envisioned a system of local involvement not unlike what he had seen in the National Youth Administration (NYA) of his early Texas days. The plan's authors, though, saw community action agencies as a means of local control and coordination of antipoverty programs and of "maximum feasible participation," in the words of the act, for the poor themselves. CAP would later become very controversial, but at the time neither it nor anything else stopped Johnson as he maneuvered the Economic Opportunity Act through Congress. To make it easier for congressmen to support the bill, LBJ funded the act at a little less than $1 billion,

enough for a skirmish, not a war, but planned to increase its appropriations later.

The tax cut, the Civil Rights Act, and the Economic Opportunity Act constituted an impressive legislative achievement, particularly since under Kennedy's leadership the first two had been stalled in Congress. Yet they only whetted Johnson's appetite for accomplishment, and during the spring of 1964 he began to define a larger domestic vision. His speechwriters had begun slipping the phrase Great Society into his speeches, and Johnson slowly adopted it as a label, like the New Deal used by his hero Franklin D. Roosevelt, for his domestic reform agenda. On May 22, in a commencement address at the University of Michigan, the president outlined what he meant by the slogan. "The challenge of the next half century," the president contended, is whether Americans have the wisdom to use their "wealth to enrich and elevate our national life, and to advance the quality of American civilization. . . . For in your time we have the opportunity to move not only toward the rich society and the powerful society, but upward to the Great Society." Such a society, he explained, would provide abundance for all, end poverty, establish racial justice, educate children, revive the cities, and beautify the environment. It would not, Johnson added, be "a safe harbor, a resting place, a final objective, a finished work. It is a challenge constantly renewed, beckoning us toward a destiny where the meaning of our lives matches the marvelous products of our labor."

That summer, LBJ established task forces, extragovernmental study groups composed of experts from various fields. They proposed much of what became the Great Society legislation, but such an undertaking would involve more than laws. In enunciating his goal, Johnson had moved beyond public opinion. He would not only have to convince Congress to enact legislation but also have to define his vision and create wide public support for it.

Johnson meets with civil rights leader Dr. Martin Luther King, Jr. *(Library of Congress)*

He would have to be, in other words, not simply the tactician he had been in the Senate but also a strategist, not simply the master of Congress but mentor for the nation as well. Whether he could do this remained to be seen. Thus far, though, Johnson had performed extremely well at managing the nation. He had secured passage of important legislation, had begun to define a broader vision for the country, and—just for good measure—in April had prevented a major rail strike through highly publicized personal intervention.

Johnson had devoted considerably less time to foreign affairs than to these domestic matters. The major foreign policy issue that he faced when he took office, and the problem that would haunt his administration, was Vietnam. Building on a commitment dating to the late 1940's, Johnson's predecessor had increased American involvement in Vietnam by providing more economic and military aid, by increasing the number of American troops there to more than sixteen thousand, and by

acquiescing in, if not supporting, a coup against the president of South Vietnam. Faced with the deteriorating situation in the wake of the coup, LBJ, no doubt following his instincts as well as continuing Kennedy's policy, in his first months in office resolved "to do more of the same but do it more efficiently and effectively." He pledged to preserve an independent, non-Communist South Vietnam, raised the number of U.S. advisers in Vietnam to more than twenty-three thousand, and provided another $50 million in economic aid. The Joint Chiefs of Staff pushed for a bombing campaign against the North as well, but Johnson only authorized them to prepare contingency studies. He also approved covert operations along the North Vietnamese coast and considered asking Congress for a resolution of support.

On August 2, 1964, the destroyer *Maddox*, conducting electronic espionage off the coast of North Vietnam, fired warning shots at rapidly approaching North Vietnamese patrol boats. The boats fired torpedoes at the *Maddox*.

When informed of the incident, Johnson ordered the destroyer *C. Turner Joy* to join the *Maddox*, and two nights later North Vietnamese patrol boats again allegedly fired on the U.S. ships. A few observers at the time, and more since, doubted whether the second attack ever occurred, suspecting that problems with sonar and panic by its operators yielded false readings. At the time, Johnson did not convey such doubts to the American people; nor did he inform them that the night of the first incident the South Vietnamese had conducted attacks against the North that the North Vietnamese could easily have assumed the *Maddox* was supporting. Instead, LBJ portrayed the incident as an unprovoked attack on American ships. He ordered air reprisals against the North and sought a resolution of support from Congress. After limited debate and with only two dissenting votes, Congress obliged with the Southeast Asia Resolution, or Tonkin Gulf Resolution, which authorized the president to do whatever necessary, including armed interven-

tion, to protect Americans and defend freedom in Southeast Asia. "Like grandma's nightgown," Johnson observed, "it covered everything." The president had not decided to send American troops or to bomb the North; indeed, he still hoped to avoid doing both. LBJ wanted a broad statement of congressional approval that would allow him to keep his options open. Moreover, his show of determination protected him from Republican charges of "softness." The 1964 presidential campaign had just begun.

Johnson's success in office had eliminated all doubt that he would receive the Democratic nomination. Only the question of who would be his running mate remained. Johnson clumsily eliminated many people's sentimental choice, Robert Kennedy, believing that Bobby would not help the ticket and wanting to escape the shadow of the Kennedys. Perhaps trying to build suspense for the convention, the president then turned the process of choosing a running mate into a public guessing game. Finally, as he left for the convention, he an-

LBJ signs the Civil Rights Act of 1964. *(National Archives)*

nounced that he had selected Hubert H. Humphrey, a former Senate ally, a dedicated liberal, and a longtime champion of civil rights.

At the convention, the sole major dispute concerned the seating of the Mississippi delegation. Only a minor incident in the Johnson administration, it nevertheless offered an epiphonal moment for understanding the gulf between the president and those who sought reform outside the system. Mississippi civil rights workers, despite the murder of some of their colleagues and the imprisonment or beating of many more, succeeded in organizing a political party and selecting convention delegates according to Democratic Party rules. Calling themselves the Mississippi Freedom Democratic Party (MFDP), these reformers asked the convention to seat their delegates rather than the regular Mississippi delegation selected without African American participation. Fearing that a floor fight over the issue would mar his convention and endanger the Democrats' chances in the South, LBJ forced through a compromise that sat the regulars if they pledged to support the ticket, allowed two representatives of the MFDP to vote in the convention, and prohibited seating in all future conventions any delegation for a state that disfranchised African Americans. Many of the civil rights workers reacted bitterly and staged a protest on the convention floor. They believed that Johnson and the liberal establishment had sold them out despite the moral authority of their cause; Johnson and his supporters thought that a politically realistic compromise had been reached that advanced the African American cause in the future. Both were correct; neither comprehended the position of the other.

The fight over the seating of the Mississippi delegation did little to disrupt LBJ's well-orchestrated celebration of his nomination. The campaign went nearly as smoothly. In the campaign, Johnson faced Republican Barry M. Goldwater of Arizona. Goldwater had publicly expressed opposition to Social Security, had

voted against the Civil Rights Act, had talked of lobbing a nuclear round into the Kremlin, and generally appeared outside the mainstream of American politics. He wanted to repeal the present and veto the future, Johnson quipped at one point in the campaign. Johnson and the Democrats shrewdly and sometimes savagely exploited Goldwater's image as a warmonger while they themselves ran on the vague promise of peace and prosperity. Vietnam never became a major issue, by agreement between the candidates, although Johnson occasionally talked about it. He emphasized his hope for a peaceful settlement, usually adding the caveat that peace depended on an end to aggression. Many of his listeners apparently missed the qualification, but the public did hear and remember when LBJ proclaimed that he had no intention of sending American boys to fight Asian wars. The only major threat to Johnson's campaign occurred in October, when Walter Jenkins, a close and longtime aide, was arrested in a Washington restroom for "disorderly conduct" with an old man. Jenkins quickly resigned, major world events soon pushed the scandal off the front pages, and it did little to damage Johnson's chances. The crowds greeting Johnson on his campaign stops were still large and enthusiastic, and in November he won one of the greatest electoral victories ever. LBJ carried forty-four states with more than 61 percent of the popular vote.

Problems of Public Perception

For a time Johnson basked in the adulation of the campaign crowds and the magnitude of his victory. The satisfaction proved short-lived, however, as older insecurities and ambitions reemerged. Johnson resolved to become the greatest president ever but also questioned whether the people really liked him. Although his victory reflected public approval of LBJ's assumption of power after Kennedy's assassination, it constituted as much a rejection of Goldwater as an endorsement of Johnson. Support for Johnson was, to use his image, like a Texas river, mighty wide but awfully shallow. The shallowness resulted partly from the fact that the public did not really know, like, or trust Lyndon Johnson. Many Americans considered him simply a Texas boor, given to wheeling and dealing, shady if not corrupt, obsessed with power and unburdened by political principles. The image—not altogether unfair—emerged from the complexity of Johnson's personality and politics. His inability to overcome it and to convey the depth and sincerity of his political philosophy proved very important to his presidency, especially during the second term.

The real Lyndon Johnson is surprisingly elusive. Even more than most politicians, Johnson remained constantly onstage, playing whatever role, political or personal, he believed the situation demanded. The fact that he presented different images to different people at different times makes it almost impossible for the historian to decide which, if any, constituted the true Johnson. Indeed, as George Reedy has suggested, he probably remained "an enigma even to himself." Most observers tried to describe him by listing numerous, often contradictory adjectives or simply by saying that he was very complex or by maintaining that he combined all that was human.

At times Johnson seemed more than merely human. He stood over 6 feet, 3 inches tall, weighed more than two hundred pounds (how much more depended on the success of his latest diet), and wore a shirt with a 17.5-inch neck and 37-inch sleeves. Many people who knew him commented on the long arms and huge hands that drew people to him. Not only his size but also his searching eyes, phenomenal intensity, and tremendous energy allowed him to dominate individuals or small groups. The "guy's just got extra glands," his friend Abe Fortas explained. Johnson also had an impressive memory and, according to many, a very agile and able mind. He turned it to little save

politics. The only other consistent interest in his life was cattle breeding, both the economics and the mechanics of it. Even in politics, his mind attacked only practical matters. He gave no thought to intellectual abstractions or theories, rendering him even more than most men a product, sometimes a prisoner, of his experience.

A few aides and friends who loved his company despite his narrow interests remained devotedly loyal. Johnson could be amazingly generous and thoughtful, inviting members of the White House staff to presidential parties, bestowing gifts, or even quietly paying the unexpected expenses of a staff member. Even some of the loyal friends, though, admitted that Johnson could also be very unpleasant. Once when LBJ himself wondered aloud why people did not like him, former Secretary of State Dean Acheson replied, "Let's face it, Mr. President, you just aren't a likeable man." Johnson bullied his staff and flew into a rage over the most inconsequential matters. He almost never apologized for his outbursts, though Lady Bird often tried to make amends and Johnson himself occasionally indirectly compensated through some great kindness. In addition to indulging his temper, Johnson apparently had a need to humiliate—at any rate, he seemed to enjoy it. Hubert Humphrey became perhaps the most prominent victim. Johnson had admirably selected a man of considerable stature as his vice president, but he toyed with him in announcing his choice, once dressed him in an oversized cowboy suit on a visit to the Johnson ranch, and inflicted many petty humiliations.

Other aspects of LBJ's public and private behavior in the White House did little to counteract stories of his attempts to humiliate and his temper. Early in his presidency, the press reported that he drank beer as he raced his Lincoln Continental around the ranch. Later, he pulled one of his beagles up by its ears and on another occasion pulled up his own shirt to display his gallbladder surgery scar—in both instances for the cameras. He bullied visitors into skinny-dipping with him in the White House pool and held conferences while he received a rubdown, sat on the toilet, or had an enema. Surely in doing so he sought not only to save time but also to intimidate and degrade. The flaunting of such behavior even suggests that the provincial enjoyed making the capital, indeed the world, aware that he had not abandoned his "country" ways. For most Americans, though, it only raised doubts about what sort of man ran the country.

LBJ's reputation as a wheeler-dealer tainted by corruption raised doubts as well. Johnson had become a very rich man while receiving only a small salary from the government. The accumulation of the Johnson fortune, estimated at anywhere from $3 million to $14 million or more when he entered the White House, began in 1943 when Lady Bird used part of her inheritance to purchase an unprofitable Austin radio station, KTBC. With occasional help from Lyndon and some of his staff as well as favorable rulings by the Federal Communications Commission, she transformed the station into a very profitable enterprise. In 1948, the FCC awarded it Austin's only television channel. Without any significant competition, KTBC television became phenomenally lucrative. With its profits and some shrewd business maneuvers, the Johnsons purchased interest in other stations and, by 1964, five thousand acres of Texas land to supplement the more than three thousand acres in Alabama that Lady Bird inherited. No one has produced evidence that Johnson overtly employed his influence to secure the favorable FCC rulings that helped make possible KTBC's success. Many have questioned the ethical propriety of a government official responsible for overseeing a regulatory agency profiting so handsomely in a regulated industry.

Just before Johnson became president, charges surfaced of financial corruption and influence peddling by Bobby Baker, secretary to Senate Democrats and former Johnson protégé. Many observers believed that Baker's problems began only after Johnson left the Senate, but instead of saying so, LBJ announced, to much incredulity, that he and Baker had never been close. Soon the public learned that in 1957 an insurance company paid Baker a sizable commission for writing two policies on the life of Lyndon Johnson, that the president of the company had then bought time on Johnson's television station, and that later its vice president had given the Johnsons an expensive television set. Johnson, by then president, maintained that the families frequently exchanged gifts, and the press let the matter drop. Baker, though, eventually served time on other charges. After the Baker affair and Jenkins's arrest, however, the Johnson administration proved remarkably free of scandal. Yet many Americans continued to think of Johnson as at least tainted by corruption.

Johnson's seemingly shady past and unattractive personality contributed to a larger problem—a public perception of LBJ as a man obsessed with power. Johnson did have, as one friend remarked, an instinct for power "as primordial as a salmon's going upstream to spawn." He sought it all his life and in the White House reveled in its attainment. Fearing his wrath, the White House staff tried to anticipate his whims by stocking gargantuan quantities of ice cream or Fresca or whatever he fancied at the moment. Johnson dispensed presidential souvenirs to almost everyone with whom he came in contact, particularly favoring an electric toothbrush bearing the presidential seal because its recipient would think of Lyndon Johnson first thing in the morning and last thing at night. He turned bill-signing ceremonies into virtual royal displays, using numerous pens and bestowing them on the honored many. On one occasion, as Johnson ran toward a group of waiting helicopters, his military guide pointed to one and suggested,

"That's your helicopter, Mr. President." Johnson stopped in his tracks and replied, "Son, they're all my helicopters."

Because of his enjoyment of the excesses of power, because of his tendency to bully and humiliate, but most especially because he sometimes appeared such a political opportunist, many Americans believed that Johnson sought power for its own sake, not to employ it to some larger public purpose. Yet Johnson's career testified to his desire to govern and, despite shifts here and there, displayed his commitment to certain basic political beliefs. They did not, however, fit easily into the traditional categories of liberal or conservative. They rested first and foremost on a faith in and fondness for "the system," in other words, for the nation's political and business establishments.

Johnson accepted, indeed relished, the cumbersome, imperfect system of politics that ruled in Washington, D.C. He talked so much of consensus and used his favorite quote "Come, then, let us reason together" so often during his presidency that people began to snicker at the words. LBJ, however, believed in them. He considered a consensus reached by reasoning together—and maneuvering and trading—a perfectly honorable and proper way to pass legislation and therefore to govern—and he sought to govern. "I have never believed," he wrote in his memoirs, "that those who are governed least are governed best. We *are* the people, as Franklin Roosevelt said. And the proper function of a government of the people, by the people, and for the people is to make it possible for all citizens to experience a better, more secure, and more rewarding life." LBJ wanted to use government to foster economic abundance and to improve the physical and social environment, but most of all, wrote George Reedy, he had "a burning desire to make life easier for those who had to struggle up from the bottom."

Johnson did not seek to ease the rise of those at the bottom by tearing down or radically restructuring the economic establishment. He had no quarrel with American capitalism; after all, it had been good to him. Throughout his career, only his advocacy of public power constituted a challenge to private ownership. As president he sponsored a tax cut that benefited business, and he rarely attacked business leaders. Some Great Society programs, particularly environmental and safety legislation, increased government regulation, but the Johnson administration did less to foster central planning or government intervention in the economy than had the New Deal. "I never wanted to demagogue against business, Wall Street, or the power companies," Johnson once said in rare criticism of his hero Roosevelt. "I thought FDR was wrong."

Rather than attacking or changing the system, Johnson sought to ease the rise of the people at the bottom by bringing them into it—and changing them, if necessary, to do so. Education always remained the reform closest to his heart, and Johnson considered it primarily a means by which the poor and disadvantaged could improve their lot in life by learning the skills of the system. When he taught in Cotulla, Johnson strove to instill in his Mexican American students the ways of the Anglo world in which, he realized, they would have to make their way. Many of OEO's programs took much the same approach. Head Start, a prekindergarten program for the disadvantaged added to OEO in 1965, and the Job Corps developed in participants the skills needed to fit into and succeed in the educational and business systems. The scholars who planned the Great Society may have operated from theories designed to overcome a "culture of poverty," but Johnson, never one for abstractions, conceived the purpose simply as teaching the poor, just as he had done in Cotulla, what they needed to enter and to advance in the business world.

Johnson also favored, though far less enthusiastically or consistently than he did pro-

In a ceremony on Ellis Island in 1965, LBJ signs an immigration bill ending the discriminatory quota system. *(Yoichi R. Okamoto, LBJ Library Collection)*

grams to bring poor people into the system, government aid to those deprived of a basic standard of living. He often said that in so rich a nation no one should be without food or medical care. In the Senate he fought to expand Social Security benefits to the disabled; in his second term he worked for medical insurance programs for the needy and elderly. Only late in his administration, however, did he support expansion of the food stamp program. Funding for these and other existing entitlement programs did rise during his years in office, but public aid as a percentage of the gross national product would be far higher at the end of the Nixon and Ford administrations than at the end of Johnson's.

Johnson, in sum, consistently, or at least as consistently as most politicians, endeavored to use his power in behalf of certain beliefs. He accepted the economic and political systems of the nation but sought to use government to increase the abundance that they produced,

to improve the environment, and to bring more people into the economic mainstream. His vision of a Great Society emerged out of these principles, but the public never completely perceived his purpose. For some people the reality and image of the president's personality—what journalists Evans and Novak called the private Johnson—overwhelmed what he did in government—the public Johnson. For others, Johnson's political craftiness led them to consider everything he did as "only politics." Especially in the White House, the fault lay with Johnson, not simply the public's perception of him. The president failed to communicate his sincerity or purpose and larger vision to the nation.

He always blamed, sometimes in incredible displays of temper and self-pity, the Northeastern intellectuals and the press. Indeed, neither group liked him very much: some intellectuals and reporters because he was not John Kennedy, others because of the private Johnson.

With journalists, the more important of the two groups, Johnson made matters worse. The man whose Senate success rested on his amazing ability to read the wants and desires of others never fathomed the goals or needs of the press. His constant changes in schedule inconvenienced them; his nearly pathological insistence on secrecy made their work difficult. As he had in the Senate, Johnson wanted to keep his options open to the very last minute and abhorred leaks that would curtail them, a reasonable attitude that he took to irrational extremes. At times LBJ changed an appointment if it was reported in the press before he announced it; on other occasions he denied any intention of doing what he then proceeded to do. Not surprisingly, the press came to distrust him and, more important, accused Johnson of creating a so-called credibility gap.

Though his poor relations with the press did not help, Johnson's problem in projecting his vision went deeper. He performed poorly on television, appearing and sounding listless. Despite repeated attempts to improve, LBJ never mastered the medium. Americans rarely saw the compelling figure described by those who met him personally or received The Treatment. Television, however, was only part of the problem; Johnson had never excelled as a formal orator. He always thought "private negotiations and compromise" more important than "public rhetoric" and, according to Reedy, considered a speech merely a "crowd pleaser" in which he had not really given his word. As president, Johnson's speaking style relied heavily on sentimentality and, part of his Southwestern style of storytelling, hyperbole. ("Hyperbole was to Lyndon Johnson," Bill Moyers once observed, "what oxygen is to life.") Sometimes the sentimentality succeeded, as in Johnson's address to Congress right after the Kennedy assassination, but more often resulted in Johnson's being labeled corny or insincere. Surely his exaggerations and numerous superlatives contributed to the credibility gap. His difficulties in public oratory, magnified by television, hindered his ability to communicate his vision of how he wanted to use his power to shape the country.

Yet Johnson had been reelected, despite these problems of personality and perception. Perhaps they would have remained, as they were in 1964, decidedly secondary to Johnson's accomplishments, but in 1965 Johnson expanded the Great Society and became embroiled in Vietnam. In undertaking both crusades, Johnson needed the full trust and support of the American people and considerable skill in shaping public opinion. His unattractive image and poor public oratory, therefore, became a greater handicap in his second term. Moreover, people angered by his crusades, particularly the war in Vietnam, often seized on and exaggerated the image of Lyndon Johnson as a boor and bully.

1965: Two Crusades

In January, 1965, aware of the dangers of overconfidence bred by his landslide victory but also of the limited lifespan of his popular mandate, Johnson went to Congress with proposals for major domestic reforms, most of them generated by the task forces established in 1964. Since his landslide victory had helped elect a large number of new liberal Democratic congressmen, his party had a more comfortable working margin over the Republicans—68 to 32 in the Senate and 295 to 140 in the House—than it had the year before. Using this majority and his legislative skills, LBJ pushed through Congress several bills, which, along with the three major ones passed in 1964, constituted the heart of his Great Society program.

First to be enacted was the $1.3 billion Elementary and Secondary Education Act. For many years Congress had debated but failed to pass a program of federal aid to primary and secondary education. This time a compromise that allowed federal aid to students in parochial schools, but not to the schools themselves, secured the support of the Roman Catholic hierarchy, which during the Kennedy administration had helped block passage of a similar measure with no aid for parochial schools. Even with the compromise and the heavy Democratic majority, the bill constituted a Johnson triumph. Congress had passed, historian and Johnson aide Eric Goldman observed, "a billion-dollar law, deeply affecting a fundamental institution of the nation, in a breath-taking eighty-seven days. The House approved it with no amendment that mattered; the Senate had voted it through literally without a comma changed."

Next, Congress passed an expanded version of a health insurance bill submitted by Johnson. It created Medicare, a program to help pay medical costs for the elderly, and Medicaid, a similar program for the poor. Other legislation followed: college scholarships, more money for housing for the needy, rent supplements, an end to the discriminatory quota system for immigrants, and the creation of the Department of Housing and Urban Development. Johnson also asked for and Congress created the National Endowments for the Arts and for the Humanities to enhance the cultural environment and stronger air and water quality acts to improve the physical environment as well as a highway beautification program, the last a personal campaign of Lady Bird.

That same spring, Johnson helped secure the passage of another major civil rights bill. The 1964 act had not satisfied the president, and later that year he ordered the attorney general to draft a voting rights bill. The "right to vote with no ifs, ands, or buts" was the key to achieving African American rights, Vice President Humphrey recalled LBJ's saying. "When the Negroes get that, they'll have every politician, north and south, east and west, kissing their ass, begging for their support." In early 1965, Johnson did not believe that the time was right to pass such legislation, but after violent police attacks on demonstrators

demanding the right to vote in Selma, Alabama, and the murder of a Northern minister there—a situation so bad that Johnson finally nationalized the Alabama National Guard to protect the protesters—Johnson decided that the time had come to enact a voting rights law.

To urge Congress to do so, Johnson delivered one of the most moving addresses of his career to a joint session and, through television, to the nation. In unequivocal language, he demanded the passage of a voting rights bill and also made the strongest statement in behalf of black equality ever offered by a president. "What happened in Selma is part of a far larger movement which reaches into every section and State of America. It is the effort of American Negroes to secure for themselves the full blessings of American life. Their cause must be our cause too. Because it is not just Negroes, but really it is all of us, who must overcome the crippling legacy of bigotry and injustice." Then he added, borrowing a line from the unofficial anthem of the Civil Rights movement, "And we shall overcome." Four months later Congress passed the Voting Rights Act of 1965, arguably the most important civil rights legislation ever enacted in the United States. It eliminated literacy tests for voting and authorized federal supervision of elections in states or voting districts where such tests had been used and fewer than half the voting age population voted or were registered to vote. Johnson's Justice Department eventually placed all or part of seven Southern states under the jurisdiction of the act, and by the end of the decade, black voter registration and office holding had risen dramatically.

In the same spring that Congress passed the Voting Rights Act and other Great Society measures, Johnson took a series of steps that substantially altered American involvement in Vietnam and rendered the war there as large a part of his legacy as domestic reform. Since the incident in the Gulf of Tonkin, Viet Cong activity and infiltration of troops and supplies from the North had increased. By December, 1964, military planners concluded that the situation was perilous and recommended a bombing campaign against the North. LBJ hesitated to undertake such an expansion of the war. He only increased economic aid and expanded various pacification programs designed to "win the hearts and minds" of the people of South Vietnam. When the situation continued to deteriorate, in early 1965 Johnson decided that a bombing campaign against the North had become necessary. Using the enemy's attack on American troops in South Vietnam as a reason, the United States in early February began an air war against North Vietnam. Soon General William Westmoreland, whom Johnson had appointed commander of American forces in Vietnam, requested troops to guard air bases there, and in March thirty-five hundred marines arrived in Vietnam. By April, Johnson had approved their employment in offensive operations. In July, after the Viet Cong had taken control of parts of the country and the fall of the government in Saigon appeared a very real possibility, the president approved sending fifty thousand more troops to Vietnam to undertake combat missions. Johnson also committed himself to send additional troops if they were needed.

Between February and July 1965, then, Johnson had begun an air war against North Vietnam, committed American troops to a direct combat role in the South, and dramatically increased the number of Americans fighting there. Perhaps one scholar exaggerated when he referred to the decisions of this period as "the Americanization of the war," for the South Vietnamese still did much of the fighting and bore much of the brunt of the war, but surely the United States had gone to war in Vietnam.

LBJ's goal in Vietnam, the survival of a stable, secure, noncommunist government in the South, was that of his predecessors Eisenhower and Kennedy. Faced with the likelihood that the government of South Vietnam would fall, however, a prospect the others had not faced, Johnson decided to use American air power and combat troops to prevent it and to inflict enough suffering, through the destruction of certain targets in the North and search-and-destroy tactics against enemy forces in the South, to force the North Vietnamese and Viet Cong to seek a negotiated settlement. Phased escalation of both the bombing and the number of American troops, Johnson and his advisers believed, would allow the United States to increase the pressure until the enemy sought peace. Few of Johnson's advisers talked of "winning" the war in any other terms. Johnson rejected an all-out bombing campaign or an invasion of the North.

The president did not decide on a policy of phased escalation in a fit of jingoistic enthusiasm or out of some innate love of battle; however, although he listened to a wide variety of opinions, he never seriously considered any other course. He rejected dramatic escalation or an all-out attack on the North because either might lead to Soviet, or more likely Chinese, intervention, a wider war, and possible nuclear confrontation. He wanted to avoid World War III at all cost; indeed, he believed that the course he chose did exactly that. Johnson's view of foreign policy had been formed in the late 1930's when, following Roosevelt, he adopted an activist view of America's role in the world. Like so many others of his generation, he looked back on the appeasement of Adolf Hitler as the cause of World War II. He therefore concluded that either aggression must be stopped or a greater danger surely encountered later. In the years after World War II, such thinking led him and much of official Washington, in which his attitudes were shaped, to the containment doctrine, which centered U.S. foreign policy on stopping Soviet and communist expansion and to the subsequent interventions in Greece and Korea. Johnson saw the war in Vietnam as another case of communist aggres-

U.S. troops in Vietnam, 1964. *(U.S. Marine Corps)*

sion, which had to be faced there or in some other place or some larger war.

Johnson also feared the domestic consequences if he abandoned South Vietnam to communism. In so many ways the product of his own political experience, he remembered well the McCarthy era. He worried that the loss of South Vietnam to communism would set off a similar period of hysteria that would be detrimental to his and the Democratic Party's political future as well as to the country. As the war continued, Johnson deeply resented his liberal critics and the young protesters, but he appeared always to fear more the wrath of the Right if he failed to keep the anticommunist faith.

Having decided that the war was necessary, however, Johnson did little to rally the American people to the cause. Instead, he took the nation to war by indirection. He sought no congressional declaration of war beyond the Tonkin Gulf Resolution and refused to call up the reserves. He did not at the time announce the April shift of U.S. soldiers to an offensive role and told the nation of the July decision for escalation during an afternoon press con-

ference. Johnson apparently feared that a fervent embrace of the war would lead to an abandonment of his first love, the Great Society. He even tried to hide the cost of the war lest it lead to a reduction in spending on reform programs. LBJ also realized that he had to mobilize people for a limited war. If he summoned them too heartily, they might demand the very wider war that he sought to avoid. To convince them to fight only the small conflict he thought appropriate demanded considerable skill in shaping public opinion. Little of Johnson's career or his political talents fitted him for the task. To make matters worse, his decision to send American troops after he had declared in the 1964 campaign that he would not do so, left many Americans distrustful of his intentions from the start. As a result of all these factors, Johnson failed to summon and sustain the national will to support his course in Vietnam, although perhaps no other president could have either.

As LBJ expanded U.S. commitments in Vietnam, he also ordered American troops into the Dominican Republic. That Caribbean nation had experienced a succession of governments after the 1961 assassination of longtime dictator Rafael Trujillo. In April, 1965, a military junta seized power but soon faced armed rebellion by leftists and constitutional forces. As the fighting in the streets increased, the U.S. ambassador requested that troops be sent to protect American lives. LBJ immediately dispatched four hundred marines. Later the same day, April 28, fearing disorder and a communist takeover, Johnson decided on armed intervention. U.S. troops, eventually numbering twenty-two thousand, went to the Dominican

Republic, stabilized the situation, and by August secured a U.S.-supported government. The following year the Dominican Republic held free elections, and in May the last American troops went home.

Some praised Johnson for restoring order and ensuring elections. Others criticized the president for undermining the only chance for noncommunist revolutionary change. They believed the intervention to be part of a larger administration policy of supporting the status quo and fostering a climate for American economic interests throughout Latin America. Even many Americans who did not go that far in their criticism remained unconvinced by Johnson's claim of communist influence among the rebels and felt misled by his early, hyperbolic accounts of the danger to Americans. His performance in the Dominican crisis reinforced the doubts of those who believed that Johnson had raced unthinkingly into Vietnam and fed growing public perception of a Johnson credibility gap.

1966 and 1967: Time of Trial

The intervention in the Dominican Republic and the escalation of the war in Vietnam marked a major turning point in the presidency of Lyndon Johnson. In 1966 and 1976 Johnson's presidency increasingly came under siege. Many Americans believed that Johnson failed to fight the Vietnam War with sufficient vigor. More vocal intellectuals and young protesters criticized him for fighting it at all. Influenced partly by this antiwar sentiment, but also by more complex factors beyond LBJ's control, some college students and other young Americans rebelled against the "establishment"— their term for an amorphous evil reaching from the suburbs through the universities and corporations to the government. As the chief symbol and proponent of the establishment, Johnson evoked their special wrath. Many African Americans embraced their own form of radicalism as black power replaced nonvio-

lence as the tactic of some in the Civil Rights movement. Both white and black radicals denounced American values and took to the streets, as did many in the nation's ghettos when rioting erupted in several cities. Many more Americans, appalled by the disorder and criticism, blamed Johnson for it, as Herbert Hoover had been blamed for the Depression. They believed that reform had gone far enough, and a few suspected that the Great Society programs contributed to the disquiet. The community action agencies, which in some cities had brought the radicalized poor into the administration of the War on Poverty, came in for special criticism.

Though he later claimed that he had already perceived the shift in public mood, in 1966 Johnson decided not to abandon domestic reform despite the turmoil and the financial demands of the war in Vietnam. He spoke of the Great Society as frequently as he had the year before and asked Congress for "guns and butter," funding for both the war and domestic reform. In 1966, Congress did enact the Model Cities Program, a major part of the Great Society. It established demonstration projects in sixty-three cities to provide slum renewal, area redevelopment, and other improvements to the urban environment. LBJ's other legislative victories that year proved more modest: a highway and automobile safety law, a rise in the minimum wage, and the creation of the Department of Transportation. In fact, Congress passed considerably fewer of Johnson's proposals than it had the year before. His legislative wizardry worked far less well as the public's willingness to support reform and the government's ability to finance it declined.

Nowhere were the changed circumstances in which the president operated more apparent than in the field of civil rights. In 1967, Johnson made an important symbolic statement when he appointed Thurgood Marshall, the lawyer who had led the fight for school desegregation, the first African American justice of the Supreme Court. In general, though, in 1966-1967 Johnson found himself less often promoting black advancement and more often reacting to black violence as summer riots in the urban centers, which had begun in 1964, became more numerous. In his public discussion of the disorders, Johnson tried to deplore the violence without endorsing reaction or abandoning his support for black equality. During the summer of 1967, he sent army troops into Detroit to reestablish order after a riot but also created a commission to study the causes of such civil disturbances. The Kerner Commission, as it came to be called after its chairman Otto Kerner, in 1968 reported severe problems in the ghettos and a fundamental division between whites and blacks in American society. Johnson simply

accepted the report and did not respond to its recommendations for new programs. He did not believe that he could secure the necessary appropriations. By then, LBJ no longer urged Congress to pass new reform initiatives but rather appealed for it to levy new taxes to curtail inflation.

As early as 1966, Johnson's economic advisers warned him of the inflationary potential of his attempt to have both guns and butter. At that time he told some congressmen that no rise in personal taxes would be necessary, though he asked for and received an increase in automobile and telephone excise taxes. When, later in the year, Johnson requested an additional increase in taxes, Congress balked. Johnson settled for a policy of budgetary restraint and appeals to business and labor to hold down prices and wages. In 1967, Johnson sought first a 6 percent and then, when the economy continued to heat up, a 10 percent tax surcharge. LBJ failed to work out a compromise with congressmen who wanted major reductions in spending to accompany the surcharge, and his bill never got out of committee. The failure to limit the federal budget deficit because of spending for both the Great Society and the Vietnam War, many economists contend, provided the initial impetus for the devastating inflation of the 1970's.

Johnson's increasing difficulties with Congress resulted not only from changing domestic and budgetary realities but also from growing opposition to his foreign policy and perhaps his own increasing involvement in world affairs. In his first two years in office, Johnson never left the continental United States; from 1966 through 1968, he made twelve trips outside it, several of them to Vietnam, Guam, or Honolulu to confer on Vietnam. The war, however, was not his only foreign policy concern. In 1967, a crisis erupted in the Middle East. In May, Egypt moved troops

The Detroit riot of July, 1967. *(Archive Photos)*

into the Sinai and closed Israel's vital water route through the Gulf of Aqaba. Johnson publicly defended Israel's right of access but also worked behind the scenes to prevent war. Some critics contended that he did not send the Israelis a strong enough signal of American opposition, but in any case, Israel, feeling threatened by the Egyptian moves, on June 5 launched a very successful attack against its old enemy. The Johnson administration announced the United States' neutrality but hastily added that it continued to support the existence and rights of Israel. The latter statement especially angered several Arab states, which quickly broke diplomatic relations with the United States. After six days, though, Israel, which had already conquered sizable amounts of Egyptian territory, signed a cease-fire. During this Six-Day War, the Israelis sank the USS *Liberty*, an intelligence-gathering ship plainly marked and clearly in international waters. Casualties included 34 dead and 171 wounded. Neither Johnson nor anyone else made much of the incident, and Israel paid indemnities to the families of the casualties. Labeled an accident by the Israelis, the sinking has never been fully explained.

During the Six-Day War, Johnson and Aleksey Kosygin, chair of the Council of Ministers of the Soviet Union, talked frequently on the hot line, thereby helping to avoid an expansion of the conflict into a larger war. Although Johnson adhered to the containment doctrine, as he demonstrated in Vietnam and the Dominican Republic as well as by his attempts to strengthen the North Atlantic Treaty Organization, he still sought to reduce Cold War tensions. He avoided unnecessary verbal attacks on the Soviet Union and kept open channels of communication. During his administration the United States and the Soviet Union signed a new consular convention and along with other countries a treaty banning weapons of mass destruction from outer space. In June, 1967, Johnson and Kosygin held at Glassboro,

New Jersey, a hastily arranged and not particularly successful summit conference. The two leaders discussed ongoing negotiations toward arms reduction but reached no agreements.

Neither relations with the Soviets nor the Six-Day War ever absorbed the president's attention or undermined his popularity the way the Vietnam War did. It came to consume his administration. By the end of 1965, 185,000 American troops were serving in Vietnam, and the war and its casualties clearly troubled Johnson. Over the Christmas holidays, he instituted a bombing halt and a well-publicized peace initiative. They failed to achieve results, and on January 31, 1966, Johnson resumed the bombing. In February, the Senate Foreign Relations Committee held televised hearings on the war, which helped fuel the growing opposition to Johnson's policy.

Johnson tried to rally popular support with bellicose patriotism and affirmations of American resolve. He held firmly to his strategy of phased escalation to prevent the overthrow of the government in the South and to force the North to negotiate. He gradually expanded the list of targets to be bombed in North Vietnam and increased the number of American troops in the South to more than five hundred thousand. The military situation had improved since 1965, and the fall of South Vietnam no longer appeared imminent, owing more to the larger American presence than to any dramatic improvement in the strength or popular support of the South Vietnamese government. The expectation that the gradual increase in pressure on the North would force it to the bargaining table proved false: With Soviet and Chinese aid, the North had met each U.S. escalation with one of its own.

Nevertheless, Johnson continued to seek a negotiated settlement. He ordered fifteen different bombing pauses in hopes of spurring negotiations and, according to a list in his memoirs, pursued seventy-two peace overtures.

Critics questioned how seriously he pursued them, and clearly the difficulties of fine-tuning military pressure and peace initiatives undermined these efforts. In the final analysis, though, the problem was that neither side was willing to make the concessions necessary to get negotiations started. Through most of his administration, LBJ insisted on a prior agreement on mutual deescalation before talks could begin and objected to any role for the Viet Cong. In late 1967, his position softened to insistence that the North would not take advantage of a bombing halt before discussions could begin. The North Vietnamese, whom Johnson probably rightly believed had little if any interest in talks, insisted on an unconditional, permanent end to the bombing before they would negotiate.

By the end of 1967, therefore, both the search for peace and the war itself seemed condemned to stalemate. Lyndon Johnson's administration did too. In 1966 and 1967, Johnson had managed to push few new reforms through Congress and worried as much about curtailing inflation as transforming America. In 1967, he rarely even used the term Great Society. His own personal popularity reached a new low that October. Protesters followed him everywhere, some chanting, "Hey, Hey, LBJ, How many kids have you killed today?" The press criticized him harshly, especially because of his credibility gap. The personal failings overlooked in 1964 now seemed so much more important. One well-known cartoon, which made fun of both his boorishness and his problems in Vietnam, pictured a saddened LBJ pulling up his shirt to show not the scar from his gallbladder operation but one in the shape of Vietnam.

In private and occasionally in public LBJ lashed out at his critics. He always suspected, according to one confidant, a conspiracy by "the intellectuals, the press, the liberals, and the Kennedys" to destroy him. When Secretary of Defense Robert McNamara, an early archi-

tect of the Vietnam policy, began to work within the administration for a change of course, Johnson quickly nominated him to be president of the World Bank. Unlike McNamara, the president in late 1967 believed that the situation in Vietnam had improved and orchestrated another campaign to convince Americans that the war was being won.

1968: Abdicating Power

In January, 1968, matters became worse rather than better. Prospects that Congress would pass the tax surcharge still did not appear good, and a British devaluation of the pound in November, 1967, had led to a drain on U.S. gold reserves that was not stopped until March. On January 23, North Korea captured the intelligence ship USS *Pueblo* and its crew of eighty-three men outside North Korea's twenty-five-mile limit. Johnson expressed his outrage, mobilized fourteen thousand members of the Air Force and Navy reserves, but did little else except begin negotiations for the return of the ship's crew. They did not succeed until the following December. Worst of all, on January 30-31, during Tet, the Vietnamese New Year, the Viet Cong and the North Vietnamese launched a major offensive.

Catching American and South Vietnamese forces off guard, the enemy attacked many hamlets, most major cities, and almost every provincial and district capital. A Viet Cong squad even penetrated the grounds of the U.S. embassy in Saigon. The American and South Vietnamese armies quickly recovered and inflicted heavy casualties on the enemy. Johnson pronounced Tet a victory, but the press had emphasized the failures, and a public grown suspicious of LBJ's pronouncements on Vietnam doubted his assessment. Many people wondered how, if the war had been going so well at the end of 1967, the enemy had launched such an extensive offensive in January. The Tet Offensive crystallized growing frustration with both Johnson and the war among those who sought to expand it as well as among those opposed to it.

The Tet Offensive also catalyzed a reassessment of Vietnam policy within the administration. Some critics of the new policy offer what amounts to a "stab in the back" thesis. They argue that the press turned the Tet victory into defeat, mobilizing public opinion against the war and forcing Johnson to abandon the escalation that would at last have won it. Such an interpretation has weaknesses. As historian George Herring observes, "That victory was within grasp," even with an increase in troops, "remains quite doubtful." Moreover, Johnson clearly listened to voices within government rather than to critics in the streets or the press. Secretary of State Dean Rusk suggested a bombing halt as a means to defuse criticism. Newly appointed Secretary of Defense Clark Clifford, formerly an ardent supporter of escalation, a group of civilians within the Defense Department, and a few close aides began to work for an end to escalation. The Wise Men, a group of establishment leaders assembled by Clifford and briefed by important officials, also urged Johnson to change his policy.

Responding to these insiders and probably to his congressional contacts as well, Johnson in March, 1968, decided on a new policy, although he did not abandon his commitment to the war. Johnson rejected Westmoreland's request for 200,000 additional troops (and soon replaced him as commander in Vietnam) and agreed to an increase of only 13,500 soldiers. He sought instead to strengthen the South Vietnamese army, initiating a program later expanded by his successor. He halted bombing over all of North Vietnam except a small strip just above the demilitarized zone where he believed it necessary to continue attacks in order to protect American troops below the zone. Finally, he resolved to undertake a new peace initiative and named a high-ranking representative to meet with the North Vietnamese.

On March 31, the president announced these measures during a nationally televised address. At its end, he linked them to a startling announcement: "I shall not seek, and I will not accept, the nomination of my party for another term as your president." Almost no one had expected it; Johnson had decided to withdraw from the coming presidential race. The debate over why he chose to do so continues. One student of the Johnson administration argues that because of his health—he had had a major heart attack in 1955 and underwent two operations while in the White House—Johnson never intended to run and had made that decision in 1965. Popular lore has it that LBJ fled from office in the face of antiwar pressure, particularly the surprisingly strong showing of peace candidate Eugene F. McCarthy in the New Hampshire primary and the subsequent announcement by Johnson's nemesis Bobby Kennedy that he, too, would challenge the president's renomination. It seems likely, however, that Johnson based his decision on more complex reasons. Sometime in early 1968, frustrated by his inability to conclude the war in Vietnam, haunted by its casualties, aware especially after New Hampshire of his unpopularity, and stymied in his efforts to pass the tax surcharge, Johnson decided that he could not govern, much less unify, a divided nation. Armed with the power of incumbency, not to mention the ability to influence the election through dramatic initiatives in Vietnam, Johnson conceivably could have retained power. Yet, realizing he could no longer use that power to govern, to accomplish what he believed needed to be done, he declined to make the effort to do so. His abdication of the presidency may offer the most convincing evidence that he did not want power only in and for itself.

When he removed himself from the presidential race, Johnson became a lame duck president who watched others fight for the right to succeed him. His administration still man-

Protesters at the 1968 Democratic National Convention, Chicago. *(Library of Congress)*

aged a few victories. After the assassination of civil rights leader Martin Luther King, Jr., and the rioting that followed it, Congress passed LBJ's last major civil rights legislation, a strong open housing law that banned discrimination in the sale and rental of most real estate. Congress also approved a Safe Streets Act that Johnson had sought since early 1967, a truth-in-lending law, and more money for housing and conservation. It even, finally, passed the tax surcharge. In July, the United States, the Soviet Union, and many other nations signed the Nuclear Nonproliferation Treaty.

Frustrations and failures, however, continued. Johnson suffered an embarrassing defeat over nominations to the Supreme Court. In 1965, Johnson had convinced Kennedy appointee and liberal Arthur Goldberg to resign from the Court in order to serve as ambassador to the United Nations. Apparently, Johnson appealed to Goldberg's patriotism, suggested that he might help bring peace in Vietnam, and hinted that he could expect to return to the Court. In Goldberg's place, LBJ appointed Abe Fortas, a very able lawyer who happened to be a very old friend. In June, 1968, Chief Justice Earl Warren offered to resign, and the president decided to elevate Fortas to chief justice. He also announced that he would appoint Homer Thornberry, a federal judge and Johnson associate, to Fortas's seat. Many in Congress, upset by Fortas's liberal record on the Court and his ill-advised conduct off the bench—including continuing to advise the president—and aghast at the cronyism implied by the Thornberry nomination, blocked Fortas's nomination with a filibuster. Johnson finally withdrew it and did not make another. His successor got to pick the next chief justice and also a replacement for Fortas, who had to resign in 1969 when it became public that while on the Court he had accepted, though later returned, a large fee from a foundation. It is difficult not to conclude that Johnson had squandered his chance to help shape the Supreme Court for the next decade.

Johnson's greatest frustration remained, as it had since 1965, Vietnam. The North Vietnamese responded to the president's March 31 proposals, but for a time nothing came of the discussions. Heavy fighting continued in the South as Johnson sought to ensure a strong bargaining position. Finally, in October the United States and North Vietnam reached an understanding by which the United States would stop all bombing of the North and North Vietnam would exercise restraint in the South and limit infiltration from the North. The plan also included a complex "your side-our side" formula to finesse the refusal of the South Vietnamese to negotiate with the Viet Cong and of the North Vietnamese and Viet Cong to talk with the government of the South. When the agreement was announced, the South Vietnamese refused to participate, probably assuming that the next administration would be more supportive. Johnson decided to proceed anyway and on October 31, announced a total bombing halt over North Vietnam, which remained in effect throughout the remainder of his term. Two weeks later, South Vietnam agreed to join the talks. By the time they began, Johnson was about to leave office. He had failed to bring peace to Vietnam.

By then his successor had been elected. During the summer the Democratic Party met in Chicago, with Lyndon Johnson not in attendance. Violent confrontations between antiwar protesters and police outside the convention hall and deep divisions within the party disrupted the convention. With Robert Kennedy having been assassinated that June and Eugene McCarthy far from popular with the party regulars, the delegates nominated Vice President Humphrey. Hurt by the discord within his party, tainted by his support for Johnson's war effort, and, for the most part, unaided by the president, Humphrey lost a very close race to Republican Richard Nixon. After a smooth transition, in January, 1969, Johnson turned over power to Nixon.

Johnson returned to the ranch near Johnson City that he had visited so often as president. The provincial had come home. According to some accounts, LBJ had trouble adjusting to life without power and went through a period of withdrawal. Soon, however, he turned his tremendous energies to the management of the ranch. He also worked with a staff writing his memoirs and closely monitored the operation of the Lyndon Baines Johnson Library and the Lyndon Baines Johnson School of Public Affairs at the University of Texas. His interest in politics eventually revived, but the former president rarely made public appearances and did not attend, and may not have been wanted at, the 1972 Democratic Convention. He spent more time with his family than he had during his career. He especially enjoyed his grandchildren; both of his daughters had married while he occupied the White House. During a visit to one of his daughters in 1972, Johnson suffered another heart attack.

Never very healthy after that, Johnson began to get his financial affairs in order. At a December, 1972, conference held at the Johnson Library, he made one last rousing speech in favor of the rights of African Americans. When a group of black radicals interrupted the scheduled program to protest, Johnson heard them out, went back to the podium, and offered a vigorous discussion of how they could make the system work. Johnson died at the ranch the following month, on January 22, 1973, one day before Richard Nixon announced a ceasefire in Vietnam.

Even before Johnson died, journalists and historians had begun to describe the Johnson presidency using words such as "irony" and "tragedy." Lyndon Johnson had held office at a time of unusual turmoil in American life, a period of rebellion by some among the young and black and poor. His administration certainly did not single-handedly foment this rebellion, but Johnson's style and the war he waged in Vietnam certainly fueled it. Both the rebels and those who resented their rebellion began to lose faith in the "system" and especially in the ability of government to meet people's needs and respond to their wishes. Perhaps the greatest irony of Johnson's presidency rested in this fact, that the man with such love for the system, who as a legislative leader could make it work so well, presided over a period in American history when so many lost faith in it. The greatest tragedy was that the style and skills that Johnson acquired within the system, in the Congress where he first learned how to make it work, poorly equipped him for the task that he faced as president. He had learned how to maneuver in secret, how to build legislative coalitions, how to pass bills. He had not learned how to be a moral leader or how to mobilize a nation. All presidents need to be able to do these things, but times of turmoil especially demand such leadership.

Even so, the skills he had acquired helped Johnson leave a legacy of domestic reform second only to that of Franklin D. Roosevelt. During Johnson's years in office, Congress passed more than two hundred pieces of legislation that created more than five hundred social programs. His attempt to create a Great Society has been rightly criticized. He may have pushed for too much too fast. He never devoted the attention to administering programs that he did to enacting them. Certainly, bringing the disadvantaged into the system proved more difficult than LBJ and many of the social theorists who staffed his task forces believed. Funding never matched promises, either. One of the major difficulties of his crusade for a Great Society, as in other aspects of his presidency, arose out of Johnson's failure to shape a national commitment to it. He talked of the Great Society with such hyperbole that many in the middle class believed that the country had been given to the poor. The poor, in contrast, heard the rhetoric but saw only the meager results of low funding and decided that the government could not or would not help them. Consequently, people in both groups turned against the president and his programs.

Despite such shortcomings, however, Johnson and his Great Society legislation made real and important contributions. Doubtless, the southern-born Johnson did more to promote the integration of African Americans into U.S. society and government than any other president, though his programs probably were more successful in dismantling the legalized biracial system in the South than ending de facto segregation throughout the nation. He had a commendable record on environmental legislation and indeed played an important role in putting the environment on the national agenda. Finally, though the War on Poverty was far from a battle to the death, the number of poor people in the nation declined during his administration. Medicaid meant that almost everyone who needed one saw a doctor, and Medicare protected many older members of the middle class from financial ruin from repeated illnesses.

Alongside the record of domestic reform, and in the minds of many people overshadowing it, Vietnam constituted the other part of Johnson's legacy. The architects of the containment doctrine that led the United States into Southeast Asia, Johnson's three predecessors who expanded involvement in Vietnam, and his successor who fought the war four more years all shared in the responsibility for the war. Yet Johnson alone decided to bomb the North and to assume a full combat role in the South. He thereby took the nation into a war that cost more than fifty-five thousand American lives (more than thirty thousand of them during Johnson's years in office) and incredible sums of money, left the nation divided, and failed in its goal of establishing a stable, secure, noncommunist South Vietnam. Though perhaps adopted for the best of motives, his policy of phased escalation simply did not achieve the desired results. Also, Johnson was not able to sustain a national commitment to the cause. Historians in the future will almost certainly criticize him for his Vietnam policy, though, like his contemporaries, some may decry his failure to fight it more aggressively whereas others may condemn his decision to fight it at all.

An accurate and fair evaluation of Johnson's record in the White House acknowledges the failure in Vietnam but also incorporates his skillful handling of the transition after Kennedy's assassination, his legislative record, his major accomplishments in the field of civil rights, and his contributions to the bettering of the lot of the poor and elderly. Something of an American original, a fascinating provincial in the capital, Johnson offers a larger-than-life reminder of the complexity of history.

Gaines M. Foster

Bibliographical References

Lyndon Johnson gives his account of his presidency in *The Vantage Point: Perspectives of the Presidency, 1963-1969*, 1971. Aides wrote much of the book, and Johnson reportedly refused to let them use the most fascinating and personal of his reminiscences. The book therefore has little of the private Johnson, though it does offer a useful compendium of his interpretation of events. Lady Bird Johnson, *A White House Diary*, 1971, and Sam Houston Johnson, *My Brother Lyndon*, 1970, also provide a perspective on Johnson.

Many biographies of Johnson have appeared, but none of them is completely satisfying. Robert A. Caro, with energies and extravagancies not unlike his subject, announced a three-volume biography. The first, *The Years of Lyndon Johnson: The Path to Power*, which in 768 pages takes Johnson only to 1941, appeared in 1982. It offers a detailed and fascinating account, marred by Caro's treatment of Johnson as virtually the embodiment of evil. The second volume, *The Years of Lyndon Johnson: Means of Ascent*, appeared in 1991. Ronnie Dugger published the first volume of his biography, *The Politician: The Life and Times of Lyndon Johnson*, 1982, which emphasizes, indeed overemphasizes, the influence of Johnson's Texas and frontier heritage on his decisions on Vietnam (even in a volume on his prepresidential years). Robert Dallek produced a scholarly two-volume biography, *Lone Star Rising: Lyndon Johnson and His Times, 1908-1960*, 1991, and *Flawed Giant: Lyndon Johnson and His Times, 1961-1973*, 1998.

The two most useful one-volume biographies are Doris Kearns, *Lyndon Johnson and the American Dream*, 1976, and Merle Miller, *Lyndon: An Oral Biography*, 1980. Kearns offers a simplistic psychological interpretation, and Miller's oral history narrative at times seems more a study of what people said about Johnson than of Johnson himself. Neither book offers sufficient information on what Johnson actually did. Consequently, Vaughn D. Bornet, *The Presidency of Lyndon B. Johnson*, 1983, though often dry and poorly organized, remains essential for understanding the events of Johnson's presidency. On the Senate years, Rowland Evans and Robert Novak, *Lyndon B. Johnson: The Exercise of Power*, 1966, is very good. Three books by former aides, each a combination of history, biography, memoir, and musings, furnish insights on Johnson: Eric F. Goldman, *The Tragedy of Lyndon Johnson*, 1969; Harry McPherson, *A Political Education*, 1972; and especially George Reedy, *Lyndon B. Johnson: A Memoir*, 1982.

For an examination of Johnson's Vietnam policy, see Brian VanDemark, *Into the Quagmire: Lyndon Johnson and the Escalation of the Vietnam War*, 1991, and Michael H. Hunt, *Lyndon Johnson's War: America's Cold War Crusade in Vietnam, 1945-1969*, 1996.

For analysis of the Johnson presidency, see Robert A. Divine, ed., *The Johnson Years*, 2 vols., 1987; Irving Bernstein, *Guns or Butter: The Presidency of Lyndon B. Johnson*, 1996; and John A. Andrew, *Lyndon Johnson and the Great Society*, 1998.

Richard M. Nixon

37th President, 1969-1974

Born: January 9, 1913
　　　Yorba Linda, California
Died: April 22, 1994
　　　New York, New York

Political Party: Republican
Vice Presidents: Spiro T. Agnew, Gerald R. Ford

Cabinet Members

Secretary of State: William P. Rogers, Henry Kissinger

Secretary of the Treasury: David M. Kennedy, John Connally, George Shultz, William Simon

Nixon's official portrait. *(White House Historical Society)*

Secretary of Defense: Melvin Laird, Elliot Richardson, James R. Schlesinger

Attorney General: John Mitchell, Jr., Richard G. Kleindienst, Elliot Richardson, William B. Saxbe

Postmaster General: Winton M. Blount

Secretary of the Interior: Walter J. Hickel, Rogers C. B. Morton

Secretary of Agriculture: Clifford M. Hardin, Earl L. Butz

Secretary of Commerce: Maurice H. Stans, Peter G. Peterson, Frederick B. Dent

Secretary of Labor: George Shultz, James D. Hodgson, Peter J. Brennan

Secretary of Health, Education, and Welfare: Robert Finch, Elliot Richardson, Caspar Weinberger

Secretary of Housing and Urban Development: George W. Romney, James T. Lynn

Secretary of Transportation: John A. Volpe, Claude S. Brinegar

Richard Milhous Nixon, born in Yorba Linda, California, on January 9, 1913, became the thirty-seventh president of the United States in 1969. On August 9, 1974, as a result of the Watergate scandal, he resigned during his second administration, becoming the first president in the country's history to leave office in this manner. The 2,026 days he spent as president were marked not only by significant achievements in domestic and foreign policy but also by a constitutional crisis of unprecedented proportions. His resignation culminated a political career plagued by controversy from its inception.

Formative Influences: Correcting Popular Misconceptions

Contrary to what most psychological historians have asserted, Nixon's formative years were not particularly traumatic or unusual for someone growing up in two small California towns near Los Angeles. The Irish ancestors of both his mother and his father dated back to the colonial period, and both parents grew up in the Midwest before migrating to California. Although Frank Nixon became a Quaker upon marrying Hannah Milhous in 1908, Nixon commented in his *Memoirs* (1978) that the type of Quakerism his family practiced—first in Yorba Linda and then in Whittier—resembled the Protestantism of the churches in the area rather than the stricter version the Milhous family had known in Butlerville, Indiana.

His father being neither a particularly good nor a lucky businessman, Nixon grew up as many boys of his generation did, poor but by no means impoverished, and imbued with the 1920's ethos which combined hard work with the dream of unlimited opportunity. Although much has been made of the deaths of his two brothers Arthur and Harold, they occurred eight years apart, when Nixon was twelve and twenty years old, respectively. While he naturally commented on their deaths, neither seemed to have negatively affected his personality or psyche. Early loss of siblings was not uncommon for Nixon's generation, nor was small-town Republicanism or the close-knit rural environment in which he was reared.

A good student and hard worker, Nixon excelled scholastically at Whittier High School and Whittier College, earning a scholarship to Duke University Law School in 1934. Although he worked equally hard in law school, graduating third in his class, he did not obtain a suitable offer from a prestigious law firm upon graduation. Instead, Nixon returned to Whittier to practice law from 1937 until 1942. Perhaps his meeting, courtship, and marriage to Thelma Catherine (Pat) Ryan between 1938 and 1940 constituted the most memorable episode in Nixon's life before he entered politics in 1946.

If anyone experienced a harsh, poverty-stricken childhood, it was Pat Ryan not Richard Nixon. Shortly after her birth on March 16, 1912, her miner father moved the family from Ely, Nevada, to Artesia, California, to become a truck farmer. By the time she was eighteen, both her parents had died. After trying several different jobs on both coasts, she returned to California to work her way through the University of Southern California. She did not complete her undergraduate education until 1937—the year Nixon finished law school. The same age as Nixon, she met him during the rehearsal of a play after she moved to Whittier to teach high school commercial subjects. Apparently Nixon impulsively decided he wanted to marry her after their first date. Even though as a young, successful lawyer he was one of Whittier's most eligible bachelors, they did not become engaged or married until three years later, in 1940.

Subsequently, World War II brought the newlyweds to Washington, D.C., where Nixon worked in the tire-rationing section of the Office of Price Administration (OPA). Quickly disillusioned with the red tape of government bureaucracy, Nixon obtained a commission and served in the South Pacific between 1942 and 1946, rising to the rank of lieutenant commander. There was nothing particularly distinguished about either his civilian or his military career during these years, and those who knew him best did not perceive any overt political ambition.

Like most American politicians, Nixon's views on government, and on domestic as well as foreign policies, appeared to be more influenced by his adult experiences beginning with World War II than with any unresolved childhood psychological crises or ideological influences which he may have experienced as a young man while going to school or establishing himself as a lawyer. As Nixon himself later said:

> I came out of college more liberal than I am today, more liberal in the sense that I thought it was possible for government to do more than I later found it was practical to do. I became more conservative first, after my experience with OPA. . . . I also became greatly disillusioned about bureaucracy and about what the government could do because I saw the terrible paper work that people had to go through. I also saw the mediocrity of so many civil servants.

In contrast to his rather nondescript background, Nixon's political career prior to assuming the presidency proved as controversial as it was meteoric. Elected to the Eightieth Congress in 1946 at the age of thirty-three, he served two terms, then ran successfully for the U.S. Senate in 1950. By 1952, at thirty-nine, he was elected vice president of the United States, and he only narrowly missed being elected president in 1960 at forty-seven. Eight years later, Nixon won the presidency in an almost equally close contest.

Preparation for the Presidency: Hard Lessons

Nixon's twenty-three years as a politician before becoming president were peppered with controversy, beginning in 1946 when he defeated the five-term liberal Democratic congressman, Jerry Voorhis, and later in 1950 when he defeated equally liberal Democrat Helen Gahagan Douglas for a Senate seat. In both campaigns, Nixon charged his opponents with having left-wing political views. In retrospect,

he probably would have defeated Voorhis and Douglas, whose government careers were basically undistinguished, without any Red-baiting because of the increasing postwar conservatism. Both remain better known for running against Nixon than for any other political achievements.

Under the direction of Murray Chotiner, a lawyer-turned-campaign-consultant for such Republican luminaries as Earl Warren and William Knowland, Nixon mounted Hollywood-style media campaigns and employed political packaging techniques (now considered commonplace) complete with innuendoes about his opponents' presumed Communist Party affiliations. Such tactics in 1946 and 1950 immediately earned for him the reputation among liberal Democrats as an opportunistic product of the Cold War and a "political polarizer" who would do anything to win an election. In 1948 Nixon, as a member of the House Committee on Un-American Activities, initiated the successful attempt to end the diplomatic and governmental career of Alger Hiss by exposing his connections with the Communist Party in the 1930's. In the same year, he proposed the Mundt-Nixon bill, which would have required individual communists and communist organizations to register with the federal government. These actions forever identified him in the American mind as a hard-line anticommunist, despite the facts that he neither became involved with the 1950's McCarthy anticommunist campaign nor made the single-minded pursuit of domestic communists a major goal of his public life.

During his years as Dwight D. "Ike" Eisenhower's vice president, from 1953 until 1960, Nixon campaigned widely for Republican candidates and in the process obtained the unenviable reputation as the party hatchet man, especially for his attacks on Adlai Stevenson, twice the Democratic presidential candidate in the 1950's. As a result, elements within the press, many academics, and liberals in general

Soviet premier Nikita Khrushchev and Vice President Nixon hold the "kitchen debate" in 1959. *(AP/Wide World Photos)*

found it easier to criticize the conservatism of the Eisenhower administrations—not by attacking a popular president, but by concentrating on the politics and personality of his vice president.

Otherwise, the 1950's were relatively quiet years for the country and for Nixon politically, despite the fact that he later placed five of his *Six Crises* (1962) in that decade. Of these, probably only one—the 1952 charge that he had created a slush fund of a little more than $18,000 to further his political career—constituted a real crisis. By going on nationwide television on September 23, 1952, Nixon successfully defended himself and forced Eisenhower to keep him on the Republican ticket as vice president. In this broadcast, he presented embarrassingly detailed information about his family's finances, including the fact that his wife, Pat,

did not own a fur coat like so many Democratic politicians' wives but only "a respectable Republican cloth coat." This speech is best remembered, however, because of his emotional statement that his children would keep a dog named Checkers although the cocker spaniel had been a political gift.

In addition to the 1952 Checkers speech, two other media events at the end of the decade enhanced Nixon's political fortunes and popularity with the general public: the stoning of his car by an anti-American mob in Caracas, Venezuela, in 1958, and his 1959 "kitchen" encounter with Soviet leader Nikita Khrushchev in which Nixon championed the American way of life during their conversations at an American home building display in Moscow. The three events did not add up to a common pattern of constant controversy or crises, as much as they represented sporadic and potentially negative incidents which Nixon turned into politically profitable opportunities in the valuable, but often discouraging, learning process he underwent during his two terms as vice president. Always outside the president's private group of advisers, and occasionally humiliated by Ike in public, Nixon bided his time and mended his own political fences by courting both moderate and conservative Republicans in order to ensure his presidential nomination in 1960.

Although Eisenhower gave him few formal responsibilities, in eight years Nixon permanently upgraded the office of vice president and gave it a much more meaningful and institutionalized role than it had ever had before. In part he accomplished this feat through several well-publicized trips abroad on behalf of the president in the 1950's. (Nixon nostalgically repeated the 1953 trip to Asia and the Far East in 1985.) The vice presidency also assumed greater importance because Eisenhower suf-

fered a heart attack in 1955, a bout with ileitis in 1956, and a stroke in 1957. Throughout all these illnesses, Nixon handled himself with considerable tact and self-effacement, while presiding over nineteen cabinet sessions and twenty-six meetings of the National Security Council (NSC).

Following his stroke, President Eisenhower worked out a plan with Nixon, Secretary of State John Foster Dulles, and Attorney General William Rogers to create the office of acting president in the event he became incapacitated from illness. This formal agreement substituted under Presidents Eisenhower and Kennedy for a constitutional amendment (which was not ratified until 1967) granting the vice president full authority to govern when the president could not discharge the powers and duties of his office.

Nixon's unsuccessful campaign against John F. Kennedy was fraught with ironies and political lessons he never forgot. Repeatedly, the press described Kennedy as a "youthful

The Kennedy-Nixon Debates, 1960. *(D.C. Public Library)*

front runner" representing a new generation, when in fact both men came from approximately the same age cohort, Nixon being only four years older than his forty-three-year-old Democratic opponent. In addition, Nixon's congressional and vice presidential records on civil rights and foreign policy were more liberal than Kennedy's, yet the press perceived them as less so. Finally, Nixon learned the hard way that television would play a most significant role in the 1960 election—the closest one in United States history since Grover Cleveland defeated James G. Blaine in 1884. As a result, Nixon perfected a television campaign style of his own in 1968 and 1972 in direct reaction to his loss of four nationally televised debates with Kennedy in September and October— losses based not on debating or substantive points but on style and image.

To his credit, Nixon did not challenge this 1960 election, which he lost to Kennedy by only 112,000 popular votes, though there was every indication that the Democrats did not legally win in either Illinois or Texas, whose combined electoral college tally tipped the election in the Democrats' favor, 303 to 219. "Our country can't afford the agony of a constitutional crisis," Nixon remarked in an unconsciously prescient moment to one reporter who had unearthed a number of voting irregularities in both states, "and I damn well will not be a party to creating one just to become President or anything else." Nevertheless, after 1960 Nixon resolved never again to take any preelection lead for granted—not in 1968 or even in 1972. All campaigns became "no holds barred" contests to him.

Temporarily retiring to private life, he wrote his first book and best-seller, *Six Crises*, in 1961, and decided to run for governor of California in 1962. Defeat in this election prompted his much-quoted remark to reporters that they would not "have Nixon to kick around anymore." It spurred him to move to New York, where at long last he joined the prestigious

law firm of his earlier dreams, and continued to build bridges between moderate and conservative factions within the Republican Party, especially after Barry Goldwater's defeat by Lyndon B. Johnson in 1964. By 1968, Richard Nixon was once again positioned to win his party's nomination for the presidency of the United States.

Unlike 1960, he faced a Democratic Party hopelessly divided over the war in Indochina and haplessly led by Hubert Humphrey in the wake of LBJ's unexpected refusal to run again, Robert Kennedy's assassination, and a strong third-party bid by George C. Wallace. Also unlike 1960, his opponent had no intrinsically better television image than he did. Instead of debating Humphrey, Nixon and his aides began perfecting thirty-second and one-minute television commercials—an innovation which eventually transformed U.S. presidential primaries and campaigns into media events rather than substantive discussions of issues—the opposite of what Nixon intended.

A Time of Transition: America on the Eve of Nixon's Presidency

Richard Milhous Nixon became president at a critical juncture in American history. Following World War II, popular and official opinion in the United States had generally agreed on two things: the effectiveness of most New Deal domestic policies and the necessity of most Cold War foreign policies. The consensus on these two crucial postwar issues began to break down during the 1960's. The war in Indochina hastened the disintegration of both consensual constructs because of its disruptive impact on the nation's political economy. By 1968 the traditional Cold War, bipartisan approach to the conduct of foreign affairs had been seriously undermined. Similarly, the "bigger and better" New Deal approach to the modern welfare state seemed to many, even many liberals, to have reached a point of diminishing returns even among liberals.

When Nixon finally captured the highest office in the land, he inherited not only Johnson's Vietnam War but also LBJ's Great Society. This transfer of power occurred at the very moment when both endeavors had lost substantial support among the people at large and—most important—among a significant number of decision makers and opinion leaders across the country. On previous occasions when such a breakdown occurred within policy-and opinion-making circles, drastic things happened. One such period preceded the Civil War; another, shorter one, occurred just before the Spanish-American War; another during the early years of the Great Depression; and another in the course of the 1960's.

A man less in tune with popular as well as elite attitudes might not have responded so quickly to manifestations of domestic discontent over the war and welfare. Nixon's sense of timing was all the more acute in 1968 and 1972 as a result of his close loss to John F. Kennedy in 1960 and his overwhelming defeat in California in 1962. By 1968, he realized that old Republican campaign slogans and traditional anticommunist shibboleths would not suffice. He deliberately kept his statements about domestic policy vague but quite palatable to the masses by talking about dispersing power. On foreign policy, however, as early as 1967, in a widely cited article, he gave notice to the tiny elite who dominate policy formulation that he had begun to question certain Cold War assumptions, such as nonrecognition of China.

Unlike the 1960 campaign, in 1968 the Democratic candidate Hubert Humphrey was clearly more liberal than Nixon except on one issue. Humphrey, the Democrat, appeared to be defending past American efforts to win the war in Vietnam more than did Nixon, the Republican many considered to be an original Cold Warrior. Thus, Nixon stressed victory in Vietnam less than Humphrey, implying that he had a "secret plan" for ending the war based on more diplomacy and less military escalation. This left Humphrey wearing the very tarnished military mantle of LBJ. Had President Johnson halted the bombing of North Vietnam and renewed peace talks in Paris before the end of October, Humphrey might have been able to squeeze by Nixon because the election results proved almost as close as in 1960. Nixon won by 500,000 popular votes and received 301 electoral votes, compared to 191 for Humphrey and 46 for Wallace.

Sensing the transitional mood of the country as it drifted away from consensus, and convinced that presidents can accomplish significant deeds only in their first administration, Nixon moved quickly on several fronts even before his inauguration. For example, he gave his approval to the reopening of the Warsaw talks with China, privately decided upon a gradual and unilateral withdrawal of American troops from Vietnam, made Henry Kissinger his national security adviser, approved a plan for reorganizing the NSC system, and concluded that Roy Ash, president of Litton Industries, should initiate a massive reorganization of the executive branch. Yet at the same time president-elect Nixon contacted Arthur Burns about becoming his deputy for domestic affairs while simultaneously deciding that Daniel Patrick (Pat) Moynihan would become head of a new Urban Affairs Council (UAC) to formulate domestic policy, even though Burns and Moynihan were at opposite ends of the political and economic spectrum. These early private actions before his inauguration clearly indicated that Nixon intended to restructure the office of the president to accomplish his domestic and foreign goals.

Nixon's Advisers: Free-Thinking Outsiders, Political Broker Insiders

One cannot look to the 1968 campaign for much advance warning about the structural and substantive changes Nixon later advocated when he called for a "decade of reform." As it turned

Presidential candidate Nixon at a Republican campaign rally in 1968. *(National Archives)*

out, he came to rely on two quite different sets of advisers: "free-thinking" outsiders who brainstormed with him on major issues, and "political broker" insiders who worked to draft and implement his legislative and administrative priorities. Initially, for example, momentum for change on most domestic and foreign affairs came after the election from such free-thinking outsiders as Robert Finch, Richard Nathan, Pat Moynihan, Henry Kissinger, and later John Connally. All these men appealed to Nixon's preference for bold action, and with the exception of Finch, Nixon had not been closely associated with any of them before being elected president.

Moynihan and Kissinger, in particular, influenced certain crucial details, but not usually the broad outlines, of domestic and foreign policies during the first administration by supporting ideas based on the concept of "linkage." Once convinced by these two men that "every-thing relates to everything," Nixon personally began to "preside over a more rapid evolution toward planning than any other President since FDR," according to historian Otis L. Graham in *Toward a Planned Society: From Roosevelt to Nixon* (1976). During his first two years in office, Nixon embarked on a planned risk-taking course in both foreign and domestic policy resulting in attempted reversals of traditional American positions on government reorganization, the idea of a guaranteed annual income, environmental considerations, revenue sharing (including block grants), the value of the dollar, the bombing of Cambodia, rapprochement with China, and détente with the Soviet Union. Thus, concepts about foreign policy as well as welfare, social service spending, the environment, economic relations between the federal government and the states, and structural reform of the executive branch all changed significantly under Nixon.

607

The impact of the free-thinking outsiders on Nixonian policies is easy to trace. Moynihan, Finch, and Nathan greatly influenced specific legislation on welfare; Kissinger carried out the president's foreign policy first as national security adviser and later as secretary of state; and Connally, whom Nixon appointed secretary of the treasury in 1971, single-handedly talked the president into imposing wage and price controls and devaluating the dollar. Connally also played a crucial role in two of Nixon's most important environmental decisions, favoring the creation of the Environmental Protection Agency and a Department of Natural Resources—both against the wishes of the farm bloc. Perhaps of all the free-thinking outsiders who advised him, Nixon was most impressed by Connally, whom he wanted for his vice president in 1968, when Connally was still a Democrat and governor of Texas; whom he wanted to succeed him had he completed his second term; and whom he favored for the vice presidency after Spiro T. Agnew resigned on October 10, 1973, when publication of information indicating that Agnew had accepted payoffs while governor of Maryland led him to plead *nolo contendere* to a single charge of federal income tax evasion. "Only three men in America understand the use of power," Nixon confided to Arthur Burns. "I do. John does. And," he grudgingly added, "I guess Nelson [Rockefeller] does."

Nevertheless, political broker insiders increasingly gained ascendancy over the flamboyant outsiders within the first Nixon administration, and his plans to reorganize the executive branch became more corporate in nature and more central to his thinking. Gray-flannel types such as John Ehrlichman and H. R. Haldeman, the president's two closest aides; Arthur Burns, counselor to the president and later head of the Federal Reserve Board; Melvin Laird, secretary of defense; George Shultz, secretary of labor and later head of the Office of Management and Budget; and

businessman Roy Ash, chair of the President's Council on Executive Reorganization—all played the role of political broker insiders. In Nixon's first years in office, Ehrlichman, Shultz (who later became Ronald Reagan's secretary of state), and Laird became dominant insiders on policy, while Haldeman and Ash concentrated on organizational matters.

Ehrlichman, for example, aided by John Whitaker, significantly influenced the content of Nixon's welfare and environmental legislation especially in connection with land-use policies. Ehrlichman was described by one forest conservation specialist as "the most effective environmentalist since Gifford Pinchot." Burns became the unexpected champion of revenue sharing within the administration. Shultz confined his advice largely to economics and labor but proved surprisingly influential in desegregation matters. Before Kissinger's ascendancy, Laird could be seen brokering on a wide variety of topics from foreign policy to such diverse issues as the volunteer draft, revenue sharing, governmental reorganization, and the situation in Vietnam. If there is a single underestimated, understudied influential figure in the first Nixon administration, it is the most diffident of the honest broker insiders, Melvin Laird.

At the same time that Nixon began relying on certain free-thinking personalities who encouraged him to make sweeping policy recommendations, he also began experimenting with changes in the decision-making process with the reorganization of the NSC and the creation of the UAC, precursor of the Domestic Council. Although he has been called a "management conscious president," Nixon had little previous management experience. In fact, his interest in establishing orderly procedures appears as much rooted in a characteristic desire to avoid personal confrontation as it was in his "preoccupation with the technology of management." From the very beginning, therefore, a tendency existed within his administration for process to become policy; for organizational reform to become a substitute for substantive considerations; for effectiveness to become more important than morality or constitutionality.

In fact, these rigid organizational expectations which characterized the Nixon administration isolated the president from opposing points of view and produced a "results at any price approach," or, at the very least, exaggerated expectations about effectiveness of structural reform. Not surprisingly, Nixon and many of his unelected top advisers began to exhibit a callous and cavalier attitude toward party politics and constitutional government. After five Republican-hired burglars were arrested on June 17, 1972, for breaking into the Watergate headquarters of the Democratic Party, the illegal and unconstitutional tendencies inherent in Nixonian attitudes about politics and government began to pollute the White House atmosphere.

President Nixon and the First Lady in Washington, D.C., in April, 1969. *(National Archives)*

Nixon once said that he thought the "mark of a leader is whether he gives history a nudge." There is no doubt that he accomplished this goal as president, but in ways he did not anticipate. Whether relying on flamboyant outsiders or honest broker insiders, he essentially took the initiative and made many of his own decisions, particularly in foreign affairs. While he and his closest advisers later disagreed on who influenced whom most, Nixon came to the Oval Office with innovative diplomatic ideas which cannot be "Kissingerized" even by Kissinger. In addition, to the dismay of many liberals and conservatives in Congress, he moved quickly into domestic reform. Given the fact that he and Bill Clinton were the only twentieth century presidents to be elected without their party having control over either house of Congress, Nixon's positive historical "nudges" in both foreign and domestic matters were truly impressive. Yet so were the negative ones.

Nixon as Domestic Reformer

Despite predictions by the media that Nixon would be a cautious, if not actually a "do-nothing," president, he proclaimed that the 1970's should become a "decade of government reform," and he actively pursued six areas of domestic reform: welfare, civil rights, growth policy, economic policy, environmental policy, and reorganization of the federal bureaucracy. These domestic programs may ultimately outlive his better-known activities in the realm of foreign policy and even transcend his negative Watergate image.

All of Nixon's attempted changes in domestic and foreign policy were aimed at establishing a conservative, yet modern, public policy. In domestic affairs, for example, faced with a jumbled, pluralist set of federal-state relations, Nixon pointed the way toward a conservative public policy to which his speechwriters and advisers later gave the name New Federalism. To understand Nixon's New Federalism, it is necessary to know how he defined a federal, as opposed to a state or local, function. Nixon applied a rule of thumb which distinguished between those activities requiring larger cash transactions and those primarily involving services. Thus, he attempted to return to the states some power over service issues (what social scientists call distributive issues) such as education, manpower training, and public health, while retaining control at the national level over cash transfers or nondistributive issues such as welfare, energy, and the environment. Above all, Nixon's New Federalism was not intended to cut federal spending programs.

Presidents usually achieve their domestic objectives in three basic ways: legislation, appeals in the mass media, and administrative actions. Nixon offered extensive legislative programs to Congress during his first administration, and when he encountered difficulty obtaining passage, resorted more and more to reform by administrative change, especially at the beginning of his abortive second term in office. His intent with most of these domestic reforms was to address national problems by redistributing federal power away from Congress and the bureaucracy. Consequently, all Nixonian domestic reforms between 1969 and 1971 were ultimately linked under the rubric of New Federalism and by overlapping personnel on various policy-making committees. All competed for attention with his well-known interest in foreign affairs. All involved a degree of boldness which he thought necessary for a successful presidency. All increased federal regulation of nondistributive public policies. All were made possible in part because he was a Republican president who took advantage of acting in the Disraeli tradition of enlightened conservatism. All offended liberals (and many conservatives), especially when it came to implementing certain controversial policies with legislation. Yet by the 1980's, many liberals wished they had Nixon's domestic legislation on environmental issues and social service

spending "to kick around" again. Most important, both his failures and his successes with domestic reform ultimately made Nixon determined to reorganize the executive branch of government with or without congressional approval.

Popular and academic opinion held that Nixon would not recommend any noteworthy social reform. Yet by the end of his first term as president, Nixon had succeeded in several major domestic reform areas, including that of civil rights. Although he was strongly criticized by liberals for employing delaying tactics and not extending busing to Northern cities, his administration achieved impressive results in the area of desegregation. In 1968, 68 percent of all African American children in the South and 40 percent in the entire nation attended all-black schools. By the end of 1972, less than 8 percent of southern African American children attended all-black schools and less than 12 percent nationwide. President Johnson expended $911 million for civil rights activities, including $75 million for civil rights enforcement during the 1969 fiscal year. For the fiscal year 1973 the Nixon administration's budget called for $2.6 billion in total civil rights outlays, of which $602 million were earmarked for enforcement through a substantially strengthened Equal Employment Opportunity Commission (EEOC).

During his first administration, with the aid of George Shultz, President Nixon also initiated the Philadelphia Plan, which set specific numerical goals for minority employment in the construction industry and extended this plan to nine other cities. While Presidents Kennedy and Johnson had employed the term "affirmative action," it "did not have much bite" until the Nixon administration required federal contractors to hire a certain number of minority workers under the Philadelphia Plan. Finally, Nixon made a special effort to encourage African American entrepreneurship by creating the Office of Minority Business Enterprise in 1969.

The Nixon administration was also attentive to the economic status of women and publicized its appointments of women to high government positions. Partially as a result of a 1970 report of a Task Force on Women's Rights and Responsibilities appointed by Nixon, Congress approved the Equal Rights Amendment (ERA) for women and submitted it to the states for ratification in 1972. Nixon's support for the ERA dated back to the beginning of his political career in 1946, and he cosponsored ERA bills as a congressman and senator and continued to support them as vice president. After the passage of the Equal Pay Act in 1963, however, he was not as enthusiastic about the ERA because he believed equality in the workplace had been guaranteed by this legislation. Nevertheless, in March, 1972, he endorsed the ERA as president of the United States.

In addition, Nixon endorsed a surprisingly enlightened rights policy for American Indians. Since World War II, white integrationists and Indian self-determinationists had debated whether American Indians had a "unique dual relationship" with the government of the United States because they were both individual citizens of the country and members of federally recognized sovereign tribes. Until the Nixon administration, the national policy had followed primarily an integrationist approach aimed at terminating tribal ties. After appointing Louis R. Bruce, a Mohawk in favor of self-determination, as commissioner of Indian affairs, Nixon quickly moved to change federal policy by declaring in a special message to Congress on July 8, 1970, that the federal government would assist American Indians in pursuing "Self-Determination without Termination." In this address the president assured "the Indian that he [could] assume control over his own life without being separated involuntarily from the tribal groups."

Nixon's determination to strengthen American Indians' sense of autonomy without threatening their sense of community became even more evident when he asked Congress to repeal the 1953 House Concurrent Resolution which had endorsed integration at the expense of self-determination. Ironically, this legislation dated from the time Nixon had been vice president. As president, however, he effectively ended the policy of forced termination of tribal status and turned over more decisions about American Indian policies to the elected tribal governments.

Thus, beginning in 1969 the Nixon administration increased the budget of the Bureau of Indian Affairs by 214 percent and requested a total, all-agency budget of $1.2 billion for Indian affairs in fiscal year 1973, an increase of $300 million in two years. Funds for improving the health of American Indians doubled under Nixon. In addition, Congress, with Nixon's approval, passed legislation strengthening existing tribal governments, restoring previously terminated tribal status, and financing tribal commercial development. With the passage of the 1975 Indian Self-Determination and Educational Assistance Act, headlines across the country declared it to be the most significant piece of American Indian legislation since 1934, and credited Nixon with having initiated his own "New Deal" for American Indians. Indeed, by 1975, Nixon appeared to have lived up to earlier praise from Bruce Willkie, the executive director of the National Congress of American Indians (NCAI), who said in 1970 that he was "the first U.S. President since George Washington to pledge that the government will honor obligations to the Indian tribes."

Nixon and Welfare

Nixon set an unexpectedly fast pace on the issue of welfare reform, in part because both Health, Education, and Welfare (HEW) Secretary Finch and UAC head Moynihan became early advocates of what came to be known as the Family Assistance Program (FAP). Had this legislation succeeded in Congress it would

"You Were Saying That You Saw A Western Movie The Other Day . . ."

A 1970 political cartoon in *The Washington Post* comments on Nixon's difficult relationship with the press. *(Library of Congress)*

have changed the emphasis of American welfare from providing services to providing income; thus, it would have replaced the Aid to Families with Dependent Children (AFDC) program, whose payments varied widely from state to state, with direct payments to families from $1,600 (initially proposed in 1969) to $2,500 (proposed in 1971) for a family of four. States were expected to supplement this amount and, in addition, all able-bodied heads of recipient families (except mothers with pre-school children) would be required to "accept work or training." If such a parent refused to accept work or training, however, only the parent's payment would be withheld. In essence, FAP unconditionally guaranteed children an

annual income and would have tripled the number of children then being aided by AFDC.

As the most comprehensive welfare reform ever proposed by a United States president, FAP's dramatic reversal of thirty-five years of incremental welfare legislation probably contributed more to its defeat than Nixon's loss of interest with the approach of the 1972 presidential election. The fundamental switch from services to income payment which FAP represented proved too much for liberals and conservatives alike in Congress, and they formed an unlikely alliance to vote it down. FAP's final defeat in the Senate in 1972 ironically led to some very impressive examples of incremental legislation that may not have come to pass had it not been for the original boldness of FAP. Congress approved, for example, Supplementary Security Income (SSI) on October 17, 1972. This measure constituted a guaranteed annual income for the aged, blind, and disabled.

The demise of FAP also led Nixon to support the uniform application of the food stamp program across the United States, better health insurance programs for low-income families, and automatic cost-of-living adjustments (COLA) for Social Security recipients to help them cope with inflation. From the first to the last budget for which his administration was responsible, that is, from 1971 through 1975, spending on all human resource programs exceeded spending for defense for the first time since World War II. All in all, there was a sevenfold increase in funding for social services under Nixon making him, not Johnson, the "last of the big spenders" on domestic programs.

Mixing Economics and Politics

Nixon appeared to reverse himself when he became president from views he held before, or at least, from views others attributed to him.

Nowhere is this more evident than on domestic and foreign economic issues. The president dramatically announced his New Economic Policy (NEP) on August 15, 1971, at the close of a secret Camp David meeting with sixteen economic advisers. His failure to obtain more revenue through tax reform legislation in 1969 and rising unemployment and inflation rates in 1970 precipitated Nixon's NEP, which tried to balance U.S. domestic concerns with wage and price controls and international ones by devaluing the dollar.

As president, Nixon did not make balancing the budget a major object of policy when faced with inflation. First he tried to deal with it in typically conservative fashion by tightening the money supply. When this monetary approach did not work and the economy appeared to be heading into a recession by 1970, the administration had to turn to fiscal policy solutions. On the advice of his Council of Economic Advisors (CEA), headed by Paul McCracken, Nixon became the first president to submit a budget based on "the high-employment budget standard." As he said in his 1971 State of the Union Message, his full-employment budget was "designed to be in balance if the economy were operating at its peak potential. By spending as if we were at full employment, we will help to bring about full employment." This full-employment budget actually justified an "acceptable" amount of deficit spending; specifically, that amount which would result if expenditures did not exceed the hypothetical revenue which would accrue if full employment existed. By setting such a limit on fine-tuning the economy and on expansion, Nixon proclaimed himself a conservative Keynesian.

Unfortunately, the business and financial communities did not endorse the president's full-employment budget. By 1971 they were more worried about the breakdown of the international economic system established in 1944 with the Bretton Woods agreement. For the

first time, therefore, they were ready to consider variable rates for international currencies. Since ending gold convertibility and allowing the dollar "to float" on international markets would cause even more inflation in the United States, such a move had to be offset by some deflationary action. Under Treasury Secretary Connally's influence, Nixon agreed that if foreign countries continued to demand ever-increasing amounts of gold for the U.S. dollars that they held, the United States would go off the gold standard, but would at the same time impose wage and price controls to curb inflation. The president's NEP perfectly reflected the "grand gesture" that Connally thought he should make on economic problems, and the post-Camp David television broadcast simply added drama to economic issues most Americans thought boring.

Although the high-handedness of the NEP with respect to traditional U.S. trading partners, especially Japan, left long-term scars, it was a short-term domestic success. The NEP initially worked so well that by early 1972 output rose sharply, unemployment fell, and inflation remained low, making Nixon the first president since World War II to bring about an economic upturn in a presidential election year—something he believed essential for solidifying a new coalition of Republican voters throughout the country. Since the Democrats remained even more disorganized behind the leadership of peace candidate George McGovern than they had been under Humphrey, Nixon's economic policies added to, but were not entirely responsible for, his victory margin of 18 million votes or 60.8 percent of the popular vote.

Long-term implementation of wage and price controls, however, revealed not only how politically motivated Nixon's commitment had been, but also how impossible it was to abandon them without exacerbating inflationary trends within the economy. Consequently one legacy of Nixon's NEP was more inflation and more federal regulation of the economy than during any other presidency since the New Deal. The administration extended federal regulation in four major areas: energy (specifically oil prices), the environment, occupational health and safety, and consumer production safety. In each instance, especially with respect to environmental legislation, Nixon tried to establish limits on the amount and expense of regulation, but usually failed to convince enough members of Congress who also mixed politics and economics without always anticipating long-range consequences.

When he was not trying to act before Congress could upstage him on regulatory issues, Nixon proposed deregulation based on free market assumptions which were more traditionally in keeping with conservative Republicanism. The administration not only devalued the dollar, but also made deregulatory recommendations for the production of food crops, for the reduction of tariff and other barriers to international trade, and for interest rates paid by various financial institutions. By and large, however, politics made Nixon more liberal on economic matters, confounding both his friends and enemies.

Governmental Reorganization Along Corporate Lines

Nixon had inherited a White House staff and executive office badly in need of reorganization because of burgeoning personnel and the fact that major departments resembled diversified holding companies more than single-function divisions. That he turned to corporate management techniques is not surprising when one considers that his Council on Executive Reorganization (known as the Ash Commission) consisted of four top corporate executives and John Connally. Nevertheless, his failure to obtain welfare reform from Congress propelled him toward a corporate presidency more quickly than otherwise would have been the case.

Nixon received recommendations based on some of the most advanced corporate theories

from the Ash Commission. Acting on its advice he introduced management by objectives into government operating procedures for the first time, and mounted several major attempts to reorganize the executive branch. His successes in these areas constitute some of his most lasting achievements. By the time he resigned from office, Nixon had replaced the Post Office Department with a public corporation less subject to political patronage; merged the Peace Corps and Vista into one agency called Action; and created five new domestic advisory boards: first, the UAC, which became the Domestic Council; the Council on Environmental Quality (established at the initiative of Congress, but effectively utilized by Nixon); the Rural Affairs Council; a Council on Executive Reorganization; and a Council on International Economic Policy (CIEP).

Nixon established the Environmental Protection Agency (EPA) and recommended that the functions of the Atomic Energy Commission (AEC) be divided into two new agencies, the Nuclear Regulatory Commission and the Energy Research and Development Administration—both of which came into existence under President Ford. He also created the Office of Child Development and the National Oceanic and Atmospheric Administration. During the Nixon administration, the Bureau of the Budget was transformed into the Office of Management and Budget, whose monitoring and investigatory powers gave it greater influence than ever before on the budgets of all government agencies and departments.

When Nixon tried to implement certain reorganizational (and ideological) ideas by impounding federal funds and eliminating the Office of Economic Opportunity (OEO), the agency established under President Johnson to aid the poor, he antagonized liberals in Congress and the country at large. Believing that the functions of OEO "should be spun off into other departments," the president first appointed Donald Rumsfeld as OEO director. For nineteen months, Rumsfeld succeeded in re-organizing the bureaucracy of the agency without unnecessarily antagonizing either moderate liberals or conservatives. He accomplished this primarily by streamlining OEO into a more efficient bureaucracy; merging, farming out, or transferring some of its programs into other cabinet departments or government agencies; lowering its public profile; and weeding out the most obvious "advocate types," such as Terry Lenzer, the head of OEO's Legal Services Division. Nixon was so pleased with Rumsfeld's performance at OEO that in December, 1970, he appointed him as counselor to the president, leaving the ultimate dismantling of OEO to Howard Phillips, who as acting director ruined his own career in the process by alienating Republican as well as Democratic supporters of the agency.

While Nixon ultimately succeeded in abolishing OEO, federal courts ruled against most of the administration's attempts to impound funds earmarked by Congress for projects which the administration either opposed or viewed as exceeding the president's recommended budget ceilings. By 1973 Nixon had withheld $18 billion of appropriated congressional funds. In 1974, the Ninety-third Congress created the Budget Reform Act which gave itself, not the president, ultimate control over spending ceilings.

There is every indication that most of Nixon's recommendations for government reorganization encouraged a blurring or merging of functions between cabinet officers and members of his executive office. Although both sets of officials were appointed, not elected, the former did require congressional approval, while the latter did not. Therefore, after Congress delayed or turned down several of his major proposals for reorganizing the executive branch, Nixon decided following his landslide election in 1972 to call for the resignation of his entire cabinet and to create a set of four special counselors to the president, or "super-secretaries," to take charge of certain domestic bureaucracies; for example, the heads of Housing and Urban Development (HUD), HEW, the Treasury, and the Agriculture Department were to be given responsibility for Community Development, Human Resources, Economic Affairs, and Natural Resources, respectively. These super-secretaries would have had direct and frequent access to Nixon and his White House staff. In addition, he wanted to create a second line of subcabinet officials consisting largely of former or current White House aides to act as presidential assistants responsible for such broad functional areas as domestic affairs, economic affairs, foreign affairs, executive management, and White House coordination. This last Nixon reorganization plan also called for these super-secretaries or counselors and presidential assistants to operate as a "super-cabinet" in order to enhance White House control over the bureaucracy.

By the end of his first administration, Nixon had also clearly decided that he needed loyal "politician managers" in these key super-secretariat positions and in many of the more than two thousand appointed "plum" managerial jobs within the executive branch. Through his appointment powers he hoped to place loyalists throughout the top levels of government to ensure the implementation of the decentralized aspects of his New Federalism such as sharing with states and local communities, welfare reform, and the impounding of federal funds earmarked for projects in excess of the president's recommended ceiling. Yet all aspects of this comprehensive reorganization, announced following the 1972 election, failed to become institutionalized as details about Watergate began to emerge in 1973 and to occupy Nixon's attention for most of his truncated second term in office.

Foreign Policy: The Geopolitics of Nixon and Kissinger

At first glance, Nixon and Kissinger, his prin-

Secretary of State Henry Kissinger meets with Chinese premier Chou En-lai in 1971. *(National Archives/Nixon Project)*

cipal foreign policy adviser, appear to be an odd couple—an American Quaker and a German Jew. In fact, however, by the time they met in 1968, they shared many similar viewpoints and similar operational styles. Both of them thrived on covert activity and decisions reached in private; both distrusted the federal bureaucracy; and both agreed that the United States could impose order and stability in foreign affairs primarily through appearing and acting tough. Neither man had previously headed any complex organizational structure, but both thought that "personalized executive control" and formalistic procedures and structures would enable them to succeed in the area of their greatest combined experiences; namely, foreign policy. Finally, each had a history of previous failure and rejection by peer or government officials which made them very sensitive to protecting themselves and their positions of power from public and private criticism. Often their concern for self-protection was reflected in their obsession with all types of eavesdropping, whether in the form of wiretaps or reconnaissance flights over communist

territory. They even eavesdropped on themselves: Nixon by installing an automatic taping system at the White House and Kissinger by having all of his phone conversations either taped or transcribed from notes.

With Nixon's approval, Kissinger quickly transformed the National Security Council system into a personal foreign policy secretariat. By subordinating the Senior Interdepartmental Group, formerly chaired by a representative of the State Department, to the Review Group, which he chaired, Kissinger effectively undercut the State Department's influence over policy making. Ultimately, he chaired six special committees operating out of the NSC. Moreover, he created interdepartmental committees that prepared policy studies which were submitted directly to his Review Group before they were presented to the NSC or to the president. He also tried to provide a "conceptual framework" for American diplomacy by establishing a series of National Security Study Memoranda (NSSM). These were drafted by the NSC staff and signed by Kissinger on behalf of Nixon. They directed various agencies and groups within the government to prepare detailed policy options, not policy recommendations, which were then passed on by Kissinger to the NSC and argued out in front of the president.

The NSSM system was designed to prevent respondents, the State Department, and other executive departments from becoming advocates. By relegating them to analysis, the new NSC system supposedly put the bureaucrats in their "proper places." Even this elaborate restructuring did not completely satisfy the desire of the president and his secretary of state to control the process of foreign policy formulation. Most covert foreign policies of the Nixon administration, for example, bypassed the NSC. This says something quite significant about policy making under Nixon and the legacy he left in foreign affairs. When a decision could be carried out which did not rely upon the civilian or military bureaucracy for implementation, the NSC was ignored, regardless of whether the action was covert. It was utilized, however, whenever the covert or overt policy required bureaucratic support.

Using this guideline, it can be determined when the NSC system was employed as a debating forum for presenting options to the president, and when it was not. The NSC did not debate the concept of Vietnamization, the Nixon Doctrine, the secret Kissinger negotiations with North Vietnam, the international aspects of Nixon's New Economic Policy announced in August, 1970, the various attempts by the Central Intelligence Agency (CIA) to undermine the elected Marxist government of Salvador Allende of Chile, or the planning of Nixon's historic trip to China to redirect U.S. Asian policy vis-à-vis the Soviet Union. All these policies or actions were presented to the NSC, if at all, as faits accomplis. Yet, the NSC did debate and approve of the secret bombing of Cambodia and the mild response of the United States to the EC-121 incident in the first year of the Nixon administration. Later it played a role in such policy decisions as the attempt to keep Taiwan in the United Nations with a "two China" policy, the decision to conduct incursions into Cambodia and Laos, the détente agreements with the Soviet Union, and Middle Eastern diplomacy before the 1973 Yom Kippur War. The key to understanding this varied track record of the NSC rests in the amount of bureaucratic support at home and abroad necessary to carry out each of the policies. Nixon not only sought greater presidential control over the process of foreign policy formulation but also wanted to alter the basic assumptions of that policy.

In Kansas City, on July 6, 1971, Nixon laid down a five-power strategy which he hoped would replace the bipolar, confrontational aspects of the Cold War since 1945. Instead of continuing to deal bilaterally with the Soviet Union, Nixon hoped to bring the five great economic regions of the world—the United States, the Soviet Union, mainland China, Japan, and Western Europe—into constructive negotiation and mutually profitable economic competition. Admitting that the United States could not long maintain its post-World War II position of "complete preeminence or predominance," Nixon outlined a "pentagonal strategy" which would promote peace and economic progress among the major superpowers.

This meant that from the beginning of the Nixon administration entire areas of the world such as southern Asia, the Middle East, Africa, and Latin America—areas commonly referred to as the Third World—occupied a secondary place in the president's (and his secretary of state's) geopolitical approach to foreign policy. In particular, Nixon and Kissinger largely ignored economic foreign policy considerations in dealing with the Third World. This neglect accounts for the seemingly erratic aspects of U.S. foreign policy in Third World areas which fell outside the parameters of pentagonal strategy. Nixon was more interested in maintaining American spheres of influence in the Third World than in the economic needs of individual countries falling within this designation. Thus, the United States promoted the overthrow of Allende in Chile; restrained Egyptian and Syrian aggression in the Middle East while ignoring the potential instability of the Shah's regime in Iran and indirectly encouraging the rise of Organization of Petroleum Exporting Countries (OPEC) oil prices; continued to oppose Fidel Castro in Cuba; and supported Pakistan against India. The grand design may have been "grand" by superpower standards, but it remained ineffectually grandiose with respect to the Third World.

Vietnam: Too Little, Too Late

Nevertheless, the first and in many ways foremost problem that Nixon faced in foreign affairs involved the Third World. He had inherited from his predecessor a war in Southeast Asia in which the United States fought to prevent the fall of the government of South Vietnam to internal communist subversion and an attack from North Vietnam which had the support of China and the Soviet Union. Although Nixon had talked in his campaign of a secret plan to end the war, he still thought the noncommunist government in the South could be, and should be, preserved even though growing domestic opposition to the war meant that he had to reduce the American role in the conflict. Nixon therefore followed a policy which came to be called Vietnamization in which greater efforts were made to strengthen the South Vietnamese army and to turn over to it more of the ground combat operations. This then allowed Nixon to reduce the number of American troops in Vietnam. Even as he pursued Vietnamization, however, Nixon still sought to prevent a communist victory in South Vietnam and soon adopted dramatic means to avoid one.

Nixon's Secretary of Defense Melvin Laird, on the other hand, had two primary goals: to end the war and to end the draft. While neither of these goals turned Laird into a dove, they made him one of the few true believers in the policy of Vietnamization—a term he coined—and the behind-the-scenes architect of the Nixon Doctrine. Vietnamization and the Nixon Doctrine are logical extensions of each other because the former called for South Vietnamese troops to replace Americans, while the latter called for American allies in general to be prepared to undertake their own ground fighting in the future. These views made him question the extension of the war into Cambodia and Laos. Unlike Nixon and Kissinger, Laird was more interested in ending the war in Vietnam than in winning it at any cost.

The Nixon Doctrine represents the internationalization of the policy of Vietnamization or, at the very least, its blanket application to the Far East. As such, its purpose was "to provide a shield if a nuclear power threatens the freedom of any nation allied with us . . . in cases involving other types of aggression we shall furnish military and economic assistance when requested in accordance with our treaty commitments. But we shall look to the nation directly threatened to assume the primary responsibility for the manpower for its defense." Clearly, the subsequent invasions of Cambodia and Laos violated the intent if not the letter of the Nixon Doctrine. Laird and others pointed out this contradiction at NSC meetings, while Kissinger reportedly insisted: "We wrote the goddam doctrine, we can change it."

The guarded secret decision to bomb Cambodia and the general widening of the war to include Laos also, can be understood only in relation to other actions which were undertaken around the same time. These included Vietnamization, the unilateral withdrawal of American troops, and stepped up negotiations with the Viet Cong in Paris. In December, 1968, under President Johnson, the Joint Chiefs of Staff had originally requested "standby authority . . . to pursue North Vietnam Army/Viet Cong (NVA/VC) Forces into Cambodia following major enemy offensives mounted and supported in Cambodia" in December, 1968. The Joint Chiefs of Staff simply reiterated this position to the new Nixon administration when asked on January 21, 1969 (NSSM no. 1), to provide a "study of the feasibility and utility of quarantining Cambodia."

Since 1966, LBJ had refused to consider a mutual, let alone a unilateral, withdrawal of American troops from Vietnam. (Whether they realized it or not, the Joint Chiefs of Staff had more bargaining power on the questions of whether to bomb and/or invade Cambodia because of Vietnamization, Nixon's private commitment to a gradual pullout of U.S. soldiers and, above all, his desire for better relations with China which precluded bombing enemy sanctuaries there.) Early attempts at rapprochement with China automatically made Cambodian sanctuaries ideal substitutes with which to placate the Joint Chiefs of Staff, who did not approve of rapid Vietnamization and troop withdrawal.

Laird, however, insisted that "because of the political implications of bombing Cambodia, the entire NSC should review the policy." This review took place on March 16, 1969, and the secret sorties began two days later under the general code name MENU with the exact target areas given the unsavory titles BREAKFAST, LUNCH, DINNER, SUPPER, DESSERT, and SNACK. From March 18, 1969, to May 1, 1970, these bombings remained secret. Thus the bombing of Cambodia was one of the few truly covert foreign policy undertakings of the Nixon administration which received full NSC consideration.

Although Nixon came to office committed to ending the war in Vietnam through negotiations, he ended up expanding and prolonging the conflict. As a result, he could never build the domestic consensus he needed to continue the escalated air and ground war, even with dramatically reduced U.S. troop involvement, and to ensure passage of some of his domestic programs. For Nixon (and Kissinger), Vietnam became a symbol of influence in the Third World which, in turn, was but one part of their geopolitical or grand design approach to international relations. Thus the war in Southeast Asia had to be settled as soon as possible so as not to endanger other elements of Nixonian diplomacy and domestic policy.

According to his book *No More Vietnams* (1985), the president viewed that conflict as military, moral, and global. Consequently, he first sought to bring military pressure to bear on the North Vietnamese in order to speed up the negotiating process. There is little indication, however, that this approach suc-

ceeded, because the Viet Cong correctly counted on opposition in the United States to the announced bombing and invasion of Cambodia in April, 1970, and of Laos in February, 1971. In like manner, Nixon's commitment to the war as a "moral cause" did not ring true, as the carnage in that civil war increased despite American troop withdrawals. Finally, the president never succeeded in convincing the country that quick withdrawal from Vietnam would "damage American strategic interests" all over the world. Congress did abolish the draft, and Nixon continued to bring U.S. troops home. These actions diminished the size of antiwar demonstrations beginning in 1971, but opposition to the war in Vietnam continued in Congress. Nixon had failed to convince many of its members and their constituents that the conflict in this tiny Third World country warranted the military, moral, and global importance he attributed to it.

Instead, the president allowed his secretary of state to become involved in secret negotiations with the North Vietnamese from August 4, 1969, to January 25, 1972 (when they were made public). As a result, only marginally better terms were finally reached in 1973 which had not been agreed to in 1969. The trade-off between Hanoi's agreement that President Nguyen Van Thieu could remain in power in return for allowing Hanoi's troops to remain in place in South Vietnam pales when compared to the additional twenty thousand American lives lost during this three-year period—especially when the inherent weaknesses of the Saigon government by 1973 are taken into consideration.

On the tenth anniversary of the peace treaty ending the war in Vietnam, Nixon acknowledged that "Kissinger believed more in the power of negotiation than I did." He also said that he "would not have temporized as long" with the negotiating process had he not been "needlessly" concerned with what the Soviets and Chinese might think if the United States pulled out of Vietnam precipitately. Because Nixon saw no way to end the war quickly in 1969 except through overt, massive bombing attacks which the public demonstrated it would not tolerate in 1970 and 1971, there was neither peace nor honor in Vietnam by the time that war was finally concluded on January 27, 1973.

Shuttle Diplomacy: The Middle East

A long overdue full-scale NSC debate over American Middle East policy took place in an all-day session on February 1, 1969. This meeting established the basic goals of the United States for the 1970's; namely, substantial Israeli withdrawal from occupied territory in exchange for contractual and practical security arrangements with Egypt. Unfortunately, however, it adopted the least successful means of the entire decade for achieving these goals, the Rogers Plan, which called for American-Soviet agreement on a comprehensive peace settlement in the Middle East and for a more "evenhanded" public posture toward both the Israelis and the Arabs. This policy of evenhandedness had been tentatively proposed by Governor William Scranton, Nixon's special, preinauguration envoy to the Middle East.

Until President Reagan and his Secretary of State George Shultz affirmed a joint military-political cooperation with Israel at the end of 1983, no American president or secretary of state formally disavowed the general principle of evenhandedness established at the February, 1969, NSC meeting. Yet these principles had been breached more than honored in the intervening fourteen years. Even the original attempt to obtain them through the Rogers Plan lasted only a year.

There are several reasons why the plan of Nixon's first secretary of state would probably have failed even if it had not been sabotaged by Henry Kissinger. From the beginning, the Rogers Plan was based on two untenable assumptions: that the Soviet Union would agree to become a joint peacemaker with the United States and would pressure Gamel Abdel Nasser of Egypt into accepting a compromise peace based on U.N. Resolution 242 which had been adopted in 1967 and called for an Israeli withdrawal from lands it had occupied, but also for peace and the recognition of the right of every state in the area to a peaceful existence; and that a publicly impartial stance toward Israel and the Arabs would enhance the American bargaining position with both sides in a way that previous pro-Israeli statements had not. Israel and Egypt both opposed the Rogers Plan when it became public at the end of 1969 because it was an obvious attempt by the Big Two (or in this case the Big One) to impose a settlement.

Aside from the Nixon Doctrine, the new Republican administration did not appear to have a positive alternative to the Rogers Plan, which was rejected by the Soviet Union in October, 1969, until after the Yom Kippur War. From the time of the 1970 crisis in Jordan through the 1973 war, the United States appeared to pursue a policy of stalemate. At the most, the stalemate policy seemed to consist of using sporadic behavior modification techniques on Israel beginning in the spring and summer of 1970. For example, on two occasions promises to Israel of more military equipment were deferred in an attempt to prevent any untoward actions against Jordan when that country appeared on the verge of falling apart.

The years from 1969 to 1973 can be considered an incubation period for the Nixon administration's Middle East policy. At the end of the Yom Kippur War, Kissinger's step-by-step disengagement policy, otherwise known as shuttle diplomacy, emerged fullblown. This approach was not only piecemeal and stopgap in nature but also essentially bilateral, although Kissinger's frantic shuttling about gave the false impression of creating multilateral arrangements. He soon fell into the post-Yom Kippur War habit of telling the Israelis and Arabs what they wanted to hear, sometimes exceeding both congressional and White House intentions. Finally, in the wake of the Yom Kippur War, Kissinger no longer called for expulsion of the Soviet Union from the area. Instead, Anwar el-Sadat's independent expulsion of Soviet personnel was viewed as a hopeful model. Rather than further polarize the Arabs into moderate and militant camps, the administration deemed it possible that Arab nationalism would assert itself against Soviet imperialism.

The 1973 Yom Kippur War broke the stalemate that since 1969 had substituted for American policy in the Middle East. "It took the war to unfreeze the positions" on both sides, Kissinger later told an aide. By the time this breakthrough occurred, the stalemate had cost the United States more than Kissinger could ever gain back, even though it freed him to play hopscotch diplomacy among Middle Eastern countries. Seyom Brown in *The Crisis of Power* (1979) and others have documented that there was little substance to show for all of Kissinger's shuttling.

Détente with China and the Soviet Union

Nixon's most lasting foreign policy achievements remain improved relations with China and the Soviet Union, including a strategic arms limitation agreement with the latter. Détente is the term most often used to describe the results of his overtures to both countries. Détente literally means "the relaxing or easing of tensions between nations." Normalization of U.S. relations with China was part of the president's grand design to bring this giant communist nation into the ranks of the superpowers. Long before Nixon sent Kissinger on a secret mission to Peking in July, 1971, to arrange the details of his visit there the following year, the administration had been indicating to the Chinese through various unilateral gestures of reconciliation that it wanted to make fundamental improvements in economic and scholarly exchanges.

Although various government officials publicly denied that Nixon courted China in order to bring pressure to bear on the Soviet Union, the president's highly publicized visit to the People's Republic of China in February, 1972 (with its attendant joint communique), did not go unnoticed by Soviet leaders. The China trip is, therefore, indirectly linked to the success of negotiations leading to the ten formal agreements between the United States and the Soviet Union in May, 1972. The most important of these agreements provided for prevention of military incidents at sea and in the air; scholarly cooperation and exchange in the fields of science and technology; cooperation in health research; cooperation in environmental matters; cooperation in the exploration of outer space; facilitation of commercial and economic relations; and, most important, arms control.

In the area of arms control, Nixon's détente strategy contained the potential not only to substitute for containment, the central premise of United States foreign policy since the 1940's which was directed at stopping Soviet expansion in the world, but also to transcend the Procrustean ideological constraints which were at the very heart of the post-World War II conflict between these two nations. This potential was never fully realized, in part because Nixon's successors proved unable to build upon the delicate balance between containment and détente which he left behind.

Nevertheless, the Strategic Arms Limitation Talks (SALT) conducted in Helsinki in 1969 and in Vienna in 1970 led to the two arms control agreements which Nixon signed in Moscow in 1972. SALT I was the only arms control agreement between the United States and the Soviet Union which the Senate approved. It included a treaty limiting the deployment of antiballistic missiles (ABMs) to two for each country, and froze the number of offensive intercontinental ballistic missiles (ICBMs) at the level of those then under production or deployed. SALT I, in essence, es-

Nixon tours the Great Wall of China, 1972. *(National Archives/Nixon Project)*

tablished a rough balance between the nuclear arsenals of the two superpowers, despite the "missiles gaps" which continued to exist between them in specific weapons. For example, when Nixon signed SALT I, the United States had a total of 1,710 missiles: 1,054 land-based ICBMs and 656 on submarines. The Soviet Union had a total of 2,358 missiles: 1,618 land-based ICBMs and 740 on submarines. SALT I by no means stopped the nuclear arms race, but it recognized that unregulated weapons competition between the two superpowers could no longer be rationally condoned.

Watergate

Despite his obvious achievements in foreign and domestic policy, a 1982 national poll of U.S. specialists rated the thirty-seventh president of the United States a failure, along with Andrew Johnson, James Buchanan, Ulysses S. Grant, and Warren G. Harding. There was one reason for this overwhelmingly negative evaluation—Watergate—a word which will forever be associated with the presidency of Richard Milhous Nixon, although not with the same emotional fervor. Watergate swept the country in 1973 and 1974 as no scandal involving the

highest officials of government had since the Teapot Dome scandal in the 1920's, and for good reason.

The cover-up by the president and his top aides of the original break-in at Democratic National Committee Headquarters in Washington, D.C., on June 17, 1972, and of related corrupt or criminal political activities ultimately resulted in the indictment, conviction, and sentencing of fifteen men, including the top White House aides to Nixon (Ehrlichman and Haldeman), the White House counsel (John W. Dean III), a special assistant to the president (Charles Colson), one former cabinet member (Attorney General John Mitchell, Jr.), and ten others who worked for the Committee for the Re-election of the President (CREEP) or the White House "plumbers'" unit which was engaged in break-ins before Watergate occurred. In addition to these men in whom public trust had been placed, four Cubans arrested in the Watergate complex also served time for their participation in the original crime.

At one level, therefore, Watergate can be viewed as dirty politics, carried to its logical and, in this instance, illegal extreme. At another level, however, Watergate is inextricably related to the war in Indochina, in particular, and in general to the wartime standards of behavior which had prevailed since the onset of the Cold War. This quasi-war atmosphere had slowly eroded public sensitivity to moral and ethical issues in foreign policy. The first wiretaps of the Nixon administration on the friends, acquaintances, and employees of Henry Kissinger were all undertaken in the name of national security. Likewise, the first break-in by the plumbers' unit at the office of

Daniel Ellsberg's psychiatrist had nothing to do with partisan politics, but with the release of the Pentagon Papers (which Ellsberg had leaked to the press) in June, 1971.

Until the mid-1960's, only a few knowledgeable Americans knew about constitutional violations incurred in the battle against communism under various presidents since World War II, and they were, for the most part, either indifferent or curiously enthusiastic. Most Americans, however, remained largely ignorant of the escalating illegal activities of the CIA, the increased spying on United States citizens by the Federal Bureau of Investigation (FBI), and the clandestine plans for overthrowing governments or assassinating their leaders under presidents Truman, Eisenhower, Kennedy, and Johnson. As the war in Vietnam dragged on with no clear-cut victory in sight, more and more Americans became aware of the inherent dangers to the Constitution in the methods for conducting U.S. foreign policy which had evolved during the decades of Cold War.

The United States has never fought a war without violating the constitutional rights of its citizens. Vietnam was no exception. What was exceptional was the increased sensitivity of people toward violations of the Constitution in the conduct of foreign and domestic policy. Many people had their consciousnesses raised about such violations because of their association with the Civil Rights movement of the late 1950's and the 1960's. When Nixon assumed office, he did so as a wartime president. As far as the White House was concerned, a wartime atmosphere prevailed that warranted traditional wartime violations of the Constitution.

By 1969, the fighting had been going on inconsequentially for too many years. Thus a

The Watergate complex in Washington, D.C., 1971. *(Copyright* Washington Post. *Reprinted by permission of D.C. Public Library)*

significant and vocal portion of the population began to question the White House and Congress about the conduct of the war. The scattered, often regionally isolated cases of antiwar protests begun during the Johnson administration became nationally coordinated and epidemic under the Nixon administration. More important than the demonstrations, however, was the fact that public-opinion leaders across the country and the elite group of opinion makers during the second Johnson administration began to disagree with one another.

It would prove easier to unite the American people behind his efforts to end the war, and even behind certain domestic policies, than it would be to reunite the elite opinion makers as he wound down the war. Nixon's real problem and the reason that he could not get away with wartime actions which disregarded the Constitution, as presidents had in the past, was that a substantial group of influential bureaucrats, policymakers, opinion leaders, and numerous students, opposed him. Largely white and middle class with draft-exempt status, these students constituted an important elite group of future American leaders.

If he ever intended to deal successfully with a divided elite, Nixon had to reestablish consensus at both the public and elite levels. His election victory in 1972 represented a partial success with the former, but it did nothing to bring around the disaffected elite groups which every president must have behind him, especially in time of war. As Nicholas Hoffman has said, "Nixon was the first American President since Lincoln to guide the nation through a war that fundamentally divided the ruling classes." Abraham Lincoln, after all, had closed down newspapers and suspended writs of habeas corpus to keep Copperheads in jail during the Civil War. Nixon did not have the luxury of such direct unconstitutional actions because the civil war he faced was in Vietnam, not in the United States. Yet his paranoia about antiwar activists was no less than Lincoln's, and

some would claim that Nixon acted as though those in opposition to the war were fomenting another civil war in the United States. At least he probably came to believe it was easier to fight an incipient civil war at home than the real one in Vietnam.

Indeed, there was a civil war going on among the American opinion leaders. Wartime presidents had traditionally silenced dissent and attacked with impunity such powerless groups as Japanese Americans, self-proclaimed socialists and communists, or assorted first-and second-generation European immigrants. Nixon, in contrast, had no choice but to take on the so-called best and brightest among the policy-making elite. His unique dilemma raises the very interesting question: What realistic avenues are open to any president who challenges an influential segment of the establishment? It was in Nixon's political and psychic self-interest to end a war that fundamentally divided many of the best and brightest.

Clearly, his aides came to the conclusion that this monumental task could be undertaken only by what has been called a "pickup team of greedy amateurs and romantics." In other words, they decided that the best and the brightest had to be defeated by the middling and the mediocre. G. Gordon Liddy and E. Howard Hunt were, at best, "second-rate second-story" men. The "third-rate" burglaries they planned and ineptly executed are a testimony to their incompetence. Apparently, Hunt and Liddy did not realize that Larry O'Brien and other Democratic Party officials had already moved the bulk of their campaign operation to Florida by the time of the second break-in on June 17. Moreover, because no strong potential candidate had emerged to oppose Nixon, the Democratic Party was in such a state of disarray by the summer of 1972 that some implied there was nothing to find out, let alone expose, at Democratic National Headquarters. All that men such as Liddy and Hunt knew how to do was to break-in, photograph, and bug, however counterproductive such acts had proven previously with Ellsberg's psychiatrist.

Although Jim Hougan suggests in *Secret Agenda: Watergate, Deep Throat and the CIA* (1984) that both James W. McCord, Jr., and Hunt were still working for the CIA to expose a sexring operation which would have compromised certain prominent Democrats, there is no conclusive proof that this was the case. A possible connection between Howard Hughes and Nixon—namely, $100,000 purportedly paid to the president's friend Charles (Bebe) Rebozo—still appears to be the most likely reason for the May and June break-ins because of the fear that O'Brien had knowledge of this transaction. No reason put forth to date satisfactorily explains the criminal break-in at the Watergate complex.

The arrest of McCord, Bernard Baker, Virgilio Gonzalez, Eugenio Martinez, and Frank Sturgis after Frank Wills, the night watchman at the Watergate, discovered adhesive tape not once, but twice, on basement doors of the expensive office and apartment complex in Washington, D.C., set off a series of events and investigations unprecedented in U.S. history. This burglary culminated a series of political dirty tricks authorized by CREEP beginning in the fall of 1971. Most of these activities, including two Watergate break-ins (the first had occurred over Memorial Day weekend), were approved by Attorney General Mitchell and presidential counsel Dean. President Nixon learned of the burglars' connections with CREEP and White House personnel on June 20, 1972, and on June 23 he agreed with the recommendations of Mitchell, Dean, and Haldeman that the CIA should prevent an FBI investigation of the Watergate break-in on grounds of national security. The CIA did not comply with the president's attempt to obstruct justice in a criminal matter and the investigation moved forward, but not until after the 1972 presidential election.

Even before the release of the "smoking gun" tape of June 23 on August 5, 1974, which revealed how early Nixon had been involved in the cover-up, the Watergate Special Prosecution Task Force headed by Texas attorney Leon Jaworski had concluded by the end of June, 1974, that

beginning no later than March 21, 1973, the President joined an ongoing criminal conspiracy to obstruct justice, obstruct a criminal investigation, and commit perjury (which included payment of cash to Watergate defendants to influence their testimony, making and causing to be made false statements and declarations, making offers of clemency and leniency, and obtaining information from the Justice Department to thwart its investigation) and that the President is also liable for substantive violations of various criminal statutes.

All these actions had taken place in the space of two years—from the summer of 1972 to the summer of 1974. Early in 1973, Federal Judge John J. Sirica used heavy-handed legal tactics by threatening the Watergate defendants with tough sentences unless they told the truth. As McCord and others began to talk about payoffs from the White House, illegal campaign contribution evidence began to surface. Nixon fired Haldeman, Ehrlichman, Dean, and Mitchell by formally accepting their resignations of April 30, after he admitted on May 22 that they had been involved in a White House cover-up without his knowledge. Dean then decided to testify before the Senate Select Committee on Presidential Campaign Activities (the Ervin Committee), and from June 25 to 29 accused the president of being involved. Among other things, testimony before this committee disclosed the existence of a White House "enemies list" of prominent politicians, journalists, academics, and entertainers, who had been singled out for various types of harassment, including Internal Revenue Service (IRS) audits. In July, Alexander Butterfield, a former White House assistant, revealed, almost inadvertently, in responding to questions from the Ervin Committee, that Nixon had a voice-activated taping system in the Oval Office.

From this point forward, various attempts to obtain these tapes from the White House failed until July 24, 1974, when the Supreme Court ruled in *United States v. Nixon* that the president could not retain subpoenaed tapes by claiming executive privilege. During this protracted struggle, Archibald Cox, the first special prosecutor appointed to investigate Watergate, acting on behalf of a federal grand jury also tried to gain access to the tapes. When Cox rejected a compromise proposed by Nixon, the president ordered both Attorney General Elliot Richardson and Deputy Attorney General William D. Ruckelshaus to fire the special prosecutor. Refusing to do so, they resigned. On October 20, 1973, an acting attorney general finally carried out Nixon's order, but this "Saturday Night Massacre" was subsequently ruled an illegal violation of Justice Department procedures in *Nader v. Bork*. This incident also created such negative public opinion that the president agreed to turn over nine subpoenaed tapes to Judge Sirica, only to announce on October 31 that two of the tapes did not exist and on November 26 that a third had an unexplained eighteen-and-a-half minute gap in it—an erasure which remains unexplained.

Finally, on October 30, 1973, the House Judiciary Committee, headed by Peter Rodino, began preliminary investigations and in April, 1974, launched a full-scale impeachment inquiry which led on July 27 to a vote recommending the impeachment of the president. Nixon resigned from office on August 9, rather than face an impeachment trial. On September 8, President Gerald Ford (whom Nixon had appointed after Vice President Agnew resigned in the midst of, but for reasons unrelated to, Watergate on October 10, 1973) unconditionally pardoned the former president for all federal crimes he may have committed or been a party

to, freeing Nixon from any criminal or civil liability in the Watergate affair. Questions about whether a deal had been struck between Ford and Nixon over this pardon before the latter resigned contributed to Ford's defeat by Democrat Jimmy Carter in the 1976 election.

The legacy of Watergate lies in the fact that it precipitated a demand for accountability on the part of government officials and a demand for greater public access to government information. Thus, Watergate directly or indirectly produced a series of reforms for elections, financing political campaigns, and for ensuring greater public access to secret or classified documents. These reforms specifically included the establishment of the Federal Election Commission (FEC), the Congressional Budget Office, the War Powers Act, the 1974 and 1978 Presidential Materials and Preservation Acts, and the 1974 amendments to the Freedom of Information Act (FOIA). In addition, Congress agreed to open conference committees to public scrutiny and the Democratic Party continued its efforts (which had begun before Watergate) to reform the primary system, with the Republican Party following suit. Unfortunately, most of these congressional acts and reforms have since been violated, watered down, or contradicted by presidential actions. Some have created unforeseen additional problems, such as the uncontrolled financing of candidates by political action committees (PACs), overly complicated ethical standard requirements, and the automatic triggering of special prosecutor investigations in response to trivial incidents.

The break-in itself was a disaster looking for a place to happen—given the decline in political ethics over many years prior to Nixon's presidency. Nixon obstructed justice thereafter for two years, and got away with it as president of the United States, a dramatic performance if ever there was one. It was hoped that Watergate's legacy would be the prevention of unconstitutional and unethical behavior.

The impeachment trial of President Bill Clinton fifteen years later raised many of the same concerns—obstruction of justice, misuse of executive power—in the context of sexual scandal. Some tried to establish direct links between the two cases, finding common ethical issues, while others pointed to differences in criminal action and scope. Whether such comparisons are valid, the Clinton impeachment led many people to revisit the "national nightmare" called Watergate.

Nixon's reputation had been revisited in the 1980's and especially following his death on April 22, 1994, in New York City, at the age of eighty-one. Clinton and former presidents Ford, Carter, and George Bush were all in attendance at his funeral (Reagan was too ill to attend), and the nation seemed ready to look at the whole picture of his political career, not merely its ignominious end.

Joan Hoff-Wilson

Bibliographical References

Even before Watergate, books about Nixon left much to be desired. Watergate only made it more difficult to find balanced accounts about his life and career. This will continue to be the case until the bulk of his papers and those of his advisers are opened. In 1974, Nixon's White House papers became subject to litigation, blocking access, and those close to him, especially Henry Kissinger and Alexander Haig, established private monopolies over their papers.

For a basic introductory account of Nixon's life, see *The Facts About Nixon: An Unauthorized Biography*, 1960, by William Costello. One of the best early works is Bela Kornitzer, *The Real Nixon: An Intimate Biography*, 1960. Another good prepresidential biography is Earl Mazo and Stephen Hess, *Nixon: A Political Portrait*, 1968. Roger Morris, *Richard Milhous Nixon: The Rise of an American Politician*, 1990, details the years from Nixon's birth in 1913 to his vice presidential campaign of 1952. Tom Wicker,

One of Us: Richard Nixon and the American Dream, 1991, examines the people, places, and events that shaped Nixon's character. Jonathan Aitken, *Nixon: A Life*, 1993, was written with full cooperation of Nixon, who granted the author interviews and access to his diaries. By far the most enduring interpretative account of his political life remains Garry Wills's *Nixon Agonistes: The Crisis of the Self-Made Man*, 1970. Christopher Matthews, *Kennedy and Nixon: The Rivalry That Shaped Postwar America*, 1996, is a fascinating study of the rivalry that began between the two men with their elections to the House of Representatives in 1946.

Of the many psychohistorical accounts which abound about Nixon, the two containing the fewest factual errors about his early life are David Abrahamsen, *Nixon vs. Nixon: An Emotional Tragedy*, 1977, which attempts to evaluate his performance as president, as well as the psychological implications of his childhood, and Fawn M. Brodie, *Richard Nixon: The Shaping of His Character*, 1981, which contains an interesting, but highly controversial psychoanalysis of his career up to 1968, but only a summary account of his presidency. Vamik D. Volkan, Norman Itzkowitz, and Andrew W. Dod, *Richard Nixon: A Psychobiography*, 1997, also applies psychoanalytic interpretation to the study of Nixon's leadership style. A short, straightforward biographical account of Nixon and 450 biographical sketches of key figures in his administration can be found in Eleanor W. Schoenebaum, *Profiles of an Era: The Nixon-Ford Years*, 1979. Richard M. Pious has written a typically negative, Watergate-dominated account of Nixon in *The President: A Reference History*, 1984, edited by Henry F. Graff. Since most of the major (and many minor) figures in the Nixon administration have written their own memoirs, it is worth consulting books by John Dean, H. R. Haldeman, John Ehrlichman, Kissinger, and Haig. An insightfully critical overview of the Nixon administration is Jonathan Schell, *The Time of Illusion*, 1976.

Among the best-documented accounts of Watergate remains *Nightmare: The Underside of the Nixon Years*, 1976, by J. Anthony Lewis, although a valuable psychoanalytical viewpoint has been provided by Leo Rangell, *The Mind of Watergate: A Study of the Compromise of Integrity*, 1980. William Safire, who served as a speechwriter for Nixon, wrote a valuable insider's account, *Before the Fall*, 1975, and so did Rowland Evans, Jr., and Robert D. Novak, *Nixon in the White House: The Frustration of Power*, 1971. The staff of the *Washington Post* published a useful annotation of the released tapes in *The Presidential Transcripts*, 1974, and the 1975 *Report* of the Watergate Special Prosecution Force (WSPF) is an excellent summary of the various investigations conducted for twenty-eight months by the Department of Justice. For a distillation of more than two hundred hours of secret Nixon tapes released in 1996, see Stanley I. Kutler, ed., *Abuse of Power: The New Nixon Tapes*, 1997. For speculation about why the Watergate break-in took place, see Jim Hougan, *Secret Agenda: Watergate, Deep Throat, and the CIA*, 1984. Two recent reevaluations of the Watergate era are Len Colodny and Robert Gettlin, *Silent Coup: The Removal of a President*, 1991, and Kutler, *The Wars of Watergate: The Last Crisis of Richard Nixon*, 1991.

There is no adequate history of Nixon's foreign policy. For two negative interpretations, see William Shawcross, *Sideshow: Kissinger, Nixon, and the Destruction of Cambodia*, 1979, which deals with the expansion of the war in Indochina, and a broader study by Seymour M. Hersh, *The Price of Power: Kissinger in the Nixon White House*, 1983. Three earlier accounts of diplomatic relations under the Nixon administration which also focus on Henry Kissinger include Roger Morris, *Uncertain Greatness: Henry Kissinger and American Foreign Policy*, 1977; *The Diplomacy of Detente: The Kissinger Era*, 1977, by Coral Bell; and Seyom Brown, *The Crisis of Power: Foreign Policy in the Kissinger Years*, 1979. Robert Litwak, *Detente and the Nixon Doctrine*, 1984, provides good detail on the relationship between the two concepts, and a general overview of Nixon's diplomatic initiatives can be found in Lloyd C. Gardner, *The Great Nixon Turn-Around: America's New Foreign Policy in the Post-Liberal Era (How a Cold Warrior Climbed Clean Out of His Skin)*, 1973. Jeffrey P. Kimball, *Nixon's Vietnam War*, 1998, provides an in-depth study of Nixon's war policy.

For an account of Nixon's postpresidential life and views, there is Robert S. Anson, *Exile: The Unique Oblivion of Richard M. Nixon*, 1984. In addition to *Six Crises*, 1962, the nine books Nixon wrote after leaving the White House: *RN: The Memoirs of Richard Nixon*, 1978; *The Real War*, 1980; *Leaders*, 1982; *Real Peace*, 1984; *No More Vietnams*, 1985; *1999: Victory Without War*, 1988; *In the Arena: A Memoir of Victory, Defeat, and Renewal*, 1990; *Seize the Moment: America's Challenge in a One-Superpower World*, 1992; and *Beyond Peace*, 1994. All are valuable for understanding his pre- and postpresidential ideas and the reasons behind attempts in the 1980's to rehabilitate his reputation.

For an overview of the legacy of the Nixon presidency, see Michael A. Genovese, *The Nixon Presidency: Power and Politics in Turbulent Times*, 1991; Gerald S. Strober and Deborah H. Strober, *Nixon: An Oral History of His Presidency*, 1994; and Martin S. Goldman, *Richard M. Nixon: A Complex Legacy*, 1998.

Gerald R. Ford

38th President, 1974-1977

Born: July 14, 1913
Omaha, Nebraska

Political Party: Republican
Vice President: Nelson A. Rockefeller

Cabinet Members

Secretary of State: Henry Kissinger
Secretary of the Treasury: William Simon
Secretary of Defense: James R. Schlesinger, Donald H. Rumsfeld
Attorney General: William B. Saxbe, Edward H. Levi
Secretary of the Interior: Rogers C. B. Morton, Stanley K. Hathaway, Thomas D. Kleppe
Secretary of Agriculture: Earl L. Butz, John Knebel
Secretary of Commerce: Frederick B. Dent, Rogers C. B. Morton, Elliot Richardson
Secretary of Labor: Peter J. Brennan, John T. Dunlop, W. J. Usery
Secretary of Health, Education, and Welfare: Caspar Weinberger, Forrest D. Mathews
Secretary of Housing and Urban Development: James T. Lynn, Carla A. Hills
Secretary of Transportation: Claude S. Brinegar, William T. Coleman

The first person to occupy both the presidency and the vice presidency without being elected to either office, Gerald Rudolph Ford, Jr., succeeded the first president to resign, fellow Republican Richard M. Nixon. Ford's unelected (and somewhat unexpected) appearance in the White House occurred in troubled times for many Americans. The domestic economy suffered from increasing unemployment and inflation. In Southeast Asia, the Saigon regime neared collapse following the almost total withdrawal of American forces from a war in Vietnam that had become equally costly, futile, and unpopular. At home, with the national bicentennial less than two years away, Americans

Ford's official portrait. *(White House Historical Society)*

629

were stunned and dismayed by the rapid decline in the credibility, and subsequent resignation under threat of impeachment, of President Nixon, who had only recently been reelected by a landslide.

Initially popular if not popularly chosen, President Ford brought with him to the White House a quarter century of experience in the House of Representatives. He also addressed his presidential responsibilities with energy, knowledge, and determination. Ford, however, retained from the discredited Nixon administration many White House advisers and cabinet officers from whom he never established sufficient independence and over whom he did not adequately impose his own initiatives and authority. Consequently, Ford himself was largely responsible for the fragmentation and turbulence of his staff, whose effectiveness was diminished by constant infighting between Nixon and Ford loyalists.

Problems soon surfaced. Less than a month after becoming president, Ford granted a "full, free and absolute pardon" to his afflicted and vulnerable predecessor, confirming the suspicions of many that Ford had concocted a deal with former President Nixon before the latter's resignation. These realities led to Democratic insinuations in 1976 that the Ford administration was an extension of the unsavory Watergate era rather than its resolution.

Two later mishaps contributed to President Ford's loss of public confidence and his ultimate failure to win the 1976 election. After his aircraft landed in Salzburg, Austria, in June, 1975, Ford slipped on a wet, rubberless metal boarding ramp, almost falling at the feet of welcoming Austrian Chancellor Bruno Kreisky. Anyone else might have taken an identical spill. A cameraman photographed the incident, and immediately newspaper cartoonists joined television comics in ridiculing the president as an uncoordinated, drink-dropping stumblebum. In reality, Ford had been a star college athlete, was an avid skier and swimmer, and

remained one of the most physically coordinated and fit of all presidents. The stumblebum image was greatly exaggerated if not false, but many Americans apparently believed it, including at least one professional historian, Irwin Unger, who still described Ford, in a 1982 textbook, as "physically awkward."

The second unfortunate event, according to one of Ford's inner circle, Robert Hartmann, writing in *Palace Politics* (1980), "was just as accidental and explicable" but one for which the president himself "must bear some of the blame." This was Ford's "incredible conclusion" in the second televised debate with 1976 Democratic presidential opponent Jimmy Carter that "there is no Soviet domination of Eastern Europe." Apparently, Ford had not meant to convey the message that his own chosen words in fact conveyed, but the remark stood and the damage was done, establishing the fear that an already bumbling Ford had also become a dangerous wanderer in a foreign affairs fantasyland.

Hartmann insists that the president's brief administration was not without substantial accomplishments but concedes that Ford may be remembered only "for never having been elected, for healing our land, for falling down steps and for pardoning Richard Nixon." Succeeded by Democratic President Jimmy Carter in January, 1977, Gerald R. Ford joined in history only four previous chief executives whose terms had been shorter than his: William H. Harrison (1841), Zachary Taylor (1849-1850), James A. Garfield (1881), and Warren G. Harding (1921-1923).

Self-Discipline and Achievement: Football, Law School, Military Service
The thirty-eighth president of the United States was born in Omaha, Nebraska, on July 14, 1913. He was originally named Leslie King, Jr., but when Ford was two years old, his parents were divorced and his mother took him with her to Grand Rapids, Michigan. There, in 1916,

The Ford family, 1960. *(Gerald R. Ford Library)*

Dorothy King married Gerald Rudolph Ford, who adopted Leslie and renamed him Gerald Rudolph Ford, Jr. His mother's second marriage gave Ford three younger half brothers—Thomas, Richard, and James. The Ford family was well balanced, close, and loving. The elder Ford was a hardworking and prosperous owner of a local paint and varnish company. Dorothy Ford actively involved herself in numerous church and community projects, in addition to being an apparently devoted mother to her four sons. The future president enjoyed a healthy, positive childhood, learning to give, take, share, win, and lose. He also learned always to do his best and to become an achiever rather than a wishful thinker. In high school, Ford played center on the football team, joined the Boy Scouts, served on the stu-

dent council, and was well liked. During the early years of the Great Depression, he worked at various part-time jobs to help his family get through the hard times. From this background, together with his Episcopalian upbringing, came Ford's widely respected honesty, openness, and reliability. He seems, finally, to have developed as a mature person with a deep sense of purpose and self-worth.

In 1931, Ford entered the University of Michigan on a football scholarship, but he had to continue working part-time in order to pay all his expenses. He joined Delta Kappa Epsilon social fraternity and made two lifelong friends at the university—John R. Stiles, who was later Ford's congressional campaign manager, and Philip Buchen, who became Ford's law partner and eventually a member of President Ford's

White House staff. Ford was named to the college all-star team after his senior season and received professional offers from both the Detroit Lions and the Green Bay Packers. He declined these invitations and instead pursued legal studies at Yale University, where he also coached the undergraduate boxing team and served as an assistant football coach.

Throughout high school, college, and law school, Ford was a consistently bright, above-average student. Future critics who delighted in pointing out that President Ford had never been a profound thinker or a straight-A student forgot that several solid presidents—Harry Truman and Dwight Eisenhower among them—had not excelled academically, and that from some points of view one of the great White House disappointments, Woodrow Wilson, had been a history professor and that mediocre president Chester A. Arthur had belonged to Phi Beta Kappa.

Several months after Ford's graduation from Yale Law School in 1940, the Japanese attacked Hawaii, bringing the United States formally into World War II and Ford into the United States Navy. As an ensign he trained recruits in North Carolina for a year and then served for the remainder of the war on the aircraft carrier USS *Monterey* in the Pacific theater. By 1946, Ford had risen to the rank of lieutenant commander and wore ten battle stars; he therefore had more combat experience than many of the war veterans who became national political figures.

Entry into Politics: A Team Player

Returning to his Grand Rapids law practice after the war, Ford became one of the young reformers of local Republican politics and in 1948 ran for the Fifth District congressional seat of Bartel C. Jonkman, an isolationist and member of the entrenched and reactionary Grand Rapids Republican establishment. A fresh and vigorous Ford campaign upset the complacent and unpopular Jonkman handily,

and later in the year, on the same national Election Day that underdog Democratic President Harry S Truman defeated Republican contender Thomas E. Dewey, Ford outpolled a Democratic congressional challenger. During the 1948 campaign Ford married Elizabeth "Betty" Bloomer. They subsequently had four children—Michael Gerald (born 1950), John Gardner (born 1952), Steven Meigs (born 1956), and Susan Elizabeth (born 1957).

From 1949 to 1973, Ford served as a diligent and loyal member of the House Republican "team," first as an apprentice congressman and after 1963 as a party leader. He did his homework conscientiously, rarely missing sessions or committee meetings. Unlike other congressional contemporaries who used their positions in the House as a means to advance to the executive branch, Ford concentrated on his House duties and responsibilities. Ford never displayed "presidential fever" and only once permitted his name to be mentioned for the vice presidency. At the 1960 Republican convention, Michigan supporters staged a brief Ford boomlet, but presidential nominee Richard Nixon chose instead Massachusetts senator Henry Cabot Lodge, Jr., as his running mate.

Ford remained in Congress, to which his admiring Fifth District constituents reelected him repeatedly, never giving Ford less than 60 percent of their votes. Chosen Republican conference chair in 1963 and House minority leader two years later, "Jerry" Ford was as much a "House man" by 1973 as Sir Winston Churchill remained a "Commons man" throughout his long and distinguished career. Whereas Michigan's Fifth District was a virtual Republican "pocket borough," as it provided Ford a secure House seat for twenty-four years, the United States was not a parliamentary democracy. The future president never had to develop or sustain a pluralistic national constituency until 1976, by which time he was the White House incumbent defending a frayed and suspect administration against a spirited attack

In March, 1952, Congressmen Ford, Robert Kean, and Norris Cotton (left to right) read a letter from General Dwight D. Eisenhower announcing that he does not plan to leave his European assignment to seek the Republican presidential nomination. *(AP/Wide World Photos)*

by the nominee of the national majority party.

Hardly any Americans outside Michigan knew of Ford at all, or even what he looked like, until he and Senate Minority Leader Everett Dirksen of Illinois appeared together on the so-called Ev and Jerry Show, a series of televised press conferences during the late 1960's in which Ford and the more oratorical Dirksen (who did most of the talking) criticized the Great Society programs of Democratic President Lyndon B. Johnson. Although Johnson had thought enough of Ford, or of his status within the Republican Party, to appoint the Michigan congressman to the Warren Commission to investigate President John F. Kennedy's assassination, LBJ was "the source of savage wisecracks that have plagued Ford to this day"—crudities such as, "Jerry's a nice guy, but he played football too long without a helmet." Johnson later directly apologized to Ford for such insensitive statements, but many Washington insiders largely agreed with them and considered Ford a person of little significance or, worse, a "lightweight."

Ford was not a lightweight. He was in fact an experienced and widely respected House minority leader among few other responsible personages in an unusually cynical and demoralized Washington. It was not Ford who publicly used abusive language to describe colleagues, peddled influence, sought to cover up felonies, or tape-recorded visitors' comments in his office without their knowledge. The only blemish on Ford's entire pre-vice presidential record was his ill considered attempt in 1969, loyally undertaken at the behest of Nixon's

White House, to impeach liberal Supreme Court Justice William O. Douglas. The movement fizzled and Ford repented. It is possible to serve honestly, intelligently, and constructively as a congressional leader without having presidential aspirations or even being "presidential timber." Dozens of persons have done so since 1789. Most of them have been forgotten by all but historians because they were only briefly, if ever, in the national spotlight. Without a presidential constitutency and lacking the presidential aura, these individuals did not seek the presidency and were not seriously considered by their parties as viable presidential contenders. Democratic House Speaker Sam Rayburn was one modern example of the type; Republican House minority leader Gerald Ford was another. Neither of these men was a lightweight.

An Accidental President

Ford made history by becoming the nation's first accidental vice president when, on October 12, 1973, President Nixon nominated him to succeed Vice President Spiro T. Agnew, whose resignation two days earlier had become necessary because of his involvement in a Maryland bribery scandal. (One previous vice president had resigned and others had died in office, but no constitutional mechanism existed for filling vice presidential vacancies until the Twenty-fifth Amendment to the Constitution was ratified in 1967.) Why did Nixon choose Ford to succeed Agnew? He chose him, first and foremost, because the Twenty-fifth Amendment required congressional confirmation of a president's vice presidential nominee, and Nixon knew that the Democratic congressional majority would confirm a "respectable" but not a "presidential" Republican. Ford was solidly respectable and equally unpresidential, a factor Ford himself was apparently compelled to reemphasize by promising Nixon that he would not seek the 1976 Republican presidential nomination. Although President Nixon was

already in difficulty with Watergate in the fall of 1973, no one could predict the events that were to follow. Nixon, Ford, and almost everyone else assumed that the president would complete his term, the Republican presidential nomination would be won by John Connally, George Bush, or perhaps Ronald Reagan, and that Vice President Ford would at last return to private life. In addition, President Nixon obviously preferred a loyal, low-profile vice president who would not attempt to overshadow or upstage his chief in the White House. No lightweight could fill such a role, which required a respectable and reliable team player—Gerald R. Ford.

Two months of congressional hearings and investigations into Ford's background and qualifications followed his nomination. Having passed congressional scrutiny, Ford took office on December 6, 1973. In his inaugural remarks that day, he said, "I am a Ford, not a Lincoln." This unpretentious, car-culture metaphor suggested that although Ford recognized his limitations when compared with the greatest of Republican presidents, the new vice president was nevertheless a durable and dependable leader in his own way. Adhering predictably to his established reputation as a team player, Ford remained in the background, permitting the White House to establish his agenda and itinerary. Until President Nixon was forced to admit that he had lied about his knowledge of the Watergate cover-up, Vice President Ford continued loyally to believe that Nixon had done nothing wrong and would complete his presidential term. It was therefore with genuinely troubled feelings that Ford beheld the rapid disintegration of Nixon's defense and personal credibility as, between December, 1973, and early August, 1974, the odds that Ford would become president rose steadily from possible to probable to certain.

On August 9, 1974, the second accident that propelled Ford into the White House occurred: Richard M. Nixon, under threat of impeachment, resigned. Before 1974, eight American vice presidents had reached the White House because their chiefs had died in office, through natural causes or assassination. Writing in 1966, Stanford professor Thomas A. Bailey described the eight as our "accidental Presidents." (In less formal classroom presentations, Bailey referred to them as "their Accidentcies.") Unlike his eight predecessors, however, Ford had not been elected to the vice presidency.

Despite having never faced the national electorate, Ford impressed the nation favorably during his first moments as chief executive. The most noteworthy of his remarks after taking the presidential oath was his since frequently quoted reference to the past agonies of Watergate: "Our long national nightmare is over," he declared, conveying a message that many Americans had been longing to hear, and to believe. (The phrase was not a Ford inspiration, although he said it convincingly; Robert Hartmann, a Ford adviser, had suggested it.) In the same speech, Ford asked fellow countrymen to pray that former President Nixon, a man "who brought peace to millions,"

could "find it for himself." Hartmann later recalled in *Palace Politics* that "no president ever started off with more friends and fewer enemies" than Ford.

A Pardon for Richard M. Nixon

President Ford's honeymoon with the American press and public, however, lasted barely a month for on September 8, Ford announced his "full, free and absolute pardon" of former President Nixon for all crimes that he had committed, or may have committed, during his tenure in the White House. The pardon meant that Nixon would never be indicted, tried, and convicted (or acquitted) in connection with Watergate or anything else that took place during his presidency; nor would the former president lose any of the perquisites of a retired chief executive—pension, staff allowances, or Secret Service protection.

Ford insisted that his reasons for pardoning Nixon were sound and valid—"It was the right thing to do." First, he felt that Nixon had suffered enough and had paid dearly for whatever he may have done. Second, Ford was sincerely concerned about Nixon's physical and mental condition at the time, believing that further criminal proceedings might break the former president altogether or even harass him into committing suicide. Third, criminal proceedings against Nixon would likely go on for months, perhaps even years, and require the reappearance as witnesses of all the Watergate participants. Such a prolonged and lurid public spectacle, Ford believed, would only add to the American people's feelings of turmoil. Finally, criminal proceedings against the former president would affect the White House

President Ford addresses the nation on his pardon of Richard M. Nixon. *(Gerald R. Ford Library)*

itself, within which many of Nixon's tapes and papers remained stored. Having to locate, sort out, copy, and furnish these materials to attorneys for both sides could paralyze Ford's presidential staff.

Unfortunately, few persons beyond Ford's intimate entourage fully accepted the president's reasons for pardoning Nixon. Many immediately concluded that the pardon was Ford's part of a deal made either directly with Nixon or through Nixon's White House chief of staff, General Alexander Haig. (Nixon, Ford, and Haig all subsequently denied that a deal was made.) Among those who continued to believe that an understanding had been reached before Nixon's resignation was former Nixon aide John Ehrlichman. Writing in *Witness to Power* (1982), Ehrlichman recalled how President Nixon might have weighed the relative advantages and liabilities of resignation and impeachment as the end drew near. A pardon, he believed Nixon concluded, would terminate *"all* the risk and would make possible a gradual rehabilitation of Nixon's influence and image. If one cared about one's place in history, the pardon route was the best. And Richard Nixon cared deeply about his place in history."

What did Gerald Ford (who could not have been oblivious to his own place in history) stand to gain by pardoning Nixon? Getting Nixon out of the White House and himself into it could not have been Ford's motive. By late July of 1974, all three men who were involved—Ford, Nixon, and Haig—must have realized that Nixon would leave the presidency, either voluntarily or by the impeachment process. If Ford agreed to pardon Nixon after he had resigned, his motives undoubtedly were, as Ford said they were, to spare both the afflicted president and the nation the agonies of both an impeachment trial and further criminal proceedings.

President Ford's controversial pardon of Nixon caused the first crisis within his own White House staff. White House press secretary

Jerald F. TerHorst resigned at once, charging that it was improper to let Nixon go free while many of the former president's loyal subordinates remained in prison for doing his bidding. According to Hartmann's assessment, "TerHorst's abrupt exit immeasurably compounded the damage done by Ford's pardon decision. . . . With his defection, the tiny phalanx of Ford people [within a White House still controlled by Nixon staffers] was weakened and Ford's own shining image was dimmed."

A Crippled Administration

Certainly, President Ford commenced his administration with a White House staff composed overwhelmingly of Nixon people. A transition team did not succeed in replacing Nixon holdovers with a majority of Ford's own people. The holdovers included cabinet members as well as many middle- and lower-rung staffers. Even at the end of his term, Ford's own appointees remained in the minority. Hartmann believed, indeed, that the "fatal" weakness in Ford's presidency was not the Nixon pardon and the public resentment of it but, as Hartmann had warned the president in a November, 1975, memorandum, "your retention of and reliance on Nixon Administration figures from a past you are trying to put behind you." The Nixonites (the more offensive of whom Hartmann called the "Praetorians" without naming them specifically) were convinced that "it was *their* White House, not Ford's. They honestly believed the new President needed them more than they needed him, and that he was incapable of running the place without them."

Ford never even responded to Hartmann's memorandum and disloyal Nixonites remained in the White House, undercutting such Ford ideas as the WIN (Whip Inflation Now) program, and ensuring repeatedly bland, punchless Ford speeches by keeping presidential speechwriters confused and edgy. One of Ford's most conscientious writers was John J. Casserly, who had come to the White House from the Commerce Department. On January 23, 1976, Casserly resigned, having reached the limit of his toleration and finding himself on bad terms with other Ford staffers. Casserly liked and admired President Ford, whom he called a "decent and good man" in his 1977 *The Ford White House*, but concluded that Ford lacked "the firmness to run the White House or the leadership to be President."

Hartmann, however, later concluded that Ford had demonstrated great leadership through his career, including the presidential years, but was deficient in command:

Much has [been] written on Presidential leadership, but command is what the Presidency is all about. . . . To put it bluntly, a President must be something of an SOB. It is not enough to surround himself with them. He must at times be *the* SOB and he must, however secretly, rather relish this role. Ford was simply too nice a guy; he boasted that he had adversaries but no enemies, and he really meant it. Sometimes he hurt people, but he hated it. Not for nothing was he called "good old Jerry." But nobody ever called our first President "good old George." A commander must be capable of shooting his own mutinous troops.

"Good old Jerry" was the joint product of a decent, religious family background and of twenty-four years within the congressional system as a team player in the minority party. Only from 1953 to 1955 were Ford and his House Republican colleagues able to initiate and push majority party legislation. From 1949 to 1953 and from 1955 to 1973, they had either to defend the programs of Republican presidents against congressional Democratic onslaughts or to oppose congressional Democratic initiatives ordered by Democratic presidents. Ford thus early in his political career developed a work mentality of compromise and adjustment, which meshed compatibly with his own personal, team-player athletic experiences. Compromise and adjustment well suit a mi-

nority member of Congress but can be lethal if maintained by an occupant of the presidency, which demands aggressive and decisive leadership at all times, as well as the ruthlessness of an "SOB," as Hartmann (and others) have observed.

Even in the Oval Office, President Ford remained essentially Congressman Ford, and "good old Jerry" seemingly did not become sufficiently skeptical, thick-skinned, or brutal to handle either the White House staff or the lonely responsibilities of presidential command. Trusting, open, optimistic, unwilling to hurt anyone's feelings—and expecting similar behavior from other White House "team players"—President Ford continued to do his best while a divided and unruled staff progressively subverted his authority and goals.

Perhaps the most successful piece of Praetorian subversion involved the man Ford appointed vice president, former New York Governor Nelson A. Rockefeller, who assumed his duties on December 19, 1974. The wealthy and multitalented Rockefeller, dean of the party's liberal and cosmopolitan eastern wing, had long been disliked if not despised by conservative Republicans from the hinterland. White House hinterlanders continually downgraded Rockefeller, kept him isolated from the president whenever possible, and sought to neutralize whatever influence he possessed. After President Ford decided to seek another term in 1976, he apparently succumbed to conservative and Praetorian pressure and in November, 1975, obtained from his vice president a statement that Rockefeller would not be on the Republican ticket during the forthcoming campaign. (The eventual Republican vice presidential nominee in 1976 was a conservative hinterlander, Senator Bob Dole of Kansas. Hartmann believed several years later that Ford would have been "unbeatable" in 1976 had his vice president been George Bush, his defense secretary Ronald Reagan, and his secretary of state Nelson A. Rockefeller.)

Domestic Legislation and Foreign Policy

Although President Ford remained ill served by a staff he failed to command, the Ford administration went dutifully and doggedly on. Among the major items of legislation Ford signed in 1974 were a $25 billion federal aid to education act (which included a restriction on busing) and the Federal Campaign Reform Act, providing public funding for the campaigns of serious presidential contenders and establishing spending limits for presidential and congressional candidates. The reform legislation had grown out of Watergate-related disclosures of illegal contributions made to President Nixon's 1972 reelection effort. As a result of the 1974 law, President Ford and his 1976 Democratic opponent, Jimmy Carter, became the first presidential candidates whose campaigns were funded largely by taxpayers. Ford also signed in 1974 a $4.8 billion federal commitment to improve public mass transit facilities. Responding to rising national unemployment which by mid-1975 had reached 9.2 percent of the workforce, the president, on June 30, approved a measure extending unemployment benefits for a maximum of sixty-five weeks.

The conservative Ford also vetoed fifty-three bills during his two-year administration, of which the Democratic Congress was able to override only nine. (Hartmann applauded the forty-four vetoes that stood, claiming they saved the taxpayers $9.2 billion and helped cut the growth rate in federal spending by one-half "for the first time in decades.") Among the measures that became law without Ford's approval were a $7.9 billion educational appropriation in 1975, plus two welfare-social services appropriations and a job bill in 1976. In opposing further federal aid to education and assistance to lower-income groups during recession, Ford may have pleased conservative Republicans, but he did so at the cost of support among voters in 1976. Not only did Ford's many vetoes likely add to his subsequent opposition but also the president's 1976 budget was, in Hartmann's view, "politically . . . suicidal" in an election year. At the same time that he supported a $28 billion cut in government spending programs already on the books, Ford proposed to reduce taxes on individuals and corporations by $28 billion. Treasury Secretary William Simon and Council of Economic Advisors Chairman Alan Greenspan energetically urged Ford to adopt this politically risky policy of economic retrenchment. (Hartmann described these Nixon holdovers as possessing two of "the best economic minds of the eighteenth century.")

Even less spectacular than Ford's domestic accomplishments were his achievements in foreign affairs. The president retained Nixon's flamboyant and brilliant secretary of state, Henry Kissinger, and Ford's foreign policy became in effect an extension of the Nixon-Kissinger pol-

As House Republican leader, Ford displays a huge gavel in September, 1968, as a symbol of the party's fight to win control of the House in the elections that fall. (*AP/Wide World Photos*)

icy. Peace among the superpowers was maintained, both Ford and Kissinger traveled extensively to confer with foreign dignitaries, but few solid or workable new initiatives emerged. A qualified exception was Kissinger's success at bringing about an Israeli-Egyptian interim peace in the Middle East in October, 1975.

Ford also had to cope with the aftermath of the Nixon-Kissinger "peace" in Vietnam—though congressional action had eliminated any further military intervention. Ford's most painful duty was to oversee the evacuation of American personnel from Saigon when the South Vietnamese regime collapsed in April of 1975. The president's most dramatic foreign policy endeavor, however, followed a month later when Cambodians of the Khmer Rouge seized the American merchant ship *Mayaguez* in the Gulf of Siam. Ford successfully used naval and military forces to rescue the crewmen. At home President Ford attempted to heal the domestic wounds of the Southeast Asian war by offering, on September 16, 1974, a clemency work program for Vietnam draft evaders and military deserters. To receive amnesty under the plan, they had to perform two years of public service work and to take an oath of allegiance. About 22,500 out of 124,000 eligibles applied for the program. Many draft evaders and deserters criticized the plan because, by not offering unconditional amnesty, it implied guilt, whereas some veterans' groups felt the president's approach was "soft."

Ford's presidency, like that of Ronald Reagan several years later, almost ended tragically. On September 22, 1975, political activist Sarah Jane Moore shot at Ford as he emerged from the St. Francis Hotel in San Francisco. A bystander deflected Moore's hand as she fired, and fortunately Ford, unlike Reagan, was not injured. Ford's luck in seeking reelection would not be as good. Almost as soon as he took office, he had to begin preparations for the race, and ill omens and difficulties burdened his efforts from the first.

The Election of 1976

Thirty-eight Republican incumbents had already met defeat in the 1974 congressional elections, enabling the Democrats to increase their House majority to 291 of the 435 members and their Senate lead to 61 of 100. Lingering disaffection over Watergate, Ford's Nixon pardon, and prevailing economic conditions were blamed for Republican losses. The Ford administration was also threatened from within. A strong challenge for the Republican presidential nomination by former California Governor Ronald Reagan jeopardized the party's fragile unity and irritated Ford. Nevertheless, the convention nominated the president by a narrow margin.

Ford's Democratic opponent, former Georgia Governor Jimmy Carter, had swept through the primaries, eliminating one better-known Democrat after another, until his nomination had become a certainty even before the party's national convention. Carter attracted voters because he was an outsider with no previous civilian experience in the federal government. No one could connect him with, or blame him for, the ongoing confusion in Washington, D.C. When Carter stressed his own personal honesty and promised "never to lie," he gained the support of many suspicious, resentful, and disenchanted Americans. Although President Ford was Carter's actual rival, former President Nixon was the implicit target of the Georgian's moralistic slogans and promises. Because Ford had pardoned Nixon and had retained many Nixon appointees, Carter sought to connect the two in as many voters' minds as possible.

Probably because he had perceived Carter's strategy at the time, Hartmann remained all the more convinced that it was Ford's failure to get rid of the White House Nixonites that finally brought about the president's defeat:

> I believe President Ford could have survived his sudden pardon of former President Nixon if he had coupled it with the dismissal of Nixon's

court and constituted one of his own choosing. Everybody expected him to do so; it is the first thing a new President does. He had the clear precedents of Harry Truman, who got rid of FDR's Praetorian Guard in short order, and of Lyndon Johnson, who hung onto Kennedy's and lived to regret it. As President, Ford boldly took the first step—and I believe pardoning Nixon was right and spared the country endless agony—but not the second step, which would have put Watergate behind us where the American people wanted it to be.

Hartmann's verdict is supported by the relatively close margin of Carter's 1976 victory—40.3 million popular votes to Ford's 38.5 million, with an edge in electoral votes of only 297 to 240. Of the six previous presidential incumbents who had been defeated in seeking reelection, only John Adams in 1800 and Grover Cleveland in 1888 lost by a smaller margin in the electoral count than Ford. Also, both Adams and Cleveland had been elected before, whereas Ford had not.

Ford's Presidency: A Tentative Assessment

Gerald R. Ford had been an able congressman and a respected House minority leader. His personal integrity, genuine commitment to public service, and forthright confrontation of critical issues restored much-needed respect to a tarnished presidency. His administration reduced the inflation rate from slightly above 12 percent to below 5 percent, "reversed the recessionary trend and increased total employment to a record high," as Hartmann recalled. President Ford also launched the nation's inner rehabilitation from the trauma of Vietnam and engaged in stabilizing discussions with the major communist powers. His administration laid the groundwork for future Middle East accords as well. He also greatly underestimated the destructive consequences of the Nixon pardon ("right" though it may have been), however, and failed either to reconstitute or to command

the White House staff. Ford was, finally, one of many recent victims of media imagery, which substitutes judgment by appearance for judgment of performance. Had he been more experienced in using visual media, as was his 1976 rival and second successor, Ronald Reagan, President Ford might have remained in the White House for the next four years.

Ford has been described as an "adequate" but "undistinguished" president. Future assessments may be slightly more favorable after the documented record of the 1970's becomes firmly established, permitting closer and less impressionistic comparisons with the administrations of both his predecessor and successor. President Bill Clinton helped this reassessment by honoring Ford with the Presidential Medal of Freedom in 1999.

Mark T. Carleton

Bibliographical References

Robert Hartmann, *Palace Politics: An Inside Account of the Ford Years*, 1980, is a thorough and critical assessment of Ford's presidency. Written by a man who served on Ford's House, vice presidential, and presidential staffs, *Palace Politics* treats Ford admiringly as a person but pulls few punches when dealing with Ford's White House years. The book also contains a comprehensive bibliography of Ford-era memoirs, biographies, and other useful works. John J. Casserly, *The Ford White House: The Diary of a Speechwriter*, 1977, is not written from Hartmann's Olympian perspective, but it presents a vivid day-by-day account of a frustrated Ford staffer. Another admiring biography of Ford is James M. Cannon, *Time and Chance: Gerald Ford's Appointment with History*, 1994. For issues-oriented collections of essays on the Ford presidency, see Kenneth W. Thompson, ed., *The Ford Presidency: Twenty-two Intimate Perspectives of Gerald R. Ford*, 1988, and Bernard J. Firestone and Alexj Ugrinsky, eds., *Gerald R. Ford and the Politics of Post-Watergate America*, 1993. The president's own account is *A Time to Heal: The Autobiography of Gerald R. Ford*, 1979. See also Betty Ford (with Chris Chase), *The Times of My Life*, 1978. For a comprehensive bibliographic overview of the Ford years, see John R. Greene, *Gerald R. Ford: A Bibliography*, 1994. For a balanced portrait of Ford's term, see Greene, *The Presidency of Gerald R. Ford*, 1995.

Jimmy Carter

39th President, 1977-1981

Born: October 1, 1924
       Plains, Georgia

Political Party: Democratic
Vice President: Walter Mondale

Cabinet Members

Secretary of State: Cyrus Vance, Edmund Muskie
Secretary of the Treasury: W. Michael Blumenthal, G. William Miller
Secretary of Defense: Harold Brown
Attorney General: Griffin Bell, Benjamin R. Civiletti

Secretary of the Interior: Cecil D. Andrus
Secretary of Agriculture: Bob S. Bergland
Secretary of Commerce: Juanita M. Kreps, Philip M. Klutznick
Secretary of Labor: F. Ray Marshall
Secretary of Health and Human Services: Joseph A. Califano, Jr., Patricia Roberts Harris
Secretary of Housing and Urban Development: Patricia Roberts Harris, Moon Landrieu
Secretary of Transportation: Brock Adams, Neil E. Goldschmidt
Secretary of Energy: James Schlesinger, Charles W. Duncan, Jr.
Secretary of Education: Shirley Hufstedler

Carter's official portrait. *(White House Historical Society)*

Campaigning for the presidency in 1976, Jimmy Carter described himself as a farmer, a Southerner, a born-again Christian, and a nuclear physicist. Although somewhat misleading, his description provided a fair index of the character and career of the man who sought to become the thirty-ninth president of the United States.

Spokesman for the New South

James Earl Carter, Jr., was born October 1, 1924, in Plains, Georgia, the first son of Lillian Gordy and James Earl Carter. Lillian was a registered nurse, Earl a prosperous businessman and farmer. Both parents stressed the importance of education to Jimmy and their other children, Ruth, Gloria, and Billy. An obedient, hardworking, enterprising youth, their eldest son not only excelled in his studies at school but also earned enough money from a boiled peanut business to invest in cotton and real estate. He was graduated from Plains High School as valedictorian of the class of 1941, spent a year each at Georgia Southwestern College and the Georgia Institute of Technology, received a coveted appointment to the United States Naval Academy, and was graduated from Annapolis in 1946, fifty-ninth in a class of 820. Though he had none of the credentials of a nuclear physicist, in the early 1950's as a young lieutenant in the United States Navy he worked for Captain Hyman G. Rickover on the *Seawolf*, one of the prototypes for the nuclear submarine. In 1953, when his father died, Carter resigned from the navy and returned to Plains to run the by-then failing family business. In partnership with his wife, Rosalynn, whom he had married in 1946, he not only revived but also expanded the enterprise and became a wealthy agribusinessman. A deacon and Sunday school teacher in the Plains Baptist Church, in 1967 he experienced a "new birth" which intensified his commitment to Christianity. Carter also gradually became involved in politics, first at the local level, where he served on the Sumter County School Board, then at the state level, where he served two terms in the Georgia Senate from 1963 to 1966.

In 1966 Carter made his first attempt to win the Georgia governorship. Campaigning as a moderate progressive, he lost to Lester Maddox, a conservative segregationist. Carter

Carter at home with his brother Billy the day before the presidential election in 1976. *(Archive Photos)*

then spent the next four years campaigning for the 1970 gubernatorial election. His experience as state senator and his 1966 congressional campaign (at the last minute he had forfeited a likely seat in the House of Representatives in order to run for the governorship) had whetted his desire for higher public office. He had become what James Wooten called the "existential politician," committed to an endless cycle of holding one office while preparing to run for another, caught up in "a process of always becoming something else."

In 1970 Carter's chief opponent was the liberal former governor Carl Sanders, rather than an extreme segregationist. With the help of political aides Jody Powell, Hamilton Jordan, Charles Kirbo, and Gerald Rafshoon, Carter mounted a grassroots campaign geared to rural, conservative, white Georgians. Although the *Atlanta Constitution* opposed him as an "ignorant, racist, backward, ultra-conservative, redneck South Georgia peanut farmer," he defeated Sanders handily in the Democratic primary runoff and went on to win over his Republican opponent in the general election, winning 60 percent of the vote. On Inauguration Day, he surprised many of his supporters by unequivocally pledging to work against racial discrimination. "I say to you quite frankly that the time for racial discrimination is over," he declared in his inaugural address. "No poor, rural, weak, or black person should ever again have to bear the additional burden of being deprived of the opportunity for an education, a job, or simple justice." Presumably, he sought to dispel the segregationist image his campaign had fostered. If so, it worked, for the address won for him national publicity as a leading voice of the "new" South. *Time* magazine featured him on its cover with the caption "Dixie Whistles a Different Tune: Georgia Governor Jimmy Carter" and proclaimed him one of a new breed of racial moderates flourishing below the Mason-Dixon line.

Carter carried out his pledge to fight racial discrimination in Georgia. Among other things, he increased state government employment of African Americans (from 4,850 when he took office to 6,684 when he left) and proclaimed Martin Luther King, Jr., Day on January 15, 1973. As governor he also worked for environmental protection, education, and tax and welfare reform. His main effort, however—and perhaps his major achievement—was the reorganization of state government. Stormy relations with the Georgia legislature made it and other legislative goals difficult to achieve. Disdaining the conventional swapping and trading, Carter frequently resorted to the veto or threat of a veto to maintain the integrity of proposed legislation. Legislators regarded him as self-righteous and stubborn. "Like a south Georgia turtle," one of them was quoted by Wooten. "He just keeps moving in the direction he's headed and it doesn't matter what you do to him. You can step on him or hit him with a stick or run over him with a pickup truck, and it doesn't faze him a bit. He just keeps on going in the way he wants to go." Another difficulty Carter faced, especially in his crusade for state reorganization, was mustering public support for rather abstract, intangible reforms. Despite such problems, he generally succeeded in streamlining the state government and in some cases saving money through zero-based budgeting. He did not win great popularity as governor, but he has been praised for helping Georgians adjust, as painlessly as possible, to necessary economic and social changes, especially in the area of civil rights.

The Campaign of 1976: An Appeal to Idealism

On December 12, 1974, shortly before his term as governor expired, Carter announced his candidacy for the presidency of the United States. He had already begun campaigning, having taken the job of chair of the 1974 Democratic Campaign Committee. It offered an ideal opportunity to meet people throughout the country while making fund-raising speeches for Democratic congressional candidates, as well as a means of enhancing his status in the national Democratic Party. Carter had also accepted an invitation to join the Trilateral Commission, a private international foreign policy organization formed in 1973 by the chairman of Chase Manhattan Bank, David Rockefeller. Later, in the presidential campaign, Carter cited his association with the commission to establish his foreign policy credentials. In his autobiography, *Why Not the Best?*, he said that membership on the commission had given him "an excellent opportunity to know national and international leaders in many fields of study concerning foreign affairs" and had provided "a splendid learning opportunity. . . . " Indeed, Carter's connection with the Trilateral Commission supplied him with more than information about foreign affairs. As Laurence Shoup has noted, it also provided or at least reinforced a major element of his campaign strategy: In a key Trilateral Commission document published in 1975, Samuel P. Huntington observed that the political history of the 1960's and 1970's showed that "the 'outsider' in politics, or the candidate who could make himself or herself appear to be an outsider, had the inside road to political office." The commission even furnished campaign support by putting Carter in touch with fund-raisers and wealthy contributors, the mass media, and various interest groups.

Carter won the Democratic nomination in 1976 because he worked longer and harder than any of the nine other candidates and, some observers said, because he wanted to be president more than any of the others did. In 1975 he spent 250 days on the road, visiting nearly every state to secure media attention and popular support. In twenty-two months of campaigning for the presidency, he made 1,495 speeches in 1,029 cities and traveled 461,240 miles. During the primaries and in the general election, he and his key aides—the foursome who had helped engineer the 1970 campaign for the governorship, plus a newcomer, pollster Patrick Caddell—devised a campaign strategy to exploit popular distrust of and alienation from government in the wake of Vietnam and Watergate. They promoted Carter as an outsider and antipolitician in their campaign against "the Washington establishment." They presented Carter's limited political experience as a state senator and one-term governor as a major asset and touted his abhorrence of political horse-trading as a virtue. Perhaps recalling his relations with the Georgia legislature, Carter said during the campaign that he had "always been inclined on a matter of principle or importance not to compromise unless it's absolutely necessary." He also said, however, that he was not disposed "to twist arms or force people to vote different from what they thought." He indicated that he might try to appeal beyond the legislature to the people. "There is a final forum that even transcends the inclination of the legislative body," he declared. "That's the people themselves."

On the campaign trail, Carter's vigor and youthfulness, even the similar shock of hair, reminded many of the late John F. Kennedy, but it was the wide, toothy grin that quickly became the Carter hallmark. Although lampooned by political cartoonists, it seemed to convey his feeling of goodwill toward others, while at the same time masking a basic shyness or, some would say, remoteness. One journalist interpreted the grin as an indication that the candidate might have a sense of humor about himself. Certainly it provided a welcome change from Richard Nixon's dour looks and Gerald Ford's blandness. Carter's soft-spoken, down-home style also contributed to his appeal as a candidate pledged to serve the people rather than the special interests.

As Elizabeth Drew observed in *American Journal: The Events of 1976*, Carter combined his antigovernment message with one of hope. Whereas the antigovernment message was grounded in an apparent enmity toward politicians, the hopeful message was based on a populistic faith in the American people. There was nothing wrong with them, Carter insisted—or, for that matter, with the system of government in the United States, which he declared to be "the best on earth." Thus at the same time that he condemned the government, he held out the possibility of redemption, of having "once again a nation with a government that is as honest and decent and fair and competent and truthful and idealistic as are the American people."

Carter promised to restore trust and pride in the government. He told the American people that he would never lie to them, never mislead them, never betray their trust. Throughout his campaign, he emphasized character over ideology or issues. He refused to be categorized as a conservative, liberal, or moderate, and when critics complained that he was "fuzzy" on the issues, he answered by making a distinction between what he called two levels of the campaign. One level was "the tangible issues" such as unemployment, inflation, the environment, health, education and welfare, taxation, agriculture, and nuclear proliferation. The other level was "the intangibles" such as integrity, compassion, and competence. Carter obviously felt more comfortable and thought it was more important—and presumably more conducive to electoral victory—talking about the intangibles than the tangible issues. When he did touch on the latter, he promised solutions without providing many details.

On November 4, Carter won the election. The vote, however, indicated no great surge of confidence on the part of the American people but rather continued apathy and skepticism. In one of the closest elections in United States history, Carter received 40,827,394 popular votes against Gerald Ford's 39,145,977. Voter turnout had declined from 62.8 percent in 1960 to 54.3 percent in 1976, which meant that less than three out of ten Americans registered to vote had cast their ballots for Carter. The close victory posed the challenge of Carter's presidency—to win the trust of the American people and prove his leadership ability.

Embattled President: Carter vs. the Washington Establishment

In the area of domestic affairs, Carter accomplished a number of objectives in education, transportation, conservation, and energy. At his behest, Congress created a separate Department of Education; deregulated the airline, trucking, and railroad industries; established a billion-dollar "superfund" to clean up abandoned chemical waste sites; and instituted a comprehensive national energy policy. Nevertheless, Carter's relations with Congress were difficult, even acrimonious at times. This situation was partly a result of the power relationship that existed between the White House and Capitol Hill. Carter's narrow election victory weakened his hand; he could hardly point to a broad popular mandate for his proposals.

At the same time, Congress continued to seek ways of regaining the power it had lost during the imperial presidencies of Lyndon Johnson and Richard Nixon.

Carter's difficulties with Congress also stemmed from his dislike of pork-barrel legislation. This led to an early confrontation with the Congress in mid-February, 1977, when Carter announced a plan to eliminate nineteen water projects around the country from the federal budget. He said he considered them a waste of taxpayers' money and threatened to take his case to the people; however, when the Congress held firm and when Carter realized that his stand on the water projects was jeopardizing other parts of his legislative program, he backed down. Later he wrote in his memoirs that the water projects battle had caused "the deepest breach" between him and the Democratic leadership in the Congress, but he continued to believe that he had been right in opposing the projects. The next year he vetoed the annual public works bill because it included some of the same projects.

Carter's fiscal conservatism also alienated some congressmen, particularly liberal members of his own party. Carter admitted feeling more comfortable with conservative Democrats and Republicans than with liberals. During the campaign he had called for comprehensive programs to create jobs and aid cities, to provide national health insurance, and to initiate welfare and tax reform. Once in office, however, he decided that inflation posed a greater threat than recession or unemployment and frequently allowed his determination to balance the budget by 1981 to take precedence over social programs. Thus he scrapped a program of significant welfare reform when Joseph Califano, the secretary of health, education, and welfare, reported that it would cost billions more than the existing program.

Carter attributed many of his difficulties with Congress to the influence that special interests wielded among the legislators. It seemed to him that members of Congress were much more vulnerable to such influence than was the president, partly because of the erosion of party discipline and consensus. "One branch of the government must stand fast on a particular issue to prevent the triumph of self-interest at the expense of the public," he declared in his memoirs. In the case of tax reform, Carter admitted that as president he had failed to marshal sufficient support among the American people to counteract the influence of the special interests. As a result, the administration's tax package had fallen victim to what he called "a pack of powerful and ravenous wolves, determined to secure for themselves additional benefits at the expense of other Americans." He thought he was much more successful standing up to another lobby, which he termed "the most formidable ever evolved in the military-industrial community," when he made the decision not to build the B-1 bomber.

The Energy Crisis: "The Moral Equivalent of War"

More than any other, the energy problem revealed the difficulties Carter encountered in working with Congress. On the president's instructions, James Schlesinger, secretary of the newly created Department of Energy, drew up a comprehensive energy program to submit to the Congress. While it was in the planning stage, Carter and Schlesinger kept the details from congressmen as well as high administration officials, fearing that if parts of it were revealed, it would be destroyed by special interest groups and lobbyists even before it reached Capitol Hill. Not surprisingly, the secrecy irritated legislators who thought they should be consulted about energy policy.

Carter unveiled his program in a speech in April, 1977, in which, borrowing a phrase from William James, he termed solving the energy crisis "the moral equivalent of war." Besides urging the American people to enlist in

a voluntary conservation effort, he sent to Congress a package of energy bills he wanted passed. Like tax reform, the energy program immediately drew fire from a wide range of special interest groups, including the oil lobby, automobile companies, consumer groups, and environmentalists. After a long struggle, the Congress passed legislation, which, among other things, eliminated waste and promoted conservation of oil and gas, in some cases through tax incentives; encouraged development and use of other sources of energy such as coal and solar power; decontrolled oil prices; and levied a windfall profits tax on oil companies. Carter termed the struggle for a national energy policy "a bruising fight" that led to "no final clear-cut victory." He insisted, however, that overall the energy program was "a good compromise" and well worth the effort it entailed.

Carter's inability to prevent Congress and the special interests from battering his legislative proposals hurt his standing in the public opinion polls. The Bert Lance affair, involving an old friend whom Carter had appointed director of the Office of Management and Budget, proved even more damaging. Early in the summer of 1977, the press, the Senate Governmental Affairs Committee, and the comptroller of the currency began raising questions about the propriety of Lance's business dealings before coming to Washington, D.C. Carter believed Lance innocent of wrongdoing, but as new findings and allegations surfaced, he became increasingly aware of the damage the charges inflicted on him and his administration. Caught between loyalty to a friend and concern for the presidency, Carter at first gave Lance an unequivocal endorsement. "Bert, I'm proud of you," Carter told him at a nationally televised press conference in August. Then, after he thought Lance had had an opportunity to exonerate himself in Senate committee hearings, he encouraged him to resign. Late in September he accepted with regret Lance's resignation.

Many observers regarded the Lance affair as a turning point in the Carter presidency. Raising the specter of Watergate, it cast a pall of suspicion over Carter and his administration. That in itself would have hurt any presidency, but it was especially damaging to Carter because he had campaigned as a man of high moral and ethical standards and had promised to restore integrity to government. The Lance affair raised the question whether Carter and his people were any more trustworthy than other politicians. The answer seemed to be that they were not, even though Lance was never convicted of any illegal activity during the Carter years. The struggles with Congress over legislation had already tarnished Carter's image by revealing his weakness in obtaining implementation of his programs. The Lance affair generated skepticism about his character as well as his competence.

Following the Lance affair, Carter began turning his attention away from domestic needs and concentrating on international affairs. In that area, he established a more impressive record, despite his lack of experience, although there, also, questions about his leadership ability dogged his efforts.

The Panama Canal Treaties

One of the most urgent foreign policy issues Carter confronted when he assumed office was the Panama Canal. Since 1964, the United States and Panama had been renegotiating the Panama Canal Treaty. Formidable opposition to any new treaty had developed in the United States, however, opposition which former California governor Ronald Reagan, among others, successfully tapped during the 1976 presidential primaries. "When it comes to the Canal, we built it, we paid for it, it's ours and we

Carter and Alejandro Orfila (center), the president of the Organization of American States, watch as Panamanian president Omar Torrijos signs the Panama Canal Treaty in September, 1977. *(AP/Wide World Photos)*

should tell Torrijos and Company that we are going to keep it!" Reagan declared, and most Americans apparently agreed with him. As late as the fall of 1977, polls showed that 78 percent of the American people did not wish to "give up" the canal; only 8 percent approved the idea. Moreover, a large number of senators had gone on record opposing any new treaty.

After six months of negotiations with Panamanian officials, Special Representative Sol Linowitz and Chief Negotiator Ellsworth Bunker succeeded in framing two treaties which were signed by President Carter and General Omar Torrijos, the leader of Panama. The treaties provided for joint operation and defense of the canal by the two countries for the rest of the century, with the United States retaining the right to use military force if necessary to keep the canal open and operating, and guaranteed the neutrality of the canal after it was turned over to Panama at the end of 1999. After the signing of the treaties, the Carter administration mounted a concerted lobbying effort to secure Senate approval. The strategy was not to try to persuade a majority of the American people to favor the treaties but, as Carter explained in his memoirs, to convince key elected officials, public opinion leaders, campaign contributors, and other influential people to give their senators "running room" on the treaty. Carter also encouraged undecided senators to visit the Canal Zone and talk with military leaders there, as well as with General Omar Torrijos, and he met privately with all but a few senators to persuade them to approve the treaties. On one occasion, Carter admitted in his memoirs, he even told a white lie in hopes of obtaining the vote of Republican senator S. I. Hayakawa. It was the day the Senate was to vote on one of the treaties. Carter got a call from some Senate leaders who were conferring with Hayakawa. "I knew he was listening when they asked me if I needed to meet occasionally with the California semanticist to get his advice on African affairs. I gulped, thought for a few

seconds, and replied, 'Yes, I really do!' hoping God would forgive me." After almost two months of debate, the Senate confirmed the two treaties by a very close margin, on March 16 and April 18, 1978, voting in each case 68 in favor and 32 opposed. The ratification process was finally completed in September, 1979, when, after another massive lobbying effort by the administration—this time in both the House and Senate—laws implementing the treaties gained approval.

Ratification of the Panama Canal treaties was a signal victory for Carter and largely the result of the kind of successful congressional lobbying he failed to muster on behalf of other programs. In the long run, however, it may have been politically damaging. Carter maintained that it "left deep and serious political wounds," and he attributed his own reelection defeat, as well as that of eighteen senators, to his and their support of the Panama Canal treaties.

The Camp David Accords
Carter's most impressive foreign policy achievement was the peace treaty ending thirty-one years of hostility between Israel and Egypt. In April, 1977, Carter began talking with the leaders of the two countries, Israeli prime minister Menachem Begin and Egyptian president Anwar el-Sadat. The culmination of the mediating process came in September, 1978, when the three men conferred at Camp David for thirteen days, during which Begin and Sadat reached final agreement on a framework for peace. That served as a basis for the peace treaty signed on March 26, 1979, in which, among other things, the two countries agreed to establish normal and friendly relations and to start negotiations on Palestinian self-rule on the West Bank and the Gaza Strip; Israel agreed to a phased withdrawal from the Sinai; and Egypt agreed to end its economic boycott of Israel and allow Israeli ships and cargoes through the Suez Canal.

Anwar el-Sadat, Carter, and Menachem Begin at Camp David. *(National Archives)*

As Haynes Johnson and Hedley Donovan have observed, Carter's success in facilitating peace between Israel and Egypt was in large measure a personal triumph. His aptitude for problem solving and absorption in detail, his religious faith and knowledge of biblical history, his sensitivity to personality differences between Begin and Sadat, his patience and stamina all paid off in his negotiations with the two Middle East leaders. His efforts, however, did little to raise his standing in the public opinion polls; and whatever luster Carter acquired upon the signing of the Egyptian-Israeli treaty dimmed when, shortly afterward, Israel began establishing new settlements on the West Bank.

Carter scored two foreign policy successes with the Panama Canal treaties and the Egyptian-Israeli Peace Treaty. He also normalized United States relations with the People's Republic of China, completing the process begun by President Richard Nixon. Relations with the Soviet Union, however, proved troublesome.

Early in his presidency Carter vowed to continue détente, but toward the end of his term he sounded and acted like a Cold Warrior. Events in places such as Cuba, Africa, and Afghanistan had much to do with his shift in policy. So did the different outlooks of his two foreign policy advisers, the pugnacious Zbigniew Brzezinski, national security adviser, and the more conciliatory Cyrus Vance, secretary of state. Even early in his term Carter seemed torn between Brzezinski's advocacy of a get-tough policy and Vance's emphasis on diplomatic accommodation. On the one hand he denounced Soviet treatment of dissidents such as Andrei Sakharov and Soviet backing of Cuban troops in Africa as well as the presence of a Soviet brigade in Cuba; he also approved construction of the MX missile system. On the other hand he encouraged the negotiations that produced the Strategic Arms Limitation Talks (SALT) II Treaty, limiting the United States and the Soviet Union to 2,250 strategic weapons each and imposing limits on the number of warheads and the development of new kinds of nuclear weapons.

After Carter and Soviet president Leonid Brezhnev signed the SALT II Treaty on June 18, 1979, the already fragile relations between the two countries deteriorated. When Soviet troops invaded Afghanistan in December of that year, Carter decided that "verbal condemnation" was not enough, that the Soviets "must pay a concrete price for their aggression." He requested the Senate to delay consideration of SALT II (which by then had little chance of passing), announced an embargo on high-technology equipment and grain sales to the Soviet Union, and organized an international boycott of the 1980 Summer Olympics in Moscow. Then, on January 23, 1980, in his State of the Union address to Congress, he announced what became known as the Carter Doctrine. Declaring that the Soviet presence in Afghanistan posed "a grave threat" to the region containing more than two-thirds of the world's exportable oil, he warned that "an attempt by any outside force to gain control of the Persian Gulf region will be regarded as an assault on the vital interests of the United States of America, and such an assault will be repelled by any means necessary, including military force." In the same address, Carter requested an increase in military spending and the resumption of draft registration. Nevertheless, Carter's sanctions and tough language failed to persuade the Soviet Union to withdraw its troops from Afghanistan. At home his efforts elicited little public enthusiasm, some criticism—from George Kennan and Senator Edward Kennedy, for example—and, in the case of the grain embargo, considerable resentment among American farmers.

Foreign Policy Initiatives: The Primacy of Human Rights

Carter's denunciation of Soviet treatment of dissidents was part of a larger program of championing human rights around the world.

In an address at Notre Dame University in May, 1977, Carter declared that a commitment to human rights was "a fundamental tenet" of his foreign policy. His administration not only protested the torture and execution of political prisoners but also sought to eliminate discrimination based on race, sex, religion, or ethnic origin and to promote freedom of travel and emigration, freedom of religion, and the right to vote, work, and be given a fair trial. In asserting the primacy of human rights, Carter repudiated the pragmatic approach associated with former Presidents Richard Nixon and Gerald Ford and former Secretary of State Henry Kissinger. Carter defended the idea of basing American foreign policy on moral principle as "a practical and realistic approach to foreign affairs." Inducing authoritarian right-wing allies and friends of the United States to protect human rights would help prevent the outbreak of leftist revolutions, he argued; championing human rights would also strengthen American influence among the unaligned nations in the Third World. Perhaps the most important reason, however, for launching the human rights campaign, at least in Carter's view, was that "it was the right thing to do."

Except for the release of a few political prisoners, Carter was unable to win much success in his crusade. Like so many of his domestic and foreign policy initiatives, it failed to fire the imagination of the American people. Perhaps Vietnam had made them wary of grandiose appeals to moral principle. Critics faulted the human rights campaign on various grounds. Some dismissed it as another instance of substituting rhetoric for action. Others criticized the administration for applying the human rights test selectively, exempting certain allies such as Iran under the shah, the Philippines, and South Korea. Still others thought the denunciations of Soviet human rights violations jeopardized a new arms limitation treaty. In his memoirs, Carter admitted that his human rights pronouncements had caused tension between the United States and the Soviet Union, but he doubted they had ever been directly responsible for any failure to reach accord on matters of common interest. "Even if our human-rights policy had been a much more serious point of contention in Soviet-American relations, I would not have been inclined to accommodate Soviet objections," he wrote. "We have a fundamental difference in philosophy concerning human freedoms, and it does not benefit us to cover it up. The respect for human rights is one of the most significant advantages of a free and democratic nation in the peaceful struggle for influence, and we should use this good weapon as effectively as possible."

Iran and the Hostage Crisis

The Iranian seizure of American hostages in November, 1979, proved to be Carter's toughest foreign policy problem. Even more than the Soviet invasion of Afghanistan, the hostage crisis made Carter appear weak and ineffectual. Upon taking office he had reaffirmed United States support of the leader of Iran, Mohammad Reza Shah Pahlavi. Early in 1979 the shah was overthrown by a religious, antimodern, popular revolution led by Ayatollah Ruhollah Khomeini. Then on November 4, militant Iranians overran the United States embassy in Tehran, took some sixty Americans hostage, and vowed not to release them until the shah, who was in New York City for medical treatment, was returned by the United States to stand trial in Iran. After a few weeks of holding the hostages, the Iranians released the women and blacks among them, leaving a total of fifty-two men in captivity; they also put forth additional demands that the United States apologize for "crimes against the Iranian people," pay financial damages, and turn over the shah's assets to Iran.

Carter refused all such demands and, when the ayatollah threatened to try some of the hostages as spies, warned that if any of the Americans were tried or harmed the United States would inflict severe punishment on Iran, including military action. Early in the hostage crisis Carter ordered a suspension of oil imports from Iran and froze billions of dollars of Iranian assets in American banks. His initial response evoked an upsurge of popular support. In the month after the crisis began, his approval rating in the polls soared from 32 to 61 percent. On December 4, he announced that he would run for a second term as president. He observed, however, that for the next few months he would not campaign, in order to devote full attention to the hostage situation.

In his memoirs, Carter wrote that during the hostage crisis he listened to every recommendation offered him, no matter how absurd, from returning the shah for trial in Iran to dropping an atomic bomb on Tehran. His administration was divided over the proper response, with Secretary of State Vance advocating reliance on diplomatic means and National Security Adviser Brzezinski favoring a military solution. Ultimately, Brzezinski won the debate when Carter and his advisers agreed to attempt the ill-fated military rescue operation of April 24 and 25, 1980. Of all Carter's advisers, only Vance opposed the mission; and he offered his resignation as secretary of state three days before the operation was launched, although it was not made public until afterward. In his memoirs, Carter wrote that he decided on the rescue mission only when intelligence information indicated there was almost no chance of the hostages being released within five or six months. No doubt Carter and his advisers had also become impatient with diplomatic efforts and economic sanctions, which had proven unavailing. Another reason that Carter and his advisers agreed to the rescue operation has been suggested by Gary Sick, the staff member on Iran in the National Security Council during the Carter presidency. As fellow government workers, they tended to identify with the imprisoned Americans and felt guilty for having left them exposed at the embassy in Tehran. Such feelings, Sick argues, encouraged "a strong impulse to do something, almost as if action was a necessary end in itself."

On April 25, Carter went on television to announce that the rescue operation had failed, with the loss of eight of the rescue team in a helicopter crash. In his brief statement, he took full responsibility for the mission and praised the courage of the volunteers who had participated in it. Five days later, on April 30, he declared that his responsibilities were now "manageable enough" for him to travel again and begin to campaign in the Democratic primaries. It seems likely that Carter and his aides were looking for an opportunity to abandon the Rose Garden strategy because it had begun to work against him politically. Critics were charging him with hiding behind the hostages to avoid debating his principal rival for the

Democratic nomination, Edward Kennedy. In a sense Carter had himself become a hostage to the crisis—he had painted himself into a corner, Patrick Caddell later remarked. Having declared that he would not travel or campaign in order to devote full attention to the hostage situation, he could not change his position lest he be thought to have lost interest in the hostages or hope for their release. Although it failed, the rescue operation seemed to provide a convenient terminus to one phase of the crisis, freeing Carter to resume a more normal schedule.

The crisis dragged on for 444 days. Not until January 20, 1981, some thirty minutes after a new president, Ronald Reagan, had taken the oath of office, did the Iranians release the fifty-two Americans. The timing was seen as one last humiliation for Carter.

Carter thought later that one of the reasons he was defeated for a second term stemmed from the "cautious and prudent policy" he had

One of the hostages is displayed to the crowd outside the U.S. embassy in Tehran, Iran, on November 9, 1979. *(AP/Wide World Photos)*

followed in the hostage crisis. Although not a disaster, his handling of the Iranian situation certainly did little to enhance his reputation as president and contrasts sharply with his remarkably successful mediation of the Camp David accords between Egypt and Israel. Why was he successful in the one case and judged to have failed in the other? As Hedley Donovan has pointed out, in the case of the Camp David talks, both Carter's abilities and the circumstances in which he operated were conducive to success. He had studied the situation in the Middle East intensively; he admired Sadat ("more than any other leaders," he wrote in his memoirs) and respected Begin. The Camp David talks were focused in time and held in a setting where Carter was in control, where the participants were isolated from the outside world, and from which the press was excluded. Although he wanted the talks to succeed, Carter could be somewhat detached since the safety of no American lives hinged on the outcome. Finally, the Camp David talks took the form of orderly, rational discourse among three men who had entered into them voluntarily and with some hope, even determination, of reaching accord. In such a situation, Carter's patient mediation facilitated the development of understanding and trust essential to any agreement between Begin and Sadat.

The Iranian hostage situation presented an entirely different situation. Carter was thrust into a potentially violent confrontation, not only with the Ayatollah Khomeini but also with the fanatic anti-American militants who demonstrated outside the United States embassy in Tehran. He had to deal with a seizure of American hostages and with a revolution as well—what one historian has described as a "man-made hurricane" that the United States, despite its might, was powerless to control. As the leader of the revolution, Khomeini pursued a policy of deliberate intransigence, against which Carter's aptitude for patient, rational negotiation proved unavailing. Patience

was the wisest policy, since release of the hostages depended finally on internal developments in Iran. Once the crisis reached an impasse, however, Carter became increasingly vulnerable to criticism for not acting to free the hostages. Saturation coverage by the media may have exacerbated popular frustration with what was seen as a weak, do-nothing policy. A few days before the 1980 presidential election, voting in the Iranian Parliament seemed to signal a breakthrough in the crisis. Nothing came of it, and it served mainly to highlight Carter's inability to secure the release of the Americans. In the end, the Iranians underscored their own control of the situation—and Carter's lack of control—by delaying the release of the hostages, after months of negotiation with the Carter administration, until just after President Reagan took office.

The questions the hostage crisis raised about Carter's leadership ability were not new. They had dogged him almost since the beginning of his presidency, but they seemed to acquire special significance in the context of the hostage situation. Not surprisingly, they dominated the 1980 presidential campaign, and voter disenchantment with Carter's performance combined with a shift toward conservatism to deny his bid for a second term.

The Carter Presidency: The Question of Leadership

The question of leadership has also been the focus of evaluations of the Carter presidency. Most of the journalists and historians who have written about Carter have judged him an intelligent, industrious, honest man who lacked the leadership ability required of an effective president. Arriving in Washington as a self-proclaimed outsider and antipolitician, he failed to develop the good working relationship with Congress he needed to implement his programs. This failure was partly because of his thinly veiled scorn for the legislators and the special interests he thought manipulated them,

Rosalynn and Jimmy Carter help build a home as volunteers for Habitat for Humanity in 1992. *(Reuters/Steve Jaffe/Archive Photos)*

partly because of the inexperience of his White House staff, and partly because of his estrangement from the Democratic Party leadership. Even after four years in office he had not made any strong alliances on Capitol Hill. Nor did Carter provide effective leadership for members of his staff. In an article entitled "The Passionless Presidency," James Fallows, chief White House speechwriter during Carter's first two years as president, observed that Carter failed to induce or inspire his staff to come up with new ideas, goals, or policies. Carter ran the White House like a bureaucracy, Fallows noted, with the result that "the White House took on the spirit of a bureaucracy, drained of zeal, obsessed with form, full of people attracted by the side-dressings of the work rather than the work itself."

Finally, Carter proved unable to lead the nation as a whole. He claimed to feel a personal,

almost mystical bond with the American people, but they did not reciprocate. Although he thought of the people as "a final forum," he was not successful in appealing to them for support. His famous "crisis of confidence" speech of July 15, 1979, is the best illustration of this fact. Carter delivered the speech in the midst of increasing public anger and frustration provoked by a severe gasoline shortage, long lines at filling stations, and huge price increases for oil and gas. Instead of focusing on the domestic energy crisis and proposing legislative remedies, Carter decided to broaden the scope of his speech. In it he contended that the problems of the nation went much deeper than gasoline lines or shortages, or inflation or recession. The true problem was "a crisis of confidence" among the American people. To solve it he called on Americans to engage in a collective act of will. Sounding not unlike Norman

Vincent Peale proclaiming the "power of positive thinking," Carter declared, "We simply must have faith in each other, faith in our ability to govern ourselves, and faith in the future of this Nation." To revive that faith, he urged Americans to rally around the "standard" of energy. "On the battlefield of energy we can win for our Nation a new confidence, and we can seize control again of our common destiny." Unfortunately, what Carter had earlier called "the moral equivalent of war" had already demonstrated scant potential for exciting enthusiasm or unity among the American people, and the July call to arms was unlikely to change matters. To be sure, after the speech Carter's approval rating in the opinion polls rose slightly, but he undermined whatever positive results the address had produced by suddenly announcing the resignation of high officials in the cabinet and White House, thereby calling attention once again to the weaknesses of his administration. In that context, the statement that had appeared to be a successful bid for support ("I realize more than ever that as President I need your help") now looked like a confession of inability to lead.

Fallows attributed Carter's inability to inspire his staff or the American people to his style of thought. Carter believed "fifty things, but no one thing," Fallows argued, noting that although Carter had well-reasoned positions on various issues, he had no "large view" of their priority or the relations among them. Fallows, and more recently Haynes Johnson, Robert Shogan, and Hedley Donovan agreed in attributing Carter's inability to lead to the absence of an overall political philosophy or ideology capable of inspiring loyalty to something larger than himself. In the 1980 campaign, he successfully dodged questions about ideology, and during his presidency he tried to substitute moralism and exhortation for ideology. During the 1980 campaign, Adam Clymer of *The New York Times* reported that although Carter had a list of goals he wanted to pursue in his second term, he still lacked any overriding vision or philosophy. That lack of vision and the resultant inability to lead gave Carter the reputation as one of the less effective presidents of the twentieth century.

Nevertheless, Carter continued to be a presence on the national and international scenes after leaving office. He became an advocate for the group Habitat for Humanity, which builds houses for poor families, and even helped construct some of them himself. He wrote books about morality and the experience of aging. He offered his talents as a peace negotiator in times of international crisis in the Middle East and elsewhere. His strong moral stance and humanitarian record came to be regarded with nostalgia in an increasingly cynical world. In 1999, he and Rosalynn were awarded the Presidential Medal of Freedom. In many ways, Jimmy Carter earned the respect that had eluded him in the White House.

Anne C. Loveland

Bibliographical References

Carter's *Why Not the Best?*, 1975, is a brief autobiography describing his early life, education, and business and political activities before the 1976 election. *Keeping Faith*, 1982, is his presidential memoirs. Peter G. Bourne, *Jimmy Carter: A Comprehensive Biography from Plains to Post-Presidency*, 1997, is an admiring biography by a close personal friend of the Carters. Kenneth E. Morris, *Jimmy Carter: American Moralist*, 1996, is a full-scale biography that explores the link between Carter's moral values and his policy decisions. For a biography by Carter's pastor, with an emphasis on the president's beliefs, see Dan Ariail and Cheryl Heckler-Fitz, *The Carpenter's Apprentice: The Spiritual Biography of Jimmy Carter*, 1996.

On Carter's governorship, see Gary M. Fink, *Prelude to the Presidency*, 1980. Patrick Anderson, *Electing Jimmy Carter: The Campaign of 1976*, 1994, is a memoir of the presidential election by one of Carter's former speechwriters. For an interesting perspective on the sources of Carter's domestic and foreign policy, see Laurence H. Shoup, *The Carter Presidency and Beyond*, 1980. Three assessments of Carter and his presidency written before he left office are James Wooten, *Dasher*, 1978; James Fallows, "The Passionless Presidency," in *The Atlantic*, May and June, 1979; and Haynes Johnson, *In the Absence of Power*, 1980. Like Fallows, former *Time* editor Hedley Donovan was an insider in the Carter administration, serving as senior adviser to the president. His *Roosevelt to Reagan*, 1985, describes his "encounters" with Carter and with eight other presidents. Robert Shogan's *None of the Above*, 1982, is also helpful in comparing Carter with his predecessors and successor. For an analysis of the Carter administration's handling of the Iranian hostage crisis, see Gary Sick, *All Fall Down*, 1985.

For an overview of the Carter presidency, see Richard C. Thornton, *The Carter Years: Toward a New Global Order*, 1991; Burton I. Kaufman, *The Presidency of James Earl Carter, Jr.*, 1993; and John Dumbrell, *The Carter Presidency: A Re-evaluation*, 1993. For an examination of Carter's postpresidential role as peace negotiator and humanitarian, see Rod Troester, *Jimmy Carter as Peacemaker: A Post-Presidential Biography*, 1996, and Douglas Brinkley, *The Unfinished Presidency: Jimmy Carter's Journey Beyond the White House*, 1998.

Ronald Reagan

40th President, 1981-1989

Born: February 6, 1911
Tampico, Illinois

Political Party: Republican
Vice President: George Bush

Cabinet Members

Secretary of State: Alexander Haig, George Shultz

Secretary of the Treasury: Donald Regan, James A. Baker III, Nicholas Brady

Reagan's official portrait. *(White House Historical Society)*

Secretary of Defense: Caspar Weinberger, Frank C. Carlucci

Attorney General: William French Smith, Edwin Meese III, Dick Thornburgh

Secretary of the Interior: James Watt, William P. Clark, Donald P. Hodel

Secretary of Agriculture: John R. Block, Richard E. Lyng

Secretary of Commerce: Malcolm Baldridge, C. William Verity, Jr.

Secretary of Labor: Raymond J. Donovan, William E. Brock, Ann Dore McLaughlin

Secretary of Health and Human Services: Richard S. Schweiker, Margaret Heckler, Otis R. Bowen

Secretary of Housing and Urban Development: Samuel Pierce

Secretary of Transportation: Andrew L. Lewis, Jr., Elizabeth Dole, James H. Burnley IV

Secretary of Energy: James B. Edwards, Donald P. Hodel, John S. Herrington

Secretary of Education: T. H. Bell, William J. Bennett, Lauro F. Cavazos

Ronald Reagan became the fortieth president of the United States on January 20, 1981. After serving two full terms in office, the first president since Dwight D. Eisenhower to do so, he was succeeded by his vice president, George Bush, in 1989.

The eight years of the Reagan administration represent a period of unprecedented domestic economic prosperity, as well as peaceful interaction between the United States and other nations. This was a period of transition, as Reagan began his administration amid growing East-West tensions, which increased with his accusations about the "evil empire" of the Soviet Union. He left office after signing the first major arms control agreement between the United States and the Soviet Union in almost a decade. In those eight years, the United States regained a forceful role internationally, an image fostered by events such as the bombing of Libya in April, 1986, in response to a terrorist bombing in Berlin which took the life of a member of the U.S. military.

Concomitantly, however, the Reagan legacy also included the largest deficit in the history of the country, a balance of payments skewed in favor of the United States' trading partners, and a marked shift in domestic political priorities.

The Early Years

Ronald Wilson Reagan was born on February 6, 1911, in Tampico, Illinois. His father, John Edward Reagan, was a New Deal Democrat who had been head of the Works Project Administration in Dixon, Illinois. His mother, born Nelle Wilson, was more conservative, a very religious woman who spent much of her time engaged in works of charity. The family moved often in Reagan's youth, but these early years were the ones that seemed to have imbued in Reagan his commitment to the American ideals of hard work, charity toward those less fortunate, and patriotism. After completing his preparatory schooling, Reagan entered Eureka College, graduating in 1932 with a major in economics.

His media career began with a job as a sports announcer with radio station WOO in Davenport, Iowa, followed by a job with station WHO in Des Moines, Iowa. In 1937, at the age of twenty-six, during a trip to California

to cover baseball spring training, he was signed by an agent for the Warner Bros. studio for a film part in which he played a radio announcer. He went on to act in more than fifty films, including *Knute Rockne—All American* (1940) and *Bedtime for Bonzo* (1951). He made his last film, *The Killers*, in 1964. In many ways, it can be argued that Ronald Reagan's early career as an actor was excellent preparation for his later political career. At ease in front of the camera, he developed a style to which the American public responded very positively, thereby earning for himself the title the "Great Communicator."

It was also during this early period in Hollywood that Reagan first became politically active: During the 1930's and 1940's, he worked for or was a member of Americans for Democratic Action, the American Veterans Committee, the United World Federalists, and the Hollywood Independent Citizens Committee of the Arts, Sciences, and Professions. He also became involved in Hollywood politics when he was elected president of the Screen Actors Guild (SAG) in 1947. He was reelected to serve five additional one-year terms. One of his primary responsibilities in his capacity as president of SAG was to represent the interests of members of the guild in negotiating union contracts and in other labor disputes. These were often bitter battles, and they contributed directly to his rethinking of many of his political and ideological convictions. As a result of his experiences in Hollywood during those early years, Reagan was converted, politically and ideologically, from a New Deal Democrat to a conservative Republican.

During this period, Reagan was married for nine years to actress Jane Wyman, with whom he had two children: a daughter, Maureen, and an adopted son, Michael. The couple divorced in 1948, and in 1952, Reagan married Nancy Davis, the daughter of a prominent physician. Reagan's bride, Nancy, was also politically conservative, and her orientation

Reagan in a scene from the film *Knute Rockne—All American. (Museum of Modern Art/Film Stills Archive)*

about politics and the role of government in the United States.

In 1954, Reagan became spokesman for the General Electric Company and host of its weekly television show. He traveled around the country on behalf of GE, preaching the corporate philosophy which blended well with his own. He spoke of the need for a strong military as the only means of assuring the nation's security, and he warned of the dangers of big government. Both these themes would figure prominently in his own political campaigns in later years. He remained as spokesman for GE until 1962, at which point he resigned in order to devote himself to the Republican Party and his own political career.

The Governor of California

Especially following Barry Goldwater's overwhelming defeat in his bid for the presidency in 1964, Reagan became increasingly active in Republican Party politics in California. Although he had little political experience beyond his activities in Hollywood, a group of California businessmen suggested that he run for the governorship of the state. He did so, and in 1966 he defeated two-term Governor Edmund G. (Pat) Brown by a margin of nearly one million votes. Reagan served two terms in the office, altering the complexion of California politics as a result. The experience also introduced him to the political realities that would help him considerably in his bid for the presidency and, subsequently, in his eight years in that office.

further encouraged the political and ideological metamorphosis of her husband. Nancy's direct influence on her husband in any number of different areas persisted through the White House years.

During Reagan's tenure in Hollywood in the 1940's and 1950's, it is possible to see the development of the themes that would later be central to his administration as president. The Cold War then being waged between the United States and the Soviet Union strengthened his anticommunist convictions. When McCarthyism and anticommunist feelings swept Hollywood in the early 1950's, Reagan became one of the leading figures in purging the alleged communists from the Screen Actors Guild. At that time, he also resigned from any liberal organization of which he was a member. In general, during this period Reagan's reputation was that of a respected and also moderate force in the anticommunist movement. These activities and events, especially against the backdrop of the Cold War, contributed to Reagan's further reevaluation of his assumptions

The three cornerstones of his administration were taxes and government spending, welfare reform, and higher education in the state. He did have an impact on all three areas, although the final outcomes were not necessarily the ones that he had initially sought. As he worked to implement changes in these areas, for six of his eight years as governor he did so with an unfriendly Democratic majority in the state legislature, a situation that would be replicated during his second term as president. Hence, his years as governor provided both the political experience that he would take to the office of president of the United States and the opportunity to see at first hand the differences between the theory and reality in first creating policies and then implementing them.

During his initial term as governor, Reagan, having inherited from Pat Brown a large state budget deficit, secured the largest tax increase in the history of the state. The increases were for corporate, personal income, and sales tax; he actually lowered property taxes. During his two terms as governor, the state budget grew from $4.6 billion to $10.2 billion, a significant portion of which was then allocated to local governments for welfare and education.

Following his victory over Democratic candidate Jesse Unruh in 1970, Reagan turned his attention to the issue of welfare, focusing on the fact that approximately one out of nine people in the state were receiving some form of welfare benefit. Reagan proposed a major welfare reform package, including the introduction of Medi-Cal, a variant of the federal Medicare program. Versions of his proposed reforms were finally adopted after lengthy debates within the state legislature.

In the area of higher education, Reagan responded to the turmoil and unrest prevalent among many college students protesting the war in Vietnam: He reduced university funding by 27 percent during his first two years in office. Once the protest movement subsided, as the war came to a halt, he reversed his position and increased funding to higher education within the state. By the time he left office

in 1974, funding for higher education had more than doubled over what it had been when he took office.

Also emerging during Reagan's tenure as governor was the social agenda that he would pursue as president, including his outspoken opposition to abortion on demand and his support for capital punishment.

The Run for the Presidency

As Reagan became more prominent nationally, his name was mentioned as a possible Republican candidate for president—first in 1968, when he did relatively well, although not well enough to secure the nomination against Richard Nixon. To become the Republican candidate in 1976, Reagan had to face incumbent president Gerald Ford, who had become president following the resignation of Nixon in August, 1974. At that time, Reagan had campaigned actively for the support needed to run as the Republican Party candidate. He fell 60 votes short of defeating President Ford for the nomination.

Reagan had another opportunity to run in 1980. He had spent the time between the election of 1976 and 1980 working on his campaign, and he reaped the rewards when he was officially nominated to be his party's candidate at the Republican National Convention in Detroit, defeating his closest rival, George Bush, by an overwhelming margin of 1,939 to 55.

In the 1980 presidential campaign against incumbent Democratic president Jimmy Carter, Reagan focused on Carter's failures during his four years in office, including an inflation rate exceeding 12 percent, the concomitantly high unemployment rates, and the apparent decline in the United States' international prestige. His campaign seemed to touch the American public: Reagan won an overwhelming victory of 489 electoral votes to Carter's 49 and about 51 percent of the popular vote to Carter's 42 percent. (The third-party candidate, John Anderson, received most of the remaining 7 percent.) Reagan declared this overwhelming victory to be his "mandate" by the American public to govern according to the policies and programs that he had outlined during the campaign.

The New Conservatism

Ronald Reagan came into the office of president of the United States determined to change the country's policies and priorities, and with the strong belief that his overwhelming margin of victory gave him the support of the American public necessary to achieve those goals. Domestically, he pledged to reduce the size of the national government, strengthen the role of the states within the framework of the federal system of government, reduce government expenditures through massive budget cuts, and lower taxes and inflation. He also sought to restructure foreign policy to make the United States more assertive and forceful internation-

ally, to enable the nation to regain its lost power and prestige, and to achieve "peace through strength." During his first term, Reagan was aided in the pursuit of his goals by a Republican majority in the Senate, the first since 1954, and by a number of Southern Democrats who supported Reagan's conservative agenda.

Reagan's key cabinet appointments, such as his appointment of Alexander Haig, former commander of the North Atlantic Treaty Organization (NATO), as secretary of state, and of former budget director Caspar Weinberger as secretary of defense, reaffirmed his commitment to a strong defense and to the perception that the United States would not yield to the Soviet Union. Donald Regan, chairman of brokerage house Merrill Lynch, was made secretary of the treasury. William French Smith, a longtime personal friend of Reagan, was named to the post of attorney general. These and the other appointments Reagan made dur-

Nancy and Ronald Reagan wave to the crowd at a campaign stop in 1980. *(Ronald Reagan Library)*

ing his first term supported his commitment to a conservative political and social agenda for the duration of his administration.

Reagan's personal popularity and his "honeymoon" period were, ironically, extended well into his first term in office when he was shot by John Hinckley, Jr., a psychotic young man, outside a hotel in Washington, D.C., in March of 1981. The incident had the effect of rallying Congress and the public behind the new president, strengthening his political position and support for his programs.

Reagan's Domestic Agenda

Reagan approached the presidency with his own conservative social, political, and economic agenda. These were articulated during his campaign in 1980 against Carter, and Reagan remained committed to them for his eight years in office. Many of the principles that he advocated were extensions of those he put forward and worked for as governor of California, and they reflected Reagan's conservatism. His two terms as president are considered among the most ideological in recent history.

Reagan came to office with a number of assumptions regarding the relationship between the economy and government. One of the primary goals that he hoped to accomplish was to "get the government off the people's backs." Specifically, Reagan's desire was to reduce government intervention in the economy, allowing government decisions to be made by business operating in a free market economy rather than by bureaucrats in government agencies in Washington, D.C. The core of this principle can be found in Reagan's belief that, when left alone to work freely, people will design, produce, and sell more because they know that they will make money by doing so. This tendency results in a cycle that creates jobs, extends prosperity to others, and benefits society on the whole by increasing productivity and creating more income through taxes. Conversely, if constricted by government, by high taxes and excessive regulation, individuals would not derive the full benefits of their achievements. Investment then dwindles, production drops, and the entire economy slumps.

In theory, according to supply-side economics as advocated by economist Arthur Laffer and others, the key to low inflation, high economic growth, low unemployment, and a balanced federal budget lies in cutting taxes and limiting government interference. The supply-siders argued that, if those things were accomplished, the economy would boom, thereby leading to an increase in revenues as more people and corporations could pay more in taxes.

This theory was adopted and implemented during Reagan's first term in office and became known as Reaganomics. Upon taking office, Reagan wanted to achieve three economic goals: reduce the size of the federal government, stimulate economic growth, and increase military spending. What Reagan discovered was that these three objectives were not totally compatible. He began by assigning a high priority to cutting taxes and keeping them cut. In his first few years in office, he worked with Congress to achieve limited tax cuts. He continued to push for tax reform, which he finally achieved with the passage of the 1986 Tax Reform Act. This bill altered the traditional approach to taxation by "tax brackets," simplifying the more than two dozen into two basic categories. It eliminated those individuals in the lowest income brackets, so that they paid no taxes at all. It increased the size of standard deductions and exemptions for individuals and couples while eliminating certain deductions for other areas. In effect, it gave the average individual lower tax rates with lower deductions, while closing many of the corporate loopholes—thereby shifting a greater portion of the tax burden onto the shoulders of the corporations.

The effect of these tax cuts was, as predicted, to stimulate the economy, which resulted in a drop in the unemployment rate and an increase in business activity. The tax cuts also contrib-

Supreme Court Justice Sandra Day O'Connor. *(Library of Congress)*

uted to an increase in the budget deficit, however—which Reagan had been determined to reduce. One of the major dilemmas facing the Reagan administration, and one which was not resolved during his eight years in office, was how to reduce the size of the deficit and balance the federal budget.

In keeping with his own priorities of building the military, starting in 1981 Reagan authorized an increase in spending for defense, resulting in a 50 percent increase in constant dollars over the next six years. While Reagan came into office determined to increase spending for the military, he was equally determined to cut or totally eliminate many domestic programs. In addition to helping to reduce the budget deficit, he claimed, such programs were detrimental because they were expensive and little benefit was derived from the investment in them. Furthermore, they contributed to the

growth of large government, which Reagan also opposed, and they made people dependent on society rather than contributors to it.

While Reagan was not willing to eliminate all types of domestic social welfare programs, he made a distinction between "the truly needy," those who could not support themselves, and "the working poor," those who could support themselves if they wished but who chose not to do so. Reagan claimed that government has an obligation to the former to ensure that they do not starve, but government is not obligated to guarantee support for those who can provide for themselves but choose not to do so.

Reagan's proposals to cut some of these programs were controversial from the beginning, specifically, whether many of the cuts proposed allowed the government to retain an adequate "safety net" for those individuals who needed government assistance. What was unclear is where that net should be. The final outcome was that there were no cuts in such publicly accepted programs as Social Security and Medicare. The biggest cuts in domestic welfare were in means-tested programs, such as Aid to Families with Dependent Children (AFDC), job training programs, Medicaid, and student loans. Even though Reagan had come into office proclaiming the need to reduce federal spending and balance the budget, it soon became apparent that, politically, the best he could accomplish was to reduce the rate of increase of federal spending for certain programs.

When he entered the White House, Reagan inherited a projected budget deficit of well over $200 billion, a number which continued to grow as the amount spent every year far exceeded the income of the government. The size of the federal deficit grew large enough for members of Congress to enact legislation in 1985, the Gramm-Rudman Balanced Budget Act, specifically to create a plan to eliminate the deficit and balance the budget. The bill was signed into law by President Reagan, who had been advocating, unsuccessfully, the need for an amendment to the Constitution to balance the federal budget. During his tenure in office, however, Reagan discovered how difficult it is to bring a budget into line when only a limited number of items can be cut and when taxes cannot be raised.

As president, Reagan advocated a conservative social agenda that supported the notion of government as responsible for legislating morality and religion. Throughout his eight years in office, Reagan supported the idea of prayer in schools and promoted the return to "old-fashioned values." He campaigned actively for the overturn of the 1973 Supreme Court decision of *Roe v. Wade*, which made abortion legal, and advocated federal legislation to ban abortion on demand. Despite the appeal that these ideas held for some Americans, Reagan was not successful in implementing any of them.

One of the legacies of the Reagan years is the change that he made in the makeup of the Supreme Court. In 1981, Reagan stunned many with his appointment of Sandra Day O'Connor to serve as the first female justice of the Supreme Court. Her impeccable credentials and record, as well as the fact that she was a woman, contributed to her relatively easy confirmation by the Senate. Five years later, Reagan made his second appointment to the Court when he nominated Antonin Scalia to be an associate justice. He, too, won Senate approval, and the orientation of the Court started to shift dramatically.

Shortly thereafter, in 1987, Reagan recommended Robert Bork to fill the next vacancy. By this time, the political climate had changed considerably, and the Senate began a very difficult and politically charged series of confirmation hearings. The verdict of the Senate was not to confirm Bork, which was seen as a major defeat for Reagan, who finally submitted the name of Anthony Kennedy to fill the vacant

post on the Court. Kennedy was confirmed by the Senate and took his seat in 1988. In addition, Reagan appointed then Associate Justice William Rehnquist as chief justice of the United States, an appointment that also was confirmed by the Senate.

These critical appointments altered the character of the Supreme Court considerably, reflecting the conservative orientation of Reagan and members of his administration.

The First Term: Foreign Policy

One of the primary goals of the Reagan administration was to restore the international power and prestige of the United States. Reagan believed that the United States had declined in power internationally, thereby clearing the way for events such as the Soviet invasion of Afghanistan in December, 1979, and the taking of the fifty-two hostages from the U.S. embassy in Tehran, Iran. Even though Reagan came into office pledging to pursue arms control negotiations with the Soviet Union, he also believed that such negotiations would be pointless unless the United States could deal from a position of strength. Further, he reiterated many of the themes, heard years earlier, of the need for a strong military to deter the aggression of the Soviet Union. To accomplish these goals, the president authorized a real increase in the defense budget, increased the size of the U.S. Navy (moving toward the goal of a "600 ship navy"), and supported the creation and deployment of new and more sophisticated weapons for the military. In conjunction with these real increases in the size and capabilities of the military, Reagan also advocated the need for the United States to be more assertive in exercising its own power in the world. Public opinion polls indicated that most American citizens were backing him at every step.

The Soviet Union was the driving force behind Reagan's foreign and national security policy. Reagan was determined to achieve a position of parity with, if not superiority to, the Soviet Union. To achieve this goal, he actively pushed for the deployment of the MX intercontinental ballistic missile, reversed Jimmy Carter's stand and agreed to the development of the B-1 bomber, and authorized research into the creation of another new long-range plane known as the Stealth bomber. This aircraft was reputed to have a highly sophisticated design that made it virtually invisible to radar. The development of two new strategic bombers was justified by the need to update the aging B-52 force.

U.S.-Soviet Relations

U.S.-Soviet relations, which started to cool under Carter, deteriorated still further during the first years of the Reagan administration. Reagan's "evil empire" rhetoric about the Soviet Union, coupled with the signals sent by his appointments of hard-line advisers, made clear the direction that his administration would take. Tensions between the two superpowers threatened to escalate following an incident occurring on September 1, 1983, when the Soviet Union shot down a routine passenger flight of a Korean Air Lines 747. Among the passengers who perished were several Americans, including a congressman.

This incident was followed two months later by the first deployment of the new intermediate-range nuclear missiles in Europe as part of NATO forces. That deployment provided the impetus for the Soviet delegation to walk out of the ongoing arms control talks in Geneva. Under the terms of the NATO agreement, signed in December, 1979, the United States was committed to pursue the dual tracks of development and deployment of the nuclear missiles while simultaneously pursuing arms control. Although Reagan was bound to uphold that decision, he also made clear his conviction that force deployment was a necessary prerequisite to arms control.

Although Reagan was personally skeptical of the value of arms control, he also believed that the time was not appropriate for reaching an agreement, given political uncertainty with the Soviet Union. The rapid succession of leaders taking office in the Soviet Union made it difficult for the Reagan administration to conduct negotiations and virtually impossible for the Soviets to formulate any consistent policy positions. When Reagan had assumed office in January of 1981, Leonid Brezhnev was premier of the Soviet Union. His illness and then death on November 10, 1982, ushered in a "succession crisis" within the Soviet Union. Brezhnev was succeeded by Yuri Andropov, who died only a year later, on February 9, 1984. He was succeeded by Konstantin Chernenko, who died on March 10, 1985, at which time Mikhail Gorbachev came to power. It was only after Gorbachev took office and introduced his policies of *glasnost* (openness) and *perestroika* (restructuring), accompanied by the dramatic arms buildup of the United States, that U.S.-Soviet relations started to ease.

The Strategic Defense Initiative

On March 23, 1983, at the end of a nationally televised speech on the defense budget, Reagan unveiled his plan for a new defense program "to counter the awesome Soviet missile threat with measures that are defensive." Reagan surprised the world by calling upon the U.S. scientific community to turn its attention to the creation of a new weapon system that would render nuclear weapons "impotent and obsolete." The Strategic Defense Initiative (SDI), or "Star Wars," as it came to be popularly known, provided a real symbolic victory in the fight to surpass the Soviet Union militarily. It also became one of the major stumbling blocks in the arms control negotiations: The Soviet Union demanded that plans for the development of SDI not go forward, claiming that it was in violation of the terms of the Antiballistic Missile Treaty of 1972 and thereby calling into question the sincerity with which the United States could enter into any new agreement.

Later that year, in October, Reagan sent another forceful signal about the power of the United States and the role that the United States would be playing globally when he ordered a surprise military attack on the Caribbean island of Grenada. Following the assassination of the prime minister of Grenada, Maurice Bishop, on October 19, a new government had been created which had strong ties to the Soviet Union and Cuba. President Reagan justified the attack, at least in part, by pointing to the need to assure the safety of American students in a medical school on the island, who, he believed, were endangered by the possibility of a communist takeover. After meeting minimal resistance, the U.S. invasion force of almost two thousand Marines and Army rangers took control of the island, deported the Cubans, and helped establish a pro-American government.

This military operation was met by criticism by some of the United States' allies, who had not been consulted in advance. The majority of Americans, however, rallied behind Reagan, and the limited military operation sent a clear signal to the Soviet Union regarding communist presence in the Western Hemisphere. Furthermore, the invasion of Grenada occurred only two days after a Muslim terrorist had driven a truck into the U.S. Marine headquarters in Beirut, Lebanon, killing 241 Americans. In the wake of that act of aggression, Reagan's decision enjoyed full public support, proving that he could, and would, act decisively in time of crisis.

Middle East Policy
The Middle East was another region that plagued Reagan during his first term in office. U.S. policy toward the Middle East during the Reagan years was in accord with his desire to revive U.S. power internationally as well as to limit Soviet influence globally. Since the creation of the state of Israel in 1948, U.S. interests in the Middle East had been tied directly to

U.S. Marines in Beirut, Lebanon, December, 1983. *(U.S. Navy)*

the security of Israel, as well as the need to assure free passage of oil through the Persian Gulf. The war between Iraq and Iran, which had begun in 1980, threatened the balance of power in the region and became a direct threat to the interests of the United States when both countries began attacking tankers in the Persian Gulf and endangering oil refineries. Furthermore, sometime in 1982, the United States had become aware of evidence that suggested that Iran was supporting terrorist groups in the Middle East, including groups engaged in the taking of American hostages. Subsequently, Reagan pointed to Iran as a sponsor of international terrorism, and the United States led the fight to stop all arms shipments to Iran.

While the Iran-Iraq war raged, Lebanon continued to be a major trouble spot. Reagan's fear was that the longer the war in Lebanon continued, the greater was the possibility that the Soviet Union would gain a stronghold in the region, at the expense of the United States and to the immediate peril of Israel. Israel's primary concern at this time was Palestinian statehood, represented by the Palestine Liberation Organization (PLO), and guarantees of the future security of Israel. The Reagan administration tacitly supported the creation of some sort of Palestinian state on the West Bank. Israel, however, sought to establish Jewish settlements on the West Bank, while Syria, Lebanon, Jordan, and the PLO could not agree as to whether a Palestinian state should exist and, if so, what form it should take.

In June, 1982, with the tacit approval of the United States, Israel invaded Lebanon, drove out the PLO, and attempted to establish a friendly Christian government. This new government soon collapsed and Reagan, fearful of the outcome if Israel withdrew from Lebanon, authorized the continued presence of U.S. Marines. In April, 1983, a powerful bomb exploded in the U.S. embassy in Beirut, killing forty-six people, including sixteen Americans. In September, 1983, Reagan stated the need for continued U.S. presence in the region and stationed naval forces off the coast of Lebanon. Then, in October of 1983, Muslim terrorists drove a truckful of explosives into the Marines' barracks, killing 241 Americans.

Reagan continued to talk about how "the United States will not be intimidated by terrorists" and announced that the United States would not "cut and run." Nevertheless, pressure at home was mounting against Reagan's policy in Lebanon. Members of Congress threatened to invoke the War Powers Act over what they saw as the increasing U.S. military buildup in the region, as well as the dangers to the members of the U.S. armed forces serving in the area. The tide of public opinion had turned as well, and, facing a reelection campaign, Reagan authorized the withdrawal of the troops by the end of February, 1984.

Policy Toward Latin America

The other major area that concerned Reagan was Latin America, specifically Nicaragua. The overthrow of Anastasio Somoza García and the subsequent rise to power of the Sandinista government raised many of the old fears of a Soviet stronghold in the region and the concomitant fear that, if not stopped, Nicaragua would become the base for exporting revolution throughout Latin America. Almost immediately upon taking office, Reagan terminated all economic assistance to Nicaragua and began a campaign to extend military and economic support to the Contras fighting to overthrow the Sandinista government. For the remainder of his term of office, Reagan would fight an ongoing battle with Congress over the issue of support for the Contras, or "freedom fighters," as Reagan preferred to call them.

What was not anticipated during Reagan's first term was the link between his policy toward Nicaragua and the Middle East that would emerge to plague him during his second term, in what became known as the Iran-Contra affair.

Foreign Policy: The Second Term

In many ways, Reagan's foreign policy in his second four years in office differed markedly from that of the first term. The arms buildup that had started during the first term had enabled Reagan to achieve his goal of asserting U.S. military and political power once again. Although American Marines had died in Beirut, the United States was not in a position of direct combat anywhere in the world. As the Republicans pointed out during the 1984 election campaign, "not an inch of territory had been seized by the Communists during the Reagan Administration." Although public support for the large defense buildup and the more bellicose foreign policies was eroding, part of the reason was that Reagan's policies during his first term in office had succeeded. The White House and the American people believed that the United States was strong once again.

As he approached his second term, Reagan did so as the first American president since Herbert Hoover not to meet with his Soviet counterpart. Polls indicated that the American public wanted an arms control agreement, which in 1984 seemed a pipe dream. Yet Reagan approached the 1984 election as one of the most popular presidents in recent history. Regardless of the number of people who disagreed with his policies, Reagan himself was able to retain his popularity and the political advantage that went with that because of this appeal to the American people.

Reagan swept the 1984 election, defeating Democratic candidate Walter Mondale by an overwhelming margin, with a 59 percent plurality in the popular vote, and a sweep of 525 to 13 electoral votes. With that degree of support, as well as the belief that the United States had regained a position of strength internationally, Reagan was able to alter some of his policies dramatically from the first term to the second.

Although Reagan's foreign policy remained focused on the Soviet Union, one of the major changes was in the type of relations that the two countries would pursue, especially after Mikhail Gorbachev came to power in March, 1985. This event was coupled with a change in Reagan's own perceptions regarding the ability of the United States to negotiate with the Soviet Union from a position of strength for the first time in many years, as well as Reagan's strong desire to achieve a permanent agreement with the Soviet Union. The result was Reagan's desire to meet with the new Soviet leader personally and to see the resumption of serious arms control negotiations.

In November, 1984, only a few weeks after Reagan's reelection, the announcement was made that arms control talks would resume the next year, and U.S. and Soviet negotiators met once again in Geneva in March, 1985. In November, Reagan and Gorbachev met for the first of what would be an annual summit meeting between the two heads of state. In the space of a few years, the course of U.S.-Soviet relations had been altered dramatically, moving from an atmosphere of hostility and Cold War to one of cooperation leading to a resurgence of détente.

The first summit meeting resulted primarily in the settlement of secondary issues, such as cultural exchanges and the resumption of air flights between the two countries, rather than any major substantive agreement. At that meeting, however, the two leaders agreed in principle to an Intermediate-Range Nuclear Forces (INF) agreement. Reagan and Gorbachev followed the first summit one year later with another held in Reykjavik, Iceland, in October, 1986. In the course of this meeting, progress seemed to be made toward the goal of achieving a verifiable arms control agreement. Movement toward this goal was thwarted shortly thereafter, when Gorbachev announced that he wanted to link an INF treaty with limits on SDI. Reagan was steadfast in his refusal to compromise on SDI, and the arms control talks collapsed again.

Reagan signs the Japanese American Internment Compensation Bill in 1988. *(Ronald Reagan Library)*

Early in 1987, Gorbachev dropped his insistence on the linkage between SDI and INF, and both sides agreed in principle to a "double-zero option," that is, the total elimination of both intermediate-range (600-3,400 miles) and short-range (300-600 miles) missiles from Europe. In addition, both sides also agreed to historic measures that were necessary to verify compliance with the agreement. These measures included not only provisions for surveillance by "national technical means," primarily spy satellites, but also, for the first time, a provision for officials and scientists to visit highly sensitive military and scientific installations on the other side to make sure that the weapons were being dismantled as agreed.

At a third summit in Washington, D.C., in December, 1987, Reagan and Gorbachev signed the INF Treaty. This agreement was the first to result in the reduction of the actual number of nuclear missiles (about 4 percent), and it

marked the first time that an entire class of nuclear weapons was eliminated. The INF Treaty was ratified by the U.S. Senate in 1988.

The final summit meeting betwen Reagan and Gorbachev took place in Moscow in May, 1988. Although both leaders talked of the need to build upon the arms control momentum started with the INF Treaty, leading toward the signing of a strategic arms agreement, nothing substantive resulted from this final summit. Nevertheless, it helped confirm the belief that relations between the two superpowers had changed considerably during Reagan's tenure in office.

The Bombing of Libya

While progress was being made in the area of arms control and U.S.-Soviet relations during Reagan's second term in office, other incidents occurred which, at times, seemed to overshadow the progress between the superpowers. In the area of U.S. foreign policy, one of the most dramatic took place in April, 1986, when Reagan authorized the U.S. military to bomb Libya in retaliation for a Libyan-backed terrorist bombing of a discotheque in West Berlin earlier in the month. Reagan previously had made the decision for, and had given approval in principle to, a U.S. military strike against suspected terrorist targets. The bombing of the discotheque, which resulted in the death of one American and a Turkish citizen, provided the reason to implement these plans.

Two U.S. flyers and at least thirty-seven Libyans, including one of dictator Muammar al-Qaddafi's daughters, were killed in the raid. In the short term, the raid caused great strife between the United States and its NATO allies, who were, with the exception of the United Kingdom, unsupportive of the raid. In fact, one of the U.S. bombs inadvertently hit and damaged the French embassy in Tripoli. In the longer term, however, it appears that Reagan's strategy paid off. Subsequent to the attack, the European countries increased their own anti-terrorist activism and diminished their relationship with Libya. The action, moreover, seemed to undermine the leadership of Qaddafi, who remained relatively silent after the episode.

Trouble Spots

One of Reagan's greatest foreign policy successes was not fully recognized until he was out of office and George Bush was inaugurated as the forty-first president. The Soviet invasion of Afghanistan in December, 1979, had renewed fears of Soviet expansion. Soviet involvement in Afghanistan had continued throughout the years of the Reagan administration, with the Soviets suffering more than forty thousand casualties in their fight against the *mujahadeen* rebels. In keeping with his anticommunist perspective and his belief that the Soviets had committed an act of aggression, Reagan backed the *mujahadeen*, extending economic and military aid. On the whole, the Congress supported

Reagan's policy in Afghanistan. In early 1988, following discussions with the United States on the issue, Gorbachev announced a plan to withdraw the Soviet troops from Afghanistan by February 15, 1989.

Through the end of the Reagan administration, the Middle East continued to be a major trouble spot. In early 1987, Reagan concluded that Iran had endangered the oil exports of Kuwait, a pro-Iraq country in the Iran-Iraq War, by threatening the free movement of the Kuwaiti tankers through the Persian Gulf. To counter this threat, Reagan put the tankers under the U.S. flag and then authorized the use of U.S. naval vessels to protect them against attack by Iranian gunboats. In 1987, an Iraqi missile struck the USS *Stark*, killing thirty-seven sailors. Then, in mid-1988, a U.S. naval commander mistook an Iranian passenger airplane for a military plane and had it shot down, killing 290 civilians. Throughout these months, members of Congress called for the need to invoke the 1973 War Powers Act and withdraw all American forces, but this did not occur. As a result of the U.S. military actions, the Persian Gulf did remain open for passage, and the U.S. Navy successfully completed its mission. Critics questioned both the wisdom and the necessity of the policies, however, given the costs. The Persian Gulf region would erupt into a larger conflict during the Bush administration following Iraq's invasion of Kuwait.

Reagan had to confront a number of other trouble spots during his second term in office. In 1986, after fourteen years of dictatorship, Ferdinand Marcos was deposed as president of the Philippines, to be replaced by Corazon Aquino, the widow of one of his murdered opponents. The United States had been formally linked to the Philippines through the Treaty of Mutual Defense, which entered into force in 1952. These ties were strengthened by the agreement to lease to the United States a naval base at Subic Bay and an Air Force base, Clark Field, for an annual rent of $500 million.

Even in the face of mounting opposition to Marcos and continued U.S. presence in the Philippines, Reagan continued to support the dictator. In February, 1986, Marcos bowed under domestic pressure and called for elections, which he won, although under questionable circumstances. Pressure from within the Philippines and finally from Reagan forced Marcos to leave the country to be replaced officially by Aquino.

The Iran-Contra Affair

Much of Reagan's success in the area of foreign policy threatened to be overshadowed by events in Central America, specifically the link between Iran and Nicaragua that unfolded as the Iran-Contra affair. While the Iran-Contra affair never had the impact on Reagan that Watergate had on Richard Nixon, it nevertheless cast some shadows on the Reagan administration and raised some very basic questions about the responsibilities of the president and the extent of the independent authority of his staff.

The event started to unfold in 1985, when it became known that Iranian-backed terrorists had seized a number of U.S. hostages in the Middle East, including some members of the State Department and the Central Intelligence Agency (CIA). Even though Reagan had often stated that he would never negotiate with terrorists, in August and September of 1985, the president worked through Israel to send anti-tank missiles and other military equipment to Iran. For the next fourteen months, shipments of weapons were sent to Iran in a highly secret operation. Simultaneously, several hostages were released, although others were seized. Reagan's national security adviser, Robert McFarlane, under Reagan's orders secretly went to Tehran to negotiate with the Iranians.

In November, 1986, this information was disclosed publicly, and Reagan told the American public that his policy was designed with the hope of opening contact with some of the Iranian "moderates." This policy was implemented despite strong protests from both Secretary of State George Shultz and Secretary of Defense Caspar Weinberger.

Approximately three weeks later, Attorney General Edwin Meese III announced that the money obtained from the arms sales to Iran had been secretly diverted to help the Contras in Nicaragua. This had occurred in 1985-1986, in direct conflict with the congressional ban on sending lethal aid to the Contras.

During the summer of 1987, joint Senate and House committees conducted nationally televised hearings on the Iran-Contra connection. In addition, Reagan assembled a special commission chaired by former Texas senator John Tower and including former secretary of state and Democratic senator Edmund Muskie and

Lieutenant Colonel Oliver North testifies on July 7, 1987, about the Iran-Contra affair. *(AP/Wide World Photos)*

Brent Scowcroft, a retired Air Force lieutenant general and Henry Kissinger's deputy on the National Security Council. The Tower Commission was empowered to investigate the role of the White House in the Iran-Contra affair. The Tower Commission concluded that "the primary responsibility for the formulation and implementation of national security policy falls on the president." It also concluded that, in this case, the staff of the National Security Council was responsible for the policies that were implemented and that President Reagan was too far removed from the policies enacted by the members of his staff. Following the revelation in 1994 of Reagan's diagnosis of Alzheimer's disease, some wondered whether this debilitating condition had begun to affect his memory and his ability to lead during his years in office.

The congressional investigation supported many of the conclusions of the Tower Commission report. Lieutenant Colonel Oliver North, an aide at the National Security Council, emerged as one of the central figures. He testified that he had worked largely under the direction of William Casey, the head of the CIA, who had died of a brain tumor months earlier. North became a hero to many Americans for his devotion to his country and president, even if that meant breaking the law.

By the end of the Iran-Contra investigations, it seemed apparent that Reagan had been unaware of much that had been done in the name of American foreign policy and the Reagan Doctrine. The incident raised important questions about who really does make policy and how much knowledge or control the president really has over a very large staff that is supposed to act in his behalf.

The Reagan Legacy

When Ronald Reagan took office in January, 1981, the presidency of the United States was in a state of decline. Humiliation over the Vietnam War, the Watergate scandal and its cul-mination in the resignation of Richard Nixon, and the perception of a series of weak leaders and poor political decisions all combined to undermine the role of the president, the power of the office, and the prestige of the United States. No president since Dwight D. Eisenhower had been able to overcome these obstacles to be elected to serve two full terms in the office. The eight years of the Reagan administration reversed many of these trends.

From the start of his first term in office, Ronald Reagan was the "Great Communicator," able to reach the American people, who believed in and supported him. With the backing of a Republican Senate during his first term in office, he could implement policies and convey a sense of leadership that enabled him to restore to the office a prestige and sense of power that had been absent for many years. Although a social conservative, he appointed Sandra Day O'Connor to serve as the first female justice of the Supreme Court, Jeane Kirkpatrick as his ambassador to the United Nations, and Elizabeth Dole as his secretary of transportation.

Domestically, Reagan promised the American people that he would get the economy moving, once again reversing the trends that had undermined the nation. He was able to control inflation and bring down unemployment, and the economy of the United States did thrive. Tied directly to this was a marked alteration in the priorities of the country, as reflected in the budget. A dramatic increase in spending for the military reflected Reagan's firm belief in the need for "peace through strength." The size of the armed forces grew dramatically, as did the readiness of those forces. Many argue that it was this increase that allowed the United States to be as successful as it was in dealing with the Soviets and in regaining its position as global leader. Some also argue that this increase was a major factor in precipitating the economic crisis tied to the breakup of the Soviet Union in 1991.

Former U.S. president Ronald Reagan and former Soviet president Mikhail Gorbachev relax at Reagan's California ranch in 1992. *(AP/Wide World Photos)*

Also reflected in the budget was the need to cut domestic programs that were not deemed essential to the United States. The cuts in many of the welfare programs illustrate clearly Reagan's conservative orientation and his belief in the need to shrink the size of the federal government. While these programs were cut amid some controversy, Reagan was able to sustain his popularity throughout the eight years in which he served as president.

In reassigning his budget priorities, Reagan also presided over the growth and acceleration of the largest budget deficit in the history of the country, which, many believe led to the 1990 recession that brought down Bush and swept Bill Clinton into office. Although critics feared that the deficit would have a disastrous impact on the future economic situation in the country, continued fiscal reform led to a balanced budget and a surplus by 1998.

During the Reagan years, another potentially dangerous trend emerged: For the first time, the United States was importing more than it exported, thereby altering the balance of payments. For the first time, the United States became a debtor nation, which would have a direct impact not only on the domestic economic situation but also on foreign policy options. Clearly, the short-term impact of Reagan's economic policies was beneficial, and the Reagan Revolution seemed to have worked. Most people had to answer "yes" in response to the question Reagan asked the American people in 1984: whether they were better off than they had been four years earlier.

In the area of foreign policy, the Reagan

administration began under the cloud of diminishing U.S. global prestige, another perception that Reagan was able to reverse in eight years. He believed in the importance of military might and in the need to negotiate from a position of strength. His national security and foreign policies were designed to underscore these points. A combination of a military buildup and an assertive policy sent unambiguous signals to the world about the resolve of the United States. By the end of his two terms in office, the result was the resurgence of the U.S. role internationally and the beginning of a new era of cooperation between the United States and the Soviet Union. This change was exemplified in the signing and ratification of the INF Treaty by the United States and Soviet Union in December, 1987, along with the commitment to pursue a more cooperative course of action in the future.

For eight years, Ronald and First Lady Nancy Reagan imposed a sense of dignity and conveyed a positive image of the United States, which in turn was reflected in the way the United States was viewed by other countries. Even after leaving office, Reagan continued to be a role model through public disclosure of his struggle with Alzheimer's disease. The "Reagan image" was especially important in boosting the pride that many Americans took in themselves and their country. To many Americans, this change in attitude was long overdue, and it represents one of the most important legacies of the Reagan years.

Joyce P. Kaufman

Bibliographical References

Lou Cannon, *Reagan*, 1982, is one of the standard sources on the early Reagan years. Kenneth T. Walsh, *Ronald Reagan*, 1997, traces Reagan's life from childhood to the presidency. Adrian Bosch, *Reagan: An American Story*, 1998, is the companion volume to the documentary on Reagan's life for the PBS series *The American Experience*. William E. Pemberton, *Exit with*

Honor: The Life and Presidency of Ronald Reagan, 1998, is a balanced biography that also includes an evaluation the Reagan presidency. J. II. Cardigan, *Ronald Reagan: A Remarkable Life*, 1995, chronicles Reagan's life from his radio broadcasting days to the presidency. Edmund Morris, *Dutch: A Memoir of Ronald Reagan*, 1998, is a biography written in the form of a first-person narrative. Reagan published his memoir, *An American Life*, in 1990. For a detailed account of the attempt on Ronald Reagan's life, see Herbert L. Abrams, *"The President Has Been Shot": Confusion, Disability, and the 25th Amendment in the Aftermath of the Attempted Assassination of Ronald Reagan*, 1992.

Robert Dallek, *Ronald Reagan: The Politics of Symbolism*, 1984, offers a critical interpretation of the first term of the Reagan administration. More sympathetic is Bob Slosser, *Reagan: Inside Out*, 1984. An insider's perspective on the formulation of Reagan's economic policies can be found in David A. Stockman, *The Triumph of Politics*, 1986, written by Reagan's first director of the Office of Management and Budget. Similarly, Alexander Haig's *Caveat*, 1984, is a bitter memoir by Reagan's first secretary of state. In-depth information on the events leading up to and surrounding the Iran-Contra affair can be found in *The Tower Commission Report*, 1987. Two of the best sources of information about the Reagan administration and arms control are both by Strobe Talbott: *Deadly Gambits*, 1984, about the INF and START talks, and *The Master of the Game*, 1988, a biography of Paul Nitze, Reagan's chief arms negotiator. For an unbiased overview of U.S. foreign policy in the Reagan administration, see Walter LaFeber, *The American Age*, 1989.

Evaluations of the Reagan presidency range from laudatory to highly critical and include David Mervin, *Ronald Reagan and the American Presidency*, 1990; Lou Cannon, *President Reagan: The Role of a Lifetime*, 1991; Deborah H. Strober and Gerald S. Strober, *Reagan: The Man and His Presidency*, 1992; Wilbur Edel, *The Reagan*

Presidency: An Actor's Finest Performance, 1993; and Dinesh D'Souza, *Ronald Reagan: How an Ordinary Man Became an Extraordinary Leader*, 1997. Peter Hannaford, ed., *Recollections of Reagan: A Portrait of Ronald Reagan*, 1997, is an illuminating collection of fifty-one essays by political associates and acquaintances. For a comprehensive reference, see Peter B. Levy, *Encyclopedia of the Reagan-Bush Years*, 1996.

George Bush
41st President, 1989-1993

Born: June 12, 1924
Milton, Massachusetts

Political Party: Republican
Vice President: Dan Quayle

Cabinet Members

Secretary of State: James A. Baker III, Lawrence Eagleburger

Secretary of the Treasury: Nicholas Brady

Secretary of Defense: Dick Cheney

Attorney General: Dick Thornburgh, William P. Barr

Secretary of the Interior: Manuel Lujan, Jr.

Secretary of Agriculture: Clayton K. Yeutter, Edward Madigan

Secretary of Commerce: Robert A. Mosbacher, Barbara H. Franklin

Secretary of Labor: Elizabeth Dole, Lynn Martin

Secretary of Health and Human Services: Louis W. Sullivan

Secretary of Housing and Urban Development: Jack Kemp

Secretary of Transportation: Samuel K. Skinner, Andrew Card

Secretary of Energy: James D. Watkins

Secretary of Education: Lauro F. Cavazos, Lamar Alexander

Secretary of Veterans Affairs: Edward J. Derwinski

George Herbert Walker Bush won the presidency at a time of transformation, at home and abroad. The Cold War was coming to an end, and for the first time in almost fifty years, people dared to dream of a genuine peace. Domestic politics was in flux; Ronald Reagan had shaken traditional electoral coalitions and had mastered the vagaries of television to pioneer a new politics

Bush's official portrait. *(White House Historical Society)*

677

of image and "character." An old-fashioned man, Bush offered voters the security of the past; they responded by electing him president of the United States. As chief executive, Bush delivered the stability he had promised. He skillfully managed America's foreign policy and endeavored to put a "kinder and gentler" face on the social and economic conservatism he inherited from his predecessor. Unfortunately for Bush, his success in liquidating the Cold War made him dispensable in an era seeking a New World Order, and his caution at home left him vulnerable to charges of indifference as the economy slipped into recession. By 1992, Bush had become an anachronism, visibly uncomfortable in an electoral realm where his opponent played the saxophone on the *Arsenio Hall Show* and bantered easily with youth on MTV. This time, voters rejected the solidity of the past for new directions. In defeat, George Bush, the last American president to have fought in World War II, gave way gracefully to William Jefferson Clinton, the first president of the baby boom generation.

Privilege, the Pacific, and Petroleum

George Bush was born into a patrician class that generally eschewed the hurly-burly of politics for the more refined strife of board rooms and country clubs. Only occasionally would a member of this elite break with convention and run for elective office. One such individual was Franklin Delano Roosevelt. Another, significantly, was Bush's father, Prescott Bush, Sr.

The elder Bush was born in Ohio into a local manufacturing family. Upon graduation from Yale University, he saw action as a captain in the field artillery during World War I. Following the war, Prescott Bush returned home and was married to Dorothy Walker of St. Louis, Missouri, daughter of a prominent businessman. Bush then embarked upon a successful career in business, which culminated in his becoming a partner in the powerful investment

banking firm of Brown Brothers, Harriman and Company. Bush believed that money was not an end in itself; for him, responsibility followed wealth. As a contemporary wrote, "Pres had an old-fashioned idea that the more advantages a man has, the greater his obligation to do public service." For two decades, Bush labored as a representative to the Greenwich, Connecticut, town meeting. In 1950, at the age of fifty-five, Prescott Bush entered the race for United States senator in Connecticut, running as a member of the internationalist, later Eisenhower, wing of the Republican Party. He lost by a narrow margin, 1,000 votes of 860,000 cast. Vindication came two years later, when Bush triumphantly captured the state's other senate seat, vacated by the incumbent's sudden death. In 1956 he won reelection, and he served until his retirement in 1963. Prescott Bush's career would be a powerful example and stimulus for his son.

George Bush was born on June 12, 1924. One of five children, Bush enjoyed what was in many ways an idyllic childhood. He grew up in Connecticut, his summers punctuated by trips to the family's vacation home at Kennebunkport, Maine. Prescott and Dorothy Bush saw to it that affluence did not spoil their children. They inculcated in George and his siblings the Puritan work ethic and a strict code of conduct. Dorothy Bush, in particular, rooted out any signs of arrogance or boastfulness which arose in her children because of their birth or their accomplishments. A keen sportswoman, she chastised her children for any signs of vaunting behavior in victory. From this background, the future president developed the mixed traits of hard work and aristocratic restraint, competitiveness and loyalty, and ambition and self-effacement that would characterize his political career.

Bush's first chance to test himself against the high standards set by his parents came with the Japanese attack on Pearl Harbor. The seventeen-year-old Bush wanted to enlist as soon as he was graduated from Phillips Andover Academy. His parents opposed his plans, urging him instead to join his older brother at Yale. The secretary of war, Henry Lewis Stimson, delivered the commencement address at Bush's school in the spring of 1942. The venerable soldier and statesman told the graduating class that the war would be a long one and that they would do their country a service by getting more schooling before joining the military. Following this address, Prescott Bush asked his son if the secretary's words had had any effect. "No, sir," was the reply, "I'm going in." The elder Bush said no more and shook his son's hand.

As soon as he came of age, George Bush joined the Navy and began a course in naval aviation. For a time, Bush at eighteen was the youngest flyer in the Navy. During World War II, he flew fifty-eight combat missions in the Pacific. His most notable exploit came on September 2, 1944, while piloting a Grumman Avenger torpedo bomber based on the carrier USS *San Jacinto*. His squadron received orders to attack a radio-communications center on the island of Chichi Jima, one of the Bonins chain, which included Iwo Jima. Enemy antiaircraft fire hit Bush's plane as he dived in to strike. Bush completed his bombing run, then ordered the other two men in the plane to bail out. Bush abandoned his plane last, successfully parachuting into the ocean. Both of his crewmen died. Floating in the Pacific, Bush experienced some frightening moments as a Japanese boat from the island raced to pick him up. Fortunately, planes from his squadron chased the Japanese away. Soon an American submarine surfaced and rescued the downed flyer. Bush then spent an adventurous month aboard the submarine before being reunited with his ship and squadron. He received a Distinguished Flying Cross for his conduct at Chichi Jima. Bush was rotated back to the United States in December, 1944. In January, he married Barbara Pierce, the beautiful daugh-

ter of an executive of the McCall Publishing Company, whom he had met at a dance during the Christmas holidays of 1941. The young war hero and newlywed was training for the expected invasion of Japan when the conflict ended in August, 1945.

Demobilized, Bush attended Yale University, majoring in economics and acting as captain of the baseball team. Already able to combine a winning amiability with a formidable capacity for work, Bush made Skull and Bones, the most prestigious and secretive club on campus, and also earned a Phi Beta Kappa key. Bush was graduated in 1948 and promptly moved his family to Texas, where he hoped to make his way in the oil industry. He began as an equipment clerk for Dresser Industries, an oil supply company in which his father had an interest. There Bush learned the rudiments of the oil business. In 1951, with the help of seed money from relatives, Bush and a friend formed the Bush-Overbey Development Company. For two years, Bush thrived as an independent oilman, seeking oil across the country, from Montana to the Gulf of Mexico. He helped found the Zapata Petroleum Corporation in 1953. The next year, he became president of a spin-off enterprise, Zapata Off-Shore Company, with its headquarters at Houston. Bush's domestic happiness matched his business success until he and Barbara were dealt a devastating blow by the loss of their three-year-old daughter Robin to leukemia. They consoled themselves in the warm relationship they maintained with their other five children. In later years, Bush would declare that he and Barbara considered their greatest accomplishment to be the fact that their children still came home.

Into Politics

Bush developed an interest in politics just as his business brought him to the threshold of wealth, but his ambition seemed doomed to frustration. A Republican, he lived in a state that had been resolutely Democratic since the days of Reconstruction. Yet, by the time Bush began to contemplate a political career, change appeared in the offing. Dwight D. Eisenhower had carried Texas in 1952 and 1956. Richard Nixon only narrowly lost the state to John Fitzgerald Kennedy in 1960. Texas was exhibiting early signs of the political realignment in the South that would challenge the traditional dominance of the Democratic Party.

Bush took advantage of this moment of opportunity. In 1962, he became chair of the Harris County Republican Party. For two years, he worked to build a Republican organization in the Houston area. He began what would become a lifelong task of seeking common ground between conservative and more moderate Republicans. Bush made a run for elective office in 1964, challenging Senator Ralph Yarborough. He campaigned effectively, but with Lyndon Johnson at the head of the Democratic ticket, it was a bad year for Republicans in Texas. Bush won the largest Republican vote in Texas history, but it was not enough to defeat the incumbent. Despite his loss, Bush enjoyed this new sphere of activity. In 1966, he resigned from Zapata to campaign for a newly created congressional seat in Houston. That fall, Bush enjoyed his first victory in a general election.

In Washington, D.C., Bush represented the opinions of his constituency, ranking as one of the most conservative members of the House of Representatives. In the area of civil rights, however, Bush braved the displeasure of his supporters. He voted for the Civil Rights Act of 1968, with its controversial provisions for open housing. Bush went home, explained his stand to the voters, and was triumphantly reelected. In his second, and final, term in the House, his most notable act was his support for the creation of the Environmental Protection Agency (EPA). In 1970, Ralph Yarborough stood for reelection. Because of his liberal voting record, the senator seemed vulnerable to a Republican challenge. Bush sacrificed his safe congressional seat and declared his candidacy in

the Senate race. Unfortunately for Bush, Lloyd Bentsen, a conservative Democrat, eliminated Yarborough in the primary election. Bentsen went on to defeat Bush in November.

Utility Man

As Bush closed his congressional office, doors opened for him elsewhere. Party leaders had marked Bush as a "comer." At the 1968 Republican Convention, he had been mentioned as a possible running mate for Richard Nixon. The president himself believed that this promising political figure deserved some recognition for his effort against Lloyd Bentsen. In December, 1970, Nixon nominated the lame duck congressman for the position of ambassador to the United Nations. The nomination came under attack because of Bush's unfamiliarity with foreign relations. Despite the criticism, the Senate confirmed Bush in February, 1971. At the United Nations, Bush began to earn his reputation as a "good soldier" by loyally supporting the administration's "two China policy." Bush fought valiantly to keep Taiwan in the United Nations, even as the Nixon administration's diplomacy with the People's Republic of China doomed his efforts.

President Nixon rewarded Bush for his service in this thankless position by asking him, in December, 1972, to take the job of chair of the Republican National Committee. Bush moved into his new office early in 1973, in time to be caught up in the storm of the Watergate scandal. Once again, Bush faithfully defended the administration, even as new revelations rendered such support increasingly untenable. Only at the end, in the summer of 1974, when he became convinced that the Republican Party could not survive an impeachment crisis, did Bush suggest that Richard Nixon resign.

Gerald R. Ford considered Bush for the vice presidency, but ultimately picked Nelson A. Rockefeller. In compensation, Ford offered Bush a choice of diplomatic posts. Bush agreed to head the United States Liaison Office in Beijing. This position held the allure of being far from the soured political atmosphere of Washington, D.C, required no senatorial confirmation, and presented the challenge of involvement in one of the most sensitive areas of American foreign policy. Bush's sojourn in China produced no significant diplomatic initiatives, but he did take advantage of the opportunity to cultivate relationships with Chinese leaders that would in time prove to have important consequences.

In November, 1975, President Ford called Bush back to Washington, D.C. In the so-called Halloween Massacre, Ford had reorganized his administration in preparation for the presidential campaign of 1976. Many Nixon appointees were asked to resign or were fired, among them William Colby, head of the Central Intelligence Agency (CIA). Ford asked Bush to take the position of Director of Central Intelligence. Bush accepted, though reluctantly. He enjoyed China and did not relish a return to Capitol Hill, fearing that the job of running the CIA would prove a political dead end. The process of winning confirmation in the Senate reinforced the unpalatability of the job. Critics charged that his appointment politicized a nonpartisan post. These attacks reflected concerns that Bush might be chosen to be Ford's running mate in 1976. To quiet such fears, the president issued a statement announcing that Bush would not be considered for the Republican vice presidential nomination. His estimate of the political cost of the post borne out by events, Bush duly received his confirmation as Director of Central Intelligence.

Bush inherited an agency riven by scandal. Congressional investigating committees had uncovered evidence that the CIA had plotted to assassinate Fidel Castro and had sponsored other disreputable activities. It fell to Bush to protect, reform, and heal the intelligence establishment. During the year that Bush headed the CIA, he replaced most of the top managers of the agency and worked to restore its tarnished public image. Although Bush served too brief a time to build a permanent institutional legacy, as he left office with the Ford administration in early 1977, he generally received high marks for his performance in a difficult job. Veteran intelligence officers praised Bush for his success in improving agency morale.

The Election of 1980

Bush's relegation to the sideline in 1976 proved a blessing in disguise. He was not forced to choose between Gerald Ford and Ronald Reagan in the bruising primary campaign of that year, and escaped any blame for the defeat in November. As a student, rather than a participant, in the election of 1976, Bush learned valuable lessons. He admired the way Jimmy Carter manipulated the primary system to transform himself from a dark horse candidate into the presidential nominee of the Democratic Party. Back home in Houston, Bush continued to watch Carter. He found less to admire in Carter's leadership as president. Bush's hopes rose with the president's political difficulties. A survey of potential Republican presidential candidates convinced Bush that he was the best man for the race. The essence of Carter's 1976 strategy had been to start early and target the first primaries. Victories in these contests would generate recognition, bringing in money and thereby more victories. Emulating Carter, Bush began early and moved fast. He started organizing a campaign and raising money in 1978, officially declaring his candidacy on May 1, 1979.

Up to a point, Bush's strategy worked. Months of diligent campaigning paid off in late 1979 as he began to win nonbinding straw polls at Republican Party gatherings. In the most important of these, in Maine, Bush upset Senator Howard Baker of Tennessee. Baker had been sufficiently confident of victory that he had flown in several reporters to record the

Bush signs the Americans with Disabilities Act of 1990. *(Joyce C. Naltchayan, White House)*

event. Instead, they described the triumph of George Bush, giving his campaign much-needed publicity. Then, in January, 1980, Bush stunned the political world by defeating Ronald Reagan, the Republican front-runner, in the Iowa caucuses. Suddenly Bush became Reagan's leading challenger. For a few heady weeks, Bush seemed capable of overtaking the popular Californian. In a famous formulation, Bush talked of his "Big Mo," or the newfound momentum behind his campaign.

The collapse of Bush's hopes came about as rapidly as their inflation. Ronald Reagan learned from his Iowa defeat and campaigned vigorously in New Hampshire, the next state to hold a primary. At a debate scheduled between Bush and Reagan at Nashua High

School, the other Republican candidates demanded seats on the stage. Reagan proved amenable to this arrangement. Bush demurred. He wanted to establish himself in the public mind as the only alternative to Ronald Reagan. An embarrassing scene ensued at the high school, as the other candidates followed Reagan and Bush to the platform. When the moderator attempted to shut down the debate because of this irregularity, Reagan uttered a telling protest, remembered from an old film: "I paid for this microphone, Mr. Green." Reagan appeared a magnanimous populist. Bush, on the other hand, seemed pettily legalistic. Reagan won a commanding victory in the primary. Bush finished second, but well behind. Thereafter, Reagan's march to the Republican presidential nomination proceeded inexorably. Bush remained in the race, suffering many defeats and gaining a few victories. Ironically, on the evening of Bush's greatest success, winning the Michigan primary in May, the television networks forecast that elsewhere Reagan had captured enough delegates to ensure his nomination. Bush withdrew his candidacy ten days later.

Bush still aspired to the secondary post that had eluded him so many times in the past. At the Republican Convention in Detroit, a highly publicized flirtation between Reagan and Gerald Ford seemed likely to dash Bush's hopes once again, but the nominee's rapprochement with the former president collapsed. Reagan then asked Bush to become his running mate, and Bush accepted. That fall he shared in Ronald Reagan's electoral triumph.

Vice President

Bush served President Reagan with his customary loyalty. He embraced Reagan's robust conservatism, despite his well-known criticisms of aspects of it during the 1980 primaries. Most notably, then-candidate Bush had branded Reagan's supply-side fiscal ideas "voodoo economics." Bush's ready adaptation to the good-soldiering role of the vice presidency contributed to a reputation for intellectual elasticity that would later haunt him as he campaigned in 1988. Nor did Bush's unswerving adherence to the administration line mollify certain hard-core conservatives in the Reagan entourage, who regarded the vice president as an ideological opportunist whose right-wing rhetoric merely camouflaged incipient apostasy. In fact, Bush came by his conservatism honestly. Adjusting to Reagan's positions on the budget, taxes, and abortion did not demand a grave distortion of his convictions. His differences with the Reaganites would always lie more in the realm of style than substance.

Bush's troubles with some of Reagan's acolytes did not extend to the man himself. Bush and Reagan developed a friendly working relationship. The vice president's position in the administration was solidified by his dignified conduct following John Hinckley, Jr.'s attempt to assassinate President Reagan on March 30, 1981. The president early on demonstrated his confidence in Bush by asking him to head a special Task Force on Regulatory Relief, charged with a mission dear to Reagan's heart. Ultimately, Bush's task force recommended the elimination of hundreds of federal regulations in an effort to cut the red tape associated with the federal bureaucracy. The vice president received other important and well-publicized responsibilities. Bush led the South Florida Task Force, and later the National Narcotics Border Interdiction System, which attempted, unsuccessfully, to stem the flow of illegal drugs into the country. He also acted as the chair of the National Security Council's crisis management team.

The president employed Bush on a number of diplomatic missions, including one to El Salvador, to warn the leaders of that nation about human rights abuses, and one to India, to improve relations with that important power. Bush played a leading role in extricating the Marines from Beirut after the debacle of American policy in Lebanon. Perhaps the vice president's greatest achievement was his tour of European capitals in February, 1983, when he helped persuade allied governments to accept the deployment of American intermediate-range nuclear missiles, a show of strength which led eventually to the Intermediate-Range Nuclear Forces (INF) Treaty with the Soviet Union. Bush was kept busy in the early 1980's attending the funerals of aged Soviet leaders, Leonid Brezhnev in 1982, Yuri Andropov in 1984, and Konstantin Chernenko in 1985. Significantly for the future, this last funeral gave Bush the opportunity to be the first high-ranking American official to meet the ambitious and reform-minded Mikhail Gorbachev after his accession to power.

Bush's activist role as vice president nearly brought him political ruin when the Reagan administration became embroiled in the Iran-Contra scandal. As controversy erupted concerning American arms sales to Iran, Bush steadfastly maintained that he was unaware that this was part of a deal to release American hostages held in Lebanon. He insisted that he was "out of the loop" concerning Oliver North's diversion of funds from these arms sales to support the Nicaraguan Contras. The vice president's claims were met with some skepticism, both because of his presence at meetings where the sales of weapons to Iran was discussed and because some of his aides were linked to fund-raising for the Contras. Though no definitive evidence ever appeared to refute his defense, questions about the Iran-Contra affair would haunt Bush for the rest of his political career.

The Election of 1988

Despite his accomplishments as vice president, Bush failed to emerge from the shadow of Ronald Reagan. He had won a reputation as the "perfect staff man" rather than as a leader. His preparatory-school mannerisms inspired a major newsmagazine to term him a "wimp." An indifferent public speaker, he was dismissed by some Democratic politicians as a man born with a "silver foot in his mouth." Consequently, Bush faced severe challenges as he prepared to run for the presidency in 1988. Even in his own party, many were unwilling to acknowledge him as the successor of Ronald Reagan. A number of Republicans entered the race for the presidential nomination, the most formidable of them being Senator Bob Dole of Kansas. When Dole inflicted an embarrassing defeat on Bush in the Iowa caucuses, it appeared as if Dole might impose on Bush the fate he had hoped to administer to Reagan in 1980. Instead, history repeated itself, with Bush's role reversed. After intense campaigning, he turned back Dole's challenge in New Hampshire. Fol-

lowing this decisive victory, Bush went on to sweep the primaries in the South, driving Dole out of the race and securing the Republican nomination.

Nevertheless, Bush's chances to prevail in the fall seemed slim. Polling indicated that he still suffered from high "negatives" with a dismayingly large percentage of the electorate. At a triumphant convention in July, the Democrats nominated Governor Michael Dukakis of Massachusetts. Dukakis emphasized his managerial expertise, counting that competence would prove a decisive weapon against a man presumed to be an ineffectual time-server. At this point in the campaign, Bush trailed Dukakis by seventeen points in the polls.

Bush, however, had advantages. The Reagan administration, despite setbacks and scandals, remained popular. The economy stayed strong, and bold diplomacy with the Soviets reduced tensions abroad. The vice president could rely on an experienced and highly skilled campaign staff, including his longtime friend James Baker and a brilliant young political strategist named Lee Atwater. Bush himself was a veteran of two presidential campaigns, and beneath his patrician manner and old-school affability was a shrewd politician. The vice president and his staff devised a campaign strategy that possessed the merit of simplicity as well as effectiveness. To counteract Bush's weaknesses, they would create weaknesses for Dukakis. Since Bush had no developed agenda, other than becoming president and continuing the Reagan era of prosperity, they decided to wage a campaign on the character and values of the candidates, concentrating on a victory rather than a mandate.

Bush presented two faces to the public. On the one hand, there was the reassuring and comfortable Bush who stood foursquare for traditional American values. This Bush, in campaign appearances and television commercials, demonstrated his sympathy with the aspirations and concerns of ordinary Americans. He extolled the family and the old moral code. He spoke of love of country and flag. He expressed his hatred of criminals and called for the death penalty for drug kingpins. He pointed with pride to his military service and called for a strong nation. He sang the praises of hard work and promised "no new taxes" that might eat away at workers' earnings. This Bush was a man of the people. On the other hand, there was the combative Bush, who aggressively attacked Dukakis for his liberalism, his membership in the American Civil Liberties Union (ACLU), and his stands on prison furloughs and school recitation of the Pledge of Allegiance. This Bush simultaneously exposed Dukakis as a man out of touch with popular opinion and proved himself tough enough for the presidency.

Governor Dukakis and his associates never developed an effective response to the Bush strategy. The politics of character became a trap for a man who either would not or could not fight Bush on Bush's terms. For most of the campaign, Dukakis dared not embrace liberalism for fear of alienating voters, while at the same time he refused to renounce his own political roots. Instead, he waffled, vainly attempting to regain the initiative he had lost to Bush. Only at the end of the campaign did Dukakis acknowledge his pride in liberalism, and by then it was too late.

Steadily over the summer and into the fall, Bush ate into Dukakis's lead and built his own. Only one misstep marred Bush's progress. His choice of Senator J. Danforth Quayle of Indiana as his running mate caused controversy. Dan Quayle was perceived as dull and inexperienced. The senator's military record came under fire, as it was charged that he had used his wealthy family's influence to win a slot in the National Guard and avoid the draft during the Vietnam War. Bush defended his running mate and refused to drop him. This liability, however, was more than made up for by the assistance of President Reagan, who cam-

paigned energetically for Bush. In the end, Bush won a commanding victory, defeating Dukakis in the popular vote by a margin of 54 percent to 46 percent and in the electoral college by 426 votes to 111.

Into the White House

George Bush entered the presidency determined to make the office his own. He and Barbara Bush brought a simpler, more easygoing style to the White House after the opulence of the Reagan years. On their first day of residence, they personally welcomed tourists to their new home. Bush made a point of playing ball with his grandchildren on the White House lawn. In an act symbolizing his independence, Bush removed the portrait of Calvin Coolidge that Ronald Reagan had placed in the Cabinet Room and replaced it with one of Theodore Roosevelt, an aristocratic statesman who served as an inspiration for the new president.

Bush filled his administration with old friends and experienced Washington operators. James A. Baker III became secretary of state. Another close associate, Nicholas Brady, became secretary of the treasury. Brent Scowcroft, who had served Gerald Ford as National Security Adviser, returned to the same post for Bush. Other familiar faces in the cabinet included Elizabeth Dole, the wife of Bush's rival in the primaries, and former congressman Jack Kemp. Bush nominated a former senator from Texas, John Tower, for the position of secretary of defense. Despite Tower's many years in the Senate and acknowledged expertise in defense matters, the nomination came under heavy attack because of Tower's alleged drinking, womanizing, and financial ties to defense contractors. Bush loyally defended his nominee, but the Senate Armed Services Committee rejected Tower. The president responded by successfully nominating Congressman Dick Cheney, a widely respected legislator and another veteran of the Ford administration.

The fight over the Tower nomination signaled that the brief honeymoon was over between Bush and the Democrats, who controlled both houses of Congress. At his inauguration, Bush called for a renewal of bipartisanship. Early in his presidency, Bush took steps to distance his administration from the ideologically confrontational style of his predecessor. He wanted to find moderate ground with Congress, on which a consensus could be built, but Bush was swimming against the tide. The intense partisan political warfare that had accompanied the Reagan Revolution continued unabated. Both parties had their grievances and martyrs. The Republicans remembered the liberal assault on Reagan's unsuccessful Supreme Court nominee Robert Bork, an event which had transformed the unfortunate judge's surname into a verb. The Democrats remembered the ruthlessness of Bush's presidential campaign. In addition, 1989 was a traumatic year for the Democratic House leadership. Majority Whip Tony Coelho resigned after being accused of financial irregularities in the purchase of a $100,000 junk bond. Jim Wright, the Speaker of the House, was also forced into retirement after being found guilty of violating House ethics rules. Republican Representative Newt Gingrich, who had orchestrated the campaign against Speaker Wright, soon found himself in turn the subject of an ethics investigation.

Thus the vicious edge to Washington politics, which would persist through the 1990's, was solidly in place as Bush took office. His hopes for bipartisanship withered in this poisoned atmosphere. Bush's relations with Congress would be rocky throughout his presidency. The president would watch cherished pieces of legislation, such as a reduction in the capital gains tax, die inglorious deaths at the hands of Capitol Hill Democrats. For his part, he stymied the legislative program of the Democrats through what the press termed the "veto strategy," exercising his veto power forty-four times. The result was gridlock and a growing sense that change was needed if pressing national business was to be addressed.

Domestic Initiatives

As Ronald Reagan's legatee, and without a clear mandate of his own, Bush pursued no Rooseveltian Hundred Days early in his presidency. His native caution, a conservative distrust of "big government," and a growing sensitivity to the budget deficit all helped preclude sweeping legislative gestures. When the president talked of a "thousand points of light" revitalizing American life, he was referring to private initiatives. Many, in both parties, criticized Bush for lacking a coherent program for his administration; the "vision thing" plagued Bush throughout his term. He repeatedly emphasized his conservative stance on taxes, trade, and government regulation, but Bush never found the rhetorical magic that had invigorated the Reagan presidency. He wanted his actions to speak for him. Ultimately this proved inadequate, and many Americans became convinced that Bush was not interested in domestic policy.

Despite this public perception, Bush's domestic record was not devoid of accomplishment. Soon after taking office, he proposed a plan to save the savings and loan industry, which had come to the brink of collapse as a result of bad loans made during the halcyon days of deregulation during the 1980's. Bush sponsored proposals to increase federal aid for child care and education. He professed a desire to be known as the "education president" and worked to focus attention on American schools. After sparring with Congress, Bush signed a bill raising the minimum wage to $4.25 and creating a special training wage for younger workers. He disappointed some conservative backers by forbidding the importation of certain types of automatic weapons favored by drug dealers. He also ended the Reagan administration's expansion of the military, cutting spending on defense as the dangers of the Cold

War receded. Two of the most significant pieces of legislation enacted with Bush's support were the Americans with Disabilities Act, which enforced new protections for citizens living with a wide range of disabilities, and the Clean Air Act, which set vigorous new standards on emissions from automobiles, utilities, and industrial plants.

Winds of Change

George Bush's greatest achievements would come in the realm of foreign policy. He successfully presided over the end of the Cold War, and inaugurated the era when the United States stood alone as the world's sole superpower. If Bush did not launch the New World Order that he proclaimed in more expansive moments, he helped shape a period of extraordinary ferment and left America more secure than it had been in over half a century.

Bush brought a distinctive style to his diplomacy. Long an assiduous networker, and famous in Washington for his Christmas card list, he cultivated strong personal ties to other world leaders. Through summits and frequent phone calls, he created bonds of trust and respect in foreign capitals that would serve American interests well in times of crisis. One of the most consequential relationships Bush developed was that with Mikhail Gorbachev.

In the first months of his presidency, Bush proceeded very cautiously in dealing with the Soviet Union. He was waiting for the completion of a policy review before taking a definitive stand on Gorbachev's efforts to reform Soviet society. Within the administration, opinion was divided between those who believed that Gorbachev was merely attempting to retool the Soviet Union for more effective competition with the United States and those who were

Crews from East and West Germany help tear down part of the Berlin Wall in November, 1989. *(Robert McClenaghan)*

convinced that he was genuinely trying to create a more open polity. In the summer of 1989 Bush put an end to this period of irresolution and began making overtures to Gorbachev. He invited the Soviet leader to a summit on Malta, which proved enormously important in forging an active partnership between the two leaders. Support of Gorbachev now became the heart of Bush's strategy for winding down the Cold War. He labored to bolster the Soviet leader against the possibility of a coup by his many internal opponents. He assured Gorbachev that the United States would not take advantage of the growing troubles within the Soviet empire. This made it easier for Gorbachev to acquiesce to the rapid collapse of the communist regimes in Eastern Europe.

First in Poland and Hungary, then in Czechoslovakia and Bulgaria, communist officials were forced to give way to newly invigorated democratic movements. Revolution came violently to Romania in December, culminating in the televised execution of the former dictator Nicolae Ceausescu and his wife on Christmas Day. The most remarkable scenes of change came in East Germany. On November 9 the East German government, reeling from internal protests, opened the Berlin Wall. The breaching of this symbol of communist tyranny electrified the world. Young Germans from both sides of the divide celebrated atop what became merely an obsolescent stretch of concrete. The dissolution of the East German state followed in short order. Sustained diplomacy by Bush and James Baker persuaded Gorbachev to accept the reunification of Germany, and its membership in the North Atlantic Treaty Organization (NATO). In return, Bush counseled moderation to the victorious democrats in former Soviet satellite states. He initially refused to recognize Lithuania's declaration of independence from the Soviet Union, fearing that the Baltic republic's attempt at succession might undermine Gorbachev's position.

Bush received scathing criticism for his refusal to back the Lithuanians. He defended his stand by arguing that he was acting in the best interests of the United States, and that he was adjusting his policy to the "overall relationship" with the Soviet Union. Bush found himself making the same sort of case regarding China. As a former envoy to China, Bush was deeply committed to the policy of improving relations with Beijing. He believed closer ties between the United States and China would promote international security. He also was deeply interested in encouraging Sino-American trade, convinced that it would provide jobs in America and prepare the way for democracy in China. Unfortunately the growing friendliness between the American and Chinese governments was brought into question on June 4, 1989, when Chinese authorities used force to disperse prodemocracy demonstrators in Tiananmen Square. Hundreds, and possibly thousands, of the demonstrators were killed. In the wake of this massacre, many more dissidents were rounded up and imprisoned. President Bush joined in the international condemnation of this brutal repression, but he refused to impose significant sanctions on the Chinese regime, despite an outcry for strong measures from Capitol Hill. Bush held that American relations with China were too important to be sacrificed to a moment of outrage. He secretly sent Brent Scowcroft and Deputy Secretary of State Lawrence Eagleburger to Beijing to explain American concerns and to urge an end to the crackdown on dissent. In coming years, Bush would successfully lobby Congress to grant China most-favored-nation (MFN) trade status.

Change came to other parts of the world as well. In 1989 F. W. de Klerk became prime minister of South Africa. De Klerk soon freed Nelson Mandela, the leader of the African National Congress (ANC). President Bush met with both De Klerk and Mandela, and supported sanctions against South Africa until

Graffiti in Panama City in January, 1990, following the U.S. invasion to overthrow General Manuel Noriega. (*Reuters/Santiago Lyon/Archive Photos*)

apartheid, its system of racial separation, was abolished. In 1991, with reform well under way, Bush lifted these sanctions. With American encouragement, Augusto Pinochet, the right-wing dictator of Chile, stepped aside in 1989, to be replaced by an elected government. In Nicaragua, Bush abandoned efforts to bring down the Sandinista government through the Contras' armed insurrection. Instead he worked for a political solution to the Nicaraguan problem and was rewarded in 1990 when an anti-Sandinista coalition won an upset victory in free elections. In neighboring El Salvador, patient diplomacy finally bore fruit, and in 1992 a guerilla war which had raged for twelve years came to an end. The government and the guerillas agreed to a package of reforms and made the commitment to resolve future difficulties through the ballot box.

Bush used less peaceful means to overthrow Manuel Noriega, the dictatorial ruler of Pan-

ama. Noriega had once been on the CIA's payroll, but by the late 1980's he had shifted his fealty from the United States to the Medellín drug cartel. He was wanted in the United States on charges of drug trafficking, gun running, and money laundering. His increasingly reckless behavior culminated in an incident in which an American soldier from the Canal Zone was killed. Noriega compounded crime with folly by threatening further actions against Americans. On December 20, 1989, Bush responded by invading Panama with twenty-five thousand troops. The Americans made short work of Noriega's forces and, after a manhunt, captured the former strongman and carried him off for trial in Miami. Twenty-three Americans died. Some five hundred Panamanians, many of them civilians, also perished. The invasion proved to be overwhelmingly popular in the United States, and even most Panamanians welcomed the Americans as liberators.

The Gulf War

Throughout the Iraq-Iran war that raged from 1980 to 1988, the United States tilted toward Iraq as a bulwark against the revolutionary Islamic fundamentalism of Iran. The American government provided the Iraqi dictator Saddam Hussein with valuable intelligence and military hardware. Even after Hussein made peace with Iran, American policymakers continued to regard Iraq as a force for stability in the Middle East. They failed to weigh adequately Hussein's well-known brutality, his militarism, and his growing economic desperation. Hence the Bush administration was taken by surprise when, on August 2, 1990, Iraqi forces invaded and occupied the neighboring principality of Kuwait, a tiny state richly endowed with oil. By taking Kuwait, Hussein was making a bold bid for international influence. His army, the fourth largest in the world, now sat poised to strike at Saudi Arabian oil fields that comprised 20 percent of the world's oil reserves.

President Bush refused to accept the Iraqi aggression as a fait accompli. He immediately began arranging a vigorous response. Within a week of the fall of Kuwait, Bush had ordered 100,000 American troops and a fleet of warplanes to Saudi Arabia, to defend the desert kingdom against any further adventuring by Saddam Hussein. He persuaded the United Nations Security Council to demand an Iraqi withdrawal from Kuwait. The Security Council imposed severe economic sanctions on Iraq as a means of pressuring the Iraqis to comply. Here Bush's patient diplomacy with China and the Soviet Union paid off handsomely. Neither former Cold War rival stood in Bush's way as

Men and women of the 608th Ordinance Company in Saudi Arabia as part of the protective Operation Desert Shield in August, 1990. *(Reuters/Faith Saribas/Archive Photos)*

he rallied international opinion against Saddam Hussein. The Soviets in particular proved cooperative. Bush met with Gorbachev in Helsinki, Finland, on September 9 to discuss Kuwait. Though the Soviets would later express deep reservations about the American military effort, Gorbachev never broke ranks on the fundamental principle that Iraq had to leave Kuwait.

Bush early on became convinced that Hussein's army would have to be ejected from Kuwait by force. He began building a grand alliance of nations committed to the liberation of Kuwait. By the time Bush was through, military units from twenty-seven countries were part of the coalition force gathering in Saudi Arabia. Other nations, including Germany and Japan, pledged financial support. In November, Bush ordered American commanders to begin planning an offensive to drive back the Iraqis. The United Nations set January 15, 1991, as a deadline for Saddam Hussein to pull his forces from Kuwait. At home, Bush faced a debate over war powers. He believed that he had the authority to launch a military offensive against Iraq. Many in Congress disputed this. A number of Democrats on Capitol Hill were convinced that the president was moving too precipitously and not giving economic sanctions enough time to work. In the end, Bush asked Congress for a resolution authorizing military action in the Persian Gulf, if necessary. The resolution passed on January 12, by a comfortable margin in the House and much more narrowly in the Senate.

Last-minute talks with Hussein's envoys failed to resolve the crisis. The January 15 deadline passed with no movement by the Iraqis. On January 16, President Bush ordered Operation Desert Storm to begin. For five weeks, Allied forces pounded the Iraqis from the air, unleashing a devastating arsenal of high-tech, precision weaponry. On February 23, General Norman Schwarzkopf ordered a ground assault. He commanded 700,000 troops, nearly 500,000 of them Americans; 200,000 of these wheeled in a great armored arc to trap and crush retreating Iraqi formations. Within four days, Kuwait had been cleared of the Iraqi invaders. As the punishment Allied forces were inflicting on the retreating Iraqis began to look like a massacre, Bush ordered an end to the war.

The Persian Gulf War was a personal triumph for George Bush. Through diplomatic skill, he had overcome a number of obstacles and struck a mighty blow for the forces of international order. Only 128 American lives were lost in battle. Iraqi casualties numbered in the tens of thousands. Critics called the victory hollow, because Saddam Hussein remained in power and even was able to crush uprisings by Shiite Muslims in the south and Kurds in the north. Bush answered by arguing that the coalition forces had no mandate to invade Iraq, and that a crusade against the Iraqi dictator would have led Americans into a bloody quagmire. He fenced in what was left of Hussein's military machine with no-fly zones in the north and south of Iraq and created a refuge for the Kurds in the north. Bush also took advantage of the momentum created by the Gulf War to encourage a peace conference between Israel and its Arab neighbors. Months of negotiating resulted in formal talks in the fall of 1991, and the beginning of a peace process.

A Time of Troubles

In the immediate aftermath of the Gulf War, President Bush enjoyed unprecedented popularity. But his poll numbers soon began to falter, as Americans focused on domestic problems. In the fall of 1990, the economy slipped into a recession. Bush was slow to acknowledge the turnaround in the economy, and when he did take steps to combat the recession, these were seen as too little, too late. The nation's economic woes focused attention on the continuing burden of the budget deficit. Facing acrimonious budget negotiations with congressional leaders, Bush decided to accept a compromise deficit reduction plan that included some tax increases. In the short run, the legislation failed to revive the economy. This and the fact that Bush had reneged on his promise to never raise taxes infuriated conservative Republicans.

In 1990, Bush had easily replaced retiring Supreme Court justice William Brennan with David Souter, a little known federal judge from New Hampshire. The retirement of the legendary African American jurist Thurgood Marshall in 1991 presented Bush with a more delicate political problem. He responded by nominating Clarence Thomas, a conservative African American judge who had headed Ronald Reagan's Equal Opportunity Commission. The Thomas nomination precipitated an unexpected political firestorm when a former employee of Thomas's named Anita Hill charged that he had sexually harassed her in the early 1980's. Bush stood behind Thomas, who won a narrow confirmation, but the ugly dispute between Thomas and Hill aggravated the polarization of American politics and created the impression that Bush was insensitive to the concerns of women. In 1990, Bush had vetoed a bill making it easier for women and minorities to sue employers for discrimination. In the wake of the Thomas scandal, he signed a new version of the bill, but this gesture failed to mollify his critics and further disgusted conservatives.

At the end of July, 1991, Bush and Mikhail Gorbachev met in Washington to sign a treaty formalizing steep reductions in American and Soviet stockpiles of nuclear weapons. A few weeks later, on August 19, Gorbachev was deposed in a coup organized by Soviet leaders frightened by his reforms. Bush initially reacted cautiously to the news. However, once it became clear that Boris Yeltsin, the president of the Russian Federation, was successfully resisting the coup, Bush began to rally international support for the charismatic Russian

leader. The coup attempt collapsed, and Gorbachev briefly returned to office, but his authority had become a shadow. Real power now lay with Yeltsin, who decided to liquidate the Soviet Union in December, 1991, replacing it with a new Commonwealth of Independent States. Bush moved quickly to build a relationship with Yeltsin, arranging financial assistance for the new regime, and signing an agreement calling for even deeper cuts in their nuclear arsenals.

The Election of 1992

In the fall of 1991, Bush pondered retirement. He was beginning to suffer from some minor ailments and was clearly tired. In the end, though, the allure of the presidency was too much, and Bush decided to grasp at the brass ring of a second term. Despite his decision to run, it quickly became clear that Bush had lost the fire of 1988. His political advisers urged Bush to launch his campaign in 1991, but he put them off until 1992. When he did at last organize his reelection effort, it displayed little of the energy and skill that had won him the presidency. Key members of his earlier team were gone. Lee Atwater had died, and James Baker was still at the State Department.

The economy continued to bedevil the president. Though it slowly began to pick up speed in 1992, the public remained more impressed with its weaknesses than its strengths. Bush devoted more time to economic issues, but he never found an economic program that sparked enthusiasm with voters. Characteristically, Bush's most significant economic initiative to stimulate the economy was an effort to encourage free trade agreements around the world. The most enduring result of this push was the North American Free Trade Agreement (NAFTA) with Canada and Mexico.

Bush faced a challenge from the right during the primary season. Patrick Buchanan, a conservative political commentator, rallied Republicans dissatisfied with Bush's lapses from Reaganite orthodoxy. Buchanan also expressed a populist distrust of big business and free trade that played well to voters concerned about their jobs. Though Buchanan never posed a serious threat to Bush's renomination, his presence in the race embarrassed the president and forced him to the right at a time when he needed to be reassuring moderate swing voters.

The Democrats nominated Governor William Jefferson Clinton of Arkansas. Bill Clinton skillfully positioned himself as a moderate and hammered away at the importance of the economy. A relatively youthful man and an exuberant campaigner, Clinton promised renewed energy and purpose for government at a time when Americans recognized themselves to be at a historical crossroads. The race between Bush and Clinton became a three-way contest when H. Ross Perot, an eccentric Texas businessman and billionaire, threw his hat into the ring. Amply funded by his immense fortune, Perot ran as a populist, capitalizing on popular distrust of the major parties by offering "commonsense" solutions to America's problems.

Bush searched in vain for an effective message to take to the people. He returned to the tactics of 1988, raising questions about Governor Clinton's character and attacking him for his equivocal behavior in avoiding the draft during the Vietnam War. The Clinton team responded energetically, raising questions about the Iran-Contra scandal. In the end, Bush's attempt to resurrect the politics of character failed. The American people were looking for new directions, and George Bush had none to offer. Clinton handily won the election, taking 43 percent of the vote to Bush's 38 percent and Perot's 19 percent.

President Bush's last months in office were busy. He launched air raids against a recalcitrant Saddam Hussein and sent thirty thousand American troops to assist famine relief in Somalia. He worked hard to ensure a smooth transfer of authority to the new administration. The transition from George Bush to Bill Clinton was widely seen as symbolic, a passing of power, and mission, from one generation to the next. Bush had ably ended the Cold War. Younger hands would guide America to the millennium. Bush retired to his homes in Houston and Kennebunkport. He devoted himself to his family and watched with pride as his sons George W. Bush and Jeb Bush continued the Bush tradition of public service.

Daniel P. Murphy

Bibliographical References

Bush's campaign autobiography, *Looking Forward: The George Bush Story* (1987), written with Victor Gold, remains useful. Herbert Parmet, *George Bush: The Life of a Lonestar Yankee*, 1997, is the only full biography of Bush. David Mervin, *George Bush and the Guardianship Presidency*, 1996, is an analytical study by a British academic. *The Bush Presidency*, 1997, edited by Kenneth Thompson, offers reminiscences by members of Bush's administration. George Bush and Brent Scowcroft, *A World Transformed*, 1998, offers insight into Bush's foreign policy. Michael Beschloss and Strobe Talbot, *At the Highest Levels*, 1993, focuses on Bush's relationship with Mikhail Gorbachev.

Bill Clinton

42d President, 1993-

Born: August 19, 1946
        Hope, Arkansas

Political Party: Democratic
Vice President: Al Gore, Jr.

Cabinet Members

Secretary of State: Warren Christopher, Madeleine Albright
Secretary of the Treasury: Lloyd Bentsen, Robert E. Rubin, Lawrence H. Summers
Secretary of Defense: Les Aspin, William J. Perry, William Cohen

Secretary of the Interior: Bruce Babbitt
Attorney General: Janet Reno
Secretary of Agriculture: Mike Espy, Dan Glickman
Secretary of Commerce: Ron Brown, Mickey Kantor, William Daley
Secretary of Labor: Robert B. Reich, Alexis Herman
Secretary of Health and Human Services: Donna Shalala
Secretary of Housing and Urban Development: Henry Cisneros, Andrew Cuomo
Secretary of Transportation: Federico Peña, Rodney Slater
Secretary of Energy: Hazel O'Leary, Federico Peña, Bill Richardson
Secretary of Education: Richard E. Riley
Secretary of Veterans Affairs: Jesse Brown, Togo D. West. Jr.

Bill Clinton. *(Library of Congress)*

William Jefferson "Bill" Clinton was born in Hope, Arkansas, on August 19, 1946. He was the son of Virginia Cassidy, a nurse, and William Jefferson Blythe III, an automobile parts salesman. Bill Clinton never knew his father. His parents, who married in Shreveport, Louisiana, in 1941, were forced to live apart during most of World War II, while Clinton's father was in the military service. On his return from the war, the best job available to him was in Chicago, so he moved there, coming to Arkansas as frequently as he could to visit his wife.

On one of these trips home, William Blythe, driving through a heavy rainstorm in Missouri, had a blowout, crashed his car into a ditch, and died. Three months later, his son was born. Virginia named the baby William Jefferson Blythe IV, after his dead father. In need of providing for herself and her infant son, Virginia, a plucky woman, set out to improve her credentials by going to New Orleans to prepare herself as a nurse-anesthetist.

Billy, as he was called, was left with his maternal grandparents in Hope. Although they were not well educated, his grandparents valued education very highly. They taught their grandson to read and to count at a very early age. By the time he was six, he was able to read the newspaper with a high degree of comprehension.

Early Years

Clinton left his grandparents' house when he was seven. His mother, finished with her training in New Orleans, returned to Arkansas, where she married Roger Clinton who, like her first husband, was a car salesman. She moved to Hot Springs, Arkansas, taking her young son with her. He attended elementary school in Hot Springs, where he was known as Bill Clinton rather than Billy Blythe. He used the name Clinton but did not change it legally until he was in his teens. He attended public schools save for two years between ages seven and nine when, despite coming from a Southern Baptist family, he was a student in a Roman Catholic elementary school.

Clinton was a precocious youth. He loved learning and was so eager a student that he once received a D grade in deportment because the nun who was his teacher believed that he did not give other students an opportunity to respond to questions. If he knew the answers, as he usually did, he blurted them out.

Life at home was far from ideal. Roger Clinton, although basically a kind and caring man, drank too much. When he was intoxicated, he sometimes struck his wife or Roger, Jr., the child he and Virginia had when Bill was ten years old. In fact, the elder Roger was so out of control at one point that he fired a gun in the house.

By the time he was fourteen, Bill had lost patience with his stepfather's antics. When Roger, quite drunk, began upbraiding his wife and younger son, Bill took control of the situation, stepping between his stepfather and his mother, warning Roger Clinton never to hit her or Roger, Jr., again. He told his stepfather that if he wanted to do anything to them, he would have to get past him first. Although Virginia and Roger Clinton separated several times, they always reunited.

The Emergence of a Leader

People soon began to recognize that Bill Clinton had a palpable charisma that made him a natural leader. He had been elected president of his junior high school class. He was a leader in his school's band and played the saxophone in a three-member group that called itself the Three Blind Mice. His involvement in extracurricular activities did not diminish his scholastic achievement. He was a finalist for a National Merit Scholarship and graduated fourth in his high school class of 323 students.

When he was seventeen, Clinton attended Boys' State, a camp where outstanding students learned about the political process. At camp, he was elected to go to Boys' Nation in Washington, D.C., as a delegate from Arkansas. This trip was perhaps the most crucial one Clinton would ever take. The young Arkansas delegate met and shook the hand of President John F. Kennedy, who had long been one of Clinton's heroes and was a distinct role model for the young man. The trip to Washington convinced the young Clinton that a life of public service was the life he wanted for himself.

Upon being graduated from high school, Clinton won a scholarship to study music in Arkansas. He opted instead, however, to go to Washington, D.C., to attend Georgetown University as an international affairs major, even though this decision placed a great financial strain upon him. Georgetown, with its cosmopolitan and multiethnic student body and politically savvy professors, opened new worlds to Clinton. Staying in school was not easy for him because of the expense, but he was determined to complete his studies at Georgetown no matter what sacrifices doing so involved on his part.

Initial Involvement in Politics

Faced with the necessity of earning money to stay in school, Clinton found part-time jobs to pay some of his college expenses. One summer, he returned to Arkansas to work for Frank Holt, who was then running for governor. Although Holt lost the election, Clinton's involvement in his campaign paid dividends for him. Holt's nephew, a justice in the Arkansas Supreme Court, recommended Clinton to Arkansas senator J. William Fulbright, who hired him to work part time in his Washington office. His work outside the university in no way impeded Clinton from being a fully involved student on campus. He was elected president of both the freshman and the sophomore classes at Georgetown, where his fellow students recognized his extraordinary devotion to his studies and appreciated his political acumen.

In 1967, while Clinton was still a student at Georgetown, Roger Clinton, Sr., became seriously ill with cancer and was obviously dying. Bill was eager to let his stepfather know that despite their differences he valued and loved him. He drove the four hours to Duke Medical Center in Durham, North Carolina, where his stepfather was being treated, every weekend until Roger died. Clinton had never quite come to grips with the loss of his own father, who died at the age of twenty-one. Now he again faced the death of someone he loved. Life in his eyes became a very uncertain affair. He became increasingly aware of his own mortality and was forced to the realization that he should do as much as he could as soon as he could.

Clinton impressed some of his Georgetown professors sufficiently that they urged him to apply for a Rhodes Scholarship, which would, following graduation, enable him to spend two years studying at Oxford University in England. Clinton held little hope of receiving this award, one of the most competitive and prestigious available to new college graduates. Despite his apprehensions, he applied and, much to his astonishment, was appointed a Rhodes Scholar.

The Oxford Experience

Completing his studies at Georgetown in 1968, Clinton soon set out for England where, for the first time in his life, he could devote his full attention to his studies. The Rhodes Scholarship covered all of his expenses, making it unnecessary for him to earn money to support himself and pay his tuition. Clinton found himself in a whole new world at Oxford. He had time to explore his huge diversity of interests. He read a book almost every day, rejoicing in the opportunity that had been afforded him. He found the pace at Oxford much more relaxed than at Georgetown, but he drove himself to accomplish as much as possible while he was there.

While Clinton was studying at Oxford, storm clouds were gathering at home. The United States, in an attempt to halt the spread of communism is southeast Asia, was waging war in Vietnam. The war was an extremely controversial and generally unpopular one. Many American youths refused to fight in it, some defecting to Canada to avoid being drafted into the United States military services. Those who refused to serve were placed in great legal jeopardy. Clinton was not in any immediate danger of being drafted because

First Lady Hillary Rodham Clinton addresses the 1996 Democratic National Convention in Chicago. *(Reuters/Luc Novovitch/Archive Photos)*

a doctorate. Such a course, however, did not coincide with his long-term plans to enter politics. He realized that the best entrée into a political career was a law degree. He applied and was admitted to the Yale University Law School, a number of whose professors had been in government service during the Kennedy presidency.

Early in his days at Yale, Clinton was smitten by a fellow classmate, Hillary Rodham, but he was too diffident to approach her and introduce himself. Rather, he stared at her in class until one day she approached him and announced that if he was going to keep staring at her, she was going to keep staring back. She told him her name, and the two became fast friends. Clinton soon considered Rodham the brightest person he had ever known. The two were inseparable. They both took leaves of absence from Yale to work in the 1972 presidential campaign of Democrat George McGovern, who was soundly defeated by Richard M. Nixon, the Republican candidate.

Upon graduating from Yale, both Bill Clinton and Hillary Rodham were offered jobs in Washington, D.C., to work on the staff of the House Judiciary Committee that was investigating Nixon's possible involvement in what soon came to be known as the Watergate scandal, an event that led to Nixon's resignation to avoid an impeachment that would surely have forced him out of office. Rodham accepted the job that was proffered, but Clinton wanted instead to return to his home state, Arkansas, and enter the political arena there.

he had a student deferment that would be good until he completed his studies.

Upon carefully considering the validity of the war, Clinton concluded that it was an unjust conflict. He helped to organize protests against the Vietnam War during his stay in Britain, an act that would come back to haunt him as his political career moved into the national arena. When his student deferment finally expired, Clinton took his chances in the draft lottery, in which the birth dates of eligible young men were drawn at random. Clinton's birth date was low on the list of those to be drafted, so he had little risk of being called for military service in a war that he strenuously opposed.

Attending Yale Law School
At the end of his second year at Oxford, Clinton could have stayed on and continued work for

The Return to Arkansas
Many people would have considered Clinton's rejection of the offer to work on the House

Judiciary Committee shortsighted or downright foolish. In returning to Arkansas, he was going back to one of the poorest, least progressive states in the country. Perhaps his work with Senator Fulbright during his years at Georgetown had inspired him to attempt to build on the liberal, progressive outlook of this notable senator. Clinton, upon relocating in Arkansas, set as his primary goal the task of bringing a new prosperity to his state.

Learning that the University of Arkansas at Fayetteville needed another law professor, Clinton applied for the job. He was still a few months shy of his twenty-ninth birthday, and his application was not taken seriously by the dean of the law school, who thought he was too young for the job. Clinton, learning of this, informed the dean that he had been too young for everything he ever tried to do. The dean was persuaded and hired the young applicant. Clinton moved to Fayetteville, a sleepy town in the Ozark Mountains, where he could have settled into an unhurried and uncomplicated life had it been his wish to do so.

Obviously, Clinton was not looking for an easy, unhurried life. Three months into his first year of teaching, he filed to run for a seat in Congress against the popular Republican John Hammerschmidt, who had the advantages of incumbency and name recognition. Few Arkansans had any idea who Bill Clinton was. This anonymity, however, was short-lived: Clinton got into his car and drove all over the state, speaking to any group he could find. He made such a favorable impression that he came within a hair's breadth of winning; Hammerschmidt commanded only 51.5 percent of the vote. Clinton did not anticipate winning the election. Rather, he wanted to see how well he could do considering the many disadvantages he had to overcome. By the beginning of 1975, Arkansans were referring to Clinton as a boy wonder who could transform Arkansas politics in time.

Early in his campaign, Hillary Rodham came to Arkansas to take a job at the University of Arkansas Law School. Her chief reason for leaving Washington, however, was to run Clinton's campaign, which she did with unswerving dedication and impressive intelligence. Although a Yankee in a southern state, she soon came to understand the people of Arkansas and to realize what it would take to win them over to Clinton and his often-heterodox positions. Clinton was far from being the "good old boy" type of southern politician that had held sway for many years in much of the South.

Once the campaign was over, Rodham expressed doubts about remaining in Arkansas. She had said that she liked a house in Fayetteville that she and Clinton had sometimes passed on their daily walks. Clinton, not wanting her to leave the state, bought the house. Before the ink was dry on the contract, he told Rodham what he had done, saying that now she had to stay and marry him. Shocked at first by his impetuousness, Rodham stayed in Arkansas and within two months became Clinton's wife.

Winning Elective Office

The year after he was defeated in his bid for Congress, Clinton, who had impressed the electorate with his near victory in the race against Hammerschmidt, ran for the office of Arkansas attorney general. By this time, he had gained sufficient popularity that Republicans, acknowledging his invincibility, did not nominate anyone to run against him. Clinton, therefore, won his first elective office with a resounding victory, garnering nearly all the votes.

As attorney general, Clinton was tireless in pursuing controversial issues that many politicians would have avoided. His doggedness and incredibly sound preparation for cases that he had to take before the court attracted the attention of influential politicians throughout the state. In 1978, they nominated him to run for governor, a position that he won handily. At age thirty-two, he was the youngest governor in the United States, a fact that was not lost on political mavens in Washington. It now appeared to many that Clinton was presidential material.

First Term as Governor

At the time, Arkansas governors did not have the usual four years in which to prove themselves; they served a two-year term. Clinton had a concrete vision of what he wished to achieve as governor. High on his list of priorities was the reform of public education in his state, which ranked close to the bottom on all national measurements of educational excellence. Clinton was convinced that the people of Arkansas were as bright as people in any other state, but that Arkansas students did not perform well on national tests because the state was not putting enough money into education.

He proposed hiring more teachers and increasing their salaries, at that time among the lowest in the United States. Linked to this proposal was one, threatening to many of his constituents, that all new teachers would have to pass competency tests to assure that those who were hired were capable of doing the job. Even more threatening was his proposal to consolidate many of the state's 382 school districts into more manageable and efficient entities. Doing so would improve the resources of many districts, but to combine four existing districts into one consolidated district would necessarily leave three superintendents out of a job. School administrators across the state balked at Clinton's proposals, and the state legislature declined to approve his budget for hiring more teachers and increasing teacher salaries.

Clinton also embarked on a much-needed road building program, raising money to finance it by increasing license fees on motor vehicles. This measure was highly unpopular with most citizens. Despite public resistance to many of Clinton's policies, however, it appeared that he would surely be elected for a second term when he ran in 1980. Much to his surprise and that of many Arkansans, the victory went not to Clinton but to his opponent, Frank White, who won by a narrow margin.

Lessons Learned from Defeat

Losing the election left Clinton somewhat dismayed and, for a time, disheartened. Never one to give up when times were difficult, he was determined to continue his political career. Many people in his situation would have abandoned all thoughts of a continuing political life, but Clinton's devotion to public service was sufficiently great to make him reassess what he was doing and to use his defeat as a learning opportunity.

As he thought through his two years as governor, he realized that he had tried to do too much too soon. He knew what he wanted to accomplish and had a solid vision of how to reach those ends. What he had failed to do was keep his constituency informed about the measures he wished to enact. He knew that he had to run again for public office but that before he could do so, he had to meet as many voters as possible. He needed to outline what he hoped to achieve but realized that it was even more important to ask questions and find out what was on the voters' minds.

It was fortunate for him that Governor White was not up to the task of running the state; he was making so many blunders that some voters referred to him as "Governor Goofy." Clinton announced his candidacy for the governorship in February, 1982, and in a humble, self-deprecating speech, told the voters that he knew he had made mistakes but that he had learned from them. He also pointed out some of the more egregious errors that Frank White had made as governor.

White also proved unequal to the task of running a successful campaign and lost to Clinton, who ran on a platform that emphasized educational reform. Clinton went even further than he had during his first term. He proposed that all teachers, those about to be hired and those who had been teaching for years, be required to pass competency tests if they were to continue teaching. The teaching profession complained loudly about this proposal, but Clinton appointed Hillary Rodham Clinton to chair a committee on educational standards, and she helped to persuade legislators and much of the citizenry that the kind of reform Clinton was proposing was much needed in the state. The legislature this time voted in favor of implementing Clinton's educational proposals. Because of a change in the law, the term of the Arkansas governor had been extended from two to four years. So with his election in 1982, he was in office until 1986, when he again won reelection.

Moving Toward the Presidency

It was clear that as he gained increasing national recognition, Clinton was viewed as someone who could win the presidency for the Democratic Party, which had been out of office since 1981. Many expected him to declare his candidacy in 1988, but he apparently considered such an early announcement premature. At the Democratic National Convention in Atlanta, Clinton was called upon to give the nominating speech for Michael Dukakis, which provided his first national presentation to a mass audience.

The speech turned out to be a disaster. The lights in the auditorium were not dimmed as they should have been. The delegates were disorderly and showed no signs of listening to Clinton's speech. Rather they chanted, "We want Mike!" Clinton's speech was much longer than it might have been. When it ended, people applauded not in approval but in relief. Talk show host Johnny Carson called Clinton a windbag, but two nights later, Clinton was on *The Tonight Show* with Carson demonstrating his quick wit, humor, and magnanimity by overlooking what Carson had said about him. He even played the saxophone. This time the audience applauded in approval.

In 1989, President George Bush appointed Clinton co-chair of a national meeting of governors to discuss educational matters. This appointment again thrust the young governor before the national eye and added greatly to his image.

A Fifth Term as Governor

In 1990, now quite secure in his position as governor, Clinton ran for his fifth term. Many voters were concerned that he would serve half his term and then resign to run for the presidency. Clinton assured them that he anticipated completing his term, which would end in 1994.

He was, nevertheless, engaging in activities that seemed destined to result in his candidacy in 1992. He was named chair of the Democratic Leadership Council, a group of party leaders mostly from the South who were deeply concerned about the course their party was taking. There had not been a Democratic president for ten years, and with Bush, the incumbent, sure to run in 1992, it seemed doubtful that a Democrat could wrest the office away from the Republicans. In 1991, Bush's popularity was considerable as a result of the Allied victory in the Persian Gulf War against Iraq.

Clinton, always a persuasive speaker and now an experienced politician, convinced the delegates to the Democratic Leadership Council that a drastic shift in emphasis was needed if the Democrats were to stand any chance of regaining the presidency and of carrying Congress. His colleagues realized the wisdom of his call for change.

The Political Climate During the Reagan and Bush Administrations

Ronald Reagan began his "Teflon presidency" with a landslide in 1980. Republicans portrayed Democrats as big spenders who were for big government. Reagan promised lower taxes and smaller government. At the end of Reagan's two terms as president, George Bush was elected in 1988 by repeating Reagan's promises.

Asked about raising taxes, Bush mouthed the famous words, "Read my lips. No new taxes." By 1991, however, this proved to be a promise on which Bush could not deliver. Bush had indeed cut taxes, but he did so mostly for the well-to-do, following the trickle-down policy that Reagan had articulated but that many voters had come to view with cynicism and contempt.

The time was ripe for someone to bring about the kind of changes for which many voters were calling. Whereas Bush in 1992 was linked in people's minds with the eastern establishment and big business, Clinton positioned himself as the populist candidate, almost a log cabin underdog who had risen to prominence through his own hard-won achievements.

The Decision to Run

During 1991, Clinton ventured away from Arkansas to make speeches and to confer with party leaders. He continually denied rumors that he was about to announce his candidacy for the presidency. In July, however, he admitted that he was considering a run for the nation's highest office. Many Arkansans were incensed that Clinton, who had promised to serve out his term, was doing exactly what they had feared. In typical Clinton style, the governor went out among the people asking that they release him from his promise because, in the long run, he told them, he would serve both Arkansas and the United States better as president than as governor. Most Arkansans who listened as Clinton made his case agreed.

On October 3, 1991, speaking from the Old State House in Little Rock, Arkansas, Clinton announced his intention to run for the presidency. He struck a responsive chord when he suggested that the United States, after eleven years of Republican leadership, was moving in a dangerous direction. The country, he contended, was losing its place as a major world power. He vowed that if he were elected, he would impose higher taxes on the rich, making possible lower taxes for the middle class and the poor. He proposed tax benefits for people who invested in ways to create jobs and resolve the unemployment problem.

Under the Reagan-Bush administrations, the nation had taken in less tax money than it spent. It had built up a staggering debt of four trillion dollars by 1991. Faced with this reality, Bush was forced to renege on his promise of no new taxes, thereby giving Clinton a decided advantage. Clinton promised to work strenuously to reduce the national debt and the ruinous interest required to service that debt. He also vowed to put the Social Security and Medicare systems, both of which were facing eventual bankruptcy, on a firmer financial footing.

Dealing with Scandal

The first stop on the campaign trail for Clinton was necessarily New Hampshire, holder of the first national primaries in U.S. elections. Clinton, who was not well known in New England, was on the Democratic ballot with five other candidates including Paul Tsongas, a former senator from Massachusetts, clearly the favorite in this contest. Although Clinton did not win the primary, he finished second, which was remarkable in the light of the opposition and especially the fact that two scandals involving him came to light during the primary. When these revelations were made public, many people dismissed his chances, remembering how other politicians had been destroyed by similar allegations.

The first allegation was that Clinton, while governor of Arkansas, had been involved in a prolonged sexual affair with a woman named Gennifer Flowers. He countered these accusations by going on national television with his wife, admitting that there had been problems in their marriage, but claiming that those problems were behind them. His candor in addressing the problem satisfied both the press and the public.

The second allegation involved a letter he had written while he was a college student in an effort to avoid being drafted. When this letter came to light, he was vilified as a draft dodger. Again, Clinton approached the public and explained away the evidence that had been presented. Although these two scandals cast a pall over the campaign and raised serious questions about Clinton's moral fiber, the public was forgiving enough to give him a near victory in New Hampshire.

The 1992 Presidential Election

The Clinton campaign after New Hampshire was one of notable victories. He easily won primaries in most of the southern states, as well as in Illinois, New York, Michigan, and Pennsylvania, all states with large numbers of electoral votes. By June, he had won California, whose electoral votes combined with the others spelled a clear victory for him at the Democratic National Convention later in the summer. Clinton judiciously selected Al Gore, Jr., of Tennessee as his running mate. An expert on environmental issues and defense, Gore was viewed as someone who could run the country adequately if anything happened to Clinton.

Although the 1992 election was a race between two major candidates, George Bush and Bill Clinton, a third, independent candidate, billionaire H. Ross Perot, somewhat muddied the waters. Essentially more conservative than either front-runner, Perot posed a threat to Republicans and Democrats, both parties fearing that he would emerge as a spoiler.

Voters had qualms about Clinton because of the scandals with which he was associated, but they had greater qualms about Bush and his administration. The national economy weakened as unemployment increased, and the national debt leapfrogged to new highs. Perot capitalized on Bush's economic woes, entering the race as a practical businessman whose lack of governmental experience would be overcome by his common sense.

Perot appeared frequently on television, but when asked pointed questions about how he would deal with specific economic problems, he always hedged. He usually stated that he wished he had known that such a question was going to be asked because he had charts he could have brought that would have clarified his answer. Perot withdrew his candidacy on the last day of the Democratic National Convention, only to declare in October, shortly before the election, that he had made a mistake and to reenter the race.

Shortly before the election, Clinton, Bush, and Perot had a debate on national television. At this point, the election seemed to be anybody's race, although a Perot victory seemed doubtful. Perot had taken votes from Bush, who was more conservative than Clinton but not conservative enough for many Republicans on the far Right. Clinton performed well in the debate and emerged as the favorite.

The final tally showed Clinton with 43 percent of the popular vote, Bush with 38 percent, and Perot trailing with 19 percent. Clinton had won in thirty-two states, Bush in eighteen. On January 20, 1993, Clinton became the third youngest elected president of the United States, three years behind John F. Kennedy and slightly older than Theodore Roosevelt had been on his inauguration day in 1905. Clinton was also the first president to be born after World War II, making him a part of the baby-boom generation. The American public had spoken, and its voice called for a new era in government, a fresh start after twelve years of Republican rule.

What Clinton Promised the People

Like all candidates, Clinton had promised the American people many things that they wanted. Now, after his inauguration as president, he tried to fulfill the promises that had brought him into office. He had vowed to bolster the nation's economy, to support gun control and crime prevention, to overhaul the

Secretary of State Madeleine Albright, the first woman to hold that office. *(Reuters/Win McNamee/Archive Photos)*

health care and welfare systems, to make the federal government more efficient, and to sign the North American Free Trade Agreement (NAFTA) and other agreements that would promote U.S. trade relations with other nations, particularly Canada and Mexico.

The first two years of the Clinton administration were very active and productive ones. The president made great progress in trying to fulfill all of his major promises. The economy began to show a renewed vigor and finally to expand in ways that affected nearly all Americans. Inflation was coming under control, free enterprise seemed to be flourishing, and unemployment was decidedly declining. On February 5, 1993, Clinton signed into law the Family and Medical Leave Act, which granted employees unpaid time off for family events such as birth, adoption, and parent-teacher conferences. On November 30, he signed the Brady

Handgun Violence Protection Act, known as the Brady bill, which imposed a five-day waiting period on those wishing to buy handguns. On December 8, 1993, he signed the highly controversial NAFTA into law.

One dark cloud that hovered over American society concerned health care. Many American families had no health insurance and little access to the medical care that one might expect to take for granted in a society as rich as that in the United States. In order to get health reform under way, the president appointed the First Lady to head a task force to investigate how the health care system in the United States could and should be altered. This appointment, although it carried no salary, raised cries of impropriety, and the final report of the task force was harshly criticized in many quarters. Nevertheless, this report opened needed dialogue about a pressing national problem and might have led to positive outcomes had not another scandal, Whitewater, erupted at about the time the report was released.

The Whitewater Problem

During their time in Arkansas's executive mansion, Bill and Hillary Clinton had taken a financial interest in a land development project called Whitewater. The Clintons were friends of James and Susan McDougal, who were principals in the Whitewater project. James McDougal was accused of misappropriating funds, and it appeared that the Clintons might have been involved in questionable activities relating to the Whitewater project. The right wing of the Republican Party called for an investigation by Congress, but the Democratic majority scuttled the investigation.

Vince Foster, the Clintons' attorney who had come to Washington with them and had an office in the White House, was under suspicion of illegal dealings relating to Whitewater. On July 20, 1993, his body was found in Fort Marcy Park near Alexandria, Virginia, with a single

Ten of Clinton's closest aides testify in the public hearings on the Whitewater investigation in July, 1994. *(Reuters/ Richard Clement/Archive Photos)*

bullet hole in the head. Foster's death, which was ruled a suicide, threw the White House into turmoil. Rumors flew in every direction. Some suspected that Foster had been murdered to keep him quiet. Hillary Clinton was accused of removing crucial papers from his office as soon as she heard of his death. Although these rumors were unsubstantiated, they raised embarrassing questions for the president and the First Lady.

Although no immediate action was taken regarding Whitewater, sentiment was growing for an investigation, and in time Independent Prosecutor Kenneth Starr was appointed by Attorney General Janet Reno. Starr was so dogged in his attempt to find evidence about presidential misconduct that many people thought he had a vendetta. The Clintons did not cooperate fully with Starr. When he subpoenaed documents from the First Lady re-

garding billing practices at the Rose Law Firm in Little Rock, with which she was associated during her husband's governorship, she claimed that the documents were misplaced and did not get them to Starr until months later, when they mysteriously surfaced.

The Paula Jones Controversy
Another scandal erupted shortly after the Whitewater problems began to surface. Two Arkansas state troopers who had worked for Clinton during his terms as governor admitted to reporters that they had arranged assignations for him in hotel rooms. This revelation generated a civil lawsuit against Clinton by Paula Corbin Jones, who claimed that the then-governor had lured her into a hotel room where he proposed that she commit a sexual act on him. Jones received financial assistance in her lawsuit from the Rutherford Institute, a con-

servative think tank that was fierce in its opposition to Bill Clinton and everything for which he stood.

A legal question now arose as to whether a sitting president could be required to defend himself against such an accusation. It was finally ruled that the suit could proceed, with the president giving a deposition under oath in answer to questions posed by the prosecuting attorney. Despite such distractions, Clinton continued to attend to affairs of state. He eventually paid a substantial financial settlement to Jones in order to close the case.

The 1996 Presidential Election

Such scandals were partly responsible for the Democrats losing their majorities in both the House and the Senate in the off-year election of 1994. Nevertheless, many Americans acknowledged that Clinton was an effective presi-

dent even though he might not be a good role model. The public consistently gave him some of the highest approval ratings ever accorded a United States president.

By the time the 1996 elections were held, the public had apparently been able to separate Clinton's private life from his professional life. Running against Republican Senator Bob Dole, Clinton won the election by a landslide. Voters were aware that he had performed such impressive political feats as bringing together the leaders of Israel and Jordan in September, 1994, to meet on neutral ground for peace talks. As genocidal wars threatened the very existence of Bosnia, Clinton and Secretary of State Warren Christopher had brought together the opponents and worked out a peace agreement. Bill Clinton won a second term handily in the face of odds that would have been daunting to most politicians.

Clinton and Vice President Al Gore celebrate in Little Rock, Arkansas, on election night, 1996. *(AP/Wide World Photos)*

The Monica Lewinsky Affair

The Paula Jones case would prove important in many ways. In order to establish his client's credibility, Jones's lawyer sought patterns of sexual misconduct by the president. Before long, his team received an anonymous telephone call suggesting that Kathleen Willey, a former White House volunteer and Clinton campaign worker, had been forced to fend off President Clinton's advances in the Oval Office on the very day her husband committed suicide.

Former White House employee Linda Tripp, who had been transferred to the Pentagon and who apparently held a grudge against Clinton, had become the friend and confidante of a twenty-one-year-old White House aide named Monica Lewinsky. Lewinsky had ingratiated herself with the president. Soon she had greater access to his office than White House aides generally are permitted. She confided in Tripp that she was sexually involved with Clinton. The story broke on January 21, 1998, after Tripp went to Kenneth Starr with tapes of Lewinsky's late-night telephone calls to her detailing sexual adventures in the pantry off the Oval Office.

Clinton went before the nation on television and denied categorically that he had had "sexual relations with that woman, Ms. Lewinsky." Starr persisted in his investigation, which was now far outside his original charge to investigate Whitewater. He would spend forty million dollars of taxpayers' money in his determined pursuit of the president.

When the Lewinsky story hit the presses, few in the White House thought that the president could survive the accusations and continue in office. His protestations of innocence were received skeptically, but he was finally backed into a corner when Lewinsky produced a blue dress stained with semen that she claimed came from the president. She had told Tripp about this dress and had been urged by her to preserve it. Clinton was forced to submit to DNA testing that proved conclusively that the semen was his.

Refusing to admit defeat, Clinton again took to the airwaves and in somber tones admitted to the public that he had acted inappropriately with Lewinsky. When he was deposed regarding this dalliance, he quibbled about what constitutes sexual contact and about ambiguities of language, but it was clear that he was guilty of the conduct of which he had been accused. Impeachment seemed all but certain.

Impeaching the President

The only president to be impeached prior to Clinton was Andrew Johnson in 1868, during Reconstruction. Richard M. Nixon avoided impeachment by resigning from the presidency in 1974 when it became clear to him that he could not emerge victorious from an impeachment hearing.

The situation looked brighter for the Clinton with the results of the 1998 congressional elections. The Republicans, many of whom relied on the impeachment issue in their campaigns, did not gain any seats in the Senate and even lost some in the House, an unusual occurrence for the opposition party in an off-year election that led to the resignation of House Speaker Newt Gingrich.

Nevertheless, in December, the House of Representatives, with its Republican majority, listened to several days of evidence and read the Starr Report that outlined in specific detail exactly what the relationship between the president and Lewinsky had been. The House voted to put the matter before the Senate, distilling the allegations to two charges: perjury before a grand jury regarding his own testimony in the Jones deposition and obstruction of justice through witness tampering and withholding of evidence, particularly Clinton's conversations with friends and employees and the return of gifts Lewinsky gave him. Because a two-thirds vote was required for conviction, it seemed certain that the president would be

A ticket to Clinton's impeachment trial in the Senate. *(AP/Wide World Photos)*

vindicated. The Senate had enough Democrats to assure victory unless some of them defected, although a small number seemed ready to do so.

After anguished hearings that went on for several days, the Senate on February 12, 1999, voted on the two articles of impeachment lodged against the chief executive. In the final vote, fifty-five senators, consisting of forty-five Democrats and ten Republicans (one whom abstained), voted against convicting the president of perjury, while forty-five, all Republicans, voted for conviction, giving the president not only the thirty-four votes he needed for acquittal but a majority as well. On the charge of obstruction of justice, the president did not fare quite as well, but he did receive an equal number of votes for acquittal and conviction. Fifty senators, including five Republicans who jumped ranks, voted against conviction. A conviction on either charge would have resulted in the president's removal from office, something that few savvy politicians wished to see happen given Clinton's high approval ratings.

Political Involvement After Impeachment

Some people feared that Bill Clinton would emerge from the impeachment hearings a toothless tiger, a president unable to serve the remainder of his term effectively. Others pointed to Clinton's way of bouncing back from adversity. They argued that his strong intellect and his ability to work persuasively with voters would permit him to complete his term of office with a degree of distinction.

The next crisis Clinton faced was the Kosovo situation, in which ethnic Albanians living in the southern part of Serbia were being systematically exterminated, much as Jews were during the Hitler regime in Germany in the 1930's and 1940's. In April, 1999, the United States, working within the framework of the North Atlantic Treaty Organization (NATO), joined other countries in trying to force the hand of the Serbian dictator Slobodan Milošević by bombing Serbia relentlessly to destroy its infrastructure. Meanwhile, the U.N. World Court indicted Milošević on charges of geno-

U.S. soldiers in Bosnia place a welcoming sign on the Croatian side of the river Sava on December 31, 1995. *(Reuters/Petr Josek/Archive Photos)*

cide, making him a criminal in the court's eyes. Just as President Clinton was gathering the Joint Chiefs of Staff to discuss waging a ground war in Serbia, Milošević capitulated, handing Clinton the victory that he needed.

Supporters claimed that were it not for the shadow cast upon Clinton's character by the scandals surrounding him, he would have been a viable candidate for the Nobel Peace Prize for his work in bringing Palestinians and Israelis together and for his successful efforts in controlling the Kosovo crisis. Both supporters and critics, however, knew that the Nobel Committee could not overlook the president's peccadilloes.

How History Will Judge Clinton

Bill Clinton ranks among the more remarkable presidents the United States has had. Clearly

an intellectual, he also displayed the ability to deal directly with people and to bring them to his way of thinking. It is impossible to know, however, how history will judge him. Just as President Nixon's reputation, which was established by his strong international policies, was sullied by Watergate and by his subsequent resignation, so might Clinton's reputation be associated more with the Paula Jones and Monica Lewinsky scandals than with the positive aspects of his administration.

Yet, for all of its blemishes, the majority of Americans continued to view the Clinton presidency as good for the United States. During his administration, the country grew in prosperity, people were employed, taxes came under control, and the Social Security and Medicare programs were reformed in an attempt to assure their future viability. The budget was balanced and, by 1998, not only had the deficit been erased but a surplus existed as well. It is telling that were it possible for Clinton to run for a third term as president of the United States, he would have stood a very good chance of being reelected.

R. Baird Shuman

Bibliographical References

Many books about the Clinton administration are carping volumes written by people who obviously detest their subject. Among them are such volumes as William J. Bennett's *The Death of Outrage*, 1998, in which the author makes moral judgments about the president in a superrighteous manner without considering fairly the positive aspects of Clinton's administration. Similar in tone is Ann Coulter's *High Crimes and Misdemeanors: The Case Against Bill Clinton*, 1998, which attempts to justify the impeachment of the president. Coulter's mind appears to have been made up before she began writing the book, which is a vitriolic outpouring of anti-Clinton sentiments. In his one-sided book *The Secret Life of Bill Clinton: The Unreported Story*, 1997, Ambrose Evans-Pritchard, a journalist credited with being the originator of nearly every devastating rumor about the Clintons, also dwells on scandals.

Other observers offer more balanced or positive portrayals. Dick Morris, Clinton's stalwart adviser during his first presidential campaign and his early years in the White House, presents a fine, three-dimensional portrait of the president in *Behind the Oval Office: Winning the Presidency in the Nineties*, 1997, published in 1998 with the subtitle *Getting Reelected Against All Odds*. Former White House aide George Stephanopoulos drew some criticism for his sincere but often-unflattering inside look with *All Too Human: A Political Education*, 1999. In *Boy Clinton: The Political Biography*, 1996, R. Emmett Tyrrell, Jr., presents valuable biographical information, but the book is slanted toward discrediting the president for his moral indiscretions. Robert Cwiklik's *Bill Clinton: President of the Nineties*, 1997, aimed at a juvenile audience, is accurate, well written, and informative, as are Elaine Landau's *Bill Clinton*, 1993, and Gene L. Martin and Aaron Boyd's *Bill Clinton: President from Arkansas*, 1993.

U.S. Constitution

We the People of the United States, in Order to form a more perfect Union, establish Justice, insure domestic Tranquility, provide for the common defence, promote the general Welfare, and secure the Blessings of Liberty to ourselves and our Posterity, do ordain and establish this Constitution for the United States of America.

Article I.

SECTION 1. All legislative Powers herein granted shall be vested in a Congress of the United States, which shall consist of a Senate and House of Representatives.

SECTION 2. The House of Representatives shall be composed of Members chosen every second Year by the People of the several States, and the Electors in each State shall have the Qualifications requisite for Electors of the most numerous Branch of the State Legislature.

No Person shall be a Representative who shall not have attained to the Age of twenty five Years, and been seven Years a Citizen of the United States, and who shall not, when elected, be an Inhabitant of that State in which he shall be chosen.

Representatives and direct Taxes shall be apportioned among the several States which may be included within this Union, according to their respective Numbers, which shall be determined by adding to the whole Number of free Persons, including those bound to Service for a Term of Years, and excluding Indians not taxed, three fifths of all other Persons. The actual Enumeration shall be made within three Years after the first Meeting of the Congress of the United States, and within every subsequent Term of ten Years, in such Manner as they shall by Law direct. The number of Representatives shall not exceed one for every thirty Thousand, but each State shall have at Least one Representative; and until such enumeration shall be made, the State of New Hampshire shall be entitled to chuse three, Massachusetts eight, Rhode-Island and Providence Plantations one, Connecticut five, New York six, New Jersey four, Pennsylvania eight, Delaware one, Maryland six, Virginia ten, North Carolina five, South Carolina five, and Georgia three.

When vacancies happen in the Representation from any State, the Executive Authority thereof shall issue Writs of Election to fill such Vacancies.

The House of Representatives shall chuse their Speaker and other Officers; and shall have the sole Power of Impeachment.

SECTION 3. The Senate of the United States shall be composed of two Senators from each State, chosen by the Legislature thereof, for six Years; and each Senator shall have one Vote.

Immediately after they shall be assembled in Consequence of the first Election, they shall be divided as equally as may be into three Classes. The Seats of the Senators of the first Class shall be vacated at the Expiration of the second Year, of the second Class at the Expiration of the fourth Year, and of the third Class at the Expiration of the sixth Year, so that one third may be chosen every second Year; and if Vacancies happen by Resignation, or otherwise, during the Recess of the Legislature of any State, the Executive thereof may make temporary Appointments until the next Meeting of the Legislature, which shall then fill such Vacancies.

No Person shall be a Senator who shall not have attained to the Age of thirty Years, and been nine Years a Citizen of the United States, and who shall not, when elected, be an Inhabitant of that State for which he shall be chosen.

The Vice President of the United States shall be President of the Senate, but shall have no Vote, unless they be equally divided.

The Senate shall chuse their other Officers, and also a President pro tempore, in the Absence of the Vice President, or when he shall exercise the Office of President of the United States.

The Senate shall have the sole Power to try all Impeachments. When sitting for that Purpose, they shall be on Oath or Affirmation. When the President of the United States is tried, the Chief Justice shall preside: And no Person shall be convicted without the Concurrence of two thirds of the Members present.

Judgment in Cases of Impeachment shall not extend further than to removal from Office, and disqualification to hold and enjoy any Office of honor, Trust or Profit under the United States: but the Party convicted shall nevertheless be liable and subject to Indictment, Trial, Judgment and Punishment, according to Law.

SECTION 4. The Times, Places and Manner of holding Elections for Senators and Representatives, shall be prescribed in each State by the Legislature thereof; but the Congress may at any time by Law make or alter such Regulations, except as to the Places of chusing Senators.

The Congress shall assemble at least once in every Year, and such Meeting shall be on the first Monday in December, unless they shall by Law appoint a different Day.

SECTION 5. Each House shall be the Judge of the Elections, Returns and Qualifications of its own Members, and a Majority of each shall constitute a Quorum to do Business; but a smaller Number may adjourn from day to day,

and may be authorized to compel the Attendance of absent Members, in such Manner, and under such Penalties as each House may provide.

Each House may determine the Rules of its Proceedings, punish its Members for disorderly Behaviour, and, with the Concurrence of two thirds, expel a Member.

Each House shall keep a Journal of its Proceedings, and from time to time publish the same, excepting such Parts as may in their Judgment require Secrecy; and the Yeas and Nays of the Members of either House on any question shall, at the Desire of one fifth of those Present, be entered on the Journal.

Neither House, during the Session of Congress, shall, without the Consent of the other, adjourn for more than three days, nor to any other Place than that in which the two Houses shall be sitting.

SECTION 6. The Senators and Representatives shall receive a Compensation for their Services, to be ascertained by Law, and paid out of the Treasury of the United States. They shall in all Cases, except Treason, Felony and Breach of the Peace, be privileged from Arrest during their Attendance at the Session of their respective Houses, and in going to and returning from the same; and for any Speech or Debate in either House, they shall not be questioned in any other Place.

No Senator or Representative shall, during the Time for which he was elected, be appointed to any civil Office under the Authority of the United States, which shall have been created, or the Emoluments whereof shall have been increased during such time; and no Person holding any Office under the United States, shall be a Member of either House during his Continuance in Office.

SECTION 7. All Bills for raising Revenue shall originate in the House of Representatives; but the Senate may propose or concur with Amendments as on other Bills.

Every Bill which shall have passed the House

of Representatives and the Senate, shall, before it becomes a Law, be presented to the President of the United States; If he approve he shall sign it, but if not he shall return it, with his Objections to that House in which it shall have originated, who shall enter the Objections at large on their Journal, and proceed to reconsider it. If after such Reconsideration two thirds of that House shall agree to pass the Bill, it shall be sent, together with the Objections, to the other House, by which it shall likewise be reconsidered, and if approved by two thirds of that House, it shall become a Law. But in all such Cases the Votes of both Houses shall be determined by Yeas and Nays, and the Names of the Persons voting for and against the Bill shall be entered on the Journal of each House respectively. If any Bill shall not be returned by the President within ten Days (Sundays excepted) after it shall have been presented to him, the Same shall be a Law, in like Manner as if he had signed it, unless the Congress by their Adjournment prevent its Return, in which Case it shall not be a Law.

Every Order, Resolution, or Vote to which the Concurrence of the Senate and House of Representatives may be necessary (except on a question of Adjournment) shall be presented to the President of the United States; and before the Same shall take Effect, shall be approved by him, or being disapproved by him, shall be repassed by two thirds of the Senate and House of Representatives, according to the Rules and Limitations prescribed in the Case of a Bill.

SECTION 8. The Congress shall have Power To lay and collect Taxes, Duties, Imposts and Excises, to pay the Debts and provide for the common Defence and general Welfare of the United States; but all Duties, Imposts and Excises shall be uniform throughout the United States;

To borrow Money on the credit of the United States;

To regulate Commerce with foreign Nations, and among the several States, and with the Indian Tribes;

To establish an uniform Rule of Naturalization, and uniform Laws on the subject of Bankruptcies throughout the United States;

To coin Money, regulate the Value thereof, and of foreign Coin, and fix the Standard of Weights and Measures;

To provide for the Punishment of counterfeiting the Securities and current Coin of the United States;

To establish Post Offices and post Roads;

To promote the Progress of Science and useful Arts, by securing for limited Times to Authors and Inventors the exclusive Right to their respective Writings and Discoveries;

To constitute Tribunals inferior to the supreme Court;

To define and punish Piracies and Felonies committed on the high Seas, and Offenses against the Law of Nations;

To declare War, grant Letters of Marque and Reprisal, and make Rules concerning Captures on Land and Water;

To raise and support Armies, but no Appropriation of Money to that Use shall be for a longer Term than two Years;

To provide and maintain a Navy;

To make Rules for the Government and Regulation of the land and naval Forces;

To provide for calling forth the Militia to execute the Laws of the Union, suppress Insurrections and repel Invasions;

To provide for organizing, arming, and disciplining the Militia, and for governing such Part of them as may be employed in the Service of the United States, reserving to the States respectively, the Appointment of the Officers, and the Authority of training the Militia according to the discipline prescribed by Congress;

To exercise exclusive Legislation in all Cases whatsoever, over such District (not exceeding ten Miles square) as may, by Cession of particular States, and the Acceptance of Congress, become the Seat of the Government of the United States, and to exercise like Authority over all Places purchased by the Consent of the Legislature of the State in which the Same shall be, for the Erection of Forts, Magazines, Arsenals, dock-Yards and other needful Buildings;—And

To make all Laws which shall be necessary and proper for carrying into Execution the foregoing Powers, and all other Powers vested by this Constitution in the Government of the United States, or in any Department or Officer thereof.

SECTION 9. The Migration or Importation of such Persons as any of the States now existing shall think proper to admit, shall not be prohibited by the Congress prior to the Year one thousand eight hundred and eight, but a Tax or duty may be imposed on such Importation, not exceeding ten dollars for each Person.

The Privilege of the Writ of Habeas Corpus shall not be suspended, unless when in Cases of Rebellion or Invasion the public Safety may require it.

No Bill of Attainder or ex post facto Law shall be passed.

No Capitation, or other direct, Tax shall be laid, unless in Proportion to the Census or Enumeration herein before directed to be taken.

No Tax or Duty shall be laid on Articles exported from any State.

No Preference shall be given by any Regulation of Commerce or Revenue to the Ports of one State over those of another: nor shall Vessels bound to, or from, one State, be obliged to enter, clear, or pay Duties in another.

No Money shall be drawn from the Treasury, but in Consequence of Appropriations made by Law; and a regular Statement and Account of the Receipts and Expenditures of all public Money shall be published from time to time.

No Title of Nobility shall be granted by the United States: And no Person holding any Office of Profit or Trust under them, shall, without the Consent of the Congress, accept of any present, Emolument, Office, or Title, of any kind whatever, from any King, Prince, or foreign State.

SECTION 10. No State shall enter into any Treaty, Alliance, or Confederation; grant Letters of Marque and Reprisal; coin Money; emit Bills of Credit; make any Thing but gold and silver Coin a Tender in Payment of Debts; pass any Bill of Attainder, ex post facto Law, or Law impairing the Obligation of Contracts, or grant any Title of Nobility.

No State shall, without the Consent of the Congress, lay any Imposts or Duties on Imports or Exports, except what may be absolutely necessary for executing it's inspection Laws: and the net Produce of all Duties and Imposts, laid by any State on Imports or Exports, shall be for the Use of the Treasury of the United States; and all such Laws shall be subject to the Revision and Control of the Congress.

No State shall, without the Consent of Congress, lay any Duty of Tonnage, keep Troops, or Ships of War in time of Peace, enter into any Agreement or Compact with another State, or with a foreign Power, or engage in War, unless actually invaded, or in such imminent Danger as will not admit of delay.

Article II.

SECTION 1. The executive Power shall be vested in a President of the United States of America. He shall hold his Office during the Term of four Years, and, together with the Vice President, chosen for the same Term, be elected, as follows:

Each State shall appoint, in such Manner as the Legislature thereof may direct, a Number of Electors, equal to the whole Number of Senators and Representatives to which the State may be entitled in the Congress: but no Senator or Representative, or Person holding an Office of Trust or Profit under the United States, shall be appointed an Elector.

The Electors shall meet in their respective States, and vote by Ballot for two Persons, of whom one at least shall not be an Inhabitant of the same State with themselves. And they shall make a List of all the Persons voted for, and of the Number of Votes for each, which List they shall sign and certify, and transmit sealed to the Seat of the Government of the United States, directed to the President of the Senate. The President of the Senate shall, in the Presence of the Senate and House of Representatives, open all the Certificates, and the Votes shall then be counted. The Person having the greatest Number of Votes shall be the President, if such Number be a Majority of the whole Number of Electors appointed; and if there be more than one who have such Majority, and have an equal Number of Votes, then the House of Representatives shall immediately chuse by Ballot one of them for President; and if no Person have a Majority, then from the five highest on the List the said House shall in like manner chuse the President. But in chusing the President, the Votes shall be taken by States, the Representation from each State having one Vote; A quorum for this Purpose shall consist of a Member or Members from two thirds of the States, and a Majority of all the States shall be necessary to a Choice. In every Case, after the Choice of the President, the Person having the greatest Number of Votes of the Electors shall be the Vice President. But if there should remain two or more who have equal Votes, the Senate shall chuse from them by Ballot the Vice President.

The Congress may determine the Time of chusing the Electors, and the Day on which they shall give their Votes; which Day shall be the same throughout the United States.

No Person except a natural born Citizen, or a Citizen of the United States, at the time of the Adoption of this Constitution, shall be eligible to the Office of the President; neither shall any person be eligible to that Office who shall not have attained to the Age of thirty five Years, and been fourteen Years a Resident within the United States.

In Case of the Removal of the President from Office, or of his Death, Resignation, or Inability to discharge the Powers and Duties of the said Office, the Same shall devolve on the Vice President, and the Congress may by Law provide for the Case of Removal, Death, Resignation or Inability, both of the President and Vice President, declaring what Officer shall then act as President, and such Officer shall act accordingly, until the Disability be removed, or a President shall be elected.

The President shall, at stated Times, receive for his Services, a Compensation, which shall neither be increased nor diminished during the Period for which he shall have been elected, and he shall not receive within that Period any other Emolument from the United States, or any of them.

Before he enter the Execution of his Office, he shall take the following Oath or Affirmation:—"I do solemnly swear (or affirm) that I will faithfully execute the Office of President of the United States, and will to the best of my Ability, preserve, protect and defend the Constitution of the United States."

SECTION 2. The President shall be Commander in Chief of the Army and Navy of the United States, and of the Militia of the several States, when called into the actual Service of the United States; he may require the Opinion, in writing, of the principal Officer in each of the executive Departments, upon any Subject relating to the Duties of their respective Offices, and he shall have Power to grant Reprieves and Pardons for Offenses against the United States, except in Cases of Impeachment.

He shall have Power, by and with the Advice and Consent of the Senate, to make Treaties, provided two thirds of the Senators present concur; and he shall nominate, and by and with the Advice and Consent of the Senate, shall appoint Ambassadors, other public Ministers and Consuls, Judges of the supreme Court, and all other Officers of the United

States, whose Appointments are not herein otherwise provided for, and which shall be established by Law: but the Congress may by Law vest the Appointment of such inferior Officers, as they think proper, in the President alone, in the Courts of Law, or in the Heads of Departments.

The President shall have Power to fill up all Vacancies that may happen during the Recess of the Senate, by granting Commissions which shall expire at the End of their next Session.

SECTION 3. He shall from time to time give to the Congress Information of the State of the Union, and recommend to their Consideration such Measures as he shall judge necessary and expedient; he may, on extraordinary Occasions, convene both Houses, or either of them, and in Case of Disagreement between them, with Respect to the Time of Adjournment, he may adjourn them to such Time as he shall think proper; he shall receive Ambassadors and other public Ministers; he shall take Care that the Laws be faithfully executed, and shall Commission all the Officers of the United States.

SECTION 4. The President, Vice President and all civil Officers of the United States, shall be removed from Office on Impeachment for, and Conviction of, Treason, Bribery, or other high Crimes and Misdemeanors.

Article III.

SECTION 1. The judicial Power of the United States, shall be vested in one supreme Court, and in such inferior Courts as the Congress may from time to time ordain and establish. The Judges, both of the supreme and inferior Courts, shall hold their Offices during good Behavior, and shall, at stated Times, receive for their Services, a Compensation, which shall not be diminished during their Continuance in Office.

SECTION 2. The judicial Power shall extend to all Cases, in Law and Equity, arising under this Constitution, the Laws of the United States, and Treaties made, or which shall be made, under their Authority;—to all Cases affecting Ambassadors, other public Ministers and Consuls;—to all Cases of admiralty and maritime Jurisdiction;—to Controversies to which the United States shall be a Party;—to Controversies between two or more States; between a State and Citizens of another State; between Citizens of different States;—between Citizens of the same State claiming Lands under Grants of different States;—and between a State, or the Citizens thereof, and foreign States, Citizens or Subjects.

In all Cases affecting Ambassadors, other public Ministers and Consuls, and those in which a State shall be Party, the supreme Court shall have original Jurisdiction. In all the other Cases before mentioned, the supreme Court shall have appellate Jurisdiction, both as to Law and Fact, with such Exceptions, and under such Regulations as the Congress shall make.

The Trial of all Crimes, except in Cases of Impeachment, shall be by Jury; and such Trial shall be held in the State where the said Crimes shall have been committed; but when not committed within any State, the Trial shall be at such Place or Places as the Congress may by Law have directed.

SECTION 3. Treason against the United States, shall consist only in levying War against them, or in adhering to their Enemies, giving them Aid and Comfort. No Person shall be convicted of Treason unless on the Testimony of two Witnesses to the same overt Act, or on Confession in open Court.

The Congress shall have Power to declare the Punishment of Treason, but no Attainder of Treason shall work Corruption of Blood, or Forfeiture except during the Life of the Person attainted.

Article IV.

SECTION 1. Full Faith and Credit shall be given in each State to the public Acts, Records, and judicial Proceedings of every other State; And the Congress may by general Laws prescribe the Manner in which such Acts, Records and Proceedings shall be proved, and the Effect thereof.

SECTION 2. The Citizens of each State shall be entitled to all Privileges and Immunities of Citizens in the several States.

A Person charged in any State with Treason, Felony, or other Crime, who shall flee from Justice, and be found in another State, shall on Demand of the executive Authority of the State from which he fled, be delivered up, to be removed to the State having Jurisdiction of the Crime.

No person held to Service or Labour in one State, under the Laws thereof, escaping into another, shall, in Consequence of any Law or Regulation therein, be discharged from such Service or Labour, but shall be delivered up on Claim of the Party to whom such Service or Labour may be due.

SECTION 3. New States may be admitted by the Congress into this Union; but no new State shall be formed or erected within the Jurisdiction of any other State; nor any State be formed by the Junction of two or more States, or parts of States, without the Consent of the Legislatures of the States concerned as well as of the Congress.

The Congress shall have Power to dispose of and make all needful Rules and Regulations respecting the Territory or other Property belonging to the United States; and nothing in this Constitution shall be so construed as to Prejudice any Claims of the United States, or of any particular State.

SECTION 4. The United States shall guarantee to every State in this Union a Republican Form of Government, and shall protect each of them against Invasion; and on Application of the Legislature, or of the Executive (when the Legislature cannot be convened) against domestic Violence.

Article V.

The Congress, whenever two thirds of both Houses shall deem it necessary, shall propose Amendments to this Constitution, or, on the Application of the Legislatures of two thirds of the several States, shall call a Convention for proposing Amendments, which, in either Case, shall be valid to all Intents and Purposes, as Part of this Constitution, when ratified by the Legislatures of three fourths of the several States, or by Conventions in three fourths thereof, as the one or the other Mode of Ratification may be proposed by the Congress; Provided that no Amendment which may be made prior to the Year One thousand eight hundred and eight shall in any Manner affect the first and fourth Clauses in the Ninth Section of the first Article; and that no State, without its Consent, shall be deprived of it's equal Suffrage in the Senate.

Article VI.

All Debts contracted and Engagements entered into, before the Adoption of this Constitution, shall be as valid against the United States under this Constitution, as under the Confederation.

This Constitution, and the Laws of the United States which shall be made in Pursuance thereof; and all Treaties made, or which shall be made, under the Authority of the United States, shall be the supreme Law of the Land; and the Judges in every State shall be bound thereby, any Thing in the Constitution or Laws of any State to the Contrary notwithstanding.

The Senators and Representatives before mentioned, and the Members of the several State Legislatures, and all executive and judicial Officers, both of the United States and of the several States, shall be bound by Oath or Affirmation, to support this Constitution; but no religious Test shall ever be required as a Qualification to any Office or public Trust under the United States.

Article VII.

The Ratification of the Conventions of nine States, shall be sufficient for the Establishment of this Constitution between the States so ratifying the Same.

Done in Convention by the Unanimous Consent of the States present the Seventeenth Day of September in the Year of our Lord one thousand seven hundred and Eighty seven and of the Independence of the United States of America the Twelfth. In Witness whereof We have hereunto subscribed our Names,

Go. Washington—Presidt and deputy from Virginia

New Hampshire { John Langdon
Nicholas Gilman

Massachusetts { Nathaniel Gorham
Rufus King

Connecticut { Wm Saml Johnson
Roger Sherman

New York { John Langdon

New Jersey { Wil Livingston
David Brearley
Wm Paterson
Jona. Dayton

Pennsylvania
~~New Jersey~~ { B Franklin
Thomas Mifflin
Robt Morris
Geo. Clymer
Thos FitzSimons
Jared Ingersoll
James Wilson
Gouv Morris

Delaware { Geo. Read
Gunning Beford jun
John Dickinson
Richard Bassett
Jaco. Broom

Maryland { James McHenry
Dan of St Tho. Jenifer
Danl Carroll

Virginia { John Blair
James Madison Jr.

North Carolina { Wm. Blount
Richd Dobbs Spaight
Hu Williamson

South Carolina { J. Rutledge
Charles Cotesworth
Pinckney
Charles Pinckney
Pierce Butler

Georgia { William Few
Abr Baldwin

Attest: William Jackson, Secretary

Amendments to the U.S. Constitution

Amendment I.

Congress shall make no law respecting an establishment of religion, or prohibiting the free exercise thereof; or abridging the freedom of speech, or of the press, or the right of the people peaceably to assemble, and to petition the Government for a redress of grievances.

[ratified December, 1791]

Amendment II.

A well regulated Militia, being necessary to the security of a free State, the right of the people to keep and bear Arms, shall not be infringed.

[ratified December, 1791]

Amendment III.

No Soldier shall, in time of peace be quartered in any house, without the consent of the Owner, nor in time of war, but in a manner to be prescribed by law.

[ratified December, 1791]

Amendment IV.

The right of the people to be secure in their persons, houses, papers, and effects, against unreasonable searches and seizures, shall not be violated, and no Warrants shall issue, but upon probable cause, supported by Oath or affirmation, and particularly describing the place to be searched, and the persons or things to be seized.

[ratified December, 1791]

Amendment V.

No person shall be held to answer for a capital, or otherwise infamous crime, unless on a presentment or indictment of a Grand Jury, except in cases arising in the land or naval forces, or in the Militia, when in actual service in time of War or public danger; nor shall any person be subject for the same offence to be twice put in jeopardy of life or limb, nor shall be compelled in any criminal case to be a witness against himself, nor be deprived of life, liberty, or property, without due process of law; nor shall private property be taken for public use without just compensation.

[ratified December, 1791]

Amendment VI.

In all criminal prosecutions, the accused shall enjoy the right to a speedy and public trial, by an impartial jury of the State and district wherein the crime shall have been committed; which district shall have been previously ascertained by law, and to be informed of the nature and cause of the accusation; to be confronted with the witnesses against him; to have compulsory process for obtaining witnesses in his favor, and to have the assistance of counsel for his defence.

[ratified December, 1791]

Amendment VII.

In Suits at common law, where the value in controversy shall exceed twenty dollars, the right of trial by jury shall be preserved, and no fact tried by a jury shall be otherwise re-examined in any Court of the United States, than according to the rules of the common law.

[ratified December, 1791]

Amendment VIII.

Excessive bail shall not be required, nor excessive fines imposed, nor cruel and unusual punishments inflicted.

[ratified December, 1791]

Amendment IX.

The enumeration in the Constitution, of certain rights, shall not be construed to deny or disparage others retained by the people.

[ratified December, 1791]

Amendment X.

The powers not delegated to the United States by the Constitution, nor prohibited by it to the States, are reserved to the States respectively, or to the people.

[ratified December, 1791]

Amendment XI.

The Judicial power of the United States shall not be construed to extend to any suit in law or equity, commenced or prosecuted against one of the United States by Citizens of another State, or by Citizens or Subjects of any Foreign State.

[ratified February, 1795]

Amendment XII.

The Electors shall meet in their respective states, and vote by ballot for President and Vice President, one of whom, at least, shall not be an inhabitant of the same state with themselves; they shall name in their ballots the person voted for as President, and in distinct ballots the person voted for as Vice-President, and they shall make distinct lists of all persons voted for as President, and of all persons voted for as Vice-President, and of the number of votes for each, which lists they shall sign and certify, and transmit sealed to the seat of the government of the United States, directed to the President of the Senate;—The President of the Senate shall, in the presence of the Senate and House of Representatives, open all the certificates and the votes shall then be counted;— The person having the greatest number of votes for President, shall be the President, if such number be a majority of the whole number of Electors appointed; and if no person have such majority, then from the persons having the highest numbers not exceeding three on the list of those voted for as President, the House of Representatives shall choose immediately, by ballot, the President. But in choosing the President, the votes shall be taken by states, the representation from each state having one vote; a quorum for this purpose shall consist of a member or members from two-thirds of the states, and a majority of all the states shall be necessary to a choice. And if the House of Representatives shall not choose a President whenever the right of choice shall devolve upon them, before the fourth day of March next following, then the Vice-President shall act as President, as in the case of the death or other constitutional disability of the President.—The person having the greatest number of votes as Vice-President, shall be the Vice-President, if such number be a majority of the whole number of Electors appointed, and if no person have a majority, then from the two highest numbers on the list, the Senate shall choose the Vice-President; a quorum for the purpose shall consist of two-thirds of the whole number of Senators, and a majority of the whole number shall be necessary to a choice. But no person constitutionally ineligible to the office of President shall be eligible to that of Vice-President of the United States.

[ratified June, 1804]

Amendment XIII.

SECTION 1. Neither slavery nor involuntary servitude, except as a punishment for crime whereof the party shall have been duly convicted, shall exist within the United States, or any place subject to their jurisdiction.

SECTION 2. Congress shall have power to enforce this article by appropriate legislation.

[ratified December, 1865]

Amendment XIV.

SECTION 1. All persons born or naturalized in the United States and subject to the jurisdiction thereof, are citizens of the United States and of the State wherein they reside. No State shall make or enforce any law which shall abridge the privileges or immunities of citizens of the United States; nor shall any State deprive any person of life, liberty, or property, without due process of law; nor deny to any person within its jurisdiction the equal protection of the laws.

SECTION 2. Representatives shall be apportioned among the several States according to their respective numbers, counting the whole number of persons in each State, excluding Indians not taxed. But when the right to vote at any election for the choice of electors for President and Vice President of the United States, Representatives in Congress, the Executive and Judicial officers of a State, or the members of the Legislature thereof, is denied to any of the male inhabitants of such State, being twenty-one years of age, and citizens of the United States, or in any way abridged, except for participation in rebellion, or other crime, the basis of representation therein shall be reduced in the proportion which the number of such male citizens shall bear to the whole number of male citizens twenty-one years of age in such State.

SECTION 3. No person shall be a Senator or Representative in Congress, or elector of President and Vice President, or hold any office, civil or military, under the United States, or under any State, who, having previously taken an oath, as a member of Congress, or as an officer of the United States, or as a member of any State legislature, or as an executive or judicial officer of any State, to support the Constitution of the United States, shall have engaged in insurrection or rebellion against the same, or given aid or comfort to the enemies thereof. But Congress may by a vote of two-thirds of each House, remove such disability.

SECTION 4. The validity of the public debt of the United States, authorized by law, including debts incurred for payment of pensions and bounties for services in suppressing insurrection or rebellion, shall not be questioned. But neither the United States nor any State shall assume or pay any debt or obligation incurred in aid of insurrection or rebellion against the United States, or any claim for the loss or emancipation of any slave; but all such debts, obligations and claims shall be held illegal and void.

SECTION 5. The Congress shall have power to enforce, by appropriate legislation, the provisions of this article.

[ratified July, 1868]

Amendment XV.

SECTION 1. The right of citizens of the United States to vote shall not be denied or abridged by the United States or by any State on account of race, color, or previous condition of servitude.

SECTION 2. The Congress shall have power to enforce this article by appropriate legislation.

[ratified February, 1870]

Amendment XVI.

The Congress shall have power to lay and collect taxes on incomes, from whatever source derived, without apportionment among the several States, and without regard to any census or enumeration.

[ratified February, 1913]

Amendment XVII.

The Senate of the United States shall be composed of two Senators from each State, elected by the people thereof, for six years; and each Senator shall have one vote. The electors in each State shall have the qualifications requisite for electors of the most numerous branch of the State legislatures.

When vacancies happen in the representation of any State in the Senate, the executive authority of such State shall issue writs of election to fill such vacancies: *Provided*, That the legislature of any State may empower the executive thereof to make temporary appointments until the people fill the vacancies by election as the legislature may direct.

This amendment shall not be so construed as to affect the election or term of any Senator chosen before it becomes valid as part of the Constitution.

[ratified April, 1913]

Amendment XVIII.

SECTION 1. After one year from the ratification of this article the manufacture, sale, or transportation of intoxicating liquors within, the importation thereof into, or the exportation thereof from the United States and all territory subject to the jurisdiction thereof for beverage purposes is hereby prohibited.

SECTION 2. The Congress and the several States shall have concurrent power to enforce this article by appropriate legislation.

SECTION 3. This article shall be inoperative unless it shall have been ratified as an amendment to the Constitution by the legislatures of the several States, as provided in the Constitution, within seven years from the date of the submission hereof to the States by the Congress.

[ratified January, 1919, repealed December, 1933]

Amendment XIX.

The right of citizens of the United States to vote shall not be denied or abridged by the United States or by any State on account of sex.

Congress shall have power to enforce this article by appropriate legislation.

[ratified August, 1920]

Amendment XX.

SECTION 1. The terms of the President and Vice President shall end at noon on the 20th day of January, and the terms of Senators and Representatives at noon on the 3d day of January, of the years in which such terms would have ended if this article had not been ratified; and the terms of their successors shall then begin.

SECTION 2. The Congress shall assemble at least once in every year, and such meeting shall begin at noon on the 3d day of January, unless they shall by law appoint a different day.

SECTION 3. If, at the time fixed for the beginning of the term of the President, the President elect shall have died, the Vice President elect shall become President. If a President shall not have been chosen before the time fixed for the beginning of his term, or if the President elect shall have failed to qualify, then the Vice President elect shall act as President until a President shall have qualified; and the Congress may by law provide for the case wherein neither a President elect nor a Vice President elect shall have qualified, declaring who shall then act as President, or the manner in which one who is to act shall be selected, and such person shall act accordingly until a President or Vice President shall have qualified.

SECTION 4. The Congress may by law provide for the case of the death of any of the persons from whom the House of Representatives may choose a President whenever the right of choice shall have devolved upon them, and for the case of the death of any of the persons from whom the Senate may choose a Vice President whenever the right of choice shall have devolved upon them.

SECTION 5. Sections 1 and 2 shall take effect on the 15th day of October following the ratification of this article.

SECTION 6. This article shall be inoperative unless it shall have been ratified as an amendment to the Constitution by the legislatures of three-fourths of the several States within seven years from the date of its submission.

[ratified January, 1933]

Amendment XXI.

SECTION 1. The eighteenth article of amendment to the Constitution of the United States is hereby repealed.

SECTION 2. The transportation or importation into any State, Territory, or possession of the United States for delivery or use therein of intoxicating liquors, in violation of the laws thereof, is hereby prohibited.

SECTION 3. This article shall be inoperative unless it shall have been ratified as an amendment to the Constitution by conventions in the several States, as provided in the Constitution, within seven years from the date of the submission hereof to the States by the Congress.

[ratified December, 1933]

Amendment XXII.

SECTION 1. No person shall be elected to the office of the President more than twice, and no person who has held the office of President, or acted as President, for more than two years of a term to which some other person was elected President shall be elected to the office of the President more than once. But this Article shall not apply to any person holding the office of President when this Article was proposed by the Congress, and shall not prevent any person who may be holding the office of President, or acting as President, during the term within which this Article becomes operative from holding the office of President or acting as President during the remainder of such term.

SECTION 2. This article shall be inoperative unless it shall have been ratified as an amendment to the Constitution by the legislatures of three-fourths of the several States within seven years from the date of its submission to the States by the Congress.

[ratified February, 1951]

Amendment XXIII.

SECTION 1. The District constituting the seat of Government of the United States shall appoint in such manner as the Congress may direct:

A number of electors of President and Vice President equal to the whole number of Senators and Representatives in Congress to which the District would be entitled if it were a State, but in no event more than the least populous State; they shall be in addition to those appointed by the States, but they shall be considered, for the purposes of the election of President and Vice President, to be electors appointed by a State; and they shall meet in the District and perform such duties as provided by the twelfth article of amendment.

SECTION 2. The Congress shall have power to enforce this article by appropriate legislation.

[ratified March, 1961]

Amendment XXIV.

SECTION 1. The right of citizens of the United States to vote in any primary or other election for President or Vice President, for electors for President or Vice President, or for Senator or Representative in Congress, shall not be denied or abridged by the United States or any State by reason of failure to pay any poll tax or other tax.

SECTION 2. The Congress shall have power to enforce this article by appropriate legislation.

[ratified January, 1964]

Amendment XXV.

SECTION 1. In case of the removal of the President from office or of his death or resignation, the Vice President shall become President.

SECTION 2. Whenever there is a vacancy in the office of the Vice President, the President shall nominate a Vice President who shall take office upon confirmation by a majority vote of both Houses of Congress.

SECTION 3. Whenever the President transmits to the President pro tempore of the Senate and the Speaker of the House of Representatives his written declaration that he is unable to discharge the powers and duties of his office, and until he transmits to them a written declaration to the contrary, such powers and duties shall be discharged by the Vice President as Acting President.

SECTION 4. Whenever the Vice President and a majority of either the principal officers of the executive departments or of such other body as Congress may by law provide, transmit to the President pro tempore of the Senate and the Speaker of the House of Representatives their written declaration that the President is unable to discharge the powers and duties of his office, the Vice President shall immediately assume the powers and duties of the office as Acting President.

Thereafter, when the President transmits to the President pro tempore of the Senate and the Speaker of the House of Representatives his written declaration that no inability exists, he shall resume the powers and duties of his office unless the Vice President and a majority of either the principal officers of the executive department or of such other body as Congress may by law provide, transmit within four days to the President pro tempore of the Senate and the Speaker of the House of Representatives their written declaration that the President is unable to discharge the powers and duties of his office. Thereupon Congress shall decide the issue, assembling within forty-eight hours for that purpose if not in session. If the Congress, within twenty-one days after receipt of the latter written declaration, or, if Congress is not in session, within twenty-one days after Congress is required to assemble, determines by

two-thirds vote of both Houses that the President is unable to discharge the powers and duties of his office, the Vice President shall continue to discharge the same as Acting President; otherwise, the President shall resume the powers and duties of his office.

[ratified February, 1967]

Amendment XXVI.

SECTION 1. The right of citizens of the United States, who are eighteen years of age or older, to vote shall not be denied or abridged by the United States or by any State on account of age.

SECTION 2. The Congress shall have power to enforce this article by appropriate legislation.

[ratified July, 1971]

Amendment XXVII.

No law, varying the compensation for the services of the Senators and Representatives, shall take effect, until an election of Representatives shall have intervened.

[ratified May 7, 1992]

Law of Presidential Succession

The following legislation was first approved July 18, 1947; it was amended September 9, 1965, October 15, 1966, August 4, 1977, and September 27, 1979:

If by reason of death, resignation, removal from office, inability, or failure to qualify there is neither a president nor vice president to discharge the powers and duties of the office of president, then the speaker of the House of Representatives shall upon his resignation as speaker and as representative, act as president. The same rule shall apply in the case of the death, resignation, removal from office, or inability of an individual acting as president.

If at the time when a speaker is to begin the discharge of the powers and duties of the office of president there is no speaker, or the speaker fails to qualify as acting president, then the president pro tempore of the Senate, upon his resignation as president pro tempore and as senator, shall act as president.

An individual acting as president shall continue to act until the expiration of the then current presidential term, except that (1) if his discharge of the powers and duties of the office is founded in whole or in part in the failure of both the president-elect and the vice president-elect to qualify, then he shall act only until a president qualifies, and (2) if his discharge of the powers and duties of the office is founded in whole or in part on the inability of the president or vice president, then he shall act only until the removal of the disability of one of such individuals.

If, by reason of death, resignation, removal from office, or failure to qualify, there is no president pro tempore to act as president, then the officer of the United States who is highest on the following list, and who is not under any disability to discharge the powers and duties of president shall act as president; the secretaries of state, treasury, defense, attorney general; secretaries of interior, agriculture, commerce, labor, health and human services, housing and urban development, transportation, energy, education, veterans affairs.

Time Line

Washington

1732, February 11:	George Washington is born in Westmoreland County, Virginia.
1755, July 9:	After General Edward Braddock's defeat near Fort Duquesne, Pennsylvania, Washington withdraws his defeated army.
1759, January 6:	Washington marries Martha Dandridge Custis, the widow of Daniel Parke Custis, in New Kent County, Virginia.
1775, June 15:	Congress names Washington as general and commander in chief of the Army of the United Colonies.
1776, March 17:	Washington forces the British to evacuate Boston.
1776, August 27:	Washington is defeated at the Battle of Long Island.
1776, December 26:	Washington defeats the Hessians at the Battle of Trenton.
1777, December 19:	The Continental Army goes into winter quarters at Valley Forge.
1781, October 19:	Lord Cornwallis surrenders to Washington at Yorktown.
1783, September 3:	A peace treaty ends the Revolutionary War.
1783, December 23:	Washington resigns his commission and returns to private life.
1787, May 25:	Washington is unanimously elected president of the Constitutional Convention.
1789, February 4:	Washington is unanimously elected the first president of the United States.
1789, April 30:	Washington is inaugurated at Federal Hall in New York City.
1789, July 4:	The first tariff act places duties on imports.
1789, August 4:	The first federal bond is issued to fund domestic and state debt.
1790, March 1:	The first U.S. census is authorized.
1790, July 16:	Congress locates the national capital in the District of Columbia.
1791, March 4:	Vermont is admitted as the fourteenth state.
1791, December 15:	The first ten amendments to the Constitution (the Bill of Rights) are ratified.
1792, June 1:	Kentucky is admitted as the fifteenth state.
1792, December 5:	Washington is unanimously reelected president.
1793, March 4:	Washington is inaugurated in Philadelphia for a second term.
1794, July–November:	The Whiskey Rebellion occurs in western Pennsylvania.
1796, June 1:	Tennessee is admitted as the sixteenth state.
1796, September 17:	Washington issues his farewell address.
1799, December 14:	George Washington dies at Mount Vernon, Virginia.

J. Adams

1735, October 30:	John Adams is born in Braintree, Massachusetts.
1764, October 25:	Adams marries Abigail Smith in Weymouth, Massachusetts.

1774, September 5- 1776:	Adams serves as a delegate to the First and Second Continental Congresses.
1776:	Adams serves on the committee to draft the Declaration of Independence.
1780, December 29:	Adams arrives as minister to the Netherlands, where he negotiates a loan and treaty.
1785, May 14:	Adams arrives as minister to England, where he serves until 1788.
1789, April 21:	Adams is inaugurated as vice president under George Washington in New York City.
1793, March 4:	Adams is inaugurated as vice president for a second term.
1796, November:	Adams is elected president.
1797, March 4:	Adams is inaugurated as President.
1798, June 25:	The Alien Act is passed.
1798, July 11:	The U.S. Marine Corps is established.
1798, July 14:	The Sedition Act is passed.
1800, April 24:	The Library of Congress is established.
1800, June 15:	The Capital of the United States is moved to the District of Columbia.
1800, November 4:	Adams is defeated for reelection by Thomas Jefferson.
1801, March 4:	Adams retires to Quincy, Massachusetts.
1818, October 28:	Abigail Adams dies in Quincy.
1826, July 4:	John Adams dies in Quincy; Thomas Jefferson dies on the same day.

Jefferson

1743, April 13:	Thomas Jefferson is born in Shadwell, Goochland (now Albemarle) County, Virginia.
1769:	Jefferson begins building his home at Monticello, Virginia.
1769, May 11:	Jefferson begins service as a member of the Virginia House of Burgesses, where he serves until 1774.
1772, January 1:	Jefferson marries Martha Wayles Skelton, the widow of Bathurst Skelton, in Williamsburg, Virginia.
1774, August:	Jefferson publishes *A Summary View of the Rights of British America*.
1775, June-December:	Jefferson serves as a delegate to the Continental Congress.
1776, June 10-July 2:	Jefferson chairs the committee to prepare the Declaration of Independence.
1779, June 1:	Jefferson is elected governor of Virginia.
1780, June 2:	Jefferson is reelected governor of Virginia.
1782, September 6:	Martha Jefferson dies at Monticello.
1783, June:	Jefferson drafts a constitution for Virginia.
1785, March 10:	Jefferson succeeds Benjamin Franklin as minister to France.
1789, September 26:	Jefferson is confirmed by the U.S. Senate as the first secretary of state.
1800, November 4:	A presidential election is held; Jefferson and Aaron Burr tie for first place, and the election is referred to the House of Representatives.
1801, February 11:	Jefferson is elected president by the House of Representatives.
1801, March 4:	Jefferson is inaugurated as president.
1801-1805:	The United States fights a war against the Barbary pirates of Tripoli.

1802, March 16:	The first U.S. military academy is authorized; it opens on July 4, 1802, at West Point.
1803, February 24:	The Supreme Court decides the case of *Marbury v. Madison*, establishing its power to declare laws of Congress unconstitutional.
1803, March 1:	Ohio is admitted as the seventeenth state.
1803, April 30:	Jefferson purchases the Louisiana Territory from France for $15 million.
1804, May 14:	Meriwether Lewis and William Clark begin their expedition to the Pacific Ocean.
1804, September 25:	The Twelfth Amendment to the Constitution is ratified, requiring the separate election of the president and vice president.
1804, November 6:	Jefferson is reelected president.
1805, March 4:	Jefferson inaugurated as president for a second term.
1807, August 7:	Robert Fulton sails the steamboat *Clermont* on the Hudson River.
1807, December 22:	The Embargo Act forbids Americans to trade with warring European powers.
1808, January 1:	The importation of slaves from Africa is prohibited.
1826, July 4:	Thomas Jefferson dies in Charlottesville, Virginia; John Adams dies on the same day.

Madison

1751, March 16:	James Madison is born in Port Conway, Virginia.
1776:	Madison drafts Virginia's guarantee of religious liberty and helps write the state constitution.
1776-1777:	Madison is active in Virginia's revolutionary government.
1780-1783 and 1786-1788:	Madison serves as a member of the Continental Congress.
1787:	Madison is made a member of the Constitutional Convention; he writes essays for *The Federalist*.
1794, September 15:	Madison marries Dolley Dandridge Payne Todd, the widow of John Todd, in Harewood, Virginia.
1801-1809:	Madison serves as secretary of state in the Jefferson administration.
1808, November:	Madison is elected president.
1809, March 4:	Madison is inaugurated as president.
1811, November 7:	General William Henry Harrison defeats American Indians at the Battle of Tippecanoe.
1812, April 30:	Louisiana is admitted as the eighteenth state.
1812, May:	Madison is renominated for president.
1812, June 18:	War is declared against Great Britain.
1812, November:	Madison is reelected president.
1813, March 4:	Madison is inaugurated as president for a second term.
1813, September 10:	Oliver Hazard Perry wins a victory on Lake Erie.
1814, August 24:	British troops capture Washington, D.C., and burn the White House.
1814, September 13:	British troops are repulsed in an attack on Fort McHenry in Baltimore; Francis Scott Key writes "The Star-Spangled Banner."
1814, December 24:	A peace treaty is signed with Great Britain.

1815, January 8:	Andrew Jackson defeats the British at the Battle of New Orleans.
1816, December 11:	Indiana is admitted as the nineteenth state.
1836, June 28:	James Madison dies in Montpelier, Virginia.

Monroe

1758, April 28:	James Monroe is born in Westmoreland County, Virginia.
1776, December 26:	Monroe is wounded at the Battle of Trenton and promoted to captain by George Washington for bravery under fire.
1776-1778:	Monroe fights in the Battles of Brandywine, Germantown, and Monmouth.
1783-1786:	Monroe is a member of the Continental Congress.
1786, February 16:	Monroe marries Elizabeth Kortright in New York City.
1788:	Monroe is a delegate to the Constitutional Convention.
1799-1803:	Monroe serves as governor of Virginia.
1803-1808:	Monroe represents the United States in France, England, and Spain.
1811-1817:	Monroe serves as secretary of state in the Madison administration.
1816, November:	Monroe is elected president.
1817:	The Rush-Bagot Agreement with Great Britain eliminates fortifications on the U.S.-Canadian border, leading to the world's longest undefended border.
1817, March 4:	Monroe is inaugurated as president.
1817, July 4:	Construction begins on the Erie Canal.
1817, December 10:	Mississippi is admitted as the twentieth state.
1818, April 4:	Congress establishes the official flag of the United States.
1818, December 3:	Illinois is admitted as the twenty-first state.
1819:	With a decision in the case of *McCulloch v. Maryland*, the Supreme Court establishes its power to declare state laws unconstitutional.
1819, February 22:	Florida is purchased from Spain.
1819, May 22:	The SS *Savannah*, the first U.S. steamship to cross the Atlantic Ocean, leaves Savannah, Georgia.
1819, December 14:	Alabama is admitted as the twenty-second state.
1820, March 3:	The Missouri Compromise prohibits slavery in the northern portion of the Louisiana Purchase.
1820, March 15:	Maine is admitted as the twenty-third state.
1820, November:	Monroe is reelected as president.
1821, March 5:	Monroe is inaugurated as president for a second term.
1821, August 10:	Missouri is admitted as the twenty-fourth state.
1823, December 2:	The Monroe Doctrine is proclaimed.
1825, March:	Monroe retires to his farm in Loudoun County, Virginia.
1830, September 23:	Elizabeth Monroe dies in Oak Hill, Virginia.
1831, July 4:	James Monroe dies in New York City.

J. Q. Adams

1767, July 11:	John Quincy Adams is born in Braintree, Massachusetts.
1794:	George Washington appoints Adams minister to the Netherlands.

1796-1797:	Adams serves as minister to Portugal and Prussia.
1797, July 26:	Adams marries Louisa Catherine Johnson in London.
1803-1808:	Adams represents Massachusetts in the U.S. Senate.
1809-1814:	Adams serves as minister to Russia.
1814:	Adams serves on a peace commission to end the War of 1812.
1815-1817:	Adams serves as minister to England.
1817-1825:	Adams serves as secretary of state.
1824, November 2:	A presidential election is held; none of the four candidates receives a majority of the electoral votes.
1825, February 9:	House of Representatives elects Adams president.
1825, March 4:	Adams is inaugurated as president.
1825, October 25:	The Erie Canal opens.
1828, November 4:	Adams is defeated for reelection by Democratic nominee Andrew Jackson.
1831-1848:	Adams serves as a member of the U.S. House of Representatives.
1848, February 23:	John Quincy Adams has a stroke on the floor of the House of Representatives and dies in Washington, D.C.

Jackson

1767, March 15:	Andrew Jackson is born in Waxhaw area, South Carolina.
1784:	Jackson studies law in Salisbury, North Carolina.
1787:	Jackson fights his first duel, with Waightstill Avery.
1791, August:	Jackson marries Rachel Stockley Donelson, the estranged wife of Lewis Robards; Jackson and Rachel later remarry on January 17, 1794.
1796-1797:	Jackson represents Tennessee in the U.S. House of Representatives.
1797-1798:	Jackson serves in the U.S. Senate for Tennessee.
1798-1804	Jackson serves as a judge of the Tennessee Supreme Court.
1806, May 30:	Jackson kills Charles Dickinson in a duel.
1814:	Jackson leads the U.S. Army in campaigns against the Creeks.
1815, January 8:	Jackson defeats British troops at the Battle of New Orleans.
1817-1818:	Jackson fights against the Seminoles in Florida.
1823-1825:	Jackson serves in the U.S. Senate.
1824:	Jackson is an unsuccessful candidate for president.
1828, November 4:	Jackson is elected president.
1828, December 22:	Rachel Jackson dies.
1829, March 4:	Jackson is inaugurated as president.
1830:	The Webster-Hayne Debates on states' rights take place.
1832, May:	Jackson is nominated for president by the Democratic Party.
1832, November 6:	Jackson is reelected president.
1832, November 24:	South Carolina declares federal tariff acts "null and void."
1832, December:	Jackson issues the Nullification Proclamation; crisis is narrowly avoided.
1833, March 4:	Jackson is inaugurated as president for a second term.
1834, March 28:	Jackson is censured by the U.S. Senate for removing public deposits from the Bank of the United States.
1836, March 1:	Texas declares its independence from Mexico.

1836, March 6:	The Alamo falls; its defenders are slaughtered.
1836, April 21:	Texans defeat Mexican general Antonio López de Santa Anna at the Battle of San Jacinto.
1836, June 15:	Arkansas is admitted as the twenty-fifth state.
1837, January 26:	Michigan is admitted as the twenty-sixth state.
1837, March:	Jackson recognizes the independence of Texas.
1837, March 16:	The Senate expunges its 1834 censure resolution.
1845, June 8:	Andrew Jackson dies in Nashville, Tennessee.

Van Buren

1782, December 5:	Martin Van Buren is born in Kinderhook, New York.
1807, February 21:	Van Buren marries Hannah Hoes in Catskill, New York.
1813-1820:	Van Buren serves in New York State Senate.
1815-1819:	Van Buren serves as attorney general for New York.
1819, February 5:	Hannah Van Buren dies in Albany, New York.
1821-1828:	Van Buren represents New York in the U.S. Senate.
1829:	Van Buren serves as governor of New York.
1829-1831:	Van Buren is secretary of state in the Jackson administration.
1833-1837:	Van Buren serves as vice president in the Jackson administration.
1836, November 1:	Van Buren is elected president.
1837, March 4:	Van Buren is inaugurated as president.
1838-1839:	The Cherokees are removed from the South to Oklahoma on the Trail of Tears.
1840, November 3:	Van Buren is defeated for reelection by Whig nominee William Henry Harrison.
1844:	Van Buren is defeated in an attempt at renomination by the Democratic Party.
1848:	Van Buren is unsuccessful as the Free-Soil Party candidate for president; he retires from public life.
1862, July 24:	Martin Van Buren dies in Kinderhook, New York.

W. H. Harrison

1773, February 9:	William Henry Harrison is born near Charles City, Virginia.
1791, August 16:	Harrison is commissioned by General George Washington.
1794-1798:	Harrison serves as a soldier in the Northwest Territory.
1795, November 25:	Harrison marries Anna Tuthill Symmes in North Bend, Ohio.
1799-1800:	Harrison serves in the U.S. House of Representatives for the Northwest Territory.
1800-1813:	Harrison serves as territorial governor of Indiana.
1811, November 7:	Harrison wins the Battle of Tippecanoe.
1812-1814:	Harrison serves as a general during the War of 1812.
1813, October 5:	Harrison defeats British troops and American Indians in the Battle of the Thames.
1816-1819:	Harrison represents Ohio in the U.S. House of Representatives.
1825-1828:	Harrison represents Ohio in the U.S. Senate.

1829:	Harrison retires to his farm in North Bend, Ohio.
1836:	Harrison is unsuccessful as the Whig candidate for president.
1839, December 4-7:	Harrison is nominated for president by the Whig Party.
1840, November 3:	Harrison is elected president.
1841, March 4:	Harrison is inaugurated as president.
1841, April 4:	William Henry Harrison dies in the White House, Washington, D.C.

Tyler

1790, March 29:	John Tyler is born in Greenway, Charles City County, Virginia.
1811-1816:	Tyler serves as a member of the Virginia House of Delegates.
1813, March 29:	Tyler marries Letitia Christian at Cedar Grove in New Kent County, Virginia.
1817-1821:	Tyler represents Virginia in the U.S. House of Representativesa.
1825-1827:	Tyler serves as governor of Virginia.
1827-1836:	Tyler represents Virginia in the U.S. Senate.
1839, December 4-7:	Tyler is nominated by the Whig Party for vice president.
1840, November 3:	Tyler is elected vice president.
1841, April 6:	Tyler takes the oath of president on the death of William Henry Harrison.
1842, September 10:	Letitia Tyler dies in the White House, Washington, D.C.
1844, June 26:	Tyler marries Julia Gardiner in New York City.
1845, March 1:	Texas is annexed by a joint resolution of Congress.
1845, March 3:	Florida is admitted as the twenty-seventh state.
1861, March 1:	Tyler serves as a member of the Virginia secession convention.
1861, July 20:	Tyler is a delegate to the Confederate Provisional Congress.
1862, January 18:	John Tyler dies in Richmond, Virginia.

Polk

1795, November 2:	James K. Polk is born in Mecklenburg County, North Carolina.
1823-1825:	Polk serves in the Tennessee House of Representatives.
1824, January 1:	Polk marries Sarah Childress in Murfreesboro, Tennessee.
1825-1839:	Polk represents Tennessee in the U.S. House of Representatives.
1835, December 7:	Polk is elected Speaker of the House of Representatives; he serves until March 3, 1839.
1839-1841:	Polk serves as governor of Tennessee.
1844, May 27-30:	The Democratic convention in Baltimore nominates Polk as the first "dark horse" candidate.
1844, November 5:	Polk is elected president.
1845, March 4:	Polk is inaugurated as president.
1845, October 10:	The U.S. Naval Academy opens in Annapolis, Maryland.
1845, December 29:	Texas is admitted as the twenty-eighth state.
1846, May 8:	The Battle of Palo Alto is fought against Mexican troops.
1846, May 13:	The United States formally declares war on Mexico.
1846, December 28:	Iowa is admitted as the twenty-ninth state.
1847:	U.S. forces conquer California.
1847, February 23:	General Zachary Taylor wins the Battle of Buena Vista.

1847, March 29:	U.S. troops under General Winfield Scott capture Vera Cruz on the Mexican coast.
1847, September 14:	General Scott captures Mexico City.
1848, January 24:	Gold is discovered in California.
1848, February 2:	The Treaty of Guadalupe Hidalgo ends the Mexican War.
1848, May 29:	Wisconsin is admitted as the thirtieth state.
1848, July 4:	Polk lays the cornerstone of the Washington Monument.
1849:	Polk declines to be a candidate for reelection; he retires to Nashville.
1849, June 15:	James K. Polk dies in Nashville, Tennessee.

Taylor

1784, November 24:	Zachary Taylor is born in Orange County, Virginia.
1808, May 3:	Taylor is commissioned a first lieutenant in the U.S. Army.
1810, June 21:	Taylor marries Margaret Mackall Smith in Louisville, Kentucky.
1812, September:	Taylor defends Fort Harrison against American Indians led by Tecumseh; he is promoted to the rank of brevet major for his gallantry.
1837, December 25:	Taylor is promoted to brevet brigadier general for distinguished service against the Seminoles.
1846, May 8:	Taylor defeats Mexican troops at the Battle of Palo Alto.
1846, May 9:	Taylor defeats Mexican troops at the Battle of Resaca de la Palma.
1846, May 18:	Taylor maneuvers the Mexican army out of Matamoros without a battle.
1846, May 28:	Taylor is promoted to brevet major general for distinguished service.
1846, June 29:	Taylor is promoted to general of the line.
1846, September 25:	Taylor captures Monterey.
1847, February 23:	Taylor defeats the Mexican army under General Antonio López de Santa Anna at the Battle of Buena Vista.
1848, July 18:	Taylor is nominated for president by the Whig Party.
1848, November 7:	Taylor is elected president.
1849, March 4:	Taylor is inaugurated as president.
1850, July 9:	Zachary Taylor dies in Washington, D.C.

Fillmore

1800, January 7:	Millard Fillmore is born in Summerhill, New York.
1826, February 5:	Fillmore marries Abigail Powers in Moravia, New York.
1829-1831:	Fillmore serves in the New York State Assembly.
1833-1835 and 1837-1843:	Fillmore represents New York in the U.S. House of Representatives.
1848, July 7-9	Fillmore is nominated for vice president by the Whig Party.
1848, November 7:	Fillmore is elected vice president.
1850, July 10:	Fillmore assumes the presidency upon the death of Zachary Taylor.
1850, September 18:	A fugitive slave law is enacted.
1852:	Harriet Beecher Stowe publishes the abolitionist novel *Uncle Tom's Cabin*.
1852, June:	Fillmore is denied nomination for president by the Whig Party.
1852, November:	Commodore Matthew C. Perry opens Japan to Western commerce.
1853, March 30:	Abigail Fillmore dies in Washington, D.C.

1856, November:	Fillmore is unsuccessful as the presidential candidate for the Know-Nothing Party.
1858, February 10:	Fillmore marries Caroline Carmichael McIntosh, the widow of Ezekiel C. McIntosh, in Albany, New York.
1874, March 8:	Millard Fillmore dies in Buffalo, New York.

Pierce

1804, November 23:	Franklin Pierce is born in Hillsborough, New Hampshire.
1829-1833:	Pierce serves in the New Hampshire House of Representatives; he serves as speaker in 1832.
1833-1837:	Pierce represents New Hampshire in the U.S. House of Representatives.
1834, November 10:	Pierce marries Jane Means Appleton in Amherst, Massachusetts.
1837-1842:	Pierce represents New Hampshire in the U.S. Senate.
1847:	Pierce enlists as a private in the Mexican War, rising to the rank of major general.
1852, June 1-5:	Pierce is nominated for president by the Democratic Party.
1852, November 2:	Pierce is elected president.
1854:	The Republican Party is founded.
1854, May 22:	Congress enacts the Kansas-Nebraska Act, nullifying the Missouri Compromise.
1854, June 30:	The Gadsden Purchase of border territory from Mexico is negotiated.
1856:	Pierce is denied renomination for president by the Democratic Party.
1863, December 2:	Jane Pierce dies in Andover, Massachusetts.
1869, October 8:	Franklin Pierce dies in Concord, New Hampshire.

Buchanan

1791, April 23:	James Buchanan is born in Mercerburg, Pennsylvania.
1814:	Buchanan serves in the War of 1812.
1814-1815:	Buchanan serves in the Pennsylvania House of Representatives.
1821-1831:	Buchanan represents Pennsylvania in the U.S. House of Representatives.
1832-1833:	Buchanan serves as minister to Russia.
1834-1845:	Buchanan represents Pennsylvania in the U.S. Senate.
1845-1849:	Buchanan serves as secretary of state in the Polk administration.
1856, June 2-6:	Buchanan is nominated for president by the Democratic Party.
1856, November 4:	Buchanan is elected president.
1857, March 4:	Buchanan is inaugurated as president.
1857, March 6:	The U.S. Supreme Court announces the Dred Scott decision, rendering the Missouri Compromise unconstitutional.
1858, May 11:	Minnesota is admitted as the thirty-second state.
1858, August-October:	The Lincoln-Douglas Debates take place.
1859, February 14:	Oregon is admitted as the thirty-third state.
1859, October 16:	John Brown seizes the federal arsenal at Harpers Ferry, Virginia.
1860, November 6:	Abraham Lincoln is elected president.
1860, December 20:	South Carolina secedes from the Union.

1861, January-February:	Mississippi, Florida, Alabama, Georgia, Louisiana, and Texas secede.
1861, January 29:	Kansas is admitted as the thirty-fourth state.
1861, February 8:	The Confederate States of America is established.
1868, June 1:	James Buchanan dies in Lancaster, Pennsylvania.

Lincoln

1809, February 12:	Abraham Lincoln is born near Hodgenville, Kentucky.
1832:	Lincoln serves in the volunteer militia during Black Hawk's War.
1835-1836:	Lincoln serves in the Illinois General Assembly.
1842, November 4:	Lincoln marries Mary Todd in Springfield, Illinois.
1847-1849:	Lincoln represents Illinois in the U.S. House of Representatives.
1858, August-October:	Lincoln debates Stephen A. Douglas in the campaign for U.S. Senate.
1860, May 16-18:	Lincoln is nominated for president by the Republican Party.
1860, November 6:	Lincoln is elected president.
1860, December 20:	South Carolina secedes from the Union.
1861, January-February:	Mississippi, Florida, Alabama, Georgia, Louisiana, and Texas secede.
1861, February 8:	The Confederate States of America is established.
1861, March 4:	Lincoln is inaugurated as president.
1861, April-June:	Virginia, Arkansas, North Carolina, and Tennessee secede.
1861, April 12:	Confederate forces fire on Fort Sumter in Charleston harbor.
1861, April 15:	Lincoln issues call for volunteers.
1861, July 21:	The Union army is routed at the First Battle of Bull Run (Manassas).
1862, March 9:	The battle between the first ironclad warships, *Monitor* and *Virginia* (*Merrimac*) takes place.
1862, April 6-7:	The Battle of Shiloh is fought.
1862, September 17:	The Battle of Antietam ends Confederate general Robert E. Lee's first invasion of the northern states.
1862, September 22:	A preliminary Emancipation Proclamation is issued.
1863, January 1:	The Emancipation Proclamation is issued.
1863, June 19:	West Virginia is admitted as the thirty-fifth state.
1863, July 1-3:	Confederate troops under General Lee are defeated at Gettysburg.
1863, July 4:	Vicksburg surrenders to Union general Ulysses S. Grant.
1863, November 19:	Lincoln delivers the Gettysburg Address.
1864, June 7-8:	Lincoln is renominated for president by the Republican Party.
1864, September 2:	Union General William Tecumseh Sherman captures Atlanta.
1864, October 31:	Nevada is admitted as the thirty-sixth state.
1864, November 8:	Lincoln is reelected as president.
1865, March 4:	Lincoln is inaugurated as president for a second term.
1865, April 9:	Lee surrenders to Grant at Appomattox Court House, Virginia.
1865, April 14:	President Lincoln is shot by John Wilkes Booth at Ford's Theater in Washington, D.C.
1865, April 15:	Abraham Lincoln dies from his wounds.

A. Johnson

1808, December 29:	Andrew Johnson is born in Raleigh, North Carolina.
1827, Mary 17:	Johnson marries Eliza McCardle in Greeneville, Tennessee.
1828:	Johnson serves as leader of the Workingmen's Party in Tennessee; he is elected alderman in Greeneville.
1830-1833:	Johnson serves three terms as mayor of Greeneville.
1835-1837 and 1839:	Johnson serves in the Tennessee legislature.
1843-1853:	Johnson represents Tennessee in the U.S. House of Representatives.
1853-1855:	Johnson serves as governor of Tennessee.
1857-1862:	Johnson represents Tennessee in the U.S. Senate.
1862-1865:	Johnson serves as military governor of Tennessee.
1864, June 7-8	Democrat Johnson is nominated for vice president on the Union Party ticket with Republican Abraham Lincoln.
1864, November 8:	Johnson is elected vice president.
1865, April 15:	Johnson assumes the presidency upon the assassination of Lincoln.
1865, April 26:	Confederate general Joseph E. Johnston surrenders to Union general William Tecumseh Sherman at Durham Station, North Carolina.
1865, May 26:	Confederate general Edmund Kirby-Smith surrenders the last major Confederate army, effectively ending the Civil War.
1865, December 18:	The Thirteenth Amendment to the Constitution is ratified, abolishing slavery.
1867:	Congress passes the Reconstruction Act against Johnson's opposition.
1867, March 1:	Nebraska is admitted as the thirty-seventh state.
1867, March 30:	The United States purchases Alaska from Russia.
1868, February 21:	The U.S. House of Representatives impeaches Johnson.
1868, March 13:	The impeachment trial begins in the Senate.
1868, May 26:	Johnson is acquitted of all charges.
1868, July 28:	The Fourteenth Amendment to the Constitution is ratified, establishing the civil rights of all citizens.
1868:	Johnson is denied nomination for president by the Democratic Party.
1874-1875:	Johnson represents Tennessee in the U.S. Senate.
1875, July 31:	Andrew Johnson dies near Carter Station, Tennessee.

Grant

1822, April 27:	Ulysses S. Grant is born in Port Pleasant, Ohio.
1839-1843:	Grant attends the U.S. military academy at West Point.
1846-1847:	Grant serves in the Mexican War and is promoted for gallant and meritorious conduct.
1848, August 22:	Grant marries Julia Boggs Dent in St. Louis, Missouri.
1854, July 31:	Grant resigns from the U.S. Army.
1854-1860:	Grant works in farming, real estate, and in his father's hardware and leather store.
1861, May 17:	Grant is commissioned a brigadier general in the U.S. Volunteers.
1862, April 6-7:	Grant wins the Battle of Shiloh, one of the bloodiest of the Civil War.
1863, July 4:	Grant captures the Confederate fortress city of Vicksburg, Mississippi.

1863, November 24-25:	Grant wins the Battle of Chattanooga.
1864, March 9:	Grant is commissioned a lieutenant general and made commander in chief of the U.S. Army.
1865, April 9:	Grant accepts the surrender of Confederate general Robert E. Lee at Appomattox Court House, Virginia.
1866, July 25:	Grant is commissioned General of the Army.
1868, May 20-21:	Grant is nominated for president by the Republican Party.
1868, November 3:	Grant is elected president.
1869, March 4:	Grant is inaugurated as president.
1870, March 30:	The Fifteenth Amendment to the Constitution is ratified, extending voting rights.
1872, January 1:	The Civil Service Act becomes effective.
1872, June 5-6:	Grant is renominated for president by the Republican Party.
1872, November 5:	Grant is reelected president.
1873, March 4:	Grant is inaugurated as president for a second term.
1876, March 10:	Alexander Graham Bell transmits a human voice over the telephone.
1876, June 25:	Sitting Bull and the Sioux defeat General George Armstrong Custer at the Battle of the Little Bighorn.
1876, August 1:	Colorado is admitted as the thirty-eighth state.
1884:	Grant's financial ruin results from bad investments.
1885:	Grant completes his memoirs four days before his death.
1885, July 23:	Ulysses S. Grant dies in Mount McGregor, New York.

Hayes

1822, October 4:	Rutherford B. Hayes is born in Delaware, Ohio.
1852, December 30:	Hayes marries Lucy Ware Webb in Cincinnati, Ohio.
1861-1865:	Hayes serves in the Union army, rising to the rank of brevet major general of volunteers.
1865-1867:	Hayes represents Ohio in the U.S. House of Representatives.
1868 and 1876-1877:	Hayes serves as governor of Ohio.
1876, June 14-16:	Hayes is nominated for president by the Republican Party.
1876, November 7:	Presidential elections are held; the results are in doubt.
1877, March 2:	An electoral commission declares Hayes the winner.
1877, March 4:	Hayes is inaugurated as president.
1878, February 19:	Thomas Alva Edison obtains the first phonograph patent.
1879, October 21:	Edison invents the first practical electric light.
1880:	Hayes declines to run for a second term as president.
1889, June 25:	Lucy Hayes dies in Fremont, Ohio.
1893, January 17:	Rutherford B. Hayes dies in Fremont, Ohio.

Garfield

| 1831, November 19: | James A. Garfield is born in Orange Township, Ohio. |
| 1857-1861: | Garfield serves as president of the Western Reserve Eclectic Institute; he teaches Latin, Greek, higher mathematics, history, philosophy, English literature, and rhetoric. |

1858, November 11:	Garfield marries Lucretia Rudolph in Hiram, Ohio.
1859:	Garfield serves in the Ohio State Senate.
1861-1863:	Garfield serves in the Union army, rising to the rank of major general of volunteers.
1863, December 5:	Garfield resigns from the army to take a seat in the U.S. House of Representatives.
1877:	Garfield serves as a member of the electoral commission that decides the disputed presidential election of 1876.
1880, June:	Garfield is nominated for president by the Republican Party.
1880, November 2:	Garfield is elected president.
1881, March 4:	Garfield is inaugurated as president.
1881, May 21:	The American Red Cross is organized.
1881, July 2:	President Garfield is shot by Charles J. Guiteau in a Washington, D.C., train station.
1881, September 19:	James A. Garfield dies in Elberon, New Jersey.

Arthur

1829, October 5:	Chester A. Arthur is born in Fairfield, Vermont.
1859, October 25:	Arthur marries Ellen Lewis Herndon in New York City.
1861-1863:	Arthur serves in the Union army.
1871-1878:	Arthur serves as collector of the Port of New York.
1880, January 12:	Ellen Arthur dies in New York City.
1880, June:	Arthur is nominated for vice president by the Republican Party.
1880, November 2:	Arthur is elected vice president.
1881, July 2:	President James Garfield is shot by Charles J. Guiteau.
1881, September 20:	Arthur assumes the presidency on the death of Garfield.
1883, March 9:	The Civil Service Commission is organized.
1884:	Arthur is the unsuccessful candidate for the Republican presidential nomination.
1885, February 21:	The Washington Monument is dedicated.
1886, November 18:	Chester A. Arthur dies in New York, New York.

Cleveland

1837, March 18:	Grover Cleveland is born in Caldwell, New Jersey.
1883-1885:	Cleveland serves as governor of New York.
1884, July 11:	Cleveland is nominated for president by the Democratic Party.
1884, November 4:	Cleveland is elected president.
1885, March 4:	Cleveland is inaugurated as president.
1886, March 22:	The first Interstate Commerce Commission is appointed.
1886, May 17:	The Haymarket Riot in Chicago leaves eleven people dead, over one hundred wounded.
1886, June 2:	Cleveland marries Frances Folsom in Washington, D.C.
1886, October 28:	The Statue of Liberty is dedicated in New York harbor.
1886, December:	The American Federation of Labor is organized.
1887, February 4:	Congress passes the Interstate Commerce Act.

1888, June 5:	Cleveland is renominated for president by the Democratic Party.
1888, November 5:	Republican candidate Benjamin Harrison defeats Cleveland.
1892, June 2:	Cleveland is nominated for president by the Democratic Party.
1892, November 8:	Cleveland is elected president, defeating Harrison.
1893, March 4:	Cleveland is inaugurated as president for a second term.
1893, July 1:	A secret operation removes cancer from Cleveland's mouth.
1894, May:	Cleveland sends federal troops to Chicago to deal with the Pullman Strike.
1894, July 4:	Hawaii declares itself a republic.
1895, February 24:	A Cuban revolt begins against Spanish rule.
1895, May 20:	The U.S. Supreme Court declares income tax to be unconstitutional.
1896, January 4:	Utah is admitted as the forty-fifth state.
1901, October 15:	Cleveland becomes trustee of Princeton University.
1908, June 24:	Grover Cleveland dies in Princeton, New Jersey.

B. Harrison

1833, August 20:	Benjamin Harrison is born in North Bend, Ohio.
1853, October 20:	Harrison marries Caroline Lavinia Scott.
1862-1865:	Harrison serves in the Union army, rising to the rank of brevet brigadier general.
1881-1887:	Harrison represents Indiana in the U.S. Senate.
1888, June 23:	Harrison is nominated for president by the Republican Party.
1888, November 6:	Harrison is elected president.
1889, March 4:	Harrison is inaugurated as president.
1889, April 22:	Oklahoma is opened for settlers.
1889, May 31:	The Great Johnstown Flood occurs in Pennsylvania.
1889, November 2:	North Dakota and South Dakota are admitted as the thirty-ninth and fortieth states.
1889, November 8:	Montana is admitted as the forty-first state.
1889, November 11:	Washington is admitted as the forty-second state.
1890, July 2:	The Sherman Antitrust Act is enacted.
1890, July 3:	Idaho is admitted as the forty-third state.
1890, July 10:	Wyoming is admitted as the forty-fourth state.
1892, June 10:	Harrison is renominated for president by the Republican Party.
1892, October 25:	Caroline Harrison dies in Washington, D.C.
1892, November 8:	Harrison is defeated for reelection by Democratic nominee Grover Cleveland.
1896, April 6:	Harrison marries Mary Scott Lord Dimmick, the widow of Walter Erskine Dimmick, in New York City.
1901, March 13:	Benjamin Harrison dies in Indianapolis, Indiana.

McKinley

| 1843, January 29: | William McKinley is born in Niles, Ohio. |
| 1861, June 11-1865: | McKinley serves in the Union army, rising from private to the rank of brevet major of volunteers. |

1871, January 25:	McKinley marries Ida Saxton in Canton, Ohio.
1877-1883 and 1885-1891:	McKinley represents Ohio in the U.S. House of Representatives.
1892-1896:	McKinley serves as governor of Ohio.
1896, June 18:	McKinley is nominated for president by the Republican Party.
1896, November 3:	McKinley is elected president.
1897, March 4:	McKinley is inaugurated as president.
1898, February 15:	The battleship USS *Maine* blows up in the harbor of Havana, Cuba.
1898, April 25:	The United States declares war on Spain.
1898, May 1:	Commodore George Dewey destroys the Spanish fleet in Manila Bay, Philippines.
1898, June 10:	U.S. Marines land in Cuba.
1898, July 7:	The United States annexes Hawaii.
1898, December 10:	The Treaty of Paris ends the Spanish-American War.
1899, April 11:	The Philippines, Puerto Rico, and Guam are formally acquired by the United States.
1900, June 21:	McKinley is renominated for president by the Republican Party.
1900, November 6:	McKinley is reelected president.
1901, March 4:	McKinley is inaugurated as president for a second term.
1901, September 6:	President McKinley is shot by anarchist Leon Czolgosz in Buffalo, New York.
1901, September 14:	William McKinley dies in Buffalo, New York.

T. Roosevelt

1858, October 27:	Theodore Roosevelt is born in New York, New York.
1880, October 27:	Roosevelt marries Alice Hathaway Lee in Brookline, Massachusetts.
1882-1884:	Roosevelt serves in the New York State Assembly.
1884, February 14:	Alice Roosevelt dies in New York City.
1886, December 2:	Roosevelt marries Edith Kermit Carow in London.
1889-1895:	Roosevelt serves on the U.S. Civil Service Commission.
1889, May 6:	Roosevelt is appointed president of the New York City Board of Police Commissioners.
1897, April 19:	Roosevelt is appointed assistant secretary of the Navy.
1898:	Roosevelt resigns his position and forms a volunteer cavalry regiment, called the Rough Riders, which serves in the Spanish-American War.
1899-1901:	Roosevelt serves as governor of New York.
1900, June 21:	Roosevelt is nominated for vice president by the Republican Party.
1900, November 6:	Roosevelt is elected vice president.
1901, March 4:	Roosevelt is inaugurated as vice president.
1901, September 14:	Roosevelt succeeds to the presidency on the death of William McKinley.
1902, May 20:	Cuba becomes a republic.
1903, November 3:	Panama declares its independence from Colombia.
1903, November 18:	The newly formed Republic of Panama grants the United States land for a canal.

1903, December 17:	The Wright brothers make the first powered airplane flight at Kitty Hawk, North Carolina.
1904, June 23:	Roosevelt is nominated for president by the Republican Party.
1904, November 8:	Roosevelt is elected president.
1905, March 4:	Roosevelt is inaugurated as president.
1905, September 5:	A Russo-Japanese peace treaty is signed in Portsmouth, New Hampshire.
1906:	Roosevelt is awarded Nobel Peace Prize for helping end the Russo-Japanese War.
1906, April 18-20:	A powerful earthquake rocks San Francisco, leaving seven hundred dead.
1907, November 16:	Oklahoma is admitted as the forty-sixth state.
1907, December 16:	The American "Great White Fleet" sets sail on an around-the-world voyage.
1912, June:	Roosevelt is denied renomination for president by the Republican Party.
1912, August:	Roosevelt is nominated for president by the Progressive Party (Bull Moose Party).
1912, November 5:	Roosevelt is defeated by Democratic nominee Woodrow Wilson.
1919, January 6:	Theodore Roosevelt dies in Oyster Bay, New York.

Taft

1857, September 15:	William Howard Taft is born in Cincinnati, Ohio.
1886, June 19:	Taft marries Helen Herron in Cincinnati.
1890-1892:	Taft serves as U.S. solicitor general.
1892-1900:	Taft serves as a federal circuit court judge.
1896-1900:	Taft serves as dean of the University of Cincinnati Law School.
1901, July 4:	Taft is appointed governor-general of the Philippines.
1904-1908:	Taft serves as secretary of war in the Roosevelt administration.
1907:	Taft is made the provisional governor of Cuba.
1908, June 19:	Taft is nominated for president by the Republican Party.
1908, November 3:	Taft is elected president.
1909, March 4:	Taft is inaugurated as president.
1909, April 6:	Robert Edwin Peary reaches the North Pole.
1910, February 8:	The Boy Scouts of America is incorporated.
1912, January 6:	New Mexico is admitted as the forty-seventh state.
1912, February 14:	Arizona is admitted as the forty-eighth state.
1912, June 22:	Taft is renominated for president by the Republican Party.
1912, November 5:	Taft is defeated for reelection by Democratic candidate Woodrow Wilson.
1913, February 25:	The Sixteenth Amendment to the Constitution is ratified, authorizing an income tax.
1913-1921:	Taft serves as a professor of law at Yale University.
1921, June 30:	Taft becomes chief justice of the U.S. Supreme Court.
1930, February 3:	Taft steps down from the Supreme Court.
1930, March 8:	William Howard Taft dies in Washington, D.C.

Wilson

1856, December 28:	Woodrow Wilson is born in Staunton, Virginia.

1870:	His family moves from Augusta, Georgia, to Columbia, South Carolina.
1885, June 24:	Wilson marries Ellen Louise Axson in Savannah, Georgia.
1890-1902:	Wilson serves as professor of jurisprudence and political economy at Princeton University.
1902, June 9:	Wilson is unanimously elected president of Princeton University.
1910, September 15:	Wilson is nominated for governor of New Jersey by the Democratic Party.
1911-1913:	Wilson serves as governor of New Jersey.
1912, July 2:	Wilson is nominated for president by the Democratic Party.
1912, November 5:	Wilson is elected president.
1913, March 4:	Wilson is inaugurated as president.
1913, May 31:	The Seventeenth Amendment to the Constitution is ratified, bringing the direct election of U.S. senators.
1913, December 23:	The Federal Reserve Act is established.
1914, August 3:	World War I begins in Europe.
1914, August 6:	Ellen Wilson dies in Washington, D.C.
1915, May 7:	A German U-boat sinks the liner *Lusitania*, with a loss of American lives.
1915, December 18:	Wilson marries Edith Bolling Galt, the widow of Norman Galt, in Washington, D.C.
1916, March:	General John Pershing pursues Mexican revolutionary leader Pancho Villa.
1916, June 16:	Wilson is renominated for president by the Democratic Party.
1916, November 7:	Wilson is reelected president.
1917, March 4:	Wilson is inaugurated as president for a second term.
1917, April 6:	The United States declares war on Germany.
1917, June 8:	The first units of the American Expeditionary Force land in England.
1918, January 8:	Wilson outlines his Fourteen Points for peace.
1918, November 11:	An armistice ends the fighting.
1919, January 29:	The Eighteenth Amendment to the Constitution is ratified, bringing Prohibition.
1919, June 28:	A peace treaty is signed with Germany at Versailles, France.
1919, September 26:	Wilson collapses in Pueblo, Colorado, while campaigning for the League of Nations.
1919, November 19:	The U.S. Senate rejects the Treaty of Versailles.
1920, January 13:	The first meeting of the League of Nations convenes with the United States not represented.
1920, August 26:	The Nineteenth Amendment to the Constitution is ratified, giving women the vote.
1920, December 10:	Wilson is awarded the Nobel Peace Prize.
1924, February 3:	Woodrow Wilson dies in Washington, D.C.

Harding

1865, November 2:	Warren G. Harding is born in Caledonia, Ohio.
1884, November 26:	Harding purchases part interest in the *Star* newspaper in Marion, Ohio.
1891, July 8:	Harding marries Florence Kling De Wolfe.
1899-1903:	Harding serves in the Ohio State Senate.

1904-1905:	Harding serves as Ohio lieutenant governor.
1915-1921:	Harding represents Ohio in the U.S. Senate.
1920, June 12:	Harding is nominated for president by the Republican Party.
1920, November 2:	Harding is elected president.
1921, March 4:	Harding is inaugurated as president.
1921, May 3:	West Virginia enacts the first state sales tax.
1921, May 19:	Congress passes the first act limiting immigration.
1921, November 11:	The Tomb of the Unknown Soldier is dedicated at Arlington National Cemetery.
1922, March 29:	The major naval powers agree on a limitation to naval armaments.
1922, October 3:	Rebecca L. Felton of Georgia becomes the first woman to serve in the U.S. Senate.
1923, January 23:	Mae Ella Nolan of California takes office as the first woman elected to Congress.
1923, August 2:	Warren G. Harding dies in San Francisco, California.

Coolidge

1872, July 4:	Calvin Coolidge is born in Plymouth, Vermont.
1905, October 4:	Coolidge marries Grace Anna Goodhue in Burlington, Vermont.
1907-1908:	Coolidge serves in the Massachusetts House of Representatives.
1912-1915:	Coolidge serves in the Massachusetts State Senate; he is president of the senate from 1914 to 1915.
1919-1920:	Coolidge serves as governor of Massachusetts.
1919:	Coolidge settles a Boston police strike.
1920, November 2:	Coolidge is elected vice president.
1921, March 4:	Coolidge is inaugurated as vice president.
1923, August 3:	Coolidge succeeds to the presidency on the death of President Warren G. Harding.
1923-1924:	Senate investigations reveal the extent of the Teapot Dome oil scandal in the Harding administration.
1924, June 12:	Coolidge is nominated for president by the Republican Party.
1924, November 4:	Coolidge is elected president.
1925, January 5:	Nellie Tayloe Ross of Wyoming becomes the first woman to be elected governor.
1925, March 4:	Coolidge is inaugurated as president.
1925, March 23:	Tennessee enacts a law making it illegal to teach the theory of evolution.
1927, May 20:	Charles Lindbergh flies solo across the Atlantic Ocean.
1928:	Coolidge decides not to seek renomination for the presidency.
1933, January 5:	Calvin Coolidge dies in Northampton, Massachusetts.

Hoover

1874, August 10:	Herbert Hoover is born in West Branch, Iowa.
1895-1913:	Hoover works as a mining engineer and consultant all over the world.
1899, February 10:	Hoover marries Lou Henry in Monterey, California.

1899-1900:	Hoover tours China with his wife; he helps defend the city of Tientsin during the Boxer Rebellion.
1914-1915:	Hoover serves as chair of the American Relief Committee in London.
1915-1918:	Hoover serves as chair of the Commission for Relief in Belgium.
1917, August-1919, June:	Hoover serves as a U.S. food administrator in Europe.
1919:	Hoover serves as chair of the Supreme Economic Conference in Paris.
1920:	Hoover serves as chair of the European Relief Council.
1921-1928:	Hoover acts as secretary of commerce during the Harding and Coolidge administrations.
1928, June 14:	Hoover is nominated for president by the Republican Party.
1928, November 6:	Hoover is elected president.
1929, March 4:	Hoover is inaugurated as president.
1929, March 16:	The first Academy Awards are presented.
1929, October 29:	The New York Stock Market crashes, beginning the Great Depression.
1931, March 3:	"The Star-Spangled Banner" is adopted as the U.S. national anthem.
1931, December 15:	Maria Norton of New Jersey becomes the first woman to chair a congressional committee.
1932, January 12:	Hattie Caraway of Arkansas becomes the first woman to serve in the U.S. Senate by election rather than appointment.
1932, May 21:	Amelia Earhart completes the first transatlantic solo flight by a woman.
1932, June 16:	Hoover is renominated for president by the Republican Party.
1932, July:	Unemployed veterans march on Washington, D.C.; they are dispersed by U.S. Army troops.
1932, November 8:	Hoover is defeated for reelection by Democratic nominee Franklin D. Roosevelt.
1933, February 6:	The Twentieth Amendment to the Constitution is ratified, changing the dates for the inauguration of the president and vice president from March 4 to January 20.
1944, January 7:	Lou Hoover dies in New York City.
1946:	President Harry S Truman appoints Hoover coordinator of the European food program.
1947-1949 and 1953-1955:	Hoover serves as chair of the Hoover Commission on the reorganization of the executive branch of the U.S. government.
1964, October 20:	Herbert Hoover dies in New York City.

F. D. Roosevelt

1882, January 30:	Franklin D. Roosevelt is born in Hyde Park, New York.
1905, March 17:	Roosevelt marries Eleanor Roosevelt in New York City.
1910, November 8:	Roosevelt is elected to the New York State Senate.
1913-1920:	Roosevelt serves as assistant secretary of the Navy in the Wilson administration.
1920, July:	Roosevelt is nominated for vice president by the Democratic Party with James M. Cox.

1920, November:	The Cox-Roosevelt ticket is defeated.
1921, August:	Roosevelt is stricken with polio while at his summer home in Campobello, Canada.
1929-1933:	Roosevelt serves as governor of New York.
1932, July 2:	Roosevelt is nominated for president by the Democratic Party.
1932, November 8:	Roosevelt is elected president.
1933, February 15:	Giuseppi Zangara attempts to assassinate Roosevelt in Miami.
1933, March 4:	Roosevelt is inaugurated as president. He appoints Frances Perkins as secretary of labor, making her the first woman to serve in the cabinet.
1933, March 5-9:	Roosevelt declares a "bank holiday" to allow U.S. financial system to reorganize.
1933, March 9- June 16:	During this period, known as the Hundred Days, Congress enacts much of the New Deal recovery measures proposed by Roosevelt.
1933, March 31:	The Civilian Conservation Corps (CCC) is established.
1933, April 12:	Roosevelt appoints Ruth Bryan Owen, the daughter of William Jennings Bryan, as minister to Denmark, making her the first woman to represent the United States abroad.
1933, May 12:	The Agricultural Adjustment Act (AAA) and the Federal Emergency Relief Act (FERA) are passed.
1933, May 13:	The Tennessee Valley Authority (TVA) is approved.
1933, June 5:	The United States rejects the gold standard as the basis for its currency.
1933, June 16:	Congress creates the Federal Deposit Insurance Corporation (FDIC) and passes the National Industrial Recovery Act (NIRA), creating the National Recovery Administration (NRA) and the Public Works Administration (PWA).
1933, November 16:	The United States diplomatically recognizes the Soviet Union.
1933, December 3:	The Twenty-first Amendment to the Constitution repeals the Eighteenth Amendment (Prohibition).
1934, June 6:	The Securities and Exchange Commission is established to regulate the stock market.
1934, June 19:	The Federal Communications Commission (FCC) is established.
1935:	The Federal Bureau of Investigation (FBI) is established, with J. Edgar Hoover as chief.
1935, April 8:	The Works Progress Administration (WPA) is established.
1935, May 27:	The U.S. Supreme Court declares the NIRA unconstitutional.
1935, July 5:	The Wagner Labor Relations Act is enacted, strengthening labor unions.
1935, August 14:	The Social Security Act is passed.
1936, January 6:	The Supreme Court declares the AAA unconstitutional.
1936, June 27:	Roosevelt is renominated for president by the Democratic Party.
1936, November 3:	Roosevelt is reelected president in a landslide victory.
1937, January 20:	Roosevelt is inaugurated as president for a second term.
1937, July 22:	The U.S. Senate defeats Roosevelt's plan to "pack" the Supreme Court by adding new justices.
1938, June 25:	The Fair Labor Standards Act is passed.
1939, September 1:	Nazi Germany invades Poland, sparking World War II.

1939, September 5:	The United States declares neutrality in the European war.
1940, May 10:	Winston Churchill becomes prime minister of Great Britain.
1940, July 18:	Roosevelt is renominated for president by the Democratic Party.
1940, September 3:	Roosevelt announces the trade of fifty World War I destroyers to Great Britain in exchange for air and naval bases in the Western Hemisphere.
1940, September 16:	The Selective Training and Service Act (the draft) is approved.
1940, November 5:	Roosevelt is reelected president for an unprecedented third term.
1941, January 6:	Roosevelt outlines the Four Freedoms in his State of the Union address.
1941, January 20:	Roosevelt is inaugurated as president for his third term.
1941, March 11:	The Lend-Lease Act providing aid to Great Britain is passed.
1941, June 22:	Nazi Germany invades the Soviet Union.
1941, August 14:	Roosevelt and Churchill issue the Atlantic Charter, their joint statement of principles for a just and lasting peace.
1941, December 7:	In a date that "will live in infamy," Japanese forces launch a surprise attack on Pearl Harbor, Hawaii, and on Guam and the Philippines.
1941, December 8:	The United States declares war against Japan.
1941, December 11:	Germany and Italy declare war against the United States.
1941, December 12:	Japanese troops capture Guam, the first U.S. territory lost during World War II.
1942, April 9:	Japan captures the Philippines.
1942, June 3-4:	The U.S. naval victory at Midway marks a turning point in the war against Japan.
1942, October-December:	Allied forces invade North Africa.
1942, August-November:	U.S. forces defeat Japanese troops in the Battle of Guadalcanal.
1942, December 2:	The Manhattan Project creates the first self-sustained nuclear chain reaction necessary to building the atomic bomb.
1943, January 14-24:	Roosevelt and Churchill meet at Casablanca in North Africa.
1943, September:	The Allies invade Italy.
1943, November 28-December 1:	Roosevelt, Churchill, and Soviet leader Joseph Stalin meet in Tehran, Iran.
1944, June 6:	Allied forces invade France, an event known as D day.
1944, June 22:	Congress approves the G.I. Bill of Rights.
1944, August-October:	The Dumbarton Oaks Conference lays the groundwork for the United Nations.
1944, July 21:	Roosevelt is renominated for president by the Democratic Party.
1944, November 7:	Roosevelt is reelected president for a fourth term.
1945, January 20:	Roosevelt is inaugurated as president.
1945, February 4-11:	Roosevelt, Churchill, and Stalin meet at Yalta in the Crimea.
1945, April 12:	Franklin D. Roosevelt dies in Warm Springs, Georgia.

Truman

1884, May 8:	Harry S Truman is born in Lamar, Missouri.

1918:	Truman serves with the American Expeditionary Force in France, rising to the rank of major.
1919, June 28:	Truman marries Elizabeth Virginia "Bess" Wallace in Independence, Missouri.
1919-1921:	Truman works in a haberdashery (men's clothing) business in Kansas City, Missouri.
1922-1924:	Truman serves as a county court judge (administrative, not judicial) in Missouri.
1935-1945:	Truman represents Missouri in the U.S. Senate.
1941-1944:	Truman serves as chair of the Special Senate Committee to Investigate the National Defense Program (Truman Committee).
1944, July:	Truman is nominated for vice president by the Democratic Party.
1944, November 7:	Truman is elected vice president.
1945, April 12:	Truman succeeds to the presidency on the death of Franklin D. Roosevelt.
1945, May 7:	Germany surrenders unconditionally to the Allies, an event known as V-E Day.
1945, June 26:	The United Nations Charter is signed in San Francisco.
1945, July 17-August 2:	Truman attends the Potsdam Conference.
1945, August 6:	The United States drops an atomic bomb on Hiroshima, Japan.
1945, August 9:	The United States drops a second atomic bomb on Nagasaki, Japan.
1945, August 14:	Japan surrenders unconditionally to the Allies, an event known as V-J Day.
1947:	The Central Intelligence Agency (CIA) is established.
1947, May 15:	Congress approves the Truman Doctrine to fight communism in Turkey and Greece.
1948, April 1:	The Soviet Union blockades Berlin; the United States begins an airlift of food and supplies.
1948, April 2:	Congress passes the Marshall Plan to rebuild European economies.
1948, July 14:	Truman is nominated for president by the Democratic Party.
1948, November 2:	Truman is elected president.
1949, January 20:	Truman is inaugurated as president.
1949, April 4:	The North Atlantic Treaty Organization (NATO) is established.
1950, June 25:	North Korea invades South Korea; the United Nations supports South Korea.
1950, July 8:	General Douglas MacArthur is named commander in chief of the United Nations forces in South Korea.
1950, November 1:	Puerto Rican nationalists attempt to assassinate Truman.
1950, November 26:	Communist China enters the Korean War on the side of North Korea.
1951, February 26:	The Twenty-second Amendment to the Constitution is ratified, limiting presidents to two terms.
1951, April 11:	Truman relieves MacArthur from command for insubordination.
1972, December 26:	Harry S Truman dies in Kansas City, Missouri.

Eisenhower

1890, October 14:	Dwight D. Eisenhower is born in Denison, Texas.

1911, June 14:	Eisenhower enters the U.S. military academy at West Point.
1916, July 1:	Eisenhower marries Marie "Mamie" Geneva Doud in Denver, Colorado.
1935-1939:	Eisenhower serves as assistant to General Douglas MacArthur in the Philippines.
1942, November 8:	Eisenhower is appointed commander in chief of the Allied forces in North Africa.
1943, July-December:	Eisenhower commands the invasion of Italy.
1944, June 6:	Eisenhower commands the D day invasion of France.
1945-1948:	Eisenhower serves as Chief of Staff for the U.S. Army.
1945, May 7:	Eisenhower accepts the unconditional surrender of Germany.
1950-1952:	Eisenhower commands the NATO forces in Europe.
1952, July 11:	Eisenhower is nominated for president by the Republican Party.
1952, November 4:	Eisenhower is elected president.
1953, January 20:	Eisenhower is inaugurated as president.
1953, June 19:	Julius and Ethel Rosenberg are executed for spying for the Soviet Union.
1953, July 27:	An armistice ends the Korean War.
1954, April 22-June 17:	The Army-McCarthy hearings are held.
1954, May 17:	The U.S. Supreme Court declares school segregation unconstitutional.
1955, April 12:	The Salk vaccine is approved for use in the prevention of polio.
1956, August 23:	Eisenhower is renominated for president by the Republican Party.
1956, November 6:	Eisenhower is reelected president.
1957, January 20:	Eisenhower is inaugurated as president for a second term.
1957, September 24:	Eisenhower sends federal troops to Little Rock, Arkansas, to enforce school integration.
1957, October 4:	The Soviet Union launches *Sputnik,* the first artificial satellite.
1958, January 31:	The United States launches its first satellite, *Explorer I.*
1959, January 1:	Fidel Castro seizes power in Cuba.
1959, January 3:	Alaska is admitted as the forty-ninth state.
1959, March 18:	Hawaii is admitted as the fiftieth state.
1969, March 28:	Dwight D. Eisenhower dies in Washington, D.C.

Kennedy

1917, May 29:	John F. Kennedy is born in Brookline, Massachusetts.
1943, August 2:	Kennedy's torpedo boat, *PT-109,* is rammed and sunk by a Japanese destroyer; he helps save crew members.
1946-1951:	Kennedy represents Massachusetts in the U.S. House of Representatives.
1952, November 8:	Kennedy is elected to the U.S. Senate.
1953, September 12:	Kennedy marries Jacqueline Lee Bouvier in Newport, Rhode Island.
1957, May 6:	Kennedy is awarded the Pulitzer Prize in biography for *Profiles in Courage.*
1960, July 13:	Kennedy is nominated for president by the Democratic Party.
1960, November 8:	Kennedy is elected president.
1961, January 20:	Kennedy is inaugurated as president.
1961, January 25:	Kennedy holds the first live presidential news conference.

1961, March 29:	The Twenty-third Amendment to the Constitution is ratified, giving residents of the District of Columbia the right to vote for president.
1961, April 17-20:	The Bay of Pigs invasion fails to oust Fidel Castro.
1961, May 5:	Alan Shepard becomes the first U.S. astronaut in space.
1961, August 12-13:	Communist East Germany builds the Berlin Wall.
1962, February 20:	John Glenn becomes the first American to orbit the earth.
1962, June 25:	The U.S. Supreme Court declares prayer in public schools unconstitutional.
1962, October:	Kennedy imposes a "quarantine" and forces the Soviet Union to withdraw nuclear missiles from Cuba, an event known as the Cuban Missile Crisis.
1963, June 19:	Kennedy proposes a strong civil rights bill to Congress.
1963, June 20:	The United States and the Soviet Union agree to a direct communication link (hot line).
1963, July 25:	The United States, Great Britain, and the Soviet Union agree to a limited nuclear test treaty.
1963, August 28:	Following the March on Washington in support of civil rights, Martin Luther King, Jr., gives his "I Have a Dream" speech.
1963, November 22:	John F. Kennedy is assassinated in Dallas, Texas.

L. B. Johnson

1908, August 27:	Lyndon B. Johnson is born in Gillespie County, Texas.
1934, November 17:	Johnson marries Claudia Alta "Lady Bird" Taylor.
1937, April 10:	Johnson wins a special election for a seat in the U.S. House of Representatives.
1941, December-1948:	Johnson serves in the U.S. Naval Reserve, rising to the rank of commander and winning the Silver Star.
1948-1961:	Johnson represents Texas in the U.S. Senate.
1953-1961:	Johnson serves as the Democratic leader in the Senate.
1960, July 14:	Johnson is unanimously nominated for vice president by the Democratic Party.
1960, November 8:	Johnson is elected vice president.
1963, November 22:	Johnson accompanies President John F. Kennedy on a visit to Dallas and is sworn in as president after Kennedy's assassination.
1963, November 29:	Johnson appoints a seven-member commission headed by Supreme Court Chief Justice Earl Warren to investigate the Kennedy assassination.
1964, January 23:	The Twenty-fourth Amendment to the Constitution is ratified, banning poll taxes.
1964, February 17:	The U.S. Supreme Court rules that congressional districts must be equal in population, known as the "one-man, one-vote" decision.
1964, March 16:	Johnson sends his legislative program for the War on Poverty to Congress.
1964, July 2:	Johnson signs the Civil Rights Act of 1964.
1964, July 18-21:	Race riots erupt in New York City.

1964, August 7:	Congress passes the Tonkin Gulf Resolution, giving Johnson approval to undertake military action in Vietnam.
1964, August 24:	Johnson is nominated for president by the Democratic Party.
1964, September 27:	The Warren Commission report names Lee Harvey Oswald as the lone assassin in the killing of President Kennedy.
1964, November 3:	Johnson is elected president in landslide victory over Republican nominee Barry Goldwater.
1965-1969:	The war in Vietnam escalates.
1965, January 4:	Johnson proposes Great Society legislative programs in his State of the Union address.
1965, January 20:	Johnson is inaugurated as president.
1965, June 3:	Major Edward White becomes the first American to walk in space.
1965, July 30:	Johnson signs the Medicare bill.
1965, August 6:	Johnson signs a voting rights bill.
1965, August 11-16:	Race riots in the Watts section of Los Angeles leave thirty-five dead, over eight hundred injured.
1966, June 13:	The Supreme Court ruling *Miranda v. Arizona* requires that arrested persons be made aware of their rights to silence and to an attorney.
1967, February 10:	The Twenty-fifth Amendment to the Constitution is ratified, establishing rules concerning presidential disability and succession.
1967, July:	During this "long hot summer," race riots flare in Newark, New Jersey, and Detroit, Michigan.
1968, January 23:	The USS *Pueblo* and its crew are seized by North Korea.
1968, March 12:	Senator Eugene McCarthy, antiwar candidate, makes a strong second place showing in the New Hampshire Democratic presidential primary.
1968, March 31:	In a nationally televised speech, Johnson announces that he will neither seek nor accept renomination for president.
1968, April 4:	Martin Luther King, Jr., is assassinated in Memphis, Tennessee; Johnson calls in federal troops to control riots in Washington, D.C.
1968, June 5-6:	Senator Robert F. Kennedy is assassinated in Los Angeles while celebrating his victory in the California Democratic presidential primary.
1968, August:	A confrontation between antiwar demonstrators and police at the Democratic National Convention leads to massive violence.
1968, October 31:	Johnson announces the complete halt to the bombing of North Vietnam.
1968, December 22:	The crew of the USS *Pueblo* is released by North Korea.
1973, January 22:	Lyndon B. Johnson dies near Stonewall, en route to San Antonio, Texas.

Nixon

1913, January 9:	Richard M. Nixon is born in Yorba Linda, California.
1940, June 21:	Nixon marries Thelma Catherine Patricia Ryan in Riverside, California.
1943-1945:	Nixon serves as a naval officer during World War II.
1946, November 6:	Nixon is elected to the U.S. House of Representatives from California.
1950, November 7:	Nixon is elected to the U.S. Senate from California.
1952, July 10:	Nixon is nominated for vice president by the Republican Party.

1952, September 23:	Nixon delivers his televised Checkers speech, in which he defends a secret fund raised by supporters and vows to keep the cocker spaniel named Checkers.
1952, November 4:	Nixon is elected vice president under Dwight D. Eisenhower.
1956, July 11:	Nixon is renominated for vice president by the Republican Party.
1956, November 6:	Nixon is reelected vice president.
1958, May:	Nixon is attacked by demonstrators while in South America on goodwill tour.
1960, July 28:	Nixon is nominated for president by the Republican Party.
1960, November 8:	Nixon is narrowly defeated by John F. Kennedy for president.
1962:	Nixon is defeated in a bid for governor of California.
1968, August 8:	Nixon is nominated for president by the Republican Party.
1968, November 5:	Nixon is elected president.
1969, January 20:	Nixon is inaugurated as president.
1969, July 20:	Neil Armstrong, Apollo 11 astronaut, becomes the first person to walk on the moon.
1970, April 30:	Nixon announces that U.S. troops will invade Cambodia.
1970, May 1:	National Guardsmen kill four students at Kent State University in Ohio during an antiwar protest.
1970, May 14:	Police kill two students at Jackson State College in Mississippi during an antiwar protest.
1970, July 9:	Nixon proposes the creation of an independent Environmental Protection Agency.
1971, April 7:	Nixon announces the withdrawal of 100,000 U.S. troops from South Vietnam by December, 1971.
1971, May 2-5:	Massive antiwar demonstrations are held in Washington, D.C.; thousands are arrested.
1971, June 10:	Nixon lifts the trade embargo on Communist China.
1971, June 13:	*The New York Times* publishes the Pentagon Papers, revealing secrets of U.S. involvement in Vietnam.
1971, July 5:	The Twenty-sixth Amendment to the Constitution is ratified, lowering the voting age to eighteen.
1972, February:	Nixon visits Communist China.
1972, June 17:	Five men are arrested in a burglary at Democratic National Headquarters in the Watergate complex in Washington, D.C.
1972, August 23:	Nixon is renominated for president by the Republican Party.
1972, November 7:	Nixon is reelected president.
1973, January 20:	Nixon is inaugurated as president for a second term.
1973, January 22:	The U.S. Supreme Court ruling in *Roe v. Wade* upholds a woman's right to an abortion during the first six months of pregnancy.
1973, January 27:	A Vietnam cease-fire agreement is signed in Paris.
1973, February 7:	The U.S. Senate establishes a committee to investigate the Watergate break-in.
1973, April 30:	Nixon announces the resignations and dismissals of major White House staff members over Watergate.

1973, July 16:	Congress learns that Nixon taped all conversations and telephone calls in his White House office.
1973, October 10:	Vice President Spiro T. Agnew resigns, pleading *nolo contendere* to charges of income tax evasion and bribery.
1973, October 12:	Nixon nominates Congressman Gerald R. Ford for vice president.
1974, July 24:	The Supreme Court rules that Nixon must surrender the tape recordings.
1974, July 27-30:	The House Judiciary Committee recommends the impeachment of President Nixon for obstruction of justice, abuse of power, and contempt of Congress.
1974, August 5:	The White House tape recordings reveal that Nixon sought to obstruct the investigation of Watergate.
1974, August 8:	In a televised address to the nation, Nixon announces that he will resign the presidency, effective August 9.
1974, September 8:	Nixon accepts a full pardon from President Ford.
1994, April 22:	Richard M. Nixon dies in New York City.

Ford

1913, July 14:	Leslie Lynch King, Jr., is born in Omaha, Nebraska.
1917:	King is renamed Gerald R. Ford, Jr., after being adopted by his stepfather.
1942-1944:	Ford serves in the U.S. Naval Reserve with forty-seven months of active service and ten battle stars.
1948, October 15:	Ford marries Elizabeth "Betty" Bloomer Warren in Grand Rapids, Michigan.
1948, November 2:	Ford is elected to the U.S. House of Representatives.
1949-1973:	Ford represents Michigan in the U.S. House of Representatives.
1963-1964:	Ford serves as a member of the Warren Commission.
1965, January 4:	Ford is elected the House minority leader.
1973, December 6:	Ford is confirmed as vice president by the Senate following the resignation of Spiro T. Agnew.
1974, August 9:	Ford succeeds to the presidency upon resignation of Richard M. Nixon.
1974, September 8:	Ford issues a full pardon to former president Nixon.
1974, December 19:	Nelson A. Rockefeller is confirmed as vice president by the Senate.
1975, April 27:	Saigon, South Vietnam, falls to the North Vietnamese.
1976, August 18:	Ford is nominated for president by the Republican Party.
1976, November 2:	Ford is defeated for president by Democratic nominee Jimmy Carter.

Carter

1924, October 1:	Jimmy Carter is born in Plains, Georgia.
1946-1953:	Carter serves in the U.S. Navy, rising to the rank of lieutenant commander.
1946, July 7:	Carter marries Rosalynn Smith in Plains, Georgia.
1971-1975:	Carter serves as governor of Georgia.
1976, July 19:	Carter is nominated for president by the Democratic Party.
1976, November 2:	Carter is elected president.
1977, January 20:	Carter is inaugurated as president.

1977, January 21:	Carter pardons Vietnam War draft resisters.
1978, June 16:	The Panama Canal Treaty is signed to return the Canal Zone to Panama.
1978, September 6:	Carter meets with Israeli prime minister Menachem Begin and Egyptian president Anwar el-Sadat at Camp David to fashion peace accords.
1978, October 16:	Polish Cardinal Karol Wojtyla is elected Pope, taking the name John Paul II.
1979, January–February:	A revolution in Iran brings Muslim fundamentalists under Ayatollah Ruhollah Khomeini to power.
1979, March 28:	The nuclear reactor at Three Mile Island in Pennsylvania threatens a meltdown catastrophe.
1979, June:	Gasoline shortages hit nationwide.
1979, November 4:	Iranians seize the U.S. embassy in Tehran and take sixty-six U.S. citizens hostage.
1980, December 27:	The Soviet Union invades Afghanistan.
1980, April 22:	The U.S. Olympic Committee votes to boycott the 1980 Olympics in Moscow to protest the Soviet invasion.
1980, August 14:	Carter is renominated for president by the Democratic Party.
1980, November 4:	Carter is defeated for reelection by Republican nominee Ronald Reagan.
1981, January 18:	Iran releases the U.S. hostages.

Reagan

1911, February 6:	Ronald Reagan is born in Tampico, Illinois.
1932-1937:	Reagan gains a national reputation as a sportscaster on the radio.
1937-1942:	Reagan makes Hollywood films, including *Knute Rockne—All American*, in which he plays "the Gipper."
1940, January 24:	Reagan marries Jane Wyman (Sarah Jane Fulks) in Glendale, California; they will divorce in 1948.
1947-1952 and 1959:	Reagan serves as president of the Screen Actors Guild.
1952, March 4:	Reagan marries Anne Frances "Nancy" Robbins Davis in Los Angeles, California.
1967-1975:	Reagan serves as governor of California.
1980, July 16	Reagan is nominated for president by the Republican Party.
1980, November 4:	Reagan is elected president.
1981, January 20:	Reagan is inaugurated as president.
1981, March 30:	Reagan is shot in the chest during an assassination attempt by John Hinckley, Jr.
1981, July 29:	The largest tax cuts in U.S. history are approved by Congress, leading to a record deficit.
1981, September 25:	Sandra Day O'Connor becomes the first woman to be appointed a justice of the U.S. Supreme Court.
1981, October 6:	Egyptian president Anwar el-Sadat is assassinated.
1982:	Great Britain and Argentina go to war over the Falkland Islands.
1983, October 23:	Terrorists blow up the U.S. Marine Corps barracks in Beirut, Lebanon.
1983, October 25:	U.S. troops invade the Caribbean island of Grenada.
1984, August:	Reagan is renominated for president by the Republican Party.

1984, November 6:	Reagan is reelected president.
1985, January 20:	Reagan is inaugurated as president for a second term.
1985, March 11:	Mikhail S. Gorbachev becomes the general secretary of the Communist Party Central Committee, thus ruler of the Soviet Union.
1985, November 19-21:	A summit meeting between Gorbachev and Reagan takes place.
1986, January 28:	The space shuttle *Challenger* explodes; it is the worst disaster in the history of the U.S. space program.
1986, November:	The administration admits to an "arms for hostages" deal with Iran.
1987:	Colonel Oliver North, Admiral John Piondexter, and others testify at hearings investigating the Iran-Contra affair, the illegal diversion of Iranian arms money to Nicaraguan rebels.
1994:	Reagan reveals that he is suffering from Alzheimer's disease.

Bush

1924, June 12:	George Bush is born in Milton, Massachusetts.
1942-1945:	Bush serves in the U.S. Navy during World War II; he is awarded the Distinguished Flying Cross and three air medals.
1945, January 6:	Bush marries Barbara Pierce in Rye, New York.
1967-1971:	Bush represents Texas in the U.S. House of Representatives.
1971-1972:	Bush serves as U.S. ambassador to the United Nations.
1973-1974:	Bush serves as chair of the Republican National Committee.
1974-1975:	Bush serves as chief of U.S. liaison office to Communist China.
1980, July 17:	Bush is nominated for vice president by the Republican Party.
1980, November 4:	Bush is elected vice president under President Ronald Reagan.
1984, August 22:	Bush is nominated for vice president by the Republican Party.
1984, November 4:	Bush is reelected vice president.
1988, August 17:	Bush is nominated for president by the Republican Party.
1988, November 8:	Bush is elected president.
1989, January 20:	Bush is inaugurated as president.
1989, March 24:	The oil tanker *Exxon Valdez* runs aground in Prince William Sound in Alaska, creating the largest oil spill in U.S. history.
1989, June 3:	Chinese troops crush prodemocracy protesters in Beijing's Tiananmen Square.
1989, August 18:	The Solidarity labor party in Poland wins free elections, ousting the Communist Party.
1989, September 21:	Hurricane Hugo strikes South Carolina, causing great damage.
1989, October 17:	A powerful earthquake hits San Francisco.
1989, November 12:	The destruction of the Berlin Wall begins.
1989, December 10:	A noncommunist government takes power in Czechoslovakia.
1989, December 20:	U.S. forces invade Panama and install a new government.
1989, December 25:	A popular revolt ousts the communist government in Romania.
1990, February 11:	Nelson Mandela, the leader of the African National Congress in South Africa, is freed after twenty-seven years in prison.
1990, August 2:	Iraqi troops invade Kuwait.

1991, January-February:	Operation Desert Storm pushes Iraqi forces out of Kuwait but stops short of ending the dictatorship of Saddam Hussein.
1991, September 6:	Estonia, Latvia, and Lithuania are recognized as independent states by the Soviet Union.
1991, December 25:	The Soviet Union is dissolved and the Commonwealth of Independent States is created, with Boris Yeltsin as president of the Russian Republic.
1992, February 1:	Bush and Yeltsin meet at Camp David and declare a formal end to the Cold War.
1992, April 29:	The acquittal of four white police officers accused of the brutal beating of an African American motorist sparks rioting in Los Angeles; Bush blames the policies of Lyndon B. Johnson's Great Society for the riots.
1992, August 19:	Bush is renominated for president by Republican Party.
1992, August 24:	Hurricane Andrew batters Florida and Louisiana.
1992, November 3:	Bush is defeated for reelection by Democratic nominee Bill Clinton.
1992, December 24:	Bush pardons six former government officials convicted or indicted for lying to Congress about arms for hostages deals with Iran during the Reagan administration.

Clinton

1946, August 19:	Bill Clinton is born in Hope, Arkansas.
1968-1970:	Clinton studies as a Rhodes scholar at Oxford University in England.
1975, October 11:	Clinton marries Hillary Diane Rodham in Fayetteville, Arkansas.
1978:	Clinton is elected governor of Arkansas.
1980:	Clinton is defeated for reelection.
1982-1992:	Clinton again serves as governor of Arkansas.
1992, July 15:	Clinton is nominated for president by the Democratic Party.
1992, November 3:	Clinton is elected president.
1993, January 20:	Clinton is inaugurated as president.
1993, February 5:	Clinton signs a family leave bill.
1993, February 26:	Terrorists bomb the World Trade Center in New York City.
1993, April 19:	Eighty cult members die in a fire at the Branch Davidian complex in Waco, Texas, following an assault by federal law enforcement officials.
1993, September 13:	The Palestine Liberation Organization (PLO) and Israel sign a peace pact at the White House.
1993, November 20:	Congress passes the North American Free Trade Agreement (NAFTA).
1994, May 6	Paula Jones files a lawsuit alleging that Clinton sexually harassed her while he was governor of Arkansas.
1994, August 5:	Kenneth Starr is appointed an independent prosecutor to investigate Clinton's role in an Arkansas real estate transaction called Whitewater.
1994, November 8:	Republicans win control of both houses of Congress for first time in forty years.
1995, April 19:	Domestic terrorists bomb the Alfred P. Murrah Federal Building in Oklahoma City, killing 169 and injuring nearly 500.

1995, December 16:	Republicans in Congress shut down the federal government in a budget disagreement with Clinton.
1996, August 29:	Clinton is renominated for president by the Democratic Party.
1996, November 5:	Clinton is reelected president.
1997, January 20:	Clinton is inaugurated as president for a second term.
1998, August:	Clinton testifies before a grand jury about his relationship with former White House intern Monica Lewinsky.
1998, August 20:	U.S. warplanes attack suspected terrorist sites in Afghanistan and Sudan in retaliation for bombings at the U.S. embassies in Kenya and Tanzania.
1998, October 23:	The Wye River Accords are signed between Israel and the PLO.
1998, December 19:	The U.S. House of Representatives votes two articles of impeachment against President Clinton, for perjury and obstruction of justice, with regard to the Lewinsky investigation.
1999, January 7:	The impeachment trial begins in the Senate.
1999, February 12:	The Senate acquits Clinton on both counts; neither count receives a majority vote, much less the two-thirds required by the Constitution for removal.
1999, March 24-June 9:	NATO launches air strikes against Serbia to stop the killing of ethnic Albanians in the Kosovo province.
2000, April 22:	Five months after surviving an escape attempt from Cuba in which his mother drowned, six-year-old Elian Gonzalez is seized from his Miami relatives by federal agents when negotiations fail to reunite the child with his father. On June 28, the U.S. Supreme Court refuses to overturn a lower court's decision in the matter, clearing the way for Elian's immediate return to Cuba with his father.

Michael Witkoski

Presidential Election Returns, 1789-1996

Year	Candidate (party)	Electoral Vote	Popular Vote
1789	**George Washington (Federalist)**	69	
	John Adams (Federalist)	34	
	Others	35	
	Not cast	8	
1792	**George Washington (Federalist)**	132	
	John Adams (Federalist)	77	
	George Clinton (Anti-Federalist)	50	
	Thomas Jefferson (Anti-Federalist)	4	
	Aaron Burr (Anti-Federalist)	1	
	Not cast	6	
1796	**John Adams (Federalist)**	71	
	Thomas Jefferson (Democratic Republican)	68	
	Thomas Pinckney (Federalist)	59	
	Aaron Burr (Democratic Republican)	30	
	Others	48	
1800	Aaron Burr (Democratic Republican)	73	
	Thomas Jefferson (Democratic Republican)	73	
	John Adams (Federalist)	65	
	Charles Pinckney (Federalist)	64	
	John Jay (Federalist)	1	
1804	**Thomas Jefferson (Democratic Republican)**	162	
	Charles Pinckney (Federalist)	14	
1808	**James Madison (Democratic Republican)**	122	
	Charles Pinckney (Federalist)	47	
	George Clinton (Democratic Republican)	6	
	Not cast	1	
1812	**James Madison (Democratic Republican)**	128	
	DeWitt Clinton (Federalist)	89	
	Not cast	1	

Year	Candidate (party)	Electoral Vote	Popular Vote
1816	**James Monroe (Democratic Republican)**	183	
	Rufus King (Federalist)	34	
	Not cast	4	
1820	**James Monroe (Democratic Republican)**	231	
	John Quincy Adams (Democratic Republican)	1	
	Not cast	3	
1824	Andrew Jackson (National Republican)	99	155,872
	John Quincy Adams (National Republican)	84	105,321
	William H. Crawford (National Republican)	41	44,282
	Henry Clay (National Republican)	37	46,587
1828	**Andrew Jackson (Democratic)**	178	647,231
	John Quincy Adams (National Republican)	83	509,097
1832	**Andrew Jackson (Democratic)**	219	687,502
	Henry Clay (National Republican)	49	530,189
	John Floyd (Independent)	11	
	William Wirt (Anti-Mason)	7	
	Not cast	2	
1836	**Martin Van Buren (Democratic)**	170	762,678
	William Henry Harrison (Whig)	73	548,007
	Hugh L. White (Whig)	26	
	Daniel Webster (Whig)	14	
	W. P. Mangum (Independent)	11	
1840	**William Henry Harrison (Whig)**	234	1,275,017
	Martin Van Buren (Democratic)	60	1,128,702
1844	**James K. Polk (Democratic)**	170	1,337,243
	Henry Clay (Whig)	105	1,299,068
1848	**Zachary Taylor (Whig)**	163	1,360,101
	Lewis Cass (Democratic)	127	1,220,544
	Martin Van Buren (Free-Soil)	—	291,501
1852	**Franklin Pierce (Democratic)**	254	1,601,474
	Winfield Scott (Whig)	42	1,386,578
1856	**James Buchanan (Democratic)**	174	1,927,995
	John C. Frémont (Republican)	114	1,391,555
	Millard Fillmore (Know-Nothing)	8	873,053
1860	**Abraham Lincoln (Republican)**	180	1,866,352
	John C. Breckinridge (Democratic)	72	845,763
	John Bell (Constitutional Union)	39	589,581
	Stephen A. Douglas (Democratic)	12	1,375,157

Year	Candidate (party)	Electoral Vote	Popular Vote
1864	**Abraham Lincoln (Republican)**	212	2,216,067
	George B. McClellan (Democratic)	21	1,808,725
1868	**Ulysses S. Grant (Republican)**	214	3,015,071
	Horatio Seymour (Democratic)	80	2,709,615
	Not counted	23	
1872	**Ulysses S. Grant (Republican)**	286	3,597,132
	Horace Greeley (Democratic, Liberal Republican)	*	2,834,125
	Thomas A. Hendricks (Democratic)	42	
	B. Gratz Brown (Democratic, Liberal Republican)	18	
	Charles J. Jenkins (Democratic)	2	
	David Davis (Democratic)	1	
	Not counted	17	
1876	**Rutherford B. Hayes (Republican)**	185	4,033,768
	Samuel J. Tilden (Democratic)	184	4,285,992
	Peter Cooper (Greenback)	—	81,737
1880	**James A. Garfield (Republican)**	214	4,449,053
	Winfield S. Hancock (Democratic)	155	4,442,035
	James B. Weaver (Greenback)	—	308,578
1884	**Grover Cleveland (Democratic)**	219	4,911,017
	James G. Blaine (Republican)	182	4,848,334
	Benjamin F. Butler (Greenback)	—	175,370
	John P. St. John (Prohibition)	—	150,369
1888	**Benjamin Harrison (Republican)**	233	5,440,216
	Grover Cleveland (Democratic)	168	5,538,233
	Clinton B. Fisk (Prohibition)	—	249,506
	Alson J. Streeter (Union Labor)	—	146,935
1892	**Grover Cleveland (Democratic)**	277	5,556,918
	Benjamin Harrison (Republican)	145	5,176,108
	James B. Weaver (Populist)	22	1,041,028
	John Bidwell (Prohibition)	—	264,133
1896	**William McKinley (Republican)**	271	7,035,638
	William Jennings Bryan (Democratic, Populist)	176	6,467,946
	John M. Palmer (National Democratic)	—	133,148
	Joshua Levering (Prohibition)	—	132,007
1900	**William McKinley (Republican)**	292	7,219,530
	William Jennings Bryan (Democratic, Populist)	155	
	Eugene V. Debs (Socialist)	—	94,768

Greeley died on November 29, 1872; his electoral votes were split among Hendricks, Brown, Jenkins, and Davis.

Year	Candidate (party)	Electoral Vote	Popular Vote
1904	**Theodore Roosevelt (Republican)**	336	7,628,834
	Alton B. Parker (Democratic)	140	5,084,491
	Eugene V. Debs (Socialist)	—	402,400
1908	**William Howard Taft (Republican)**	321	7,679,006
	William Jennings Bryan (Democratic)	162	6,409,106
	Eugene V. Debs (Socialist)	—	402,820
1912	**Woodrow Wilson (Democratic)**	435	6,286,214
	Theodore Roosevelt (Progressive)	88	4,126,020
	William Howard Taft (Republican)	8	3,483,922
	Eugene V. Debs (Socialist)	—	897,011
1916	**Woodrow Wilson (Democratic)**	277	9,129,606
	Charles Evans Hughes (Republican)	254	8,538,221
	A. L. Benson (Socialist)	—	585,113
1920	**Warren G. Harding (Republican)**	404	16,152,200
	James M. Cox (Democratic)	127	9,147,353
	Eugene V. Debs (Socialist)	—	917,799
1924	**Calvin Coolidge (Republican)**	382	15,725,016
	John W. Davis (Democratic)	136	8,385,586
	Robert M. La Follette (Progressive, Socialist)	13	4,822,856
1928	**Herbert Hoover (Republican)**	444	21,392,190
	Alfred E. Smith (Democratic)	87	15,016,443
	Norman Thomas (Socialist)	—	267,420
1932	**Franklin D. Roosevelt (Democratic)**	472	22,821,857
	Herbert Hoover (Republican)	59	15,761,841
	Norman Thomas (Socialist)	—	884,781
1936	**Franklin D. Roosevelt (Democratic)**	523	27,751,597
	Alfred M. Landon (Republican)	8	16,679,583
	Norman Thomas (Socialist)	—	187,720
1940	**Franklin D. Roosevelt (Democratic)**	449	27,244,160
	Wendell L. Willkie (Republican)	82	22,305,198
	Norman Thomas (Socialist)	—	99,557
1944	**Franklin D. Roosevelt (Democratic)**	432	25,602,504
	Thomas E. Dewey (Republican)	99	22,006,285
	Norman Thomas (Socialist)	—	80,518
1948	**Harry S Truman (Democratic)**	303	24,179,345
	Thomas E. Dewey (Republican)	189	21,991,291
	Strom Thurmond (States' Rights)	39	1,176,125
	Henry A. Wallace (Progressive)	—	1,157,326
	Norman Thomas (Socialist)	—	139,572

Year	Candidate (party)	Electoral Vote	Popular Vote
1952	**Dwight D. Eisenhower (Republican)**	442	33,936,234
	Adlai E. Stevenson (Democratic)	89	27,314,992
1956	**Dwight D. Eisenhower (Republican)**	457	35,590,472
	Adlai E. Stevenson (Democratic)	73	26,022,752
	Walter B. Jones (Democratic)	1	
1960	**John F. Kennedy (Democratic)**	303	34,226,731
	Richard M. Nixon (Republican)	219	34,108,157
	Harry F. Byrd (Democratic)	15	
1964	**Lyndon B. Johnson (Democratic)**	486	43,129,484
	Barry Goldwater (Republican)	52	27,178,188
1968	**Richard M. Nixon (Republican)**	301	31,785,480
	Hubert H. Humphrey (Democratic)	191	31,275,166
	George C. Wallace (American Independent)	46	9,906,473
1972	**Richard M. Nixon (Republican)**	520	47,169,911
	George McGovern (Democratic)	17	29,170,383
	John Hospers (Libertarian)	1	
	John G. Schmitz (American)	—	1,099,482
1976	**Jimmy Carter (Democratic)**	297	40,830,763
	Gerald R. Ford (Republican)	240	39,147,973
	Ronald Reagan (Republican)	1	
	Eugene McCarthy (Independent)	—	756,631
1980	**Ronald Reagan (Republican)**	489	43,899,248
	Jimmy Carter (Democratic)	49	36,481,435
	John Anderson (Independent)	—	5,719,437
1984	**Ronald Reagan (Republican)**	525	54,455,075
	Walter Mondale (Democratic)	13	37,577,185
1988	**George Bush (Republican)**	426	48,886,097
	Michael Dukakis (Democratic)	111	41,809,074
	Lloyd Bentsen (Democratic)	1	
1992	**Bill Clinton (Democratic)**	370	44,909,889
	George Bush (Republican)	168	39,104,545
	Ross Perot (Independent)	—	19,742,267
1996	**Bill Clinton (Democratic)**	379	47,402,357
	Bob Dole (Republican)	159	39,198,755
	Ross Perot (Independent)	—	8,085,402

Vice Presidents

Administration	Vice President (term)	Political Party	Born-Died	State
Washington	John Adams (1789-1797)	Federalist	1735-1826	Massachusetts
J. Adams	Thomas Jefferson (1797-1801)	Democratic Republican	1743-1826	Virginia
Jefferson	Aaron Burr (1801-1805)	Democratic Republican	1756-1836	New York
	George Clinton (1805-1809)	Democratic Republican	1739-1812	New York
Madison	George Clinton (1809-1812)	Democratic Republican		
	Elbridge Gerry (1813-1814)	Democratic Republican	1744-1814	Massachusetts
Monroe	Daniel D. Tompkins (1817-1825)	Democratic Republican	1774-1825	New York
J. Q. Adams	John C. Calhoun (1825-1829)	National Republican	1782-1850	South Carolina
Jackson	John C. Calhoun (1829-1832)	Democratic		
	Martin Van Buren (1833-1837)	Democratic	1782-1862	New York
Van Buren	Richard M. Johnson (1837-1841)	Democratic	1780-1850	Kentucky
W. H. Harrison	John Tyler (1841)	Whig	1790-1862	Virginia
Tyler	none	—	—	—
Polk	George M. Dallas (1845-1849)	Democratic	1792-1864	Pennsylvania
Taylor	Millard Fillmore (1849-1850)	Whig	1800-1874	New York
Fillmore	none	—	—	—
Pierce	William R. D. King (1853)	Democratic	1786-1853	Alabama
Buchanan	John C. Breckinridge (1857-1861)	Democratic	1821-1875	Kentucky
Lincoln	Hannibal Hamlin (1861-1865)	Republican	1809-1891	Maine
	Andrew Johnson (1865)	Democratic	1808-1875	Tennessee
A. Johnson	none	—	—	—
Grant	Schuyler Colfax (1869-1873)	Republican	1823-1885	Indiana
	Henry Wilson (1873-1875)	Republican	1812-1875	Massachusetts
Hayes	William A. Wheeler (1877-1881)	Republican	1819-1887	New York
Garfield	Chester A. Arthur (1881)	Republican	1830-1886	New York
Arthur	none	—	—	—
Cleveland	Thomas A. Hendricks (1885)	Democratic	1819-1885	Indiana
B. Harrison	Levi P. Morton (1889-1893)	Republican	1824-1920	New York
Cleveland	Adlai E. Stevenson (1893-1897)	Democratic	1835-1914	Illinois

Administration	Vice President (term)	Political Party	Born-Died	State
McKinley	Garret A. Hobart (1897-1899)	Republican	1844-1899	New Jersey
	Theodore Roosevelt (1901)	Republican	1858-1919	New York
T. Roosevelt	Charles W. Fairbanks (1905-1909)	Republican	1852-1918	Indiana
Taft	James S. Sherman (1909-1912)	Republican	1855-1912	New York
Wilson	Thomas S. Marshall (1913-1921)	Democratic	1854-1925	Indiana
Harding	Calvin Coolidge (1921-1923)	Republican	1872-1933	Massachusetts
Coolidge	Charles G. Dawes (1925-1929)	Republican	1865-1951	Illinois
Hoover	Charles Curtis (1929-1933)	Republican	1860-1936	Kansas
F. D. Roosevelt	John Nance Garner (1933-1941)	Democratic	1868-1967	Texas
	Henry A. Wallace (1941-1945)	Democratic	1888-1965	Iowa
	Harry S Truman (1945)	Democratic	1884-1972	Missouri
Truman	Alben W. Barkley (1949-1953)	Democratic	1877-1956	Kentucky
Eisenhower	Richard M. Nixon (1953-1961)	Republican	1913-1994	California
Kennedy	Lyndon B. Johnson (1961-1963)	Democratic	1908-1973	Texas
L. B. Johnson	Hubert H. Humphrey (1965-1969)	Democratic	1911-1978	Minnesota
Nixon	Spiro T. Agnew (1969-1973)	Republican	1918-1996	Maryland
	Gerald R. Ford (1973-1974)	Republican	1913-	Michigan
Ford	Nelson A. Rockefeller (1974-1977)	Republican	1908-1979	New York
Carter	Walter Mondale (1977-1981)	Democratic	1928-	Minnesota
Reagan	George Bush (1981-1989)	Republican	1924-	Texas
Bush	Dan Quayle (1989-1993)	Republican	1947-	Indiana
Clinton	Al Gore, Jr. (1993-)	Democratic	1948-	Tennessee

Cabinet Members by Administration

Washington

Secretary of State
Thomas Jefferson (1789-1794)
Edmund Randolph (1794-1795)
Timothy Pickering (1795-1797)
Secretary of the Treasury
Alexander Hamilton (1789-1795)
Oliver Wolcott, Jr. (1795-1797)

Secretary of War
Henry Knox (1789-1795)
Timothy Pickering (1795-1796)
James McHenry (1796-1797)
Attorney General
Edmund Randolph (1789-1794)
William Bradford (1794-1795)
Charles Lee (1795-1797)

J. Adams

Secretary of State
Timothy Pickering (1797-1800)
John Marshall (1800-1801)
Secretary of the Treasury
Oliver Wolcott, Jr. (1797-1801)
Samuel Dexter (1801)

Secretary of War
James McHenry (1797-1800)
Samuel Dexter (1800-1801)
Secretary of the Navy
Benjamin Stoddert (1798-1801)
Attorney General
Charles Lee (1797-1801)

Jefferson

Secretary of State
James Madison (1801-1809)
Secretary of the Treasury
Samuel Dexter (1801)
Albert Gallatin (1801-1809)
Secretary of War
Henry Dearborn (1801-1809)

Secretary of the Navy
Benjamin Stoddert (1801)
Robert Smith (1801-1809)
Attorney General
Levi Lincoln (1801-1805)
John Breckinridge (1805-1807)
Caesar Rodney (1807-1809)

Madison

Secretary of State
Robert Smith (1809-1811)
James Monroe (1811-1817)
Secretary of the Treasury
Albert Gallatin (1809-1814)
George Campbell (1814)
Alexander J. Dallas (1814-1816)

William H. Crawford (1816-1817)
Secretary of War
William Eustis (1809-1813)
John Armstrong (1813-1814)
James Monroe (1814-1815)
William H. Crawford (1815-1817)

Secretary of the Navy
Paul Hamilton (1809-1813)
William Jones (1813-1814)
Benjamin Crowninshield (1814-1817)

Attorney General
Caesar Rodney (1809-1811)
William Pinckney (1811-1814)
Richard Rush (1814-1817)

Monroe

Secretary of State
John Quincy Adams (1817-1825)
Secretary of the Treasury
William H. Crawford (1817-1825)
Secretary of War
George Graham (1817)
John C. Calhoun (1817-1825)

Secretary of the Navy
Benjamin Crowninshield (1817-1818)
Smith Thompson (1818-1823)
Samuel Southard (1823-1825)
Attorney General
Richard Rush (1817)
William Wirt (1817-1825)

J. Q. Adams

Secretary of State
Henry Clay (1825-1829)
Secretary of the Treasury
Richard Rush (1825-1829)
Secretary of War
James Barbour (1825-1828)

Peter B. Porter (1828-1829)
Secretary of the Navy
Samuel Southard (1825-1829)
Attorney General
William Wirt (1825-1829)

Jackson

Secretary of State
Martin Van Buren (1829-1831)
Edward Livingston (1831-1833)
Louis McLane (1833-1834)
John Forsyth (1834-1837)
Secretary of the Treasury
Samuel Ingham (1829-1831)
Louis McLane (1831-1833)
William John Duane (1833)
Roger B. Taney (1833-1834)
Levi Woodbury (1834-1837)
Secretary of War
John Henry Eaton (1829-1831)

Lewis Cass (1831-1837)
Benjamin Butler (1837)
Secretary of the Navy
John Branch (1829-1831)
Levi Woodbury (1831-1834)
Mahlon Dickerson (1834-1837)
Attorney General
John M. Berrien (1829-1831)
Roger B. Taney (1831-1833)
Benjamin Butler (1833-1837)
Postmaster General
William Barry (1829-1835)
Amos Kendall (1835-1837)

Van Buren

Secretary of State
John Forsyth (1837-1841)
Secretary of the Treasury
Levi Woodbury (1837-1841)

Secretary of War
Joel R. Poinsett (1837-1841)
Secretary of the Navy
Mahlon Dickerson (1837-1838)
James K. Paulding (1838-1841)

Attorney General
    Benjamin Butler (1837-1838)
    Felix Grundy (1838-1840)
    Henry D. Gilpin (1840-1841)

Postmaster General
    Amos Kendall (1837-1840)
    John M. Niles (1840-1841)

W. H. Harrison

Secretary of State
    Daniel Webster (1841)
Secretary of the Treasury
    Thomas Ewing (1841)
Secretary of War
    John Bell (1841)

Secretary of the Navy
    George E. Badger (1841)
Attorney General
    John J. Crittenden (1841)
Postmaster General
    Francis Granger (1841)

Tyler

Secretary of State
    Daniel Webster (1841-1843)
    Hugh S. Legaré (1843)
    Abel P. Upshur (1843-1844)
    John C. Calhoun (1844-1845)
Secretary of the Treasury
    Thomas Ewing (1841)
    Walter Forward (1841-1843)
    John C. Spencer (1843-1844)
    George M. Bibb (1844-1845)
Secretary of War
    John Bell (1841)
    John C. Spencer (1841-1843)
    James M. Porter (1843-1844)

    William Wilkins (1844-1845)
Secretary of the Navy
    George E. Badger (1841)
    Abel P. Upshur (1841-1843)
    David Henshaw (1843-1844)
    Thomas Gilmer (1844)
    John Y. Mason (1844-1845)
Attorney General
    John J. Crittenden (1841)
    Hugh S. Legaré (1841-1843)
    John Nelson (1843-1845)
Postmaster General
    Francis Granger (1841)
    Charles A. Wickliffe (1841-1845)

Polk

Secretary of State
    James Buchanan (1845-1849)
Secretary of the Treasury
    Robert J. Walker (1845-1849)
Secretary of War
    William L. Marcy (1845-1849)
Secretary of the Navy
    George Bancroft (1845-1846)

    John Y. Mason (1846-1849)
Attorney General
    John Y. Mason (1845-1846)
    Nathan Clifford (1846-1848)
    Isaac Toucey (1848-1849)
Postmaster General
    Cave Johnson (1845-1849)

Taylor

Secretary of State
    John M. Clayton (1849-1850)
Secretary of the Treasury
    William M. Meredith (1849-1850)

Secretary of War
    George W. Crawford (1849-1850)
Secretary of the Navy
    William B. Preston (1849-1850)

Attorney General
Reverdy Johnson (1849-1850)
Postmaster General
Jacob Collamer (1849-1850)

Secretary of the Interior
Thomas Ewing (1849-1850)

Fillmore

Secretary of State
Daniel Webster (1850-1852)
Edward Everett (1852-1853)
Secretary of the Treasury
Thomas Corwin (1850-1853)
Secretary of War
Charles M. Conrad (1850-1853)
Secretary of the Navy
William A. Graham (1850-1852)

John P. Kennedy (1852-1853)
Attorney General
John J. Crittenden (1850-1853)
Postmaster General
Nathan K. Hall (1850-1852)
Sam D. Hubbard (1852-1853)
Secretary of the Interior
Thomas McKennan (1850)
A. H. H. Stuart (1850-1853)

Pierce

Secretary of State
William L. Marcy (1853-1857)
Secretary of the Treasury
James Guthrie (1853-1857)
Secretary of War
Jefferson Davis (1853-1857)
Secretary of the Navy
James C. Dobbin (1853-1857)

Attorney General
Caleb Cushing (1853-1857)
Postmaster General
James Campbell (1853-1857)
Secretary of the Interior
Robert McClelland (1853-1857)

Buchanan

Secretary of State
Lewis Cass (1857-1860)
Jeremiah S. Black (1860-1861)
Secretary of the Treasury
Howell Cobb (1857-1860)
Philip F. Thomas (1860-1861)
John A. Dix (1861)
Secretary of War
John Floyd (1857-1861)
Joseph Holt (1861)

Secretary of the Navy
Isaac Toucey (1857-1861)
Attorney General
Jeremiah S. Black (1857-1860)
Edwin M. Stanton (1860-1861)
Postmaster General
Aaron V. Brown (1857-1859)
Joseph Holt (1859-1861)
Horatio King (1861)
Secretary of the Interior
Jacob Thompson (1857-1861)

Lincoln

Secretary of State
William H. Seward (1861-1865)

Secretary of the Treasury
Salmon P. Chase (1861-1864)
William P. Fessenden (1864-1865)

Hugh McCulloch (1865)
Secretary of War
    Simon Cameron (1861-1862)
    Edwin M. Stanton (1862-1865)
Secretary of the Navy
    Gideon Welles (1861-1865)
Attorney General
    Edward Bates (1861-1864)

James Speed (1864-1865)
Postmaster General
    Horatio King (1861)
    Montgomery Blair (1861-1864)
    William Dennison (1864-1865)
Secretary of the Interior
    Caleb Smith (1861-1863)
    John P. Usher (1863-1865)

A. Johnson

Secretary of State
    William H. Seward (1865-1869)
Secretary of the Treasury
    Hugh McCulloch (1865-1869)
Secretary of War
    Edwin M. Stanton (1865-1867)
    Ulysses S. Grant (1867-1868)
    John M. Schofield (1868-1869)
Secretary of the Navy
    Gideon Welles (1865-1869)

Attorney General
    James Speed (1865-1866)
    Henry Stanbery (1866-1868)
    William M. Evarts (1868-1869)
Postmaster General
    William Dennison (1865-1866)
    Alexander Randall (1866-1869)
Secretary of the Interior
    John P. Usher (1865)
    James Harlan (1865-1866)
    O. H. Browning (1866-1869)

Grant

Secretary of State
    Elihu B. Washburne (1869)
    Hamilton Fish (1869-1877)
Secretary of the Treasury
    George S. Boutwell (1869-1873)
    William A. Richardson (1873-1874)
    Benjamin H. Bristow (1874-1876)
    Lot M. Morrill (1876-1877)
Secretary of War
    John A. Rawlins (1869)
    William Tecumseh Sherman (1869)
    W. W. Belknap (1869-1876)
    Alphonso Taft (1876)
    James D. Cameron (1876-1877)
Secretary of the Navy
    Adolph E. Borie (1869)

George M. Robeson (1869-1877)
Attorney General
    Ebenezer R. Hoar (1869-1870)
    Amos T. Akerman (1870-1871)
    G. H. Williams (1871-1875)
    Edwards Pierrepont (1875-1876)
    Alphonso Taft (1876-1877)
Postmaster General
    John A. J. Creswell (1869-1874)
    James W. Marshall (1874)
    Marshall Jewell (1874-1876)
    James N. Tyner (1876-1877)
Secretary of the Interior
    Jacob D. Cox (1869-1870)
    Columbus Delano (1870-1875)
    Zachariah Chandler (1875-1877)

Hayes

Secretary of State
    William M. Evarts (1877-1881)

Secretary of the Treasury
    John Sherman (1877-1881)

Secretary of War
George M. McCrary (1877-1879)
Alexander Ramsey (1879-1881)
Secretary of the Navy
Richard W. Thompson (1877-1881)
Nathan Goff, Jr. (1881)

Attorney General
Charles A. Devens (1877-1881)
Postmaster General
David M. Key (1877-1880)
Horace Maynard (1880-1881)
Secretary of the Interior
Carl Schurz (1877-1881)

Garfield

Secretary of State
James G. Blaine (1881)
Secretary of the Treasury
William Windom (1881)
Secretary of War
Robert Todd Lincoln (1881)
Secretary of the Navy
William Hunt (1881)

Attorney General
Wayne MacVeagh (1881)
Postmaster General
Thomas James (1881)
Secretary of the Interior
S. J. Kirkwood (1881)

Arthur

Secretary of State
Frederick T. Frelinghuysen (1881-1885)
Secretary of the Treasury
Charles J. Folger (1881-1884)
Walter Q. Gresham (1884)
Hugh McCulloch (1884-1885)
Secretary of War
Robert Todd Lincoln (1881-1885)
Secretary of the Navy
William E. Chandler (1881-1885)

Attorney General
Benjamin J. Brewster (1881-1885)
Postmaster General
Thomas James (1881)
Timothy O. Howe (1881-1883)
Walter Q. Gresham (1883-1884)
Frank Hatton (1884-1885)
Secretary of the Interior
Henry M. Teller (1881-1885)

Cleveland (1st Administration)

Secretary of State
Thomas F. Bayard (1885-1889)
Secretary of the Treasury
Daniel Manning (1885-1887)
Charles S. Fairchild (1887-1889)
Secretary of War
William C. Endicott (1885-1889)
Secretary of the Navy
William C. Whitney (1885-1889)

Attorney General
A. H. Garland (1885-1889)
Postmaster General
William F. Vilas (1885-1888)
Don M. Dickinson (1888-1889)
Secretary of the Interior
L. Q. R. Lamar (1885-1888)
William F. Vilas (1888-1889)
Secretary of Agriculture
Norman J. Colman (1889)

B. Harrison

Secretary of State
James G. Blaine (1889-1892)
John W. Foster (1892-1893)
Secretary of the Treasury
William Windom (1889-1891)
Charles Foster (1891-1893)
Secretary of War
Redfield Procter (1889-1891)
Stephen B. Elkins (1891-1893)

Secretary of the Navy
Benjamin F. Tracy (1889-1893)
Attorney General
W. H. H. Miller (1889-1893)
Postmaster General
John Wanamaker (1889-1893)
Secretary of the Interior
John W. Noble (1889-1893)
Secretary of Agriculture
Jeremiah M. Rusk (1889-1893)

Cleveland (2d Administration)

Secretary of State
Walter Q. Gresham (1893-1895)
Richard Olney (1895-1897)
Secretary of the Treasury
John G. Carlisle (1893-1897)
Secretary of War
Daniel S. Lamont (1893-1897)
Secretary of the Navy
Hilary A. Herbert (1893-1897)
Attorney General
Richard Olney (1893-1895)

Judson Harmon (1895-1897)
Postmaster General
Wilson S. Bissel (1893-1895)
William L. Wilson (1895-1897)
Secretary of the Interior
Hoke Smith (1893-1896)
David R. Francis (1896-1897)
Secretary of Agriculture
J. Sterling Morton (1893-1897)

McKinley

Secretary of State
John Sherman (1897-1898)
William R. Day (1898)
John Hay (1898-1901)
Secretary of the Treasury
Lyman J. Gage (1897-1901)
Secretary of War
Russell A. Alger (1897-1899)
Elihu Root (1899-1901)
Secretary of the Navy
John D. Long (1897-1901)

Attorney General
Joseph McKenna (1897-1898)
John W. Griggs (1898-1901)
Philander C. Knox (1901)
Postmaster General
Joseph Gary (1897-1898)
Charles E. Smith (1898-1901)
Secretary of the Interior
Cornelius N. Bliss (1897-1898)
E. A. Hitchcock (1898-1901)
Secretary of Agriculture
James Wilson (1897-1901)

T. Roosevelt

Secretary of State
John Hay (1901-1905)
Elihu Root (1905-1909)

Robert Bacon (1909)
Secretary of the Treasury
Lyman J. Gage (1901-1902)

Leslie M. Shaw (1902-1907)
George B. Cortelyou (1907-1909)
Secretary of War
Elihu Root (1901-1904)
William H. Taft (1904-1908)
Luke E. Wright (1908-1909)
Secretary of the Navy
John D. Long (1901-1902)
William H. Moody (1902-1904)
Paul Morton (1904-1905)
Charles J. Bonaparte (1905-1906)
Victor H. Metcalf (1906-1908)
T. H. Newberry (1908-1909)
Attorney General
Philander C. Knox (1901-1904)
William H. Moody (1904-1906)

Charles J. Bonaparte (1906-1909)
Postmaster General
Charles E. Smith (1901-1902)
Henry C. Payne (1902-1904)
Robert J. Wynne (1904-1905)
George B. Cortelyou (1905-1907)
George von L. Meyer (1907-1909)
Secretary of the Interior
E. A. Hitchcock (1901-1907)
James R. Garfield (1907-1909)
Secretary of Agriculture
James Wilson (1901-1909)
Secretary of Commerce and Labor
George B. Cortelyou (1903-1904)
Victor H. Metcalf (1904-1906)
Oscar S. Straus (1906-1909)

Taft

Secretary of State
Philander C. Knox (1909-1913)
Secretary of the Treasury
Franklin MacVeagh (1909-1913)
Secretary of War
Jacob M. Dickinson (1909-1911)
Henry L. Stimson (1911-1913)
Secretary of the Navy
George von L. Meyer (1909-1913)
Attorney General
George W. Wickersham (1909-1913)

Postmaster General
Frank H. Hitchcock (1909-1913)
Secretary of the Interior
Richard A. Ballinger (1909-1911)
Walter L. Fisher (1911-1913)
Secretary of Agriculture
James Wilson (1909-1913)
Secretary of Commerce and Labor
Charles Nagel (1909-1913)

Wilson

Secretary of State
William Jennings Bryan (1913-1915)
Robert Lansing (1915-1920)
Bainbridge Colby (1920-1921)
Secretary of the Treasury
William Gibbs McAdoo (1913-1918)
Carter Glass (1918-1920)
David F. Houston (1920-1921)
Secretary of War
Lindley M. Garrison (1913-1916)
Newton D. Baker (1916-1921)
Secretary of the Navy
Josephus Daniels (1913-1921)

Attorney General
James C. McReynolds (1913-1914)
Thomas W. Gregory (1914-1919)
A. Mitchell Palmer (1919-1921)
Postmaster General
Albert Burleson (1913-1921)
Secretary of the Interior
Franklin K. Lane (1913-1920)
John P. Payne (1920-1921)
Secretary of Agriculture
David F. Houston (1913-1920)
E. T. Meredith (1920-1921)

Secretary of Commerce
William C. Redfield (1913-1919)
J. W. Alexander (1919-1921)

Secretary of Labor
William B. Wilson (1913-1921)

Harding

Secretary of State
Charles Evans Hughes (1921-1923)
Secretary of the Treasury
Andrew W. Mellon (1921-1923)
Secretary of War
John W. Weeks (1921-1923)
Secretary of the Navy
Edwin Denby (1921-1923)
Attorney General
Harry M. Daugherty (1921-1923)
Postmaster General
Will H. Hays (1921-1922)

Hubert Work (1922-1923)
Harry S. New (1923)
Secretary of the Interior
Albert B. Fall (1921-1923)
Hubert Work (1923)
Secretary of Agriculture
Henry C. Wallace (1921-1923)
Secretary of Commerce
Herbert Hoover (1921-1923)
Secretary of Labor
James J. Davis (1921-1923)

Coolidge

Secretary of State
Charles Evans Hughes (1923-1925)
Frank B. Kellogg (1925-1929)
Secretary of the Treasury
Andrew Mellon (1923-1929)
Secretary of War
John W. Weeks (1923-1925)
Dwight F. Davis (1925-1929)
Secretary of the Navy
Edwin Denby (1923-1924)
Curtis D. Wilbur (1924-1929)
Attorney General
Harry Daugherty (1923-1924)
Harlan F. Stone (1924-1925)
John G. Sargent (1925-1929)

Postmaster General
Harry S. New (1923-1929)
Secretary of the Interior
Hubert Work (1923-1928)
Roy O. West (1928-1929)
Secretary of Agriculture
Henry C. Wallace (1923-1924)
Howard M. Gore (1924-1925)
William Jardine (1925-1929)
Secretary of Commerce
Herbert Hoover (1923-1928)
William F. Whiting (1928-1929)
Secretary of Labor
James J. Davis (1923-1929)

Hoover

Secretary of State
Henry L. Stimson (1929-1933)
Secretary of the Treasury
Andrew Mellon (1929-1932)
Ogden L. Mills (1932-1933)
Secretary of War
James W. Good (1929)

Patrick J. Hurley (1929-1933)
Secretary of the Navy
Charles Francis Adams (1929-1933)
Attorney General
William D. Mitchell (1929-1933)
Postmaster General
Walter Brown (1929-1933)

Secretary of the Interior
  Ray Lyman Wilbur (1929-1933)
Secretary of Agriculture
  Arthur M. Hyde (1929-1933)
Secretary of Commerce
  Robert Lamont (1929-1932)

Roy D. Chapin (1932-1933)
Secretary of Labor
  James J. Davis (1929-1930)
  William N. Doak (1930-1933)

F. D. Roosevelt

Secretary of State
  Cordell Hull (1933-1944)
  E. R. Stettinius, Jr. (1944-1945)
Secretary of the Treasury
  William H. Woodin (1933-1934)
  Henry Morgenthau (1934-1945)
Secretary of War
  George H. Dern (1933-1936)
  Harry H. Woodring (1936-1940)
  Henry L. Stimson (1940-1945)
Secretary of the Navy
  Claude A. Swanson (1933-1940)
  Charles Edison (1940)
  Frank Knox (1940-1944)
  James V. Forrestal (1944-1945)
Attorney General
  H. S. Cummings (1933-1939)
  Frank Murphy (1939-1940)

Robert Jackson (1940-1941)
Francis Biddle (1941-1945)
Postmaster General
  James A. Farley (1933-1940)
  Frank C. Walker (1940-1945)
Secretary of the Interior
  Harold Ickes (1933-1945)
Secretary of Agriculture
  Henry A. Wallace (1933-1940)
  Claude R. Wickard (1940-1945)
Secretary of Commerce
  Daniel C. Roper (1933-1939)
  Harry L. Hopkins (1939-1940)
  Jesse Jones (1940-1945)
  Henry A. Wallace (1945)
Secretary of Labor
  Frances Perkins (1933-1945)

Truman

Secretary of State
  James F. Byrnes (1945-1947)
  George C. Marshall (1947-1949)
  Dean Acheson (1949-1953)
Secretary of the Treasury
  Fred M. Vinson (1945-1946)
  John W. Snyder (1946-1953)
Secretary of War
  Robert P. Patterson (1945-1947)
  Kenneth C. Royall (1947)
Secretary of the Navy
  James V. Forrestal (1945-1947)
Secretary of Defense
  James V. Forrestal (1947-1949)
  Louis Johnson (1949-1950)
  George C. Marshall (1950-1951)

Robert A. Lovett (1951-1953)
Attorney General
  Tom C. Clark (1945-1949)
  J. Howard McGrath (1949-1952)
  James P. McGranery (1952-1953)
Postmaster General
  R. E. Hannegan (1945-1947)
  Jesse M. Donaldson (1947-1953)
Secretary of the Interior
  Harold Ickes (1945-1946)
  Julius A. Krug (1946-1949)
  Oscar L. Chapman (1949-1953)
Secretary of Agriculture
  C. P. Anderson (1945-1948)
  C. F. Brannan (1948-1953)

Secretary of Commerce
W. A. Harriman (1945-1948)
Charles Sawyer (1948-1953)

Secretary of Labor
L. B. Schwellenbach (1945-1948)
Maurice J. Tobin (1948-1953)

Eisenhower

Secretary of State
John Foster Dulles (1953-1959)
Christian A. Herter (1959-1961)
Secretary of the Treasury
George Humphrey (1953-1957)
Robert B. Anderson (1957-1961)
Secretary of Defense
Charles E. Wilson (1953-1957)
Neil H. McElroy (1957-1959)
Thomas S. Gates (1959-1961)
Attorney General
H. Brownell, Jr. (1953-1957)
William P. Rogers (1957-1961)
Postmaster General
A. E. Summerfield (1953-1961)

Secretary of the Interior
Douglas McKay (1953-1956)
Fred Seaton (1956-1961)
Secretary of Agriculture
Ezra T. Benton (1953-1961)
Secretary of Commerce
Sinclair Weeks (1953-1958)
Lewis L. Strauss (1958-1961)
Secretary of Labor
Martin Durkin (1953)
James P. Mitchell (1953-1961)
Secretary of Health, Education, and Welfare
Oveta Culp Hobby (1953-1955)
Marion B. Folsom (1955-1958)
Arthur S. Flemming (1958-1961)

Kennedy

Secretary of State
Dean Rusk (1961-1963)
Secretary of the Treasury
Douglas Dillon (1961-1963)
Secretary of Defense
Robert McNamara (1961-1963)
Attorney General
Robert F. Kennedy (1961-1963)
Postmaster General
J. Edward Day (1961-1963)
John A. Gronouski (1963)

Secretary of the Interior
Stewart L. Udall (1961-1963)
Secretary of Agriculture
Orville Freeman (1961-1963)
Secretary of Commerce
Luther Hodges (1961-1963)
Secretary of Labor
Arthur Goldberg (1961-1962)
W. Willard Wirtz (1962-1963)
Secretary of Health, Education, and Welfare
Abraham Ribicoff (1961-1962)
Anthony Celebrezze (1962-1963)

L. B. Johnson

Secretary of State
Dean Rusk (1963-1969)
Secretary of the Treasury
Douglas Dillon (1963-1965)
Henry H. Fowler (1965-1968)
Joseph W. Barr (1968-1969)

Secretary of Defense
Robert McNamara (1963-1968)
Clark Clifford (1968-1969)
Attorney General
Robert F. Kennedy (1963-1965)
N. de B. Katzenbach (1965-1967)
Ramsey Clark (1967-1969)

Postmaster General
John A. Gronouski (1963-1965)
Lawrence F. O'Brien (1965-1968)
W. Marvin Watson (1968-1969)
Secretary of the Interior
Stewart L. Udall (1963-1969)
Secretary of Agriculture
Orville Freeman (1963-1969)
Secretary of Commerce
Luther Hodges (1963-1965)
John T. Connor (1965-1967)
Alexander B. Trowbridge (1967-1968)

C. R. Smith (1968-1969)
Secretary of Labor
W. Willard Wirtz (1963-1969)
Secretary of Health, Education, and Welfare
Anthony Celebrezze (1963-1965)
John W. Gardner (1965-1968)
Wilbur J. Cohen (1968-1969)
Secretary of Housing and Urban Development
Robert C. Weaver (1966-1968)
Robert C. Wood (1968-1969)
Secretary of Transportation
Alan S. Boyd (1966-1969)

Nixon

Secretary of State
William P. Rogers (1969-1973)
Henry Kissinger (1973-1974)
Secretary of the Treasury
David M. Kennedy (1969-1970)
John Connally (1970-1972)
George Shultz (1972-1974)
William Simon (1974)
Secretary of Defense
Melvin Laird (1969-1973)
Elliot Richardson (1973)
James R. Schlesinger (1973-1974)
Attorney General
John Mitchell, Jr. (1969-1972)
Richard G. Kleindienst (1972-1973)
Elliot Richardson (1973)
William B. Saxbe (1974)
Postmaster General
Winton M. Blount (1969-1971)
Secretary of the Interior
Walter J. Hickel (1969-1971)
Rogers C. B. Morton (1971-1974)

Secretary of Agriculture
Clifford M. Hardin (1969-1971)
Earl L. Butz (1971-1974)
Secretary of Commerce
Maurice H. Stans (1969-1972)
Peter G. Peterson (1972)
Frederick B. Dent (1972-1974)
Secretary of Labor
George Shultz (1969-1970)
James D. Hodgson (1970-1973)
Peter J. Brennan (1973-1974)
Secretary of Health, Education, and Welfare
Robert Finch (1969-1970)
Elliot Richardson (1970-1973)
Caspar Weinberger (1973-1974)
Secretary of Housing and Urban Development
George W. Romney (1969-1973)
James T. Lynn (1973-1974)
Secretary of Transportation
John A. Volpe (1969-1973)
Claude S. Brinegar (1973-1974)

Ford

Secretary of State
Henry Kissinger (1974-1977)
Secretary of the Treasury
William Simon (1974-1977)
Secretary of Defense
James R. Schlesinger (1974-1975)

Donald H. Rumsfeld (1975-1977)
Attorney General
William B. Saxbe (1974-1975)
Edward H. Levi (1975-1977)
Secretary of the Interior
Rogers C. B. Morton (1974-1975)

Stanley K. Hathaway (1975)
Thomas D. Kleppe (1975-1977)
Secretary of Agriculture
Earl L. Butz (1974-1976)
John Knebel (1976-1977)
Secretary of Commerce
Frederick B. Dent (1974-1975)
Rogers C. B. Morton (1975)
Elliot Richardson (1975-1977)
Secretary of Labor
Peter J. Brennan (1974-1975)

John T. Dunlop (1975-1976)
W. J. Usery (1976-1977)
Secretary of Health, Education, and Welfare
Caspar Weinberger (1974-1975)
Forrest D. Mathews (1975-1977)
Secretary of Housing and Urban Development
James T. Lynn (1974-1975)
Carla A. Hills (1975-1977)
Secretary of Transportation
Claude S. Brinegar (1974-1975)
William T. Coleman (1975-1977)

Carter

Secretary of State
Cyrus Vance (1977-1980)
Edmund Muskie (1980-1981)
Secretary of the Treasury
W. Michael Blumenthal (1977-1979)
G. William Miller (1979-1981)
Secretary of Defense
Harold Brown (1977-1981)
Attorney General
Griffin Bell (1977-1979)
Benjamin R. Civiletti (1979-1981)
Secretary of the Interior
Cecil D. Andrus (1977-1981)
Secretary of Agriculture
Bob S. Bergland (1977-1981)
Secretary of Commerce
Juanita M. Kreps (1977-1979)

Philip M. Klutznick (1979-1981)
Secretary of Labor
F. Ray Marshall (1977-1981)
Secretary of Health and Human Services
Joseph A. Califano, Jr. (1977-1979)
Patricia Roberts Harris (1979-1981)
Secretary of Housing and Urban Development
Patricia Roberts Harris (1977-1979)
Moon Landrieu (1979-1981)
Secretary of Transportation
Brock Adams (1977-1979)
Neil E. Goldschmidt (1979-1981)
Secretary of Energy
James Schlesinger (1977-1979)
Charles W. Duncan, Jr. (1979-1981)
Secretary of Education
Shirley Hufstedler (1979-1981)

Reagan

Secretary of State
Alexander Haig (1981-1982)
George Shultz (1982-1989)
Secretary of the Treasury
Donald Regan (1981-1985)
James A. Baker III (1985-1988)
Nicholas Brady (1988-1989)
Secretary of Defense
Caspar Weinberger (1981-1987)
Frank C. Carlucci (1987-1989)
Attorney General
William French Smith (1981-1985)

Edwin Meese III (1985-1988)
Dick Thornburgh (1988-1989)
Secretary of the Interior
James Watt (1981-1983)
William P. Clark (1983-1985)
Donald P. Hodel (1985-1989)
Secretary of Agriculture
John R. Block (1981-1986)
Richard E. Lyng (1986-1989)
Secretary of Commerce
Malcolm Baldridge (1981-1987)
C. William Verity, Jr. (1987-1989)

Secretary of Labor
Raymond J. Donovan (1981-1985)
William E. Brock (1985-1987)
Ann Dore McLaughlin (1987-1989)
Secretary of Health and Human Services
Richard S. Schweiker (1981-1983)
Margaret Heckler (1983-1985)
Otis R. Bowen (1985-1989)
Secretary of Housing and Urban Development
Samuel Pierce (1981-1989)
Secretary of Transportation
Andrew L. Lewis, Jr. (1981-1983)

Elizabeth Dole (1983-1987)
James H. Burnley IV (1987-1989)
Secretary of Energy
James B. Edwards (1981-1983)
Donald P. Hodel (1983-1985)
John S. Herrington (1985-1989)
Secretary of Education
T. H. Bell (1981-1985)
William J. Bennett (1985-1988)
Lauro F. Cavazos (1988-1989)

Bush

Secretary of State
James A. Baker III (1989-1992)
Lawrence S. Eagleburger (1992-1993)
Secretary of the Treasury
Nicholas F. Brady (1989-1993)
Secretary of Defense
Richard Cheney (1989-1993)
Attorney General
Dick Thornburgh (1989-1992)
William P. Barr (1992-1993)
Secretary of the Interior
Manuel Lujan, Jr. (1989-1993)
Secretary of Agriculture
Clayton K. Yeutter (1989-1991)
Edward Matigan (1991-1993)
Secretary of Commerce
Robert A. Mosbacher (1989-1992)
Barbara H. Franklin (1992-1993)

Secretary of Labor
Elizabeth Dole (1989-1991)
Lynn Martin (1991-1993)
Secretary of Health and Human Services
Louis W. Sullivan (1989-1993)
Secretary of Housing and Urban Development
Jack Kemp (1989-1993)
Secretary of Transportation
Samuel K. Skinner (1989-1992)
Andrew Card (1992-1993)
Secretary of Energy
James D. Watkins (1989-1993)
Secretary of Education
Lauro F. Cavazos (1989-1991)
Lamar Alexander (1991-1993)
Secretary of Veterans Affairs
Edward J. Derwinski (1989-1993)

Clinton

Secretary of State
Warren Christopher (1993-1996)
Madeleine Albright (1996-   )
Secretary of the Treasury
Lloyd Bentsen (1993-1995)
Robert E. Rubin (1995-1999)
Lawrence H. Summers (1999-   )
Secretary of Defense
Les Aspin (1993-1994)
William J. Perry (1994-1996)

William Cohen (1997-   )
Secretary of the Interior
Bruce Babbitt (1993-   )
Attorney General
Janet Reno (1993-   )
Secretary of Agriculture
Mike Espy (1993-1995)
Dan Glickman (1995-   )
Secretary of Commerce
Ron Brown (1993-1996)

Mickey Kantor (1996-1997)
William Daley (1997-   )
Secretary of Labor
Robert B. Reich (1993-1997)
Alexis Herman (1997-   )
Secretary of Health and Human Services
Donna Shalala (1993-   )
Secretary of Housing and Urban Development
Henry Cisneros (1993-1997)
Andrew Cuomo (1997-   )
Secretary of Transportation
Federico Peña (1993-1997)

Rodney Slater (1997-   )
Secretary of Energy
Hazel O'Leary (1993-1997)
Federico Peña (1997-1998)
Bill Richardson (1998-   )
Secretary of Education
Richard E. Riley (1993-   )
Secretary of Veterans Affairs
Jesse Brown (1993-1998)
Togo D. West, Jr. (1998-   )

First Ladies

President	First Lady	Born-Died	Marriage Year	State
Washington	Martha Dandridge Custis	1732-1802	1759	Virginia
J. Adams	Abigail Smith	1744-1818	1764	Massachusetts
Jefferson	Martha Wayles Skeleton*	1748-1782	1772	Virginia
Madison	Dorothy "Dolley" Payne Todd	1768-1849	1794	North Carolina
Monroe	Elizabeth Kortright	1768-1830	1786	New York
J. Q. Adams	Louisa Catherine Johnson	1775-1852	1797	Maryland
Jackson	Rachel Donelson Robards	1767-1828	1791	Virginia
Van Buren	Hannah Hoes*	1783-1819	1807	New York
W. H. Harrison	Anna Symmes	1775-1864	1795	New Jersey
Tyler	Letitia Christian	1790-1842	1813	Virginia
	Julia Gardiner	1820-1889	1844	New York
Polk	Sarah Childress	1803-1891	1824	Tennessee
Taylor	Margaret Mackall Smith	1788-1852	1810	Maryland
Fillmore	Abigail Powers	1798-1853	1826	New York
Pierce	Jane Means Appleton	1806-1863	1834	New Hampshire
Buchanan	none (never married)	—	—	—
Lincoln	Mary Todd	1818-1882	1842	Kentucky
A. Johnson	Eliza McCardle	1810-1876	1827	Tennessee
Grant	Julia Dent	1826-1902	1848	Missouri
Hayes	Lucy Ware Webb	1831-1889	1852	Ohio
Garfield	Lucretia Rudolph	1832-1918	1858	Ohio
Arthur	Ellen Lewis Herndon*	1837-1880	1859	Virginia
Cleveland	Frances Folsom	1864-1947	1886	New York
B. Harrison	Caroline Lavinia Scott	1832-1892	1853	Ohio
McKinley	Ida Saxton	1847-1907	1871	Ohio
T. Roosevelt	Alice Hathaway Lee*	1861-1884	1880	Massachusetts
	Edith Kermit Carow	1861-1948	1886	Connecticut
Taft	Helen Herron	1861-1943	1886	Ohio

Died before her husband took office.

The American Presidents

President	First Lady	Born-Died	Marriage Year	State
Wilson	Ellen Louise Axson	1860-1914	1885	Georgia
	Edith Bolling Galt	1872-1961	1915	Virginia
Harding	Florence Kling DeWolfe	1860-1924	1891	Ohio
Coolidge	Grace Anna Goodhue	1879-1957	1905	Vermont
Hoover	Lou Henry	1875-1944	1899	Iowa
F. D. Roosevelt	[Anna] Eleanor Roosevelt	1884-1962	1905	New York
Truman	Bess Wallace	1885-1982	1919	Missouri
Eisenhower	Mamie Geneva Doud	1896-1979	1916	Iowa
Kennedy	Jacqueline Lee Bouvier	1929-1994	1953	New York
L. B. Johnson	Claudia "Lady Bird" Alta Taylor	1912-	1934	Texas
Nixon	Thelma Catherine "Pat" Ryan	1912-1993	1940	Nevada
Ford	Elizabeth "Betty" Bloomer Warren	1918-	1948	Illinois
Carter	Rosalynn Smith	1927-	1946	Georgia
Reagan	Anne Frances "Nancy" Robbins Davis	1921-	1952	New York
Bush	Barbara Pierce	1925-	1945	New York
Clinton	Hillary Rodham	1947-	1975	Illinois

Presidential Libraries

Rutherford B. Hayes Presidential Center and Library

Opened in 1916 as the Rutherford B. Hayes Memorial Museum and Library, it was the first of its kind in the United States. It holds more than one million manuscripts and books and has exhibits of objects including weapons used by Hayes as a Union general during the Civil War. The 25-acre site includes the Hayes family home.

CONTACT INFORMATION:
1337 Hayes Avenue
Fremont, OH 43420
Ph.: (419) 332-2081
Web site: www.rbhayes.org

The Herbert Hoover Presidential Library

Dedicated on August 10, 1962, this 178-acre site includes the library, Hoover's birthplace, a reconstruction of his father's blacksmith shop, the Quaker meeting house that Hoover attended as a child, a schoolhouse, and the gravesite of Hoover and his wife. In addition to the library collection itself, life-size figures and interactive displays present the story of Hoover's life.

CONTACT INFORMATION:
PO Box 488
West Branch, IA 52358
Ph.: (319) 643-5301
Web site: www.hoover.nara.gov

Franklin D. Roosevelt Library and Museum

Dedicated on June 20, 1941, the Franklin D. Roosevelt Library is the oldest of the presidential libraries. The library was the conception of President Roosevelt himself, who realized the importance of keeping intact historic collections of official presidential papers and documents. Roosevelt helped design the building and donated land at his family estate at Hyde Park for its location. The library contains Roosevelt's papers and those of his wife, Eleanor, as well as the papers of over one hundred friends and associates. Exhibits re-create the White House during Roosevelt's tenure as president and present FDR's life story. The Eleanor Roosevelt Gallery, added to the original library building in 1972, commemorates the president's active wife and her own many accomplishments. The 290-acre Franklin D. Roosevelt National Historic Site also includes the family home and Roosevelt's gravesite.

CONTACT INFORMATION:
511 Albany Post Road
Hyde Park, NY 12538
Ph.: (914) 229-8114
Web site: www.academic.marist.edu/fdr/

The Harry S Truman Library

Officially dedicated on July 6, 1957, the library holds Truman's presidential papers and other documents relating to his life and career. There are also collections of books, periodicals, and other printed materials, as well as displays and objects including automobiles and a re-creation of the Oval Office while Truman was president. The gravesites of Truman and his wife, Bess Wallace Truman, are in the library's courtyard. The Truman Library is unique in that for many years the former president used it as his working office, sitting behind his desk from the White House.

CONTACT INFORMATION:
US Highway 24 and Delaware
Independence, MO 64050
Ph.: (816) 833-1400
Web site: www.trumanlibrary.org

The Dwight D. Eisenhower Library

Dedicated on May 1, 1962, the Eisenhower Library is part of a site that includes the family home on its original site, a museum, visitors' center, and the Place of Meditation, which has the graves of Eisenhower, his wife, Mamie, and their first son. The library holds documents relating to Eisenhower's presidency and life, especially his long military career. It contains over eleven million pages of manuscripts and thousands of photographs, books, and recordings. In addition are abundant audiovisual materials, in large part because the Eisenhower presidency was the first to be extensively covered by television.

CONTACT INFORMATION:
Abilene, KS 67410
Ph.: (913) 263-4751
Web site: redbud.lbjlib.utexas.edu/
  eisenhower/ddehp.htm

The John Fitzgerald Kennedy Library

Designed by internationally acclaimed architect I. M. Pei and dedicated on October 20, 1979, the Kennedy Library was substantially expanded and reopened in 1993 to better present the life and accomplishments of President John F. Kennedy to a new generation of Americans. The library makes extensive use of visual and audio presentations, many of them featuring the image and voice of President Kennedy. Exhibits re-create important moments of Kennedy's life and presidency, including the famous televised debate with Richard Nixon during the 1960 election. The library holds massive collections of Kennedy's own papers and those of other major figures of the twentieth

century, over forty-two million manuscript pages in all. There are almost 200,000 photographs, 6 million feet of film and videotape, and 1,000 audiotapes. The library has also collected almost all the known existing manuscripts of Nobel Prize-winning author Ernest Hemingway, including his original drafts for the novels *A Farewell to Arms* (1929) and *For Whom the Bell Tolls* (1940). The Kennedy Library's site at Columbia Point overlooks Boston Harbor, and the library is unique in that it can be reached by boat.

CONTACT INFORMATION:
Columbia Point
Boston, MA 02125
Ph.: (617) 929-4523
Web site: www.cs.umb.edu/jfklibrary

The Lyndon Baines Johnson Library

Dedicated on May 22, 1971, the Lyndon Baines Johnson Library is on the grounds of the University of Texas at Austin, and the library is associated with the university's graduate school of public affairs. The library holds the official papers of Johnson throughout his career as U.S. congressman, senator, vice president, and president. There are some forty million pages of manuscript. In addition, the library contains papers of Johnson's friends and associates, including his presidential cabinet. The extensive audiovisual files include numerous hours of oral history interviews. The displays and exhibits include dramatic presentations of the aftermath of President John F. Kennedy's assassination in Dallas in 1963, the escalating war in Vietnam, and the politics of the 1960's. Because of its location and the wealth of its holdings, the Johnson Library is the most visited and used of all presidential libraries.

CONTACT INFORMATION:
2313 Red River Street
Austin, TX 78705
Ph.: (512) 482-5137
Web site: www.lbjlib.utexas.edu

The Richard Nixon Library and Birthplace

Dedicated on July 19, 1990, this library sits on a 9-acre site that includes part of a California orange grove once worked by the president's parents and the small wooden farmhouse where Nixon was born. The library's manuscript holdings contain materials from Nixon's public service, as well as papers and materials from his associates. Exhibits trace Richard Nixon's political career, including his meetings with world leaders and such triumphs as the establishment of détente with the Soviet Union and his historic visit to the People's Republic of China. One section presents the Watergate affair that led to Nixon's resignation in the face of impeachment. Richard Nixon and his wife, Pat, are buried in a formal garden on the grounds.

CONTACT INFORMATION:
18001 Yorba Linda Boulevard
Yorba Linda, CA 92686
Ph.: (714) 993-3393
Web site: www.nixonfoundation.org

The Gerald R. Ford Library

Dedicated on September 18, 1981, the Gerald R. Ford Library is on the campus of Ford's alma mater, the University of Michigan at Ann Arbor. The bulk of the library's holdings focus on Ford's years as president, but they also contain records of his brief time as vice president and his service in the House of Representatives. In addition, the papers of Betty Ford and of various advisers and associates are included in the collection. A companion facility, the Gerald R. Ford Museum, is located in Grand Rapids, Michigan. Exhibits trace Ford's political career, including his position as the first vice president and president to serve without being elected to those positions. There is also an exhibit on the United States' Bicentennial, celebrated during Ford's presidency.

CONTACT INFORMATION:
Library
1000 Beal Avenue
Ann Arbor, MI 48109-2114
Ph.: (313) 741-2218
Museum
303 Pearl Street, NW
Grand Rapids, MI 49504
Ph.: (616) 451-9263
Web site: www.lbjlib.utexas.edu/ford/
   index.html

The Jimmy Carter Library

Dedicated on October 1, 1986, the Jimmy Carter Library is located on 30 acres of natural landscape near downtown Atlanta and features a peaceful, contemplative air. Conceived as an educational resource for students of the American presidency, the library highlights the development of that office during the twentieth century through films and exhibits. The library's collection is based on materials from the Carter presidency and includes manuscripts and papers from the president's wife, Rosalynn, and their staffs. Documents and materials for the period are included; these holdings are being increased systematically.

CONTACT INFORMATION:
One Copen Hill Avenue
Atlanta, GA 30307
Ph.: (404) 331-0296
Web site: carterlibrary.galileo.peachnet.edu/

The Ronald Reagan Library

Dedicated on November 4, 1991, the Reagan Library is set in a landscape of unspoiled beauty and is designed in traditional California style. The library has a complete collection of all official records from the Reagan White House, including the records of many of the cabinet officers during the Reagan administration. In addition are numerous personal documents of the president and Nancy Reagan. There are more than forty-seven million documents in all. Photographs, videotapes, films, and audiotapes are part of the collection. Displays and exhibits trace Reagan's life and career, emphasizing his achievements as president. A gallery displays some of the thousands of gifts that Reagan and his wife received from foreign governments.

CONTACT INFORMATION:
40 Presidential Drive
Simi Valley, CA 93065
Ph.: (805) 522-8444
Web site: www.cyber-pages.com/reagan/ index.html

The George Bush Presidential Library

Groundbreaking ceremonies for the George Bush Presidential Library were held on November 30, 1994. Situated on the grounds of Texas A&M University, the library contains over thirty-eight million pages of personal papers and official documents from Bush's vice presidency and presidency. There is also an extensive audiovisual and photographic collection, as well as over sixty thousand historical objects, including gifts from foreign nations and American citizens. The library has a classroom, the first of its kind in the presidential libraries network.

CONTACT INFORMATION:
1000 George Bush Drive West
College Station, TX 77845
Ph.: (409) 260-3770
Web site: csdltamu.edu/bushlib/ bushlibrary.html/

Michael Witkoski

Glossary

AAA: the Agricultural Adjustment Act. Passed in 1933 as part of Franklin Roosevelt's New Deal, it intended to reduce farm production in order to increase farm income. Declared unconstitutional by the Supreme Court in 1936.

Alien and Sedition Acts: laws passed by the Federalist Party in 1789 that authorized the president to deport "undesirable aliens" and imprison persons who criticized the government or its officials. Widely unpopular, as well as unconstitutional, the acts were among the reasons the Federalists lost the 1800 elections.

American Independent Party: third party established in 1964 by George Wallace, governor of Alabama, as a protest against Democratic and Republican policies, but which helped tilt the election in favor of Richard Nixon, the Republican candidate.

amnesty: the authority of the president to grant a pardon to members of a group who have violated federal law. *See* **pardon.**

Australian ballot: a secret ballot which allows voters complete confidentiality. It did not come into general use in the United States until the 1880's.

balanced ticket: the nomination of presidential and vice presidential candidates who appeal to the widest spectrum of potential voters—for example, having one candidate from the East Coast and the other from the Midwest or West.

bandwagon: a political campaign that is perceived as a winner. Uncommitted or undecided delegates or voters are encouraged to "jump on the bandwagon" instead of backing a losing candidate.

Bay of Pigs: the term used to describe the abortive anti-Castro invasion of Cuba in 1961.

Bill of Rights: the first ten amendments to the Constitution which guarantee the rights of individuals and of the states.

bloody shirt: a campaign technique used by Republicans in the years following the Civil War to remind voters that many members of the Democratic Party had opposed the war.

boss: the leader of a political organization, sometimes called a "machine," that can deliver votes in a specific area.

Buck Stops Here, The: the sign which Harry S Truman had on his desk in the Oval Office, indicating that ultimate responsibility rests with the president.

Bull Moose Party: the party which nominated Theodore Roosevelt for president in 1912. *See* **Progressive Party.**

bully pulpit: a phrase made popular by Theodore Roosevelt for the use of the presidency to inspire or lead.

cabinet: the heads of the major departments of the executive branch, such as state, treasury, defense, and commerce. Their dual purposes are to administer their specific agencies and to advise the president. Cabinet members are appointed by the president with the advice and consent of the Senate but can be removed at any time by the president.

Camp David: a presidential retreat in the Maryland countryside. Named by Dwight D. Eisenhower after his grandson.

Camp David accords: the agreement signed by Israeli prime minister Menachem Begin and Egyptian president Anwar el-Sadat on September 17, 1978, as mediated by President Jimmy Carter. The accords, which began the peace process in the Middle East, were named after the presidential retreat where the negotiations took place.

campaign: the activities associated with seeking public office, starting from announcing one's candidacy, through the nomination to canvassing for votes in the general election. It includes fund-raising and the preparation and placement of advertising.

Checkers speech: the nationally televised address delivered by Republican vice presidential candidate Richard M. Nixon on September 23, 1952, in which he defended accepted special and secret contributions. Nixon claimed that the funds were used purely for political purposes and that the only gift kept by the Nixon family was their cocker spaniel, Checkers.

chief executive: the term for the president's role in implementing the decisions of Congress in particular and the federal government in general.

Civil Rights Act of 1964: a far-ranging civil rights law proposed by President John F. Kennedy and enacted under his successor, Lyndon B. Johnson. It outlawed discrimination in voter registration, public accommodations such as hotels and restaurants, and employment. It also gave the federal government the authority to take action to ensure these provisions. The most powerful civil rights act since Reconstruction, it was enacted only after the longest debate in Senate history to date (eighty-three days).

Civil Rights Act of 1968: legislation that prohibited discrimination in housing.

Civil Rights movement: a broad term to cover the different campaigns by African Americans from the late 1940's onward to secure their rights as American citizens. Its legis-lative results included the Civil Rights Acts of 1964 and 1968.

civil service reform: the replacement of the spoils system of awarding public offices with employment of government workers on the basis of open, competitive examinations. The Civil Service Act of 1883 was the original legislation in this effort.

closed primary: a primary election restricted to registered voters of the specific party conducting the election.

coalition: the uniting of various political groups to achieve electoral victory. For example, a traditional Democratic coalition consists of African Americans, urban ethnic groups, and organized labor.

code words: seemingly innocent words or phrases that carry a meaning which a candidate wishes to communicate to certain voters but not openly express. "Law and order" and "states' rights" as synonyms for "anti-civil rights" are examples.

Cold War: a period of hostility, but not actual warfare, between communist nations and the United States and its allies from 1948 to 1989.

commander in chief: as designated by the Constitution, the president as the person in charge of the armed forces of the United States.

conscription and selective service acts: the laws by which the federal government drafts citizens into the armed forces. Conscription acts were enacted during the Civil War (1862) and World War I (1918). A peacetime draft was established in 1940 and again in 1948. The draft was ended during the Nixon administration, although mandatory registration was retained.

conservative: as used in American politics, the term for those who generally favor the status quo, or existing situation, and who wish to make few if any changes, and then make them as deliberately as possible. Generally, conservatives reject or limit the role for government in addressing most social ills but favor a strong "law and order" approach to crime and a reduction of taxes, especially on business and the wealthy.

Constitution: a written document that establishes the procedures by which the United States is governed. The original Constitution was drafted in 1787 and ratified by 1788. It has been amended numerous times since.

Constitutional Union Party. *See* **Know-Nothing Party**

convention: a meeting of members (delegates) of a political party to nominate candidates and to write and adopt a party platform. Presidential candidates are nominated at the national political conventions, held once every four years.

"corrupt bargain": the charge made against John Quincy Adams and Henry Clay by supporters of Andrew Jackson after the presidential election of 1824. Although Jackson had received a plurality of the popular and electoral votes, no candidate received a majority. When the House of Representatives decided the election, Clay's supporters voted for Adams. Later, Adams appointed Clay as his secretary of state.

cross of gold: the dramatic phrase used by William Jennings Bryan at the 1896 Democratic Convention in support of using more available silver as the basis for U.S. currency.

Cuban Missile Crisis: the confrontation between the United States and the Soviet Union over the presence of Soviet missiles based in Cuba. The Soviets withdrew the missiles after President John F. Kennedy placed a naval embargo around Cuba.

dark horse: the descriptive name for a person who seems to have little chance of winning a nomination or an election.

Democratic Party: in modern American politics, one of the two major parties. The oldest continuous political party in the world, it was founded prior to 1800 by Thomas Jef-

ferson as the Democratic Republican Party; the name was changed by the time of Andrew Jackson. In general, it supports the traditional freedoms guaranteed under the Constitution along with government action to improve economic and social conditions.

Dixiecrat Party: a group of southern Democrats angered by the civil rights platform of the 1948 Democratic Party who nominated Strom Thurmond of South Carolina for president. Officially known as the States' Rights Party.

draft: to nominate by popular acclaim, generally at a national political convention, a person who has not been an announced candidate for president.

electoral college: the body of persons selected from each state to cast that state's electoral votes for president and vice president. According to the Constitution, each state has the same number of electoral votes as it has senators and representatives in Congress. The electoral votes of a state go to the candidate who wins the popular vote of that state.

Emancipation Proclamation: a wartime measure issued by Abraham Lincoln that abolished slavery in all states "in rebellion against the United States." Slavery was officially ended in the United States with the ratification of the Thirteenth Amendment in 1865.

Era of Good Feelings: the name given to the second term of James Monroe, who was reelected without opposition and with only one dissenting vote in the electoral college.

executive order: a directive from the president based on powers granted to the president by Congress.

executive privilege: the asserted right of the president, as chief executive, to withhold information from Congress. Invoked by Richard M. Nixon during the Watergate crisis and Bill Clinton during the Lewinsky investigation but strongly restricted by the Supreme Court.

Fair Deal: the name given by President Harry S Truman in his 1949 state of the union address to his domestic policies. The name deliberately evoked Franklin D. Roosevelt's New Deal.

favorite son: a candidate for president whose support comes largely from his or her own state. Sometimes indicating a serious candidate, it is more often a way to control a bloc of votes for bargaining purposes.

Federalist Party: the political party that formed around Alexander Hamilton during the administration of George Washington. It favored a strong central government and protection of wealth and property rights. It faded after John Adams's defeat by Thomas Jefferson in 1800.

filibuster: the debating of a bill at great length in Congress (or other legislative body) in order to defeat it. It is generally used by opponents who lack the votes to defeat a bill outright. The most notable use of the filibuster is in the Senate, whose rules allow almost unlimited debate.

fireside chats: the informal radio addresses used by Franklin D. Roosevelt to discuss issues directly with the American public.

First Lady: the traditional popular title for the wife of the president.

Fourteen Points: conditions prepared by Woodrow Wilson for drawing up a peace treaty following World War I. They formed the basis for the League of Nations.

gerrymander: to redraw political boundary lines, such as those for congressional districts, to favor one party over another. Named after Elbridge Gerry, who was governor of Massachusetts in 1812 when such a district was established. An editorial cartoonist drew the district to resemble a salamander and renamed it a "gerrymander."

Gettysburg Address: Abraham Lincoln's brief but eloquent remarks at the dedication of the National Cemetery at the site of the Civil War battlefield at Gettysburg. In his address, Lincoln redefined the United States as a union of people, rather than independent states, and thus undercut the legal arguments for secession and extreme states' rights.

Good Neighbor Policy: the term used by Franklin D. Roosevelt to describe the relations between the United States and Latin America.

GOP: an abbreviation for Grand Old Party; a nickname for the Republican Party.

Great Depression: the severe breakdown in the economy which began with the collapse of the stock market in 1929 and resulted in high unemployment, bank failures, bankruptcies, and intense social unrest. The measures of Franklin D. Roosevelt's New Deal were designed to address these conditions.

Great Society: the term used by Lyndon Johnson to describe his ambitious social programs proposed during 1965 and 1966, including the War on Poverty.

"Happy Days Are Here Again": the song played at Franklin D. Roosevelt's nomination at the Democratic Convention of 1932. Since then, it has been the unofficial theme of the Democratic Party.

"Happy Warrior, the": the nickname given to Governor Alfred E. Smith of New York by Franklin D. Roosevelt in his speech nominating Smith for the presidency at the 1928 Democratic Convention.

hat in the ring: a term meaning that a political candidate has officially announced his or her intentions to run for office. It derives from early boxing and wrestling matches, where a person would throw his hat into the ring to indicate that he was ready to fight.

Hatch Act: a 1939 federal law that prohibited political parties from forcing federal employees to contribute money or involuntarily take an active role in campaigning.

He Kept Us Out of War: the slogan used by Democratic presidential candidate Woodrow Wilson in the 1916 campaign. World War I had begun in Europe in 1914, and Wilson had pursued a course of strict neutrality.

Hundred Days, the: the period following the inauguration of Franklin D. Roosevelt in 1933, during which much of the New Deal legislation was enacted. The term has since become a convenient measuring point for the progress of any new administration.

I Like Ike: the popular slogan to express support for Dwight D. (Ike) Eisenhower in the presidential elections of 1952 and 1956.

impeachment: a formal accusation of wrongdoing against a public official. The Constitution provides that the House of Representatives has the power to impeach a president for "high crimes and misdemeanors." If impeached, the president is tried by the Senate.

In Your Heart, You Know He's Right: the slogan used by supporters of conservative Republican nominee Barry Goldwater in 1964. Democrats and independents countered with the rejoinder "Yes—extreme right."

inauguration: the formal action that installs the president in office.

incumbent: a candidate in an election who holds the office being voted on.

Interstate Commerce Commission: the oldest independent regulatory agency of the federal government, established in 1887 to regulate trade within the United States, set minimum standards of service and safety, and ensure fair prices.

Jacksonian democracy: a political and social movement, reaching its peak with the presidency of Andrew Jackson, that expanded the role of the average citizen in government.

Jeffersonianism: a belief in a limited government that respects the rights of individuals and does the least possible to restrict their liberties.

Keep Cool with Coolidge: the Republican slogan during 1924 presidential campaign used to make a virtue of the candidate's taciturn style.

Kennedy-Nixon Debates: the first televised presidential debates, held during the 1960 election. John F. Kennedy is widely credited with having won the debates, which helped propel him to a narrow victory over Richard M. Nixon in the November election.

Kitchen Cabinet: an informal group that provides the president with advice. The term was popularized during the presidency of Andrew Jackson.

Know-Nothing Party: an antiforeign, anti-Catholic party (also called the Constitutional Union Party or the American Party) formed during the 1850's. Its members, when asked about the organization, responded "I know nothing."

lame duck: a politician serving out a term who is not eligible for reelection. Traditionally, lame ducks are seen as handicapped by their status.

Lame Duck Amendment: the Twentieth Amendment to the Constitution, which changed the presidental inauguration date from March 4 to January 20 and set the beginning of congressional terms on January 3 instead of March 4.

law and order: during the 1960's and 1970's, a code word used by politicians to signal an antiliberal, anti-civil rights position.

League of Nations: an international assembly to regulate disputes between states and preserve peace. Proposed by Woodrow Wilson at the end of World War I, it proved ineffective, largely because of lack of U.S. support.

liberal: in American politics, the term used to describe those who favor a stronger role of government in addressing issues and solving problems facing the nation as a whole. Traditionally, liberals have been concerned with civil rights and individual liberties, are tolerant of the views of others, and support progressive movements.

Lincoln-Douglas Debates: a series of public appearances by Democrat Stephen A. Douglas and Republican Abraham Lincoln during the 1858 Illinois senatorial campaign. These debates made Lincoln a force in national politics and helped him gain the Republican nomination for president in 1860.

line-item veto: the authority of the president to veto specific portions of an appropriation bill without having to reject the entire bill.

Ma, Ma, Where's My Pa?: the derogatory chant used by Republicans against Democratic nominee Grover Cleveland, who as a young man may have fathered a child out of wedlock. Upon Cleveland's election, the Democratic response was "Gone to the White House, Ha-Ha-Ha."

machine: the name given to a political organization on the state or local level that is well organized and efficient in providing votes and public support for its candidates. The term is generally associated with big cities, such as the Daley Machine in Chicago or Tammany Hall in New York.

March on Washington: the massive, peaceful demonstration of supporters of civil rights legislation who converged on the capital in August, 1963. It was at this event that Dr. Martin Luther King, Jr., gave his famous "I Have a Dream" speech.

Medicaid: a health insurance program established in 1960 to assist poor persons who need medical care.

Medicare: a health insurance measure enacted in 1965 to provide medical care to the elderly.

missile gap: an issued raised by Democratic nominee John F. Kennedy in the 1960 election about a supposed shortfall in U.S. military capability relative to the Soviet Union.

Monroe Doctrine: a statement of U.S. foreign policy by President James Monroe in 1823 which declared that the Western Hemisphere was no longer subject to colonization or control by European powers.

muckrakers: journalists and other writers who expose illegal, dangerous, or improper activities by large corporations, government bodies, or government officials. They were especially influential during the late nineteenth and early twentieth centuries.

mugwumps: persons who are formally associated with one political party but who support another party. The term was first used to describe Republicans who refused to support their party's presidential candidate James G. Blaine.

New Deal: the term given to the policies of Franklin D. Roosevelt in fighting the Great Depression, especially during his first two administrations.

New Federalism: a term used by Richard M. Nixon to describe his plan to move much of the responsibility and authority of the federal government to the state governments.

New Freedom: the term used by Woodrow Wilson in the election of 1912 and during his first term as president to describe greater activism by the federal government and more involvement in public policy by citizens.

New Frontier: the popular name for the policies of John F. Kennedy during his presidency. Following his assassination and the inauguration of Lyndon B. Johnson, the New Frontier was replaced by the Great Society.

"no third term": a popular tradition in American presidential politics, originating with George Washington, that no president should serve more than two terms. The tradition was broken by the unprecedented four terms of Democrat Franklin D. Roosevelt and restored in 1951 with the passage of the Twenty-second Amendment. Ironically, two presidents who could have probably overcome the tradition of "no third term" were Dwight Eisenhower and Ronald Reagan, both Republicans.

NRA: the National Recovery Act. Part of the New Deal of Franklin D. Roosevelt, it helped address the Great Depression but was declared unconstitutional by the Supreme Court in 1935.

nullification: the theory that a state can nullify, or declare void within its borders, an act of Congress or a decision of the Supreme Court. The doctrine is in clear violation of the Constitution.

open primary: a primary election open to all registered voters of whatever party. Also known as a cross-over primary. *See* **closed primary.**

Oval Office: the personal office of the president, often used to represent the presidency. This is an example of the rhetorical devices of synecdoche (the part stands for the whole), in which the office of the president signifies the White House, and metonymy (an object stands a larger concept), in which the White House signifies the presidency itself.

pardon: the authority of the president to grant release from punishment or legal consequences of a crime before or after conviction. A pardon may be individual, as when President Gerald R. Ford pardoned former president Richard M. Nixon for crimes that he may have committed while in office, or general, as the blanket pardon that President Jimmy Carter granted to Vietnam draft evaders. *See* **amnesty.**

plank: a part of a platform that deals with a specific issue.

platform: the official statement of principles and goals by a political party, generally drafted and adopted by the party at its national convention.

"Plumed Knight, the": the nickname for Republican presidential candidate James G. Blaine.

pocket veto: an automatic veto that takes place if Congress adjourns after sending a bill to the president and the president refuses to sign it.

popular vote: as distinct from the electoral vote, the number of individual voters who cast their ballots for a particular presidential candidate. Because of the electoral college system, a president can be elected with a majority of the electoral vote without a majority of the popular vote. This is especially true during elections featuring a strong third party. Abraham Lincoln, Woodrow Wilson, Harry S Truman, John F. Kennedy, Richard M. Nixon, and Bill Clinton all won the presidency in this fashion. Rutherford B. Hayes and Benjamin Harrison won a majority of the electoral vote and an absolute minority of the popular vote, and thus were elected president.

Populist Party: a party loosely organized in the agricultural South and West during the late 1800's seeking greater representation and better treatment for farmers. For all practical purposes, it merged with the Democratic Party in 1896 with the nomination of William Jennings Bryan, who championed many of its causes.

president-elect: the term for the candidate who has been selected by the electoral college to be the next president but who has not yet been inaugurated.

presidential succession: the order in which the office of president is filled in case of death or disability. According to the Presidential Succession Act of 1947, the vice president, Speaker of the House, president pro tempore of the Senate, and the secretary of state are the first four in line of succession.

primary: a process which allows voters to select the delegates to a party's presidential nominating convention in a special state election.

The delegates chosen in such primaries are generally pledged or committed to voting for their candidate.

Progressive Party: although used by several parties in U.S. political history, a term most often referring to the party organized in 1912 to support the presidential candidacy of Theodore Roosevelt, who had been denied renomination for president by the Republican Party. Because of its close association with Roosevelt, it was popularly known as the Bull Moose Party.

Prohibition: the national ban on the sale of alcoholic beverages, as instituted by the Eighteenth Amendment in 1918. The Twenty-first Amendment, adopted in 1933, repealed the Eighteenth Amendment and ended national Prohibition, but it left states and counties with the power to enact local prohibition statutes.

Radical Republicans: during the Civil War and its immediate aftermath, those Republicans who favored immediate emancipation of slaves, vigorous prosecution of the war, and harsh treatment of the defeated Southern states.

Reconstruction: the period following the Civil War in which the states of the former Confederacy were brought back into the Union.

Republican Party: one of the two major parties in modern U.S. politics. It was founded in the 1850's in opposition to slavery. Traditionally, it has opposed greater government intervention, especially in social welfare, health care, and education, and has favored the reduction of taxes, especially on big business and capital gains.

Rum, Romanism, and Rebellion: a description of the Democrats as the party identified with "Rum [alcohol], Romanism [Catholicism], and Rebellion [the Civil War]" by minister Samuel D. Burchard in a statement supporting Republican James G. Blaine for president in 1884. The offensive words helped defeat Blaine in the election.

runoff primary: a second primary election held if no candidate in the first primary receives a majority of votes cast. It was originally used in a number of Southern states during the period when there was no substantial Republican Party and nomination in the Democratic primary was tantamount to election.

segregation: the policy of keeping races separated in housing, education, and other facilities, either by law (de jure) or custom (de facto).

Share the Wealth: the slogan used by Senator Huey P. Long during the 1930's as he contemplated a campaign for the presidency.

smoke-filled room: the popular shorthand term to describe the private deals made by professional politicians to nominate candidates and pass legislation. The term was coined at the 1920 Republican Convention, where party leaders nominated Warren G. Harding as a compromise candidate for president.

Social Security: legislation passed in 1935, as a major part of Franklin D. Roosevelt's New Deal, to provide public assistance to the elderly and disabled. The program has since been expanded and is a cornerstone of the domestic policy of the United States.

Southern strategy: a term to describe the approach, used by Richard M. Nixon in 1968 and subsequent Republican presidential candidates, to court Southern voters by covert attacks on the pro-civil rights policies of the Democratic Party.

split-ticket voting: voting for candidates of two or more parties for different offices. *see* **straight-ticket voting.**

spoils system: the practice of hiring public officials according to their political affiliation, based on the premise that "to the victors belong the spoils."

State of the Union address: an annual message to Congress, required by the Constitution, during which the president customarily presents a legislative program for the coming year.

states' rights: the doctrine that the powers of the individual states are equal or superior to those of the federal government. This concept was used extensively by Southerners prior to the Civil War to justify secession and after it to defend segregation.

States' Rights Party: the official name for the Dixiecrat Party.

straight-ticket voting: voting only for the candidates of a single party. *See* **split-ticket voting.**

Tammany Hall: the popular name for the Democratic Party machine in New York City, especially during the nineteenth century. It was named after the building in which the organization members met.

Teapot Dome scandal: the 1929 bribery conviction of Albert B. Fall, secretary of the interior under Warren G. Harding, for taking money to grant valuable oil leases, including those at Teapot Dome in Wyoming. The case became a symbol of corruption in the Harding administration.

third party: in modern American politics, an influential political party other than the Democratic Party or Republican Party. Generally arising over a specific issue and often representing no more than a protest against existing conditions, third parties can sometimes influence the outcome of presidential elections.

ticket: the name given to the candidates for a political party running in a single election. For example, the Democratic ticket consists of all Democratic nominees for offices from the presidency to local offices.

Tippecanoe and Tyler Too: the slogan used by Whigs during the presidential election of 1840 to express support for William Henry Harrison, victor of the Battle of Tippecanoe, and his vice presidential running mate, John Tyler.

Tonkin Gulf Resolution: a measure passed by Congress in 1964 giving President Lyndon B. Johnson the authority to respond to attacks on U.S. forces by North Vietnam.

United Nations: an international body, formed after World War II, to secure the peaceful resolution of international disputes and to develop global cooperation. It was the successor to the earlier League of Nations.

veto: the act of the president returning a bill to Congress so that it does not become law. Two-thirds of the members present and voting are required to overturn a presidential veto.

vice president: the constitutional officer who assumes the presidency upon the death or incapacity of the president and who presides over the Senate, although voting only to break a tie.

Voting Rights Act of 1965: legislation that expanded the right to vote, especially to African Americans, by prohibiting the use of literacy tests to discriminate against potential voters. The act also expanded federal supervision of restrictions on voting, especially in Southern states that had traditionally set barriers to participation by African Americans.

VP, the Veep: informal names for the vice president.

War on Poverty: the popular name given to efforts of Lyndon B. Johnson's Great Society programs to improve social conditions in the United States. Specifically, the Economic Opportunity Act of 1964 declared "war on poverty" by assisting poor communities in the undertaking of antipoverty programs involving job training, vocational education, and job development.

Warren Commission: the body authorized by the Senate on December 13, 1963, to investigate and report on the assassination of John F. Kennedy. Named for Chief Justice Earl Warren, who headed it, the commission consisted of members of the Senate and

House of Representatives (including future President Gerald R. Ford), former Central Intelligence Agency head Allen Dulles, and John McCloy, the former high commissioner of Germany. On September 28, 1964, the commission issued a report finding that Lee Harvey Oswald acted alone in the assassination of President Kennedy.

Watergate: the popular term for the burglary of Democratic National Committee headquarters in 1972 and the following cover-up and obstruction of justice that were orchestrated by the Nixon White House.

Whig Party: a major party in the United States from about 1834 to 1854. It was established by opponents of Democratic president An-

drew Jackson who opposed his strong presidency. After winning the presidency in 1849 and 1848, it faded after 1852 and many of its members joined the new Republican Party.

WPA: the Works Project Administration. This part of the New Deal was designed to stimulate the economy through employment in public projects ranging from highways to the arts.

Yellow Dog Democrat: the name given to a voter who is so loyal to the Democratic Party that he or she would "vote for a yellow dog if it ran on the Democratic ticket."

Michael Witkoski

Bibliography

General References

Bennett, Anthony J. *The American President's Cabinet: From Kennedy to Bush*. New York: St. Martin's Press, 1996.

Gilbert, Robert E. *The Mortal Presidency: Illness and Anguish in the White House*. 2d ed. New York: Fordham University Press, 1998.

Graff, Henry F., ed. *The Presidents: A Reference History*. 2d ed. New York: Charles Scribner's Sons, 1996.

Hyland, Pat. *Presidential Libraries and Museums: An Illustrated Guide*. Washington, D.C.: Congressional Quarterly, 1995.

Kane, Joseph N. *Facts About the Presidents: A Compilation of Biographical and Historical Information from George Washington to Bill Clinton*. 6th ed. New York: H. W. Wilson, 1993.

Michaels, Judith E. *The President's Call: Executive Leadership from FDR to George Bush*. Pittsburgh: University of Pittsburgh Press, 1997.

Neustadt, Richard E. *Presidential Power and the Modern Presidents: The Politics of Leadership from Roosevelt to Reagan*. 4th ed. New York: Free Press, 1990.

Simpson, Brooks D. *The Reconstruction Presidents*. Lawrence: University Press of Kansas, 1998.

The Presidency

Burton, David H. *The Learned Presidency: Theodore Roosevelt, William Howard Taft, Woodrow Wilson*. Rutherford, N.J.: Fairleigh Dickinson University Press, 1988.

Campbell, Colin. *The U.S. Presidency in Crisis: A Comparative Perspective*. New York: Oxford University Press, 1998.

Congressional Quarterly. *Powers of the Presidency*. 2d ed. Washington, D.C.: Author, 1997.

Cronin, Thomas E., and Michael A. Genovese. *The Paradoxes of the American Presidency*. New York: Oxford University Press, 1998.

Freidel, Frank B., and William Pencak. *The White House: The First Two Hundred Years*. Boston: Northeastern University Press, 1994.

Frendreis, John P., and Raymond Tatalovich. *The Modern Presidency and Economic Policy*. Itasca, Ill.: F. E. Peacock, 1994.

Hart, John. *The Presidential Branch: From Washington to Clinton*. 2d ed. Chatham, N.J.: Chatham House, 1995.

Hess, Stephen. *Presidents and the Presidency: Essays*. Washington, D.C.: Brookings Institution, 1996.

Kessler, Ronald. *Inside the White House: The Hidden Lives of Modern Presidents and the Secrets of the World's Most Powerful Institution*. New York: Pocket Books, 1995.

Kiewe, Amos, ed. *The Modern Presidency and Crisis Rhetoric*. Westport, Conn.: Praeger, 1994.

Levy, Leonard W., and Louis Fisher, eds. *Encyclopedia of the American Presidency*. New York: Simon & Schuster, 1994.

Lorant, Stefan. *The Glorious Burden: The American Presidency*. Lenox, Mass.: Author's Editions, 1976.

Martin, Fenton S., and Robert Goehlert. *How to Research the Presidency*. Washington, D.C.: Congressional Quarterly, 1996.

Nelson, Michael. *Guide to the Presidency*. 2d ed. Washington, D.C.: Congressional Quarterly, 1996.

————. *The Presidency and the Political System*. 4th ed. Washington, D.C.: CQ Press, 1995.

Nichols, David K. *The Myth of the Modern Presidency*. University Park: Pennsylvania State University Press, 1994.

Ragsdale, Lyn. *Vital Statistics on the Presidency: Washington to Clinton*. Washington, D.C.: Congressional Quarterly, 1996.

Riccards, Michael P. *The Ferocious Engine of Democracy: A History of the American Presidency*. Lanhan, Md.: Madison Books, 1994.

Smith, Craig A., and Kathy B. Smith. *The White House Speaks: Presidential Leadership as Persuasion*. Westport, Conn.: Praeger, 1994.

Thomas, Norman C., Joseph A. Pitka, and Richard Watson. *The Politics of the Presidency*. 4th ed. Washington, D.C.: CQ Press, 1997.

Thompson, Kenneth W. *Twenty Years of Papers on the Presidency*. Lanham, Md.: University Press of America, 1995.

Tsongas, Paul E. *Journey of Purpose: Reflections on the Presidency, Multiculturalism, and Third Parties*. New Haven, Conn.: Yale University Press, 1996.

Zernicke, Paul H. *Pitching the Presidency: How Presidents Depict the Office*. Westport, Conn.: Praeger, 1994.

Presidential Campaigns and Elections

Boller, Paul F. *Presidential Campaigns*. Rev. ed. New York: Oxford University Press, 1996.

Congressional Quarterly. *Presidential Elections, 1789-1996*. Washington, D.C.: Author, 1997.

————. *Selecting the President: From 1789 to 1996*. Washington, D.C.: Author, 1997.

Davis, James W. *U.S. Presidential Primaries and the Caucus-Convention System: A Sourcebook*. Westport, Conn.: Greenwood Press, 1997.

Hacker, Kenneth L. *Candidate Images in Presidential Elections*. Westport, Conn.: Praeger, 1995.

Haskell, John. *Fundamentally Flawed: Understanding and Reforming Presidential Primaries*. Lanham, Md.: Rowman & Littlefield, 1996.

Havel, James T. *U.S. Presidential Candidates and the Elections: A Biographical and Historical Guide*. New York: Macmillan, 1996.

Jamieson, Kathleen H. *Packaging the Presidency: A History and Criticism of Presidential Campaign Advertising*. 3d ed. New York: Oxford University Press, 1996.

McGillivray, Alice V., and Richard M. Scammon. *America at the Polls: A Handbook of American Presidential Election Statistics*. Washington, D.C.: Congressional Quarterly, 1994.

Morris, Richard S. *Behind the Oval Office: Winning the Presidency in the Nineties*. New York: Random House, 1997.

Palmer, Niall A. *The New Hampshire Primary and the American Electoral Process*. Westport, Conn.: Praeger, 1997.

Pika, Joseph A., and Richard A. Watson. *The Presidential Contest: With a Guide to the 1996 Presidential Race*. 5th ed. Washington, D.C.: CQ Press, 1995.

Polsby, Nelson W., and Aaron B. Wildavsky. *Presidential Elections: Strategies and Structures of American Politics*. 9th ed. Chatham, N.J.: Chatham House, 1996.

Schantz, Harvey L., ed. *American Presidential Elections: Process, Policy, and Political Change*. Albany: State University of New York, 1996.

Southwick, Leslie H. *Presidential Also-Rans and Running Mates, 1788 Through 1996*. 2d ed. Jefferson, N.C.: McFarland, 1998.

Tenpas, Kathryn D. *Presidents as Candidates: Inside the White House for the Presidential Campaign*. New York: Garland, 1997.

Troy, Gil. *See How They Ran: The Changing Role of the Presidential Candidate*. Rev. ed. Cambridge, Mass.: Harvard University Press, 1996.

Woodward, Bob. *The Choice: How Clinton Won*. New York: Simon & Schuster, 1997.

Wright, Russell O. *Presidential Elections in the United States: A Statistical History, 1860-1922.* Jefferson, N.C.: McFarland, 1995.

First Ladies and Presidential Families

Baker, Jean H. *Mary Todd Lincoln: A Biography.* New York: W. W. Norton, 1987.

Brendon, Piers. *Ike, His Life and Times.* New York: Harper & Row, 1986.

Bush, Barbara. *Barbara Bush: A Memoir.* New York: Charles Scribner's Sons, 1994.

Caroli, Betty B. *The Roosevelt Women.* New York: Basic Books, 1998.

Carter, Rosalynn. *First Lady from Plains.* Boston: Houghton Mifflin, 1984.

David, Lester. *Ike and Mamie: The Story of the General and His Lady.* New York: Putnam, 1981.

Fields, Joseph E., ed. *Worthy Partner: The Papers of Martha Washington.* Westport, Conn.: Greenwood Press, 1994.

Geer, Emily A. *First Lady: The Life of Lucy Webb Hayes.* Kent, Ohio: Kent State University Press, 1984.

Gelles, Edith B. *First Thoughts: Life and Letters of Abigail Adams.* New York: Twayne, 1998.

Keller, Rosemary S. *Abigail Adams and the American Revolution: A Personal History.* New York: Arno Press, 1982.

Kerr, Joan P., ed. *A Bully Father: Theodore Roosevelt's Letters to His Children.* New York: Random House, 1995.

Kilian, Pamela. *Barbara Bush: A Biography.* New York: St. Martin's Press, 1992.

King, Norman. *The Woman in the White House: The Remarkable Story of Hillary Rodham Clinton.* New York: Carol, 1996.

Klein, Edward. *All Too Human: The Love Story of Jack and Jackie Kennedy.* New York: Pocket Books, 1996.

Levin, Phyllis L. *Abigail Adams: A Biography.* New York: St. Martin's Press, 1987.

Miller, Nathan. *The Roosevelt Chronicles.* Garden City, N.Y.: Doubleday, 1979.

Milton, Joyce. *The First Partner, Hillary Rodham Clinton: A Biography.* New York: William Morrow, 1999.

Monk, William F. *Theodore and Alice, A Love Story: The Life and Death of Alice Lee Roosevelt.* Interlaken, N.Y.: Empire State Books, 1994.

Morris, Sylvia J. *Edith Kermit Roosevelt: Portrait of a First Lady.* New York: Coward, McCann & Geoghegan, 1980.

Nagel, Paul C. *The Adams Women: Abigail and Louisa Adams, Their Sisters and Daughters.* New York: Oxford University Press, 1987.

Radcliffe, Donnie. *Hillary Rodham Clinton: A First Lady for Our Time.* New York: Warner Books, 1993.

Ross, Ishbel. *Grace Coolidge and Her Era: The Story of a President's Wife.* New York: Dodd, Mead, 1962. Reprint. Plymouth, Vt.: Calvin Coolidge Memorial Foundation, 1988.

Saunders, Frances W. *Ellen Axson Wilson: First Lady Between Two Worlds.* Chapel Hill: University of North Carolina Press, 1985.

Schreiner, Samuel A. *The Trials of Mrs. Lincoln: The Harrowing Never-Before-Told Story of Mary Todd Lincoln's Last and Finest Years.* New York: Donald I. Fine, 1987.

Shachtman, Tom. *Edith and Woodrow: A Presidential Romance.* New York: Putnam, 1981.

Tribble, Edwin, ed. *A President in Love: The Courtship Letters of Woodrow Wilson and Edith Bolling Galt.* Boston: Houghton Mifflin, 1981.

Truman, Margaret. *Bess W. Truman.* New York: Macmillan, 1986.

Van der Heuvel, Gerry. *Crown of Thorns and Glory: Mary Todd Lincoln and Varina Howell Davis, the Two First Ladies of the Civil War.* New York: E. P. Dutton, 1988.

Warner, Judith. *Hillary Clinton: The Inside Story.* New York: Signet, 1993.

Withey, Lynne. *Dearest Friend: A Life of Abigail Adams.* New York: Free Press, 1981.

Young, Jeff C. *The Fathers of American Presidents: From Augustine Washington to William Blythe and Roger Clinton.* Jefferson, N.C.: McFarland, 1997.

Presidential Quotations

Boritt, G. S., ed. *Of the People, by the People, for the People and Other Quotations by Abraham Lincoln*. New York: Columbia University Press, 1996.

Brallier, Jess M. *Presidential Wit and Wisdom: Maxims, Mottoes, Sound Bites, Speeches, and Asides—Memorable Quotes from America's Presidents*. New York: Penguin, 1996.

Frost-Knappman, Elizabeth, ed. *The World Almanac of Presidential Quotations: Quotations from America's Presidents*. New York: Pharos Books, 1993.

Gallen, David, ed. *The Quotable Truman*. New York: Carroll & Graf, 1994.

Kaminski, John P., ed. *Citizen Jefferson: The Wit and Wisdom of an American Sage*. Madison, Wis.: Madison House, 1994.

Lott, Davis N. *The President Speaks: The Inaugural Addresses of the American Presidents from Washington to Clinton*. New York: Henry Holt, 1994.

The White House

Abbott, James A., and Elaine M. Rice. *Designing Camelot: The Kennedy White House Restoration*. New York: Van Nostrand Reinhold, 1998.

Caroli, Betty Boyd. *Inside the White House: America's Most Famous Home, the First Two Hundred Years*. Garden City, N.Y.: Doubleday, 1992.

Freidel, Frank B., and William Pencak, eds. *The White House: The First Two Hundred Years*. Boston: Northeastern University Press, 1994.

Seale, William. *The White House: The History of an American Idea*. Washington, D.C.: American Institute of Architects Press, 1992.

The Presidents:

GEORGE WASHINGTON

Brookhiser, Richard. *Founding Father: Rediscovering George Washington*. New York: Free Press, 1996.

Callahan, North. *Thanks, Mr. President: The Trail-Blazing Second Term of George Washington*. New York: Cornwall Books, 1991.

Clark, E. Harrison. *All Cloudless Glory: The Life of George Washington*. Washington, D.C.: Regnery, 1995.

Dalzell, Robert F. *George Washington's Mount Vernon: At Home in Revolutionary America*. New York: Oxford University Press, 1998.

Edgar, Gregory T. *Campaign of 1776: The Road to Trenton*. Bowie, Md.: Heritage Books, 1995.

Hirschfeld, Fritz. *George Washington and Slavery: A Documentary Portrayal*. Columbia: University of Missouri Press, 1997.

Lewis, Thomas A. *For King and Country: The Maturing of George Washington, 1748-1760*. New York: HarperCollins, 1993.

Randall, Willard S. *George Washington: A Life*. New York: Henry Holt, 1997.

Smith, Richard N. *Patriarch: George Washington and the New American Nation*. Boston: Houghton Mifflin, 1993.

JOHN ADAMS

Adams, John. *John Adams: A Biography in His Own Words*. Edited by James B. Peabody. New York: Harper & Row, 1973.

Brown, Ralph. *The Presidency of John Adams*. Lawrence: University Press of Kansas, 1975.

East, Robert A. *John Adams*. Boston: Twayne, 1979.

Ellis, Joseph J. *Passionate Sage: The Character and Legacy of John Adams*. New York: W. W. Norton, 1993.

Ferling, John E. *John Adams: A Bibliography*. Westport, Conn.: Greenwood Press, 1994.

———. *John Adams: A Life*. Knoxville: University of Tennessee Press, 1992.

Shepard, Jack. *The Adams Chronicles: Four Generations of Greatness*. Boston: Little, Brown, 1975.

Thompson, C. Bradley. *John Adams and the Spirit of Liberty*. Lawrence: University Press of Kansas, 1998.

THOMAS JEFFERSON

Adams, William H. *The Paris Years of Thomas Jefferson*. New Haven, Conn.: Yale University Press, 1997.

Ambrose, Stephen E. *Undaunted Courage: Meriwether Lewis, Thomas Jefferson, and the Opening of the American West*. New York: Simon & Schuster, 1996.

Bedini, Silvio A. *Thomas Jefferson: Statesman of Science*. New York: Macmillan, 1990.

Burstein, Andrew. *The Inner Jefferson: Portrait of a Grieving Optimist*. Charlottesville: University Press of Virginia, 1995.

Ellis, Joseph J. *American Sphinx: The Character of Thomas Jefferson*. New York: Alfred A. Knopf, 1997.

Gaustad, Edwin S. *Sworn on the Altar of God: A Religious Biography of Thomas Jefferson*. Grand Rapids, Mich.: Wm. B. Eerdmans, 1997.

Gordon-Reed, Annette. *Thomas Jefferson and Sally Hemings: An American Controversy*. Charlottesville: University Press of Virginia, 1997.

Lautman, Robert C. *Thomas Jefferson's Monticello: A Photographic Portrait*. New York: Monacelli Press, 1997.

Lerner, Max. *Thomas Jefferson: America's Philosopher-King*. New Brunswick, N.J.: Transaction, 1996.

Mapp, Alf J. *Thomas Jefferson: Passionate Pilgrim*. Lanham, Md.: Madison Books, 1991.

Miller, Douglas T. *Thomas Jefferson and the Creation of America*. New York: Facts on File, 1997.

Randall, Willard S. *Thomas Jefferson: A Life*. New York: Henry Holt, 1993.

Risjord, Norman K. *Thomas Jefferson*. Madison, Wis.: Madison House, 1994.

Shackleford, George G. *Thomas Jefferson's Travels in Europe, 1784-1789*. Baltimore: The Johns Hopkins University Press, 1995.

Stein, Susan. *The Worlds of Thomas Jefferson at Monticello*. New York: Harry N. Abrams, 1993.

JAMES MADISON

Banning, Lance. *The Sacred Fire of Liberty: James Madison and the Founding of the Federal Republic*. Ithaca, N.Y.: Cornell University Press, 1995.

Goldwin, Robert A. *From Parchment to Power: How James Madison Used the Bill of Rights to Save the Constitution*. Washington, D.C.: AEI Press, 1997.

Ketcham, Ralph L. *James Madison: A Biography*. New York: Macmillan, 1971.

McCoy, Drew R. *The Last of the Fathers: James Madison and the Republican Legacy*. New York: Cambridge University Press, 1989.

Madison, James. *James Madison: A Biography in His Own Words*. Edited by Merrill D. Peterson. New York: Harper & Row, 1974.

Matthews, Richard K. *If Men Were Angels: James Madison and the Heartless Empire of Reason*. Lawrence: University Press of Kansas, 1995.

Miller, William L. *The Business of May Next: James Madison and the Founding*. Charlottesville: University Press of Virginia, 1992.

Moore, Virginia. *The Madisons: A Biography*. New York: McGraw-Hill, 1979.

Rakove, Jack N., and Oscar Handlin. *James Madison and the Creation of the American Republic*. Glennview, Ill.: Scott, Foresman, 1990.

Rutland, Robert A., ed. *James Madison and the American Nation, 1751-1836: An Encyclopedia*. New York: Simon & Schuster, 1994.

————. *James Madison: The Founding Father*. New York: Macmillan, 1987.

————. *The Presidency of James Madison*. Lawrence: University Press of Kansas, 1990.

JAMES MONROE

Ammon, Harry. *James Monroe: A Bibliography*. Westport, Conn.: Meckler, 1991.

————. *James Monroe: The Quest for National Identity*. New York: McGraw-Hill, 1971.

Cunningham, Noble E. *The Presidency of James Monroe*. Lawrence: University Press of Kansas, 1996.

JOHN QUINCY ADAMS

Hargreaves, Mary W. M. *The Presidency of John Quincy Adams*. Lawrence: University Press of Kansas, 1985.

Hecht, Marie B. *John Quincy Adams: A Personal History of an Independent Man*. New York: Macmillan, 1972.

Nagel, Paul C. *John Quincy Adams: A Public Life, a Private Life*. New York: Alfred A. Knopf, 1997.

Parsons, Lynn H. *John Quincy Adams*. Madison, Wis.: Madison House, 1998.

_____. *John Quincy Adams: A Bibliography*. Westport, Conn.: Greenwood Press, 1993.

Richards, Leonard L. *The Life and Times of Congressman John Quincy Adams*. New York: Oxford University Press, 1986.

Shepherd, Jack. *Cannibals of the Heart: A Personal Biography of Louisa Catherine and John Quincy Adams*. New York: McGraw-Hill, 1980.

ANDREW JACKSON

Cole, Donald B. *The Presidency of Andrew Jackson*. Lawrence: University Press of Kansas, 1993.

Davis, Burke. *Old Hickory: A Life of Andrew Jackson*. New York: Dial Press, 1977.

Marszalek, John F. *The Petticoat Affair: Manners, Mutiny, and Sex in Andrew Jackson's White House*. New York: Free Press, 1997.

Remini, Robert V. *Andrew Jackson: A Bibliography*. Westport, Conn.: Meckler, 1991.

_____. *Andrew Jackson and the Course of American Democracy*. New York: Harper & Row, 1984.

_____. *The Jacksonian Era*. 2d ed. Wheeling, Ill.: Harlan Davidson, 1997.

_____. *The Life of Andrew Jackson*. New York: Harper & Row, 1988.

Sellers, Charles G., comp. *Andrew Jackson: A Profile*. New York: Hill & Wang, 1971.

Williams, Frank B. *Tennessee's Presidents*. Knoxville: University of Tennessee Press, 1981.

MARTIN VAN BUREN

Cole, Donald B. *Martin Van Buren and the American Political System*. Princeton, N.J.: Princeton University Press, 1984.

Mushkat, Jerome, and Joseph G. Rayback. *Martin Van Buren: Law, Politics, and the Shaping of Republican Ideology*. DeKalb: Northern Illinois University Press, 1997.

Niven, John. *Martin Van Buren: The Romantic Age of American Politics*. New York: Oxford University Press, 1983.

Wilson, Major L. *The Presidency of Martin Van Buren*. Lawrence: University Press of Kansas, 1984.

WILLIAM HENRY HARRISON

Peterson, Norma L. *The Presidencies of William Henry Harrison and John Tyler*. Lawrence: University Press of Kansas, 1989.

Stevens, Kenneth R. *William Henry Harrison: A Bibliography*. Westport, Conn.: Greenwood Press, 1998.

JOHN TYLER

Chidsey, Donald B. *And Tyler Too*. Nashville: Thomas Nelson, 1978.

Merk, Frederick. *Fruits of Propaganda in the Tyler Administration*. Cambridge, Mass.: Harvard University Press, 1971.

Morgan, Robert J. *A Whig Embattled: The Presidency Under John Tyler*. Lincoln: University of Nebraska, 1954. Reprint. Hamden, Conn.: Archon Books, 1974.

Peterson, Norma L. *The Presidencies of William Henry Harrison and John Tyler*. Lawrence: University Press of Kansas, 1989.

JAMES K. POLK

Bergeron, Paul H. *The Presidency of James K. Polk*. Lawrence: University Press of Kansas, 1987.

Haynes, Sam W., and Oscar Handlin. *James K. Polk and the Expansionist Impulse*. New York: Longman, 1997.

Williams, Frank B. *Tennessee's Presidents*. Knoxville: University of Tennessee Press, 1981.

ZACHARY TAYLOR

Bauer, K. Jack. *Zachary Taylor: Soldier, Planter, Statesman of the Old Southwest.* Baton Rouge: Louisiana State University Press, 1985.

Smith, Elbert B. *The Presidencies of Zachary Taylor and Millard Fillmore.* Lawrence: University Press of Kansas, 1988.

MILLARD FILLMORE

Dix, Dorothea L. *The Lady and the President: The Letters of Dorothea Dix and Millard Fillmore.* Edited by Charles M. Snyder. Lexington: University Press of Kentucky, 1975.

Grayson, Benson L. *The Unknown President: The Administration of President Millard Fillmore.* Washington, D.C.: University Press of America, 1981.

Rayback, Robert J. *Millard Fillmore: Biography of a President.* Buffalo, N.Y.: Buffalo Historical Society, 1959.

Smith, Elbert B. *The Presidencies of Zachary Taylor and Millard Fillmore.* Lawrence: University Press of Kansas, 1988.

FRANKLIN PIERCE

Bisson, Wilfred J., and Gerry Hayden. *Franklin Pierce: A Bibliography.* Westport, Conn.: Greenwood Press, 1993.

Gara, Larry. *The Presidency of Franklin Pierce.* Lawrence: University Press of Kansas, 1991.

Nichols, Roy F. *Franklin Pierce, Young Hickory of the Granite Hills.* Rev. ed. Philadelphia: University of Pennsylvania Press, 1964.

JAMES BUCHANAN

Binder, Frederick M. *James Buchanan and the American Empire.* Cranbury, N.J.: Associated University Presses, 1994.

Birkner, Michael, ed. *James Buchanan and the Political Crisis of the 1850's.* Selinsgrove, Pa.: Susquehanna University Press, 1996.

Cahalan, Sally S. *James Buchanan and His Family at Wheatland.* Lancaster, Pa.: James Buchanan Foundation, 1988.

Smith, Elbert B. *The Presidency of James Buchanan.* Lawrence: University Press of Kansas, 1975.

ABRAHAM LINCOLN

Bak, Richard. *The Day Lincoln Was Shot: An Illustrated Chronicle.* Dallas: Taylor, 1998.

Burlingame, Michael. *The Inner World of Abraham Lincoln.* Urbana: University of Illinois Press, 1994.

Chadwick, Bruce. *The Two American Presidents: A Dual Biography of Abraham Lincoln and Jefferson Davis.* Secaucus, N.J.: Carol, 1999.

Donald, David H. *Lincoln.* New York: Simon & Schuster, 1995.

Einhorn, Lois J. *Abraham Lincoln, the Orator: Penetrating the Lincoln Legend.* Westport, Conn.: Greenwood Press, 1992.

Freedman, Russell. *Lincoln: A Photobiography.* New York: Clarion Books, 1987.

Garrison, Webb B. *The Lincoln No One Knows: The Mysterious Man Who Ran the Civil War.* Nashville, Tenn.: Rutledge Hill Press, 1993.

Good, Timothy S., ed. *We Saw Lincoln Shot: One Hundred Eyewitness Accounts.* Jackson: University Press of Mississippi, 1995.

Hamilton, Charles. *Lincoln in Photographs: An Album of Every Known Pose.* Dayton, Ohio: Morningside, 1985.

Hanchett, William. *Out of the Wilderness: The Life of Abraham Lincoln.* Urbana: University of Illinois Press, 1994.

Harrell, Carolyn L. *When the Bells Tolled for Lincoln: Southern Reaction to the Assassination.* Macon, Ga.: Mercer University Press, 1997.

Harris, William C. *With Charity for All: Lincoln and the Restoration of the Union.* Lexington: University Press of Kentucky, 1997.

Holzer, Harold, ed. *The Lincoln-Douglas Debates: The First Complete, Unexpurgated Text.* New York: HarperCollins, 1993.

Kunhardt, Philip B., Jr., Philip B. Kunhardt III, and Peter W. Kunhardt. *Lincoln: An Illustrated Biography.* New York: Alfred A. Knopf, 1992.

Matthews, Elizabeth W. *Lincoln as a Lawyer: An Annotated Bibliography*. Carbondale: Southern Illinois University Press, 1991.

Neely, Mark E. *The Abraham Lincoln Encyclopedia*. New York: McGraw-Hill, 1982.

———. *The Last Best Hope for Earth: Abraham Lincoln and the Promise of America*. Cambridge, Mass.: Harvard University Press, 1993.

———. *The Lincoln Family Album*. New York: Doubleday, 1990.

Oates, Stephen B. *Abraham Lincoln: The Man Behind the Myths*. New York: Harper & Row, 1984.

Paludan, Phillip S. *The Presidency of Abraham Lincoln*. Lawrence: University Press of Kansas, 1994.

Peterson, Merrill D. *Lincoln in American Memory*. New York: Oxford University Press, 1994.

Platt, Thomas B. *Abraham Lincoln: A Biography*. New York: Book of the Month Club, 1986.

Rawley, James A. *Abraham Lincoln and a Nation Worth Fighting for*. Wheeling, Ill.: Harlan Davidson, 1996.

Reck, W. Emerson. *A. Lincoln: His Last Twenty-four Hours*. Jefferson City, N.C.: McFarland, 1987.

Simon, Paul. *Lincoln's Preparation for Greatness: The Illinois Legislative Years*. Urbana: University of Illinois Press, 1989.

Williams, Frank J., William Pederson, and Vincent Marsala. *Abraham Lincoln: Sources and Style of Leadership*. Westport, Conn.: Greenwood Press, 1994.

Wills, Garry. *Lincoln at Gettysburg: The Words That Remade America*. New York: Simon & Schuster, 1992.

Wilson, Douglas L. *Lincoln Before Washington: New Perspectives on the Illinois Years*. Urbana: University of Illinois Press, 1997.

ANDREW JOHNSON

Benedict, Michael L. *The Impeachment Trial and Trial of Andrew Johnson*. New York: W. W. Norton, 1973.

Brabson, Fay W. *Andrew Johnson: A Life in Pursuit of the Right Course, 1808-1875*. Durham, N.C.: Seeman Printery, 1972.

Castel, Albert E. *The Presidency of Andrew Johnson*. Lawrence: Regents Press of Kansas, 1979.

Gerson, Noel B. *The Trial of Andrew Johnson*. Nashville: Thomas Nelson, 1977.

McCaslin, Richard B. *Andrew Johnson: A Bibliography*. Westport, Conn.: Greenwood Press, 1992.

Mantell, Martin E. *Johnson, Grant, and the Politics of Reconstruction*. New York: Columbia University Press, 1973.

Nash, Howard P. *Andrew Johnson: Congress and Reconstruction*. Rutherford, N.J.: Fairleigh Dickinson University Press, 1972.

Rehnquist, William H. *Grand Inquests: The Historic Impeachments of Justice Samuel Chase and President Andrew Johnson*. New York: William Morrow, 1992.

Sefton, James E. *Andrew Johnson and the Uses of Constitutional Power*. Boston: Little, Brown, 1980.

Smith, Gene. *High Crimes and Misdemeanors: The Impeachment and Trial of Andrew Johnson*. New York: William Morrow, 1977.

Trefousse, Hans L. *Andrew Johnson: A Biography*. New York: Norton, 1989.

———. *Impeachment of a President: Andrew Johnson, the Blacks, and Reconstruction*. Knoxville: University of Tennessee Press, 1975.

ULYSSES S. GRANT

Arnold, James R. *Grant Wins the War: Decision at Vicksburg*. New York: John Wiley & Sons, 1997.

Goldhurst, Richard. *Many Are the Hearts: The Agony and the Triumph of Ulysses S. Grant*. New York: Reader's Digest Press, 1975.

Grant, Julia Dent. *The Personal Memoirs of Julia Dent Grant*. New York: Putnam, 1975.

Grant, Ulysses S. *Memoirs and Selected Letters: Personal Memoirs of U. S. Grant, Selected Let-*

ters 1839-1865. New York: Library of America, 1990.

Kaltman, Al. *Cigars, Whiskey, and Winning: Leadership Lessons from General Ulysses S. Grant.* Paramus, N.J.: Prentice Hall, 1998.

McFeely, William S. *Grant: A Biography.* New York: W. W. Norton, 1981.

Perret, Geoffrey. *Ulysses S. Grant: Soldier and President.* New York: Random House, 1997.

Scaturro, Frank J. *President Grant Reconsidered.* Lanham, Md.: University Press of America, 1998.

Simpson, Brooks D. *Let Us Have Peace: Ulysses S. Grant and the Politics of War and Reconstruction.* Chapel Hill: University of North Carolina Press, 1991.

RUTHERFORD B. HAYES

Barnard, Harry. *Rutherford B. Hayes and His America.* Indianapolis: Bobbs-Merrill, 1954.

Davison, Kenneth E. *The Presidency of Rutherford B. Hayes.* Westport, Conn.: Greenwood Press, 1972.

Hoogenboom, Ari A. *The Presidency of Rutherford B. Hayes.* Lawrence: University Press of Kansas, 1988.

————. *Rutherford B. Hayes: Warrior and President.* Lawrence: University Press of Kansas, 1995.

Williams, T. Harry, ed. *Hayes: The Diary of a President, 1875-1881.* New York: David McKay, 1964.

JAMES A. GARFIELD

Bates, Richard O. *The Gentleman from Ohio: An Introduction to Garfield.* Durham, N.C.: Moore, 1973.

Booraem, Hendrik. *The Road to Respectability: James A. Garfield and His World, 1844-1852.* Lewisburg, Pa.: Bucknell University Press, 1988.

Clark, James C. *The Murder of James A. Garfield: The President's Last Days and the Trial and Execution of His Assassin.* Jefferson, N.C.: McFarland, 1993.

Doenecke, Justus D. *The Presidencies of James A. Garfield and Chester A. Arthur.* Lawrence: Regents Press of Kansas, 1981.

Leech, Margaret, and Harry J. Brown. *The Garfield Orbit.* New York: Harper & Row, 1978.

Peskin, Allan. *Garfield: A Biography.* Kent, Ohio: Kent State University Press, 1978.

Rupp, Robert O. *James A. Garfield: A Bibliography.* Westport, Conn.: Greenwood Press, 1997.

Shaw, John, ed. *Crete and James: Personal Letters of Lucretia and James Garfield.* East Lansing: Michigan State University Press, 1994.

CHESTER A. ARTHUR

Doenecke, Justus D. *The Presidencies of James A. Garfield and Chester A. Arthur.* Lawrence: Regents Press of Kansas, 1981.

Reeves, Thomas C. *Gentleman Boss: The Life of Chester Alan Arthur.* New York: Alfred A. Knopf, 1975.

GROVER CLEVELAND

Hollingsworth, J. Rogers. *The Whirligig of Politics: The Democracy of Cleveland and Bryan.* Chicago: University of Chicago Press, 1963.

Marszalek, John F. *Grover Cleveland: A Bibliography.* Westport, Conn.: Meckler, 1988.

Tugwell, Rexford G. *Grover Cleveland.* New York: Macmillan, 1968.

Vexler, Robert I., ed. *Grover Cleveland, 1837-1908: Chronology, Documents, Bibliographical Aids.* Dobbs Ferry, N.Y.: Oceana, 1968.

Welch, Richard E. *The Presidencies of Grover Cleveland.* Lawrence: University Press of Kansas, 1988.

BENJAMIN HARRISON

Socolofsky, Homer E., and Allan B. Spetter. *The Presidency of Benjamin Harrison.* Lawrence: University Press of Kansas, 1987.

WILLIAM MCKINLEY

Bristow, Joseph L. *Fraud and Politics at the Turn of the Century: McKinley and His Administration as Seen by His Principal Patronage Dispenser and Investigator.* New York: Exposition Press, 1952.

Damiani, Brian P. *Advocates of Empire: William McKinley, the Senate, and American Expansion, 1898-1899*. New York: Garland, 1987.

Gould, Lewis L. *The Presidency of William McKinley*. Lawrence: Regents Press of Kansas, 1980.

_____. *The Spanish-American War and President McKinley*. Lawrence: University Press of Kansas, 1982.

Gould, Lewis L., and Craig H. Roell. *William McKinley: A Bibliography*. Westport, Conn.: Meckler, 1988.

Johns, Wesley A., and Paul Avrich. *The Man Who Shot McKinley*. South Brunswick, N.J.: A. S. Barnes, 1970.

Leech, Margaret. *In the Days of McKinley*. New York: Harper, 1959. Reprint. Westport, Conn.: Greenwood Press, 1975.

McElroy, Richard L. *William McKinley and Our America: A Pictorial History*. Canton, Ohio: Stark County Historical Society, 1996.

Spielman, William C. *William McKinley, Stalwart Republican: A Biographical Study*. New York: Exposition Press, 1954.

THEODORE ROOSEVELT

Berman, Jay S. *Police Administration and Progressive Reform: Theodore Roosevelt as Police Commissioner of New York*. New York: Greenwood Press, 1987.

Brands, H. W. *T.R.: The Last Romantic*. New York: Basic Books, 1997.

Burton, David H. *Theodore Roosevelt*. New York: Twayne, 1972.

Cadenhead, Ivie E. *Theodore Roosevelt: The Paradox of Progressivism*. Woodbury, N.Y.: Barron's, 1974.

Collin, Richard H. *Theodore Roosevelt's Caribbean: The Panama Canal, the Monroe Doctrine, and the Latin American Context*. Baton Rouge: Louisiana State University Press, 1990.

Cutright, Paul R. *Theodore Roosevelt: The Making of a Conservationist*. Urbana: University of Illinois Press, 1985.

Egloff, Franklin R. *Theodore Roosevelt, an American Portrait*. New York: Vantage Press, 1980.

Gardner, Joseph L. *Departing Glory: Theodore Roosevelt as Ex-President*. New York: Charles Scribner's Sons, 1973.

Gould, Lewis L. *The Presidency of Theodore Roosevelt*. Lawrence: University Press of Kansas, 1991.

Grant, George. *Carry a Big Stick: The Uncommon Heroism of Theodore Roosevelt*. Nashville, Tenn.: Cumberland House, 1996.

Harbaugh, William H. *Power and Responsibility: The Life and Times of Theodore Roosevelt*. Rev. ed. New York: Octagon Books, 1975.

Hart, Albert B., Herbert R. Ferleger, and John A. Gable, eds. *Theodore Roosevelt Encyclopedia*. 2d ed. Westport, Conn.: Meckler, 1989.

Jeffers, H. Paul. *Colonel Roosevelt: Theodore Roosevelt Goes to War, 1897-1898*. New York: John Wiley & Sons, 1996.

McCullough, David G. *Mornings on Horseback*. New York: Simon & Schuster, 1981.

Markham, Lois. *Theodore Roosevelt*. New York: Chelsea House, 1985.

Meltzer, Milton. *Theodore Roosevelt and His America*. New York: Franklin Watts, 1994.

Miller, Nathan. *Theodore Roosevelt*. New York: William Morrow, 1992.

Morris, Edmund. *The Rise of Theodore Roosevelt*. New York: Coward, McCann & Geoghegan, 1979.

Norton, Aloysius A. *Theodore Roosevelt*. Boston: Twayne, 1980.

Ornig, Joseph R. *My Last Chance to Be a Boy: Theodore Roosevelt's South American Expedition of 1913-1914*. Mechanicsburg, Pa.: Stackpole Books, 1994.

Renehan, Edward J., Jr. *The Lion's Pride: Theodore Roosevelt and His Family in Peace and War*. New York: Oxford University Press, 1998.

Samuels, Peggy. *Teddy Roosevelt at San Juan: The Making of a President*. College Station: Texas A&M University Press, 1997

Wilson, Robert L. *Theodore Roosevelt, Outdoors-*

man. Agoura, Calif.: Trophy Room Books, 1994.

WILLIAM HOWARD TAFT

Anderson, Judith I. *William Howard Taft: An Intimate History*. New York: Norton, 1981.

Burton, David H. *William Howard Taft: In the Public Service*. Melbourne, Fla.: R. E. Krieger, 1986.

Coletta, Paolo E. *William Howard Taft: A Bibliography*. Westport, Conn.: Meckler, 1989.

Mason, Alpheus T. *William Howard Taft, Chief Justice*. New York: Simon & Schuster, 1965.

Minger, Ralph E. *William Howard Taft and United States Foreign Policy: The Apprenticeship Years, 1900-1908*. Urbana: University of Illinois Press, 1975.

WOODROW WILSON

Buckingham, Peter H. *Woodrow Wilson: A Bibliography of His Times and Presidency*. Wilmington, Del.: Scholarly Resources, 1990.

Clements, Kendrick A. *The Presidency of Woodrow Wilson*. Lawrence: University Press of Kansas, 1992.

_____. *Woodrow Wilson, World Statesman*. Boston: Twayne, 1987.

Cooper, John M. *The Warrior and the Priest: Woodrow Wilson and Theodore Roosevelt*. Cambridge, Mass.: The Belknap Press of Harvard University Press, 1983.

Esposito, David M. *The Legacy of Woodrow Wilson: American War Aims in World War I*. Westport, Conn.: Greenwood Press, 1996.

Heater, Derek B. *National Self-Determination: Woodrow Wilson and His Legacy*. New York: St. Martin's Press, 1994.

Heckscher, August. *Woodrow Wilson*. New York: Charles Scribner's Sons, 1991.

Knock, Thomas J. *To End All Wars: Woodrow Wilson and the Quest for a New World Order*. New York: Oxford University Press, 1992.

Mulder, John M., Ernest M. White, and Ethel S. White. *Woodrow Wilson: A Bibliography*. Westport, Conn.: Greenwood Press, 1997.

Saunders, Robert M. *In Search of Woodrow Wilson: Beliefs and Behavior*. Westport, Conn.: Greenwood Press, 1998.

Stid, Daniel D. *The President as Statesman: Woodrow Wilson and the Constitution*. Lawrence: University Press of Kansas, 1998.

Thorsen, Niels. *The Political Thought of Woodrow Wilson, 1875-1910*. Princeton, N.J.: Princeton University Press, 1988.

Weinstein, Edwin A. *Woodrow Wilson: A Medical and Psychological Biography*. Princeton, N.J.: Princeton University Press, 1981.

WARREN G. HARDING

Anthony, Carl S. *Florence Harding: The First Lady, the Jazz Age, and the Death of America's Most Scandalous President*. New York: William Morrow, 1998.

Downes, Randolph C. *The Rise of Warren Gamaliel Harding, 1865-1920*. Columbus: Ohio State University Press, 1970.

Ferrell, Robert H. *The Strange Deaths of President Harding*. Columbia: University of Missouri Press, 1996.

Frederick, Richard G. *Warren G. Harding: A Bibliography*. Westport, Conn.: Greenwood Press, 1992.

Mee, Charles L. *The Ohio Gang: The World of Warren G. Harding*. New York: M. Evans, 1981.

Murray, Robert K. *The Harding Era: Warren G. Harding and His Administration*. Minneapolis: University of Minnesota Press, 1969.

Russell, Francis. *The Shadow of Blooming Grove: Warren G. Harding in His Times*. New York: McGraw-Hill, 1968.

Sinclair, Andrew. *The Available Man: The Life Behind the Masks of Warren Gamaliel Harding*. New York: Macmillan, 1965.

Trani, Eugene P., and David L. Wilson. *The Presidency of Warren G. Harding*. Lawrence: Regents Press of Kansas, 1977.

CALVIN COOLIDGE

Booraem, Hendrik. *The Provincial: Calvin Coolidge and His World, 1885-1895*. Lewisburg, Pa.: Bucknell University Press, 1994.

Ferrell, Robert H. *The Presidency of Calvin Coolidge.* Lawrence: University Press of Kansas, 1998.

Greene, J. R. *Calvin Coolidge's Plymouth, Vermont.* Dover, N.H.: Arcadia, 1997.

McCoy, Donald R. *Calvin Coolidge: The Quiet President.* Lawrence: University Press of Kansas, 1988.

Sobel, Robert. *Coolidge: An American Enigma.* Washington, D.C.: Regnery, 1998.

HERBERT HOOVER

Barber, William J. *From New Era to New Deal: Herbert Hoover, the Economists, and American Economic Policy, 1921-1933.* New York: Cambridge University Press, 1985.

Best, Gary D. *Herbert Hoover, the Postpresidential Years, 1933-1964.* Stanford, Calif.: Hoover Institution Press, 1983.

————. *The Politics of American Individualism: Herbert Hoover in Transition, 1918-1921.* Westport, Conn.: Greenwood Press, 1975.

Burner, David. *Herbert Hoover: A Public Life.* New York: Alfred A. Knopf, 1979.

Burns, Richard D. *Herbert Hoover: A Bibliography of His Times and Presidency.* Wilmington, Del.: Scholarly Resources, 1991.

Eckley, Wilton. *Herbert Hoover.* Boston: Twayne, 1980.

Fausold, Martin L. *The Presidency of Herbert C. Hoover.* Lawrence: University Press of Kansas, 1985.

Hoff-Wilson, Joan. *Herbert Hoover, Forgotten Progressive.* Boston: Little, Brown, 1975.

Krog, Carl E., and William R. Tanner., eds. *Herbert Hoover and the Republican Era: A Reconsideration.* Lanham, Md.: University Press of America, 1984.

Liebovich, Louis. *Bylines in Despair: Herbert Hoover, the Great Depression, and the U.S. News Media.* Westport, Conn.: Praeger, 1994.

Nash, George H. *The Life of Herbert Hoover.* 3 vols. New York: W. W. Norton, 1983.

Nye, Frank T., Jr. *Doors of Opportunity: The Life and Legacy of Herbert Hoover.* West Branch,

Iowa: Herbert Hoover Presidential Library Association, 1988.

Olson, James S. *Herbert Hoover and the Reconstruction Finance Corporation, 1931-1933.* Ames: Iowa State University Press, 1977.

Robinson, Edgar E. *Herbert Hoover, President of the United States.* Stanford, Calif.: Hoover Institution Press, 1975.

Rosen, Elliot A. *Hoover, Roosevelt, and the Brains Trust: From Depression to New Deal.* New York: Columbia University Press, 1977.

Smith, Richard N. *An Uncommon Man: The Triumph of Herbert Hoover.* New York: Simon & Schuster, 1984.

Sobel, Robert. *Herbert Hoover at the Onset of the Great Depression, 1929-1930.* Philadelphia: J. B. Lippincott, 1975.

Tracey, Kathleen. *Herbert Hoover, a Bibliography: His Writings and Addresses.* Stanford, Calif.: Hoover Institution Press, 1977.

Walch, Timothy, and Dwight M. Miller, eds. *Herbert Hoover and Franklin D. Roosevelt: A Documentary History.* Westport, Conn.: Greenwood Press, 1998.

FRANKLIN D. ROOSEVELT

Abbott, Philip. *The Exemplary Presidency: Franklin D. Roosevelt and the American Political Tradition.* Amherst: University of Massachusetts Press, 1990.

Alsop, Joseph. *FDR, 1882-1945: A Centenary Remembrance.* New York: Viking Press, 1982.

Buhite, Russell D, and David W. Levy, eds. *FDR's Fireside Chats.* Norman: University of Oklahoma Press, 1992.

Davis, Kenneth S. *FDR: Into the Storm, 1937-1940: A History.* New York: Random House, 1993.

————. *FDR: The New Deal Years, 1933-1937: A History.* New York: Random House, 1986.

————. *FDR: The New York Years, 1928-1933.* New York: Random House, 1985.

Ferrell, Robert H. *The Dying President: Franklin Delano Roosevelt, 1944-1945.* Columbia: University of Missouri Press, 1998.

Freidel, Frank B. *Franklin D. Roosevelt: A Rendezvous with Destiny*. Boston: Little, Brown, 1990.

Goldberg, Richard T. *The Making of Franklin D. Roosevelt: Triumph over Disability*. Cambridge, Mass.: Abt Books, 1981.

Goodwin, Doris Kearns. *No Ordinary Time: Franklin and Eleanor Roosevelt: The Home Front in World War II*. New York: Simon & Schuster, 1994.

Graham, Otis L., and Meghan Wander, eds. *Franklin D. Roosevelt, His Life and Times: An Encyclopedic View*. Boston: G. K. Hall, 1985.

Langston, Thomas S. *Ideologues and Presidents: From the New Deal to the Reagan Revolution*. Baltimore: The Johns Hopkins University Press, 1992.

Leuchtenberg, William E. *The FDR Years: On Roosevelt and His Legacy*. New York: Columbia University Press, 1995.

Maney, Patrick J. *The Roosevelt Presence: A Biography of Franklin Delano Roosevelt*. New York: Twayne, 1992.

Miller, Nathan. *FDR: An Intimate History*. Garden City, N.Y.: Doubleday, 1983.

Morgan, Ted. *FDR: A Biography*. New York: Simon & Schuster, 1985.

Mortimer, Edward. *The World That FDR Built: Vision and Reality*. New York: Charles Scribner's Sons, 1989.

Rozell, Mark J., William D. Peterson, eds. *FDR and the Modern Presidency: Leadership and Legacy*. Westport, Conn.: Praeger, 1997.

Ryan, Halford R. *Franklin D. Roosevelt's Rhetorical Presidency*. New York: Greenwood Press, 1988.

Thompson, Robert S. *A Time for War: Franklin Delano Roosevelt and the Path to Pearl Harbor*. New York: Prentice Hall, 1991.

Underhill, Robert. *FDR and Harry: Unparalleled Lives*. Westport, Conn.: Praeger, 1996.

Ward, Geoffrey C. *Before the Trumpet: Young Franklin Roosevelt, 1882-1905*. New York: Harper & Row, 1985.

_____, ed. *Closest Companion: The Unknown Story of the Intimate Friendship Between Franklin Roosevelt and Margaret Suckley*. Boston: Houghton Mifflin, 1995.

_____. *A First-Class Temperament: The Emergence of Franklin Roosevelt*. New York: Harper & Row, 1989.

HARRY S TRUMAN

Burns, Richard D. *Harry S Truman: A Bibliography of His Times and Presidency*. Wilmington, Del.: Scholarly Resources, 1984.

Donaldson, Gary. *Truman Defeats Dewey*. Lexington: University Press of Kentucky, 1998.

Donovan, Robert J. *Conflict and Crisis: The Presidency of Harry S Truman*. Columbia: University of Missouri Press, 1996.

_____. *Tumultuous Years: The Presidency of Harry S Truman, 1949-1953*. New York: W. W. Norton, 1982.

Ferrell, Robert H. *Choosing Truman: The Democratic Convention of 1944*. Columbia: University of Missouri Press, 1994.

_____. *Harry S Truman: A Life*. Columbia: University of Missouri Press, 1994.

_____, ed. *Harry S Truman and the Bomb: A Documentary History*. Worland, Wyo.: High Plains, 1996.

_____. *Harry S Truman and the Modern American Presidency*. Boston: Little, Brown, 1983.

_____. *Harry S Truman: His Life on the Family Farms*. Worland, Wyo.: High Plains, 1991.

_____, ed. *Off the Record: The Private Papers of Harry S Truman*. Columbia: University of Missouri Press, 1997.

_____. *Truman: A Centenary Remembrance*. New York: Viking Press, 1984.

Gullan, Harold I. *The Upset That Wasn't: Harry S Truman and the Crucial Election of 1948*. Chicago: Ivan R. Dee, 1998.

Hamby, Alonzo L. *Man of the People: A Life of Harry S Truman*. New York: Oxford University Press, 1995.

Kirkendall, Richard S., ed. *The Harry S Truman Encyclopedia*. Boston: G. K. Hall, 1989.

McCoy, Donald R. *The Presidency of Harry S Truman*. Lawrence: University Press of Kansas, 1984.

McCullough, David G. *Truman*. New York: Simon & Schuster, 1992.

Maddox, Robert J. *From War to Cold War: The Education of Harry S Truman*. Boulder, Colo.: Westview Press, 1988.

Merrill, Dennis, ed. *Documentary History of the Truman Presidency*. 23 vols. to date Bethesda, Md.: University Publications of America, 1995-   .

Miller, Richard L. *Truman: The Rise to Power*. New York: McGraw-Hill, 1986.

Pemberton, William E. *Harry S Truman: Fair Dealer and Cold Warrior*. Boston: Twayne, 1989.

Poen, Monty M., ed. *Strictly Personal and Confidential: The Letters Harry Truman Never Mailed*. Boston: Little, Brown, 1982.

Sand, G. W. *Truman in Retirement: A Former President Views the Nation and the World*. South Bend, Ind.: Justice Books, 1993.

Stone, I.F. *The Truman Era, 1945-1952*. Boston: Little, Brown, 1988.

Thompson, Kenneth W., ed. *The Truman Presidency: Intimate Perspectives*. Lanham, Md.: University Press of America, 1984.

Wainstock, Dennis. *The Decision to Drop the Atomic Bomb*. Westport, Conn.: Praeger, 1996.

Walker, J. Samuel. *Prompt and Utter Destruction: Truman and the Use of Atomic Bombs Against Japan*. Chapel Hill: University of North Carolina, 1997.

DWIGHT D. EISENHOWER

Ambrose, Stephen E. *Eisenhower*. 2 vols. New York: Simon & Schuster, 1983.

_____. *The Victors: Eisenhower and His Boys, the Men of World War II*. New York: Simon & Schuster, 1998.

Beschloss, Michael R., and Vincent Virga. *Eisenhower: A Centennial Life*. New York: HarperCollins, 1990.

Bowie, Robert R., and Richard H. Immerman. *Waging Peace: How Eisenhower Shaped an Enduring Cold War Strategy*. New York: Oxford University Press, 1998.

Burk, Robert F. *Dwight D. Eisenhower, Hero and Politician*. Boston: Twayne, 1986.

Ewald, William B. *Eisenhower the President: Crucial Days, 1951-1960*. Englewood Cliffs, N.J.: Prentice Hall, 1983.

Ferrell, Robert H., ed. *The Eisenhower Diaries*. New York: W. W. Norton, 1981.

Hold, Daniel D., and James W. Leyerzapf, eds. *Eisenhower: The Prewar Diaries and Selected Papers, 1905-1941*. Baltimore: The Johns Hopkins University Press, 1998.

Kinnard, Douglas. *Ike, 1890-1990: A Pictorial History*. Washington, D.C.: Brassey's, 1990.

Lasby, Clarence G. *Eisenhower's Heart Attack: How Ike Beat Heart Disease and Held on to the Presidency*. Lawrence: University Press of Kansas, 1997.

Lee, R. Alton. *Dwight D. Eisenhower: A Bibliography of His Times and Presidency*. Wilmington, Del.: Scholarly Resources, 1991.

_____. *Dwight D. Eisenhower, Soldier and Statesman*. Chicago: Nelson Hall, 1981.

Mayer, Michael S., ed. *The Eisenhower Presidency and the 1950's*. Boston: Houghton Mifflin, 1998.

Pach, Chester J., and Elmo Richardson. *The Presidency of Dwight D. Eisenhower*. Rev. ed. Lawrence: University Press of Kansas, 1991.

Pickett, William B. *Dwight D. Eisenhower and American Power*. Wheeling, Ill.: Harlan Davidson, 1995.

Warshaw, Shirley Anne. *Reexamining the Eisenhower Presidency*. Westport, Conn.: Greenwood Press, 1993.

Wykes, Alan. *The Biography of General Dwight D. Eisenhower*. Greenwich, Conn.: Bison Books, 1982.

JOHN F. KENNEDY

Andersen, Christopher P. *Jack and Jackie: Portrait of an American Marriage*. New York: William Morrow, 1996.

Benson, Michael. *Who's Who in the JFK Assassination: An A-Z Encyclopedia.* Secaucus, N.J.: Carol, 1993.

Brogan, Hugh. *Kennedy.* New York: Longman, 1996.

Chomsky, Noam. *Rethinking Camelot: JFK, the Vietnam War, and U.S. Political Culture.* Boston: South End Press, 1993.

Claflin, Edward, ed. *JFK Wants to Know: Memos from the President's Office.* New York: William Morrow, 1991.

Damore, Leo. *The Cape Cod Years of John Fitzgerald Kennedy.* New York: Four Walls Eight Windows, 1993.

Duffy, James P. *The Assassination of John F. Kennedy: A Complete Book of Facts.* New York: Thunder's Mouth Press, 1992.

Giglio, James N. *John F. Kennedy: A Bibliography.* Westport, Conn.: Greenwood Press, 1995.

_____. *The Presidency of John F. Kennedy.* Lawrence: University Press of Kansas, 1991.

Goldman, Martin S. *John F. Kennedy, Portrait of a President.* New York: Facts on File, 1995.

Hamilton, Nigel. *JFK, Reckless Youth.* New York: Random House, 1992.

Hellmann, John. *The Kennedy Obsession: The American Myth of JFK.* New York: Columbia University Press, 1997.

Hersh, Seymour M. *The Dark Side of Camelot.* Boston: Little, Brown, 1997.

Mailer, Norman. *Osawld's Tale: An American Mystery.* New York: Random House, 1995.

Matthews, Christopher. *Kennedy and Nixon: The Rivalry That Shaped Postwar America.* New York: Simon & Schuster, 1996.

May, Ernest R., and Philip Zelikow, eds. *The Kennedy Tapes: Inside the White House During the Cuban Missile Crisis.* Cambridge, Mass.: The Belknap Press of Harvard University Press, 1997.

Posner, Gerald L. *Case Closed: Lee Harvey Oswald and the Assassination of JFK.* New York: Random House, 1993.

Reeves, Richard. *President Kennedy: Profile of Power.* New York: Simon & Schuster, 1993.

Salinger, Pierre. *John F. Kennedy, Commander in Chief: A Profile in Leadership.* New York: Penguin, 1997.

Schwab, Orrin. *Defending the Free World: John F. Kennedy, Lyndon Johnson, and the Vietnam War, 1961-1965.* Westport, Conn.: Praeger, 1998.

Scott, William E. *November 22, 1963: A Reference Guide to the JFK Assassination.* Lanham, Md.: University Press of America, 1999.

Sorensen, Theodore C. *The Kennedy Legacy.* New York: Macmillan, 1993.

Strober, Gerald S., and Deborah H. Strober, eds. *Let Us Begin Anew: An Oral History of the Kennedy Presidency.* New York: HarperCollins, 1993.

Thompson, Robert S. *The Missiles of October: The Declassified Story of John F. Kennedy and the Cuban Missile Crisis.* New York: Simon & Schuster, 1992.

LYNDON B. JOHNSON

Andrew, John A. *Lyndon Johnson and the Great Society.* Chicago: Ivan R. Dee, 1998.

Bernstein, Irving. *Guns or Butter: The Presidency of Lyndon Johnson.* New York: Oxford University Press, 1996.

Bornet, Vaughn D. *The Presidency of Lyndon B. Johnson.* Lawrence: University Press of Kansas, 1983.

Califano, Joseph A. *The Triumph and Tragedy of Lyndon Johnson: The White House Years.* New York: Simon & Schuster, 1991.

Caro, Robert A. *The Years of Lyndon Johnson.* New York: Alfred A. Knopf, 1982.

Dallek, Robert. *Flawed Giant: Lyndon Johnson and His Times, 1961-1973.* New York: Oxford University Press, 1998.

_____. *Lone Star Rising: Lyndon Johnson and His Times, 1908-1960.* New York: Oxford University Press, 1991.

Divine, Robert A., ed. *The Johnson Years.* 2 vols. Lawrence: University Press of Kansas, 1987.

Henggeler, Paul R. *In His Steps: Lyndon Johnson*

and the Kennedy Mystique. Chicago: Ivan R. Dee, 1991.

Hunt, Michael H., and Eric Foner. *Lyndon Johnson's War: America's Cold War Crusade in Vietnam, 1945-1968—A Critical Issue.* New York: Hill & Wang, 1996.

Muslin, Hyman L. *Lyndon Johnson, the Tragic Self: A Psychohistorical Portrait.* New York: Insight Books, 1991.

Redford, Emmette S., and Richard T. McCulley. *White House Operations: The Johnson Presidency.* Austin: University of Texas Press, 1986.

Reedy, George E. *Lyndon B. Johnson: A Memoir.* New York: Andrews & McMeel, 1982.

Roell, Craig, comp. *Lyndon B. Johnson: A Bibliography.* 2 vols. Austin: University of Texas Press, 1984.

Rulon, Philip R. *The Compassionate Samaritan: The Life of Lyndon Baines Johnson.* Chicago: Nelson-Hall, 1981.

Schulman, Bruce J. *Lyndon B. Johnson and American Liberalism: A Brief Biography with Documents.* Boston: Bedford Books of St. Martin's Press, 1994.

VanDemark, Brian. *Into the Quagmire: Lyndon Johnson and the Escalation of the Vietnam War.* New York: Oxford University Press, 1991.

RICHARD M. NIXON

Aitken, Jonathan. *Nixon: A Life.* Washington, D.C.: Regnery, 1993.

Colodny, Len, and Robert Gettlin. *Silent Coup: The Removal of a President.* New York: St. Martin's Press, 1991.

Genovese, Michael A. *The Nixon Presidency: Power and Politics in Turbulent Times.* New York: Greenwood Press, 1990.

Goldman, Martin S. *Richard M. Nixon: A Complex Legacy.* New York: Facts on File, 1998.

Kimball, Jeffrey P. *Nixon's Vietnam War.* Lawrence: University Press of Kansas, 1998.

Kutler, Stanley I., ed. *Abuse of Power: The New Nixon Tapes.* New York: Free Press, 1997.

_____. *The Wars of Watergate: The Last Crisis*

of Richard Nixon. New York: Alfred A. Knopf, 1990.

Matthews, Christopher. *Kennedy and Nixon: The Rivalry That Shaped Postwar America.* New York: Simon & Schuster, 1996.

Morris, Roger. *Richard Milhous Nixon: The Rise of an American Politician.* New York: Henry Holt, 1990.

Nadel, Laurie. *The Great Stream of History: A Biography of Richard M. Nixon.* New York: Atheneum, 1991.

Nixon, Richard M. *Beyond Peace.* New York: Random House, 1994.

_____. *In the Arena: A Memoir of Victory, Defeat, and Renewal.* New York: Simon & Schuster, 1990.

Parmet, Herbert S. *Richard Nixon and His America.* Boston: Little, Brown, 1990.

Strober, Gerald S., and Deborah H. Strober. *Nixon: An Oral History of His Presidency.* New York: HarperCollins, 1994.

Volkan, Vamik D., Norman Itzkowitz, and Andrew W. Dod. *Richard Nixon: A Psychobiography.* New York: Columbia University Press, 1997.

Wicker, Tom. *One of Us: Richard Nixon and the American Dream.* New York: Random House, 1991.

GERALD R. FORD

Cannon, James M. *Time and Chance: Gerald Ford's Appointment with History.* New York: HarperCollins, 1994.

Casserly, John J. *The Ford White House: The Diary of a Speechwriter.* Boulder: Colorado Associated University Press, 1977.

Firestone, Bernard J., and Alexej Ugrinsky, eds. *Gerald R. Ford and the Politics of Post Watergate America.* Westport, Conn.: Greenwood Press, 1993.

Ford, Gerald R. *A Time to Heal: The Autobiography of Gerald R. Ford.* New York: Harper & Row, 1979.

Greene, John R. *Gerald R. Ford: A Bibliography.* Westport, Conn.: Greenwood Press, 1994.

_____. *The Limits of Power: The Nixon and Ford Administrations.* Bloomington: Indiana University Press, 1992.

_____. *The Presidency of Gerald R. Ford.* Lawrence: University Press of Kansas, 1995.

Hartmann, Robert T. *Palace Politics: An Inside Account of the Ford Years.* New York: McGraw-Hill, 1980.

Howell, David, Margaret Mary Howell, and Robert Kronman. *Gentlemanly Attitudes: Jerry Ford and the Campaign of '76.* Washington, D.C.: HKJV, 1980.

Reeves, Richard. *A Ford, Not a Lincoln.* New York: Harcourt Brace Jovanovich, 1975.

Schoenebaum, Eleanora W. *The Nixon/Ford Years.* New York: Facts on File, 1979.

TerHorst, Jerald F. *Gerald Ford and the Future of the Presidency.* New York: Third Press, 1974.

Thompson, Kenneth W., ed. *The Ford Presidency: Twenty-two Intimate Perspectives of Gerald R. Ford.* Lanham, Md.: University Press of America, 1988.

Jimmy Carter

Anderson, Patrick. *Electing Jimmy Carter: The Campaign of 1976.* Baton Rouge: Louisiana State University Press, 1994.

Ariall, Dan, and Cheryl Heckler-Feltz. *The Carpenter's Apprentice: The Spiritual Biography of Jimmy Carter.* Grand Rapids, Mich.: Zondervan, 1996.

Bourne, Peter G. *Jimmy Carter: A Comprehensive Biography from Plains to Post-Presidency.* New York: Charles Scribner's Sons, 1997.

Brinkley, Douglas. *The Unfinished Presidency: Jimmy Carter's Journey Beyond the White House.* New York: Viking, 1998.

Dumbrell, John. *The Carter Presidency: A Reevaluation.* New York: St. Martin's Press, 1993.

Glad, Betty. *Jimmy Carter: In Search of the Great White House.* New York: W. W. Norton, 1980.

Hyatt, Richard. *The Carters of Plains.* Huntsville, Ala.: Strode, 1977.

Jordon, Hamilton. *Crisis: The Last Year of the Carter Presidency.* New York: Putnam, 1982.

Kaufman, Burton I. *The Presidency of James Earl Carter, Jr.* Lawrence: University Press of Kansas, 1993.

Kraus, Sidney, ed. *The Great Debates: Carter vs. Ford, 1976.* Bloomington: Indiana University Press, 1979.

Lasky, Victor. *Jimmy Carter, the Man and the Myth.* New York: R. Marek, 1979.

Mazlish, Bruce, and Edwin Diamond. *Jimmy Carter: A Character Portrait.* New York: Simon & Schuster, 1979.

Morris, Kenneth E. *Jimmy Carter: American Moralist.* Athens: University of Georgia Press, 1996.

Neyland, James. *The Carter Family Scrapbook: An Intimate Close-up of America's First Family.* New York: Grosset & Dunlap, 1977.

Richardson, Don, ed. *Conversations with Carter.* Boulder, Colo.: Lynne Rienner, 1998.

Stroud, Kandy. *How Jimmy Won: The Victory Campaign from Plains to the White House.* New York: William Morrow, 1977.

Thornton, Richard C. *The Carter Years: Toward a New Global Order.* New York: Paragon House, 1991.

Troester, Rod. *Jimmy Carter as Peacemaker: A Post-Presidential Biography.* Westport, Conn.: Praeger, 1996.

Wooten, James T. *Dasher: The Roots and the Rising of Jimmy Carter.* New York: Summit Books, 1978.

Ronald Reagan

Abrams, Herbert L. *"The President Has Been Shot": Confusion, Disability, and the Twenty-fifth Amendment in the Aftermath of the Attempted Assassination of Ronald Reagan.* New York: W. W. Norton, 1992.

Bosch, Adriana. *Reagan: An American Story.* New York: TV Books, 1998.

Cannon, Lou. *President Reagan: The Role of a Lifetime.* New York: Simon & Schuster, 1991.

Cardigan, J. H. *Ronald Reagan: A Remarkable Life*. Kansas City, Mo.: Andrews & McMeel, 1995.

Davis, Patti. *Angels Don't Die: My Father's Gift of Faith*. New York: HarperCollins, 1995.

D'Souza, Dinesh. *Ronald Reagan: How an Ordinary Man Became an Extraordinary Leader*. New York: Free Press, 1997.

Edel, Wilbur. *The Reagan Presidency: An Actor's Finest Performance*. New York: Hippocrene Books, 1992.

Hannaford, Peter, ed. *Recollections of Reagan: A Portrait of Ronald Reagan*. New York: William Morrow, 1997.

Levy, Peter B. *Encyclopedia of the Reagan-Bush Years*. Westport, Conn.: Greenwood Press, 1996.

Mervin, David. *Ronald Reagan and the American Presidency*. New York: Longman, 1990.

Morris, Edmund. *Dutch: A Memoir of Ronald Reagan*. New York: Random House, 1998.

Pemberton, William E. *Exit with Honor: The Life and Presidency of Ronald Reagan*. Armonk, N.Y.: M. E. Sharpe, 1998.

Reagan, Ronald. *An American Life*. New York: Simon & Schuster, 1990.

———. *A Shining City: The Legacy of Ronald Reagan*. Edited by Erik D. Felen. New York: Simon & Schuster, 1998.

Strober, Deborah H., and Gerald S. Strober. *Reagan: The Man and His Presidency*. New York: W. W. Norton, 1992.

Walsh, Kenneth T. *Ronald Reagan*. New York: Park Lane Press, 1997.

GEORGE BUSH

Duffy, Michael. *Marching in Place: The Status Quo Presidency of George Bush*. New York: Simon & Schuster, 1992.

Hyams, Joe. *Flight of the Avenger: George Bush at War*. San Diego, Calif.: Harcourt Brace Jovanovich, 1991.

Levy, Peter B. *Encyclopedia of the Reagan-Bush Years*. Westport, Conn.: Greenwood Press, 1996.

Parmet, Herbert S. *George Bush: The Life of a Lone Star Yankee*. New York: Charles Scribner's Sons, 1997.

Rozell, Mark J. *The Press and the Bush Presidency*. Westport, Conn.: Praeger, 1996.

Smith, Jean E. *George Bush's War*. New York: Henry Holt, 1992.

Stinnett, Robert B. *George Bush: His World War II Years*. Missoula, Mont.: Pictorial Histories, 1991.

Tarpley, Webster G., and Anton Chaitkin. *George Bush: The Unauthorized Biography*. Washington, D.C.: Executive Intelligence Review, 1992.

Valdez, David. *George Herbert Walker Bush: A Photographic Profile*. College Station: Texas A&M University Press, 1997.

BILL CLINTON

Allen, Charles F., and Jonathan Portis. *The Comeback Kid: The Life and Career of Bill Clinton*. New York: Birch Lane Press, 1992.

Campbell, Colin, and Bert A. Rockman, eds. *The Clinton Presidency: First Appraisals*. Chatham, N.J.: Chatham House, 1996.

Carpozi, George. *Clinton Confidential: The Climb to Power, the Unauthorized Biography of Bill and Hillary Clinton*. Del Mar, Calif.: Emery Dalton Books, 1995.

Clinton, Roger. *Growing Up Clinton: The Lives, Times, and Tragedies of America's Presidential Family*. Arlington, Tex.: Summit, 1995.

Coulter, Ann. *High Crimes and Misdemeanors: The Case Against Bill Clinton*. Washington, D.C.: Regnery, 1998.

Denton, Robert E., Jr., and Rachel L. Holloway, eds. *The Clinton Presidency: Images, Issues, and Communication Strategies*. Westport, Conn.: Praeger, 1996.

Drew, Elizabeth. *On the Edge: The Clinton Presidency*. New York: Simon & Schuster, 1994.

Dumas, Ernest, ed. *The Clintons of Arkansas: An Introduction by Those Who Know Them Best*. Fayetteville: University of Arkansas Press, 1993.

Gallen, David, and Philip Martin. *Bill Clinton as They Know Him: An Oral Biography*. New York: Gallen, 1994.

Hohenberg, John. *The Bill Clinton Story: Winning the Presidency*. Syracuse, N.Y.: Syracuse University Press, 1994.

Maraniss, David. *First in His Class: A Biography of Bill Clinton*. New York: Simon & Schuster, 1995.

Metz, Allan. *Bill Clinton's Pre-Presidential Career: An Annotated Bibliography*. Westport, Conn.: Greenwood Press, 1994.

Morris, Dick. *Behind the Oval Office: Getting Reelected Against All Odds*. Los Angeles: Renaissance Books, 1999.

Morris, Roger. *Partner's in Power: The Clintons and Their America*. New York: Henry Holt, 1996.

Oakley, Meredith L. *On the Make: The Rise of Bill Clinton*. Washington, D.C.: Regnery, 1994.

Odom, Richmond. *Circle of Death: Clinton's Climb to the Presidency*. Lafayette, La.: Huntington House, 1995.

Renshon, Stanley A., ed. *The Clinton Presidency: Campaigning, Governing, and the Psychology of Leadership*. Boulder, Colo.: Westview Press, 1995.

Stephanopoulos, George. *All Too Human: A Political Education*. Boston: Little, Brown, 1999.

Stewart, James B. *Blood Sport: The President and His Adversaries*. New York: Simon & Schuster, 1996.

Tyrrell, R. Emmett. *Boy Clinton: The Political Biography*. Washington, D.C.: Regnery, 1996.

Walker, Martin. *The President We Deserve: Bill Clinton, His Rise, Fall, and Comebacks*. New York: Crown, 1996.

Woodward, Bob. *The Choice: How Clinton Won*. New York: Simon & Schuster, 1997.

Kevin J. Bochynski

The American Presidents

Revised Edition

Index

AAA. *See* Agricultural Adjustment Act

ABMs. *See* Antiballistic missiles

Abolitionist movement; and Lincoln, 261; and Polk, 207; and Van Buren, 167

Abortion, 665

Acheson, Dean, 519, 583

ACLU. *See* American Civil Liberties Union

Acting president, 604

Adams, Abigail, 55, 121

Adams, Charles Francis, 454

Adams, John, **47-61**; as J. Q. Adams's father, 121; appointment of judges, 70; as a diplomat, 122; and the election of 1796, 3; legacy of, 4; opinion of J. Q. Adams, 122; opinion of Madison, 102; as vice president, 31

Adams, John Quincy, **121-134**; and the campaign of 1824, 118, 141; and the campaign of 1828, 141; and the election of 1824, 5, 190; and the Holy Alliance, 115; opinion of Jackson, 114; opinion of Monroe, 107, 119; opinion of Polk, 190; opinion of Van Buren, 167; as secretary of state, 108; and slavery, 112; and Van Buren, 164

Adams, Sherman, 531, 538, 557

Adamson Act, 416

Addison's disease, 557, 559

AFDC. *See* Aid to Families with Dependent Children

Affirmative action, 610

Afghanistan, 651, 671

African Americans; and Coolidge, 446; and Hoover, 460; in the military, 523; rights of, 368; and the Seminoles, 169; in the South, 515; voting rights of, 319, 588

African National Congress, 688

Agnew, Spiro T., 608, 634

Agricultural Adjustment Act, 475

Agricultural Marketing Act, 455

Agriculture, 445, 455, 475

Aguinaldo, Emilio, 364, 369

Aid to Families with Dependent Children, 612

Air Commerce Act of 1926, 444

Alabama claims, 297, 303

Alaska, 284

Albanians, 708

Albany Regency, 164

Aldrich, Nelson W., 398

Algeciras Conference, 392

Alger, Horatio, 8

Alger, Russell A., 360, 364

Alien and Sedition Acts, 4, 44, 55, 68

Allen, Henry J., 463

Allende, Salvador, 617

Alliance for Progress, 549

Alliance of 1778, 69

Allied Powers (World War I), 421

Allies (World War II), 492, 498

Allison, David, 138

Allison, William Boyd, 322

Amendments, 24. *See also* individual amendments

American Civil Liberties Union, 685

American Civil War. *See* Civil War

American Federation of Labor, 415

American Indians; assimilation of, 76; and Cleveland, 344; in Florida, 113; and W. H. Harrison, 178; and Hayes, 323; and Hoover, 459; Jackson's opinion of, 140; and Nixon, 611; policies under Jackson, 143, 145; removal of, 118, 130, 143, 145, 169; self-determination of, 611; treaties with, 118, 143, 145; and Western settlement, 34

American Revolution. *See* Revolutionary War

American System, 130, 146, 149, 192, 244

Americans with Disabilities Act, 687

Ames, Fisher, 30, 42, 54

Ames, Oakes, 306

Anderson, John, 661

Anderson, Robert, 239

Andropov, Yuri, 666, 683

Antiballistic missiles, 621, 666

Antietam, Battle of, 262

Anti-Masons, 149, 217

Antitariffites, 149

Antiwar protests, 597, 624, 661, 697

Apartheid, 689

Appropriation, 109

Aquino, Corazon, 671

Arab countries, 620

Argentia Conference, 492

Arkansas, 697

Armistice, 426

Arms control, 621, 666, 669

Arms reductions, 461
Armstrong, John, 90, 95, 97
Army, U.S., 54
Army Appropriations Act, 284
Aroostook River, 169
Arthur, Chester A., **332-337**; and the campaign
    of 1880, 329; as New York Customhouse
    collector, 323
Article 231, 429
Articles of Confederation, 22, 65, 86
Arts patronage, 484
Ash, Roy, 606, 608
Ash Commission, 614
Ashley, James, 285
Assassination; of Garfield, 331, 333; of Kennedy,
    568, 571; of Lincoln, 274, 280; of McKinley,
    370, 379
Assassination attempt; against Ford, 639; against
    Reagan, 663, 683
Aswan Dam, 546
Atlantic Charter, 492, 498
Atomic bomb, 496, 508, 519
Atomic Energy Commission, 539-540, 614
Attorney general, 26
Atwater, Lee, 684, 692
Axis powers, World War II, 497
Ayatollah, the. *See* Khomeini, Ayatollah Ruhollah

B-1 bomber, 647, 666
Babcock, Orville E., 302, 308
Baker, Bobby, 584
Baker, Howard, 681
Baker, James A., III, 684-685, 692
Baker, Newton D., 414
Balanced budget, 613, 664
Ballinger, Richard H., 399
Ball's Bluff, Battle of, 265
Baltic republics, 688
Baltimore, Md., 97
Bancroft, George, 195, 197, 209, 275
Bank of the United States, 28, 32, 71, 92, 102,
    110, 130, 148, 151, 184, 192; Jackson's veto of
    recharter bill, 149; Tyler's veto of recharter
    bill, 186
Bank War, 153, 163, 184
Banking crisis, 474
Banking reform, 415
Banknotes, 298
Bankruptcy, 174
Banks, 170. *See also* Bank of the United States;
    National banks; State banks
Barbary pirates, 38, 72, 101
Barbour, James, 127

Barnburners, 224
Barnett, Ross, 566
Barron, James, 79
Barry, William Taylor, 143
Bates, Edward, 250
Batista, Fulgencio, 549
Battles. *See* names of individual battles
Bay of Pigs, 563
Begin, Menachem, 649
Beijing, 688
Beirut, 667-668
Belknap, W. W., 308
Bell, John, 7, 249
Bennet, William S., 402
Benton, Thomas Hart, 139, 142, 155, 162, 166
Bentsen, Lloyd, 680
Bering Sea, 357
Berlin, 513, 549, 564
Berlin Decree, 80
Berlin Wall, 564, 688
Berrien, John M., 142
Biddle, Nicholas, 111, 149, 151, 153
Big Stick Diplomacy, 387-388, 392
Big Three, 498, 501
Bill of Rights, 24, 86
Birmingham, Ala., 567
Birney, James G., 196
Bishop, Maurice, 667
Black, Hugo L., 478
Black, Jeremiah S., 233, 239
Black Friday, 302
Black Hawk's War, 145, 211
Black suffrage, 280, 283
Black Tuesday, 456
Blaine, James G., 9, 309, 315, 329, 334-335, 337,
    342, 356
Blair, Francis Preston, 148, 160
Blair, Montgomery, 250
Bland-Allison bill, 322
Bleeding Kansas, 227
Bliss, Cornelius N., 359
Blockade; of Berlin, 513; of Cuba, 564; by Great
    Britain, 79, 95
Bloody shirt, 304
Blount, William, 137
Blount, Willie, 139
Blum, John Morton, 373, 387
Bohlen, Charles, 540
Bolsheviks, 427
Bomb. *See* Atomic bomb; Hydrogen bomb;
    Nuclear weapons
Bombing; in Beirut, 668; of Cambodia, 617, 619;

of Japan, 508; of Libya, 659, 671; of North Vietnam, 589; of Quemoy and Matsu, 545
Bonaparte, Napoleon. *See* Napoleon I
Bonds, 298, 348
Bonus riot, 463
Booth, John Wilkes, 274, 280
Borah, William E., 429
Borden, Robert L., 402
Border states, 252, 261
Bork, Robert, 665, 686
Boulder Dam, 444
Bourbon Democrats, 336, 342, 348
Boutwell, George S., 300-301
Boxer Rebellion, 369, 452
Boycotts, 542
Braddock, Edward, 20
Bradley, Joseph P., 316
Brady, Nicholas, 685
Brady bill, 703
Branch, John, 142
Brandeis, Louis D., 413, 415
Breckinridge, John C., 7, 237, 249, 279
Brennan, William, 692
Brewster, Benjamin J., 335
Brezhnev, Leonid, 651, 666, 683
Briand, Aristide, 448
Brinkmanship, 538, 543
Bristow, Benjamin H., 308-309, 315
Britain. *See* Great Britain
British West Indies. *See* West Indies
Broken voyage concept, 78
Brooks, Preston, 226
Brown, Pat, 660
Brown, Walter, 454
Brown v. Board of Education of Topeka, Kansas, 542
Browne, William E., 238
Bruce, Louis R., 611
Bryan, William Jennings, 10, 350, 359, 411, 413, 415
Brzezinski, Zbigniew, 650, 652
Buchanan, James, 230-240; and the election of 1856, 6; legacy of, 300; and Mexico, 202; as secretary of state, 197
Buchanan, Patrick, 692
Buchen, Philip, 631
Budget and Accounting Act, 435
Budget deficit. *See* Deficit; National debt
Budget Reform Act, 615
Buena Vista, Battle of, 212
Buffalo, N.Y., 340
Bulge, Battle of the, 499
Bull Moose Party. *See* Progressive Party

Bull Run, First Battle of, 258; Second Battle of, 262
Bureau of Indian Affairs, 459, 611
Burleson, Albert, 414
Burlington Treaty, 324
Burns, Arthur, 606, 608
Burnside, Ambrose E., 265
Burr, Aaron, 30, 44, 59, 68; conspiracy of, 81; duel with Alexander Hamilton, 74; and the election of 1800, 3, 60; and Jackson, 139; trial of, 82
Burt, Silas W., 324
Bush, George, **677-693**, 700; and the campaign of 1980, 661; and the campaign of 1992, 702; and Clinton, 700; and the election of 1992, 16; legacy of, 16
Bush, Prescott, 678
Businessman's Cabinet, 354
Butler, Anthony, 155
Butler, Benjamin F., 259, 285, 287, 300, 304, 306
Butterfield, Alexander, 625
Byrnes, James F., 505

Cabinet, 26, 148, 445, 615; of J. Adams, 51, 127; of Arthur, 334; of Buchanan, 233, 238-239; of Bush, 685; of Cleveland, 343; of Coolidge, 442; of Eisenhower, 537; of Garfield, 329; of Grant, 300; of Harding, 435; of B. Harrison, 354; of Hayes, 318; of Hoover, 454; of Jackson, 142, 145, 148; of Jefferson, 70; of A. Johnson, 284-285; of Kennedy, 560; of Lincoln, 249, 265; of McKinley, 359, 361; of Madison, 88; of Monroe, 108; of Pierce, 224; of Reagan, 662; of Van Buren, 167; of Washington, 26; of Wilson, 413
Cabot, George, 74
Caddell, Patrick, 645
Calhoun, John C., 108, 123, 132, 142, 145-147, 150, 172, 214, 218
Califano, Joseph, 646
California, 197, 200-201, 206, 213-214, 218, 482, 660
Cambodia, 617-618; bombing of, 619
Camelot, 554, 568
Camp David Accords, 649, 654
Campaign of 1796, 49
Campaign of 1800, 59, 68
Campaign of 1808, 397
Campaign of 1824, 118, 123, 141
Campaign of 1828, 132, 141
Campaign of 1832, 149
Campaign of 1836, 156, 166
Campaign of 1840, 175, 179

Campaign of 1844, 194, 196
Campaign of 1848, 212
Campaign of 1852, 219, 222
Campaign of 1856, 220, 231
Campaign of 1860, 237, 248, 279
Campaign of 1864, 7, 268, 271, 279
Campaign of 1868, 289, 296
Campaign of 1872, 305
Campaign of 1876, 309, 315
Campaign of 1880, 310, 329
Campaign of 1884, 337, 341
Campaign of 1888, 346, 353
Campaign of 1892, 347
Campaign of 1896, 359
Campaign of 1900, 369
Campaign of 1912, 393, 403, 410
Campaign of 1916, 417
Campaign of 1920, 430, 434
Campaign of 1924, 443
Campaign of 1928, 449, 454
Campaign of 1932, 464, 472
Campaign of 1936, 485
Campaign of 1940, 490
Campaign of 1944, 499
Campaign of 1948, 514, 517, 524
Campaign of 1952, 525, 537
Campaign of 1956, 557
Campaign of 1960, 558, 576, 604
Campaign of 1964, 568, 581
Campaign of 1968, 595, 605-606
Campaign of 1976, 630, 634, 637, 639, 644-645, 661, 681
Campaign of 1980, 653, 661, 681
Campaign of 1988, 684
Campaign of 1992, 692, 701
Campaigns, 5, 15, 180, 684
Canada; border with, 112, 123; and McKinley, 360; support for rebellion in, 168; and Taft, 401; and the War of 1812, 95
Canning, George, 80, 89, 114
Cannon, Joseph G., 381, 399
CAP. See Community Action Program
Capitol, 60, 105; burning of the, 97
Caroline affair, 168
Carranza, Venustiano, 418-419
Carter, Jimmy, **642-657**; Bush's opinion of, 681; and the campaign of 1976, 639; and the campaign of 1980, 661; and the election of 1976, 15
Carter Doctrine, 651
Casey, William, 673
Cass, Lewis, 148, 213, 224, 233
Casserly, John J., 636

Castlereagh, Viscount, 95, 98
Castro, Fidel, 549, 563, 681
Catholicism, 556, 568
Caucuses. See Congressional party caucuses
CCC. See Civilian Conservation Corps
Ceausescu, Nicolae, 688
Censure; of Jackson, 153, 155; of Joseph McCarthy, 575
Central America, 214
Central High School, 542
Central Intelligence Agency, 563, 617, 623, 681
Central Powers, 421
Chamberlain, Daniel, 319
Chamberlain, Neville, 489
Chandler, William E., 335
Chandler, Zach, 316, 318
Chase, Salmon P., 214, 250, 266, 268, 287, 293
Chase, Samuel, 75
Checkers speech, 15, 603
Cheney, Dick, 685
Chernenko, Konstantin, 666, 683
Cherokees, 119, 144, 169
Chesapeake. See USS Chesapeake
Chiang Kai-shek, 448, 521, 546
Chief justice of the United States, 406
Chile, 617, 689
China, 186, 369; and Bush, 681, 688; conquest by Japan, 461; and Coolidge, 448; and Eisenhower, 546; and Hayes, 324; and the Korean War, 521; and McKinley, 368; and Nixon, 606, 617, 621; Nixon's visit to, 621; and T. Roosevelt, 388; and Taiwan, 546; treaties with, 324; and Truman, 518
Chinese immigration, 324
Chotiner, Murray, 602
Chou En-lai, 546
Churchill, Winston, 449, 492, 497-498, 544
CIA. See Central Intelligence Agency
CIO. See Congress of Industrial Organizations
Civil rights, 522, 541, 588; and Carter, 644; and L. B. Johnson, 576; and Kennedy, 566; and Nixon, 610; and Truman, 516
Civil Rights Act of 1957, 558, 575-576
Civil Rights Act of 1964, 578
Civil Rights Act of 1968, 680
Civil Rights movement, 516, 542-543, 588, 591; and Kennedy, 562
Civil service reform, 299, 303, 305-306, 322, 326, 337
Civil War, 8, 252, 273, 295, 314
Civilian Conservation Corps, 476
Clark, Champ, 402, 410
Clark, William, 72

Clay, Henry, 5-6, 92, 113, 123, 125, 127, 141, 149, 172, 185, 192, 194, 196, 214, 218, 244
Clayton Act, 416
Clayton-Bulwer Treaty, 214, 368
Clean Air Act, 687
Clemenceau, Georges, 427-428
Cleveland, Grover, **338-350**; and the campaign of 1888, 353; and the election of 1884, 9; as New York governor, 336; and Spain, 362
Clifford, Clark, 515-516, 595
Clinton, Bill, **694-709**; and the campaign of 1992, 693; and the election of 1992, 16; impeachment of, 17, 627
Clinton, DeWitt, 95, 127, 164
Clinton, George, 31, 87, 92
Clinton, Hillary Rodham, 697-698, 703
Coal mines, 384
Cobb, Howell, 233-234
Coelho, Tony, 686
Cohn, Roy, 540
Colby, William, 681
Cold War, 427, 508-509, 527, 543, 565, 605, 617, 650; cost of the, 546; end of the, 687-688
Colfax, Schuyler, 293
Colombia, 389, 437; treaties with, 389
Colonialism, 115, 498
Colorado River, 444
Colson, Charles, 622
Columbia University, 536
Commander in chief, 255
Commercial treaties, 128
Committee for the Re-election of the President, 622, 625
Committee on Public Information, 425
Commonwealth of Independent States, 692
Communism, 447, 524; in Eastern Europe, 688; expansion of, 544, 589; in the United States, 523, 540, 602, 660
Communist Party during World War II, 493
Community Action Program, 579
Compromise of 1850, 214, 218-219, 222, 278
Confederate army, 258
Confederate States of America, 249
Confederation, 23
Confiscation acts, 259-260
Congress; conflict with Jackson, 152; election of the president, 1; founding of, 25; and Lincoln, 255; power over territories, 112; role in internal improvements, 109
Congress of Industrial Organizations, 485
Congressional party caucuses, 5, 40, 118
Conkling, Roscoe, 315, 323, 329, 333
Connally, John, 607-608

Conner, Fox, 534
Connor, Bull, 567
Conscientious objectors during World War I, 425
Conscription Act of 1863, 267
Conscription Act of 1917, 425
Conservation, 386, 399, 458-459, 475
Conservatism, 479, 663; dynamic, 538; and F. D. Roosevelt, 479
Conservatives, 166
Constitution, 238
Constitution, U.S., 1, 23, 32, 86, 254, 711-724; amendments to the, 3, 24, 68, 263, 272, 281-283, 406, 634; interpretation of the, 32; presidential succession in the, 185; ratification of the, 24
Constitutional Convention, 3, 26
Constitutional Union Party, 7, 249
Constitutions, 49
Containment, 511-512, 518, 538, 589, 621
Continental Army, 21
Continental Congress, 21, 24, 48, 64, 86
Contraction of the currency, 298
Contras, 668, 672, 684, 689
Convention of 1818, 112
Conventions, 5, 245. *See also* Constitutional Convention; Convention of 1818; Democratic National Conventions; Hartford Convention; Philadelphia Convention
Coolidge, Calvin, **440-450**; legacy of, 11
Copperheads. *See* Peace Democrats
Cornell, Alonzo B., 323
Corrupt bargain, 5, 125, 141, 190
Corruption, 237, 306, 308, 311, 438; in war production, 506
Cortelyou, George B., 361, 370
Cost-of-living adjustments, 612
Coughlin, Charles, 482
Council of Economic Advisors, 514, 613
Council on Environmental Quality, 614
Council on Executive Reorganization. *See* Ash Commission
Covode, John, 237
Cox, Archibald, 626
Cox, Jacob D., 294, 300, 303
Cox, James M., 430, 434, 471
Coxey, Jacob S., 348
Cramer, Charles F., 438
Crash of 1929. *See* Stock market crash of 1929
Crawford, William H., 108, 123, 127, 141
Credibility gap, 587
Crédit Mobilier scandal, 306
Credit system, 172
Creek War, 139

Creeks, 119, 139
Creel, George, 425
CREEP. See Committee for the Re-election of the President
Creeping socialism, 538
Creswell, John A. J., 300
Crime of '73, 321
Crittenden, John J., 219
Crittenden Resolution, 258
Cross of gold speech, 10
Crowninshield, Benjamin, 108
Cuba, 129, 297, 361; acquisition of, 224, 227, 237; and Cleveland, 349; and Eisenhower, 549; and Grant, 302; invasion of, 549, 563; and Kennedy, 563; and McKinley, 364, 367; revolution in, 549; and T. Roosevelt, 391; and Taft, 397
Cuban Missile Crisis, 564
Currency, 28, 156, 166, 170, 297, 301, 321, 415; contraction of the, 298; debasement of, 156; paper, 172
Currency Act of 1874, 294
Cushing, Caleb, 225
Custis, Martha Dandridge, 20
Czechoslovakia, 489-490, 513
Czolgosz, Leon, 370

D day invasion, 499, 536
Dallas, Alexander J., 98
Dana, Francis, 122
Daniels, Josephus, 414
Dark horse candidates, 6, 193, 222, 681
Daugherty, Harry M., 435, 438, 442
Davis, David, 316
Davis, James J., 443, 454
Davis, Jefferson, 211, 224, 272, 278, 280
Davis, John W., 443
Dawes, Charles G., 443
Dawes Act of 1887, 344
Dawes Plan, 443, 448
Day, William R., 360
Dean, John W., III, 622, 625
Deane, Silas, 48
Dearborn, Henry, 70, 95
Debs, Eugene V., 349, 411, 425, 436
Debt. See Deficit; National debt; State debts; War debt
Declaration of Independence, 48, 64, 257
Defense industry, 495
Defense of the Constitutions of the United States of America, A, 49
Defense spending, 518, 664
Deficit, 16, 487, 664, 674, 691, 708

Deficit spending, 487-488, 613
De Klerk, F. W., 688
De Lafayette, Marquis, 21, 119
De Lesseps, Ferdinand. See Lesseps, Ferdinand de
Demilitarized Zone, 543
Democracy, 257
Democratic National Convention; of 1844, 194; of 1964, 582; of 1968, 15, 597
Democratic Party, 3-5, 8; and Buchanan, 236; and Carter, 646; and the Civil War, 266; and Cleveland, 340; and Clinton, 700; factions in the, 222; founding of the, 132; and Jackson, 154; and A. Johnson, 279; and F. D. Roosevelt, 488; in the South, 516; split of the, 248; and Truman, 505; and Tyler, 184. See also Democratic Republican Party; National Republican Party
Democratic Republican Party, 3, 30, 40, 55, 86; factions in the, 118; and Jefferson, 81
Dependents' Pension Act, 347, 356
Depression, 347, 456. See also Great Depression
Depression of 1819, 110, 124
Depression of 1857, 234
Deregulation, 614, 683
De Santa Anna, Antonio López, 205, 212
Desegregation; of the armed forces, 522; of public schools, 542, 562, 610
Détente, 565, 569, 621, 669
Devens, Charles A., 318
Dewey, George, 364, 377
Dewey, Thomas E., 13, 14, 499, 517
Díaz, Porfirio, 324, 418
Diem, Ngo Dinh. See Ngo Dinh Diem
Dienbienphu, 544-545
Dillon, Douglas, 560
Dingley tariff, 360
Dinwiddie, Robert, 20
Direct vote, 1
Dirksen, Everett, 578, 633
District of Columbia, 213-214, 260
Dix, John A., 224
Dixiecrat Party. See States' Rights Party
Dixon, Edgar, 539
Dixon-Yates issue, 539
Dodge Commission, 365, 368
Dole, Bob, 637, 684, 706
Dole, Elizabeth, 673, 685
Dollar Diplomacy, 403, 406
Dolliver, Jonathan P., 399
Domestic Council, 608
Dominican Republic, 391, 590. See also Santo Domingo

Domino theory, 544
Donelson, Andrew Jackson, 148
Donelson, John, 137
Doughboys, 425
Doughfaces, 6, 111
Douglas, Helen Gahagan, 602
Douglas, Stephen A., 7, 214, 218, 225, 235, 237, 248-249, 279
Douglas, William O., 634
Douglas-Lincoln Debates. *See* Lincoln-Douglas Debates
Douglass, Frederick, 283, 293, 323
Draft, 425; and Clinton, 697, 702
Draft evaders, 639, 696, 702
Draft riots, 267
Dred Scott decision, 233, 260
Duane, William John, 152
Dukakis, Michael, 684-685
Dulles, Allen, 563
Dulles, John Foster, 538, 543
Dupuy de Lome, Enrique, 362
Duties, 334
Dynamic conservatism, 537

Eagleburger, Lawrence, 688
East Berlin, 549
East Florida, 77, 92-93, 113
East Germany, 688
Eastern Europe, 510, 548, 688
Eaton, John Henry, 143, 145
Eaton, Peggy, 145
Eaton scandal, 145, 148
Eavesdropping, 616
Economic Opportunity Act, 579
Education, 587, 699
Egypt, 546, 592, 620, 649
Ehrlichman, John, 608, 622, 636
Einstein, Albert, 496
Eisenhower, Dwight D., **530-552**; and the campaign of 1948, 517; and the campaign of 1952, 526; and the election of 1952, 14; and L. B. Johnson, 575; and Nixon, 602; in World War II, 499
Eisenhower, Mamie, 533
Eisenhower Doctrine, 548
El Salvador, 683, 689
Election laws, 320
Election of 1796, 3, 44, 50
Election of 1800, 3, 60, 68
Election of 1804, 74
Election of 1808, 83, 87, 397
Election of 1812, 95
Election of 1816, 106

Election of 1824, 5, 125, 141, 190
Election of 1828, 5, 133, 142
Election of 1832, 150
Election of 1836, 156, 167
Election of 1840, 175
Election of 1844, 6, 186, 196
Election of 1848, 209, 213
Election of 1852, 6, 223
Election of 1856, 6, 231
Election of 1860, 7, 237, 248
Election of 1864, 272
Election of 1868, 8
Election of 1874, 307
Election of 1876, 8, 310, 316
Election of 1880, 8, 324, 329
Election of 1884, 9, 343
Election of 1888, 353
Election of 1892, 347, 357
Election of 1896, 10, 359
Election of 1904, 11, 385
Election of 1910, 400
Election of 1912, 11, 405, 412
Election of 1920, 434
Election of 1924, 443
Election of 1928, 454
Election of 1930, 463
Election of 1932, 12, 464
Election of 1936, 12
Election of 1938, 488
Election of 1940, 13, 491
Election of 1944, 13, 499
Election of 1948, 13-14
Election of 1950, 525
Election of 1952, 14, 526
Election of 1956, 543
Election of 1960, 14, 559, 605
Election of 1964, 15
Election of 1968, 597, 606
Election of 1972, 613
Election of 1976, 640, 646
Election of 1980, 661
Election of 1984, 669
Election of 1992, 16, 693, 702
Election of 1996, 706
Election of 1998, 706
Elections, 1, 5-6, 191
Electoral college, 3, 26, 44, 51, 68, 191
Electors, 3
Electric power, 539
Elementary and Secondary Education Act, 587
Ellsberg, Daniel, 623
Ellsworth, Oliver, 30
Emancipation Proclamation, 255, 261-262, 267

Embargo, 651
Embargo Act, 80, 88, 122
Emergency Relief Appropriation Act, 484
Emory, William H., 287
Employment Act of 1946, 514
Energy, Department of, 647
Energy crisis, 647
England. *See* Great Britain
Enlightenment, 63
Environmental Protection Agency, 608, 614, 680
EPA. *See* Environmental Protection Agency
Equal Employment Opportunity Commission, 610
Equal Pay Act, 611
Equal Rights Amendment, 611
ERA. *See* Equal Rights Amendment
Era of Good Feelings, 108, 123, 164
Era of Sectionalism, 125
Erskine, David, 88-89
Ervin Committee, 625
Espionage Act of 1917, 425
Essex Junto, 74
Establishment, the, 591
Europe, 421, 448, 461; aid following World War II, 512
Eustis, William, 88
Ev and Jerry Show, 633
Evarts, William M., 287, 318, 335
Evil empire, 666
Excise taxes, 42
Executive Order 8802, 495
Executive power, 25
Executive privilege, 83
Exodusters, 320
Expansion. *See* Western expansion

Factions. *See* Parties
Fair Deal, 522-523
Fair Employment Practices Commission, 495
Fair Labor Standards Act, 487
Fairfax, Thomas Lord, 19
Fairfield, John, 169
Fall, Albert B., 435, 439
Fallen Timbers, 35
Fallows, James, 655
Family and Medical Leave Act, 703
Family Assistance Program, 611
FAP. *See* Family Assistance Program
Farewell address, 157; of Jackson, 157; of Truman, 526; of Washington, 43, 47, 69
Farm relief, 444, 455, 475
Faubus, Orville, 542
FBI. *See* Federal Bureau of Investigation

FDR. *See* Roosevelt, Franklin D.
Federal Bureau of Investigation, 623
Federal Campaign Reform Act, 638
Federal deficit. *See* Deficit; National debt
Federal Emergency Relief Administration, 476
Federal Employment Stabilization Board, 458
Federal Farm Board, 455, 458
Federal Farm Loan Board, 416
Federal government, role of the, 28, 610
Federal Reserve Act, 415
Federal Reserve System, 415
Federal Trade Commission, 416, 446
Federalist Party, 4, 25, 30, 68; and J. Adams, 47; and the Louisiana Purchase, 74; and Washington, 41, 44; and the XYZ affair, 54
Federalist, The, 86
Federated American Engineering Societies, 453
Fenno, John, 30
FEPC. *See* Fair Employment Practices Commission
FERA. *See* Federal Emergency Relief Administration
Fessenden, William Pitt, 288
Fifty-four Forty or Fight, 199
Filibusters, 523, 562, 576, 578
Fillmore, Millard, **216-221**
Finch, Robert, 607
Fireside chats, 442, 474
First Bank of the United States. *See* Bank of the United States
First Battle of Bull Run. *See* Bull Run, First Battle of
First Continental Congress. *See* Continental Congress
First World War. *See* World War I
Fish, Hamilton, 302-303
Fisk, Jim, 301
Flood Control Act of 1928, 445
Florida, 43, 77, 91, 93, 113, 141
Flowers, Gennifer, 701
Floyd, John, 237
Folger, Charles J., 336, 341
Forbes, Charles, 438-439
Force Act, 184
Ford, Gerald R., **629-641**; and the campaign of 1976, 661; and the campaign of 1980, 683; pardon of Nixon, 626
Foreclosures, 477
Forest Service, 386
Formosa Resolution, 545
Forney, John W., 225
Forsyth, John, 168
Fort Duquesne, 20

Fort Sumter, 239, 252
Fortas, Abe, 596
Foster, Augustus J., 92, 95
Foster, Vince, 703
Founding Fathers, 1
Four Freedoms, 491
Fourteen Points, 426, 428, 492
Fourteenth Amendment, 282-283, 516
France, 36; and J. Adams, 51, 57; Half-War with, 54; and Indochina, 544; and Jackson, 155; and Jefferson, 72; Jefferson in, 65; and Madison, 90; seizure of American ships by, 38, 86, 89; trade with, 90; and Washington, 37
Franco, Francisco, 489
Franklin, Benjamin, 49, 65
Fredericksburg, Battle of, 265
Free market economy, 663
Free-Soil Party, 213, 225
Freedmen's Bureau, 281
Freedom of Information Act, 626
Freeman, Orville, 560
Frelinghuysen, Frederick T., 335
Frémont, John C., 6, 259, 269, 272
French Revolution, 36, 50
Freneau, Philip, 31
Fries, John, 57
FTC. See Federal Trade Commission
Fugitive Slave Act, 259
Fulbright, J. William, 560

Gadsden, James A., 228
Gadsden Purchase, 228
Gag rule (slavery), 168, 207
Gage, Lyman J., 359
Gallatin, Albert, 70, 88-89, 96
Garfield, James A., 328-331; and the election of 1876, 317; and the election of 1880, 9, 325; opinion of Grant, 293, 296
Garner, John Nance, 473
Garrison, Lindley M., 414
Gary, Joseph, 359
Gas shortage, 655
Gazette of the United States, 30
Geary, John W., 227
General Electric, 660
Genet, Edmond, 37
Genet v. Sloop Betsy, 37
Geneva Disarmament Conference, 444, 462
Georgia, 119, 144, 301, 643
Germany, 422, 489; reunification of, 688; surrender of, 507
Gerry, Elbridge, 52, 57, 95
Gettysburg Address, 264, 268

Ghent, Treaty of, 100, 123
Gingrich, Newt, 17, 686, 706
Girondists, 37
Glasnost, 666
Glass, Carter, 415
Godoy, Manuel de, 43
Gold, 10, 299, 301, 321, 348
Gold standard, 308, 321, 348, 355, 613
Gold Standard Act of 1900, 360
Goldberg, Arthur, 560, 596
Goldwater, Barry, 15, 551, 568, 582
Gompers, Samuel, 415
Good Neighbor Policy, 437, 447, 461
Good, James W., 454
Gorbachev, Mikhail, 666, 669, 683, 687, 692
Gore, Al, Jr., 702
Gould, Jay, 301
Gramm-Rudman Balanced Budget Act, 664
Granger, Francis, 217
Grant, Ulysses S., 292-312; and the campaign of 1868, 289; and the campaign of 1880, 329; and the Civil War, 268, 273; and the election of 1868, 8; and A. Johnson, 283; as secretary of war, 284, 286; and slaves in the Civil War, 259
Great Britain; aid in World War II, 491; and American expansion, 34; blockade by, 79, 95; border dispute in Oregon, 198; and Cleveland, 350; and Coolidge, 449; 1812 war with, 95-97, 99, 139, 179, 211; and Grant, 302; and Jefferson, 78; and McKinley, 360; and Madison, 88; and Monroe, 112; search for deserters by, 79; seizure of American ships by, 38, 58, 78, 86; support for the Confederacy, 297; trade with, 38-39, 88; treaties with, 38, 79, 100, 112, 200, 214, 368; and Van Buren, 168
Great Communicator, 659, 673
Great Depression, 12, 456-457, 471, 474, 495
Great Emancipator, 262
Great Society, 15, 484, 569, 579, 587, 591, 598, 606
Great War. See World War I
Greece, 511
Greeley, Horace, 8, 261, 305
Green, Duff, 148
Greenback Party, 9
Greenbacks, 298, 301, 306, 321
Greenspan, Alan, 638
Greenville, Treaty of, 36
Gregory, Thomas W., 413
Grenada, invasion of, 667
Groton School, 468
Guadalcanal, Battle of, 497

Guadalupe Hidalgo, Treaty of, 206
Guiteau, Charles Julius, 331, 333
Gulf War. *See* Persian Gulf War
Gunboat Diplomacy, 461
Guthrie, James, 224

Habeas corpus, 254, 266
Habeas Corpus Act, 267
Haig, Alexander, 636, 662
Haiti, 73, 78
Haldeman, H. R., 608, 622, 625
Half-Breeds, 315
Half-War with France, 54
Hall, Nathan K., 217
Halleck, Henry Wager, 265
Halloween Massacre, 681
Hamilton, Alexander, 27-30, 86; as commander
    of the army, 54-55; conflict with J. Adams,
    50, 54; conflict with Jefferson, 65; creation of
    the Bank of the United States, 32; defense of
    the electoral college, 2; duel with Aaron
    Burr, 74; and Great Britain, 39; view of the
    French Revolution, 36; and the Whiskey
    Rebellion, 42
Hamilton, Paul, 88, 96
Hamlin, Hannibal, 248
Hammerschmidt, John, 698
Hampton, Wade, 319
Hancock, Winfield Scott, 9, 285, 329
Hanna, Mark, 10, 359-360, 379, 385
Hannegan, Robert, 506
Hard money, 156, 166, 299, 308, 321, 355
Harding, Warren G., **433-439**; and Coolidge, 441;
    and the election of 1920, 430; legacy of, 11;
    and Taft, 406
Harlan, John Marshall, 323
Harrison, Benjamin, **351-357**; and the campaign
    of 1888, 346; and the election of 1888, 9
Harrison, William Henry, **177-181**; and the
    campaign of 1836, 156; and the campaign of
    1840, 175; and the election of 1840, 5; as B.
    Harrison's grandfather, 351; and the Indian
    wars, 93; as Indiana Territory governor, 72;
    and Jackson, 160; and the War of 1812, 95
Hartford Convention, 99
Hartmann, Robert, 630, 635, 636
Harvard University, 469
Hawaii, 349, 357, 360, 364, 494
Hay, John, 331, 361, 365, 370
Hay-Herran Treaty, 389
Hay-Pauncefote Treaty, 368-369
Hayakawa, S. I., 649
Hayes, Lucy Ware Webb, 314

Hayes, Rutherford B., **313-327**; and the
    campaign of 1876, 310; and the election of
    1876, 8; opinion of Garfield, 328; opinion of
    Grant, 293
Hazlett, Swede, 533, 536
Head Start, 585
Health insurance, 588, 703
Health, Education, and Welfare, Department of,
    539
Hell's Canyon, 539
Henry, Patrick, 44
Hepburn Railroad Act, 385
Hermitage, 138
Herrera, José Joaquín, 201
HEW. *See* Health, Education, and Welfare,
    Department of
High crimes and misdemeanors, 288
Hill, Anita, 692
Hinckley, John, Jr., 663, 683
Hiroshima, 508
Hiss, Alger, 602
Hitler, Adolf, 13, 488-489, 499, 507
Ho Chi Minh, 544
Hoar, Ebenezer R., 303
Hodges, Luther, 560
Hofstadter, Richard, 373, 375-376, 381
HOLC. *See* Home Owner's Loan Corporation
Hollywood, 659
Holocaust, 499
Holt, Joseph, 239, 280
Holy Alliance, 114, 129
Home Owner's Loan Corporation, 477
Homestead Act of 1862, 268
Hoover, Herbert, **451-466**; and the campaign of
    1928, 449; and the campaign of 1932, 473;
    and the election of 1928, 12; and F. D.
    Roosevelt, 472; as secretary of commerce,
    435, 442; and Wilson, 430
Hoover Dam, 459
Hoover Moratorium, 457, 461
Hoover Plan, 462
Hopkins, Harry, 476, 484
Hostage crisis, 652, 654
Hostages, 652, 654, 672, 684
House Committee on Un-American Activities,
    602
House of Burgesses, 20, 64
House of Representatives; and the election of
    1824, 125, 141; role in treaty making, 40;
    Speaker of the, 399
House, Edward M., 413
Housing Act of 1949, 522

Housing and Urban Development, Department of, 588
Houston, David F., 414
Huerta, Victoriano, 418-419
Hughes, Charles Evans, 417, 435-436, 443, 447
Hull, William, 95
Human rights, 651
Humphrey, George, 537
Humphrey, Hubert H., 15, 516, 558, 582-583, 597, 605-606
Humphrey, William E., 446
Hundred Days, 12, 476, 484
Hungary, 548
Hunt, E. Howard, 624
Hunt, William, 330
Hunter, David, 259
Hussein, king of Jordan, 548
Hussein, Saddam, 16, 690-691, 693
Hyde, Arthur M., 454
Hydrogen bomb, 519

I Like Ike, 531
ICBMs. See Intercontinental ballistic missiles
ICC. See Interstate Commerce Commission
Ickes, Harold, 478
Ike. See Eisenhower, Dwight D.
Illinois, 243
Immigration from China, 324
Impeachment, 75, 288, 707; of Samuel Chase, 75; of Clinton, 17, 627, 706-707; of William O. Douglas, 634; of A. Johnson, 285, 287; of Nixon, 626, 697; of John Pickering, 75; of Tyler, 186
Imperialism, 387
Importation from Great Britain, 80
Impressment, 79
Improvements, internal, 126, 146-147, 208, 227; role of Congress in, 109
Inaugural address; of J. Q. Adams, 126; of Buchanan, 233; of Grant, 300; of Hayes, 317; of Jefferson, 76; of Kennedy, 561; of Lincoln, 250, 254, 273; of Monroe, 107; of Polk, 196; of F. D. Roosevelt, 474; of Van Buren, 167
Inauguration; of Grant, 293; of W. H. Harrison, 180; of Jefferson, 69; of Lincoln, 249, 279; of Monroe, 105; of Taft, 398; of Van Buren, 162
India, 683
Indian affairs. See American Indians
Indian Defense Association, 459
Indian Self-Determination and Educational Assistance Act, 611
Indian wars, 35
Indiana, 72, 93

Indiana Territory, 178
Indochina, 520, 544-545. See also Vietnam
Industrialization, 107
INF Treaty. See Intermediate-Range Nuclear Forces Treaty
Inflation, 170, 298, 305, 592, 646
Ingham, Samuel, 142
Intercontinental ballistic missiles, 550, 621
Intermediate-Range Nuclear Forces Treaty, 669, 683
Internment of Japanese Americans, 496
Interstate Commerce Commission, 385, 400, 446
Iowa, 682
Iran, 652, 668, 671, 684; hostage negotiations with, 652, 654, 672
Iran-Contra affair, 672-673, 684
Iraq, 668, 671, 690-691
Irish Mafia, 557
Isolationism, 13, 387, 489, 507, 509
Israel, 547, 593, 620, 649, 667-668
Italy, 489; surrender of, 498

Jackson, Andrew, 135-161; and the campaign of 1824, 123; and the campaign of 1828, 132; and the election of 1824, 5, 125, 190; and the election of 1828, 5; and Lincoln, 243, 250; and Mexico, 201; and Monroe, 114; and Polk, 188, 192; and the Seminoles, 113; and Tyler, 183; and Van Buren, 164; at Van Buren's inauguration, 162; and the War of 1812, 98, 100
Jackson, Francis James, 89
Jackson, Rachel Donelson Robards, 137, 142
Jacksonians, 130-132
Jacksonville agreement, 446
Jacobins, 36
James, Thomas, 330
Japan, 519; conquest of China, 461; and T. Roosevelt, 388, 491, 493; surrender of, 508; and Truman, 507
Japanese Americans, 496
Jardine, William, 443
Jaworski, Leon, 625
Jay, John, 27, 39, 86
Jay Treaty, 39-40, 77
Jefferson, Thomas, 32, 51, 62-65, 68-84, 86; conflict with Alexander Hamilton, 31; and the Democratic Republican Party, 3, 30; and the election of 1796, 3, 44; and the election of 1800, 3, 59-60; and Great Britain, 38; legacy of, 4; and Monroe, 106; opinion of J. Adams, 48-49; opinion of J. Q. Adams, 127;

opinion of Madison, 85, 101; view of the French Revolution, 36; and Washington, 31
Jenkins, Walter, 582
Jesup, Philip, 170
Jim Crow laws, 517
Job Corps, 579, 585
Johnson, Andrew, **277-291**; and Hayes, 314; legacy of, 300
Johnson, James Weldon, 447
Johnson, Lady Bird, 572, 584
Johnson, Louis, 518
Johnson, Lyndon B., **571-599**; and the campaign of 1960, 558; and the Civil Rights movement, 543, 558; and the election of 1964, 15; and Kennedy's legacy, 569; opinion of Ford, 633; as vice president, 562
Johnson, Richard M., 166
Joint Chiefs of Staff, 618
Joint Committee on Reconstruction, 281
Joint Committee on the Conduct of the War, 255, 265
Jones, Paula, 704-705
Jones, William, 96
Jones lawsuit, 704-705
Jonkman, Bartel C., 632
Jordan, 620
Jordan, Hamilton, 643
Judicial review, 70
Judiciary Act of 1789, 26, 70
Judiciary Act of 1801, 70
Judiciary Act of 1802, 70, 82

Kansas, 225, 234; slavery in, 234
Kansas crisis, 226
Kansas-Nebraska Act, 226, 233, 246
Keating-Owen Act, 416
Kefauver, Estes, 557
Kellogg, Frank B., 443, 447
Kellogg-Briand Pact, 448
Kelly Act of 1925, 444
Kemp, Jack, 685
Kendall, Amos, 148, 152
Kennedy, Anthony, 665
Kennedy, Edward, 653
Kennedy, Jacqueline Bouvier, 557, 561
Kennedy, John F., **553-570**; and the campaign of 1960, 550, 576, 604; and the election of 1960, 14
Kennedy, Joseph P., 554, 556, 560
Kennedy, Robert, 557, 560, 576, 581, 595, 597, 605
Kennedy-Nixon Debates, 559, 605
Kentucky Resolutions, 68, 86
Kerner Commission, 592

Key, David M., 318
Keynes, John Maynard, 427, 487
Khomeini, Ayatollah Ruhollah, 652, 654
Khrushchev, Nikita, 547-548, 564, 603
King, Martin Luther, Jr., 542, 567, 596
King, Rufus, 30, 102, 127
King, William R., 232
Kirbo, Charles, 643
Kirkpatrick, Jeane, 673
Kissinger, Henry, 606-607, 616, 618, 638
Kitchen Cabinet, 148
KKK. See Ku Klux Klan
Klan, the. See Ku Klux Klan
Kleberg, Richard M., 572
Know-Nothing Party, 220
Knox, Frank, 490
Knox, Henry, 27, 30, 58
Konoye, Fumimaro, 493
Korean War, 520, 523, 528; end of the, 543
Kosovo, 708
Kosygin, Aleksey, 593
Ku Klux Klan, 303-304, 447, 482
Ku Klux Klan Act, 304
Kuomintang, 448
Kuwait, 671, 690-691

Labor movement, 383
Lafayette. See De Lafayette, Marquis
Laffer, Arthur, 663
La Follette, Robert M., 403, 443, 482
Laird, Melvin, 608, 618
Lamont, Robert, 454
Lance, Bert, 647
Land Act of 1796, 43
Land speculation, 33, 111, 156
Landon, Alfred M., 485
Landrum-Griffin Act of 1959, 558
Lane, Franklin K., 414
Lansing, Robert, 413
Laos, 565, 618
Latin America, 113-114, 128-129, 335, 391, 436, 461, 548, 668
Laurier, Wilfrid, 402
Lawyers, 243
LBJ. See Johnson, Lyndon B.
League of Nations, 11, 429-430, 437, 448
Lebanon, 548, 667-668
Leclerc, Charles, 72
Lecompte, Samuel, 226
Lecompton constitution, 235
Lee, Charles, 58
Lee, Henry, 42
Lee, Robert E., 262, 273

Legal Tender Act, 306
Lend-Lease Act, 491
Lenin, V. I., 428
Lenzer, Terry, 615
Lesseps, Ferdinand de, 324
Lewinsky, Monica, 706
Lewinsky investigation, 706
Lewis, John L., 496
Lewis, Meriwether, 72
Lewis and Clark expedition, 72, 77
Liberal Republicans, 8, 305, 315
Liberalism, 685; and F. D. Roosevelt, 479
Liberty League, 480
Liddy, G. Gordon, 624
Lincoln, Abraham, **241-276**, 624; and the election
    of 1860, 7; and A. Johnson, 279; legacy of, 8,
    300
Lincoln, Levi, 70
Lincoln, Robert Todd, 334
Lincoln-Douglas Debates, 248
Literacy tests, 588
Lithuania, 688
Little Ben, 352
Little Rock, Ark., 542
Livingston, Robert, 72
Lloyd George, David, 427-428
Lodge, Henry Cabot, 377, 429
Lodge, Henry Cabot, Jr., 557-558
Logan, George, 89
London Naval Treaty, 460
Long, Huey P., 483, 485
Long, John D., 359, 377
Louisiana, 43, 72, 74, 81, 307, 309, 319, 483;
    slavery in, 74
Louisiana Purchase, 72, 74, 106
Loyalty oaths, 280
Luce, Clare Booth, 492
Lusitania, 422
Lynchings, 447, 460

McAdoo, William Gibbs, 413
MacArthur, Douglas, 463, 521, 534
McCammant, Wallace, 445
McCarran Internal Security Act of 1950, 524
McCarran-Walter Immigration and Nationality
    Act, 524
McCarthy, Eugene, 595, 597
McCarthy, Joseph, 524-525, 540, 556, 575
McCarthyism, 523, 541, 556, 602, 660
McClellan, George B., 7, 260, 262, 264-265, 271
McCord, James W., Jr., 625
McCormack, John W., 562
McCracken, Paul, 613

McCrary, George M., 318
McDougal, James and Susan, 703
McDowell, Irvin, 264
McFarlane, Robert, 672
McGovern, George, 613
McHenry, James, 51, 60
Machine politics, 299, 330, 506
McKenna, Joseph, 359
McKinley, William, **358-371**; legacy of, 10, 355,
    377
McKinley tariff, 347 348, 355, 359
McLean, John, 127
McNamara, Robert, 560, 594
McNary-Haugen bills, 445
Macon, Nathaniel, 89
Macon's Bill No. 2, 90
McReynolds, James C., 413
MacVeagh, Wayne, 330
Madawaska River, 169
Maddox, Lester, 643
Madero, Francisco, 418
Madison, Dolley, 97, 103
Madison, James, **85-104**; conflict with Alexander
    Hamilton, 30-31; at the Constitutional
    Convention, 26; and William Marbury, 70;
    and Monroe, 106; opinion of the presidency,
    26; opposition to congressional elections, 1;
    as secretary of state, 70; view of the French
    Revolution, 37; view on national debt, 29;
    and the Virginia and Kentucky Resolutions,
    55; and the War of 1812, 4
Maine, 111; border with New Brunswick, 168
Maine, sinking of the, 362, 377
Manassas, First Battle of. *See* Bull Run, First
    Battle of
Manchuria. *See* China
Mandela, Nelson, 688
Manhattan Project, 496
Manifest destiny, 227-228
Mansfield, Mike, 562
Manufacturing, 118
Marbury, William, 70
Marbury v. Madison, 70
March on Washington, 567
Marcos, Ferdinand, 671
Marcy, William L., 224
Marshall, George C., 512, 535
Marshall, John, 52, 58, 60, 82
Marshall, Thurgood, 591, 692
Marshall Plan, 512-513
Maryland, 213
Mason, Stevens Thomson, 39
Mass media, 442

Massachusetts, 441
Massive retaliation. *See* Brinksmanship
Mathews, George, 92-93
Matsu, 545
Matthews, J. B., 540
Matthews, Stanley, 317, 323
Maynard, Horace, 323
Mayo, Henry T., 419
Maysville Road, 109, 147, 192
Meat Inspection Act, 385
Medicaid, 588, 598
Medi-Cal, 661
Medicare, 588, 598
Meese, Edwin, III, 672
Mellon, Andrew, 443, 454
Mellon Plan, 443
Mencken, H. L., 373
Mendès-France, Pierre, 544
Mercer, Lucy, 471, 501
Meredith, James, 566
Mero District, 136
Merritt, Edwin A., 324
Merry, Anthony, 81
Mexican-American War. *See* Mexican War
Mexican Revolution, 418-419
Mexican War, 6, 189, 203, 211; and Lincoln, 244, 246
Mexico, 81, 200, 418; and Buchanan, 236; and Coolidge, 447; and Hayes, 324; and Jackson, 155, 201; and Polk, 198, 201; and Taft, 418; treaties with, 206, 237; and Van Buren, 168; and Wilson, 418
Middle East, 620, 650, 667
Milan Decree, 80
Military, 520; African Americans in the, 523
Military buildup, 519-520, 665
Military-industrial complex, 496
Militia, 42, 89; in Maine, 169; in Tennessee, 138; in Virginia, 20
Miller, Thomas, 439
Milosevic, Slobodan, 707
Minh, Ho Chi. *See* Ho Chi Minh
Minimum wage, 487, 686
Mining, 446, 452
Minnesota, 482
Missile gap, 550, 559
Missiles. *See* Antiballistic missiles; Intercontinental ballistic missiles
Missionaries in Oregon, 198
Mississippi, 309
Mississippi Freedom Democratic Party, 582
Mississippi River, 43
Mississippi Valley; secession of the, 82

Missouri, 111, 505; slavery in, 111, 259
Missouri Compromise line, 207
Missouri Compromise of 1820, 111, 124, 206, 233, 247; repeal of the, 225
Mitchell, John, Jr., 622, 625
Mitchell, William, 444
Mitchell, William D., 454
Model Cities Program, 591
Mohammad Reza Shah Pahlavi, 652
Moley, Raymond, 473-474
Mondale, Walter, 669
Money. *See* Currency; Hard money; Specie
Mongrel Tariff of 1883, 334
Monopolies, 416
Monroe, James, 52, **105-120**; conflict with Jackson, 141; and the election of 1816, 4, 102; negotiation of the Louisiana Purchase, 73; negotiation with Great Britain, 79; as secretary of state, 88
Monroe Doctrine, 115, 123, 200, 350, 390, 403, 461, 549
Monterrey, 211
Montgomery, Ala., 542
Monticello, 68, 83
Moore, John Bassett, 419
Moore, Sarah Jane, 639
Morality, 381, 665
Morgan, J. P., 384
Mormons, 236
Morrill Land Grant Act, 268
Morris, Robert, 30, 33-34
Morrow, Dwight, 443-444
Morton, Oliver P., 315, 318
Motley, John Lothrop, 302-303
Mount Vernon, 19-20
Moynihan, Daniel Patrick, 606-607
Mr. Madison's War, 101
Muckrakers, 381
Mugwumps, 342
Mundt-Nixon bill, 602
Murchison letter, 346
Murphy, Charles F., 470
Muscle Shoals, 444, 476
Muskie, Edmund, 672
Mussolini, Benito, 489

NAACP. *See* National Association for the Advancement of Colored People
NAFTA. *See* North American Free Trade Agreement
Nagasaki, 508
Nagy, Imre, 548
Napoleon I, 72, 77, 80, 86, 89-90

Napoleonic Wars, 76

NASA. *See* National Aeronautics and Space Administration

Nasser, Gamel Abdel, 546, 620

Nathan, Richard, 607

National Aeronautics and Space Administration, 561

National Association for the Advancement of Colored People, 447, 459, 515

National Bank. *See* Bank of the United States

National Banking Act of 1863, 218

National banks, 298

National Building Survey Conference, 456

National Business Survey Conference, 456

National Credit Association, 457

National debt, 27, 29, 495, 701; under Grant, 301; under Monroe, 108

National Defense and Education Act of 1958, 558

National Drought Committee, 457

National Endowment for the Arts, 588

National Endowment for the Humanities, 588

National Gazette, 31

National Guard, 542

National Industrial Recovery Act, 478

National Labor Relations Act, 485

National Labor Relations Board, 478

National Recovery Administration, 478

National Republican Party, 123

National Security Act of 1947, 518

National Security Council, 604, 616, 673

National Security Council-68, 519

National Security Study Memoranda, 616

National Union Party, 282

National Youth Administration, 573, 579

Nationalism, 101

NATO. *See* North Atlantic Treaty Organization

Natural resources, 386

Navigation Acts of 1818 and 1820, 116

Navy, 460

Navy, U.S., 54; search by Royal Navy, 80

Nazi Party, 489, 492, 499

Nebraska, 225

NEP. *See* New Economic Policy

Neutrality, 37, 421

Neutrality Act, 489

New Brunswick, border with Maine, 169

New Deal, 12, 460, 465, 473, 476, 479, 505, 605; and L. B. Johnson, 573; and Truman, 506

New Deal, second, 484

New Echota, Treaty of, 169

New Economic Policy, 613

New England, secession of, 74, 99

New Federalism, 609

New Freedom, 11, 414

New Frontier, 554, 559, 561

New Hampshire, 682

New Jersey, 410

New Mexico, 206, 213-214

New Nationalism, 400, 411, 416

New Orleans, Battle of, 100-101, 139

New World Order, 678, 687

New York Customhouse, 323

New York State, 341, 378, 470, 472

Newell, Frederick, 386

Newlands Reclamation Act of 1902, 386

Newsreels, 442

Ngo Dinh Diem, 545, 565

Ngo Dinh Nhu, 565

Nhu, Ngo Dinh. *See* Ngo Dinh Nhu

Nicaragua, 668, 672, 689; and Coolidge, 447

Nicholls, Frances T., 319

Nicholson, A. O. P., 225

1950's, 531

1960's, 606

NIRA. *See* National Industrial Recovery Act

Nixon, Dixon and Yates, 539

Nixon, Pat, 601

Nixon, Richard M., **600-628**; and Bush, 680; and the campaign of 1960, 558; and the election of 1960, 15; and the election of 1968, 15; and Ford, 634; and Kennedy, 556; pardon of, 630, 634; resignation of, 629, 634

Nixon Doctrine, 618

Nixon-Kennedy Debates. *See* Kennedy-Nixon Debates

Nobel Peace Prize, 392

Noblesse oblige, 374, 387, 468

Non-Importation Act, 80

Nonintercourse Act of 1809, 88, 90

Noriega, Manuel, 689

Normalcy, 11, 430, 434

Normandy, 499

Norris, George W., 399, 446-447, 476

Norris-LaGuardia Act, 458

North American Free Trade Agreement, 692, 703

North American Land Company, 33

North Atlantic Treaty Organization, 519, 536, 564, 666, 707

North Carolina, 24

North Korea, 520, 543

North Vietnam, 589; negotiations with, 619

North, Oliver, 673, 684

Northwest Territory, 35, 178

Notes on the State of Virginia, 65

Novanglus essays, 48

NRA. *See* National Recovery Administration

NSC. *See* National Security Council
NSC-68. *See* National Security Council-68
Nuclear Nonproliferation Treaty, 596
Nuclear Regulatory Commission, 614
Nuclear Test Ban Treaty, 565
Nuclear treaties, 565, 596, 621, 670
Nuclear weapons, 519, 622; in Vietnam, 544
Nullification, 146-147, 150, 183, 192
NYA. *See* National Youth Administration

Oath of office. *See* Presidential oath
Obregón, Álvaro, 420
O'Brien, Lawrence, 557, 624
O'Connor, Sandra Day, 665, 673
O'Donnell, Kenneth, 557
OEO. *See* Office of Economic Opportunity
Office of Economic Opportunity, 614
Office of Management and Budget, 614
Office of Minority Business Enterprise, 610
Office of Price Administration, 601
Ohio, 36, 72, 314
Oil, 647, 690
Old Guard Republicans, 482, 485
Old Hickory, 179
Old Republicans, 111
Old Rough and Ready, 213
Old Tippecanoe, 179
Olds, Robert, 447
Olney, Richard, 349
Olson, Floyd, 482
Open Door notes, 368
Operation Desert Storm, 691
Operation Mongoose, 563
Operation Overlord, 498, 535
Operation Torch, 497
Operation Vulture, 544
Oppenheimer, J. Robert, 540
Orders in Council, 80, 88, 90, 94-95
Oregon Country, 112, 114, 195; border dispute
    with Great Britain, 198
Oregon Trail, 198
Osceola, 170
Ostend Manifesto, 227, 233
Oswald, Lee Harvey, 568, 577
Otis, Harrison Gray, 55, 99
Otis, James, 48
Overton, John, 137

Packard, Stephen B., 319
PACs. *See* Political action committees
Pahlavi, Mohammad Reza Shah. *See*
    Mohammad Reza Shah Pahlavi.
Pakenham, Edward, 139

Palestine Liberation Organization, 668
Palestinians, 649, 668
Panama, 389-390, 437, 648; invasion of, 689
Panama Canal, 324, 388, 397, 447, 648
Panama congress, 129
Pan-American Congress, 357
Pan-American Union, 357
Panic of 1819, 109-110, 189
Panic of 1837, 163, 170
Panic of 1873, 305, 321
Panic of 1893, 347
Panic of 1907, 402
Panic session, 153
Paper currency, 172
Pardons, 280; of Nixon, 626, 630, 635
Paredes, Mariano, 202
Paris, Treaty of, 48
Parker, Alton, 385
Parker, John J., 463
Parks, Rosa, 542
Parochial schools, 556, 558-559, 562, 587
Parrott, William S., 202
Parties, 26, 30, 40, 68, 131, 164, 245; and J. Q.
    Adams, 126, 131; and Jackson, 165; and
    Monroe, 107; rise of, 5; and Van Buren, 131,
    165
Partisan press, 30
Patents, 126
Patronage, 250, 283, 299, 306, 311, 331
Paul, Randolph, 499
Payne-Aldrich Tariff Act, 399
Peabody, Endicott, 468
Peace Corps, 569, 614
Peace Democrats, 266, 271
Peace movement (Civil War), 266
Peace of Paris. *See* Kellogg-Briand Pact
Pearl Harbor, 494
Pendergast, Tom, 506
Pendleton, George H., 314
Pendleton Act, 337
Pennsylvania, 42, 234
Pensions, 344, 356
Pentagon Papers, 623
Pentagonal strategy, 617
Peress, Irving, 540
Perestroika, 666
Perot, Ross, 16, 693, 702
Perry, Matthew C., 219
Perry, Oliver Hazard, 95
Pershing, John J., 420, 534
Persian Gulf, 668
Persian Gulf War, 16, 691
Petticoat politics, 147

Philadelphia Convention, 1, 23
Philadelphia Plan, 610
Philippines, 364-365, 367, 369, 396, 534, 671
Philippines Commission, 367, 396
Phillips, Howard, 615
Pickering, John, 75
Pickering, Timothy, 50-51, 60, 74, 99
Pierce, Franklin, **222-229**; and the election of 1852, 5
Pike, Zebulon M., 77
Pinchot, Gifford, 386, 399
Pinckney, Charles Cotesworth, 52, 60, 74, 83, 87
Pinckney, Thomas, 43-44, 50
Pinkney, William, 79, 90, 92
Pinochet, Augusto, 689
Piracy, 38, 72, 101; slave trade as, 117
Platt Amendment, 367, 369, 397
Platt, Thomas, 330, 355, 379
Pledge of Allegiance, 685
PLO. See Palestine Liberation Organization
Plumbers' unit, 622
Plumed Knight, 356
Pocket veto, 271
Poinsett, Joel R., 167
Poland, 498, 500-501, 548
Polio, 471
Political action committees, 626
Political parties. See Parties
Polk, James K., **188-209**; and the election of 1844, 6; and Jackson, 160; and Lincoln, 245
Polk, Sarah Childress, 190
Pope, John, 262, 265, 285
Porter, John Addison, 361
Portsmouth Conference, 392
Postal service, 323
Postal system, 330
Potomac Company, 33
Potter investigation, 322
Powell, Jody, 643
POWs. See Prisoners of war
Prayer in schools, 665
Preemption Act, 186
Presidency, 1-17, 334, 359-360, 380, 673; election to the, 2; establishment of the, 25, 45; power of the, 25, 245, 250, 254, 330, 386; rituals and the, 25
Presidential campaigns. See Campaigns
Presidential elections. See Elections
Presidential oath, 254
Presidential power. See Presidency, power of the
Presidential succession. See Succession
President's Emergency Committee for Employment, 457

President's Organization on Unemployment Relief, 457
Press; partisan politics and the, 30; relationship with the president, 360, 442, 587
Press conferences, 442, 561
Primaries, 10
Princeton University, 410
Prisoners of war in the Korean War, 543
Privateers, 37
Proclamation of Amnesty and Reconstruction, 270
Proctor, Redfield, 363
Profiles in Courage, 123, 557
Progressive Party, 11, 404, 411
Progressive Republican League, 403
Progressivism, 11, 382, 400, 416, 451, 453, 465
Prohibition, 437, 455, 460
Prophet, The, 178
Protectionism, 446
Protective tariffs. See Tariffs
Protests. See Antiwar protests
PT 109, 555
Public debt. See National debt; State debts; War debt
Public works, 478, 539
Public Works Administration, 478, 573
Puerto Rico, 129, 369
Pullman Strike, 349
Pure Food and Drug Act, 385
PWA. See Public Works Administration

Qaddafi, Muammar al-, 671
Quakers, 452, 601
Quay, Matthew, 353, 355
Quayle, Dan, 685
Quemoy, 545
Quids, 81
Quitman, John, 227

Race relations, 515, 575
Racism, 320, 495; and T. Roosevelt, 388
Radford, Arthur, 544
Radical Republicans, 268, 280, 296
Radio, 442
Radio Act of 1927, 444
Rafshoon, Gerald, 643
Railroad, 320, 349, 384
Railroad, transcontinental, 228, 268
Railroad strike of 1877, 320
Railway Labor Act, 444
Rambouillet Decree, 89
Randolph, A. Philip, 517
Randolph, Edmund, 27, 30, 40

Randolph, John, 75, 81, 88, 143
Rawlins, John A., 302
Rayburn, Sam, 562, 572-573, 634
Reagan, Nancy, 659
Reagan, Ronald, **658-676**, 700; and Bush, 683;
    and the campaign of 1976, 639; and the
    campaign of 1980, 682; legacy of, 16, 677;
    and the Panama Canal, 648
Reagan Revolution, 674, 686
Reaganomics, 663
Rebozo, Bebe, 625
Recession of 1990, 691
Reciprocity with Canada, 401
Reconstruction, 274, 280-281, 283, 296, 299, 301,
    308, 319; and Lincoln, 269, 273
Reconstruction Acts, 283-284, 287
Reconstruction Finance Corporation, 457, 539
Red Army, 497
Red Scare, 426, 523-524, 540
Redfield, William C., 414
Reed, Thomas B., 355
Reeder, Andrew, 226
Regan, Donald, 662
Regulation, 614
Rehnquist, William, 665
Relief Act of 1821, 111
Relief programs, 476, 484
Reorganization, 614
Reparations; for Civil War claims, 297; for
    World War I, 429, 448, 461
Report on Manufactures, 28
Republican National Committee, 680
Republican Party, 6, 8, 220; and Arthur, 333; and
    Buchanan, 231; and the election of 1870, 303;
    founding of the, 226, 248; and Garfield, 329;
    and Hoover, 461; and A. Johnson, 279, 282;
    and Lincoln, 264, 271; and Reagan, 660; and
    T. Roosevelt, 379; in the South, 307, 309, 319;
    and Taft, 398; and Texas, 680
Research Committee on Social Trends, 454, 459
Resignation; of Spiro T. Agnew, 608, 634; of
    Nixon, 626, 630
Resumption Act, 321
Revolutionary War, 21, 50, 106, 121, 136, 257
Reykjavik summit, 669
Rhode Island, 24
Ribicoff, Abraham, 560
Richardson, Elliot, 626
Richmond, 269
Riots, 463; draft, 267; race, 282, 592
Rives, William C., 166-167, 172
Robertson, William H., 329
Rockefeller, Nelson, 568, 608, 637

Rodham, Hillary. *See* Clinton, Hillary Rodham
Rodino, Peter, 626
Rodney, Caesar, 88
Roe v. Wade, 665
Rogers Plan, 620
Romania, 688
Romney, George, 568
Roosevelt, Eleanor, 470
Roosevelt, Franklin D., **467-503**; and the
    campaign of 1932, 464; and the campaign of
    1944, 505-506; and Hoover, 464; and L. B.
    Johnson, 573; legacy of, 8, 12; and the Soviet
    Union, 509
Roosevelt, Theodore, **372-394**; and the campaign
    of 1900, 369; and the campaign of 1912, 403,
    411; and the election of 1904, 11; and the
    election of 1912, 11; and the elections of
    1910, 400; and B. Harrison, 354; opinion of
    Tyler, 182; as F. D. Roosevelt's cousin, 469;
    and Taft, 396, 398-399, 404; and trusts, 402;
    and Wilson, 417
Roosevelt Corollary, 390
Root, Elihu, 359, 361, 461
Rosenberg, Julius and Ethel, 540
Rough Riders, 377
Ruckelshaus, William D., 626
Rule of 1756, 78
Rules Committee, 399
Rum, Romanism, and Rebellion, 342
Rumsfeld, Donald, 614
Runaway slaves, 213
Rush, Richard, 127, 130
Rusk, Dean, 560, 595
Russell, Richard, 574
Russia, 123; and Wilson, 427. *See also* Soviet
    Union
Russian Revolution, 423, 427
Rutherfurd, Lucy Mercer. *See* Mercer, Lucy

Sachs, Alexander, 496
Sackville-West, Lionel, 346
Sadat, Anwar el-, 621, 649
St. Clair, Arthur, 35, 72
St. John River, 168
St. Lawrence River, 459
Salary grab, 306
SALT. *See* Strategic Arms Limitation Talks
Samoan Islands, 357
San Juan Hill, 365
San Lorenzo, Treaty of, 43
Sanders, Carl, 643
Sandinistas, 668, 689
Sandino, Augusto, 447

Santo Domingo, 302-303. *See also* Dominican Republic
Saturday Night Massacre, 626
Saudi Arabia, 690
Savings and loan industry, 16, 686
Scalia, Antonin, 665
Scandals, 438, 701, 703-704, 706. *See also* Crédit Mobilier scandal; Eaton scandal; Iran-Contra affair; Jones lawsuit; Lewinsky investigation; Teapot Dome scandal; Watergate scandal; Whitewater investigation
Schine, G. David, 540
Schlesinger, James, 647
Schofield, John M., 288
Schurz, Carl, 318, 323
Schwarzkopf, Norman, 691
Scott, Thomas A., 317
Scott, Winfield, 6, 169, 204-205, 211, 220, 264
Scowcroft, Brent, 673, 685, 688
Scranton, William, 620
Screen Actors Guild, 659
SDI. *See* Strategic Defense Initiative
Secession, 150, 239, 270, 281; of the Mississippi Valley, 82; of New England, 74, 99; of the South, 7, 214, 218, 249, 279
Second Bank of the United States. *See* Bank of the United States
Second Battle of Bull Run. *See* Bull Run, Second Battle of
Second Continental Congress. *See* Continental Congress
Second Declaration of Independence, 174
Second Industrial Conference, 453
Second party system, 172, 176
Second World War. *See* World War II
Secretary of commerce, 453
Secretary of the treasury, 152
Securities, 27, 33
Sedgwick, Theodore, 30
Sedition Act of 1798, 55
Sedition Act of 1918, 425
Segregation, 14, 516, 522; in the armed forces, 517
Segregationists, 643
Seminoles, 113, 141, 145, 169, 211
Senate, 48, 58; confirmation of cabinet positions, 445; rejection of Charles B. Warren, 445; rejection of John Tower, 685; rejection of Robert Bork, 665; rejection of William Short, 88; role in foreign policy, 72; vote on impeachment, 75
Serbia, 707
Settlement. *See* Western settlement

Settlers, 198
Seven Days' Battles, 265
Seven Years' War, 20
Seventeenth Amendment, 406
Sevier, John, 137
Seward, William H., 7, 214, 217, 248, 250, 266, 284, 290
Seymour, Horatio, 8, 267
Shafter, William R., 365
Shah of Iran, the. *See* Mohammad Reza Shah Pahlavi.
Shannon, Wilson, 226
Shays's Rebellion, 86
Shenandoah Valley, 19
Shepherd, Alexander H., 306
Sheppard-Towner Act, 435
Sheridan, Philip, 271, 284
Sherman, John, 317-318, 321-322, 329, 355, 360
Sherman, William Tecumseh, 269, 271, 273, 283
Sherman Antitrust Act, 355, 384, 396, 402, 415
Sherman Silver Purchase Act, 347-348, 355
Short, William, 88
Shultz, George, 608
Shuttle diplomacy, 620
Sick, Gary, 652
Silver, 321, 348, 355
Silver Democrats, 350
Simon, William, 638
Sinclair, Upton, 482
Sirica, John J., 625
Sit-ins, 543
Six-Day War, 593
Six Nations, 35
Sixteenth Amendment, 406
Slave trade, 117
Slavery, 5, 7, 206, 258; abolition of, 260; and Buchanan, 232; and expansion, 228; and Great Britain, 39; and A. Johnson, 278; in Kansas, 234; and Lincoln, 247; in Louisiana, 74; and Madison, 103; and the Mexican War, 213, 218; in Missouri, 111, 259; and Monroe, 112; and Pierce, 224; and Polk, 207; and Taylor, 215; and Van Buren, 167
Slidell, John, 202, 233
Smith, Alfred E., 12, 454, 472-473
Smith, Jesse M., 438
Smith, Robert, 70, 88
Smith, Samuel, 97
Smith, William French, 662
Smith, William Loughton, 30
Smoot-Hawley Tariff, 457
Social Security, 485, 539, 575, 612
Social service system, 459

Socialism, 482

Solid South, 9, 336, 414

Somalia, 693

Sorensen, Theodore, 557, 561

Soulé, Pierre, 227

Souter, David, 692

South; and African Americans, 515; civil rights protests in the, 542; Democratic Party in the, 516; and protective tariffs, 146; Republican Party in the, 307, 309, 319; secession of the, 7, 214, 218, 249, 279; violence in the, 304; voting fraud in the, 307

South Africa, 688

South Carolina, 60, 150, 184, 239, 252, 319

South Korea, 520, 543

South Vietnam, 589

Southard, Samuel, 127

Southeast Asia Resolution. *See* Tonkin Gulf Resolution

Southeast Asia Treaty Organization, 545

Soviet Union, 447, 508, 666; and Bush, 687; and Carter, 650; coup in the, 692; and Eisenhower, 550; end of the, 692; and Germany, 490; as joint peacemaker with the United States, 620; and Kennedy, 564; and Nixon, 621; and the Persian Gulf War, 690; and Reagan, 665-666, 669; and F. D. Roosevelt, 493, 509; and Truman, 509; and World War II, 509

Space program, 561, 575

Spain, 489; and J. Adams, 56; and American expansion, 34; border with, 113, 123; and Cleveland, 362; end of New World empire, 129; and Grant, 302; and Jefferson, 77; and McKinley, 362; and Monroe, 112; treaties with, 43, 366

Spanish-American War, 361, 364, 377

Speaker of the House of Representatives, 399

Special interests, 646

Specie, 170-171, 298, 301, 321

Specie circular, 157, 170

Speculation, land, 33, 111, 156

Spoils system, 143, 323, 337

Spooner Amendment, 369

Springfield Junto, 244

SSI. *See* Supplementary Security Income

Stalin, Joseph, 497, 498-499

Stalingrad, Battle of, 497

Stalwarts, 315, 318, 323, 329, 333

Stamp Act, 48

Stanbery, Henry, 284, 287

Stanton, Edwin M., 239, 280, 284-285

Star Route case, 323, 330, 335

Star Wars. *See* Strategic Defense Initiative

Starr, Kenneth, 17, 704, 706

State banks, 172

State debts, 27, 29

State governments, role of, 610

State legislatures, 1

State of the Union address; of Cleveland, 346; of Madison, 92, 102

States' rights, 50, 55, 81, 109, 150

States' Rights Party, 14, 517

Stealth bomber, 666

Stevens, Ted, 540

Stevens, Thaddeus, 281, 284, 287

Stevenson, Adlai E., 14, 526, 543, 557, 560, 602

Stewart, Alexander T., 300

Stiles, John R., 631

Stimson, Henry L., 443, 454, 490, 679

Stimson Doctrine, 462

Stock market crash of 1929, 456

Stoddert, Benjamin, 58

Stone, Harlan F., 446

Strategic Arms Limitation Talks, 621, 650

Strategic Defense Initiative, 666, 669

Strikes, 320, 349, 441, 482, 487

Stuart, Gilbert, 21

Stump speech, 282

Submarine warfare, 422

Submerged Lands Act, 539

Succession, 185

Suez Canal, 546

Suffrage. *See* Black suffrage; Universal suffrage; Woman suffrage

Summit meetings, 669

Sumner, Charles, 226, 281, 284, 302-303

Superpowers, 617

Supplementary Security Income, 612

Supply-side economics, 663, 683

Supreme Court; appointments by Bush, 692; appointments by L. B. Johnson, 596; appointments by Reagan, 665; and civil rights legislation, 516, 522; and the Dred Scott decision, 233; establishment of the, 26; and the New Deal, 484; and F. D. Roosevelt, 486

Surplus, 344, 347

Surratt, Mary, 280

Swartwout, Samuel, 143

Symington, Stuart, 558

Taft, Robert A., 14, 513, 536

Taft, William Howard, **395-407**; and the campaign of 1912, 411; as chief justice, 446; and the election of 1912, 11; and the League

of Nations, 430; and Mexico, 418; and T. Roosevelt, 393
Taft-Hartley Act, 556, 574
Taggart, Samuel, 90
Taiwan, 545-546, 617, 680
Talleyrand, 52, 57, 77
Tallmadge, James, Jr., 111
Tallmadge, Nathaniel P., 172
Tammany Hall, 341, 470
Taney, Roger, 148, 152-153, 266
Tariff commission, 446
Tariff of Abominations, 130, 184
Tariff reform, 234, 345, 348, 414
Tariffs, 28, 102, 118, 130, 146, 150, 183, 192, 208, 299, 345-346, 355, 360, 398, 446
Tax reform, 647, 663
Tax Reform Act of 1986, 663
Taxes, 16, 444; cutting of, 567, 578, 663; elimination of, 71; under L. B. Johnson, 592; role of federal, 28; on the wealthy, 485; during World War II, 495
Taylor, Zachary, **210-215**; and the election of 1848, 6, 209, 246; and Fillmore, 218; and the Mexican War, 202, 204-205
Teapot Dome scandal, 439
Tecumseh, 178
Television, 14-15, 558, 561, 605
Television commercials, 605
Teller Amendment, 364, 367
Temperance, 305
Tennessee, 137, 189, 278
Tennessee River, 444, 459
Tennessee Valley Authority, 444, 476, 539
Tenure of Office Act, 284, 286-287, 300
TerHorst, Jerald F., 636
Territories, 112
Terrorism, 668, 671-672
Tet Offensive, 594-595
Texas, 572; annexation of, 6, 160, 168, 186, 194, 197, 201; attempts to purchase, 155; claims in New Mexico, 214, 218; and the Republican Party, 680
Third parties, 6, 8
Third term, 12
Third World, 548, 617
Thirteenth Amendment, 263, 272, 281
Thomas, Clarence, 692
Thomas, Lorenzo, 287
Thompson, Jacob, 233, 238
Thompson, Richard W., 318
Thornberry, Homer, 596
Thousand points of light, 686
Thurman, Allen G., 314

Thurmond, Strom, 14, 517
Tiananmen Square, 688
Tilden, Samuel J., 8, 308, 310, 316
Tippecanoe, 93, 178
Tippecanoe and Tyler Too, 175, 180, 184
Todd, John Payne, 103
Tollgates, 109
Tonkin Gulf Resolution, 581
Torrijos, Omar, 649
Tower, John, 672, 685
Tower Commission, 673
Townsend, Francis, 482
Townsend Plan, 482
TR. *See* Roosevelt, Theodore
Trade, 128; conflict with Great Britain over, 78; with France, 78, 90; with Great Britain, 38-39, 88; in the West Indies, 116, 128
Trail of Tears, 145, 169
Transcontinental railroad, 228, 268
Transcontinental Treaty of 1819, 114
Transportation, 107, 109
Treason, 83
Treasury, U.S., 27-28, 71, 98, 163, 171; independence of the, 173, 197, 208; secretary of the, 152
Treasury reserve, 348
Treaties, 40, 401; with American Indians, 118, 143, 145; with China, 324; with Colombia, 389; commercial, 128; with Great Britain, 38, 79, 100, 112, 200, 214, 368; with Mexico, 206, 237; nuclear, 565, 596, 621, 670; with Panama, 649; with Spain, 43, 366. *See also* individual treaties
Treatment, the, 574
Trilateral Commission, 644
Tripoli, 71
Tripp, Linda, 706
Trist, Nicholas, 205
Truman, Harry S, **504-529**; and the campaign of 1944, 499; and the election of 1948, 13; legacy of, 12; opinion of Germany and the Soviet Union, 493
Truman Doctrine, 512
Trumbull, Lyman, 288
Trusts, 355, 382, 384, 398, 402, 405
Tsongas, Paul, 701
Turkey, 511
TVA. *See* Tennessee Valley Authority
Twelfth Amendment, 3, 68
Twenty-fifth Amendment, 634
Two China policy, 617, 680
Two-party system, 158
Tyler, John, **182-187**; annexation of Texas, 198;

and the campaign of 1840, 175; and the election of 1844, 5

U-2 incident, 550
UAC. *See* Urban Affairs Council
Underwood-Simmons Tariff Act, 414
Unemployment, 638
Union army, 258
Union Party, 485
Unions, 383, 485, 495, 558
United Mine Workers, 446
United Nations, 500, 680; founding of the, 507
United Nations Security Council, 690
United States Telegraph, 147
United States v. Nixon, 626
Universal suffrage, 296; and Lincoln, 244
University of Mississippi Law School, 566
Urban Affairs Council, 606
USS *Chesapeake*, 79
Utah, 214, 236

Vallandigham, Clement L., 267
Valley Forge, 22
Van Buren, Martin, **162-176**; and the American System, 146; and the campaign of 1828, 132, 142; and the campaign of 1836, 156; and the campaign of 1844, 194; and the Eaton scandal, 146; and the Free-Soil Party, 213; legacy of, 5; opinion of J. Q. Adams, 127; and political parties, 131; as secretary of state, 142
Vance, Cyrus, 650, 652
Vandenberg, Arthur, 462, 513
Vera Cruz, invasion of, 419
Versailles, Treaty of, 427, 429-430, 462
Veterans, 344, 347, 356; from the Civil War, 344; from World War I, 463
Veterans Bureau, 435, 438
Veto, 151, 245, 271, 334, 638
Vice presidency, 49, 441, 576, 604; election to the, 2
Viet Cong, 588, 594
Vietnam; and Eisenhower, 544; and L. B. Johnson, 580, 589; and Kennedy, 565, 569. *See also* Indochina
Vietnam War, 588, 591, 593, 596, 598, 618-619; and the campaign of 1968, 606; and Clinton, 696; end of the, 620; lack of declaration of, 590
Vietnamization, 618
Villa, Pancho, 418-419
Virginia, 57, 64, 85
Virginia dynasty, 62, 102, 106

Virginia House of Burgesses. *See* House of Burgesses
Virginia Plan, 86
Virginia Resolutions, 44, 86
Voice of America, 540
Voodoo economics, 683
Voorhis, Jerry, 602
Voting rights, 588
Voting Rights Act of 1965, 588

Wade, Benjamin F., 288
Wade-Davis bill, 270
Wade-Davis Manifesto, 271
Wagner, Robert, 446, 458, 485
Wagner Act, 485
Walker, Robert J., 234
Wallace, George, 566, 605
Wallace, Henry A., 14, 499, 505-506, 511-512, 514
Wanamaker, John, 354
War Between the States. *See* Civil War
War debt; from the Revolutionary War, 27-28; from the War of 1812, 98; from World War I, 447, 462
War Democrats, 266
War Hawks, 88
War of 1812, 95-97, 99, 139, 179, 211
War of Independence. *See* Revolutionary War
War on Poverty, 569, 579, 591, 598
War powers, 253, 255
War Powers Act, 447
Ward, Ferdinand, 310
Warren, Charles B., 445
Warren, Earl, 542, 577, 596
Warren Commission, 568, 577, 633
Wars. *See* Civil War; Korean War; Mexican War; Persian Gulf War; Spanish-American War; Revolutionary War; Vietnam War; War of 1812; World War I; World War II
Washington, George, **18-46**; legacy of, 3; and political parties, 3; reinstatement as commander in chief, 54; retirement of, 47
Washington Conference, 436
Washington, D.C., 60, 63, 96, 253; burning of, 97
Washington Globe, 147
Washington Union, 225
Watergate scandal, 15, 609, 615, 622, 635, 680; legacy of, 626
Wayne, Anthony, 35, 178
Webster, Daniel, 149, 156, 172, 214, 218-219
Webster-Ashburton Treaty, 169, 186
Weed, Thurlow, 217
Weinberger, Caspar, 662
Welfare reform, 611, 661

Welles, Gideon, 250
West Bank, 649, 668
West Berlin, 549, 564
West Florida, 77, 91
West Indies, 116, 128
West Point, 294, 533
Western expansion, 107, 197; and the Mexican War, 203
Western settlement, 33-34, 43
Westmoreland, William, 589, 595
Wheeler, Burton K., 491
Wheeler-Rayburn Act, 485
Whigs, 6, 153, 156, 165-166, 172, 174, 179, 184, 186, 212, 247; and Lincoln, 244-245; and Tyler, 186
Whiskey Rebellion, 42
Whiskey Ring, 308
Whitaker, John, 608
White, Frank, 699
White, Hugh Lawson, 156
White House, 97, 105, 334, 360, 381; burning of the, 97; remodeling of the, 561
White House staff, 361; of Eisenhower, 538; of Kennedy, 561
White Leagues, 307
Whitewater investigation, 17, 703-704
Whitman, Walt, 268
Whitney, William C., 341, 344
Why England Slept, 554
Wickersham, George W., 402
Wilbur, Ray Lyman, 454
Wilkinson, James, 82, 95
Willey, Kathleen, 706
Willkie, Bruce, 611
Willkie, Wendell L., 13, 490
Wilmot, David, 207
Wilmot Proviso, 207, 218, 225
Wilson Dam, 476
Wilson, Edith Galt, 410
Wilson, Ellen Axson, 410
Wilson, Henry, 308
Wilson, Henry Lane, 418
Wilson, William B., 414
Wilson, Woodrow, 408-432; and the campaign of
1912, 404; legacy of, 11, 380; and T. Roosevelt, 382, 393, 471
Wilson-Gorman bill, 348
Winder, William H., 96
Windom, William, 330, 355
Wirt, William, 97, 108, 127
Wisconsin, 482
Wise Men, 595
Wolcott, Oliver, Jr., 51
Woman suffrage, 412
Women's rights, 611
Wood, Leonard, 377
Woodbury, Levi, 148
Work, Hubert, 443
Work relief, 484
Works Progress Administration, 484, 573
World Court, 448, 461
World War I, 11, 393, 417, 421, 424, 436; and Hoover, 453
World War II, 13, 490-491, 497-499; and Bush, 679; and Eisenhower, 535-536; home front during, 494; impact on the Soviet Union, 509; impact on the United States, 509; and Kennedy, 555; and Truman, 506
WPA. See Works Progress Administration
Wright, Jim, 686
Wright, Silas, 195
Writ of habeas corpus. See Habeas corpus
Wythe, George, 64

XYZ affair, 52

Yalta Conference, 500, 509, 540
Yarborough, Ralph, 680
Yates, Eugene, 539
Yazoo land companies, 33-34, 81
Yeltsin, Boris, 692
Yom Kippur War, 620
Young, Owen D., 461
Young Hickory, 188

Zapata, Emiliano, 418
Zimmerman, Alfred, 423
Zweicker, Ralph, 540